THE CAMBRIDGE HISTORY OF
SOUTH AFRICAN LITERATURE

*

South Africa's unique history has produced literatures in many languages, in oral and written forms, reflecting the diversity in the cultural histories and experience of its peoples. The *Cambridge History* offers a comprehensive, multi-authored history of South African literature in all the country's eleven official languages (and more minor ones), produced by a team of over forty international experts, including contributors drawn from all of the major regions and language groups of South Africa. It will provide a complete portrait of South Africa's literary production, organised as a chronological history from the oral traditions existing before colonial settlement to the post-apartheid revision of the past. In a field marked by controversy, this volume is more fully representative than any existing account of South Africa's literary history. It will make a unique contribution to Commonwealth, international and postcolonial studies, and serve as a definitive reference work for decades to come.

DAVID ATTWELL is Professor of English in the Department of English and Related Literature at the University of York. He has published widely on anglophone African literature, South African literature and postcolonial studies.

DEREK ATTRIDGE is Professor of English at the University of York and a Fellow of the British Academy. He has published many books on literary theory, poetic form, Irish literature and South African writing.

THE CAMBRIDGE
HISTORY OF
SOUTH AFRICAN
LITERATURE

*

Edited by
DAVID ATTWELL
and
DEREK ATTRIDGE

CAMBRIDGE
UNIVERSITY PRESS

CAMBRIDGE UNIVERSITY PRESS
Cambridge, New York, Melbourne, Madrid, Cape Town,
Singapore, São Paulo, Delhi, Tokyo, Mexico City

Cambridge University Press
The Edinburgh Building, Cambridge CB2 8RU, UK

Published in the United States of America by Cambridge University Press, New York

www.cambridge.org
Information on this title: www.cambridge.org/9780521199285

First published 2012

Printed in the United Kingdom at the University Press, Cambridge

A catalogue record for this publication is available from the British Library

Library of Congress Cataloguing in Publication data
The Cambridge history of South African literature / edited by David Attwell and Derek Attridge.
p.   cm.
Includes index.
ISBN 978-0-521-19928-5 (hardback)
1. South African literature – History and criticism.   I. Attwell, David.   II. Attridge, Derek.
PL8014.S6C36   2011
809'.8968 – dc23   2011037990

ISBN 978-0-521-19928-5 Hardback

Contents

v

Contents

Contents

Contents

PART VI

SOUTH AFRICAN LITERATURE: CONTINUITIES
AND CONTRASTS

Contents

Notes on contributors

DEREK ATTRIDGE was born in South Africa, and completed degrees at the Universities of Natal and Cambridge. He has taught in the UK, France and the USA, and is currently Professor of English at the University of York and a Fellow of the British Academy. Among his books are *Writing South Africa* (co-edited with Rosemary Jolly, 1998), *The Singularity of Literature* (2004) and *J. M. Coetzee and the Ethics of Reading* (2004).

DAVID ATTWELL was born in South Africa and studied at the Universities of Natal, Cape Town and Texas at Austin. He is currently Professor of English at the University of York. His books are *Doubling the Point* (with J. M. Coetzee, 1992), *J. M. Coetzee: South Africa and the Politics of Writing* (1993), *Rewriting Modernity* (2005) and *Bury me at the Marketplace, Es'kia Mphahlele and Company, Letters 1946–2006* (with N. Chabani Manganyi, 2010).

RITA BARNARD is Professor of English and Comparative Literature at the University of Pennsylvania and Professor Extraordinaire at the University of Stellenbosch. She is the author of *Apartheid and Beyond: South African Writers and the Politics of Place* (2006) and *The Great Depression and the Culture of Abundance* (1995). She is the editor of *Safundi: The Journal of South African and American Studies* and the forthcoming *Cambridge Companion to Nelson Mandela*.

PETER BLAIR studied at the Universities of Oxford and York, and completed some of his doctoral research at the University of KwaZulu-Natal, Durban. He has published on various aspects of South African literature, and is Senior Lecturer in English at the University of Chester and co-editor of *Flash: The International Short-Short Story Magazine*.

ELLEKE BOEHMER is the author of four novels – *Screens again the Sky* (1990), *An Immaculate Figure* (1993), *Bloodlines* (2000) and *Nile Baby* (2008) – and of *Colonial and Postcolonial Literature* (1995, 2005), *Empire, the National and the Postcolonial, 1890–1920* (2002), *Stories of Women* (2005) and *Nelson Mandela* (2008). She is Professor of World Literature in English at the University of Oxford.

MBONGISENI BUTHELEZI lectures in the Department of English at the University of Cape Town. He is currently conducting research on the use of oral poetry in the revival of precolonial memory and identity in contemporary southern Africa.

LAURA CHRISMAN is Nancy K. Ketcham Endowed Chair of English at the University of Washington. Her publications include *Postcolonial Contraventions: Cultural Readings of Race, Empire and Transnationalism* (2003), *Rereading the Imperial Romance* (2000) and *Colonial Discourse and Postcolonial Theory: A Reader* (1993). Her current research explores transnational relations between black South African and black American intellectuals of the early twentieth century.

STEPHEN CLINGMAN is Professor of English at the University of Massachusetts, Amherst. His books include *The Novels of Nadine Gordimer: History from the Inside* (2nd edn 1992), *Bram Fischer: Afrikaner Revolutionary* (1998, winner of the 1999 Sunday Times Alan Paton Award) and *The Grammar of Identity: Transnational Fiction and the Nature of the Boundary* (2009).

CARLI COETZEE is a South African-born academic currently teaching at SOAS in London; she has published on archives and memory in South Africa and is the co-editor of *Negotiating the Past: The Making of Memory in South Africa* (1998).

MARGARET J. DAYMOND is Emeritus Professor in English Studies at the University of KwaZulu-Natal and a Fellow of the University. Her publications are mostly on writing by African women, fictional and non-fictional narrative and questions of gender.

LEON DE KOCK is Professor and Head of English at the University of Stellenbosch. He is a poet, translator and academic who has published numerous books, including *Civilising Barbarians* (1996), *Bloodsong* (poems, 1997), *South Africa in the Global Imaginary* (2004, with Louise Bethlehem and Sonja Laden), *gone to the edges* (poems, 2006) and *Bodyhood* (poems, 2010).

DOROTHY DRIVER taught for twenty years in the English Department of the University of Cape Town, where she is now an Emeritus Professor, and currently teaches part-time at the University of Adelaide.

IAN GLENN is Professor of Media Studies and Director of the Centre for Film and Media Studies at the University of Cape Town. He studied at the Universities of KwaZulu-Natal, York (UK) and Pennsylvania, where he took a Ph.D. in modern British and American literature. He has published widely on South African literature, culture and media.

MICHAEL GREEN is Professor of English and Creative Writing at Northumbria University. He is the author of *Novel Histories: Past, Present, and Future in South African Fiction* (1997), and (under the name Michael Cawood Green) works of fiction, including *Sinking: A Verse Novella* (1997) and *For the Sake of Silence* (2008). In 2009 he was inducted into the Society of the Fellows of the University of KwaZulu-Natal, and he has won the University of Natal Book Prize and the Olive Schreiner Prize.

MANIE GROENEWALD is Associate Professor in the Department of African Languages at the University of Johannesburg. He specialises in performed verbal art in isiZulu.

PETER HORN is a poet and critic whose works include *Poems 1964–1990* (1991), *An Axe in the Ice* (1992) and *Writing my Reading: Essays on Literary Politics in South Africa* (1994). He is Honorary Professorial Research Associate (Witwatersrand) and Honorary Life Fellow (Cape Town), and has won the Alex La Guma/Bessie Head Award, the Herman Charles Bosman Prize and the Lifetime Achievement Literary Award.

DAVID JOHNSON is Senior Lecturer in the English Department at the Open University. He is the author of *Shakespeare and South Africa* (1996) and *Imagining the Cape Colony* (2011), the principal author of *Jurisprudence: A South African Perspective* (2001) and the coeditor of *A Historical Companion to Postcolonial Literatures in English* (2005).

RUSSELL H. KASCHULA is Head of the School of Languages and Professor of African Language Studies at Rhodes University, specialising in isiXhosa literature and Applied Language Studies. His academic books include the co-authored *Communicating across Cultures in South Africa* (1995) and *The Bones of the Ancestors are Shaking: Xhosa Oral Poetry in Context* (2002). He has also authored award-winning short stories and novels for young adults.

DIRK KLOPPER is Professor of English at Rhodes University. He publishes regularly on aspects of South African literature in various journals, and is co-author, with Gareth Cornwell and Craig Mackenzie, of *The Columbia Guide to South African Literature in English since 1945* (2010). His current research focuses on nature writing in South African literature.

LOREN KRUGER is the author of *The National Stage* (1992), *The Drama of South Africa* (1999) and *Post Imperial Brecht* (2004) as well as numerous journal articles. She has served as editor of *Theatre Journal* and contributing editor of *Theatre Research International*, and is currently on the advisory boards of *Modern Drama* and the *South African Theatre Journal*, among others. She teaches at the University of Chicago.

NHLANHLA MAAKE is currently the Dean of the Faculty of Humanities at the University of Limpopo. He has held lectureship and professorial positions at the Universities of the Witwatersrand, London (SOAS), Pretoria, Vista and North-West. He has published twenty books of fiction and non-fiction. His most recent book is *Barbarism in Higher Education: Once Upon a Time in a University*.

CRAIG MACKENZIE teaches in the English Department at the University of Johannesburg. His most recent book publication is *The Columbia Guide to South African Literature in English since 1945* (2010), co-written with Gareth Cornwell and Dirk Klopper.

MOKGALE MAKGOPA is Associate Professor and Dean of the School of Human and Social Sciences at the University of Venda in South Africa. He holds a D. Litt. et Phil. in African Languages from UNISA, has published papers in leading journals, and has participated in regional and international conferences in the following areas of specialisation: literature, indigenous knowledge systems, folklore and sociolinguistics.

NTONGELA MASILELA is Professor of English and World Literature and Professor of Creative Studies at Pitzer College in Claremont (Los Angeles), California. He is the author of *The Cultural Modernity of H. I. E. Dhlomo* (2007), and is the architect of the website New African Movement about the making of South African modernity throughout the twentieth century.

PETER D. MCDONALD is Fellow of St Hugh's College and Professor of English at the University of Oxford. His principal publications include *British Literary Culture and Publishing Practice, 1880–1914* (1997), *Making Meaning: 'Printers of the Mind' and Other Essays by D. F. McKenzie*, co-edited with Michael Suarez (2002), and *The Literature Police: Apartheid Censorship and its Cultural Consequences* (2009).

THENGANI H. NGWENYA is the Director of the Centre for Excellence in Learning and Teaching (CELT) at Durban University of Technology.

GERRIT OLIVIER is Professor of Afrikaans and Dutch Literature and previous Dean of the Faculty of Humanities at the University of Witwatersrand. He is currently located in the School of Arts and is focusing most of his attention on postgraduate supervision and a study of the importance of land in Afrikaans literature.

BHEKIZIZWE PETERSON is Professor of African Literature at the University of the Witwatersrand. He is the author of *Monarchs, Missionaries and African Intellectuals* (2000) and co-authored the screenplays for the films *Fools* (1997), *Zulu Love Letter* (2004) and *Zwelidumile* (2010).

TLHALO RADITLHALO lectures in English Literary Studies at the University of South Africa, specifically in the field of South African and African literatures. He was part of the editorial panel for *Es'kia* (2002), *Es'kia Continued* (2004) and *Eskia: May you Grow as Big as an Elephant* (2006), and was the compiler of Njabulo S. Ndebele's *Fine Lines from the Box: Further Thoughts about our Country* (2007). He is a contributor to the forthcoming *Cambridge History of South Africa*, volume II.

DANIEL ROUX is currently Senior Lecturer in the Department of English at the University of Stellenbosch. His research focuses largely on writing from and about the prison in postcolonial Africa.

MEG SAMUELSON is Associate Professor in the Department of English at the University of Stellenbosch. She has published widely on South African literature, including the book *Remembering the Nation, Dismembering Women? Stories of the South African Transition* (2007). She is currently co-authoring, with Dorothy Driver, a study of South African literatures focusing on land, sea and city and exploring representations of Oceanic Africa.

MATTHEW SHUM lectures in the Department of English at the University of KwaZulu-Natal in Durban. He works primarily in the area of Romanticism and colonialism and is currently working on a monograph entitled *Improvisations of Empire: Thomas Pringle in Scotland, the Cape Colony and London, 1789–1832*.

CHRISTIAAN SWANEPOEL taught African Languages at UNISA (Pretoria) for twenty-eight years, serving ten simultaneously as Vice-Dean. He became Vice-Principal Academic and Research in 2001 until retirement at the end of 2006, when he was appointed Professor Emeritus and Research Fellow. He co-authored *Southern African Literature in African Languages* with D. B. Ntuli, and co-edited, with Albert Gérard and colleagues, *Comparative Literature and African Literatures*.

MICHAEL TITLESTAD lectures in the Department of English at the University of the Witwatersrand, Johannesburg. He is the author of *Making the Changes: Jazz in South African Literature* (2005). Currently he writes essays about South African fiction, contemporary music, and literatures of the sea. He is currently working on a volume of essays concerning the representation of the shipwreck.

HEDLEY TWIDLE grew up in Namaqualand, studied at Oxford and York and is now a lecturer in the Department of English at the University of Cape Town.

H. P. (HENNIE) VAN COLLER is Chair of the Department of Afrikaans and Dutch, German and French at the University of the Free State and a Distinguished Professor. He is the editor of a three-part literary history, *Perspektief en Profiel* (1998–2005), an award-winning literary critic, a translator and a former chairperson of Die Suid-Afrikaanse Akademie vir Wetenskap en Kuns.

ANDREW VAN DER VLIES, a native of the Eastern Cape, was educated at Rhodes University and at the University of Oxford and presently teaches at Queen Mary, University of London. He has published widely on South African writers and on South African and postcolonial book history and print cultures, and is the author of *South African Textual Cultures* (2007).

MALVERN VAN WYK SMITH is Professor Emeritus in the Department of English at Rhodes University. His publications include *Drummer Hodge: The Poetry of the Anglo–Boer War* (1978), *Shades of Adamastor* (1988) and *Grounds of Contest: A Survey of South African English Literature* (1990), as well as articles in many journals. His book *The First Ethiopians: The Image of Africa and Africans in the Early Mediterranean World* appeared in 2009.

LOUISE VILJOEN is Professor in the Department of Afrikaans and Dutch at Stellenbosch University and works in the field of Afrikaans literature and literary theory with a special focus on postmodernism, postcolonialism, gender, identity and (auto)biographical writing. She has published a book on the work of Antjie Krog, *Ons Ongehoorde Soort. Beskouings oor die Werk van Antjie Krog* (2009).

ANDRIES VISAGIE is Professor in Afrikaans and Dutch Literature at the University of Pretoria. His publications are mostly devoted to representations of masculinity and sexuality in Afrikaans fiction, and to autobiographical writing.

TONY VOSS was born in Namibia and educated in South Africa and the USA and is now a Research Associate of the University of KwaZulu-Natal, Durban. He has published on Shakespeare, the eighteenth century, South African literature, the unicorn and the Mazeppa motif.

HEIN WILLEMSE is Professor of Literature in the Department of Afrikaans at the University of Pretoria. He has been the editor-in-chief of *Tydskrif vir Letterkunde* since 2003.

CATHERINE WOEBER lectures in English Studies on the Pietermaritzburg campus of the University of KwaZulu-Natal. She has a Ph.D. in African Literature from the University of the Witwatersrand, and has published on black South African autobiographical and political writing and African modernity

Acknowledgements

The editors wish to thank the British Academy for a significant contribution to the costs of this research. Our thanks for support are also due to the University of York and the F. R. Leavis Fund, which is administered by the university's Department of English and Related Literature.

The editors owe a particular debt of gratitude to Hedley Twidle, who has served not only as one of our authors but who has been an astute and tireless web technician, research assistant and copy-editor, working closely with us from the inception of the project. Hedley's versatility and resourcefulness have been, quite simply, indispensable.

We also wish to thank Wendy Williamson, who provided additional web support, and Karlien van der Schyff, who contributed to the copy-editing. Mbongiseni Buthelezi, also one of our authors, was generous with his time and expertise when we needed additional guidance with regard to oral culture and literature in some of the African languages. Many of our contributors played a role in the shaping of the volume, either through the initial workshop or in subsequent correspondence, making this history a genuinely collaborative project.

Note on racial nomenclature and languages

The history of racial classification in South Africa makes it necessary to use terms referring to different racial groups; this is done without any implication that these categorisations have a scientific basis. The terms 'black' and 'African' are used to refer to the indigenous Bantu language speakers and their descendants, 'white' to European immigrants and their descendants, and 'coloured' (without capitalisation or quotation marks) to what the apartheid legislators called 'Coloured' or 'mixed-race' peoples. The largest group of Asian South Africans identify themselves as Indian.

In opposition to the official vocabulary of apartheid, '"coloured"' in quotation marks and 'so-called coloured' were widely used, but the term can now be employed without any stigma. During the ascendancy of the Black Consciousness movement, 'black' or 'Black' was often used collectively with reference to African, coloured and Indian peoples, but that is less frequently the case today.

The earliest inhabitants of the country, when encountered by European settlers, were called 'Hottentots' (a pastoral people of the western and northern Cape) and 'Bushmen' (hunter-gatherers widespread through the country). The former are referred to as the 'Khoikhoi', the latter as the 'San' or 'Bushmen' (see Chapter 1, note 2, on these terms). The two groups are closely related and are known collectively as the 'Khoi-San' or 'Khoisan' peoples. Only small populations survive in South Africa today.

Numerous languages are spoken in South Africa, eleven of which have been declared 'official languages' (see Introduction, p. 2, and note 2). The names of the indigenous languages are formed with prefixes: thus the Zulu people speak isiZulu. Similarly, Xhosa: isiXhosa; Ndebele: isiNdebele; Swazi: Siswati; Tswana: Setswana; Tsonga: Xitsonga; Venda: Tshivenda. The Sotho language, Sesotho, is distinguished from Northern Sotho (Sesotho sa Leboa), which is also referred to as Sepedi.

Introduction

DAVID ATTWELL AND DEREK ATTRIDGE

The names of a small number of South African writers are familiar around the globe: they include Olive Schreiner, Alan Paton, Athol Fugard, Nadine Gordimer, André Brink, Wilbur Smith and J. M. Coetzee. Others, such as Zakes Mda, Damon Galgut, Njabulo Ndebele, Antjie Krog, Marlene van Niekerk, Ivan Vladislavić and Zoë Wicomb, have growing international reputations. Earlier periods recorded fame for writers whose stars have now faded, among them Sarah Gertrude Millin, Daphne Rooke and Laurens van der Post. Many South Africans have gone on to make names for themselves in other countries: among authors well known in the United Kingdom, for instance, are Dan Jacobson, Barbara Trapido, James McClure, Christopher Hope, Justin Cartwright and Tom Sharpe.

A roll-call of this sort, however, gives very little sense of the range and richness of South Africa's literary output. Several literary traditions, oral and written, have fed into the complex array of verbal productions charted in this volume, at times influencing or infiltrating one another, and at other times ignoring or challenging one another. From indigenous folk-tales to European elite art, these traditions have been constantly reworked and reinvented, creating an extensive body of literary art that continues to grow, despite the smallness of the home market and the very limited financial means of most potential readers. South Africa's fraught political history, with its continual inroads into the lives of ordinary people, has given rise to remarkable literary achievements while at the same time skewing the institutional processes whereby works of literature are produced and disseminated. The establishment of a democratic system of government and the ending of state-sponsored racism make it possible to offer a survey of the entire history of South African literature from a vantage point that was formerly unavailable. This is not to say that the present moment is a plateau of serenity; the challenges that face the reborn nation remain considerable, and South Africa's writers, while not averse to an occasional celebratory moment, continue to explore the difficulties and dangers of twenty-first century life, at once intensely local and inescapably global.

Readers of *The Cambridge History of South African Literature* will therefore find South Africa's literary culture extraordinarily diverse in histories, voices and traditions. The source of the diversity is the country's social range and multilingualism. Since the disposition of the languages is fundamental to what follows, a brief description is in order. South Africa may not have as many languages as other postcolonial societies like India or, to restrict ourselves to the African continent, Nigeria, but what is unusual is the granting of official status to the eleven most commonly spoken languages in the country, a position inscribed in the post-apartheid Constitution in direct response to the situation prior to 1994, when only English and Afrikaans enjoyed this status.[1] The egalitarian vision behind the constitutional provision for the indigenous African languages will be slow to realise in practice, given the hegemonic status of English, but the legal position shared by the predominant languages reflects current political aspirations. In numerically descending order of their mother-tongue speakers, the official languages of South Africa are isiZulu, isiXhosa, Afrikaans, Sepedi, Setswana, English, Sesotho, Xitsonga, siSwati, Tshivenda and isiNdebele.[2] Whilst English is used as a second, third or even a fourth language by many speakers, it is currently dominant in education, commerce and government.

Since each of the languages has a literature – and in the case of the indigenous languages, an orature and a literature in symbiosis – the country's literary range is so extensive that it places the idea of a national literature in question. In this respect, South Africa's literature is an extension of its national culture. It is no accident that following the first democratic elections in 1994, the framers of the symbolism of state chose for the national motto – *!ke e:/xarra//ke*, 'people who are different joining together' – an ancient language (|Xam, from the Khoi-San group), which is no longer spoken. A consensus around the desire for indigeneity and authenticity could be secured more easily by using

1 See www.info.gov.za/documents/constitution/1996/96cons1.htm
2 The names given here for the African languages are those employed by the language users themselves. In some cases the prefix is dropped in the adjectival form (isiZulu becomes 'Zulu poetry', etc.). 'Sepedi' is widely used, although the Pan-South African Language Board (PanSALB) prefers 'Sesotho sa Leboa' (Northern Sotho), of which Sepedi is one dialect among others. Khoi-San will be used to refer collectively to the Khoi and San groups of languages, the hyphen indicating that they are historically differentiated. There are arguments for Khoe, Khoesan and Khoe-San, but these variants are less common. Other languages used in the country and acknowledged in the constitution are, in addition to the Khoi-San groups, sign language, Arabic, German, Greek, Gujarati, Hebrew, Hindi, Portuguese, Sanskrit, Tamil, Telegu and Urdu, and several local creoles and pidgins. See http://pansalb.org.za/index.html for further information.

a language which had no claim to being a *lingua franca*, although it has a greater claim than most to longevity in the country. With the literature, similarly, there is no overriding, definitive principle of unity, although there have been several attempts to find a metaphor in which a principle of unity-in-diversity might be instantiated.

The challenge of producing a collective description of South Africa's literary past has given rise to a series of particularly lively attempts over the past three decades, of which only the high points can be considered here.[3] In the late 1970s, Stephen Gray took the lead in offering both ontological and functional descriptions which remain useful points of reference. The whole field, he wrote in *South African Literature: An Introduction*, 'is like an archipelago. The islands with their peaks protrude in set positions, even if one does not readily see the connections between them and the surface' (p. 14). Referring to English-language writing, he continued: 'it is related to adjacent landmasses . . . the mainland of English literature; diminishingly, the British Commonwealth of literature; and increasingly, the continent of Africa which gives it its active nourishment' (p. 14). The archipelago metaphor is appealing because it enables one to imagine the distinctive qualities of each of the literatures while positing the unity of the underlying landmass to which each is attached; nevertheless, one suspects that its usefulness has something to do with its continuing to obscure rather than map the underlying unity. As if acknowledging this, Gray proposed that what was needed was the study of how each of the islands was shaped by the forces that linked them: 'what it is necessary to chart now is what tides and drifts and spins, what internal connections, have made them what they are' (p. 14).

The question Gray was wrestling with – the one that confronts all literary history in South Africa and, indeed, any multilingual society – is whether a literature should be defined by its relationship to a particular language, or whether the shaping influences cut across language barriers.[4] If the emphasis is to fall on immanent developments within the literature of a particular language, then certain satisfactions will follow: the opportunity to create

---

3 Literary-historiographical literature in South Africa has roots in the nineteenth century, and begins to express nationalist sentiment in the early twentieth (see Andries Walter Oliphant, 'Nonidentity and Reciprocity' and 'Fabrications and the Question of a National South African Literature').

4 Oliphant classifies past literary historiography into *monolingual*, *bilingual* and *multilingual* models. The bilingual is earliest and reflects the post-1910, Union position of the white colonial state seeking to unite English and Afrikaans. The monolingual is ethnic-nationalist and is expressed most forcefully in Afrikaans literary history, although it finds its way into English as well. Oliphant supports the multilingual position (associated with Gray, Albert Gérard, Michael Chapman, D. B. Ntuli and C. F. Swanepoel and others), which is also adopted here.

linear narratives as one author or generation follows another, in patterns of continuity and reaction. This version of literary history, with its roots in the traditions of literary criticism, is certainly valid and has produced some of the most useful accounts of South African literature: for example, A. C. Jordan's *Towards an African Literature* (1973) on literature in isiXhosa; Malvern van Wyk Smith's *Grounds of Contest* (1990) on literature in English; and J. C. Kannemeyer on Afrikaans literature in *Die Afrikaanse Literatuur, 1652–2004* (2005, with earlier editions).

When viewed from a wider, or world-historical, perspective, useful though it may be, single-language literary history seems essentially nostalgic. Its roots lie in the German romantic philosophy of Wilhelm von Humboldt and Johann Gottfried Herder and the view that national character is expressed in a national language. Albert Gérard, whose pioneering example is important to the present volume, believed that even in most European countries, let alone African ones, the single-language approach obscures a real plurality of national cultures and tends to be associated with powerful metropoles ('Towards a National History', p. 92). In the present context, he argued that 'the study of any "national literature" in Africa is bound to be effected on a translinguistic basis' (p. 97). *The Cambridge History of South African Literature*, though written in English for a wide international readership, is multilingual in the attention it gives to South Africa's literatures. It takes the view that the story of each of the country's literatures appears in a different light when viewed in the context of the others.[5] In taking this position as editors we do not see our task as especially revisionist; it is, rather, the fulfilment of a long-held aspiration.

In developing this position we find ourselves in agreement with literary historians in comparable postcolonial situations. Sisir Kumar Das, for example, in the multi-volume *A History of Indian Literature*, argues convincingly that the language–literature equation, valuable though it is, is not a *sufficient* condition for understanding literary history in a multilingual society. If the defining element in a national literature is said to be not just the relationships between languages and their literatures, but the relationships between *people and their forms of expression*, then the need to embrace multilingualism becomes obvious. Das argues that political unity, like language, is also a useful but insufficient

---

5 This is true of all the literatures, including those written in European languages. It is generally accepted that postcolonial literatures in the European languages (Caribbean, Australian, Canadian, New Zealand, South African) should be studied as constituents of their national literary cultures rather than as supplements to their European origins. This position assumes the influence of history, geography and the multilingualism of postcolonial nation-states. See Riemenschneider's collection, *The History and Historiography of Commonwealth Literature*, which includes a number of essays on this theme, including Jürgen Schäfer's, 'Nation or Language?'

criterion for defining the communality that informs literary history in national terms; what defines the idea of a unitary Indian literary history for Das are forms of communality which are essentially cultural. In this regard, he mentions several religious and literary traditions reaching back to the concept of *Bhāratavarsa* mentioned in the *Mahābharata*, in which a 'unified cultural zone' is defined and in which a number of the ancient languages of the subcontinent cross one another (pp. 1–4).

Does South Africa, notoriously divided against itself, have anything comparable to the traditions Das describes? It would seem not: if there are grounds for describing the relationships existing amongst the literatures of South Africa in national terms, they would have to be found elsewhere than in ancient, scripted tradition. But we could begin to delineate such grounds by mentioning the following three factors.

Firstly, there is undoubtedly a unifying history which has produced some powerful national narratives; it would be fair to say, a national mythology. To say this is not to assert a uniformity of experience, nor a consensus, not to mention a common identity, but it is to affirm that South Africans generally understand what they disagree about. A shared history has produced politicised discursive reflexes that are commonly understood. South Africa might be radically heterogeneous in linguistic and cultural terms, but a common history has been imposed on it, a history which is the product of its violent absorption into the modern world-system. Colonialism and then apartheid do not define all of South Africa's history, certainly not its cultural origins, but it is axiomatic that European expansion from the seventeenth to the nineteenth centuries set in train the processes that would lead to the development of the nation-state. In many postcolonial societies, particularly in Africa, national cultures are unevenly mapped on to nation-states; nevertheless, in South Africa's case the peculiarly aggressive form of modernity that was imposed on the region – racial capitalism abetted by the state in successive forms – has had the effect of creating pan-ethnic forms of association in the fields of labour, the economy, political life and cultural expression. We would agree with Michael Chapman that this spine of historical event provides the basic points of reference for a collective history of the country's many literatures.[6]

6 Literary historiography has raised the question of the instability of national borders, which are crossed by several languages and by patterns of economic migration. Michael Chapman goes as far as to include the literatures of all South Africa's neighbours in his *Southern African Literatures*. The decision we have taken is to focus on the juridical (and bibliographic) entity known as South Africa, which is marked by a particular historical experience, but we do take migrant cultures (such as Sotho orature) into account when they have become an established part of national life. We take comfort from the fact that boundary definitions around what constitutes English literature would be just as difficult to define.

Secondly, there is the question of translingual influence, which is a persistent feature of South Africa's cultural landscape. (To gauge the translingual influences on the English language alone, one need only spend a few hours perusing the *Dictionary of South African English on Historical Principles*.) In South African literary studies, however, it is not generally agreed that the multilingualism of the country's speech communities translates into the kind of cross-pollination that we might associate with literary influence. In 1996, two years after the democratic transition, Van Wyk Smith (the author of *Grounds of Contest*, mentioned earlier, and one of the contributors to the present volume) delivered a memorable critique of a rather premature and celebratory form of national multiculturalism. Taking his point of reference from Harold Bloom in coining the phrase 'the anxiety of non-influence', Van Wyk Smith argued that there was little literary substance to the forms of interracial and cross-linguistic influence that did exist in South Africa, certainly not much that would satisfy Bloom's criterion of influence, in which authors feel an intimate connection with the work of their predecessors. Where cross-cultural connections were apparent, they were merely a function of writers' 'exploring the same subject matter because they happen to have been written in the same part of the world' ('White Writing/Writing Black', p. 75).

In the era of rainbow-nation euphoria, this critique felt like a cold shower, although on its own terms it was well illustrated and persuasive. Now that the dust has settled on the 1990s, it seems that what was wrong with the argument was that its terms were too narrow: to argue that an immanent sense of tradition, as Bloom describes it, should be *the* measure of cross-cultural influence in a country where the languages are as knotted together as they are in South Africa, is to look for roses amongst the thickets of thorn trees and foreign scrub that make up South Africa's cultural scene. If cross-cultural influence is seldom discernible at the level of the individual author responding to a particular genius, it is unmistakeable in broader generic and rhetorical terms. Communally defined traditions *do* travel across the language barriers in South Africa: biblical allegory finds its way into African-nationalist historical fiction; Shakespearean tragedy shows up in radio drama in isiZulu; praise poetry migrates into imperial romance; oral tales migrate into modernist short stories; the Anglo-American lyric enters Soweto poetry, etc. – the list could be endlessly extended. These connections are not those of the private study but of colonial modernity's encounters in places like the mission school classroom, the colonial kitchen, the political meeting, the frontier courtroom, the shebeen, the apartheid jail, the rehearsal room, the radio studio, the suburban writers' group, the editorial desks of dozens of arts magazines and publishers. Admittedly, the precise itineraries of these generic migrations are difficult to trace but such is the nature of the culture and the work that it demands of its literary historians.

Thirdly, a development from the foregoing, there are widespread practices of translingual writing and translation which reveal the extent to which multilingualism is constitutive of the field. By translingual writing we mean writing done by authors who work in more than one language and whose writing is informed by knowledge of several languages. Amongst their number are generations of leading authors: Sol T. Plaatje, Eugene Marais, Louis Leipoldt, the Dhlomo brothers, Herman Charles Bosman, André Brink, J. M. Coetzee, Antjie Krog. The category of translingual writing could be extended to include writing in which the reader is invited to hear, overhear, or imagine languages being spoken or written which are not actually the language of the text. Such writing, which seeks to capture social texture, is endemic in South African literature. In *White Writing*, Coetzee has explored what he calls processes of linguistic 'transfer' in which non-English speech (Afrikaans and isiZulu, in his examples from Pauline Smith and Alan Paton) is rendered in simplified forms of English in order to build ideological capital. But this is only one form of translingual practice in a diverse and complex field which includes Coetzee's own writing in English and Afrikaans (*In the Heart of the Country*). In each of the stories in Njabulo Ndebele's landmark collection of short fiction, *Fools*, we are expected to imagine multilingual conversations taking place in Charterston township; the text is thus already an act of translation.

Stephen Gray was therefore right when he identified cultural translation as a defining feature of the literature: 'the [South African] writer is always forced into a position of having to negotiate between extremes in crossing the language–colour barrier; he or she can only be a syncretist and hybridizer'; 'the basic act of writing is of carrying information across one or other socio-political barrier, literally of "trading"'; 'trading of literary forms – like the lullaby, the praise-poem, the elegy, and the letter – is shown to be part of the continuing business of a shared literary system that is bigger than the sum of its parts'. In this view, translation 'is more than the technical transposition of a work across from one language to another. It is an act of unblocking channels of communication to insist on the reciprocity of human feelings . . . the arrangement of the work foregrounds translation itself as a major, life-sustaining activity' ('Some Problems of Writing Historiography', pp. 20–1). Cultural translation is an important point of focus for South African criticism, theory and historiography; even if some of the humanist leanings of Gray's description have been questioned (as they are in Leon de Kock's chapter on translation in this volume), his argument remains generally valid.

De Kock's own contributions to South Africa's literary historiography have been provocative. Taking his point of reference from Noël Mostert's monumental history of the Eastern Cape, *Frontiers* ('if there is a hemispheric seam to the world between the Occident and the Orient, it must be along the eastern seaboard of Africa', *Frontiers*, p. xv), De Kock proposed in 2001 that the *seam* is a defining metaphor because it identifies a site where incommensurate elements are stitched together. (De Kock's language is less benign when he writes of the seam as a scar requiring suturing, the nib of the pen being the suturing instrument.) The seam, he argues, is the place where 'difference and sameness are hitched together' – 'always uneasily' because the seam continues to mark the place of difference ('South Africa in the Global Imaginary', pp. 272–6). Here we have a more sceptical version of Gray's trading metaphor, but a similar concept. More recently (2005), De Kock has posed the question 'Does South African Literature Still Exist?', by which he means that the counterhegemonic, didactic version of literary studies that prevailed in the English-language academy during the apartheid period has become tired; he welcomes the passing of politicised versions of South African literary studies while ushering in their successor, a looser notion of 'literature *in* South Africa'. Despite the playfulness of De Kock's exaggerations, his rhetoric still reproduces the pressures of the local debate.

As De Kock implies, literary historiography in South Africa, like other areas of its national life, is bedeviled by the recent past. The debate over the relative merits of the language–literature equation as against a multilingual perspective is a case in point. As has been mentioned, for decades a multilingual, collective literary history has been the stated goal of many a literary historian and editor. Gérard went as far as to suggest that the fact that South Africa had not produced a 'polyethnic' literary history was indicative of the effects of apartheid on the country's intellectual life (*European-Language Writing*, p. 172). Once the era of formal apartheid came to an end, the project was attempted: Michael Chapman led the way with his encyclopedic work, *Southern African Literatures* (1996, 2003). Despite its scale and political credentials, it was to meet with opposition from conservative English quarters for its tendentiousness, and from non-English quarters for its apparent foreshortenings and implicit anglocentrism. This was followed by Christopher Heywood's *A History of South African Literature* (2004), a book which has not entered the debate in any serious sense because its historiography is too idiosyncratic and it is flawed by persistent factual errors. In their introduction to the recent *Columbia Guide* to *South African Literature in English since 1945* (2010), Cornwell, Klopper and MacKenzie go as far as to say that existing attempts to write 'integrative' histories – Gray, Chapman, Heywood – succeed only in demonstrating the failure of their intentions; they are 'an optimistic gesture in the optative mood – the expression of a political ideology rather than an objectively existent state of affairs' ('South African Literature in English', p. 3). For these editors, such gestures are merely reactive in their desperation to put behind them the racial and linguistic separatism of apartheid.

The historiography adopted by Cornwell and colleagues, which develops from the argument made by Van Wyk Smith, insists that properly literary history is only interested in what they call 'idiogenetic' processes, that is, the processes of 'formal exhaustion and renewal' that are internal to a particular tradition. The 'allogenetic', which is the history of 'social and political events and conditions', is regarded as falling outside of the domain of literary history. Their preference for the idiogenetic over the allogenetic, or internal over external causality, serves their purpose of justifying the *Columbia Guide*'s focus on English, but it would surely be in conflict with the sources informing their terms, which lie in the aesthetic theory of Marx and Engels. Dialectical theory would normally assume that literary history, like any interpretive narrative, would be comprised of *both* elements, just as Saussure would argue of language in general, which developed under the pressure of both internal and external events. Saussure was, of course, mainly interested in the systemic properties of language and chose to emphasise the internal for his own purposes, but his recognition of the nature of language change as involving both internal and external factors is clear. (His recognition of the effects of colonialism on language change is especially interesting in the present context; *Course in General Linguistics*, pp. 21–2.) Similarly, literary history and historiography need a dialectical position in which the parts can be seen in all their uniqueness but in the context of the whole. The various literatures in South Africa do speak to one another but when they *fail* to do so, this failure is no less significant as we seek to understand the complexity of the picture.

The position adopted in the *Cambridge History* is in broad agreement with Oliphant, who has theorised the demands of literary historiography from the point of view of 'the multilingual fact' of South Africa ('Nonidentity and Reciprocity', p. 241). Citing Ntuli and Swanepoel, he argues that the 'political developments which reversed the attitudes of separateness and exclusivity', and which have steered towards 'national unity and inclusiveness', will 'eventually render all segregationist approaches anachronistic' (p. 249). In this position, the theoretical complexity of the field is deferred to history itself:

South African modernity has consistently produced centrifugal forces which have undermined separatism. This historical fact translates into the pragmatism which recognises, in Oliphant's words, that 'the object of South African literary studies may therefore be defined as consisting of all the literatures in the languages spoken within the borders of South Africa as specified in the Constitution of 1996' (p. 252).

In a second essay on this theme, Oliphant asks whether the accommodating position just described is sufficient for the purpose of defining South African literature in properly *national* terms. His answer is no: 'a national literature does not exist in South Africa' because the country does not have a common national culture ('Fabrications', p. 22). On the face of it, Oliphant's conclusions in these two essays seem to contradict one another: on one hand, the object of South African literary studies is simply the literatures of all the languages spoken in the country; on the other hand, the adjective 'South African' has no force in pointing to a common, national identity. There is no contradiction if we accept the strictness of what Oliphant means by a national literature or culture. For him, a 'national' literature would involve, 'minimally', a 'single all-embracing narrative with a nationalist theme in which all the literatures are shown to have participated over time' (pp. 22–3). Such a narrative clearly does not exist in South Africa, as he correctly points out, certainly not at present, although as he suggests it may develop in future (p. 23). But is this strict definition of a national culture sustainable? As Oliphant recognises (p. 13), *nowhere* is the nation state, as the juridical and geopolitical entity, underpinned by a common national culture. The pragmatic definition of national literature which Oliphant proposes, which we have accepted, and which simply uses the plural, should not allow itself to be haunted by a chimera of cultural unity which is simply not currently a historical possibility.

How might we translate this broad, accommodating definition of what constitutes South African literary studies into practice? The solution is firstly, to cede authorship to a collective. With the best will in the world, a multilingual literary history is unlikely to be written by a single author, who is more likely to produce a monolingual account of a multilingual situation. The practice we have followed is proposed by Gérard, who speaking specifically of Ghanaian literary history but with all of Africa's literatures in mind, said,

> Literary history on a national scale can only be carried out by a team of . . . scholars, capable of providing a well-informed and correlated account of all creative writing produced in English and in the . . . African languages. The approach is bound to be multilingual and any satisfactory overall survey

will have to be rooted in an intimate knowledge of the cultural background of the societies concerned, including their oral tradition and recent social history. ('Towards a National History', p. 96)

The *Cambridge History* meets Gérard's standards in bringing together a team of forty-three authors (from South Africa, Europe, Australia and the United States) who are representative of current scholarship in the field and who have appropriate expertise in the country's various languages and cultural traditions. The literary history presented here is appropriately multi-voiced, so much so that on occasion, similar material is treated with different emphases by two or more authors. More than just a gathering of information available elsewhere, this volume also represents a significant research endeavour in a number of areas. The project has been collaborative from an early stage: a workshop with the majority of the contributors was held in Johannesburg on 2 August 2008 and a website has been used to share information, circulate drafts and invite comments. Contributors have also been invited to consider other essays in the volume and to cross-refer where appropriate.

The approach has been to combine a broad historical perspective with analysis which is specific to each of the literatures under discussion. To avoid forcing a single developmental narrative, Part I ('Oratures, oral histories, origins') ranges across periods in its consideration of oratures in indigenous languages, while the four broadly chronological Parts II to V ('Exploration, early modernity and Enlightenment at the Cape, 1488–1820', 'Empire, resistance and national beginnings, 1820–1910', 'Modernism and transnational culture, 1910–1948', and 'Apartheid and its aftermath, 1948 to the present') allow for particular foci as well as overlaps and cross-period connections. The final section, Part VI ('South African literature: continuities and contrasts') is devoted to topics traced over a longer historical span, and in which the comparative method becomes more prominent. Each section begins with an extended headnote providing historical context, identifying major trends and locating points of comparison. The chapters that follow pursue particular histories, focusing on specific themes or groups of writers. We trust that the approach and methodology chosen for this volume will be useful to the growing global interest in South Africa's literatures and their history. Readers will appreciate that it is not possible to be absolutely even-handed or completely representative in covering so extensive a field, and it is inevitable that there will be objections to the relative lack of attention given to particular writers, performers, genres or periods; nevertheless, it is our hope that *The Cambridge History of South African Literature* will serve a useful purpose as the most fully representative collection of historical scholarship on the country's extensive literary production yet to have been published.

Bibliography

Chapman, M. *Southern African Literatures*, 2nd edn, Pietermaritzburg: University of KwaZulu-Natal Press, 2003.

Coetzee, J. M. *In the Heart of the Country*, Johannesburg: Ravan, 1978.

White Writing: On the Culture of Letters in South Africa, Johannesburg: Radix (in association with Yale University Press), 1988.

Cornwell, G., D. Klopper and C. MacKenzie. 'South African Literature in English since 1945: Long Walk to Ordinariness', in G. Cornwell, D. Klopper and C. MacKenzie (eds.), *The Columbia Guide to South African Literature in English since 1945*, New York: Columbia University Press, 2010, 1–42.

Das, S. K. *A History of Indian Literature, 1800–1910: Western Impact, Indian Response*, New Delhi: Sahitya Akademi, 1991.

De Kock, L. 'Does South African Literature Still Exist? Or: South African Literature is Dead, Long Live Literature in South Africa', *English in Africa* 32:2 (2005), 69–83.

'Introduction', *Poetics Today*, special issue on 'South Africa in the Global Imaginary', 22:2 (2001), 263–98.

A Dictionary of South African English on Historical Principles: South African Words and their Origins, Cape Town: Oxford University Press, 1996.

Gérard, A. *European-Language Writing in Sub-Saharan Africa*, Budapest: Akadémiai Kiadó, 1986.

Four African Literatures: Xhosa, Sotho, Zulu, Amharic, Berkeley: University of California Press, 1971.

'Towards a National History of Ghanaian Literature: A Case Study in Methodology', in Riemenschneider, *History and Historiography of Commonwealth Literature*, 91–8.

Gray, S. 'Some Problems of Writing Historiography in Southern Africa', *Literator* 10:2 (1989), 16–24.

South African Literature: An Introduction, Cape Town: David Philip, 1979.

Heywood, C. *A History of South African Literature*, Cambridge University Press, 2004.

Herder, J. G. *Philosophical Writings*, ed. M. N. Forster, Cambridge University Press, 2002.

Jordan, A. C. *Towards an African Literature: The Emergence of Literary Form in Xhosa*, Berkeley: University of California Press, 1973.

Kannemeyer, J. C. *Die Afrikaanse Literatuur, 1652–2004*, Cape Town: Human & Rousseau, 2005.

Mostert, N. *Frontiers: The Epic of South Africa's Creation and The Tragedy of the Xhosa People*, London: Jonathan Cape, 1992.

Ndebele, N. *Fools and other Stories*, Johannesburg: Ravan, 1983.

Ntuli, D. B., and C. F. Swanepoel. *Southern African Literature in African Languages: A Concise Historical Perspective*, Pretoria: Acacia, 1993.

Oliphant, A. W. 'Fabrications and the Question of a National South African Literature', *Journal of Literary Studies* 20:1–2 (June 2004), 5–24.

'Nonidentity and Reciprocity in Conceptualising South African Literary Studies', *Journal of Literary Studies* 19:3–4 (December 2003), 237–54.

Riemenschneider, D. (ed.). *The History and Historiography of Commonwealth Literature*, Tübingen: Gunter Narr Verlag, 1983.

Saussure, Ferdinand de. *Course in General Linguistics*, Peru, IL: Open Court, 1986.

Van Wyk Smith, M. *Grounds of Contest: A Survey of South African English Literature*, Cape Town: Juta, 1990.

'White Writing/Writing Black: The Anxiety of Non-Influence', in J. A. Smit, J. van Wyk and J-P. Wade (eds.), *Re-Thinking South African Literary History*, Durban: Y Press, 1996, 72–83.

Von Humboldt, W. *On Language*, ed. Michael Losonsky, Cambridge University Press, 1999.

ORATURES, ORAL HISTORIES, ORIGINS

South Africa's indigenous orature is marked, on one hand, by its longevity, since it includes the oral culture of hunter-gatherer societies now known collectively as the San; on the other hand it is marked by its modernity, because oral performance in South Africa is continually being reinvented in contemporary, media-saturated environments. This range is fully represented in the research collected in Part I, as is the linguistic and generic variety of the oral cultures of the region.

These chapters bear out Liz Gunner's observation about recent research in African orature in *The Cambridge History of African and Caribbean Literature*:

> the older model of freestanding oral genres, manifested in the often very fine collections of single or relatively few genres of 'oral literature' from a particular African society such as those published by the pathbreaking Oxford Library of African Literature series in the late 1960s and the 1970s . . . has been superseded by theories of orality that embrace a far more interactive and interdependent sense of cultural practices and 'text'.
>
> (F. Abiola Irele and S. Gikandi, eds., Cambridge University Press, 2004, p. 11)

The research collected here demonstrates this trend, with each chapter paying particular attention to the ways in which prevailing social, cultural, economic and political conditions have shaped the genres under discussion. Whilst the chapters are organised on a linguistic basis in an effort to cover all the major indigenous languages of the region, the authors have been concerned to move away from notions of oral culture as tied to fictions of stable ethnic identities, or to an understanding of oral genres as being passed down from one generation to the next in a state relatively untouched by historical circumstance.

Our general introduction refers to the intensity and violence of the region's encounters with colonialism. The effects of this history on South Africa's oral cultures are marked, but two points need to be made clear. Firstly, instead of an implication that oral expression and performance have been rendered obsolete by aggressive modernisation, the opposite is in fact the case: oral cultures have proved to be remarkably adaptive, with their practitioners reinventing traditional genres and their forms of transmission in order to negotiate the rapid and far-reaching social changes taking place around them. Secondly, the region provides telling illustrations of the epistemic and aesthetic complexities involved in the recording, translation and dissemination of oral discourse through print and other media. South Africa's oral and print-based cultures interact in countless ways – often in the work of a single practitioner – and the history of cultural translation, beginning with nineteenth-century philology and folklore studies and continuing down to post-apartheid poetry's cross-cultural explorations is foregrounded in the research that follows.

The most striking example of colonial science's encounters with indige-nous orality is undoubtedly the collection discussed by Hedley Twidle in Chapter 1, involving the German linguist Wilhelm Bleek and, in particular, his English sister-in-law Lucy Lloyd. Between 1870 and 1884, in conversation with convicts on parole from the Breakwater Prison at the Cape Town docks, they produced over 150 notebooks of phonetic transcriptions with English transla-tions of |Xam and !Kung language and folklore, in what is now regarded as one of the richest archives of its kind in the world. (Much of it has been digitised and is available at http://lloydbleekcollection.cs.uct.ac.za/index.html) The appeal, but also the difficulty of the collection lies in the fact that although it is a product of a complex set of cultural forces, readers have assumed that it offers direct access to the language and culture of societies which had been in existence for thousands of years before settler encroachment and then geno-cide all but destroyed them. The loss of the culture itself (and with it, the disappearance of a supposedly premodern subject) has fuelled further waves of encroachment, as philology, ethnography, travel and fictional narratives, and finally contemporary poetry, have successively reinvented it on their own terms. The whole history, from the recording of San speech to its afterlives in South African literature, comprises a complex and moving cultural legacy.

Chapters 2 to 5 discuss oral cultures in contemporary indigenous African languages. It has proved to be impossible to give equal weight to the oratures of all these languages because research amongst them is unevenly distributed. Historically, the most intensively researched of the indigenous oral cultures (and this pattern is generally true of written literature) are those in the Nguni languages, isiXhosa and isiZulu, the former spoken predominantly in the Eastern Cape (though increasingly also in the Western Cape and Cape Town) and the latter in KwaZulu-Natal and Gauteng (including Johannesburg). Sesotho orature is reasonably well served in the scholarship, but the oral expression of the languages spoken in the provinces of Limpopo and Mpumalanga, isiNdebele, Xitsonga, Tshivenda and siSwati, have been relatively under-researched and deserve further attention. Interestingly, this was recognised by Es'kia Mphahlele on his return from exile in 1977 when he embarked on a project to record and translate oral poetry in Tshivenda; however, the volume failed to appear in print (N. C. Manganyi and D. Attwell, eds. *Bury me at the Marketplace*, Witwatersrand University Press, pp. 344, 371, 400, 404, 443). Nevertheless, in Chapter 5, Manie Groenewald and Mokgale Makgopa seek to fill the gaps in their absorbing and wide-ranging account of the oratures in these languages, although the focus of their work is on poetry and performance in isiNdebele.

Despite the limitations on the linguistic range of existing research, the present collection goes a long way towards documenting the state of existing scholarship (which in the case of isiZulu begins as far back as the 1830s) and exploring how the country's indigenous oral cultures have developed under various historical pressures in the course of the past two centuries. In Chapter 2, Russell H. Kaschula discusses changes that have taken place in the Xhosa tradition of praise poetry known as *izibongo*. The genre became internationally visible through the performance of Zolani Mkiva at the inauguration of President Nelson Mandela in 1994, but it has been a central taproot in Xhosa oral performance for centuries. In Xhosa literature, the oeuvres of early twentieth-century figures like Nontsisi Mgqwetho and S. E. K. Mqhayi, who performed as *iimbongi* while also publishing in the mission and commercial press, have recently been published and continue to fuel research. Kaschula uses the particular example of Bongani Sitole to explore the technical inventiveness of the contemporary *imbongi*, and he illuminates the ways in which the poet's craft is influenced by changing power bases and the forms of patronage associated with them, with a shift over time from praises of royalty to the concerns of ordinary citizens.

This pattern, of diffusion and democratisation, is consistent across all the languages. In his discussion of Sotho orature in Chapter 3, Nhlanhla Maake discusses a similar trajectory, with traditional songs and royal praises being adapted and transformed in *difela*, the songs of Basotho migrant workers travelling between Lesotho and South Africa. So pervasive a feature of Sotho culture have the *difela* become that Maake is able to show how they have been taken up in self-referential ways, including self-parody. In Chapter 4, Mbongiseni Buthelezi ranges widely across a number of genres in isiZulu, while also focusing on the development of praising – the *izithakazelo*, or kinship group praises, and the *izibongo* or praises of individuals. Buthelezi's revealing account of how 'new meanings have been created for old forms and new forms have mutated out of older ones' follows the fortunes of traditional performances into the church, the mine hostel, the labour union rally and the political meeting. Particularly significant is the dynamic capacity of the *izibongo* 'to unleash social energy in new directions' and to facilitate new forms of public participation in the political process.

I

'The Bushmen's Letters': |Xam narratives of the Bleek and Lloyd Collection and their afterlives

HEDLEY TWIDLE

In the special collections of the University of Cape Town library are over 150 notebooks filled with columns of Victorian handwriting: phonetic notations of the languages once spoken by southern Africa's |Xam and !Kung peoples with English translations alongside that run to some 13,000 pages. The record of a unique instance of cross-cultural interaction within the history of the Cape Colony, the Bleek and Lloyd Collection is widely considered to be one of the world's richest ethnographic archives, and the most important textual record of indigenous oral expression on the subcontinent. Indicative of the symbolic charge this particular culture has come to assume in contemporary South Africa, the national coat of arms unveiled by President Thabo Mbeki on 27 April 2000 carries as its motto a sentence written in |Xam, preserving the nineteenth-century orthography of the notebooks to record its various clicks. *!ke e:|xarra ||ke* is officially translated as 'Unity in Diversity', glossed more carefully from a language no longer spoken by any living South African, it can be rendered as 'people who are different come together'.[1]

The disparate assemblage of texts, correspondence, photographs, water-colour sketches and other material traces that make up the collection resulted from the convergence of two very different groupings of people in late nineteenth-century Cape Town. One was the unorthodox household of the German linguist Wilhelm Bleek, his English wife, and his sister-in-law Lucy Lloyd; the other was a succession of individuals from four extended fami-lies of |*Xam-ka !ei*, a people descended from one branch of the indigenous

The support of the NRF Research Initiative in Archive and Public Culture at the University of Cape Town, and the suggestions of its participants, are gratefully acknowledged.

1 In the orthography adopted by Bleek, ! is the cerebral click now rendered (in written isiXhosa, for example) as q ('iqhira'); | is the dental click written as c ('nceda'); || is the lateral click written as x ('amaXhosa'). Bleek gives a description of these in his *Comparative Grammar of South African Languages* (1862), pp. 12–13.

inhabitants of southern Africa who had no collective name for themselves, but were known to the Dutch as *Bosjemans*, to the English as Bushmen, and to the cattle-owning Khoikhoi as Sonqua, Soaqua or San.[2] Like many others drawn into the violence of the colony's northern frontier, several |Xam men had been displaced from their homes and sentenced to hard labour in Cape Town's Breakwater Prison. Following a request from Bleek to the governor Sir Philip Wodehouse, certain individuals were transferred to the genteel suburb of Mowbray between 1870 and 1884. Here they were received first as convicts on parole, servants and 'native informants' for Bleek's abstruse philological enquiries, yet increasingly as valued teachers, storytellers, artists and (in Lloyd's phrase) 'givers of native literature' (Bleek and Lloyd, *Bushman Folklore*, p. x).

Transcribed, translated and edited with uncommon diligence and foresight by Bleek and Lloyd, the words of individuals like |A!kúnta (Klaas Stoffel), Diä!kwain (David Hoesar), |Han≠kass'o (Klein Jantje), ||Kabbo (Oud Jantje Tooren) and Kweiten-ta-||ken (Griet) reach us now as dense, digressive and often confusing fragments of text. 'The Mantis assumes the form of a Hartebeest', 'The Moon is not to be looked at when Game is shot', 'A Woman of the Early Race and the Rain Bull', '||Kabbo's Capture and Journey to Cape Town' – the titles given to the dictations are grouped under headings like 'Mythology, Fables, Legends and Poetry', 'Customs and Superstitions' and 'Personal History' in Bleek and Lloyd's reports to the Cape parliament of the 1870s and 1880s. Yet the narrators themselves seem to have made little distinction between the various *kukummi* they related in the drawing rooms and on the verandas of colonial Mowbray: it was a word which could refer to lively creation narratives as well as accounts of daily life in the northern Cape thirstland, and which seemed to encompass 'anything told'. Occasionally the *kukummi* depart from the tales of the mantis |Kaggen, of rain animals, stars and hunting methods to record the brutal intrusion of settlers and pastoralists in an area which, according to recent genetic and archaeological evidence, had

2 Although both terms are in common use today, neither 'Bushmen' nor 'San' are words that can be employed without reservations. As well as its obvious sexist limitations, the former carries with it the racist overtones of eighteenth- and nineteenth-century usage, but has in recent decades been to some degree reclaimed, acquiring meanings associated with resistance and self-determination. Although initially used by the Khoikhoi in a pejorative sense for those peoples who 'gathered wild food' and did not possess cattle, 'San' (popularised by Isaac Schapera through his 1930 magnum opus, *The Khoisan Peoples of South Africa*) is often preferred in that it is relatively free of colonial connotations. For a sense of the long and complex debate on terminology with regard to the Khoi-San (Khoi, Ju and !Ui-Taa) language families in southern Africa, see Gordon, *The Bushman Myth*, and the website of the South African San Institute (SASI), www.sanculture.org.za/body.htm, which states: 'Today San people prefer to be identified as San or by their ethnic community names' (accessed 1 October 2009).

been inhabited by anatomically 'modern' humans for around 100,000 years when herder groups, pastoralists and *trekboers* arrived from the north and south.

The very names of the five principal narrators listed above embody a history of forced acculturation, genocidal violence and language death that resulted from colonial settlement meeting with a hunter-gatherer economy in the arid regions south of the Orange River. In 1863 the magistrate of Namaqualand, Louis Anthing, wrote of 'a wholesale system of extermination' being carried out against the Cape San by armed, mounted settler bands known as commandos (Report, p. 5). In 1910, while her aunt prepared selections of the |Xam and !Kung material for publication in *Specimens of Bushman Folklore* (1911), Bleek's daughter Dorothea visited the Kenhardt and Prieska districts where the narrators had once lived. Writing in 1929, she recalled that 'Fifty years ago every adult Bushman knew all his people's lore. A tale begun by a person from one place could be finished by someone from another place at a later date'; yet at the beginning of the twentieth century, 'not one of them knew a single story . . . the folklore was dead, killed by a life of service among strangers and the breaking up of families' ('Bushman Folklore', p. 311).

!Khwe‖na s'o !kwe: from 'First Peoples' to the 'Early Race'

For almost a century these 'Bushman researches' received little scholarly attention from anyone outside of the Bleek family,[3] but in recent decades steadily more of the archive's narrative and visual material has been brought into the public domain by visual artists, curators, writers, anthologists and, most recently, digital scanning.[4] Read in dialogue with contemporary fieldwork amongst Ju|'hoansi and Nharo communities in Namibia and Botswana, the nineteenth-century records have become a fragmentary, speculative yet vitally important means of reconstructing a wider indigenous expressive culture which once existed throughout the subcontinent.[5] Yet as in so many contexts involving the recovery and representation of autochthonous or precolonial

3 The series of articles on 'Customs and Beliefs of the |Xam Bushmen' by Dorothea Bleek, which appeared in *Bantu Studies* in the 1930s, are collected in Hollman, *Customs and Beliefs*.
4 A large part of the archive, including all the |Xam and !Kung notebooks, was scanned and placed online by Pippa Skotnes between 2005 and 2007. See 'The Digital Bleek and Lloyd', http://lloydbleekcollection.cs.uct.ac.za/ (accessed March 2010).
5 Major works here include Vinnicombe, *People of the Eland*; Lewis-Williams, *Believing and Seeing*; Hewitt, *Structure, Meaning and Ritual*; Guenther, *Bushman Folktales*. For a comprehensive overview of the ways in which these different explicators approach the |Xam texts, see Wessels, *Bushman Letters*.

identities, the process has been a contested and controversial one. Curators have been accused of appropriation and poets of plagiarism (Skotnes, 'Museum Display'; Watson, 'Annals of Plagiarism'); historians revealing Bleek's proximity to social Darwinism and his theories of racial difference have reacted against idealised visions of cultural exchange in the garden village of Mowbray (Bank, *Bushmen in a Victorian World*; Dubow, *Scientific Racism*; Moran, *Representing Bushmen*; Wessels, *Bushman Letters*).

'The Lost World of the Kalahari', 'The Harmless People', 'The Little People' – such well-worn phrases from the twentieth century reveal a recurring tendency to sentimentalise the indigenous inhabitants of southern Africa as prehistoric, isolated hunter-gatherers in a way which obscures the complex cultural transactions of the frontier and masks a fierce resistance to colonial encroachment (Penn, 'Fated to Perish'). The 'Bushman', J. M. Coetzee remarked, is a literary figure 'whose romance has lain precisely in his belonging to a vanishing race' (*White Writing*, p. 177). As a result, when portrayed as a quaint, childlike presence, this personage somehow removed from the ambit of human history could safely be seen as 'the truest native of South Africa' by colonial writing from the travelogues of William Burchell and Thomas Pringle to the international bestsellers of Laurens van der Post. Perhaps even the commemoration of the |*Xam-ka !ei* on the coat of arms – the symbolic reinstatement of this and similar 'First Peoples' as part of the post-apartheid national project – risks ignoring a legacy of rural poverty and land disputes still all too evident in Namibia, Botswana and the resettlement camps of contemporary South Africa (Gordon, *Bushman Myth*; Robbins, *On the Bridge of Goodbye*).

Yet the painful autobiographical testimony contained in this archive and the particular circumstances of its creation mean that it can hardly be considered as a nostalgic access to a premodern existence or, as Bleek put it in his second *Report* of 1875, as 'pictures of the native mind in its national originality' (p. 2). Instead, it is most valuably approached as a language event of great complexity, difficulty, beauty and unexpectedness.[6] As a collaborative enterprise of a depth, detail and material richness which has been able to support a wide variety of cultural afterlives, the Bleek and Lloyd Collection is best explored not as an ethnographic document evoking a vanished, mythic past, but rather as a body of work continually expanding to include adaptations, translations

---

6 See Barnard for an account of how a phrase used for the national motto, *!ke e:|xarra* ('people who are different'), appears coincidentally and cryptically in one of the kukummi related by |Han≠kass'o in 1878, where it is translated as 'strangers' ('Multiple Origins', pp. 243–50).

and literary recastings: diverse strands of writing and rewriting which do not so much explicate from a distance as become part of the archive itself.

In a context where the colonial register of occupation or the transplanted European forms of the nineteenth century hardly seem adequate points of departure given the age and extent of the earliest expressive cultures in the region, the complex interplay between the oral and the written which one finds in |Xam texts has led to their being explored as both a site of origin for, and a persistent presence in, South African literary history (Brown, *Voicing*, pp. 33–74; Chapman, *Southern African Literatures*, pp. 21–37; Van Vuuren, 'Orality in the Margins', pp. 129–35). They emerge as a fitting prologue to an irrevocably divided national literature, yet one in which, as Gray remarks, there emerges the recurring motif of writer cast in the role of transcriber, shaper and 'amanuensis of the spoken word': 'the shift from the spoken to the written persists as our major event' (*Southern African Stories*, p. 10).

As a result, this entry into the |Xam records attempts to balance the possible antiquity which they gesture towards against the specific, context-bound details of their transcription, and to suggest both the similarities and discontinuities between these narratives and the mythologies of those Khoi-San cultures, which have gone largely unrecorded. The unbridgeable historical distance between a modern reader and an individual like ||Kabbo ('Dream') is set against his own insistence that *kukummi* – news, stories, customs, gossip – owed their existence to being told and retold. He was a narrator who, Lloyd recalled, 'much enjoyed the thought that the Bushman stories would become known by means of books' yet also voiced his longing to return to a part of the country where a story is 'like the wind, it comes from a far-off quarter, and we feel it' (*Bushman Folklore*, pp. x, 301). One of the most famous fragments in the collection, '||Kabbo's Intended Return Home', hauntingly evokes the universality of the impulse to narrate, setting its speaker's confinement in a colonial household against the fluidity of spoken tales – their tendency to 'float' between people and places – all of it rendered in the deliberately archaic English of Bleek and Lloyd's translation:

> Thou knowest that I sit waiting for the moon to turn back for me, that I may return to my place. That I may listen to all the people's stories, when I visit them; that I may listen to their () stories, that which they tell . . . Then I shall get hold of a story from them, because they (the stories) float out from a distance; while the sun feels () a little warm; while I feel that I must altogether visit, that I may be talking with them, my fellow men.
>
> (*Bushman Folklore*, p. 301)

Rock, art, writing

'Africa is everywhere inscribed', writes Alain Ricard, remarking that 'one needs a stubborn and narrow-minded commitment to alphabetic writing to deny that the continent has left graphic marks of its history everywhere' ('Africa and Writing', p. 153). From the engraved pavements of the Orange River and pecked dolerite boulders of the northern Cape to the processions of ochre figures in the Cederberg and the shaded polychromatic elands of the Drakensberg, the rock art of South Africa bears out the truth of this observation. Drawing attention to its variation and extent, Brown describes some panels as possessing a 'script' of extraordinary beauty and complexity, one that 'uses an array of symbols, signs, colours, shapes and images in making its meaning, and which demands intelligent "reading"' (*To Speak of this Land*, pp. 21–2). So too, in a way that is suggestive of where a study of southern African 'writing' might properly begin, rock art researchers have explained their debt to the Bleek and Lloyd Collection not as a simple means of decoding the paintings, but as a source of apprehending the deep metaphoric structures of rain-making, trance and shamanic potency which run through the narratives and across the rock surfaces of what has been called the longest continuous artistic tradition in human history (Lewis-Williams, *Believing and Seeing* and *The Mind in the Cave*).

Rock art in southern Namibia has been dated at over 27,000 years before the present, yet panels throughout the South African escarpment showing European ships, then wagons and soldiers could only have been painted in the last decades of the colonial era (Deacon and Deacon, *Human Beginnings*, p. 165). This immense time depth of cultural production remains a challenge in any attempt to consider what an 'indigenous oral tradition' might be, particularly when an archaeological label like 'late Stone Age people' seems inadequate for societies that worked in ochre, haematite, ostrich shells, animal skins and even copper. Historical and ethnographic accounts of the Khoi-San describe a social organisation based on small mobile bands in which an absence of stratification and an abundance of 'leisure time' afforded by the pattern of hunting, gathering or transhumance pastoralism allowed for the development of the highly verbal culture evoked by ‖Kabbo, a culture which placed great value on 'spokenness' and the telling of stories. Without recourse to an idea of primordial hunters or herders, one can suggest that many of the *kukummi* emerge from and embody a distinctive cultural response to life in the arid and challenging environment of the southern African interior.

The Bleek and Lloyd notebooks contain considerable amounts of zoological and botanical information, from the sketches of edible plants and animal spoor provided by the !Kung boys !Nanni and Tamme, to descriptions relating to the ritualistic sharing of vital resources like meat, water and *veldkos* (wild food). Yet quite apart from this, even in the most convoluted and (to a contemporary reader) most surreal narratives of the therianthropic (part-human, part-animal) beings of the 'Early Race', one can discern an oblique meditation on social interaction. The lawless, unmannerly doings of the *!Khwe‖na s'o !kwe* – the 'First at Sitting People'– provide a medium through which to explore the importance of kinship bonds, rites of passage and the danger of incompetence in human relations. In his analysis of the collection's deep narrative grammar, Hewitt writes that 'this fictive early period is thought of as a formative one for the San', offering to the reflective performer a mass of motifs, plot structures and character galleries in which 'the raw materials of life, both cosmological and social, were constantly interacting, rearranging themselves, revealing social truths and the natural order of things' ('The Oral Literature of the San', p. 654).

Yet if folklorists and ethnographers have tended to dwell on the mythological plane of the narratives, other readers of the collection have been drawn to the evocations of specific sites in the Northern Cape, depictions of the home territory of the |Xam informants which intimate a sense of place entirely different to the feminised landscapes or depopulated vistas of colonial writing (Deacon, 'Home Territory'; Martin, *Millimetre*). In an excerpt entitled 'Bushman Presentiments', ‖Kabbo explained the 'springbok sensation': the 'tapping' or 'beating of the flesh' through which hunters identified with their quarry. It is a passage which suggests how an ability to read signs and auguries in the natural environment constituted an intimate and extensive corpus of knowledge, a form of cultural memory which revealed itself at an embodied, even somatic level:

> The Bushmen's letters are in their bodies. They (the letters) speak, they move, they make their (the Bushmen's) bodies move. They (the Bushmen) order the others to be silent; a man is altogether still, when he feels that () his body is tapping (inside). A dream speaks falsely, it is (a thing) which deceives. The presentiment is that which speaks the truth; it is that by means of which the Bushman gets (or perceives) meat, when it has tapped.
>
> (*Bushman Folklore*, pp. 331–3)

Yet even as this metaphor of literacy is used to imagine the unwritten, it underscores the multiply translated, mediated form in which ‖Kabbo's words now appear, and reminds us how any attempt to access the imaginative content of the narratives becomes inseparable from their textual history.

Khoi-San oratures: a comparative approach

As Bleek's wide-ranging philological enquiries prior to 1870 emphasise, the earliest written information about the Khoi-San language families is inevitably the product of colonial records: the word lists of seventeenth-century mariners (Herbert, 1638) and later the narratives of foreign travellers like Kolb (1719), Le Vaillant (1790), Barrow (1801), Lichtenstein (1810; English translation, 1812–15) and Burchell (1824).[7] Between 1857 and 1859, Bleek worked to catalogue Sir George Grey's extensive library of 'traditional literature' in Cape Town, and in the process drew up a table of twenty-eight different orthographies which had been used to notate the oldest southern African languages. As well as being a summary of the linguistic information contained within early accounts of the Cape, it provides the spectacle of a colonial taxonomy trying to apprehend and codify the sheer foreignness of the Khoi, Ju and !Ui-Taa language families, all of them characterised by a complex array of clicks, gutturals and shifting intonations.

As Elphick remarks, their position at a vital stopping point on Europe's sea route to the East meant that in the seventeenth and eighteenth centuries, the Western Cape Khoikhoi were perhaps 'the most frequently observed and intensively discussed' of all the preliterate peoples in the eastern hemisphere (*Kraal and Castle*, p. xvi). Scattered through French, Dutch and English accounts one finds occasional speculations about the Khoi deities 'Tsui-Goab', 'Gaunab' and 'Haiseb', but for the most part this is a literature of dismissal and disgust, often comprised of tropes recycled by authors who had never set foot at the Cape. Notable exceptions, however, include the more sympathetic travelogues of Dapper (1668), Tachard (1688), Kolb, Le Vaillant and Burchell, as well as (a text not listed by Bleek) the 1779 *Berigt* of Hendrik Jacob Wikar, a Swedish deserter from the Dutch East India Company who lived with societies of the Orange River. Within a journal unusual for its imaginative entry into the lifeways of various Khoi-San groups is perhaps the earliest recorded indigenous narrative of southern Africa: the fable explaining the origin of death among mankind. In most versions it is the Moon which tells the Hare to give a message to humans saying that they would come to life again after death. The Hare distorts the message, bringing mortality into the world, and

7 See Chapter 8 in this volume for a fuller account and bibliography of this travel and ethnographic literature at the Cape.

is struck a blow across the face which results in its split lip. In Wikar's version it is the deity 'Tzoekoab of God' ('Tsui-Goab or God') who gives 'een boodschap aan den haas' ('a message to the hare'), recorded in a language that was already moving some way from Dutch towards a proto-Afrikaans (Mossop, *Journals*, p. 139).

Recorded in over seventy variants throughout southern Africa, this narrative is one of the most compelling suggestions that a pan-Khoi-San myth complex once extended throughout the region (Schmidt, 'Folktales', 'Relevance' and *Catalogue*; Guenther, *Tricksters and Trancers*). A version of it appears in the first significant collection of 'Hottentot Fables and Tales', compiled in 1864 after Bleek wrote to missionaries like Theophilus Halm, J. G. Krönlein, H. Tindall and C. F. Wuras requesting collections of 'Native Literature'. Bleek's sycophantic dedicatory preface to Sir George Grey remarks that the various animal and mood songs interspersed through the collection will be of little interest, yet it is just such chanted refrains which are excerpted by Jack Cope and Uys Krige for their 1968 *Penguin Book of South African Verse*:

Hyena's Song to her Children

The fire threatens
The sling-stone menaces me
The assegais threaten
The gun points death at me
Yet you howl around me for food
My children!
Do I get anything so easily?   (p. 254)

Among evocative narratives of 'Fish-Stealing' and 'Cloud-Eating', the tales in the 1864 collection concerning the exploits of Jackal and the 'ǀ Icitsi Eibip' (Haiseb) reveal two incarnations of the trickster figure who forms the second major link between the different oratures.

An embodiment of ambiguity who is, according to Guenther, 'as ubiquitous as he is multifarious' (*Tricksters and Trancers*, p. 97), this favoured antihero of Khoi-San folklore assumes a bewildering array of identities. The Haiseb and Jackal figures of Heiǁom, Nama and Damara oratures find their closest analogue in the |Xam *kukummi* as |Kaggen, or 'Cagn' as J. M. Orpen transcribed it from his 'Maluti Bushman' informant Qing in 1874 ('Mythology of the Maluti Bushmen'). Although most often portrayed as a flying Mantis with magical powers, |Kaggen was also associated with the large, revered antelopes like the hartebeest or eland, and simultaneously personified as a foolish, cowardly and lascivious old man (some of whose lewd catchphrases remain tellingly untranslated in Bleek and Lloyd). As with the Ju|'hoansi narratives recorded by Biesele (*Women Like Meat*), in the Nharo and G|wi folktales collected by Guenther in Botswana the exploits of the trickster Pisamboro – which include the 'flashing' of young women – suggest how the bawdy elements of oral performances might have been largely effaced during the making of the Bleek and Lloyd records.

In compiling the most comprehensive twentieth-century archive of folklore from Namibia, Schmidt also tracks the changing identity of the more sinister !Kung figure of !O!otsi|dasi (who appears in the |Xam narratives as !Goe|weiten), a protagonist with an eyeless face but eyes between its toes or on the back of its ankles. Sometimes a trickster-being, and at other times his victim, 'Eyes-on-his-Feet' is in turn conflated with the man-eating ogres of Nguni folklore by some storytellers, and enters the Afrikaans folk tradition as the bogey-man 'Voetoog' (Foot-Eye) (Schmidt, *Märchen aus Namibia*; 'The Relevance of the Bleek/Lloyd Folktales'). At other moments in the Nama and Dama records, it is evident how an infusion of biblical narratives concerning 'Jesso Kreste' and the Devil began to alter Khoi-San narrative performance at the very moment when it was first being recorded by missionaries; certain stories even seem to appropriate and recast figures like 'Till Eulenspiegel' and 'Reineke Fuchs' from Dutch and German folk traditions.

'How the alphabet was made': the creation of the archive

Viewed against this history of constant borrowing, bilingualism and cultural barter, the title of Bleek's 1864 collection, *Reynard the Fox in South Africa*, signals his comparative ambitions – an attempt to see the figures from southern African oratures as local embodiments of universal mythological 'types' – even as it reveals the impossibility of identifying 'pure survivals' in such oratures. Yet although such overweening comparative philology is an obsolete discipline, and despite the representational and all too actual violence that permeates so many of the colonial records from which he worked, the attention devoted to vocabulary and orthography was to prove vital when Bleek and Lloyd came to recording the words of skilled narrators like Diä!kwain, |Han≠kass'o and ||Kabbo. In 1866 a series of interviews in Cape Town's Roeland Street jail served as a kind of dress rehearsal for the dictations of the 1870s; the words and short sentences transcribed and translated from Adam Kleinhardt, son of a Bushman woman and a Korana man, make up the early pages of the notebooks:

heart of ox;
thy heart;
my heart is;
  sore
ox lungs;
ox lung;
my lungs are
  sore;

. . .

the Bushmen
eat the cattle
of the Boers;
the Boers take
the children of
the Bushmen (Bleek Collection, 151 A1 4)

By the time |A!kunta arrived in Mowbray in August 1870, Bleek had com bined further work on Bushman vocabulary and orthography with a recording method which he had first experimented with when collecting Zulu folklore in Natal as far back as 1855. Right-hand pages were divided into two columns, with the |Xam text entered in one and the other reserved for translation, which was done over a period of days, weeks or even months, then checked with the narrators. Further observations or clarifications offered by them during this process were entered on the left-hand pages of the notebooks, becoming in the printed text a bewildering array of asterisks and footnotes which make the accounts confusing and sometimes contradictory, yet also greatly richer and more nuanced.

In a finely detailed reconstruction of the recording process, Bank shows how this attempt to record every aspect of the circling, digressive perfor mances constitutes a 'thick description' that is as much script as transcript: a 'grammar of performance' or diary of daily life and learning (*Bushmen in a Victorian World*, p. 83). Far from being a perfect exchange of words for things in a colonial garden, the process of establishing vocabulary using household objects, children's books, illustrated travelogues and even a visit to the nat ural history museum was a procedure characterised by partial recognition, misrecognition and constant negotiation. Yet despite an ongoing reluctance to claim credit for her primary role in the making of the archive, Lloyd's apti tude for the work soon became apparent, and it is her less theoretical, more empathetic approach that elicits the personal testimony which now seems more compelling than Bleek's abstract catalogues of mythology. |A!kunta's remark in the notebooks that 'de bushman tal praat is baie swer die noi' ('speaking the Bushman language is very difficult for the young lady') reveals too how a broken form of Dutch was often used by the narrators and transcribers (BC 151 L124, cited Bank, p. 84) making the notebooks a complex tissue of linguistic registers. Farmyard animals appear as 'beest' (cow) and 'huhness' ('hoenders' – chickens) and even in the evocation of 'the Bushman's letters' in the printed volume of 1911, ‖Kabbo explains that ‖gu means 'de bloem tijd' ('the flowering time') of the Northern Cape (*Bushman Folklore*, p. 337).

No doubt, the entire collection could in one sense be regarded as an extended example of the observer's paradox; as Chapman remarks, 'it is difficult to decide whether the circularity of the tale betokens the style of the oral imagination or the patience of the tellers in accommodating themselves to the laborious process of . . . longhand transcription . . . The emphasis, one way or another, is probably a fine one' (*Southern African Literatures*, p. 23). Is the aberrant grammar (where present tense fragments are embedded in longer past tense narratives) an example of inbuilt dramatisation, evidence of the seamlessness of a pre-Cartesian cosmology, or merely a result of problems in transcription? Abstracted from the living, communal context of oral performance, a fidelity to the process of story dictation must often have worked against the larger narrative arc: Lloyd describes in her preface how ‖Kabbo 'watched patiently until a sentence had been written down, before proceeding with what he was telling' (*Bushman Folklore*, p. x). Nonetheless, as many of those who have worked with the texts remark, the contributions of the different 'givers of native literature' do emerge as distinct, each with a set of narrative traits all of their own (Hewitt, *Structure, Meaning and Ritual*). Even as twentieth-century anthologists and poets have drawn on the collection, seeking to make its lengthy transcriptions more readable and accessible, the very stiltedness and archaism preserved in the records perhaps serves as a necessary reminder of the artificial circumstances in which they were created, and also of the singularity and awkward delicacy of this linguistic encounter.

The breaking string: the archive and the poets

> People were those who
> Broke for me the string
> Therefore,
> The place () became like this to me,
> On account of it,

Because the string was that which broke for me.
Therefore,
The place does not feel to me,
As the place used to feel to me,
On account of it.
For,
The place feels as if it stood open before me,
() Because the string has broken for me.
Therefore,
The place does not feel pleasant to me,
On account of it.

Reproduced as it appears on page 237 of *Specimens of Bushman Folklore*, across from the notation of the |Xam words spoken to Lucy Lloyd by Diä!kwain in July 1875, 'The Broken String' is a language event that has reverberated in the poetic imagination even when the Bleek and Lloyd Collection was all but forgotten. A version of it appears in Cope and Krige's 1968 anthology, and again in that edited by Stephen Gray in 1989, though classified here as a 'traditional' San song, a label which does not indicate the painful, personal circumstances of its telling. Asterisks in Bleek and Lloyd explain how !Nuin-|kuïten, a *!giten* ('sorcerer' according to the original transcribers, now more accurately rendered as 'shaman'), had been on an out-of-body journey in the form of a lion and had killed 'a Boer ox'. The farmer raised one of the local, mounted bands known as a commando, pursued and shot him in reprisal. Mortally wounded, he limped back to the camp and described with his last breath how these people had destroyed his connection to the water bull resident in the sky, urging Diä!kwain's father Xa:ä-tin to continue singing the old songs, making rain in the old way: 'Now that "the string is broken", the former "ringing sound in the sky" is no longer heard by the singer, as it had been in the magician's lifetime.'

How can such a distanced and delicate fragment be approached? Enlisting the aid of structural anthropology and rock art research developed from the 1970s onwards, one could note its blend of real and non-real components, or the conflation of ancient and modern as narrators' attempts to relate 'traditionary' material for Bleek and Lloyd became ineluctably entangled with the violence of the colonial frontier. Perhaps one could attempt to chart the horizontal and vertical axes of |Xam cosmology, from camp to hunting ground, and earth to the heavens, 'mediated by water which both wells up in waterholes and falls from the sky' (Lewis-Williams, '"A Visit to the Lion's House"', p. 126). Or describe it instead as that 'great and complex web of *signs* that wrote themselves across the landscape and into the lives and bodies of those capable of understanding them' (Bennun, *Broken String*, p. 234). Yet at the same time a fragment like 'The Broken String' cannot but suggest the disruption to |Xam culture created by the very breakage or breach through which we have entered. As with the Aranda song cycles adapted by the likes of Theodor Strehlow and Bruce Chatwin, the Bleek and Lloyd material throws into relief the technical challenges and ethical dilemmas of bringing such material into modern literary currency.

For an English-speaking readership both within South Africa and abroad, the most influential interpreter of 'Bushman' culture during the twentieth century was undoubtedly Laurens van der Post. His often fabricated but immensely influential works drew heavily on the archive: in *The Heart of the Hunter* (1961) he described *Specimens of Bushman Folklore* and Dorothea Bleek's whimsical 1924 collection for children, *The Mantis and his Friends*, as 'the authorised version of what is a sort of stone age Bible to me' (p. 12). Van der Post's imaginative entry into the world of the myths and his evocations of rock art in the Tsodilo Hills have in recent years been revisited as an early attempt to treat San cultures with a requisite attention and empathy, and also as an anticipation of the post-apartheid national identity fashioned from notions of indigeneity by a political project like Mbeki's African Renaissance (Masilela, 'White South African Writer').

Yet his incorrigibly mystic turn of phrase, and a dedication of the 1961 volume to Jung – 'because of his great love of Africa and reverence for the life of its aboriginal children' – suggests how this was an approach intent on collapsing very different cultures into a single entity, one which was then infantilised and rendered as a source of spiritual rejuvenation untouched by modernity. In later books, Van der Post would place the stories in the mouths of fictional creations and living individuals whom he claimed to have met, transferring the folklore and narrative from its point of origin to an entirely different location in the Kalahari. A similar transposition occurs in the 1956 and 1971 collections compiled from the Bleek and Lloyd records by Arthur Markowitz, who acknowledges a large debt to the archive in his introduction, yet does not seem to realise that its narrators had little to do with the Nharo, !Kung, G|wi or G||ana peoples further north (*With Uplifted Tongue* and *The Rebirth of the Ostrich*).

By contrast, Stephen Watson's 1991 collection of 'Versions from the |Xam', *Return of the Moon*, brought together colonial historiography, ethnographic information and scholarly accounts of rock art in an attempt to situate the |Xam narratives within their particular, disturbing historical moment, while at the same time making their aesthetic more accessible to a modern audience. Whilst Markowitz limited himself to recorded 'Bushman vocabulary' in compiling his volume, and while Alan James's scrupulously contextualised 2001 collection *The First Bushman's Path* was praised for the degree to which its author allowed his versions of |Xam texts to *resist* his own voice, *The Return of the Moon* is a selection where the transcriptions are carefully brought into a modern idiom, interacting with the 'framing device' of Watson's own poetics and enabling him 'to cast into relief certain features which would almost certainly have been lost even in the best prose translation' (*Return of the Moon*, p. 16)

In a detailed introduction, he remarks how what seemed the purely technical challenges of the source material – a verbal surface of shifting tenses, syntactical spirals and 'word-salads', the 'natural surrealism' of many of the extracts – led to a more acute sense of what Skotnes called the 'perceptual abyss' between received twentieth-century ideas about the 'Bushmen' and the rich detail of the |Xam records ('"Civilised off the face of the earth"', p. 312). Of all the stereotypes which threaten to fill such absences, the most insistent temptation for the contemporary poet, he suggests, is a tendency to wistfulness and melancholy that results from knowing the historical fate of the |Xam, so that the elegiac mode 'comes to have the force of gravity whenever one sets to work' (p. 17). In his version, 'The Song of the Broken String' is given as a series of overlapping variations in four stanzas, where the explanatory glosses of Bleek and Lloyd's 1911 volume are incorporated into a single poem that accentuates a subtext of psychic and cultural dislocation:

> Because
> of this string,
> because of a people
> breaking the string,
> this earth, my place
> is the place
> of something –
> a thing broken –
> that does not
> stop sounding,
> breaking within me.   (pp. 59–60)

A different approach is taken by Lewis-Williams in his 2000 volume, *Stories that Float from Afar*, a more sober, stripped down anthology which includes ||Kabbo's account of watching a procession in honour of the Governor of the Cape of Good Hope, Sir Bartle Frere, at Cape Town's Grand Parade in

June 1879. It is a previously unpublished extract which offers a rare reversal of the colonial gaze, and an oblique perspective on the city as a seat of high empire. Concerned to emphasise the historicity of the records, the editor suggests that it is prose which best brings out their difficulty and digression, and that versification risks a 'prettification' of the texts (pp. 36–8). Yet in her 2004 volume of 'selected and adapted' |Xam poetry, *the stars say 'tsau'* (published simultaneously in Afrikaans as *die sterre sê 'tsau'*), Antjie Krog describes how she employed 'the natural way in which the narratives "fell" into verse' (p. 10), preserving the found poetry of the Bleek and Lloyd transcriptions: a jagged *vers libre* created as the English translation was strictly aligned with |Xam dictation, never able to evolve into grammatically coherent sentences, punctuated at random by commas which create drifting clauses and adverbial phrases.

As a result, 'the song of the broken string' which opens her (English) collection remains virtually unchanged from its original incarnation, appearing alongside a sepia photograph and short biography of its narrator, the man sentenced for killing a farmer who had threatened his family, yet known in suburban Mowbray as the Bleeks' 'pet murderer' on account of his gentleness. With Krog's Afrikaans version of 'die gebreekte snaar' however, one witnesses another link in a far-reaching chain of translation and retranslation: the words of the collection have now passed from the |Xam via broken Dutch into Victorian English and now into the Afrikaans of a South African author who writes and publishes simultaneously in two languages:

> mense was dit
> wat die snaar vir my gebreek het
> daarom
> het die plek vir my só geword
> as gevolg daarvan   (p. 13)

The stilted diction of the nineteenth-century texts – 'as gevolg daarvan' (on account of it) – is retained here, and in her introduction Krog claims to identify with an Afrikaans substructure present in convoluted phrases like, 'Hold thou strongly fast for me the hartebeest skin' (*Bushman Folklore*, p. 3). In the plagiarism scandal which ensued after she was accused by Watson of barely altering Lloyd's transcriptions, Krog asserted that her prime motivation for the collection had been to bring the poems back into Afrikaans, pointing to the work of Eugene Marais and a long history of drawing on Khoi-San orality in its literature.

'The Bushmen's letters': literary afterlives and beyond

Marais's preface to his *Dwaalstories* of the early 1920s leaves one in no doubt that the Bleek and Lloyd Collection is a major presence at a formative moment of Afrikaans lyric poetry, yet even before this a writer of the *Eerste Taal Beweging* (First Language Movement), Gideon Retief von Wielligh, had translated and anthologised excerpts in his *Boesman-Stories*. Published in four volumes between 1919 and 1921, the last of these makes explicit reference to Bleek and Lloyd and translates into early Afrikaans passages entitled 'Boesmans in die Breekwater' and 'Uit die Breekwater huis-toe'. So too, his recollections of totally bilingual |Xam narrators in Namaqualand, Bushmanland and the Hantam between 1870 and 1883 bear out Marais's claim of how 'when the Bushman language was dying out, the narrators transferred the stories into their own *eienaardige* (idiosyncratic) Afrikaans' (*Dwaalstories*, p. i).

Unlike those of Von Williegh, Markowitz or Van der Post, the *Dwaalstories* are not simple relocations and retellings of the Bleek and Lloyd material. They are, however, permeated by its metaphors and narrative structures: in footnotes we are told about 'dinksnare' (the 'thinking strings' through which the narrators expressed a model of consciousness), 'Die Rëenbul' ('the Rain Bull') and the belief that each individual was associated with a particular wind which would efface their footsteps from the earth after death (p. 29), a belief related by Diä!kwain in August 1875 in one of his many *kukummi* concerning mortality during that year. As Kannemeyer suggests in his history of Afrikaans literature, it is this flexible, transformative attitude to the tradition of the *Boesmanvertelling* (Bushman tale) rather than any quest for folkloric purity that gives the collection its unity, and makes it such an important influence on later writers: the graphic language, 'irrational' imagery and spoken feel are regarded as a foreshadowing of the experimentalism of Jan Rabie, Uys Krige and Breyten Breytenbach in the 1950s and 1960s (*Geskiedenis*, p. 234).

Whilst the shifting incarnations of specific fragments can be tracked through the twentieth century and up to the present, it is more difficult to give a sense of the residual orality evoked by Marais, an infusion of linguistic and narrative energy which extends from the earliest Afrikaans poetry to the post-apartheid novels of André Brink. In works such as *The First Life of Adamastor* (1993) and *Praying Mantis* (2007), Khoi-San narrative modes and mythology interact with a South African strain of magic realism to create playful, postcolonial rewritings of the country's various contact zones. So too, there have been many poets who do not explicitly rewrite the material, but rather elaborate on or weave it in to their own work. Cope's 'Rock Painting' (included in his 1968 Penguin anthology) joins a literary strand of rock art *ekphrasis* that runs from Olive Schreiner's *The Story of an African Farm* (1883) through the short fiction of William Plomer to meditative poetry like that of Peter Sacks's *In these Mountains* (1986), the 'parched, cryptic ones' of Douglas Livingstone's 1991 collection *A Littoral Zone* (p. 45), as well as Jeremy Cronin's imaginative inhabiting of archaeological sites in a 'Venture into the Interior' entirely unlike that of Van der Post:

> mouth or
>   cave-site of word
> root, birdbone,
>   shells of meaning
> left in our mouths
> by thousands of years of
>   human occupation.   (*Inside*, p. 37)

More recently, the verbal suggestiveness of isolated fragments inspires poems in P. R. Anderson's *Foundling's Island* (2007), while an historical novelist like Yvette Christiansë acknowledges her debt to the archive as a means of recreating the texture of nineteenth-century Khoi and Afrikaans diction in *Unconfessed* (2006).

Yet of course, such literary afterlives constitute only one medium through which the Bleek and Lloyd Collection has been extended and celebrated. The varied work of the graphic artist and curator Pippa Skotnes attempts to convey not simply the textual matter of the archive, but also its materiality, its striking imagery and entire aesthetic. The three-year process of digitally scanning not only the content of notebooks but also their marbled covers, as well as drawings, watercolours, landscapes, blotting papers, slips for the 'Bushman Dictionary' and all manner of other material traces is offered not as an interpretation of indigenous thought, but rather as an attempt to present (as far as this is possible) 'the archive itself' (*Claim to the Country*, p. 41). This, she adds, should not be thought of as a dusty, forgotten repository but a dynamic, even chaotic space 'in which one can never be a passive participant, where one must constantly be alert to new possibilities, to different insights, to other ways of understanding the complexities of the past' (p. 41). As in her installations for the South African National Gallery and Museum – where an absence of information panels and the lack of any prescribed route meant that the viewer was required to adopt a personal, non-linear way through – there is in her publications a sense of merely bringing objects into relation and allowing them to stand for themselves. The notion of editor as curator enables an array of historical artefacts to be left intact and immanent to a remarkable degree given the limitations of a two-dimensional page.

In another publication attuned to the visual grammar and intense formal beauty of this archive, *My Heart Stands in the Hill* (2005), film-maker Craig Foster and archaeologist Janette Deacon project photographic portraits of the narrators on to the land where they once lived: one sees images of Diä!kwain, |Han≠kass'o and ||Kabbo superimposed on aloes, kokerbooms, tortoiseshells and the cracked mud of the Bitterpits in an environment where, as the authors remark, the uneven surfaces transform the anthropometric photographs into distended, layered images not unlike the hallucinatory visions of rock art. Several others who have worked with the archive have spoken of the need to visit the homes of the informants in the Northern Cape, reimagining the lone quest of colonial romance in terms of pilgrimage and silent vigil.

One hopes that such diverse, ongoing afterlives fulfil the wishes of the master-narrator ||Kabbo, who in his testimony evoked so powerfully how *kukummi* borne by the natural conduits of wind and water and felt almost as a bodily presence by those attuned to them, provided the most vital links between the dispersed, dispossessed bands of the |*Xam-ka !ei*. The truth of his historical experience and that of his extended family is surely all but irrecoverable in the multiply translated language through which we now approach it. Yet the embodied understanding of place that so many of the extracts intimate perhaps finds a distant correlative in the unforeseen workings of its poetry on the readers of today, material that, once it has begun to act on the auditory imagination, cannot easily be forgotten:

> I must go together with the warm sun, while the ground is hot. For a little road it is not. For, it is a great road; it is long. I should reach my place, when the trees are dry. For I shall walk, letting the flowers become dry while I follow the path.
>
> Then, autumn will quickly be (upon) us there; () when I am sitting at my (own) place. For, I shall not go to other places; for, I must remain at my (own) place, the name of which I have told my Master; he knows it; he knows, (having) put it down. And thus () my name is plain (beside) it.
>
> (*Bushman Folklore*, p. 317)

Bibliography

Anderson, P. R. *Foundling's Island*, University of Cape Town Press, 2007.

Anthing, L. Cape Parliamentary Papers: Report A39, Cape Town: Government House, 1863.

Bank, A. *Bushmen in a Victorian World: The Remarkable Story of the Bleek-Lloyd Collection of Bushman Folklore*, Cape Town: Double Storey, 2006.

Barnard, A. '!Ke e: |xarra||ke: Multiple Origins and Multiple Meanings of the Motto', *African Studies* 62:2 (2003), 243–50.

Barrow, J. *Travels into the Interior of Southern Africa, in the Years 1797 and 1798*, London: T. Cadell and W. Davies, 1801.

Bennun, N. *The Broken String*, London: Viking, 2004.

Biesele, M. *Women Like Meat: The Folklore and Foraging Ideology of the Kalahari Ju/'hoan*, Johannesburg: Witwatersrand University Press, 1993.

Bleek, D. F. *A Bushman Dictionary*, New Haven: American Oriental Society, 1956.

   'Bushman Folklore', *Africa* 2 (1929), 302–13.

   The Mantis and his Friends, Cape Town: Maskew Miller, 1924.

Bleek, W. H. I. *A Comparative Grammar of South African Language*, Parts I and II, London: Trübner & Co., 1862 and 1869.

   The Library of His Excellency Sir George Grey, K.C.B., London: Trübner & Co., 1858.

   Report of Dr Bleek Concerning his Researches into the Bushman Language and Customs, Cape Town: House of Assembly, 1873.

   Reynard the Fox in South Africa, or Hottentot Fables and Tales, London: Trübner & Co., 1864.

   Second Report Concerning Bushman Researches: A Brief Account of Bushman Folk-Lore and other Texts, Cape Town: Government Printer, 1875.

Bleek, W. H. I., and L. C. Lloyd. *Specimens of Bushman Folklore*, London: George Allen, 1911.

Brink, A. *The First Life of Adamastor* [1993], London: Vintage, 2000.

   Praying Mantis, London: Secker & Warburg, 2005.

Brown, D. *To Speak of this Land: Identity and Belonging in South Africa and Beyond*, Pietermaritzburg: University of KwaZulu-Natal Press, 2006.

   Voicing the Text: South African Oral Poetry and Performance, Cape Town: Oxford University Press, 1998.

Burchell, W. *Travels in the Interior of Southern Africa*, London: Longman, Hurst, Rees, Orme and Brown, 1822–4.

Chapman, M. *Southern African Literatures*, new edn, London: Longman, 2003.

Christiansë, Y. *Unconfessed*, Cape Town: Kwela Books, 2006.

Coetzee, J. M. *White Writing: On the Culture of Letters in South Africa*, New Haven: Yale University Press, 1988.

Cope, J., and U. Krige (eds.). *The Penguin Book of South African Verse*, Harmondsworth: Penguin, 1968.

Cronin, J. *Inside* [1983], London: Jonathan Cape, 1987.

Dapper, Olfert. *Naukeurige Beschrijvinge der Afrikaensche Gewesten*, Amsterdam: Jacob van Meurs, 1668.

Deacon, H. J., and J. Deacon. *Human Beginnings in South Africa: Uncovering the Secrets of the Stone Age*, London: AltaMira Press, 1999.

Deacon, J. '"My place is the Bitterpits": The Home Territory of Bleek and Lloyd's |Xam San Informants', *African Studies* 45 (1986), 135–55.

   'A Tale of Two Families: Wilhelm Bleek, Lucy Lloyd and the |Xam San of the Northern Cape', in Skotnes (ed.), *Miscast*, 93–113.

Deacon, J., and T. A. Dowson (eds.). *Voices from the Past*, Johannesburg: Witwatersrand University Press, 1996.

Deacon, J., and C. Foster. *My Heart Stands in the Hill*, Cape Town: Struik, 2005.

Dubow, S. *Scientific Racism in Modern South Africa*, Cambridge University Press, 1995.

Elphick, R. *Kraal and Castle: Khoikhoi and the Founding of White South Africa*, New Haven: Yale University Press, 1977.

Gordon, R. *The Bushman Myth: The Making of a Namibian Underclass*, Boulder, CO: Westview Press, 1992.

Gray, S. (ed.). *The Penguin Book of Southern African Stories*, Harmondsworth: Penguin, 1985. *The Penguin Book of Southern African Verse*, Harmondsworth: Penguin, 1989.

Guenther, M. *Bushman Folktales: Oral Traditions of the Nharo of Botswana and the |Xam of the Cape*, Stuttgart: Steiner-Verlag Wiesbaden, 1989.

Tricksters and Trancers: Bushman Religion and Society, Bloomington: Indiana University Press, 1999.

Herbert, T. *Some Yeares Travels into Divers Parts of Asia and Afrique . . .*, London: 1638.

Hewitt, R. 'The Oral Literature of the San and Related Peoples', in B. W. Andrzejewski et al. (eds.), *Literatures in African Languages: Theoretical Issues and Sample Surveys*, Cambridge University Press, 1985, 650–72.

'Reflections on Narrative', in Skotnes (ed.), *Claim to the Country*, 161–7.

Structure, Meaning and Ritual in the Narratives of the Southern San, Hamburg: Helmut Buske Verlag, 1986.

Hollman, J. C. (ed.). *Customs and Beliefs of the |Xam Bushmen*, Johannesburg: Witswatersrand University Press, 2004.

James, A. *The First Bushman's Path*, Pietermaritzburg: University of KwaZulu-Natal Press, 2001.

Kannemeyer, J. C. *Geskiedenis van die Afrikaanse Literatuur*, vol. 1, Cape Town and Pretoria: Academica, 1978.

Kolb, P. *Caput Bonae Speii hodiernum . . .*, Nuremberg: 1719.

Krog, A. *die sterre sê 'tsau' and the stars say 'tsau'*, Cape Town: Kwela Books, 2004.

Lewis-Williams, D. *Believing and Seeing: Symbolic Meanings in Southern San Rock Art*, London: Academic Press, 1981.

The Mind in the Cave: Consciousness and the Origins of Art, London: Thames & Hudson, 2002.

Stories that Float from Afar, Cape Town: David Philip, 2000.

Le Vaillant F. *Voyage dans l'intérieur de l'Afrique par le Cap de Bonne-Espérance*, 2 vols., Paris: Leroy, 1790.

Lewis-Williams, J. D. '"A visit to the Lion's House": The Structures, Metaphors and Sociopolitical Significance of a Nineteenth-Century Bushman Myth', in Deacon and Domson, *Voices from the Past*, 122–41.

Lichtenstein, H. [Martin Heinrich Carl]. *Travels in Southern Africa in the Years 1803, 1804, 1805 and 1806*, 2 vols., trans. Anna Plumptre, London: Henry Colburn, 1812–15.

Livingstone, D. *A Littoral Zone*, Cape Town: Carrefour Press, 1991.

Lloyd, L. C. 'A Short Account of Bushman Material Collected', *Third Report Concerning Bushman Researches*, London: David Nutt, 1889.

Marais, E. *Dwaalstories* [1927], Cape Town: Human & Rousseau, 1959.

Markowitz, A. *The Rebirth of the Ostrich, and other Stories of the Kalahari Bushmen told in their manner by Arthur Markowitz*, Gaborone: National Museum and Art Gallery, 1971.

    With Uplifted Tongue: Stories, Myths and Fables of the South African Bushmen told in their manner, Cape Town: Central News Agency, 1956.

Marshall, L. '!Kung Bushman Religious Beliefs', *Africa* 32 (1962), 221–52.

Martin, J. *A Millimetre of Dust: Visiting Ancestral Sites*, Cape Town: Kwela Press, 2007.

Masilela, N. 'The White South African Writer in our National Situation', in G. V. Davis, J. Jansen and M. Manaka (eds.), *Matatu*, special issue on '*Towards Liberation: Culture and Resistance in South Africa*', 2:3–4 (1988), 48–75.

Moran, S. *Representing Bushmen: South Africa and the Origin of Language*, University of Rochester Press, 2009.

Mossop, E. E. (ed.). *The Journals of Wikar, Coetsé and Van Reenen*, vol. xv, Cape Town: Van Riebeeck Society, 1935.

Orpen, J. M. 'A Glimpse into the Mythology of the Maluti Bushmen', *Cape Monthly Magazine* 9 (1874), 1–13.

Penn, N. '"Fated to Perish": The Destruction of the Cape San', in Skotnes, *Miscast*, 81–91.

Ricard, A. 'Africa and Writing', in F. A. Irele and S. Gikandi (eds.), *The Cambridge History of African and Caribbean Literature*, vol. i, Cambridge University Press, 2003.

Robbins, D. *On the Bridge of Goodbye: The Story of South Africa's Discarded San Soldiers*, Johannesburg: Jonathan Ball, 2007.

Sacks, P. *In these Mountains*, London: Collier Macmillan, 1986.

Schapera, I. *The Khoisan Peoples of South Africa: Bushmen and Hottentots*, London: Routledge & Kegan Paul, 1930.

Schmidt, S. *Catalogue of the Khoisan Folktales of Southern Africa*, 2 vols., Hamburg: Helmut Buske Verlag, 1989.

    'Folktales of the Non-Bantu Speaking Peoples in Southern Africa (Bushmen, Khoikhoi, Dama)', *Folklore* 86:2 (summer 1975), 99–114.

    Märchen aus Namibia, Düsseldorf and Cologne: Eugen Diederich Verlag, 1981.

    'The Relevance of the Bleek/Lloyd Folktales to the General Khoisan Traditions', in Deacon and Dowson, *Voices from the Past*, 100–21.

Skotnes, P. '"Civilised off the face of the earth": Museum Display and the Silencing of the |Xam', *Poetics Today* 22:2 (summer 2001), 299–321.

Skotnes, P. (ed.). *Claim to the Country: The Archive of Wilhelm Bleek and Lucy Lloyd*, Johannesburg: Jacana and Athens: Ohio University Press, 2007.

    'The Digital Bleek and Lloyd', http://lloydbleekcollection.cs.uct.ac.za/, 2005–7, accessed January 2011.

    Miscast: Negotiating the Presence of the Bushmen, University of Cape Town Press, 1996.

    Sound from the Thinking Strings: A Visual, Literary, Archaeological and Historical Interpretation of the Final Years of |Xam Life, Cape Town: Axeage Private Press, 1991.

Sparrman, A. *A Voyage to the Cape of Good Hope . . . from the Year 1772 to 1776*, trans. G. Forster, London: 1785.

Stow, G. W. *The Native Races of South Africa; A History of the Intrusion of the Hottentots and Bantu into the Hunting Grounds of the Bushmen, and the Aborigines of the Country* [1905], Cape Town: Struik, 1964.

Tachard, G. *A Relation of the Voyage to Siam . . . by Six Jesuits . . . in the Year 1685*. London: F. Robinson and A. Churchill, 1688.

Van der Post, L. *The Heart of the Hunter* [1961], London: Chatto & Windus, 1969.

The Lost World of the Kalahari [1958], London: Chatto & Windus, 1988.

Vinnicombe, P. *People of the Eland: Rock Paintings of the Drakensberg Bushmen as a Reflection of their Life and Thought*, Pietermaritzburg: University of Natal Press, 1976.

Von Wielligh, G. R. *Boesman Stories*, vols. I–IV, Cape Town: Nasionale Pers, 1919–21.

Van Vuuren, H. 'Orality in the Margins of Literary History: Prolegomena to a Study of Interaction between Bushmen Orality and Afrikaans Literature', in J. A. Smit, J. van Wyk and J-P. Wade (eds.), *Rethinking Literary History in South Africa*, Durban: Y Press, 1996, 129–35.

Watson, S. 'Annals of Plagiarism: Antjie Krog and the Bleek and Lloyd Collection', *New Contrast* 33:2 (2005), 48–61.

Return of the Moon: Versions from the |Xam, Cape Town: Carrefour Press, 1991.

Wessels, M. *Bushman Letters: Interpreting |Xam Narrative*, Johannesburg: Witwatersrand University Press, 2010.

2

A contextual analysis of Xhosa *iimbongi* and their *izibongo*

RUSSELL H. KASCHULA

Southern African oral literature

Southern African oral literature has conventionally been grouped into three primary genres: oral poetry (praise poems and songs); narrative material (folk-tales, myths, legends, fables); and wisdom-lore (idioms, riddles and proverbs) (Lestrade, 'Domestic and Communal Life'). An analysis of these various genres and how they relate to aspects of modern-day African existence such as music, gender, medicine, theatre, cinema, religion, politics and history can be found in my edited work, *African Oral Literature* (2001). This chapter begins by outlining some of the most important early works in the narrative genre of the folk-tale and then moves on to oral poetry, the main focus of this chapter.

A number of seminal works over the years have emphasised the importance of southern African oral literature and offered different approaches to analysis. A few of these dealing with the folk-tale in southern Africa are contained in my edited work, *Foundations in Southern African Oral Literature* (1993). Collected in that volume is a broad-based essay dating from 1930 by G. H. Franz, which deals generally with the preliterary period as well as the development of modern written literature in Lesotho. Franz looks at oral poetry, *lithoko*, as well as folk-tales, *litsomo*. He traces the development of Christian and school literature and includes a valuable analysis of writings concerning folklore and custom. In the same volume, P. D. Cole-Beuchat (1958) provides a contextualised analysis of various oral literary genres (riddles, folk-tales and proverbs) among the Tsonga-Ronga peoples.

Further seminal works dealing with oral poetry and song include E. W. Grant's 1927 contribution on praise poems in honour of important Zulu chiefs such as Senzangakhona, Shaka, Dingane and Mpande, and P. A. W. Cook's similar work of 1931, where he analyses the praises produced in honour of Swazi chiefs. B. W. Vilakazi's 1938 analysis of the development of poetry in isiZulu is also important. Vilakazi analyses poetical expression in isiZulu, drawing on traditional poetry and song. He offers some comment on the future of Zulu poetry, which he maintains must reflect the indomitable Zulu spirit. S. K. Lekgothoane and N. J. van Warmelo (1938) provide a fascinating collection of animal praises in Northern Sotho. They include praises of the elephant, baboon, lion and so on. All these works are included in my *Foundations*, as is G. Fortune's 1948 original and substantial analysis of recurrent structures in Shona oral poetry, which draws on extensive fieldwork. Presenting an idiosyncratic approach, H. I. E. Dhlomo ('African Drama and Poetry', 1939) seeks to explore the relationship between oral poetry and drama. By providing various examples of dramatic presentations, he attempts to prove that many *izibongo* were dramatic and produced for the purposes of entertainment. Already, then, this speaks to the question of the mixing of genres, discourses and styles, thereby suggesting that oral literature does not necessarily fall into clearly definable genres. This is what Gunner refers to as 'genre boundary jumping' in relation to worker poetry ('Mixing the Discourses', pp. 68–75).

In more recent times, a number of scholars have contributed to the scholarly analysis of oral narrative in southern Africa. These include Duncan Brown, Noverino Canonici, David Coplan, Ruth Finnegan, Manie Groenewald, Liz Gunner, Isobel Hofmeyr, R. H. Kaschula, W. F. Kuse, Mokgale Makgopa, Mashudu C. Mashige, M. I. P. Mokitimi, S. J. Neethling, Jeff Opland, Harold Scheub and N. S. Turner. Scheub, for example, contributed significantly to the understanding of the use of expansible images and parallel image sets in isi-Xhosa folk-tale performances ('Technique of the Expansible Image'). Neethling has provided a contribution which is an example of analysing the sociocultural factors underpinning the Xhosa folk-tale ('Eating Forbidden Fruit'). Canonici has provided extensive work on the Zulu narrative tradition and included an analysis of the folk-tale and its functions (*Zulu Folktale Tradition*). I now concentrate on one form of oral literature, namely Xhosa *izibongo*.

Introducing the Xhosa *imbongi*

Definitions are in essence anachronistic and require constant revision. In my definition of the *imbongi* provided in my book on Xhosa oral poetry, *The Bones of the Ancestors are Shaking*, it is suggested that the contemporary *imbongi* can be classified as a person involved in the oral production of poetry using traditional styles and techniques in any given context where they are recognised as mediator, praiser, critic and educator and accepted by the audience as such (p. 47). However, there is no mention of technology which would need to form part of a contemporary definition. Today the discourse used by *iimbongi* is moulded within both the physical and technological contexts in which they find themselves. This is clearly illustrated by the case study presented later in this chapter.

Archie Mafeje, in 'A Chief Visits Town', defined the *imbongi* as 'a praise poet who frequented the chief's great place and travelled with him in traditional Nguni society. His distinctive feature is that he can recite poems without having prepared them beforehand' (p. 91). If one bears in mind the socioeconomic, political and technological changes which have taken place in South African society since the colonial era, this definition no longer reflects the reality of the situation. In *Xhosa Oral Poetry*, Opland acknowledges the fact that 'The actual situation today is complicated by social processes such as urbanisation, assimilation, and formal education' (p. 33).

A definition of the contemporary Xhosa *imbongi* would need to consider recent developments such as the Internet, the role of the music industry in the commercialisation of this oral art, and more importantly the influence on the tradition of shifts in contemporary political power, for example to female political leadership in South Africa.

Iimbongi and the early colonial era

Some of the earliest recorded *izibongo* (1827) were produced by Ntsikana kaGaba. He was one of the first Xhosa Christian converts and he praised God as he would have done a chief, thereby producing a number of Xhosa hymns, including *Ulo Thixo Omkhulu Ngosezulwini* (He, the Great God in Heaven) (Hodgsen, *God of the Xhosa*, p. 24). The Reverend Lordwyck Xozwa is perhaps an example of a modern-day *imbongi* that operates in the tradition of Ntsikana (Kaschula, *Bones of the Ancestors*, pp. 110–25).

Another early and relatively unknown Xhosa poet who operated in the *izibongo* tradition is Nontsizi Mgqwetho. Her work has been collected and published in Opland's *The Nation's Bounty* (2007). In accordance with the modern-day tradition, Hofmeyr, in the foreword to Opland's book, asserts: 'Central to Mgqwetho's concerns lie questions of leadership and there are few organisations which escape her stern admonishment for lack of direction, strategy and purpose in the face of colonial oppression, on the one hand, and greed and materialism on the other ("our people slip / on slopes with carpets of cash")' (p. x). Arguably, this poetry remains extremely relevant in modern-day South Africa. Another great oral poet who performed and wrote in the late 1800s and early 1900s, a contemporary of Mgqwetho, was S. E. K. Mqhayi. He was responsible for the crossover from orality to literacy and remains one of the most recognised Xhosa *imbongi*. Opland, in *Xhosa Oral Poetry*, provides a succinct summary of Mqhayi's life and work in the early 1900s. Mqhayi began praising his childhood companions and the cattle that they were herding. He later began writing for a Xhosa newspaper, *Izwi Labantu*, and so began his career as an author. Opland has also recently translated sixty-eight pieces of Mqhayi's writing into English in *Abantu Besizwe: Historical and Biographical writings of S. E. K. Mqhayi, 1902–1944*. These literary texts, published both in the original isiXhosa with English translations in this book, serve to highlight the complex link between literature and history in South African society.

Iimbongi and the apartheid era, 1948–94

One of the greatest South African poets to emerge during the apartheid era was D. L. P. Yali-Manisi, who, in Opland's words, 'wears the mantle of S. E. K. Mqhayi' (video recording, University of Natal Oral Documentation and Research Centre). Manisi lived in the Khundulu valley in the Eastern Cape. As a result of his relationship with Opland, he worked as a researcher at Rhodes University as well as the University of Transkei. Opland's research on Yali-Manisi culminated in his 2005 work *The Dassie and the Hunter: A South African Meeting*. This book contains an extensive analysis of Yali-Manisi and his poetry, primarily against the sociopolitical backdrop of apartheid. In one of his more famous poems, 'The bird of the forest grows restless', performed during the height of apartheid in 1985, he refers to the colonisers as 'Things who don't fear death / Who crossed the sea leaning on cannon and breach-loader / They came to Africa and raped it' (Kaschula, *Bones of the Ancestors*, p. 247). Opland provides a slightly different translation for the last line: 'They entered and forced the abortion of Africa' (*Dassie*, p. 250).

Melikhaya Mbutuma was another poet who operated during apartheid, often producing poetry which was critical of the homeland system as designed by apartheid leaders. He once referred to Chief K. D. Matanzima, the homeland leader of Transkei, as an *iqaqa* (polecat) and *uxam* (leguan or monitor lizard). A polecat is both black and white, while the lizard lives on both land and water. These animal metaphors indicate that Matanzima was trying to get the best of both worlds. The poet concludes by stating that Matanzima would come out of the water 'rotten and stinking', thereby referring to Matanzima's ultimate political demise as part of the downfall of apartheid (Kaschula, *Bones of the Ancestors*, pp. 136–7).

In order to understand the form and function of isiXhosa oral poetry as produced for example by poets such as Yali-Manisi and Mbutuma, it is important to have some historical perspective on how the tradition operated in past times. But it is equally important to locate the tradition within a contemporary environment in order to avoid the tradition being romanticised and from being studied as a dead tradition. Gunner argues similarly by placing this form of poetry in a contemporary context. She refers to the southern African tradition as follows: 'Both Zulu and Xhosa praise poetry . . . because they exploit powerful cultural symbols with such ease, appeal in a very direct way to their listener's emotions and attitudes. They intrinsically combine political and aesthetic appeal and perhaps for this reason represent valuable "property" in any ideological struggle' ('Dying Tradition', p. 33). The notion of 'ideological' significance over the years, and the sense that this poetry represents 'valuable property', are interesting ideas. With regard to the source of power and poetic function, Vail and White point out that in southern Africa, 'it is not the poet that is licensed by literary convention, it is the poem' (*Power and the Praise Poem*, p. 56). But it can be argued that it is the tradition itself that needs to be recognised. This tradition includes the poet, the poem and the context – the performance as a whole, as with the example of Mbutuma provided above. Is it not within the tradition itself that the importance and power lies, hence its possible 'manipulation' by those who seek to control the function of the tradition for their own benefit? Arguably, it is within the tradition as a whole that the function of the oral poet as social, historical and political commentator can be found. On one hand, the power of oral poetry and of the poet lies in the tradition as a whole, on the other hand, it exists in relation to those who are in control – there is a dependency relationship between the poet and those who hold power. The past and present function can be looked at as continually changing, partly in accordance with the popular support enjoyed by the authorities, and partly in accordance with the extent to which the authorities are able to appropriate the tradition, thereby manipulating it and informing its function. Mbutuma was often harassed by the apartheid security police and refused to be manipulated. Another example of such a poet would be Qangule. He was also opposed to the homeland system and he was ultimately exiled to Zambia due to his anti-apartheid stance.

Over the years the narrative tradition of the *imbongi* or Xhosa oral poet has never been a static one. As Opland puts it, 'the dynamic element is necessary in our approach since the tradition of Xhosa oral poetry has clearly changed and is continuing to change with changes in Cape Nguni society. Tradition is not a lifeless thing; it alters and adapts to new social circumstances' (*Xhosa Oral Poetry*, p. 236).

Iimbongi and the emergence of a new democracy

Many elements of the tradition have been dropped or adapted. Nevertheless the concept of singing praises still retains an identifiable character which is based on the tradition in the past. The *imbongi*'s relationship with the audience and the role which their poetry plays within that particular society are of utmost importance. Any analysis of the tradition will therefore have to take into account the context of the performance, the audience itself and the function and role of the *imbongi* in a society which is subjected to constant sociocultural, political and technological pressure. What follows in this chapter is a case study of the late Bongani Sitole, in order to show how the tradition has adapted to a technologised, globalised world. Reference will also be made to other 'struggle' *iimbongi* as well as those representing the era of political freedom and democracy.

The role of the *imbongi* as mediator and as political and social commentator of the power base within which they operate has been retained over time. For example, whilst Yali-Manisi largely represented the interest of the Thembu chiefdom, Alfred Qabula, an *imbongi* who operated within the Congress of South African Trade Unions (COSATU), saw his role as that of mediator between the people and the union which he represented, in the same way that the traditional *imbongi* mediated between the people and the chief. Sitole saw his role as mediator between organisations or chiefs with differing viewpoints and also as an adviser to such organisations or chiefs. Sitole and Qabula also saw their roles as including the awakening of political consciousness. Gunner states that 'The *izibongo* are a unique tool in raising workers' consciousness of their union and its role in their lives as workers. Yet they are also quite clearly an expression of a strong and old art form with its roots deep in social and political awareness' ('Dying Tradition', p. 35). In the 1990s the tradition proved to be extremely dynamic. Urbanisation, the impact of education, the formation and later disbanding of the independent homelands, the changing nature of the chieftainship, the emergence of black nationalism during apartheid, the subsequent release of political prisoners and unbanning of organisations in the early 1990s, South Africa's transition to democracy, shifts in political power especially since about 2000, as well as the rapid emergence of new technologies all had their effect on the tradition. In his book *In the Time of Cannibals*, Coplan analyses changes in performance creativity and culture over the years in South Africa and provides concrete evidence of the adaptability of tradition, with specific reference to the Sotho tradition. He states that 'the production and reproduction of performances must be located within the set of political, economic, social and cultural, relations between performers and the total context in which they perform' (p. 242).

In accordance with Coplan's methodology, this chapter will contextualise some of Sitole's performances. This will provide a more holistic impression of only one important *imbongi*, but my analysis will also outline the factors which have contributed to change in the tradition within the reality of globalisation and increasing reliance on what one could term technologised literacy or 'technauriture'. His life and work is analysed in *The Bones of the Ancestors are Shaking*, as well as in another book containing an introduction to Sitole's life, work and selected poetry *Qhiwu-u-u-la!* (see below).

Sitole was born at Mqhekezweni near Mthatha in the Eastern Cape (Transkei) on 21 June 1937. At this time the area was under the control of Chief Jongintaba Dalindyebo. From 1959 until 1976 Sitole worked as a migrant worker in the Johannesburg area as well as in Port Elizabeth. He then returned to Mthatha, where he resided until his death in 2003. He had retired from the then University of Transkei where he worked as a research assistant in the Bureau for African Research and Documentation.

According to Sitole, he began praising while he was still at school in about 1954. He would praise at various school functions such as school concerts. Sitole's poetry shows that, although the themes of the poetry have changed or been added to, they have been adapted to accommodate new pressures and new power bases. The traditional *iimbongi* (attached to chiefs) were concerned mainly with events which were taking place in the immediate area where the chief lived, hence it can be argued that the poetry of Yali-Manisi, Mbutuma and Mqhayi is rich in genealogical references. Historical themes also permeated their poetry. Today, modern *iimbongi* are concerned with contemporary events; Sitole's poetry was therefore fuelled by events immediately prior to the 1994 general elections, and the audience's response. It also contains historical perspectives regarding the origins of the struggle against apartheid. Again, the adaptation of themes reflects changes in 'textual elements', those features which, according to Opland, are reflected in a transcribed text (*Xhosa Oral Poetry*, p. 241). The themes have changed because the political and social environment on which poetry is a commentary has changed. Changes in themes are also linked directly to changes in what Opland terms 'contextual elements' (p. 253). The context in which the poetry is performed is no longer limited to the chief. The use, for example, of political rallies and meetings as well as contemporary open mike sessions as platforms for the performance of *izibongo* have also encouraged a change in the thematic repertoire of poets such as Sitole and the more recently acknowledged 'President's Poet', Zolani Mkiva (see below) (Kaschula, '*Imbongi* and Griot', pp. 64–5). The repertoire now often reflects the new power bases which were legitimised with the emergence of a democratic South African society as well as shifts in power within these respective power bases.

Sitole stated in interviews conducted in the 1990s that his inspiration for producing oral poetry depended entirely on the occasion at which he found himself together with a particular group of people. The occasion and the audience largely determined whether or not he felt inspired to produce. When in the mood, Sitole burst forth, producing poetry in an inspired state he accounted for as *ukuthwasa*, where he moved into a state of 'emotional intensity' which was associated with Xhosa ritual and religious expression. Sitole's performance was always a spontaneous one, of which he kept no record. In his article '"Even under the Rine of Terror..."', Jeremy Cronin makes the following general comments with regard to this type of protest oral poetry produced in the 1980s and 1990s:

> The poetry is, clearly, largely a poetry of performance. The bodily presence of the poet becomes an important feature of the poetics. Arm gestures, clapping, and head nodding are often used expressively and deictically. The poets also draw freely from the current political lexis of gestures: the clenched fist salute of people's power (*Amandla ngawethu*); the index finger pointing emphatically down to signal *Ngo!* ('Here and now!') after the chanted call *Inkululeko* ('Freedom'); or the slow, hitchhiker-like thumb sign to signal 'Let it come back' (*Afrika ... Mayibuye*). (pp. 18–19)

Although the modern *imbongi* normally holds a microphone, which can be an inhibiting factor, there is still a lot of movement and the *imbongi* is never stationary. Gesture is therefore still an important part of the performance. The performance as a whole plays an integral part in keeping the audience's attention. It also enhances or supports much of what the *imbongi* is saying.

In terms of what Opland refers to as 'contextual elements' (those features which an audience can see and hear but which are not reflected in a transcribed text), some changes have taken place. Individual poets such as Sitole adapted dress in order to suit their particular power base; they have therefore reacted differently over time to these 'contextual elements'.

Shouts of *amandla* accompanied by audience response were common in Sitole's poetry, again indicating the political power base from which Sitole sometimes operated as commentator. This political dimension was also clearly supported by the content of his poetry. In an interview in May 1990, Sitole stated that the *iimbongi imbongi* would align themselves with a policy with which they agreed. He stated: 'There is the African National Congress (ANC) and the Pan African Congress (PAC), so I don't function with the PAC, their system does not agree with me' (video recording, Bureau for African Research and Documentation, 'Changing Praises'). Although he may not have been inspired to praise the PAC as such, he was still in a position to try and join the two together: 'What I could do is join together the PAC [Pan African Congress] and ANC [African National Congress], and show the road on which we should go.' Sitole therefore aligned himself with a particular power base in the 1990s with which he felt comfortable.

Contemporary *iimbongi* do not necessarily have a uniform dress, or any particular style of dress for that matter. It depends entirely on the individual performer. The *imbongi* no longer wears the traditional animal-skin robe and animal-skin hat. Traditionally they also used to carry a spear. However, one often sees *iimbongi* wearing remnants of the traditional dress, such as an animal-skin hat, while dressed in a suit. According to Cronin,

> The clothing of the performer should also be noted. As often as not it is unexceptional. However, quite a few poets, especially those who adopt a more bardic tone, don dashikis as an integral part of their performance. The several trade union praise poets also tend to wear special clothing, traditional skins and ornamentation, or a modern-day facsimile of the kind already noted. ('"Rine of Terror"', p. 19)

Sitole was more traditional in his dress, choosing to wear a fully-fledged traditional animal skin and animal hat. He also carried a knobkerrie (a traditional short club). But the skin was braided with the ANC colours and the stick was beaded in ANC colours. Also, he would often wear an ANC T-shirt under his skins. These skins were finally placed alongside his coffin in his grave at his burial.

The poetry in Sitole's book was initially recorded on tape and video, with more than one hundred recordings made, reflecting the volatile pre-election period of 1990–4. The poetry was then transcribed into isiXhosa by the performer. Together with co-author Mandla Matyumza, all three of us then worked together to translate the material into English. The book *Qhiwu-u-u-la!! Return to the Fold!!* (ed. Kashula and Matyazuma), containing fifteen selected poems in isiXhosa and English, was published by Via Afrika in 1995 and then reissued in 2006.

Sitole's work is diverse and dynamic. Take the following extract produced at the reburial of Chief Sabata Dalindyebo (an opponent of the independent homeland system). Chief Sabata died in exile in Zambia during the Matanzima era in Transkei. He was now being buried at his rightful burial place, with the blessing of the then new military leader, Major-General Bantu Holomisa, who was pro-ANC at that time. Also present was regional ANC representative for Transkei and councillor to the royal Dalindyebo family, A. S. Xobololo. The full version of this poem appears in *Qhiwu-u-u-la!!* (pp. 62–3).

> *Amandla!* Power!
> The grandchild of Xobololo is going to stand up,
> Xobololo's going to peel the tree bark until gum appears,
> Xobololo's trying,
> Xobololo's suffering from asthma,
> His buttocks are chafed due to being jailed because of Daliwonga (Matanzima).

Sitole is critical of Chief K. D. Matanzima, who is blamed for much hardship experienced by the ANC and its members in this region during earlier days. By condemning the action of Matanzima, the *imbongi* is emphasising the power base of the ANC. This is especially true if one bears in mind that Matanzima was never an ANC supporter and that he always aligned himself with the previous apartheid regimes.

The following extracts are taken from poems produced during Mandela's first visit to Transkei after his release from prison:

> It's a dream of the dead,
> It's a dream that people thought would never come true,
> People cried till they gave up,
> How many souls are under the ground?
> How many corpses because of Mandela?
> Mand-e-e-e-la Mand-e-e-e-la
> Mand-e-e-e-la Mand-e-e-e-la.
> (Kaschula, 'Mandela comes Home', p. 9)

The *imbongi* here refers to those comrades who died in the struggle in order to get Mandela released. The poet also refers to those comrades who died, never thinking that freedom would be so near. In lines 6 and 7 the *imbongi* moves from one side of the stage to the other, shouting Mandela's name in a praising way, and, in the process, emphasising Mandela's power and that of the ANC. The poem continues:

> They call him even if they don't know him,
> They call him even if they've never seen him before,
> That's why we need to be humble and respect one another,

Because we have seen him at last.
An example of Jesus followed by many people,
He's come with them in truth and dignity,
That's where we can hear and witness his words,
That's where we've confirmed that his words are true.

The *imbongi* here plays a mediating role, asking people to respect one another, and the integration of Christian mythology and imagery within contemporary political discourse is innovative and significant. Christianity is regarded as one of the cornerstones of Xhosa society. The church wields significant power within Xhosa communities. Many *iimbongi* also operate within the church, praising God in the same way as a chief would have been praised. As mentioned earlier in this chapter, Hodgsen, in *The God of the Xhosa*, notes that the first Christian *imbongi* to praise God using the traditional *izibongo* style was Ntsikana. The use of Christian mythology by Sitole is further proof of the adaptability of the tradition. Sithole continues:

Things are approached with skill,
Things are approached carefully if they're to succeed,
They're not approached with vigour,
They're not approached with speed,
He's steady,
The son of Ngubengcuka of Ngangelizwe,
He's steady,
He's accompanied by his disciples,
Like Jesus,
He's accompanied by Sisulu and Mbeki,
He's accompanied by Mhlaba,
He's accompanied by worthy men.

This extract sees the furthering of the biblical metaphor with Sisulu and others being described as disciples. Mandela is again compared to Jesus leading his people and accompanied by his disciples. Again this enhances the image of power within the ANC. There is also some reference to genealogy, namely 'the son of Ngubengcuka of Ngangelizwe'. This is common in traditional Xhosa *izibongo* and serves to strengthen the legitimacy of the individual being praised.

In another poem Sitole comments on the relationship between Mandela and Sisulu, from the early days up to the present. He also portrays the Rivonia trial and the law as follows:

He finished his education and they joined in the law of truth,
Imagine, lawyers representing themselves.
They just stood and defended themselves,
Because the truth couldn't be perverted.

(Kaschula, *Bones of the Ancestors*, p. 145)

Sitole comments here on the early involvement of Oliver Tambo and Nelson Mandela in the legal fraternity in Johannesburg before the banning of the ANC. This extract makes an interesting play on the word *gqwetha* (lawyer), bearing in mind that Mandela represented himself at the Rivonia trial. Mandela is presented as a lawyer of truth The power base of the ANC and its leaders is portrayed as truthful. This serves to subvert the power that was implicit in the South African legal system during the 1960s. Reference to the Rivonia trial can also be seen as an attempt by the poet to preserve aspects of history. The poem continues:

We'll never change,
Shangaans, Sothos, Malawains, Xhosas, Vendas, Tswanas,
And Zulus as well,
We are black people.
Please!
Please, son of Mandela,
Please go and fetch Gatsha Buthelezi and arrest him,
The problem is there.

In this extract Sitole appeals for unity. He calls for the arrest of Chief Buthelezi in order to create a climate for unity in the struggle. This is an excellent example of where the poet juxtaposes two power bases, and, in turn, makes use of this opportunity in order to legitimise the ideological power base from which he is operating at the time.

Stylistically, Sitole's poetry bears many similarities to traditional poetry produced about chiefs, for example by earlier poets such as Yali-Manisi. Those techniques which are generally associated with the production of traditional *izibongo* include personification, use of metaphor and simile, particularly the use of animal imagery. Examples of this would be where Sitole metaphorically compares Mandela to Christ, or to a black bull which is all powerful. Cronin states: 'The most notable verbal stylistic features are those commonly associated with principally oral cultures: the style tends to additive, aggregative, formulaic, and "copious" . . . The repetitive and formulaic features assist the performing poet mnemonically. But these features also assist the audience to hear and understand the poem' ('"Rine of Terror"', pp. 19–20).

The use of parallelism or repetition is interesting and useful. It allows the *imbongi* to develop a particular idea, either by initial, final or oblique linking in a sentence. Such repetitions assist the audience in their understanding of the meaning of the poem. Through the use of repetition, the poet also reinforces the power base from which he draws.

Opland refers to elements associated with stylistic technique as 'textual elements'. Clearly, certain of these textual elements have been retained over time, though they may have been adapted. The use of *amandla* as an opening formula is as example of such an adaptation. Again, the adaptation reflects affiliation to a particular power base, but at the same time is rooted within the tradition as it existed in the past. The use of animal metaphor and anaphoral repetition also reflects the retention of 'textual elements' found in traditional *izibongo*. According to Opland, metaphors involving *inkunzi*, 'a bull', were often used traditionally in order to refer to chiefs. In a poem of 1991 about Mandela, Sitole refers to Mandela as 'A bull that kicks up dust and stones' (*Qhiwu-u-u-la!*, pp. 56–61). Likewise, Meshack Masumpa makes use of this traditional animal metaphor in order to refer to COSATU [Congress of South African Trade Unions], as is clear from the title of the poem *UCosatu Inkunzi' Emnyama* (Cosatu, Black Bull). The metaphor is used throughout this poem. Past and present stylistic techniques are therefore interlinked (see Oliphant, *Ear to the Ground*, p. 88).

The tradition described above, together with the poet's stylistic techniques, have in recent times been transported into the realm of technology. This represents another leap in the revitalisation of oral tradition. The tradition was adapted from conventional uses in the 1990s, with political liberation, and it is now being allowed to reinvent itself within the realms of technology, such as the Internet and the music industry.

One of the *iimbongi imbongi* who has been at the cutting edge in this regard is Zolani Mkiva. He represents a new type of poet in the present democracy. Mkiva produced poetry in honour of both Nelson Mandela at his presidential inauguration as well as at the inauguration of Thabo Mbeki. As a result he became known as the 'President's Poet' or the 'Poet of the Nation'. His poetry has also been performed to the accompaniment of hip-hop contemporary music and he has a website on which he is represented. This places him within the realms of modern-day technology. He regards himself as a 'traditional praise singer who is dynamic' (Kaschula, *Bones of the Ancestors*, p. 92). The digitisation of oral literature within the ambit of modern technology requires further elaboration.

Towards a new definition: 'technauriture'

In late 2004 with a project team from elearning4Africa, a vision to collect, collate and digitise oral literature and tradition was espoused. This led to the initiation of the www.oralliterature.co.za project development plan. Through local, national and international linkages, it was envisaged that an open source platform would make the Sitole material accessible for the widest possible audience: from learners in schools across the country using the material as a learning resource, through to graduate students collecting oral traditions and writing teaching resources for post-graduate certificates and degrees, through to tourists learning about the 'real' history of the places they aim to visit.

It is access to technology that has created and encouraged a global culture of immediate access to information. From the above we can see that orality, literacy and technology are developing a special relationship. It may be argued that the idea of computers as machines is being replaced by that of computers as companions, facilitating the ability to speak, interact and even translate from one language to another, thereby enabling communication to take place, and, in many cases, community development. Performance poets are taking advantage of this new form of technologised orality, thereby giving rise to what is termed 'technauriture' in this chapter, in other words the developing relationship between technology, auriture and literature. Mkiva, for example, is a university graduate who makes use of corporate culture: he recently appeared in a television advertising campaign where he produced praises about a major corporation, as well as the 2010 soccer World Cup held in South Africa. He has also released a number of compact discs containing his poetry, which is set to music.

The interaction between orality and literacy is now more complex than one would expect. It would seem to be dependent on the individual performers and where they find themselves on a continuum between orality, literacy and technology. Hofmeyr rightly points out that there is an 'appropriation' of the oral into the literate, and the extent of this process depends on the individual performer ('*We Spend our Years*'). This appropriation is now often taken one step further, namely into the arena of technology. In fact, those extralinguistic elements, which are often lost in the transmission of orality into literacy, can again be recaptured through technology where soundbites or videoclips are uploaded. The reaction of the audience, the performer's intonation, voice quality and emphasis, the effects of rhythm, context and speed of perfor-mance are lost in the written version, but can once again come alive through the technologised version. This renders a performance of differing impact and intensity, a performance based in technauriture. The differences between individual poets further complicates the debate surrounding appropriate literary criticism of transcribed oral texts (Yai, 'Issues in Oral Poetry', pp. 62–3). Added to this would now be a literary criticism which incorporates aspects of technology. The dialectic between print, popular performance, technology and primary orality differs both in terms of individual performers, as well as the culture-specific community of, for example, Sitole's world as described in this chapter.

The interaction of national literatures with global literature is also apparent through technauriture. The Internet site www.litnet.co.za contains sections such as *Isikhundla Sababhali* (The Writer's Den) and *Phezulu* (From Above) which publish isiXhosa and isiZulu works, including poetry in traditional form, though only in transcribed written form. Alongside these sites representing indigenous works, one finds a critique of Afrikaans and English literature, thereby bringing together the local and the global through technology. This technauriture is illustrated by the fact that Microsoft bought a snippet of a poem by Sithole in honour of Nelson Mandela for its Encarta Encyclopaedia, thereby facilitating oral poetry's further absorption into the modern technological era.[1]

Increasingly, technology is opening up the field of oral literature in terms of commercialisation of the discipline in relation to the emergence of globalisation. With the advent of technauriture, it is important that the rights of the performers be protected contractually. This is a field which requires further exploration in relation to oral poetry as technauriture. Galane concludes as follows in regard to the Sepedi oral tradition of Kiba song and dance:

> Dance and drum designs are not . . . protected by any copyright law . . . Kiba and other forms of classical art and culture are continually being recorded by various radio stations . . . The royalty accrued on these songs should be paid back to the communities through a foundation or directly to the group that has performed the recorded and broadcast text . . . The institutional memory of South African . . . communities needs to be protected.
>
> ('Critical Analysis of the Kiba', pp. 147–9)

The proposal of a 'foundation' should be commended and needs further exploration. A question for the poets and their present and future marketing

---

1 Microsoft License Agreement, Sound Recording (single product), contract no. 16630.

agencies is: how does one go about placing a financial value on the oral, recorded word, even more so the oral, recorded, technologised word?

In their attempts to remain relevant amidst socioeconomic and political changes in South Africa, many *iimbongi* such as Mbutuma and Sitole moved away from those chiefs who were associated with apartheid. Directly linked to these changes is the fact that the power bases from which the *iimbongi* draw have also changed. The modern *iimbongi* are attracted to power bases which represent the interests of the average man in the street. The power of the *imbongi* should be given a holistic interpretation in terms of the tradition itself, together with all its contextual and ever-changing technological facets, rather than in relation to any single aspect of tradition. Gunner states:

> In an era of globalisation, orality has not disappeared but has often adapted itself in its many different forms to become a vehicle of the expression of the fears and hopes of new generations of Africans ... In many cases the electronic media ... have played an important role in enabling new genres to emerge, or adaptations of old genres to continue.
>
> ('Africa and Orality', pp. 70–1)

In adapting to changing power bases in southern Africa, *iimbongi* such as the late Bongani Sitole and the young Zolani Mkiva have proven the adaptability of culture and tradition in the face of drastic societal, political and technological changes. In the midst of societal change, the voice of the *iimbongi* link the traditions of the past to new directions and visions of the future.

In this chapter the term *technauriture* has been encouraged in order to highlight the complex nature of oral literature in the contemporary global reality. No poet remains untouched by the influence of radio, television, the Internet and the constant interaction between the oral and written word. In Africa, television and particularly radio remain the driving technological influences promoting the oral word. From this will follow the emergence of technauriture as an established discipline in the rest of the world. There is no longer any society which is not affected by what Walter Ong refers to as 'secondary orality' (*Orality and Literacy*, p. 68). The influence of technology on both the oral and written word has reached a point where both are inextricably linked, where both feed off each other in a symbiotic fashion – hence the chapter argues for the legitimisation of technauriture as a discipline in its own right – a term which links the past and the present.

Bibliography

Bureau for African Research and Documentation. 'Changing Praises: The Xhosa Imbongi Today', video recording, University of Transkei, n.d.

Canonici, N. *The Zulu Folktale Tradition*, Pietermaritzburg: University of Natal Press, 1993.

Coplan, D. *In the Time of Cannibals. The Word Music of South Africa's Basotho Migrants*, Johannesburg: Witwatersrand University Press, 1994.

Cronin, J. '"Even under the Rine of Terror . . . "': Insurgent South African Poetry', *Research in African Literatures* 19:1 (1988), 12–23.

Dhlomo, H. I. E. 'African Drama and Poetry', *South African Outlook*, 1 April 1939, 88–90.

Galane, S. 'A Critical Analysis of the Kiba (Song-Dance-Drama) Discourse', MA thesis, University of Cape Town, 2003.

Gunner, E. 'Africa and Orality', in T. Olaniyan and A. Quayson (eds.), *African Literature: An Anthology of Criticism and Theory*, Oxford: Blackwell, 2007.

'A Dying Tradition', *Social Dynamics* 12:2 (1986), 31–8.

'Mixing the Discourses: Genre Boundary Jumping in Popular Song', in E. Sienaert and M. Lewis (eds.), *Oral Tradition and Innovation: New Wine in Old Bottles*, Pietermaritzburg: University of Natal Oral Documentation and Research Centre, 1991, 68–75.

Hodgsen, J. *The God of the Xhosa: A Study of the Origins and Development of the Traditional Concepts of the Supreme Being*, Cape Town: Oxford University Press, 1982.

Hofmeyr, I. *'We Spend our Years as a Tale that is Told': Oral Historical Narrative in a South African Chiefdom*, Johannesburg: Witwatersrand University Press, 1993.

Kaschula, R. H. 'Imbongi and Griot', *Journal of African Cultural Studies* 12:1 (1999), 64–5.

'Mandela comes Home: The Poets' Perspective', *Journal of Ethnic Studies* 19:1 (1991), 1–19.

Kaschula, R. H. (ed.). *African Oral Literature. Functions in Contemporary Contexts*, Cape Town: New Africa Books, 2001.

The Bones of the Ancestors are Shaking: Xhosa Oral Poetry in Context, Cape Town: Juta, 2002.

Foundations in Southern African Oral Literature, Johannesburg: Witwatersrand University Press, 1993.

Kaschula, R. H., and M. Matyumza. *Qhiwu-u-u-la!! Return to the Fold!!* [1995], Pretoria: Via Afrika, 2006.

Lestrade, G. P. 'Domestic and Communal Life', in I. Schapera (ed.), *The Bantu-Speaking Tribes of South Africa*, Cape Town: Maskew Miller Longman, 1959, 119–28.

Mafeje, A. 'A Chief Visits Town', *Journal of Local Administration Overseas* 2 (1963), 91.

Neethling, S. J. 'Eating Forbidden Fruit', *South African Journal of African Languages* 11:1 (1991), 83–7.

Oliphant, A. (ed.). *Ear to the Ground: Contemporary Worker Poets*, Fordsburg: COSAW in association with COSATU, 1991.

Ong, W. *Orality and Literacy: The Technologising of the Word*, London: Methuen, 1982.

Opland, J. *Abantu Besizwe: Historical and Biographical Writings of S. E. K. Mqhayi, 1902–1944*, Johannesburg: Witwatersrand University Press, 2009.

The Dassie and the Hunter: A South African Meeting, Pietermaritzburg: University of KwaZulu-Natal Press, 2005.

The Nation's Bounty: The Xhosa Poetry of Nontsizi Mgqwetho, Johannesburg: Witwatersrand University Press, 2007.

Xhosa Oral Poetry: Aspects of a Black South African Tradition, Cambridge University Press, 1983.

Scheub, H. 'The Technique of the Expansible Image in Xhosa Ntsomi-Performances', *Research in African Literatures* 1:2 (1970), 119–46.

Sienart, E. *Zulu and Xhosa Oral Poetry Performed and Explained. Guide to the Nguni Oral Poetry*, Durban: Oral Documentation and Research Centre, University of Natal, 1985.

Vail, L., and L. White. *Power and the Praise Poem: Southern African Voices in History*, London: James Currey, 1991.

Yai, O. 'Issues in Oral Poetry', in *Discourse and its Disguises: The Interpretation of African Oral Texts*, Centre for West African Studies, University of Birmingham, 1989, 62–3.

3

'I sing of the woes of my travels':
the *lifela* of Lesotho

NHLANHLA MAAKE

Sotho folk literature, like that of other Bantu or indigenous languages spoken in South Africa, has been in existence since time immemorial, and has been passed by word of mouth from one generation to the succeeding, until in the latter half of the nineteenth century when it was transcribed by the Paris Evangelical Missionary Society, whose members arrived in Lesotho around 1833. Poetry in particular is a salient genre of this folk tradition. The literature in general is composed of a variety of genres, namely myths and legends (*ditshomo*), riddles (*dilotho*), proverbs and idioms (*maele le maelana*), folk-songs (*dipina*), hymns (*dikoma*), praises (*dithoko*) (Guma, *Likoma* and *Form, Content and Technique*), and through evolution to modern poetry (*dithothokiso*). *Dikoma* and *dithoko* are predominant forms of Sotho literature and perhaps the oldest recognisable form of poetry. However, they are not *sui generis*, as they are also found in the oral tradition of other languages, for example isiZulu and isiXhosa, as discussed in Chapters 2 and 4 of this volume.

The word *dithoko* (singular: *thoko*) is derived from the verbal root, *ho roka* (to praise). Later I shall illustrate how *dikoma* and *dithoko*, the oldest forms of poetry, have resonance in a later form of poetry that gained the somewhat curious term of *difela tsa ditsamaya naha* (also written as *lifela tsa litsamaea naha* in the orthography of Lesotho), which literally means 'songs of veteran travellers'. The singular of *difela* is *sefela*, which literally translates as 'hymn' in modern Sesotho.

Difela form a unique genre within the Sotho oral tradition. It developed from the migrant labour system and is not extant in the literary tradition of any of the other Bantu languages spoken in South Africa, or southern Africa as a whole for that matter. It has been argued that 'Basuto participation in the labour markets of southern Africa during the years between the diamond and gold discoveries . . . during the middle and the late nineteenth century was not atypical of other southern African peoples' (Kimble, 'Labour Migration in Basutoland', p. 119). Perhaps the question which begs an answer is why this particular migrant experience resulted in the development of a unique genre such as *difela* in only one language group. Perhaps its uniqueness, as I shall argue and demonstrate in this chapter, derives from the landlocked location of the Kingdom of Lesotho (formerly Basutoland up to independence in 1966), within the Republic of South Africa.

It seems strange that while the migrant labour system – where a mass labour force migrated to South Africa for the purposes of supplying labour in the industrialised areas of the country and, up to a point, farms – affected other southern African countries such as Swaziland, Botswana (formerly Bechuanaland), Mozambique, Zimbabwe (formerly Southern Rhodesia and then Rhodesia) and Malawi (formerly Nyasaland), it is only Lesotho and the national language of the country which produced *difela*. And whilst there is perhaps a need to explore this phenomenon further, this chapter can go only as far as to suggest hypothetically that it is the Basotho mode of travel and the landscape to be traversed that gave rise to this anomaly, especially through the then Boer 'republic' of the Orange Free State, which was characterised by hostility to their passage. The farmers of the republic, who were in dire need of labour, saw the Basotho as potential, but tantalisingly unavailable, workers who were allowed to pass through to the mines. The main objective of this chapter, however, will be to undertake a sociocritical study of the *difela* genre and to relate it to other Sotho literary forms, including traditional folk and modern genres.

A sociohistorical background

The Sotho language is part of the Southern Eastern Bantu languages, belonging to the Sotho group (Sesotho, Setswana and Sepedi). It is widely spoken in South Africa and is also the national language of the Kingdom of Lesotho, where it is spoken as the mother tongue by more than 95 per cent of subjects of the king. The second official language is English. The kingdom came into being in the nineteenth century, when King Moshoeshoe I united several tribes during the reign of Shaka, which had resulted in the scattering of tribal groups – an event that was to become known as *difaqane* or *mfecane* in Sesotho and the Nguni languages respectively (see Thompson, *Moshoeshoe*). When the Boers attempted to annex Lesotho to the Boer Republics of the Orange Free State and Transvaal, Moshoeshoe asked for protection from the British government; as a result, the kingdom, together with Swaziland and Botswana (Bechuanaland), became British protected colonies or protectorates, until they all gained independence in the mid twentieth century.

The Kingdom of Lesotho, being landlocked in a country which became the Union of South Africa in 1910 and a republic in 1961, was absorbed into the latter's socioeconomic sphere of influence, more so because the former's resources were not sufficient to carry its population, even though subsistence farming had thrived to the level of self-sufficiency and competition with the Orange Free State in the nineteenth century. The discovery of diamonds and gold in the 1880s created a need for mass labour in the industrialising and mining towns of South Africa, Kimberley and Johannesburg. Up to that point there had been influx and efflux of Basotho into South Africa in the nineteenth century. A major part of economically active Basotho men gravitated towards South African farms, towns and newly developing black townships in search of labour opportunities on a large scale, due to various economic needs. According to Kimble, 'By the time of their original annexation in 1868, Basotho had been renowned for over four decades as good workers on white-owned farms, and in colonial towns and ports . . . From the earliest of Moshoeshoe's reign in Lesotho, general migratory movements of homesteads had taken place' ('Labour Migration', p. 120). She also suggests that they formed a considerable if not the largest part of the population of migrant labour in South Africa.

The migrant workers migrated with a part of the Basotho popular culture. Some of the men had been to initiation schools (*lebollo* or *mophato*), in accordance with Sotho culture, where they had learned *dithoko* and composed their own panegyrics, *dithoko tsa makolwane* (songs of the initiates). In accordance with Guma (*Likoma*) and Kunene (*Heroic Poetry of the Basotho*), this chapter will illustrate that there is a strong structural and thematic affinity between *dithoko tsa makolwane*, *dithoko* and *dikoma*. The latter had a strong influence on *dithoko* and also on Sotho modern poetry, *dithothokiso*.

As mentioned above, it is plausible to argue that the development of the genre of *difela* has its origin in the long walks which the migrant workers took from Lesotho to South Africa, travelling through the then province of the Orange Free State. Sometimes the migrant workers spent several nights on the way, stopping overnight wherever they could find a place to rest. In the complex environment through which they had to travel, passes and restrictions were at times imposed. It was during the trials and tribulations of these journeys that workers reminisced about home and anticipated the challenges they had to contend with, both on their way and at their destination: the mine compounds where they had to live far away from home and family. They drew courage from the oral folk tradition, perhaps in a manner akin to the African-American spiritual songs of the nineteenth century in the plantations.

Amongst those who had been to the initiation schools the closest experience was *dikoma* and *dithoko*, genres which I will discuss as a progenitor of *difela*.

Dikoma: songs of the initiates

Guma is arguably one of the first literary scholars to collect *dikoma*. His 1966 anthology is not accessible to English readers because it is written in Sesotho. In the introduction he defines the etymology of the word *koma*, the singular of *dikoma*, as follows.

> As it is often said, *koma* is the truth. You will remember that sometimes it is said that a man is a man par excellence – a real man. Moreover, it is often said that he is a real Mosotho-of-koma, which means that he is a full blooded Mosotho. These descriptions are in accordance with what the Basotho really mean by *koma*, when they say it is the truth.
>
> Sometimes they refer to them as hymns of the Basotho. But as you know, these two words, Hymn and *Dikoma*, are generally used to refer to the songs which are sung in church.   (Guma, *Likoma*; my translation)

He then goes on to explain that this semantic shift in the words came about as a result of the missionaries' arrival in Lesotho and the spread of Christianity and their gospel. As far as he was concerned the 'hymns of the Basotho' and *dikoma* are synonymous. He explains that there are two types of *dikoma*, long and short ones. The former were meant to teach young Basotho boys a respectable lifestyle: to behave well, to respect elderly people, to respect their leaders (p. ii) and also, as Wells adds, as 'instruction in certain practical skills' (*Introduction to the Music*). The content of the shorter type of *dikoma*, according to Guma, was composed of the history of the Basotho, which had faded in memory and only fragments remained in this type of *dikoma*.

Guma further explains that the structure of *dikoma* is related to its mode of delivery, and that they were meant 'for the ear but not the eye . . . recited to be listened to and then repeated in the form of song' (p. 24). He explains that the first line of the poem, which ran on into the second to complete a sentence, introduced the main theme, which would then recur through subsequent lines until the end of the poem. The inherent characteristics of *dikoma* are defined by Guma as consisting mainly of an opening sentence that introduces the theme, lexical and syntactic reiteration where the word that closes a line is repeated in the following line, echoing of a noun or name at the end of a line and in verbal form at the beginning of the next line, apposition, use of ideophones, repetition of certain lines in one *koma* or through several *dikoma*, use of heavy intonation on particular syllables and freedom in coining words.

The language of the collection of *dikoma* which are recorded in Guma's anthology is mainly archaic and obscure. In order to illustrate both the structure and language, let us consider the first few stanzas of the first *koma* in the anthology, entitled *Konyana tsa Leboya* (Lambs of the North):

> Modimo wa rona,
> Modimo wa borare, o a utlwa.
> Tshakajwe tsa lata,
> Tsa lata dikgwesha,
> Kgwesha, morokolo
>
> Our God,
> God of our ancestors, you hear us.
> Tshakajwe went to fetch,
> Went to fetch dikgwesha,
> Kgwesha, morokolo.

The words which I have not translated are archaic and obscure, like many words in *dikoma*. Guma also does not translate them, but only gives footnotes which define *morokolo* as *ya besang mollo* (he who makes fire). The word *borare* (forebears / forefathers) is fossilised in Sesotho and exists in the modern version of another Sotho group language, Setswana. The opening of this *koma* sounds like the opening of a supplication to *Modimo* (God). In terms of structure the reiteration of the phrase 'Modimo wa borona' (God our father) and 'Modimo wa borare' (God of our forebears) in lines 1 and 2 and 'went to fetch' in lines 3 and 4 and the word '*(di)kgwesha*' in lines 4 and 5 of the above stanza, are a stylistic feature which Kunene, in his study of *dithoko*, refers to as horizontal line repetition in the first instance and as oblique line right-to-left parallelism in the second (*Heroic Poetry*, p. 73). This is a feature which *dithoko* inherited abundantly from *dikoma*, as will later be demonstrated. The reference to *Leboya* (The North) in the title is obscure, but according to Tladi, it might refer to the migration of the Basotho and other Bantu groups from the North (*Mehla ea Boholo-holo*).

One would like to suggest that *dikoma*, due to the archaism of their language, preceded *dithoko* in chronological development and also that the content, structure and style of the latter drew from the former. Guma makes an authoritative affirmation of *dikoma* as the prototype of other Sotho poetic forms: '*Dikoma* are followed by the praises of the initiates, which boys composed while they were still on the mountain [initiation school], then follows the praises of kings and stalwarts. Dikoma are the foundation; the praises of the initiates [are] the wall and the kings [are] the roof' (p. 32; my translation).

Dithoko: within living memory

In her 1971 account of *Oral Literature in Africa*, Finnegan suggested that 'Self-praises, created and performed by the subject himself, are not uncommon. Among the Sotho all individuals (or all men) are expected to have some skill in the composition and performance of self-praises . . . [the performer] must find inspiration in a particular episode, compose a topical and personal praise poem based on it, and add it to his repertoire' (p. 116). Guma, as already mentioned, suggests that *dikoma* is the harbinger of *dithoko* as a genre. He explains that the difference between the two is that the former were learned and repeated in secrecy (*bolotseng*) while the latter were learned and recited in the public domain (*Likoma*, p. 32). He does not give reasons for the secrecy of *dikoma*. With regard to content, he explains that '*Dikoma* repeat the narrative of the ancient days, which we in modern times only see vaguely, while *dithoko* narrate the recent, when the nation finds itself where it is now'. *Dithoko* are 'traditional praises of chiefs and warriors. They are based on actual deeds or actions connected with the particular individual who is praised . . . Chiefs either composed their own praises or were praised by their official praisers, *diroki*, with the singular *seroki*, from *roka*, praise' (*Form, Content and Technique*, pp. 151–2). Kunene adds that 'Their chief purpose is to praise – extol the virtues of manly prowess; of courage, valour, and of fighting skills' (*Heroic Poetry*, p. 1). It is therefore obvious that such a genre should thrive during the kinds of conflict prevalent in nineteenth-century Lesotho and southern Africa in general. The *difaqane* or *mfecane*, set in domino motion by the conquering King of the Zulus, Shaka, unleashed a series of wars which devastated the subcontinent. Lesotho fought various wars of annexation in this period, among them the Gun War (1880–1) against the government of the Cape Colony, which resulted when colonial authorities attempted to disarm the Basotho. The Basotho royals resisted disarmament and the British were subjected to a humiliating defeat by the well-armed Basotho. This conflict was followed by a succession of civil disputes within the kingdom. It was thus that the genre of *dithoko* and *izibongo* developed among the Sotho and Nguni groups, respectively, and indeed thrived, reaching unprecedented heights in that era of belligerence.

In order to illustrate the above I will draw from an example of a *thoko*, which is explicated by Kunene:

> Ba *Matsieng* ba phokaka *ditsie*,
> Ba phoka *tsie* tse kgubedu-kgubedu
> Ba tswatswile ba re ba a di phoka,
> Tsa tloha tsa hana, tsa ba hlobolela dikobo
> Tsa tloha tsa senya talane ya bona.
>
> Ba ha *Mahao* ba *hahola* dikobo,
> Ba senya kobo tsa bana ba Fitori,
> Tse ntle, tse rekwang Makgoweng.
> Ha ba a di tseba dikobo tsa marena
> Tse ntle, tse rekwang Makgoweng,
> Eba hona ba ntseng ba di senya!   (*Heroic Poetry*, pp. 95–6)

Kunene's translation renders the above excerpt in literal translation as follows:

> Those of Matsieng were busy whisking away the locusts,
> They whisked away the locusts that were bright red.
> While vainly they tried to whisk them away,
> They (the locusts) suddenly grew obstinate and doffed their
> Blankets
> They suddenly destroyed their yet-ripening millet.
>
> Those of Mahao tore their blankets,
> They laid waste to the blankets of the children of Fitori,
> The beautiful ones that are bought at the whiteman's place,
> In spite they lay them waste.

Kunene brings our attention to the fact that the praise singer uses punning, which is, 'one might almost say, accidental; by which we mean that the poet is suddenly struck by the possibility of a pun, and he seizes the opportunity without any sign that it was deliberate or premeditated' (p. 95). In the above the punning is found in the word *Matsieng* (the King's palace, derived from the personal and royal name *Letsie*) and *tsie* (locust); and also in *Mahao* (personal name) and *hahola* (ripping or tearing apart). Another salient feature of the poem is that when it praises the valour and prowess of the protagonist, as Kunene mentions, it also evokes his genealogy:

> Ba ha Sebatli ba batlile dipere,
> Ba batlile dipere tsa mor'a Mokhachane.   (p. 96)

Those of Sebatli looked for the horses.
They looked for the horses of the son of Mokhachane.

(Kunene's translation)

Ke ne ke re ba hlapanyetsa Moshoeshoe,
Masia le yena, ngwan'a Pshabane, ka utlwa a ana,
Ka utlwa a re, 'Ka Moroke a shwele!'
A bile a re, 'Ka 'Masefunelo!'
E le ngwana weso, ngwana wa Pshabane.   (pp. 96–7)

I thought I'd swear to their detriment, by Moshoeshoe,
When Masia too, the child of Pshabane, I heard him swear,
I heard him say, 'By Moroke who is dead!'
And further he said, 'By 'Masefunelo!'
Yet being my mother, the child of Pshabane.

(Kunene's translation)

In the two stanzas quoted above we find puns, for example Sebatli (personal name) and Batla (look for/search) as well as reference to the ancestors of the protagonists, by whom they swear, namely Moshoeshoe, Pshabane, Moroke and 'Masefunelo, who are evoked in both the authorial narrative of the poet and the direct speech of the protagonists.

This *thoko* encompasses most of the distinguishing thematic features of this genre as explicated by Kunene in his all-embracing analysis: 'Those which proclaim the hero, either calling the hero's attention of the audience to him as the subject of the poem . . . or reminding the audience who the poem is about . . . [and] calling the attention of the hero to the words addressed to him' (p. 54). The style tends to include a wide range of figurative aspects – 'pictures, symbols, comparisons and all manner of indirect (or poetic) representations' (p. 102). These are features which *dithoko* share with the praises of other languages, Setswana (see Schapera, *Praise Poems*) and isiZulu (see Cope, *Izibongo*; Rycroft, 'The Question of Metre', 'Melodic Features' and 'Zulu and Xhosa Praise-Poetry'; Gunner and Gwala, *Musho!*). So too, the *thoko* can be said to have a beginning, middle and end (Damane and Sanders, *Lithoko*).

With regard to the influence of *dithoko* on modern Sotho poetry, *thothokiso*, Kunene cites poets such as J. J. Machobane (who in his epic praises a bull in the language and style of the *thoko*) and B. M. Khaketla. In this vein he also refers to the use of this genre by prose writers such as Thomas Mofolo, the renowned writer of *Chaka* (*Heroic Poetry*, pp. 133–50), a novel which has been translated into several European languages, and others, including poets. I shall refer to Mofolo and Khaketla later in this chapter.

Difela tsa ditsamaya naha: songs of travellers

There is a link between *difela tsa ditsamaya naha* and *dithoko tsa makolwane* (songs of the initiates). As already mentioned, the latter were the praises which the initiates composed while they were at the initiation schools. According to Guma, they were recited with intervals of chanting. Composed in the first person, they were largely comprised of self-description by the initiates, but in some cases employed the third person for satirical purposes (*Likoma*, pp. 41–2). It could be argued that this was meant to enhance the status of the first person, as in this *thoko ya makolwane*:

> Majakane ho nona a matshehadi,
> A matona me mekotatsie.
> Maqai le mathisa phuthehang,
> Suthang ka moyeng le a nkga;
> Qai le nkga sa podi ya phooko,
> Thisa le nkga sa kolobe ya motswetse. (pp. 42–3)

> Among the converted the fat ones are females
> The males are storks.
> [You] the uninitiated, both male and female come closer together,
> Get out of the wind's way because you smell;
> The uninitiated male smells like a he goat,
> The uninitiated female smells like a pig which has littered.

In describing himself the initiate finds it necessary to denigrate those who have not been to the *lebollo* (initiation school). The word *majakane* refers to those who have been converted to Christianity. It is derogatory, in reciprocation for the word *bahetene* – heathens. The words *maqai* and *mathisa*, which refer to the uninitiated, male and female respectively, are also insulting. Letele suggests that *dithoko tsa makolwane* are 'the efforts of one who is not necessarily gifted in any sense as a poet, nor do they necessarily refer to events and exploits which actually took place' ('Some Recent Publications'). That is to say, the composition of *dithoko tsa makolwane* was not judged according to any particular skill or competence; any composition was accepted. They also did not necessarily refer to real events but could simply be the composer's flight of imagination. The earliest known collection of the genre of *dithoko tsa makolwane* was made by Jankie (*Lithoko tsa Makoloane*, 1930).

Describing oneself and one's plight is a predominant feature of the content of *difela*. Kunene defines *sefela* as 'a song of a person whose emotions are triggered for several reasons. Much about *lifela* talk about mysteries of life, it is why the word *sefela* (hymn) was seen as appropriate for the songs of the European missionaries'. In an *en passant* comparison between *difela* and *dithoko*, Mokitimi and Phafoli state that although the genres derive from the same poetic tradition, they differ in their performance and content. They summarise the themes of *difela* succinctly as 'poverty . . . dehumanisation . . . disruption in family life' ('Orality in Worker Movements', pp. 225–8). When considering the life imposed by industrialisation and its impact on Lesotho, it is easy to see why these themes would be paramount in the poetry of the migrants, in which they sing mainly of the woes of their journey, what they have left behind at home, and the problems with which they are going to contend in a new world. This prospective experience was also drawn from the practical experience of those who had been to and come back from the mines.

Mokitimi and Phafoli sum up the definition of *difela* as 'literature expressing the social, economic, political, and cultural issues of the Basotho society of migrant workers'. The plight of the Basotho workers includes poverty and its attendant humiliation. Mokitimi and Phafoli illustrate this theme via the following *sefela*:

> Kajeno lena ke se tlohetse sekolo.
> Ke se ke bile ke khasa ka tlas'a majoe.
> Ken e ke ile sekolong Thabana-Morena,
> Mount Rabor Secondary.
> E ile eare ha ke fihla heso lapeng,
> Ka fumanakhaitseli ea ka a lla.
> A re: 'M'e nthekele kobo ke hlobotse,
> Ha ke na le sa nketlana mahetleng.'
> (Makakane in Mokitimi and Phafoli, p. 225)

The translation by Mokitimi and Phafoli renders the *sefela* as follows:

> Nowadays I've been impoverished by lack of schooling
> I find myself under knees under rocks.
> I attended school at Thabana-Morena
> At Mt Tabor Secondary School,
> When I came home,
> I found my sister in tears.
> Saying: 'Mother buy me a blanket.
> I am wearing rags,
> I haven't even a small piece on my shoulder.'

The essential features of the *difela* are described by Wells as follows:

> The singer begins his song with an account of his home town . . . Having established his identity through the description of his home town, the singer proceeds to the next section of his musical narrative . . . switch[ing] between the past and present tense . . . The whole piece is framed within the standard opening formula 'My fathers, I greet you all' . . . These techniques seek to unite individual and collective experience, crossing boundaries of performer and audience in a manner similar to the concept of *tumellano*, harmonious interaction, in Sesotho dance songs.   (*Introduction to the Music*, pp. 275–6)

This genre has also been studied by several scholars (Coplan, *In the Time of Cannibals*; Swanepoel, *Sotho Dithoko*) whose works supplement one of the earliest treatments, Moloi's 'The Germination of Southern Sotho Poetry'.

Sesotho modern poetry and the novel

Arguably the most influential historical factors operating on Sotho literature are labour migration and World Wars I and II. These factors are echoed in the themes of both poetry and prose in Sotho. The first novel in Sotho (Segoete, *Monono ke Moholi ke Mouoane* [Riches are like Mist, Vapour], 1910), written by one of the early converts, is a case in point. Other novels were to follow suit, where the protagonist leaves Lesotho to seek manual labour opportunities in the then Union of South Africa. The theme echoed through to the 1940s and beyond (e.g. Nqheku, *Arola Naheng ya Maburu* [Arola in the Land of the Boers], 1942).

The themes of the two world wars were also taken up by the two most prominent poets of Lesotho in the twentieth century, namely K. E. Ntsane and B. M. Khaketla. Khaketla's poetry is often melancholic, while Ntsane tends to the satirical. The poetry of both, each via their own distinctive style, tends to draw from the stylistic features of *dithoko*, and also from *difela tsa ditsamaya naha*. A selection of samples of their writing is given below to illustrate this point. Khaketla wrote about World Wars I and II and of the liberation wars of the African continent. In the poem 'Ntwa ya Jeremane' (The German War), he narrates:

> Hlwaya tsebe o mamele wa nkgono,
> O mamele masisimosa-mmele:
> Taba tsa banna di mosenekeng,
> Di batla ho reetswa ka tsebe lethwethwe.

E ne le le ka kgwedi ya Phato, selemong
Meya, Lesotho, e foka, e puputla,
Ho thunya marole a mafubedu tlere!
Ka hohle ho utlwahala lepukupuku.   (*Dipjamathe*, p. 30)

Lend me your ears, son of my grandmother,

And listen to the news which makes the body tremble with fear:
The news about men is bad,
They need to be listened to with a sharp ear.

It was in the month of August, in the year,
Winds in Lesotho were blowing, raging
The whirling dust was red, like blood!
All over the winds roared and raved.

The opening lines of the poem have not only borrowed from the stylistic features of *dithoko*, but also set the scene for war as in the mood of the genre. In the following stanzas the poet describes the protagonists who participated in the war with typical *thoko* panegyric:

Na o ka kgutsa mora Lerotholi,
Setlolo sa Kgodu le sa Fitoria?
A hana hehehe a latola bosehla,
A bolela: yaba ha e tjhe a le teng.   (p. 31)

Could he have remained silent, [Paramount Chief Griffith] Lerotholi,
The grandson of Kgodu and [Queen] Victoria?
He refused totally,
And gave command: then it [the war] could not have raged in his presence
[without him picking up the gauntlet].

The protagonists who are mentioned in the poem are praised and their genealogy is evoked. However, Khaketla also mourns the fact that in the end the conflict brought nothing for the Basotho, despite the loss of their kin.

Ntsane laments the ravages of World War II in a poem entitled 'Selemo sa 1939' (The Year 1939):

Ha thwasa lemo sa ditsietsi,
Lemo sa ho kgaba ka tlokotsi;
Lefatshe kaofela la hwasa la duma,
Matshwafo a batho a phahama, a uba;
Tau tsa hotetsa hlaha mawatleng,
Tsa hloka kutlwano makgotleng.

The year of trouble blossomed,
The year which bloomed with grief;
The whole world sighed and trembled,
People's lungs heaved heavily;
Lions ignited conflagrations in the seas,
And there was no understanding among them in war councils.

Ntsane here uses repetition and parallelism in a manner which is typical of *dithoko*. In the first line we see the word 'year' – '[se]lemo', then repeated in the second line. The poet also adopts the couplet rhyme of English poetry. In the fourth and fifth stanzas he resorts to the *thoko* mode of praise by referring to the protagonists of the war:

A o baka moferefere Switlane;
A bua le ntja tse thata Majeremane:
Ntho tsa ithafatsa dipelo,
Tsa tela tsohle, tsa tela bophelo,
Tsa labalabela madi a motho,
Tsa nyorelwa madi a batho.

Tjhambalene, Tona e kgolo ya Engelane
A tshela lewatle ho bua le Switlane;
Ba etsa wa motona morero,
Wa fela ka tsatsi la boraro   (Ntsane, *Musapelo* I, p. 6)

Switlane [name obscure in the source language] caused real havoc;
He spoke to the tough beasts of Germany:
The beasts hardened their hearts,
They gave up on everything, they gave up on life,
They thirsted for human blood,
They hankered for blood.
Chamberlain the Great Minister of England
Crossed the sea to speak to Switlane;
They drew a great strategy,
Which they completed on the third day.

Another war which seems to have fascinated Sotho poets is the Ethiopian War of Independence. Khaketla and another Sotho major poet and novelist, A. S. Mopeli-Paulus, composed poems about this conflict. That of Khaketla is entitled 'Ntwa ya Abisinia' (The War of Abyssinia) and that of Mopeli-Paulus 'Ethiopia'. Both draw from *difela* and *dithoko* as prototypes, in terms of stylistic features. The opening stanza of Mopeli-Paulus's poem reminisces on the persona's past visit to Ethiopia, and then introduces the war theme:

Abyssinia, joale ka ha bacha ba e rehile kajeno
E bakile mohono esita mose, ha Mussolini.
Monongoaha Italy e itekela ho koeba poho-ntso,
Poho-ntso dinaka e li khotse, li setse khoaling,
Hara motse ho koekoetla mohlankana, se-jara-lerumo,
O tsetsema joalo ka phokojoe e tsomile dinkonyana.

Abyssinia, as it is has been named by youth nowadays
Evoked greed abroad, even in Mussolini.
This year Italy is trying to bellow like a black bull,
A black bull is too full with its horns, it left them at war council,
A young man, carrier-of-a-spear walks around the village,
He skulks like a wolf hunting lambs.

The predominant feature of the poem is the use of the common *thoko* metaphor, *poho* (bull), which is repeated in slanting parallelism in the third and fourth lines via the animal metaphors and compound nouns such as 'se-jara-lerumo' (carrier-of-a-spear). Throughout the poem Haile Selasse is referred to several times as 'Tau' (Lion) and 'Tau-tona' (Male Lion).

Let us return to Ntsane to see how he uses the *difela* mode in parody. In a poem entitled 'Ha re ya Lejweleputswa' (When we Travel to the Rand Mines) the persona narrates the plight of a recruited miner: the trials and tribulations from when he and his companions start preparations for the long journey from Lesotho to the mines of Johannesburg. It is narrated in the first person:

Ra lala re phehile mefaho
Re phehile mefaho ka la maobane,
Merwalo re e tlamme, ntja tsa batho
Ntja tsa moreneng ma-lala-laotswe.
Loala, morena, re lokile,
Re loketse ho kena mekoting ya ditadi;
Tadi tsena di maoto mane, di a bua,
Di bua tjhomi, di bua Sekgowa.   (Ntsane, *Musapelo 1*, p. 61)

We prepared our provisions
Prepared our provisions the night before,
Our baggage readily bound, we poor dogs
Dogs of our chief, ever ready.
Give command oh chief, we are ready,
Ready to creep into the rat hole;
These four footed rats can speak,
They speak in foreign tongues, they speak English.

73

The persona describes how he and his peers had to prepare their bag and baggage, provision and all, the night before their journey. He speaks collectively for the group which he is going to travel with by using the first person plural, *re* (we), repeatedly. He describes their departure from home: how they had to give up the comforting company and communion of their closest relatives, who are figuratively referred to as *mme* (mother) and *nkgono* (grandmother). The journey takes them to the recruitment office, where they have to sign documents which hand their labour to the mining companies. He says satirically: 'Ra saena Tshu re sa mo tsebe' ('We even signed "Q" despite our illiteracy').

In a sequel to the first anthology of his poetry, Ntsane uses the *difela* prototype in a satirical poem entitled 'Hwenene' (Home-Brewed Beer), which lampoons the journey of a drunkard who staggers from a tavern, where he has overindulged in home-made liquor. The journey is made out to be very difficult, but in this case it is because the persona is his own undoing. On his way he utters a monologue:

> Hae ra fihla neng e le bosiu?
> Hae re tlohile tsatsi le qeta ho dikela,
> Shwalsane e tshwara re tshwere dikala,
> Jwale re kgitla bosiu mphiphi,
> Le enwa monga hiki tjhelete e feta boroko,
> Roko bo ka tla jwang soka di kena?
> Re ka ya hae jwang hiki e eso fele?
> Faki motsheo di sa tletse hwenene?
>
> Ka re ka ema ka boela faatshe,
> Qetellong ka kgasa sa ngwana lesea,
> Ka lekisa ngwana ka etsa mehlolo.
> Wa horeng a tholana le nna a utlwa monate,
> A utlwa monate Mosotho a tsheha,
> Athe re tauwe ho tshwana re tjhele motjhalla ruri,
> Fofu tsa tataisana tsa utlwa monate,
> Tsa wa bobedi tsa wa bohlaswa   (Ntsane, *Musapelo II*)

How late did we arrive home?
Home we left after the sun had set,
Dusk caught us with beer containers in our hands,
Now it's late and pitch dark and night,
[To] this beer seller money is better than sleep,
How can sleep come when sixpenny coins are flowing in?
How can we go home when the beer is not yet finished?
While casks in the far corner are still full?

I tried to stand up but I fell down,
I gave up and crawled on my knees like a baby,
Like a baby and performed wonders.
I met a stranger on the road and we kept each other sweet company,
The Mosotho found my company and felt good,
The Mosotho felt good and had a good laugh,
Whereas we were both equally drunk and perpetual drunkards,
The blind showed each other the way and it felt good,
They both fell down like in recklessness.

The poem is a parody of *difela*. The trials and tribulations which the persona experiences in this poem are not imposed by necessity, as are those of the veteran traveller and composer of *difela*. He has imposed his misery upon himself and without any heroism, he narrates his journey home, after a heavy drinking spree, in a mock heroic mode.

An interesting question to pursue is whether these apparently pervasive forms of oral art, *dithoko* and *difela*, have encroached upon modern popular culture in Lesotho and South Africa. In this regard Mokitmi and Phafoli suggest that one of the predominant forms of popular music in Lesotho is accordion music. They assert that it is in this genre where *difela* has made its mark, and where it has evolved into protest songs levelled at some of the acts of tyranny manifested by the Lesotho government of the day. They also illustrate how it has influenced Sotho popular accordion music in Lesotho. What I would like to observe is that in South Africa, Sotho *dithoko* and their modern versions have not carved a niche in modern popular culture, as have Xhosa and Zulu *izibongo*. How some popular musicians who sing in Sesotho (e.g., Tau ya Matshekha, Tshepo Tshola and Bhudaza) have made inroads in this regard would be the subject of another study.

Bibliography

Cope, A. T. *Izibongo: Zulu Praise-Poems*, Oxford: Clarendon Press, 1968.
Coplan, D. B. *In the Time of Cannibals: The Word Music of South Africa's Basotho Migrants*, University of Chicago Press, 1994.
Damane, M., and P. B. Sanders (eds.). *Lithoko: Sotho Praise-Poems*, Oxford: Clarendon Press, 1974.
Finnegan, R. *Oral Literature in Africa*, Oxford University Press, 1971.
Guma, S. M. *Form, Content and Technique in Traditional Literature in Southern Sotho*, Pretoria: Van Schaik, 1967.
Likoma, Pietermaritzburg: Shuter & Shooter, 1966.
Gunner, L., and M. Gwala. *Musho! Zulu Popular Praises*, East Lansing: Michigan State University Press, 1991.

Jankie, H. E. *Lithoko tsa Makoloane*, Morija: Morija Sesuto Book Depot, 1930.

Khaketla, B. M. *Dipjamathe*, Johannesburg: Bona Press, 1954.

Kimble, J. 'Labour Migration in Basutoland', in S. Marks and R. Rathbone (eds.), *Industrialisation and Social Change in South Africa: African Class Formation, Culture and Consciousness 1870–1930*, New York: Longman, 1982, 117–41.

Kunene, D. P. *Heroic Poetry of the Basotho*, Oxford: Clarendon Press, 1971.

Letele, G. L. 'Some Recent Publications in Languages of the Sotho Group', *African Studies* 13:1 (1944), 161–71.

Mokitimi, M., and L. Phafoli. 'Orality in Worker Movements: A Case of Lifela', in R. H. Kaschula (ed.), *African Oral Literature. Functions in Contemporary Contexts*, Cape Town: New Africa Books, 2001, 221–33.

Moloi, A. J. 'The Germination of Southern Sotho Poetry', *Limi* 8 (June 1969), 28–59.

Nqheku, A. *Arola Naheng ya Maburu*, Morija: Morija Sesuto Book Depot, 1942.

Ntsane, K. E. *Musapelo I*, Morija: Morija Sesuto Book Depot, 1947.

   Musapelo II, Afrikaanse Pers Beperk, Morija: Morija Sesuto Book Depot, 1947.

Rycroft, D. K. 'Melodic Features in Zulu Eulogistic Recitation', *African Language Studies* 1 (1960), 60–78.

   'The Question of Metre in Southern African Praise Poetry', in P. J. Wentzel (ed.), *Third African Languages Conference*, Pretoria: University of South Africa Press, 1980, 289–312.

   'Zulu and Xhosa Praise-Poetry and Song', *African Music* 3 (1962), 798.

Schapera, I. *Praise Poems of Tswana Chiefs*, Oxford: Clarendon Press, 1965.

Segoete, E. L. *Monono ke Moholi ke Mouane*, Morija: Morija Sesuto Book Depot, 1910.

Swanepoel, C. F. *Sotho Dithoko tsa Marena: Perspectives on Composition and Genre*, 2nd edn. Pretoria: Mmuelli, 1991.

Thompson, L. *Moshoeshoe: Survival in Two Worlds*, Oxford University Press, 1975.

Wells, R. E. *An Introduction to the Music of the Basotho*, Lesotho: Morija Museum and Archives, 1994.

4

Praise, politics, performance: from Zulu *izibongo* to the Zionists

MBONGISENI BUTHELEZI

As South Africa hurtled towards its third national democratic election in 2009 an old anti-apartheid struggle song jostled with poetry and songs from the long oral tradition to bolster the public images of politicians. At rallies the leader of the largest political party led supporters in singing 'Umshini wami' ('My machine [gun]'), a song with a long career in the underground camps of the liberation struggle. The song was imbued with new meanings and sung with relish by those seeking to voice popular dissatisfaction with the perceived failures of the state and of political leadership (Gunner, 'Jacob Zuma', pp. 28, 30). The same song had in the preceding months been transformed into countless cellular telephone ringtones by entrepreneurs seeing a popular cultural phenomenon out of which to score sales. Sound and video clips of singing crowds were also heard and seen on radio and television. At the same time debate raged under trees, in offices, on numerous blogs, news websites, and on radio and television talk shows about the public uses of a song with an illustrious history of galvanising fighters for justice by a politician whose post-liberation character was allegedly dubious. To add to the maelstrom of reinvented cultural idioms and symbols, some of the politicians were being lauded in praise poetry, *izibongo*, and songs in the *maskanda* genre performed at live concerts. The poetry and music were recorded and disseminated through fast-selling compact discs. The same compact discs were simultaneously being illegally reproduced on isolated computers and the songs and poetry circulated via cellular phones in even the remotest parts of South Africa.

A few weeks earlier, in a remaking of the praise tradition, the internationally acclaimed Ladysmith Black Mambazo *isicathamiya* music group had won a Grammy award for *Ilembe: Our Tribute to King Shaka* (2007), their honouring of Shaka Zulu, the early nineteenth-century empire builder who melded together

The support of the Wenner-Gren Foundation, English Studies at the University of KwaZulu-Natal, and the NRF Research Initiative in Archive and Public Culture at the University of Cape Town at various stages of research is hereby gratefully acknowledged.

the Zulu kingdom. In yet another renewal of praise poetry, the praise poet, *imbongi*, of the incumbent Zulu king, Buzetsheni Mdletshe, had put music to the praises of the entire lineage of Zulu kings from Shaka onwards and produced a compact disc, *Wena Wendlovu Bayede!* (2008).

The artistic forms and products noted above – *izibongo*, the album in honour of Shaka, the liberation struggle song and *maskanda* – are either praise genres or borrow aspects of the praise tradition towards new ends. Since one of the first written descriptions of Zulu *izibongo* in 1837 by American missionary the Revd George Champion (Brown, *Voicing the Text*, p. 75), the praise tradition has continued to be used in ways that are close to the use Champion observed at the royal court of Dingane, Shaka's successor. The form also has time and again been remade in the mouths as well as the singing and dancing bodies of people who have created new forms of expression out of it. Such remakings have ranged from an old oral poem such as Zulu king Shaka's praises being declaimed in a new setting and thus taking on new meanings or the performance by praise poets of the praises of the current Zulu king, to the importation of the imperative of praising that is at the core of praise poetry to produce a music album by the internationally acclaimed Ladysmith Black Mambazo. The emergence of new forms over the past century points to the capacity of traditional South African, and African, oral forms for renewal as successive generations of people find uses for, and meaning in, earlier poems, songs, stories, riddles and other forms. As the society has changed so have people's popular expressive forms evolved while maintaining continuity with earlier forms. This confirms the often repeated point about the dynamism of traditions against earlier assumptions of the stasis of African cultures (Vail and White, *Power and the Praise Poem*; Hofmeyr, '*We Spend our Years*'; Brown, *Voicing the Text*; Gunner, 'Africa and Orality'; Finnegan, *Oral and Beyond*). This chapter introduces in their range the Zulu language performance forms intent on praise that have emerged in the past century and a half.

Nineteenth-century backgrounds

Praise forms have a long history in Zulu society. *Izithakazelo*, kinship group praises, and *izibongo*, praise poetry, are two of the earliest known forms from which later ones have been derived (Vilakazi, 'Conception and Development'). Several forms have been created from *izibongo* over the past century and a half and continue to exist alongside *izibongo* today even as ever newer forms mutate from older ones. On a daily basis Zulu speakers continue to greet one another using *izithakazelo*. During weddings, funerals or any ceremonies conducted in commemoration of ancestors, the *izibongo* of the specific individuals being remembered are declaimed by family historians to address the dead. Identified by its *isibongo*, surname, each kinship group that makes up the Zulu *isizwe* or ethnic group has its *izithakazelo*, which it sometimes shares with groups that historically broke away from it to form their own chiefdoms. The *izithakazelo* are a series of names that canonise some of the most significant male figures of the particular kinship group in line with the traditional patrilineal practices of Zulu society. The figures that are canonised can be leaders who founded the group and/or its chiefdom, who fought great wars in the kinship group's collective memory, or who led great treks in search of freedom from oppressing powers. The praises can also describe the topography where the group has resided in its history and/or the geography traversed by the group as it searched for land to settle away from hostile nature and/or human enemies. Overall, these praises build up the central group's greatness, regardless of its numerical size or the magnitude of its past achievements. Thus people of the Mchunu surname praise one another and are praised as:

> Macingwane kaLubhoko.
> UMacingwan' engowaseNgonyameni.
> Dladlama mfokaMajola,
> UMajol' aphuma khon' eMachunwini.
> Ndabezitha!
> Mnguni!
> Lembe[d]e!   (Sithole, *Izithakazelo*, p. 61)

> Macingwane (son) of Lubhoko.
> Macingwane who is of Ngonyameni.
> Dladlama of (the) Majola (people),
> Majola having come out of Chunwini.
> Ndabezitha!
> Mnguni!
> Lembe[d]e!

Macingwane was the leader of the Chunu chiefdom who was forced to flee as Shaka's Zulu group was advancing on his chiefdom in the early nineteenth century. The praises of the Chunu remember him foremost as the Chunu people are generically praised as 'Macingwane'. Macingwane's father was Lubhoko and Macingwane had his capital at Ngonyameni near the headwaters of the Mhlathuze River in the north of the present-day KwaZulu-Natal province. The Majola with whom the Chunu are associated in the praises are historical relations of the Chunu, as are the Lembede. The Chunu are finally assigned greatness in calling them Ndabezitha and Mnguni, terms that defined high status for those being thus named prior to Shaka's limitation of the terms' use to Zulu royalty (Wright, 'Politics', p. 108).

Kinship group praises can also borrow fragments of the personal *izibongo* of the leaders who are canonised in the group praises. The praises of the Ndwandwe chief, Zwide kaLanga, who is remembered as the consolidator of the Ndwandwe confederacy that was destroyed by Shaka's Zulu forces in 1826, are incorporated into the kinship group praises. All the Ndwandwe people are 'nina bakaNonkokhel' abantu bahlatshwe njengezinkomo' ('you [descendants] of "leader of the people until they are stabbed like cattle"'). This is an extract from the personal praises of Zwide (Msimang, *Kusadliwa Ngoludala*, p. 403), the meaning of which is obscure due to the surviving record of the praises providing no gloss on it. Yet when an Ndwandwe person is greeted or addressed in conversation as 'Zwide' today the history of the confederacy and the kinship group are recalled. Zwide himself, the erstwhile leader, is not particularised or remembered in great detail: in this recalling 'Zwide' becomes a term that has been largely emptied of references to a specific historical personage. Only Zwide as a reminder of former Ndwandwe greatness remains; yet these praises were once part of a corpus of a living person's praises, used to praise him in his lifetime – from when he was a child through his leadership of the Ndwandwe confederacy.

Zwide's praises are part of the long tradition of praising using *izibongo* that continues in Zulu-speaking society. In the past the set of praises a person came to bear in adult life formed part of a line of poetic and narrative composition associated with her/him that began before s/he was born and lasted throughout her/his life. The praises accumulated during a person's life eventually would outlive her/him, being used to praise the dead person at her/his funeral and in later commemoration ceremonies. Creative composition would begin before the child's birth with a mother's composition of *izangelo*, songs combined with poetry about the mother's experiences of married life with her husband, co-wives and the extended unit in a polygynous and multi-generational family living together in a homestead. The songs and poems sometimes would lead to the child's name being derived from the *izangelo*. Names given to children carried significance as records of important events that occurred around children's births or of states in which families or societies were when the children were born. Names could also pass comment from the perspective of the parent naming the child (often the father) on goings-on in the family or the society. Hence South African president Jacob Zuma is Gedleyihlekisa because his father named him thus to pass comment on people whom he considered to be harming him while feigning friendliness ('Motlanthe').

Once the child was born it would be welcomed into the world and the ancestors of the family enjoined to guide and protect the person throughout her/his life (Msimang, *Kusadliwa*, p. 210). Thus the child joined the kinship group, tied to the living and to those who had lived before s/he was born through the kinship group praises, *izithakazelo*. The initial *izangelo* sung to the child would gradually give way to another form of song and praises, *imilolozelo* (lullabies) which would often combine playful praise of the child for her/his physical beauty and hope for the moral and social values the child would come to exhibit in later life. Out of these lullabies would grow the child's early personal praise poems, *izibongo*, which would be added to by siblings, relatives and neighbours as the child grew. Gender roles came to be defined by a separation in the development of personal praises when children began to participate in chores in the homestead. At approximately the age of 7 boys would start herding the family's goats while girls participated in household chores. At this stage a boy's heroic deeds in play and in dispensing his duties would assume public prominence as friends composed praises for him based on any notable actions on his part while girls' actions were confined to the relative obscurity of the private sphere inhabited by women. An ethos of heroism was hence instilled in boys. Their praises would be declaimed by their peers when they were playing games in the veld such as stick fighting.

The accumulation of praises would continue through the boy's joining of an *ibutho*, age set, his growth into manhood and throughout his adult life. During communal dances, collective hunting expeditions and when he participated in battles he would be egged on by his peers using his praises. These *izibongo* would be geared towards praising a person and bolstering his public image. In addition to being given to a person by those observing her/his actions, praises could also be self-composed. This was often the case with praises of women who, as they grew from childhood, tended to move further from the public sphere, as mentioned earlier. Women would use the praises to comment on their circumstances in life vis-à-vis marriage and the treatment they received at the hands of their husbands and in-laws, or to comment on aspects of their public lives in the communities in which they lived. Mcasule Dube, for instance, refers to herself as follows:

Ng'uSidlukuya-dlwedlwe besihlukuza abafazi namadoda.
Bathi bamphe ngaphansi bamphe ngaphezulu.
Dlula bedlana o'nto zawonina.
Abayosala emhlabeni bayosala bedl' amakhanda e'nyoni.
Wombuza uthanathana kanyoko
Ngoba ngiyesab' amazondo.

I am the Wild Staff-Shaker shaken by women and men.
They say, 'They've given it to her down below and they've given it to her
    up above.'
She passes as they are having sex, those lousy private parts of their mothers.
Those who remain on the earth will live long and be wealthy.
You go and ask that little private parts of her mother because I myself am
    afraid of the ill-feeling.   (Gunner, 'Clashes of Interest', pp. 192–3)

Dube uses a martial praise and extends it 'to provide a riposte to liars and
gossips who ruin reputations with whispers' (p. 192).

On the other hand, the men would be praised in public, thus developing a
public profile as stated above. The praises of a man could also borrow lines
from those of his ancestors whom he was said to resemble in action or in
appearance. It would be said that such and such an ancestor has come back
in the form of that particular person. The person could then inherit some of
the ancestor's praises as early as birth, any later additions being to the base
of praises that had been carried over from the life of the ancestor. In some
cases, the child would even be named after the ancestor before inheriting
her/his praises. The borrowing of the praises of forebears was, and remains,
particularly pronounced in royal *izibongo*. Rulers are legitimated in *izibongo*
by the calling up of their lineages. In a way which draws obvious parallels
between Zulu king Zwelithini's rise to the throne and that of Shaka, the
former is praised as follows:

> Unesibindi Buthelezi ngokukhuthazela
> UmntakaNdaba bemthuka bemcokofula,
> bethi, 'UZwelithini kayikubusa kayokuba nkosi',
> kanti bamgcoba ngamafuth' empepho.

> Buthelezi was brave in his encouragement.
> They insulted the child of Ndaba, they pecked at him
> saying, 'Zwelithini will never rule, will never be king',
> whereas he was anointed with the sacred oil of kings.
>   (Gunner and Gwala, *Musho!*, pp. 55–6)

Nevertheless, there was hardly a structural distinction between the early development of royals and other people in the society. *Abantwana*, royals, would only begin to be distinguished from ordinary people once they began to assume positions of national responsibility and elevated status, for example being leaders of *amakhanda*, regional royal homesteads. At such a juncture a royal would wield significant power. With power went its trappings, including being praised in more elaborate fashion on public occasions such as festivals, *inqina* hunts and *ukuviva* (drills/dances in preparation for war). A royal homestead sometimes would have an *imbongi*, praise poet, attached to it whose responsibility it would be to perform the chief's/king's praises. However, a praise poet would often be tied to a leader, travelling with him wherever he did in order to be present to declaim praises whenever an occasion calling for praising arose. The position of such an *imbongi* was not an official one nor was it remunerated in any way similar to the reward of poets in cultures with traditions of retaining court poets. An *imbongi* would grow into the position based on public acclaim. Several *izimbongi* would praise the leader in the early part of his leadership. It was only through public acclaim that one or two would eventually grow to quasi-official status (Brown, *Voicing the Text*, p. 89).

The efficacy of *izibongo* in bolstering the public image of their subject derives from the formal elements of the poem which lend themselves to energising performance. To evoke greatness *izibongo* use metaphor, allusion and parallelism profusely. Leaders are likened to fierce wild animals in powerful images that build one upon the other. An image can be contained in a brief epithet of a few words or it can be developed and elaborated over a few lines. Because *izibongo* are a series of epithets, the lines are interchangeable depending on either the *imbongi*'s strategy or on the order in which he remembers lines. In performance the *imbongi* can choose to foreground certain epithets to promote a particular image of the subject. This can be achieved after the *imbongi* opens a performance with an opening formula that captures the audience's attention. *Izibongo* are often performed during events characterised by a lot of noise. When the chief or king appears the *imbongi* seizes the public's attention by repeatedly shouting an opening praise that calls for a response, usually a line of *izithakazelo* or a royal salute that is then repeated by the audience, for example:

IMBONGI: Ndabezitha!
AUDIENCE: Ndabezitha!
IMBONGI: Bayede
AUDIENCE: Bayede!

The *imbongi* then launches into a declamation of the king's praises at the top of his voice, walking up and down in front of his audience in his traditional finery. It is in this early part of the praises, before the audience returns to its chatter, that the *imbongi* can insert particular epithets that build the image of the king for which he is aiming. The *imbongi* then builds up a rhythm using, among other devices, repetition of phrases, and parallelism by having a succession of epithets that start with the same words in order to emphasise the magnitude of the king's achievements. This style of delivery is characteristic of the long praises of royalty. The *izibongo* of common people are often a few lines declaimed during vigorous dancing to the accompaniment of singing and clapping at feasts.

The 1880s and beyond: growth of art and scholarship

The wide use of the praises has only recently been given serious recognition in scholarship, the bulk of earlier commentary having created the impression that the genre of *izibongo* was reserved for royalty. This impression was created largely because of the earliest documented commentary that came in the early stages of contact between Europeans and Zulu-speaking communities from traders and adventure travellers who commented on the sensational aspect of the tradition. This sensationalisation was further fuelled by the development of the discipline of anthropology through the 1960s (Vail and White, *Power and the Praise Poem*, p. xi). The more rigorous and most influential early contribution to the study of *izibongo* came from James Stuart, who collected 'oral testimony and *izibongo* from Zulu informants' over a period of more than thirty years from 1888 to 1922 (Gunner, 'Ukubonga', p. 15). To date, Stuart's methodology and the volume of the *izibongo* he collected, accompanied by explanatory notes, remain a touchstone in the study of *izibongo*. Nevertheless, Stuart focused his collection of ethnographic information on the Zulu monarchy. Hence his collection provides scholars with only small fragments of information regarding other descent groups and almost nothing of their praise poetry.

Further fragments were provided by A. T. Bryant in his problematic *Olden Times in Zululand and Natal* (1929). Bryant's work further contributed to the focus of early scholarship on royal *izibongo*. It was B. W. Vilakazi who eventually attempted to introduce the wider range of Zulu oral artistic forms into scholarly discourse in his 1938 article 'The Conception and Development of Poetry in Zulu'. Yet influential books such as Trevor Cope's *Izibongo: Zulu*

Oral Literature (1968) continued to reinforce the dominance of royal *izibongo* in scholarship. Not until the publication of Ruth Finnegan's *Oral Literature in Africa* (1970) did scholars take seriously the need to widen their focus beyond the oral forms of the elite in African societies. Furthermore, the decolonisation of African countries in the 1960s resulted in an increase in contributions to the field by Africans where previously oral forms had been studied predominantly by European anthropologists and folklorists who often did not speak the languages in which the forms circulated. Since the late 1970s Liz Gunner has contributed to the growing sophistication of the study of Zulu language oral forms. In the 1980s the University of Natal's Oral Documentation and Research Centre continued the work of collecting these forms. It produced timely research work such as that probing the effects of formalised education on oral forms in *Oral Tradition and Education* (eds. Sienaert and Bell, 1988). Further, Isabel Hofmeyr takes stock of the growth of oral literary studies in the 1990s in 'Making Symmetrical Knowledge Possible: Recent Trends in the Field of Southern African Oral Performance Studies' (1999). However, in spite of the recent growth of oral literary studies, we have no evidence of the practice of praising before the 1820s and can therefore only speculate that it was relatively similar to what we know from the late 1820s.

Overlapping in time with the work of recording and preserving testimonies that Stuart was conducting was the development of new modes of using the old forms of *izibongo* and new forms drawing from *izibongo*. Two such examples are *maskanda* (from the Afrikaans *musikant* for musician) music and the hymns and praises of the Church of the Nazarites, or the Shembe Church, as it is commonly known. In these and later forms what is transferred to new contexts are products – songs and poems – as well as formal aspects, aesthetic principles and functions of praise genres. The mobile elements are deployed in new situations or new forms. The mobility of such elements is the realisation in diverse cultural sites of an aesthetic Leroy Vail and Landeg White, following Hugh Tracey, have termed 'poetic license' (*Power and the Praise Poem*, p. 45). Whereas writers like H. I. E. Dhlomo, Pallo Jordan and others had previously insisted that it was the praise poet who was licensed to criticise the ruler in performance, in Vail and White's interpretation poetic license means 'it is not the *poet* who is licensed by the literary conventions . . . it is the *poem*' (p. 56); 'it is *not* the performer who is licensed; it is the *performance*' (p. 57). The emphasis on the poem/performance being privileged leads Vail and White to recognise that poetic license 'permits, for instance, the assumptions legitimating the *imbongi* [to criticise the ruler in performance] to be carried not only into the village, the dancing arena, the homestead, the township, the spirit-possession ceremony, but also into the plantation, the township, the mining compound, or the black trade union meeting' (p. 57). Furthermore, Liz Gunner asserts:

> Africa teems with the temporal and spatial journeying of various kinds of song. They travel, they metamorphose, they die, sometimes they are reborn and they give birth. They are the midwives to new ideas and to new social visions. They summon up collective memory with amazing speed. They can provide platforms for debate and for an evolving discourse on a range of topics. Often the electronic media have facilitated rather than hampered such journeyings, sometimes with unpredictable results.   ('Jacob Zuma', p. 36)

What follows below is a tracing of the journeying of assumptions underlying oral poetry and cognate forms into *maskanda* music, Shembe hymns and later poetry.

Maskanda is one of the best-selling types of music in South Africa today, especially popular in rural areas of eastern South Africa and among migrant workers in urban centres like Johannesburg and Durban who hail from rural areas. *Maskanda* 'has always maintained the right of those on the far edges of power to comment on the social and political and to represent the voices of those who might otherwise go unheard' (Gunner, 'Jacob Zuma', p. 44). The genre 'began in the late nineteenth century as a musical expression of self-propelling individuality, as courting songs sung "on feet" (as isiZulu puts it) by young men on amorous walk-about' (Coplan, 'Sounds of the "Third Way"', p. 112). *Maskanda* was the music of young men, sung as they travelled across the land in search of sweethearts. A young man would sing about the landscapes of his home district, the cattle his family has to pay *ilobolo* (bridewealth) for the women he was courting, and apostrophise himself as a great lover and/or warrior, calling out some of the *izibongo* he had accumulated since childhood or making up new ones. However, the form grew out of women's music in which they sang about themselves and their experiences while accompanying themselves on the *umakhweyana* or the *ugubhu* bow and gourd. Princess Magogo Buthelezi, master *ugubhu* player and composer until her death in 1984, remains the best-known practitioner of the original incarnation of the form. Once it became a men's form, however, *maskanda* gradually migrated to urban centres like Johannesburg with the absorption of more and more Zulu men into the labour market. For a long while during this interregnum it maintained its identity as a travelling form or one of the 'cultures of mobility', as David Coplan terms it, a form of 'practice not only transported by but formulated "on the road" within the context of multisited, mobile networks of kin, homeboys and girls, and reciprocal friendships' ('Sounds of the "Third Way"', p. 112).

New *maskanda* songs were made up and sung on the road by men migrating to seek work in the cities; hence it was a culture of mobility. Songs expressed disconnection from, and longing for, the landscapes and people back home. These young men accompanied their singing on homemade guitars fashioned out of old oil cans, fishing line and wood. *Izibongo* remained a centrepiece of male *maskanda* songs, expressing aggressive and virile masculinity. The tin guitars came gradually to be replaced by guitars purchased from shops in the urban centres. The form settled in economically depressed urban sites of migrant settlement, for example barrack-style men's hostels. It circulated more widely as the expressive cultural form of dispossessed labourers who gathered together on weekends to sing and dance together in these hostels of Johannesburg, Durban and Kimberley, among other places.

Throughout the 1920s homeboys (and a few homegirls who had made it to the cities) would gather together during their leisure time to perform. Solo guitar, violin or concertina players competed against one another at these gatherings in a manner similar to veld stick fights in which boys engaged while they were herding cattle in the rural areas. Over time the form came to incorporate more than the individual self-accompanying singer. According to Coplan, in the 1930s when early recording companies went into the migrants' hostels in search of products for the African market, *maskanda* was transformed into ensemble music. Later still, with urban *maskanda* concerts becoming established, dancers were added to the ensembles (Coplan, 'Sounds of the "Third Way"', p. 112). The new elements can be identified as deriving from rurally based traditional dance forms like *ingoma* and *indlamu*. The lead singer-guitarist came to stand in a similar position as the *igoso* who leads the singing and dancing in an *ingoma* or *indlamu* group. Hence was established the *maskanda* aesthetic that remains popular to this day. Until his death in 2004 and more so afterwards, the most popular *maskanda* musician was Mfaz' Omnyama. He praised himself variously in his songs as:

> UMfaz' omnyama nezingane zakhe,
> Qoma ntombi ngafa inhlamba kanyoko.
> Wuy' umfan'ozalwa yinyanga kanti nay' uyinyanga,
> Ugogo wakhe isangoma, umfowabo umthakathi.
> Yil' inxele likaMgquzula leli,
> Phezulu kwaNongoma laph' engiqhamuka khona,
> Umful' engiwuphuzayo ngiphuz' eVuna,
> La emanxiweni obabamkhulu.
> (Mfaz' Omnyama, *Ngihlanze Ngedela*, 2001)

> Black woman and his children,
> Say yes to a suitor, maiden, I'm tired of your mother's insults.
> This is the boy whose father is a healer and this boy is also a healer,
> His grandmother is a diviner and his brother a wizard.
> This is the left-handed one of Mgquzula here,
> Up in Nongoma is where I hail from,
> The river (the waters of which) I drink is the Vuna,
> Here at my forefathers' former homesteads.

Coterminous with the early development of *maskanda* was a new use of praise poetry in Zulu by Isaiah Shembe, founder of the Church of the Nazarites. This church was founded in 1910 by Shembe at a time when Zulu monarchical authority had finally been broken down by the increasing assertion of colonial power after the Anglo-Zulu War of 1879 and rapid urbanisation from the 1860s onwards in southern Africa. According to Duncan Brown the environment created by such a flux opened up space for new Zulu leaders to emerge (*Voicing the Text*, p. 119). Thus emerged Shembe as the leader of a new African Independent Church at a time when, as African nationalism was growing, many black Christians were dissatisfied with the racist arrogance of white missionaries on matters of theology and doctrine such as polygamy and belief in the existence of ancestors (p. 132). Shembe was a modern leader, combining aspects of a traditional chief with those of a Christian prophet in his conduct. His vision for his church yielded a hybridised religious and cultural practice that combined, among other things, the calling out of his praises and the singing of hymns that he had composed through his career as a prophet, which was similar to that of the early nineteenth-century Xhosa prophet Ntsikana (Hodgsen, *The God of the Xhosa*, p. 24). Orality and literacy combined in a synthesis of disparate symbols and practices from Zulu culture and Christian worship. Shembe's praises borrow from those of Shaka images of a martial hero, which are then combined in an inventive way with symbols that had become significant in the lives of Shembe's followers, the Gospel in this case:

> Spear which is red even at the handle,
> you attacked with it at Mpukunyoni
> because you attacked by means of the Gospel.

Even successors of the founder of the church are often referred to by their praise names: Isaiah Shembe's son Johannes Galilee is iLanga (Sun) who was succeeded by Amos, iNyangayezulu (Moon of the Heavens) after whom came Vimbeni, uThingo lweNkosazana (Rainbow of the Princess) (Gunner, *The Man of Heaven*, p. 3).

The hymns, *amahubo*, of the Shembe church are a similarly syncretic form to the *izibongo*. They combine the tradition of church hymns brought from the mission churches, from which early African Independent Church leaders broke away, with elements of traditional indigenous modes of religious expression. Moreover,

> the hymns of Isaiah Shembe and the Church of the Nazarites treat many of the most pressing issues of twentieth-century Zulu history in particular, and modern South African history in general: ownership and occupation of land; economic dispossession; African nationalism and ethnicity; the ideological and educational role of the missionaries. (Brown, *Voicing the Text*, p. 124)

Examples include hymn no. 219 in which God is referred to as 'Babamkhulu' (forefather) and in which is enunciated a long-standing difficulty of conversion (ostensibly due in the contemporary moment to missionary control of matters of biblical interpretation):

> Thousands of generations
> stand here
> oh! Babamkhulu
> they found your world difficult
> oh! Babamkhulu
> make soft thy word
> oh! Babamkhulu.
> (Oosthuizen quoted in Brown, *Voicing the Text*, p. 134)

Taken together with Shembe's *izibongo* that were, and continue to be, declaimed during services, this hymn demonstrates the coextensiveness of praising the living and the ancestors. There is a fusion of the Zulu concept of *uMvelinqangi* as the all-powerful being to whom appeals can only be made through the departed ancestors as intermediaries and the Christian model of making direct appeal to God in prayer and song. God has become 'Babamkhulu', the figure to whom prayers are addressed and who, in Zulu cosmology, has the power to touch the affairs of the living.

We can view Nazarite hymns as remakings of Zulu *amahubo*. *Amahubo* in Zulu are a kind of solemn hymn sung during some ceremonies of family and/or national importance. Each *isibongo* (surname) has its own *ihubo lesizwe* ('national' hymn) that is sung, for example, when a woman is being led out of her family home to go and marry into another family. As Gcob-hoza Ndwandwe said in an interview, the *ihubo* is a prayer to the ancestors (Buthelezi, 5 May 2008). When she is led out of the house on the afternoon of the day before the wedding, the hymn is sung in that sombre moment as she walks with the elders of her family to the cattle enclosure. In the cattle enclosure the ancestors of the family are called up and informed that their daughter will soon be leaving the family. The ancestors are enjoined to guide and guard her in her new family. They are requested to collaborate with their new relatives, the ancestors of the family into which their daughter is marry-ing, to protect her. Each important departed member of the lineage of the extended family is briefly praised using his *izibongo* as he is addressed and the living male elders of the patrilineal family unit also have their praises called out as the 'parents' of the 'child' that is being ceremonially 'taken out' of the home. Hence the praises of the living and the dead are coextensive with the *ihubo lesizwe* in a similar way to the Shembe use of the leader's *izibongo* and the hymns that address God as 'Babamkhulu'. God is the ancestor to whom prayer is addressed in the hymn. The differences from the Zulu ceremony described above are that there are no praise poems addressed to God and that the praise is conducted in a religious ceremony rather than the kind of social situation in which most Zulu communion with the ancestors occurs.

Shembe hymns and praise poetry strongly demonstrate the mobility of features of traditional praise forms as argued by Vail and White and by Gunner. It has also been shown how in the 1970s poets, galvanised by ideas of Black Consciousness and radicalised by the events that began with the student uprising of June 1976, sought to affirm their blackness in the face of oppression by a racist state apparatus by returning to traditional African cultural models (Brown, *Voicing the Text*, pp. 165–211). By reinventing oral poetry through combining it with music in some cases, performance poets were able to negate state censorship: 'poems could be memorised, passed on, and performed in a variety of contexts' (p. 183). Poems such as Ingoapele Madingoane's 'black trial' borrow formal elements from *izibongo*, using parallelism and building up to rhetorical climaxes in a similar way to the royal *izibongo* discussed earlier. The praise imperative featured strongly in the work of most Soweto poets as the group of poets from this era of radical poetry have been named (Chapman, *Soweto Poetry*). Praises were sung to heroes from the African past as well as to landscapes.

At the same time as the study of Zulu oral forms deepened with the work of the likes of Liz Gunner in the 1980s, further innovation expanded the range of forms that were oriented towards praise. Where *izibongo* traditionally had been about praising and criticising individuals, a new form came into being that combined the group praise orientation of *izithakazelo* with the declamatory style of *izibongo*. Enterprising poets performed praises alongside plays and political speeches at trade union rallies. This was a new genre of oral poetry in which trade unions were praised for the work they were doing fighting for the rights of workers, and in which the leadership of the resistance movement was praised for its work, thus being similar to *izithakazelo* in praising a large collective and in the same poem singling out particular leaders. In this poetry the collective being praised was a group of co-participants in the struggle for justice and freedom. Similarly to *izibongo*, the poems gave sometimes veiled, sometimes overt criticism and warning to apartheid authorities about the consequences of oppressing the black majority of the people of South Africa. Whereas the Shembe and other African Independent Churches were oppositional to white authority in subtle ways in their song and dance, the tradition of song and dance came increasingly to be used as a mode of shouting opposition to apartheid state policies in the 1980s. Alfred Themba Qabula is credited with originating the employment of performance poetry as part of the cultural aspect of the industrial workers' struggle for rights in Durban (Brown, *Voicing the Text*, p. 215).

Drawing on his acquaintance with the poetic license of Xhosa (and Zulu) *izibongo* to praise and admonish, Qabula first performed 'A Poem for FOSATU' as part of the *Dunlop Play* created by workers in the Dunlop tyre factory in Durban in 1983. In the socioeconomic environment of the time the relationship the praise poet mediated was no longer between a ruling leader and the ruled populace but a much more oppositional one between exploitative employers forming part of a larger state-sponsored system of exploitation and a group of workers organised into a trade union. The role of the poet had thus been altered from being one of praising the ruler for his achievements as a leader and attempting to correct faults in his conduct through criticism, to praising the union for its achievements in organising workers into a stronger collective. The poet also warned the leadership of the union to remain vigilant while at the same time criticising the employers for the poor working and living conditions that workers were forced to endure. However, in this new role Qabula still deployed the formal strategies of *izibongo* familiar to his audiences that comprised people most of whom were users of *izibongo* and *izithakazelo* and some of whom listened to *maskanda* music and/or were members of the Shembe church.

'Praise poem for FOSATU' remains emblematic. Once Qabula had made the initial attempt, the responses of the thousands of union members in front of whom he performed encouraged the growth of the form. The form was taken up by more poets, becoming a central part of union mass gatherings. Poets performing to large crowds had the benefit of amplification so that they no longer needed to perform like the *izimbongi*, being less flamboyant in their movements in order to remain within the range of a microphone and no longer needing to project their voices. Moreover, the poets combined orality, writing and print in innovative ways, writing their poems before performing them and often publishing them in union newsletters and pamphlets. *Black Mamba Rising* (ed. Sitas, 1986), containing the poetry of Qabula, Nise Malange and Mi Sdumo Hlatshwayo, was one of the products of this period of creative explosion.

Izibongo continue to be a vibrant form: the tradition of Zulu royal poetry has continued unbroken among Zulu royalty from the founding of the Zulu kingdom until today. Whilst ordinary people continue to compose and declaim their own *izibongo*, the tradition has significantly contracted with the hybridisation of the cultures of Zulu speakers as they have encountered and sought accommodation with other cultures. Nevertheless, while fewer people use *izibongo* in their daily lives, the form has gained more prominence beyond the confines of Zulu culture through new technologies that have been used by *izibongo* practitioners. The Zulu king's *imbongi*'s CD is one example. Since the 1880s the assumptions legitimating the *imbongi* to praise and criticise have journeyed to new contexts – the Shembe church, the migrant hostel compound, the soccer stadium during a labour union mass meeting, and others – as new meanings have been created for old forms and new forms have mutated out of older ones – *maskanda*, hymns, performance poetry and other forms. Today in South Africa we are seeing forms deriving from *izibongo* being midwives to other social visions. *Maskanda* has been at the forefront of voicing the dissatisfaction of those left behind by uneven post-apartheid socioeconomic development who found common cause with Jacob Zuma when he was fired as deputy president of the country in 2005. Popular *maskanda* group Izingane ZoMa's 2005 album, *Msholozi*, in praise and support of Zuma, found popular success as allusive criticism of the government of the day and then president Thabo Mbeki. Even the title of the album is the praise name of the Zuma kinship group. At the same time Zuma himself was able to harness 'Umshini Wami', a song that had had very different meanings among exiled anti-apartheid fighters, to capture the hopes of the disaffected. Deriving from another traditional form, *amahubo empi* or war chants, and sharing *izibongo*'s poetic licence assumptions, the song has further reinvigorated the ability of *izibongo* and coextensive forms to unleash social energy in new directions. Similarly, popular rapper Zuluboy has teamed up with *maskanda* musician Bhekumuzi Luthuli and produced hits that combine the two musical forms to speak poignantly about HIV/AIDS, poverty and *maskanda*'s traditional subject – courtship. Musicians and poets in the society created out of this social energy may yet create new pathways for the poems, songs and aesthetic assumptions that we know to have been in motion since the nineteenth century.

Bibliography

Brown, D. *Voicing the Text: South African Oral Poetry and Performance*, Cape Town: Oxford University Press, 1998.

Bryant, A. T. *Olden Times in Zululand and Natal: Continuing Earlier Political History of the Eastern-Nguni Clans*, London: Longmans, Green & Co., 1929.

Buthelezi, M. Interview with Gcobhoza and Mahlanza Ndwandwe, 5 May 2008, unpublished.

Chapman, M. (ed.). *Soweto Poetry*, Johannesburg: McGraw-Hill, 1982.

Cope, T. *Izibongo: Zulu Oral Literature*, Oxford: Clarendon Press, 1968.

Coplan, D. 'Sounds of the "Third Way": Identity and the African Renaissance in Contemporary South African Popular Traditional Music', *Black Music Research Journal* 21:1 (2001), 107–24.

Finnegan, R. *The Oral and Beyond: Doing Things with Words in Africa*, London: James Currey, University of Chicago Press and Pietermaritzburg: University of KwaZulu-Natal Press, 2007.

Oral Literature in Africa, Oxford University Press, 1970.

Gunner, E. A. W. 'Ukubonga Nezibongo: Zulu Praising and Praises', Ph.D. thesis, University of London, 1984.

Gunner, L. 'Africa and Orality', in F. A. Irele and S. Gikandi (eds.), *The Cambridge History of African and Caribbean Literature*, 2 vols. Cambridge University Press, 2004, vol. I, 1–18.

'Clashes of Interest: Gender, Status and Power in Zulu Praise Poetry', in G. Furniss and L. Gunner (eds.), *Power, Marginality and African Oral Literature*, Cambridge University Press, 1995.

'Jacob Zuma, the Social Body and the Unruly Power of Song', *African Affairs* 108:430 (2008), 27–48.

The Man of Heaven and the Beautiful Ones of God: Isaiah Shembe and the Nazareth Church, Pietermaritzburg: University of KwaZulu-Natal Press, 2004.

Gunner, L., and M. Gwala. *Musho!: Zulu Popular Praises*, Johannesburg: Witwatersrand University Press, 1994.

Hodgsen, J. *The God of the Xhosa. A Study of the Origins and Development of the Traditional Concepts of the Supreme Being*, Cape Town: Oxford University Press, 1982.

Hofmeyr, I. 'Making Symmetrical Knowledge Possible: Recent Trends in the Field of Southern African Oral Performance Studies', in Duncan Brown (ed.), *Oral Literature and Peformance in Southern Africa*, London: James Currey, 1999, 18–26.

'We Spend our Years as a Tale that is Told': Oral Historical Narrative in a South African Chiefdom, Johannesburg: Witwatersrand University Press, 1993.

Mfaz' Omnyama, Ngihlanze Ngedela, Gallo Record Company, 2001.

'Motlanthe swearing in likely to be delayed', Mail and Guardian, 3 May 2009, www.mg.co. za/article/2009-05-06-motlanthe-swearing-in-likely-to-be-delayed, accessed 6 May 2009.

Msimgang, C. Kusadliwa Ngoludala [1975], Pietermaritzburg: Shuter & Shooter, 1991.

Sienaert, E., and N. Bell (eds.). Oral Tradition and Education, Durban: Natal University Oral Documentation and Research Centre, 1988.

Sitas, A. (ed.). Black Mamba Rising: South African Worker Poets in Struggle, Durban: Worker Resistance and Culture Publications, 1986.

Sithole, E. T. Izithakazelo Nezibongo ZakwaZulu, Ashwood: Mariannhill Mission Press, 1982.

Stuart, J. The James Stuart Archive, vols. I–V, Pietermaritzburg and Durban: University of KwaZulu-Natal Press and Campbell Collections, 1976–2001.

Vail, L., and L. White. Power and the Praise Poem: Southern African Voices in History, Charlottesville: University of Virginia Press and London: James Currey, 1991.

Vilakazi, B. W. 'The Conception and Development of Poetry in Zulu', Bantu Studies 12 (1938), 105–34.

Wright, J. 'Politics, Ideology and the Invention of the Nguni', in T. Lodge (ed.), Resistance and Ideology in Settler Societies, Johannesburg: Ravan, 1986.

5

IsiNdebele, siSwati, Northern Sotho, Tshivenda and Xitsonga oral culture

MANIE GROENEWALD AND MOKGALE MAKGOPA

Traditional contexts

While the oral cultures in southern Africa may share the same oral genres and performance strategies, different contexts provide for peculiarities. A few of these contexts will be mentioned before elaborating on aspects of Ndebele verbal art as an illustration of the range and evolution of oral discourse in South Africa.

In her study on Hananwa[1] and Lobedu oral performance, Annekie Joubert gives an idea of the vibrancy of their song culture in particular:

> Almost every phase and event in the yearly cycle of the Hananwa and Lobedu are accompanied and embraced with song. Men sing as they manufacture various crafts, execute strenuous physical work, relax around the fire in the evenings, at beer-drinking gatherings, or over weekends when they perform the drum-flute ensembles. The women sing as they perform household tasks, when they gather to assist one another to perform communal tasks, in the relaxing hours of the evening, during periods of drought and subsequently when the rain has fallen, at church gatherings and at festivities.
>
> (*Power of Performance*, p. 267)

The annual rainmaking ceremony performed by the people of 'the rain queen' Modjadji of the Lobedu showcases the most important ceremony. Joubert's study, however, gives a view of the daily struggles and pastimes of men, but especially those of women. Secluded on the plateau of the Blouberg, a mountain in the north-west of the country, Lobedu women sing about their cares as they are left behind by their migrant husbands. Debra James, giving a view on migrant labour, shows that the migrant workers do not simply transpose their rural songs to the city but activate 'a new world of experience which bridges the gap between past and present, town and

---

1 Hananwa, Lobedu, and Sepedi are a few of the dialects of the Northern Sotho language.

country' (*Metropoles and Satellites*, p. 13). The drum-flute ensembles mentioned by Joubert, known to some Northern Sotho speakers as *kiba*, are performances unique to Northern Sotho men and illustrate another kind of development in traditional performance, namely how it has become semi-professional as performers perform on request for payment.

Joubert gives an impressive list of different types of praise poetry amongst Hananwa and Lobedu speakers, types that may be found among many Northern Sotho speakers (*Power of Performance*, p. 387). The praise poem for a Hananwa leader, for example, is lofty in style and recalls the war waged by the Zuid-Afrikaanse Republiek (ZAR) government against the Hananwa in 1894, and although the Hananwa lost the war the intention of the poem is to instil ethnic pride by reminding the people of their brave leader's efforts. The praise poetry for a leader will be performed on auspicious occasions; the praise poetry for diviners and their craft, probably the most prevalent type of praise poetry, is performed daily in many places.

In the past the narrating of folk-tales in the evenings, especially by women, was also a common event and, apart from being educational and entertaining, it afforded women the opportunity to protest against, for instance, abusive behaviour by their husbands. As the narrating of folk-tales as a means of complaint has largely been lost, singing remains a genre that fulfils a variety of functions – it is a vehicle for complaint; it mediates rituals; expresses personal and social concerns; mediates political change. The traditions of *khekhapa* (performed by Lobedu men and women), *tshigombela* (performed by Venda women), and *xibelani* (performed by Tsonga women) – all of which are in the Limpopo Province – are a few of the many examples illustrating the vibrancy of song. *Khekhapa*, like *kiba*, has emerged as a type that has little or no ritual intent and is performed mostly for the entertainment of the singers and their audience on various social occasions and as a small source of income. Singers organise themselves into groups, each with its own name and distinctive clothing. Although the material used is factory-made, its link with commercialism is softened by bleaching – note the Lobedu word *dituku* derived from the Afrikaans '*doek*' (headscarf) to refer to the cloth. Makgopa notes that the cloth is spread out in the sun on the roof of a house for about a week, or is bleached before the garments are sewn ('Origin and Context', p. 57). Many *khekhapa* songs refer to labour injustices, and infidelity on the part of the husband; in the following song the women lament the fact that a husband seeks the company of another woman while working in Pretoria, yet pride in the traditional space is still there (lines 9–15):

Pretoria at Mamelodi of Tshwane
At Mamelodi of Tshwane, at the place of Ndebeles
Because to Pretoria I will no longer go
At Mamelodi of Tshwane, at the place of Ndebeles
Anyone with problems let him/her[2] report at Mamelodi of Tshwane
Because I am not a fool
At Mamelodi of Tshwane
I am relocating and returning to Mohlatlareng at Seroto's place
I am longing for our own area
Our mountain Marobong
The mountain with a scar on the forehead
I am returning to the Bokgaga people where I come from
I am a true Mokgaga [I belong to the clan whose totem is the pangolin . . .]
Who washes with soft porridge which is bitter
I don't wash with water, I am afraid of becoming pale.
                    ('Origin and Context', p. 63; translation by Manie Groenewald)

In traditional rural societies the role of women was circumscribed; in contemporary society, women are freer to express themselves in song. In the following song women allude to the fact that they have the right to vote and to make a difference:

We are the children of Mandela
We are the children of Mandela
The old man has fought for us, he has been brave
Even when he steps down, we do that with him
We are looking for someone new whom we don't know as yet.
                    ('Origin and Context', p. 64; translation by Mogale Makgopa)

Using the example of siSwati praise poetry for King Sobhuza, Vail and White show how oral art can be rendered politically subservient: 'Sobhuza captured poetry, and it became a "traditional" means of propaganda in the service of a state that overtly espouses "tradition" in support of a "traditional" monarchy' (*Power and the Praise Poem*, p. 192). The rule by traditional monarchy in Swaziland, they argue, has given prominence to cultural practices (over good governance) which serve to enhance political power. This is also illustrated in an unpublished study by Thwala on the songs of women groups who call themselves *lutsango*; Thwala notes that one of the most important festivals in Swaziland, the *incwala* (feast of the first fruits), serves to entrench the power of the king ('Lutsango', p. 5). Equally prominent is the *umhlanga*

2 The idea is that the person should report to Mamelodi to resolve the issue.

(the festival of the reed, popularly known as the annual reed dance), when thousands of unmarried girls congregate and bring a reed for the building or repairing of fences and when King Mswati III may view the girls should he choose to take another wife. Such is the hegemony of the traditional monarchy in Swaziland that much of *lutsango* singing idealises traditional practices and encourages people to attend these ceremonies. But not all siSwati performance is conservative. The vitality of oral performance does find a creative outlet in the form of songs and praises for buses, to mention one example. Ntuli notes that 'Buses are so much part of the community that they seem to be perceived as "human beings" who should be praised in the same traditional way as prominent heroes are praised' ('Bus Naming', p. 319).

Modern contexts

Oral culture should not be read solely in terms of ethnic divisions as it is a continually adapting tradition which speaks to the present. Sangoma and political performances are two examples that transcend ethnic boundaries and adapt to changing contexts. Political songs, for example, are performed all over the country by singers belonging to a variety of ethnic groups. Whilst pre-1994 songs were performed in an effort to topple the apartheid government, many of the same songs are sung post-1994 to celebrate freedom or to criticise leaders of the new dispensation. In the following song former Gauteng Premier Bhazima Shilowa and former President Thabo Mbeki were criticised for their approval of privatisation:

> Shilowa, you don't know what you want
> We gave you the hand
> We even gave you the arm
> We gave you the breasts
> You don't know what you want
> Mbeki, you don't know what you want
> We took you from the bush
> We gave you the vote
> We put you in parliament
> You don't know what you want.
> > (Recorded by Sikwebu, 'Strike Hit Parade', p. 13,
> > translated by Manie Groenewald)[3]

3 In an interview on 24 January 2002, Jeremy Cronin recalls that the same song was sung by disaffected members of the crowd at the funeral of Govan Mbeki, held in the township of Zwide outside Port Elizabeth on 8 September 2001. See Gevisser, *Thabo Mbeki*, p. 771.

In February 2006, during hearings of then Deputy President Jacob Zuma when he was defending himself against an accusation of rape, a small band of activists associated with POWA (People Opposing Women Abuse) made their sentiments known in this song:

> When POWA When POWA strikes them strikes them
> You Zuma You Zuma go overseas go overseas
> Don't cry Don't cry you woman you woman
> POWA is here POWA is here it will strike them it will strike them.[4]

Performances connected to various types of traditional healers are varied and abundant. The different types of healers have their own variant of a particular ceremony – be it to identify the call to become a healer, performances of the training phase, or that of healing – while ceremonies may take place in rural and urban environments.

Ndebele oral culture

The early history of the amaNdebele (henceforth Ndebele) concerns the origin and consolidation of the polity as well as inter- (and intra-) cultural conflict (1500s–1845). The later history includes contact with whites and its results (1845–83); dispersion (1883–1922); struggle for recognition (1922–85); the conflict over homeland independence (1985–8); and the question of identity in post-apartheid South Africa (1988 to the present). Today the Ndebele (or Southern Ndebele, as opposed to the amaNdebele of Zimbabwe), governed by a democratically elected government, are a typically decentred group. Whilst the Ndebele people living in rural areas north-east of Pretoria live closer to their traditional chieftaincies (of which there are six), other Ndebele speakers are spread out in surrounding townships, towns and cities. From the time of the founding monarchs who can be recalled from oral tradition, twenty-five Ndzundza Ndebele and thirty-four Manala Ndebele monarchs or regents have ruled. (The Ndzundza and the Manala are the two larger Ndebele groups.)

A history of oral performance in isiNdebele is to a large extent a history of scientific texts on the Ndebele people, written by ethnographers, anthropologists and historians. Given the varied nature of these texts based on their differing objectives, a seamless diachronic narrative of oral performance is not possible; at best, one may perhaps refer to general phases that most oral cultures pass through. Thus one can refer to a primary, secondary and tertiary

---

4 The response following the call is underlined. The song is translated from the original as recorded by Manie Groenewald in 2006.

phase. Primary refers to the precolonial context with minimal foreign influence. In the secondary phase significant changes and the loss of some practices have taken place due to contact with another culture. Tertiary would describe a culture of which most 'original' cultural practices have become obsolete; remnants of oral art are confined to text, and ceremonies are symbolic rather than efficacious. The earliest study on the Ndebele people is a 1921 thesis by Hermanus Fourie on the Ndzundza section entitled *Amandebele van Fene Mahlangu en hun Religieus-Sociaal Leven* (The AmaNdebele of Fene Mahlangu and their Social-Religious Life).[5] Fourie wrote at a time when the oral culture of the Ndebele was in transition from a primary to a secondary phase. At this point the Ndebele people were divided into the two larger sections (the Manala and the Ndzundza) with other smaller groupings. The war in 1883 with the ZAR government was most damaging as the Ndebele under the kingship of Ndzundza were evicted from their land and families were indentured to white farmers of the area, marking the end to a life of relative unity and independence. Even so, it is clear from Fourie's commentary that activities and ceremonies in this community at the time of writing were still efficacious and elaborate and considered vital for social coherence and identity.

Consider, for instance, Fourie's account of a wedding characterised by typical traditional activities, in which what he calls the 'bruiloftsrede' ('wedding address') played a vital part (*Amandebele*, p. 104). Fourie calls the recorded texts the 'wedding addresses' of the Mahlangu family. The texts consist of the praise poems of the very first known leaders (before the great split between the Manala and the Ndzundza sections) and subsequently of the Ndzundza kings. He lists twenty-three praise poems. Praise poetry remains one of the iconic genres of oral art in most of the African language communities in South Africa and Fourie is no exception in canonising it when he says: 'Een verzameling van familie-bonga's zou een aardige bijdrage zijn tot de Bantu-letterkunde' ('A collection of family praises would be a notable contribution to Bantu literature') (p. 114). A moment of social division within the Ndebele polity could be considered a major event and could find expression in oral art. A major split occurred sometime in the 1500s in the present day area of Pretoria, when the Ndebele were united under Musi, who was preparing to appoint a successor. The rivalry between the two major contenders, Manala and Ndzundza, is captured in a curious legend of origin closely resembling the biblical Esau and Jacob story. Although Fourie is adamant that the narrators

---

5 Hermanus Cornelis Marthinus Fourie was a minister in the Nederduits Hervomde Kerk and a Bible translator. He completed his doctorate on the Ndebele at the University of Utrecht.

of the legend knew nothing of the Bible and that the Ndebele people since the reign of Musi had been living an isolated life (*Amandebele*, p. 3), the legend has too many resemblances with the biblical story to be discounted as foreign influence. One thus has to question Fourie's insistence of no foreign influence and accept that somehow this story was adopted and adapted to the context in the nineteenth century to make sense of a significant event in the life of the community. The story is told that when Musi felt that his time to die was near he summoned his sons to appear before him at the first crow of the rooster. Manala however went hunting because as the firstborn he expected to receive the kingship. Ndzundza was the first to appear before Musi, who was blind by this stage. Since Manala was a hairy man, Ndzundza covered himself with animal skin and so Ndzundza received the symbols of kingship after which he fled with his following fearing reprisal by Manala.

Today the Ndebele people, living in a modern, developing, democratic African state, can perhaps be described as possessing a culture whose oral performance is in a secondary phase exhibiting some tertiary tendencies. In this culture modern institutions have supplanted the need for certain types of oral art. Schooling, for instance, has replaced the need for the performance of riddles to sharpen the wits of children; radio, television and other media have supplanted the narration of stories as a means of entertainment and moral edification. Thus, when Groenewald recorded Ndebele oral performance (see 'Ndebele Verbal Art') between 1986 and 1993 the performance of folk-tales, riddles and songs connected to ceremonies now obsolete (for instance that of the first fruits) had all but ceased so that such texts are found mainly in written collections. And although there remains an appreciable core of culture-defining performances, they are practised with a fluid interpretation of the rules while at the same time being influenced or eroded by extracultural elements, as will be shown in a few examples.

The *iqude*, or initiation ceremony for girls, is probably the most frequently held traditional ceremony among Ndebele people today. Whilst some families may still observe the *umchaso* (an optional ceremony held to announce that a girl has become physically mature and to rejoice in this fact), the first significant event of the *iqude* proper after the girl has menstruated for the first time is her seclusion. According to Janse van Vuuren ('Aard en Betekenis', p. 380), the initiate is secluded on a Friday morning while another girl, a specially chosen instructor, and her helpers will start preparing for the drum-beating ceremony that evening. Towards late afternoon the girls of the area will assemble and sing and dance through the night. The adaptability of a secondary oral culture is clearly illustrated by the inclusion of the emergent practice of the so-called *spit kops* ('speed cops'). They consist of a group of married women who arrive with a goat as a gift to the initiate and who 'fine' the men in the vicinity. Early the following morning the girls will go to a river to perform a ceremonial washing while the initiate is hidden in their midst. When they return later that morning, they will be met at the gate by the mothers who will praise the girl with extracts of the family praises. There will be feasting as guests arrive throughout the day. The next day (Sunday) is spent presenting gifts to the girl. After singing and dancing (also by the men assembled there) the people will feast. After a period of thirty days of seclusion the *ukuhlubula* ceremony will take place, consisting of the removal of the old blanket to induct the girl into adult life. This part of an *iqude* was attended by Groenewald and associates at the place of Jim Ntuli on 5 March 1988. The ceremony was held for his granddaughter.

When we arrived on the Saturday morning, Ntuli and other male relatives were spending the time leisurely drinking beer. From time to time one of the senior men would stand up and *giya* (perform a men's dance), and from time to time they sang songs. Often, after a song, the *thamba* was performed. This is a mock fight performed with a shield and sticks. The *thamba* was invariably followed by a 'combat formula' consisting of a praise line, unique to each individual, part of which is always repeated by the audience as the man dances. The *thamba*, in turn, often led to another song. One spokesperson referred to these songs as *amasino*, songs sung when men gather to drink, sing and dance. Another spokesperson denied that such a term existed. This shows how songs are redefined as knowledge of the primary context is lost. The singing of a popular religious song during this ceremony also shows that a ceremony that surely was, and still largely is, characterised by rigid procedure becomes open to include non-core songs. It should be clear from this terse description that songs were abundant, showing that the ceremony is still productive and not merely a fragment of the past. Songs follow the well-known pattern of call and response. The fact that songs carry contemporary content, albeit presented in the usual illusionary way, also testifies to the fact that the ceremony is not simply a relic from the past. Shortly after our arrival at Ntuli's house the men began singing this song:

> Angikhaleli ngiyabalabala: <u>wo woo</u>
> Wo:lele wolelele: <u>wo woo</u>
> Etc.
>
> I am not complaining, I am fretting <u>wo woo</u>, etc

Despite its apparent negative message (probably about the political situation at the time), the song has a pleasant tune, sung with great enjoyment and clapping of hands and repeated for quite some time. After forty-two repetitions Ntuli ends the song by shouting 'Okay!', and he utters his *thamba* formula:

Nang' owam', nang' owam', nang' owam', Masinda- Masindakulu akoSelephi Masindakulu akoSelephi! Masindakulu akoSelephi!

Here is mine [common introduction to *thamba* formulae], Masindakulu of Selephi's place.

Whilst Ntuli subsequently performs his mock charges, the other men repeat the *thamba* lines. He then announces the feast, both to those present and to the ancestors. Notice how he includes sections of his clan praises (underlined; only the translation is given):[6]

You of the chief!
This is Ntuli's place, at Ntuli's place who is aligned to the sun
Here we are at Ntuli's place who is aligned to the sun
We are at Mphemba's place who made fire
At the place of the hyena
Oh father we plead, today we have a feast here at home; we are glad, the child is here at home
At Masindakulu of Selephi's place
Now, her father is Red Cow of Bafikisaphi's place.

In the life of a traditional healer there are three major events or stages: the call, the training, and lastly the occupational stage. These events, in turn, have different ceremonies in which songs, chants, and praise poetry may feature. The training phase culminates in two ceremonies: the graduation ceremony, called *ukudla ithwaso* (eating/enjoying the fulfilment) or *ukugeza idaka* (washing off the clay) by other groups, followed by the ceremony held 'to take the healer home', namely to have a ceremony at the healer's place of birth where the ancestors are. The graduation ceremony is probably the most elaborate of all healing ceremonies. It usually commences on a Friday evening when people gather to sing and when the trainees (*amathwasa*) present themselves to the people. The beat of drums at the place of gathering determines the routine of the night. When the drums stop beating it is the sign for the trainees to assume a kneeling position at which time they could come into contact with the ancestors, which is characterised by loud shouts of *Yawuu!* and shooting upright on the knees. At the commencement of

6 In contrast to songs, clan praises are fixed texts preserving content from a distant past when the content still made sense.

the drums they sit again while a song is initiated until it is again drowned by the drums. When a healer (or even a member of the audience) exhibits signs of entering into trance s/he will chant the *thokoza* discourse. It is a performance resembling a praise poem, which is uttered to another participant who assumes a kneeling position. The following day is spent on divining, slaughtering and cleansing activities. Healers are prolific singers and songs are invariably sung to a relatively fast tempo and are typically one-liners divided into the call and response. For example in the song 'Sengikhalela inyongo yami' (I am crying for my gall bladder) the call is 'Inyongo yami, inyongo' (My gall bladder). 'Sengikhalela inyongo yami' is the response. Many of the healing ceremonies are characterised by openness. Men and women participate on an equal footing; children witness most of the activities while language is also not an issue. At the performances attended we witnessed how songs were sung in isiNdebele, isiZulu and Northern Sotho. Then there is also the incorporation of songs from other types of experience, such as religion. At one ceremony the song 'The holy names will be called out' was performed with great delight and enthusiasm by healers and participants alike.

Even the wedding of a leader or important culture figure exhibits foreign influence. The wedding of *Ingwenyama* (a respectful term for an Ndebele king meaning 'lion') Mabhena of the Manala took place between 11 and 17 December 1989. It would not be uncommon to hear work songs in the preparatory stages of weddings as people are preparing the venue. A well-known work song among Ndebele was recorded during these preparations; it illustrates the master–slave situation in colonial and apartheid times and the contempt the worker had for the master and *induna* (black foreman). The song is sung when an object has to be lifted. As the workers look for a place to grip the leader says:

Sandla fun' indawo <u>hm hm hm</u> (Hand, look for a place. *Repeated as often as is necessary*)

Having all found a place they say:

ʼphelele ʼphelele ʼphelele ([It is] complete – *repeated*)

They lift the object:

Dubula, dubula <u>ziyasha, ziyasha</u> (Shoot, shoot! They [cows?] are burning, they are burning, things are hectic)

When the object is lifted the workers say:

Ngomsa ngomsa ngomsa (With care – *repeated*)
Abelungu ngodem, ngodem (Whites say 'damn')
Abelungu ngoshit, ngoshit basibiza ngoshit (Whites say 'shit', they call us 'shit')
Induna amasend' enduna (The induna, testicles of the induna)

When the workers put the object down they say:

Phasi phasi phasi (Down)

A 'traditional' African wedding is often divided into the 'traditional' part (or rather: the part with some traditional elements) – which often takes place on a Saturday; this is called the *isikhethu* ('our culture') – and the modern part (*isikhuwa* – 'white culture'), which takes place on a Sunday. *Ingwenyama* Mabhena hired the Mathjirini Boys (a local band) and the Mamelodi Brass Band to lead his entourage to his homestead. After many speeches and songs the *Ingwenyama* appeared and a Manala praise poet commenced to praise the Manala chiefs of old. One example reads as follows:

(For Nsele or: Sele)

Ayeeela!
Take this cow
It is that of Sele, Sele there he is yonder
On the plain of the mountain
5 All the nations
Are stretching themselves towards him
He is stretched for by those of Tsheme and of Doyi
He was stretched for by those of Nhlathu and of Mamba
For a long time we have said Sele should go to his father
   (*Shouts of* Bayethe! Ngonyama!)
10 We have said the guy is bad; he should be killed
Sele, for liking the seat of the chief
This Sele
The hands (= care) of his father he doesn't know
He knows those of his mother
15 Of Mbokazi
NaMayisa.

As is clear here, the praise poem does not only recall heroic attributes (lines 5–8) but also vilifies Sele's lust for power (line 11).

The first song we recorded expressed reverence for the chiefs. The lead singer sang a complete line and the responders took up the call after which the lead singer would use one or two words of the song to prompt the call, as follows: 'When I look at the chiefs of KwaNdebele I cry tears. Tears, father, I cry tears'. In a society that has experienced the reduction of their culture in the context of colonialism and apartheid there is often the anxiety of loss, as can be seen in this song.

The Ndebele *ingoma* (initiation of boys), also referred to as *ukuwela* (to cross over), is very important from an historical perspective. Janse van Vuuren states that it proved to be nothing less than a means of social cohesion and even political survival: 'Concerning the organisation of the boys' initiation, Ndzundza informants maintain that it had a centralised character up to the Mapoch war of 1883, and they point to the fact that after the attack by Mzilikazi the *ingoma* kept the Ndzundza together' ('Aard en Betekenis', p. 472; our translation).

But needless to say, its historical centralised nature and its traditional four-year cycle have been subject to change in recent years. There are now at least three main centres authorising different *ingoma*. The increasing number of young men to be initiated and the financial potential of *ingoma* have probably led to changes in its frequency. For performance purposes, the ceremonies can be divided into four main parts (Janse van Vuuren, 'Aard en Betekenis', p. 334, speaks of nine smaller sections): the pre-initiation rendezvous, the initiation period itself, the post-initiation rendezvous, and lastly, the receiving of the initiated at his home. Pre-initiation is characterised by belligerent groups of initiates making their way to the meeting place where they will engage in duals with quince switches. In a secondary oral society primary knowledge increasingly dissipates and *ukuwela*, important as it is, is no exception. On the occasion of the 1989 *ukuwela* witnessed at *Ingwenyama* Mabhoko's place, we learned that the *Amarudla* regiment was being formed, at least this is what some spokesmen said – the person we asked first, *Ingwenyama* Mabhoko's personal attendant, did not know. Each initiation cycle has a particular name (known as an *intanga*, regiment) of which there are fifteen. Thus after fifteen cycles, or forty-five years, the names will repeat themselves. According to Philemon Buti Skhosana, at the time Chief Cultural Officer, the boys are taught moral issues, for example how a man has to conduct himself. They are also taught the songs that have been in circulation in previous initiation schools while each boy composes his own praise poem, which, curiously, is in Northern Sotho, from which the practice was obviously adopted, possibly in precolonial times.

Fourie refers to *ikwabo* (*AmaNdebele*, pp. 125–6) as the four-year period prior to *ukuwela* when boys served the king in cultivating fields, and in other duties. Today *igwabo* simply refers to the post-initiation celebration. Having left the 'mountain' or the 'bush' (metaphors used for the initiation period), the young men gather in purpose-built enclosures where they stand singing in subdued fashion. They still wear the leather loin skin but as they leave later in the day each man will receive the colourful Ndebele blanket. During *ukuwela* all activities are meant to inculcate endurance, even the singing. One song will serve as example. At an *igwabo* held on 15 August 1988 at *Ingwenyama* Makhosoke's place, we observed that the young men, under watchful oversight by instructors, sang a particular song intermittently until about 14:00. This epitomises the test of endurance these young men have been subjected to during their stay in the veld for about two months in the winter. (These days the period is shorter as *ukuwela* has to coincide with the school holidays.) Since the words of the song are repeated and last for hundreds of lines; only a few lines are illustrated here:

> Hha:yi hhayi hhayi hha:yi Ha ha ha::[7]
> Hha:yi bobaba beniyephi na?
> (No fathers, where have you gone to?)
> Hha:yi hhayi hhayi hha:yi
> (Hhayi means 'no', but this could simply be embellishment)
> Hha:yi indlovu zing'dlele
> (The elephants have eaten to my detriment [= have caused damage])
> Aina aina aina
> Hha:yi Malimele ndlelen'
> (Mr Cultivator-in-the-footpath)
> Hha:yi indlovu zing'dlele
> Hha:yi zidl' amabel' wam'
> (They have eaten my sorghum)
> Hha:yi hhayi hhayi hha:yi
> Hha:yi Malimele-ndlelen'
> Hha:yi bobaba beniyephi?
> (Oh, fathers were have you gone?)

However, *ukuwela* is also characterised by relief and freedom: as the men leave for their homes they break out in songs characterised by more modern content and pleasant melodies as they celebrate their manhood.

Among the Ndebele people there are two national ceremonies. The Manala hold a national day towards the end of February or the beginning of March each year, and the Ndzundza regard 19 December as their national day, the day the leader Nyabela died in 1903. Annually the Ndzundza Ndebele gather

7 The underlined part is the fixed response repeated after each line; colons and double colons indicate relative syllable length.

near the cave near Roossenekal where a statue of Nyabela was unveiled on 19 December 1970. Oral discourse comes in many genres and forms: theorists have spoken of rite, game, festival, spectacle, commemoration, and so forth. The activities on Nyabela Day can be divided into two main sections. First there is the formal, commemorative part that ends with speeches and prayer as well as the singing of the national anthem. The second part can be called festivity; it is a joyous celebration by the ordinary folk after most of the officials have left. During this time people enjoy their meals and listen to performers. One of the most popular activities is the singing and dancing by bands. Even traditional healers take the opportunity to sing their songs and perform their dance routines. Although these ethnic 'national days' – see also Shaka Day among the Zulu people – are reactions to the exhibition of 'national' pride by previous apartheid governments and are clearly modelled on their form, they provide opportunity for celebration and expression of ethnic pride, and in some cases they are rare opportunities to engage in oral performance.

Ndebele verbal art also occurs on what one may call 'ad hoc' occasions (apart from modern contexts such as church services, funerals, parties and cultural festivals). Special mention must be made of political meetings that occurred during the late 1980s when the Ndebele people were deeply divided over the question of independence for a homeland that would be called KwaNdebele. At this time (between 1986 and 1990) when there was a national state of emergency, a number of political meetings took place where the royalists (those who supported *Ingwenyama* Mabhoko, ruler of the Ndzundza at the time) campaigned against independence. Four types of verbal art manifested themselves at these meetings: song, *amahubo* (revered royal battle songs), *thamba* formulae and *iimbongo* (praise poetry). The latter were utilised the most because of the fact that praise poetry can be easily adapted by a creative praise poet to serve as protest poetry. The praise poet was Mbulawa Amos kaCitha Mahlangu, popularly known as Sovetjheza, and honoured as the *imbongi yakwaMabhoko*, praise poet of Mabhoko's place. It was these political meetings which proved Sovetjheza's ability not only to perform commemoratively, as happens at the annual Nyabela Day where praises of the kings of old are recited, but also to compose new praise poetry for political leaders, as exemplified in the praise poem for Prince James Mahlangu (now deceased), younger son of *Ingwenyama* Mabhoko. Prince James Senzangakhona was the most vociferous of the 'amaradicals' (the radicals, as the anti-independence campaigners were called) during the political campaigning. He was the one, according to the praise poet, who 'brought down the two walls of Imbokodo (a violent vigilante group) and independence'.[8] He was praised as follows at one of the political meetings:

> The bull gored with its horn right inside Magezini the earth tore
>   open and we saw the fleeing of men.
> (Musho! – 'Tell him / praise!' *is the standard crowd response.*)
> Senzangakhona of Mabusa has a long arm
> Which is strong. It is able to push over
> 5   It pushed over the two walls supported by Imbokodo and
>   independence and they fell.
> (Musho! *Hand clapping and cheering*)
> I am afraid to say he is still a lad
> You who brought the kingship back from Magezini
> Stop you criminals
> (Stop) taking the kingship of the old mamba of our people of
>   Mayisha and placing it at Magezini.
> (*Applause*)
> 10 You danced and it was befitting for you child of Mabusa
> In the legislative assembly of KwaNdebele
> All the nations have seen him
> The whole world has seen his dancing
> It has clapped hands for him and ululated for him
> 15 On televisions
> And in the newspapers
> And over the radio.
> (*Applause*)
> The assembly of criminals is lying.
> It says Senzangakhona of Mabusa will eventually die in jail.
> 20 We heard through the rumours of the women of the criminals
> They say Senzangakhona's perm will wither in jail.
> (*Applause*)
> The hands and feet of Senzangakhona are wounds
> As result of being bound with handcuffs
> Day after day
> 25 Days on end.
> (*Applause*)
> The long-legged bull of the married daughter of Ndala
> Of the place of the mother of Mthunywa

8 'Imbokodo' in a few Nguni languages simply refers to a smooth round or oval rock which is used as a grinding stone. It is the feature of grinding which appeals to speakers and thus the 'grinding stone' has been used as a symbol by many groups and institutions to warn adversaries that they are dealing with a formidable opponent. Recall for instance the famous march by women of South Africa to the Union Buildings in 1956 to protest against the pass laws; on this occasion they sang 'Wathint' abafazi wathint' imbokodo' – 'You strike the women you strike a rock'.

When he was tied by his hands and feet
He smiled
30   Your friends said: 'Senzangakhona why are you laughing?'
And he said: 'I'm doing so because they don't know what they
    are doing.'
Bayethe!

This praise poem of Prince James presents an image of an unstoppable defender of the chieftaincy as well as an image of a most forgiving sufferer. The first nine lines, speaking of the securing of the chieftaincy, portray Senzangakhona as one with extraordinary power, effectiveness and bravery. Praise poetry, all scholars will agree, relies on exaggeration. The praise poet attributes the victory over Imbokodo and the KwaNdebele Legislative Assembly to Prince James, whereas it is known that it was the youth, organised by a certain Timothy Skhosana, who brought the downfall of Imbokodo, which operated from their 'torture centres' – such as eMagezini' (Kwaggafontein Small Industrial Park [line 8]). Line 11 alludes briefly to his career as member of the KwaNdebele Legislative Assembly. Much attention is given to his 'dancing' from line 10 to 17. The line refers literally to the fact that he liked to *gida* (dance) with the people whenever there was an opportunity. But his 'dancing' also alludes to the value of his public service. His imprisonment is illustrated in the same striking manner, with reference to a personal aspect, namely his famous hairstyle, that will wither in jail (lines 19–21). The motifs of James's wounds, a picture of his suffering (lines 22–5), are very important in his presentation as one who had suffered much for a just cause. The bleeding hands and feet motif is a messianic metonym. His long suffering (lines 26–31) illustrated in the motif 'they know not what they are doing' has the same effect.

The 'literature from below', or oral performance, of African-language speakers in South Africa in its largely secondary phase functioning in the twenty-first century is still remarkably extensive. On the one hand these cultures are hemmed in by the demands of modernity – note for instance how ceremonies are mostly confined to weekends so as not to clash with one's job – on the other hand modern aspects afford it wider popularity as we see, for instance, how orally composed songs and praises are being produced and distributed by studios. Not only are occasions for oral performance still abundant, but at each occasion there is an abundance of verbal art forms, especially songs. The indications of earlier forms of orality are there, such as group performance in the call and response style, while the songs are highly repetitive. Although repetitive, not one song copies another exactly in form or in melody and this clearly shows the vitality of the genre. For the foreseeable future, 'literature from below', especially song, will remain a vibrant oral genre in its secondary phase in South African society.

The larger part of this chapter has concentrated on Ndebele oral performance so as to illustrate the development of this oral culture from its primary phase to its present secondary phase. As Ndebele oral culture develops further, into a tertiary phase, most of its oral culture will be known through texts only. The Ndebele situation has been described in some detail to illustrate this evolution, which is characteristic of other oral cultures in South Africa.

Bibliography

Fourie, H. C. M. *AmaNdebele van Fene Mahlangu en hun religieus-sociaal leven*, published thesis, Zwolle: La Rivièra & Voorhoeve, 1921.

Gevisser, M. *Thabo Mbeki: The Dream Deferred*, Johannesburg: Jonathan Ball, 2007.

Groenewald, H. C. 'Ndebele Verbal Art with Special Reference to Praise Poetry', D.Litt. and Phil. thesis, Johannesburg: Rand Afrikaans University, 1998.

James, D. 'Metropoles and Satellites: The Dancing of Identity by Northern Transvaal Migrants on the Reef', paper presented at the 38th annual meeting of the African Studies Association, Orlando, Florida, 3–6 November 1995.

Janse van Vuuren, C. J. 'Die Aard en Betekenis van 'n Eie Etnisiteit Onder die Suid-Ndebele', D.Phil. thesis, University of Pretoria, 1992.

Joubert, A. *The Power of Performance: Linking Past and Present in Hananwa and Lobedu Oral Literature*, Berlin: Mouton de Gruyter, 2004.

Makgopa, M. A. 'The Origin and Context of Khekhapa: A Cultural Performance of the Balobedu of South Africa', *South African Journal for Folklore Studies* 16:2 (2006), 52–77.

Ntuli, D. B. 'Bus Naming as a Communication Strategy – a Swaziland Experience', in R. Finlayson (ed.), *African Mosaic*, Pretoria: UNISA Press, 1999, 311–28.

Sikwebu, D. 'The Strike Hit Parade', *SA Labour Bulletin* 25:6 (2001), 13–16.

Thwala, J. J. 'The Thematic Explication of Lutsango Songs', unpublished paper, 2009.

Vail, L., and L. White. *Power and the Praise Poem*, London: James Currey, 1991.

EXPLORATION, EARLY MODERNITY AND ENLIGHTENMENT AT THE CAPE, 1488–1820

As we move from indigenous cultural forms to Europe's writing about southern Africa from the fifteenth to the eighteenth centuries, we encounter discourses shadowed by deep uncertainties. There are good reasons why three and a half centuries of European writing are contracted into just three chapters in Part II. The textual record of European exploration and settlement in southern Africa has density and complexity but it is a record, initially, of wild speculations and mythic patterns revealing anxieties that refuse to be quelled. Once the Dutch settlement is established in 1652, it becomes a record of carefully guarded strategic knowledge and impersonal descriptions of countless encounters with the new and the strange. By the end of the eighteenth century it has become fledgling science, trying to bring knowledge of the new terrain and its peoples into a kind of order.

The peculiarities of Europe's attempts to grasp the specificities of southern Africa can best be understood by contrasting the western and the southern expansions into the Atlantic during Europe's phase of early modernity. The voyages of discovery to the Americas and to India via the southern tip of Africa are almost simultaneous: of the same generation as Columbus but five years before he sailed across the Atlantic, Bartholomeu Dias embarked from Lisbon in 1487 to chart the route to India. He succeeded in rounding the Cape in

January 1488 (though unwittingly, having been forced eastwards in a southern Atlantic storm). After reaching what is now Kwaaihoek, east of Algoa Bay, he was forced to return by a rebellious and sceptical crew. Columbus's story may also be full of accident but in the long run the difference between the overall success of his voyage and Dias's failure actually to reach India speaks to subsequent generations. As the centuries of expansion unfold, it becomes irresistible, as Noël Mostert does in *Frontiers* (Jonathan Cape, 1992), to contrast the 'underlying optimism' of the American frontier with the 'doubts and moral ambiguities' of the settlement at the Cape. 'More than any other settlement point during the ages of the oceanic expansion of Europe, it was along the frontier line of confrontation in the Cape Colony that uneasy questioning of the dark side of universal involvement became lodged' (p. xvi).

We should bear in mind, however, that while Europe's southern Atlantic expansion carried these anxieties, the Indian Ocean to which it aspired had for centuries supported a lively trade between the East Coast of Africa, Arabia and Asia. At issue was less the founding of new colonies than the opportunity for Europe to participate in the Indian Ocean's already established economy. The fact that Dias's failure prepared the way for Vasco da Gama's more successful voyage from Lisbon in 1497 does not change the argument that the southern expansion was less propitious than the western. That perception was reinforced by the appearance of what Dias calls the 'Cabo Tormentosa', the Cape of Storms, in the pivotal fifth canto of Luis Vas de Camões's famous Homeric poem about maritime Portugal, *The Lusiads*. Camões's mythic figure of Adamastor, challenging the mariners in their hubris as they round the Cape, survives as a multivalent symbol in later literature, most notably in early and mid twentieth-century modernism – just at a point when African nationalism is becoming more vocal. Malvern van Wyk Smith charts the legacy of the *Lusiads* in South African literature in Chapter 6, showing not only how Camões lives on into the twentieth century, but also how the patterns of representation of Africa that came to be consolidated during the Renaissance have their roots in the classical Mediterranean world.

Portuguese, English and Dutch ships put in regularly at the Cape until the Dutch East India Company (the VOC, or Vereenigde Oost-Indische Compagnie) established a refreshment station there under Jan van Riebeeck. For the next century and a half, from 1652 until 1795, the Company's purposes at the Cape were entirely commercial, since the colony was simply a strategic hinge in its management of a vast trading enterprise that made it the largest joint-stock company in existence and perhaps the world's first global multinational. The cultivated arts – with the exception of viticulture which was introduced by the Dutch and developed following the arrival of French Huguenots – were scarcely a priority. In Chapter 7, Carli Coetzee gives an account of the functional literature of the Cape in Dutch hands, showing the extent to which it was guarded by the VOC and determined almost entirely by profit accumulation in Amsterdam. She also explores the various ways in which contemporary novelists of the late- and post-apartheid periods have visited the archives in order to reimagine both past and present.

The VOC's control over the production of knowledge about the Cape was far from absolute, however. Throughout the eighteenth century European travellers – explorers, naturalists and venture capitalists – surveyed the region and published their findings in English, German, Swedish and French. In Chapter 8, Ian Glenn explores this literature, demonstrating its range and richness. Of particular interest is the extent to which the natural science and nascent anthropology of the period were able, thanks to a handful of exceptional intellectuals, to free themselves from complete subordination to the prevailing commercial and political interests. In doing so, some of the naturalists, notably Robert Gordon and François Le Vaillant, through their influence on Diderot and Rousseau, played a part in the French Enlightenment.

The control of the Cape by the Netherlands came to an end in 1806. By 1795 the British had taken possession in order to prevent revolutionary French naval and commercial ships from rounding the Cape. In a short period during the Batavian Republic in Holland, from 1803 to 1806, the Cape was handed back to the Dutch; then it was repossessed by Britain in order to prevent Napoleon from assuming control. The British occupation began where the Dutch had left off, as an instrumental affair motivated by the desire to control a strategic sea-route. As Part III demonstrates, however, the British presence would soon develop into a properly imperial enterprise, introducing a settler-colonial English culture and provoking in due course the Afrikaner and African nationalisms that would so profoundly determine the directions of the twentieth century. The relevance of 1820 to our periodisation is that it marks the beginning of a long-term British settlement and, consequently, the development of an English-language print culture.

6

Shades of Adamastor: the legacy of
The Lusiads

MALVERN VAN WYK SMITH

From a European perspective southern Africa was invented before it was discovered. As the giant spectre of Adamastor declaims to Vasco da Gama in William Atkinson's 1952 translation of Luis Vaz de Camões's *Lusiads*: 'I am that mighty hidden cape, called by you Portuguese the Cape of Storms, that neither Ptolemy, Pomponius, Strabo, Pliny nor any other of past times ever had knowledge of' (v, 50).[1] Yet almost two thousand years earlier in the *Meteorologica* Aristotle had speculated that the northern temperate world of the Mediterranean had to be matched by a similar region south of the 'uninhabitable' equatorial wilderness of Africa. That this domain and its inhabitants might be the opposite, in every sense of the word, of the known ancient *oecumene* remained a subject of speculation throughout the Christian Middle Ages and beyond until Dias and da Gama at last stood face to face with the Khoikhoi.

By then a virtual consensus had been reached in patristic discourse that these southerners, who walk 'with feet opposite to ours' (hence Antipodeans) would be anti- or pseudo-human caricatures of northern humanity. The baneful effect that such thinking would have on the earliest European encounters with sub-Saharan Africans and notably with the Khoikhoi cannot be pursued here (see Van Wyk Smith, '"Most wretched of the human race"'), but the conceit of a southern anti-human world, intrinsically hostile to Mediterranean civilisation and its harbingers, is fundamental to the trope of Adamastor as deployed by Camões and as variously echoed, refurbished or contested in the work of numerous southern African writers of the twentieth century.

More specifically, the ambivalent and unresolved encounter of the Portuguese explorers with the peoples and terrain of southern Africa, envisaged by Camões as an allegorical rite of passage under the baneful curse of a

---

1 Unless otherwise specified, all incidental citations of *The Lusiads* are from this edition and are cited by canto and page.

hostile avatar of Africa, found ample resonance in the imaginations of a generation of mid twentieth-century English (some would want to say 'settler') poets becoming increasingly aware of their marginalised position between a rampant and appropriative Afrikaner nationalism and an emergent spirit of African liberation and resistance. The fraught drama of uncertain domicile, the ongoing arbitration between cultural memories of Europe and the harsh challenges of a resistant Africa, impelled these poets towards the rich lode of tensions and contradictions in the Adamastor mythos.

On most speculative world maps preceding the Portuguese voyages, Africa is depicted as crescent shaped or squarish, with Ptolemy's terminal 'Promontorium Prassum' placed in the far south-east (Randles, *L'Image du sud-est Africain*, pp. 21–3). When Dias reported that the southern African coast continued endlessly eastward, as Ptolemaic maps predict, he only confirmed that the Portuguese still had to achieve the crucial rounding of the continent. What was needed, moreover, was some confirmation of the full symbolic import as against the merely geographical importance of Dias's discovery.

It was da Gama who provided the proof that Africa had been rounded, and Camões who developed the symbolism of a great rite of passage from west to east, from hardship to riches, from damnation to salvation, and from one kind of Africa to another. Dias, on the contrary, perishing off the Cabo Tormentoso in 1500, became for the poets a figure of haunting uncertainty, his failure an instance of paradise forfeited.

Furthermore, the Portuguese circumnavigation of Africa at the end of the fifteenth century was still deeply conceptualised in terms of a binary and allegorical apprehension of the continent that went back to Homer. When Homer spoke in the *Odyssey*, 1.22–4, of two kinds of 'Ethiopian, who dwell . . . some where Hyperion sets and some where he rises', he might have intended no more than a very general reference to all dark-complexioned people known to inhabit a great southern arc from Mauretania to India, but his stark division became one of the great ethnogeographic templates of classical, medieval and even early Renaissance talk about Africa.

For Herodotus, Diodorus Siculus, Strabo, Pliny and Ptolemy, writing between the fifth century BC and the second AD and all invoking Homer, the 'eastern Ethiopia' was the powerful Kushite empire of the Nubian Nile and its successor states based on Napata and Meroe, once powerful enough to conquer Egypt, and whose inhabitants were thought to be favoured by the gods. To the west and the south-west, however, inhabiting the Sahara and beyond, were the 'other Ethiopians', or, in the words of Herodotus, 'the dog-faced creatures, and the creatures without heads, whom the Libyans declare to have their eyes in their breasts; and also the wild men, and wild women' (*Histories*, 1.iv.191). Later Diodorus Siculus would add that 'they are entirely savage and display the nature of a wild beast'; in short, 'they present a striking contrast when considered in the light of our own customs' (*Library of History*, 3.8.2–3). One does not need to labour the point. The 'fabulous Ethiopians' of the east and the 'savage Ethiopians' of the west became set pieces of African geoethnography. Homer's division developed into one of the most powerful European myths about Africa (see Van Wyk Smith, *Shades of Adamastor* and *The First Ethiopians*).[2]

Camões's Cape

There can be little doubt that Luis Vaz de Camões was well aware of the special symbolic significance of the moment da Gama rounded the Cape and turned his face towards the east. Camões had himself sailed around the Cape, had spent many years in east Africa and India, and had personally suffered much of the hardship the *Lusiads* describes (Atkinson, *Lusiads*; Bullough, *Lusiads in Sir Richard Fanshawe's Translation*). He thus handles the Cape of Good Hope sequence in terms of baroque allegory, as an encounter between man and demigod.

The major adversary of the Portuguese in their epic endeavour is Bacchus, who is cast in the role of an African deity, chief instigator of Moorish perfidy against the Portuguese. He becomes the very spirit of darkness and ignorance against whom 'Portugal was engaged in a fight for the true faith, for the spiritual values of Europe' (Atkinson, p. 21). Repeatedly it is disguised as a Moor that Bacchus appears in the poem, plotting against da Gama, and Adamastor is effectively one of the many avatars of Bacchus.

It is in the course of a lengthy flashback, occupying three of the poem's ten cantos, that da Gama introduces his encounter with Adamastor, the Spirit of the Cape. The full significance of this meeting only dawns on the reader when he realises that it marks the major rite of passage in the poem, and that it is da Gama's bold handling of Adamastor that earns him access to the *alterum orbem*, the new world anticipated by ancient myth. Furthermore, in his treatment of the Cape of Good Hope Camões seeks to reconcile the paradise of expectation with the tempestuous headland of the seafarers' experience.

2 Most of the poems discussed in this chapter can be found in my 1988 *Shades of Adamastor* anthology.

For though medieval geo-allegorical speculation might have wanted a paradise at the tip of Africa (Van Wyk Smith, 'Ptolemy, Purgatory and Paradise', pp. 83–97) the notorious changeability of Cape weather often led to the experience of nightmare. Hence, framing the central tableau of da Gama's confrontation with Adamastor are two archetypically different encounters with the continent and its people.

The first, on the west coast, is fraught with suspicion, misunderstanding and treachery; the second landfall, at São Braz after the rounding of the Cape, is triumphant and pastoral. Camões celebrates 'fat, sleek flocks', 'dusky women on the backs of lazy oxen' and 'pastoral songs, rhyming and unrhymed, to the accompaniment of rustic flutes, as did Tityrus long ago' (v, 63), thus inviting a comparison with the familiar pastoral allegory of Europa riding a bull. He invokes Fernão Lopes de Castanheda's lyrical version of the encounter, in which da Gama lands in a southern Eden: the country is 'very pleasant with trees and waters'; the navigator is astonished by 'the gentleness of those black people', and on hearing their flute music 'in four sundry voices' orders the trumpets to be blown and all to join in dancing and feasting (Castanheda, *History of the East Indies*, fo. 9). Thus Cabo Tormentoso becomes the portal to a prospect of Good Hope that would be fully realised in India.

Adamastor the African

Until the appearance of Landeg White's excellent translation of the *Lusiads* in 1997, Camões had not been fortunate in his English translators, and the fault lies partly with the *Lusiads* itself. Whilst Camões claims to have taken Virgil's austere *Aeneid* as his model (II, 45), the poem is actually cast much more in the flamboyant baroque idiom of the propagandistic anti-Muslim romance epics of Ariosto and Tasso. Much of the supernatural machinery is merely fanciful, if not foolish, and Camões was lucky in his creation of the figure of Adamastor (whose name first appears in Rabelais), at once portentous and pathetic, who would so exactly capture for subsequent generations of South African poets their sense of the ambivalent demands and threats of Africa.

For our purpose here, William Julius Mickle's version of 1778 is particularly relevant. Mickle abandons the stanzaic verse of Camões's romance epic in favour of the more solemn measure of Augustan heroic couplets. The result is that his Adamastor, a bewildered and grotesque outcast demi-deity in Camões, becomes the vast menacing spirit of a continent resisting the imperial mission:

> I spoke, when rising through the darken'd air,
> Appall'd we saw an hideous Phantom glare;
> High and enormous o'er the flood he tower'd,
> And thwart our way with sullen aspect lour'd. (p. 198)

It was this translation that first introduced Roy Campbell to Camões's epic (Alexander, *Roy Campbell*, p. 74), and the above rendering of Adamastor has some telling implications for Campbell's subsequent treatment of the figure.

It also anticipates a verse translation of the southern African section of the *Lusiads* by Guy Butler, written at the time of the contentious Dias Quincentenary of 1988 (Van Wyk Smith, *Shades of Adamastor*, pp. 47–63). Imagined at a moment when the destiny of South Africa seemed bloody and unresolvable, Butler's Adamastor is neither god nor allegory but a tormented being, possessed of more power, hatred and prophecy than he knows how to deal with:

> While I yet spake, under that sombre cowl
> A horrid form took shape before our gaze:
> A figure huge and strong, with heavy jowl
> And unkempt beard, whose sullen eyes, ablaze
> From caves beneath the beetling forehead, scowl
> With hate enough to frighten and amaze –
> Grey and clay-matted was his shock of hair;
> Yellow his teeth in his black mouth appear. (p. 51)

The earliest Adamastors

Adamastor's very ambivalence has thus for many readers been his greatest attraction, and any discussion of what may be called the 'Portuguese connection' in South African English poetry must pursue the protean permutations of the Adamastor motif, from an image of hostile confrontation to be overcome by the European conquistador to an emblem of resistance to such conquest. Furthermore, much poetry about the Cape of Good Hope and Table Mountain is thematically closely related to verse that explicitly invokes the motifs of the Portuguese and Adamastor. Whilst not every poem about Table Mountain is a poem about Adamastor, many are, and the rite of passage theme is continued in numerous poems that place this dramatic and magnificent mountain or its great peninsula thrusting boldly into southern seas on a frontier to an *alterum orbem* of human experience. John II's purported revision of Dias's

'Cabo Tormentoso' to 'Cabo de Boa Esperança' would come to encapsulate a sharp dichotomy at the very heart of the European perception of southern Africa and of the poetry generated by that experience.

Simplistic contrasts developing the motif of paradise and desolation dominate early English poetry featuring the Cape of Good Hope. Most appearances of Table Mountain or the southern extremity of Africa, while not always explicitly heralding either Adamastor or paradise, are never far from either or both. George Marshall in 1812 invoked Claude, Poussin, Titian, Correggio and Michaelangelo to describe 'this second Paradise':

> Now glowing gems the eastern skies adorn,
> And joyful Nature hails the op'ning morn;
> From Afric's point the goddess bids me sing
> Elysian fields, an ever-blooming spring!
>
> (*Epistles in Verse*, p. 99)

Yet Marshall's Eden is an embattled place – 'Forth from their dens, impatient of delay / The savage monsters prowl in search of prey' (p. 113) – while the inhabitants of this paradise are presented as 'untutored natives' and 'scarce human'. Such thinking left a vigorous and dangerous legacy in South African discourse. The Caliban-like 'squalid figure' of 'scarce human form', confined to 'darkness' and 'instinct', merges easily with (indeed, is often inspired by) Camões's Adamastor to become the threatening spirit of a continent menacing the European settler seeking to legitimise his possession and enjoyment of paradise, whether discovered or created. There is ample evidence, from an early stage, of a tendency to alienate the natural inhabitants of the Cape from their environment and to sanitise the landscape at the expense of the people. Given the utter distinction that the early colonists perceived between themselves and the indigenes of the Cape, early writers found it seductively easy to inscribe the landscape with a welcoming code while excluding the inhabitants from it. Thus Adamastor became not just the barbaric spirit of the Cape but the barbarian himself.

By the time of the abolitionist debate of the late eighteenth century, Adamastor had evolved into the figure of the shackled African, to be redeemed not only from slavery without but also from darkness within. Thomas Pringle's 'The Cape of Storms' (*African Sketches*) is one of the better among many poems that reveal such a redemptive reading of the Cape in which a hostile setting, clearly conceived in the shadow of Camões's Adamastor and matched by the 'sin and sorrow and oppression stark' of a racial encounter already highly problematic, is nevertheless salvaged by the endeavours of a civilised (settler) human community: 'Loved Kindred and congenial Friends sincere'.

Pringle's 'Cape of Storms' is also a poem of valediction. In this as in so many other ways he anticipated a major subgenre of southern African verse – what one might call 'exodus' poetry. From this poem, through numerous nineteenth-century occasional colonial pieces of salutation and valediction, burgeoning in Campbell's 'Rounding the Cape' and reappearing in the work of almost every prominent mid twentieth-century South African English poet, a pronounced motif of departure (and sometimes return), based on the Cape and often alluding explicitly to Adamastor, runs through South African literature, registering white English-speaking South Africans' calamitous ambivalence about the European-African antinomies in their heritage and commitments. In Guy Butler's words:

> In all of us two continents contend;
> Two skies of stars confuse us, on our maps
> The long- and latitudes contort and rend
> Our universe to twenty-acre scraps.
>
> ('Elegy II', *Collected Poems*, p. 142)

Much of the verse generated after Pringle and before Campbell by the topos of Adamastor readily falls into the categories suggested so far. William Rodger Thomson's 'Cape of Good Hope' (*Poems, Essays and Sketches*) and D. C. F. Moodie's 'Adamastor, or the Titan shape of the mighty Cape' (*Southern Songs*) are valedictory poems dedicated to a paradisal world established through heroic settler endeavour. William Scully's 'Table Mountain' (*Poems*) and Lance Fallaw's 'The Watchers of the Cape' (*Silverleaf and Oak*) and 'Land's End of Africa' (*An Ampler Sky*) offer a suitably tamed Adamastor, still alarming but essentially sympathetic to settler enterprise. Joseph Forsyth Ingram's 'The Discovery of Natal' (*Poems of a Pioneer*), Lance Fallaw's 'Prester John' (*Silverleaf and Oak*) and 'The Navigators' (*Ampler Sky*), 'Vasco da Gama' by one 'J.R.' (Crouch, *Treasury of South African Poetry and Verse*) and Mary R. Boyd's 'Table Mountain' (*Table Mountain*) are celebratory narratives or panegyrics, conferring on the Portuguese voyages the status of national legend.

Numerous volumes of verse published at the Cape in the nineteenth century, as well as the many ambitious literary journals of the Victorian colony, are littered with poems of this kind. Nor was this vein of highly affirmative verse inhibited by the appearance of Campbell's *Adamastor* (1930). Harold Sampson's 'Table Mountain' (Slater, *New Centenary Book of South African Verse*), Adèle Naudé's 'Cabo Tormentoso' (*Pity the Spring*), F. D. Sinclair's charmingly classical vision of the Cape in several poems in *The Nine Altars* and *Lovers and Hermits* and Juliet Marais Louw's 'Portuguese Gold' (*Selected Poems*) all still encourage an essentially unproblematic view of Adamastor as countenancing the establishment here of a world that looks firmly to Europe for its origins. In a minor key, poems such as Hugh Evans's 'A Voyager' (Alder, *Veldsingers' Verse*), A. S. Cripps's 'Beira Bay' (*Lake and War*), Mary Morison Webster's sonnet 'As mariners by dark and treacherous gales' (*Silver Flute*) and Adèle Naudé's fragile 'April at the Cape' (*Only a Setting Forth*) embroider on the Portuguese theme to express personal delight, a principle that still underlies Douglas Livingstone's playfully topographic eroticism in 'Giovanni Jacopo meditates on an early European navigator' (*Rosary of Bone*).

Campbell's Adamastor

Campbell's 'Rounding the Cape', published in *Adamastor* (1930), inaugurated the most important phase of Camões's legacy in South African literature. As Stephen Gray has remarked, 'the figure of Adamastor is at the root of all the subsequent white semiology invented to cope with the African experience' (*Southern African Literature*, p. 27). The poem has attracted considerable debate (Gray, *Camoens and the Poetry of South Africa*; Cronin, 'Turning Around'; Chapman, 'Roy Campbell', pp. 79–93), and not only is its very ambivalence likely to ensure that it will continue to do so, but so too are vital features of its provenance. At the heart of controversy about the poem is a question of Campbell's social conscience: does his poem confront and accept responsibility for the colonial subjection of Adamastor and consequent sociopolitical disasters, or does its invocation of Camões's allegorical mode in fact fend off culpability? One needs to look again at the Adamastor Campbell knew.

Firstly, Campbell's Adamastor is Mickle's 'terrific shade', a horrendous but austerely authoritative figure; he is neither Camões's spiteful fallen Titan nor the Renaissance grotesque of baroque translations. As with Mickle's, there is nothing pathetic or quaint about Campbell's Adamastor.

Secondly, Campbell has remembered what many of his and Camões's readers tend to forget, namely that 'the Shade of the Cape's' primary function in the *Lusiads* is to pronounce a curse on the Portuguese voyagers and all their European successors in the appropriation of Africa:

> In thunder still his prophecies are spoken,
> In silence, by the centuries, fulfilled.

If curses mean what they say, all South Africans of European descent still live under that of Adamastor:

> Hear from my lips what direful woes attend,
> And bursting soon shall o'er your race descend.
>
> (Mickle, p. 201)

Thirdly, the poem should be read in conjunction with a companion piece, 'Tristan da Cunha', in which the lonely Adamastor-like island, also associated with Portuguese discoverers, is seen as a persona of the poet himself:

> Exiled like you and severed from my race
> By the cold ocean of my own disdain.   (*Adamastor*, p. 65)

Thus the Adamastor of 'Rounding the Cape' contains more than just a hint of Campbell's tormented other self, as his valediction makes clear:

> I watch the phantom sinking in the sea
> of all that I have hated or adored.

Cambell is profoundly aware of the ambivalent severance he is dramatising here, not simply from Africa and its people, but more alarmingly from a darkly fructifying inner source. Though he might 'go free' in one sense, in another the 'powers of darkness' within him will always owe allegiance to Adamastor.

K. K. Ruthven has remarked that 'a successful mythology is one which encourages people to invent new and more reputable reasons for believing in it after the old ones are no longer tenable' (*Myth*, p. 60). So from a mythic point of view it matters little to the continuing power of Campbell's poem what specific sociopolitical reality his Adamastor is supposed to represent. Jeremy Cronin has rightly warned against the invocation of Adamastor figures in our literature to shift responsibility for real sociopolitical evils into a realm of satanic destiny and thus beyond the bounds of human agency. Nevertheless, Campbell's poem cannot be condemned for plunging into an abyss of profound personal as well as general white South African doubt and guilt without coming up with a precise solution. As we shall see, black African poets have had no difficulty with Adamastor's curse: it expresses their exact verdict on the whole European colonial enterprise in Africa.

Campbell provided South African English poetry with its central informing myth over the next few decades and even beyond. In 1983 Stephen Watson lambasted South African 'liberal humanist' poetry for its failure to develop and sustain a vital mythology ('Recent White English South African Poetry'), but he should have considered the brooding and still vivifying presence of the Adamastor topos in much of South African verse since Campbell. Indeed, it may have been such a recognition that led to Watson's subsequent renunciation of his former position (Gardner, *Four South African Poets*), since his own 'The Mountain' *(In this City)* gains much of its power from an evocative and unmistakable reworking of the resonances of Camões and Campbell: 'the shadow, huge of something else, beyond itself'.

Campbell's heirs

The half-century between Campbell and Watson produced the bulk of the significant poetry on the Dias/da Gama/Adamastor theme. It was also the period during which white English-speaking South Africans had to come to terms with the continent of their birth and decide whether they were Europeans or Africans. Those who realised with Guy Butler that 'I have not found myself on Europe's maps' ('Home Thoughts', *Collected Poems*) found in Campbell's Adamastor a potent symbolism – 'The legends and the currents ran together', as Anthony Delius put it ('At the Cape', *Corner of the World*). Ironically, though it is a valediction – indeed, an exorcism – 'Rounding the Cape' made available to Campbell's successors several productive metaphors for their own internal and public debates about the terms on which they belonged to (South) Africa. Again, Anthony Delius speaks for them all:

> Looking back
> I see the Cape was always hidden
> In our thoughts, rising out of the deeps
> Of our minds, coming out of the mists
> Of water, of paper, always a shapelessness
> Dreaming a shape.   (*Black South Easter*, n.p.)

Campbell's Cape of Good Hope, or Table Mountain, has remained a site of agonised self-appraisal. The great peninsula thrusting out into the southern seas conjures a metaphysic of the confrontation between known and unknown, conscious and unconscious, familiar and alien, just as the startling bulk of Table Mountain, turning round on its axis and facing north (to the perennial confusion of visitors), elicits a rhetoric of challenge and defiance. Clustered round this central topos are the motifs of quest and discovery, the courage and skill of the navigator in unknown seas, the epiphany of Southern Cross and stranger stars, the elemental trauma of shipwreck on barren shores, and, above all, the haunting memories of those earliest encounters between the peoples of the north and the south when, just for a moment, as the Khoi flutes sounded 'in four voices' and da Gama's trumpets blew in response, harmony rather than disaster seemed a possibility.

Not only in its subject matter did Campbell's poem prefigure much of subsequent South African poetry. Its elegiac tone and ominous, pessimistic conclusion anticipates the sense of gathering dusk in much of the later verse. The wide-eyed innocence with which the observers in, say, Lance Fallaw's 'The Navigators' and William Lipsett's 'Cape Point (Cape of Good Hope)' (*The Glen [Camp's Bay] and other Poems*) watch from the edge of the continent the arrival of the ships of Europe becomes the suspicion in the mind of an F. D. Sinclair that the event heralds:

> a later growing story, one that tells
> of such a landscape but of smaller men,
> of such a beauty but a poor delight.
> ('Neo-Classical landscape', *Lovers and Hermits*, p. 60)

The disappearance of Henry the Navigator's great maritime establishment at 'the limit of Europe' ('Here nothing breathes except rock and some lizards') anticipates for David Wright the eventual disappearance of another European outpost at the edge of another continent ('Cape St Vincent from Sagres', *Adam at Evening*). Manfred Jurgensen ('At the Cape', *South African Transit*) and Noel Brettell ('Prospect: Cape Point', *Four Voices*) finally look out from the peninsula into a void that refuses to yield any future at all.

The treatment of the symbolism of Table Mountain has followed a similar downward vector. Still magisterially disdainful of mere humanity in Harold Sampson's poem, already domesticated in Naudé's 'Cabo Tormentoso', it becomes the devalued real estate of Delius's *The Last Division* and the petty suburbia (home of Mr Adam Astor) of Douglas Livingstone's *The Sea my Winding Sheet*. Counterpointing this decline, however, are the forceful reverence of Sydney Clouts's Table Mountain poetry (*One Life*), the virulence of David Farrell's *Charlie Manson False Bay Talking Rock Blues* – 'where the homes of the soon dead hang from their privilege' – and the reinstatement of the mountain's numinous presence in Watson's 'The Mountain' (*In this City*). In the words of Gareth Cornwell, reviewing Watson's work: 'so familiar to the eye as to be practically invisible, so hoary a symbol in the poetic tradition, the mountain here bulks into appalling otherness, edging the surreal' ('Beauty with Cruelty', pp. 36–44).

Moreover, shadowing this real mountain in much South African verse, one senses again and again, is the image of that other legendary southern massif, Dante's Mount Purgatory, whose sheer physical presence is never lost sight of in the *Purgatorio*. Indeed, like southern Africa itself, Table Mountain could be said to have been invented before it was discovered. Related to both southern massifs are the stars above them. When Dante and Virgil arrive in the southern hemisphere, at the beginning of the *Purgatorio*, it is the strange stars that attract their immediate attention:

> Right-hand I turned, and, setting me to spy
> That alien pole, beheld four stars, the same
> The first men saw, and since, no living eye.
> (1.i.8, trans. Sayers)

From then until Thomas Hardy during the Anglo-Boer War invoked 'strange-eyed constellations' to guard over Drummer Hodge, the southern night sky has remained for the European observer a graphic reminder of cosmic displacement, and hence for the white South African poet a challenging ingredient in the rhetoric of appropriation – or alienation. A few stanzas before his arrival at the Cape, Camões's da Gama 'said good-bye to the familiar constellations of the northern world', and many a subsequent poem has recorded his successors' attempts to familiarise those of the south.

Sydney Clouts, in the wake of Dante, not only directs our attention to the inevitably questlike nature of these voyages of discovery, but also alerts us to an increasingly problematic assurance about what was actually discovered. His Prince Henry and his sea captains are anxious spiritual venturers, gazing on a fearful darkness: 'At the summit of perception a blackness starts to rise' ('The Navigator', *One Life*). As Ruth Harnett has pointed out ('Some Poems'), although Clouts's 'Discovery' poems are concerned with 'the journey of the mind' rather than with maritime exploration, he did respond powerfully to the symbolism of the navigator's simultaneously terrifying and exhilarating venture deep into the unknown, where the 'raw images of darkness . . . that can torment the sturdy mind' are transformed into 'night's huge and driving breath [which] ordains the heart of knowledge' ('The Navigator').

Clouts is not alone. The 'unfamiliar sounds' that Adèle Naudé's listener tries to interpret in 'Africa' (*No Longer at Ease*) but still fails to understand even when they become 'deep-throated warnings', may be heard in poem after poem. Alan Lennox-Short's Dias finds that the meaning of his discovery ultimately evades him – 'thrust back, his prize denied' ('Dias', *Brief Candle*).

'Who confessed to hope?' asks Delius ('At the Cape', *Corner of the World*), and again:

> How did we come, cursing our luck,
> Upon this see-saw slope of time?

while his Dias admits

>   a cross
> Looked out from a virgin headland
> Over the width of my failure.   (*Black South Easter*)

Roy MacNab's 'ancient mariner' contemplating his conquest 'never discovered that deep within was the beat of an African heart' ('The Road to Bologna', *Man of Grass and other Poems*). In his reworking of Fernando Pessoa's elegiac treatment of these imperial themes, Charles Eglington must eventually ask:

> How could there ever come a time
> For guilt, expiation and remorse?
>   ('Lourenço Marques', *Under the Horizon*)

Vernon Forbes's 'Kwaaihoek, 12th March 1488', in so many ways an affirmative treatment of the site where Dias had planted his terminal padrão – 'Upon this summit stood assertively / A milestone of two thousand hard won leagues' – nevertheless ends with 'small brown men' viewing the cross, 'stark harbinger of doom / For all their kind in centuries to come'. Visiting Dias's Kwaaihoek with Guy Butler, David Wright finds 'all solitude as when [Dias] came' and the 'sunlit water wringing hands' ('A letter from Westmorland to Isabella Fey', *Selected Poems*). And though the choruses from Butler's own 'Natal Cantata' (*Songs and Ballads*) proffer a hopeful vision of the continents of the Three Kings meeting in harmony at the tip of Africa on Christmas Day, 1497, his later work, *A Pilgrimage to Dias Cross*, raises more distressing questions about a southern African history that begins with Dias:

> How can an ageing man with glimmerings of belief
> Get rid of his futile fury, his embitterment of grief?   (p. 11)

His Dias fails to guess

> What destinies of consciousness,
> Fleets, empires, tribes, tongues, gods
> Hung in his rotten rigging,   (p. 14)

and must finally confess 'I have no words to meet your need', apart from echoing Portuguese doubts of five centuries ago:

> You are nowhere near your farthest east,
> Still have to double your Cape of Storms.   (p. 51)

Other poets who, in Clouts's words, have strained to 'hear all warning men but no man's voice so loud' ('Cape of Good Hope') as that of the disappointed Dias include Mike Nicol –

> How sad
> Prince Henry must be now:
> all was in vain and a violent
> land spits in his Catholic face   ('Ilha do Sal', p. 18)

– Peter Wilhelm, whose Dias is irreverently 'stuffed with lyricism and wine' (*White Flowers*), and finally Alan James, most bemused of all commentators confronting the cryptic message of 'Landscape at Kwaaihoek Dunerock' and aware of an elemental alienation that not even Dias could have shared:

> So then. Strangers here. At
> a place, aliens. What
> to make of that.   (*Producing the Landscape*, p. 7)

What several poets have 'made of that' has been to advance the emblems of voyage and discovery into the realm of metaphysics. Walt Whitman had already done so in his 'Passage to India' in 1868 (*Leaves of Grass*) where Columbus, Vasco da Gama and others become the carriers of spiritual injunctions:

> We too take ship, O soul,
> Joyous we too launch out on trackless seas . . .
> For we are bound where mariner has not yet dared to go.
>   (1926 edn; pp. 342–50)

South African poets have continued in Whitman's orbit. Robert Dederick sees the lack of a star-marked southern astral pole in contrast to the fixed North Star as a virtue, a pointer towards ampler codes of cognition and experience ('The Dark Focus', *Quest and other Poems*), also hinted at in Bruce Hewett's 'The Navigator' – in uncharted waters

He knows
a man must overcome
darkness, chaos
before he has the Light.   ('Dawn of Song', p. 8)

For Charles Eglington it is Dias's encompassment of 'the fear of unknown things' that is the greater achievement, and his reaching of 'the ultimate small beach' a confirmation of 'the pure / Aesthetic of horizons' in the human mind ('Homage to Fernando Pessoa', *Under the Horizon*). Once more we are in Clouts territory, the persistent reminder in all his 'Discovery' poems that the 'shorter kingdom' is Portugal while the greater world of exploration is 'the deliberate gulf of man'.

Adamastor's demise

If we attempt, finally, to assess just why the themes of Dias, da Gama and Adamastor remained so productive in South African English poetry until at least the 1980s, we are forced back to the great divide which is nevertheless also a nexus: that between Europe and Africa in the psyche of white English-speaking South Africans. 'We kept returning to those Portuguese' ponders Guy Butler in 'Elegy for a South African Tank Commander' (*Collected Poems*, pp. 76–96), and he speaks for many. David Wright invokes Adamastor as his muse in a poem that explicitly confesses the speaker's divided attachments to Europe and Africa:

Aware we are looking back no longer to
Where we have come from, but must begin to plan
Arrival at those places to which we go.
('A Voyage to Africa', *Monologue of a Dead Man*, p. 14)

Roy MacNab, echoing poems by Eglington, Delius, Butler and Wright, could speak for all –

O how this sea-blown symmetry
Proclaims the Africa in me,
And binds me with the years' intent
Heart and mind to this continent!
('Entering Table Bay', *Man of Grass and other Poems*, p. 11)

All, however, would also share Wright's bewilderment of feeling 'Claimed and disowned, disowning, peculiarly belonging here' ('Flying to Africa, December 1969', *South African Album*). They might decry this 'spectacular home of mediocre visionaries' ('Cape Town, 1937: Embarking for England', *South African Album*) even while yearning for the visionary assuredness of a Clouts: 'We know where we are' ('Around this Coast', *One Life*). A chilling variation on the theme is Geoffrey Haresnape's 'Ocean Voyage – A Return to RSA':

> The Africa to which we slide
> crouches tense beyond the phosphorescence . . .
> Why do we return? (p. 43)

By way of an answer, the searchlight beam of the moon funnels whatever can be said into claustrophobic silence.

Beyond such silence, what voices remain? It is unlikely that Adamastor will again enjoy the ascendancy of the post-Campbell years. The quincentenary of Dias's arrival in 1988 was marked by ambivalence and controversy about the Portuguese legacy to a degree that confirmed in contemporary South African discourse a resolution to distance itself from the exploits of conquistadors. As Butler's *Pilgrimage* envisaged, Dias would in 1988 return to his ship for the last time and leave his pilgrims stranded.

Insofar as the Dias legacy might fuel a poetry of protest and outrage, it has retained some life. The weary disillusion of Stephen Gray's version of 'Rounding the Cape' – 'I don't believe in goodwill trade plenty / it's hard to tack around and try' (*It's About Time*) – and the caustic import of Gilbert Horobin's 'The African is the equal of the Portuguese' (*African Notes and other Poems*) gesture in possible directions, some of which have been pursued by black poets. The missionary zeal with which the South African black poet Allan Kirkland Soga in the 1890s celebrated the planting of Dias's cross ('Santa Cruz: The Holy Cross', in Chapman and Dangor, *Voices from Within*) would now be unthinkable. Whilst David Rubadiri might concede that 'the tide that from the west / Washes Africa to the bone' (Kgositsile, *Word is Here*) may once have 'washed a wooden cross' of redemption, he has to insist that it was also the cross of the conquistador and that his own response can only be one of outrage; it 'Boils in my marrow, / Dissolving bone and sinew'. Mbella Sonne Dipoko's 'To Pre-Colonial Africa' (*Black and White in Love*) confirms the verdict.

Adamastor in Afrikaans

Afrikaans literature reveals a much more slender tradition of meditations on the Adamastor topos than does its English counterpart, for the obvious reason that Afrikaans authors have not usually (or at least not till recently) thought of their position as one of exile. In both Afrikaner history and world-view the attractions and ancestral connections of the culture's European origins had sunk below its conceptual horizons by the end of the eighteenth century, and would be ousted from Afrikaner symbology by the much more powerful *mythoi* of Slagtersnek (1815), Great Trek (1836–8), Anglo-Boer War (1899–1902), the recognition of the Afrikaans language and, of course, the temporary triumph of its racist ideologies. C. Louis Leipoldt's 'Voorspel vir 'n Afrikaanse Heldedig' (Prelude to an Afrikaans Epic) anticipated a projected celebration of the southern African environment and Afrikaner history in heroic terms, starting with Dias and da Gama but ignoring the threat of both Adamastor and the Khoikhoi (*Uit Drie Wêrelddele*). The verse is lively and competent, the vision pedestrian.

More substantial treatments of the Dias/da Gama/Adamastor motif are D. J. Opperman's *Joernaal van Jorik* (Jorik's Journal) and N. P. van Wyk Louw's *Dias*, a radio play in blank verse inspired by the Van Riebeeck Festival of 1952. For Van Wyk Louw, Dias sets out as the emissary of God's will, but his venture ends (contrary to the nationalist sentiment of 1952) in existential disillusion – no God, no mission, no certainty. Opperman's *Joernaal* is the more impressive treatment of the theme. A densely allusive narrative in ballad measure, it evinces the modernist impact of Ezra Pound and T. S. Eliot in its anxieties about history and faith, the anonymity of the city, and the devaluation of the individual. Its protagonist is an Everyman figure, trapped into re-enacting the heroic feat of Dias confronting 'Die horingdier van berg wat staan en bak' ('The horned beast of mountain baking in the sun' – i.e. Table Mountain), but suffering the fate of Kafka's Joseph K.: anonymous and ignominious execution for sins not his. Produced in the late 1940s, at the end of World War II and on the eve of half a century of National Party rule, *Joernaal* questions the heroic and 'official' version of Afrikaner history as much as it anticipates that history's disastrous denouement over the decades to follow.

What may well turn out to be the terminal treatment in our literature of the Adamastor theme, appropriately as farce and in both Afrikaans and English renderings, is André P. Brink's *Die Eerste Lewe van Adamastor* or *The First Life of Adamastor*. Brink's prologue suggests that he may originally have intended a much more ambitious project of satirical import in which a protean Khoi Adamastor would review five centuries of historical miscarriage in South Africa ('How would *he* look back from the perspective of the late twentieth century, on that original experience?'), but instead we have a priapic farce in which the Adamastor narrator, T'Kama (whose name, we are told, means

Big Bird but is surely also a pun on da Gama), has surrealist trouble with an ever-growing 'member' and can thus never consummate his passion for Thetis, an abductee from the Portuguese ships. The whole myth is spoofed, from Camões to Khoi 'ritual', but the substance is slight. More significantly, Brink's *Adamastor* inspired a giant mural by Cyril Coetzee in the Cullen Library of the University of Witwatersrand and further elaborations of the theme in *T'Kama-Adamastor: Inventions of Africa in a South African Painting*, edited by Ivan Vladislavić.

Bibliography

Alder, A. et al. (eds.). *Veldsingers' Verse*, London: J. M. Dent, 1910.

Alexander, P. *Roy Campbell: A Critical Biography*, Cape Town: David Philip, 1982.

Aristotle. *Meteorologica*, ed. and trans. H. D. P. Lee, Loeb Classical Library, London: Heinemann, 1962.

Atkinson, W. C. 1952. *See* Camões.

Boyd, M. R. *Table Mountain*, Cape Town: Maskew Miller, 1926.

Brettell, N. 'Prospect: Cape Point', in Molony et al., *Four Voices*, 93.

Brink, A. P. *Die Eerste Lewe van Adamastor*, Cape Town: Saayman & Weber, 1988.

    The First Life of Adamastor, London: Secker & Warburg, 1992.

Bullough, G. 1963. *See* Camões.

Butler, G. *Collected Poems*, Cape Town: David Philip, 1999.

    A Pilgrimage to Dias Cross, Cape Town: David Philip, 1987.

    Songs and Ballads, Cape Town: David Philip, 1978.

    Stranger to Europe, Cape Town: Balkema, 1960.

Butler, G. (trans.). *Lusiads*, canto 5, in Van Wyk Smith, *Shades*, 47–63.

Butler, G., and C. Mann (eds.). *A New Book of South African Verse in English*, Cape Town: Oxford University Press, 1979.

Camões, Luis Vaz de. *The Lusiads, in Sir Richard Fanshawe's translation* [1655], ed. G. Bullough, London: Centaur, 1963.

    The Lusiad; or, The Discovery of India, trans. W. J. Mickle, 2nd edn, Oxford: Jackson & Lister, 1778.

    The Lusiads, trans. W. C. Atkinson, Harmondsworth: Penguin, 1952.

    The Lusiads, trans. L. White, New York: Oxford University Press, 1997.

Campbell, R. *Adamastor* [1930], London: Faber and Cape Town: Paul Koston, 1950.

Castanheda, F. L. de. *The First Book of the History of the Discovery and Conquest of the East Indies*, trans. N. L. [N. Litchfield], London: 1551–82.

Chapman, M. 'Roy Campbell, Poet: A Defence in Sociological Times', *Theoria* 68 (1986), 79–93.

Chapman, M., and A. Dangor (eds.). *Voices from Within: Black Poetry from Southern Africa*, Johannesburg: Ad Donker, 1982.

Clouts, S. *Collected Poems*, Cape Town: David Philip, 1984.

    One Life, Cape Town: Purnell, 1966.

Cornwell, G. 'Beauty with Cruelty', *New Coin* 22:2 (1986), 36–44.

Cortesão, A. *History of Portuguese Cartography*, 2 vols., Coimbra: Junta de Investigacoes do Ultramar Lisboa, 1969–71.

Cripps, A. S. *Lake and War*, Oxford: Blackwell, 1917.

Cronin, J. 'Turning Around: Roy Campbell's "Rounding the Cape"', *English in Africa* 11:1 (1984), 65–78.

Crouch, A. H. (ed.). *A Treasury of South African Poetry and Verse*, Cape Town: Juta, 1907.

Dante Alighieri. *The Divine Comedy*, trans. D. L. Sayers, 3 vols., Harmondsworth: Penguin, 1949–62.

Dederick, R. *The Quest and Other Poems*, Cape Town: Purnell, 1967.

Delius, A. *Black South Easter*, Grahamstown: New Coin 1:3, supplement (1965).

    A Corner of the World, Cape Town: Human & Rousseau, 1962.

    The Last Division, Cape Town. Human & Rousseau, 1959.

Diodorus Siculus. *Library of History*, trans. C. H. Oldfather et al., 12 vols., Loeb Classical Library, London: Heinemann, 1933–67.

Dipoko, M. S. *Black and White in Love*, London: Heinemann, 1972.

Eglington, C. 'Lourenço Marques', in J. Cope (ed.), *Under the Horizon: Collected Poems*, Cape Town: Purnell, 1977.

Evans, Hugh. 'A Voyager', in Elder.

Fallaw, L. *An Ampler Sky*, London: Macmillan, 1909.

    Silverleaf and Oak, London: Macmillan, 1906.

Farrell, D. *The Charlie Manson False Bay Talking Rock Blues*, Johannesburg: Bateleur, 1974.

Fereira, O. J. O. *Adamastor: Gees van die Stormkaap*, Pretoria: privately published, 1975 (Includes Afrikaans translation of the southern African section of *The Lusiads*.)

Forbes, V. 'Kwaaihoek, 12th March 1488', *New Coin* 8:1 (1972).

Gardner, S. (ed.). *Four South African Poets: Interviews with Robert Berold, Jeremy Cronin, Douglas Reid Skinner and Stephen Watson*, Grahamstown: National English Literary Museum, 1986.

Glenn, I. 'Sydney Clouts: Our Pen insular Poet', *English Academy Review* 3 (1986), 127–34.

Gray, S. *Camoens and the Poetry of South Africa*, Camoens Annual Lectures 1, Johannesburg: Oppenheimer Institute for Portuguese Studies, 1980.

    It's About Time, Cape Town: David Philip, 1974.

    Southern African Literature: An Introduction, Cape Town: David Philip, 1979.

Gray, S. (ed.). *Theatre One: New South African Drama*, Johannesburg: Ad Donker, 1978.

Haresnape, G. 'Ocean Voyage – A Return to RSA', *Contrast* 53 14:1 (1982).

Harnett, R. 'Some Poems by Sydney Clouts', *English in Africa* 11:2 (1984), 108–61.

Herodotus. *Histories*, trans. G. Rawlinson, ed. E. H. Blakeney, 2 vols., London: J. M. Dent, 1910.

Hewett, Bruce (ed.). New Coin, special issue of 'The Dawn of Song', 20:2 (1984).

Homer. *Odyssey*, trans. A. T. Murray, 2 vols., London: Heinemann, 1919.

Horobin, G. *African Notes and other Poems*, Athens: Anglo-Hellenic, 1974.

Ingram, J. F. *Poems of a Pioneer*, Pietermaritzburg: P. Davis, 1893.

James, A. *Producing the Landscape*, Rondebosch: Upstream, 1987.

Jurgensen, M. *South African Transit*, Johannesburg: Ravan, 1979.

Kgositsile, K. (ed.). *The Word is Here: Poetry from Modern Africa*, New York: Doubleday, 1972.

Leipoldt, C. L. *Uit Drie Wêrelddele*, Cape Town: Nasionale Pers, 1923.

Lennox-Short, A. *Brief Candle*, Cape Town: Purnell, 1971.

Le Roux, S. W., and O. J. O. Fereira. 'Camões in Afrikaans: Vertaling van die Gedeelte uit *Os Lusiadas* wat oor die Suidpunt van Afrika Handel', *Tydskrif vir Geesteswetenskappe* 48:1 (2008), 95–110.

Lipsett, W. *The Glen (Camp's Bay) and other Poems*, Cape Town: Cape Times, c. 1940.

Livingstone, D. 1964. *The Sea my Winding Sheet*, in S. Gray (ed.), *Theatre One*.

A Rosary of Bone, Cape Town: David Philip, 1975.

Louw, J. M. *Selected Poems*, Cape Town: Maskew Miller, 1981.

Louw, N. P. van Wyk. *Dias*, Cape Town: Nasionale Boekhandel, 1952.

MacNab, R. *The Man of Grass and other Poems*, London: St Catherine, 1960.

Marshall, G. *Epistles in Verse . . . Descriptive of a Voyage to and from the East Indies*, Newcastle: the author, 1812.

Molony, R., et al. *Four Voices: Poetry from Zimbabwe*, Bulawayo: Books of Zimbabwe, 1982.

Moodie, D. C. F. *Southern Songs*, Cape Town: Juta, 1887.

Naudé, A. *No Longer at Ease*, Cape Town: Balkema, 1956.

Only a Setting Forth, Cape Town: Human & Rousseau, 1965.

Pity the Spring, Cape Town: Balkema, 1953.

Nicol, M. 'Ilha do Sal', *New Coin* 12:3 (1976).

Opperman, D. J. *Joernaal van Jorik*, Cape Town: Nasionale Pers, 1949.

Pringle, T. *African Sketches*, London: Edward Moxon, 1834.

Randles, W. G. L. *L'Image du sud-est Africain dans la littérature européenne au XVIe siècle*, Lisbon: Centro de Estudos Historicos Ultramarinos, 1959.

Ruthven, K. K. *Myth*, Critical Idiom Series, London: Methuen, 1976.

Scully, W. *Poems*, London: Fisher Unwin, 1892.

Sinclair, F. D. *Lovers and Hermits*, Cape Town: Balkema, 1957.

The Nine Altars, Cape Town: Unie-Volkspers, 1945.

Slater, F. C. (ed.). *The New Centenary Book of South African Verse*, Cape Town: Longmans, Green, 1945.

Thomson, W. R. *Poems, Essays and Sketches*, Cape Town: Juta, 1868.

Van Wyk Smith, M. *The First Ethiopians: The Image of Africa and Africans in the Early Mediterranean World*, Johannesburg: Witwatersrand University Press, 2009.

'"The most wretched of the human race": The Iconography of the Khoikhoin (Hottentots)', *History and Anthropology* 5:3–4 (1992), 91–104.

'Ptolemy, Purgatory and Paradise: Portugal and the African imaginary', in Vladislavić (ed.), *T'Kama-Adamastor*, 83–97.

Van Wyk Smith, M. (ed.). *Shades of Adamastor: Africa and the Portuguese Connection*, Grahamstown: Institute for the Study of English in Africa and National English Literary Museum, 1988.

Vladislavić, I. (ed.). *T'Kama-Adamastor: Inventions of Africa in a South African Painting*, Johannesburg: Witwatersrand University Press, 2000.

Watson, S. *In this City*, Cape Town: David Philip, 1986.

'Recent White English South African Poetry and the Language of Liberalism', *Standpunte* 36:2 (1983), 13–23.

Webster, M. M. *The Silver Flute*, London: Poetry Bookshop, 1931.

Whitman, W. *Leaves of Grass* [1871], ed. Emory Holloway, Garden City, NY: Doubleday, 1926. (First edition to include 'Passage to India'.)

Wilhelm, P. *White Flowers*, Johannesburg: Bateleur, 1977.

Wright, D. *Adam at Evening*, London: Hodder & Stoughton, 1965.

   Monologue of a Dead Man, London: André Deutsch, 1958.

   Selected Poems, Johannesburg: Ad Donker, 1980.

   A South African Album, Cape Town: David Philip, 1976.

7

In the archive: records of the Dutch settlement and the contemporary novel

CARLI COETZEE

This chapter attempts an overview of the Dutch record of settlement, and traces the development of a Dutch-language writing tradition at the Cape. Before the mid seventeenth century writing about the Cape had appeared in English, French, German, Portuguese and other European languages; but in the writing produced at the Cape itself Dutch was the dominant language until the end of the eighteenth century, when the Cape came under British rule. In the period subsequent to this, Dutch retained some official role (for example in schooling and the church) until the late nineteenth century, when the movement for the formalisation of Afrikaans and eventual replacement of Dutch started (see Chapter 13 below).

The early Cape Dutch record raises a number of issues for someone trying to understand the development of writing about, and in, South Africa. In his influential *White Writing: On the Culture of Letters in South Africa*, J. M. Coetzee has written about the reasons for the absence of a 'myth of a return to Eden' in writing about the Cape (p. 2). The present chapter has a different focus, namely to examine the nature of reading and writing at the Dutch Cape (or in most cases their absence), as well as the enduring presence of this period and its archives in contemporary South African literature. For a different perspective, which deals with the Portuguese-language response to Africa, see Chapter 6 in this volume.

Many of the documents that now constitute the Dutch-language archive of the Cape were written for a limited, and in most cases closed, readership. The Dutch East India Company (VOC), a trading company with profit as its main aim, established the Cape as a refreshment station for ships on their way to the East, and made it compulsory for all of its ships to stop over at the Cape. The Company required of its commanders to keep meticulous accounts, and to write journals and reports that were regularly despatched, in multiple sealed copies, to offices in Batavia (the present-day Jakarta) and in the Netherlands. These accounts were regarded as secret, for the eyes of the Company only; trade routes and information about potentially profitable ventures were guarded, and sometimes even written in code to prevent others from gaining this knowledge.

Significantly, then, the intended audience of writing at the early Cape often (even typically) excluded those living at the Cape. Thus in the discussion of this early period of colonial settlement, questions of literacy and communities of readers are perhaps different from those in many other chapters, where the connections between different local writing and reading traditions are examined. This chapter attempts to give an outline of the development of a literary tradition at the Dutch Cape and the reasons for its not being more substantial. It aims to distinguish between writing produced for an (often official) audience in Europe, and later, more private, texts written with a local audience as primary consumers. For a discussion of a very different body of work, in which Enlightenment values are to be found, see Ian Glenn's discussion in Chapter 8 below.

The limited availability of many of the records written during the Dutch period of rule is not a hindrance to a modern reader (of Dutch or Afrikaans) who wants to get the flavour of these texts. Conradie's *Hollandse Skrywers uit Suid-Afrika* (published in two volumes between 1934 and 1949) was long the standard history. More recently Siegfried Huigen has published an overview that supplements Conradie's work ('Nederlandstalige Suid-Afrikaanse Letterkunde'), correcting also some of her political slant. A large number of the texts from the Dutch period have been transcribed and published in widely available editions. The reception and publication history of these texts is a revealing one. The early interest in these documents was closely linked with political developments in South Africa, initially in an effort to associate with the Dutch (pre-British) period, later for Afrikaner nationalists to write their particular national narrative. More recently there has been an attempt to place the Dutch Cape within a larger Indian Ocean world (see the work of Worden), and to show how the Cape formed part of larger knowledge networks (see the edited collection by Huigen, de Jong and Kolfin, *The Dutch Trading Companies*).

The nature of the South African written archive of early settlement is, as is the case with many archives (in particular in colonial settings), a vexed one. The texts are inevitably written from a particular point of view – in this case the prescribed point of view of the VOC, which required of its officials, and of its official scribes, to see the world through eyes intent on profit. Only knowledge that could increase the profit of the Company was to be regarded as important, and this information had to be protected against other eyes and ears (for English-language discussions of the world of the VOC see, for example, Boxer's *The Dutch Sea-Borne Empire* and Sleigh's *Jan Compagnie: The World of the Dutch East India Company*).

In the writing on this encounter, historians and artists have of necessity responded to the texts produced at the time, since they are the only documents accessible to us now. So this record has been scrutinised not only for what it seems to yield with ease, but also for that which it cannot communicate. In particular, readers have attempted to find in these documents information about the indigenous inhabitants of South Africa, and how they viewed the colonial encounter (see for example Elphick's *Khoikhoi and the Founding of White South Africa*). There are a number of instances in the documents of the time when a Khoi representative is quoted, or where the words and understanding of an encounter is that of a Khoikhoi individual. Not surprisingly, these are the moments in the texts that we as contemporary readers find most interesting, and which have formed the basis for much recent historical and fictional writing.

The contact zone

When European ships started rounding the Cape in the fifteenth century, the captains of these ships represented the rulers of highly literate cultures; they were equipped with maps and route plans, and they were obliged to document their discoveries and experiences. Thus was Africa, like the East, produced as a commodity for those in Europe desirous of enriching themselves through trade and conquest.

Writing at the Cape has a history predating Dutch settlement at the Cape (for an overview of this material, as well as examples, see Raven-Hart's *Before van Riebeeck* (1967) and Malvern van Wyk Smith's *The First Ethiopians: The Image of Africa and Africans in the Early Mediterranean World* (2009), in many ways a reappraisal of Raven-Hart's methodology and selection). The early travellers at the Cape encountered the Khoikhoi (or 'Hottenots' as they were called at the time, a collective term used to describe the groups of indigenous people who lived at the Cape). In the contact zone between these groups, the map-making and contract-writing Europeans gained the upper hand over the Khoikhoi. The early encounters between these groups involved writing, in some cases writing on the land itself.

It would seem that from the Khoi point of view, Europeans were initially seen as migratory beings, who posed little real threat since they always moved on again. The marks and letters left on the landscape by passing ships' captains confirmed this pattern of temporary residence. The messages typically contained information about safe routes, confirmations that a particular ship had passed safely, or instructions to ships about increasing their safety by sailing together. A range of methods was used for leaving messages. In some cases a stone (or wooden cross) would be engraved to show a ship had been there. In other cases a rock would be engraved with an instruction that mail was buried under or near it. In these cases the letters might be wrapped in linen bags, red woollen cloths and sometimes even sandwiched in lead to prevent them from rotting. The letters would lie waiting for the men of passing ships to read them, sometimes leaving them again with annotations; sometimes enclosing them in packets of letters to be returned either to Europe or to stations in the East.

By July 1607 a passing English captain commented on the fact that a local man had managed to remember some English (Raven-Hart, *Before van Riebeeck*, p. 34). By 1638 communication between local men and passing English and Dutch ships had become so successful that there were attempts to appoint local individuals as agents of the English and the Dutch. The use of Khoikhoi individuals as postal agents foreshadows the later work of intermediaries and interpreters in the service of the VOC (Raven-Hart, *Before van Riebeeck*, p. 149).

The journal of Jan van Riebeeck

The text that is most often cited, by historians and by artists responding to the Dutch period, is the set of documents collected together during the first ten years of the VOC's presence at the Cape, which is now referred to as Jan van Riebeeck's *Journal*. The definitive published version of the journal was issued in 1952 (the tercentenary celebration of Jan van Riebeeck's arrival at the Cape) in two different language editions. In one version one finds a translation into modern English, in the other a slightly edited version of the seventeenth-century official Dutch in which it was written. The two editions appeared with separate introductions, and in fact acrimonious debate ensued between the two editors on the character of Jan van Riebeeck.

The VOC required of all commanders to keep accurate accounts and to compile reports, on a daily basis, of the progress of the settlements. Each official had to report on expenses, trade and profit, as well as on disciplinary methods meted out to men in the Company's employ. The text, which to a modern reader appears unified, never existed in this form during Van Riebeeck's time. In order to publish the 1952 version, the editors and translators had to collate the multiple (and sometimes different) versions held in archives in Cape Town and in The Hague (a third copy had to be sent to the offices of the Council of the Indies in Batavia). The fact that multiple copies existed, and that these copies formed part of the VOC's archives, confirms the fact that what we now call the *Journal* was not intended for circulation beyond the group of official readers under whose administrative control the Cape fell.

Van Riebeeck found the Khoikhoi reluctant to trade (and describes this reluctance in the journal as theft from the Company, whose right it is to trade and profit), and the letters to the Company repeatedly ask for permission (ever denied) to take action against them. In terms of planting and growing food, the weather also seemed not to favour Van Riebeeck. As he grew despondent about the wind, the rain, and the uncooperative Khoikhoi, he became ever more interested in another aspect of his project, namely the exploration of the country beyond the Cape. These expeditions were commissioned by the VOC, the explorers were obliged to be employed by them, and anything discovered was to be reported to the Company. These travel accounts are included in the papers sent to Amsterdam and Batavia, and in the published version they are inserted as part of the narrative.

The fabled empire of Monomotopa had been written about long before the VOC settled on the Cape as an outpost. According to the accounts, the European source of which is often said to be Jan Huygen van Linschoten in his *Itinerario* (1596), there was a city of gold in the African interior. In some versions of this story, it is ruled by a tribe European in appearance and dress. To Van Riebeeck, trained in the discourse of profit and commodification, the discovery of this city held great allure. To the VOC, disappointed with trade relations with the Khoikhoi, and ever on the lookout for new trade and profit opportunities, this was a particularly interesting part of Van Riebeeck's posting. Equipped with the map included in the *Itinerario*, expeditions set off in search of the city of gold. (For a fuller discussion of Monomotopa, see Huigen, 'Travellers to Monomotopa' and *De Weg Naar Monomotopa*.)

Some notable expeditions, whose accounts are embedded in the journal, include those of Pieter van Meerhoff. Van Meerhoff was a Danish surgeon who struggled with Dutch. Nevertheless, his accounts are described as well written, and he had the further recommendation of being experienced at sketching. His reports were transcribed into the official journal, and rewritten in the official (though as yet unstandardised) seventeenth-century Dutch preferred by the VOC. His account of his 1661 expedition is representative of the six expeditions in search of the fabled Vigiti Magna (or city of gold), each of which he accompanied.

Under the later governors more travel accounts are included. With the submission of these reports a complex system of copying and transcribing develops, which at first may seem to encourage a community of readers and writers. Some of these reports are dictated by 'writers' who are illiterate, and whose words are written down (and edited) by a clerk. Even these oral accounts were to be held secret, and the process of copying served instead to contain and standardise reports.

Some significant travel journals are those written (by the Swede Olof Bergh) of journeys undertaken in 1682 and 1683, and by the Dutch-born Isac Schrijver of a journey made in 1689. An account exists of a journey by a certain Jacobus Coetsé, who claimed to be the first European to have crossed the Orange River. Significantly, Coetsé could not write, and his report was dictated to the secretary of the council. The language used in his report (one of the very few native Dutch-speaking explorers) is thus filtered through the official Dutch of the scribe.

An interesting case is that of the Swede Hendrik Jacob Wikar, who was employed as a scribe (making copies of documents) in the VOC's hospital. He deserted his post at the Cape, remaining for four years among the Khoikhoi. Upon his return in September 1779, he handed a letter to the then governor Joachim van Plettenbergh. In return for the information included in his report, he was pardoned and reinstated in the employ of the VOC. Various versions of this report exist, some written in the bureaucratic Dutch favoured by the VOC.

What is striking about this group of texts written by travellers during the Dutch period is how few of the travellers were native speakers of Dutch. Of the ones who were native speakers, not all were literate, and so their texts are dictated and written down by clerks who are used to writing in the specialised language of the VOC. The practice of transcribing documents also influences the versions of documents we find in archives, since clerks would improve and edit, aiming for a cohesion in the documents sent along as the official version of the outpost's chronicle.

Representations of and by 'Hottentots'

Reading Raven-Hart's anthology *Before van Riebeeck: Callers at South Africa from 1488 to 1652*, as well as the work of later historians of the Khoikhoi like Elphick, Newton-King, Penn and Viljoen, it is striking to note that comments on the 'Hottentots' by Dutch callers are consistently unfavourable, although van Wyk Smith's *The First Ethiopians* challenges this perception. In descriptions of South Africa by early travel writers, the concern was often that there was relatively little to say about the indigenous people. Early writers about the Cape comment on their lack of religion, lack of mores, lack of industriousness and lack of language. The Cape seemed to offer little opportunity for profit: the inhabitants and their culture could not easily be commodified, and the Cape did not offer the kinds of products that made trade with the East profitable. The solution arrived at by many travel writers on the Cape was to recycle endlessly anecdotes about the Khoikhoi, through this repetition of paucity of material reinforcing the idea that these people were not worthy of interest. Many later writers refer to this discourse and quote from it. In fact, many of the commentators on the 'Hottentots' had never been to the Cape but had merely read reports or seen etchings made by artists who also had never travelled beyond their home towns, such as the famous Olfert Dapper.

Another strand of discourse about the 'Hottentots' does exist, though. Glenn in his article 'Classical Black' has traced a trend in this alternative tradition, in which references borrowed from antiquity are used to describe the 'Hottentots'. These accounts, most famously those by Willem ten Rhyne and Johannes de Grevenbroek are written not in Dutch, but in Latin.

In Van Riebeeck's journal there are a striking number of scenes in which Khoikhoi are described engaging the Dutch on land rights and the legitimacy of Dutch claims to the Cape. The official journal documents the progressive mapping of the land, accompanied by the planting of Dutch flags and the division of farming lands. Thus the knowledge the VOC employees gained about the land contributed to the displacement of the Khoikhoi, pushing them into progressively less inhabitable lands. During one of these unequal truces between Van Riebeeck and the Khoikhoi, he orders them to remove themselves somewhere outside the eye of the Dutch settlement, thus forcing them off the 'map'.

The reason provided by the Khoikhoi for their diminishing willingness to trade is supplied by the journal of February 1655: 'they let us understand that we were on their land and that they saw that we were happily settling without the intention of ever leaving, and for this reason they were unwilling to trade any animals with us since we also took the best grazing for ourselves' (Bosman's edition of the journal, 1, p. 287, my translation from the Dutch). In another reported conversation, the Goringhaikona chief Autsumao (named Herry in the journal) made claim to the land, and the journal refutes this as 'a pretence of ownership of the land'. In contrast with this 'pretence' at ownership, the Company's own, legitimate (in its view) methods for keeping the land 'in possession for itself' are stated. The diarist writes that the land had been 'fortified . . . etc.', the 'etc.' perhaps implying that it is unnecessary even to state such well-established legitimating methods (II, p. 38; my translation).

In February 1657 the freeburghers were allowed to choose land, conclusively proving (in the Company's eyes) that the land had not been under anyone's ownership before. The diarist notes that Herry and 'the fat captain with some other elders came to the fort to inquire if we wanted to build houses there and break the land as they noticed we intended to, where then would they live, since at the moment they were living on the land that the freeburghers had selected' (II, p. 98; my translation).

In answer to the Dutch allegation that there was not grazing enough for both groups, Herry and the elders responded that, in that case, the Caepmans had the prior right to the land and could forbid the Dutch to keep cattle: 'Who then is obliged to leave, the true owner or the foreign invader?' With the Khoikhoi appealing to natural rights to the land, the journal states, 'at last the word had to be spoken'. The words that can be uttered at last are that the land had been lost in battle, that the Caepmans had lost their say in the matter, and that henceforth they had no claim to the land.

A few Khoikhoi individuals did learn to speak (and write) Dutch, and continued the tradition of acting as agents for the Dutch started before 1652. Two of the most significant figures in this regard are Doman and Krotoä, both of whom had careers as interpreters to the VOC, and both of whom were accused by their own people of being traitors. Krotoä is significant in another way, as she was the first Christian convert at the Cape (christened Eva by Van Riebeeck and his wife), and also learnt to read (an essential part of religious conversion in the Dutch reformed religion of the time). Eva's story is one to which many have returned, and in the final section of this chapter some of this material is discussed.

When Eva's voice is found transcribed in the colonial archives, it is most often articulating her loyalty to the Dutch and their superior ways. Eva's desire to please her patrons moved her to report the existence of a group who lived in stone houses, wore clothes of fine white cloth, and prayed to God in churches just as the Dutch do. (She married that searcher for the city of gold, the Dane Pieter van Meerhoff.)

European audiences, local audiences

In his work on Jan van Riebeeck's journal ('The Role of Writing in the First Steps of the Colony'), Adrien Delmas writes that the function of the journal resided primarily in linking places – the Cape, Batavia and Amsterdam. Thus

writing and reading at the Cape did not tie people together in a local community; instead it reinforced links with a world outside, and all communication
was redirected through offices in Batavia and Amsterdam.

Writing at the Cape remained the domain of a limited number and these
were with few exceptions men who had been employed by and schooled in the
discourse of the VOC. The Company recruited its officials in the Netherlands,
and was not particularly concerned with education in the outposts. Small
attempts were made to educate the children of officials, but generally literacy
was limited to the ability to read the catechisms. Some elite sons were sent
back to the Netherlands for their education, thus reinforcing the idea of all
knowledge and culture being transmitted from Europe, and at the same time
limiting the formation of local knowledge communities.

All the texts discussed so far are produced by educated European men,
for consumption by men like themselves, in Europe. In some cases, such as
the official journals, this audience is small and even closed. In fact, the VOC
insistence on secrecy was so severe that they readily dismissed employees
from their service for talking or sharing information.

The VOC employed, as merchants and clerks, some men with high levels of
learning and literacy. Some of these men were naturalists and collectors, who
saw in the VOC service an opportunity to further their own research. In the
period 1670 to 1710, a number of educated and intellectual Company employees
conducted researches at the Cape. But like the Company's trade secrets, this
learning was not encouraged to become rooted locally. An interesting case
in point is the career of the German chemist Heinrich Claudius, who arrived
at the Cape in 1682. Cook, in *Matters of Exchange: Commerce, Medicine, and
Science in the Dutch Golden Age*, writes about how this young botanist, sent to
draw and paint the Cape and its plants, and to start a herbarium on behalf of
the VOC, made the mistake of sharing some of his sketches and observations
with some passing Jesuits. His punishment was severe: banishment for treason
(p. 323).

As in all things, however, all profit had to accrue to the Company. Knowledge was not encouraged to circulate, and literacy at the Cape remained low.
Locally produced newspapers were banned, thus actively discouraging the
development of intellectual life. The lack of a local printing press also meant
no newspapers could be produced at the Cape. All profit had to be channelled
back to the Netherlands, and all learning and knowledge was encompassed
within the greater aims of the Company.

Different from the documents discussed so far is the private diary of Adam
Tas, a freeburgher born in the Netherlands, but representative of a new group

of immigrants whose identity was not tied up with the VOC. Tas acted as the secretary to a group of farmers who were dissatisfied with the monopolistic practices of the then governor Willem Adriaan van der Stel. On behalf of a group of signatories he wrote a letter of complaint to the Heeren XVII (the governing body of the VOC, literally the 'Lords Seventeen') in Amsterdam, a document which was smuggled out of the country on a passing ship. When the content of this letter became known, Tas was arrested and carried to the Castle along with his desk and its contents. In his desk were found papers, some of which we now refer to as his diary. For the court case against him, copies were made of this diary, in order to be sent along as evidence to Amsterdam. Tas was held in the Castle for more than a year awaiting trial, during which time he was denied pen and paper. Subsequent to his release, he applied a number of times to have his diary returned to him, but it never was.

Tas's diary is significant for a number of reasons. It was written for private use, and not as an official document. Hence the language is not that of the official VOC documents, but rather a freer language that some have argued reflects language use at the Cape. Huigen, however, points out that his language is instead the language common in the western part of the Netherlands, and not Cape Dutch (private communication). The diary provides a rare reflection on views of the VOC, not from the official point of view. It also provides a rare picture of Stellenbosch society, including gossip and descriptions of drinking and smoking parties. Most interesting for the discussion here are references to his reading practices and his books. Tas makes notes on lending books to others (or sometimes transcribes relevant sections for a friend), significant at a time when there were as yet no libraries or bookshops at the Cape. He refers to a number of theological texts, perhaps the most common kind of reading done at the Cape, but also to some other historical and literary texts. Most interestingly he refers to a monthly newsletter, produced in the Netherlands, in which extracts appear of new books published in Europe.

Tas's diary is unique as an example of private writing at the early Cape. Its preservation was due to the trial against Tas, and the transcription of it into the case prepared against him. It is possible that letters were written from the Cape – the Dutch side of some such correspondences exists in copies. At the time even personal correspondence was subject to censorship by the VOC, and it is from the VOC records that we get references to private letters that were smuggled on to passing ships.

Whereas there was little in the way of local intellectual life, society was highly stratified according to (VOC) status. Clothing, food and social interaction were regulated according to strict rules of etiquette. Many passing commentators were struck by the lack of printing presses, libraries and book-shops; and also by the superficiality of life at the Cape, with endless rounds of visits and social events, where little beyond local gossip was discussed. Common activities for men included card and board games, drinking and smoking, while the women were reported to gossip, knit and sew (Worden et al., *Cape Town*, p. 78).

For the first one hundred and fifty years of Dutch settlement, that is from 1652 until 1795, this remained the case. New, educated officials were imported, and no attempt was made at a local dissemination of knowledge. Book possession actually declined in the eighteenth century, and passers-by refer often to one exception, that of the collector Joachim von Dessin. In 1761 he bequeathed his collection (which he had acquired partly from auctions at the Cape) to the public. It was not the library of a discerning collector, and in any case, as Boxer writes, there is evidence indicating that practically none of the residents at the Cape used the library for the next fifty years (*Dutch Sea-Borne Empire*, p. 179).

The end of the VOC period

In 1795 the Cape slipped from the VOC's control. The short British occupation lasted until 1803, to be resumed in 1806. The three short years before the second, decisive and conclusive British occupation are known as the Batavian reign, and it saw reports written in a style and approach far removed from the VOC and its narrowly commercial viewpoint. Instead, influenced by revolutionary and Enlightenment ideals in Europe, this period is characterised by a strong interest in reform and transformation. The Batavians intended to make real and permanent changes at the Cape, reversing what was seen as the decadence and moral decay of the VOC period. Jacob Abraham de Mist was appointed to compile a report, his *Memorandum, Containing Recommendations for the Form and Administration of Government at the Cape of Good Hope*, and subsequently as Commissioner-General to the Cape to oversee the implementation of this project.

In his memorandum on the state of the country, De Mist laments the laziness and lack of application of the young people he met, and argues for the need for local schools, a little museum and a printing press. The Batavian period was short-lived, however, and it fell to the British to bring about a new social order. Of De Mist's travels into the interior, two interesting accounts exist. One is written by the German naturalist Hinrich Lichtenstein, whose rivalry with his predecessor John Barrow neatly mirrors De Mist's own distrust of the British rulers who preceded him. The other is a slight volume written by De Mist's daughter, and is an example of the kind of writing a cultured young European woman might have produced. Whilst limited in its scope, and conventional in most aspects, it contrasts usefully with the lack of any comparable education or literary production at the Cape.

Religious fervour was the catalyst for another set of texts produced at the Cape and, significantly, written to be read at the Cape. The English-language mission discourse is the subject of another chapter (Chapter 10), and its literary influence continues to be felt in South Africa. Whilst the Dutch-language authors mentioned here were conversant with English-language writing (corresponding with John Newton of Olney, for example), and sympathetic to the aims of the newly founded London Missionary Society, the writing discussed here was produced in Dutch. Central to the circle of missionary sympathisers at the Cape were the sister and brother Catharina Aldegonda van Lier (1768–1801) and Helperus Ritzema van Lier (1764–93). Their reading and writing is part of a tradition of spiritual self-examination, with an emphasis on emotion and a mystical union with God.

Their circle met to discuss religious texts, and also to read one another's letters and diaries. Both died young, and a cult sprang up around Catharina's notebooks, which she had prepared for publication before she died. These were printed in the Netherlands, and are very monotonous to the modern reader, but the diarising of fluctuating emotions is representative of the small circle who clustered around the missionaries. Significant is the lack of reference to a social world.

Slightly different, in that he was not born in Europe, is the autobiography of the Reverend Michiel Christiaan Vos (1759–1825), written in epistolary form, and describing his emotional and spiritual development (see Huigen, 'Michiel Christiaan Vos' – Vos is described as 'the first black writer in South Africa' because of his mixed European and Asian parentage). Linked to this tradition of pietist autobiography is a little novel which has sometimes been called the first Afrikaans-language text (some of the dialogue is written in Cape Dutch vernacular, while the narrative is in Dutch). *Benigna van Groenekloof of Mamre* purports to be the autobiography of a convert of the Moravian brethren at Mamre mission station. The text was in fact written by a certain Hermann Benno Marx as an exemplary life story, thus providing another version of the auto-surveillance of the VOC and missionary journals. (For a discussion of some of the language debates around this text, see Deumert, *Language Standardisation*, and Koch, 'Hermann Benno Marx'.)

Religious texts and the Company's discipline of journal writing inform the writings by a small group still using Dutch – the literate members of the Great Trek. Their education level was not high, but if they deviated from standard Dutch it was certainly not intentional. Some of these texts were written during the emigration, while others were prepared years later when they had settled in Natal. The diary of Louis Trichardt shows a strong influence of biblical language. Whilst some have used this as evidence of the fact that the Trekkers saw themselves as a biblical Israel (for English-language discussions, see Akenson, *God's Peoples* and Templin, *Ideology on a Frontier*), this may be a later reinterpretation of these works. It is worth remembering that the Boer emigrants were on the whole not highly literate, and that the little book learning they had would have been limited to the catechisms and the Bible. With little writing and reading practice, it seems natural that language borrowed from their only reading matter would suggest itself.

Accompanying the Boer emigration was the Dutch-born missionary Erasmus Smit, whose missionary training would have prepared him for journal writing (the missionary societies, like the VOC, required regular reports). He uses standard Dutch, but his writing is not representative of the group he accompanied (for a fuller discussion of this material, and Smit's self-styling as the religious leader of the Trek, see Carli Coetzee, 'Individual and Collective Notions'). More interesting are the (unpublished) journals of his wife, Susanna Catharina (sister of the Trekker leader Gerrit Maritz).

These journals, compromising a series of eighteen small notebooks in which Smit writes in a neat, consistent hand, are dated between 1843 and 1850 and have handwritten numbers between 1 and 43 on the covers. Whether there were notebooks for the historically perhaps more interesting period of the emigration is not clear; nor is it evident who numbered the hand-bound volumes, or whether the numbering implies some are missing from the series. The style and content of these writings remind one of the pietist writings produced at the Cape, and contain hardly any references to a wider social world, but do attempt some discussion of theological debates. The lack of reference to a wider context is all the more striking given that Susanna Smit is famous as the woman who confronted the British Commissioner in Natal, Henry Cloete, locking him up and asserting that the Trekker women would rather cross the Drakensberg barefoot than return to the colony. (For an account of the events, see Bird's *Annals of Natal*. For a discussion of these events as the first example of feminist consciousness among Afrikaner women, see Kruger, 'Gender, Community and Identity'). What the journals do contain are repeated comparisons between her own and her husband's plight – housework dominates her existence, and she has no room of her own. The journals recount a number of dreams, often dreams in which domestic disorder (dust, insects, dirt) act as metaphors for the unexamined state of her own spiritual being:

> I have no money, no possessions to give to your poor, also no vineyard in which to labour, I am a poor woman confined and constricted in the intestines of my meagre home, and the sorrows of life oppress the abilities of my soul. I do write on pieces of paper, ponder the wonders of your mercy, and suppose hereby to provide my soul with some solace and thus to praise you. But for whom is it, who will read it? Presented by a spirit lacking in talent, undecorated by any skill in the art of writing, left behind by a poor unrespected person, it will soon be torn up as dirty paper, and so the only glory I attempt to bring my dear Lord in my weakness, will be lost. And thus I walk away from the scene of life where god has blessed me so mercifully, patiently and lovingly, and no trace of your goodness, shown to me in such large measure, is to be found.
>
> (*Dagboeke*, Booklet xxxv, pp. 29–30, entry for 29 October 1845; my own transcription and translation)

Continuity and the historical turn

In the last decades there has been a renewed interest in the Dutch period, as revisionist historians scrutinise the record in an attempt to reinterpret the early colonial encounter. The written tradition in Dutch was used, at various times, in political debates around identity. In the 1930s, when the development of Afrikaner nationalism needed to be served by literary historians, these early documents were reinterpreted as an early expression of a pre-English, national *volk* identity (see Conradie, *Hollandse Skrywers*). Ciraj Rassool and Leslie Witz have documented the changes in the way the arrival of the Dutch in 1652 has been commemorated, showing that Van Riebeeck has remained 'the figure around which South Africa's history is made and contested' ('Constructing and Contesting', p. 467). The body of creative literature which is set during the early Dutch period, or engages with characters from that period, continues to grow.

One of the earliest poems written in Afrikaans (published in 1897) is S. J. du Toit's 'Hoe die Hollanders die Kaap Ingeneem het' ('How the Dutch Invaded the Cape'), a dramatic monologue interestingly imagined from the point of view of a Khoikhoi (or Griqua, as the poem has him identify himself), Danster. More in line with the politics of their time are the early stage plays *Susanna Reyniers* (1908) by Francken and *Die Laaste Aand* (The Last Evening, 1930) by

Leipoldt. In these pieces, both of which are set at the early Cape settlement, there is no attempt to imagine an indigenous viewpoint. (Leipoldt's work is interesting, however, in its romanticisation of a mystical East.) A number of popular and romantic historical fictions are set at the early Cape, typically focused exclusively on the Dutch-speaking population.

A few notable early novels that exhibit features of the archival turn are J. M. Coetzee's *Dusklands* (1974) and André Brink's *An Instant in the Wind* (1976; first published in Afrikaans as *'n Oomblik in die Wind* in 1975). The two novels approach the archives very differently, and this difference has persisted as a trend in work set at the early Cape. Coetzee's work is interested in the textuality of the archive, and to this end he uses an actual travel account by an illiterate traveller (that of Jacobus Coetsé mentioned earlier), but frames it in a complex web of textual commentary. Thus the reader is never tempted to accept the narrator's voice as that of a realistic person. Coetzee's novel uses the travel account as much more than historical background for a narrative.

On the other hand André Brink, ever interested in developing analogies that will illuminate contemporary political questions, uses the archival material as background to a romance that is described in late twentieth-century erotic terms. His treatment of the material guides the reader to understand the present through the country's history. This is the trend that persists in much of the literature today, with the early Cape used as a vehicle for reflecting on the changing past.

A number of novels appeared in the early 1990s, at a time of political change that necessitated a new engagement with what constitutes the record. The early Cape archives seem to have held a particular fascination for authors, a number of whom chose Krotoä/Eva as their focus. Some of these novels, in an attempt perhaps at excavating Krotoä's point of view, have her present her side of the story, speaking with the values and emotions of a post-transformation South African. Examples of such novels include Bloem's *Krotoä-Eva* and Matthee's *Pieternella van die Kaap*. In my 'Krotoä Remembered: A Mother of Unity, a Mother of Sorrows?', I analyse how some Afrikaner artists have appropriated Krotoä as 'our mother' in an attempt at forging an 'African' identity through identification with Krotoä. In some of these works the conflict of the past is elided to present a world of acceptance and inclusion for white South Africans.

A different version of Krotoä's significance is to be found in the work of Yvette Abrahams, an historian who describes herself as 'brown' and has written about Krotoä's history in terms of conflict and rape, rather than acceptance and inclusion. The most complex engagement with Krotoä's life is that found in the work of Karen Press, whose 'Krotoä's Story' forms part of a collection of poems (*Bird Heart Stoning the Sea*) that asserts its revolutionary credentials. Press also wrote a children's version of Krotoä's life, to be included in a series that focuses on South African heroines.

André Brink's later novels develop the historical turn of *An Instant in the Wind*, often with an interest in the textuality of the past. So, in *On the Contrary* (1993; also published as *Inteendeel* in 1993) he creates a voice based on the travellers' tales of searching for Monomotopa. In his *Imaginings of Sand* (1995; also published as *Sandkastele* in 1995), *Rights of Desire* (2000; also published as *Donkermaan* in 2000) and *Praying Mantis* (2006; published originally as *Bidsprinkaan* in 2005) he uses figures from the Dutch period, often recreating their stories in magical realist fables that aim to echo the indigenous storytelling traditions while at the same time reflecting on the present.

Another writer who has made a significant contribution to historical writing in South Africa is Karel Schoeman, who has published widely and whose recent works on the first decades of the Cape settlement have added greatly to our understanding of the period. He is also one of the leading Afrikaans-language novelists, and in his novel *Verkenning* (Exploration), provides a sensitive reflection on the craft of the novelist who tries to recreate the world in which his historical characters move. Schoeman's novel is set at the turn of the eighteenth century and draws on the discourses of exploration and of religious and spiritual life. A similar world is that created in Elsa Joubert's *Missionaris* (Missionary) of 1988, in which the Van Liers appear as characters, alongside London Missionary Society sympathisers like Machtelt Schmidt. Karel Schoeman has also written a biography of Susanna Smit (*Die Wêreld van Susanna Smit, 1799–1863*), in which he places Smit (about whom not much is known apart from her confrontation with Cloete) in her religious and historical context. Schoeman chooses for his epitaph the section quoted above, his biography an answer to her question as to who would ever read her diaries. Different in tone and in the use made of Susanna Smit is the 1981 collection of poetry by Antjie Krog, *Otters in Bronslaai* (Otters in Watercress), which includes a cycle of six poems based on the historical figure of Susanna Smit and on her diaries. Whereas Schoeman is intent on placing Smit in her own context, Krog's poems find in her writings and life contemporary resonances.

A very successful recent novel is the subtly postmodern *Eilande* (translated into English as *Islands*) by Dan Sleigh (who has also written historical works on the period). In his novel, Sleigh uses de Grevenbroek as his final voice, and we read a text claiming to be by him, in which he reflects on the craft of the historian.

In the last decades, VOC studies have undergone a dramatic transformation. Seemingly at risk of falling out of fashion due to political changes, a new wave of historiography has instead provided a new context for this material. Significant work on the Khoikhoi was done in the 1980s by historians like Elphick and Malherbe, which refocused attention at the early Cape away from the Dutch settlers. More recently, with the work of Delmas and Penn, historians like Worden and Ward, and literary historians like Huigen, the Dutch Cape is being reinterpreted as part of a greater Indian Ocean world.

Bibliography

Abrahams, Y. 'Was Eva Raped? An Exercise in Speculative History', *Kronos* 23 (1996), 3–21.

Akenson, D. *God's Peoples: Covenant and Land in South Africa, Israel and Ulster*, Ithaca, NY: Cornell University Press, 1992.

Bergh, O. *Journals of the Expeditions of the Honourable Ensign Olof Bergh (1682 and 1683) and the Ensign Isaq Schrijver (1689)*, trans. and ed. E. E. Mossop, Cape Town: Van Riebeeck Society, 1931.

Bird, J. *The Annals of Natal 1405 to 1845*, 2 vols., Pietermaritzburg: P. Davis & Sons, 1888.

Bloem, T. *Krotoä-Eva: The Woman from Robben Island*, Cape Town: Kwela Books, 1999.

Boxer, C. R. *The Dutch Sea-Borne Empire* [1965], Harmondsworth: Penguin, 1990.

Brink, A. P. *Imaginings of Sand*, London: Secker & Warburg, 1996.

    An Instant in the Wind [1976], London: Minerva, 1991.

    On the Contrary, London: Secker & Warburg, 1993.

    Praying Mantis, London: Secker & Warburg, 2005.

    The Rights of Desire, London: Secker & Warburg, 2000.

Coetzee, C. 'Individual and Collective Notions of the "Promised Land": The "Private" Writings of the Boer Emigrants', *South African Historical Journal* 32 (1995), 48–65.

    'Krotoä Remembered: A Mother of Unity, A Mother of Sorrows?', in S. Nuttall and C. Coetzee (eds.), *Negotiating the Past: The Making of Memory in South Africa*, Cape Town: Oxford University Press, 1998, 112–19.

    'Visions of Disorder and Profit: The Khoikhoi and the First Years of the Dutch East India Company at the Cape', *Social Dynamics* 20:2 (1994), 35–66.

Coetzee, J. M. *Dusklands*, Johannesburg: Ravan, 1974.

    White Writing: On the Culture of Letters in South Africa, New Haven, CT: Yale University Press, 1988.

Conradie, E. J. M. *Hollandse Skrywers uit Suid-Afrika, 'n Kultuur-historiese Studie*, 2 vols., Pretoria: J. H. de Bussy, 1934–49.

Cook, H. J. *Matters of Exchange: Commerce, Medicine, and Science in the Dutch Golden Age*, New Haven, CT: Yale University Press, 2007.

De Jongh, P. S. *Die Lewe van Erasmus Smit*, Cape Town: HAUM, 1977.

Delmas, A. 'The Role of Writing in the First Steps of the Colony: A Short Enquiry in the Journal of Jan van Riebeeck, 1652–1662', in N. Worden (ed.), *Contingent Lives: Social Identity and Material Culture in the VOC World*, Cape Town: Royal Netherlands Embassy, 2007, 500–12.

Delmas, A. and Penn, N. (eds.). *Written Culture in a Colonial Context: Africa and the Americas, 1500–1900*. Cape Town: University of Cape Town Press, 2011.

De Mist, A. U. 'Dagverhaal van eene reis naar de Kaap de Goede Hoop en in de binnelanden van Afrika door Jonkvr. Augusta Uitenhage de Mist, in 1802 en 1803', in *Penélopé of Maandwerk aan het vrouwelijk geslacht toegewijd 8*, Amsterdam: Beijerinck, 1835.

Diary of a Journey to the Cape of Good Hope and the Interior of Africa in 1802 and 1803, trans. Edmund Burrows, Cape Town: Balkema, 1954.

The Memorandum of Commissary J. A. de Mist Containing Recommendations for the Form and Administration of Government at the Cape of Good Hope, Cape Town: Van Riebeeck Society, 1920.

*Relation d'un voyage en Afrique et en Amerique par Madame *****, Namur: D. Gerard, 1821.

Deumert, A. *Language Standardization and Language Change: The Dynamics of Cape Dutch*, Amsterdam: John Benjamins, 2004.

'Variation and Standardisation – The Case of Afrikaans', Ph.D. thesis, University of Cape Town, 1999.

Elphick, R. *Khoikhoi and the Founding of White South Africa*, Johannesburg: Ravan, 1985.

Francken, A. *Susanna Reyniers*, Amsterdam and Pretoria: J. H. de Bussy, 1908.

Glenn, I. 'Classical Black', *English in Africa* 34:2 (2007), 19–33.

Huigen, S. 'Michiel Christiaan Vos: De Eerste Zwarte Schrijver in Zuid-Afrika', *Tydskrif vir Nederlands en Afrikaans* 4:2 (1997), 162–8.

'Natural History and the Representation of South Africa in the Eighteenth Century', *Journal of Literary Studies* 14:1–2 (1998), 67–79.

'Nederlandstalige Suid-Afrikaans Letterkunde, 1652–1925', in H. P. van Coller (ed.), *Perspektief en Profiel*, vol. III, Pretoria: Van Schaik, 2005, 3–42.

'Travellers to Monomotopa: The Representation of Southern Africa by the Dutch in the Seventeenth Century', *History and Anthropology* 9 (1996), 207–30.

De Weg Naar Monomotapa: Nederlandstalige Representasies van Geografische, Historische en Sociale Werkelijkheden in Zuid-Afrika, Amsterdam University Press, 1996.

Huigen, S., J. L. de Jong and E. Kolfin. *The Dutch Trading Companies as Knowledge Networks*, Leiden: Brill, 2010.

Israel, J. I. *Dutch Primacy in World Trade, 1585–1740*, Oxford University Press, 1989.

Joubert, E. *Missionaris*, Cape Town: Tafelberg, 1988.

Koch, J. 'Hermann Benno Marx (1827–1917) – Auteur van *Benigna van Groenckloof of Mamre* (1873)', *Werkwinkel* 1:1 (2006), 1–30.

Krog, A. *Otters in Bronslaai*, Cape Town: Tafelberg, 1981.

Kruger, L. 'Gender, Community, and Identity: Women and Afrikaner Nationalism in the Volksmoeder Discourse of Die Boerevrouw (1919–1931)', MA thesis, University of Cape Town, 1991.

Leibbrandt, H. C. V. *Letters and Documents Received, 1649–1662*, 2 vols., Cape Town: Richards, 1898–9.

Precis of the Archives of the Cape of Good Hope, Cape Town: Richards, 1896–1906.

Resolutien van den Commandeur en Raden van het Fort de Goede Hoop, 1652–1662, Cape Town: Richards, 1898.

Riebeeck's Journal, Cape Town: Richards, 1896.

Leipoldt, C. L. *Die Heks en die Laaste Aand*, Cape Town: Tafelberg, 1981.

Marx, H. B. *Benigna van Groenekloof of Mamre*, Genadendal: Moravian Press, 1873.

Matthee, D. *Pieternella van die Kaap*, Cape Town: Tafelberg, 2000.

Newton-King, S. *Masters and Servants on the Cape Eastern Frontier, 1760–1803*, Cambridge University Press, 1999.

Penn, N. *The Forgotten Frontier: Colonist and Khoisan on the Cape's Northern Frontier in the 18th Century*, Cape Town: Double Storey, 2005.

Preller, G. S. (ed.). *Dagboek van Louis Trichardt (1816–1838)*, 2nd edn, Cape Town: Nasionale Pers, 1938.

Voortrekkermense ii, Cape Town: Nasionale Pers, 1920.

Voortrekkermense iii, Cape Town: Nasionale Pers, 1922.

Voortrekkermense v, Cape Town: Nasionale Pers, 1938.

Press, K. *Bird Heart Stoning the Sea*, Cape Town: Buchu, 1990.

Krotoä, Pietermaritzburg: Centaur, 1990.

Rassool, C., and L. Witz. 'The 1952 Jan van Riebeeck Tercentenary Festival: Constructing and Contesting Public National History in South Africa', *Journal of African History* 34 (1993), 447–68.

Raven-Hart, R. *Before van Riebeeck: Callers at the Cape from 1488 to 1652*, Cape Town: Struik, 1967.

Samuelson, M. *Remembering the Nation, Dismembering Women? Stories of the South African Transition*, Pietermaritzburg: University of KwaZulu-Natal Press, 2007.

Schapera, I. (ed.). *The Early Cape Hottentots, described in the Writings of Olfert Dapper (1668), Willem ten Rhyne (1686) and Johannes Gulielmus de Grevenbroek (1695)*, Cape Town: Van Riebeeck Society, 1933.

Schoeman, K. *Armosyn van die Kaap: Voorspel tot Vestiging, 1415–1651*, Cape Town: Human & Rousseau, 1999.

Armosyn van die Kaap: Die Wêreld van 'n Slavin, 1652–1733, Cape Town: Human & Rousseau, 2001.

Kinders van die Kompanjie: Kaapse Lewens uit die Sewentiende Eeu, Pretoria: Protea Boeke-huis, 2006.

Verkenning, Cape Town: Human & Rousseau, 1996.

Schoon, H. F. (ed.). *The Diary of Erasmus Smit*, trans. W. G. A. Mears, Cape Town: Struik, 1972.

Sleigh, D. *Islands*, trans. A. P. Brink, London: Secker & Warburg, 2004.

Jan Compagnie: The World of the Dutch East India Company, Cape Town: Tafelberg, 1980.

Smit, S. *Dagboeke, Herinneringe en Briewe van Susanna C Smit, 1843–1859*, Pietermaritzburg Archives Repository, K.S.U. III/1/4.

Tas, A. *The Diary of Adam Tas, 1705–1706*, Cape Town: Van Riebeeck Society, 1970.

Templin, J. A. *Ideology on a Frontier: The Theological Foundation of Afrikaner Nationalism, 1652–1910*, Westport, CT: Greenwood Press, 1984.

Van Riebeeck, J. *Daghregister gehouden by den opperkoopman Jan Anthonisz. van Riebeeck*, ed. D. B. Bosman, 3 vols., Cape Town: A. A. Balkema, 1952.

Journal of Jan van Riebeeck, ed. H. B. Thom, Cape Town: Balkema for the Van Riebeeck Society, 1952–8.

Van Wyk Smith, M. *The First Ethiopians: The Image of Africa and Africans in the Early Mediterranean World*, Johannesburg: Witwatersrand University Press, 2009.

Viljoen, R. *Jan Paerl, a Khoikhoi in Cape Colonial Society, 1761–1851*, Leiden: Brill, 2006.

Vos, M. C. *Merkwaardig Verhaal aangaande het leven en lotgevallen van Michiel Christiaan Vos*, Amsterdam: A. B. Saakes, 1824.

Ward, K. *Networks of Empire: Forced Migration in the Dutch East India Company (Studies in Comparative World History)*, Cambridge University Press, 2008.

Wikar, H. J. *The Journal of Hendrik Jacob Wikar (1779): with an English translation by A. W. van der Horst and the Journals of Jacobus Coetsé Janz: (1760) and Willem van Reenen (1791)*, ed. E. E. Mossop, Cape Town: Van Riebeeck Society, 1935.

Worden, N. 'New Approaches to VOC History in South Africa', *South African Historical Journal* 59 (2007), 3–18.

Worden, N. (ed.). *Contingent Lives: Social Identity and Material Culture in the VOC World*, Cape Town: Royal Netherlands Embassy, 2007.

Worden, N., E. van Heyningen and V. Bickford-Smith (eds.). *Cape Town: The Making of a City*, Cape Town: David Philip, 1999.

8

Eighteenth-century natural history, travel writing and South African literary historiography

IAN GLENN

Travel writing in South Africa in the eighteenth and early nineteenth centuries was a highly self-conscious genre, aimed at the European elite, and closely linked to the leading intellectual and political movements of its time. Its major protagonists came from a variety of countries and many were major figures in scientific discovery. The German Peter Kolb(e)(n) (1675–1725/6) and Frenchman Nicholas Louis de La Caille (Delacaille, de la Caille, De Lacaille) (1713–62) were astronomers; the Swedes Anders Sparrman (1748–1820) and Carl Thunberg (1743–1828) were naturalists with a particular interest in botany; the Scot William Paterson (1755–1810) was a soldier and botanist; the Surinam-born Frenchman François Le Vaillant (also known as Levaillant) (1752–1824) was primarily an ornithologist. Other figures had strong links to colonial administration: Johannes de Grevenbroek was the secretary of the Dutch East India Company Political Council at the Cape in the late seventeenth century; Robert Gordon (1743–95) was of Scots origin but working for the Dutch government as a military commander at the Cape; while the Englishman John Barrow (1764–1848) was a geographer and colonial civil servant with a strong interest in land surveying. There were other important travel writers, notably the only important female figure, Lady Anne Barnard (1750–1825), wife of the British Governor in the late eighteenth and early nineteenth centuries, whose work has enjoyed more attention than any of the other figures although her diaries remained unpublished until the twentieth century.

At no other time has writing about South Africa been so influential in the history of ideas or in shaping European ideas about itself. Siegfried Huigen suggests part of the reason when he observes that during this period 'To be taken seriously in Europe, the traveller had to have a thorough scientific education' (*Knowledge and Colonialism*, p. 16). We thus have travel accounts that are strongly linked to major developments in European thought and form part of the elite discourse of their time. These links can be observed most closely in the ways in which this literature sees itself as linked to positivist science, remains in dialogue with the Enlightenment, forms part of the emerging discipline and discourse of anthropology, and helps develop an anti-colonial critique. In terms of style, its rhetoric is anti-rhetorical, claiming for itself the simplicity of observation and experience.

In my analysis, I turn for evidence in the first instance to what the travellers said about themselves, particularly as their sophisticated and self-conscious prefaces and publicity material demonstrates how ideologically sophisticated they were. (See also Huigen, *Knowledge and Colonialism*, pp. 119–21, for a study of how important the opening plates were in establishing the credentials and attitudes of the author.)

The ideals of science

How did these travellers see their work? We have, in their prefatory remarks, publicity for their travels, and their critiques of other travellers, a fairly consistent set of views, which show that they regarded themselves as providing serious and reliable material for the consideration and contemplation of a European audience. Each writer in turn, in what might now be regarded as a convention of the academic essay, presents the work as an accurate correction of the regrettable errors of the past. In his translator's preface to the French edition of Kolb (*Description du cap de Bonne-Esperance*, p. i), the translator, identified by Good as Jean Bertrand ('Construction of an Authoritative Text', p. 90), opens on a typical note:

> Il y a peu de Livres aussi généralement goûtés, que les Voyages; lors du moins qu'ils sont exacts, fidèles, détaillés . . . Aussi les a-t-on appellés les Romans des honnêtes-gens.

> There are few books as widely enjoyed as travel accounts, as long as they are exact, faithful, detailed . . . Thus they have been called novels for respectable people.   (My translation)

Bertrand continues by insisting on Kolb's accuracy but also admits that he has had to abridge the work – a literary decision that was so successful that the French edition was used as the basis for later German editions.

Kolb's tactic of complaining about the inaccuracies of previous authors and allegations that they based their work on hearsay was very influential to judge by the number of times it was used against him – by Gordon, De Lacaille and Le Vaillant among others. But the notion of the literature of travel as a more respectable form of diversion than the novel also merged with a greater ambition: to be seen as scientifically valid.

Sparrman's prefatory remarks may be regarded as typical, though the English and French translators provide intriguingly different versions:

> Now every authentic and well-written book of voyages and travels is, in fact, a treatise of experimental philosophy.   (Sparrman and Forster, pp. iii–iv)

> Tous les voyages authentiques peuvent être considérés comme autant de traités de physique expérimentale. (All authentic voyages may be considered as so many treatises of experimental physics.)
>
>   (Sparrman and Le Tourneur, p. i)

I prefer the French version, where the cheerfully positivist view reminds us that much travel writing has a strongly referential function. For Sparrman and most of the other scientific travel writers coming to South Africa, the quest was to observe behaviour in the field or to find new objects: stars, plants, birds, mammals. In doing this, they were engaged in an exercise of scientific discovery that was at once competitive and collaborative; this in turn shaped their accounts, which were in large measure a corollary to these discoveries, partly adduced as additional proof, or as map of the terrain, or laboratory notes of sorts.

Whilst the influence or importance of these writers is not simply a factor of their referential adequacy, they certainly presented their work as valuable in relation to their truthfulness, and scholars such as Vernon Forbes and Kees Rookmaaker have gave to great pains to track their travels to ascertain the validity of their claims (Forbes, *Pioneer Travellers*; Rookmaaker, *Zoological Exploration*). In their scientific fields, the travellers' standing has usually depended on how accurate and reliable their descriptions were. Thus, in the case of Le Vaillant, Forbes spent considerable energy and time tracking down how far north Le Vaillant had in fact gone on his second voyage, eventually admitting in his chapter in the two-volume parliamentary collection that evidence suggested that Le Vaillant had indeed reached the Orange River.

Elsewhere, Erwin Stresemann, who sees Le Vaillant as the first great ornithologist, points to his discovery (in his voyage north to the Orange) that the Rosy Lovebird utilises the nests of Sociable Weavers – a behaviour only recorded in formal ornithology a century later (*History of Ornithology*, p. 97). And, equally, the reason that Le Vaillant has never earned the reputation he, arguably, deserves as social critic, ornithologist, or travel writer stems from the dubious claims and scientific misinformation, if not simple deception, that marked some of his later work in particular.

Most of the writers show considerable sophistication in explaining why their observations may not accord with those of earlier observers. When they make discoveries, they typically refer to earlier accounts to correct or confirm information. They may criticise earlier writers but in doing so they are working with conventions that are distinctively modern, both as scientists and as social critics.

Dialogue with the Enlightenment

The scientific travel writers saw themselves as being on a mission set by the scientific classifiers like Linnaeus and Buffon, but were also in an ongoing dialogue with figures like Rousseau and Diderot who regarded voyages into unknown countries as being the experimental fieldwork of discovering human nature itself. Rousseau read widely in the travel compendiums of his day, drawing on these accounts to formulate his theories of human development.

In the case of Diderot, a key moment came in his meeting with Robert Gordon, perhaps the most intriguing and knowledgeable of late eighteenth-century travellers to southern Africa. Gordon helped and influenced Paterson and Le Vaillant and, although he did not publish a full account of his travels at the time, he certainly influenced Enlightenment thought. Patrick Cullinan shows that Diderot, in his account of the meeting, contrasts Gordon's knowledge of the 'Hottentots' and his understanding of their language with the bias of his other interlocutor, Doctor Robert, and with the prejudice of Kolb. Cullinan argues that Diderot's contribution to Raynal's 1780 edition of *A Philosophical and Political History of the Settlements and Trade of the Europeans in the East and West Indies*, where he defended the Khoikhoi and attacked the Dutch settlers, thus stemmed more or less directly from Gordon's views (*Robert Jacob Gordon*, pp. 22–4).

The key frontispiece illustration of Rousseau's *Discours sur l'Inegalité* of the 'Hottentot' returning to his people and renouncing the ways of the white colonisers which he had experienced showed how central the Cape reports were to social theorising in France in particular, and how this story took on different resonances and interpretations throughout the century (see Merians, *Envisioning the Worst*). Rousseau had lain down the challenge to produce a new kind of travel writing and a new, non-ethnocentric view of the world in his Note x of the *Discourse on the Origins of Inequality*:

For the three or four hundred years since the inhabitants of Europe have inundated the other parts of the world, and continually published new collections of voyages and reports, I am persuaded that we know no other men except the Europeans; furthermore, it appears, from the ridiculous prejudices which have not died out even among Men of Letters, that under the pompous name of the study of man everyone does hardly anything except study the men of his country. In vain do individuals come and go; it seems that Philosophy does not travel. In addition, the Philosophy of each People is but little suited for another . . . All of Africa and its numerous inhabitants, as distinctive in character as in colour, are still to be examined.   (My translation)

Elsewhere Rousseau complained that the travellers who had given accounts were by definition unreliable because they were soldiers or missionaries or traders – all of whom were disqualified by their missions from having the properly disinterested attitudes necessary for a proper account.

This insistence that they were sharing a larger scientific and social investigation linked many of the travellers. Huigen remarks that 'what all travellers had in common was that they wanted to establish the exact facts; however, in accumulating knowledge the scientific travellers lacked an instrumentalist objective' (*Knowledge and Colonialism*, p. 3). The travellers in fact often insisted on the purity of their scientific motives by explicitly denying any instrumentalist role. William Paterson, travelling in the late 1770s, insisted on his motivation not being either imperial or commercial, and thus implicitly claimed for himself the proper attitude of scientific and academic detachment:

But if ambition did not tempt the conquerors of the world to extend their empire across the dreary deserts of Africa, nor commerce induce mankind to examine a country, the external appearance of which presents few allurements to the mere lovers of gain, to compensate for the dangers of exploring dreary and scorching regions, inhabited by ravenous beasts and noxious reptiles; yet there is one description of men to whom, with all their terrors, they will afford the most ample gratification. The admirer of Nature has, in this country, a wide field for investigation: here he will discover objects amply sufficient to satisfy the most inquisitive taste: here he will find every object, simple and unadorned; and will behold, in the uncivilized Hottentot, those virtues, which he, perhaps, sought for in civilized society in vain.

Impressed with these sentiments, and incited by the prospect of a country, the productions of which were unknown, I left England with a view to gratify a curiosity, which, if not laudable, was at least innocent.

(*Narrative of Four Journeys*, p. 3)

Mary Louise Pratt reads this claim of innocence suspiciously, as an example of 'anti-conquest' literature, supposedly denouncing imperialism but in fact complicit with it (*Imperial Eyes*, p. 57). The Guelkes, following Forbes, rather more plausibly, read the claim to innocence as Paterson's disavowal, given his later military service, that he had in fact been on a spying mission (Guelke and Guelke, 'Reassessing Travel Narratives', pp. 22–3). But if we keep Rousseau in mind, it seems as though Paterson is in fact stating his credentials for being the proper inquirer into Nature, including the Nature of man.

Le Vaillant too, both in the publicity sent out for his first volume of travels and in the work itself, insisted on his ability to judge based on his disinterested and impartial stance: 'Neither commercial speculation, nor fondness for any sort of service took me to the Cape. Only the impulse of my character and the desire to discover new things directed my wanderings in this part of the world. I got there free and with an independent mind' (*Travels*, p. 142).

Another ongoing theme of these travellers is their critical relationship to the metropolitan authorities, whether social or scientific. In Sparrman's work, he turns on Buffon:

> It frequently becomes necessary for me to correct in this manner, the volu-
> minous works of this illustrious author; which, indeed merit this correction
> so much the more, as the errors in them, being in other respects not unfre-
> quently dressed up in an elegant style, have, in fact, imposed on many with
> charms which ought to be the attendants on pure genuine truth only, and
> unadulterated nature. It is therefore probable, that the sportive genius of M.
> De Buffon, must at times have operated in imposing likewise on its owner;
> but I am willing to hope, that this gentleman being *by profession* the interpreter
> of nature and truth, will on this account see with the greater pleasure, any
> strictures and remarks which are necessary to preserve the science of nature
> from falsehood and error.   (*Voyage to the Cape of Good Hope*, ii, p. 88)

When Le Vaillant's first *Voyage* was on the point of publication, his editors sent out a 'Prière d'Inserer' or what we would now call a press release ('Voyage de M. Le Vaillant'). This shows a highly self reflective sense of the truth claims and theoretical value of this travel account but seems, particularly, to speak to the errors of the metropolitan theorists or 'genius' like Rousseau:

> This is a series, as varied as it is touching, of the adventures, the setbacks, the
> pleasures, the thoughts, of all the affections of a man of feeling in the midst of
> the wilderness, and in the home of wild beasts. In a word, this work becomes
> a solid and upright reference point for the philosopher and the savant who
> up till now have only been able to study the savages and the marvels of
> nature through risky comparisons, false perceptions, or through frivolous

novels. This is the correction, if it may be said, of the imposing errors of the genius, all the more accredited as the homage given to him is general and public.   (My translation)

Le Vaillant throughout his writing reacts critically, as this barb against the theoretical genius suggests, to the claims of the metropolitan critic or theorist in his study to be able to generalise about reality in the abstract instead of working from the knowledge and experience of the observer in the field. Yet this does not mean that he rejects the authority but rather that he wants to set it on the right track. Similarly, Le Vaillant at points seems to reject the authority of Buffon, just as Sparrman does.

Elsewhere in this publicity statement, Le Vaillant is presented as a figure who is properly disinterested, independent, raised outside of France and marked by a proto-Rousseauistic sensibility and the ability to judge freely and properly. When Le Vaillant named one of his sons Jean-Jacques Rousseau, he may have been cannily showing his sympathy with the revolutionary times but he was also paying tribute to a major influence.

Le Vaillant knew and drew on Gordon for help and advice and he too criticised Kolb, as Gordon had Diderot, and repeated the critiques of colonial cruelty and defence of the traditional indigenous way of life that Diderot invoked in his additions to Raynal's work or in the *Supplément au voyage de Bougainville*. We thus have an ongoing exchange of impressions and theory between those in the Cape and those in Europe.

Anthropology

The major unsettling achievement of many of these eighteenth-century writers was to provide the materials for the theoretical critique of ethnocentric observation by figures like Rousseau and Diderot but also to put these precepts into practice in the field. Earlier observers give Rousseau the data to call for a 'philosophy that travels', while later writers accept the challenge of finding such knowledge. In many ways, then, these texts are the founding texts or pre-texts of anthropology, as Anne Good ('Construction of an Authoritative Text'), Huigen (*Knowledge and Colonialism*), Tania Manca ('Voyages européens') and I (Le Vaillant, *Travels*) have argued. At the outset, writers like Dapper and Kolb provide the materials, in collections like that of the Abbé Prévost, for the Enlightenment social thinkers to use as data; then the Cape thinkers meet the philosophers, as in the case of Gordon meeting Diderot; then the critical works of Rousseau become the theoretical and methodological guide for a new generation of travellers.

In a final movement, a figure like Le Vaillant returns to France, joins the Idéologues and is present when Degérando sets out his formal theoretical basis for anthropology, intended in part as a guide for Le Vaillant, who was thought to be intending a third journey into the African interior (Copans and Jamin, *Aux origines*, p.73).

Duchet, rather than J. M. Coetzee or Pratt, looks most closely at the links between travel writing and the Enlightenment but her text has a strong period Marxist feel to it. She admits that most of the Enlightenment figures were strong critics of colonialism: 'Certes, il n'est pas un philosophe qui ne condamne les crimes les conquistadores, l'atroce commerce des esclaves, la cruauté des colons' ('Admittedly, there is no philosopher who does not condemn the crimes of the conquistadors, the horrible commerce of slavery, the cruelty of the colonisers') (*Anthropologie et histoire*, p. 23). Yet, she argues that none of the travellers or philosophers was able to abandon their own civilised perspective to enter into the view of modern ethnography (pp. 16, 88). Duchet's demand that eighteenth-century travellers should meet the standards of modern ethnography seems obtuse because it ignores how much the writers in fact did to unsettle ethnocentric perception. It is Le Vaillant who comes closest to the self-critical view of European society that represents the true beginnings of anthropology, but Duchet relied on the heavily censored Boulenger edition of Le Vaillant and would not have seen the relevant material.

Kolb was in many ways the first powerful voice of Enlightenment self-critique and a sceptical observer of any claims of western perfection. Though he very often starts by granting that the hostile critical views of the 'Hottentots' had some justification, he then often undermines or makes such claims dubious. The first lengthy account in the English or French editions is the story of Claas, a worthy Hottentot who displays Job-like patience as he is treated appallingly and unjustly by the Dutch authorities and his own people alike.

In his preface to a 1968 reprint edition, anthropologist Peter Carstens notes that 'throughout his text one is repeatedly struck by his satirical attacks on the European way of life when he is comparing the two cultures' (p. ix). Good notes that in the original text of Kolb, he 'crafted his description of the Khoikhoi to talk back to European culture' ('Construction of an Authoritative Text', p. 85). Good points out that what happened fairly systematically in later versions of Kolb was that sensational facts or incidents were taken out of his original context where they might have made more sense as cultural comparisons with events in European culture.

In his concluding remarks on the 'Hottentot' character and its strengths and weaknesses in the English edition, Kolb set down his overall sense of their virtues, and this passage is probably the single most powerful example of the trend Carstens and Good note; it goes a long way to explaining not only the ways in which eighteenth-century travel accounts fed into ideas of the Noble Savage, but also why they presented such a threat to later white settler identity and self-justification:

> The Integrity of the *Hottentots*, their Strictness and Celerity in the Execution of justice, and their Chastity are Things in which they excell all or most other Nations in the World. A most beautiful Simplicity of Manners runs through All the Nations of 'em. and Numbers of 'em have told me, that the Vices they saw prevail among the Christians; their Avarice, their Envy and Hatred of one another, their restless discontented Tempers, their Lasciviousness and Injustice were the Things that principally kept the *Hottentots* from Hearkening to Christianity.   (*Present State*, p. 336)

Le Vaillant went even further in that he took what European culture had said back to the people described when he describes asking the Khoi travelling with him about earlier ethnographic descriptions:

> I especially asked them lots of questions about Kolb and different authors, about their religious beliefs, their laws, their customs. They laughed at me openly. Sometimes I saw they were stung by what was said and become indignant, shrug their shoulders and burst into angry exclamations.
>
> (*Travels*, p. 72)

Le Vaillant is certainly not, systematically, a modern ethnographer, and one can see this direct question as methodologically naive while elsewhere he retreats into notions of western superiority over the 'sauvages'. Yet it is worth noting that Margaret Shaw called his description of the Gonaqua the best anthropological account we have of them (Quinton et al., *François Le Vaillant*).

Le Vaillant, as I have argued elsewhere, was in many ways an exemplary ethnographer, working as the different disciplines of ethnology and ethnography emerged (Glenn, 'Primate Time'). He fulfilled what Lévi-Strauss, in his description of Rousseau, saw as a central function of the anthropologist: an observer who moves between societies and reflects that tension. In his lengthy description of the Gonaqua, Le Vaillant addresses many of the major sensationalist claims about them and deals with them by agreeing that in some cases they may be true, but he rejects claims of widespread incest sharply and interestingly. Whilst some other observers claim that the Khoikhoi are subhuman, Le Vaillant argues that the incest taboo among the Khoikhoi gave them a fully human status.

We can judge just how radical and unsettling this anthropological detachment of the early writers was when we see how difficult European or white South African readers found it to accept. (In retranslating Le Vaillant's work, I was struck by how often the two rival 1790 translations into English err in not accepting just how detached and critical an observer of European civilisation and Dutch colonisation Le Vaillant was.)

There is another reason the eighteenth-century observers may have been more able to judge the indigenous peoples they met sympathetically. In many cases, their response, based on biblical or classical reference, was to see Africans as people from an ancient civilisation, perhaps Jews or a lost tribe of Israel (in the case of Kolb) or as Egyptians (in the case of Barrow). Whilst this may seem condescending or misguided, the result was, throughout this period, a widespread use of classical imagery, both verbally and visually, to describe indigenous peoples (Glenn, 'Classical Black'). Travellers could be open to the aesthetic qualities of black bodies, seen as being as strikingly powerful as a Hercules or as beautiful as one of the Graces. The nineteenth century's framing of African society in strongly Christian terms as heathen or in social Darwinist terms as backward made a spirit of ethnographic openness much more difficult.

Colonial critique

Eighteenth-century travel writers had, the evidence above suggests, several loyalties and implicit audiences, but none of them were to local political or social groups. That was at once the source of their descriptive power as disinterested and impartial outsiders, but also the source of their subsequent fall from local grace and influence and the reason they were neglected in an increasingly nationalistic and jingoistic European and settler context. In short, these authors were for the most part simply too critical of white colonialism to form an easy part of a subsequent settler literature. This also helps explain much of the subsequent neglect by white South African scholars in a nationalistic era but cannot explain their neglect when, from the 1970s on, those critics uneasy with the pieties of the settler tradition might have used these authors as the bases for a more widely shared literary culture.

Grevenbroek is, as Katherine George observed, the first author to present a sustained literary critique of white colonialism ('Civilized West', p. 69). He does this explicitly through direct statement when he notes: 'Candore animi multis nostratium superiores sunt' ('In whiteness of soul they are superior to many of our countrymen') (Schapera, *Early Cape Hottentots*, pp. 174–5). But his more complex critique of the nature of white colonialism comes when he writes, in Latin, of what happened to an English sailor, wrecked on the *Stavenisse*, who was subsequently rescued and in being rescued left behind the African woman with whom he had a child. To try to understand white colonialism and its psychic cost for coloniser and colonised, Grevenbroek compares the sailor's story to Virgil's story of Aeneas and his desertion of Dido. As I conclude in a fuller analysis elsewhere:

> Thus Grevenbroek's classical allusion gives a dual sexual-political possibility for the white man: to found a new city as Aeneas does in Rome by putting the classical imprint of Iulus on the 'Barbara'; or to return to another duty and way of life. The tragedy of white colonial identity is that he cannot do the former fully, by staying and founding a new hybrid culture; while the latter comes in the account to seem like an irresponsible and inhumane action. This passage uses the classical model and anticipates the scene in which Kurtz leaves the native woman in *Heart of Darkness*, but seems more humanely and humanly affected by what has happened than Conrad's Marlow was to be. ('Classical Black', p. 22)

It is rare, in fact, to find any of the eighteenth-century travellers expressing a consistent sense of white racial superiority though there are certainly moments and passages like that. (Huigen argues that firm racial categories only get established during the nineteenth century [*Knowledge and Colonialism*, p. 22].) Whether it is in regarding Gordon, De Lacaille or Sparrman, who after his trip to the Cape helped in an anti-slavery expedition and publication (Wadström, *Observations on the Slave Trade*), we generally confront a view of colonial expansion and dispossession that is far from celebratory and triumphalist. Even Barrow, the explicit agent of British colonialism, took much from Le Vaillant's critique and was clearly horrified by settler brutality, as Nigel Penn has highlighted ('Onder Bokkeveld Ear Atrocity').

Le Vaillant, however, is the most marked and striking case and certainly qualifies as the first strongly anti-colonial writer to emerge from South Africa. The revolutionary fervour around the time of his collaboration and the pro-Republican sympathies of his collaborator Casimir Varon helped produce a text which served as a damning indictment of Dutch settler mores and of colonial brutality.

Le Vaillant's first major revision of Kolb's generally positive review of the achievement of Dutch colonialism comes when he produces an attack on Van Riebeeck:

> Riébek soon arrived in Table Bay. His shrewd policy was to appear as an able peacemaker and he used all the devious means necessary to attract the good will of the Hottentots, and covered the lip of the poisoned cup with honey. These masters of this whole portion of Africa by imprescriptible right, these savages, were won over by these cruel lures, and did not see at all how this culpable debasement was taking away their rights, their authority, their peace, and their happiness. Why should these men, indolent by nature, unattached to any particular piece of land, like true cosmopolitans, not in the least inclined to agriculture, be concerned that some strangers had come to take a little piece of useless and often uninhabited land? They thought that a little further, or a little nearer, was immaterial. It didn't matter where their flocks, the only wealth worthy of their note, found their food, as long as they found some. The Dutch held out great hopes for their greedy policy after such a peaceful beginning, and as they are especially skilful and tougher than others in seizing the advantages given by chance, they did not fail to finish off the work, by offering to the Hottentots two highly seductive lures: tobacco, and brandy. From this moment on, no more liberty, no more pride, no more nature, no more Hottentots, no more men. These unfortunate savages, enticed by these two baits, stayed as close as they could to the source providing them. On the other side, the Dutch who could get an ox for a pipe of tobacco or a glass of brandy, tried to keep, as much as possible, such valuable neighbours. Imperceptibly the colony spread and got stronger. Soon one saw rising on foundations that it was too late to destroy, this redoubtable power which dictated laws to this whole part of Africa, and rejected violently all that might resist its ambitions and greedy advancement.
>
> (*Travels*, pp. 121–2; original footnote omitted)

What is noteworthy here is the language of human rights (the 'imprescriptible' found in the French of Rousseau and the English of Thomas Paine) that move between countries and contexts and also of the anthropological sophistication that makes it clear that Dutch and indigenous understanding of property and land rights are necessarily very different.

When Le Vaillant reached the eastern frontier, still ravaged by the traces of the most recent Frontier Wars, he sought local opinion from one Hans, the 'son of a white man and a Hottentot woman' who had 'spent most of his life among the Caffres'. Hans gives an account of the origins of conflict and the conduct of the warfare that seems to have traumatised Le Vaillant as much as any security police atrocity related to the South African Truth and Reconciliation Commission two centuries later did its reporters:

> What he told me confirmed me in my opinion that the Caffres are generally peace loving and calm, but he assured me that as they were constantly harassed, robbed, and slaughtered by the whites, they had had no choice but to take up arms in self-defence. He told me that the colonists reported them far and wide to be a barbarous and bloodthirsty race to justify the robberies and atrocities they perpetrated on the Caffres every day and which they misrepresented as retaliation. Under the pretext that a few head of cattle had been stolen, they had exterminated whole hordes of Caffres, regardless of sex or age, stolen all their oxen, and laid their country to waste. This way of getting cattle was quicker than breeding them for themselves and they had used it so indiscriminately that in a year they had shared more than twenty thousand and mercilessly slaughtered anyone who had attempted to defend the livestock. Hans assured me that he had witnessed an incident, which I report here as he told it to me. A band of colonists had just destroyed a Caffre village. A young lad of twelve or so had escaped and hidden in a hole. Unfortunately he was discovered by one of the colonists who wanted to have him as a slave and took him to the camp with him. The commander took a fancy to the boy and declared that he was going to have him. The man who had captured the boy obstinately refused to give him up. Tempers ran high on both sides. Then the commander, in a blind rage, making for his innocent victim like a madman, yelled out to his opponent: 'If I can't have him, you won't have him either.' In the same instant he fired a shot into the chest of the young child who dropped dead.
>
> I was also told that these criminals would on occasion amuse themselves by placing their prisoners some distance away from them and compete who among them would be the best at hitting the target. I would never stop if I wanted to report in detail the shocking atrocities which are indulged in every day against these unfortunate savages who have no protection and no support. Particular considerations and powerful motives silence me and, besides, what can the voice of a sensitive individual do against despotism and force? One must groan and know how to be silent. I have said enough for everyone to know what the colonists are doing in that part of Africa while the indolent government gives free rein to their excesses and even fears to punish them. In this place all the horrors invented in hell are committed, in a republican state that stands out above all the others by its simple manners and philanthropic spirit. The most sinful iniquities go unpunished because it is just too much of an effort to look beyond the immediate surroundings. If the governor occasionally gets wind of such dreadful wrongdoings, distance, the time it takes for the reports to get to him, and perhaps other reasons which it is more prudent not to delve into, bring them in such disfigured and disguised forms that they hardly get discussed.   (pp. 141–2)

In his review of Le Vaillant, Nicolas Chamfort made a point which we may see as the very basis of postcolonial ideological critique. Chamfort asked himself why Le Vaillant had reached such different conclusions on the Khoikhoi from earlier writers and commented:

> It is a very remarkable thing to see the majority of modern travellers in opposition to the former ones who painted in horrible colours the savage, the man of nature, that others have since seen in a more favourable light. Bacon said that one had to re-start human understanding, a rather painful enterprise after so many lost centuries. It is not impossible that in the same way we will have to re-start observations, the basis for the ideas of some philosophers on human nature, that they represent as evil and made so as always to be so. (Chamfort, 'Voyage', p.79; my translation)

If Bacon is the founder of ideological criticism, and Chamfort one of the major influences on Nietzsche, then we can see how strongly Le Vaillant's account stands as one of the texts that shook any self-confident and self-congratulating colonial ideology. Huigen is quite right to say that 'Le Vaillant was an early postcolonial author' (*Knowledge and Colonialism*, p. 122).

The case of the two writers most closely linked to the British occupation of the Cape, John Barrow and Lady Anne Barnard, is particularly interesting. They occupy a transitional space from the detached critique of the largely foreign visitors to a defensive and self-justifying settler literature: at once sharing the critical distance of a Le Vaillant or Sparrman from the behaviour of the colonists, yet starting to justify a meliorative British colonial mission. Barnard's case as wife of a colonial official, not writing for publication, has interested later feminist critics in particular, but her marginality and allegiances differ from those of the earlier writers.

The critical debate

Over half a century ago, Katherine George wrote an article in which she surveyed the travel accounts of voyagers to Africa from 1400 to 1800. After noting that Grevenbroek broke sharply with previous negative accounts and was 'the first champion of the natives of South Africa before the world' ('Civilized West', p. 69), she quoted him at length. She then continued by arguing that the strand represented by Grevenbroek came to dominate in the eighteenth century:

Accounts of African travel in the eighteenth century are more numerous than in any previous era, and they are also more various ... There are missionaries, traders, and officials, as in the past, but in addition there are numbers of an entirely different breed, men who, with a considerable background of education in the philosophical and scientific thought of the day, came to Africa primarily to explore and to observe. It is in the reports of such men as these, Thunberg, Sparrman, Le Vaillant, Bruce, Mungo Park, and others, that the new spirit, barely indicated in seventeenth-century accounts, achieves its full development. So persuasive and powerful was this new spirit, however, that almost all eighteenth-century reports of travel to primitive Africa show it.

The two components of this spirit, an increased regard for accuracy of reporting, and an unprecedented sympathy for the primitive and his culture, which consistently tend to reinforce one another, cooperate in stimulating active criticism of previous prejudice and error, so commonly found in eighteenth-century accounts.   (p. 70)

George goes on to examine the link of these writers to ideas of the Noble Savage and a new spirit of anthropological self-critique and concludes her article with a eulogy to the Enlightenment spirit:

If one considers these eighteenth-century accounts, however, in comparison with the earlier literature, one is struck by a crucial change. A decisive expansion of human interests and sympathies has occurred. Real progress in the direction of a fuller understanding of man and his culture has been made. Indeed, I know of no body of data which compels one more forcibly and directly to an admiration for the intellectual and moral magnificence of the eighteenth century.   (p. 72)

Her views contrast sharply with influential postcolonial critiques of eighteenth-century travel writing such as those of Michelle Duchet or Mary Louise Pratt, but as the first part of this chapter suggests, her view has been unjustly neglected as her emphasis on the links between eighteenth-century Enlightenment thinking and the travel accounts is the central, most important issue in assessing them.

Pratt's claims have been particularly influential. In her view, influenced by Foucault and Said, the eighteenth century marks the growing influence of a scientific discourse set in place by Linnaeus that sets up the European scientific viewer as the 'imperial eye' of her title. For her, Peter Kolb was the only writer to show something of the Enlightenment sympathy and self-critique, writing 'with a humanism not found in later writers' (*Imperial Eyes*, p. 43).

Several scholars have reacted to the views of Pratt in defence of individual authors, while Huigen makes a more general attack (*Knowledge and Colonialism*, p. 28) on her ideological bias with pointed commentary on her treatment of Le Vaillant, Barrow and others. Scholarship since her publication also casts doubt on her central thesis. For William Beinart, Pratt treats Anders Sparrman and William Burchell unjustly while the Guelkes, starting with a respectful reading of Pratt, argue that her consideration of Kolb, Sparrman, William Paterson and John Barrow is basically unjust and they 'concur with Beinart that [these explorers] did not erase indigenous people – indeed, were receptive to Native positions, and that they construed masculinity in terms of outdoor adventure' ('Reassessing Travel Narratives', p. 19). They point out that Pratt reads selectively and omits crucial evidence, remarking justly on 'the extent to which the search for literary tropes and structures to frame an anti-conquest thesis becomes a Procrustean Bed for naturalists' recollections, stretched or trimmed according to structural requirements of fiction genres' (p. 22). The Guelkes also note a problem in Pratt's use of sources and a tendency for scholarly short cuts: unable to locate Paterson's original English text, she found a French text which she personally retranslated. They note that her 'translation is somewhat more favorable to her case than Paterson's original' (p. 23).

In my work on François Le Vaillant, I was highly surprised by the account of Le Vaillant that emerges in Pratt and by her claims that, for example, consideration of the Khoikhoi more or less disappeared by the late eighteenth century (*Imperial Eyes*, pp. 52–3) and by her neglect of the strong anti-colonist view in Le Vaillant. Here, Pratt's scholarly short cut is far more damaging than in the case of her neglect of Paterson's original text. As I argue in my introduction to the critical edition of Le Vaillant:

> Le Vaillant's texts had gone out of print and the only easily available reprint came in 1932, in a text edited by Boulenger, who combined the first and second Voyages into one abridged version. Boulenger claims (1:xvii) that his work is an accurate summary of the original with all omissions indicated faithfully and this claim has in effect been accepted by critics such as Michelle Duchet and Mary-Louise Pratt who take their Le Vaillant from Boulenger. As Boulenger's preface makes clear, however, he is hostile to the Rousseauistic and anti-colonial strands of Le Vaillant's thought, and he has edited correspondingly. We thus face our final irony. It seems that it suits Marxist theorists such as Duchet and post-colonial and feminist discourse theorists such as Pratt to rely on bad right-wing scholarship because it simplifies the complexity of past texts so admirably. (Le Vaillant, *Travels*, pp. lviii–lix; original notes omitted)

Whilst Pratt may have distorted evidence by relying on bad texts or omitting large sections of them, she was also unaware of evidence brought to light by more recent scholarship, such as several editions of the very positive account of Xhosa society by the 'French boy', known either as Chalezac or Laujardiere, who survived the wreck of the *Stavenisse* (Lanni, *Fureur et barbarie*; Chalezac, *Guillaume Chenu de Chalezac*; Laujardiere, *Relation d'un voyage*), or of Patrick Cullinan's work that established the Enlightenment links and credentials of Robert Gordon, demonstrating the ways in which he influenced Diderot's critique of colonialism, or indeed of Le Vaillant's strong links to the Idéologues and to the French Revolution (Boisacq, 'Mythe du bon sauvage Hottentot'; Rookmaaker et al., *François Levaillant and the Birds of Africa*.) Nor could she take into account recent historical work by Nigel Penn and Andrew Bank, among others, who show how strongly travel writing influenced social policy that aimed to improve the lot of indigenous South Africans in criticising the behaviour of colonists. Nevertheless, it is difficult, finally, to demur from Huigen's irate dismissal (*Knowledge and Colonialism*, pp. 28–30) of her scholarship as fatally flawed.

Whilst later scholarship and specialist knowledge has invalidated many of Pratt's claims or revealed how wildly speculative many of her readings (particularly the Freudian excursions) were, her interpretive drive has had some beneficial results in, for example, stimulating research into figures like Lady Anne Barnard. But we do not yet have any very persuasive overview of the period, in part because so much scholarship remains to be done.

Kolb and Le Vaillant were undoubtedly the most influential writers of the period and did the most to shape European perceptions and other writers, yet there is no fully reliable scholarly text of either and the original texts are out of print. In the case of Kolb, the translations in French and English (both of which abridged the original text) have been attacked as inaccurate and biased by Good, Huigen and Merians. Huigen notes severely that 'It is remarkable that none of the researchers mentioned in this note even deemed it necessary to consult the full Kolb text when they set out to characterise his work. It is not customary to approach canonised literature with such a degree of carelessness' (*Knowledge and Colonialism*, p. 35, n. 2). Furthermore, Kolb's original notebooks have not had adequate scholarly attention and a proper reassessment of him must await a scholarly re-edition.

Other important figures like De Lacaille and Barrow also need scholarly attention, and so a general survey at this point must be regarded as provisional. A further complication is that some important scholarly work (on Gordon, Paterson and Le Vaillant, for example) has been published in expensive Africana publications with limited editions and thus remains out of reach for the general academic or reading public (Cullinan, *Robert Jacob Gordon*; Rookmaaker et al., *François Levaillant and the Birds of Africa*; Paterson et al., *Paterson's Cape Travels*).

The influence of travel writing

I have elsewhere repeatedly argued for the influence, both formal and thematic, of the eighteenth-century travel writers, and particularly Le Vaillant ('Wreck of the Grosvenor'; 'Future of the Past'; 'Man who Invented Safaris'; 'Francois Levaillant and the Mapping of Southern Africa'; 'Classical Black'; Le Vaillant et al., *Voyage into the Interior*, 2007). In my view, most of what emerges in South African literature later, whether in adventure writing, the hunting narrative, the spiritual safari into the wilderness, interracial sexuality, the colonial erotic or the exposé of colonial brutality has its roots in eighteenth-century travel writing. These accounts also did much to shape other influential genres such as the illustrated and mapped first person travel account, cartography, illustrated bird books and ethnology. In his recent monograph, Huigen provides a more systematic account of the travellers during the period of Dutch rule, showing both their intellectual background and openness of spirit. Much more comparative work on the respective merits and influence of South African travellers with those elsewhere is necessary.

Attention to the travel writers complicates the common view that South African literature began with Olive Schreiner, a view that inhibits a proper consideration of the formal development and ideological range of early South African writing. What Merians makes clear is that Le Vaillant's work, in particular, was immediately an ideological flashpoint in British responses in particular. She notes that 'Le Vaillant's work received an enthusiastic reception from Britain's more liberal literary and political circles' (*Envisioning the Worst*, p. 171) and that 'the very fact that Le Vaillant's romantic vision of "Hottentots" earned such a number of strong responses suggests the level to which it threatened a conservative agenda and program for the nation' (p. 174). David Johnson too shows how conservative British satirists of Rousseau and the Noble Savage took Le Vaillant's account as a target ('Representing the Cape "Hottentots"').

Literary scholars who neglect travel writing miss or misread much of its influence. For much of the first half of the nineteenth century and even beyond, writing about South Africa took much of its tone from Le Vaillant.

In the first significant South African novel, *Makanna* (1834), the hero, Paul Laroon, is based on Le Vaillant and, as a French agent hostile to British interests in South Africa, he helps Makanna, a character based on the Xhosa rebel Makanna, in his anti-colonial struggle. (Makanna was so well known at the time that the island, used for political prisoners, was also known as 'Makana's' or 'Makanna's Island' and retained this name for many political prisoners.) Though we do not know who wrote *Makanna*, it seems clear that the author, dealing with events of the late eighteenth and early nineteenth century, permitted anachronisms in mixing the era of the French Revolution with Xhosa rebellion and Makanna's presence because he still saw Le Vaillant as a contemporary.

The anthropological awareness of cultural and political differences influenced literature, with books like Kendall and Bone's *The English Boy at the Cape: An Anglo-African Story* (1835) showing many facets of Cape society by having a young English boy make his way through almost every element in it. Even at mid century, texts like *Everard Tunstall* (1851), with its thoughtful preface on the difficulties of judging colonial wars, or *The Adventures of Mrs Colonel Somerset* (1858), a South African fictive capture narrative where a shipwrecked heroine finds herself in Xhosa society during their war with the British and in essence takes the Xhosa side, kept alive the critical view of colonial expansion. It is an indictment that South African literary scholarship has spent so little time on these texts. In terms of social influence, too, the role of the travel writers has begun to receive reassessment. Directly, and through figures like the Revd Philip, they did much to present a view of South African colonialism that became and remained critical and sceptical. (See Bank, 'Great Debate'; Penn, 'Mapping the Cape'; Penn, *Forgotten Frontier*; Huigen, *Knowledge and Colonialism*.)

In conclusion, then, we should note that a reassessment of the achievement of eighteenth-century naturalists and travel writers gives us a much sounder and longer view of South African literature and culture and the debates surrounding it. The theoretical irony, for anybody trying to grasp the overall shape of South African literature, is that the writers and observers who did most to shape a postcolonial critique, by their observations, the records they left at the time and their self-critical reflections, have been the most shabbily treated by those wielding the late twentieth-century version of that legacy. We need to return to the long view that Katherine George set out and see how much of South African writing and culture, thematically and formally, starts in eighteenth-century travel accounts.

Bibliography

Anon. *Makanna; or, The Land of the Savage*, 3 vols., London: Whittaker & Co., 1834.

Bank, A. 'The Great Debate and the Origins of South African Historiography', *Journal of African History* 38:2 (1997), 261–81.

Barnard, A. L., and H. D. Melville. *The Letters of Lady Anne Barnard to Henry Dundas, from the Cape and Elsewhere, 1793–1803, Together with her Journal of a Tour into the Interior, and Certain other Letters*, Cape Town: Balkema, 1973.

Barnard, A. L., D. Driver, M. Lenta and A. M. L. Robinson. *The Cape Journals of Lady Anne Barnard, 1797–1798*, Cape Town: Van Riebeeck Society, 1994.

Beinart, W. 'Men, Science, Travel and Nature in the Eighteenth- and Nineteenth-Century Cape', *Journal of Southern African Studies* 24:4 (1998), 775–99.

Boisacq, M-J. 'Le Mythe du bon sauvage Hottentot', *Literator* 14:2 (1993), 117–31.

Chalezac, G. C. de, and R. Vigne. *Guillaume Chenu de Chalezac, the 'French Boy': The Narrative of his Experiences as a Huguenot Refugee, as a Castaway among the Xhosa, his Rescue with the Stavenisse Survivors by the Centaurus, his Service at the Cape and Return to Europe, 1686–9*, Cape Town: Van Riebeeck Society, 1993.

Chamfort, N. 'Littéraires: Voyage de M. Le Vaillant dans l'intérieur de l'Afrique . . .', *Mercure de France* 138:12 (1790), 57–81.

Coetzee, J. M. *White Writing: On the Culture of Letters in South Africa*, New Haven, CT: Yale University Press, 1988.

Copans, J., J. Jamin and Société des Observateurs de l'Homme. *Aux Origines de l'anthropologie francaise: les memoires de la Societe des Observateurs de l'Homme en l'an VIII*, ed. rev. and corrected edn, Paris: Jean Michel Place, 1994.

Cullinan, P. *Robert Jacob Gordon 1743–1795: The Man and his Travels at the Cape*, Cape Town: Struik Winchester, 1992.

Diderot, D., and D. Lanni. *Supplément au voyage de Bougainville*, Paris: Flammarion, 2003.

Duchet, M. *Anthropologie et histoire au siècle des Lumières*, Paris: Albin Michel, 1995.

Forbes, V. S. *Pioneer Travellers in South Africa*, Cape Town and Amsterdam: Balkema, 1965.

George, K. 'The Civilized West Looks at Primitive Africa: 1400–1800; A Study in Ethnocentrism', *Isis* 49:1 (1958), 62–72.

Glenn, I. 'Classical Black', *English in Africa* 34:2 (2007), 19–33.

'François Levaillant and the Mapping of Southern Africa', *Alternation* 14:2 (2007), 25–39.

'The Future of the Past in English South African Literary History', *Quarterly Bulletin of the South African Library* 51:1 (1996), 38–46.

'The Man who Invented Safaris', *New Contrast* 33:2 (2005), 64–70.

'Primate Time: Rousseau, Levaillant, Marais', *Current Writing* 18:1 (2006), 61–77.

'The Wreck of the Grosvenor and the Beginning of English South African Literature', *English in Africa* 22:2 (1996), 1–18.

Good, A. 'The Construction of an Authoritative Text: Peter Kolb's Description of the Khoikhoi at the Cape of Good Hope in the Eighteenth Century', *Journal of Early Modern History* 10:1–2 (2006), 61–94.

Guelke, L., and J. K. Guelke. 'Imperial Eyes on South Africa: Reassessing Travel Narratives', *Journal of Historical Geography* 30:1 (2004), 11–31.

Huigen, S. *Knowledge and Colonialism: Eighteenth-Century Travellers in South Africa*, Leiden: Brill, 2009.

Johnson, D. 'Representing the Cape "Hottentots", from the French Enlightenment to Post-Apartheid South Africa', *Eighteenth-Century Studies* 40:4 (2007), 525–52.

Kolb, P. *The Present State of the Cape of Good Hope... With a new introduction by W. Peter Carstens*, New York: Johnson Reprint Corp., 1968.

Lanni, D. *Fureur et barbarie. Récits de voyageurs chez les Cafres et les Hottentots (1665–1721)*, Paris: Cosmopole, 2003.

Laujardiere, G. C. de C., et al. *Relation d'un voyage à la côte des Cafres (1686–1689)*, Paris: Éditions de Paris/Max Chaleil, 1996.

Le Vaillant, F., I. Glenn, I. Farlam and C. Lauga du Plessis. *Travels into the Interior of Africa via the Cape of Good Hope*, vol. 1. (2nd series, no. 38), Cape Town: Van Riebeeck Society, 2007.

Lévi-Strauss, C. 'Jean-Jacques Rousseau: fondateur des sciences de l'homme', in S. Baud-Bovy et al. (eds.), *Jean-Jacques Rousseau*, Neuchâtel: Baconnière, 1962, 239–48.

Manca, T. 'Voyages européens en Afrique Subsaharienne (xviiie et xixe siècles): poétique d'un genre, variantes et évolutions d'un discours: François Le Vaillant, Carlo Piaggia et Mary Kingsley', Ph.D. thesis, Sorbonne-Paris iv, 2005.

Merians, L. *Envisioning the Worst. Representations of 'Hottentots' in Early Modern England*, Newark: University of Delaware Press, 2001.

Paterson, W. *A Narrative of Four Journeys into the Country of the Hottentots, and Caffraria; in the Years One Thousand Seven Hundred and Seventy-Seven, Eight, and Nine*, London: printed for J. Johnson, 1789.

Paterson, W., V. S. Forbes and J. P. Rourke. *Paterson's Cape Travels, 1777 to 1779*, Johannesburg: Brenthurst Press, 1980.

Penn, N. *The Forgotten Frontier: Colonist and Khoisan on the Cape's Northern Frontier in the Eighteenth Century*, Athens: Ohio University Press and Cape Town: Double Storey, 2005.

'The Onder Bokkeveld Ear Atrocity', *Kronos* 31 (2005), 62–106.

Pratt, M. L. *Imperial Eyes: Travel Writing and Transculturation*, London and New York: Routledge, 1992.

Quinton, J. C., A. M. Lewin Robinson and P. W. M. Sellicks. *François Le Vaillant, Traveller in South Africa, and his Collection of 165 Water-Colour Paintings, 1781–1784*, Cape Town: Library of Parliament, 1973.

Rookmaaker, L. C. *The Zoological Exploration of Southern Africa 1650–1790*, Rotterdam: Balkema, 1989.

Rookmaaker, L. C., P. Mundy, I. Glenn and E. Spary. *François Levaillant and the Birds of Africa*, Johannesburg: Brenthurst Press, 2004.

Rousseau, J-J., and J. Starobinski. *Discours sur l'origine et les fondements de l'inégalité parmi les hommes*, Paris: Gallimard, 1969.

Schapera, I. *The Early Cape Hottentots Described in the Writings of Olfert Dapper (1668), Willem Ten Rhyne (1686) and Johannes Gulielmus de Grevenbroek (1695)*, trans. I. Schapera and B. Farrington, Cape Town: Van Riebeeck Society, 1933.

Sparrman, A., and J. G. A. Forster. *A Voyage to the Cape of Good Hope, Towards the Antarctic Polar Circle, and Round the World*, trans. J. G. A. Forster, London: Robinson, 1785.

Sparrman, A., and P. Le Tourneur. *Voyage au Cap de Bonne-Espérance, et autour du monde avec le capitaine Cook, et principalement dans le pays des Hottentots et des Caffres*, Paris: Buisson, 1787.

Stewart, W. E. *Die Reisebeschreibung und ihre Theorie im Deutschland des 18. Jahrhunderts*, Bonn: Bouvier Verlag, 1978.

Stresemann, E. *Ornithology from Aristotle to the Present*, Cambridge, MA: Harvard University Press, 1975.

'Voyage de M. Le Vaillant', *Journal Encyclopédique* 8:3 (1789), 496–502.

Wadström, C. B. *Observations on the Slave Trade, and a Description of some Part of the Coast of Guinea, During a Voyage, made in 1787, and 1788, in Company with Doctor A. Sparrman and Captain Arrehenius* [i.e. Arrhenius], London: J. Phillips, 1789.

PART III

*

EMPIRE, RESISTANCE AND NATIONAL BEGINNINGS, 1820–1910

Beginning in the third decade of the nineteenth century a slow evolution of new literary cultures and social imaginaries can be observed, in the indigenous languages, in English and in Afrikaans. In Chapter 9, Matthew Shum describes the early literature of the British settlement after 1820, when the colony sought to establish a white agricultural economy by settling 4,000 British citizens on the Eastern Cape frontier that it was steadily extending against Xhosa resistance. Like the literature of the Dutch settlement, much of this writing, consisting of journals, diaries, reports and letters, reflects what Shum calls the 'hard pragmatics' of early colonisation. Its most ambitious literary undertaking is associated with Thomas Pringle, who, having settled his Scottish family near Grahamstown, moved to Cape Town to take a post as a government librarian, found a school and launch a career in publishing. Pringle had been the founding editor of the *Edinburgh Monthly Magazine*, and he now started a newspaper and the more literary *South African Journal*; but if the idea was to introduce to the Cape a version of the civil culture he had known in Edinburgh, the autocratic administration of Lord Charles Somerset made this an impossible task through its strict control over all reporting on colonial governance. Pringle left after only six years to become secretary of the Anti-Slavery Society in London, where he died in 1834, leaving a small but influential body of poems and related writings, much of it informed by the abolitionist movement.

Pringle's thwarted ambitions seem emblematic of the difficulties encountered by all the emerging literate cultures of the region, which struggled not only with the ideological restrictions of empire but also with the basic essentials of literacy and print. In Chapter 10, Catherine Woeber describes the emergence of print cultures in the African languages, a process driven entirely in its early years by missionaries who created the phonetic orthographies and stilted grammars that enabled them to reduce these languages to writing and, ultimately, to produce a devotional literature. After many translations of the Bible and of Bunyan's *The Pilgrim's Progress*, the mission presses began printing newspapers and a secular literature from which developed the writing that came to be associated with early African nationalism. Tiyo Soga looms large as a figure whose career encompasses each of these phases. Typically, it took at least half a century for an editorially and financially independent journalism to develop from such beginnings. The publication of fiction in both the African languages and English by black writers continued to be managed by the mission presses until well into the twentieth century.

In Afrikaans, it is difficult to pinpoint a precise date of origin because the parturition of the language from Dutch was slow and took place within the complex social mix of the Cape from the seventeenth century onwards. In Chapter 13, H. P. van Coller discusses the history (and historiography) of Afrikaans literature alongside the history of the language, marking the highpoints when an indigenised sensibility clearly emerges. In the post-apartheid period, there has been a lively revision of Afrikaans's history, leading to general acceptance of its status as a creole influenced by Cape slaves and their descendants. By 1875 a group of intellectuals in Paarl near Cape Town, led by the teacher Arnoldus Pannevis, formed the Genootskap van Regte Afrikaners (Association of True Afrikaners), recognising that Afrikaans had become a distinctive language separate from Dutch. Somerset had sought to anglicise the Cape Colony and declared English the official language in 1822. The founding of the Genootskap half a century later is an unsurprising, long-term consequence.

The tentative and impecunious conditions that governed the development of indigenous literary cultures were in stark contrast with the rampant and lucrative market for imperial adventure fiction in Britain. In Chapter 11, Laura Chrisman describes this literature, which thrived in the last quarter of the nineteenth century and survived into the first quarter of the twentieth (with a longer legacy in popular culture, which is far from over to this day). The appetite for the genre of imperial romance, whose most famous example is Rider Haggard's *King Solomon's Mines*, was formidable and served to protect

British metropolitan readers from the disintegration of imperial ideology long after it ceased to be relevant either at home or abroad. Olive Schreiner famously demurred when the genre's popularity surfaced in the London reviews of her novel of 1883, *The Story of an African Farm*. Responding, in a preface to the second edition, to reviewers who would have preferred stories of 'wild adventure; of cattle driven into inaccessible "krantzes" by Bushman; of encounters with ravening lions, and hair-breadth escapes', she said they were 'best written in Piccadilly or The Strand'. Imperial romance provides a revealing cultural archaeology of attitudes to race, caste and gender in Britain's high imperial phase in South Africa.

It would seem that the literary cultures of the missions, of the English settlement, and of Afrikaans developed in parallel universes, but the co-presence of imperial adventure fiction should encourage us to think twice before concluding that these were entirely autonomous developments. Since the 1980s historical writing about South Africa in the nineteenth century has tended to emphasise the integrative effects of empire. The most striking example of this trend is the revised interpretation of what has been called the *mfecane* in isiXhosa and isiZulu, or the *difaqane* in Sesotho. This term, loosely translated as 'the crushing' or 'the scattering', is used to describe the forced migration of several indigenous communities following the formation of the Zulu kingdom under King Shaka. In its crudest form, however, the *mfecane* became a theory useful to settler historiography because it provided an Afrocentric explanation for the depopulation of regions in the centre and north-east of the country, thereby legitimising settler encroachment. It is now accepted that the migrations of the 1820s and 1830s were influenced by twin pressures from the south and the north-east: the Cape Colony's relentless demands for land, labour and cattle, and the effects of large-scale slave-trading by the Portuguese from Delagoa Bay (now Maputo). A further, key migration involved the departure of *trekker* parties from the British-controlled Cape into the interior, from which eventually were to emerge the Afrikaner republics of the Orange Free State and the Transvaal. These competing, largely agrarian political economies were to be transformed again in the latter half of the century, with the discoveries of diamonds near Kimberley (in 1866) and gold in Johannesburg (in 1886), which led to industrialisation at breakneck speed. Even as the industrial economy was developing, the last of the conflicts between the British and the indigenous kingdoms was being played out in Natal and Zululand in the Anglo-Zulu Wars. During the course of the nineteenth century, then, a number of relatively autonomous communities were forced into the relationships that make up modern South Africa. By the early twentieth century, as he wrote his novel *Mhudi* in London, Sol T. Plaatje could look back on the early to mid nineteenth century and discern in it a process of national formation: with restrained, Edwardian irony he could narrate a story in which Boer, Rolong-Tswana and Ndebele people could meet and negotiate their various destinies.

The nineteenth century was to end in conflagration. In Chapter 12, Elleke Boehmer discusses the literature of the Second Anglo-Boer War (also known as the South African War). On the pretext of defending the rights of foreign citizens in the Boer republics, Britain sought to gain control over their vast mineral wealth. The war that followed was brutal, in fact industrial, in the scale of its violence. Boehmer's chapter traces the representation of the war in poetry, journal writing and fiction in English and Afrikaans. The literature of the Anglo-Boer War speaks of a degree of anguished national self-recognition, an appropriate outcome following a century of collisions. The political settlement which it led to, however, namely the Act of Union of 1910, which united the former British colonies of the Cape and Natal with the Boer republics, further divided the country because it excluded Africans from full citizenship. Union, which served to consolidate a white settler-colonial state, led to an African National Convention and the founding, in 1912, of what became the African National Congress. The larger reckoning was still to come.

9

Writing settlement and empire: the Cape after 1820

MATTHEW SHUM

The period from the 1820s to the 1870s is a problematic one for South African literary history written in English. With the notable exception of the poetry of Thomas Pringle, not much happens in the official genres and no single literary work survives as anything other than a period piece. If, however, one broadens the boundaries of literary history to include a variety of genres conventionally overlooked or marginalised by it – diaries/journals, letters, articles in the periodical press, politically motivated writing, for example – then the 'field' enlarges significantly. Envisaged in this way, literary history also intersects with the expanding civic infrastructure of schools, libraries, art galleries, museums, learned societies, newspapers and periodicals. In effect, since early colonial literary activity is simply too sporadic to generate those forms of continuity which we associate with a national literature, it is necessary to expand the remit of literary history to include diverse forms of print production and cultural practice. For similar reasons, the work of outsiders commenting on South African affairs may be regarded as indigenous insofar as these writers enter into the currents of intellectual life and contribute to the formation of colonial identity. The best known and most influential of these works was Anthony Trollope's two-volume *South Africa*, an account of a five-month visit to the country published in 1878. The book provoked widespread debate among colonial readers – in itself an indication that colonial South Africans were beginning to conceive of themselves as a distinctive national group rather than merely a province of empire.

The most comprehensive documentation of print production in nineteenth-century colonial South Africa is a bibliographical record of the private library of Cape bibliophile Sidney Mendelssohn, first published in 1910 as *Mendelssohn's South African Bibliography*. Whilst the *Bibliography* was not systematically amassed, it is still very considerable, recording hundreds and hundreds of volumes. In the back of the second volume there is a tabulated section entitled 'South Africa in General', which divides the entries into general categories: column after column on Botany and Forestry, Hydrology and Irrigation, Trade, Natives, Farming and Agriculture, and so on. Then there are the entries for 'Fiction' and 'Poetry'. The former gives us, for the years 1720–1907, a scant fifty volumes; the entry on poetry records only thirty-one volumes for the period 1858–1908. These figures might not be entirely accurate, for we know of other works published in this period which the *Bibliography* does not record, but the very scarcity of literary material in relation to what we might call the empirical prose of settlement speaks for itself: the writing of imagination or sentiment was entirely marginal to the hard pragmatics of early colonisation.

Beginnings: Thomas Pringle

If one excludes the travel literature written in English prior to the settlement in 1820 (when, for the first time, a significant number of English-speaking immigrants arrived to settle as permanent residents), then the work of Thomas Pringle occupies a place of inaugural importance. It is crucial, however, to understand Pringle's work, and in particular his poetry, as the product of overlapping influences and territorial locations. Pringle arrived in the Cape Colony with a settler party in 1820 and left in 1826, following well-documented disputes over freedom of the press with Sir Charles Somerset, the autocratic Tory governor. Much of Pringle's South African writing was either written or revised in London from 1826 to 1834 (the year of his death). It was strongly inflected by his roles as secretary to the Anti-Slavery Society and editor of a widely read annual, *Friendship's Offering*, which targeted the genteel, female end of the literary market – and in which many of his poems were published for the first time. One has further to consider that Pringle was, in certain respects, a colonial Scot, who fashioned his literary career as an assimilated Englishman rather than writing in the vernacular Scottish tradition. He stands, therefore, as a paradigmatic instance of those early nineteenth-century colonial writers who, as Katie Trumpener observes, 'describe . . . the experience of empire in terms of the transcolonial consciousness and transperipheral circumstances of influence it creates' (*Bardic Nationalism*, p. 289).

These diffuse affiliations do not necessarily imply a limitation to Pringle's status as a specifically South African writer. It is surely self-evident that colonial writing in English in the nineteenth century is in various ways derivative, or that it owes its character to complex circulations between the imperial centre and its numerous colonial peripheries. In the case of Pringle, it could be argued that his work continues to engage contemporary readers precisely because of its enactment of the perceptual and generic dissonances which characterise the displacements of colonial experience. In addition, the sheer range of Pringle's writing – as poet, editor, diarist, journalist and pamphleteer, and as the author of *A Narrative of a Residence in South Africa* (1834), in which all these roles coalesce in a prose account of his colonial experience – uncannily anticipates the shape of future South African literature written in English, where the impulse towards the fictional and the imaginative is tempered by the realist imperatives of testimony and reportage.

The usual sequence in the settler literatures (I refer here to the British settlements in Australia, New Zealand, Canada and South Africa) was for a national literature to develop in tandem with the growth of national consciousness and a more distinct sense of national identity. Whilst Pringle might not have created such an identity, his contribution towards it was considerable, and it was only in the final two decades of the century that similarly significant voices began to be heard in the work of Olive Schreiner and, to a lesser extent, H. Rider Haggard. This inversion of the customary sequence of colonial literary history should not, I think, be understood as a uniquely local phenomenon. It was unusual for a highly literate, university-educated person with experience in literary journalism (Pringle was the first, short-lived editor of *Edinburgh Monthly Magazine*, the precursor of the much better known *Blackwood's Edinburgh Review*) and a reputation as a minor poet to find himself leading a party of agricultural settlers to a far-flung and hostile colonial frontier. Pringle's 'prematurity' is probably best explained by happenstance.

Settler poetry

A further issue to be considered is the simple fact that so much of the poetry produced subsequent to Pringle has had very little purchase on literary memory. The first anthology of South African verse, *Poetry of the Cape of Good Hope, Selected from the Periodical Journals of the Colony*, came out in 1828, and it was to be over half a century before the 1887 publication of another anthology, *The Poetry of South Africa*, in which Pringle, with twenty-three poems, was still the major contributor. This is not to imply that other poetry produced during this period was worthless, but that its claims upon our attention are limited. In a 1989 anthology, for example, Stephen Gray included a number of settler poets alongside Pringle, and in his *Southern African Literature: An Introduction* he argues that the verse drama by Andrew Geddes Bain, *Kaatje Kekkelbek, or Life among the Hottentots* (1838), with its creolised Dutch-English diction and its inclusive colonial focus, marks the inception of a 'multilingual African literature' rather than a literature attuned to metropolitan norms (p. 57). For this reason, Gray nominates Bain as a 'more appropriate transitional figure' for South African literature than Pringle, who never strayed in any substantial way from conventional verse forms. Gray's claim is, however, contested in Michael Chapman's *Southern African Literatures*. Whilst Chapman concedes that Bain is innovative in his use of 'localised speech' (p. 110), he finds both *Kaatje Kekkelbek* and other work by Bain to be diminished by its tendency to confirm settler 'prejudices' (p. 101). More recently, Damian Shaw has added weight to this appraisal by assembling archival evidence that in *Kaatje Kekkelbek* Bain deliberately sought to slander humanitarians such as Philip and Pringle ('Origins of *Kaatje Kekkelbek*'). Whatever the case may be, Bain's work, like other settler verse of this period besides Pringle's, remains tangential to South African literary history. It is seldom anthologised, long out of print, and rarely acts as a reference point in the critical literature. For the most comprehensive record of the poetry of this period, readers may consult G. M. Miller and H. Sergeant's *Critical Survey of South African Poetry in English* (1957).

Fictional forms: the hunter romance and the novel

The development of the fictional novel in the first phase of colonial settlement is similarly intermittent and uneven, but it does offer more coherent lines of continuity than are to be found in settler poetry. The extensive literature of travel and exploration dating back to periods well before the British settlement provided a template for later fictional and quasifictional writing, and in particular for what Stephen Gray describes as the 'hunter romance', the precursor to the imperial romance, the dominant genre of the late nineteenth and early twentieth century. Colonial travel and exploration literature, despite its ostensible grounding in the empiricism of fact and observation, frequently offers readers a variation on the quest romance, with its familiar motifs of a lone, heroic figure overcoming obstacles on the path to the attainment of a specific set of goals. If this scaffolding remains implicit in the earlier literature, in the hunter romance it is far more visible as the male protagonists venture forth to test their mettle in the African wilds. In its origins this genre was dominated by the immensely popular reminiscences of professional hunters such as William Cornwallis Harris, Gordon Cumming and Fredric Selous, but as the century progressed it soon expanded into more fully fictionalised forms (for a useful anthology see Haresnape, *The Great Hunters*). Gray makes some interesting observations on the intersections of the hunter romance with one of the central motifs of Victorian juvenilia, the initiation into manhood, as well as its persistently disingenuous claims to plain speech despite obvious literary embellishment. He further observes that while the hunter romance began to lose its allure at approximately the same time as increased occupation of the land put restraints on the practices of professional hunters, variants of the genre have proved remarkably durable. In contemporary times the illustrative example is Wilbur Smith, whose best-selling novels exploit the ongoing attraction of this genre. 'It has to be a comment on the nature of Southern African English literature', writes Gray, 'that this genre alone is the one that has produced the most works, and endured the longest' (*Southern African Literature*, p. 111). To this one might add that game parks and the 'Big Five' still remain integral to the global tourist marketing of a South African imaginary.

The hunter romance is by no means an unproblematic genre: it is generally perfunctory in its treatment of indigenous peoples and its militaristic ethos often produces an unfortunate conflation between the hunting of animals and the slaughter of people. Indeed, the genre's preoccupation with the exercise of dominance may be said to model, in an unadulterated or ideal form, the predations of colonial conquest itself. Beyond the hunter romance, no other genre emerges as notable, though David Livingstone's immensely popular *Missionary Travels and Researches in Southern Africa* (1857) successfully drew on the conventions of missionary literature and there were innumerable, lesser-known books of an adjacent sort where 'travels and researches' were motivated by other factors, such as the search for natural resources. Only a handful of fictional novels from this period have merited anything other than a mention in the scholarly literature. Of these, *Makanna; or, The Land of the Savage*, a three-decker published anonymously in London in 1834, is perhaps the best known. Indeed, Gray regards it as a precursor to *The Story of an African Farm* (1883) because its 'detailed, if somewhat windy, style of effective realism' succeeds in conveying 'the essential feelings of its characters' (*Southern African Literature*, p. 139). As Gray concedes, however, *Makanna* remains 'utterly lost', and while it is now available online there have apparently been no concerted attempts to rescue it from critical oblivion. Which is perhaps not altogether surprising: *Makanna* is a prolix and melodramatic text in which the colony and certain historical characters function as adjuncts to a fantastically contrived set of circumstances. Whilst certain passages, such as an extended description of a Boer dwelling in Volume II, at least aspire to realism, these are simply interludes in the unfolding of a plot whose central historical fabulation (an alliance between Makanna and a creole agent of the French government) is highly improbable. 'Independently of the strange absurdities of the plot', wrote Thomas Pringle shortly after the book's publication, 'and of the liberty taken with history and geography, the descriptions of South African scenery and manners given in this work do not bear even a remote resemblance to the reality' (*Narrative of a Residence*, p. 288). I see no reason to dissent from this judgement.

A more appropriate area for renewed critical interest might be the novels of Harriet Ward: *Helen Charteris* (1848), *Jasper Lyle* (1851), *Lizzy Dorian: The Soldier's Wife* (1854) and *Hardy and Hunter* (1858). The best known of these novels (long out of print and not always available even in specialist libraries) is *Jasper Lyle*, whose eponymous protagonist detours through a number of experiences (including being a Chartist leader in Britain) before being transported to Australia. He is wrecked on the Cape coast and becomes a gun-runner, supplying weapons to opponents of the government in the course of a frontier war. The novel ends with, among other things, his crucifixion at the hands of the Xhosa. In commenting on *Jasper Lyle*, Malvern van Wyk Smith makes the point that, despite being 'much blemished by Victorian sentimental romance and melodrama' (*Grounds of Contest*, p. 10), the novel is more referentially grounded than previous fiction (invariably written by outsiders), and displays tensions and ambivalences that suggest a veiled critique of the colonial order. In the only full-length study of Ward to date, Valerie Letcher supports Van Wyk Smith's contention that Ward 'wrote better than she knew' and discerns in the novel a 'subtle incitement to the reader to condemn British imperialism and racism' ('Trespassing Beyond the Borders', p. 267). Other critics are more cautious in their appraisals. Jenny de Reuck (1995), for example, warns against too easy a recuperation of Ward's writings, while Gray finds her fiction to be beset with 'frankly propagandistic intentions' (*Southern African Literature*, p. 117). However we might adjudicate between these differing responses to Ward's work, they are at least an indication that it is, in different ways, intriguing to contemporary critical sensibilities. When we further consider that in addition to her fiction, Ward was a widely published journalist at a time when the field was utterly dominated by males, then the case for renewed recognition of her work is surely a plausible one – especially given the common perception that the fictional novel has to wait for Schreiner and Haggard in the 1880s before it can be taken seriously.

It would seem that the experience of living in a new country is itself so novel that the writing of fictional or quasifictional work in the early stages of colonial settlement has an inevitably close relationship with 'factual' or documentary writing. Harriet Ward, for example, made her debut appearance with a chronicle of life on the frontier entitled *Five Years in Kaffirland* (1848), and the later fictional work derives some of its detail from this account. In a similar manner, and in a different genre, the footnotes in Pringle's poetry frequently direct the reader towards relevant factual material in his *Narrative*. In attempting to account for the prolific production of texts concerned in various ways with either the affairs or the resources of the colony, one has to be selective. Obviously those texts relating to directly empirical matters have tangential relevance for a literary history, no matter how generously it is conceived. But those texts which focus on the cultural and political life of the colony, or which recount the day-to-day experiences of the coloniser, such as diaries and letters, deserve some consideration since they supply the substrate out of which a more formal literature arises.

The writings of the humanitarians and their antagonists

The first prose genre to emerge in a distinct way from the literature of travel and exploration might be characterised as an early, anglophone version of what came to be known as 'protest writing'. In the 1820s and 1830s there were a number of polemical works by humanitarians attacking colonial treatment of indigenous peoples: John Philip's *Researches in South Africa* (1828), Saxe Bannister's *Humane Policy* (1830), Pringle's *Narrative of a Residence* (1834), and *The Wrongs of the Caffre Nation* (1837) by 'Justus' (Robert Mackenzie Beverley). Although Pringle's *Narrative* has a much broader scope than the other publications, it has in common with them a combination of advocacy and testamentary evidence that marks the inception of an enduring line of literature engaged with the ethics of colonial conduct. Counterposed against these works are settler writings such as Godlonton's *A Narrative of the Irruption of the Kaffir Hordes* (1835) and Donald Moodie's intensively researched and still consulted *The Record: or, A Series of Official Papers Relative to the Condition and Treatment of the Native Tribes of South Africa* (1838–41), which offer an account of colonial events more sympathetic to settler interests. The works of the humanitarian reformers and their antagonists also formed an important contribution to South African historiography. Their conflicting accounts of colonial events established a frame of reference that later historians, such as G. M. Theal, could not ignore (see Saunders, *Making of the South African Past*, part 1). This interventionist genre did not survive its political moment (the ascendancy of the humanitarian lobby in British politics) and it gave way to a more racially inflected consensus on the governance of indigenous people.

Yet while its heyday may have been brief, the humanitarian movement was a critical precursor to the later formation of Cape liberalism and its associated texts.

Allied to these humanitarian critiques of colonial government, and in some ways a direct result of their attempts to influence colonial policy, are documents such as the 1834 *Report from the Select Committee on Aborigines (British Settlements)*, a parliamentary hearing conducted at the instigation of the Thomas Fowell Buxton's Select Committee on Aborigines. Formed after the model of similar committees for the abolition of slavery, this committee of humanitarians was influenced by the example of the Cape Colony, and the transcriptions of its proceedings, in which both colonisers and indigenes gave testimony on relations between them, offer us a fascinating glimpse into how these groups of people conceived their worlds. Though there is evidence that indigenous testimony was, to some extent, orchestrated by officials from the London Missionary Society, the hearings of the committee marked the first time in which the voices of the colonised were represented in British parliamentary discourse.

Settler diaries and journals

Settler diaries and journals (hereafter given as journals), as well as settler letters, chronicles and 'reminiscences', are without doubt the most profuse genre of writing produced in this initial phase of settlement. Specialist publishers (in particular the Van Riebeeck Society and A. A. Balkema, in collaboration with Rhodes University) have issued limited editions of settler accounts of this period and a number have also been privately published; there doubtless remain many more such manuscripts in the archive or in the attic, awaiting future researchers. Journals (one must again stress the fluidity of this genre) covered a widely disparate range of experiences. There are collections of excerpts from journals devoted entirely to the activities of military men stationed in the colony (Boyden, *British Army in the Cape Colony*) and collections dealing with the experience of growing up on the frontiers of settlement (Butler, *When Men were Boys*). However, a methodological problem arises: what kind of valency can we grant such writings? In what ways do they constitute a 'literary history'? The journals, for example, were not explicitly written for a wider audience and were invariably published decades after the deaths of their authors and then only for a limited, specialist readership. In addition, besides its standardised temporal structuring, the journal is employed in differing ways: some journals seldom venture beyond the merely notational, others are richly detailed. Despite this unevenness, such writings can be understood as a nascent form of life writing or autobiography, the conceptualising or creating of a colonial self in contexts removed from the country of origin. Then there is the curiously interstitial and unofficial nature of this writing: the inscriptions of identity in a journal or a letter do not necessarily affirm the authorised version of the colonial project; indeed, they often attest to its failure or its fracture. The genre is also shaped by its diversity of address. The archive of missionary journals, many unpublished, is in part conditioned by the obligation on practitioners in the field to send reports to missionary headquarters, while letters 'home' often require the construction, or the maintenance, of a persona consistent with the expectations of the recipients. The private journal, on the other hand, is frequently a form of self-communing deliberately hidden from the eyes of others.

Any attempt to itemise the plethora of journals and collections of letters written during this period would serve no purpose other than tabulation. Among those which have received a more than usual share of interest are, in no particular order: the journals of the astronomer John Herschel, who played a leading role in the colony's cultural and institutional life in the 1830s; the letters of the upper-class settler Thomas Philipps, with their astute and nuanced observations on frontier life in the 1820s; the journal of the Methodist missionary John Ayliff, which records, with moving directness, the difficulties of mission work in the first decade of settlement; the letters of William Porter, the liberal Attorney-General who drew up the colony's first constitution (which, despite its failure substantively to alter the pattern of racial politics, was formally free of racial bias and its franchise more democratic than its British counterpart). Since space is limited, I will focus attention on two journals which illustrate very different experiences of settlement.

The first of these is the *Chronicle of Jeremiah Goldswain*, described by its editor as 'probably the fullest' (p. ix) record of the settlement, and as notable for its idiosyncratic orthography as it is for its class positioning. Goldswain was a sawyer from Buckinghamshire who came out in a party headed by a merchant named William Wait. The opening sections of the *Chronicle* provide a detailed description of how Goldswain (then aged 18) and the other indentured labourers engaged in a protracted battle to be discharged from the employment of their obviously exploitative master. Goldswain's account of the settlement is fascinating not only for its detailed revelation of colonial class relationships, but also for its unschooled candour. Whilst Goldswain has an unerring eye for the injustices meted out to lower-class settlers by masters and colonial officials alike, his descriptions of indigenous peoples display either scorn or incredulity. Thus 'Hottentots' are described as 'the most dispisable creatours that ever I saw' (p. 20), while the elongation of the bare breasts of Xhosa women attracts a fascinated revulsion: 'When the child is older they women throw thear Brest over thear shoulder and after they have had three or four Children thear Brestes will ang down like two pieces of skin' (p. 101). The racism of the *Chronicle* is consistent with an ingenuousness which tells us much about the lived experience of colonial life, and in particular the fears and apprehensions experienced by the poorer class of settler when they were forced into participation in the Frontier War of 1834.

In one moving section, worth quoting in full, Goldswain describes an incident in which a Mrs Forbes and her six children watched as her husband was stabbed to death. 'I Cannot beter describe their fealings and their sorrow than stating of it as folows' (p. 80), writes Goldswain, and in an unexpected shift of genre, he offers his readers the rough eloquence of a poem:

> In the year 1834 when I think of
> that eve it grieves my Hart sore
> when the blacks came on ous
> that dwelt in the east
> to burn and to murder
> and to drive of our beast
>
> when theas savages first
> in our borders they came
> they seased Mrs Forbes that
> dwelt on the plain
> poor Alick he ruen the cause
> to inquire they stabd him
> to the hart and set his house all on fier
> he think of her Loss her greaf
> and her payn Six Fatherless
> Babes and her House all in flames
> no foud and no Clothing and
> and they kaffers all in site
> and nought but they woods
> two sleep in all night.   (pp. 80–1)

Goldswain's *Chronicle* is a valuable reminder of just how threatened and precarious early settler existence could be, pitched into a future that offered no guarantees of eventual success. In a 1970 paper Guy Butler made the throwaway remark that the *Chronicle* 'is the most remarkable settler document in print... Goldswain comes through to me as a character of far greater interest than anyone in South African fiction to date' ('Non-Fictional Prose', p. 228). Whatever the merits of Butler's claim, the fact remains that Goldswain's *Chronicle* has generated no significant critical interest, nor has it been the subject of any fictional appropriation. Nonetheless, these remarks provide further impetus towards a reconsideration of this neglected text. Whilst the diary loses some of its tensions in the second volume as Goldswain's fortunes become more secure, there is still a great deal of interesting detail on the critical period from after the 1834 war until the Cattle-Killing of 1856–7. Precisely because it lacks any sense of a polite register and the constraints of the permissible, and is not beholden to metropolitan patterns of expectation, the *Chronicle*, I would argue, takes us more deeply into the experiential tenor of settler experience than any other journal of this period.

By way of contrast we might consider the *Journals of Sophia Pigot*, which represent the other end of the social and expressive spectrum of settler writing. Pigot was the daughter of a Major George Pigot, who arrived at the Cape as the head of his own party and with influential connections amongst the colonial elite. His aim was to establish a country estate in Albany, and he brought with him a large retinue of servants and dependents. An earlier journal of Sophia Pigot's, which she had written before her arrival, evoked, her editor tells us, 'a social milieu reminiscent of the novels of Jane Austen' (*Journals*, p. 2). Pigot's South African journal starts in December 1819 on the voyage over (she was 15 or 16 at the time) and ends in 1821. Although Pigot's observations are in many ways entirely unremarkable and most of the entries, often prefaced with 'Very fine day', simply specify her daily activities, they give us a fairly detailed sense of the social clustering of the middle- and upper-class settlers. Even though a late entry acknowledges that Pigot had at times to 'lay aside the accomplishments of the Drawing Room for those of the kitchen and farm yard' (p. 93), there is very little sense of her life being anything other than a more makeshift version of what she had recorded in the earlier diary: a constant stream of visitors, visits, and social gatherings with settlers of their own class and colonial or military officials, interspersed with activities such as reading and walking. Indeed, the journal is remarkable for its omission of the pressing realities of colonial life; the only references to indigenous people, for example, are fleeting and commonplace. No doubt this journal would have taken a different form were it extended into the adulthood of Sophia Pigot, but it serves to remind us how diverse and differentiated the class experiences of settlement could be. Pigot's journal is in addition atypical insofar as writing by women settlers in this genre very often offers a narrative of colonial life at odds with the proscriptions of the imperial mission and with the patriarchal and masculinist bias informing it. Indeed, it is only the journals of settler women that have attracted any significant attention from literary critics, chiefly feminist scholars.[1]

Finally, we must single out for special consideration the journal of Tiyo Soga, the first black man to be ordained as a minister in the colony. Whilst Soga's work is generally regarded as consequential within that strand of South African writing which records the rise of a black literary tradition, there is a case to be made for placing him, at least partially, within a discursive tradition shaped by British settlement. For Soga's *Journal and Selected Writings*, which cover the years 1857 to 1871, is in most respects governed by protocols of representation that had become familiar to him through his mission education and his Scottish training for the ministry. In Soga's hands, forms such as the journal and the letter book undergo a significant reshaping, as they lend themselves to the expression of a sensibility in which racial and cultural divides become unstable and hence open to very different registers of experience. Considered in their totality, the profuse number of journals and related writings of this period constitute a rich and diverse account of the experience of settlement. The historian Noël Mostert has remarked how the 'differing opinions' to be found in these records 'illustrate a unique aspect of the British arrival. From a variety of minds and outlooks, there is a flow of simultaneous observation, a collective scrutiny of the South African frontier at this dramatic point of change in its history from sharply contrasting points of view' (*Frontiers*, p. 530).

Periodical publications and cultural institutions

Then there are those writings which enter the public domain in more direct ways in such forms as periodical publications and newspapers, as well as the developing infrastructure of educational institutions, learned societies, libraries and museums which these writings facilitated and promoted. Periodical publication began with the two editions of the *South African Journal* edited by Pringle and his Scottish associate John Fairbairn in 1824, and continued through a line that included the *Cape of Good Hope Literary Gazette* and the *Cape of Good Hope Literary Magazine*, before consolidating with the *Cape Monthly Magazine* in 1857. The *Monthly* was by far the most prestigious of

---

1 See for example De Reuck, 'Women on the Frontier'; Dagut, 'Construction of Social Distance'; and Woodward, 'Marginal Midwifery'. For a bibliographic database of 'Women Travellers, Explorers and Missionaries to Africa', see www.africabib.org.

the nineteenth-century periodicals, and provided a forum for the exchange of intellectual, scientific and artistic ideas amongst the colonial elite at a time (the transition from representative government in 1853 to responsible government in 1872) when the colony was beginning to develop a more coherent sense of local identity.

Pringle and Fairbairn's *South African Journal*, short-lived as it was, provided the framework within which similar periodical publications would assert their utility to the colonial project. The *Journal* announced in its 'Prospectus' that it sought to contribute to the 'self-respect and home importance, in which the prosperity of every Country has it foundation' (*Journal* 1, 1824, n.p.). It further promoted the belief that 'this *first* literary journal' could facilitate a network of affiliated practices in the fields of religion, education, literature and science which would 'unite men together by means of their happiest feelings, and gradually transmute their coarse antipathies'. Though these speculations are offered in the subjunctive mode, the underlying intent is clear: the creation of an enlightened body of public opinion essential to an incipient civil society and the 'consolidation of native feelings, sentiments and views into a distinct and pervading character'. From the start, such scenarios were problematic in their exclusiveness; they envisaged no affiliation with indigenous structures of thought other than the codification of language and lore and posited as their primary readership a narrow class cohort which the 'Prospectus' identified as 'men of capital and ability'. In addition, as the first editorial put it, the social formations envisaged in the *Journal* were premised on an economic base of laissez-faire capitalism or free trade, 'the active spirit of commerce, with all the arts in its train'. But free trade, as Pringle himself acknowledged in a later article, was precisely what the colony lacked, controlled as it was by monopolies and mercantile interests under the patronage of Sir Charles Somerset.

Somerset's increasingly anachronistic determination not to allow the public articulation of any interests that did not coincide with his own resulted in the shutting down of both the *Journal* and the *South African Commercial Advertiser*, a newspaper, again edited by Pringle and Fairbairn, which also commenced publication in 1824. However, the impetus towards freedom of the press could not be halted, and by the end of the decade restrictions of the sort imposed by Somerset (recalled from his post in 1826, the same year in which Pringle left the colony) were lifted and newspaper and periodical publication resumed, protected by the Cape Ordinance of 1829 which revoked the obligation to seek the approval of the governor for such activities. From about this time a modest cultural infrastructure also began to establish itself: the South African Library, in existence since 1822, acted as a base for the expansion of cultural activities; a museum tentatively established in 1825 was bolstered by the establishment of the South African Institution in 1829, which explored the geography, natural history and general resources of the colony; in the same year the *South African Quarterly Journal* was issued with featured articles relevant to the work of the institution. The year 1829 also saw the establishment of the South African College and the founding of a civic theatre. A few years later the South African Institution merged with the South African Literary Society (an earlier Literary Society established by Pringle had been shut down by Somerset) to form the South African Literary and Cultural Institution. All these developments were directly modelled on British, and often specifically Scottish, precedents for the cultural mobilisation of the educated middle class, carving out a civic space unrestrained by patronage or legislative coercion. As such they shared, with little significant variation, the predispositions and the cultural values of the models they emulated.

From the beginning the periodical press was inextricable from this interlocking set of institutions. Its subscribers, as well as its contributors and editors, were drawn from the small pool of people who kept these enterprises going. Various 'literary' journals (the word referred to a miscellany of topics) succeeded Pringle and Fairbairn's initial effort. The most prominent of these was the *Cape of Good Hope Literary Gazette*, edited by Alexander Jardine, the man who took over the South African library after Pringle's resignation. Readership figures indicate that there was no significant increase in circulation: in 1824 the *Journal* had 130 subscribers and a decade later the figure was 200 for the *Gazette* (Lewin Robinson, *None Daring*, p. 232). The *Gazette* ceased publication in 1835 and it was not until 1847 that a journal with similar aspirations was published. A lengthy 'Introductory Address' to the first issue of the *Cape of Good Hope Literary Magazine* decried the long absence of a literary publication and saw itself as responding to the needs of the 'literary public of the colony' (pp. 1–2), which it felt to be sufficiently large to support such an undertaking. 'We propose to take up a position not yet occupied – to supply a deficiency not yet filled up', the address declared, adding that 'The character to which we aspire is, to be the Champion of South African Literature' (p. 3). Whilst there is no indication that the *Magazine* was ever 'instrumental in evoking some hidden talent' (p. 2), the express desire for a 'national' literature, though short of any specifics, was moving beyond the merely notional. Despite the flourish of its ambitions, the *Magazine*, like its predecessors, faded away.[2] It was not

---

2 A. M. Lewin Robinson (*None Daring to make us Afraid*) provides a detailed breakdown of the contents of Cape periodical publications from 1824 to 1835.

until the establishment of the *Cape Monthly Magazine* in 1857 that a periodical publication aimed at the general reader gained sustained momentum among both subscribers and contributors.

Some (very simplified) considerations of context are also relevant here. By the late 1840s the economy had been boosted by the expansion of sheep farming in the Eastern Cape; a rising commercial class, no longer bound by the old monopolising practices, became more assertive in the colony's affairs and more intolerant of indigenous resistance to their financial interests. The agitations of 1849, when Dutch and British colonists in Cape Town united in their refusal to countenance the use of the colony as a dumping ground for convicts, strengthened intracolonial bonds and the demand for greater self-representation. More baleful developments on the frontier also played their part: the war of Mlanjeni in the early 1850s, by far the most retributive of any of the many frontier clashes, considerably weakened Xhosa polities in the area and a few years later the Cattle-Killing broke the back of resistance to colonial rule in the region. The granting of representative government in 1853 acted as a further stimulus to economic growth since it enabled easier access to capital and loans for colonial businessmen. In the final stages of the decade the colony had a far more assured sense of itself and its future than ever before and this confidence extended to cultural achievement as well. The *Monthly* was 'notably more ambitious and successful than any of its periodical predecessors', writes Saul Dubow (*Commonwealth of Knowledge*, p. 71), an indication that there existed a network of print connections among the educated classes able to support a 'sustainable critical mass of middle class readers and opinion-formers' (p. 73). As Dubow points out, this readership advocated, and to some extent constituted, the virtues of material and cultural 'improvement'; it was also a readership that valued 'aesthetic and cultural sensibility' (p. 73). In a distant colonial echo of Coleridge's distinction between cultivation and civilisation, the first editorial of the *Cape Monthly Magazine* cautioned against the dangers of merely 'material' improvement and warned that 'A community that gives no signs of even a nascent literature of its own is still far from civilisation' (1857, p. 1). Despite the fact that the *Monthly* signalled the existence of a more numerous class of educated people, and marked a decisive shift in the development of a colonial intelligentsia, there is surely no doubt that, as Edna Bradlow has commented, the mid-century 'intellectual tone' at the Cape 'was undistinguished. The white elite was too small and too thinly spread . . . to produce a vigorous influential intelligentsia . . . The colonists did not draw on their culturally diverse society to develop their own sensibilities, but imported Anglo-Saxon artistic and intellectual assumptions, as they imported their material requirements' ('Culture of a Colonial Elite', p. 396). We should remember, too, that when literary writing coming out of South Africa in the nineteenth century did finally attract international recognition, it was sharply divided in its focus. Rider Haggard, an upper-echelon colonial bureaucrat, wrote novels that were rooted in rococo imperial fantasies rather than colonial realities; the writing of Schreiner, on the other hand, gained part of its compelling power from its depiction of the solitude and insular incivility of colonial life – the very qualities which would seem inimical to the growth of a 'national' literature.

Outsiders: Anthony Trollope

In 1878 the British novelist Anthony Trollope, widely known in the English-speaking world for his fictional evocations of the rural gentry, published a book on South Africa. The astonishingly prolific Trollope had already 'done' Australia, New Zealand, America, Canada and the West Indies, so his South African production was awaited with some wariness by the local settler population: losing colonial face was not a prospect to be welcomed. Whilst for the contemporary reader there might be obvious limits to Trollope's rather buccaneering brand of journalism, with its tendency to dispense quick and untroubled judgement and its unperturbed confidence in transposing British values to other parts of the world, the book still retains considerable interest. Trollope's vivid, impressionistic style carries a narrative of ambitious if dis-jointed scope: by carriage, cart, ship and rail, the 62-year-old author traversed all the varied regions of the expanded colony in the space of just six months. For the first time a composite sense of the entire country emerges, with all the peculiarities and perversities of its race relations, its straggling growth of towns and settlements, its chequered past and uncertain future. Trollope was by no means an unsympathetic observer of the local scene, but time and again he would revert to a comparative colonial judgement he found unavoidable and unsettling:

> I am driven again to assert the difference between South Africa, and Canada, or Australia, or New Zealand. South Africa is a land peopled by coloured inhabitants. These other places are lands peopled with white men. I will not again vex my readers with numbers . . . He will perhaps remember the numbers, and bethink himself of what has to be done before all those negroes can be assimilated and digested and made into efficient parliamentary voters. A mistake has been made; – but I do not think that because of that mistake the troops should be withdrawn from the colony.   (*South Africa*, p. 158)

South Africa was an error: a colony of a special type, in which the usual guarantees of white security and supremacy could not be assured. Although this insight was central to Trollope's understanding of the country, he could not have foreseen how this 'mistake' would be greatly compounded, and then deferred, by imminent historical events. The book contains numerous fine descriptive set pieces, one of the most memorable being an account of open-cast mining at the 'Big Hole' in Kimberley. The sight leads to an extended meditation on the rhythms of industrial work and the efficacy of wage earning, rather than religion or philanthropy, as the 'great civiliser of the world' (p. 368). The 'love of money', Trollope avers, 'works very fast' (p. 368), and he finds Kimberley 'one of the most interesting places on the face of the earth' (p. 369) because he believes it to be a kind of industrial laboratory developing the blueprint for the future social evolution of what he routinely refers to as the 'savage' races.

In its time Trollope's *South Africa* was enormously influential in shaping public opinion both in South Africa and the United Kingdom. Sections of it were serialised in metropolitan and colonial newspapers even before its final publication, and views and reviews were numerous. *South Africa* also ran through numerous abridgements and additions, making it, as Davidson comments in his introduction, 'possibly the most widely read book on the country since Livingstone's *Missionary Travels and Researches* in 1857' (p. 18). Significantly, the book appeared at a time when South African affairs were beginning to shift away from an exclusive preoccupation with the Cape towards the complications of the Dutch republics and the economic opportunities opened up by the discovery of precious minerals. In short, South Africa was beginning to assume both its present territorial extent and the contours of the industrial modernity which would define its future. The country was also starting its long career as an international conundrum: in 1878 British prime minister William Gladstone memorably described South Africa as 'the one great unsolved, perhaps unsolvable, problem of our colonial system' (quoted in Davidson's, 'Introduction', p. 18). The achievement of Trollope's book was to conduct 'a national audit of a country in the making' (Dubow, *Commonwealth*, p. 132), to offer an assessment of the colony in which it might begin to discern some of the patterns which would shape its future.

Bibliography

Anon. *Makanna; or, The Land of the Savage*, 3 vols., London: Whittaker & Co., 1834.

Ayliff, J. *The Journals of John Ayliff*, ed. Peter Hinchcliff, Cape Town: Balkema, 1971.

Bannister, S. *Humane Policy, or Justice to the Aborigines of New Settlements Essential to a due Expenditure of British Money, and to the Best Interests of the Settlers, with Suggestions How to Civilise the Natives by an Improved Administration of Existing Means* [1830], London: Dawsons, 1968.

Boyden, P. B. *The British Army in the Cape Colony: Soldiers' Letters and Diaries, 1800–1858*, London: Society for Army Historical Research, 2001.

Bradlow, E. 'The Culture of a Colonial Elite: The Cape of Good Hope in the 1850s', *Victorian Studies* 29:3 (1986), 387–403.

Butler, G. 'Non-Fictional Prose, with Special Reference to Early Diaries and Reminiscences in English', *English Studies in Africa* 13:1 (1970), 221–33.

When Men were Boys, Cape Town: Oxford University Press, 1969.

Chapman, M. *Southern African Literatures*, Scottsville: University of Natal Press, 2003.

Dagut, S. 'Gender, Colonial "Woman's History" and the Construction of Social Distance: Middle Class British Women in Later Nineteenth-Century South Africa', *Journal of Southern African Studies* 26:3 (2000), 555–72.

De Reuck, J. 'Women on the Frontier: Self Representations of the Conqueror: Which Frontier? Conqueror of What?', *Current Writing* 7:1 (1995), 34–45.

Dubow, S. *A Commonwealth of Knowledge, Science, Sensibility and White South Africa, 1820–2000*, Cape Town: Double Storey, 2006.

Godlonton, R. A. *A Narrative of the Irruption of the Kaffir Hordes, 1834–1835* [1836], Cape Town: Struik, 1965.

Goldswain, J. *The Chronicle of Jeremiah Goldswain, Albany Settler of 1820*, vols. I and II, ed. U. Long, Cape Town: Van Riebeeck Society, 1949.

Gray, S. *Southern African Literature: An Introduction*, Cape Town: David Philip and London: Rex Collings, 1979.

Haresnape, G. *The Great Hunters*, London: Parnell, 1974.

Herschel, J. *Herschel at the Cape: Diaries and Correspondence of Sir John Herschel, 1834–1838*, ed. D. Evans et al., Cape Town: Balkema, 1969.

Letcher, V. H. 'Trespassing Beyond the Borders: Harriet Ward as Writer and Commentator on the Eastern Cape Frontier', Ph.D. thesis, Rhodes University, Grahamstown, 1996.

Lewin Robinson, A. M. *None Daring to make us Afraid: A Study of English Periodical Literature in the Cape Colony from its Beginnings in 1821 to 1835*, Cape Town: Maskew Miller, 1962.

Livingstone, D. *Missionary Travels and Researches*, London: John Murray, 1857.

Mackenzie, B. ('Justus'). *The Wrongs of the Caffre Nation*, London: James Duncan, 1837.

Mendelssohn, S. *Mendelssohn's South African Bibliography*, London: Kegan Paul, Trench & Trübner, 1910.

Miller, G. M., and H. Sergeant. *A Critical Survey of South African Poetry in English*, Cape Town: Balkema, 1957.

Moodie, D. *The Record: Or, A Series of Official Papers Relative to the Condition and Treatment of the Native Tribes of South Africa* [1838–41], Cape Town: Balkema, 1960.

Mostert, N. *Frontiers: The Epic of South Africa's Creation and the Tragedy of the Xhosa People*, London: Pimlico, 1992.

Pigot, S. *The Journals of Sophia Pigot*, ed. M. Rainer, Cape Town: Balkema, 1974.

Philip, J. *Researches in South Africa Illustrating the Civil, Moral and Religious Condition of Native Tribes*, London: James Duncan, 1828.

Porter, W. *The Touwfontein Letters of William Porter*, ed. K. Schoeman, Cape Town: South African Library, 1993.

Pringle, T. *African Poems of Thomas Pringle*, ed. M. Chapman and E. Pereira, Scottsville: University of Natal Press, 1989.

   A Narrative of a Residence in South Africa [1834], Cape Town: Struik, 1966.

Saunders, C. *The Making of the South African Past: Major Historians on Race and Class*, Cape Town: David Philip, 1988.

Shaw, D. 'Two "Hottentots", some Scots and a West Indian Slave: The Origins of *Kaatje Kekkelbek*', *English Studies in Africa* 52:2 (2009), 4–14.

Soga, T. *Journal and Selected Writings of the Reverend Tiyo Soga*, Cape Town: Balkema, 1983.

Stapleton, R. J. (ed.). *Poetry of the Cape of Good Hope, Selected from the Periodical Journals of the Colony*, Cape Town: Greig, 1828.

Trollope, A. *South Africa* [1878], ed. J. H. Davidson, Cape Town: Balkema, 1973.

Trumpener, K. *Bardic Nationalism: The Romantic Novel and the British Empire*, Princeton University Press, 1997.

Van Wyk Smith, M. *Grounds of Contest: A Survey of South African Literature*, Cape Town: Juta, 1990.

Ward, H. *Five Years in Kaffirland, with Sketches of the Late War in that Country, to the Conclusion of Peace. Written on the Spot*, London: Henry Colburn, 1848.

   Hardy and Hunter: A Boy's Own Story, London: George Routledge & Co., 1858.

   Helen Charteris. A Novel, 3 vols., published anonymously, London: Richard Bentley, 1848.

   Jasper Lyle: A Tale of Kaffirland, 2 vols., London: George Routledge & Co., 1851.

   Lizzy Dorian, the Soldier's Wife: A Tale, London: John Henry Jackson, 1854 (no copies in existence).

Wilmot, A. (ed.). *The Poetry of South Africa*, Cape Town: Juta, 1887.

Woodward, W. 'Marginal Midwifery: Hannah Dennison and the Textualising of the Feminine Settler Body in the Eastern Cape, 1834–1838', *Current Writing* 7.1 (1995), 18–33.

10

The mission presses and the rise
of black journalism

CATHERINE WOEBER

Throughout a roughly fifty-year period in the late nineteenth century which saw the emergence of African nationalism, articulated in the black press by the rising Christian elite, there were specific nodes that facilitated early black print culture. What Switzer ('Introduction', p. 22) has called 'the African protest press' was nurtured in indigenous Christian communities that emerged from rural stations which European and American missionary societies first estab-lished in southern Africa during the early nineteenth century. The mission schools of the various societies working among the indigenous peoples created literate (*kholwa*) communities on mission stations, and their presses gradually produced a literature in the vernacular among the amaXhosa and Batswana in the Cape Colony, the Basotho in Basutoland (Lesotho) and the southern Orange Free State, and the amaZulu in Natal and Zululand.

Whilst the spoken languages of the various indigenous peoples were highly developed and their traditional lore abundant, none had a written alphabet, so the task before the early missionaries from various missionary societies was to provide orthographies for the different vernaculars, to initiate a culture of reading and writing, and to disseminate the Scriptures and other religious material to an increasingly literate readership. 'The preaching and teaching ministry', notes Switzer in *Power and Resistance* (p. 119), 'were dependent on the mission's control and manipulation of literate culture.' Most mission stations acquired a printing press in order to publish devotional and evangelical litera-ture and to assist in the industrial training of new male converts. Newspapers and periodicals would issue from these presses, originally under missionary editorship but increasingly, as the century progressed, under black editorship.

By the mid 1880s an independent, secularised and increasingly rebellious press had begun. The reasons for that transition have been fully documented over the last three decades by Switzer (most recently in his extensive intro-duction to *South Africa's Alternative Press*), and it is now understood that the ethos and forms of mission literacy and print production defined the terms on which local black written literatures were to emerge (see De Kock, *Civilising Barbarians*, pp. 64–104). The mission-educated newspapermen fulfilled the roles of what Anderson (*Imagined Communities*, p. 65) has termed 'pilgrim functionaries' and 'provincial printmen', by moving between metropole and colony (and perhaps 'forward' towards modernity), even as they were located in specific areas and communities, and were to generate a new nationalist consciousness by the start of the twentieth century.

Mission-sponsored translations and monographs

Early missionaries were, in the main, Protestant evangelical nonconformists from the revivals that had swept through Britain and parts of western Europe and north America in the late eighteenth and early nineteenth centuries. The two texts which were invariably translated into the main vernaculars were the Bible and the *Pilgrim's Progress*. Because the *Pilgrim's Progress* encapsulated the evangelical message, the book virtually became a fetish in the mission system, and was widely considered a substitute for the Scriptures themselves. The earliest translations of the Scriptures into the vernacular were done by Robert Moffat of the London Missionary Society (Congregationalist) at his mission station at Kuruman, in the northern Cape Colony. In 1830 he published the Gospel of Luke in Setswana, the printing being done at the government printers in Cape Town. In 1840 his Setswana translation of the New Testament appeared in London (with 500 copies being brought to the Cape by his son-in-law David Livingstone), and the Old Testament followed in 1857. Moffat's Setswana version of the *Pilgrim's Progress*, the first in any African vernacular on the African mainland, was published in London in 1848.

Twenty years later, the isiZulu translation, done by Bishop John William Colenso, and probably William Ngidi, between 1865 and 1868, was published by a commercial press in Pietermaritzburg, Natal. Because white missionaries were second-language speakers – even though Colenso was a considerable linguist and would publish his *Zulu–English Dictionary* in 1884 – they were dependent on first-language converts with whom they worked, so that mission translation was routinely a joint affair. The New Testament in isiXhosa was completed by the Glasgow Missionary Society (Presbyterian) at Tyumie in the eastern Cape Colony in 1838 and published in 1846, and it was followed by the Old Testament in 1857. The complete Bible in isiXhosa was published in 1865, and revisions undertaken by the Glasgow Missionary Society were completed in 1887. Tiyo Soga, the first black clergyman, participated in the revision process before his early death in 1871. He himself translated into isiXhosa the

New Testament, and the first part of the *Pilgrim's Progress* as *Uhambo lo Mhambi*. Begun during his theological training in the United Presbyterian Church in Glasgow in the 1850s, it was published by Lovedale Press in 1868; the second part was translated by his son, John Henderson Soga, and published in 1929.

Soga's fine translation was to exercise an influence on written Xhosa literature comparable to that of the Authorised Version on English literature. It was, moreover, doctrinally precise, 'no easy task for a translator working with a recently minted Christian terminology and an unsteady orthography' (Hofmeyr, *Portable Bunyan*, p. 118). The text went through countless editions, and was prescribed, together with the original version, as a set work at Lovedale in the Eastern Cape from 1883. Lovedale Institution, the alma mater of so many of the black Christian elite drawn from across southern Africa, was established as a mission station by the Glasgow Missionary Society in 1824, later rebuilt on a new site near the Tyumie River, and opened in 1841. The *Pilgrim's Progress* appealed to the *kholwa* elite at the time, because of their preoccupation with ideas of 'betterment', 'progress', and 'improvement', and 'the story became an alembic that could distill these broader debates and provide an image fluid enough to accommodate very different ideas of where one might be headed' (Hofmeyr, *Portable Bunyan*, p. 116). Tiyo Soga was undoubtedly the pioneer literary figure in what Attwell has termed the 'transculturation of enlightenment', comprising the recasting of European forms into African terms, 'a historical and archival reality of black print culture in South Africa' (*Rewriting Modernity*, p. 21). Soga composed several hymns, first published by the Glasgow Mission Society in 1864, and later included in most other Protestant hymnals. One entitled *Lizalis' idinga lakho, Thixa Nkosi yenyaniso* (Fulfil Thy Promise, Lord God of Truth) has been described by T. S. N. Gqubule as 'almost a national anthem' (Switzer, *Power and Resistance*, p. 121).

Even if 'devotional, evangelical, and primary educational themes acceptable to the missionaries continued to dominate book and pamphlet production in the vernacular' (Switzer, *Power and Resistance*, p. 121), local indigenous literatures owe an indisputable debt to the early mission presses. The New Testament in Sesotho appeared in 1855, and the whole Bible in 1883, while the Sesotho translation of the *Pilgrim's Progress*, done by a Swiss missionary, Adolphe Mabille, and Filemone Rapetloane of the Paris Evangelical Mission Society in Basutoland, was published by Morija Press in 1872. Although R. H. W. Shepherd, last superintendent of Lovedale, considered translation of the Scriptures to have 'generally served the secondary purpose of setting standards for purity of language' ('African Literature', p. 603), Solomon Tshekiso

Plaatje – according to Switzer, 'perhaps the most prominent linguist, translator, literary figure and pioneer investigative journalist of his generation' ('Introduction', p. 27) – called missionaries' orthography into question, and the dynamics of reducing indigenous languages to writing, particularly when those languages had multiple dialects, were fraught.

Because missionaries 'claimed the right to "own" and codify African languages', the result, as Hofmeyr has noted, was often 'a mission-made language not always fully recognisable to its speakers and a world of racially supervised literary and cultural production' (*Portable Bunyan*, p. 22). The Reverend J. Tom Brown, for example, had compiled the first Setswana dictionary, *Lokwalo loa Mahoku a Secwana le Seeneles*, in 1876, the year of Sol Plaatje's birth, and it was updated in several editions, the last being the 'official' *Secwana Dictionary* of 1925. Aware of its inadequacies, Plaatje began lexicographical work towards an authoritative dictionary, but all that survives is his annotated copy of the 1925 edition. 'Plaatje's handwritten comments in this, though, are of considerable interest,' according to Willan ('Sol T. Plaatje', p. 92), 'revealing as they do more of his reasons for the dissatisfaction with the existing compilation as well as containing a hundred or so words that Plaatje had added to it.' Plaatje attributed the lack of standardisation in his tongue to disagreement among the various missionary societies working across scattered Batswana territory – and, importantly, their ignoring the native speakers of the language. Although Setswana had been one of the very first vernaculars to be committed to writing, by the 1920s it was being overtaken by work that had been done in the others, particularly isiXhosa and Sesotho.

The standardisation achieved in isiXhosa and Sesotho was largely owing to the influential missions at Lovedale in the Eastern Cape, and at Morija in Basutoland, the latter established by the Paris Evangelical Missionary Society, which were responsible for most of the material published in the respective vernaculars from the 1860s well into the twentieth century. Both Lovedale (in 1861) and Morija (in 1874) would become fully fledged commercial printing and publishing concerns, comprising a book-binding department, book depot and distribution agencies. Morija Printing Works eventually produced publications in forty-five African languages for countries across the continent, 'probably a unique achievement for a mission press' (Switzer and Switzer, *Black Press*, p. 3). Lovedale Mission Press initially concentrated on religious and educational publications, such as hymn books and devotional books, primary school Readers, grammars and dictionaries. However, the early twentieth century saw the entry of indigenous traditions into print, a domain which had tended to be condemned and sidelined by the various missions. Under

R. H. W. Shepherd, Lovedale became the major publishing centre for African literatures in the subcontinent, printing mainly in English and isiXhosa.

The first collection of customs and proverbs in Sesotho, Azariele M. Sekese's *Mekhoa ea Basotho le maele le litsomo*, had appeared just before the turn of the century in 1893, and Thomas Mofolo's Sesotho novel, *Moeti oa Bochabela* (Traveller to the East) was published by Morija Press in 1907. Notwithstanding the influence of the *Pilgrim's Progress* on Mofolo's novel, its use of Sesotho oral tradition has been recognised by Hofmeyr, and 'a brief glance through the text reveals poems, songs, passages, and oral narratives dropped as direct quotation into the text' (*Portable Bunyan*, p. 171). Also indebted to Bunyan's allegory was the first isiXhosa novel, H. M. Ndawo's *Uhambo lukaGqobhoka* (Christian's Journey), published by Lovedale Press in 1909. In 1906, Walter B. Rubusana's 500-page anthology of traditional isiXhosa poetry and lore, *Zemk' inkomo Magwalandini* (Preserve your Heritage; or, more literally, There go your Cattle, you Cowards) – which included material collected from oral tradition as well as that culled from the pages of early black newspapers – was published privately in London; a second edition appeared in 1911. London was also the place of publication of Sol Plaatje's 1916 collection, *Sechuana Proverbs with Literal Translations and their European Equivalents* – and, as Plaatje states in the introduction, he 'decided to adopt in this book the language and orthography used by the Sechuana newspapers' (in Willan, *Selected Writings*, p. 220). This illustrates the influence the black press had on the reduction of indigenous traditions to writing, especially when a book of proverbs was published beyond the aegis of the mission presses and their contentious orthography.

Newspapers and serial publications

Basutoland (Lesotho)

The Paris Evangelical Missionary Society had first begun producing evangelical tracts in Sesotho at Beerseba, in the southern Orange Free State, during the 1840s and later, during the 1860s, at Bethesda (now Maphutseng) and Masitise in Basutoland. The first serial publication, *Moboleli oa Litaba* (The Preacher of the News), appeared in four issues from October 1841 to May 1846. The original mission press, which had been under the control of Frederic Ellenberger, was moved to Morija where Adolphe Mabille had established his own press in 1861, and the two merged to form the Morija Printing Works in 1874 – thirteen years after Lovedale Mission Press was established. In the same year the Paris

Evangelical Mission adopted as its own newspaper *Leselinyana la Lesotho* (Little Light of Lesotho), which Mabille had started in November 1863. Published monthly or fortnightly until 1908, when it became a weekly in English and Sesotho (a separate English edition appeared for six years from January 1872), it is the oldest, continual serial publication in Lesotho. *Leselinyana* reflected the broader political, social and economic realities of life in Basutoland and became an important forum for the country's literary elite. Mofolo's *Moeti oa Bochabela* was serialised in the paper from January 1907, as were works by Zakes Mangoaela, Edward Motsamai, and Azariele M. Sekese – who was a contributor of historical articles from 1892 to 1925.

A Sesotho newspaper which seems to have offered an alternative to the editorial policies of *Leselinyana la Lesotho* at this time was the short-lived *Lentswe la Batho* (Voice of the People), edited in Maseru in 1899 by Josiel Lefela. Less ephemeral was *Naledi ea Lesotho* (Star of Lesotho), a fortnightly newspaper in Sesotho founded in February 1904 by Solomon Monne in Mafeting, but which moved to Maseru in 1919. It ran as a weekly from 1911 to April 1937, when it was incorporated in the notable Sotho paper *Mochochonono* (The Comet), which had been launched by Abimaele Tlale in Maseru in 1911. *Naledi* and *Mochochonono* 'are the only known publications independent of the missionary societies, British colonial government and other white individuals and institutions' (Switzer and Switzer, *Black Press*, p. 4).

Western Cape Colony

The Cape Colony's first mission station, Genadendal, was actually established in the west by the Moravian Mission in 1738 – although it only took root early in the nineteenth century, along with its outstation Mamre, founded in 1808 – and a priority in seeking to entrench the Protestant culture of Scripture reading and the primacy of the written word was to acquire a press to print religious literature. An early novel in Afrikaans, *Benigna van Groenekloof of Mamre: Een verhaal voor de Christen kleurlingen van Zuid-Afrika* (Benigna of Groenekloof, or Mamre: A Story for the Coloured Christians of South Africa) was written anonymously by Hermann Benno Marx, a German missionary, and seen through the press in 1873 by W. F. Bechler, the white superintendent of Genadendal at the time. It tells the story of the coloured 'mother of Mamre', Benigna Johannes, one of the first Louwskloof converts and founder of the powerful Johannes clan in Mamre (see Chapter 7 in this volume). Prescribed in the Genadendal primary school, the novel was based on a serialised life story which had appeared in 1860 in the mission-printed monthly newsletter, *De Bode* (The Messenger), first issued on a simple wooden printing press which had been given to the mission in 1834 by friends in Holland, but only assembled in 1859. It also printed liturgical and catechismal books, school books, music books, books in isiXhosa, pamphlets and tracts.

Two years later, the Society for the Propagation of the Gospel donated an Albion press, which required at least five people to work it, along with book-binding equipment. On it was printed *Die Huisvriend* (The Friend of the Home), a religious journal published monthly from 1868 to 1914 in Dutch and, later, Afrikaans. The Moravian stations were multiracial until 1863 when, under pressure from white settlers, future settlement at Genadendal was limited to coloureds. From 1869 the Moravian missions in the Cape Colony were administered separately – six in the Western Cape (largely coloured) and three in the Eastern Cape (largely Xhosa). One of the latter, Shiloh, founded in 1828, is assumed to have produced the first female Xhosa newspaper poet and correspondent, Nontsizi Mgqwetho, whose idiosyncratic body of poetry and essays was published throughout the 1920s in various Johannesburg newspapers (see Chapter 36). Hermann Benno Marx's words in 1860 sound the refrain echoed by most mission stations in the nineteenth century, that 'if we can get them to read tracts, books and magazines, printed expressly for them, and adapted for their use, the beneficial effect on their minds will by the blessing of the Lord, be very great' (in Balie, *Geskiedenis*, p. 105). In 1885 Messrs Harrild & Sons donated a superior Bremner press, and male students from the Training School assisted in the afternoons with both printing and binding, a pattern which was repeated on mission stations across the country.

Eastern Cape Colony

The Wesleyan Methodist Missionary Society was operating a press at Grahamstown in the eastern Cape Colony as early as 1833, but it was moved to other towns along the frontier, before returning to Grahamstown in 1876. *Umshumayeli Wendaba* (Preacher of the News), an irregular serial published in isiXhosa between July 1837 and April 1841, is regarded as the earliest black periodical in southern Africa. It was followed by another Xhosa periodical, *Ikwezi* (Morning Star), published in association with the Wesleyan Methodists, but actually founded by the Glasgow Missionary Society at Tyumie. Four issues, from August 1844 to December 1845, were republished in *A Kaffir Reading Book* (1850); in it there appeared in print the story of the legendary seer Ntsikana as set down by his son, William Kobe Ntsikana. Some of the *Ikwezi* material was used by John Knox Bokwe, a Lovedale clergyman and noted hymn composer, in his English version of the legend which he published in various forms, including *Ntsikana, The Story of an African Hymn* (Lovedale, c. 1904) and *Ntsikana, The Story of an African Convert* (Lovedale, 1914). The Wesleyan Methodist Mission also started the first English–isiXhosa serial, *Isitunywa Sennyanga* (The Monthly Messenger), for the 'literary and religious advancement of the Xhosa', which ran from August to December 1850.

However, the first significant newspaper to be published in English and isiXhosa was launched in August 1862 by the Glasgow Missionary Society at Lovedale. The monthly *Indaba* (News) contained general interest as well as religious news, a third being in English for the 'intellectual advancement' of the reader. Both English and Xhosa sections were under the control of white editors on the Lovedale staff. Among its correspondents was Tiyo Soga who, under the pseudonym 'Nonjiba Waseluhlangeni' (Dove of the Nation), published a Xhosa letter in the first issue of *Indaba* wishing the new journal well and expressing high hopes for its preservation of traditional lore and poetry: 'Let us resurrect our ancestral fore-bears who bequeathed to us a rich heritage. All anecdotes connected with the life of the nation should be brought to this big corn-pit our national newspaper *Indaba* (The News)' (in Switzer, *Power and Resistance*, p. 161). By the time *Indaba* ceased publication in February 1865, however, Soga's hopes were unrealised, for the 'big corn-pit' never carried a Xhosa poem. It was left to its successor, *Isigidimi Sama-Xosa* – in a relatively late issue (1 October 1884) – to publish the first poem in isiXhosa, included in a letter from Thomas Mqanda, to use the form and style of oral tradition. 'Mqanda exploits the new technology of printing and the new medium of publication', notes Opland ('Isolation', p. 181), 'to reach an audience potentially wider than the *imbongi* [praise poet] could reach through oral performance.'

Isigidimi Sama-Xosa (The Xhosa Messenger, or Herald), was the most important newspaper produced in the first fifty years of the mission-sponsored press. Initially a supplement from October 1870 to December 1875 in the *Kaffir Express*, the Glasgow Mission's flagship journal, *Isigidimi* was to appear as a separate monthly – and at intervals between 1879 and 1884 as a fortnightly – until its demise in December 1888. Under James Stewart's editorship, *Isigidimi* published Xhosa poetry for the first time, but it was exclusively moral or lyrical, and written in English metres quite foreign to the oral *izibongo* (praise poetry). Elijah Makiwane, editorial assistant to Stewart, who continued editing the *Kaffir Express* (renamed the *Christian Express* in January 1876), was given the task of editing *Isigidimi*. In 1881 Makiwane was succeeded as editor by John Tengo Jabavu, a teacher and Methodist lay preacher, who would soon become a key figure in Cape politics. William Wellington Gqoba, a well-known poet and orator, took over from Jabavu in late 1884 and ran *Isigidimi* until his death, whereupon it ceased publication. By this time, the disillusionment of many of the *kholwa* elite, who were finding themselves increasingly alienated from mission culture as the missions began to support colonial society, had become evident.

In the last months of Jabavu's editorship, *Isigidimi* (1 February 1884) published a bitter Xhosa poem, 'Some thoughts till now ne'er spoken', by Jonas Ntsiko, a blind catechist from St John's Anglican mission in the Transkei, writing as 'uHadi Waseluhlangeni' (Harp of the Nation). Isaac Wauchope, under the pseudonym of I. W. W. Citashe, had earlier published the now iconic Xhosa poem, 'Your cattle are gone, my countrymen!' in *Isigidimi* (1 June 1882), in which he urged black resistance to colonial society no longer with the breechloader, but with the pen. What has been termed the 'secondary resistance' of the pen included 'aspects of colonial modernity such as education, Christianity, journalism, and political organisation' (Attwell, *Rewriting Modernity*, p. 5). Besides providing the space for disaffected poetry and political debate, *Isigidimi*'s last two editors would use their leaders and columns to persuasive, and often divisive, effect. 'Jabavu sensed that the depths of protest had hardly been tapped', notes Switzer in *Power and Resistance* (p. 147), 'He brought his readers' grievances nearer the surface and got the newspaper involved in settler politics.' This was too much for Stewart, and Jabavu resigned. In November 1884 he started *Imvo Zabantsundu*, the first black-owned newspaper in southern Africa.

The story of Jabavu's groundbreaking establishment of the weekly *Imvo Zabantsundu* (African Opinion) in King William's Town, with white financial support, has been well documented (see, for example, Switzer, 'African Christian Community', pp. 455–76; De Kock, *Civilising Barbarians*, pp. 105–40). The launching of *Imvo* marks a watershed in early black journalism, dividing it into two roughly equal phases: the religious publications initiated by the missions during the 1830s, and the black-run newspapers established from the 1880s onwards. These years also saw the development of black political pressure groups, and the driving force behind the formation of several of these was Jabavu himself, whose newspaper 'sought to articulate and unify the interests and needs of a modernising elite, which by this time had emerged as a distinct social class' (Switzer, *Power and Resistance*, p. 148). *Imvo* provided both an outlet for political discussion and a medium for new forms of writing in English, such as the lecture, the essay, the anonymous editorial and the letter, which often initiated heated debate. In addition to the new 'literary' form of the didactic obituary, the earliest poems in English by black writers appeared in its pages. The first of these, 'To us a son is born', was published in *Imvo* (19 May 1892) by 'I. W. W.' (Isaac Wauchope, who by then had become an ordained minister). Some years afterwards, 'Ntsikana's Vision', a poem by 'A. K. S.' (Alan Kirkland Soga, son of Tiyo Soga), was published in *Imvo* (28 October 1897), and this was soon followed by others (republished in Couzens and Patel, *Return of the Amasi Bird*, pp. 16–19). During the South African War of 1899–1902, Jabavu's neutral, pacifist stance made him and his newspaper very unpopular with sections of colonial society. The white-owned press in King William's Town that printed *Imvo* withdrew its contract, and the paper was temporarily shut down in August 1901. Upon resumption in October 1902, it was plagued by financial problems so that, by the end of the nineteenth century, *Imvo*'s best days were over.

Other black intellectuals, of course, supported the British war effort, particularly those who had formed the South African Native Congress (SANC) in King William's Town in December 1891, and sustained black political opposition to Jabavu had begun. Since *Imvo* was increasingly perceived to be an organ of the Afrikaner Bond, Cecil John Rhodes's party, the Progressives, was looking for a newspaper to support its interests among black voters. The SANC believed in parliamentary democracy and had faith in Rhodes, who in 1898 would declare himself an advocate of 'equal rights for every civilised man'. So Rhodes's offer to help fund the launching of *Izwi Labantu* (Voice of the People) in East London in November 1897 was gratefully accepted. The Eagle Printing Press Company was formed, and the first editors of *Izwi*, a weekly in English, isiXhosa and Sesotho, were Nathaniel Umhalla and George Tyamzashe, who had started out as a journalist with *Imvo*.

Izwi soon proved a spirited competitor to *Imvo* in both poetry and politics. Within fifteen months, Umhalla was succeeded by A. K. Soga, who ran *Izwi* for the first decade of the new century and came to rival Jabavu as a protest journalist. Tyamzashe's successor was S. E. K. Mqhayi, who also wrote for *Izwi* under the pseudonym of 'Imbongi YakwaGompo' (The East London Poet). Together with his *Izwi* colleague, Walter Rubusana, a Congregationalist minister, Mqhayi pioneered the publication of books of Xhosa poetry in the early decades of the twentieth century. Rubusana was *Izwi*'s most important political writer, and became Jabavu's political foe. Although *Izwi* broke *Imvo*'s monopoly, so enhancing the black press's role as a forum for the coordination of political activity, it always struggled financially. When Rhodes died in 1902, his party stopped subsidising it, partly owing to Soga's increasingly anti-capitalist editorial line. The closure in April 1909 of the mouthpiece which 'had concretised the ideas and attitudes of its readers and translated them into viable political action programs' (Switzer, *Power and Resistance*, p. 174), dealt the SANC a virtual death blow.

Izwi Labantu actively supported the Native Press Association (NPA), formed in January 1904, but which did not survive beyond that year. Nonetheless, it represented a pioneering attempt to provide a news agency for the young black press. Sol Plaatje and F. Z. S. Peregrino – editor of the *South African Spectator*, a fortnightly English–Dutch newspaper, with an occasional column in isiXhosa, serving mainly the coloured community in Cape Town from December 1900 to 1912 – together initiated the NPA, which may have been modelled on the Negro Press Association in the United States. The constitution sent to the Principal Native Commissioner, Orange River Colony on 1 February 1904 (reproduced in Willan, *Selected Writings*, pp. 81–3), lists as its president A. K. Soga, editor of *Izwi*; its vice president, F. Z. S. Peregrino, editor of the *South African Spectator*; its treasurer, Chief Molema, proprietor of *Koranta ea Becoana*; and its secretary, Sol Plaatje, editor of *Koranta ea Becoana*. Its motto was 'Defence, not Defiance', and its aim, to protect the interests of 'the Native People's Newspaper Press of South Africa'. Its membership was confined to 'Native Africans who are British Subjects, and engaged as Editors, Publishers or Compositors, on newspapers devoted to the interest of the Native races of Africa'. ('Native' obviously encompassed both black and coloured subjects.) The possibility of reviving the NPA was mooted in 1908, but nothing concrete emerged from the discussions.

Natal Colony

Robert Grendon, the influential poet and journalist of Irish–Herero parentage, cut his printing teeth on *Inkanyiso* (The Enlightener), the first mission newspaper to be outspoken against Natal society. Started by the Anglican St Alban's College in Pietermaritzburg as a monthly in April 1889, increasing to a fortnightly later that year, and to a weekly from 1891 onwards, *Inkanyiso* was a four-page newspaper in English and isiZulu. Entitled *Inkanyiso* from its inception to February 1891 and *Inkanyiso yase Natal* (Natal Light) from March 1891 to June 1896, it was subtitled 'the first native journal in Natal' (12 March 1891), but the mistake was corrected in a later edition (9 April 1891), where it was acknowledged that 'American Missionaries on the coast' had issued a 'Native paper' as early as 1861. This was *Ikwezi* (Morning Star), a monthly Zulu religious and educational newspaper founded by Josiah Tyler of the American Board Mission (Congregationalist), which ran from April 1861 to December 1868. Printed initially in Pietermaritzburg, and later on the press at Esidumbini mission station, north of Durban, it was succeeded by a Zulu fortnightly, *uBaqa Lwabantwana* (Light of the Children), printed from January 1877 to May 1883 on the press at Umvoti. The editor of *Inkanyiso* was the Reverend Francis Green, son of the Dean of Pietermaritzburg, and copy was supplied by the staff and students of St Alban's College. An early statement of intent (*Inkanyiso*, 12 March 1891) indicated that 'by having a column or two in English, we wish to give publicity to our thoughts, in the hope that, as our English friends become more acquainted with "Native opinion", a better understanding between us may be created' (in Christison, 'African Jerusalem', p. 247). The newspaper, which provided both religious news and social and political comment, by September 1891 could claim 2,500 subscribers. In January 1895 *Inkanyiso yase Natal* was bought out by a black syndicate and, as Natal's first black-run newspaper, was published and edited by Solomon Kumalo, a teacher at St Alban's. In the last eighteen months of its life, until the withdrawal of the government subsidy to St Alban's forced its closure, *Inkanyiso yase Natal* became 'a relatively vociferous protest paper' (Switzer and Switzer, *Black Press*, p. 249).

Grendon was probably seconded from Zonnebloem College in Cape Town, where he had matriculated, to join Sikweleti Nyongwana in operating the new press, which had been supplied, as was the Albion press at Genadendal, by the Society for the Propagation of the Gospel. Zonnebloem, established by the Anglican Church in 1857 for the sons of chiefs and offering a fine academic education, boasted a non-racial student body until the early twentieth century and had an industrial school with its own printing press. Grendon was attached to the St Alban's printing department for two months from September 1889, and may well have been responsible for *Inkanyiso*'s becoming a fortnightly publication. *Inkanyiso yase Natal* would become a mouthpiece for *Funamalungelo*, an important pressure group for articulating political grievances and 'progressive' aspirations. Founded in 1887, *Funamalungelo* was a precursor to later political bodies, such as the Natal Native Congress, regional forerunner of the South African Native National Congress (SANNC) formed in 1912, and enabled the *kholwa* elite to consolidate its identity and pursue the modernity from which certain groups – traditional chiefs, mission institutions, and white settlers – wished to exclude it. 'One pressing need in such circumstances', as Hofmeyr has noted, 'was to fashion a public sphere through which an emerging elite might rehearse and refine a self-definitional repertoire of ideas, images, and discourses' (*Portable Bunyan*, p. 116). Over the years newspaper columns and epistolary networks became spaces for self-fashioning, as the demands of an industrialising society increasingly marginalised new generations of the black Christian elite and prevented them from sharing fully in colonial society.

A decade after *Inkanyiso yase Natal*'s closure, the Church of Sweden Mission (Lutheran) at Dundee started *Isithunywa* (The Messenger), a monthly devotional and evangelical publication in isiZulu only. It was produced initially by the Dundee mission's Ebenezer Press from 1905 to December 1909, before the Lutheran Church Conference publishing efforts were centralised in Durban. *Inkanyiso yase Natal* would appear to have had more in common with the weekly English–isiZulu newspaper, *Izwe la Kiti* (Our Country), launched jointly in September 1912 by the Lutheran Mission and Natal Missionary Conference, a Protestant missionary body founded in 1877, as 'an inter-denominational united Christian, educational and political newspaper for the Zulu people' (*Izwe*, 9 September 1912). Although relatively short-lived, *Izwe* was an important vehicle for the expression of black opinion in Natal at that time. Fragments of Grendon's poem, 'Dinizulu, ex-King of Zululand', and his more provocative prose appeared in the newspaper over a few months in early 1914, before *Izwe* ceased publication in June 1915 (one poetic fragment, 'A Tribute to Miss Harriet Colenso', is republished in Couzens and Patel, *Return of the Amasi Bird*, pp. 41–4). It is likely that *Izwe la Kiti* was started to counter publications appearing from the Roman Catholic mission press, particularly the influential newspaper for black readers launched in October 1910, *Izindaba Zabantu*.

Izindaba Zabantu (People's Topics) hailed from Mariannhill, the Trappist monastery founded outside Pinetown by the German, Father Franz Pfanner, in December 1882. Within a month of the mission station's founding, a hand-press was established in the Abbot's own quarters, and there 'soon appeared (January 1883) the mission-paper known as *"Fliegende Blätter"*, which circulated in Europe for the benefit of the mission', according to an issue of the *Catholic Magazine* in 1911 (see *Mission Work of the Trappists and Mariannhill*, p. 222). At the same time, a small Sotho catechism was printed for Bishop Jolivet, who had invited Pfanner to Natal. Catechisms in several vernaculars, prayer books, hymnals, as well as other publications for the use of the Trappist community were printed on that hand-press. Some dedicated brothers worked as printers and bookbinders on what became the St Thomas Aquinas Press for half a century. The *Catholic Magazine* reported that the 'most important branch of our industries is the printing and bookbinding establishment, with which is connected stereotype, electrotype, and type of foundry work' (*Mission Work*, p. 33). A later issue noted that Mariannhill was believed to have the only type foundry in southern Africa, and that music printing was 'a speciality with the Trappists' (*Mission Work*, p. 88). Within five years of the mission's founding, two newspapers were started, which are regarded as the first for black readers published by the Roman Catholic Church in southern Africa.

Ingelosi Yenkosi (The Angel of the Lord) was a monthly devotional publication launched in 1888 by Anthony T. Bryant, an Englishman and the son of a printer, who arrived at Mariannhill towards the end of the first year of its existence, and took the name Father David upon his ordination in 1886. The Zulu newsletter ran for only a few years, as did its secular counterpart, *Izwi Labantu* (Voice of the People), launched by Father Franz Pfanner at the same time, but this was an English–isiZulu newsletter, more in keeping with the Abbot's eclectic outlook, and it ceased publication along with its counterpart. Bryant, who built up a reputation as an authority on Zulu customs and traditions, published his extensive, but not uncontroversial, *Zulu–English Dictionary* through the mission press in 1905. The real flagship of the St Thomas Aquinas Press, however, was *Izindaba Zabantu*, which became *Umafrika* (The African) in December 1928. Originally a fortnightly general interest isiZulu–English newspaper, it became a weekly in 1911 and early in its history also contained pieces in Afrikaans, Sesotho and isiXhosa. Under Bryant's editorship for the first five years, and afterwards (its editorial directors would always be white Trappists), *Izindaba Zabantu* established a reputation for its accurate mirroring of events of interest to communities in Natal and, in due course, nationally.

Between the demise in June 1896 of *Inkanyiso* through political interference and the start of *Ipepa lo Ilanga* (The Paper of the Nation) in 1898 or 1899, Natal had no black-run newspaper. It was only in June 1898 that the three proprietors of the Zulu Publishing Syndicate, Limited announced their intention to launch *Ipepa*, a weekly in English and isiZulu, in Pietermaritzburg. *Ipepa*'s contributors were, in most cases, founder members of the Natal Native Congress, and prominent members of the Wesleyan Methodist mission at Edendale, outside Pietermaritzburg – which itself for a few months in 1893 had published *Umsizi Wabantu* (The Helper of the People), a weekly English–isiZulu religious and educational journal. The first editor of *Ipepa* was Mark Samuel Radebe, who had been educated at Lovedale and was active in both Wesleyan Methodist circles and *Funamalungelo*. He would be succeeded by Cleopas Kunene, who, although a local man like Radebe, had been educated at Healdtown, the Methodist mission school established near Fort Beaufort in the Eastern Cape in 1853, which John Tengo Jabavu also attended. Robert Grendon published half a dozen poems in *Ipepa* between 1901 and 1904, including the first three parts of his epic, *Paul Kruger's Dream*, which he serialised before the poem's publication in Pietermaritzburg in 1902. In 1901, by which time the newspaper had 550 subscribers, pressure from the Natal Native Affairs Department resulted in the proprietors deciding not to renew their publication licence, and *Ipepa* – Natal's first non-missionary paper – ceased, like *Imvo Zabantsundu*, in August 1901. It resumed publication in April 1903, only to coincide, unfortunately, with the debut of the weekly, *Ilanga lase Natal*, and shut down for good a year later.

The first editor of *Ilanga lase Natal* (The Natal Sun) was John Langalibalele Dube, the most prominent black educator at the time. *Ilanga* was published at his famous Zulu Christian Industrial School (Ohlange College), north of Durban. John Dube had received his education at the American Board's Inanda mission, established in 1847, also north of Durban, before finishing at the prestigious Amanzimtoti Institute – later named Adams College – founded in 1865 south of Durban. *Ilanga* was established some years after Dube returned from theological training at the Union Missionary Seminary in Brooklyn, at a critical time for Natal, and also national, politics. Some of the issues which dominated its pages during its first decade were the strategies employed by the Christian elite to hold their own against an increasingly hostile colonial society, questions around their place in the discriminatory constitutional framework when Union was established in 1910, and the implications of the Natives' Land Act of 1913 for the *kholwa* community who still largely worked in rural areas in the colony.

Ilanga lase Natal began as a four-page weekly in English and isiZulu, the first page of which was usually given over to advertisements. Sikweleti Nyongwana is usually taken to be the earliest known editor other than Dube, but evidence has now come to light that Grendon – who taught at Ohlange from November 1903, and was also an English sub-editor on *Ilanga* – was at the helm for fifteen months from February 1904 to May 1905, when Dube was in the United States. His inflammatory editorials and leader articles during this period call into question any generalisation that the newspaper 'ranks as one of the major outlets for moderate opinion in the history of the black press' (Switzer and Switzer, *Black Press*, p. 39). Textual and circumstantial evidence proves that, in Dube's absence, Grendon authored *Ilanga*'s English editorials, pieces 'of extraordinary value, from aesthetic, ideological, and historical points of view' (Christison, 'African Jerusalem', p. 544). Immediately after Dube's return, however, Grendon disappeared from the pages of *Ilanga*, in part owing to a fierce dispute arising over the reception of Bryant's new *Zulu–English Dictionary* which, according to *Ilanga* (7 April 1905), was 'not reckoned authoritative as far as educated natives are concerned'. In his editorial on his return (*Ilanga*, 19 May 1905), Dube took care to mollify Bryant and the broader Natal missionary establishment by pronouncing that 'men like him of European birth can be regarded as authorities on the Zulu language'. In another editorial, Dube repudiated much of what had been published by the English sub-editor while he was abroad (*Ilanga*, 9 June 1905), and he obviously felt that Grendon had gone a step too far.

Ilanga 'played an important part in the development of Zulu literature by providing useful training ground for Zulu writers' (C. L. S. Nyembezi in Christison, 'African Jerusalem', p. 527), but it also fostered the development of English literary talent. Grendon's mature poetry appeared regularly, sometimes under pseudonyms, in *Ilanga*, which also has the distinction of carrying the earliest written poem clearly attributable to a black woman, 'Africa: My Native Land'. This was published on 31 October 1913, shortly after the promulgation of the Natives' Land Act in June, and the day on which the Zulu king Dinizulu was buried. Its author, Adelaide Dube (Tantsi), had studied at Inanda Seminary, founded by the American Board Mission in 1869, and later at Wilberforce University in Ohio. She married a son of John Dube, and taught at Ohlange for many years. Though indebted to the English poetic lexicon and literary tradition, her style is consistent with that of other mission-educated writers who expressed themselves in what was taught in the schools as 'good English'. Like the didactic obituary, which became a popular form before the turn of the century – 'a kind of moral example to be followed by the reader' (Couzens, 'Widening Horizons', p. 69) – Dube's poem is an exhortation to recover Africa's lost freedom The relatively late date of the piece underlines the extent to which the world of the early black press was overwhelmingly male – from typesetters, printers and binders, to correspondents, journalists, editors and proprietors. The editors of *Women Writing Africa*, a 2003 anthology of texts by southern African women in contexts of transculturation, point out that 'print culture is "modern" in more ways than one' (Daymond et al., p. 2), and that black women in the nineteenth century never considered entering the world of print. As the twentieth century got under way, however, they grasped their opportunity – so much so that ever more publications are being uncovered.

Northern Cape Colony and southern Orange Free State

It is clear that, while not all mission publications were confined to religious matters only, 'the missionary *zeitgeist* had a profound and lasting impact at every level of the black experience and this was reflected in its serial publications' (Switzer and Switzer, *Black Press*, p. 2). The first recorded serial publication has been identified as a set of religious tracts in Setswana produced in the mid 1830s by the London Missionary Society at Kuruman in the northern Cape Colony, but the oldest Tswana periodical was *Mokaeri oa Becuana, Le Muleri oa Mahuku* (The Teacher of the Bechuana, and The Herald of the News), founded in October 1857 by William Ashton of the Kuruman mission. A four-page general interest monthly, it ran until May 1859, and included translations of colonial regulations and news of the Eastern Cape Frontier wars. The first English–Setswana periodical, *Molekoli oa Becuana* (The Bechuana Visitor), was published from May 1856 to April 1858 (and in Sesotho from June 1857). In his introduction to *Sechuana Proverbs* (1916), Sol Plaatje says that one of his 'most valued treasures' is a file of – in his spelling – *Molekudi ua Bechuana*, 'the first newspaper published in the Sechuana language, from 1856 to 1857. It was a partly religious, partly political and social monthly issued by the Rev Mr. Ludorf of the Wesleyan Mission, from the Mission Press at Thaba Nchu' in the Orange Free State (in Willan, *Selected Writings*, p. 215).

The London Missionary Society at Kuruman nevertheless could claim the substantial serial publication, *Mahoko A Becoana* (Bechuana News). This was an eight-page newspaper in Setswana which ran from January 1883 to July 1896 (but was suspended for two years from August 1887). A monthly digest of current events, but also giving mission news and topics of devotional and evangelical interest, 'the little sheet [which] increased in size and popularity until it became a fair-sized periodical with a very smart cover' was praised by Sol Plaatje a generation later:

> During the first week of every month the Native peasants in Bechuanaland, and elsewhere, used to look forward to its arrival as eagerly as the white up-country farmers now await the arrival of the daily papers. How little did the writer dream, when frequently called upon as a boy to read the news to groups of men sewing karosses under the shady trees outside the cattle fold, that journalism would afterwards mean his bread and cheese.
>
> (Willan, *Selected Writings*, p. 216)

Plaatje's whimsical approbation suggests that 'a few mission journals appear to have had some success in making the transition to publishing critical news and opinion on contemporary events' (Switzer, 'African Christian Community', p. 468), although this was not characteristic of the mission press as a whole.

In his introduction to *Sechuana Proverbs*, Plaatje claims that the 'first Native-owned newspaper was *Koranta ea Becoana* (The Bechuana Gazette), founded by Chief Silas Molema in 1901. It appeared weekly, was printed partly in

English and ran for seven years at Mafeking' (Willan, *Selected Writings*, p. 216). Plaatje was either not aware of the initiatives regarding black owner-ship of *Inkanyiso* and *Ipepa lo Hlanga* already under way in Natal in the mid to late 1890s or, perhaps, was blinkered in favour of his own tongue, for it was certainly the first black-owned newspaper in Setswana, and the one on which he learnt his trade. Although founded in what is now Mafikeng by George Whales, proprietor of the *Mafeking Mail*, in April 1901, Silas Molema bought the newspaper in August, and expanded it to two pages, including material in English. A year later Molema and Plaatje started the Bechuana Printing Works to print the English–Setswana newspaper which until then had been printed for them by the *Mail*, and launched *Koranta ea Becoana*, consisting of four pages of political and general interest news. It was dedicated to 'the amelioration of the Native', and committed to the principles of 'Labour, Sobriety, Thrift and Education'. It built up a weekly circulation of nearly 2,000 copies, mainly in the Bechuanaland Protectorate, Cape Colony, and Orange River Colony. The 'select band of black pressmen' to which Plaatje belonged 'regarded it as their duty to provide in the columns of these newspapers a forum for the expression and formulation of "native opinion"' (Willan, *Selected Writings*, p. 16), and, just as the generation before them, they were determined to expose their readers to the values and beliefs of the educated elite. Financial difficulties, however, owing mainly to the still low level of literacy among its potential readership forced the newspaper to appear less frequently from about 1905. Efforts to obtain capital from a syndicate under Badirile Montsoa were unsuccessful and, when Whales (who had bought the publication rights in February 1907) went bankrupt, *Koranta ea Becoana* ceased publication a year later.

Plaatje founded *Tsala ea Batho* (The People's Friend), originally entitled *Tsala ea Becoana* (Friend of the Bechuana), when he moved from Mafeking to Kimberley in the Northern Cape in 1910. Financed largely by relatively wealthy black farmers (the 'Tsala' Syndicate) in the Thaba Nchu district of the southern Orange Free State, and advertised as 'an independent newspaper', the English–Setswana weekly remains one of the few surviving organs of black political news and opinion for the turbulent period of its existence (June 1910 to July 1915). The early activities of the SANNC, of which Plaatje was secretary general, are recorded in the newspaper, which added material in Sesotho, isiXhosa and Sepedi when it became virtually a national newspaper, *Tsala ea Batho*, in October 1912. Plaatje left for Britain in May 1914, on the brink of World War I, as a member of the SANNC deputation protesting the

Natives' Land Act, and *Tsala ea Batho* came to an end during the prolonged time he was forced to spend overseas.

'The Voice of the Native Races of South Africa'

With the establishment of Union in May 1910, and the formation of the SANNC in January 1912, the time was ripe for a national newspaper. *Abantu-Batho* (The People), whose masthead proclaimed it 'The Voice of the Native Races of South Africa', was founded as a weekly in Johannesburg in late 1912 with a grant from the Queen Regent Labotsibeni of Swaziland on the advice of Pixley ka Izaka Seme, then a solicitor to the Swazi monarchy. Pixley Seme purchased a printing press for his new paper – possibly that of the recently defunct *Times of Swaziland* – and installed it at Sophiatown in Johannesburg. Seme, who would become president of the SANNC's successor, the African National Congress (ANC) in the 1920s, staffed the first black national newspaper with the talented black elite who would join him in the ANC, and the newspaper itself became its official organ in 1929 until it folded, probably in July 1931. As befitting a national newspaper, it carried material in English, isiZulu, Sesotho, isiXhosa and Setswana, and it incorporated two Johannesburg papers, *Moromioa* (The Messenger) – formerly *Motsoalle* (The Friend) – a Setswana–Sepedi weekly edited by D. S. Letanka, and *Umlomo wa Bantu* (Mouthpiece of the People), an English–isiXhosa weekly edited by Saul Msane, within its first few years.

D. S. Letanka and Cleopas Kunene were *Abantu-Batho*'s first joint editors, and they were followed by T. D. Mweli Skota, Saul Msane, R. V. Selope Thema and Robert Grendon. With the exception of Selope Thema, all of the English and Zulu editors of *Abantu-Batho* up to 1918 had strong ties to the Wesleyan Methodist *kholwa* community at Edendale. The national newspaper attracted prominent contributors, playing an important part in the struggle against the Natives' Land Act, and subsequently campaigning victoriously against the pass laws for women in the Orange Free State during World War I. Virtually no copies have survived of what the Switzers call 'possibly the most influential of the black protest journals of the era' (*Black Press*, p. 25), and none before 1920. However, those 'clippings and transcriptions from *Abantu-Batho* as have been located in various archival collections show that the Swazi cause received thorough treatment in the early volumes' (Christison, 'African Jerusalem', p. 775). Cleopas Kunene was succeeded as editor in December 1915 by another staunch defender of 'the Swazi cause', Robert Grendon. However, Grendon was dismissed in mid 1916, along with Saul Msane, after a dispute relating to allegations of mismanagement by John Dube of funds meant for the SANNC deputation to Britain in 1914. This issue had been broached by Sol Plaatje, who was part of the delegation stranded overseas, in a letter to *Abantu-Batho* on 30 September 1915, and provoked a heated exchange over some three months, which Grendon, as editor, unpopularly fuelled in the interests of revealing the truth – and, perhaps, to punish Dube for his dismissal from *Ilanga*. It is clear, however, that Grendon's brief tenure as editor of *Abantu-Batho* 'showed that he, for one, appreciated the proper role and independence of the fourth estate' (Christison, 'African Jerusalem', p. 794).

'Writers like Plaatje or Grendon at the turn of the century were drawing on an audience of no more than a couple of hundred thousand', remarks Couzens in 'Widening Horizons' (p. 74), and he even admits this figure is exaggerated. But in response to the steady growth of literacy in the new century, successful national newspapers would be launched, like the *Bantu World* in 1932 (with a circulation of nearly 6,000), and the popular magazine *Drum* in 1951 (see Chapters 14, 16 and 19 in this volume). None of the early black newspapers, however, exceeded a circulation of 4,000 and, until *Abantu-Batho*, 'even the militant African-owned protest press remained provincial in its audience if not in its outlook' (Switzer and Switzer, *Black Press*, p. 24). At different times and in different areas across the country the pioneer press-men 'tried to organise public discourse and provide a platform that would embrace the imagined interest of the majority population' (Switzer, *Power and Resistance*, p. 147). Though initially limited by language and locale, their endeavours, apparent in mission journals like *Indaba* onwards, were accompanied by a growing nationalist consciousness which reached its apogee around Union, culminating in the launch of an independent national press with *Abantu-Batho*. Shortly after the draft Act of Union was published in early 1908, delegates to the newly formed South African National Convention meeting in Bloemfontein proposed amendments to the exclusionary provisions of the draft and elected an executive committee, all leading politician-editors: Walter Rubusana and A. K. Soga were chosen president and general secretary of the organisation, and John Dube was elected vice president. At the follow-up conference in March 1910, Rubusana and Dube were again elected to their posts. And when the SANNC was founded in January 1912, it was Sol Plaatje who replaced Soga as secretary general, and Dube became president. If one considers that the 'pilgrim functionaries' of the national political body were also pioneer 'provincial printmen', one clearly sees the instrumental role that the emergence of an independent black press in the late nineteenth century had on the coming of age of both politics and literature in South Africa in the twentieth century.

Bibliography

Abrahams, L., and E. Hellman (eds.). *Handbook on Race Relations in South Africa*, Cape Town: Oxford University Press, 1949.

Anderson, B. *Imagined Communities: Reflections on the Origin and Spread of Nationalism* [1983], rev. edn, London and New York: Verso, 1991.

Attwell, D. *Rewriting Modernity: Studies in Black South African Literary History*, Pietermaritzburg: University of KwaZulu-Natal Press, 2005.

Balie, I. *Die Geskiedenis van Genadendal 1738–1988*, Cape Town: Perskor, 1988.

Christison, G. 'African Jerusalem: The Vision of Robert Grendon', Ph.D. thesis, University of KwaZulu-Natal, 2008.

Couzens, T. 'Widening Horizons of African Literature, 1870–1900', in Couzens and White, *Literature and Society in South Africa*, 60–80.

Couzens, T., and E. Patel (eds.). *The Return of the Amasi Bird: Black South African Poetry 1891–1981*, Johannesburg: Ravan, 1982.

Couzens, T., and L. White (eds.). *Literature and Society in South Africa*, Pinelands: Maskew Miller Longman, 1984.

Daymond, M. J., et al. (eds.). *Women Writing Africa: The Southern Region*, vol. 1, New York: Feminist Press at the City University of New York, 2003.

De Kock, L. *Civilising Barbarians: Missionary Narrative and African Textual Response in Nineteenth-Century South Africa*, Johannesburg: Witwatersrand University Press, 1996.

Friedgut, A. J. 'The Non-European Press', in Abrahams and Hellman, *Handbook on Race Relations in South Africa*, 484–510.

Hofmeyr, I. *The Portable Bunyan: A Transnational History of* The Pilgrim's Progress, Princeton University Press and Johannesburg: Witwatersrand University Press, 2004.

The Mission Work of the Trappists and Mariannhill as recorded in the South African Catholic Magazine 1891–1924: A Documentation, facsimile edition, Ashwood: Mariannhill Mission Press, 1977.

Mofolo, T. *Moeti oa Bochabela*, Morija: Morija Sesuto Book Depot, 1907.

Ndawo, H. M. *uHambo lukaGqoboka*, Alice: Lovedale Press, 1952.

Opland, J. 'The Isolation of the Xhosa Oral Poet', in Couzens and White, *Literature and Society in South Africa*, 175–95.

Plaatje, S. T. *Sechuana Proverbs with Literal Translations and their European Equivalents*, London: Kegan Paul, 1916.

Rubusana, W. B. *Zemk'inkomo Magwalandini*, Alice: Lovedale Press, 1964.

Sekese, A. M. *Mekhoa ea Basotho le maele le litsomo*, Morija: Morija Sesuto Book Depot, 1953.

Shepherd, R. H. W. 'African Literature', in Abrahams and Hellman, *Handbook on Race Relations in South Africa*, 599–611.

Soga, T. *Uhambo lo Mhambi*, Alice: Lovedale Press, 1889.

Switzer, L. 'The African Christian Community and its Press in Victorian South Africa', *Cahiers d'Etudes Africaines* 96: 24(4) (1984), 455–76.

'Introduction', in L. Switzer (ed.), *South Africa's Alternative Press: Voices of Protest and Resistance 1880–1960*, Cambridge University Press, 1997, 1–53.

Power and Resistance in an African Society: The Ciskei Xhosa and the Making of South Africa, Pietermaritzburg: University of Natal Press and Madison: University of Wisconsin Press, 1993.

Switzer, L., and D. Switzer. *The Black Press in South Africa and Lesotho: A Descriptive Bibliographic Guide to African, Coloured and Indian Newspapers, Newsletters and Magazines 1836–1976*, Boston, MA: G. K. Hall, 1979.

Willan, B. 'Sol T. Plaatje and Tswana Literature', in Couzens and White, *Literature and Society in South Africa*, 81–100.

Willan, B. (ed.). *Sol Plaatje: Selected Writings*, Johannesburg: Witwatersrand University Press and Athens: Ohio University Press, 1996.

II

The imperial romance

LAURA CHRISMAN

The South African imperial romance was a major cultural phenomenon. It peaked between 1885 and 1925, when writers published, and frequently reprinted, over one hundred romances. Rider Haggard's *King Solomon's Mines* (1885) established the prototype, with its British chivalric heroes, magnificent African warriors, faithful African servants, demonic African 'witchdoctors', big game hunting, hidden treasure and ancient civilisations. Haggard uses standard narrative features of the romance mode: a regenerative quest, marvellous episodes, coincidences, hazardous landscape, limited characterisation, and heroic triumph over a series of increasingly difficult challenges. To romance's socially conservative ethos he, and subsequent writers, added the particular racial and national inflections of British imperialism, which glorify the British as the epitome of bravery and humane paternalism. English and, at times, Scottish and Irish heroes embody these imperial-national characteristics, and operate as agents of morality, justice and order.[1]

Some prolific romancers, such as Bertram Mitford and Ernest Glanville, specialised in the South African region. Other equally prolific authors devoted only a few volumes to the country, out of their multinational range; these include British juvenile writers such as Lieutenant-Colonel F. S. Brereton, Janet Gordon, G. A. Henty, W. H. G. Kingston, Bessie Marchant, Frederick Wishaw and May Wynne. Contributing to the romance industry were writers with no personal experience of South Africa, such as these juvenile writers (with the exception of Brereton); those who had spent time in the country, including one-time government administrators Haggard and John Buchan; and those who were native or adoptive South Africans, including A. Elizabeth Douglas, Glanville, Anna Howarth, Charlotte Mansfield, Annabella Bruce Marchand, Mitford, Charlotte Moor, Thirza Nash, Olive Schreiner, Rosamond

My thanks to Ram Prasanak and Michael Zeigler for their generous research assistance.
1 A significant number of Scottish writers were active in imperial romance production, including F. S. Brereton, John Buchan, R. M. Ballantyne, Janet Gordon, Hume Nisbet and Annie S. Swan.

Southey, Jane H. Spettigue, Nora Stevenson, Elizabeth Charlotte Webster, and Atherton Wylde (the pseudonym of Frances Colenso).

The juvenile imperial romance market was considerable and its authors abundant. Parallel with Baden-Powell's scouting movement, they endeavoured to inspire and prepare a future generation of colonists, instructing youth in the techniques and ideals of empire-building and featuring adolescents or young adults as protagonists. Some authors, such as Glanville, did double-duty, producing both adult- and juvenile-directed romances. Some were 'crossover' writers who were writing, as the dedication of Haggard's *King Solomon's Mines* indicates, for 'all the big and little boys who read it'.

The classic Haggardian genre favours male imperial heroes whose masculinity is tested and proved in the course of the narrative. Yet a large number of women writers produced both adult and juvenile variants of the genre. As well as the writers mentioned above, they include Anna de Brémont, Richard Dehan (pseudonym of Clotilde Graves) and Annie S. Swan.[2] Readership of both adult and juvenile romances was diverse and multicontinental, even if publishers largely operated from within Britain and the genre's target audience was metropolitan. As Michael Chapman observes, the books were widely reviewed and consumed within a South Africa that modelled itself upon the metropole (*Southern African Literatures*, p. 129).

Historical overview and context

King Solomon's Mines was formative, but it was not the first fiction to render South Africa a site of imperial adventure. One of the earliest examples is Captain Marryat's novel of 1845, *The Mission*; subsequent works include Harriet Ward's *Jasper Lyle* (1851), A. W. Drayson's *Among the Zulus* (1868), R. M. Ballantyne's *The Settler and the Savage* (1877), Kingston's *Hendricks the Hunter* (1879) and Charles Eden's *Ula, in Veldt and Laager* (1879). These earlier narratives indicate that there was already plenty to attract writers to the region, dynamic and dramatic as it was with British–Xhosa Frontier Wars, migrations of colonial settlers, the consolidation of the Zulu kingdom, the discovery of diamonds in Griqualand and more generally, expansion of missions, trade and ethnographic enquiry. The raw materials of South Africa, then, were already a boon for writers, who were able to exploit these materials more fully from the 1880s, following developments in literacy and the mass production of affordable single-volume books.

2 See Letcher, 'A Bibliography of White Southern African Women Writers 1800–1940'.

As the fiction market expanded, so did the British Empire in southern Africa, characterised by major military aggression, armed resistance by local peoples, and political-economic upheaval. The more turbulent South Africa's reality became, the more urgently grew the need to idealise and legitimate British domination, and to demonise or discredit its adversaries. The romance answered this need. The mode belongs to a metaphysical, absolutist universe that is peopled with heroes and villains; as Northrop Frye suggests of romance, its 'moral polarizing provides the same kind of emotional release that a war does' (*Secular Scripture*, p. 36).

Writers and publishers responded rapidly to the numerous British–black African and British–Afrikaner conflicts. The Anglo-Zulu War of 1879 was among the first of this period, and quite popular, inspiring the Revd H. C. Adams's *Perils in the Transvaal and Zululand* (1887), Brereton's *With Shield and Assegai* (1899), Glanville's *The Lost Heiress* (1891), Henty's *The Young Colonists* (1885) and Mitford's *The Gun-Runner* (1893), *The Curse of Clement Waynflete* (1894) and *The Luck of Gerard Ridgeley* (1894). As the annexation of the Transvaal and resulting First Anglo-Boer War (1880–1) occurred shortly after the Anglo-Zulu War, writers often condensed both conflicts into the pages of one romance, as can be seen in the volumes of Adams, Brereton and Henty. George Fenn's *A Dash from Diamond City* (1901) and Janet Gordon's *Jacob Jennings* (1884) also address the First Anglo-Boer War.

When Cecil Rhodes and his chartered British South African Company extended imperial aggression northwards into Matabeleland and Mashonaland, the immediate results were the First Matabele War (1893–4) and the First Chimurenga (1896–7). This expansion and repeated black African resistance stimulated Mitford's writing in particular, resulting in *John Ames, Native Commissioner* (1900), *The Triumph of Hilary Blachland* (1901), *In the Whirls of the Rising* (1904) and *A Legacy of the Granite Hills* (1909). Other fictional coverage includes James Chalmers's *Fighting the Matabele* (1898) and Wishaw's *The White Witch of the Matabele* (1897). Olive Schreiner's novella *Trooper Peter Halket of Mashonaland* (1897) is an important and complex fictional intervention against Rhodesian violence, which radically challenges empire and simultaneously upholds ideals associated with the British imperial romance.

The Second Anglo-Boer War (1899–1902) prompted a fictional deluge. Inevitably, Brereton (*With Rifle and Bayonet*, 1901; *One of the Fighting Scouts*, 1902), Glanville (*The Despatch Rider*, 1900; *Max Thornton*, 1901; *The Commandant*, 1902; *A Beautiful Rebel*, 1902), Henty (*With Buller in Natal*, 1901; *With Roberts to Pretoria*, 1902) and Mitford (*Aletta*, 1900) contributed to the flood. A miscellany of writers that includes Dehan (*The Dop Doctor*, 1910), Howarth (*Nora*

Lester, 1902), Arthur Laycock (*Steve, the Outlander*, 1900), Moor (*Marina de la Rey*, 1903), Hume Nisbet (*The Empire Makers*, 1900), Southey (*Hugh Gordon*, 1915) and Swan (*Love Grown Cold*, 1902) joined them.[3] The indefatigable Mitford was again active in portraying the final armed conflict of this period, the Natal Uprising of 1906, in *The White Hand and the Black* (1907), *Forging the Blades* (1908), *A Dual Resurrection* (1910) and *Seaford's Snake* (1912). This conflict is also thought to have inspired Buchan's *Prester John* (1910).

As this suggests, the imperial romance fixed upon and reified contemporary South African events. It did likewise with the past; romancers developed historical and current topics in tandem. Independent nineteenth-century black South African nations proved a popular subject. Haggard and Mitford both produced series on the Zulu and Ndebele, set largely during the precolonial era of their sovereignty, populating them with noble warriors as well as allegedly despotic leaders modelled upon historic leaders such as Shaka, Dingaan and Mzilikazi. Haggard's 1892 *Nada the Lily* is a stand-alone 'Zulu epic'; he subsequently produced his Zulu trilogy: *Marie* (1911), *Child of Storm* (1912) and *Finished* (1917). Mitford's Zulu/Ndebele tetralogy comprises *The King's Assegai* (1894), *The White Shield* (1895), *The Induna's Wife* (1898) and *The Word of the Sorceress* (1902). Early and mid nineteenth-century white 'pioneer' history was also of interest. Douglas's *The End of the Trek* (1923); Howarth's *Katrina* (1898) and *Sword and Assegai* (1899) explore this subject matter, as does Spettigue's *A Trek and a Laager* (1901).[4]

Another significant impetus to the genre was the rapid development of monopoly capitalism, epitomised in South African's diamond and gold mining industries. Whilst a few romances dealt directly with the mining industry, many more mediated the subject through the motif of individuals questing for hidden gold or diamonds. The blunt titles of these romances signal both their topic and its commercial appeal: Haggard's *King Solomon's Mines*, De Brémont's *The Gentleman Digger* (1891), A. W. Drayson's *Diamond Hunters of South Africa* (1889), Glanville's *The Golden Rock* (1895), *The Fossicker* (1891) and *The Diamond Seekers* (1903), Mitford's *Renshaw Fanning's Quest* (1894), and Elizabeth Webster's *Potholes: An Adventure of the Diamond Fields* (1928) and *Bullion: A Tale of Buried Treasure and the Bush* (1933).

Romance's archaic form and idealist value system contradict its operation as a contemporary commodity. Such authors as Haggard present the genre as

---

3 See Weinstock, 'The Two Boer Wars and the Jameson Raid'.
4 See also Mitford's coverage of British–Xhosa Frontier Wars: *A Romance of the Cape Frontier; The Fire Trumpet* (1889); *'Tween Fire and Snow* (1892); *A Veldt Official* (1895); *A Veldt Vendetta* (1903); *Harley Greenoak's Charge* (1906); *A Border Scourge* (1910); *The River of Unrest* (1912).

a regenerative force for a metropolitan population physically and spiritually disabled by industrialisation and scientific enquiry ('About Fiction', pp. 172–80). Yet the mass-produced romance emerges from that same modernity. Such contradictions do not diminish but rather enhance romance's function as an instrument of colonial recruitment and imperial domination. Rather than encourage readers to develop a critical relationship to the material realities of imperialism, it instead seeks to escape, justify or mystify those realities.[5]

Although allied with the agendas of imperial governance, practitioners of the romance frequently deplore state administration and policies. Ballantyne criticises the early nineteenth-century Cape governor General Somerset, while Brereton, Buchan, Haggard, Henty and Mitford almost ritualistically criticise the late nineteenth- and early twentieth-century British state for poor leadership and judgement, particularly in military matters, resulting in the state's inadequate service to empire and the avoidable loss of life. The alleged cause is metropolitan ignorance, bureaucracy, arrogance and failure to heed the counsel of white settlers. The romance promotion of 'local' knowledge and authority reflects, as Hannah Arendt argues, historical tensions between metropolitan and colonial polities ('Imperialism'). At the same time, it operates as part of the ideological disparagement of 'politics' per se, in favour of a transcendent authoritarian ruling power. This project imaginatively demotes the British state and appoints in its place an ideal autonomous white settler nation, unmediated by the apparatus of formal government, and unaccountable to such.

Imperial heroics: nation, class and caste

Gentlemen heroes propel the narratives of imperial romance. The genre loosely transforms contemporary British class identities into the pre-industrial castes of the three estates. Within the fantasised romance environment of the colony, any white British male, potentially, can emerge as a gentleman, and enjoy a corollary acquisition of property and wealth. Significantly, it is the man's innate characteristics, rather than his socioeconomic formation or origins, that confer his potential for colonial nobility. Late nineteenth-century social Darwinist and eugenicist thought, with its emphasis upon biological determinism, supported this imaginary reconfiguration.[6]

---

5 See Chrisman, *Rereading the Imperial Romance*.
6 See Kidd, *Social Evolution*, and Pearson, *National Life*. See also Jones, *Social Darwinism and English Thought*.

The majority of imperial romances, however, do not extend the possibility of nobility to British working-class or artisan subjects, who occupy the margins of the fiction if present at all. An exception is the eponymous Jacob Jennings, in Gordon's novel, who is an apprentice cabinet-maker before his arrival in South Africa. Another is Laycock's eponymous Steve, who is the only Boer War hero of proletarian origins, according to Michael Rice ('Hero in Boer War Fiction'). Regarding the other end of the social spectrum, romance can give unflattering representations of those born to the upper classes. Adams includes a decadent family of the gentry, the Bostocks, who are now impoverished gamblers and villains. Ballantyne's Skyd brothers are an incompetent gentry family – described as 'Ready for anything, and fit for nothing!' – that fails in its attempts at farming. Against these, Haggard's Sir Henry Curtis is an English baronet who does fulfil all the criteria of imperial nobility; however, his unsuccessful younger brother indicates that high birth itself is no guarantee of high calibre.

Frequently, gentlemanly character surfaces in traders, hunters, prospectors and farmers, in protagonists who hail from either the British mainland or South Africa. Their natural rank takes various expressions, but skill in battle is an essential requirement, and often the culmination of the narrative itself. Martin Green argues that the imperial romance constitutes a fusion of trade and military castes:

> The mercantile hero continued to be dominant in English adventure tales right through to the days of John Buchan. But . . . England had a military caste [which] made its claims felt, in the form of a demand for romance, from Scott's time on; and if military heroes are rarely to be found in novels, there are often adventures which turn the merchant into a temporary soldier. (*Dreams of Adventure*, p. 26)

Haggard's *King Solomon's Mines* literally and figuratively unites the British forces of trade (Allan Quatermain), the military (Captain Good) and the gentry (Sir Henry). The trio's ultimate vindication as gentlemen occurs in their successful war against the despotic black African King Twala. In Henty's *The Young Colonists*, his heroic youthful traders supply goods to the government forces before, inevitably, becoming directly involved in fighting Zulus and Boers. As with Davey Crawfurd in Buchan's *Prester John*, their trading skill itself demonstrates their natural high rank, but their social capital increases with their graduation to battle. At the same time, the novel takes pains to emphasise the nobility and martial heroism of trade itself. Mr Harvey, the professional merchant, relays his and the boys' perilous trading experiences to the Colonel who immediately equates commercial and military domains: 'Your life is indeed an adventurous one . . . It needs endurance, pluck, coolness, and a steady finger on the trigger. You may truly be said . . . to carry your lives in your hands' (p. 129).

The endowment of British individuals with gentlemanly status is also, in romance, the endowment of the British nation as a whole. Britain is itself the 'natural' personification of aristocracy, but as Arendt observes, it is only within the colonies that this 'essential' racial-national character can fully exist for ideological consumption, freed from internal complications of class ('Imperialism'). Within the romance genre, British social-Darwinian supremacy emerges in direct contrast to other competing European and black African presences, past and present.

When reading romantic transformations of British gentlemen into violent, virile fighters, popular nineteenth-century anthropology needs to be borne in mind.[7] Authors such as Haggard followed modern ethnographic tenets when they construed the heroic exercise of British arms as an opportunity for the protagonists and readers to obtain psychic, physical, and sociocultural regeneration, through a controlled and temporary regression to a 'primitive' state of being. Militarism is a necessary expression of imperial character, but it is not sufficient. Unlike the Zulu people whom romance completely confines to the essentialised role of warrior supreme, British gentlemen heroes are fundamentally versatile. As well as superior fighting qualities of bravery, discipline, strength and fitness, their skill set includes enterprise and initiative; engineering and construction skills; medical know-how; canniness and quick wits; acting, make-up and physical disguise abilities; multilingualism, and ethnographic knowledge of 'the native'. They exercise restraint in both military and economic pursuits. Rarely do they instigate battles; they fight in reaction to aggression against their community or else on behalf of Africans who require or deserve their paternal defence.

It is not only against, or through, the medium of warrior Zulus that British heroes establish their superior rank. It is also by contrast with Afrikaners who typically feature as rigid patriarchs, and as racists who abuse and exploit black servants. Afrikaners' illiberal, treacherous and clannish characteristics signal their ineligibility for gentlemanliness, notwithstanding their casting as brave fighters and hunters. A significant number of 'good' Afrikaners are also present in this same fiction, but they are defined by their proximity to the British-identified qualities of fair-mindedness, commitment to justice, and liberal

7 See Lubbock, *The Origin of Civilisation* (1870), and Tylor, *Primitive Culture* (1871).

paternalism. Such qualities, as well as their friendship with British heroes, and their proven willingness to protect the British from hostile Afrikaners or Africans, differentiate them from their home community. Adams, Ballantyne and Jacobs (whose book was later retitled *My Boer Chum*) are among the writers that include such honorary British gentlemen Afrikaners.

Noble heroes create, or uphold, the rule of law. Romances often highlight this legality through its antithesis, anarchic criminality, which claims both white and black subjects who gamble, steal, defraud, speculate, engage in illicit diamond trading, rustle cattle, murder and form gangs, as work by Adams, Ballantyne, Buchan, De Brémont, Marchant and Mitford suggests. Industrial modernity contributes to lumpen life choices, fomenting greed, corruption and alcoholic depravity. However, lawlessness also develops in rural environments. In the hinterland setting of Ballantyne's *The Settler and the Savage*, a Malay slave Jemalee, Booby the 'Bushman' shepherd and Ruyter the 'Hottentot' run off and join a band of robbers. Likewise, in Mitford's *Renshaw Fanning's Quest* the rural Cape hosts two criminal black Africans, Muntiwa and Booi, who rustle cattle and kill 'Hottentot' families on their escape from jail.

Imperial British stature requires recognition by racial or national others who demonstrate self-sacrificing loyalty to that authority. Recognition can resemble deification, as for instance occurs in *King Solomon's Mines*, when the Kukuana venerate the English trio. The trope of the white boy raised by black Africans provides automatic recognition and elevation of the white gentleman, as we see in Drayson's *The White Chief of the Caffres* (1887) and Wishaw's *The White Witch of the Matabele* (1897). Romance's convergence of mystical and national authority ultimately turns the British not only into natural gentlemen but also into divinely entitled kings. As Buchan puts it in *Prester John*: 'That is the difference between white and black, the gift of responsibility, the power of being in a little way a king' (p. 225).

Gendering empire

Gender politics of the imperial romance have stimulated considerable critical discussion. That the genre validates and thematises patriarchal masculinity is unarguable. More open to debate is the view that the genre itself originates from a desire to dominate and police women, or to symbolically control their reproductive power (see McClintock, *Imperial Leather*). Another view posits the romance as a homosocial project, which seeks to exclude women, and active heterosexuality, from the colonial arena, as threats to the operations of empire (Smith, 'Every Man').

Scrutiny of South African imperial romance suggests, however, the irreducibility of the genre to a monolithic sexual impulse, anxiety or explanation. Different romances assign different functions to women, sexuality and nuclear-familial domesticity, all of which reinforce an imperial agenda. What does emerge, across the genre, is that gender identities and functions are racially specific. Haggard's map to King Solomon's Mines provides a feminised landscape, which critics such as McClintock cite to support claims about the general sexual symbolism of empire. Yet this map is also racialised: the mountains that the heroes must climb are 'Sheba's Breasts', which pronounces their association with the ancient African queen. Masculinity is also racially specific in its representations, as *King Solomon's Mines* indicates. Umbopa has offered to travel with the trio. Sir Henry asks him to stand up, and he does, simultaneously slipping off his clothes. Quatermain observes: 'He certainly was a magnificent-looking man; I never saw a finer native. Standing about six foot three high he was broad in proportion, and very shapely.' Sir Henry walks up to Umbopa, looks into Umbopa's 'proud, handsome face' and remarks in English: 'I like your looks, My Umbopa, and I will take you *as my servant*' (emphasis added). It is to this servile inscription of his masculinity that Umbopa responds, in isiZulu: '"It is well", and then with a glance at the white man's great stature and breadth, "we are men, thou and I"' (p. 70).

For some writers, romance permits the fantasy of a womanless adventure that frees men to bond and fight together, uninterrupted by the responsibilities of domesticity or the distractions of heterosexuality. Haggard and Buchan exemplify such homosocial yearning, which frequently shifts into a homoerotic register. All-male activity is, however, regularly threatened or dissolved by inescapable forces of heterosexual desire in Haggard's work: thus, Sir Henry couples with Nyleptha in *Allan Quatermain*; Captain Good is tempted to romance with Foulata; in *She* both Holly and Leo fall under the spell of Ayesha. Only the first example culminates in union, marriage and procreation; significantly, Nyleptha is the only white female listed here.

For Haggard and Buchan, then, imperial romantic adventure provides a satisfying but finite escape from hetero-normativity. For Adams, Ballantyne and Mitford, adventure by contrast facilitates white heterosexual union and colonial settlement; the romance narrative is a combination of these elements. For others, such as Webster in *Potholes*, or Brereton in *With Shield and Assegai*, adventure creates the material conditions for colonially empowered males to return to Britain (Scotland in these two instances) and marry.

Indeed, white womanhood can, in the imperial romance, play a crucial role in literally and figuratively reproducing empire. Mitford, in particular, underscores the value of white female agents of empire. In *Renshaw Fanning's Quest*, Mitford has Marian, the young ideal future wife for Fanning, arm herself and use the gun as a fatal instrument to defend the household against marauding criminal black men. Model imperial femininity for Mitford generally includes martial ability, fitness, bravery, level-headedness and enterprise, which are also, unsurprisingly, properties of British gentlemen. Mitford contrasts Marian with young Violet, signalling her unfitness for South African settlement and reproduction by her hysterical conduct during this crisis.

Mitford's fiction renders white women as complementary, albeit subordinate, to white males, whose function is to protect and provide for these mates and mothers in the process of establishing empire. Marchant's fiction extends the reach of imperial femininity to include heroic girls and young women, demonstrating their suitability for colonial South African life, marriage and motherhood with their triumph through a series of challenging adventures. The eponymous Molly of One Tree Bend, for instance, saves drowning women, rescues babies, drives mules in a thunderstorm, and even lies atop her wagon in the storm to prevent the wind from blowing the goods away. Her moral heroism is equally developed; she bravely confronts her uncle and guardian about the immorality of his livelihood. Unlike the boys in Henty's *The Young Colonists*, Molly does not get to kill large animals and people, though she does save a banker from being shot by throwing herself at the assailant and pushing his gun upwards.

Marchant places a large emphasis on female entrepreneurship and self-reliance, encouraging girls to develop the farming and trading skills to support themselves. Throughout the novel (and in *Held at Ransom* also), Marchant presents the majority of men as physically – or ethically – challenged, and inferior to women upon whom they depend. The list includes Bertie, who dies young, an invalid from rheumatic fever; Molly's reprobate and finally reformed uncle, who never recovers from a broken leg; the one-armed male 'Kaffir' servant who pushes Bertie's wheelchair about in Johannesburg. The novel concludes with Molly's engagement to Tom and the display of her successful flower-growing business, achieved by the time she is age 20; within this business, and household, her uncle is merely an auxiliary, and Tom will be also.

Marchant's fiction is saturated with anti-black racism; her support for white female empowerment is consistent with her support for colonial expansion.

Her example suggests that white women writers are not, by virtue of their gender, necessarily predisposed towards anti-racist or anti-imperialist perspectives. It is, however, worth pointing out that among imperial romance writers, two women, Schreiner and Colenso (writing as Atherton Wylde) display the most liberal attitudes towards recently dispossessed black Africans, while they remain within the racist framework of the romance genre. It is also among white women writers such as Howarth, Marchand and Spettigue that sympathetic representations of Afrikaners are most pronounced.

British–Afrikaner intermarriage and reproduction is a significant feature of imperial romance, occurring too frequently (and across several decades of Anglo-Afrikaner conflict) to be inconsequential. Most foregrounded are unions between British heroes and Afrikaner women: in Adams, Annchen Vander Heyden marries George Rivers; in Ballantyne, Bertha Marais marries Charlie Considine; in Haggard's *Marie*, Marie Marais marries Allan Quatermain. Adams and Howarth (in *Nora Lester*) also sympathetically portray adult men who are the offspring of a British father and Afrikaner mother. (Marriage between Afrikaner men and British women also takes place, among more secondary characters: in Ballantyne, Gertie Brook marries Hans Marais; Jacobs's 'good' Afrikaner Hendrik de Merwe marries a Scottish woman, while in Adams's novel George's widowed mother has married an Afrikaner.)

Such intermarriage usually occurs only after the prospect has met with initial resistance by the Afrikaner girl's patriarch (who often has another Afrikaner suitor in mind). This pattern establishes, through contrast, the preferable romantic liberalism of white British males. That they eventually triumph and marry suggests the utility (for the authors) of intermarriage, as a means to promote both British domination and an Anglo-Afrikaner coalition of whiteness. Such a coalition seems to rest upon a eugenic and a pragmatic political understanding; reproduction across British and Afrikaner families will promote superior racial health as well as assist in conflict resolution. The prominence of 'natural' familial ideology more broadly serves as a trope for the 'naturalness' of white occupation of South Africa.

Romance carefully stages its presentation of threatening black females, not only containing the threat but also rendering it a means to reinforce its racial and patriarchal-familial agendas. Nubile African women (Foulata, for example, in *King Solomon's Mines*) raise one threat, miscegenation. Another threat is emasculation, provided by senior African women who have assumed political and spiritual power rather than submit to the protocols of domesticity and motherhood (Gagool and her *isanusis* in *King Solomon's Mines*; Ayesha in Haggard's *She* is a complicated Arabian variant of this). Haggard solves both threats by the women's death, which converts them into imperial assets. Foulata's death safely transforms sexual threat into an affirmation of empire; it establishes her selfless devotion to the imperial trio and thus confirms their supremacy. The heroes use Gagool's superior knowledge, the result of her antiquity and unwomanly political authority, to gain access to the mines. At the same time, her political opposition to the British Empire is compromised by her representation as an unnatural female who has transgressed the natural patriarchal order. Her resistance to the trio becomes as unnatural as her rejection of normative femininity.

Schreiner, in *Trooper Peter*, however, presents black womanhood in a radically different way. She critically highlights white men's rape and sexual exploitation of African women as a central feature of Rhodesian imperial conquest. Schreiner also positively represents the political agency of African women in resisting colonisation. The Shona women Peter has appropriated as concubines and domestic workers escape, taking Peter's gun and ammunition with them, to assist the first *Chimurenga*.

Romantic racism

Racism is foundational to the imperial romance, as it was to British domination; it justifies the conquest, dispossession and exploitation of indigenous peoples. Within romance all representations of black Africans – whether minor or major characters, whether romantically elevated, casually patronised, or vilified – are vehicles for white supremacy, 'self-consolidating Other[s]' in the words of Gayatri Spivak ('Three Women's Texts', p. 254). The imperial romance is indeed an ideal medium for racist ideology: its hero–villain dualism suits an imperial condition of fundamental and absolute opposition between white and black, which anti-colonial thinker Frantz Fanon famously termed 'colonial Manicheism' (*Wretched of the Earth*, pp. 41–52). The romantic dimension of the genre adds a further twist through its frequent use of 'noble savage' imagery; this is most pronounced in the representations of Zulu and Ndebele peoples as supreme antagonists. Some critics find in 'noble savage' representation – with its positive account of black warrior cultures and bodies – strong evidence for imperial self-doubt, and conclude from this that the imperial romance is a genre that threatens to disrupt the tenets of imperialism (see for example Poon, *Enacting Englishness*). The view taken here, however, is that noble savage mythology supports empire. It helps to articulate and then resolve anxieties created by black South Africa's strenuous and repeated political resistance to white rule.

Imperial romances advance a rigid hierarchy of black South African peoples. 'Bushmen' are the lowest on the evolutionary ladder, repulsive to look at, inclined to murderous hostility, generally inassimilable into empire; examples of derogatory representations are in Ballantyne, Drayson's *White Chief*, Mitford's *Renshaw Fanning* and Wylde. Second lowest are 'Hottentots', 'Koranna', 'Griqua', who are equally repulsive but can be loyal servants, in possession of good 'animal' skills of scent and sound; examples include Ballantyne, Haggard's *King Solomon's Mines* and Mitford's *Renshaw Fanning*. Xhosa people (often termed 'Kaffirs') feature as good warriors, and as loyal or as treacherous servants, but do not receive the same widespread romantic elevation as Zulus; examples include Drayson's *White Chief*, Marchant, Mitford and Ward. Sotho peoples surface intermittently in the imperial romance, often as servants, as with 'Jim' in Haggard's *King Solomon's Mines*. Wylde is atypical in characterising the Sotho as extraordinary warriors; they are merely mediocre scouts in Buchan. At the pinnacle are the 'warrior' Zulus and Ndebele, who can be credited with physical beauty, oratorical gifts, shrewd reasoning skills, and celebrated for their bravery and fighting skills, nostalgically evoked. Examples abound across authors, but Haggard and Mitford provide the most prolific coverage.

The romantic elevation of Zulu peoples operates with strict conditions. Their beauty must be rendered an anomaly among black African peoples, and associated with allegedly lighter skin, straighter hair, and angular rather than flat noses. Romance codes such features as a heritage of Semitic or North African peoples. Buchan describes the Zulu anti-hero Reverend Laputa as one who 'had none of the squat and preposterous Negro lineaments, but a Hawk nose like an Arab' (*Prester John*, p. 19). Notably, Haggard withholds beauty from the two Kukuana (fictionalised Zulu) who actively oppose the British Empire, Twala and Gagool, who instead are ugliness personified. The widespread erotic fetishisation of male Zulu bodies – especially evident in Buchan, Haggard and Mitford – participates in a dynamic of racist objectification and consumption. The desire that speaks through it is not transgressive of imperial capitalism but is, instead, its product.

Another condition of representation is that Zulus originate elsewhere than South Africa. Romance generally characterises them as a people from the north, whose southern 'invasion' occurred in distant history. This geographical difference, like their physical appearance, fictionally distinguishes Zuluness from generic black South Africanness. It also works to establish the alleged imperialist dimensions of Zulu polity. Not only nineteenth-century Shaka and Mzilikazi but their ancient forefathers become empire builders who violently subdued indigenous populations and who are as alien to the territory as contemporary Europeans, or more so. Romances frequently describe Shaka as a black Napoleon, as we see in Adams, Buchan and Haggard.

The noble imperial savage is, then, a device that turns Zulus into a fantasised mirror, reflecting back to the British an idealised valour and virility that they wish for themselves. Michael Lieven argues, of Mitford's historical Zulu tetralogy, that it

> validates the virtues and values of a warrior caste at a time of wars of conquest by black kingdoms, both through the nature and form of the genre itself and through the glorification of supposed Zulu qualities. [This] also validates, by extension, the British warrior caste, insofar as that caste can match the heroic and aggressive qualities of this 'imagined' Zulu nation. It is this validation of the imperial project which underlies much of the mythologizing, in British popular culture, of the Zulu people.   ('Contested Empire', unpaginated)

Not only Zulu militarism but also the alleged absolutism of Zulu royal leadership appeals to romancers such as Haggard and Mitford. This representation allows them to project on to Zulu polity their desire for British imperial authoritarianism, and at the same time to condemn Zulu leaders for despotism. It is such despotism – in itself or in conjunction with succession disputes, uncontrollable self-destructive bloodlust and a fatal weakness for beautiful women – that dooms the kingdom to extinction as a sovereign power. This applies not only to earlier nineteenth-century historical romances, focused largely on internecine Zulu conflict (with the Retief massacre a further addition), but also to romances concerned with the recent Anglo-Zulu war. The Zulu warriors can then be rendered the tragic victims of a tyrannical ruler who cannot act other than as his racialised essence dictates. The downfall of the noble Zulu kingdom becomes a matter of fate rather than white imperial aggression.

British affirmation of Zulu military-imperial greatness occurs in the safe aftermath of their historical defeat (1879), when after a formidable resistance they became a colonised people. Their kingdom then becomes available for romantic elegy and nostalgia. And only then do fictional individual survivors such as Haggard's Umslopogaas gain admission to the adventure unit of the British, as fighting allies and faithful servants. By the time of Buchan's *Prester John* (1910), romance cannot countenance even an imaginary loyal Zulu; Buchan's racial reasoning takes segregation to the next level.

The representational differences between *King Solomon's Mines* and *Prester John* reveal some shifts within racist South African culture. In Haggard's romance, the British trio operates as kingmaker, aiding Umbopa/Ignosi to gain the crown of Kukuanaland (a fictionalised Zululand) from the usurper Twala. In Buchan, Davie Crawfurd and Captain Arcoll are, on the contrary, king killers. They effectively eliminate the threat of the militant, university-educated, ordained Zulu Reverend Laputa, who, claiming the African crown of Prester John, organises a mass movement to reclaim South Africa from white power and reinstate traditional black culture and society. Approaching his death, Laputa calls himself the last African king. Upon his suicidal leap into the water, wearing the legendary gem-studded collar of royalty, Davie and Arcoll also acknowledge Laputa as a king, whose death is furthermore, they state, the death of romance. By 1910 the threat of black nationalism is such that even the romantic apparatus of 'noble savagery' has itself to be symbolically terminated.

Buchan's termination is wholesale; it targets African oral expression. Haggard confidently includes Zulu oratory, lauding Umbopa's eloquence for its poetic and metaphysical properties, and offering it for British readers' consumption. Buchan, however, registers such oratory as fundamentally dangerous; Laputa's rhetorical ability seduces Davie, disguised as one of Laputa's followers, to the point of (temporary) rapturous surrender. Consequently the charismatic source, Laputa, needs elimination. Buchan also targets 'traditional' political culture. Haggard concludes *King Solomon's Mines* with Kukuanaland's entry into the 'indirect rule' of British Empire promoted by Theophilus Shepstone; this system maintains the trappings of Zulu traditional polity while subjecting the kingdom to imperial control. Such an arrangement is unthinkable for Buchan, who promotes, instead, all surrender of African polity to direct white domination, in the form of a college which will give 'the Kafirs the kind of training which fits them to be good citizens of the state. There you will find every kind of technical workshop, and the finest experimental farms, where the blacks are taught modern agriculture' (*Prester John*, p. 230). Pointedly the college administrator, a Scot like Crawfurd, turns the region into an image of Scotland: 'the loch on the Rooirand is stocked with Lochleven trout', he writes, and the Machudi area, where Laputa's movement was strong, is now 'white with sheep' (p. 232).

Natural capital

Romance idealises imperial acquisition of wealth and property. The treasure quest is one of its most salient devices. British adventurers succeed in locating and removing uncut diamonds from the earth, as in Marchant's

Held at Ransom, and Mitford's *Renshaw Fanning's Quest*, or where they have already been mined and stored in chests, as in *King Solomon's Mines* and *Prester John*. To diamonds, Buchan and Haggard add gold, which has been turned into coins, neatly combining the two major mineral commodities of South Africa. Romantic presentation mystifies the process of capital accumulation, removing the mining industry from view. Instead of corporations, unaided individuals extract the stones. The severe challenge of accessing and exiting the treasure caves becomes an heroic life-endangering trial whereby the representatives of empire prove their entitlement to the treasure. In Haggard and Buchan, the heroes are further entitled by their service to empire; Haggard's trio 'earns' the wealth by restoring order and rightful rule to the Kukuanas; Buchan's Davie is awarded a share of the treasure by the British government, for 'saving the country' from black overthrow.

Heroic entitlement to treasure rests upon the assumption that the indigenous populations lack entitlement. Haggard and Mitford suggest that black South Africans do not appreciate the economic value of the stones and instead accord them only cultural-symbolic value; because of this, they do not merit a share in the wealth that results. Their own archaic traditions, rather than imperial capitalism, prevent them from gaining profits. At the same time, imperial romance often reveals its heroes to be dependent upon black assistants, whose resources of topographical knowledge (Gagool, Laputa), food provision (Foulata) and manpower (Marchant's Koos) are crucial to white treasure acquisition.

However the notion of economic profit, of surplus, threatens to debase romantic idealism, and consequently romances develop a variety of techniques to dissociate their heroes' wealth acquisition from the taint of materialistic greed. The heroes typically do not obtain the full treasure, but only a fitting proportion of it, enough to enable a comfortable rather than extravagant existence. Marchant, however, denies her heroine Judy even that much; she loses all of her proceeds from the diamonds in a fire. Mitford takes a much more lenient stance; he allows his villain Sellon to escape South Africa taking the huge Eye diamond and an adulterous relationship with him. His hero, Fanning, receives a gentlemanly share of wealth from the smaller diamonds in the crater.

Haggard softens the taint of materialism by associating acquisition of the stones with natural instinct of self-preservation. Allan Quatermain explains, on their exiting the cave, that 'If it had not, from the habits of a lifetime, become a sort of *second nature* with me never to leave anything worth having behind, if there was the slightest chance of my being able to carry it away, I am sure I should not have bothered to fill my pockets' (*King Solomon's Mines*, p. 226). Quatermain describes the largest diamonds as resembling 'pigeon eggs', another way to naturalise and justify accumulation (p. 217). Diamonds become food rather than profit.

Mineral commodities require a degree of fictional moderation and modification to fit the idealistic template of imperial romance. But romance openly harnesses black human bodies to the processes of capital accumulation. One of the most telling instances is the death of the Zulu manservant Khiva during a hunting expedition, who in saving the life of Captain Good is torn in two by an elephant. Allan Quatermain first records that it took two days to remove and bury the tusks, then enthuses about the quality and weight of the ivory, before relaying: 'As for Khiva himself, we buried what remained of him in an ant-bear hole, together with an assegai to protect himself with on his journey to a better world' (p. 79). Although Khiva's life and death further the heroes' wealth, his burial is of secondary importance; Haggard unselfconsciously prioritises commodity extraction. The black body is a 'natural' instrument of imperial economic gain.

Bill Schwarz argues that 'Within the colonial sensibilities of the English especially, South Africa has functioned as both the fantasised frontier of the nation and as the utopian image of what actually-existing England, destroyed by the mundane forces of an unforgiving modernity, is not' ('Romance of the Veld', p. 65). The imperial romance played a primary role in establishing South Africa's imaginary function for the metropole. Its continued British currency is evident in the popularity of John Wilcox's South African romances. The geographical reach of the genre extended, in the early twentieth century, to what is now Zimbabwe. The Rhodesian imperial romance, whose early authors include Gertrude Page and Cynthia Stockley, retains currency in the hands of Wilbur Smith. Within South African literature itself, the imperial romance quickly became entrenched as a major popular form that even serious novelists could not ignore. Sol Plaatje and Peter Abrahams, in the first half of the twentieth century, adopted and subverted elements of the genre to fashion a black nationalist aesthetic, in their respective novels *Mhudi* (1930) and *Wild Conquest* (1950). The late twentieth-century fiction of Nadine Gordimer and J. M. Coetzee incorporates and criticises the imperial romance. In particular, it is their 1970s works – Gordimer's *The Conservationist* (1974), Coetzee's *Dusklands* (1974) and *In the Heart of the Country* (1977) – that most overtly engage with the genre. Through rapid digitalisation, nineteenth-century South African romances are now entering a new and global phase of consumption.

Bibliography

Adams, H. C. *Perils in the Transvaal and Zululand*, London: Griffith, Farran, 1887.

Arendt, H. 'Imperialism', in *The Origins of Totalitarianism* [1951], London: André Deutsch, 1986.

Ballantyne, R. M. *The Settler and the Savage: A Tale of Peace and War in South Africa*, London: Nisbet, 1877.

Brereton, F. S. *One of the Fighting Scouts: A Tale of Guerrilla Warfare in South Africa*, London: Blackie, 1902.

  With Rifle and Bayonet: A Story of the Boer War, London: Blackie, 1901.

  With Shield and Assegai: A Tale of the Zulu War, London: Blackie, 1899.

Buchan, J. *Prester John* [1910], West Valley City: Waking Lion Press, 2006.

Chalmers, J. *Fighting the Matabele*, London: Blackie, 1898.

Chapman, M. *Southern African Literatures*, London: Longman, 1996.

Chrisman, L. *Rereading the Imperial Romance: British Imperialism and South African Resistance in Haggard, Schreiner and Plaatje*, Oxford University Press, 2000.

De Brémont, A. *The Gentleman Digger: A Study of Johannesburg Life*, London: Sampson, Low, 1891.

Dehan, R. [Clotilde Graves]. *The Dop Doctor*, London: Heinemann, 1910

Douglas, A. E. *The End of the Trek: A Story of South Africa*, London: Melrose, 1923.

Drayson, A. W. *Among the Zulus: The Adventures of Hans Sterk, South African Hunter and Pioneer*, London: Griffith & Farran, 1868.

  Diamond Hunters of South Africa, London: Griffith & Farran, 1889.

  The White Chief of the Caffres, London: Routledge, 1887.

Eden, C. *Ula, in Veldt and Laager: A Tale of the Zulus*, London: Marcus Ward, 1879.

Fanon, F. *The Wretched of the Earth*, trans. R. Philcox, New York: Grove Press, 2005.

Fenn, G. M. *A Dash from Diamond City*, London: Nister, 1901.

Frye, F. *The Secular Scripture and other Writings on Critical Theory 1976–1991*, ed. J. Adamson and J. Wilson, University of Toronto Press, 2006.

Glanville, E. *A Beautiful Rebel*, London: Long, 1902.

  The Commandant, London: Digby, Long, 1902.

  The Despatch Rider, London: Methuen, 1900.

  The Diamond Seekers: A Tale of Adventure by Veld and River, London: Blackie, 1903.

  A Fair Colonist, London: Chatto & Windus, 1894.

  The Fossicker: A Romance of Mashonaland, London: Chatto & Windus, 1891.

  The Golden Rock, London: Chatto & Windus, 1895.

  The Lost Heiress: A Tale of Love, Battle and Adventure, London: Chatto & Windus, 1891.

  Max Thornton, London: Chatto & Windus, 1901.

Gordon, J. *Jacob Jennings, The Colonist; Or, The Adventures of a Young Scotchman in South Africa*, Edinburgh: Oliphant, Anderson & Ferrier, 1884.

Green, M. *Dreams of Adventure, Deeds of Empire*, London: Routledge, 1979.

Haggard, H. R. 'About Fiction', *Contemporary Review* 51 (February 1887), 172–80.

  Child of Storm, London: Cassell 1912.

  Finished, London: Ward, Lock, 1917.

  King Solomon's Mines [1885], ed. G. Monsman, Peterborough: Broadview Press, 2002.

Marie: An Episode in the Life of the Late Allan Quatermain, London: Cassell, 1911.

Nada the Lily, London: Longmans, Green, 1892.

She, London: Longmans, Green, 1887.

Henty, G. A. *With Buller in Natal; Or, A Born Leader*, London: Blackie, 1900.

With Roberts to Pretoria: A Tale of the South African War, London: Blackie, 1902.

The Young Colonists, London: Routledge, 1885.

Howarth, A. *Katrina: A Tale of the Karoo*, London: Smith, Elder, 1898.

Nora Lester, London: Smith, Elder, 1902.

Sword and Assegai, London: Smith, Elder, 1899.

Jones, G. *Social Darwinism and English Thought: The Interaction Between Biology and Social Theory*, Brighton: Harvester, 1982.

Kidd, B. *Social Evolution*, London: Macmillan, 1894.

Kingston, W. H. G. *Hendricks the Hunter; Or, The Border Farm, a Tale of Zululand*, London: Hodder & Stoughton, 1879.

Laycock, A. *Steve, the Outlander: A Romance of South Africa*, London: Digby, Long, 1900.

Letcher, V. 'A Bibliography of White Southern African Women Writers 1800–1940', *English in Africa* 31:2 (2004), 121–71.

Lieven, M. 'Contested Empire: Bertram Mitford and the Imperial Adventure Story', *Paradigm* 25 (1998), available at http://faculty.ed.uiuc.edu/westbury/paradigm/lieven2.html

Lubbock, J. *The Origin of Civilisation and the Primitive Condition of Man: Mental and Social Condition of Savages*, London: Longmans, Green, 1870.

McClintock, A. *Imperial Leather: Race, Gender and Sexuality in the Colonial Contest*, London: Routledge, 1995.

Mansfield, C. *Gloria. A Girl of the South African Veld*, London: Holden & Hardingham, 1916.

Marchand, A. B. *Dirk: A South African*, London: Longmans, Green, 1913.

Marchant, B. *Held at Ransom: A Story of Colonial Life*, London: Blackie, 1900.

Molly of One Tree Bend: A Story of a Girl's Heroism on the Veldt, London: Butcher, 1910.

Marryat, F. *The Mission; Or, Scenes in Africa*, London: Longman, Brown, Green & Longmans, 1845.

Marwick, E. *The City of Gold: A Tale of Sport, Travel and Adventure in the Heart of the Dark Continent*, London: Tower, 1896.

Mitford, B. *Aletta: A Tale of the Boer Invasion*, London: White, 1900.

A Border Scourge, London: Long, 1910.

The Curse of Clement Waynflete: A Tale of Two Wars, London: Ward, Lock, 1894.

A Dual Resurrection, London: Ward, Lock, 1910.

The Gun-Runner: A Tale of Zululand, London: Chatto & Windus, 1893.

Harley Greenoak's Charge, London: Chatto & Windus, 1906.

In the Whirls of the Rising, London: Methuen, 1904.

The Induna's Wife, London: White, 1898.

John Ames, Native Commissioner: A Romance of the Matabele Rising, London: White, 1900.

The King's Assegai: A Matabili Story, London: Chatto & Windus, 1894.

A Legacy of the Granite Hills, London: Long, 1909.

The Luck of Gerard Ridgeley: A Tale of the Zulu Border, London: Chatto & Windus, 1894.

Renshaw Fanning's Quest: A Tale of the High Veldt, London: Chatto & Windus, 1894.

The River of Unrest, London: Ward, Lock, 1912.

A Romance of the Cape Frontier, London: Heinemann, 1889.

Seaford's Snake, London: Ward, Lock, 1912.

The Triumph of Hilary Blachland, London: Chatto & Windus, 1901.

'Tween Fire and Snow, London: Heinemann, 1892.

A Veldt Official: A Novel of Circumstance, London: Ward, Lock & Bowden, 1895.

A Veldt Vendetta, London: Ward, Lock, 1903.

The White Hand and the Black: A Story of the Natal Uprising, London: John Long, 1907.

The White Shield, London: Cassell, 1895.

The Word of the Sorceress, London: Hutchinson, 1902.

Moor, C. *Marina de la Rey*, London: Digby, Long, 1903.

Nash, T. *The Ex-Gentleman*, London: Jarrolds, 1925.

Nisbet, H. *The Empire Makers: A Romance of Adventure and War in South Africa*, London: White, 1900.

Pearson, K. *National Life from the Standpoint of Science*, London: A & C Black, 1901.

Poon, A. *Enacting Englishness in the Victorian Period: Colonialism and the Politics of Performance*, Aldershot: Ashgate, 2008.

Rice, M. 'The Hero in Boer War Fiction', *English in Africa* 12:2 (1985), 63–81.

Schreiner, O. *Trooper Peter Halket of Mashonaland*, London: Fisher Unwin, 1897.

Schwarz, B. ''The Romance of the Veld', in A. Bosco and A. May (eds.), *The Round Table, Empire/Commonwealth, and British Foreign Policy*, London: Lothian Foundation Press, 1997, 65–125.

Smith, C. 'Every Man must Kill the Thing he Loves: Empire, Homoerotics, and Nationalism in John Buchan's *Prester John*', *Novel* 28:2 (winter 1995), 173–200.

Southey, R. *Hugh Gordon: A South African Novel*, London: Duckworth, 1915.

Spettigue, J. *A Trek and a Laager: A Borderland Story*, London: Blackie, 1901.

Spivak, G. 'Three Women's Texts and a Critique of Imperialism', *Critical Inquiry* 12:1 (1985), 243–61.

Stevenson, N. *African Harvest*, London: Butterworth, 1928.

Swan, A. S. *Love Grown Cold*, London: Methuen, 1902.

Tylor, E. B *Primitive Culture*, London: John Murray, 1871.

Ward, H. *Jasper Lyle: A Tale of Kaffirland*, London: Routledge, 1851.

Webster, E. *Bullion: A Tale of Buried Treasure and the Bush*, London: Eldon, 1933.

Potholes: An Adventure of the Diamond Fields, London: Chapman & Hall, 1928

Weinstock, D. 'The Two Boer Wars and the Jameson Raid: A Checklist of Novels in English', *Research in African Literatures* 3:1 (1972), 60–67.

Wishaw, F. *The White Witch of the Matabele*, London: Griffith, Farran, Browne, 1897.

Wylde, A. [F. Colenso]. *My Chief and I; Or, Six Months in Natal after the Langabibalele Outbreak*, London: Chapman, Hall, 1880.

Wynne, M. *The Girls of the Veldt Farm*, London: Pearson, 1922.

12

Perspectives on the South African War

ELLEKE BOEHMER

The twentieth century's first modern war

The Second Anglo-Boer or South African War (1899–1902), commencing in the final months of the nineteenth century and overshadowing the beginning of the war-ridden and genocidal twentieth, represented the first modern war, as is now widely recognised.[1] In terms of its participants, its political and economic impact, and also its literary representation, the war was international in scope in large-scale ways that other late nineteenth-century conflicts like the Crimean and the Spanish-American wars had anticipated but did not match. In technological and military terms, too, the war cast long shadows across twentieth-century world history. In the major formal battles of the war's first pre-guerrilla phase – Elandslaagte, Modder Rivier, Colenso, Magersfontein – modern devices such as the field telephone, hot-air balloon reconnaissance, and the smokeless rifle were used in combination with conventional drill-block advances for the first time. The empire's volunteer army numbered up to a million men, many of them literate and educated, drawn from all corners of the globe – Canada and New Zealand, Ireland and Australia – and the Boers, too, drew on diverse international support, including from France, Russia, the Netherlands, and, again, Ireland. Correspondents hailing from as many countries again reported on activities on both sides. The powerful long-range weaponry, barbed-wire fortified trenches, and, notoriously, concentration camp installations that marked the war, and also the guerrilla tactics the Boers deployed from June 1900, represented critical, even shocking, new departures in the annals of warfare, whose destructive impact, on a mass scale, the 1914–18 conflict only magnified. As for the pessimistic Thomas Hardy pondering his 'blast-beruffled' 'Darkling Thrush' in December 1900, the turn-of-the-century hostilities, which he controversially opposed, harboured grave

---

1 See, amongst others, the work of Lowry, *The South African War Reappraised*; Pakenham, *The Boer War*; Spies, *Methods of Barbarism?*; Warwick, *Black People and the South African War*.

portents of global devastation despite the promise that mass industrialisation had once seemed to hold.[2]

Within the international arena, especially across the British Empire, the South African War represented a body blow to British imperial morale and Liberal idealism. As Britain's major war between the Napoleonic campaigns in the early nineteenth century and the First World War (1914–18), the conflict irrevocably changed perceptions of empire as making possible a world-encompassing and inviolable Greater Britain beyond the seas, dedicated to the social and spiritual upliftment of native peoples. Moreover, the war's final phases of attrition waged against the Boers, which blatantly contravened the 1899 Hague Conventions on military engagement, were quickly perceived as raising serious ethical questions with transnational implications. From the first year of the war, 'South Africa' became a humanitarian and human rights issue for people within the country and abroad, including on the European continent, and amongst anti-colonial nationalist groups within the empire, as it would once again during the international campaign against apartheid from the 1960s.[3]

Regionally, too, within the South African subcontinent where the political entity 'South Africa' did not yet formally exist, 1899–1902 had long-term implications for the political and cultural history of that country-to-be – implications that would unfold right across the twentieth century. The conflict informed vocabularies of rights and community representation amongst Britons and Boers, black Africans and South African Indians alike – as recorded for example by M. K. Gandhi in his account of his divided responses to the war in his *Autobiography* (1927).[4] The South African War not only shaped the colonial vision of the influential anglophile architects of the united new South Africa inaugurated in 1910; it also honed the rhetoric and resistance tactics of the anti-colonial nationalists who were to interrogate its all-white make-up. As the historian Bill Nasson observes, this war was South Africa's 'Great War' insofar as it was in crucial ways a highly fissiparous civil struggle, internally dividing the different participant communities into frangible factions and fractions, as much as they were divided from one another – for example, the Cape Afrikaners against the Transvaal Boers (see Nasson, *Abraham Esau's War*). For this reason, among historians across a broad range, from the canonical Thomas Pakenham through to the more contemporary Greg Cuthbertson,

2 Boehmer, 'A War of White Savages', pp. vii–xiv.
3 See Harlow, 'Boers and Bores', pp. 90–102.
4 He identified with the Boers' nationalism; yet he wished to show loyalty as a citizen of the British Empire – hence his ambulance corps work at Ladysmith. See Gandhi, *An Autobiography*, pp. 156–7.

Albert Grundlingh or Liz Stanley, the 1899–1902 conflict is now often called the South African War alongside the more common term 'Anglo-Boer', as it indeed was at the time of its unfolding. Though the term remains contentious, the war also having been long considered a 'white man's war', which officially involved only white combatants (and also called 'die Engelse oorlog' by Afrikaners), it is now generally perceived as having impacted on all South Africa's peoples, and on men, women and children alike. As a 'war that would be crucial to the historical formation of modern South Africa as were the Civil Wars to England and the [USA]' (Nasson, 'Tot siens to all that?', p. 192), and a 'war as difficult as any nation has passed through',[5] it moulded both the geopolitical and the imagined shape of the nation-in-formation. In the 1994 'new' South African dispensation, the aftershocks of 1899–1902 were registered in the extraordinary dismantling of Transvaal province, and not of Free State (which only lost the 'Orange' in its name) – the Transvaal having retained in the twentieth century the shape of the old and most powerful of the two Boer republics.

With its international cast list of key players, the South African War burst emphatically into imaginative literature both across the empire and within the region. First in journalism and poetry, then in memoirs and prose fiction, the nation-making as well as nation-breaking repercussions of the conflict found symbolic expression, not only at the time (in the pre-1914 period) but in ensuing decades, in national literatures in English and Afrikaans, along their different trajectories of formation. As the pitched propaganda battle in British publications of the time reveals (as between W. T. Stead in his excoriating *Methods of Barbarism* [1901], and Arthur Conan Doyle in his riposte, *The War in South Africa* [1902]), 1899–1902 had ramifying effects across the literary spectrum, including in middle-brow and popular forms. It was in diverse literary media, far more persuasively than in, say, the imperialist rhetoric of Cape High Commissioner Alfred Milner, that the war was conceived as unfolding in regional, international but especially national dimensions, and as having an impact on all communities. Literature also registered in sensitive and revealing ways the private, shifting and morally divided subjectivities of South Africans across the protracted period of conflict – and literature in this sense should again be broadly defined as embracing journalism and campaigning letters to the press, as well more conventional literary writing.

5 Jan Smuts's words in his 'Preface' to Reitz's *Commando*, p. ix.

Within mere days of its commencement on 11 October 1899, the war was widely espoused as a crucial moral as well as political problem across the English-speaking world. Steered by campaigners like Stead and Emily Hobhouse, and underpinned by the anti-imperialist (and prewar) analyses of Olive Schreiner, the pro-Boer Liberal lobby in Britain expressed concerns that a mighty power was perpetrating a shameful injustice against a small people, on the pretext of restoring justice on that power's terms. The poetic world, too, was divided, with poets otherwise as far apart as Alfred Austin and Algernon Charles Swinburne urging England and the empire to 'Rise', take arms and 'Scourge these dogs', against Thomas Hardy's lamentations in his 'War Poems' over the futility of war, and the senselessness of aggressive patriotism.[6] Lyrics of 1899 by Hardy, such as 'Drummer Hodge' and 'A Christmas Ghost Story, in striking ways prefigured the anti-war literature of 1914–18, and in their pungent evocations of the distant 'broad Karoo' deserve to be considered as forming a key part of South African War writing.

As for imaginative writing within the country, those nation-making or nation-prefiguring narratives and poems to which postcolonial criticism in the wake of Benedict Anderson's *Imagined Communities* has given pride of place: the Boer War was especially important for the development of these forms. Since 1899–1902 marked a traumatic phase in the clash between a number of the subcontinent's emergent and rival nationalisms, it rapidly became a crucible for the formation of new and newly defined national identities, as war novels from Douglas Blackburn's early comedic but prescient *A Burgher Quixote* (1903) onwards recognised. (Blackburn's anti-hero Sarel Erasmus stumbles into involvement first with the Boers, then with the British, and with both against his better judgement: see Chapter 18 in this volume.) Now, British designs upon a united English-speaking South Africa and its wealth came decisively up against Afrikaner defensiveness concerning their land, language and customs (including the oppression of black Africans) – a set-to registered from the perspective of the former by Kipling, and from that of the Boers by Denys Reitz. As is perhaps not surprising, literature in the emergent language of Afrikaans, the literature of the war's beaten yet spiritually undefeated people, has maintained a particularly intense and lasting involvement with 1899–1902, as will be seen. But the war also fostered increasingly more determined moves to self-determination among African peoples, whose frustrations over their representation and rights both during the war and in the years following are

---

6 Boehmer, 'The South African War', pp. 275–97; Hardy, 'War Poems'.

registered in movingly restrained form in Solomon T. Plaatje's *Mafeking Diary* (1973).

The rest of this chapter surveys the counterpoised nationalist and imperial emotions that the South African War raised in British and some South African writing of the period, as already extensively documented by Malvern van Wyk Smith in his 1978 book *Drummer Hodge*. It also traces that crux which is represented by the convergence of British, Afrikaner and black African perceptions about the conflict in the work of Rudyard Kipling, Denys Reitz and Solomon Plaatje – texts which the events of the war interestingly juxtapose. These three authors, who in time built international reputations in part through their writing of the war's bitternesses, in their different ways recognised the conflict for what it was, a crisis over what it meant to be South African – at once a citizen of empire and a South African nationalist. Following their work, the impact of the war moved in subterranean and mediated but no less powerful ways through South African literature, cropping up in Boer War novels published across the twentieth century, especially towards its end, the time of the war's centenary.

A thumbnail sketch of the progression of the war is appropriate at this point, to give a rough time-chart against which the responses to the war from soldiers and campaigners, poets and memoirists, might be measured. As with the first Anglo-Boer War of 1880–81, the South African War began as a textbook expansionist war, in the name of 'elementary freedom for all white men', as Kipling put it with characteristic frankness (Lycett, *Rudyard Kipling*, p. 320). A diplomatic campaign in favour of the rights of British and other settlers in the Boer republics of the Transvaal and Orange Free State (the Uitlanders) was used as a front for the assertion of British supremacy over the strategically important subcontinent, especially the republics' valuable gold and diamond mines. On the British side it was confidently predicted that this would be a short war against a band of unruly Afrikaners, entailing a mere 'taking of tea' (and involving 500,000 troops against 50,000 farmers). Yet the British Cabinet and the army's generals had not reckoned with the Boers' fierce patriotism, or their skills as riflemen and bush fighters. In the retrospective words of Churchill, 'utterly insufficient resources' were pitched against an adroit and powerful enemy in terrain where 'every advantage lay with the Boer' (Pakenham, *Boer War*, p. 125; Conygham, *Desecration of the Graves*, p. 138). In the first months of the war the British sustained a number of heavy and demoralising defeats, several concentrated in the 'Black Week' of December 1899, which drove them into the expensive investment of three towns widely spaced along the snaking line of the front, Ladysmith, Kimberley and Mafeking (now Mafikeng). The first of these would throw Gandhi, Churchill, Jameson and Reitz into close proximity; the second would see Rhodes physically standing guard over his diamond fields. The third would give birth to the idea of Scouting as civilian military preparedness training in the mind of its prankster man-in-command, Colonel Robert Baden-Powell.

At around six to nine months into the conflict Boer forces began steadily to buckle under the massively reinforced British Army, now supplied from across the white empire. Field Marshall Lord Roberts, an old 'India hand', replaced the by now discredited Sir Redvers ('Reverse') Buller. Yet the Boers' defeat by conventionally organised troops only stiffened their resistance; in mid 1900 they met the departure of the army's generals and the colonial troops with a shrewdly waged guerrilla warfare. It took a further two full years of terrible attrition against the entire Boer community – 'burnt earth' farm burning and the herding of thousands of civilians into camps (where 28,000 died, mainly children) – before the bitter 'no compromise' Peace of Vereeniging was concluded in May 1902. Though Britons and Boers had agreed on one thing, that this should be a war waged by whites, the near three years of the conflict had disrupted the lives of most southern Africans, not least blacks. Working as servants, hard labourers, dispatch riders and informal spies in the wake of all the war's military actions, black South Africans also suffered their own refugee camps, where there were over 14,000 fatalities. Out of the molehills that had first moved the conflict forwards in 1899, an 'alp of unforgiveness', in the words of William Plomer, had been built in South Africans' hearts (*Collected Poems*, p. 20).

Initial responses

As regards how literary writing takes up cataclysmic events like war and acts of terror, it tends to be the case that smaller scale, impressionistic forms, lying closer to a culture's oral tradition, like the lyric poem, will be the first to register the impact of such crises. Journalism, too, offers channels of immediate reaction, whereas the novel responds in more considered, incremental ways. Symptomatically, D. H. Lawrence in *The Rainbow* (1915) and James Joyce in *Ulysses* (1922) – both novels being set during or not long after 1899–1902 – allow the main characters' awareness of the Boer War to percolate gradually into their lives, or lightly to touch its margins. In the British press, certainly, and in music-hall songs, the outbreak of the Anglo-Boer War, coming swiftly after the celebration of Queen Victoria's Diamond Jubilee in 1897, triggered a strident burst of jingoism not witnessed on this scale before, as deplored by

Hardy. Yet, as it became apparent that the war would not be over by Christmas, and that it might require the massed forces of the British Empire effectively to overcome the Boers, this overweening confidence within months broke down into tremulous uncertainty, as again expressed in poetry of the time. Profound disillusionment marks the later war poems of Britons William Watson and A. E. Housman, and the always prescient Kipling, while Irish nationalist songs of the same period, sung at pro-Boer rallies in Dublin and during periods on commando with the Boers themselves, applauded courage and resilience and crowed over the empire's weaknesses.

Called the 'watchman of our Empire' by H. Rider Haggard, and its bard by countless others, Rudyard Kipling was an enthusiastic yet curiously obtuse proponent of the imperial 'go-fever' which he believed England needed in powerful doses, in order to rise as a truly great nation.[7] Some significant time before the outbreak of the Anglo-Boer War, he had taken it as his task to incite and defend Britain's sense of imperial mission. To him, the expansion of British power was a good in itself, which, however, demanded the exercise of a duty of care towards its colonised territories and peoples (the 'White Man's Burden'), such as the Transvaal Uitlanders demanded and deserved. His poem 'Recessional', which appears to ring darkly with the kind of foreboding and exhausted responsibility that might emanate from over-ambitious imperial exploits and hard-won victory, was in fact published as early as 1897, Victoria's Diamond Jubilee year, in response to the excessive confidence he then witnessed on London's streets.

However, as Kipling himself fully acknowledged, he wrote on empire and war in schizophrenic fashion, from 'two sides of his head' ('Recessional' itself appears to exalt what it condemns). The poem concerned with 'the far-flung battle-line' of South Africa that followed close on 'Recessional' was the massively popular, music-hall style 'Tommy song' 'The Absent-Minded Beggar' (1899), written and widely disseminated (on tea towels, handkerchiefs, mugs, jugs, etc.) to raise money for the Soldiers' Families Fund. The poem's catchy exhortation to 'pay-pay-pay' transmitted a starkly realistic if also comic picture of the unequal economic and moral balance sheets on which the task of 'saving the Empire' rested:

> Let us manage so as, later, we can look him in the face,
>   And tell him – what he'd very much prefer –
> That, while he saved the Empire, his employer saved his place,
>   And his mates (that's you and me) looked out for *her*.

7 For a detailed account of Kipling's involvements in the war, see Lycett, *Rudyard Kipling*, pp. 288–345.

He's an absent-minded beggar and he may forget it all,
 But we do not want his kiddies to remind him
That we sent 'em to the workhouse while their daddy hammered Paul,
 So we'll help the homes that Tommy left behind him!
Cook's home – Duke's home – home of a millionaire,
 (Fifty thousand horse and foot going to Table Bay!)
Each of 'em doing his country's work
 (and what have you got to spare?)
Pass the hat for your credit's sake,
   and pay – pay – pay!

As this final stanza of the poem conveys, 'The Absent-Minded Beggar' brought the war to the attention of the British public in energetic and unforgettable ways, even leaking into the consciousness of Bloom and Stephen in Joyce's *Ulysses*, where the conflict is itself called 'absentminded' (15.795, a term which plays also on the historian J. R. Seeley's well-known phrase that the repressive British Empire was acquired by Liberal Britain in a 'fit of absence of mind').

It is broadly true to say that English writing of the Boer War is infused with Kipling's complex, urgent cadences. These echoes extend from W. E. Henley's indignant 'Remonstrance' (1900) that a once proud England has been 'put on the run' by an 'old mad burgher man', to the more considered yet no less patriotic war histories of Churchill or A. Conan Doyle. But Kipling had as many direct as indirect imitators also, among them Edgar Wallace and T. W. H. Crosland, whose *The Five Notions* (1903) took off Kipling's Boer War collection *The Five Nations* in the same year. Though in this period Kipling's more nuanced writing was dedicated to the Indian spaces that, for all his love of the dusty expanses of southern Africa, would continue to claim his heart (in *Kim,* 1901), South Africa for a period of time captured his patriotic imagination and imperialist idealism. His sense of high imperial duty is transmitted in a different form again in the poem 'The Lesson' of 1902, which offers an uncompromising lecture on the consequences of the British military ineptitude that the war had exposed.

In particular, Kipling felt 'pulled' to his mentor Rhodes's vision of an integrated, self-governing South Africa, reflected in his penning not only of rollicking anthems of Tommy experience (like 'Boots'), but also letters home on behalf of star-struck troops met at the front, and bemused journalism for Bloemfontein's *Friend*. Working on the *Friend* in the newly 'liberated' Orange Free State capital for about a month in early 1900, to rally the troops' morale, Kipling contributed propagandistic verse, reportage and 'Kopje-Book Maxims'. He also lost no opportunity to hail the 'equal war' as the crucible of 'one' South Africa, and Kruger as an ironic 'Empire-builder'– as if he were still mentally engaged in debate with an interlocutor like Thomas Hardy concerning the political and moral consequences of the conflict.

Yet Kipling's Boer War writing was not merely devoted to 'steam and patriotism', to cite Henry James's judgement on his work at the time. Marked perhaps by his own direct experience of the front, especially at Karee-Siding on 28 March 1900 (when a journalistic excursion undertaken by Kipling and others to this advance British position came under surprise Boer fire), his short stories inspired by the war are often interestingly textured and conflicted, and are respectful of the experiences of shellshock and loss that the conflict wreaked. In particular, the stories trace the shifting loyalties generated by the war, and the motley, 'ringstraked' make-up of those involved (as Reitz and Plaatje in their ways do, too). 'The Outsider' (1900) and 'The Comprehension of Private Copper' (1902) from different angles lambast British ignorance of South Africa, born of presumption and complacency. 'The Captive' (1902) indicts the 'effete system' of the British Army, while also clearly favouring mavericks, on both sides, who show technological skill and initiative. But Kipling's most interesting story of the conflict is 'A Sahib's War' (1901), a monologue delivered by a Sikh trooper of the Indian Army, Umr Singh, who has followed his 'master' to South Africa. The story lays bare the racially coded ambiguities of a 'white man's war', in which a brown-skinned soldier may not fight, yet consistently considers himself superior to the duplicitous, less than white 'Boer-*log*' and, when pressed, takes up arms in defence of his Sahib. Kipling's stories of the war also repeatedly acknowledge the reliance on the technologies of rail and heliograph that connected the two sides in a common dependence, and the crying need on the British side for more training in the basic techniques of tracking and survival ('The Way that he Took', 1900). Where Kipling's work on the South African War is particularly prescient is in his acute sense that the conflict would create not so much a more bellicose England, self-conscious about its imperial mission, but rather a unified South Africa, matching a vision that Rhodes had first instilled in him.

At the opposite end of the political spectrum to Kipling, one of the more telling testimonies to the crisis of the South African War, especially to its mass civilian suffering, is found in the work of the Liberal campaigner, Emily Hobhouse (1860–1926). Long considered a virtual saint amongst Afrikaners, she was deemed 'unspeakable' by Kipling, who can be taken to have relayed the views of the imperial authorities at the Cape in saying this. Her vivid reports on the 'refugee camps', expressed in letters and gathered in *The Brunt of the War and Where it Fell* (1902), and the posthumous *War without Glamour*

(1927), show keen awareness of the war's damage to future national morale and community relations, if not to imperial ideals generally. Hobhouse's protests against the conflict moved through several phases, as reflected in her letters and memoirs. Following on from her organisation of committees and protest meetings in the first months of the war, she visited the 'harsh and cruel' 'refugee' camps at Bloemfontein in early 1900, and attempted to bring about improvements in sanitation and general hygiene (Hobhouse, *Boer War Letters*, p. 42). Martial law was invoked to prevent her from revisiting the camps in 1901, which suggests that the painful truth of her exposés of this 'very great wrong', as in her *Report of a Visit to the Camps* (1901), was registered in the highest halls of power (*Boer War Letters*, p. 50).

Her writing on the camps makes an impact even today for its stark and relatively unsentimental realism, and for her unflinching insight into the moral damage brought by empire triumphant and the harmful consequences of patriotism. '[The camps are] such a wholesale cruelty', she wrote, 'and one of which England must be ashamed. It can never be wiped out of the memories of people here' (p. 50). And again: 'It is almost impossible to describe the moral atmosphere of [Bloemfontein] . . . like being in continual disgrace or banishment or imprisonment. Some days I think I must cut and run' (p. 55). Or, 'Everything is censored – spies abound – barbed wire and picquets surround the town' (p. 53). To be pro-Boer, she averred, was to be a pro-Englander, defending English values of justice and fair play. She also conceived in visionary ways the promise that continued to exist, even in the terrible camps, for the achievement of an internally integrated and healed South Africa, seeing this as demonstrated in particular through cooperation between individuals. In many ways ahead of her time, Emily Hobhouse nevertheless shared with her Boer friends and hosts, and most other whites, an inability to regard black South Africans as fully human; their suffering, if registered at all, was seen as merely collateral to that of whites. Yet this blindness of Hobhouse's is broadly typical, and paradoxically links her to Kipling, for whom the black 'Hubshis' of South Africa were either invisible or repellent (as in 'A Sahib's War'). For Denys Reitz, too, the presence of his black servant Charley to cook his meals and look after his horses while on commando is part of the natural order of things. It was precisely this invisibility to which blacks were relegated, that galvanised Plaatje into the enumeration of some of his grievances in his *Diary*.

The work of Hardy and Kipling, and perhaps more surprisingly of Lawrence and Joyce, presents rich testimony to the impact of the South African War across the seas. However it was on the land, within the country, and in the writing of its peoples that the conflict, divisive as it was, was viewed first and foremost as forging bonds of belonging and a sense of who belonged. The next section will take this literature as its focus – the literature that by addressing war conditions within the war-torn colonies and republics themselves, can be seen as beginning to write the nation South Africa.

Later reflections

Apart from the work of Kipling, the larger-scale, more reflective narrative accounts of the Anglo-Boer War which were revised or rediscovered years after its end have proved more influential in informing twentieth-century perceptions of the conflict than writing produced in its immediate aftermath. Of these apparently retrospective works, still the most striking is Denys Reitz's *Commando* (1929), first written in early Afrikaans as a war diary entitled 'Of Horses and Men' while transport riding in Madagascar in 1903, and later self-translated by the observant and apparently fearless guerrilla-fighter-turned-diplomat. *Commando* is now widely considered *the* Boer War classic for its high-adventure action and evocative reportage, relayed as if in the white heat of action at Spioenkop (Spion Kop) or in the thick of Smuts's forays into the Cape. Yet it is also strongly memorable for the profound humanness and compassion of its combatant's eye-view.

It was Denys Reitz's great good fortune as a soldier-writer to have lived through and survived three of the war's major phases, which he describes with a kind of spirited equanimity: the Natal campaign, the middle-period skirmishing in the western Transvaal, and the desperate endgame action of Smuts's Cape column. His writing is notable, too, for rendering not only the sweep and mass scale of different battles – 'great clouds of dust billowed over the veld' (p. 42) – but also its small, telling details, the 'acrid green' fumes of lyddite (p. 61), the thudding of the guns, the haphazard formations of the Boers. His references to his 'deserted tent' after Spioenkop (p. 80), all his comrades having fallen, and, at Talana, to 'the ashen faces and staring eyeballs' of the dead (pp. 30–1), stripped of the war glory he expected, anticipate what Wilfred Owen would later distil as the 'pity' of war. Perhaps not surprisingly, *Commando* was consulted in the early 1960s as a manual on guerrilla tactics by a Nelson Mandela keen to read up on unconventional methods of warfare, persuasively explained.

Following the fortuitous discovery of the manuscript of *Mafeking Diary* (1973) in 1969, Reitz's *Commando* deserves to be read as a 'plain tale' of the war alongside this equally striking and perhaps even more remarkable buried testimony, from the rare perspective of a black man, court reporter Sol Plaatje. In a notebook unwittingly preserved across seven decades by his descendants, the later journalist and nationalist-to-be Plaatje recorded his day-to-day observations on the war's longest (117-day) siege, sketching its elongated trajectory, noting its early enthusiasms and, later, its declining mood. Although Plaatje breaks off suddenly in March 1900, about two months before the siege of Mafeking finally ended, his often bemused account covers a varied and representative range of experiences, demonstrating, like Reitz, an eye for the telling, contradictory detail, especially seen from the perspective of the Barolong *stadt*.

As poignantly observed by Plaatje, smaller, poorer-quality rations were meted out to blacks than to the inhabitants of the white town, presided over by the 'Colonel Commanding' Robert Baden-Powell. Yet the entire besieged community was dependent on the supply lines of food and news unofficially maintained by black cattle rustlers and dispatch riders, and on the protection of its 'Black Watch', as he does not fail to notice. Plaatje's writing is memorable, too, for the auditory landscapes of the siege that it creates, the textured, onomatopoeic renditions of the Boer guns, the evocations through creolised wordplay of the multiple cultural interfaces that the siege conjoined: 'Haikonna terror', 'tutaing' (toing and froing) ambulances (*Mafeking Diary*, pp. 23, 37, 29). Read with hindsight, Plaatje's trust in British bravery and honour, offset by the Boers' heavy-handed ineptitude as besiegers, rings somewhat hollow, as none of their assurances to his Barolong people of protection and support as reward for their good services were ever met. Yet in this, again, Plaatje's *Diary* demonstrates a sideways percipience, a residual awareness, born out in his *Native Life in South Africa* (1916), that loyalty so fulsomely bestowed, demanded some answer if it was not to foment even deeper feelings of pariah-hood than the Boers were soon to express. The ambivalences of Plaatje's position as court interpreter, diarist and (conjecturally) British spy, have been provocatively drawn in Andries Oliphant's 'The Interpreter', a fictional reconstruction of the final twenty blank pages of the Mafeking notebook (pp. 1–12).

To the same degree as their humiliation at British hands honed and sharpened the Boers' nationalist spirit, the war experience also contributed to transforming their language, a hybridised version of Dutch, as discussed by H. P. van Coller in Chapter 13 below, into a supple new medium of nationalist self-expression, as Afrikaans poetry of the war's aftermath testifies. Taken together, this restrained, often mournful work – by Eugène Marais, Jan F. E. Celliers, J. D. du Toit (Totius) and C. Louis Leipoldt – provides another definitive perspective on the South African War, though pitched from vantage points seemingly far removed from its central action. Whereas the majority of Afrikaners in the 1890s comprised a rural people deeply attached to what they considered to be their God-given land, and loyal to their powerful oral traditions based in communal prayer, stirring song, and storytelling, often drawn from the Bible, the years of reconstruction post 1902 drew many onetime Boers to the cities, and provided improved educational opportunities as well as new occasions for the building of political and cultural solidarities out of a core of shared war memories. It is an irony of the war that the camps had triggered this development, by introducing the Boers to formal literacy in larger numbers than urban schools had been able to achieve. So, whereas Afrikaans writing produced during the war was confined to the military memoirs of heroes like Christiaan de Wet (*Strijd tussen Boer en Brit/The Three Years War*, 1902), and unremarkable, sometimes humorous newspaper verse, the nationalist and linguistic chemistry of its aftermath generated an entirely new poetic approach. The Afrikaans literary renaissance from 1905 is distinguished in particular by its meditative yet also highly mediated and subtle reflections on the pathos of a militarily defeated yet spiritually defiant people. These range from Marais's nuanced, expressionist 'Winternag' (1905) and Celliers's telegraphic evocations of veld landscapes and Boer heroes (as in 'Die Vlagte'), to Totius's and Leipoldt's dramatic mythologisations of Afrikaner history.

As anticipated, the second half of the twentieth century and the coming of the 1899 centenary saw the emergence of a number of retrospective novels tracing back to the Boer War experience, some of the most powerful coming from Afrikaans writers. An influential forerunner, Etienne Leroux's *Magersfontein, O Magersfontein!* (1976) draws parallels between the 1899 Battle of Magersfontein, a disastrous defeat for the British, who had failed to reconnoitre Boer positions, and the reconstruction of these events by a foreign film company at Magersfontein in the present day. Flash floods ultimately disrupt the film project yet miraculously deliver two of the characters from the mundane messiness of history via hot-air balloon. Not long before the war's centenary, Christoffel Coetzee's *Op Soek na Generaal Mannetjies Mentz* (1998), in part a postmodern reflection on the vagaries of story, in part a multivoiced family saga, follows the circuitous pathway of the vengeful eponymous rebel, styled as an embodiment of Boer viciousness. With every atrocity committed by the general, whose pathway takes him from the hidden fortifications of the Golden Gate to the slopes of Kilimanjaro, a retreat for Boer rebels, the novel begs the question implied by his everyman name: in what does human nature consist?

In the same year, 1998, Karel Schoeman published *Verliesfontein*, an historical reconstruction of the Free State commandos' daredevil invasion of the Cape Colony. The novel rounds off with the dark reflection, set in some unspecific later time, but full of resonance for the post-apartheid era, that their war experience taught the Boers nothing of forgiveness, and doomed them to repeating history's cycles of violence and revenge. Ingrid Winterbach's testing but highly suggestive word-play, as in *Belemmering* (1990) and *Niggie* (2002; translated as *To Hell with Cronjé*, 2007), also questions how heroic myths of the past might be disrupted to forge new, more constructive futures, as if in line with the processes of the 1996 Truth and Reconciliation Commission. Further back, at the half-century, the time of the Second World War, and emerging from an anglophone if self-consciously indigenised narrative tradition, Herman Charles Bosman's short stories that address the Boer War – 'Mafeking Road', 'The Affair at Ysterspruit', 'The Rooinek'– draw bifurcated commemorative contours in looking back to the conflict (Bosman, *Mafeking Road* and *Selected Stories*). Whereas the narrative voice acknowledges 'the stubborn and elemental strength' of the Boers, the stories' situational and dramatic ironies speak of the *volk*'s experiences of internal division, betrayal, disloyalty and irreparable loss.

Towards the end of the century, in English, John Conyngham's *The Desecration of the Graves* (1990), a fictionalised report on a research project, Ann Harries's imaginatively charged *Manly Pursuits* (1999), on the Cape's Boer War, and Elleke Boehmer's century-straddling narrative collage *Bloodlines* (2000), too, find in the retrieval of the clashes and cleavings of the Anglo-Boer War period, the means of investigating and in some cases resolving troubled relations in the present day. Drawing heavily on the rich newspaper and photographic archive of the war, the British writer Giles Foden's *Ladysmith* (1999), too, tells the multitiered tale of that famous if dreary siege in which a number of prominent figures of modern world history – Churchill, Gandhi, Reitz himself – had a walk-on part. The texture of Foden's reportage narrative is evocatively interwoven with the characteristic phrases, sayings and *bon mots* of the conflict: 'the rattle of Mausers', 'Johnny Boer' being 'only a farmer'; Kruger to Milner, 'What you really want is my country'. The siege of Ladysmith as a microcosm of South Africa's remarkably tight entanglements of history, race and community – some of the legacies of which are only being worked out today – is central also to Boehmer's more metafictional *Bloodlines*.[8] One hundred years on, the South African War continues

---

8 See Nuttall, *Entanglement*, 2008.

to inform South African literary imaginations, providing occasion after occasion not only to interrogate but also to catalyse new notions of South African nationhood.

Bibliography

Anderson, B. *Imagined Communities: Reflections on the Origin and Spread of Nationalism* [1983], rev. edn, London and New York: Verso, 1991.

The Spectre of Comparisons: Nationalism, Southeast Asia and the World, London and New York: Verso, 1998.

Blackburn, D. *A Burgher Quixote*, London: Blackwoods & Sons, 1903.

Boehmer, E. *Bloodlines*, Cape Town: David Philip, 2000.

Empire, the National and the Postcolonial 1890–1920, Oxford University Press, 2002.

'The South African War', in Boehmer, *Empire Writing*, 275–97.

'A War of White Savages, and other Stories: Introduction', in Boehmer, 'South African War?', vii–xiv.

Boehmer, E. (ed.). *Empire Writing*, Oxford University Press, 1998.

'South African War? 1899–1902', special issue of *Kunapipi* 21:3 (1999).

Bosman, H. C. *Mafeking Road* [1947], Johannesburg: Dassie Books, 1957.

Selected Stories, ed. S. Gray, Cape Town: Human & Rousseau, 1980.

Celliers, J. F. E. *Die Vlakte en Ander Gedigte*, rev. edn, Pretoria: Volkstem, 1917.

Chrisman, L. *Rereading the Imperial Romance*, Oxford University Press, 2000.

Coetzee, C. *Op Soek na Generaal Mannetjies Mentz*, Cape Town: Queillerie, 1998.

Conyngham, J. *The Desecration of the Graves*, Johannesburg: Ad Donker, 1990.

Cuthbertson, G., A. Grundlingh and M-L. Suttie (eds.). *Writing a Wider War: Rethinking Gender, Race and Identity in the South African War 1899–1902*, Athens: Ohio University Press, 2002.

Doyle, A. C. *The Great Boer War*, London: Thomas Nelson & Sons, 1900.

The War in South Africa: Its Cause and Conduct, Toronto: Morang & Co., 1902.

Foden, G. *Ladysmith*, London: Faber & Faber, 1999.

Gandhi, M. K. *An Autobiography; or, The Story of my Experiments with Truth*, trans. Mahadev Desai, Ahmedabad: Navajivan Publishing House, 1958.

Hardy, T. 'War Poems', in *Poems of the Past and the Present*, London: Macmillan, 1901.

Harlow, B. 'Boers and Bores: International Delegations and Internal Debates', in Boehmer, 'South African War?', 90–102.

Harries, A. *Manly Pursuits*, London: Bloomsbury, 1999.

Hobhouse, E. *Boer War Letters*, ed. Rykie van Reenen, Cape Town: Human & Rousseau, 1984.

The Brunt of the War and Where it Fell, London: Methuen, 1902.

War without Glamour. Women's War Experiences Written by Themselves. Bloemfontein: Nationale Pers, 1927.

Joyce, J. *Ulysses*, ed. H. W. Gabler, Harmondsworth: Penguin, 1996.

Kipling, R. *War Stories and Poems*, ed. A. Rutherford, Oxford University Press, 1990.

Lawrence, D. H. *The Rainbow*, intro. R. Aldington, Harmondsworth: Penguin, 1955.

Leroux, Etienne. *Magersfontein, O Magersfontein!* Cape Town: Human & Rousseau, 1976.

Lowry, D. (ed.). *The South African War Reappraised*, Manchester University Press, 2000.

Lycett, A. *Rudyard Kipling*, London: Weidenfeld & Nicolson, 1999.

Marais, E. *Versamelde Gedigte*, Pretoria: Van Schaik, 1933.

Nasson, B. *Abraham Esau's War: A Black South African War in the Cape, 1899–1902*, Cape Town: David Philip, 1991.

'*Tot siens* to all that? South Africa's Great War, 1899–1902', *South African Historical Journal* 32 (1995), 191–205.

Nuttall, S. *Entanglement: Literary and Cultural Reflections on Post-Apartheid*, Johannesburg: Witwatersrand University Press, 2008.

Oliphant, A. 'The Interpreter', in Boehmer, 'South African War?', 1–12.

Pakenham, T. *The Boer War*, 2nd edn, London: Abacus, 1992.

Plaatje, S. T. *Mafeking Diary: A Black Man's View of a White Man's War*, ed. J. Comaroff, London: James Currey, 1991.

Plomer, William. *Collected Poems*, London: Jonathan Cape, 1960.

Reitz, D. *Commando: A Boer Journal of the Boer War*, Halfway House: Southern Books, 1983.

Schoeman, K. *Verliesfontein*, Pretoria: Human & Rousseau, 1998.

Schreiner, O. *Thoughts on South Africa*, London: T. Fisher Unwin, 1923.

Trooper Peter Halket of Mashonaland, London: T. Fisher Unwin, 1897.

Spies, J. B. *Methods of Barbarism?: Roberts and Kitchener and Civilians in the Boer Republics*, Cape Town: Human & Rousseau, 1977.

Stanley, L. *Mourning Becomes . . . Post/memory and Commemoration of the Concentration Camps of the South African War 1899–1902*, Manchester University Press, 2006.

Stead, W. T. *Methods of Barbarism: 'War is War' and 'War is Hell': The Case for Intervention*, London: Mowbray House, 1901.

Van Wyk Smith, M. *Drummer Hodge: The Poetry of the Anglo-Boer War*, Oxford: Clarendon Press, 1978.

Warwick, P. *Black People and the South African War, 1899–1902*, Cambridge University Press, 1983.

Willan, B. *Sol Plaatje: South African Nationalist 1876–1932*, London: Heinemann, 1984.

Winterbach, I. *Belemmering*, Johannesburg: Taurus, 1990.

Niggie, Cape Town: Human & Rousseau, 2002; translated as *To Hell with Cronjé*, Cape Town: Human & Rousseau, 2007.

13

The beginnings of Afrikaans literature

H. P. VAN COLLER

In 1975 the Afrikaans Language Monument was completed. It stands on the southern slopes of Paarl Mountain, overlooking the site where the Genootskap van Regte Afrikaners (GRA) (Association of True Afrikaners) first came together a century before to help standardise Afrikaans and to promote Afrikaans literature. It is an abstract-style monument with sharp lines designed by the architect Jan van Wijk: to the left the colonnade symbolises the languages and cultures of western Europe; encircling the front and right the podium represents Africa; and the low wall between the African and European elements symbolises the Malayan language and culture. The main column rises from the confluence of these structures and represents Afrikaans: distinct yet rooted in these diverse linguistic and cultural traditions. On its right, a column symbolising the Republic of South Africa stands free, yet remains part of the structure. As Van Wyk Louw's inscription reads:

> Afrikaans is the language that connects Western Europe and Africa . . . It forms a bridge between the large, shining West and the magical Africa . . . And what great things may come from their union – that is maybe what lies ahead for Afrikaans to discover. But what we must never forget, is that this change of country and landscape sharpened, kneaded and knitted this newly-becoming language . . . And so Afrikaans became able to speak out from this new land . . . Our task lies in the use that we make and will make of this gleaming vehicle.

The Afrikaans Language Monument embodies not only the diverse roots of Afrikaans, but being abstract, it also invites an official narrative as well as subjective interpretations and reactions. So it is with the language and literature as well: developing an official narrative during its early years, and with the democratisation of the political and cultural spheres in later years, new interpretations came to light. Differing views exist regarding the origin of Afrikaans:

Afrikaans and Dutch share a common past in terms of language structure and vocabulary. Modern Afrikaans is a relatively spontaneous continuation of Dutch, which differentiated further from the latter in the seventeenth century because of creolising influences. Much of what was written in Dutch or Afrikaans in South Africa (colonial texts included) has to be seen as belonging to the Afrikaans literary system, specifically where there is a so-called South African perspective present. This view regards the origin of Afrikaans literature as the first Dutch writings at the Cape, such as Jan van Riebeeck's *Daghregister* (December 1651–May 1662), as mentioned by Antonissen (*Afrikaanse Literatuur*, p. 7). Nienaber (*Perspektief en Profiel*) focuses on texts that are regarded as written in proto-Afrikaans. Kannemeyer (*Afrikaanse Literatuur 1652–2004*) focuses on a few Dutch and Afrikaans texts in chronological terms before devoting more time to the First Afrikaans Language movement. February ('Klein Begin', 1998) is similarly selective, while Huigen ('Nederlandstalige Suid-Afrikaanse Letterkunde, 1652 tot 1925') systematically analyses Dutch South African writing. Many of the Dutch authors (such as De Lima, Boniface and Gordon) found in schematic versions of other Afrikaans literary histories (such as Antonissen, *Die Afrikaanse Letterkunde van Aanvang tot Hede*), also occur in Huigen, indicating that although theoretical approaches differ, practice often leads to similar selections.

The opposing viewpoint holds that Afrikaans had a long history as a spoken variant of Dutch, but only emerged in a written form in the latter half of the nineteenth century as the bearer of a literary culture. According to this approach, this period represents the actual beginning of Afrikaans literary history, and can be found in a few Afrikaans literary histories (Beukes and Lategan, *Skrywers en Rigtings*, 1952; Dekker, *Afrikaanse Literatuurgeskiedenis*, 1935, 1967 and Lindenberg et al., *Inleiding tot die Afrikaanse Letterkunde*, 1965). Although Dekker argues that the establishment of the Dutch colony at the Cape by Jan van Riebeeck in 1652 constitutes the obvious origin of Afrikaans literature, he discusses the early Dutch texts in a cryptic and incomplete manner (*Afrikaanse Literatuurgeskiedenis*, 1961 edn, p. 3).

All texts from and in reference to South Africa, including precolonial documents in for instance Portuguese, and with a specific focus on the South African subcontinent – even rock art as narrative – should be regarded as part of South African literature. This view is particularly common amongst proponents of an inclusive South African literary system, mirroring political unity after 1994 (see also Willemse, *Aan die Anderkant*, p. 37 and further).

The origins and development of Afrikaans literature need to be understood in relation to the development of the language. Grebe (in 'Wij Spreken' and 'Die Taal') argues that the internal history of Afrikaans has been represented too simplistically. He questions whether standard Afrikaans is based upon one relatively uniform vernacular that was already stabilised by the end of the eighteenth century, and which replaced Dutch in its higher functions because of political and social factors ('Wij Spreken', p. 1). He considers standard Afrikaans as a construction with political and ideological undertones, in which Afrikaner nationalism played a significant role. Grebe rejects theories that regard the sociolect, Eastern Border Afrikaans ('Oosgrensafrikaans'), as the basis for Afrikaans.[1] Furthermore, he rejects theories of the South African philological school (such as Raidt, *Afrikaans en sy Europese Verlede*, p. 174) that regard Afrikaans as the result of the codification and elaboration of an existing uniform vernacular that was already stabilised by 1775.

Grebe's theory of the origin of Afrikaans is based primarily upon the views of international linguists (Den Besten, 'From Khoekhoen Foreigntalk', p. 198; Roberge, 'Formation of Afrikaans', and particularly Deumert, *Language Standardization and Language Change*). In Deumert's view, language change at the Cape did not lead to a rigid system of diglossia, with on the one hand as *high variant* Dutch and its acrolectic variants and on the other as *low variant* basilectic variants of Cape Dutch. According to Deumert (quoted in Grebe, 'Wij Spreken', p. 2) the development of Afrikaans to a standard form can therefore not be reduced to the replacement of Dutch by a lower variant, that is, a specific form of Afrikaans that had lain in wait for a century: she argues that language stratification is much more complex. In this regard, it is important to note that most standard languages are the result of multiple selections – a complex recombination of characteristics from various dialects ('Wij Spreken', p. 2).

Deumert notes that most standard languages have an origin in diverse language variants and come into existence through various forms of language contact and through the interdependent contact between the written and spoken versions of a language. Grebe therefore argues that Deumert's research indicates that Afrikaans developed much more laboriously than was originally conceived (by for instance the South African philological school). A written tradition originated slowly at the Cape during the nineteenth century, with the

<hr/>

1 See Van Rensburg, *Die Afrikaans van die Griekwas in die Tagtigerjare*, p. 514; *Soorte Afrikaans*, pp. 436–67; and *Taalvariëteite en die Wording van Afrikaans*, pp. 66–7; Ponelis, 'Die Eenheid van die Afrikaanse Taalgemeenskap', p. 9; Du Plessis, 'Aspekte van Suid-wes-Afrikaans', p. 108 and *Variasietaalkunde*, p. 144.

notable use of the most distinct characteristics of the Cape Dutch vernacular in an attempt to depict this dialect. Literary texts are, however, seldom linguistically authentic since they often use stereotypes, and are therefore in fact satirical imitations. Characters in literary texts such as Arme Boer, Boereseun, Klaas Waarzegger and Kaatje Kekkelbek are according to Deumert examples of stylised linguistic and social prototypes, portraying the ordinary farmer and rural population as symbolic opposites of the haughty colonial Englishman and urbanite (Grebe, 'Wij Spreken', p. 4).

Grebe notes that the standardisation process requires selecting between concurrent forms and constructions. In pursuit of linguistic purity, different views existed from the perspective of Afrikaner nationalism that aimed at delimiting Afrikaans as other than a 'Hotnot-language' (variants associated with brown speakers of Afrikaans were scorned and marginalised, [Grebe, 'Wij Spreken', p. 8]), but also as different from Dutch.[2] According to Grebe, an example of these norms of purity can be found in the early Afrikaans poem, 'Di Afrikaanse Taal' by J. Leon Cachet (1838–1912) (reprinted in Brink, *Groot Verseboek*, p. 12). Naturally, a substantial amount of variation remained for some time in terms of lexical items, spelling and grammar.

Conventionally, the 'true' origin of Afrikaans literature has been located in the latter half of the nineteenth century when Afrikaans was established as a language suitable for literary culture. Brink also accepts this date when discussing the evolution of Afrikaans literature against the backdrop of post-colonial thought (*Afrikaans: Op Pad na 2000*; see also Amuta, *Theory of African Literature*, and Ashcroft, *Empire Writes Back*). Such an evolution takes place in three stages, Brink argues, namely emancipation through the appropriation of the dominant culture's forms and traditions, decolonisation through amongst others a challenging nationalism, and thirdly complete emancipation through a reconciliation between Africa and Europe.

This model is useful, but too anchored in the binary structure of power relations: appropriation is also the (re)creation of a literary tradition; capitalising on European models is not merely emulation, but also conscious connection with another tradition. It is the literary tradition that colours an author's work with echoes and expectations. This has a direct bearing on major interpretative and evaluative difficulties with regards to works from the beginning phase of Afrikaans literature, when the nuances of these works would be overlooked in Brink's model.

2 It should however be noted that the move towards standardisation resulted in Afrikaans moving closer to Dutch, underscoring Deumert's theories, which are obviously not ideologically neutral.

It is clear that the standard Afrikaans literary canon (as in fact the concept 'literature') is a construction referring to a corpus of texts that are considered literary within a specific time and place.[3] It is therefore not surprising that the process of canonisation is often likened to mere ideological power play. Nevertheless, even if there was a sanctioned standard variant of Afrikaans, this did not mean that other variants disappeared; many are still in existence today. This applies to literature also: outside the canon there were viable alternative traditions that have survived to the present (see Willemse et al., *Reis na Paternoster*).

The statement that standard Afrikaans is a political and ideological *construction* with the goal of embodying certain ideals is of particular importance to the question of where the origin of Afrikaans literature can be located. From the beginning, Afrikaans literature has been entwined with Afrikaner nationalism and it has been argued that Afrikaans literature, with a few exceptions, is the literary representation of the white Afrikaans-speaking population (Willemse et al., *Die Reis na Paternoster*, p. 9).

In light of the above statements, the following discussion of the origins of Afrikaans literature is premised on the suggestion that no definite point of origin for the Afrikaans language can be determined; it is a slow process of language change, selection and replacement that preceded standardisation. Similarly, there is no definite origin for Afrikaans literature. Although the founding of the Association of True Afrikaners on 14 August 1875 was an important structural step towards the standardisation of Afrikaans and its eventually canonisation, it cannot be seen as the beginning of the Afrikaans language or literature. Just as earlier statements and texts already exhibited traces of Afrikaans and as such can be regarded as proto-Afrikaans, certain literary contributions reveal characteristics of what were later regarded as Afrikaans literature and these texts are noted in this overview.

From Dutch to British at the Cape: 1652–1806

Antonissen (*Afrikaanse Letterkunde*, p. 7) refers to the lively style of van Riebeeck, who in his *Daghregister* composes a gripping narrative that focuses attention on ordinary daily activities and incorporates much tragedy, drama and humour. Although written in Dutch, it expresses a desire for settlement with an emphasis on the land that should not only be explored, but is often

3 See Huigen, *De Weg naar Monomotapa* (p. 95), who refers to an anonymous writer who, in 1897, alleged that only texts written in Afrikaans or Dutch after 1806 should be regarded as part of the South African literary corpus; earlier texts belong to the Dutch literary corpus.

seen in antagonistic terms; it is a struggle to turn space into *place*. Naturally, naming of the terrain plays an important role in such a colonial appropriation.

Claassens (*Die Geskiedenis van Boerekos*, 2006, p. 44 and further) indicates how the sourcing of sufficient fodder, and particularly meat, was a substantial problem the settlers faced from the outset. Van Riebeeck introduced almost every well-known herb and spice from Europe and the East, and widely employed these at the Cape through Dutch recipes and customs. Arguably, what would later become known as Cape 'Malaysian cuisine' in fact has its roots in Dutch cuisine, which in turn is based on other traditions (Claassens, *Geskiedenis van Boerekos*, p. 365 and further). In the same manner literary and linguistic models and styles from elsewhere were adapted to life at the Cape (Huigen, *De Weg naar Monomotapa*), but naturally this process was not unidirectional. Thus acculturation because of contact with indigenous groups not only produced new agricultural methods and new treatments for illnesses, but also a new language, Afrikaans (see also Davids, 'Afrikaans – die Produk van Akkulturasie').

Huigen, in *De Weg naar Monomotapa*, provides an overview of writings produced at the Cape and notes numerous 'land journeys' – of inland recon-naissance – that were undertaken (by for instance Pieter van Meerhoff, Olof Bergh and J. G. de Grevenbroek). The journals of these forays often provide a wealth of knowledge of fauna and flora, and some of these explorers – such as Pieter van Meerhoff and J. G. de Grevenbroek – would later become well known. Van Meerhoff appears in eminent Afrikaans novels (Dalene Matthee's *Pieternella van die Kaap*, 2000, and Dan Sleigh's *Eilande*, 2002), and according to Antonissen, the learned Latinist, J. G. de Grevenbroek (1644–1726), writes a well-styled report (1686–94) that later serves as canvas for Dan Sleigh's comprehensive novel (*Afrikaanse Letterkunde*, p. 8). Antonissen in particular regards the *Daghregister* (1705–6) of Adam Tas (1668–1722) as containing some of the best Dutch in this period. Tas's writings are central to John Miles's novel *Voetstoots: 'n Episode* (As it Stands: An Episode) published in 2009 (see also Chapter 7 on early writings at the Cape).

In 1776, Pieter Cloete explored the interior with the son of Governor Swellengrebel. His report deviates from the expected factual or scientific account and focuses on human activities and experiences rather than on merely being a description of nature, and is written in a language pep-pered with strong Afrikaans characteristics (Antonissen, *Afrikaanse Letterkunde*, p. 9). Afrikaans spelling differs from Dutch, in both vowels (e.g. *i* for *ij* as in Dutch *wonderlijk*, Afrikaans *wonderlik*) and consonants (e.g., the Dutch *z* is substituted with *s*). Nouns are not grammatically gendered in Afrikaans, nor do cases influence inflections. Afrikaans furthermore simplifies tenses: the use of the simple past (Dutch *imperfektum* or *preteritum*) is very limited, and the pluperfect or past perfect (Dutch *plusquamperfectum*) is seldom used. Afrikaans mainly uses the present tense and present perfect (Dutch *perfektum*), the latter with the construct *het ge* + *verb* (*het* is the Afrikaans equivalent of Dutch *heb*, *hebt*, *heeft*, *hebben*). Whilst the use of strong verbs in particular is limited in Afrikaans, unlike in Dutch, the verb *to be* (Afrikaans *is*, Dutch *zijn*) remains the same regardless of the number or persons (first, second or third) it refers to, whereas Dutch inflects it *ben, bent, is, zijn*.

Johanna Margaretha Duminy (1757–1807) wrote a lively journal of her daily experiences on a farm near Caledon. Claassens (*Geskiedenis van Boerekos*) refers to Duminy's journal numerous times, particularly her descriptions of hunting and eating habits and the preparation of country dishes (*boeregeregte*). Susanna Catharina Smit (1799–1863) had limited schooling and wrote Dutch with difficulty. The stark influence of seventeenth- and eighteenth-century Dutch pietism underlies her unpublished diary, which deals mainly with her religious life and contains sixty-six poems, some of them depicting erotic and mystical feelings (Huigen, 'Nederlandstalige Suid-Afrikaanse Letterkunde', pp. 20–1). Her work is of particular importance in light of the literary wake it produced: Antjie Krog's 'Die Leeu en die Roos-Siklus' ('The Lion and the Rose Cycle') in *Otters in Bronslaai* (Otters in Watercress, 1981), which is based on Susanna Smit's diary; Margaret Bakkes's novel *Susanna die Geliefde* (Susanna the Beloved, 1988); Karel Schoeman's biography *Die Wêreld van Susanna Smit, 1799–1863* (The World of Susanna Smit: 1799–1863) and Brink's 1995 *Sandkastele* (*Imaginings of Sand*). (Smit is also discussed in Chapter 7 of this volume.)

In the anonymous 'Lied ter ere van de Swellendamsche en diverse andere helden bij de bloedige actie van Muisenberg in dato 7 Aug. 1795' conscious use is made of the Swellendam language – a form of proto-Afrikaans – in an attempt to portray this community as ridiculous. Important also is the *Dagboek* (Diary) of the Voortrekker leader, Louis Trichardt (1783–1838), especially since the language already shows characteristics of Afrikaans. Trichardt focuses on the human element and humour occupies a central role. This diary is considered a seminal text in Afrikaans literature because of references to it by D. J. Opperman (the poem 'Clat Boek' in *Blom en Baaierd* [Flower and Chaos, 1956], and the drama *Voëlvry* [Outlawed, 1968]) and Jeanette Ferreira's novel, *Die Son Kom aan die Seekant Op* (The Sun Rises over the Ocean, 2007) in which the Trichardt trek from the Cape Colony to Delagoa Bay (the later Lourenco Marques, currently Maputo) is described.

From British hegemony to the GRA: 1806–75

Apart from referring to Trichardt, Antonissen (*Afrikaanse Letterkunde*, p. 14) also mentions the diary of Erasmus Smit, with its lyrical passages, as well as the journal of Sarel Cilliers as foundational to settler memoirs, a literary form that is widely found in the early phases of all literatures. Charles Etienne Boniface (1787–1853) is a notable figure of the period who wrote dramas in various languages. His resentment towards the missionary Dr Philip inspired him to write sharp satirical pieces, such as the sketch of Hendrik Kok (Nienaber, *Perspektief en Profiel*, p. 16) and his best-known work, *De Nieuwe Ridderorde of de Temperantisten* (The New Knightly Order or the Knights Templar) of 1832, which contains large sections written in early Afrikaans. Antonissen sees this piece of burlesque writing as exemplary drama and a specially true depiction of 'coloured folk' (*Afrikaanse Letterkunde*, p. 17), while Nienaber notes the successful use of 'raw folk language' and language realism in general (*Perspektief en Profiel*, p. 17). According to Keuris ('Uitbeelding'), the primary reason for the continuing relevance of Boniface's works lies in his early depiction of Hottentots-Afrikaans.

Kaatje Kekkelbek, or Life among the Hottentots of around 1835 is a comical and satirical drama by Andrew Geddes Bain and G. Rex, and also targets Dr Philip. Gray calls Kaatje, the main character, 'the first indigenous women character in South African theatre' ('Women in South African Theatre', p. 76). Not only does Kaatje boast about the Hottentots' manipulation of Philip and the like, but they are stereotypically depicted as lazy ne'er-do-wells who pilfer and get drunk. In this sketch English and Afrikaans are used alternately by the main character:

> My name is Kaatje Kekkelbek,
> I come from Kat River
> Daar's van water geen gebrek, (There is no scarcity of water)
> But scarce of wine and beer.
> My ABC in Ph'lipes school,[4]
> I learned a kleine beetje, (I learned a little bit)
> But left it just as great a fool
> As gekke Tante Mietje. (As mad Aunt Mietje)

Margaret Lenta adds that 'though the poem puts words into the mouth of a black woman, there is not even an attempt to claim that Bain's purpose is mimetic' ('Speaking for the Slave', p. 116). Kaatje is required for the purposes of

---

4 The school of the controversial missionary, Dr Phillips.

political and comic effect to convict herself of drunkenness, promiscuity and theft. Shaw ("Two "Hottentots"") also notes the link between *Kaatje Kekkelbek* and *De Nieuwe Ridderorde of de Temperantisten*. He argues that the Khoikhoi are depicted in a negative way as a marginalised community in both texts, with a specific focus on their (supposed) alcoholism.

In the same vein, L. H. Meurant (1811–93) writes a series of letters in *The Cradock News-Het Cradockse Nieuwsblad* (1861), but he is principally known for his *Zamenspraak tusschen Klaas Waarzegger en Jan Twyfelaar over het onderwerp van Afscheiding tusschen de Oostelyke en Westelyke Provincie* (Negotiations Between Klaas Waarzegger and Jan Twyfelaar on the Issue of the Separation Between the Eastern and Western Province), published in 1861. In this piece he widely uses 'Dopper-Hollands', a form of proto-Afrikaans. Especially in the first two chapters, Meurant's main character, Klaas Waarzegger, uses strikingly vigorous and vivid language, which sometimes attains a comical effect. Nienaber, however, sees the fictive and satirical reporting on the Cape parliament as Meurant's best work (*Perspektief en Profiel*, p. 19). In the same year, an Afrikaans poetry anthology also saw the light. Following P. J. and G. S. Nienaber, it was subsequently called the anthology of 'missing' poetry, probably referring to verses by D. C. Esterhuyse (Antonissen, *Afrikaanse Letterkunde*, p. 19, and almost identically in Kannemeyer, *Afrikaanse Literatuur*, p. 33). These poems were, however, almost exclusively in Dutch and of a low quality (Nienaber, *Perspektief en Profiel*, p. 20).

A noteworthy writer of this period is Samuel Zwaartman, the alias of H. W. Cooper (1842–93), who wrote *Boerenbrieven uit Fraserburg* and *Kaapsche Schetsen*, all in the Afrikaans idiom (see Antonissen, *Afrikaanse Letterkunde*, p. 19 and Nienaber, *Perspektief en Profiel*, p. 21). The aesthetic function (Jakobson, 'Concluding Statement') is never dominant in these works. However, in poetry the aesthetic function regains prominence: firstly in 'Klaas Geswint en syn Perd' ('Klaas Geswint and his Horse') by F. W. Reitz (1844–1934) in 1870 – a reworking of Robert Burns's 'Tam O' Shanter' – and later in 'Gert Beyers'[5] and 'Di Steweltjiis fan Sanni' ('Sanni's Boots'), also by F. W. Reitz, Jr. In 1873, Adam de Smidt (1836–1910) published 'Dopper Joris en Zijn Zijltje' ('Calvinist Joris and his Sail') under the pseudonym 'Pulvermacher'; it is regarded as one of the best poems from the era before the First Language Movement (see Scholtz, *Afrikaner en Sy Taal*). In addition, Pikkedel's 'Op Hartebeesfontein' is a comprehensive and skilful poem that bears a strong

---

5 According to Nienaber, this is F. W. Reitz senior, father of the more well-known poet and state president (*Perspektief*, p. 33).

resemblance to Bredero's 'Boerengeselschap' ('Boer conversation') in its razor-sharp registration of farming types in action and speech, and in the portrayal of a country festival that leads to a fight (see also Louw, *Versamelde Prosa 1*, p. 589).

Building on the work of Du Plessis (*Afrikaans in Beweging*), which in turn is based on the work of Van Rensburg (*Afrikaans van die Griekwas in die Tagtigerjare*) and Muller ('Die Maleier-Afrikaanse Taalbeweging'), Koch distinguishes between the different 'language movements': Eastern Border, Malay, Bible translations, and so on (*Historia Literatury Poludniowafrikanskiej*, pp. 249–373). It is argued that the Eastern Border Language movement of the 1860s was the first true language movement in Afrikaans, because it connected Afrikaans with the Secession Movement (Du Plessis, *Afrikaans in Beweging*, p. 25). In 1862, Sheik Abu Bakr Effendi (1835–80) launched a deliberate attempt to promote Islam within the Malaysian community at the Cape through what became known as the Malay Language Movement. Abu Bakr was instrumental in the erection of an Afrikaans Madrasah, and in 1869 completed the 354 pages of *Bayan al-Dîn* (The Explanation of the Religion),[6] consisting of the *matn* (text) and *sharâ* (commentary), although it was only published in 1877. Whilst the *matn* is in Arabic, the *sharâ* is a phonetic rendering of Afrikaans in Arabic script, which aimed at communicating subjects of Islamic law to local Muslims (Argun, 'Life and Contribution', p. 69). This was the earliest attempt to use Afrikaans as a literary language, and since it was so intricately tied to religion, it is comparable with early translations of the Bible. Although the need to translate the Bible into Afrikaans is traditionally seen as part of the First Language Movement, Du Plessis (*Afrikaans in Beweging*, p. 39) argues instead for a distinction between the Bible translation movement (predominantly religious in nature) and the Afrikanerbond movement (predominantly political in nature). The fact that Du Plessis needs to argue this view in contrast with traditional perceptions, however, indicates how intricately the political and religious motivations were enmeshed. From 1872 to 1878 the first attempts were made to translate the Bible into Afrikaans, and from 1886 to 1898 Afrikaans was employed for plainly political goals by the Afrikanerbond movement. This movement established the first Afrikaans school and Afrikaans businesses, and published *Di Patriot*; Du Plessis (*Afrikaans in Beweging*, p. 52) notes that this was the most successful of the early Afrikaans language movements.

February ('Klein Begin', pp. 8–10) and Koch (*Historia Literatury Poludniowafrikanskiej*, p. 298 and further) refer to the role played by the mission

---

6 *Bayan al-Dîn* was translated into English by Mia Brandel-Syrier in 1960 (Argun, 'Life and Contribution ', p. 70).

station at Genadendal in promoting Afrikaans. Previously, the diaries of the Hernhutter missionaries were neglected in Afrikaans literary histories. In favour of intelligibility, these German missionaries used an Afrikaans variant of Dutch. From 1859 *De Bode van Genadendal: Een Godsdienstig Maand-Blad voor Christelijke Huisgezinnen* (The Genadendaal Bulletin: A Devotional Monthly Paper for Christian Households) was published (it was renamed *Die Huisvriend* in 1914). *Benigna van Groenekloof of Mamre*, written by Hermann Benno Marx, was published in 1873, before Hoogenhout's novella, *Catharina, die Dogter van die Advokaat* and Cachet's 'Di Geldduiwel' of 1882 (see also Chapter 7). Although written in Dutch, albeit with Afrikaans lexis used sporadically in dialogues, this novel is regarded as important by Kannemeyer because it deviates from the stereotypical and caricatured depictions of coloured characters and is the first novel in South Africa that criticises a social organisation based on colour differences (see Kannemeyer, *Afrikaanse Literatuur*, p. 31).

What is sometimes referred to as the Bible translation movement (Du Plessis, *Afrikaans in Beweging*, p. 37 *passim*; Koch, *Historia Literatury Poludniowafrikanskiej*, p. 335 *passim*) was in fact an earnest appeal for an Afrikaans translation of the Bible. Du Plessis goes so far as to claim that the translation of the Bible into Afrikaans was the main motivation behind the founding of the GRA, while others argue for a national motivation (see Antonissen, *Afrikaanse Letterkunde*, p. 30). Willemse notes that the motivation of the most outstanding proponent of the translation of the Bible into Afrikaans, Arnoldus Pannevis, was that he could reach coloured people, among others (*Aan die Anderkant*, p. 48).

The central role-players in this movement, Pannevis, C. P. Hoogenhout and S. J. du Toit, produced pioneering work and attempts at translation that laid the foundation for the first proofs in 1889, the later proofs of 1922 and the eventual translation of the Bible in 1933. The latter event was not only a standardisation landmark, but also had a profound influence on Afrikaans literature.

The First Afrikaans Language Movement is embodied in the founding of the GRA on 14 August 1875 in the home of Gideon Malherbe in Paarl (currently a museum exhibiting the diversity of Afrikaans). This event was the result of a significant Afrikaans culture in Paarl at the time. Arnoldus Pannevis, a linguist and lecturer at the Paarl Gymnasium, was one such important role-player, and under the guidance of G. W. A. van der Lingen this institution was a hotbed of (Afrikaner) nationalism. Pannevis greatly influenced his students – such as Du Toit, J. Lion Cachet and Hoogenhout – in favour of Afrikaans, and they all became important role-players in the First Afrikaans Language Movement as well as influential writers and promoters of Afrikaans.

The GRA released the monthly paper, *Die Afrikaanse Patriot* (later *Di Afrikaanse Patriot*), from 1876 and a magazine, *Ons Klyntji*, from 1896. Both published creative work and although not always of the highest quality, these publications became an important publishing platform for Afrikaans. From 1880 it even became the platform for the Afrikanerbond (see Du Plessis, *Afrikaans in Beweging*, p. 51 and further). Perhaps more importantly, the *Eerste Beginsels van die Afrikaanse Taal* (First Principles of the Afrikaans Language, 1876) contributed to the process of standardisation, and so did *Die Geskiedenis van Ons Land, in die Taal van Ons Volk* (The History of our Country, in the Language of our People, 1877), which enriched the ties between Afrikaans and the Afrikaner.

From the First Afrikaans Language Movement to official language: 1875–1919

Exemplary works from the period of the First Afrikaans Language Movement are few and far between, but include the poems of F. W. Reitz, Hoogenhout's novella *Catharina* (1879) as well as some (mostly anonymous) folk poetry (see Brink, *Groot Verseboek*, pp. 23–9). Folk poetry in this period is exceedingly diverse, but the playful verses are praiseworthy in particular (see Kannemeyer, *Afrikaanse Literatuur*, p. 52). One of the most outstanding of these is Cachet's allegorical and satirical 'Die Afrikaanse Taal' ('The Afrikaans Language'), which Nienaber considers an early example of 'real poetry' ('Eerste Letterkundige Pogings', p. 24). Nienaber also refers to a satirical poem by Piet Faure (Hoogenhout) and P. D. Rossouw's mocking of John Mackenzie in 'Stellaland'. In his later reappreciation of a dancing song, N. P. van Wyk Louw (*Versamelde Prosa 1*, pp. 588–95) notes characteristics that are often regarded as fundamental to folk poetry: its cryptic nature, ambiguity, cruelty and the like. One finds these characteristics – and others such as the irrational and illogical, the erotic, a sense of mortality and especially the manner in which language is utilised – in experimental poetry. C. W. Joubert's 'Nuttige Reseppe' ('Handy Recipes') for instance satirises the tradition of *boererate* (home remedies), and others hark back to the Watcher's/Dawn song (the so-called *daeraadslied* in Middle Dutch literature, of which the most familiar English example is in Shakespeare's *Romeo and Juliet*) and often depict the confounded lover (see also Grobbelaar, 'Half Vergete Lied').

Nienaber discusses the folk-song 'Wanneer Kom ons Troudag, Gertje?' ('When is our Wedding Day, Gertjie?'), and shows the wealth of original as well as translated and adapted folk-songs in Afrikaans ('Eerste Letterkundige Pogings', pp. 13–15). His remark that the original title, 'Plaatje', was changed to 'Danie' in the later 'canonical' version because Plaatje was probably considered a coloured name, begs the question whether the song had originally been a coloured song. February indicates the role of the Malay community in preserving the Old Dutch song ('Klein Begin', p. 12). The best-known Cape song in Afrikaans is probably 'Daar kom die Alibama' (Here comes the Alabama),[7] which has its origins in the slave community at the Cape, as do many other folk-songs (see also Koch, *Historia Literatury Poludniowafrikanskiej*, p. 125, for examples of ghomma songs).

S. J. du Toit (1847–1911) published his travel journal, *Sambesia, of Salomo's Goudmijnen Bezocht* (The Zambezi, or a Visit to Solomon's Goldmines) in 1894, and his historical novel, *Di Koningin van Skeba, of Salomo's syn Oude Goudvelde in Sambesia* (The Queen of Sheba, or Solomon's Goldmines in the Zambezi) in 1896–8. Nienaber (*Perspektief en Profiel*, p. 29) is critical of this novel as it seems hastily written and disjointed. Nevertheless, fact and fiction are adeptly entwined in this hybrid work that contains poetry in addition to the main narrative, and it would later be regarded as a seminal text in the tradition of the historical novel. In addition, *Magrieta Prinsloo* (1896) is not a completely successful novel, although paving the way for van Wyk Louw's *Die Dieper Reg* (The Deeper Right, 1938) and *Donkerland* (Dark Land, 1996) by Deon Opperman, both profound reflections on the Afrikaner and the Groot Trek, and both with a scenic presentation.

Another fine work is *Sewe Duiwels en Wat Hulle Gedoen Het* (Seven Devils and their Deeds) by Cachet (1838–1912). Five chapters were published in *Di Afrikaanse Patriot* (1882–92) and two in *Ons Klyntji* (1897 and 1898). This work is not faultless either, and Antonissen, above all, indicates numerous shortcomings: a plethora of allegory, a lack of psychological portrayal, overemphasis and

---

7 The *Alabama* referred to in this song is generally believed to be the legendary Confederate Steam Ship (CSS) *Alabama*, used by the Confederate navy during the American Civil War. Launched in 1862, she visited Table Bay harbour in August and September 1863, causing much excitement and capturing the Union bark, the *Sea Bride*, just off Green Point. On her way back from the East Indies she again visited Table Bay harbour in March 1864, and van Niekerk ('The Story of the CSS', p. 175) claims that the general view holds that the song dates to this second visit. The CSS *Alabama* was eventually sunk by the USS *Kearsarge* on 19 June 1864. Van Niekerk ('The Story of the CSS', p. 250), however, cites another possible origin of the song: in the middle of the nineteenth century, a small, flat-bottomed sailing cutter transported thatching reed and string, and in particular a type of reed used in the manufacture of beds specially made for Cape Malay brides. The song is then supposed to refer to this ship, also called the *Alabama*, and since the song refers to a reed-bed, van Niekerk regards this explanation as 'altogether more plausible'.

geniality (*Afrikaanse Letterkunde*, pp. 48–9). However, the work is redeemed by its apt characterisation of town personages, striking dialogue and satire. No wonder, then, that it was later mentioned in discussions of Etienne Leroux's satire *Sewe Dae by die Silbersteins* (*Seven Days at the Silbersteins*, 1962), and that Anna M. Louw's *Kroniek van Perdepoort* (Chronicle of Perdepoort, 1975) also ties in with Cachet's work as it builds on the seven deadly sins.

The work of G. R. von Wielligh (1859–1932) is important because of its documentary nature. He published numerous works, including *Jacob Platje*, parts of which were published between 1896 and 1906, and *Dierestories* (Animal Stories, 1907), a work on animals and 'Hotnots' that regards both as curiosities of the South Africa environment in a eurocentric mode. Von Wielligh finds the oral narratives he reports 'the gift of an uncivilised people' (Willemse, *Aan die Anderkant*, p. 41). In his narratives he often focuses on the comical aspect of indigenous peoples and in the process portrays them in a stereotypical manner, which is a simplification 'not because it is a false version of reality, but because it is a fictional form of representation' (Willemse, *Aan die Anderkant*, p. 64). This type of portrayal we find later in depictions of the 'jolly Hotnot' (Gerwel, *Literatuur en Apartheid*) and in the portrayal of black workers in the Afrikaans *plaasroman* (farm novel).

Anthologising poetry is a central canonisation practice. Kannemeyer (*Geskiedenis van die Afrikaanse Literatuur*, I, p. 61) calls Reitz the first Afrikaans poetry anthologist who published *Vyftig Uitgesogte Afrikaanse Gedigte* (Fifty Selected Afrikaans Poems) in 1888. This anthology saw two further editions (in 1897 and 1909), both with additional works included, and was so popular that it was reprinted five times. It is accompanied by a short preface by Reitz, in which his objective of showcasing Afrikaans as more than just 'kitchen- or Hotnot-language' is clear. Because Reitz compiled these poems from works published in newspapers and magazines, many of the names of the authors are missing (see also Burger, *F. W. Reitz*, p. 99).

Despite Kannemeyer's claim that Reitz's anthology was the first of its kind in Afrikaans, D. F. du Toit and colleagues released *Afrikaanse Gedigte (Eerste Versameling)* (Afrikaans Poems [First Collection]) in 1878. A second collection was published in 1881 with subsequent editions in 1882, 1883, 1885, 1889 and 1901. Following this, *Afrikaanse Gedigte, 'Byeenversameld uit wat in di laaste 30 Jaar Ferskyn is, 1876–1906'* (Afrikaans Poems, 'Collected from what was Published in the Last 30 years, 1876–1906') was published. In his 1987 introduction, Pheiffer is seemingly unsure of who the compiler was, for he quotes Kannemeyer (*Geskiedenis van die Afrikaanse Literatuur*, I, p. 56), who names Du Toit. The compiler was, however, 'Oom Jan wat Versies Maak'

(Oom Jan who Composes Verses) (Hoogenhout), as argued by Nienaber (*Mylpale*, p. 117).[8]

Another anthology published before that of Reitz is *Klaas Gezwint en Zijn Paert and Other Songs and Rijmpies of South Africa* (1884), probably compiled by J. Noble. This collection of English and Afrikaans poems is an obvious precursor to the much later bilingual collection, *S. A. in Poësie / S. A. in Poetry* (1988).

Thomas Francois Burgers (1834–81) was a minister in the Dutch Reformed Church, and from 1871 to 1877 president of the Zuid-Afrikaansche Republiek (ZAR), later the Transvaal. During his study at Utrecht, he was exposed to the humoristic tradition in Dutch literature. In his work, *Toonelen uit ons Dorp* (Scenes from our Town; initially published in *Het Volksblad*, 1866–69 and later republished by Praamsma, *Dorp in het Onderveld*, 2004), he provides a realistic albeit lightly ironical view of his townsmen, with dialogues that are often in Afrikaans. Burgers was a controversial theologian (confirmed as minister in Hanover in 1859) whose modern theological thinking brought him into opposition with orthodox church leaders. He was suspended and numerous court proceedings followed, in which he was always found to have been in the right. During this time, he wrote tales about his life in a small-town milieu, tales that indicate his aversion to orthodox and parochial ministers and to members of the congregation (Burgers in Praamsma, *Dorp in het Onderveld*, p. 126). In addition, his *Schetsen Uit de Transvaal* (Sketches from the Transvaal) is considered thorough journalism and a clever drawing of nature (Antonissen, *Afrikaanse Letterkunde*, p. 21).

Die Patriot continued until 1904 and *Ons Klyntji* until 1906. Despite the Anglo-Boer War in the north (1899–1902), many continued to publish (Du Toit, Cachet, Von Wieligh and Reitz). After the Peace of Vereeniging, Anglicisation was vigorously implemented (Antonissen, 'Afrikaanse Letterkunde van 1906–1966', p. 37), but there nevertheless emerged a strong nationalism. Between 1896 and 1998, J. F. van Oord (pseudonym D'Arbez) published a dozen literary histories in the Zuid-Afrikaansche Historie-Bibliotheek (South African Historical Library) series. Huigen (*Weg naar Monomotapa*, pp. 95–124) sees these works as some of the most important of the period, particularly because they depict history from an Afrikaner perspective (although written in Dutch). Some of these works were translated into Afrikaans, such as *Mooi Annie*, and were best-sellers; of the latter text, 24,000 copies were sold in 1936

---

8 The question remains if this was not J(an) L. Cachet.

(Huigen, *Weg naar Monomotapa*, p. 97). In this historiography fact and fiction are inextricably entwined, and thus it constitutes a pioneering work in what is today called 'literary non-fiction' (see Myburgh, 'Vierde Genre').

Although numerous poets were actively writing at the time, many of their works were not published. The Afrikaans movement was supported by various expressions: J. H. Hofmeyr's speech, 'Is't Ons Ernst?' ('Is it our Serious Intent?') in March 1905, Gustav Preller's articles, 'Laat't ons toch Ernst Wezen' ('Let it be our Serious Intent/Endeavour') in April 1905, and D. F. Malherbe's piece '*Is Afrikaans 'n Dialect?*' (Scholtz, 'Wording en Ontwikkeling', pp. 16–18); nevertheless Antonissen quotes Langenhoven who laments how generation after generation of 'Vondels and Goethes and Miltons' went to their graves silently in the absence of a written language ('Afrikaanse Letterkunde', p. 39). There is a notable absence of black and female voices in early Afrikaans literature, and one can attribute their absence to the specific sociopolitical environment of the day. One way of rectifying the matter is to 'discover' authors who had previously been ignored or undervalued for ideological or poetical reasons. This is done by Willemse (*Aan die Anderkant*, pp. 62–88) and February ('Klein Begin') when they reinterpret and re-evaluate the statements made by Piet Uithalder in 'Straatpraatjies' ('Street Conversations', columns from 1909 to 1922 in the magazine *A. P. O.*, the official mouthpiece of the Afrikaansche Politieke Organisatie). In particular, his opposition to colonial stereotypes is highlighted as undermining the ruling hegemony.

Language impotence and language inferiority certainly did play a role in creating an absence of female and black voices in the literature of these early years, as did social and political factors. It is striking that the most prominent figures after the Second Anglo-Boer War (Jan F. E. Celliers, Totius, D. F. Malherbe and C. Louis Leipoldt) spent a considerable amount of time overseas, and that the first three later dedicated themselves heartily to the Afrikaans movement. One of the reasons for their diligence was probably their contact with the European situation where many language variants developed into fully-fledged languages over time, sometimes also as an extension of nationalism.

Gustav S. Preller is an important author of historical works (such as his biography on Andries Pretorius), founder of Afrikaans literary criticism and skilled journalist. He published *Land en Volk* (1902–8) with Eugène Nielen Marais (1871–1936) and was appointed editor of *De Volkstem* from 1903. Furthermore, he was the patron of Marais, whose poem 'Winternag' ('Winter

Night', published in *Land en Volk*, 23 June 1905) is often regarded as the beginning of Afrikaans literature of international standard. The opening lines are amongst the most familiar in Afrikaans literature:

O koud is die windjie	O cold is the slight wind
en skraal.	and sere.
En blink in die dof-lig	And gleaming in dim light
En kaal,	and bare,

(trans. Butler in Grové and Harvey, Afrikaans Poems with English Translations, p. 7)

Marais was a tragic figure, addicted to opiates, who later committed suicide. Although his first collection of poetry, *Gedigte* (Poems, 1925), was published much later, the appearance of 'Winternag' and 'Is Daar Nog Trane?' ('Are there more Tears?'), was certainly meaningful in this initial phase of Afrikaans literature. His scientific work, such as *Die Siel van die Mier* (1934, translated as *The Soul of the White Ant* in 1937), is admirable, and his short stories, *Dwaalstories* (Wandering Tales, 1927) remain highlights in Afrikaans prose (see Chapter 1).

The very first collection of Afrikaans poetry after the turn of the century was *Die Vlakte en ander Gedigte* (The Plains and other Poems) by Jan F. E. Celliers (1908), which is widely regarded as his most accomplished poetry collection. Though marred by heavy-handed rhetoric and allegory, the title poem contains stunning descriptions of nature and effective auditory experiments. Furthermore, numerous expressionistic 'manly' verses embody Boer soldiers in a striking manner. In Afrikaans literature, 'Dis Al' ('That's All') has, alongside other poems such as Leipoldt's 'Oom Gert Vertel', become synonymous with the Anglo-Boer War, as poems by Wilfred Owen and Siegfried Sassoon have become associated with the First World War:

Dis die blond,	Gold
dis die blou:	blue:
dis die veld,	veld,
dis die lug;	sky;
en 'n voël draai bo in eensame vlug –	and one bird wheeling lonely, high –
dis al.	that's all.
Dis 'n balling gekom	An exile come back
oor die oseaan,	from over the sea;
dis 'n graf in die gras,	a grave in the grass
dis 'n vallende traan-	a tear breaking free;
dis al.	that's all.

(trans. Butler in Grové and Harvey, Afrikaans Poems with English Translations, p. 13)

Totius (J. D. du Toit, 1877–1953) was the son of S. J. du Toit, and, like his father, a theologian. He later became one of the final translators of the 1933 Bible, a contributor to the versification of the Psalms, and a respected academic. According to Antonissen, the prominent Flemish priest-poet Guido Gezelle influenced Totius ('Afrikaanse Letterkunde', p. 44). His debut collection, *By die Monument* (At the Monument, 1908) was slight in scope and depth, and his verses are saturated with symbolism. There are constant comparisons between the human and extra-human (*buite-menslike*), the actual and the historical, the profane and the biblical-historic (Antonissen, 'Afrikaanse Letterkunde', p. 45); allegory and the emblematic are the warp and weft of his work.

D. F. Malherbe's poetry collection, *Karooblommetjies* (Karoo Flowers, 1909), is not considered to be on a par with the poetry of his peers, and it is only later as novelist that he became acclaimed. Although his ornate style prevented critics from generally holding him in high esteem, *Die Meulenaar* (The Miller, 1926) constitutes a seminal work within the tradition of the Afrikaans *plaasroman*, as do his historical novels within this subgenre (see John, 'Afrikaanse Historiese Roman').

Although written earlier, C. Louis Leipoldt's poems were only published in 1911 as *Oom Gert Vertel en ander Gedigte* (Oom Gert Tells and other Poems), collected and edited by his friend and dictionary compiler, J. J. Smith. Whereas many of the other poets emphasised suffering on the side of the Boers during the war, Leipoldt broadened his view to a 'universal' depiction of the consequences of war. He avoided strident patriotism, heavy rhymes and rigid versification in favour of a conversational tone, irony and a dramatic element. In conjunction with a few sonnets – some of the first in Afrikaans – twenty-odd 'slampamperliedjies' are also contained in the collection. In these poems he reflects on life in terms of the natural elements, asks questions about the mystery of existence, his place in the world, and sometimes delivers a personal confession (Kannemeyer, *Afrikaanse Literatuur*, p. 84).

In general, Afrikaans literature from the late nineteenth century onwards conformed to older, European models (as did Dutch and English literature) while adapting to the local context. Consider how well-known Afrikaans poems, such as Reitz's 'Klaas Geswind en Zijn Paard' and Celliers's 'Die Vlakte', were free translations or rather adaptations of the well-known English poems 'Tam O' Shanter' (Robert Burns) and 'The Cloud' (Percy B. Shelley) respectively. Reitz's reworking is more an adaptation than a translation into Afrikaans, as in verse six:

But pleasures are like	Plesiir is nes 'n jong	Pleasure is like a
poppies spread-	komkommer,	young cucumber,
You seize the flo'r, its	As jy hom pluk ferlep	If picked, it easily
bloom is shed;	hy sommer;	withers;
Or like the snow falls	Of nes 'n skulpad in	Or like a tortoise in
in the river;	syn dop in,	its shell,
A moment white –	Soos jy hom fat dan	When grasped, he
then melts	trek hy kop in.	retracts his head.
forever . . .		

Here, the imagery used by Burns is adapted to the African context. In a comparable manner, Abu Bakr Effendi's *Bayan al-Dîn* utilised an established literary model by being 'a classical example of traditional Islamic writing' (Argun, 'Life and Contribution of the Osmanli Scholar', p. 69), with the important difference that the commentary was adapted to South Africa by being mainly in Afrikaans. Whereas Bakr's text is religious, the literary works of Reitz and Celliers also build on established models and adapt them to South Africa, and more specifically, Afrikaans.

I return to the message of the Afrikaans Language Monument near Paarl: like the monument, Afrikaans literature bears witness to a variety of styles and influences – some western European, some African, some Malayan. As the monument symbolises in terms of language, Afrikaans literature was the product of the confluence of these diverse cultural and literary traditions. Perhaps intentionally, the flowing lines of the monument make it difficult to pinpoint the exact moment where the main column symbolising Afrikaans rises from its roots, and it never separates from them. This is true of the language and literature also: defining the origins of the Afrikaans language and therefore literature depends on the view taken, for with every change of rubric, the answer to the question of beginnings seems to change. For this reason, the chapter heading refers to the *beginnings* of Afrikaans literature, not the *beginning*. Various early Afrikaans texts have been discussed in an attempt to show not precisely *when* Afrikaans literature developed, but rather *how*.

Bibliography

Afrikaanse Gedigte, Byeenfersameld uit wat in di Laaste 30 Jaar Verskyn is, 1876–1906: Verkleinde Faksimileeherdruk met 'n Inleiding deur Prof. R. H. Pheiffer en Registers, Cape Town: Suid-Afrikaanse Biblioteek, 1987.
Amuta, C. *The Theory of African Literature*, London: Zed Books, 1989.

Antonissen, R. *Die Afrikaanse Letterkunde van Aanvang tot Hede*, Cape Town: Nasionale Boekhandel, 1956.

'Die Afrikaanse Letterkunde van 1906–1966', in Nienaber, *Perspektief en Profiel*.

Argun, S. 'The Life and Contribution of the Osmanli Scholar, Abu Bakr Effendi, towards Islamic Thought and Culture in South Africa', MA thesis, University of Johannesburg, 2000.

Ashcroft, B., Gareth Griffiths and Helen Tiffin. *The Empire Writes Back: Theory and Practice in Post-Colonial Literatures*, London and New York: Routledge, 1989.

Bain, A. G., and G. Rex. *Kaatje Kekkelbek; or, Life among the Hottentots* [1835], Cape Town: Van Riebeeck Society, 1949.

Bakkes, M. *Susanna die Geliefde*, Pretoria: HAUM, 1988.

Besten, Den H. 'From Khoekhoen Foreigntalk via Hottentot Dutch to Afrikaans', in Pütz and Dirven, *Wheels within Wheels*, 185–230.

Beukes, G. J., and F. V. Lategan. *Skrywers en Rigtings*, Pretoria: Van Schaik, 1952.

Brink, A. P. *Afrikaans: Op Pad na 2000 (Acta Varia 1)*, Bloemfontein: University of the Free State Press, 1991.

Sandkastele, Cape Town: Human & Rousseau, 1995; *Imaginings of Sand*, London: Secker & Warburg, 1996.

Brink, A. P. (ed.). *Groot Verseboek*, Cape Town: Tafelberg, 2008.

Burger, C. J. S. *F. W. Reitz: Outobiografie, Toegelig deur J. C. Moll, Met sy Twee en Sestig Uitgesogte Afrikaanse Gedigte*, Cape Town: Tafelberg, 1978.

Burgers, T. F. *Dorp in het Onderveld: Zuid-Afrikaanse Verhalen*, ed. O. Praamstra, Amsterdam: Athenaeum–Polak & Van Gennep, 2004.

Cachet, J. L. 'Di Geldduiwel', Paarl, *Di Afrikaanse Patriot*, 1882.

Sewe Duiwels en Wat Hulle Gedoen Het, Potchefstroom: Het Western Drukkerij, 1911.

Celliers, J. F. E. *Die Vlakte en ander Gedigte* [1908], Cape Town: Nationale Pers, 1920.

Chapman, M. *Southern African Literatures*, Durban: University of Natal Press, 2003.

Claassens, H. W. *Die Geskiedenis van Boerekos 1652–1806*, Pretoria: Protea Boekhuis, 2006

Conradie, E. *Hollandse Skrywers uit Suid-Afrika: 'n Kultuurhistoriese Studie, Deel I (1652–1875)*, Cape Town and Pretoria: HAUM, 1934.

Hollandse Skrywers uit Suid-Afrika: 'n Kultuurhistoriese Studie, Deel II (1875–1905), Cape Town and Pretoria: HAUM, 1949.

Davids, A. 'Afrikaans – die Produk van Akkulturasie', in Olivier and Coetzee, *Nuwe Perspektiewe*, 110–19.

De Smidt, A. 'Dopper Joris en Zijn Zijltje', Bloemfontein, *Het Volksblad*, 1873.

Dekker, G. *Afrikaanse Literatuurgeskiedenis* [1935], Cape Town: Nasionale Boekhandel, 1961.

Afrikaanse Literatuurgeskiedenis [The Literary History of Africans], twaalfde uitgawe, bygewerk tot 1966, eerste uitgawe 1935 [12th edn, collected to 1966, 1st edn 1935], Cape Town: Nasou.

Deumert, A. *Language Standardization and Language Change: The Dynamics of Cape Dutch*, Amsterdam: John Benjamins, 2004.

Du Plessis, H. 'Aspekte van Suid-wes-Afrikaans met Spesifieke Verwysing na die Afrikaans van die Van der Merwes', Pretoria, RGN Report, 1987.

'Taalvariasie in Afrikaans', in Olivier and Coetzee, *Nuwe Perspektiewe*, 120–9.

Variasietaalkunde, Pretoria: Serva, 1987.

Du Plessis, H., and T. du Plessis (eds.). *Afrikaans en Taalpolitiek*, Pretoria: HAUM. Opvoedkundige Uitgewery, 1987.

Du Plessis, L. T. *Afrikaans in Beweging*, Bloemfontein: Patmos, 1986.

Du Plessis, T., and A. van Gensen (eds.). *Taal en Stryd 1989–1999: Gedenkbundel: Geselekteerde Bydraes van die Taal en Stryd-kongres*, Pretoria: Van Schaik, 1999.

Du Toit, S. J. *Di Koningin van Skeba, of Salomo's syn Oude Goudvelde in Sambesia*, Paarl: D. F. du Toit, 1896–8.

   Magrieta Prinsloo, of Liifde getrou tot in di Dood: 'n Historiese toneelstuk uit di tyd van di Grote Trek, Paarl: D. F. du Toit, 1896.

   Sambesia, of Salomo's Goudmijnen Bezocht [1894], Paarl: D. F. du Toit, 1895.

February, V. 'Klein Begin is Aanhou Wen', in van Coller, *Perspektief en Profiel*, vol. I, 3–20.

   Mind your Colour. The 'Coloured' Stereotype in South African Literature, London: Kegan Paul, 1981.

Ferreira, J. *Die Son Kom aan die Seekant Op*, Cape Town: Human & Rousseau, 2007.

Gray, S. 'Women in South African Theatre', *South African Theatre Journal* 4:1 (1990), 75–87.

Gerwel, G. J. *Literatuur en Apartheid*, Kasselsvlei: Kampen-uitgewers, 1983.

Grebe, H. P. 'Die Taal is Gans het Volk – Taalstandaardisatie en de Constructie van Identiteit', *Internationale Neerlandistiek* 47:1 (February 2009), 21–34.

   'Wij Spreken zo niet Onder ons – Taalstandaardisasie en die Konstruksie van Identiteit', unpublished lecture, Nederelandistiekberaad, University of Johannesburg, 21 February 2009.

Grobbelaar, P. W. 'Half Vergete Lied Werp Nuwe lig op ou Dansterm', *S. A. Tydskrif vir Kultuurgeskiedenis / S. A. Journal of Cultural History* 11:1 (May 1997), 1–8.

Grové, A. P., and C. J. D. Harvey. *Afrikaans Poems with English Translations*, Cape Town: Oxford University Press, 1962.

Hoogenhout, C. P. *Catharina, die Dogter van die Advokaat, deur Klaas Waarsegger Jr*, Paarl: D. F. du Toit, 1879.

Huigen, S. 'Nederlandstalige Suid-Afrikaanse Letterkunde, 1652 tot 1925', in van Coller, *Perspektief en Profiel*, vol. III, 3–42.

   De Weg naar Monomotapa: Nederlandstalige Representasies van Geografische, Historische en Sociale Werkelijkheden in Zuid-Afrika, Amsterdam University Press, 1996.

Jakobson, R. 'Concluding Statement: Linguistics and Poetics', in T. A. Sebeok (ed.), *Style in Language*, Cambridge, MA: MIT Press, 1960, 350–77.

John, P. 'Die Afrikaanse Historiese Roman en die Literêre Kritiek: Aspekte van die Verhouding tussen Literêr-Kritiese Perspektief en Literêre Tradisie', D.Litt. thesis, Stellenbosch University, 1998.

Kannemeyer, J. C. *Die Afrikaanse Literatuur 1652–2004*, Cape Town: Human & Rousseau, 2005.

   Geskiedenis van die Afrikaanse Literatuur, vol. I, Cape Town and Pretoria: Academica, 1978.

Keuris, M. 'Die Uitbeelding van Khoisan-karakters in Boniface en Bains se werk', unpublished lecture delivered at the biannual conference of the Afrikaans Literary Society, Port Elizabeth, 2010.

Koch, J. *Historia Literatury Poludniowafrikanskiej. Literatura Afrikaans* XVII–XIX *Wiek*, Warsaw: Dialog, 2004.

Kok, Hendrik. *De Nieuwe Ridderorde of de Temperantisten*, 1832.

Krog, A. *Otters in Bronslaai*, Cape Town: Human & Rousseau, 1981.

Lenta, M. 'Speaking for the Slave: Britain and the Cape, 1751–1838', *Literator* 20:1 (1999), 103–17.

Leroux, E. *Sewe Dae by die Silbersteins*, Cape Town: Human & Rousseau, 1962; *Seven Days at the Silbersteins*, trans. C. Eglington, Cape Town: Central News Agency, 1964.

Lindenberg, E., et al. *Inleiding tot die Afrikaanse Letterkunde*, Pretoria and Cape Town: Academica, 1965.

Louw, A. M. *Kroniek van Perdepoort*, Cape Town: Tafelberg, 1975.

Louw, N. P. van Wyk, *Die Dieper Reg: 'n Spel van die Oordeel oor 'n Volk*, Cape Town: Tafelberg, 1938.

Versamelde Prosa 1, Cape Town: Tafelberg, 1986.

Malherbe, D. F. *Karooblommetjies, Afrikaanse gedigte*, Cape Town: Van de Sandt de Villiers Drukpers Maatschappij, 1909.

Die Meulenaar, Bloemfontein: Nasionale Pers, 1926.

Marais, E. N. *Dwaalstories* [1927], Cape Town: Human & Rousseau, 1959.

Gedigte, Cape Town: Nasionale Boekhandel, 1925.

Die Siel van die Mier [1934], Pretoria: Van Schaik, 1938; translated as *The Soul of the White Ant*, London: Methuen, 1937.

Matthee, D. *Pieternella van die Kaap*, Cape Town: Tafelberg, 2000.

Meurant, L. H. *Zamenspraak tusschen Klaas Waarzegger en Jan Twyfelaar over het onderwerp van Afscheiding tusschen de Oostelyke en Westelyke Provincie*, 1861.

Miles, J. *Voetstoots: 'n Episode*, Cape Town: Human & Rousseau, 2009.

Morrison, T. 'Playing in the Dark', in J. Rivkin and M. Ryan (eds.), *Literary Theory: An Anthology*, 2nd edn, Oxford University Press, 2004, 1005–16.

Muller, P. J. 'Die Maleier-Afrikaanse Taalbeweging', *Tydskrif vir Volkskunde en Volkstaal* 13:1 (1962), 1–11.

Myburgh, H. M. M. 'Die Vierde Genre: De Plaag (Van Reybroeck) as Voorbeeld van Nie-fiksie', MA thesis, University of South Africa, 2009.

Nienaber, G. S. 'Die Eerste Letterkundige Pogings in Afrikaans', in Nienaber, *Perspektief en Profiel*.

Nienaber, P. J. *Mylpale in die Geskiedenis van die Afrikaanse Taal en Letterkunde*, Johannesburg: Afrikaanse Pers-Boekhandel, 1951.

Nienaber, P. J. (ed.). *Perspektief en Profiel*, Johannesburg: Perskor, 1982.

Noble, J. *Klaas Gezwint en zijn paert and other Songs and Rijmpies of South Africa in English and Dutch*, Cape Town: Juta, 1884.

Olivier, G., and A. Coetzee (eds.). *Nuwe Perspektiewe op die Geskiedenis van Afrikaans, Opgedra aan Edith H. Raidt*, Halfweghuis: Southern Uitgewers, 1994.

Opperman, D. J. *Blom en Baaierd* [1956], Cape Town: Nasionale Boekhandel, 1967.

Donkerland, Cape Town: Tafelberg, 1996.

Voëlvry; Kroniekspel van 'n Voortrek, Cape Town: Human & Rousseau, 1968.

Pheiffer, R. H. 'Inleiding', *Byeenfersameld uit wat in di laaste 30 jaar ferskyn is 1876–1906, Verkleinde faksimileeherdruk met 'n inleiding deur prof. R. H. Pheiffer en registers*, Cape Town: South African Library, 1987.

Ponelis, F. A. 'Die Eenheid van die Afrikaanse Taalgemeenskap', in Du Plessis and Du Plessis, *Afrikaans en Taalpolitiek*, 3–17.

Prinsloo, K. P., and M. C. J. Van Rensburg. *Afrikaans: Stand, Taak, Toekoms*, Pretoria: HAUM Opvoedkundige Uitgewery, 1984.

Pütz, M. and R. Dirven. (eds.). *Wheels within Wheels*, Frankfurt-on-Main: Peter Lang, 1989.

Raidt, E. H. *Afrikaans en sy Europese Verlede*, Cape Town: Nasou, 1989.

Reitz F. W. 'Klaas Geswint en syn Perd', *Het Volksblad*, 1870.

Reitz, F.W. (ed.). *Vijftig uitgesogte + Afrikaanse gedigte (met prentjes)*, Cape Town: 'Argus' Drukkers en Uitgevers Maatschappij Beperk, 1888.

Roberge, P. T. 'The Formation of Afrikaans', in R. Mesthrie (ed.), *Language and Social History: Studies in South African Sociolinguistics*, Cape Town: David Philip, 1995, 68–87.

Rosengren, K. E. 'Time and Literary Fame', *Poetics* 14 (1985), 157–72.

Schoeman, K. *Verkenning*, Cape Town: Human & Rousseau, 1996.

Die Wêreld van Susanna Smit, 1799–1863, Cape Town: Human & Rousseau, 1995.

Scholtz, J. du P. *Die Afrikaner en sy Taal 1806–1875*, Cape Town: Nasou, 1964.

'Ons Eerste Poësie', *Huisgenoot*, 29 April 1938.

'Wording en Ontwikkeling van Afrikaans', Cape Town: Tafelberg, 1980.

Semmes, R. *The Cruise of the Alabama and the Sumter, as published in 1864*, 2 vols., London: Otley & Co., 1864.

Shaw, D. 'Two "Hottentots", some Scots and a West Indian Slave: The Origins of Kaatje Kekkelbek', *English Studies in Africa* 52:2 (2009), 4–14.

Sleigh, D. *Eilande*, Cape Town: Tafelberg, 2002; *Islands*, trans. A. Brink, London: Secker & Warburg, 2004.

Tas, A. *Daghregister*, 1705–6 or 1668–1722.

Van Aswegen, H. J. *Geskiedenis van Suid-Afrika tot 1854*, Pretoria and Cape Town: Academica, 1989.

Van Coller, H. P., and B. J. Odendaal. 'Die Verhouding van die Afrikaanse en Nederlandse Literêre Sisteme. Deel 1: Oorwegings vir 'n Beskrywende Model', *Stilet* 15:3 (September 2005), 1–17.

Van Coller, H. P. (ed.). *Perspektief en Profiel*, vol. i, Pretoria: Van Schaik, 1998; vol. iii, 2006.

Van den Heever, R. *Tree na Vryheid: 'n Studie in Alternatiewe Afrikaans*, Kasselsvlei: Kaapse Professionele Onderwysunie, 1987.

Van Niekerk, J. P. 'The Story of the CSS ('daar kom die . . . ') Alabama', *Fundamina, A Journal of Legal History* 13:2 (2007), 175–250.

Van Rensburg, C. 'Die Ontstaan van Afrikaans in 'n Intertaal Konteks', in Olivier and Coetzee, *Nuwe Perspektiewe*, 166–79.

Van Rensburg, M. C. J. *Die Afrikaans van die Griekwas in die tagtigerjare*, Pretoria: RGN Report, 1984.

'Soorte Afrikaans', in T. J. R. Botha (ed.), *Inleiding tot die Afrikaanse Taalkunde*, Pretoria and Cape Town: Academica, 1989, 436–67.

Taalvariëtiete en die Wording van Afrikaans, Bloemfontein: own publication, 1990.

Van Rensburg, M. C. J. (ed.). *Afrikaans in Afrika*, Pretoria: Van Schaik, 1997.

Van Riebeeck, J. *Daghregister* (December 1651–May 1662).

Van Selms, A. *Arabies-Afrikaanse Studies. Mededelingen der Koninklijke Nederlandse Academie voor Wetenschapppen*, Afdeling Letterkunde, Nieuwe Reeks 14:7, Amsterdam: NV Noord-Hollandse Uitgeversmaatschappij, 1951.

'Abu Bakr se "Uiteensetting van die godsdiens"', *Mededelingen der Koninklijke Nederlandse Academie voor Wetenschapppen*, Afdeling Letterkunde, Nieuwe Reeks 101, Amsterdam: North-Holland Publishing Company, 1979.

Von Wielligh, G. R. *Dierestoriis (Soos deur Hottentots Verteld)*, Paarl: Paarlse Drukpers, 1907. *Jacob Platje*, parts of which were published between 1896 and 1906.

Willemse, H. *Aan die Anderkant: Swart Afrikaanse Skrywers in die Afrikaanse Letterkunde*, Pretoria: Protea-Boekhuis, 2007.

Willemse, H., M. Hattingh, S. van Wyk and P. Conradie. *Die Reis na Paternoster: 'n Verslag van die Tweede Swart Afrikaanse Skrywersimposium gehou op Paternoster vanaf 29 September tot 1 Oktober 1995*, Bellville: University of the Western Cape Press, 1997.

PART IV

*

MODERNISM AND
TRANSNATIONAL CULTURE,
1910–1948

The formation of Union in May 1910 was the constitutional expression of attempts to reconcile Boer and Briton following the Second Anglo-Boer or South African War. As a white arrangement it may have been a false start in the development of South Africa's nation-statehood; nevertheless, the period 1910–48 sees a series of engagements in all the major languages with the idea of national culture. Herman Charles Bosman, iconically South African and very popular amongst local English-language readers, was convinced by the late 1940s that a sea change had started: 'South African English writing is at the present moment passing through an interesting stage in its development from a "colonial" literature into a nationally conscious art' ('Preface', *Veld trails*, unpaginated). The sentiment would not have been controversial amongst most writers of his generation. It is as if Union and its failures established the national question as an irresistible, if still elusive, point of reference for much of South Africa's intellectual life.

The failures of Union were certainly a catalyst for black writers working both in English and the indigenous languages, as Bhekizizwe Peterson shows in Chapter 14. The state after 1910 produced a series of measures which prepared the way for the even more draconian legislation associated with apartheid after 1948. Peterson lists the most relevant Acts of Parliament: they curtailed African land ownership, regulated African labour and movement between towns and cities, and restricted the franchise. The intellectuals who responded to this climate included a number of writers like Thomas Mofolo, Sol Plaatje, John Dube and later A. C. Jordan, who, having been schooled in the missions and then in journalism, produced compelling historical fiction which looked back to the nineteenth century with its sovereign kingdoms and their encounters with empire in order more fully to comprehend and reconfigure the present. In Chapter 16, Ntongela Masilela explores the broader cultural activism of the 'New Africans' who included Selby Msimang, R. V. Selope Thema, H. I. E. Dhlomo, S. E. K. Mqhayi, D. D. T. Jabavu and B. W. Vilakazi. Modelling themselves to some degree on the achievements of African-Americans of the Harlem Renaissance, the task faced by this generation was immense: to reinvent colonial modernity by making it more racially inclusive. Masilela makes a powerful case about the work of the English-language writers having delivered at best an incomplete transformation; in his view, the twenty-first century must turn to indigenous-language models if what is sought is a properly self-defining intellectual history.

This generation regarded literary inventiveness as an index of national self-definition and achievement. In this respect, they shared common terrain with some of the key Afrikaans figures, notably N. P. van Wyk Louw and then D. J. Opperman, as Gerrit Olivier shows in Chapter 15. National restitution following a period of dispossession and the destruction of an agrarian way of life: these themes reach across the racial and language barriers between black writing in English and the indigenous languages, and white writing in Afrikaans. Whilst the black writers tended towards narrative and the revisionist appeal of historiography, the Afrikaans poets, especially, sought to refine the national language and sensibility. Olivier focuses on two noteworthy features of the Afrikaans literature of the 1930s, the poetry of the *Dertigers* (and with it, Van Wyk Louw's cultural philosophy) and the *plaasroman* or farm novel. In both instances, he discusses the lasting significance of these movements, and in the case of the farm novel its enduring fascination for contemporary novelists including Karel Schoeman, Marlene Van Niekerk and J. M. Coetzee. In his comparative analysis of these years Tony Voss, in Chapter 17, compares and contrasts the poetic careers of Roy Campbell, van Wyk Louw and H. I. E. Dhlomo, whose paths intersect and diverge in revealing ways. All three were romantic individualists and interpreters of their respective cultures, embracing different versions of modernism.

In Chapter 18, Craig MacKenzie discusses the lives and careers of predominantly English-language writers 'between the metropolitan and the local'.

From this position, there was little compulsion to develop the ambitious cultural philosophy which drove figures like Van Wyk Louw or Herbert Dhlomo. Nevertheless, Douglas Blackburn, Pauline Smith and William Plomer spent formative periods in South Africa and their major work was deeply engaged with the country's rural life, in Smith's case entirely so. Blackburn, to some extent Plomer, but especially Bosman represent another major trend of this period: satire aimed mainly (though not exclusively) at rural venality and bigotry. Of this group of writers, Bosman is the most locally rooted, although in his case the American humorists provided a model which was easily adapted.

In the general election of 1948 Jan Smuts and the United Party were defeated and the National Party assumed power under D. F. Malan. Union-era politics had given prominence to the reconciliation of English and Afrikaner, an ideal whose ascendancy came to an end with the resurgence of Afrikaner nationalism. Racial segregation, which had built on colonial policy, was extended during the Union period but after 1948 it was codified and written into law as apartheid. These developments catalysed African nationalist and other forms of resistance, most prominently in the Youth League of the ANC in which Nelson Mandela had become prominent. The second half of the twentieth century would be dominated by the most notorious conflict of South Africa's history, between apartheid and the struggle for democracy.

14

Black writers and the historical novel: 1907–1948

BHEKIZIZWE PETERSON

The start of the twentieth century witnessed the first explorations of the novel form by black South African writers. Between 1907 and 1948 many important novels were published that despite their various themes seemed predicated on some degree of engagement with aspects of South Africa's complex and contested history. Amongst many other concerns, three historical developments informed the dominant concerns of the novelists. The first was the large-scale social upheaval, migration and dislocation that occurred across southern Africa in the early decades of the nineteenth century and that is referred to as the *mfecane*.[1] The second was the final defeat of the last independent African polities in the decades before the end of the nineteenth century and their replacement with neotraditional forms of authority under the patronage of colonialism. Then there was the formation of Union in 1910 with the unification of the four colonial provinces into a unitary state. Union consolidated the development of South Africa as a society structured on racial dominance and exploitation and typified by various forms of dispossession and disenfranchisement that afflicted Africans in the twentieth century. It is not surprising, then, that parts of the thematic subtexts of many of the novels reflect on the ways in which the African elite should construct its senses of group and class identity and aspirations, especially in relation to the chiefly classes and colonial administrators.

Since the social, cultural and political experiences that the novels narrate are overdetermined in sociopolitical and economic terms, the authors adopt and engage with a range of political, ethical and literary preoccupations and strategies that are visionary and incendiary, as well as paradoxical and

---

1 For debates on the *mfecane* and whether the changes in Southern African were the results of 'state-building' amongst different polities in the region and, in particular, the Zulu kingdom under Shaka *circa* 1820–36, or whether they were precipitated by the disruptions unleashed by the labour demands of Cape colonists and slave traders based at Delagoa Bay, see Hamilton, *The Mfecane Aftermath*.

contradictory. Some of the key issues that are explored in this regard include the challenges of narrating restorative senses of self amidst the tensions and ambiguities that informed the intelligentsia's experiences of the politics of tradition and modernity, and, in particular, colonial modernity's violent and exclusionary unfolding in South Africa. Even though the novelists cast themselves as modernisers (also demonstrated in their valorisation of literature and the aesthetic as markers of their status as modern citizens), they were compelled to rehabilitate 'the past' by engaging in cultural and literary processes of retrieval and reconstruction, hence the thematic focus on precolonial polities and the tropes of the *mfecane* and Shaka. The past was approached as a mnemonic site, where through its memorialisation in prose, senses of politics, culture and identity could be excavated and offered as parabolic and allegorical parallels, lessons and armour for the present. And when writers explored their contemporary contexts and experiences (narrated through the horrors of industrialisation, urbanisation and forms of sociopolitical and cultural alienation), the present, in the title of R. R. R. Dhlomo's novella, was nothing less than *An African Tragedy* (1928). As for the future, there was no getting away from willing it into being through political mobilisation and the evocation of Janus-like narratives, looking both to the past and to the future.

Tracing the foundations for the novel

Written literature amongst black South Africans owed its emergence to the spread of mission education and its concomitant endeavours with studying, classifying and codifying African languages in the nineteenth century (see Chapter 10 in this volume). The new African intelligentsia were the products of mission schools and they exhibited well into the twentieth century ambiguous and paradoxical relations with missions, Christianity, the 'civilising mission', the 'Enlightenment' and colonial modernity. The establishment of centres such as Lovedale in 1841 and the college at Fort Hare in 1916, with their more systematic teaching of the three Rs and studies of local cultures and languages, were to prove seminal in the emergence and growth of literature. The emergent African elite saw itself as part of the vanguard in the spread of education and Christianity amongst Africans. The latter spirit manifested itself in the high regard given to the acquisition of literacy and the cultivation of 'taste' and 'discrimination' as, ostensibly, manifested in the production and consumption of written literature that is 'exalted'. B. W. Vilakazi cautioned against what he saw as the 'broad application' of the notion of 'Bantu Literature' and instead he preferred a more selective use of the term to distinguish that cultural development with its own vehicle of communication and its own technique of expression, used by the Bantu in their own individual way, spontaneous or studied. It implies further, the communication of the Bantu mind and heart in the revelation of those things of art which we call beauty, with their aesthetic pleasure for both writer and reader, in which the Bantu passes a test and proves his fitness for what Emerson calls 'the ability of man to stand alone'. ('Oral and Written Literature in Nguni', pp. 269, 278)[2]

Newspapers provided the space for the most sustained apprenticeship in writing for Africans, and landmarks in the development of journalism and creative writing amongst Africans can be linked to a number of key newspapers. Lovedale launched *Ikwezi* (The Morning Star, 1844–5) and *Isigidimi* (The Herald, 1870–88). Morija Press in Lesotho started *Leselinyana la Lesotho* (The Little Light of Lesotho) in the 1860s. The Eastern Cape witnessed the appearance of *Imvo Zabantsundu* (Native Opinion, launched in 1884) and *Izwi labantu* (Voice of the People, launched in 1897). In the new century *Koranta ea Bechuana* (Newspaper of the Tswana, Mafikeng, 1902), *Ilanga Lase Natal* (The Natal Sun, 1903) and the Johannesburg-based *Abantu-Batho* (The People, 1912–31) and *Umteteli wa Bantu* (Mouthpiece of the People, 1920–56) were to launch the stellar careers of, amongst others, William Wellington Gqoba, John Tengo Jabavu, John Knox Bokwe, Walter Rubusana, John Langalibalele Dube, Solomon Tshekisho Plaatje, Nontsizi Mgqwetho, R. R. R. Dhlomo and H. I. E. Dhlomo (Opland, *Xhosa Poets and Poetry*, pp. 236–51).

The preferred genres before the forays into extended prose were the short story, essay, poetry and the different forms of indigenous orature and performance traditions. Together with the latter, other key catalysts in the emergence of the novel are the translations of selected books from the Bible and, more importantly, of John Bunyan's *The Pilgrim's Progress*. Biblical parables and Bunyan's text were to serve as important templates for the prose fiction by black writers, especially in their deployment of the aesthetics and politics of allegory.[3] Tiyo Soga's translation of the first part of *Pilgrim's Progress*

---

2 See also pp. 356–7 where, after his assessment of a 'half-a-century' of Nguni literature, Vilakazi declares that 'It is questionable as yet whether any Nguni works can be given the title of "Classics". By "classics" is understood those . . . literary works of the first rank and acknowledged excellence, based upon their artistic quality'. Vilakazi is also concerned with what he perceives to be a tendency towards a superficial and impressionistic assessment of the literary merits of work. Hence the lack of appropriate critical criteria with which to appreciate Bantu literature: 'As yet there lack critical opinions of men of taste and knowledge, whose qualifications would enable them to judge a work by certain positive standards . . . The real decision rests with posterity based on critical knowledge and independent opinions of men of taste and knowledge'.

3 With regard to the Bible, Vilakazi intones that 'no modern literature worthy of the name can ignore the influence of the Bible as a great literary factor in the moral and religious progress of mankind' ('Oral and Written Literature in Nguni', p. 273).

appeared in 1867 as *Uhambo lo Mhambi*; the translation of the second part by his son, John Henderson Soga, appeared in 1927. The Pniel Lutheran Mission School issued a Tswana version in 1848 and Morija issued a Sotho version in 1872. The influence of Bunyan's text can be seen in Thomas Mofolo's *Moeti oa Bochabela* (1907, translated as *The Traveller of the East*, 1931), Everitt Lechesa Segoete's *Monono ke Moholi ke Mouoane* (Riches are like Mist, Vapour, 1910), Sol T. Plaatje's *Mhudi* (1930) and countless variations in the twentieth century on the 'Jim comes to Jo'burg' theme. Other important sources for historical and literary information and style included works by James A. Stuart, Hugh Bryan, Josiah Tyler, Bishop John W. Colenso, Father Anthony T. Bryant and Rider Haggard.[4]

Inasmuch as the first generations of educated black intelligentsia saw themselves as modernisers, they were also keenly aware and concerned with asserting the cultural integrity of their backgrounds. As a result they compiled and wrote hymnals, poems, journalistic articles and books that traced and valorised the history, language, folklore and customs of their respective African nationalities and polities in South Africa and Lesotho. In the genre of hymnals, the output of converts such as Ntsikana (*c.* 1783–*c.* 1820) and Isaiah Shembe (*c.* 1870–1935) were to be deeply influential, the thematic concerns of their hymns often revisited in the twentieth century. Key amongst pioneering texts with an historical and anthropological orientation are Azariele M. Sekese's collection of articles, *Buka ea Pokello ea Mekhoa ea Basotho le Maele le Litsomo* (Book that is a Collection of the Customs of the Basotho, and their Proverbs and their Folktales; see Kunene, 'African-Language Literatures', 295), Isaiah Bud-Mbelle's *Kafir Scholar's Companion* (1903), W. B. Rubusana's *Zemk'inkomo Magwalandini* (There go your Cattle, you Cowards, 1906), S. M. Molema's *The Bantu Past and Present* (1920), Magema ka Magwaza M. Fuze's *Abantu abamnyama, lapha bavela ngakhona* (Black People and from whence they came, 1922), John Henderson Soga's *The South-Eastern Bantu* (1930) and *The Ama-Xosa: Life and Customs* (1931).

Archibald C. Jordan has observed that from the 1880s there is a discernible disenchantment with the evangelical and colonial projects amongst the African intelligentsia. This is in the wake of the Basutoland Gun War in 1880–1; the last Frontier War in the Eastern Cape, starting in 1887, that led to the final subjugation of the Xhosa; and, in the same year, the British assault on the Zulu kingdom that concluded in the defeat of Cetshwayo in 1879. 'The African

---

4 Vilakazi describes Stuart's Readers as 'a mine for many writers of the future. I am safe in saying that most of the Zulu authors have been roused to action by Stuart's books' ('Some Aspects of Zulu Literature', pp. 270, 274).

writers', Jordan suggests, were 'now face to face with the military conqueror who lurked behind the missionaries. The earliest writers saw no connection between the two' (*Towards an African Literature*, p. 89). He notes that 'the few short stories written at this period make depressing reading. The rapid changes are undermining the African's manhood in all walks of life, and the writers are concerned with this rather than with entertainment' (p. 88). Amongst the oral poets, the associations of evangelism and education with conquest and colonialism, the Bible and the book with treaties and the gun, were long-standing (see Opland, *Xhosa Poets and Poetry*, chapter 14).

The novel and history

Many of the novels published between 1907 and 1940 can be described as historical novels. There is, firstly, the persistent interest in drawing on key historical experiences, events and characters as the raw material for fictional endeavours. In particular, the widespread warfare and social dislocation that resulted from the *mfecane* and the 1856–7 Cattle-Killing amongst the Xhosa, were tropes that were frequently revisited by writers. In 1857 Nongqawuse, a young prophet, claimed that the ancestors implored the people to destroy their grain and kill their cattle. Upon the completion of the ancestral injunction, the dead warriors, the corn and the cattle would rise again and the white men would be defeated and driven into the sea (see Peires, *Dead will Arise*). The latter did not come to pass and the episode was figured by writers and politicians as tantamount to a 'national suicide'.

It is understandable, then, that the epochal historical upheavals of the nineteenth century provided the recurring historical tropes within or against which the narratives were set. Consequently, and interestingly, the history that is drawn upon, scrutinised and imaginatively depicted is often one that is pre-colonial and frontier rather than contemporary. Furthermore, the authorial point of view is interested in the elaboration of collective rather than individual social destinies. Also, in their recourse to history, the authors emphasise the links between the past and the present by creating narratives that enter into a dialogic representation of past, present and future. It is in this sense that the resultant narratives were intended to speak deeply to the historical developments and struggles of the day and age in which the writers found themselves. In this regard, the strengths and weaknesses of preconquest African polities are interrogated and contrasted with the inequalities and disfranchisement which typify white oligarchies that emerge in the wake of the post-Union, settler-colonial state. The latter, however, is evoked and negotiated through the use of allegory and a complex marshalling of aesthetics and strategies drawn from orature and not simply through realism and social realism, as was the case in the European historical novel.

A striking feature of the narratives is that, despite their different authors, contexts and concerns, and the use of genre conventions that range from the epic to the romance and historical novel, there is a deep and permeating sense of historical focus. Mofolo's *Moeti oa Bochabela* was serialised in 1907 in the *Leselinyana* before appearing as a book later the same year. It is reputed to be the first novel published by an African. Mofolo's *Pitseng* (In the Pot) was also serialised in *Leselinyana* before its publication in 1910 and *Chaka* was published in 1925, though it is speculated that the novel was completed by 1909 but only appeared in 1925 because some members of the Paris Evangelical Missionary Society 'construed it as an apology for pagan superstitions' (Gérard, *African Language Literatures*, p. 191). Chaka was translated into English in 1931 and into French in 1940, and Gérard regards it as 'the first major African contribution to world literature' and 'the earliest modern Bantu classic'.

Henry Masila Ndawo's *uHambo lukaGqoboka* (Christian's Journey, 1909) is regarded as the first Xhosa novel. Samuel Edward Krune Mqhayi, an influential figure in oral poetry, augmented his status as a poet with the writing of important novels such as *Ityala lamawele* (The Lawsuit of the Twins, 1914), which he followed up with his allegorical novel *UDon Jadu* (1929). Letitia Kakaza, the first woman to make forays into extended prose, wrote two Xhosa novellas *Intyatambo yomzi* (The Flower of the Home, 1913) and *Tandiwe wakha Gcaleka* (Tandiwe, a Maiden from Gcaleka) (see Opland, *Xhosa Poets and Poetry*, p. 196.) Enoch Sillinga Guma's *UNomaliso* (which is another exploration of the 'evils of the city' theme) was translated from isiXhosa into English as *Nomaliso, or The Things of this Life are Sheer Vanity*, appearing in 1928. Sol Plaatje's *Mhudi* – probably completed by 1920 – was published in 1930 and is regarded as the first novel in English written by a black South African. John L. Dube's *UJeqe Insila kaShaka* (1933) is the first novel in isiZulu. It was followed by a series of novels that were to become landmarks in Zulu literature, by R. R. R. Dhlomo and Benedict W. Vilakazi. Dhlomo wrote five historical novels on the lives of Zulu kings starting with *UDingane* (1936), *UShaka* (1937), *UMpande* (1938), *UCetshwayo* (1952) and *UDinuzulu* (1968). He returned to the concerns he treated in *An African Tragedy* in *Idlela Yababi* (The Way of the Wicked, 1946). Vilakazi's oeuvre – in addition to his seminal poetry in the anthologies *Inkondlo kaZulu* (Zulu Songs, 1935) and *Amal'ezulu* (Zulu Horizons, 1945) – includes the novels *Noma Nini* (For Ever, 1935), *UDingiswayo ka Jobe* (Dingiswayo, Son of Jobe, 1939) and *Nje-Nempela* (Truly, Indeed, 1949). Davidson Pelman Moloto wrote the first novel in Setswana, *Mokwena*, in 1937, which was an ethnographical representation of the customs of the Bakwena as encapsulated in the life story of one of their chiefs. Daniel Cornel Marivate's novella in Xitsonga, *Sasavona*, on the perennial comparison between tradition and Christianity, appeared in 1938. The 1940s were ushered in with the publication of A. C. Jordan's seminal *Ingqumbo Yeminyanya* (translated by the author as *The Wrath of the Ancestors*, 1940) and E. H. A. Made's Zulu novel, *Indlalifa yase Harrisdale* (1940). Both novels explore the 'conflict of cultures' theme, with Made's novel also drawing on the motif of the prodigal son. One of Jordan's contemporaries and master Xhosa poet, J. J. R. Jolobe, published another revisiting of the Chaka theme, *Elundini loThukela* (On the Horizon of the Thukela Valley) in 1959. The period demarcated for this study closes with the emergence of the next generation of writers, led by Peter Abrahams, who produced *Song of the City* (1945), *Mine Boy* (1946), *The Path of Thunder* (1948) and *Wild Conquest* (1950).

The allure and treachery of history

Albert Gérard has surmised that for the black writers who emerged in the first two decades of the twentieth century 'the historical novel . . . was an oblique and politically innocuous way of conveying the lessons that the past held in store for the present' (*African Language Literatures*, pp. 195–6). When considering the larger sociopolitical motivations that probably informed the turn towards the historical novel amongst the 'New Africans', two observations are in order. As Gérard notes with regards to Mofolo's *Chaka*, the responses of the missionary presses to the emerging novels were far from innocuous. We know, in some detail, that the publication of two seminal novels, Mofolo's *Chaka* and Plaatje's *Mhudi*, were occasions for what is tantamount to editorial skirmishes between the writers and their respective publishers.[5] It is also important to grasp that the seemingly cautious political ideas and actions of black writers reflected a much deeper and symptomatic weakness within the African elite as an embryonic class. Elsewhere, drawing on Phillip Bonner's writing on black politics in the interwar years, I have argued that the ambiguities and paradoxes of African nationalism stemmed from the various forms of

5 For discussions of the fractious publication histories of such texts see the following: Gérard, *Four African Literatures*, where he suggests that the delay in the publication of *Chaka* was due to its negative reception by priests such as the Revd H. I. Dieterlen (pp. 116, 127–8); and Kunene, *Thomas Mofolo*, pp. 142–52; and for *Mhudi* see Gray, *Southern African Literature*, pp. 127–8, 172–82. See also Opland, *Xhosa Poets and Poetry*, chapters 11 and 12, for discussions of the fraught relations between missionaries and African writers at Lovedale.

dependency that informed the African elite in South Africa (Peterson, *Monarchs, Missionaries and African Intellectuals*, pp. 15–18, 171–82). I suggested that the limited size and social power of the new African intelligentsia predisposed them to engaging with colonial society on the level of ideas and consciousness. In doing so I drew on Laclau's proposition that 'the more separated is a social sector from the dominant relations of production, and the more diffuse are its "objective interests" and consequently, less developed its "class instinct" – the more the evolution and the resolution of the crisis will tend to take place on the ideological level' (Laclau, *Politics and Ideology in Marxist Theory*, p. 104).

Narrative and historiography seemed extremely attractive tools and sites with which to challenge colonial accounts on South African society and history. Narrative, it would seem, was one ideological site that the African intelligentsia felt was, firstly, under its relative control and, secondly, allowed for contesting colonial historiography. Such a demeanour was necessitated by the frequency with which colonial ideologues invoked an Africa without history, culture or civilisations as part of rationalising the colonial project. As H. I. E. Dhlomo remarked, 'time and again our position and future have been prejudiced and made insecure by reference to our past', a past that was dismissed by white historians as primitive and barbaric ('Evolution II'). It is important to emphasise that the authors had fairly nuanced and troubled perspectives on the concept and treacherous politics of historiography. Furthermore, another challenge was the novelist's reliance on the very colonial historical archive that they sought to contest, recast and even displace. The thematic and aesthetic consequences of such tensions are key in an understanding of the thematic preoccupations and aesthetic strategies of the novelists. At any rate, history, in their opinion, was far from being an objective bedrock that provided the 'back-story' against which they could measure their experiences and narratives.

Dhlomo, in one of his most prescient essays, 'The Evolution of the Bantu', presents the challenges that writers and historians need to overcome if they are to present accounts that transcend the limitations of colonial discourses. Dhlomo identifies two weaknesses in colonial historiography. The first is the ethnocentric assumption that 'the writing of the history of backward people is very simple work'. As a result, crucial aspects of African life (such as ethics, philosophy, art and religion) have no bearing on the histories that are proffered. Secondly, and important for our purposes, is the weak appreciation of what Dhlomo regards as the principal craft of the historian, 'the art of narrative'; that is, the recourse to narrative in order to 'combine fragments into living whole' and to 'find a general law in a mass of scattered facts' ('Literary

Theory and Criticism', p. 19) – facts that were open to being 'given various interpretations . . . depending on the bias of the writer or reader' ('History and Human Behaviour'). Mindful of the discursivity of historiography, Dhlomo emphasised that 'our ideas of the past, present and future do not rest on a firm and unchanging impregnable rock of finality or perfection, but are dependent upon the shifting sands of conditions and doctrines and thoughts' ('Evolution III'). Such a sense of the partial and contested nature of history is implicit in Plaatje's observations in his preface to *Mhudi* where he notes that 'South African literature has hitherto been almost exclusively European' and that 'in all the tales of war I have ever read, or heard of, the cause of the war is invariably ascribed to the other side'.[6] His intention in writing the novel was, consequently, 'to interpret to the reading public one phase of "the back of the Native mind"' (*Mhudi*, p. 21).

The next challenge, over and above the contestation of colonial historiography, resided in the historical and sociopolitical perspective of the writers as well as their literary inventiveness and abilities. For instance, Vilakazi, even though he was impressed with the writings of African writers, felt that 'their historical understanding is not yet deep enough'. On the one hand, he notes, approvingly, that

> the shifting facets of an African author's opinions represent intellectual growth in the adjustment of his literary methods and approach. The writers who began by moralising and judging all heathen conduct on a western ethical basis now have turned back critically, and take pride in their past, in the same way as the West glories in the achievements of its classical period.

However, he continues, often

> the flow of the narrative is encumbered by an undue amount of historical and anthropological information, it is also quite possible that to the author this was the core of his message, which he tried to convey more attractively and more efficiently by embodying it in some love story derived, perhaps, from fashionable western interest in such matters.
>
> ('Oral and Written Literature in Nguni', p. 371)[7]

---

6 Vilakazi in the prefaces to *Noma Nini* and *Nje-Nempela* links the need to create a canon of Zulu literature with the imperative to remind contemporary generations of the history and warriors of the past. For a fuller treatment of the tactical uses of prefaces by black writers to negotiate and circumvent possible readings, readerships and the 'thresholds of native life', see Peterson, 'Sol Plaatje's *Native Life in South Africa*'.

7 Interestingly, Vilakazi's own novels have been accused of similar tendencies. See Khumalo, 'Plot and Character'.

Then there were the complexities that arose as a result of the different demands of literature and history. The imagination and the demands of narration (in the creative sense) were not always consistent with the factual and forensic demands and claims of historiography. In such cases, not only was historical detail open to different interpretations but, often, writers consciously privileged the imagination over facts. So, for instance, in response to criticism concerning perceived historical inaccuracies in *Chaka*, Mofolo responded:

> I believe that errors of this kind are many in the book *Chaka*; but I am not very concerned about them because I am not writing history. I am writing a tale, or I should rather say I am writing what actually happened, and from which a great deal has been removed, so that much has been left out, and much has been written that did not actually happen, with the aim solely of fulfilling my purpose in writing this book. (p. xv)

Furthermore, 'the events in Chaka's life were overwhelming because they were so numerous and of such tremendous import; they were like great mysteries which were beyond the people's understanding. But since it is not our purpose to recount all the affairs of his life, we have chosen only one part which suits our present purpose' (p. 153). Mofolo's historical infidelity, according to Kunene, 'is to build up greater intensity in plot, and to increase dramatic tensions by creating new juxtapositions of highly volatile events and situations' (Mofolo, *Chaka*, p. xv).

Similarly, in his reading of Peter Abrahams's intentions and narrative point of view in *Wild Conquest*, Es'kia Mphahlele suggests that 'Abrahams has introduced "a new will into the past time", thus bending history in order to tell more of the truth than the historian. This "unhistorical will" operates within a short space of time in history, so that the characters produce short-lived effects' (*African Image*, p. 215). Part of Abrahams's 'unhistorical will', evidently, results from the writer 'trying to break away from the Rider Haggard tradition of bloodthirsty witch-doctors (Ntongolwane in *Wild Conquest* is like Gagool the witch-doctor in *King Solomon's Mines*)' (p. 216). Interestingly, Mphahlele regards *Wild Conquest* as a rewrite of *Mhudi*: 'He takes up Plaatje's story twenty years later and blows it up so that Mzilikazi and Gubuza attain life-size proportions' (*African Image*, p. 214).

Allegory, the ruins of history and redemption

I have noted that such historical and allegorical novels do not simply reflect a world that is past but that they seek to interact in very intricate ways with the contemporary world that is being inhabited by authors and readers. The novelists, in their preoccupation with establishing the continuities and discontinuities between past, present and future, turn to the politics and aesthetics of allegory in the texts. Allegories tend to flourish in periods experiencing profound social transformation, when the certitudes of old beliefs and epochs are violently called into question and where future directions and possibilities have yet to crystallise. In Walter Benjamin's pithy statement, 'allegories are, in the realm of thoughts, what ruins are in the realm of things' (*Origin of German Tragic Drama*, p. 178).

At the most basic level, historical allegories posit multiple, parallel frames of reference where the characters, events and experiences that are in the narrative proper are, over and above their coherence and meaning within a specific frame, meant to signify another correlated set of actions, agents, historical periods and meanings. It is in this sense that novels such as *Chaka*, *Insila kaShaka*, *Mhudi*, *UDingiswayo Ka Jobe* and *Wild Conquest* are set in the time between 1820 and 1848. The historical setting allows the authors to scrutinise the *mfecane*, the great social and political upheavals that played themselves out across southern Africa in the wake of a complex set of interconnected developments. The two key contributing factors to the *mfecane* were the territorial colonial expansion by British and Afrikaner forces in the aftermath of victories scored in numerous frontier wars, and the growth and militarisation of the Zulu state, initially under the leadership of Shaka.[8] In both instances, the chain of wars that were unleashed from the 1820s resulted in a large-scale destruction of kingdoms, the appropriation of land and the use of indentured labour. These developments, in turn, initiated considerable environmental pressures and demographic shifts following the widespread migration of people. All in all, violence, plunder, the loss of land, political power and rights meant that access to the means and quality of life by Africans was deeply compromised.

The novelists draw on what they regard as the Shakan legacy in order to posit analogies with and to critically interrogate their contemporary experiences in the twentieth century. Firstly, in the latter regard, black writers considered the role the *mfecane* played in facilitating the defeat of the remaining independent African polities, including the Zulu kingdom. The crucial questions posed concerned whether Shaka, for instance, should be regarded as a great unifier and symbol of black unity, or whether his exploits and

8 Shaka has been the subject of diverse creative treatments across the continent, including Leopold Senghor's *Chaka* (1956), S. Badian's *La Mort de Chaka* (The Death of Chaka, 1961), Condetto Nenekhaly-Camara's *Amazoulou* (1970) and Djibril Niane's *Chaka* (1971). See Gérard *Afrian Languages Literatures*, p. 192. For a fascinating account of the depiction of Shaka in the white imaginary, see Wylie, *Savage Delight*.

the internecine warfare that followed his demise facilitated colonial conquest because they dissipated black energy, focus and unity. In H. I. E. Dhlomo's view, Shaka's rule and policies 'gave birth . . . to the adverse conditions prevailing in Natal today' ('Tshaka: A Revaluation'); or, expressed differently, the formation of the centralised Zulu state, ironically, laid 'the basis for its substitution by a new colonial power' (Marks and Atmore, *Economy and Society*, p. 18). As a catalyst in both history and in the novels, the Zulu monarch is depicted as the supreme being, the link between nature, man and the gods. This is especially so in the historical and quasibiographical novels of Zulu kings that R. R. R. Dhlomo wrote. Generally, the representation of Shaka, and subsequent Zulu kings, is informed by a tyrant–martyr dichotomy. Most African authors start by scrutinising the leadership qualities and style of Zulu monarchs in relation to their own Christian and 'democratic' sensibilities, and the author finds the monarch to be tyrannical or wanting because of their authoritarian rule. However, as soon as colonial forces start to encroach on a monarch's domain and mindful of the demonisation of black leaders by colonial ideologues, these writers institute a corrective change in the way they represent the monarch as the narrative progresses. The tyrant is then rehabilitated into a martyr whose previous despotism is attributed to various conditioning factors that range from psychological, cultural and sociopolitical influences that stem from childhood experiences, the defence of African independence and dignity, to the gallant and sacrificial bravery that makes them try and halt the relentless march of colonialism. In his preface to *Dingane*, R. R. R. Dhlomo observed that 'today it is very easy for us to dismiss the deeds of the past as bad ones; we do not see much that is good in them'. The reason is that Africans 'interpret things through . . . the eyes of learning and Christian beliefs, and of civilisation. Today the deeds that disturb us are those that were performed by our chiefs' (*UDingane*, p. i). Mphahlele, in response to the paradoxes that informed black writing, perceptively described the tension between a traditional ethos and a Christian ethos as 'a dialogue of two selves'.[9] The other thematic areas in which such a conflicting orientation revealed itself in the novels is in the ambiguous representation of *lobolo* (dowry), polygamy, traditional healers and medicine.

It is clear that the development of South Africa into an oppressive and exploitative white oligarchy had its roots in developments and events predating the twentieth century. Then, of course, there are the many sociopolitical

9 See the essays 'African Literature: A Dialogue of Two Selves and the Voice of Prophecy – 1975' and 'Landmarks of Literary History in South Africa: A Black Perspective – 1980' in Mphahlele, *Es'kia*.

parallels between 1820–48 and the period 1910–48. The successive post-Union governments implemented a Native Policy that entrenched racial segregation, repression, subjugation, disenfranchisement and exploitation of black South Africans. The crucial legislation that was promulgated included the Native Labour Regulation Act of 1911 that classified the breaking of job contracts as a criminal offence; the Native Land Bill of 1911 and the Land Act of 1913 which set aside 7.3 per cent of land for occupation by blacks; the Masters and Servants Act and the Native Service Contract Act of 1932, the Native Administration Act of 1927 and the Native (Urban Areas Act) of 1932 and its Amendment Act of 1935, all of which regulated the movement of Africans; and the Hertzog Bills of 1936 which removed Africans from the Cape common voters role. In *Mhudi*, Plaatje draws explicit parallels between the past, the present, and their implications for the future. He critiques the expansionist dreams of King Mzilikazi in language which recalls Cecil John Rhodes's own imperial visions: 'This was his dream of many years, but now he saw the imperial structure of his super expansionist dream shattered and blown away like so many autumn leaves at the mercy of a violent hurricane' (pp. 170–1). There is also, of course, an intimation of the ways in which, as is amply affirmed by South Africa's history, violence begets violence.

African oppositional politics in the interwar years were as much marked by the striving for unity as by fractious tendencies, underpinned by a conservative, middle of the road approach by the African National Congress. Vilakazi suggests that the search for unity is an underlying thematic thread in the literary endeavours of writers since Rubusana's *Zemk'Inkomo Magwalandini*:

> [Magema] Fuze visualises a united black people of the future in the light of their past history. The Congress stood for this unity. Dr Rubusana in his book *Zemk' Inkomo Magwalandini* has already seen this, and the whole air of his book is a protest againt Bantu disunity. Stuart's records of the Zulu rebellion of 1906 seems to confirm my idea that the political unity of which the Black peoples felt the urge, found itself in all the books of that period, 1905–1925. But as this period drew to a close, Dr Dube's vision of an accomplished unity seems to dwindle, and experience had taught him that the failure of black people is not wholly to be laid at the White man's door, but that most of it could be accounted for in the Black man's insincerity to one another. Hence the title of his book *Isitha somuntu*.
>
> (Vilakazi, 'Some Aspects of Zulu Literature', pp. 271–2)

Following the promulgation of the Hertzog Bills, a broad coalition of black oppositional groups, under the chairmanship of D. D. T. Jabavu, convened in Bloemfontein on 16 December 1935 under the banner of the All African

Convention (AAC). The African National Congress appealed to 'African leaders and masses to unite, and to bury all political differences in this time of national crisis' (Jabavu, *Criticism of the Native Bills*, p. 24). Yet, ultimately, despite the occasional pronouncements of 'fire and brimstone', the AAC, in the sharp observation of Jack and Ray Simons, suffered from the fact that 'a people's front so widely based was bound to cheer the radicals and follow the moderates' (*Class and Colour in South Africa*, p. 493).

It is important to note that allegorical evocations of the past extend beyond their significance in the setting of conditions for the present and the future. The past, as an allegorical motif, becomes 'not merely a sign of what is to be known but it is in itself an object worthy of knowledge' (Benjamin, *Origin of German Tragic Drama*, p. 184). It becomes a mnemonic site where the allegorist can search and excavate the ruins of history and in H. I. E. Dhlomo's terms, 'assemble the broken gourds' and show how and when 'the gourds were broken' (*Collected Works*, p. 93). It is in this sense that all the novels that are set in the nineteenth century, whatever their specific themes and narratives, engage in various ways and to various degrees with the processes of social, political and cultural retrieval and reconstruction. In the first edition of Lovedale's *Indaba* in August 1862, Tiyo Soga, 'writing as Unonjiba waseluhlangeni (the dove of the nation)', implored readers and writers to use the newspaper as 'a beautiful vessel for preserving stories, fables, legends, customs, anecdotes and history of the tribes... Everything must be imparted to the nation as a whole'. Furthermore, 'let us bring to life our ancestors... Let us resurrect our ancestral forebears who bequeathed to us a rich heritage' (Opland, *Xhosa Poets and Poetry*, pp. 237–8).

On the level of form, the novels draw on, or use as eulogies, cultural repertoires from orature and make frequent use of folk-tales, legends, myths, hunting tales, historical narratives, praise poetry, proverbs and clan names. Furthermore, precolonial societies, whatever their limitations, are presented in novels such as *Ityala lamawele* and *Mhudi* as well-structured polities with cohesive, integrated and complex forms of governance, judicial systems, cultures, cosmologies and epistemologies. The past as heritage is in itself a critique of conquest and the inequities of the present. In setting the scene of the Barolong before conquest, Plaatje writes, 'strange to relate, these simple folk were perfectly happy without money or silver watches. Abject poverty was practically unknown; they had no orphanages because there were no nameless babies' (*Mhudi*, p. 27). No wonder that Ra-Thaga in his poetic paean to Mhudi, says, 'Give back the palmy days of our early felicity / Away from the hurly burly of your city' (p. 71). Writing in a different context and many decades later, Chinua Achebe was compelled to state that 'I would be quite satisfied if my novels (especially the ones I set in the past) did no more than teach my readers that their past – with all its imperfections – was not one long night of savagery from which the first Europeans acting on God's behalf delivered them' (*Morning yet on Creation Day*, p. 72).

Next to the depiction of precolonial life, the majority of novels explore the entanglements of the contact zones where tradition and modernity encounter each other in intricate and ambiguous ways. The earlier, straightforward treatments of conversion and its benefits that were presented in accounts such as Mofolo's *Moeti oa Bochabela*, *Pitseng* and Ndawo's *uHambo lukaGqoboka* are superseded by more complex and layered reflections on the contradictions and paradoxes that inform the experiences of the educated and Christianised African elite who are caught between African and western modes of living. Vilakazi's *Noma Nini* and *Nje-Nempela* and Jordan's *Ingqumbo Yeminyanya* are classic explorations of the latter themes. Importantly, they do so in a manner that shows the personal and social consequences that flow from the contending social groups, cosmologies and epistemologies in ways that challenge the usual notions of 'tradition' and 'modernity', 'collaboration' and 'resistance'.

A similar approach and development is discerned in the treatment of urbanisation and its discontents. The city, initially, was presented as the antithesis of both African and Christian values and life. In novels such as *An African Tragedy* town life is associated with moral laxity, alcohol abuse, gangsterism, prostitution and all the evils that suggest the breakdown of traditional and Christian familial and cultural values. The appearance of Mqhayi's *UDon Jadu* in 1929 ushered in a more socially rather than simply morally grounded understanding of the various forms of alienation that blacks were experiencing in the cities. Don Jadu's journeys impress upon him that poverty, alienation, violence and racial intolerance are widespread and can be found in the 'reserves' as well as in the cities. Since there is no pristine 'homeland' to retreat to (given the instances of serfdom that Don Jadu witnesses), Mqhayi imagines a future, utopian, non-racial and egalitarian society, where there is respect and work for everyone: a place that he tellingly calls *Mnandi*, that is, bliss or sweetness. It was to be in Abrahams's *Song of the City* and *Mine Boy*, and in the novels by the next generation of black writers, that the permanency of black people in the cities of South Africa was accepted and urban life, with all its pains and pleasures, embraced.

Bibliography

Abrahams, P. *Mine Boy*, London: Heinemann Educational, 1978.

    The Path of Thunder, Cape Town: David Philip, 1984.

    Song of the City: A Novel, London: Dorothy Crisp, 1945.

    Wild Conquest, New York: Anchor Books, 1971.

Achebe, C. *Morning yet on Creation Day*, London: Heinemann Educational, 1975.

Benjamin, W. *The Origin of German Tragic Drama*, trans. J. Osborne, London: Verso, 1985.

Bud-Mbelle, I. *Kafir Scholar's Companion*, Alice: Lovedale Press, 1903.

Dhlomo, H. I. E. *The Collected Works of H. I. E. Dhlomo*, Johannesburg: Ravan, 1985.

    'The Evolution of the Bantu ɪ', *Umteteli wa Bantu*, 14 November 1931.

    'The Evolution of the Bantu ɪɪ', *Umteteli wa Bantu*, 21 November 1931.

    'The Evolution of the Bantu ɪɪɪ', *Umteteli wa Bantu*, 28 November 1931.

    'History and Human Behaviour', *Umteteli wa Bantu*, 24 September 1932.

    'Literary Theory and Criticism', ed. N. Visser, special issue of *English in Africa* 4:7 (1977).

    'Tshaka: A Revaluation', *Umteteli wa Bantu*, 18 June 1932.

Dhlomo, R. R. R. *An African Tragedy*, Lovedale: Lovedale Press, 1928.

    Indlela Yababi, Pietermaritzburg: Shuter & Shooter, 1962.

    UCetshwayo kaMpande, Pieteramaritzburg: Shuter & Shooter, 1952.

    UDingane kaSenzangakhona, Pietermaritzburg: Shuter & Shooter, 1966.

    UDinuzulu, Pietermaritzburg: Shuter & Shooter, 1968.

    UMpande, Pietermaritzburg: Shuter & Shooter, 1949.

    UNomalanga kaNdengezi, Pietermaritzburg: Shuter & Shooter, 1947.

    UShaka, Pietermaritzburg: Shuter & Shooter, 1970.

Dube, J. *UJeqe: Insila kaShaka*, Mariannhill: Mariannhill Mission Press, 1985.

Fuze, M. M. *Abantu abamnyama, lapha bavela ngakhona*, Pietermaritzburg: University of Natal Press, 1979.

Gérard, A. *African Language Literatures: An Introduction to the Literary History of Sub-Saharan Africa*, London: Longman, 1981.

    Four African Literatures, Berkeley: University of California Press, 1971.

Gray, S. *Southern African Literature: an Introduction*, Cape Town: David Philip, 1979.

Guma, E. S. *UNomalizo or 'The Things of this Life are Sheer Vanity'*, London: Sheldon Press, 1928.

Hamilton, C. *The Mfecane Aftermath: Reconstructive Debates in Southern African History*, Johannesburg: Witwatersrand University Press, 1995.

Jabavu, D. D. T. *Criticisms of the Native Bills*, Alice: Lovedale Press, 1935.

Jolobe, J. J. R. *Elundini loThukela*, Johannesburg: Educum, 1984.

Jordan, A. C. *Ingqumbo Yeminyanya*, Alice: Lovedale Press, 1940.

    Towards an African Literature: The Emergence of Literary Form in Xhosa, Berkeley: University of California Press, 1973.

    The Wrath of the Ancestors, Johannesburg: Ad Donker, 2004.

Khumalo, J. S. M. 'Plot and Character in Vilakazi's Novels', *Limi* 14 (1972).

Kunene, D. P. 'African-Language Literatures of Southern Africa', in F. A. Irele and S. Gikandi (eds.), *The Cambridge History of African and Caribbean Literature*, 2 vols., Cambridge University Press, 2004, vol. ɪ, 289–305.

    Thomas Mofolo and the Emergence of Written Sesotho Prose, Johannesburg: Ravan, 1989.

Laclau, E. *Politics and Ideology in Marxist Theory*, London: Verso, 1987.

Made, E. H. A. *Indlalifa yase Harrisdale*, Pietermaritzburg: Shuter & Shooter, 1940.

Marivate, D. C. *Sasavona*, Johannesburg: Swiss Mission in South Africa, 1938.

Marks, S. and R. Atmore (eds.). *Economy and Society in Pre-Industrial South Africa*, London: Longman, 1980.

Mofolo, T. *Chaka*, trans. D. P. Kunene, London: Heinemann, 1989.

Moeti oa Bochabela, Morija: Morija Sesuto Book Depot, 1907.

Pitseng, Morija: Morija Sesuto Book Depot, 1930.

Molema, S. M. *The Bantu Past and Present*, Cape Town: Struik, 1963.

Moloto, D. P. *Mokwena*, Cape Town: Via Afrika, 1961.

Mphahlele, E *The African Image*, London: Faber, 1974.

Es'kia: Education, African Humanism and Culture, Social Consciousness, Literary Appreciation, Cape Town: Kwela Books, 2002.

Mqhayi, S. E. K. *Ityala lamawele*, Alice: Lovedale Press, 1947.

UDon Jadu, Alice: Lovedale Press, 1944.

Ndawo, H. M. *uHambo lukaGqoboka*, Alice: Lovedale Press, 1952.

Opland J. *Xhosa Poets and Poetry*, Cape Town: David Philip, 1998.

Peires, J. B. *The Dead will Arise: Nongqawuse and the Great Xhosa Cattle Killing Movement of 1856–57*, Johannesburg: Ravan, 1989.

Peterson, B. *Monarchs, Missionaries and African Intellectuals: African Theatre and the Unmaking of Colonial Marginality*, Johannesburg: University of the Witwatersrand Press, 2000.

'Sol Plaatje's *Native Life in South Africa*: Melancholy Narratives, Petitioning Selves and the Ethics of Suffering', *Journal of Commonwealth Literature* 43:1 (2008), 79–95.

Plaatje, S. T. *Mhudi* [1978], London: Heinemann, 1982.

Rubusana, W. B. *Zemk'inkomo Magwalandini*, Alice: Lovedale Press, 1964.

Segoete, E. L. *Monono ke Moholi ke Mouoane*, Mojira: Mojira Sesuto Book Depot, 1926.

Simons, J., and R. Simons. *Class and Colour in South Africa, 1850–1950*, London: International Defence and Aid Fund, 1983.

Soga, J. H. *The Ama-Xosa: Life and Customs*, Alice: Lovedale Press, 1932.

The South-Eastern Bantu, Johannesburg: Witwatersrand University Press, 1930.

Soga, T. *Uhambo lo Mhambi*, Alice: Lovedale Press, 1889.

Vilakazi, B. W. *Amal'ezulu*, Johannesburg: Witwatersrand University Press, 1945.

Inkondlo kaZulu, Johannesburg: Witwatersrand University Press, 1944.

Nje-Nempela, Mariannhill: Mariannhill Mission Press, 1985.

Noma Nini, Mariannhill: Mariannhill Mission Press, 1962.

'The Oral and Written Literature in Nguni', Ph.D. thesis, University of the Witwatersrand, 1945.

'Some Aspects of Zulu Literature', *African Studies* 1:4 (1942), 270–4.

UDingiswayo ka Jobe, Mariannhill: Mariannhill Mission Press, 1939.

Wylie, D. *Savage Delight: White Myths of Shaka*, Pietermaritzburg: University of KwaZulu-Natal Press, 2000.

15

The Dertigers and the *plaasroman*: two brief perspectives on Afrikaans literature

GERRIT OLIVIER

Afrikaans writers of the 1930s

The two main figures who interpreted the renewal brought to Afrikaans literature by the Dertigers (Poets of the Thirties) were N. P. van Wyk Louw (1906–70), the most prominent Dertiger, and D. J. Opperman (1914–85), who appeared on the literary scene about a decade after him. Both these poets were also academics and men of letters. Due to their erudition and sound judgement their views on Afrikaans literature and its historical development gained lasting authority. Van Wyk Louw entered the discursive arena at key moments to decisively shift the debate, as he did at the beginning of the 1960s in *Vernuwing in die Prosa* (Innovation in Fiction). Opperman's defining anthology *Groot Verseboek* (Great Book of Verse), first published in 1951, survives up to the present and has had a huge influence in shaping literary tastes. In different ways Van Wyk Louw and Opperman established a canon that would remain virtually unchallenged for many years. As late as 1969, for example, Ernst van Heerden's essay on nationalism and literature ('Nasionalisme en Literatuur', pp. 22–44) largely reiterates ideas formulated by Van Wyk Louw thirty years earlier.

Van Wyk Louw and Opperman were key figures in the establishment of a new cast in the Afrikaans literary world: that of the literary critic. In their writings and those of contemporaries such as H. A. Mulder (1906–49), W. E. G. Louw (1913–80) and Gerrit Dekker (1887–1973), the patriotically supportive literary culture of previous generations was replaced by a more erudite, demanding, combative and comparative approach.

Thus the appearance of the Dertigers marked two emancipatory developments that would help define the landscape of Afrikaans literature. Complementing the rapid growth of a more cosmopolitan and technically accomplished literature, there came into being a professional discourse around that literature. A new generation of commentators, the most prominent of whom were all university teachers, created an impressive body of criticism.

The rivalry between Van Wyk Louw and Opperman as poets and critics greatly enriched Afrikaans literature. Whereas in the 1960s Van Wyk Louw (see Chapter 17) emphasised the primacy of the aesthetic, in the 1950s he pleaded for a more rigorous scholarly approach in which the investigation of influences or 'the person behind the book' would be replaced by a focus on the text itself as the object of study. This was a confident rebuke to existing amateurish practices. But Opperman's *Digters van Dertig* (1953), the most impressive single piece of literary analysis to have appeared in Afrikaans by then, was in effect a silent repudiation of Van Wyk Louw's formalism, containing many freely made claims about biographic, bibliographic and contextual influences on authors and texts. The debate between text-centred and more contextually sensitive approaches to literature would reappear in many subsequent publications of a critical nature.

Although in his comprehensive Afrikaans literary history Kannemeyer (*Geskiedenis van die Afrikaanse Literatuur*, 2 vols., 1978 and 1983) offers various divisions into literary periods (see also Dekker, *Afrikaanse Literatuurgeskiedenis*, 1935, and Antonissen, *Afrikaanse Letterkunde*, 1955), only the Dertigers and the Sestigers (Writers of the Sixties) became generally accepted as representing a distinct phase of renewal, accompanied by a meaningful overlap of ideas among the main figures. 'The poets of the first generation' (Jan F. E. Celliers, Totius and C. Louis Leipoldt) and 'the poets of the second generation' (Eugène N. Marais, Toon van den Heever, A. G. Visser and a few minor figures) are largely classifications of convenience. Attempts at inventing a generation of Tagtigers never gained ground despite the appearance of a journal called *Tagtiger*.

When Afrikaans literary experts refer to the innovation of Dertig they largely have Van Wyk Louw in mind. Apart from producing the most striking renewal with his collection of poetry *Die Halwe Kring* (The Half Circle) in 1938, he also articulated, in the essays of *Berigte te Velde* (Dispatches from the Front, 1939) and *Lojale Verset* (Loyal Resistance, 1939), a manifesto of ideas aimed at making the new poetry intelligible to the Afrikaner elite (see Chapter 17).

Van Wyk Louw's seminal intervention marked the point at which Afrikaans literature started turning away from its preoccupations with war, suffering and a rural Afrikaans way of life. An important part of his critical activities was the re-evaluation of poets from previous generations, each of whose work he interpreted within his idealist and Hegelian notion of organic development towards a 'true' national literature. Thus he helped create a shared tradition for new initiatives in the present, in response to which others, including Opperman, would produce their own perspectives and rebuttals. He depicted Jan Celliers's poetry as the embodiment of 'our old Boer civilisation', and identified in C. Louis Leipoldt, the most important poet preceding the Dertigers, the first signs of a literature aspiring to complexity and universal values.

In 'Die Rigting van die Afrikaanse Letterkunde' ('The Direction of Afrikaans Literature') and 'Die Jonger Afrikaanse Literatuur' ('The Newer Afrikaans Literature') Van Wyk Louw insisted that Afrikaans literature had to start measuring itself against the best world literature could offer. This implied several things. Technical accomplishment and aesthetic refinement, exemplified by the unity of form and content, would be a *sine qua non*. The full complexity of modern existence should be faced: the end of a mainly agrarian economy, the effects of industrialisation and urbanisation, individual anguish, racial tensions, the work environment, the relationship between man and woman, and so forth. Afrikaans literature should also abandon the paternalistic attitudes that were prevalent in 'gemoedelike lokale realisme' ('good-natured local realism') and focus on life as it was lived *unmittelbar zu Gott* (unmediated before God) and in relation to eternal values. This amounted to a plea for a spiritual transformation and emancipation that would accompany the Afrikaner's entry into a modern, industrial and urbanised world.

These *desiderata* posed a challenge to the Afrikaans literary orthodoxy of the time. In his attack on what was previously understood to be 'national literature', Van Wyk Louw depicted the kind of literature that sought to exemplify an 'Afrikaans' way of life as 'colonial' for its lack of awareness of itself as an independent source of meaning and value (for a fuller analysis see Olivier, *N. P. van Wyk Louw*). Instead, he posited the ideal of a national literature that would be rooted in the spiritual unity of the *volk* and would thus encompass all diversity a priori. If there was an unbreakable spiritual bond between the writer and the nation, all literary expressions, even those considered too 'individualistic' or 'sickly' by a critic like F. E. J. Malherbe (1894–1979), would by definition form part of the new edifice called 'national literature'. For Van Wyk Louw, the excellence of that literature and other cultural expressions would endow the nation with the right to exist, which could not be based on mere biological necessity. In its Platonic and Romantic search for beauty, the new literature would remove the need for any author to address certain themes in order to be deemed a true Afrikaner.

Fifteen years after the appearance of the Dertigers, Opperman would chart the social, artistic and literary influences upon them in *Digters van Dertig*. Some of the older Afrikaans writers (Celliers, Totius and particularly Leipoldt) were well read and well travelled. Opperman illustrated how the Dertigers brought a deliberate new international perspective to their literary activities, an interest in other art forms, and a conscious attempt to match the best from European literatures.

Of the poets discussed by Opperman, Van Wyk Louw would dominate the Afrikaans literary landscape for several decades and also have a lasting impact on intellectual discourse. To begin with the latter: while his passionate defence of an Afrikaans national literature was rooted in German idealism, Romantic notions of beauty and a Nietzschean concept of the extraordinary individual who lives life to the fullest, even to the extremes, Van Wyk Louw's later essays contained an equally passionate plea for rationality and 'die oop gesprek' ('the open discussion'). His argument for a more scholarly approach to the literary text as an autonomous linguistic and aesthetic utterance paved the way for a generation of scholars inspired by Russian Formalism, New Criticism and the Dutch-based 'stylistics on linguistic principles', a form of close reading developed in Amsterdam by Wytze Hellinga (1908–85) and H. van der Merwe Scholtz (1924–2005) during the decade that Van Wyk Louw was a professor in the Netherlands. In his essays on politics, Van Wyk Louw postulated nationalism as a universal principle originating in western European humanism (Olivier, 'Loyal Resistance'). His influential idea of 'liberal nationalism' resulted from the conviction that a dialogue between the principles of nationalism and liberalism, as represented by R. F. A. Hoernlé, could produce a reconciliation of conflicting claims to power and rights in South Africa.

By turning nationalism into a supposedly universal principle, Van Wyk Louw was embarking on what Sanders calls 'a violent cognitive remapping of the polity in postwar Afrikaner-nationalist thinking' (*Complicities*, p. 70). For if nationalism was unassailably universal, then the question of racial cohabitation was reduced to how one should accommodate a variety of ethnic nationalisms within a single territory. Despite this limitation, Van Wyk Louw's writings became a source upon which dissident discourse would draw repeatedly in the future, with the strongest impulses emerging from his concept of 'loyal resistance' and his view that Afrikaner nationalism must be able to justify itself with reference to 'universal principles' and the justice it was able to deliver to all citizens.

Despite the nationalist beliefs expressed in his essays, Van Wyk Louw was able to explore fascinating new poetic territory in each of his collections (Olivier, '*Tristia* in Dialoog'; see also Chapter 17). His nationalist preoccupations are qualified and sometimes even rebutted by his restless intellect and by the huge historical sweep, the syncretism, inclusivity and humanism of especially his later poetry. The genius of his poetry resides in the fact that new philosophical themes were always combined by a search for new language and new forms.

Against the numerous traces of European influences and heroic individualism in *Die Halwe Kring*, a more disillusioned and anxious voice can be heard in the cryptic poems of *Gestaltes en Diere* (Figures and Beasts, 1942), a collection exploring the unconscious layers of the human psyche in deeply disturbing ways, especially in the enigmatic 'Die Swart Luiperd' ('The Black Leopard') and the dramatic monologue of an intellectually and emotionally torn inquisitor in 'Die Hond van God' ('The Hound of God').[1] This new uncertainty no doubt resulted from an awareness of the irrational forces unleashed by the outbreak of the Second World War. His accomplished epic poem *Raka* (1941), written in rhymed free verse, deals in complex ways with the position of the heroic leader in the battle between the forces of civilisation and barbarism. In *Nuwe Verse* (New Poems, 1953) one encounters a much more conciliatory approach to the perceived tension between the sensual pleasures of earthly life and the demands of metaphysics ('the higher, colder paths' of the introductory poem to *Die Halwe Kring*). In the fragments collected in the series 'Klipwerk' ('Stonework') he became the first major Afrikaans poet to explore the capacity of the Western Cape regional language to capture elementary human experiences. His greatest accomplishment as a poet is *Tristia* (1962), a huge collection of 'fugues' and 'preludes' drawing upon Ovid's work as exile on the shores of the Black Sea. Here the pervasive themes of exile and yearning are combined with a very specific view of the poem as a sign (never a self-advertising symbol) of an ultimately unreachable and unimaginable 'godliness', 'holiness' or 'fullness'. With its variety of voices, the huge amount of historical and contemporary material it incorporates and its numerous poems dedicated to poetics and art, this collection establishes the philosophical and artistic apparatus underpinning its own relentless quest for meaning and consolation. That meaning, however, is of necessity always provisional, inadequate and therefore subject to adjustment, as in the last line of 'Groot Ode' ('Great Ode'): 'other names still slumber'. Despite the elegiac depiction of human existence as unfulfilled and alienated from whatever is godly, *Tristia* speaks in a sharp voice about the 'bont prosessie' ('colourful procession') of

---

1 For poems by Louw and Opperman, see their *Versamelde Gedigte* and *Versamelde Poësie* respectively.

history. It also movingly celebrates the reconciliation of mind and spirit that is seen as characteristic of the Mediterranean world in a heartbreaking poem such as 'Groet in Bruin' ('Farewell in Brown').

The poetry of Elisabeth Eybers (1915–2007) also underwent various transformations (see Chapter 21). She developed beyond her initial status as the female voice of the thirties, as Opperman characterised her somewhat patronisingly in *Digters van Dertig*. In her remarkable oeuvre, which spans more than six decades of sustained quality, she exploits everyday situations in immaculately constructed poems. Her unassuming realism manages to capture moments of wonder and insight in ways that are reminiscent of much modern Dutch poetry and even of seventeenth-century painters such as Vermeer and de Hooch. As an immaculate wordsmith, Eybers responded to the universal themes of the Dertigers by increasingly seeing language as an instrument for constructing meaning out of everyday experience: love, the process of adjustment to a foreign country and the ravages of old age. After her emigration to Amsterdam in the early 1960s she became the first major poet of exile and the harbinger of the diasporic poet in Afrikaans literature. As Ena Jansen has shown, the tension between South Africa and the Netherlands in Eybers's work is reflected in a unique 'in-between language' (*Afstand en Verbintenis*). Eybers gradually became an adopted Dutch poet, winning the most prestigious of Dutch literary awards, the P. C. Hooft Prize, in 1991.

The third major poet of the 1930s was Uys Krige (1910–87), who found his sources of inspiration in Spanish and French rather than in the Germanic, Dutch and English literature which had such a major impact on other Dertigers. This 'trekvoël' ('migratory bird') of Dertig used freer forms, writing songs and ballads. His uniquely valuable contribution to Afrikaans literature includes accomplished translations from poets such as Lorca, Neruda, Éluard and Villon. In contrast to the high seriousness of the Louws, Krige's work displays a charming Romantic melancholy that forgivingly embraces all humankind, even though he could also produce the most devastating sarcasm in his balladesque poem about the Spanish Civil War, 'Lied van die Fascistiese Bomwerpers' ('Song of the Fascist Bombers'). Together with Van Wyk Louw, he was the only Dertiger to try his hand at drama as well. The difference between Krige's *Die Goue Kring* (The Golden Circle, 1955) and Van Wyk Louw's drama *Germanicus* (1956), which was to be followed by many texts written for the radio, confirms that in Krige and Van Wyk Louw we have the two opposing poles of the Dertigers. In fact, Krige always found himself on the margins of the 'movement' of which Van Wyk Louw was the undisputed leader; he was the opposite of the team man.

Of lesser significance are W. E. G. Louw – who contributed some beautiful sonnets and 'sensitivist' poems to Afrikaans literature, but whose work seldom reaches the heights of his brother N. P. van Wyk – and C. M. van den Heever (1902–57), in whose poems Opperman detected the first signs of a new sensibility that would flourish in the work of other Dertigers. Dertig produced only one work of prose in its early years: the scorching confessional novel *Sy Kom met die Sekelmaan* (She comes with the Crescent Moon, 1937) by Hettie Smit (1908–13). The focus of this work, with its sensitive and expressive style, is on the self and the battle for equilibrium between intellect and emotion.

The importance of the Dertigers is located not only in the exceptional poetry they produced. They set a standard against which their successors would measure themselves or react against. Thus the poetry of Opperman, who debuted in 1947 with *Heilige Beeste* (Holy Cattle), constituted a movement away from the more esoteric Dertiger preoccupations towards a focus on the South African landscape (particularly Zululand) and sociopolitical themes (see Chapter 21). Ernst van Heerden (1916–97), who started off as something of a Dertiger epigone in *Weerlose Uur* (Defenseless Hour, 1942), would in his many subsequent collections of poetry establish a more independent style (see Chapter 21). Peter Blum (1925–90), the most important debutant of the 1950s, would respond parodically to what he saw as the self-aggrandisement of Dertiger themes, particularly the 'geding met God' ('dispute with God'). This remarkable poet, who came to South Africa as a 12-year-old exile from Trieste, spoke several European languages and then, having learnt Afrikaans at school, turned to poetry and exploited the Afrikaans language in etymological ways using 'sprung rhythms' reminiscent of Gerard Manley Hopkins. His work is infused with an all-encompassing scepticism, in terms of which creative endeavour constitutes no more than 'brewwe ligmomente' ('brief moments of light') against the darkness and destruction of history (see Chapter 21). The most important – and radically different – poet to have emerged after him is Breyten Breytenbach (1939–), whose work falls outside the scope of this chapter (see Chapter 22).

Most of the Dertigers and their successors had an uneasy relationship with Afrikaner orthodoxy. Van Wyk Louw started off as an idealistic supporter of nationalism, but insisted that it be more than a set of slogans and sentiments; in the last phase of his life he responded negatively to the materialism and puritanism he perceived around him. He initially acted as a strident opponent of censorship, and later on, when the introduction of the Publications Act had become a fait accompli, agitated for at least the appointment of literary experts as censors (McDonald, *Literature Police*, p. 38). In the 1960s he was famously lambasted in public by the then prime minister Hendrik Verwoerd because his play *Die Pluimsaad Waai Ver* (The Plumed Seed Blows Far, posthumously published in 1972) supposedly did not depict Afrikaner heroes in a sufficiently positive light.

Eybers and Krige were sceptical towards nationalism from early on, and some of Eybers's later poems contain a strong humanistic criticism of apartheid. Opperman's poetics, in terms of which the poet as a Keatsian chameleon would identify with all the elements of creation and seek to discern universal patterns of good and evil in contemporary circumstances, prevented a direct engagement with politics (see Chapter 21). Despite this, his carefully constructed, multilayered symbolic poetry displays a deep awareness of the South African landscape and the country's complicated social and political circumstances; it also contains moments of great beauty and emotion. In both his poetry and some of his essays there are signs of a pervasive discomfort with the insular tendencies of Afrikanerdom. The collections *Dolosse* (Witch Doctor Bones, 1963), *Kuns-mis* (Compost/Art-Manure, 1964), *Edms. Bpk.* (Pty. Ltd., 1970) and *Komas uit 'n Bamboesstok* (Comas from a Bamboo Shoot, 1979) are more pessimistic than his earlier work, but also more playful, with strong elements of parody and more supple in form than the 'klein konstellasies vers' ('little constellations of verse') which used to be his forte. Against this background the call by some Sestigers for a *littérature engagée* marked a move towards a much more direct challenge to the government of the day and a step away from the 'lojale verset' that was, in a variety of forms, evident in the attitudes of their predecessors (see Chapter 21).

The farm novel in Afrikaans

The *plaasroman* (farm novel) in Afrikaans literature is yet to be fully investigated as both a literary and a broader discursive phenomenon. The best point of departure is the work of C. M. van den Heever, a contemporary of Van Wyk Louw, whose novels were given prominence in J. M. Coetzee's *White Writing* (pp. 82–114). Coetzee criticises the canonised view in Kannemeyer (*Geskiedenis*, I, pp. 299–313) that Van den Heever's work hovers uncomfortably between realism and romanticism by showing that this hybridity relates to a central creative problem: how to invest protagonists who have a limited intellectual horizon with the kind of consciousness that would embody a set of sophisticated concepts. In Coetzee's analysis, Van den Heever's farm novels are seen to generate an ideological justification for ownership of the farm. This depended on the farmer reaching a state of awareness in which Romantic notions of nature are combined with the experience of a symbiotic relationship between nature and agricultural endeavour. Together with the notion of stewardship, Coetzee argued, such an awareness would signify the right to ownership and continuity over generations. In *Laat Vrugte* (Late Fruit, 1939), for example, Oom Sybrand's eventual acceptance of his son's accession to the land also is an acceptance of old age, death and human embeddedness in the seasonal patterns of nature.

Coetzee's contribution to our understanding of the *plaasroman* rests on the insight that this type of fiction represents a creative and symbolic appropriation; that it is, therefore, never simply a descriptive genre. Within a wider political and social framework, the *plaasroman* must be understood against the background of the dispossession and destruction brought about by the Anglo-Boer (or South African) War. From this perspective, as pointed out by Van Wyk Louw in his early essays, the farm novel and related idyllic evocations of a 'Boere past' belong to a genre of restitution. Of key importance, too, is that during the thirties the idea of an idyllic and productive farm existence was threatened by social developments. Drought, the growth of industry, urbanisation and the appearance of an Afrikaans proletariat underscored the tenuousness of small-scale farming. One could say that the spectre of 'poor white' destitution always haunted the farm novel. The *Ampie* trilogy (1924, 1928, 1942), by Jochem van Bruggen (1881–1957), one of the most famous examples of the genre, is notable for its reinstatement of the rural idyll in the face of relentless pressures on a putative traditional way of life.

The farm novel was effectively marginalised by the Dertigers' interest in poetry and their more cosmopolitan attitudes, with Van Wyk Louw's term 'gemoedelike lokale realisme' ('good-natured local realism') hanging disdainfully over the genre for many years. The Dertigers saw themselves as citizens of the world; their orientation was away from the small-town and agrarian concerns that characterised so much of the literature before them. In its purest form, the poetry defended by Van Wyk Louw is individualistic in its approach and symbolist in its execution, creating a complex unit of expression and sound that retains only a spiritual link with the material concerns of the nation. Whilst his great successor Opperman incorporated many aspects of the South African landscape and sociopolitical conditions in a much more concrete poetry, these elements were almost always seen *sub specie aeternitatis*, and in Opperman's multilayered metaphorical approach subsumed into a metaphysical scheme. Some of Blum's poetry would be a taunting response to both Louw and Opperman. The arrival of the Sestigers initially marked a new phase of cosmopolitanism and inspiration derived from Europe and elsewhere: Surrealist and Zen influences in Breyten Breytenbach (1939–); explorations of existentialist philosophy and the Theatre of the Absurd in André P. Brink (1935–), parables of Jungian individuation in Etienne Leroux (1922–89) (see Chapters 21 and 22).

Yet in the midst of these developments realism would continue, and the farm would retain its potential to be a site of symbolic contestation. Right up to the present, many prominent Afrikaans works, including Marlene van Niekerk's *Agaat* (2004; English translation 2006 – outside South Africa, this translation appears under the title *The Way of the Women*), engage in complex and often parodic ways with the themes, values and historical vision of the farm novel (Devarenne, 'Nationalism and the Farm Novel'; Prinsloo and Visagie, 'Postkoloniale Plaasroman'). *Triomf*, Van Niekerk's other great work from 1994, tells the stories of a forgotten generation of Afrikaners who were marginalised socially and whose lives never found their way into the canon of Afrikaans literature. The Benades are part of the people who became urban dwellers and found themselves betrayed by the grand narratives of Afrikanerdom.

In trying to explain why the farm novel returned to the mainstream from the beginning of the 1970s, one could argue that given the importance of territorial expansion, occupation and contestation around land in Afrikaner history, authors would almost naturally see the farm novel as a vehicle for challenging hegemony, investigating official morality or questioning the future. There is some irony in the fact that the tradition of writing about the farm displays an ambiguous relationship to the land from the earliest texts. The themes of occupation and dispossession, gain and loss, are already evident in the epic poetry of Jan F. E. Celliers (1865–1940) in *Martjie* (1911) and Totius (1877–1953) in *Trekkerswee* (Trekker Woe, 1915). Against the celebratory occupation and exploitation of the land there are the memories of past loss (primarily associated with the Anglo-Boer War) and the fear of impending loss through poverty or appropriation by outsiders. Thus the farm always is a place of triumph as well as vulnerability, a place of happiness as well as anxiety. Aspects of commemoration can be discerned in texts which depict in symbolic form the utopia of a land finally under control. Later engagements with the rural archive would include works in search of new symbolic territories providing an escape from both a tainted history and the perceived deprivations, fears and political pressures of the present. Thus John Miles's *Die Buiteveld* (The Outfield/Outer Pasturage, 2003) creates an imaginary, almost ahistoric, space of individual liberation. Dan Roodt's clumsy *Moltrein* (Underground, 2004) locates the hero in the Paris metro, a kind of last refuge from a decaying western civilisation by which he feels betrayed.

Amongst later works situated on the farm, Leroux's *Sewe Dae by die Silbersteins* (Seven Days at the Silbersteins, 1962) depicts an extremely modernised farm, an emblem of industrialised existence (see Chapter 21). This becomes the backdrop for Leroux's main themes: the relationship of the individual to society and processes of integration and individuation (see Chapter 21). The farm Welgevonden is largely a symbolic milieu – and yet the novel is important within the tradition as a forerunner for new treatments of the farm. What happens on Welgevonden, especially after sunset, is very far removed from the propriety of van den Heever.

At the same time, there exist a large number of farm stories from the thirties onwards in which vexed issues such as ownership, economic well-being, history and the future are not problematised. A rich vein of memoir literature in Afrikaans contains loving descriptions and nostalgic scenes from farm life. M. E. R. (1875–1957), C. G. S. de Villiers (1894–1978), Boerneef (1897–1967), Alba Bouwer (1920–2010) and Hennie Aucamp (1934–) are only a few of the more accomplished authors in the field of *kontreiliteratuur* (regional literature), with Aucamp doing much to encourage and anthologise such writing. Interesting though they may be, these writings lie outside the more polemic strand of farm writing that is the focus here. Many of these texts, however, do provide a correction to the racial and class hierarchies of van den Heever and van Bruggen by portraying black farm inhabitants (for example Toiings and Matewis and Meraai in the work of Mikro [1903–68], and Dirk Ligter in Boerneef) as interesting and dignified characters in their own right.

The first pivotal text after van den Heever to deliberately re-engage with the tradition and ideological burden of the farm novel is Karel Schoeman's *Na die Geliefde Land* (1972; *Promised Land*, 1978). This is a farm novel in inversion (see Chapter 21). The protagonist George's visit, in some unspecified future, to the family farm Rietvlei (which has been destroyed by the new regime for having served as a hideaway in the planning of resistance) is a harbinger of later, more apocalyptic visions in the farm novel and elsewhere. Dystopian perspectives, too, are evident in later texts by Eben Venter and Van Niekerk. The inversion of established power relations, with white farm inhabitants being repressed by (presumably black) security forces, would have had a familiar ring to many readers and has understandably been read as a political warning. The most striking aspect of the novel is how Schoeman's future world is frozen in past habits of patriotism and allegiance to an agrarian existence. The parties that are held, the songs that are sung, the poem recited by Raubenheimer, are all a desperate invocation of a lost world; even when Carla and Paultjie read a book together, it sounds like a farm idyll. The futile clinging to historically shaped habits in changed circumstances is repudiated in the figure of Carla, who insists that life must be lived in the present. George, however, has already chosen a different direction:

> 'You were born here,' Gerhard says [to George]. 'You can resume your life where it was broken off.'
> 'No, it is no longer possible; it is too long ago, too much has happened in the meantime. There is nothing left that has remained the same.'
> 'The earth is the same.'
> 'I am not a farmer, and I don't want to be one.'
> 'The land is the same.' (p. 125; my translation)

Significantly, the passage distinguishes between the land or earth and the farm, thus breaking the essential determinant of meaning in van den Heever's farm novels. George finds himself in the long line of people who have 'betrayed' the soil for an urbanised existence, ranging from farmers who left their land in the 1930s to the émigrés in *Agaat* and Venter's *Horrelpoot* (2006; *Trencherman*, 2008), who return to the farm in the role of ethnographic observers before finally leaving it all behind.

Later farm novels address the silences in Van den Heever, Van Bruggen and others. Wilma Stockenström's *Uitdraai* (with the title itself – 'turn off' or 'turning away' – providing a metafictional key to the novel) is an impressive example of themes that would be reworked in later novels (see Chapters 21 and 22). Foregrounding miscegenation across the farm boundary, Stockenström reverses the dominant themes in *Laat Vrugte*, of which her novel is undoubtedly a parody. Whereas in Van den Heever's novel it comes as some surprise for the reader to realise that the romantic scene between Henning and Johanna has in fact led to impregnation, Cornelie and the neighbour's son Flip enjoy some quick and urgent sex in the parental bedroom. In *Laat Vrugte* the illegitimate offspring is finally accepted into the family's bosom; *Uitdraai*, in contrast, shows us a sordid backroom abortion, dramatically visualised by one of those present vomiting up the figs she has consumed. Over this exposé of rural hypocrisy presides an omniscient narrator who is unsparingly sardonic in her comment.

In their focus on the black presence, later farm novels would follow Stockenström's lead in exposing intimacies that disturb the official ideology of class differences and separation. Such hierarchical patterns are classically represented in *Die Meulenaar* (The Miller, 1926) by D. F. Malherbe (1881–1969), which Kannemeyer (*Geskiedenis*, 1, pp. 163–4) singles out as the first Afrikaans farm novel. Yet these patterns are not as simple as they might seem on the surface. One the one hand, one encounters overt racism in the discourse: 'Kyk die volk maak so met mekaar – hulle rand mekaar aan – maar witmense, ordentlike witmense, doen dit mos nie!' ('You see, the blacks do that to each other – they assault each other – but white people, decent white people, surely don't do that! [pp. 92–9]). On the other hand, there is more than a little unintended irony in the fact that the black characters are more vivid and interesting than their white counterparts; the clumsy and naive Faans even experiences a strong element of rivalry in his observation of a farm worker's romantic success: 'En waarom sal jy nie ook Leonore se hart wen as jy aanhou nie? Sal jy dan nie kan doen wat 'n Masbieker reggekry het nie' ('And why would you not capture Leonore's heart, too, if you persevered? Wouldn't you be able to do what a Masbieker has succeeded in doing?' [p. 119]).

Whilst restoring the bodily and sexual presence of black characters, later farm novels also explore the situation on the farm as a product of past injustices and transgressions. In this way, the farm becomes a critical microcosm of South African society. *Kroniek van Perdepoort* (Chronicle of Perdepoort, 1975) by Anna M. Louw (1913–2003), for example, introduces a vast array of characters and combines the tradition of the generational novel ('Der Verfall einer Familie', as Thomas Mann subtitles his *Buddenbrooks*) with complex individualised reflections on sin and retribution. In his *Toorberg* (1986; *Ancestral Voices*, 1989) Etienne van Heerden effects a considerable complication of the farm milieu, with two families ('die familie' and 'die skaamfamilie' or 'family of shame') living side by side and interlinked through Floris Moolman, a member of the Moolman dynasty, having had a child with Ouma Kitty Riet. In this very skilfully constructed novel, the past and present exist simultaneously; living people and ghosts all make their appearance in the futile attempts to save the life of Noag du Pisani, who has fallen into a borehole. Noag or 'Druppeltjie' ('Droplet') is the only member of the last generation of Moolmans living on Toorberg. To the enmeshed history of the farm inhabitants is added a further dimension by the presence of a magistrate who has come to investigate Noag's death, and who finally reaches the conclusion that nobody can be held directly responsible for it. Ironically, Noag's bizarre fate also dramatises the recurrent metaphorical themes of drought and water. The novel ultimately suggests that the past can be reconciled not through identifying any culprit, but through the assumption of moral responsibility, understanding and forgiveness.

Van Heerden's *Die Stoetmeester* (The Stud Master, 1993) and Venter's *Foxtrot van die Vleiseters* (Foxtrot of the Carnivores, 1993) both appeared towards the end of the apartheid regime and provide perspectives on an era of privilege and material well-being. Within the context of the farm novel, Venter's text is refreshing for its irreverence and occasional wild humour, yet unambiguous in depicting the activities on the farm as the last convulsions of a 'time of grace'. His *Horrelpoot* (see Chapter 22) is much more ambitious and ponderous, but fascinating for the way in which the returning émigré of Schoeman's novel makes a reappearance. Venter's main characters (Marlouw and Koert) and some dominant themes echo Conrad's *Heart of Darkness*. Unfortunately, the use of this intertext ultimately becomes an awkward importation instead of a means of creating a productive dialogue. Translating Conrad's alluring but unfathomable 'darkness', which appears to lie in a psychological and metaphysical realm beyond the symbolic order, into a too literal moral universe leads to a somewhat facile parable of destruction and decay that fails to engage fully with the apocalyptic post-apartheid world that is imagined here.

A broader treatment of the farm novel would have to encompass South African writing in English as well. One key text, however, must be mentioned. In *Disgrace* (1999), Coetzee produces a compelling contemporary version of the farm novel he has so eloquently analysed (see also Chapter 31). Locating the main events on the historical frontier of the Eastern Cape, Coetzee depicts a series of significant inversions. Whilst Petrus gradually promotes himself from 'bywoner' ('tenant farmer') and 'handlanger' ('handyman') to farmer and authority figure, it becomes clear that Lucy's continued existence on the land would depend on her subservience and his protection. It would appear that in *Disgrace*, historical justice implies retribution and the acceptance of a new racial order. Whether David Lurie ever escapes from his state of disgrace is a matter for debate; one reading certainly could be that the only refuge from humiliation lies in aesthetic escapism.

At the end of the trajectory of the farm novel in Afrikaans thus far stands Marlene van Niekerk's monumental *Agaat*: an encyclopaedic recapitulation of the genre (see Chapters 22, 35 and 36). Obsessively detailed and textually dense, the novel focuses on the relationship between the servant-girl Agaat and her mistress Milla as it is re-enacted at the latter's deathbed. This is the most intimate and multilayered negotiation between master and servant in the history of the farm novel, but it is more than that: in mourning Milla, Agaat is also grappling with the loss of a mother figure and her own sense of abandonment. Through its many mirror images and inversions, the process of mourning and commemoration in *Agaat* suggests the tantalising possibility that through their interaction Milla and Agaat may be improvising a new relationship that might transcend the boundaries and traumas of the past. On the metafictional level, *Agaat* is an extended wake at the deathbed of the farm novel, raising the question whether at the end of the mourning process a new relationship to the land, to other people and to the tradition of Afrikaans literature could be found. Or will the author perhaps become, like Milla's son Jakkie, an uprooted nomad, a curator and chronicler of a vanishing culture? This is a question that surely extends beyond Afrikaans literature, whatever its future may turn out to be.

Despite Van Wyk Louw's comments about the tradition of realism in Afrikaans and the limitations of earlier works in the genre, the farm novel has proven to be resilient. It survived because, given the contested nature of land in South Africa, it has shown itself to be a vehicle for exploring what Van Niekerk ('Kind in die Agterkamer', p. 116) calls 'nasionale erfenis en etniese lot' ('national heritage and ethnic fate'). At the beginning of the account offered in this chapter stands Van Wyk Louw, triumphantly announcing the birth of a new Afrikaans literature. At the end we have Van Niekerk questioning the very possibility of writing in Afrikaans, talking about the 'pathetic self-overestimation' of the 'romantic artist' and 'the transience of his legacy in a constantly diminishing minority language'. The 'dialogue' between these two authors provides one strand of fascinating continuity and change in Afrikaans literature.

Bibliography

Antonissen, R. *Die Afrikaanse Letterkunde van Aanvang tot Hede* [1955], 3rd edn, Cape Town: Nasou, 1965.

Brink, A. P. (ed.), *Groot Verseboek*, 3 vols., Cape Town: Tafelberg, 2008. (First published in 1951 with D. J. Opperman as editor.)

Celliers, Jan F. E. *Martjie*, Kampen: J. H. Kok, 1911.

Coetzee, J. M. *Disgrace*, London: Secker & Warburg, 1999. Translation by F. Olivier as *In Oneer*, Cape Town: Umuzi, 2009.

   White Writing: On the Culture of Letters in South Africa, New Haven: Yale University Press, 1990.

Dekker, G. *Afrikaanse Literatuurgeskiedenis* [1951], 14th edn, Cape Town: Nasou, 1980.

Devarenne, N. 'Nationalism and the Farm Novel in South Africa, 1883–2004', *Journal of Southern African Studies* 35:3 (2009), 627–42.

Jansen, E. *Afstand en Verbintenis. Elisabeth Eybers in Amsterdam*, Pretoria: Van Schaik, 1996.

Kannemeyer, J. C. *Geskiedenis van die Afrikaanse Literatuur*, vol. I, Cape Town and Pretoria: Academica, 1978.

Geskiedenis van die Afrikaanse Literatuur II, Cape Town and Pretoria: Academica, 1983.

Krige, U. *Die Goue Kring*, Cape Town: Balkema, 1956.

Leroux, E. *Sewe Dae by die Silbersteins*, Cape Town: Human & Rousseau, 1962. Translation by C. Eglington as *To a Dubious Salvation: A Trilogy of Fantastic Novels*, Harmondsworth: Penguin, 1972.

Louw, A. M. *Kroniek van Perdepoort*, Cape Town: Tafelberg, 1976.

Louw, N. P. van Wyk. *Germanicus*, Cape Town: Nasionale Boekhandel, 1956.

Die Pluimsaad Waai Ver, of Bitter Begin, Cape Town: Human & Rousseau, 1972.

Versamelde Gedigte [1981], Cape Town: Tafelberg/Human & Rousseau, 2002.

Versamelde Prosa I, Cape Town: Tafelberg, 1986.

Versamelde Prosa II, Cape Town: Human & Rousseau, 1986.

McDonald, P. D. *The Literature Police: Apartheid Censorship and its Cultural Consequences*, Oxford University Press, 2009.

Malherbe, D. F. *Die Meulenaar*, Bloemfontein: Nasionale Pers, 1926.

Opperman D. J. *Digters van Dertig*, Cape Town: Nasou, 1953.

Versamelde Poësie, Cape Town: Tafelberg, 1987.

Olivier, G. '"Loyal Resistance": N. P. van Wyk Louw (1906–1970) and the Intellectual', *Social Dynamics* 36:1 (2010), 202–13.

N. P. van Wyk Louw: Literatuur, Filosofie, Politiek, Cape Town and Johannesburg: Human & Rousseau, 1992.

'Tristia in Dialoog met N. P. van Wyk Louw se Oeuvre', *Tydskrif vir Literatuurwetenskap* 24:2 (2008), 45–70.

Prinsloo, L., and A. Visagie. 'Die Representasie van die Bruin Werker as die Ander in Marlene van Niekerk se Postkoloniale Plaasroman *Agaat*', *Stilet* 19:2 (2007), 43–62.

Roodt, D. *Moltrein*, Johannesburg: PRAAG, 2004.

Sanders, M. *Complicities: The Intellectual and Apartheid*, Durham, NC: Duke University Press, 2002.

Schoeman, K. *Na die Geliefde Land*, Cape Town: Human & Rousseau, 1972. Translation by M. Friedmann as *Promised Land*, London: J. Friedmann, 1978.

Smit, H. *Sy Kom met die Sekelmaan*, Cape Town: Nasionale Pers, 1937.

Stockenström, W. *Uitdraai*, Cape Town and Pretoria: Human & Rousseau, 1976.

Totius. *Trekkerswee*, Potchefstroom: A. H. Koomans, 1915.

Van Bruggen, J. *Ampie: die Kind*, Cape Town: Nasionale Pers, 1942.

Ampie: die Meisiekind, Amsterdam: Swets & Zeitlinger, 1928

Ampie: die Natuurkind, Amsterdam: Swets & Zeitlinger, 1924.

Van den Heever, C. M. *Laat Vrugte* [1939], Pretoria: Van Schaik, 1972.

Van Heerden, E. 'Nasionalisme en Literatuur', in *Die Ander Werklikheid: Letterkundige Beskouings*, Cape Town: Nasionale Boekhandel, 1969.

Weerlose Uur, Cape Town: Nasionale Pers, 1942.

Van Heerden, E. *Die Stoetmeester*, Cape Town: Tafelberg, 1993.

Toorberg, Cape Town: Tafelberg, 1986. Translation by M. Hacksley as *Ancestral Voices*, Harmondsworth: Penguin, 1989.

Van Niekerk, M. *Agaat*, Cape Town: Tafelberg 2004. Translation by M. Heyns, Jeppestown and Cape Town: Jonathan Ball and Tafelberg, 2006.

'Lambert Benade van Triomf en Agaat Lourier van Grootmoedersdrift: Die Kind in die Agterkamer as die Sjamaan van die Familie', in E. Jansen, R. de Jong-Goossens and G. Olivier (eds.), *My Ma se Ma se Ma: Zuid-Afrikaanse Families in Verhalen*, Amsterdam: Suid-Afrikaanse Instituut, 2008.

Triomf, Pretoria and Cape Town: Quellerie, 1994. Translation by L. de Kock, Johannesburg: Jonathan Ball, 1999.

Venter, E. *Foxtrot van die Vleiseters*, Cape Town: Tafelberg, 1993.

Horrelpoot, Cape Town: Tafelberg, 2006.

16

New African modernity and the New African movement

NTONGELA MASILELA

In the early years of the twentieth century African people were confronted with the hegemony of European modernity, which had violently entered African history through the social formation of capitalism and the political systems of imperialism and colonialism. They came to the gradual realisation that colonial modernity, which was a variation of European modernity, had to be engaged with, even if principally in opposition, since modernity as a worldly experience was a 'historical necessity', as Jameson was to argue in several of his writings in the closing years of the twentieth century where he retroactively traced the historical passageways from modernity to postmodernity (*Postmodernism* and *A Singular Modernity*).

Since European modernity in the form of imperialism had jettisoned African people from African history into European history, the historical challenge for them became how to revert back to African history, as Amilcar Cabral astutely observed in the revolutionary decade of the 1960s (*Return to the Source*). In this era of social upheaval, Cabral postulated the national liberation struggle as an effective instrument for reversion back to African history. In contrast to the moment of Cabral, in the early decades of that century, when imperialism and colonialism were hegemonic and consequently had the monopoly of power regarding state violence, many New African intellectuals sought to master the complexity of European modernity with the intent of subverting it to a form of modernity that would emerge from the democratic imperatives of African history. These imperatives came into being as a consequence of opposition to European domination. The historic position was classically formulated in 1904 by Pixley ka Isaka Seme in an essay ('The Regeneration of Africa') that Kwame Nkrumah was to celebrate half a century later in the early years of the postcolonial era as an ideological position that gave intellectual authorisation to the decolonisation process.

One of the philosophical credos developed by Seme in this landmark essay was that the twentieth century would be the beginning of an engagement with the historical meaning and significance of modernity by African people. Seme's prescience forecast the cultural and intellectual phenomenon of the New African Movement in South Africa, consisting of New African intellectuals, political and religious leaders, writers and artists, whose objective was to construct a counternarrative to European modernity by inventing New African modernity. The entrance of European modernity into African history ensured that the contestation between the European colonisers and the colonised Africans, and the practice of European domination, would be around particular constructs: religion, politics and language. Other constructs of contestation between the dispossessors and the dispossessed in the modernisation process emerged in the 1930s: culture, arts, film and aesthetics. The last will not concern us here. The valences of the previous three will concern us, although they were disproportional to each other in the struggle of New African intellectuals to 'overcome' the deleterious effects of European modernity. The profound paradox is that the *modern* incarnation of these constructs, as the great invention of Europeans who reconstituted them in the non-European lands they conquered, ensured that they served *simultaneously* as instruments or philosophies of oppression and of liberation. This dialectical unity of opposites is what enabled New African intellectuals to invent New African modernity against European modernity, while at the same time situating the earlier generations of these intellectuals, the most brilliant by far over succeeding ones, in a state of permanent crisis concerning their ambivalence about the role of missionaries in the colonial enterprise of modernisation. H. I. E. Dhlomo and R. V. Selope Thema were just two of the New African intellectuals who were caught in the contradictory nature of this relationship. (For a representative sample, see H. Selby Msimang, 'Bantu Intellectuals' and 'Mr Hay and Bantu Intellectuals'; R. V. Selope Thema, 'Bantu Intellectuals' and 'Intellectuals and the Chiefs'; H. I. E. Dhlomo, 'Bantu and the Church', 'The Period of Evangelisation' and 'Developments and Achievements in the Field of Culture [and] Literature'.)

Language seems to have been more durable than religion and politics in the construction of New African modernity and in facilitating the making of a national identity, for the simple reason that African religious systems and political practices in a true sense never survived the violent trauma of the transition from tradition to modernity. This is not to deny that New African intellectuals in their making of New African modernity around religion and politics invented Ethiopianism or Shembeism or African nationalism, and so on, but rather I wish to indicate their momentary and ideological nature in contrast to the durability of language (here meaning African languages). This is all the more surprising since African languages were never facilitators of the entrance into European modernity, that role being played by European languages. Yet they were central in the displacement or conversion of European modernity into New African modernity; moreover, they enabled the later *participation* of New African masses in modernity. Modernity, then, is an endless system of paradoxes.

Given the fact that the English language had facilitated the entrance of many generations of Africans into the historical experience of modernity, who thereby became the New African intellectuals of the New African Movement, it is understandable that many of them valorised the importance of language over politics. This gave rise to a passionate debate throughout the trajectory of the New African Movement from the late nineteenth century to the middle of the twentieth century as to the contrasting values of language and politics, and whether matters of language superseded the practices of constricted politics: the debates between Elijah Makiwane and Pambani Jeremiah Mzimba in the 1880s; S. E. K. Mqhayi against William Wellington Gqoba in 1910s; Clement Martyn Doke against Solomon T. Plaatje in the 1920s; Benedict Wallet Vilakazi against H. I. E. Dhlomo in the 1930s; Mazisi Kunene against the *Drum* writers in the 1950s. These debates continued abroad in exile when the apartheid state terminated the New African Movement at the moment of the Sharpeville massacre in 1960. The historical question of language or politics was bisected by another issue that also emerged as the consequence of the violent entrance of European modernity into African history: the creation of *written literatures* which were oppositional to each other, African literature in the African languages and African literature in the European languages. In the precolonial era there were *oral forms* of literary expression, all of them realised or articulated in the African languages (see Chapters 2 to 5). The monumental undertaking by missionaries of reducing the African languages into written form created a paradoxical revolution of modernising them while simultaneously subordinating them to European literary forms of expression. A hundred-page report, 'A Preliminary Investigation into the State of the Native Languages of South Africa with Suggestions as to Research and the Development of Literature', assembled by Doke with the assistance of other scholars (for example, G. P. Lestrade), examined how missionaries, later followed by European scholars of African languages, had revolutionised African-language studies in South Africa by identifying their grammatical, phonetic and lexicographical structures through formidable scholarship and hard work (Doke, 'Preliminary Investigation'). It was such extraordinary undertakings that made most of the New African intellectuals of earlier generations pay homage to the missionaries' role in *modernising* Africa, despite their complicity with imperialism and colonialism.

In the first three decades of the twentieth century, New African intellectuals wrote voluminous essays about the necessity for South Africa (and by extension Africa) to modernise, about creating distinct variants of modernity in accordance with decolonising imperatives then emergent, and making certain that modernity 'triumphed' over tradition. This ideological and political perspective was expressed and articulated in the leading New African newspapers of the time: *Umteteli wa Bantu* (Mouthpiece of the People), *Izwi Labantu* (Voice of the People), *Imvo Zabantsundu* (African Opinion) and *Ilanga lase Natal* (Sun of Natal). It is necessary here to undertake an abbreviated and stenographic examination of the writings of the following five major New African intellectuals on this matter of the making of modernity in South Africa: Henry Selby Msimang, R. V. Selope Thema, H. I. E. Dhlomo, D. D. T. Jabavu and Benedict Wallet Vilakazi.

Five New African intellectuals

In a series of articles written throughout the 1920s, Henry Selby Msimang endorsed modernity, which he characterised variously as a 'hybrid civilisation' of the 'New Age', as an historical necessity that would enable African people to break the political power of African chiefs whom he viewed as representing the interests of 'provincialism', 'sectionalism' and 'tribalism' so endemic of traditional societies. Against the destructive forces of 'ignorance', 'apathy' and 'selfishness', which he believed were promulgated by the chiefs, he endorsed the political view that African intellectuals should be in the forefront of forging a 'national spirit' that would articulate the 'national aspirations of the people' ('The Bantu Nation?'). Like other New African intellectuals of the moment, he thought it imperative that the ideology of African nationalism be constructed in order for African people not only to accept the idea of progress, but also to consolidate their national interests against those of the white people who were oppressing them. The main focus of these articles was the social responsibility of New African intellectuals to the emergent modern African 'Nation'. The transformative power of modernity convinced Msimang that the African people must participate wholly in the creation of a 'new civilisation' of industrialism ('Bantu Destiny'). In this accelerated temporality of modernity, New African intellectuals sought to define not only their social responsibilities to the African people, but also to articulate new forms of artistic representation and new modes of historical representation.

R. V. Selope Thema and H. I. E. Dhlomo, separately and two decades apart, constructed the idea of the 'New African' to indicate that a new historical consciousness had emerged among African people in accordance with the imperatives of modernity. These imperatives necessitated the invention of the ideology of Nationalism, new modes of artistic expression, new political practices, among many other new things. Thema proposed the fundamental characteristic of the New African as being the endless search for knowledge to overcome the oppression of colonial modernity and simultaneously to facilitate the emergence of the African genius. This inquisitiveness would lead the New African on an intellectual journey in search of an answer as to how and why colonial modernity had falsely forced Africans into European history, to live it as though it were their own. The knowledge that would emerge from this enquiry would make Africans understand the compelling need for modernity and thereby enable them to invent their particular form of New African modernity. Dhlomo's take on the construct of the New African was slightly different. He emphasised the transformation of political attitudes among those Africans who were aware of their situational context, emphasising that they should possess a representative, progressive and democratic national consciousness that would enable them to build national organisations, whether political, cultural or social. Being a progressive moderniser, in contrast to Thema who was clearly a conservative moderniser, Dhlomo pointed to the importance of the linkages between the New African intellectuals and the New African masses. He argued for synchrony with the accelerated temporality of New African modernity as one of the best attributes of a New African, whose patriotism was engaged with national issues and values, not with race or colour ('Racial Attitudes').

Simultaneous with the development of a national consciousness of the New African, made possible by the haltingly progressive replacement of European modernity by New African modernity, if not its transformation, was the greater bifurcation of South African literature into African literature in the African languages and African literature in the European languages. Throughout the literary history of the country, African literature in the European languages stemmed from and aligned itself with the political hegemony of European modernity, while African literature in the African languages aligned itself with the contradictory democratic impulse of New African modernity. The conscious decision of S. E. K. Mqhayi to write all of his creative products, including his great poetry, *exclusively* in isiXhosa precipitated a fundamental literary revolution in South African literary history in that arguably the most distinguished poets the country has produced across the twentieth century wrote in the African languages: following on from him the lineage continued with Nontsizi Mgqwetho (isiXhosa), J. J. R. Jolobe (isiXhosa), Benedict Wallet Vilakazi (isiZulu), S. K. Ntsane (Sesotho), David Livingstone Phakamile Yali-Manisi (isiXhosa) and Mazisi Fakazi Mngoni Kunene (isiZulu). The achievement was so remarkable that at the height of Mqhayi's productivity, in the 1920s and in the 1930s, language and culture seemed to have held politics at bay, however hegemonic the latter continued to be. The literary revolution and the tradition that Mqhayi launched in the pages of *Izwi Labantu* in the early 1900s seems to have terminated with the death of Kunene in 2006, who was accorded recognition as a great poet by André Brink and J. M. Coetzee, in a conjointly edited 1986 anthology, *A Land Apart*.

Mqhayi's conscious historical choice of writing in isiXhosa rather than English, as spelled out in the preface to his novella, *Itywala lamawele* (The Case of Twins, 1914), was made with the intent of showing that an African language was just as capable as any, including any European language, of representing the complex historical experience of modernity. (An abridged version of *Ityala Lamawele* and the preface rendered in English translation by C. August appeared in the January 1966 issue of *The New African*.)

In arguing for the priority of African languages over the English language, Mqhayi was undoubtedly criticising his predecessors, the Xhosa intellectuals of the 1880s (Elijah Makiwane, Pambani Jeremiah Mzimba, William Wellington Gqoba, John Knox Bokwe, William Isaac Wauchope, John Tengo Jabavu, Walter Benson Rubusana), many of whom seemed to have accepted fatalistically the hegemony of the English language since it was this very language that had been a cultural facilitator of their entrance into European modernity, discovering therein Shakespeare, Francis Bacon and Chaucer, whom they considered to be the holy trinity of English literary culture. For some of them the English language epitomised the qualitative superiority of European modernity and relegated African languages to the backwardness they abhorred in traditional societies. They were among the first Africans to receive a missionary education in South Africa, which, astonishingly, consisted of Classics, Theology, Ethics and History, the very same kind of education that was given in public schools in England before the emergence of English Studies in the late nineteenth century. It was some of these Xhosa intellectuals who argued that language (albeit European languages) should be given primacy over politics, a theme that was to repeat itself in various forms throughout the trajectory of the New African Movement.

Writing a decade later after Mqhayi, Clement Martyn Doke, arguably South Africa's foremost scholar of African languages in the twentieth century, postulated the thesis that the African languages possessed their own particular genius, as unique as that of any other language in the world. This remarkable document ('A Call to Philological Study') by the great linguist was one of the defining documents of the New African Movement. It was written at a time when there was beginning to be a resurgence in the development of African literature in the African languages. In fact, this manifesto of New African modernity appeared in the same year as the publication of the great novel *Chaka* (1925), written in Sesotho by Thomas Mofolo, arguably the finest novel written by a black South African in the past century: a true classic of African literature.

But much more importantly, the essay by Doke coincided with the first formulations of the *idea* of African literature within the New African Movement. The idea of African literature consisted of two aspects: construction of the descriptive literary history of its genesis, and development of the literary criticism of its essential qualities. Writing an encapsulated literary history of this emergent literature in a 27-page pamphlet (*Bantu Literature*), D. D. T. Jabavu argued that its historical parameters were circumscribed by the fact that it was written in the *African languages* and, by implication, it *had* to be written in those languages. At the time of the writing of this literary history, in 1921, he thought that its predominant form was only in two languages: in Sesotho and in isiXhosa. Jabavu tabulated its structure into five categories: novels, history and folklore; translations; biblical matter; manuscripts awaiting publication; dictionaries, school books and newspapers. He emphasised that these two literatures had been made in their written form by the missionaries who had established printing presses, one in the city of Alice, known as the Lovedale Press, and the other in Maseru, designated as the Morija Press (see Chapter 10). For each of the literatures, he singled out the novelistic form as their distinctive achievement: for Sotho literature, Mofolo's *Moeti oa Bochabela* (1907, The Traveller of the East) and *Pitseng* (1910, the name of a village); for Xhosa literature Mqhayi's *Ityala lamawele*. Although emphasising the novelistic form, Jabavu was quick to indicate that the strength of Sesotho literature had been enabled by Azariele Sekese's *Mekhoa le Maele a Basotho* (1907), a compendium of customs, traditions and proverbs that had been serialised in the columns of the missionary newspaper *Lesilinyana La Lesotho* ('The Little Light of Lesotho) in the late nineteenth century. For inexplicable reasons, Jabavu does not mention Rubusana's *Zemk' inkomo magwalandini* (1906, Preserve your Culture), a landmark anthology of poems and prose pieces by important Xhosa writers such as Mqhayi, Gqoba and Wauchope, which many scholars consider to have been the foundation stone of modern Xhosa literature.

D. D. T. Jabavu felt compelled to write *Bantu Literature* when he overheard a white South African blithely pronounce in public that 'Bantu [Africans] have no literature'. But perhaps the real reason for the booklet was his fear, also expressed by Mqhayi in the preface to *Ityala lamawele*, that without modern African literature written in the African languages, vernacular African literary cultures would atrophy and die through being denied modern consciousness and modern sensibilities. In all probability, another reason for the pamphlet was to contest and challenge the notion that only literature written by Europeans (whites) in the European languages constituted South African literature, in total exclusion of that written by Africans in the African languages, let alone oral literature, which was falsely seen as located only in traditional societies and thereby automatically expressible in the latter languages. The thesis of *Bantu Literature* was easier to formulate than it would have been later, since in the early stages of the emergent modern literature in South Africa, written African literature in the African languages was not completely ruptured from the poetics of oral literature and its *otherness* was defined by African literature written in the European languages, invariably by white South Africans. Through the influence of New Negro modernity (in the United States) in the making of New African modernity (in South Africa), actualised in the literary sphere by the impact of the Harlem Renaissance of the 1920s on South Africa in the 1930s, there emerged for the first time in a serious and *collective* manner an African literature in European languages by black South Africans. The concept or structure of otherness was fundamentally altered by this new invention. Now the otherness for African literature in the African languages was African literature in the European languages written by both white and black South Africans. The conduit for this seminal development was *The Bantu World* launched by R. V. Selope Thema in 1932.

The one project on which Selope Thema never wavered during his half a century of intellectual life was the call for the destruction of African traditions, which he passionately despised since he associated them with 'backwardness', 'heathenism' and all sorts of 'foolishness'. It should be remembered that in emulation of his 'master', Booker T. Washington, who had written an autobiography, *Up from Slavery*, Thema in the 1930s wrote an incomplete and unpublished memoir with the title of 'Up from Barbarism'. In other words, tradition was synonymous with barbarism. New Negro modernity, which he absolutely adored, except for jazz which he despised like the other conservative New African modernisers, was to be the instrument with which to destroy African traditions. All the major participants in the creation of this 'new' literature – H. I. E. Dhlomo, Peter Abrahams, Walter B. M. Nhlapo, Todd Matshikiza and Henry Nxumalo – were the acolytes of Thema, working under his guidance and being trained and/or inspired into journalism in the pages of *Bantu World*. Although not involved in the making of African literature in the European languages, the other brilliant young New African intellectuals also apprenticed by Thema in this newspaper at the time were R. R. R. Dhlomo, Guy Bundlwana Sinxo and Jordan Ngubane. It would seem that in the 1930s everything cultural, if not political, was predetermined: the Sophiatown Renaissance decade of the 1950s, so vaunted in our cultural history, was largely a celebration, a dancing and singing to a tune written two decades earlier.

Having pledged allegiance to the great conservative journalist, his protégés made decisions and discoveries in this decade that were to have far-reaching cultural and literary consequences for the rest of the century. One central theme that Thema propagated in his editorials and in 'Special Correspondent' pieces was that the key to resolving most of the problems in the making of New African modernity in South Africa lay in absorbing and digesting the historical lessons of New Negro modernity in the United States. This was an edict that his students took very seriously. Seemingly inexplicably (since, in hindsight, we have the counterexample of Vilakazi, who only wrote in isiZulu), H. I. E. Dhlomo in 1932 wrote a short piece in *Ilanga lase Natal* in which he explained that he would not write creative literature in an African language (Zulu specifically) but would do so in the English language since it would afford him a much bigger audience, especially overseas ('Mr Vilakazi'). Immediately thereafter he commenced writing poetry which was as much influenced by the Romantics as it was by Countee Cullen and James Weldon Johnson of the Harlem Renaissance (sometimes known as the New Negro Renaissance). All of his plays written in this decade, which were influenced by Elizabethan drama (particularly Shakespeare), were an attempt to resolve the tension and unity between tradition and modernity. Dramas with such strange titles as *The Girl who Killed to Save: Nongqause the Liberator* could not resolve this historical conundrum; Nongqause had to kill tradition in order to successfully save it from itself. Dhlomo's brilliant essays of this decade on literary theory, which were in effect a social theory of modernity in an African context, could not untangle this contradictory unity. Notwithstanding the delay of six years, when Vilakazi struck at Dhlomo in a famous 1938–9 intellectual duel, Vilakazi was clearly aware by then that Dhlomo was succeeding or had succeeded in capsizing African literature in the African languages in favour of African literature in the European languages. This was the real historic importance of this duel between these very close friends, both of whom were great intellectuals.

African literature in English

In discovering the Harlem Renaissance through *The New Negro* (1925), edited by Alain Locke, and *The Souls of Black Folk* (1903) by W. E. B. du Bois on the shelves of the Bantu Men's Social Centre library in Johannesburg in this important decade (of which he was to inform us in his autobiography *Tell Freedom* [1954]), Peter Abrahams brought to young New African intellectuals of the New African Movement such as Ezekiel Mphahlele, Todd Matshikiza, Henry Nxumalo, Walter B. M. Nhlapo (older than himself) the poetics, arts and music of New Negro modernity. This emphasis was in contrast to the politics, religion and philosophy of the New Negro Movement that had informed the awakening modernistic imagination of senior New African intellectuals such as Thema, Dube, Plaatje and Seme in the late years of the nineteenth century and in the early years of the twentieth century. Although Abrahams left South Africa permanently in 1939 at the age of 19 (residing in Britain from 1939 to 1956 and in Jamaica from 1956 to the present), his intervention was, for several reasons, more decisive than that of Dhlomo in overthrowing the dominant position of African literature in the African languages in the imagination of black South Africans in preference of African literature in the European languages. In part, Abrahams's position reinvented a tradition started in South Africa by two Xhosa intellectuals, William Wellington Gqoba and William Isaac Wauchope, who switched back and forth between writing poetry in isiXhosa and in English in the late nineteenth century.

First, the example of Abrahams's short stories *Dark City* (1942) and novel *Mine Boy* (1946) was central in persuading *Drum* magazine to switch from celebrating 'tradition' in its earliest copies to emphasising 'modernity', thereby capturing the zeitgeist of the 1950s. This can be inferred not only from the serialisation of parts of *Wild Conquest* (1951) in *Drum* magazine, but also from the intellectual portrait written by Nxumalo for the magazine following Abrahams's 1952 visit sponsored by the London *Observer* newspaper for a series of reports on apartheid ('Peter Abrahams'). In the following year Abrahams assembled the reports in the book *Return to Egoli* (1953). What is so revealing about the book, reading it today, is not so much its denunciation of apartheid, which is unstinting, but its revelling in the memory of the intellectual atmosphere around *Bantu World* in the 1930s, of which H. I. E. Dhlomo, Nxumalo and Abrahams himself were a part, under the tutelage of Thema. Dhlomo and Nxumalo are portrayed superbly in the book.

Secondly, Abrahams's introduction of Langston Hughes and Richard Wright into South African literary history through his own poetic and novelistic practice had a profound influence on Mphahlele, Bloke Modisane and Lewis Nkosi. Mphahlele in his autobiography *Down Second Avenue* (1959) recalled twenty years after the fact that his first encounter with the Harlem Renaissance at St Peter's College (High School) was through Abrahams. Thema's influence on Walter B. M. Nhlapo and on Jordan Ngubane was of a different order. One of the defining characteristics of the 1930s was the beginnings of a serious definition and articulation of African nationalism by Isaka Seme, Allan Kirkland Soga and Isaiah Bud-M'Belle in *Umteteli wa Bantu* and Thema in *Bantu World*. The construction of this ideology by these conservative modernisers was partly necessitated by the emergence of Marxism within the New African Movement brought in by revolutionary modernisers such as Albert Nzula, J. B. Marks, James La Guma and E. T. Mofutsanyana. It was in the context of the struggle between nationalism and Marxism that there appeared in the late 1930s for the first time in *Bantu World* a serious appreciation and evaluation of marabi music and intermittently of American jazz written by Nhlapo. The singular contribution of Nhlapo was that of tracing the metamorphosis of marabi music from South African 'popular culture'. This popular culture was part of the urban culture that transformed the historical consciousness of the peasantry into that of the proletariat. What Nxumalo and Matshikiza brought from the 1930s to the *Drum* magazine of the 1950s was the literary style of writing in the English language that sought to articulate and express emergent popular forms, and it was in synchrony with the desire for modernity by the newly formed working class. Casey Motsisi, Arthur Maimane, Can Themba and Modisane made this literary style hegemonic by making it representative of what African literature in modernity should be.

In becoming dominant, this literary style and its constituents succeeded in displacing African literature in the African languages from the literary imagination of the New African Movement, replacing it with African literature in the European languages. The defeat of African literature in the African languages went hand in hand with the defeat of Marxism by African nationalism across the 1930s and the 1940s. The founding of the African National Congress Youth League in 1944 by Anton Lembede, Jordan Ngubane, Nelson Mandela, Oliver Tambo, A. P. Mda, William Nkomo and others expressed the triumph of nationalism as the guiding ideology of the national project of New African modernity. Ngubane, as editor of the newspaper *Inkundla ya Bantu*

(Bantu Forum) in the 1940s and as a major contributor to *Indian Opinion* in the 1950s, was the principal proponent of the ideology of nationalism in those two decades.

The publication of H. I. E. Dhlomo's epic *Valley of a Thousand Hills* (1941) made possible the emergence of the first serious literary criticism by Ngubane within the New African Movement. Though there were epics written by New African intellectuals earlier than the one by Dhlomo – for instance Robert Grendon's *Pro Aliis Damnati* (Condemned for Others) which was published in *Ilanga lase Natal* from 14 October 1904 to 15 May 1905 and consisted of 4,412 lines with twenty long stanzas – all of them appeared before the coalescence of a national consciousness and a national artistic sensibility. In many ways *Valley of a Thousand Hills* consolidated the unity of this consciousness and sensibility. This is how Ngubane viewed the epic in his appreciation ('*Valley of a Thousand Hills*'), whose fundamental merit is that it examined the poem principally on its artistic qualities rather than on its ideological correctness. Ngubane saw the epic as articulating a 'national spirit' of the valley that had been traversed by Shaka in earlier times in the process of creating a unified Zulu nation leading towards building a unified Africa. The epic was a symbolic representation of the progress achieved by African people in modernity. Ngubane assessed the publication of the epic as a landmark in the self-definition of the African people in the struggle against oppression and domination.

Although the poetic work of H. I. E. Dhlomo has been central in establishing the singularity of African literature in the European languages within the history of the New African Movement, it should be contrasted with the poetic form of African literature in the African languages, for instance that of Nontsizi Mgqwetho (*The Nation's Bounty*), in order to have a complete view of the complex range of South African cultural history. In this regard, Mgqwetho's achievement can be characterised in the following manner. She had an uncanny consciousness of history in the making, of complex ideologies shaping the outcome of historical processes. She sought to capture the unending form of history as perpetual change determined by the contending forces of permanence and transience. She wanted to convey the qualitative nature of her historical moment. In this sense, she was a modern poet with a depth that perhaps no other poet previous to her had, and this is equally true of poets who were to emerge in her wake in our cultural and intellectual history. Many of her poems were shaped by two ideological forces, which paradoxically were seemingly in opposition to each other and yet were mutually reinforcing: Christianity (ethics) and African Nationalism (African languages). Her poetry is characterised by a dialectical talking-through of issues in order to facilitate a praxis in resolving them, rather than a meditative singing voice contemplating the supposedly ordained nature of things. Her speaking voice in its poetic form articulated that things are changeable through action because they are historically made; this defines her understanding of modernity and her practice of modernism within the New African Movement, of which she was a pre-eminent member.

An holistic perspective on the history of the New African Movement makes it clear that the current, and seemingly hegemonic, predominance of African literature in the European languages over African literature in the African languages in South Africa emanates from the colonial political consequences of the incomplete transformation of European modernity by New African modernity. Aesthetically and cognitively, African literature in the African languages is supreme in relation to African literature in the European languages, as the appearance of the voluminous unpublished poetry of Mqhayi and Kunene in the unfolding decades of the twenty-first century will make abundantly clear. It may well be that this century will belong to African languages despite the fact that at present they are still ideologically oppressed.

Bibliography

Abrahams, P. *Mine Boy*, London: Dorothy Crisp, 1946.
    Return to Egoli, London: Faber, 1953.
    Tell Freedom, London: Faber, 1954.
    Wild Conquest, New York: Anchor Books, 1971.
Brink, A., and Coetzee, J. M. *A Land Apart*, New York: Viking, 1987.
Cabral, A. *Return to the Source*, New York: Monthly Review Press, 1974.
Dhlomo, H. I. E. 'African Attitudes to The European', *Democrat*, 1 December 1945.
    'Bantu and the Church', *Umteteli wa Bantu*, 30 August 1930.
    Collected Works, ed. N. W. Visser and T. Couzens, Johannesburg: Ravan, 1985.
    'Developments and Achievements in the Field of Culture [and] Literature', *Ilanga lase Natal*, 13 June 1953.
    'Mr Vilakazi and Writers', *Ilanga lase Natal*, 1 January 1932.
    'The Period of the Evangelisation', *Umteteli wa Bantu*, 19 December 1931.
    'Racial Attitudes: An African Viewpoint', *Democrat*, 17 November 1945.
    Valley of a Thousand Hills, Durban: Knox Publishing Co., 1941.
Doke, C. M. 'A Call to Philological Study and Research in South Africa', *South African Quarterly* (July 1925–February 1926).
    'A Preliminary Investigation into the State of the Native Languages in South Africa with Suggestions as to Research and the Development of Literature', *Bantu Studies* 7 (1933).
Jabavu, D. D. T. *Bantu Literature: Classification and Reviews*, Lovedale: Book Department, 1921.

Jameson, F. *Postmodernism; or, The Cultural Logic of Late Capitalism*, Durham, NC: Duke University Press, 1991.

A Singular Modernity, London: Verso, 2002.

MacNab, R. (ed.). *Poets in South Africa: an Anthology*, Cape Town: Maskew Miller, 1958.

MacNab, R., and C. Gulston. *South African Poetry: A New Anthology*, London: Collins, 1948.

Mgqwetho, N. *The Nation's Bounty: The Xhosa Poetry of Nontsizi Mgqwetho*, ed. and trans. J. Opland, Johannesburg: Witwatersrand University Press, 2007.

Mqhayi, S. E. K. *Ityala Lamawele*, abridged and trans. C. August, *The New African*, January 1966.

Mofolo, T. *Moeti oa Bochabela*, Morija: Morija Sesuto Book Depot, 1907.

Pitseng, Morija: Morija Sesuto Book Depot, 1930.

Msimang, H. S. 'Bantu Destiny', *Umteteli wa Bantu*, 18 July 1927.

'Bantu Intellectuals', *Umteteli wa Bantu*, 17 October 1925.

'The Bantu Nation?', *Umteteli wa Bantu*, 14 July 1923.

'Intellectuals and Chiefs', *Umteteli wa Bantu*, 3 September 1927.

'Mr Hay and Bantu Intellectuals', *Umteteli wa Bantu*, 26 May 1928.

Ngubane, J. 'Valley of a Thousand Hills: Story of Feeling, Hope and Achievement', *Ilanga lase Natal*, 29 November 1941.

Nxumalo, H. 'Peter Abrahams', *Drum* (December 1955).

Rubusana, W. B. *Zemk'inkomo Magwalandini*, Alice: Lovedale Press, 1964.

Sekese, A. *Mekhoa le Maele a Basotho*, Morija: Morija Sesuto Book Depot, 1931.

Seme, Pixley ka Isaka. 'The Regeneration of Africa', *African Affairs, Journal of the Royal African Society* (July 1906).

Thema, R. V. S. 'Bantu Intellectuals', *Umteteli wa Bantu*, 12 September 1925.

'Intellectuals and the Chiefs', *Umteteli wa Bantu*, 3 September 1927.

17

Refracted modernisms: Roy Campbell, Herbert Dhlomo, N. P. van Wyk Louw

TONY VOSS

Roy Campbell (1901–57), Herbert Dhlomo (1903–56) and N. P. van Wyk Louw (1906–70) are the three most eminent South African early twentieth-century writers in English and Afrikaans: Campbell the expatriate settler, the first South African writer since Olive Schreiner to achieve an international reputation; Dhlomo the black Zulu-speaking African nationalist, who chose English as the medium of his work in drama, poetry, narrative and criticism; and Van Wyk Louw the Afrikaner, who remained at the forefront of his people's spiritual life from his leadership of the Digters van Dertig (Poets of the Thirties) until his death (see Chapter 15).

If *modernism* is European and Anglo-American in origin, and parades from *Prufrock* in 1917 to the complete *Cantos* of 1970, then its synchronous and historical refraction as it reaches South Africa complicates our reading of writers of this period, from the immediate aftermath of the Anglo-Boer War of 1899–1902 through the initiation of the armed struggle to the eve of the collapse of apartheid; through industrialisation and two world wars to the first hopes of a post-apartheid state. Given the medium of refraction, colonial (or dominion) modernism would never be mere imitation:[1] neither Campbell nor Dhlomo nor Van Wyk Louw committed themselves unequivocally to the conventional formal devices of modernism – free verse, discontinuity, the epiphany. Van Wyk Louw mastered canonical verse forms early in his career, but in his last volume explored a prosody that recalls Mallarmé. Dhlomo fashioned his verse style from post-Romantic poetic diction and from African American writers of the early twentieth century,[2] and Campbell his from Tennyson, the Symbolistes and Robert Service. Van Wyk Louw builds on

I thank Helize van Vuuren, Duncan Brown and Colin Gardner for their help.
1 'No national culture . . . is the cultural centre of the world' (N. P. van Wyk Louw in 1951; *Versamelde Prosa* I, p. 413).
2 See the section of Ntongela Masilela's website devoted to Dhlomo and the New African Movement (1900–60) – http: // pzacad.pitzer.edu / NAM /

Afrikaner proto-nationalism and an oral folk culture, encountering Europe early via his Dutch ancestry and the study of German at the University of Cape Town. Campbell rejects Freud, but with Van Wyk Louw, invokes Nietzsche. Dhlomo had some engagement with Marx, but aligned himself with African nationalism rather than communism.

Yet all respond actively to their own moment of modernity, to 'the currently governing concept of what it means to be a subject of history' (Attwell, *Rewriting Modernity*, p. 3). This suggests technological competence, submission to the protection or dominance of a centralised state, an identification with the values of the Enlightenment and the bourgeois revolutions of the late eighteenth and early nineteenth centuries: all of which raised difficulties for both Campbell and Van Wyk Louw. Usually, but not always, the imagined modernist setting is urban (which Campbell, and Van Wyk Louw in a sense rejected) and its viewpoint individualist (which both Van Wyk Louw and Campbell – extravagantly – embraced). Whilst the more common modernist response is to turn away from the repetition and sensation of mass democratic society, the proletarianisation and commodification of work, Dhlomo moves from gradualist, progressive and elitist to a populist conception of the artist's social role, a trajectory following that of the ANC and its predecessors (Thompson, *History of South Africa*, pp. 174, 156). In his conception of the aristocratic artist, raised above the masses but in tune with the *volkswil* (people's will), Van Wyk Louw attempts to reconcile the hierarchical society with the class divisions of modern Afrikanerdom, but seems to assume the possibility of a just implementation of 'separate development'. Dhlomo embraced the African nationalism of the ANC, Van Wyk Louw Afrikaner nationalism; perhaps sensing that in South Africa these alternatives were irreconcilable, Campbell chose the rootless nomadism of the *diasporado*.

Although its origins coincide closely with the First World War, it is difficult to see that conflict as the sole cause of modernism. For the Afrikaner the war of 1899–1902 may have equalled in trauma what 1914–18 meant to Europe. In a sense, continuous historical disjuncture is as much the condition of the colony as the metropolis, and the modernisation of South Africa is inextricably bound up with colonisation. Oppression and separation worked to subject black people to the deprivations and indignities of modernity while denying them the advantages, a process which Dhlomo attacked and of which Campbell and Van Wyk Louw were on occasion critical.[3] Resistance to the colonial project

---

3 'Afrikaner nationalism had given very little attention, in the heat of its struggle for survival, to the survival of other groups in South Africa as separate nations' (Louw, *Versamelde Prosa* I, p. 500).

could be either traditional or modern, while the modernity of colonial rule was defensive and exploitative. The Bambatha Rebellion of 1906 could be seen as the last movement of traditional armed resistance, and the 'struggle', after 1960, as its modern resurgence. Campbell and Dhlomo write in a language of the coloniser; Dhlomo's mother tongue was isiZulu, but his choice of English is his modern gesture.[4] Campbell wrote in the language he was born to but turned it into an idiom of his own, 'an English re-invented and deterritorialized' (Pechey, '"Poetry in the World"', p. 10). Van Wyk Louw's Afrikaans is also a language of the coloniser, but from a *volksnasionaal* perspective a tongue to be protected against recolonisation, and he draws on oral resources throughout his career. In this respect, Van Wyk Louw's enterprise has something in common with the attempts by S. E. K. Mqhayi (1875–1945) and B. W. Vilakazi (1906–47) to establish national traditions in isiXhosa and isiZulu.[5]

One feature of European modernism was its recognition of the colonial or exotic other, both an anthropological discovery and an artistic appropriation. Campbell, without a folk culture of his own, identified with the vestigial equestrian culture of his youth, and invokes the various mythologies of the Terrapin, the Zulu, Mithraism and tauromachy, and gypsies. Dhlomo identifies with the tribal culture and cosmology of his own people's past (and their urban present). Van Wyk Louw calls on the orality / oral culture of the rural *volk*, the imaginary pastoral-hunting economy of *Raka* and later in *Tristia* the urban underworld of whores and pimps. For Van Wyk Louw and Campbell this is a recognisably modernist exploitation of myth, whereas Dhlomo accesses myth though eulogy and incorporates it into his poetic. All show a modernist interest in science and evolution and in eugenics. Van Wyk Louw was drawn to national socialism, and Campbell to Spanish fascism and shotgun anti-Semitism. None of these writers seems strongly to follow any modernist move to gender equality and women's liberation, while acknowledging both individual women and the archetypal feminine.

Modernism is partly an engagement with religion. Campbell rejected the Presbyterianism of his inheritance and became a Catholic, a move which Van Wyk Louw too seems to have considered; but in the year of his death Van Wyk Louw wrote a festival poem for the Nederduitse Gereformeerde Kerk

4 See Masilela (Chapter 16 in this volume) for the tension between African-language and English-language modernity in late nineteenth- and early twentieth-century South Africa.
5 The maturation of a colonial education system may link these writers across the barriers of race and language (Durban High School, Adams Mission, South African College School, Lovedale, Mariannhill). The mission schools would have promoted 'a relatively liberal Western tradition' (Thompson, *A History of South Africa*, p. 156), perhaps more so than the white schools.

parish of which he was a member. Dhlomo held on to his Protestant faith, the monotheism of which was tempered by his sense of the link between the living and the dead as 'one genealogical continuum' (Opland, *Xhosa Oral Poetry*, p. 148).

All share further the mode of existence of the modern writer, in a negotiated relationship with their readers, to whom they were occasionally obliged to explain their work. They were familiar with recording and/or broadcasting studios: Van Wyk Louw was a pioneer in radio drama. Campbell, Dhlomo and van Wyk Louw were critics, even teachers, publishers, editors and promoters of their own and others' work. Under patronage Campbell edited *Voorslag* and, later, *The Catacomb*, a Catholic journal. Mqhayi and Dhlomo were professional journalists. Van Wyk Louw was one of the founders of the *Vereniging van die Vrye Boek* in 1935, and of *Standpunte* in 1945. Like Van Wyk Louw, Mqhayi, whose career displays an energy as versatile as that of any of the other writers, is thought of by his audience as his people's voice, fashioning his whole career on effecting a just continuance of his language and culture, embracing print, the medium of modernity, in order to sustain, perhaps even to revive and extend the tradition of the oral *imbongi* (Opland). In addition to the virtuosity of his attempts to adapt isiZulu to formal demands of rhyme and metre, Vilakazi, like Van Wyk Louw an academic, also working at a theoretical and historical framework for the literature of his mother tongue, strives for and achieves a more disembodied 'vatic' voice, as much in his nature poetry as in his poetry of social protest (Attwell, *Rewriting Modernity*, p. 108). Both Dhlomo and Van Wyk Louw wrote on literary and philosophic topics for the middle-class popular press.

Roy Campbell

> I am a pure modernist . . . I don't mean that I acquiesce in all the supposed triumphs of our civilisation – the sentimental destructiveness of the howitzer, the hysterical cacophony of the gramophone, or the inane garrulity of the radio entertainment.
> ('How I Began to Write' [1925], *Collected Works*, IV, p. 171)

> The mob passes: the individual remains.
> ('Fetish Worship in South Africa' [1926], *Collected Works*, IV, p. 216)

Campbell was age 23 when *The Flaming Terrapin* was published by Jonathan Cape in 1924. With this poem he established his style, of 'alien poetry: written in English but not English by nature' (Anon., 'Vaquero in Vacuo', p. 672), after he had explored, in Oxford, a number of modernist modes that were abroad in the immediate aftermath of the First World War: imagism, surrealism, the *vers de café* of Verlaine, the 'objective correlative' imagery of Eliot. A genuine original, an emergent, a brief epic of creation, struggle and survival, in which the Terrapin tows the ark about the world from south to north, Campbell's poem recalls *The Waste Land* and Eliot's 'mythical method', without the disillusionment and world-weariness, but Campbell puts himself in the myth, together with Noah, Chaka and the 'Angel Horsemen'. The civilisation of which he felt himself to be a part, cut back by war and corrupted by complacency, is to be revived by its outriders: the north by the south, the old by the young, the central by the peripheral, the industrial by the pastoral, the mechanical by the equestrian. This is the first of Campbell's manifestoes, a figuration of himself as 'the dreamer that remains, / The Man, clear-cut against the last horizon' (*Collected Works*, I, p. 63).

Campbell's versatile creativity continued on his triumphal return from Britain to his birthplace in Durban in 1924. Philosophical interests are evident in the lectures he gave in Pietermaritzburg: 'Modern Poetry and Contemporary History'. His allegiances are to Shaw, John Davidson and Lucretius, to a creative evolutionism, although his commission here, and in *Voorslag*, seems to have been to explicate the new poetry to his colonial audience. Campbell wrote a brief but path-breaking and admiring account of *The Waste Land*, in which he heard 'the crash of falling ruins, the querulous expostulation of the old ideals and idols against the powers of an inscrutable darkness . . . the agonised searching questions of youth'. The younger poet sensed a colleague in 'the great work of reconstruction' that he had imagined in *The Flaming Terrapin* (*Collected Works*, IV, pp. 199–201), attacking both 'the fetish that rules this country – Colour Prejudice' (p. 212) in a *Voorslag* essay, and the mundane violence of racial politics in the epigram on Smuts:

> In a country like ours . . . the laws are based on the white man's mental superiority to the native – a superstition which was exploded by science ten years ago and by Christianity two thousand years before.
>
> (*Collected Works*, IV, p. 202)[6]

In identifying with a progressive oppositional tradition that included Bishop John William Colenso (1814–83), Olive Schreiner (1855–1920) and Mohandas Karamchand Gandhi (1869–1948), Campbell and his colleague William Plomer

---

6 During his first term as prime minister (1919–24), Smuts authorised violent suppression of black resistance at Bulhoek in the Eastern Cape in 1921 and in Warmbad (in what is now Namibia) in 1922, in which hundreds were killed.

(1903–73) 'were thinking far beyond any of their metropolitan contemporaries' (Pechey, '"Poetry in the World"', p. 10; see also Chapter 18 in this volume).

But Campbell was straining under the burden of the modern poet; fidelity to his own vision (both poetic and political), a didactic responsibility to a readership of his countrymen, and obligations to patrons. Before he left South Africa in December 1926 came visionary poems on the implications of colonialism ('The Zulu Girl' and 'The Serf'), and projections of himself as *isolato* in 'Tristan da Cunha', 'The Making of a Poet', 'To a Pet Cobra' and 'Mazeppa', and his Lucretian love poem to Mary 'From Thee, Goddess . . .' He completed most of *The Wayzgoose*, his light-hearted satirical revenge on 'South Africa and my fellow colonials', which would be published in 1928.

Campbell bade farewell to his native land in 'Rounding the Cape', never to live in South Africa again, but he always called himself a South African, identifying himself with its writers, English especially, but Afrikaans and Zulu too.[7] Although his political attitudes shifted, he published in South African journals and newspapers all his life and returned for the last time in 1954, when he was awarded an honorary doctorate by the University of Natal.

The return to England proved unhappy. But by May 1928 the family had settled in Martigues where Campbell 'entered one of the happiest periods of his life' (Alexander, *Roy Campbell*, p. 90). The poet acknowledged his debt to his wife in 'Dedication, to Mary Campbell', dated January 1929, the first poem of *Adamastor*, published in April 1930. The volume includes 'Early Poems' (concluding with 'Rounding the Cape'; see Chapter 6 in this volume) and 'Satirical Fragments', but the central section which gives the volume its title combines the visionary and radical South African poems with the sacramental celebrations of the life in Provence, the wild horses, bull-fighting and fishing.

Michael Chapman suggests that given the pathology of much of Campbell's later politics and poetry, all that is worth saving 'for South African literature' are 'the striking *Adamastor* poems of Campbell's youth' (*Southern African Literatures*, p. 182). But there is a continuity, even a beginning, in poems such as 'Mass at Dawn' and 'The Secret Muse' (the latter from *Poems*, 1930), which takes Campbell through bluster and braggadocio into quietism and piety. The strain resumes in *Flowering Reeds* (1933) and *Mithraic Emblems* (1936).

Continuity in Campbell is neither visceral reactionary polemic nor a vision of 'apocalyptic liberation'. Perhaps we can both acknowledge our 'concern

7 In 1953 the Afrikaans poet and academic D. J. Opperman acknowledged Campbell's championing of the Afrikaans language and its literature, and his influence on the Afrikaans poets of the 1930s (*Digters van Dertig*, pp. 61–7).

with the politics' (Chapman, *Southern African Literatures*, p. 181) of Campbell's poetry but 'detach him from simplistic ideological gut-reactions' (Pechey, '"Poetry *in* the World"', p. 3).

Campbell's early allegiance to the paganism and iconoclasm of Lucretius and Davidson continues as a variety of humanist materialism. For Campbell, 'middle-class education, after a century in the hands of Democracy . . . aims at producing a certain type of idealist'. The process 'manages to derange in the young many of the more natural perceptions that result in the generation of materialistic desires, ambitions and emotions, and diverts them away from the material universe into the realms of abstract thought' (*Collected Works*, IV, p. 244). Campbell's modernist (perhaps Nietzschean) materialism embraces an idea with 'a long history in the Western philosophical tradition': selfhood, the concept of 'an own self', is 'a form of self-experience intensely physical in kind and expression',[8] setting him apart from 'the predominant emphasis in the European tradition of philosophy and political thought on idealism' (Kenney, *Lucretius*, p. 38). Campbell's early modern, pre-Freudian concept of the self, like his prosody, is a further aspect of what seems to set him out of time with modernity.

Roy Campbell is often read for sensation rather than for thought, but Nicholas Meihuizen proposes that Campbell embraces 'the paradox [of] the form of the endless' (*Ordering Empire*, p. 159): futurism, vorticism, Lucretian Epicureanism, Mithraism, perhaps fascism, thus seem to lead almost inevitably to Campbell's and his wife's conversion to Catholicism in Toledo in 1936. This spiritual homecoming may have fulfilled the poet's Orphic conception of his craft as the creation of a world of words, a naive and primitive energy which powers both the lyrical and the satirical extremes of Campbell's work.

> My verse was nourished by Toledo's sun
> In whose clear light Ray, Sword and Pen are one.
>
> ('Talking Bronco')

In fact, neither modernity nor modernism, *tout court*, could offer Campbell an idiom. His prosody was determined by an allegiance to 'the traditional poetic frame . . . the dynamos of poetic form which have been left to us by men who actually depended for their livelihood upon the generation of mental electricity' (*Collected Works*, IV, p. 247). Throughout his life Campbell opposed, with his friend Wyndham Lewis, what he called the modern 'religion of

---

8 Katherine Maus, quoted by Gail Kern Paster, 'The Tragic Subject and its Passions', p. 143.

"time'" (*Collected Works*, III, p. 37), [9] an instrumental, future-directed historicist sense:

> We do not make appointments with the clock,
> But rooted in the Past from which we came
> Live in the moment as the light in flame.
>
> ('The Family Vault')

Campbell's thinking of himself as 'a pure modernist' does not clear his idiom of the dross of history or his own psychology. Yet, with Schreiner, he has 'an assured place in any comprehensive account of international modernism' (Pechey, '"Poetry *in* the World"', p. 11).

This lyrical strain of 'pure art' persists in Campbell for forty years, from Durban to his last home in Sintra: from 'Now, like a ghost . . . ', through 'The Secret Muse', 'Mass at Dawn', 'The Palm', 'The Flowering Reed', to 'The Gum Trees' and beyond. In these poems intense personal feeling is transcended as Campbell acknowledges fully the world beyond the self, truly attuned not only to the feelings of others but to his own. Often both the world and the inspiration are his love for Mary, but the feeling is not always contentment, often it is 'dread' at the transience of his gift or awe at the frailty of the verses he offers against the relentless passage of time, a counterpoint to the triumphal invocation of 'rust' in 'To the Survivors', 'Rust' and 'Junction of Rails: Voice of the Steel'. In addition to those admitted to the activist register, these other poems are part of a wider lyrical canon. In 1935 Campbell appeared in Yeats's *The Oxford Book of Modern Verse 1892–1935* but not in Michael Roberts's *The Faber Book of Modern Verse* the next year. [10]

Campbell's last two decades were unsettled, although service in the Second World War fulfilled what seems to have been a lifelong fantasy of soldiering. The reception of *Mithraic Emblems* (1936) was disappointing, and Campbell never regained the acclaim that *Adamastor* had received. The Francoist *Flowering Rifle* (1939) was generally denounced and *Talking Bronco* (1946) hardly noticed. Since his encounters with the Symbolistes in his early twenties, Campbell had been learning from European poetry, and in 1951 he published the translations of the *Poems of St John of the Cross*, on which he had started work in Toledo in the 1930s and which gave expression to his lyrical gift and his Catholic faith. There followed *Poems of Baudelaire: Les Fleurs du Mal* in

9 From Campbell's essay *Wyndham Lewis* (*Collected Works*, IV, p. 37). Frederic Jameson contrasts 'the commitment to temporality as an experience, the valorization of historicity and *durée*' with 'the timeless objectivity of the lived present' (*Fables of Aggression*, p. 124).
10 Campbell may have been omitted by Roberts for asking too high a fee. See Van der Vlies, *South African Textual Cultures*, pp. 64–5.

1952. 'Fragment, from "The Golden Shower"', Campbell's final manifesto, a Catholic, quietist love poem to Mary, was a revision of the Lucretian, materialist and erotic 'From thee Goddess . . .' (1926) made in 1956, the year before he died in Portugal, from injuries sustained in a motor accident.

H. I. E. Dhlomo

> My creative writing is the greatest thing I can give to my people, to Africa . . . It will endure and speak truth even if I perish . . . I have chosen the path to serve my people by means of literature, and nothing will deflect me from this course.
>
> (Herbert Dhlomo, letter to Charles Mpanza, 16 October 1941,
> Couzens, New African, p. 350)

As distinct from thirty years of journalism, a creative achievement in itself,[11] Herbert Dhlomo's literary Collected Works consist of plays, verse and prose fiction. From The Girl who Killed to Save: Nongqause the Liberator, published by Lovedale Press in 1935, arguing that the Xhosa Cattle-Killing of 1856–7 was 'beneficial since it destroyed tribalism and brought people into a modern age' (Collected Works, p. xi), to Dingane, produced in Durban in 1954, together with Ntsikana, Cetshwayo and Moshoeshoe, Dhlomo created a sequence of 'histories' whose heroes (Xhosa, Zulu, Sotho) evoke a national rather than tribal identity and the integrity of traditional life. By 1941 his sense of history was radical rather than progressive: in a production of Shaw's Saint Joan at his alma mater, Adams College, Dhlomo saw them burn 'the St Joan of Africa. She still burns . . . horror! horror! It was not St Joan they were burning! It was I!' (Couzens, New African, p. 340); Cetshwayo attacks the Shepstone system of the 1860s as anticipating Hertzog's segregation bills of the 1930s, portraying John Dunn as a grasping colonial and the assassin of Cetshwayo.[12] In 1942 Dhlomo identified the themes of Dingane and Cetshwayo as the 'Decay and Collapse of Zulu power' (Couzens, New African, p. 339). In Nongqause, Kreli

---

11 In The Cultural Modernity of H. I. E. Dhlomo, Ntongela Masilela argues that many of Dhlomo's essays are in fact Baudelairean 'prose poems' giving expression to 'the African soul, conscience and mind in encounter with the modern city' (p. 145), which 'much more than his plays and/or verse merit inclusion in the cultural geography of African modernism in the twentieth century' (p. 142). Masilela plans a monograph on 'The Literary Modernism of H. I. E. Dhlomo' (p. x), and has collected much of Dhlomo's work on his website, www.pitzer.edu/new_african_movement. The Campbell Collections of the University of KwaZulu-Natal hold substantial Dhlomo manuscripts.

12 John Dunn (1830–95): freebooter and frontiersman. For his treachery the British Empire rewarded Dunn with one of the largest of the thirteen chiefdoms into which Zululand was divided after the war of 1879.

claims 'Individuals must lose themselves in the race' (Dhlomo, *Collected Works*, p. 15). But in *Cetshwayo*, tragically, the king discovers his own individuality only in the moment before he is ingloriously shot down: 'Of myself as myself I never thought. I always thought of myself in the light of the people. I never was I . . . Now that I am lost, I know that I am a person. I am I. I am a soul' (*Collected Works*, p. 175). *Moshoeshoe* celebrates the Sotho king's creation of an independent nation, which serves as a model for the aspirations of the 'New African' of the 1930s, while implementing Dhlomo's own theories of 'tribal drama'.

Among the plays on contemporary themes in contemporary settings, *The Living Dead* (pre-1941) is a *Grand Guignol* in which the middle-class urban Mkhize family is visited by the matriarch Ruth '*shrouded in burial linen*', come to teach her impious children that 'The dead must be remembered' (*Collected Works*, p. 188). *Malaria* (1932) attacks inadequate health services for Africans, through 'a heroic self-help scheme' founded and run by mission-educated Ruromba and his family. Ruromba is part preacher, part healer, and the cooperation between black and white mark the play as 'progressive'. Yet again the tone is complex, from the comedy of the opening exchange to the transcendental conclusion. *The Pass (Arrested and Discharged)* dramatises the experience of many millions of urban Africans: arbitrary arrest, detention and trial under the pass laws. There is a vestigial progressive emphasis, but the hero seems to speak for Dhlomo: 'Daily they turn innocent souls like me into defiant and cynical fatalists, reckless criminals, and even bitter and unreasoning enemies . . . How long, O Lord, how long!' *The Workers* (1940–1) is certainly 'his most radical play, at least in terminology' (Couzens, *The New African*, p. 188), dramatising the resistant syndicalisation of labour and the unity of intellectuals and workers. As Walter Nhlapo wrote, these are 'plays of ideas' (Couzens, *New African*, p. 348), the later, activist, scripts particularly recalling US socialist drama of the 1930s.

Most of Dhlomo's poetry dates from the 1940s. *Valley of a Thousand Hills*, published in Durban in 1941, shortly after his move from Johannesburg, is a brief epic, in which the poet retreats from the harsh world of modernity to his 'native vale',[13] the organic tribal community, identifying with those who 'Forever strove and struck, themselves to wrench from domination foreign', figures from the tribal past aligned with those who 'rise and strike for right'. The poet thus identifies with both 'the Band of bards of old' and the African Mineworkers' Union, founded in 1941.

---

13 ' . . . a whole picture of the African as disoriented man, of his landscape as wasteland' (Mphahlele, *The Voice of the Black Writer*, p. 5).

Dhlomo gathered his shorter poems as 'A Gourd of African Milk' ('the breaking of the gourd' is a recurring image of dissension and crisis). The earliest poems invoke God and nature with Romantic echoes:

> From chaos God made order and from sin
> Salvation, from discord sweet concord, in
> All things changed bad to good. So men can too
> If serve they will the Beautiful and True.
>
> ('Reflections', *Collected Works*, p. 323)[14]

'Renunciation' suggests a radical break as Dhlomo turns from 'singing songs / Of Nature's beauty' in order to dedicate his 'entire life to these mass struggles of the oppressed'. He takes heart from John L. Dube and Vilakazi, but there is a note of deep despair, which threatens the conviction of his calling in later poems such as 'Sweet Mango Tree' and 'Ikehla', and doubt about the future in 'Inanda'. The 'Patriotic and Protest Poems' sound an occasional note of hope ('On Munro Ridge, Johannesburg') and poems of anger and frustration derive their power from the fusion of the emotional and the political ('The Harlot', 'Because I'm Black').

That Dhlomo is a writer of ideas is also apparent from his short stories. For example, 'Drought' features two 'progressive' Africans, an old farmer and a young extension officer (a Dhlomo figure). In 'Farmer and Servant' (1948), which may be in part a response to the Bethal convict labour scandal first reported in June 1947, a farm worker becomes a World War II hero. In the postwar conclusion he dies from a shot aimed at his white woman unionist colleague by her ex-fiancé, a poor white who was once the hero's employer. In 'An Experiment in Colour' (1935–8) Frank Mabaso, inspired by the speech he hears at his Fort Hare graduation, devotes himself to the discovery of a serum which will turn skin from black to white, and its antidote which will reverse the process. The point is that colour is the only difference: as black or white Frank is in all other respects the same man. When he demonstrates (and destroys) his discovery at a public meeting Frank is shot and killed by an insane white racist. 'Euthanasia by Prayer' sets materialism against religion: in forging an elegant reconciliation, the story is the culmination of Dhlomo's lifelong interest in science.

The integrity of Dhlomo's *oeuvre* can be read from his essays in literary theory and criticism, which both expound the principle and practice of African

---

14 Dhlomo's sonnets 'The Nile' and 'The Ocean' may recall Keats's 'To the Nile' and 'On the Sea' and Shelley is ironically evoked in 'Not for Me'. Dhlomo's work alludes throughout to the Bible.

literature and serve as a guide to his writing. In the 1930s the focus is on drama: arguing for the African roots of his own dramatic work as well as for the dramatic potential of the matter of Africa, Dhlomo makes African drama the generator of a whole cultural process of archives, libraries, academic research and performance. In the 1940s (as in the exchange with Vilakazi; see Attwell, *Rewriting Modernity*, pp. 77–110) Dhlomo addresses questions of language and form in African poetry, the appropriateness of English prosody to African languages, and the 're-creation' (an important term) of the African past in modern literature. The third group of essays deals explicitly with the role of the modern South African writer, and suggests both Marxism and African Nationalism. 'Masses and the Artist' is the poet's revolutionary appeal to and identification with his people, an expression of allegiance and a claim for the social power of art, at a time when Dhlomo was campaigning for Chief Luthuli and the Youth League. Literature is neither 'art for art's sake' nor propaganda, its function, both recreative and recreational, as of all human endeavour, to make human life more just, beautiful, healthy, harmonious.

> As long as the fruits of life are not malleated out to reach all and sundry,[15] so long will there be upheavals and wars which are the result of oppression, frustration, despondency. In other words, these chronic explosions are but the tangible and palpable forms of humanity's cry for freedom, for happiness.
>
> ('Literary Theory', p. 61)

This fusion of aesthetics and activism (and individual faith) emerges in 'The Expert', a fragmentary and unpublished play, in which Christ appears successively as '"a common black worker", then in the abstract garb of Truth, Beauty and Goodness, and thirdly as "a talented, independent, bold patriotic African thinker"' (Couzens, *New African*, p. 215).

Although Dhlomo is remembered by many for politics rather than style, in his best poems (such as 'Because I'm Black', 'The Question' and the sonnets) the metre is sturdy and the diction straightforward. The literary essays consistently probe and engage. From the plays, consider exchanges between Hugh and the Missionary in *Nongqause*, Shepstone and Park in *Cetshwayo*, the Commissioner and his assistant in *Malaria*, the king and Mohlomi in *Moshoeshoe*; from the stories the description of the Highveld Afrikaner family in 'Farmer and Servant', Mabaso's dying speech in 'An Experiment in Colour' and the conclusion to 'Euthanasia by Prayer'.

Dhlomo's dedication to literature is the central feature of his modern achievement, for all the versatility of his working life, as teacher, journalist,

---

15 Malleated: 'hammered, beaten thin'; in the original misprinted as 'mallenated'.

musician, librarian, activist. The fact of his *writing* is as important as the *writings* which are his legacy.

N. P. van Wyk Louw

The writer knows . . . that all pain and need and longing which remain wordless, must disappear and that he can give them enduring form only through his word.

('The Newer Afrikaans Literature' [1938], *Versamelde Prosa*, i, p. 156)

N. P. van Wyk Louw sustained a capacity for surprise throughout his writing life. His debut, *Alleenspraak* (Soliloquy, 1936), is given an individual twist by the fact that the three sections are presented in reverse chronological order: a headlong love story is interwoven with intense self-examination and response to the natural world, mostly in strict stanzaic forms, including the sonnet, with an unerring rhythmic sense; intense spiritual struggle, from ecstasy to despair, recalls the European metaphysical poets of the seventeenth century. The poet figures implicitly as both the Moses of 'Opstand' ('Resistance') and 'Die Speelman' ('The Fiddler'). *Die Halwe Kring* (The Half Circle, 1938) extends the historical reference and intensifies the religious struggle. 'Die Profeet' ('The Prophet') in blank verse comes to a rugged acceptance of God's 'other mercy', while in the unrhymed alexandrines of 'Aan die Skoonheid' ('To Beauty') Van Wyk Louw declares his faith in beauty as the responsibility of the artist, the condition of full human life and the manifestation of God's 'eternal being and His own joy'. 'Gedagtes, Liedere en Gebede van 'n Soldaat: 1935–1937' ('Thoughts, Songs and Prayers of a Soldier') are militantly nationalistic. Transfiguring acceptance informs the sonnets which close *Die Halwe Kring*, 'Vier Gebede by Jaargetye in die Boland Mei–Julie 1937' ('Four Prayers for Seasons in the Boland, May to July 1937').

Van Wyk Louw's early essays, collected in *Berigte te Velde* (Dispatches from the Front) and *Lojale Verset* (Loyal Resistance; both 1939), develop an historical and theoretical framework for Afrikaner nationalism and *geestelike lewe* (spiritual life): the aristocratic ideal, the interconnection of individual (artist) and *volk*, and the sense that the *volk* was always becoming, never completely achieved.[16] Afrikaans had moved from a patriotic to a people's literature

---

16 Louw's essays are gathered in the two volumes of *Versamelde Prosa* (Collected Prose). Johan van Wyk's English translation of 'Die Rigting van die Afrikaanse Letterkunde' (Direction in Afrikaans Literature, 1936), was published in *Alternation* 11:1 (2004), pp. 71–8. The translator 'thought that the ANC nation-building culture debate was uncannily repeating some of Van Wyk Louw's ideas' (Shane Moran, personal communication).

(*volksliteratuur*) to a national literature for the Afrikaner, 'simply a modern person in an Afrikaans environment' (*Versamelde Prosa*, I, p. 9). Although tempted by national socialism, Van Wyk Louw put his faith in Platonic notions of poetic 'form', the word, and the moral values of beauty, truth and justice ('skoonheid, waarheid en geregtigheid'), espousing an hierarchical idea of society, itself seen as part of the vertical order of nature. (For the racist implications of Van Wyk Louw's defence of Afrikaner nationalism, see Sanders, *Complicities*, pp. 57–92.)

Nationalism inspires *Die Dieper Reg, 'n Spel van die Oordeel oor 'n Volk* (The Deeper Right, a Play on the Judgment of a People), commissioned for the Great Trek centenary in 1938. In this choric, ritual drama 'the Voice of Justice decrees that the powerful and simple deed (of the Trekkers) is its own justification before God, and that as a people the Afrikaner will continue in the land which they conquered' (p. 9). This has been called an 'essentially amoral idea of justification' (Olivier, 'N. P. van Wyk Louw', p. 622), unbalanced and ahistorical (Renders, 'Dramatise Werke', p. 3).

It is tempting to read nationalism into *Raka*, a tragic 'brief epic' (*klein epos*) published in 1941. The story of Raka 'die aapmens' ('the ape-man') who takes over the tribe after killing the lonely hero, Koki, is open to many interpretations, as Van Wyk Louw himself ironically acknowledged in the last year of his life (*Versamelde Prosa*, I, pp. 545–6). But the complexity, detachment and narrative skill of the verse make the meaning at once powerful and elusive: the evanescence of high ideals, the fragility of community and civility?

Gestaltes en Diere (Figures and Beasts, 1942) includes some of Van Wyk Louw's most memorable work: ironic urban ballads and a dark transgressive Jungian bestiary (The Beach Hyena, the Black Leopard, Three Beasts).[17] Whereas the poetry of the 1930s was strongly confessional, these poems are more symbolic, their psychology and form more obsessive, and their theology more complex: as Gerrit Olivier observes, Van Wyk Louw has found in these figures Eliot's 'objective correlative' for his own struggles ('N. P. van Wyk Louw', p. 622). In the powerful dramatic monologue 'Die Hond van God' – central to the volume and to Van Wyk Louw's work as a whole – the struggle of the late sixteenth-century inquisitor is 'a clash – humanly impure as all spiritual clashes are – between two eras or two worlds' (*Versamelde Gedigte*, p. 139: Van Wyk Louw's headnote), but his torture of the heretic is also self-torture.

---

17 Louw's psychic beasts are more visionary than Campbell's observed or imagined creatures, but in 'Reflections' Campbell sees a series of animals in the mirror image of himself.

The heroes of *Dias* (written for the van Riebeeck festival of 1952) and the verse drama *Germanicus* (1956) also straddle historical eras. Dias seeks both to challenge God and to implement His will, by extending the boundaries of the known world. Ironically, before dying at sea with his crew, he accepts that he will not fulfil his ambition. Germanicus, the aristocratic soldier and intellectual condemned to inaction by his own scruples, dies a martyr's death, holding fast to super-temporal ideals in the face of the corruption of the empire.

From 1950 to 1958 Van Wyk Louw held a chair in South African Literature and History at the University of Amsterdam, and Europe features strongly in *Nuwe Verse* (New Poems, 1954), but the collection opens with 'Nog een maal wil ek . . . ' ('Once again I want . . . '), not simply 'a little poem of a man's longing for the world of his childhood' (*Versamelde Prosa*, I, p. 579) but also a poem about *poesis*, of the direct creativity of youth, the poetic inspiration which comes from and returns to nature. Among grim tight-lipped poems of fear, apprehension, frustration, there are candid evocations of the created world, free of any search for meaning, and the poet's craft shifts from crusade or burden to 'Die Ambag' ('The Trade'), yet 'our art lives close to God'. The poet speaks through 'Die Doper in die Woestyn' ('The Baptist in the Desert') rather than through an Old Testament prophet, or wryly as 'Die Digter' ('The Poet'):

> The great day will find me sleeping
> by Vanity my sweet friend
> and near us in his cradle:
> a rhyme, our unchurched child.

This is immediately followed by 'Die Beiteltjie' ('The Chisel'), a symbol of the unexpected consequences of human action (Olivier, 'N. P. van Wyk Louw', p. 628) but also the tool of the poet's trade, with which he seems to achieve a reverse re-enactment of creation. *Nuwe Verse* includes the striking sequence 'Klipwerk' ('Stonework'), evoking the world of the poet's youth in demotic (sometimes scatological) vocabulary and folk verse forms. After two Mediterranean 'Elegiac Verses' ('Arlésiennes' and 'Meretrix Tarraconensis'), *Nuwe Verse* concludes with 'Beeld van 'n Jeug: Duif en Perd' ('Evocation of a Youth: Horse and Pigeon'), a poem of exquisite pace and impressive range, recalling his childhood home in Sutherland. In the sunshine the young boy reads of Hannibal, recalling Cortes and Montezuma, as his pigeons feed and fly and a groom stables his horse. Sketching a Roman sword, the Aztec axe and the Cross in the sand, then lightly erasing the images, he thinks of Abel, of Abraham and Isaac, of the Crucifixion, until he sees that all creation forms 'a great and single fiction / concerning him and us, recounted by Himself . . .' (trans. Butler in Grové and Harvey, *Afrikaans Poems*, p. 195). *Nuwe Verse* thus looks back to youth and earlier volumes, and, in its elegiac and ironic tones and a new sense of unity, anticipates Van Wyk Louw's last collection and magnum opus.

Among the Ovidian echoes of *Tristia* (1962), an enigmatic, oracular and variously interpretable work, are both exile from the homeland and alienation from its politics. Van Wyk Louw returns to the struggle with God, the life of the artist, meaning and being, the discovery of Latin Europe, and human love, in strict stanzaic verse and the sonnet, but also in demanding experimental forms, seeking absolute precision in elaborate punctuation (or its omission), repetition, syllabification, orthography and etymology. Into its melancholy prospect of the 'gekeerde lewe' of humanity in the 'bont prosessie' ('motley procession') of history *Tristia* integrates South Africa,[18] as in 'Karoo-dorp: Someraand' ('Karoo Village: Summer Evening') and recurring reminiscences of 'Klipwerk', demonstrating that as the language of a national literature Afrikaans had achieved a universal relevance (*Versamelde Prosa*, I, p. 164). The volume becomes a coda to Van Wyk Louw's engagement with Europe: he had confronted early modernity, Romanticism, the Enlightenment and the Renaissance: *Tristia* embraced the medieval: the aesthetic is Gothic, levelling all sorts and conditions of humanity. As Dryden said of Chaucer, 'here is God's plenty'. *Tristia* concludes with 'Great Ode' an 'enigmatic modernist poem of high complexity' and 'remarkable intertextuality with *The Waste Land*' (van Vuuren, 'From "Burning City" to "Death's Crevice"', p. 2), inspired by a visit to the Altamira caves.[19]

Whilst *Tristia* suggests little about apartheid *per se*, 'Nuusberigte: 1956' ('News Reports: 1956'; *Versamelde Gedigte*, p. 316) denounces the corruption of wealth and power and the divisions of class (although the poet also requests

---

18 *Versamelde Gedigte*, pp. 326, 273. But 'gekeerde' means both 'frustrated' and 'orientated' (Olivier, 'N. P. van Wyk Louw', p. 631).

19 Many South African writers have been inspired by the rock art of their home country. In choosing Altamira, perhaps Van Wyk Louw, who asked in 1947 why the Bushman should be closer to the true South Africa than the modern Afrikaner (*Versamelde Prosa* I, p. 524), was suggesting the primacy of European rock art. In the nineteenth century, Bleek and Stow had claimed a bond between Bushman aboriginal and European settler, which was not there between European and Bantu. 'The poet . . . must be aware that the mind of Europe – the mind of his own country – a mind which he learns in time to be much more important than his own private mind – is a mind which changes, and this change is a development which abandons nothing *en route*, which does not superannuate either Shakespeare, Homer, or the rock drawing of the Magdalenian draughtsmen' (T. S. Eliot, 'Tradition and the Individual Talent', cited in Moran, *Representing Bushmen*, p. 118).

mercy for himself). Van Wyk Louw identified 'nationalist... "writ small"' with Kantian 'personal liberalism' (*Versamelde Prosa*, I, p. 426), rather than with social democracy, and 'was an ardent Nationalist all his life' (*Dictionary of South African Biography*). South Africa should not become 'a formless stew of peoples' (*Versamelde Prosa*, I, p. 458)[20] since the country was never 'a multiracial people but a multi-national [and multi-lingual] community, like Europe' (*Versamelde Prosa*, II, p. 510). Van Wyk Louw's stated principle was 'voortbestaan in geregtigheid' ('survival in justice') (*Versamelde Prosa*, I, p. 462), yet the historical dramas of his last years are written as if apartheid, or separate development, with *geregtigheid* were achievable without white domination.

Insisting that Afrikaans literature, to survive, had to guarantee its readers 'the satisfaction of their deepest longings ... and something not to be obtained in any other language' (*Versamelde Prosa*, I, p. 164), Van Wyk Louw alternately (or simultaneously) ventures forth into European culture and history, for both political justification and literary sustenance, and returns to his Afrikaans folk roots: in search of a 'universal' national literature, and the maintenance of its local African origins.

Modernism in postmodern times

In 1958, Campbell, Dhlomo and Van Wyk Louw were all taken up in Roy MacNab's *Poets in South Africa: An Anthology*.[21] Yet it is difficult now to think of them as having a single national South African readership. In one view, 'The great white South African writers contemporaneous with the New African intellectuals and artists constituted an extension of European modernism in Africa, rather than African modernism' (Masilela, *Cultural Modernity*, p. 143).[22] Nor, in South Africa itself, may Dhlomo himself fare any better. In 1998 Es'kia Mphahlele wrote that 'the reading culture Dhlomo lived in is dying or already dead in most circles' (Masilela, *Cultural Modernity*, p. 214). Van Wyk Louw is still engaged with by poets of the generations who have followed him, an

---

20 "'n vormlose volksbredie': 'bredie' recurs in *Tristia* (*Versamelde Gedigte*, p. 296). Addressing the British royal family in 1947, Campbell called South Africa 'a Babel of tongues and breeds', unified only 'in our joint allegiance to your crown' (*Collected Works* I, p. 614). For Louw, 'volk' was a transcendent category: 'We believe that the human is revealed only in national form – nowhere on earth is there a "general person", only and always concrete persons who belong to a particular *volk* and speak a particular language' (*Versamelde Prosa*, I, p. 45).
21 MacNab also included translations of work by Mqhayi and Vilakazi. In 1948 MacNab had edited *South African Poetry: A New Anthology*: the change of emphasis in the title *may* suggest a shift in the conception of the South African polity after ten years of National Party rule.
22 Masilela also claims that 'Campbell is appalling' for his 'unparalleled ... hatred of Africans' (*Cultural Modernity*, p. 143). Campbell's anti-Semitism was much more virulent.

annual lecture at the University of Johannesburg bears his name, and theses and journal articles on his work continue to appear (see Viljoen, 'Digterlike Gesprekke').

South African history may have vindicated Dhlomo's African Nationalism, even if it has lost him his middle-class readership. But the age in which Campbell could claim imperial citizenship and the status of *vaquero* is over, as perhaps is the political, as opposed to the cultural, viability of Van Wyk Louw's concept of the Afrikaner *volk*. Dhlomo had the advantage of 'a philosophy which defined the person in universally valid terms' (Ngubane, *Forty Years of Black Writing*, p. 11), while in Campbell and perhaps Van Wyk Louw we must face 'the lifelong affirmation of the intellectual inequality of human beings and the even more disturbing fascination with racial categories' (Jameson, *Wyndham Lewis*, p. 20). We accept either what for many is a central tenet of modernism, the radical disjuncture between art and life, or that when the artist is true to herself or himself *qua* artist, the art goes beyond its maker's ideology. At its best, the work of these three writers expresses 'a desire for some solid truth while at the same time mourning its elusiveness' (Eagleton, 'Determinacy Kills', p. 9). When the solid truth loses its elusiveness, the work loses its conviction.

Campbell, Dhlomo and Van Wyk Louw are African or Africanised post-Romantics, seeking to validate the power and capacity of art to define the individual and traditional mythic systems they invoke and create. For these poets the aesthetic carries communal energies amenable to the shaping work of the artist. In these respects at least they are all touched by metropolitan modernism.

Bibliography

Alexander, P. *Roy Campbell: A Critical Biography*, Cape Town: David Philip, 1981.

Anon. 'Vaquero in Vacuo', *Times Literary Supplement*, 8 November 1957, 672.

Attwell, D. *Rewriting Modernity: Studies in Black South African Literary History*, Pietermaritzburg: University of KwaZulu-Natal Press, 2005.

Campbell, R. *Collected Works*, ed. P. Alexander, M. Chapman and M. Leveson, 4 vols., Johannesburg: Ad Donker, vols. I and II, 1985; vols. III and IV, 1988.

'Uncollected Verse', in Tony Voss, 'Roy Campbell: Uncollected Verse', *English in Africa* 32:2 (October 2005), 9–38.

Campbell, R., W. Plomer and L. van der Post, (eds.). *Voorslag 1–3* [1926]. Facsimile reprint, ed. Colin Gardner and Michael Chapman, Pietermaritzburg and Durban: University of Natal Press and Killie Campbell Africana Library, 1985.

Chapman, M. *Southern African Literatures*, Johannesburg: Ad Donker, 1996.

Couzens, T. *The New African: A Study of the Life and Work of H. I. E. Dhlomo*, Johannesburg: Ravan, 1985.

Dhlomo, H. I. E. *Collected Works*, ed. N. W. Visser and T. Couzens, Johannesburg: Ravan, 1985.

    Dictionary of South African Biography, ed. W. J. de Kock, Pretoria: National Council for Social Research, 1968.

    'Literary Theory and Criticism of H. I. E. Dhlomo', ed. N. Visser and T. Couzens, special issue of *English in Africa* 4:2 (1977).

Eagleton, T. 'Determinacy Kills', *London Review of Books* 19:6 (2008), 9–10.

Eliot, T. S. 'Tradition and the Individual Talent' [1919], in *The Sacred Wood: Essays on Poetry and Criticism* [1920], London: Methuen, 1969, 47–59.

Grové, A. P., and C. J. D. Harvey (eds.) *Afrikaans Poems with English Translations*, Cape Town: Oxford University Press, 1962.

Jameson, F. *Fables of Aggression: Wyndham Lewis, the Modernist as Fascist*, Berkeley: University of California Press, 1979.

Kenney, E. J. *Lucretius*, Greece and Rome, New Surveys in the Classics no. 11, Oxford: Clarendon, 1977.

Louw, N. P. van Wyk. *Asterion*, Cape Town: Human & Rousseau, 1965.

    Berei in die Woestyn, Cape Town: Nasionale Boekhandel, 1968.

    Blomme vir die Winter, Cape Town: Human & Rousseau, 1974.

    Dagboek van 'n Soldaat, Johannesburg: Afrikaanse Pers-Boekhandel, 1961.

    Dias, Kaapstad: Tafelberg, 1952.

    Die Dieper Reg, 'n Spel van die Oordeel oor 'n Volk [1938], Cape Town: Tafelberg, 1978.

    Germanicus, Cape Town: Nasionale Boekhandel, 1956.

    Die Held, Johannesburg: Afrikaanse Pers, 1962.

    Koning-Eenoog of Nic vir Geleerdes, Cape Town: Nasionale Boekhandel, 1963.

    Kruger Breek die Pad Oop, Cape Town: Human & Rousseau, 1966.

    Lewenslyn, Cape Town: Human & Rousseau, 1971.

    Die Pluimsaad Waai Ver, of Bitter Begin, Cape Town: Human & Rousseau, 1972.

    Die Val van 'n Regvaardige Man, Cape Town: Human & Rousseau, 1976.

    Versamelde Gedigte [1981], Cape Town: Tafelberg and Human & Rousseau, 2002.

    Versamelde Prosa, vol. I, [1986], Cape Town: Tafelberg, 2005.

    Versamelde Prosa, vol II, Cape Town: Human & Rousseau, 1986.

MacNab, R. (ed.). *Poets in South Africa: An Anthology*, Cape Town: Maskew Miller, 1958.

MacNab, R., and C. Gulston (eds.). *South African Poets: A New Anthology*, London: Collins, 1948.

Masilela, N. *The Cultural Modernity of H. I. E. Dhlomo*, Trenton, NJ: Africa World Press, 2005.

Meihuizen, N. *Ordering Empire: The Poetry of Camões, Pringle and Campbell*, Bern: Peter Lang, 2007.

Moran, S. *Representing Bushmen: South Africa and the Origin of Language*, Rochester, NY: University of Rochester Press, 2009.

Mphahlele, E. Afterword to Masilela, *Cultural Modernity of H. I. E. Dhlomo*, 211–23.

    'Landmarks of Literary History in South Africa', in Mphahlele and Couzens, *Voice of the Black Writer in Africa*, 1–8.

Mphahlele, E., and T. Couzens (eds.). *The Voice of the Black Writer in Africa*, Senate Special Lectures, Johannesburg: University of Witwatersrand Press, 1980.

Mqhayi, S. E. K. *Aggrey umAfrika*, translation of Charles Kingsley Williams, *Aggrey of Africa*, London, 1935.

I-bandla laBantu, Alice: Lovedale Press, 1923.

Idini, Johannesburg: Caluza, 1928.

Imihobe nemibongo yokufundwa ezikolweni, London: Sheldon Press, 1927.

Inzuzo Bantu Treasury [1943], rev. edn, Johannesburg: Witwatersrand University Press, 1957.

Isikhumbuzo zom-Polifiti u-Ntsikana, Johannesburg: Caluza, 1926.

Ityala Lamawele, Alice: Lovedale Press, 1914.

uAdonisi waseNtlango, translation of G. C. and S. B. Hobson, *Kees van die Kalahari*, Alice: Lovedale Press, 1945.

UDon Jadu: Ukuhamba Yimfundo, Alice: Lovedale Press, 1929.

U-mhlekazi u-Hintsa, Alice: Lovedale Press, 1937.

uMquayi wase Ntab'ozuk, Alice: Lovedale Press, 1939.

uSamson, Alice: Lovedale Press, 1907.

uSo-Gqumahashe, Alice: Lovedale Press, 1921.

Ngubane, J. K. 'Forty Years of Black Writing', in Mphahlele and Couzens, *Voice of the Black Writer in Africa*, 11–16.

Olivier, G. 'N. P. van Wyk Louw (1906–1970)', in van Coller, *Perspektief en Profiel*, 615–35.

Opland, J. *Xhosa Oral Poetry: Aspects of a Black South African Tradition*, Johannesburg: Ravan, 1983.

Xhosa Poets and Poetry, Cape Town: David Philip, 1998.

Opperman, D. J. *Digters van Dertig*, 3rd edn, Cape Town: Nasionale Opvoedkundige Uitgewery Beperk, 1953.

'Roy Campbell en die Suid-Afrikaanse Poësie', *Standpunte* 8:3 (March 1954), 4–15.

Paster, G. K. 'The Tragic Subject and its Passions', in Claire McEachern (ed.), *The Cambridge Companion to Shakespearean Tragedy*, Cambridge University Press, 2001.

Pechey, G. '"Poetry in the World": Roy Campbell's Rhyming Universe', unpublished paper delivered at the 'Campbell in Context' Colloquium, University of Durban-Westville, July 2002.

Renders, L. 'Die Dramatiese Werke van N. P. van Wyk Louw met Volk-wees as Inspirasie', http://litnet.co.za/cgi-bin/giga (2002), accessed 26 May 2009.

Roberts, M. (ed.). *The Faber Book of Modern Verse*, London: Faber, 1936.

Sanders, M. *Complicities: The Intellectual and Apartheid*, Durham, NC: Duke University Press, 2002.

Taylor, D. 'Unbroken Record – A Study of Roy Campbell', *Trek* 2:13 (10 October, 24 October and 7 November 1941).

Thompson, L. *A History of South Africa*, New Haven, CT: Yale University Press, 1990.

Van Coller, H. P. (ed.). *Perspektief en Profiel: 'n Afrikanse Literatuurgeskiedenis*, vol. II, Pretoria: Van Schaik, 1999.

Van der Vlies, A. *South African Textual Cultures: White, Black, Read All Over*, Manchester: Manchester University Press, 2007.

Van Vuuren, H. 'From "Burning City" to "Death's Crevice": Modernism in T. S. Eliot's *The Waste Land* (1922) and N. P. van Wyk Louw's "Great Ode" (1962)', paper delivered at ICLA, Pretoria, 2000.

Viljoen, L. 'Digterlike Gesprekke met Van Wyk Louw', *Tydskrif vir Geestes-Wetenskappe* 48:3 (September 2008), 267–96.

Yeats, W. B. (ed.). *The Oxford Book of Modern Verse: 1892–1935*, Oxford: Clarendon, 1935.

18

The metropolitan and the local: Douglas Blackburn, Pauline Smith, William Plomer, Herman Charles Bosman

CRAIG MACKENZIE

Like colonial subjects in other British colonies, South African writers have for centuries felt the tug of the metropole. Olive Schreiner went to London to seek a publisher for her *African Farm*, and almost without exception late nineteenth-century and early twentieth-century South African writers followed suit. This trend has continued to the present: local publishing houses established themselves firmly enough in the years that followed World War II to offer writers a viable local market, but the prestige of publication in London or New York (and other major metropolitan centres), and the global reach that this brings, sees South African writers continuing to send their manuscripts abroad.

The writers examined here were active from the last years of the nineteenth century to the middle of the twentieth, a period that saw a decisive shift from a situation in which there was no viable alternative to being published in Britain to one in which a writer could choose. The change was remarkable: Douglas Blackburn's turn-of-the-century novels were published and reviewed in London and Edinburgh, generated some interest in the wake of the Boer War, and then vanished almost without trace; not fifty years later, Herman Charles Bosman's *Mafeking Road* (1947) was released by a local publisher, remaining in print and immensely popular through half a dozen local editions and innumerable impressions before finally making an inconspicuous entry into the British and American markets in 2008. In different ways William Plomer and Pauline Smith successfully straddled the two worlds of the local and the metropolitan, both achieving success in London before being recuperated into the local literary tradition via South African editions of their work in the postwar years, and particularly in the 1980s.

Douglas Blackburn: interpreter of the
Boer character

London-born Douglas Blackburn (1857–1929) came to South Africa in the early 1890s and returned to England only in 1908, thus spending nearly two (immensely eventful) decades in the country. In his extensive journalistic and creative output Blackburn was to prove himself a shrewd and incisive interpreter of South African society in the turbulent years spanning the Jameson Raid (1895) and Union (1910). In many ways a pioneer of the satirical turn in South African literature, particularly in his treatment of the Afrikaner as subject, Blackburn enjoyed a brief vogue in the first two decades of the twentieth century, but is now almost completely forgotten.

First and foremost a pressman, Blackburn was the precocious young editor of the *Brightonian* before its bankruptcy in 1884, worked in Fleet Street as a drama reviewer for nearly a decade, and then came out to South Africa in the 1890s to work on the *Star*. At the time of the Jameson Raid he became the proprietor-editor of the weekly newspaper *The Sentinel*, and during the Boer War years worked on both sides of the front as a correspondent.

As editor-journalist as well as novelist, he was staunchly anti-imperialistic and pro-republican. In his 'Open Letter to a Prominent Krugersdorp Jingo', published in the *Sentinel* on 31 October 1896, he begins by berating an unidentified jingoistic Englishman for denigrating the country (South Africa) that had 'made' him 'with a fraction of the effort and energy that would have been required of you in England' (Blackburn, 'Open Letter', p. 15). He then goes on to assert that 'the Boers have every right and excuse for being jealous of the Uitlander [foreigner]' because 'their history is one long record of oppression and injustice at the hands of the representatives of the country to which you and I belong' (p. 15).

It is these sentiments that infuse his novels, the most important of which are *Prinsloo of Prinsloosdorp: A Tale of Transvaal Officialdom* (1899), *A Burgher Quixote* (1903) and *Leaven: A Black and White Story* (1908). The last of these is an early example of the 'Jim comes to Jo'burg' genre and is dealt with elsewhere in this volume. The first two are pertinent to the discussion here since they are precursors in style and theme to the work of Smith and Bosman.

The foreword to *Prinsloo*, in which the narrator, Sarel Erasmus, lays out his motivation for writing the tale, begins as follows:

> The removal of my father-in-law, Piet Prinsloo, to a better world by dropsy, and of myself to Rhodesia by the machinations of the Hollander clique in Pretoria, have given me occasion and leisure to write and publish in safety

much that is necessary for the vindication of the character of a father of his country and founder of the *dorp* that bears his name. At the same time I take the opportunity to show how the presence of the Hollander and Uitlander in the Transvaal has ruined the character of the Afrikander.

(Blackburn, *Prinsloo*, unpaginated)

This is an early indication that what follows will be a self-serving attempt at exculpation. Once the reader tumbles to the slyly ironic narrative angle of the account, it becomes clear that Sarel Erasmus's 'vindication' of his esteemed father-in-law actually amounts to a revelation of the full extent of the latter's venality and criminal incompetence as a *landdrost* (magistrate). Indeed, what the novel turns out to be is a series of diverting anecdotes about small-town *verneukery* (swindling and fraud). This act of unconscious sabotage on Erasmus's part is in fact achieved before the foreword has been concluded:

I think that the fair-minded, *oprecht* [upright] man will be bound to confess that if Piet Prinsloo had faults ... they were not part of his nature, but came from the seed of bad example, from temptation to which he had not been used, and the smallness of the salaries paid by the Transvaal Government.

Ernest Pereira remarks that the prototype of Bosman's Oom Schalk Lourens should perhaps be sought in Blackburn's novel: 'This unjustly neglected satire has its origins in the clichéd caricature of the unsophisticated Takhaar [bump-kin] Boer, whose cunning and avarice are matched only by his naivety and ignorance – a combination calculated to render him an easy dupe for the Jewish speculator or his traditional enemy, the Rooinek Englishman' ('Tall Tellers', p. 109). Pereira goes on to draw attention to Erasmus's role as both commentator and narrator, pointing out that, 'as in the Bosman stories, it is the narrator's unconscious self-revelations that give ironic force to the humour' (p. 109).

In *A Burgher Quixote*, Sarel Erasmus as narrator takes centre stage and relates his picaresque Boer War adventures: being press-ganged into joining the Boer forces, the various scrapes he manages to survive and how he rises to be commandant. His loyalty throughout is to himself, however, and, while he tries to present himself as an '*oprecht* burgher' (upright citizen), we come to see that he is a Falstaffian character who survives only by being expedient, and, when that fails, by allowing himself to be the dupe of the British forces who capture him. Cervantes's and Blackburn's Quixotes are both inept bunglers, but where Don Quixote is a misguided do-gooder, Sarel Erasmus looks out for himself alone.

Blackburn's satire, then, targets both sides (English and Afrikaner). British colonial rapacity and ruthlessness are undoubtedly exposed, but so are Afrikaner turpitude in the form of various frauds and deceptions by the state authorities, and expediency (if not outright cowardice) in the Anglo-Boer War. Indeed, among the profusion of characters one encounters in *A Burgher Quixote*, there are very few exceptions to the norm of self-serving, often craven, behaviour in the face of danger.

Blackburn shows remarkable insight into the character of the turn-of-the century Afrikaner and the various disadvantages (poverty, illiteracy, isolation) that he tries to overcome by being *'slim'* (cunning, smart). Blackburn's evocation of various South African settings in telling detail and, above all, the ironic humour that pervades his Sarel Erasmus stories are memorable. But it is perhaps his larger vision, which goes beyond English–Afrikaner rivalry, that makes him important. For in the no quarters given struggle for riches between Boer and Briton it is the country's black inhabitants who are presented as the real losers: 'the true schlemiels of *Prinsloo* are not the Boers but the ultra-gullible Blacks, dispossessed by taxes, herded into recruitment camps, and reduced to labour units in the background' (Gray, 'Piet's Progress', p. 35).

Pauline Smith: romantic realist

Pauline Smith (1882–1959) was born in Oudtshoorn (Cape Province) to British parents. Her father, a medical doctor who came out to South Africa for the sake of his health, had established a practice in the town. Smith attended schools in South Africa and Britain, but her education was interrupted by ill health (from which she suffered intermittently her whole life), and she never completed her schooling. The death in 1898 of her father, to whom she was very close, meant that she never returned to the Cape permanently, and lived for most of her life in Dorset, making return trips to South Africa when health and finances allowed.

Thus, whereas Blackburn spent two intense decades as an adult in South Africa, immersed himself in the country and its culture and wrote prolifically about it while he was here, Smith spent only her early years in the country, and had to rely on childhood memories, updated by experiences from her later visits, for her depictions of South Africa and its people. Writing decades after Blackburn, Smith created characters that hark back to an earlier, more settled era prior to the massive disruptions of the two Anglo-Boer Wars, the First World War and the rapid industrialisation of South Africa in the first half of the twentieth century.

Her first story, 'A Tenantry Dinner', appeared in 1902 in the Aberdeen *Evening Gazette* under the pseudonym Janet Tamson. Other 'non-South African' stories and poems followed. In 1904 she returned to South Africa, where she started a diary in which she recorded observations about South African society and landscape. In 1908, on a visit to Switzerland, she met the writer Arnold Bennett, who was henceforth to encourage her in her writing. It is likely that her entire literary orientation, which she frankly admitted to being 'not . . . particularly bookish' ('Why and how', p. 151), was given direction by him. Noting that Bennett's favourite writers included Gissing, Flaubert, Zola, Chekhov, Dostoevsky, Turgenev and Tolstoy, Dorothy Driver remarks that Smith 'represents . . . a different school of fiction from the one represented by Virginia Woolf, born in the same year as Smith and writing in strong reaction against the realism of such writers' ('Introduction', p. 22).

Smith's next trip to South Africa in 1913 was nearly a year in duration, much of it spent in the Little Karoo area, in which she again recorded incidents and observations of people she met. She spent the First World War years in England, and published the first of her Little Karoo stories, 'The Sisters', in the *New Statesman* in 1915. In the early 1920s, with Bennett's assistance, five other stories, including 'The Pain' and 'The Schoolmaster', appeared in the *Adelphi*, where they attracted the attentions of the London literati, including T. S. Eliot. The *Adelphi* was edited by John Middleton Murry, Katherine Mansfield's husband and literary executor, and Smith thus made her literary debut in the very heart of London's literary world.

In 1925 *The Little Karoo* was published (with an introduction by Bennett). At this stage it was a collection of eight stories; the revised 1930 edition would add two more ('Desolation' and 'The Father'). Less than a year later her novel *The Beadle* (1926) was published. This was to be her last major work, although several other pieces appeared, both in her lifetime and posthumously.

In 1929 the BBC broadcast Smith's play *The Last Voyage* and readings of several stories from *The Little Karoo*; extracts from *The Beadle* followed in the late 1940s. In 1933 she published *A. B. ' . . . a minor marginal note'*, her memoir of Arnold Bennett (who had died two years earlier). Towards the end of this year she made another trip to South Africa, this time staying for over two years. Her collection of children's stories, *Platkops Children* (1935), appeared at this time. Her 1937–8 trip to South Africa was to be her last. The Second World War intervened, and Smith spent these years in England, depressed and in increasingly poor health. She struggled from 1949 onwards to complete her second novel, *Winter Sacrament*, but, dogged by ill health (neuralgia and chronic heart problems), she was forced eventually to abandon it.

The stories of *The Little Karoo* exemplify Smith's remarkable ability to capture the stark, elemental quality of her Dutch-Afrikaans characters and the ponderous biblical cadences of their speech. Her skill at catching their speech was less mimicry than artistry, however. As J. M. Coetzee persuasively argues, Smith had contact with Afrikaans, 'an indigenous language . . . close enough to her own English in some of its characteristic structures to be domesticated simply by the process of *faux-naif* translation'. This, he concludes, combined with 'access to stylistic resources available only in a language with a long written history' enabled her 'to create in the echo chamber of the English prose tradition felicitous effects that cohere neatly with the Afrikaner's myth of himself as Israelite' (*White Writing*, p. 126).

Smith's characters spend their lives wresting the barest of yields from the reluctant earth, and their austere Protestant faith and the tragic dimension in their human fallibilities are oppressively dominant. The compatibility of the stories that make up the story cycle in terms of their themes and setting has established Smith as one of South Africa's foremost 'regional' writers.

In 'The Pain' (often considered Smith's best story), Juriaan van Royen undertakes a journey to Platkops *dorp* (town) to seek help for his terminally ill wife at the newly established hospital there. The humble, rustic lifestyle of the simple peasant couple – a life closely tied to the soil and the elements, and presided over by a benign but frugal God – comes up against a newer world of modern medicine and impersonal efficiency, a world with novel rhythms and rationales. In this bewildering setting, Juriaan's God deserts him and the central irony of the story unfolds: Deltje's physical pain, which persuaded them to undertake the journey, is not cured in hospital but is merely eclipsed by the greater pain of spiritual suffering. The couple secretly resolve to leave the hospital, and the closing passage sees them on their way back to their isolated homestead, where Deltje will await a lingering death, and with her passing (the reader is left to presume) will come Juriaan's own demise.

'The Schoolmaster' concerns the youthful, selfless love Engela feels for Jan Boetje, a man on the run from his past. Jan Boetje becomes the teacher to the young children on Engela's grandparents' farm. He teaches the children and Engela about the far-off wonders of Europe, while Engela instructs him in local veld-lore. One day, in a fit of rage (which signifies something about his troubled past), Jan Boetje blinds a pair of mules when they refuse to cross a stream. In deep remorse, he banishes himself to a life of hardship, buying and selling goods to eke out an existence. In the depths of her anguish upon his departure, Engela draws comfort from the thought that what she taught him about the veld would help him in the physical and spiritual wilderness that he has damned himself to inhabit for life. In a tragically ironic final twist, the family discovers that Jan Boetje has drowned in a flood at the drift near the farm. The story illustrates Smith's immense power as a writer in the tragic mode, and marks her position in this tradition in South African literature.

The Beadle shares *The Little Karoo*'s setting and thematic concerns. Andrina, the central character, is a warm-hearted and innocent young girl who works for the Van der Merwe family on their farm Harmonie in the Aangenaam (Pleasant) valley area of the Little Karoo. In much the same pattern as 'The Schoolmaster', a stranger comes into this caring, God-fearing household: he is the self-centred and feckless Englishman Henry Nind, who seduces Andrina before leaving the district. Finding herself pregnant, Andrina leaves Harmonie in search of Nind, who is believed to be in the north of the country.

In the same community lives the beadle, a morose and embittered man whose story shadows Andrina's own: it emerges that he is Andrina's secret father, having forced himself on her mother, who died in childbirth. He has for years been watching his daughter grow up and now nurses an intense hatred of the young Englishman, whom he sees as a version of himself, committing the same errors and ruining a young girl's life. Andrina's plight precipitates the beadle's confession of guilt to the community, the Englishman goes back to England, and the end of the novel sees father and daughter reconciled, with Andrina quite unashamed of giving birth to a child under these circumstances. Smith thus offers a highly sympathetic rendering of the 'fallen woman' theme, and presents at the novel's conclusion a sense of hope and regeneration largely absent in her unrelievedly tragic short stories.

Blackburn and Smith both took as their principal subject the Dutch-Afrikaans settler, but their representations of this figure are strikingly different. Where Blackburn is ironic and satirical and attempts to catch his characters in all of their historical specificity, Smith imbues her characters with a timeless, emblematic quality. The reason for this is not hard to find. In 'Why and how I Became an Author' (drafted in 1927) Smith makes the following remark about the Little Karoo inhabitants whom she encountered as a child:

> In those unhustled days ... the Dutch farmers among whom my father's work as a doctor lay, still lived in a primitive simplicity close to their God. Among these people we had many friends and all their way of life, and their slow and brooding talk which fell so naturally in translation into the English of the Old Testament, was full of interest to us.   (p. 151)

In Smith's view of the South Africa of her childhood, misted over by the distance of some 6,000 miles and frozen into the last decades of the nineteenth century, her characters thus take on larger than life proportions.

This is certainly posterity's view of Pauline Smith, but there is another – minor – side to her that remained hidden for many years and that suggests a more direct link to Blackburn and Bosman. In 1993 a collection of her miscellaneous works appeared under the title *The Unknown Pauline Smith*. This includes the *Winter Sacrament* fragment, extracts from her diaries and several out-of-print stories. Among the last are her Koenraad tales ('The Cart' and 'Horse Thieves'), which employ a narrator, Koenraad, and deal with the pranks of farmers in the Little Karoo district in a manner that is strikingly reminiscent of Blackburn and that also anticipates Bosman's Oom Schalk Lourens stories. Interestingly, these pieces first appeared in a local newspaper, *The Cape Argus* (in December 1925 and January 1927), which perhaps suggests that they were deemed by her to be more ephemeral in nature and also more suited to local consumption. Indeed, they are no more than light-hearted diversionary yarns, and as such are markedly different from the stark, tragic stories for which she is better known.

William Plomer: an Englishman abroad

Whereas Smith's South African childhood was seen by her in later years as idyllic, and was one upon which she could productively draw for all her major work, the creative trajectory of William Plomer (1903–73) tended in the other direction: his African experience may loom disproportionately large in his oeuvre, but he was, in the words of Stephen Gray, 'one of those rare cosmopolitans who defy categorisation – an English writer in the African colonies, or the Far East, or Abroad on the Mediterranean, but an English writer pre-eminently' ('Introduction', *Selected Stories*, p. viii). By the age of 26, this precocious talent had five books published by the Hogarth Press. He also later collaborated with Benjamin Britten as librettist for *Gloriana* (1953) and three other operas, and became Chairman of the English Poetry Society. And, in the wake of the appearance of his *Collected Poems* (1960), he was awarded the Queen's Gold Medal for Literature (1963) and the CBE (1968). William Plomer's story, then, is that of a man who climbed clear of his remote colonial origins to ascend to the very top ranks of the metropolitan literary world.

Born in the far northern Transvaal town of Pietersburg to English parents, Plomer spent his early years in this region, but his South African childhood was regularly punctuated by visits to England, some of them lengthy in duration. Indeed, his peripatetic youth is likely to have given rise to his later sense of being a citizen of the world, although he seems not to have thought of it in these terms at the time: he felt merely rootless and abandoned. He began to have homosexual encounters with other schoolboys, and his biographer, Peter Alexander, argues that this was partly a response to the regime he had to endure under the dictatorial headmaster Clement Bode during his three years at Beechmont in Kent: 'In later life Plomer was to feel that Bode's tinpot tyranny had inculcated in him a lasting subversiveness which was to show itself subtly in his writing, and less subtly, but more secretively, in his sexual life' (*William Plomer*, p. 27). Being separated from his parents, moving about from school to school and having holidays with various relatives (instead of his own parents) made for a very fragmented and insecure childhood, and accounts for the position of 'observing outsider' that Plomer was later to adopt in his life and work alike.

After completing school at Rugby and, when the war ended and the family returned to South Africa, at St John's in Johannesburg, in 1921 the 19-year-old Plomer took a job as an apprentice farmer in the Molteno district of the Eastern Cape. As a farmhand in the Stormberg, an impressive mountain range in the Molteno district, the young man was already profoundly convinced of two things: that he was deeply and irrevocably estranged from colonial society (in attitudes to race and sex above all), and that the world of art and literature, represented by literary London, provided a more nurturing and valuable haven.

Plomer's father had a chequered career as a colonial administrator and government official, and finally moved to Zululand (in the north-eastern part of what was then Natal Province) in 1922, where the family ran a trading store. This provided the setting for some of Plomer's most important fiction, including his controversial novel *Turbott Wolfe* (1926) and the stories 'Ula Masondo' (1927) and 'The Child of Queen Victoria' (1933). The physical beauty of the almost naked young African men made a powerful impression on the young Plomer: 'their mere presence was to me deeply and agreeably disturbing' (*Double Lives*, p. 146), he later remarked. He gave expression to this in his poem 'The Black Christ', which, like the many others he wrote during this time, he sent to Harold Monro, founder of the Poetry Bookshop and publisher of the Georgian Poetry series and the poetry magazine the *Chapbook*, which published new poetry by emerging writers. Although there were numerous exchanges between the two men spanning some months, it all came to nothing in the end: Monro stopped replying to his eager young correspondent in

Zululand, and Plomer's hopes of being published by Monro's Poetry Book-shop died. The significant point, here, though, is the direction of Plomer's literary aspirations: to be published in London and rub shoulders with the likes of Rupert Brooke, D. H. Lawrence, Walter de la Mare, Siegfried Sassoon and Robert Graves, all of whom appeared in the Georgian Poetry volumes (1912–22).

Turbott Wolfe, which Plomer had started when he was 19 and completed by the time he was 21, is a work that stirred white society at the time. It was published by the Hogarth Press, run by Leonard and Virginia Woolf, and the modernist tendencies of the novel are conspicuous. It takes the form of a frame narrative (in the style of Joseph Conrad), has a fractured, episodic form, and is held together by powerful visual images and sense impressions rather than plot and verisimilitude.

The novel purports to be the narrative of the eponymous Turbott Wolfe, as told to 'William Plomer', and concerns the former's experiences in Africa, whence he has come to England to die (although still a young man). Wolfe (often taken by critics as a representation of the author himself) is employed in a trading store in Lembuland (north-eastern Natal) and encounters a range of people, including the missionary Rupert Friston, storekeeper Caleb Msomi and his cousin Zachary, who marries Mabel van der Horst and thus introduces the theme of 'miscegenation'. This group styles itself 'Young Africa' and has lengthy discussions about how to shape Africa's future. Wolfe falls foul of the police authorities, however, and returns to England. His own attraction to a young African girl also broaches the topic of forbidden love across the colour bar, but the relationship is never consummated. (This subject is later handled more maturely in 'The Child of Queen Victoria'.) Episodic and fragmented, the novel is frequently criticised for being unsure of its own direction, for attempting too much and resolving too little. The central character himself is also insufficiently developed and motivated, and yet the novel has a raw power and sense of urgency that has elicited much debate and controversy.

Given the numerous similarities between Turbott Wolfe and the young Plomer himself, it is significant that Wolfe was, in his own words, 'suddenly ordered to Africa by some fool of a doctor' (*Turbott Wolfe*, p. 10). His cultural base is England, he is sent out to Africa, and there contracts a disease that will shortly kill him. His trajectory is precisely the opposite of Plomer's, and perhaps represents what Plomer would have liked for himself: a thoroughly English, metropolitan upbringing and education. At least as striking as the self-consciously innovative style of the novel is the overwhelming sense of alienation the protagonist feels in colonial society: in matters of taste and decorum as much as attitudes to race and class, Wolfe is an outsider figure. His narrative is marked by deep disdain for the barbarism (as he sees it) of colonial South African society, whose representatives are reduced to crude caricatures, while his admiration and aesthetic appreciation for the 'nobler' aspects of untainted African culture are equally pronounced.

Alexander argues convincingly that the novel is saturated with frustrated homosexual desire, and points out that if one substitutes female characters for male ones (the androgynous yet beautiful Mabel van der Horst for the author himself, most crucially), the novel makes emotional sense:

> The triumph of *Turbott Wolfe* lay in the fact that Plomer had found a vehicle that allowed him to yoke his intense sexual frustration to a protest at South Africa's racial situation, to link an inner with an outer struggle. This was what gave the novel the force of a scream, and has kept it in print ever since its first publication. (*William Plomer*, p. 83)

Whilst the provocative *Turbott Wolfe* was being prepared for the press, Plomer met Roy Campbell and was invited to spend some time with him and his wife Mary at their home on the Natal south coast. There he met Laurens van der Post, and the three men collaborated on producing the literary magazine *Voorslag* (Whiplash), the first issue of which appeared in June 1926. The magazine was to founder soon afterwards, but, before it did, it provoked controversy almost the equal of *Turbott Wolfe*'s reception in South Africa. With the magazine's avowedly non-political stance (itself a bold political statement in 1920s South Africa) and its declaration of non-racialism in its editorial policy, it constituted a frontal attack on the pillars of white South African society, with its assumption of European superiority, its complacency at racial separation and the differential treatment of the races, its narrowness and aesthetic boorishness.

Making matters worse, as far as its more conservative readers were concerned, was the appearance in the launch issue of *Voorslag* of the first part of Plomer's 'Portraits in the Nude', which attacked white (and especially Afrikaner) brutality and immorality. (The second and third issues of the magazine published the remainder of the novella.) After a stormy interview with the magazine's manager and its financier, Campbell abruptly resigned as editor even before the third issue appeared, and the three *enfants terribles* of South African letters thus needed to find a new outlet. In September 1926 Plomer and van der Post impulsively took a ship to Japan, where Plomer was to live until 1929. During this time his collection of stories *I Speak of Africa* and *Notes for Poems* (both 1927) appeared. Later volumes of short stories are *Paper Houses* (1929), a set of stories about Japan, and *The Child of Queen Victoria* (1933), set in South Africa, Greece and France. Plomer later made a selection of his stories entitled *Four Countries* (1949); the posthumous *Selected Stories* (1985), edited by Stephen Gray, is a gathering of Plomer's African stories.

I Speak of Africa contains the well-known 'Ula Masondo', a tale in the 'Jim comes to Jo'burg' mould. Ula Masondo leaves his home village in Lembuland for the goldfields of Johannesburg, symbolically wrapped in a traditional African blanket. He soon falls into bad company and a life of crime, abandons his earlier ways, and at the story's end returns to the village dressed in 'European' clothes and with a changed attitude. The twist at the end is that it is he who rejects his family and former way of life, rather than the other way round, and becomes a pathetic, deracinated figure. The title story of *The Child of Queen Victoria* centres on the dilemma of a traditional Englishman whose attraction to a young African woman in rural Natal threatens to disrupt his conceptual and moral universe.

In 1929 Plomer left Japan for England, where he was to live out the rest of his life, working for the publishing house Jonathan Cape. These years, in which he became a distinguished man of letters and knew many of the important literary figures of the day, including the Woolfs and other members of the Bloomsbury group, are recounted in his two volumes of autobiography *Double Lives* (1943) and *At Home* (1958). These were later revised and combined into one volume entitled *The Autobiography of William Plomer* (1975); the sections dealing with his life in South Africa were republished separately as *The South African Autobiography* (1984). His literary connections stretched beyond elite circles like Bloomsbury: he persuaded Cape to publish Ian Fleming and edited several of his novels in the 1950s and 1960s.

Despite the considerable standing he ultimately achieved in the metropolitan literary world, he actively participated in and supported local literary culture, publishing some of his earliest poems in the mainly Zulu-language newspaper *Ilanga lase Natal*, and in the process becoming acquainted with the newspaper's remarkable founder, the Reverend John L. Dube. And his connections with South Africa did not diminish with the years: he wrote a highly perceptive foreword for Lionel Abrahams's important selection of Bosman's stories (*Unto Dust*, 1963), supplied an introduction for Guy Butler's second poetry collection *South of the Zambesi: Poems from South Africa* (1966), and helped translate a posthumous selection of Ingrid Jonker's poetry (published in 1968).

Herman Charles Bosman: 'An indigenous South African culture is unfolding'[1]

Born in Kuils River near Cape Town a little more than a year after Plomer, Herman Charles Bosman (1905–51) spent most of his life in the Transvaal, and it is the Transvaal milieu that permeates almost all of his writing. He was educated in Johannesburg at Jeppe Boys' High School, the University of the Witwatersrand and Normal College, where he qualified as a teacher. In January 1926 he received a posting as a newly qualified teacher to the Groot Marico in the remote Western Transvaal (today the North-West Province).

In the Marico Bosman encountered a community poor in material wealth but rich in the art of storytelling. Sent out to convert the people of the region to the alphabet and literacy, he was instead won over by their own impressive mastery of oral narrative. Stories about the Anglo-Boer and Native Wars, about life in the Boer republics of Stellaland, Goshen and Ohrigstad, about local legend and lore, were all eagerly absorbed by the young schoolteacher over coffee on the farm *stoep* (veranda) or in the *voorkamer* (parlour). The American humorous tradition – epitomised by Mark Twain, Bret Harte and Stephen Leacock, for example – was a strong influence on Bosman, as he was later to acknowledge in his essays of the 1940s, and his Marico experience gave this inspiration a local context in which to play itself out. He would deploy it to great effect, writing more than one hundred and fifty stories over some twenty years, work that established his reputation as one of South Africa's most popular and enduring writers. It also brought a unique region of the country to the public's attention: 'There is no other place I know,' Bosman later remarked, 'that is so heavy with atmosphere, so strangely and darkly impregnated with that stuff of life that bears the authentic stamp of South Africa' ('Marico Revisited', p. 145).

In July 1926, near the end of a mid-year vacation in Johannesburg, he became embroiled in a family quarrel, which led to his shooting and killing his stepbrother David Russell. In November he was tried for murder and sentenced to death, a sentence that was later commuted to imprisonment for ten years with hard labour. He eventually served four years and was released on parole in September 1930.

Upon his release Bosman embarked on a series of journalistic ventures with Aegidius Jean Blignaut. Thus began a literary partnership between the two men that was to last until 1934 (when Bosman left for London) and that

---

1 The title of an article by Bosman originally published in *South African Opinion* in April 1944 (see Bosman, *A Cask of Jerepigo*, pp. 46–51).

was to have important consequences for Bosman's development as a writer. Together the two men launched a series of short-lived periodicals, including *The Touleier* (1930), *The New L. S. D.* (1931) and *The New Sjambok* (1931), the last two being vain attempts at reviving journals originally run by the pioneering dramatist and satirist Stephen Black (1880–1931).

Interestingly enough, Black was one of the first to publish a piece by Bosman – the languorous poem 'Perhaps some Day', smuggled out of prison in 1929. Other Bosman items would appear in Black's satirical paper *The Sjambok* in 1930. Thus Black had a hand in the launching of a career that would rapidly eclipse his own. Indeed, Black's role in South African literature is as forgotten as that of Blackburn, and, like the latter, he also enjoyed a brief but glorious vogue. His first major stage success was the play *Love and the Hyphen* (first performed in 1908), which broke all records at the time as South Africa's longest-running show (Gray, 'Introduction', *Stephen Black*, p. 9). Other plays would follow: *Helena's Hope, Ltd.* (1910), *The Flapper* (1911), *The Uitlanders* (1911) and *A Boer's Honour* (1912). He was also the author of *The Dorp* (1920), a bitingly humorous novel of small-town life that anticipates Bosman's *Jacaranda in the Night* (1947) and *Willemsdorp* (*c.* 1949/50; first published 1977) and Alan Paton's *Too Late the Phalarope* (1953).

The journals that Bosman and Blignaut launched carried some literary material, including, in the first edition of the *Touleier* (December 1930), Bosman's first Oom Schalk Lourens story, 'Makapan's Caves'. With very few exceptions, this 'local' trend in Bosman's writing – which runs counter to that of the other writers discussed here – continued for the rest of his short life: almost all of his work was carried by local periodicals, several of which he had a hand in launching and editing. The editorial in the first issue of the *Touleier* described the periodical's role as 'burn[ing] like a storm-lamp through the darkness of the night' (Gray, *Herman Charles Bosman*, p. 6) – in other words, blazing a trail in uncharted territories (something suggested by the journal's name, and also by the illustration on the cover of the launch issue of a young *touleier* leading an ox-wagon across a river and gazing into the unexplored terrain beyond).

Like so many of his country men and women before and since, Bosman left South Africa in 1934 to seek fame and fortune abroad. Although he found neither, and returned rather ignominiously on borrowed funds just after the start of World War II, some of his most famous stories (including 'Veld Maiden', 'In the Withaak's Shade', 'The Music Maker' and 'Mafeking Road') were written while he was in London. Homesick but doggedly exploiting the sharpness of vision that distance can bring, he sent these stories (and over a dozen more) in a steady stream back to Johannesburg, where they appeared in the *South African Opinion*. They are among the best-known and best-loved stories in the entire canon of South African literature, and it would not be an exaggeration to say that they played a large role in establishing a local literary tradition.

In the late 1940s Bosman began the most productive period of his career: he released *Mafeking Road* (1947) and produced some thirty other Marico stories, his prison memoir *Cold Stone Jug* (1949) and the 'Voorkamer' (Parlour) series, which appeared regularly in the South African weekly the *Forum* until the writer's sudden death from heart failure. Numbering eighty in all, the Voorkamer stories, which take place in Marico farmer Jurie Steyn's *voorkamer*, are conversation pieces: various characters, whom we get to know as the series unfolds, participate in desultory discussions on topics of current interest.

All but one of the twenty-one stories in *Mafeking Road* feature the wily backveld raconteur Oom Schalk Lourens, through whom Bosman is able to reflect ironically on the prejudices and weaknesses of the Marico community, a community that he nonetheless evokes with great sympathy and under-standing. It is clear, despite the regional setting and localised humour, that Bosman's concerns in these stories are not confined to the Groot Marico but touch upon wider issues that extend to the entire South African population and beyond.

Many of the stories in *Mafeking Road* contain references to events that are staple items in Boer folk history. These mainly concern the two Anglo-Boer Wars and the various wranglings between the Boer community and the British authorities (see also Chapter 12). Here again, however, Bosman's vision extends beyond sympathy only with the Boer cause. The opening passages of 'The Rooinek' (first published in 1931) describe the Second Anglo-Boer War and the devastation caused to Boer farms in the course of hostilities. The concentration camps into which the British herded many Afrikaner women and children are also briefly alluded to. However, the bulk of the story concerns the actions of a young Englishman – the *rooinek* (redneck) of the story's title – who comes to settle in the Marico in the midst of a community who are bitterly hostile to the English. He strikes up a friendship with a Boer couple to whose baby daughter he grows extremely attached. When the couple decide to trek to German West Africa after the *miltsiek* (anthrax) has laid waste to their cattle, he goes with them. The family dies in the Kalahari Desert, and the Englishman's body is discovered with them, clutching a bundle of rags he evidently believed in his feverish state to be the little girl.

Unto Dust (1963), the second collection of Bosman's bushveld stories to appear, also features Oom Schalk Lourens prominently (in all but four of the twenty-four stories). The title story about two dead men – one white, one black – whose bones become inextricably intermingled is a sustained piece of satire that targets Afrikaner prejudice against the black man. It is the subtle complexity of Bosman's style that enables him to carry off this indictment of racial prejudice with the most dexterous of touches.

Interestingly, two major Afrikaans writers of the period under discussion here evince in their life and work a straddling of the metropole–colony divide not unlike that of their English-language counterparts. The poet, short-story writer, essayist and naturalist Eugène Marais (1872–1936) worked as a newspaper editor in the Transvaal Republic before studying medicine and law in London. He fought in the Anglo-Boer War on the side of the Boers and thereafter practised as a country doctor and lawyer. His books on nature (*Die Siel van die Mier*, 1934, translated as *The Soul of the White Ant*, 1937; and *Burgers van die Berge*, 1938, translated as *My Friends the Baboons*, 1939, and reissued as *The Soul of the Ape* in 1969) are probably what he is best remembered for, certainly in the English-speaking world, but it as a poet and short-story writer in Afrikaans that he is best known among Afrikaans speakers.

C. Louis Leipoldt (1880–1947) similarly had a foot in both worlds. He is now chiefly remembered as a major Afrikaans poet of the 1930s, but his early writing – mainly journalistic contributions to local and British newspapers – was almost exclusively in English. Like Marais, Leipoldt was a journalist before turning to medicine (he studied at Guy's Hospital in the year immediately following the Anglo-Boer War), and he spent several productive years as a medical inspector in various rural parts of South Africa from 1914 to the mid 1920s. This experience he later recounted in his autobiographical *Bushveld Doctor* (1937). Along with several medical and historical works he published over the years, during World War II he wrote numerous poems in English – published posthumously as *The Ballad of Dick King and other Poems* (1949). Another posthumous publication is what has become known as his 'Valley Trilogy' – a series of historical novels dealing with the Clanwilliam area of the Western Cape from the slave days of the colony through the Victorian era (*Chameleon on the Gallows*, c. 1930s; first published 2000) and on to the ravages of the Anglo-Boer War (*Stormwrack*, c. 1930s; first published 1980, new edition 2000). The final volume in the series, *The Mask* (c. 1930s), was first published together with the other two novels as *The Valley* in 2001. Stephen Gray, one of Leipoldt's editors, sums up the writer's extraordinary cosmopolitanism: 'this all-round literary gentleman . . . who quoted screeds of Horace and Kipling . . . had become an Empire-supporting commonwealth figure of no mean standing. He had become, in a sense, the epitome of the Cape liberal humanists of his times, a literary establishment in one' ('Introduction', *Stormwrack*, p. 9).

Plomer outlived both Smith and Bosman and was in a position, in his mature years, to bestow upon both his imprimatur. He wrote appreciative prefaces to both *The Little Karoo* and *Unto Dust*. 'South Africa has produced three outstanding writers of short stories', he observed in the latter: 'Pauline Smith, Nadine Gordimer and Herman Charles Bosman. Bosman has this in common with Pauline Smith, that he was able, at an impressionable age, to observe and identify himself emotionally with a homogeneous society of which the moods and manners were not complicated by artifice, and in which every person was as conspicuous as in some remote, pre-industrial village' ('Foreword', p. ix).

It is an arresting thought that at precisely the time (the early 1920s) that Smith was crafting enduring portraits of her Dutch-Afrikaans subjects, in which they are cast for the most part as noble and tragic characters, their human failings notwithstanding, Plomer was drafting his acerbic 'Portraits in the Nude'. In sharp contrast to Smith's almost reverential depictions, Plomer foregrounds the raw and lascivious side to his characters – their lust and brutality, their desire to appease their animal appetites, the sham and hypocrisy of their religious beliefs. Not long afterwards, Bosman would publish his first major stories, 'Makapan's Caves' and 'The Rooinek', in which the historical events of Chief Makhapane's defeat by a vengeful Boer commando and the ill-fated Dorstland Trek are treated with sympathy, but are also stripped of the mythical status they hold in Boer folklore. Three views of the Afrikaner: three writers positioning themselves in relation to South African locals and their culture.

In his preface to *Veld-trails and Pavements* (1949), a compilation of South African stories, Bosman remarked:

> South African English writing is at the present moment passing through an interesting stage in its development from a 'colonial' literature into a nationally conscious art. In prose – and more especially through the medium of the short story – we are beginning to witness the rise of an authentically South African school of letters . . . It is, above all else, incumbent on our writers to remain true to their own environment and traditions.

Each of the four writers forming the main focus of discussion here witnessed, and contributed in different ways to, the development of a local tradition. Blackburn's satirical, though not unsympathetic, representations of locals had their moment, but could not persist in an era in which South Africans themselves began increasingly to write for and about fellow South Africans. For the most part, Smith, against her will, wrote from a distance, but her stories about the Little Karoo bear all the marks of a deep love for and intimate understanding of the region, and have remained trenchant to this day. Plomer left South Africa with some hauteur and achieved status in the metropolis, from where he was able to assist other South African writers, among them Smith and Bosman. His sense of the dislocation and incongruity of twentieth-century South African society is perhaps achieving a new resonance in the more innovative examples of post-apartheid literature. And Bosman, by the time of his premature death in 1951, had already achieved iconic status as a local writer. Although he has never achieved fame outside of the country, he has a local reputation that has grown stronger with each passing decade.

Bibliography

Alexander, P. *William Plomer: A Biography*, Oxford University Press, 1989.

Black, S. *Stephen Black: Three Plays*, ed. S. Gray, Johannesburg: Ad Donker, 1984.

Blackburn, D. *A Burgher Quixote*, London: Blackwood, 1903; Cape Town: David Philip, 1984.

    English in Africa, special issue on Douglas Blackburn, 5:1 (1978), 1–47.

    Leaven: A Black and White Story, London: Alston Rivers, 1908; Pietermaritzburg: University of Natal Press, 1991

    'An Open Letter to a Prominent Krugersdorp Jingo' [1896], reprinted in *English in Africa* 5:1 (1978), 14–16.

    Prinsloo of Prinsloosdorp: A Tale of Transvaal Officialdom, London: Dunbar, 1899; Cape Town: South African Universities Press, 1978.

Bosman, H. C. *A Cask of Jerepigo: Sketches and Essays*, Cape Town: Central News Agency, 1957; Cape Town: Human & Rousseau, 2002.

    Cold Stone Jug, Johannesburg: Afrikaanse Pers Beperk, 1949; Cape Town: Human & Rousseau, 1998.

    Homecoming: Voorkamer Stories (II), Cape Town: Human & Rousseau, 2005.

    Idle Talk: Voorkamer Stories (I), Cape Town: Human & Rousseau, 1999.

    Jacaranda in the Night, Johannesburg: Afrikaanse Pers Beperk, 1947; Cape Town: Human & Rousseau, 1999.

    Mafeking Road, Cape Town: Central News Agency, 1947; Cape Town: Human & Rousseau, 1998.

    'Marico Revisited', in S. Gray (ed.), *My Life and Opinions*, Cape Town: Human & Rousseau, 2003, 142–5.

    'Preface', *Veld-trails and Pavements*, Johannesburg: Afrikaanse Pers Beperk, 1949, unpaginated.

    Unto Dust, Cape Town: Human & Rousseau, 1963; 2002.

Willemsdorp, Cape Town: Human & Rousseau, 1977; 1998.

Campbell, R., W. Plomer and L. van der Post (eds.). *Voorslag: A Magazine of South African Life and Art* [facsimile reprint of numbers 1, 2 and 3 (1926)], ed. C. Gardner and M. Chapman, Durban: Killie Campbell Africana Library, 1985.

Coetzee, J. M. *White Writing: On the Culture of Letters in South Africa*, New Haven, CT: Yale University Press, 1988.

Driver, D. 'Introduction', *Pauline Smith*, ed. Driver, 21–31.

Driver, D. (ed.). *Pauline Smith*, Johannesburg: McGraw-Hill, 1983.

Gray, S. 'Introduction', *Selected Stories*, by William Plomer, ed. S. Gray, Cape Town: David Philip, 1984, vii–x.

'Introduction', *Stephen Black: Three Plays*, ed. S. Gray, Johannesburg: Ad Donker, 1984, 7–41.

'Introduction', *Stormwrack*, by C. L. Leipoldt, Cape Town: Human & Rousseau, 2000, 5–17.

'Piet's Progress: Douglas Blackburn's Satire on the Foundation of the Transvaal', *English Studies in Africa* 24:1 (1981), 24–36.

Gray, S. (ed.). *Herman Charles Bosman*, Johannesburg: McGraw-Hill, 1986.

Stephen Black: Three Plays, Johannesburg: Ad Donker, 1984.

Leipoldt, C. L. *The Ballad of Dick King and other Poems*, Cape Town: Stewart, 1949.

Bushveld Doctor, London: Jonathan Cape, 1937; Johannesburg: Lowry, 1980.

Chameleon on the Gallows, ed. S. Gray, Cape Town: Human & Rousseau, 2000.

Stormwrack, ed. S. Gray, Cape Town: David Philip, 1980; Cape Town: Human & Rousseau, 2000.

The Valley, ed. T. S. Emslie and P. L. Murray, Cape Town: Stormberg, 2001.

Marais, E. N. *Burgers van die Berge*, Pretoria: Van Schaik, 1938. Translated as *My Friends the Baboons*, London: Methuen, 1939.

Die Siel van die Mier, Pretoria: Van Schaik, 1934. Translated as *The Soul of the White Ant*, London: Methuen, 1937.

Pereira, E. 'Tall Tellers of Tales: Some Fictional Narrators and their Function in the South African Short Story in English', in S. Gray, ed., *Herman Charles Bosman*, 103–15.

Plomer, W. *At Home: Memoirs*, London: Jonathan Cape, 1958.

The Autobiography of William Plomer, London: Jonathan Cape, 1975.

The Child of Queen Victoria, London: Jonathan Cape, 1933.

Collected Poems, London: Jonathan Cape, 1960.

Double Lives: An Autobiography, London: Jonathan Cape, 1943.

'Foreword', *Unto Dust*, by H. C. Bosman, vii–ix.

Four Countries, London: Jonathan Cape, 1949.

I Speak of Africa, London: Hogarth Press, 1927.

Notes for Poems, London: Hogarth Press, 1927.

Paper Houses, London: Hogarth Press, 1929.

Selected Stories, ed. S. Gray, Cape Town: David Philip, 1984.

The South African Autobiography, Cape Town: David Philip, 1984.

Turbott Wolfe, London: Hogarth Press, 1926; Johannesburg: Ad Donker, 1993.

Smith, P. A. B. '. . . *a minor marginal note*', London: Jonathan Cape, 1933.

The Beadle, London: Jonathan Cape, 1926; Cape Town: Balkema, 1956.

Douglas Blackburn, Pauline Smith, William Plomer, Herman Charles Bosman

The Little Karoo, London: Jonathan Cape, 1925; 1930; Cape Town: Balkema, 1981.

Platkops Children, London: Jonathan Cape, 1935; Cape Town: Balkema, 1981.

The Unknown Pauline Smith: Unpublished and Out of Print Stories, Diaries and other Prose Writings, ed. E. Pereira, H. Scheub and S. Scholten, Pietermaritzburg: University of Natal Press, 1993.

'Why and how I Became a Writer', *English Studies in Africa* 6:2 (1963), 150–3.

PART V

*

APARTHEID AND ITS AFTERMATH, 1948 TO THE PRESENT

The year 1948 marks one of the most significant transitions in South Africa's political, social and economic life: D. F. Malan's National Party was voted into power on a platform of increased racial separation – *apartheid* – by an almost entirely white electorate, and set about passing a series of acts of parliament to entrench white domination. The cultural effects of this change of government, too, were to be profound, but took some time to register. For several years, multiracial exchange and cross-fertilisation produced a rich cultural dividend; geographically, two sites were especially symbolic of this ferment, Sophiatown, in Johannesburg, and District Six, in Cape Town. The 1950s saw a remarkable flourishing of the short story in English, notably in the pieces produced for *Drum* magazine by a number of black writers, and in the early work of white authors such as Nadine Gordimer and Dan Jacobson (see Dorothy Driver's discussion in Chapter 19). Novels were largely the preserve of white writers in this period, including the two just mentioned, though Peter Abrahams, writing from outside South Africa, was an important exception. The year 1948 saw the publication of what was to be for a long time South Africa's most famous novel, Alan Paton's *Cry the Beloved Country*; thus, ironically, the apartheid era was ushered in by a widely heard, if not widely heeded, warning of the destructive effects of racism. A liberal outlook was dominant in this body of work, described by Peter Blair in Chapter 23 in conjunction with a number of other literary oeuvres by white and black writers.

The destructive consequences of apartheid became more and more visible as the decade passed. The bills enacted by the Nationalist government to extend white power and enforce racial segregation included, in 1950, the Population Registration Act, requiring that every South African be classified as belonging to a particular racial category; the Group Areas Act, assigning different racial groups to different districts; the Suppression of Communism Act, which defined communism as any attempt to effect political change by 'the promotion of disturbance or disorder'; and the Immorality Act, which rendered sexual relations between whites and non-whites illegal. In 1953 the Bantu Education Act extended racial separation to all educational institutions. These laws – which were expanded and added to over the following years – were met with widespread resistance, including a non-violent defiance campaign launched by the ANC in 1952. Meanwhile, in 1955, Sophiatown was declared a white zone and its non-white residents expelled. (District Six was to suffer a similar fate in 1966.) Apartheid had a direct impact on the lives and work of all South African writers, and the creative potential of a multiracial South Africa was increasingly dimmed.

In March 1960, the end of the decade and of any promise it might have held were dramatically marked by the massacre by police of sixty-nine African demonstrators at Sharpeville. The countrywide protests that followed were met with a fierce clampdown by the state: the ANC and the Pan Africanist Congress (the organisers of the Sharpeville demonstration) were declared illegal organisations, detention without trial was introduced, censorship became more draconian, bannings and house arrests increased. The ANC, now operating underground in South Africa and increasingly abroad, initiated a campaign of sabotage; many of its leading activists were imprisoned, including Nelson Mandela. Among the many who left the country during these years were some of the leading black writers, resulting in a substantial literature of exile, much of which could not be read by South Africans because of censorship. (This literature is discussed by Tlhalo Raditlhalo in Chapter 20). Two of the most important African-language writers, A. C. Jordan (in isiXhosa) and Mazisi Kunene (in isiZulu), left South Africa; and two of the most illuminating black autobiographies, Es'kia Mphahlele's *Down Second Avenue* and Bloke Modisane's *Blame me on History*, were written in exile, their authors having departed the country not long before the Sharpeville massacre.

In South Africa itself, the 1960s saw the rise of engaged literature in response to the increasingly heavy-handed imposition of state power. In the theatre,

Athol Fugard's plays explored the effects of apartheid on individuals, while novels by Alex La Guma and Gordimer dealt with the underground resistance (and were consequently banned). Less politically committed but more formally experimental, the group of Afrikaans writers known as the Sestigers wrote innovative poetry and fiction (see Hein Willemse's Chapter 21, on Afrikaans literature between 1948 and 1976). The iron grip of apartheid showed no sign of loosening as the 1970s began, and a significant shift took place in black political resistance: Black Consciousness emerged as a powerful force, promoting the view that all white opposition was inevitably compromised. A number of black poets writing in English saw themselves as engaged, through their writing, in the struggle; after the 1976 Soweto uprising (a movement which began as a protest against the imposition of Afrikaans as the medium of school instruction and which spread throughout the country) the appellation 'Soweto poets' took on a particular resonance. The literature of resistance of this period is discussed by Thengani H. Ngwenya in Chapter 24, while writing from and about prison is the subject of Daniel Roux's Chapter 26. Fugard collaborated with black actors to produce powerful anti-apartheid theatre (see Loren Kruger's Chapter 27 on theatre in the apartheid and post-apartheid periods). Other black and coloured voices emerged, including women (notably Miriam Tlali and Bessie Head, by this time exiled in Botswana). A more radical note was to be heard among novelists, one example being André Brink's *Kennis van die Aand* (1973), the first Afrikaans novel to be banned. A number of new publishers committed to oppositional writing emerged, including David Philip, Ravan Press and Ad Donker. After 1976, as Louise Viljoen indicates in Chapter 22, Afrikaans writing became increasingly oppositional, partly in response to the heightened stigma attached to the language after the Soweto uprising.

The unworkability of grand apartheid began to be evident even to the country's leaders in the early 1980s, and State President Botha attempted (and failed) to co-opt coloureds and Indians with an offer of very limited political representation. Instead, resistance grew more widespread, and the founding of the United Democratic Front in 1984 (a proxy for the banned ANC) began to put real pressure on the government. The literature of this period of gathering tension was richly varied, including subtle engagements with South Africa's political and social tensions by Gordimer and J. M. Coetzee; fictional endorsements of the ANC's campaign in the townships by Tlali, Mongane Serote and Sipho Sepamla; a contrasting emphasis on the daily dramas of township life by Njabulo Ndebele; lively black protest theatre; and more memorable writing, including poetry, by political prisoners. Much of this work was banned. This period also saw the rise of popular protest poetry, written to be performed at mass rallies, as described by Peter Horn in Chapter 25. The increasing activism provoked the government into the declaration of a State of Emergency in 1986, and from this moment on the huge and complex edifice of apartheid began to come apart at the seams.

The literature of the 1980s and the early 1990s, before democracy was secured by the first non-racial election in 1994, is sometimes referred to as 'interregnum writing', picking up on a phrase used by Gordimer in 1983, and is the subject of Chapter 30 by Stephen Clingman. As political life grew more uncertain, characterised by blatant state violence side by side with a loosening of racist restrictions and different factions jockeying for power, writers found a number of different means to express the sense of impending change. Protest theatre of various kinds continued to flourish, the Market Theatre in Johannesburg being the most prominent venue for this work (see Chapter 27). Writers of fiction explored direct and indirect ways of engaging with the unfolding drama of South African history in the making, from Coetzee's oblique yet forceful narratives to Gordimer's evocations of imaginings of the country's future to Ndebele's and Zoë Wicomb's portraits of life away from the great dramas of the period.

Although some Afrikaans writing took an uncritical stance towards the state's repressive policies, the work of Brink and Breyten Breytenbach stands out for the strength of its resistance. Writing in African languages suffered, as it did throughout the apartheid period, from the dearth of opportunities (school textbooks being the major outlet for African-language writing), though a significant moment in Xhosa literature was the 1980 translation by R. L. Peteni of his own novel *Hill of Fools* (see Christiaan Swanepoel's discussion of the literatures of the indigenous languages in Chapter 29). The period saw the rise of gay and lesbian literature, and the Congress of South African Writers published an important anthology in 1993. As Dirk Klopper shows in Chapter 28, poetry of this period exhibits the same variety, with some poets concentrating on the natural world and personal issues and only implicitly engaging with political developments, while others turned the lyric towards the large questions of the day.

Nineteen ninety-four, another date that stands out in twentieth-century South African political history along with 1910 and 1948, saw the triumph of the African National Congress (ANC) as the first democratically elected government, and of Nelson Mandela as the first leader of the country chosen by all its citizens. Racial discrimination was outlawed, the censorship apparatus was dismantled (and its archives made available to researchers), and the

Truth and Reconciliation Commission investigated human rights abuses that had occurred after 1960. The post-apartheid literary landscape is constantly evolving, yet some definite contours and preoccupations have undoubtedly emerged in the last decade, such as the fraught visions of young black writers in the metropolis (K. Sello Duiker, Phaswane Mpe) (see Chapter 32, by Michael Titlestad), the sounding of untold narratives of the liberation struggle (Wicomb, Henk van Woerden), the registering of the growing cultural force of Islam (Achmat Dangor, Rayda Jacobs), and the challenge of representing AIDS, a pandemic which arguably represents as extreme a set of demands on the writer-as-witness as apartheid ever did (Jonny Steinberg).

Since 1994, authors have felt much freer to take the personal and the lyrical as their canvas, implementing the recommendation made by Albie Sachs in a much discussed presentation to the ANC in 1989. In Chapter 31, Rita Barnard traces some of the ways in which writers have committed themselves to making a contribution to the new nation, including both celebrations and warnings. The large Indian community, based largely in Natal, which produced some outstanding writers in English during the apartheid years, including Ahmed Essop, Ronnie Govender and Essop Patel, has continued to contribute significantly to South Africa's literary richness; among the new generation of Indian writers are Imraan Coovadia, Aziz Hassim and Praba Moodley. The new Constitution's protection of same-sex rights notwithstanding, homophobia remains widespread, and the important body of gay and lesbian writing of recent years (Steinberg, Hennie Aucamp, Damon Galgut, Joan Hambidge, Michiel Heyns and many more) is not all celebratory. These and other varied voices reveal South Africa as a site embodying in an acute form the dynamics of an interaction between the West and the 'global South'; in terms of literary historiography, a formidable but exhilarating set of contradictions and possibilities where existing notions of the 'postcolonial' will always be stretched.

19

The fabulous fifties: short fiction in English

DOROTHY DRIVER

In the 1950s the most popular literary form for publication was the short story: stories were not only the staple of magazines, which themselves formed a staple of entertainment before the advent of television, but were also frequently gathered into anthologies, often for schools. Black writers' attraction to the form has usually been explained by its hospitality to those who lacked the domestic space, privacy and leisure time, and perhaps the literary confidence, too, required for novels, but crucial, also, in the 1950s was the publishing opportunity provided by *Drum* magazine, which has given to this period the name the '*Drum* decade'. However, Lewis Nkosi's term 'fabulous' in his essay 'The Fabulous Decade' encapsulates the period's extraordinary atmosphere of romantic self-construction. Young black intellectuals, writing in English, were entering a modernity that seemed, still, theirs for the taking, and a small white avant-garde (mostly English-speaking but also including young Afrikaners) were eager to associate with them or to affiliate through writing, as if their combined presence could reverse – like a fable – the effects of apartheid.

Underpinned as it was by a liberal humanist ethos, the predominant mode of the English-language culture of the 1950s was literary realism of the kind that valorised witness and protest: art was subjugated to life. (The term 'realism' includes Georg Lukács's critical or bourgeois realism, naturalism, social realism and other variants.) But what primarily distinguished the fifties' fiction from that of earlier decades was the move from the countryside – the land or farm as home base, or the veld as the site of romance – to the city or small town. The urban settings and revised urban–rural relations brought into being different kinds of fictional characters and concerns, and then also different perspectives and conventions: apartheid's sinister sequences of dispossession (of land, home, mobility, education, career and so on) meant that white and black writers – drawing on their entirely different experiences of the rural and urban – produced a literature that was racially distinctive, although the black writers' education in English also brought them to share, if then sometimes to resist, the values and conventions of that English tradition.

South African realism had long been served by the use of contrasting perspectives – racial, political, economic, religious, generational and sexual – with race or racial attitudes often functioning as the fundamental opposition. Yet when Nkosi called some of the period's black writing 'journalistic fact parading outrageously as imaginative literature' (Nkosi, *Home and Exile*, p. 132), he identified a key problem not only for black writers but also for all contemporary writers of realism – to distil the deeper significances of a world whose surface realities needed nonetheless to be mapped in the new complexities created by apartheid. For a counterexample to mere 'journalistic fact', Nkosi marshalled something more than simply an irony of contrasting perspectives: he commended a story by Alex La Guma for its 'suggestive language' and for a sustained irony that revealed the 'absurdity' of life under apartheid (*Home and Exile*, pp. 137–8). In a similar frame, Ezekiel (later, Es'kia) Mphahlele claimed in his own writing a shift from the escapism of *Man must Live* (1946) first into protest and later into 'the ironic meeting between protest and acceptance in their widest terms' (*Down Second Avenue*, p. 205). Nkosi and Mphahlele thus not only developed ironic ambiguity as an indicator of excellence but also foregrounded what would in South African literary criticism become a major question relating to 1950s fiction and beyond: is it, or should it be, escape or protest or art?

The explosion of Alan Paton's *Cry, the Beloved Country* (1948) on to the world stage had created an international readership eager to learn more about South African apartheid, which encouraged the production of texts engaged with truth-telling. At the same time (whatever the actual relevance of realism at this moment of ethical crisis), local political exigencies produced a dissident literary culture that was then, and later, mostly appreciative of novels that – as Lukács put it – 'sharpen[ed] the edge of social contradictions' and produced 'change and development' in characters' agency or self-recognition, or perhaps (*pace* Lukács) in the readers' consciousness instead, rather than simply adhering to what Lukács saw as the more 'static' representations of naturalistic realism (Lukács, *Studies in European Realism*, pp. 170–1; *Meaning of Contemporary Realism*, pp. 34–5), or – on the other hand entirely – to an art that eschewed politics. Critical expectations around realism became equally complex and ideologically loaded in relation to the short story.

The short story is often considered to be more obedient to convention than the novel: it is said to require temporal and spatial unity, for instance, along with singleness of event and effect. However, the ironic strategies available through what Nadine Gordimer has instead called the short story's 'fragmented and restless form' (Gordimer, 'Flash of Fireflies', p. 180) arguably helped give birth to an African modernism on South African soil as distinctive, if also as variable, as that of the Harlem Renaissance, but open to a non-ethnic definition of 'African'. This interest in experimentalism was short-lived. In the Black Consciousness writing of subsequent decades (whether for writers or for critics speaking on their behalf) the preference would be for a social realism or naturalism without the tonal complexities that developed irony as ambiguity rather than retaining it as mere contrast. Thus while the self-aware (self-ironising) turn to irony was one of the products of apartheid it was also one of its casualties, stifled by ideological shifts as well as the censorship and bannings that threatened the existence of black writing in English. However, for Gordimer and Jacobson, the deft, ironic, tonal play driving, especially, their short fiction was part of what accounted for the flourishing of their literary careers.

White English-language writers

Novelists and short-story writers had already measured their distance from racism, African dispossession under colonialism and the bourgeois hegemony of 'Englishness', but apartheid brought some new directions. For instance, Paton's 'Death of a Tsotsi' (*Trek*, March 1952) shifted from the 'distorted, sentimental, if meliorative vision' offered in his pre-apartheid novel (Nkosi, *Home and Exile*, p. 5), and his 'A Drink in the Passage' (*Africa South* 4:3 [1960]) took up with a new acuteness and capacity for nuance the complex dynamic between an African sculptor and an Afrikaner who has invited him for a drink. If, as his biographer puts it, apartheid meant that 'iron had entered Paton's soul' (Alexander, *Alan Paton*, p. 328), a new irony had too.

Herman Charles Bosman offers a second case in point. Well established by 1948 as an English-language-short story-writer with an ambiguous cultural affiliation to rural Afrikaners, Bosman had celebrated the National Party victory as a triumph against British cultural imperialism (see Chapman, *Southern African Literatures*, pp. 191–2). His early stories were deeply ironic yet depicted a securely rooted Afrikaner rural community. Now, just before his untimely death in 1951, Bosman published a set of 'inconclusive voorkamer debates' in Lily Rabkin's *Forum* (Siebert, '"A More Sophisticated Bosman"', p. 74); these appeared weekly between 15 April 1950 and 12 October 1951 (*voorkamer* is Afrikaans for *front room* or *parlour*). This generically experimental story sequence disrupts communal coherence through the use not simply of conflicting perspectives but also of formal fragmentation (see Gray, 'Tale Larger', and also Chapter 18 in this volume).

Four of the major white fiction writers of the 1950s were Jewish: Nadine Gordimer, Dan Jacobson, Phyllis Altman and Harold Bloom. If English-speaking South African writers were already politically alienated from Afrikaner nationalists, then Jewish writers were additionally alienated through the publicly articulated pro-German sympathies of many leading Afrikaner politicians (although it must be said that anti-Semitism was also to be found among English-speaking South Africans, as was anti-black racism among Jewish and other white South Africans). For Nkosi, one of the youngest *Drum* journalists and the period's most astute cultural critic, Jews brought a 'cultural vitality' to the 'desert' of a white South Africa 'immune to all the graces of African tribal life and to the contemplative pleasures of European cultural life', and their 'mitigating human presence' made a fusion seem possible between 'African native talent and European discipline and technique' (*Home and Exile*, pp. 13–14). Nkosi would have been thinking in part of Gordimer's friendship with various *Drum* writers – *A World of Strangers* (1958) and *Occasion for Loving* (1963) are strongly marked by this association – and of Bloom's co-authorship, with Todd Matshikiza and others, of the screenplay for the musical *King Kong* (see Matshikiza, *Chocolates for my Wife*, pp.121–2). Bloom's political involvement as a defence lawyer also fed into the presented world of his fiction, as did Altman's political activism into hers.

Gordimer, Jacobson and Jack Cope were the leading English-language short-story writers who established themselves in the 1950s. (Altman, Bloom and Daphne Rooke were primarily novelists and their short-story publication was scant.) Early stories by Gordimer, Jacobson and Cope appeared in some of the few local outlets, but mostly in prestigious international magazines such as the *New Yorker* (Gordimer, Jacobson), *Paris Review* (Gordimer and Cope) and *Harper's* (all three). Gordimer published her first volume of stories, *Face to Face*, in Johannesburg in 1949, and two further short-story volumes of this decade, *Soft Voice of the Serpent* (1952) and *Six Feet of the Country* (1956), in London and New York, the former reprinting most of the first volume. Jacobson's twinned novellas, *The Trap* (1955) and *A Dance in the Sun* (1956), were published internationally, as with his stories, which were collected first in *A Long Way from London* (1958) and then in *The Zulu and the Zeide* (1959) (the second volume, published in Toronto and New York, mostly repeats the first). Cope's 1950s stories were collected into *The Tame Ox* (1960), also published internationally. Paton's magazine publication remained local, although his first and only short-story collection, *Debbie Go Home* (1961), was published internationally and was well received, its US title, *Tales from a Troubled Land*, standing as a reminder of the marketability of South African fiction that told the 'truths' about apartheid. Common to this writing was an engagement with the social transformations wrought by apartheid and its social engineering, or by the related processes of urbanisation, with setting often functioning as an agent in the production of character and plot. The writers all reveal more or less anxious efforts to represent what a reviewer in the 1950s astutely called 'their common measure, the voiceless African' (H. V. L. S., review, p. 174), although there is interest as well in other kinds of human relations, usually implicitly informed by the political context.

Gordimer, who had produced over fifty stories by the time she turned 35, published more than half of these internationally (unlike Bosman, who had specifically refused to publish other than locally). Her first three stories accepted by the *New Yorker* barely register a South African context, and thereafter those that focus on race more or less alternate with those that do not, confirming that her earliest aspirations were not to define herself as a specifically South African writer but rather to set herself on a modernist world stage. Her stories show an increasing technical capacity to reconcile aesthetics and politics, the intensity of the form giving her excellent opportunity to stress the discontinuities of whiteness in its encounter with its other, which appears to have been an important part of what to her was 'an experience that had scarcely been looked at' (Gordimer, *Essential Gesture*, p. 20). In many stories, the narrator confronts her black fellows in order to know herself as white, and, sometimes simply as human. Her stories often give us to understand that the opposite of an 'outsider's perspective' is not necessarily or only an 'insider's perspective' but may instead be constituted through a dialectic between outside and inside.

As with Gordimer, so Jacobson's South African writing is concerned with the depiction of a world that seemed to him 'never to have been described at all' (Jacobson, 'Dan Jacobson Talks to Ian Hamilton', p. 26), and with the moral implications of racism. His novellas are single-plot stories whose events flow from a single dramatic incident, underwriting the impression that racism – running back from apartheid to the arrival of the Europeans – is the single most important occurrence feeding into the fiction. More emphatically than the early Gordimer, Jacobson's early fiction was preoccupied with the impact of that disastrous intrusion into Africa, and either with the missed opportunities for its undoing – as in the human connections whites might have forged, but did not forge, with blacks – or the small gestures of redemption manifesting in the barest and most ironic moments of epiphany, for either the character or the reader. These displaced epiphanies exacerbate the experience of rootlessness, dissociation and alienation – whiteness intersecting with a Jewish immigrant experience – in which his modernism makes itself most strongly felt.

Jacobson's short stories were path-breaking in their sensitive treatment of South African Jews and the ambiguities arising out of the nexus of their historical consciousness, their social position and current attitudes. He was not part of the Johannesburg group, but his modernism, like Gordimer's, would have been partly what Nkosi meant when he spoke of 'European discipline and technique', depending as it did on the wider, cosmopolitan reading habits and intellectual curiosity whose absence among other members of the 'civilised' Europeans was a source of amusement and mockery to Nkosi and his *Drum* colleagues (see Nkosi, *Home and Exile*, pp. 22–3). He left South Africa in the early 1950s, but continued for a while to set stories in South Africa, specifically in Kimberley in the Northern Cape; he also published two South African novels that decade (*The Price of Diamonds*, 1957, and *The Evidence of Love*, 1959). However, he soon dropped the South African setting and then also the short story: it was the novel, rather, that became the vehicle for his experiments in narrative technique and form. His story 'Fresh Fields' (published in *Encounter* in 1961) marks the moment of departure: what seems to have been felt as the rut of apartheid and anti-apartheid writing is metonymised in 'Fresh Fields' through the recycling engaged in by two writers, one older, the other younger, of each other's stale stories.

Cope stood with Gordimer and Jacobson in the 1950s in terms of literary reputation, and was an important literary entrepreneur, too, as founding editor of *Contrast* in 1960, but his star aligns now rather more with that of Rooke, that once popular and admired but now minor figure. His earliest stories, set either in South Africa (mostly Natal) or its bordering countries, include deftly handled portrayals of black and white characters in precarious moments of self-awareness or mutual recognition. The apparent ease of the narrative shift into the consciousness of blacks now seems innocent, and perhaps dated, the incipient patronisation being unleavened by an ironic self-consciousness. This innocence is shared by Rooke's writing, and by Altman's and Bloom's too, as well as by Dora Taylor's. Taylor was active in Western Cape Trotskyite politics and cultural activism from the 1930s to the 1950s, and her short stories – written in the 1950s but published long after her death in a volume called *Don't Tread on my Dreams* (2008) – were more concerned to convey the material trials undergone by blacks than with the moral impact of racism upon white sensibilities.

Two further short-story publications fit largely by accident into the 1950s. The stories in Bertha Goudvis's *The Mistress of Mooiplaas and other Stories* (1956) were written in the 1940s (see Leveson, 'Bertha Goudvis', p. 63), and stand at the end of Goudvis's literary career (her published plays date from the 1920s and 1930s, and her novel *Little Eden* from 1949). They recall Pauline Smith's quiet interweaving, in the 1910s and 1920s, of idyllic romance and social critique. Sarah Gertrude Millin's *Two Bucks without Hair and other Stories* (1957) also comes at virtually the end of her career. Its stories were mostly published in the London *Athenaeum* and *Adelphi* in the 1920s and 1930s, but the two she adds, 'Two Spades Deep' and 'Rosie and the Queen's Washerwoman', are newly motivated by a desire to play with the distance between author, narrator and text. They nonetheless mark the limit to Millin's ironic self-reflection, a limit dependent primarily on her failure to root the characters historically and sociologically. The stories thus put into question the development of a newly self-critical stance on whiteness among white English-speaking writers, and even the capacity of the 'restless form' of the short-story genre, referred to earlier, to flourish in the stultifying context of apartheid. They also point, by default, to the symbiotic relation of truth-telling and irony in the modernist tradition, a relation being affirmed just at that time by some of the black short-story writers, who were associated either with Sophiatown in Johannesburg or District Six in Cape Town.

The Sophiatown writers and *Drum* magazine

By a trick of history, Sophiatown remained exempt from resettlement longer than other black areas. Proclaimed a freehold zone in 1903, it was the oldest of the African townships, close against Johannesburg's city centre, and home to a heterogeneous population: families settled for generations lived alongside migrant workers, and Africans mingled with coloureds and Indians and a sprinkling of white traders in an amalgam of classes from the relatively wealthy to the unemployed (see Hart and Pirie, 'Sight and Soul of Sophiatown'). Ongoing government repression and increasing poverty in the cities had already brought into being a variety of oppositional movements, with the ANC Youth League, for instance, rejecting what it saw as the ethic of accommodation and dialogue of the past, and in other ways, too, older patriarchal structures had been giving way to newer structures consistent with migrant labour hostel life and the demise of the extended family. After the 1954 Natives Resettlement Act, Sophiatown was bulldozed, and between 1955 and 1959 its African population was relocated mostly to a newly built, segregated township called Meadowlands. By 1963 all the tenants had been evicted, and a suburb for low-income white Afrikaners, called (without irony) 'Triomf', was built in its place. The most important literary reflection of Sophiatown's fertile cultural mix was the journalism and fiction that appeared in *Drum* magazine, most of whose leading writers lived in the city.

Drum magazine was established by a three-man directorate in Cape Town in early 1951 under the title *The African Drum*. Its early issues mostly represented Africans as rural and tribal, but also contained Matshikiza's essays on jazz and a remarkable story of the city by Bloke Modisane called 'The Dignity of Begging' (September 1951). By early 1952, under the advice of black readers and an advisory committee, the magazine was transformed into a thoroughly urban production, based in Johannesburg and under the sole proprietorship of Jim Bailey (the son of a Johannesburg gold-mining magnate). Its circulation figures rose from 20,710 in 1951 to 60,024 in 1953 (Bailey, quoted in Manoim, 'Black Press', p. 32). *Drum* was above all a commercial venture. Dominated by advertisements, usually in comic-strip format, it ran tips on beauty, conduct and health, with advice columns and beauty contests, all geared to develop a middle-class, consumer culture. But the magazine was also a spirited amalgam of essays, columns and photographs on politics, boxing and ball sports, crime, gangs and jazz, models and housewives, and a monthly short story or two that brought into its pages virtually all the black writers of note. Covering political leaders, major international visitors and local stars from different spheres of life, *Drum* also drew on the Durban-based South African Indian community, the Cape coloured community, continental Africa and African-America. It established West and East African editions, its 'media empire' carrying back and forth across the continent images of a new, multicultural black urban identity (see Fleming and Falola, 'Africa's Media Empire', and J. Matshikiza, 'Instant City', p. 485).

Drum had four white editors in the 1950s – Bob Crisp (1951–2), Anthony Sampson (1952–5), Sylvester Stein (1956–8) and Tom Hopkinson (1958–61) – and, in Johannesburg, a staff of African journalists and columnists, of whom the dominating figures were Henry Nxumalo (1951–6), Arthur Maimane (1952–8), Matshikiza (late 1951–60), Can Themba (1953–9), Casey Motsisi (1954–62; 1974–7), Modisane (1955–9), Mphahlele (1955–7), Nkosi (1956–61) and Nat Nakasa (1958–9). Most of them had had a mission education, and several a Fort Hare University degree; Nxumalo had written for *Bantu World*, Nkosi for *Ilange lase*

Natal (taking over from H. I. E. Dhlomo), Mphahlele had been a secondary school teacher and Modisane a bookshop employee. In the Cape Town office was James Matthews, who also contributed four short stories to *Drum*; in the Port Elizabeth office, Jimmy Matyu, who published a single story in *New Age* (February 1957); and in the Durban office G. R. Naidoo, who contributed a short story in the 1960s.

Although there was overlap, *Drum*'s political heyday occurred under Sampson's editorship, and its literary heyday under Stein's. The first five years featured essays by Nelson Mandela, Selope Thema and Albert Luthuli among others, and path-breaking political exposés researched and usually written by Nxumalo ('Mr Drum'). (Later, under the name George Magwaza, Nxumalo wrote the column 'Talk o' the Rand'.) But political reportage remained bold even after 1955, covering, for instance, the women's anti-pass campaigns, the formation of the PAC, the increasingly assertive politics of both the PAC and the ANC, and the Sophiatown and other removals. Sampson initiated the annual short-story competitions, and gave first space to Matshikiza's and Motsisi's lively columns; however, it was under Stein, with Mphahlele as fiction editor and Themba as assistant editor, that the magazine published its most impressive array of short stories and non-fiction essays, the latter written by Themba in a story-telling style that prefigured American New Journalism.

Stein left in 1958 after a political disagreement with Bailey, and under Hopkinson's editorship *Drum* became a mostly pictorial magazine. In 1961 Bailey turned *Drum* into a monthly supplement to his other venture, a popular Sunday paper called *Golden City Post* (the two publications, now edited by Cecil Eprile, had for some time shared resources and space; several of the *Drum* journalists also wrote for *Post*). The magazine of later years shares little with the *Drum* of the *Drum* decade. Banned by the South African government from 1965 to 1968, it kept on after 1968 as an autonomous monthly, Naidoo from Durban becoming its first black editor in 1969. In 1984 Bailey sold it to Nasionale Pers, and all vestige of dissidence disappeared.

Drum's contents signalled an affiliation with modernity, not least in the use of English, which – Nakasa later said – assisted in 'the process of eliminating tribal division with all its unwelcome consequences' (Nakasa, *World of Nat Nakasa*, p. 79). It is in this context that some of the *Drum* writers apparently claimed not to speak – or feel at home in – any African language: researchers mention Themba, Motsisi, Maimane and even Modisane (Rabkin, '*Drum* Magazine', pp. 109, 113; Van Dyk, 'Short Story Writing', pp. 62, 102; Nicol, *Good-looking Corpse*, pp. 179, 341; see also Nakasa, *World*, p. 77). Thus the history of *Drum* through the 1950s has to do with the creation not only of a black South African writing but also of a black South African reading public. A close study of its circulation figures suggests that its major appeal was political reportage, with its urban audience having 'more in common with readers of working-class and radical papers in Britain in the last century, than with those of the *Daily Mirror* in ours' (Rabkin, '*Drum* Magazine', p. 56), even while Bailey and Sampson continued to include pin-ups, sex and crime. Still, at a time when *Bantu World* was dropping virtually all its literary content (reviews, literary news) (Maake, 'Publishing and Perishing', p. 152), *Drum* was encouraging imaginative writing, its first competition in 1953 attracting over a thousand entrants (perhaps in part for the considerable £50 prize), even if the short stories themselves were not read widely by black readers, as is sometimes claimed (Rive, 'Interview', p. 52). Yet it was in response to the Bantu Education Act (with its reduced education, and reduced teaching of English) that Hopkinson so radically transformed *Drum*, more or less submitting to its competition with *Zonk*, a mass-market English-language pictorial magazine founded in 1950 that focused entirely on entertainment and ran brief short stories only occasionally.

The *Drum* writers responded with wit to apartheid legislation. At a time when beaches were being segregated, *Drum* photographed Dolly Rathebe posing in her bikini on a mine dump; at a time when blacks were excluded from parliamentary representation, *Drum* ran its own '*Drum* Parliament'; at a time when education was being limited, *Drum* ran its own '*Drum* School Quiz', offering to its readers an informal, mostly political, education; at a time when theatres were for whites only, township street life and the shebeens were rendered as dramatic as the stage (in real life, a frequently recounted occurrence is about *tsotsis* – gangsters – forcing their victims to recite Shakespeare). Through *Drum* the African journalists made Johannesburg their own; indeed, tried to make the world their own in contradiction to exclusive white ownership.

Nkosi argued that when his generation repudiated the kind of hero typified in Paton's emollient African character Kumalo and cast about for alternative heroes, they seized upon the 'cacophonous, swaggering world of Elizabethan England [as] the closest parallel to our own mode of existence' (*Home and Exile*, p. 18). 'The world of Shakespeare reaches out a fraternal hand to the throbbing heart of Africa', added Themba ('Through Shakespeare's Africa', p. 150). The creative use of Shakespearean allusions articulates 'a complex resistance to the notion of the "native" as less "civilized"' (Distiller, 'South African Shakespeare', p. 26; see also Johnson, *Shakespeare and South Africa*, pp. 173–6); such resistance, moreover, self-consciously partakes of the erudition found to be lacking in white South Africans and a moral universe felt to be closer to current African experience than to the culturally thin and morally enervated one the black writers found in white South Africa. Themba's 'Mob Passion' (April 1953) is surely in part designed to demonstrate to bewildered whites how extensively he can quote the Bard. At the same time, his photo-strip story 'Baby come Duze' (April 1956) shows off his facility with *tsotsitaal* (the township street argot, mixing several languages) and serves as a reminder of the Africanness that was at the same time being produced.

The modern urban individual depicted in *Drum* is informed by a multi-plicity of cultural contexts, including not just the life of the streets (itself informed by the Hollywood B-movies from which the young gangsters took their lead), but also a range of reading: notably, British and American detective fiction (Peter Cheyney and Damon Runyon) and the Harlem Renaissance (Richard Wright, Willard Motley). The latter, which reassessed the American dream through the lens of an enforced marginality, helped the *Drum* writers to present themselves as 'iconoclastic, independent, and ineradicably cosmopoli-tan' (Nixon, 'Harlem, Hollywood and the Sophiatown Renaissance', p. 16). Sophiatown was South Africa's Greenwich Village. There, Nakasa said, 'you were more likely to walk into a conversation centred around James Joyce or John Osborne or Langston Hughes instead of local names like Gertrude Millin or Olive Schreiner' (Nakasa, *World of Nat Nakasa*, p. 80). Modisane's 'The Dig-nity of Begging' is indebted to American modernism in its anti-heroic, even Dadaist, guise; his character Nathaniel or Nathan is but one gesture made to Nathanael West's *Miss Lonelyhearts*, which appeared in its first British edition in 1949.

Drum fiction was markedly mixed in genre and subject matter. Paton's *Cry, the Beloved Country* and Peter Abrahams's *Wild Conquest* and *Tell Freedom* were serialised in *Drum*'s early years; some of the other fiction consisted of stories from the annual prize winners and runners-up (judged by figures as various as Paton, Abrahams, Gordimer, Jordan Ngubane, R. R. R. Dhlomo and Langston Hughes), with a handful of stories from outside the country. In the early years, the symbolic and educative short narratives of the African oral tradition were deflected through mission influence into moral tales about the adverse effects of urban life on rural innocents, in much the manner of R. R. Dhlomo. Many stories reached for a novelistic range rather than the concentration typical of the modern short story, while others took the form of sketches whose fleeting manner spoke to the inappropriateness of developing a narrative in so 'fugitive' a culture (Mphahlele's term, quoted in Attwell, *Rewriting Modernity*, p. 24). Motsisi's monthly columns – 'If Bugs were Men' (February

1958) and others in the 'Bugs' series, with their jokes about bloodsucking and consanguinity, along with 'On the Beat' – offered brief episodes: a life lived in snatches. Maimane's detective series, running monthly through 1953 under the Americanised pseudonym J. Arthur Mogale (part of his name), provided a comic, ironic treatment of police corruption and criminal power in 'hard-boiled' style. Themba's stories, also using Americanised nominalisation (D. Can Themba), were '"yellow press" situations . . . pushed toward serious confrontation' (Chapman, 'Drum' Decade, p. 208), depicting a world in which morality, family feeling, honesty and love struggled to survive in an urban order corrupt at its core, and where horizontal violence (it was occasionally hinted) substituted for political revolt. Mphahlele's stories made a similar suggestion, but they are otherwise very different, mostly sketching a Newclare community (part of greater Sophiatown) that incorporated a traditional, rural ethos into its urban fabric. Mphahlele thus contradicted the image propagated by the government presses of a rural world with nothing to offer modernity, and he portrayed continuity between the urban and rural rather than the rupture depicted elsewhere in Drum. His stories also treated the changed position of women in the city in a less fraught way than did some of the other Drum pieces.

Drum has been remembered through a considerable literary infrastructure of marketable accounts, including editors' memoirs,[1] anthologies combined with commentary,[2] and collections of photographs, interviews and reminiscences,[3] and it has continued to be kept alive through theatre, film and nostalgic media references. It is also the subject of numerous book chapters and journal articles,[4] academic theses and university courses. Whilst Drum fiction only occasionally makes it to the more general anthology selections,[5]

---

1 Sampson, Drum: The Making of a Magazine (slightly revised from Drum: A Venture into the New Africa); Hopkinson, In the Fiery Continent; Hopkinson, Under the Tropic; see also Stein's Second-Class Taxi and Who Killed Mr Drum?
2 Chapman's The 'Drum' Decade includes an essay, 'More than Telling a Story', pp. 183–232, and a select bibliography at pp. 233–8; Nicol, A Good-looking Corpse, has interspersed commentary.
3 For example, Stein and Jacobson, Sophiatown Speaks; Schadeberg, with Gosani et al., The Fifties People; Naidoo, The Indian in Drum Magazine in the 1950s.
4 A sample list would include Addison, 'Drum Beat'; Barnett, A Vision of Order'; Choonoo, 'The Sophiatown Generation'; Clowes, 'Masculinity, Matrimony and Generation'; Driver, 'Drum (1951–9) and the Spatial Configurations of Gender'; Fenwick, '"Tough guy, eh?"'; Gready, 'The Sophiatown Writers of the 1950s'; Hannerz, 'Sophiatown'; Helgesson, 'Shifting Fields'; Maughan Brown, '"The Anthology as Reliquary?"'; Mzamane, 'An Unhistorical Will into Past Times'; Ndebele, 'The Ethics of Intellectual Combat'; Nixon, 'Harlem, Hollywood and the Sophiatown Renaissance'. See also Woodson, Drum: An Index.
5 For example, Raising the Blinds: A Century of South African Women's Stories included one of three South African stories Drum published under female signature, although these appear to have been written by men (see Driver, 'Drum', pp. 236, 241 n. 12).

collections of the writing of some of its key figures also help keep the *Drum* myth alive, although the particular writers are represented by pieces published elsewhere too.[6]

In some critical accounts, the musical *King Kong* rather than the magazine is named as the 'ultimate achievement and final flowering' of Sophiatown's cultural enterprise (Coplan, *In Township Tonight!*, p. 175) for it represents a new urban African aesthetic forged out of a complex cultural interaction that *Drum* only reached for. In other accounts, the short-story writers themselves are the achievers. Mphahlele, Modisane and Nkosi are seen as the young African intellectuals of the New African movement, the culmination of a line running from H. I. E. Dhlomo through Peter Abrahams, drawing into Africa the poetics of the Harlem Renaissance and giving to the period the name 'Sophiatown Renaissance'.[7] But Themba is by general agreement the iconic *Drum* figure, partly on account of his strong identification with the city, and specifically with shebeen and outlaw culture. Nkosi called him 'the supreme intellectual *tsotsi*' (Nkosi in Themba, *Will to Die*, p. x). His insouciance is taken as *Drum* style. Themba is also used, specifically in Chapman's anthology, to foreground the heterogeneric quality of the *Drum* story (Chapman includes journalism, fiction and columns, plus Themba's comic-strip story).

Drum style is characterised, then, in part by the bravado with which the writers voiced their refusal to submit to the versions of blackness (both rural and urban) being delivered by apartheid, and in part by linguistic and generic experimentalism. The magazine has been credited with producing an African English in the making, inflected variously by a creative colloquialism and a *tsotsitaal*, along with a vocabulary of erudition and literary allusion, as well as inventive neologisms and vigorous syntactical structures that commentators have associated with jazz: 'Matshikese', *Drum* called it, after Matshikiza's monthly jazz columns (see Titlestad, 'Jazz Discourse and Black South African Modernity'). The descriptions of Sophiatown gave expression to an often carnivalesque urban experience and what is generally called a 'shebeen camaraderie'[8] that belied the incessant fracturing of communal existence at a time of increasingly repressive and brutal apartheid legislation. In the face of a

6 These include Motsisi, *Casey & Co.*; Nakasa, *The World of Nat Nakasa*; and Themba, *The World of Can Themba* and *The Will to Die*.
7 Visser, 'South Africa: The Renaissance that Failed'; Nixon, 'Harlem, Hollywood and the Sophiatown Renaissance'; see also Masilela's informative website, 'New African Movement' for his entry on 'Sophiatown Renaissance 1952–1960': http://pzacad.pitzer.edu/NAM/sophia/writers/sr.shtml
8 The term is a favoured one, used for example by Adey et al., *Companion to South African Literature*, p. 188; Cornwell et al., *Columbia Guide to South African Literature in English*, p. 87; and Chapman, *Drum*, p. 221.

tendency to sentimentalise *Drum*, we need to recall its images of urban horror: a 'hit and run mislife', as Themba's story 'Marta' puts it (July 1956), whose most frequent expression is either domestic or township violence (Themba, 'Mob Passion', April 1953) or African-Indian warfare (Jordan Ngubane, 'Man of Africa', August 1956; Mphahlele, 'Lesane', February 1957), or a complex 'cry of fear, of hurt, of sorrow and of all the bitter memories stored in a suffering heart' (Mbokotwane Manqupu, 'Love Comes Deadly', January 1955).

Whilst *Drum* should probably be thought of as an encouragement to the Sophiatown writers, their subsequent publications do not always reflect well on the magazine. Modisane revised 'The Dignity of Begging' for republication in Peggy Rutherford's *Darkness and Light* in such a way as to draw further attention to the constructed, artful nature of his tale and its deep satire; Nakasa's weekly columns in the *Rand Daily Mail* were, for Gordimer, 'the best writing he did' (Gordimer, *Essential Gesture*, p. 70); and by far Themba's most intricate short story, 'The Suit', was published not in *Drum* but in *The Classic*. La Guma's 'Battle for Honour' was, he said, ruined by *Drum* (La Guma in Abrahams, *Memories of Home*, p. 19), and he published a different version in *The New African*.

The story of *Drum* should not inhibit a fuller look at the rise and fall of the black short story in other magazines of the day.[9] Of the Sophiatown writers, only Maimane and Mphahlele published elsewhere during the 1950s, Maimane in *Africa South* (2:3 [1958]), and Mphahlele in *Purple Renoster* (2 [1957]), *Black Orpheus* (4 [1958]), and (under the pseudonym Bruno Esekie) in *Standpunte* (8:4 [1954]), *Fighting Talk* (June 1955) and *Africa South* (2:2 [1958]). Most of the others contributed stories to other magazines, but had to stop in the 1960s when censorship kicked in.

The District Six writers

Among the writers published in *Drum* were some of those associated with the District Six quarter in Cape Town either by birth and residence (Rive, La Guma) or place of work (Matthews) or association (Peter Clarke). Alf Wannenburgh was a close associate of the group; he published short stories in the 1960s, not in *Drum* but in *Black Orpheus* and *The New African* (his classification as white is one of the many ambiguities of apartheid). Like its

9 Local independent magazines that ran one or more stories by black writers in the 1950s and early 1960s were (with magazine start dates included) *Fighting Talk* (1946), *Standpunte* (1952), *New Age* (1954), *Africa South* (1956), *The Purple Renoster* (1956), *Contrast* (1961), *The New African* (1962), *The Classic* (1963).

Sophiatown counterpart, the District Six group was disparate – intellectually, politically and in class terms – but the writers were linked through friendship, a shared interest in writing (Rive and De Vries, 'Interview', pp. 45–6), and in some cases political activism. But for 'Willie-Boy!' (*Drum* [April 1956]), a three-hander by Rive, Matthews and Clarke, the magazine was incidental to their connection. Not only did they publish other short stories elsewhere – Rive in *New Age* (September 1955) and *Fighting Talk* (December 1955, January 1956 and January 1957); La Guma in *Fighting Talk* (October 1956), *New Age* (January 1957) and *Africa South* (3:1 [1958]); Matthews in *Africa South* (3:1 [1958]) – but they were also more overtly political than the Sophiatown group, and seen as chiefly responsible for sustaining the protest tradition in black South African fiction.

In the Western Cape, where the racial atmosphere had in the past been relatively relaxed, a new militancy had already started expressing itself through the Non-European Unity Movement, the major political force among coloured intellectuals (see Lodge, *Black Politics*; Alexander, 'Aspects of Non-Collaboration in the Western Cape', pp. 183–4). Opposition politics became increasingly fraught after the Communist Party was forced to disband in 1950 and as increasingly harsh apartheid laws and practices took root, many of which created or exacerbated hierarchical distinctions among those designated 'non-European'. La Guma, the major writer in this group, and the most deeply politically engaged, had been an active member of the Young Communist League. He subsequently joined the South African Coloured People's Organisation, and between 1956 and 1960 was a defendant in the notorious Treason Trials; he was acquitted, finally, with the other accused, but spent the next years in and out of prison.

La Guma's writing, like Rive's and Matthews's, was centred on District Six. The area received its name as the last of the six municipal districts created in and around Cape Town in 1867. Although it was mostly a working-class coloured community, its proximity to the city and docks in addition to its multinational origins gave it a multiracial, multiclass and cosmopolitan atmosphere, for it was home to numerous Indians and Chinese, some whites and those few Africans who had permits to be there, or else lived as illegals, and it also attracted those who wanted to share in its political activism and night life (sex and jazz).[10] For Rive, District Six 'cultivated a sharp, urban inclusivity,

10 See Bickford-Smith, 'The Origins and Early History of District Six', p. 37. The Africans who continued to live in District Six occupied what was known as 'The Building', according to Fortune, *The House in Tyne Street*, p. 100. See Ngcelwane, *Sala Kahle District Six*, for an account of the removal of an African family from District Six in the 1960s.

the type which cockneys have in the East End of London and black Americans in Harlem' (Rive, 'District Six', p. 112), and his writing, like that of the others, was concerned with what it meant to be classified as coloured under apartheid, exploring the varieties of racism (white racism, African racism towards coloureds, and colour consciousness among coloureds) both within and beyond the community. Their realist and often naturalist tales depict characters struggling more or less weakly against the world of poverty, discrimination and crime into which destiny has driven them. Sympathy is often focused on women. In most of the stories, squalid conditions take on a life of their own, often stressing what was a strong theme in *Drum* as well, that the *skollie* (the Cape version of the *tsotsi*) is made and not born.

La Guma was employed as a journalist on *New Age* from 1955, which meant that, unlike the *Drum* writers, he wrote for a magazine whose editorial policy was consonant with his political beliefs. (Alfred Hutchinson, a fellow Treason Trialist, also published short stories in *New Age*.) La Guma's major journalistic project was to report on District Six, and his columns ('Up my Alley') fed into his stories, which were centred on slum-dwellers and petty gangsters who acted through necessity rather than choice, and some of whom he represented as figures of morality, sensitivity and honour. Of the novella *A Walk in the Night* (1962), largely completed during the 1950s, La Guma said he had tried to depict 'a people struggling . . . to see something new, other than their experiences in this confined community' (La Guma in Abrahams, *Alex La Guma*, p. 49), and his short stories, too, treat the possibility of political or intellectual awakening, though this is usually given over to the reader. His stories are structurally as sophisticated as those of any other writer of the 1950s, and his dialogue meets Themba's for deftness, not least in its use of Kaaps (Cape coloured vernacular, often mixing English and Afrikaans). He also produced in *New Age* a remarkable comic strip, 'Little Libby: The Adventures of Liberation Chabalala', published in weekly instalments through much of 1959, thus for a moment making *New Age* a little more like *Drum* (see Field, *Alex La Guma*, p. 92); this has been reprinted, along with La Guma's other pieces in *New Age*, in A. Odendaal and R. Field's, *Liberation Chabalala* (1993).

Proclamations for resettlement under the Group Areas Act started in 1957, and by 1965 over 30,000 coloured people had been shifted to the Cape Flats, radically reducing the number of those with a municipal vote (see Pinnock, 'Ideology and Urban Planning', p. 163). (In all, 60,000 people were removed from District Six; see Bickford-Smith et al., *Cape Town in the Twentieth Century*, p. 183.) In 1966 District Six was officially proclaimed white. It was bulldozed in 1980, but, unlike Sophiatown, massive public outcry meant that the area was not redeveloped. Like Sophiatown, District Six has been celebrated in South African cultural memory as the kind of community that might have persisted, and spread, had it not been for apartheid's atomisation (see, for example, Willemse, *More than Brothers*). With the classification of coloureds into five subsections under the Population Registration Act, one memoirist recalls, the members of her extended family were resettled in five different townships (Hettie Adams, in Adams and Suttner, *William Street District Six*, pp. 55–6).

The District Six writers produced a new body of writing, the first stories of their place. The coloured population, which accounted for well over half of the city's total, had hitherto spawned only one notable literary figure, the Afrikaans writer Adam Small. But Cape culture did not spring from nowhere. It tapped into a long-standing musical and performance tradition: dance bands, choirs and particularly the ironic, mocking and self-mocking posturing of the New Year carnival parades, with their *ghoemaliedjies* (a blend of Dutch and Indonesian folk-songs) and blackface minstrel performances (adapted from African America), two forms in which satire and masquerade combined (see Winberg, 'Satire, Slavery', p. 93). Although the short stories sometimes focus on characters exploiting a tension between the reality produced under apartheid and an alternative way of being, and sometimes refer to the carnival or elements of it, the carnival cannot on the whole be said to define District Six style. This leads us to consider a distinction between it and at least some of the Sophiatown writing. Nowhere in the District Six short stories does one distinguish the kind of modernist instability opened up in Modisane's writing, and to a lesser extent in Maimane's, through their self-conscious play with the relation between the represented and the real; nor can they be characterised by the same self-consciously aestheticised, experimental manner sometimes associated with *Drum*. On the other hand, a different kind of irony, as well as expressionist elements, connects La Guma's short stories to Mphahlele's: their realism expands well beyond the merely representational, and they both orient themselves within a stable vernacular culture, which gives them their lasting stature as writers. However, on yet another hand, La Guma's generic departures expanded the range of the vernacular through reference to the satirical powers of popular culture, notably in the 'Little Libby' comic strip; and in his sketches in the *New Age* columns, fact masquerades absurdly as fiction, in a way which recalls (and extends the ambit of) *Drum*'s experimentalism.

As a literary period, the 1950s came to an untidy end. Apartheid drove several of the Sophiatown writers into exile in the late 1950s or early 1960s – Maimane,

Modisane, Mphahlele, Nakasa, Nkosi and Themba – and some of the white writers: Altman, Bloom, Cope, Jacobson, Rooke and, later, Taylor (see Chapter 20). Apartheid may also be blamed for driving two to an early death, Nakasa in 1965, Themba in 1968. La Guma had already been banned under the Suppression of Communism Act, and in 1966 an amendment to the act was used to ban a further group, including six of the Sophiatown set: Matshikiza, Modisane, Mphahlele, Nakasa, Nkosi and Themba. The District Six writers' careers continued through the 1960s and beyond. Clarke, who published only one more story (in *The New African*), went on to become a graphic artist. Matthews, who would later found and run a Cape Town publishing house, was banned several times but established himself internationally through short stories and poetry. Rive, armed with a university degree, had a successful career as an academic, editor and writer until his death aged 58.

Some of the black writers continued to publish stories locally, sometimes under pseudonym: in *The Classic*, which Nakasa founded and edited from 1963 (Themba, Motsisi, Mphahlele, Nkosi and Rive), *Fighting Talk* (Maimane, Nkosi), and *Contrast* (Nkosi, Rive). Themba's remarkable story 'The Urchin' went into *Drum* in April 1963.[11] International journals were also hospitable – *Africa South in Exile* (La Guma, Themba and Mphahlele), *Transition* (Rive, Maimane, Matthews and Nkosi), *Présence Africaine* (Nkosi and Matthews), *The New African* (La Guma, Nkosi), *Frontier* (Nkosi) and *Negro Digest* (Rive). La Guma also published, in Portuguese translation only, a story in the Brazilian journal *Cadernos Brasileiros*. Mphahlele, co-editing *Black Orpheus*, took five stories from La Guma, and single stories from Maimane, Modisane and himself. He also played a leading role in the Mbari Publishing House (Nigeria), developing a Pan-African list and helping launch La Guma on his international career. Besides becoming a major literary critic and producing some poems, libretti and remarkable short stories, Nkosi established himself as a literary editor in the 1960s (editing *The New African*), also becoming a dramatist and novelist of note. Rive produced his first short-story volume, *African Songs* (1963), and edited *Quartet* (1963), which contained four stories each by himself, La Guma, Matthews and Wannenburgh, dedicating it to Mphahlele 'in admiration and regard for his work for literature' on the African continent as well as in South Africa. But, like the memoirs so many of them would write in the 1960s, their short stories became close to non-existent for the next generation. Anthologies published in or marketed for South Africa had to exclude many of them; moreover, local magazine publication was either

---

11 This was not published in *The Classic*, despite what various sources say.

proscribed or difficult, writers, publishers and readers being intimidated, even if sometimes unconsciously, into habits of literary caution.

Bringing together the Sophiatown and District Six writers, and then these together with white writers, tempts one to reconsider the period through the reputation and career of two women writers marginal to the larger group: M. K. Jeffreys, a Cape writer who wrote at the end of the decade a set of path-breaking essays for *Drum*, and also some poems, about racial passing and cultural interaction; and Bessie Head, who lived for a short time in District Six and was loosely associated with *Drum* by virtue of working in first Cape Town and then Johannesburg for *Golden City Post* as a journalist and columnist. Jeffreys has had to wait until this century to be 'discovered'; and Head was able to begin publishing (initially mostly in *Africa South*) only after she had left the country (see also Chapter 20). Writing of *Drum* and *Post* first in *The Cardinals* and then, briefly, in *A Question of Power*, Head strove in Botswana to address the racial and gender constraints she had experienced as a journalist and aspirant fiction writer, and to make the connections with African village life that had been either lost or unavailable to those *Drum* writers so carefully measuring their distance from white constructions of tribalism.

Whereas *Drum* – its white editors and black journalists, but also the very context it sprang from and represented – arguably failed women writers, it helped concretise a historical moment through and against which black South African writers and readers would define and redefine themselves. The black writing of the 1950s carries within it the promise of a literature that might have developed differently had it not been for the limiting aspects of Bantu Education, the censorships and bannings, and the other apartheid repressions. As Nkosi put it, 'the fifties . . . finally spelled out the end of one kind of South Africa and foreshadowed the beginning of another' (*Home and Exile*, p. 6). Including the white writing too, the literature of the decade hangs heavy with history, carrying like a massive hinge the weight of the half-century past and the one to come.

Bibliography

Sources of stories published in magazines are given in the text.

Abrahams, C. A. *Alex La Guma*, Boston: Twayne, 1985.

Abrahams, C. A. (ed.). *Memories of Home: The Writings of Alex La Guma*, Trenton, NJ: Africa World Press, 1991.

Adams, H., and H. Suttner. *William Street District Six*, Diep River: Chameleon Press, 1988.

Addison, G. 'Drum Beat: An Examination of Drum', *Speak* 1:4 (1978), 4–8.

Adey, D., R. Beeton, M. Chapman and E. Pereira (comps.). *Companion to South African English Literature*, Johannesburg: Ad Donker, 1986.

Alexander, N. 'Aspects of Non-Collaboration in the Western Cape, 1943–1963', *Social Dynamics* 12:1 (1986), 1–14.

Alexander, P. F. *Alan Paton: A Biography*, Oxford University Press, 1994.

Attwell, D. *Rewriting Modernity: Studies in Black South African Literary History*, Pietermaritzburg: University of KwaZulu-Natal Press, 2005.

Barnett, U. A. *A Vision of Order: A Study of Black South African Literature in English (1914–1980)*, Cape Town: Maskew Miller Longman, 1983.

Bickford-Smith, V. 'The Origins and Early History of District Six', in S. Jeppie and C. Soudien (eds.), *The Struggle for District Six: Past and Present*, Cape Town: Buchu, 1990, 35–43.

Bickford-Smith, V., E. van Heyningen and N. Worden. *Cape Town in the Twentieth Century: An Illustrated Social History*, Cape Town: David Philip, 1999.

Chapman, M. (ed.). *The 'Drum' Decade: Stories from the 1950s*, Pietermaritzburg: University of Natal Press, 1989.

Southern African Literatures, London and New York: Longman, 1996.

Choonoo, R. N. 'The Sophiatown Generation: Black Literary Journalism during the 1950s', in L. Switzer (ed.), *South Africa's Alternative Press: Voices of Protest and Resistance, 1880s–1960s*, Cambridge University Press, 1997, 252–65.

Clowes, L. 'Masculinity, Matrimony and Generation: Reconfiguring Patriarchy in *Drum* 1951–1983', *Journal of Southern African Studies* 34:1 (2008), 179–92.

Cope, J. *The Tame Ox*, London: William Heinemann, 1960.

Coplan, D. *In Township Tonight!*, London: Longman, 1985.

Cornwell, G., et al. *Columbia Guide to South African Literature in English since 1945*, New York: Columbia University Press, 2010.

Distiller, N. 'South African Shakespeare: a Model for Understanding Cultural Transformation?', *Shakespeare in Southern Africa* 15 (2003), 21–7.

Driver, D. '*Drum* (1951–1959) and the Spatial Configurations of Gender', in K. Darian-Smith, L. Gunner and S. Nuttall (eds.), *Text, Theory, Space: Land, Literature and History in South Africa and Australia*, London: Routledge, 1996, 227–38.

Fenwick, M. '"Tough guy, eh?": The Gangster-Figure in *Drum*', *Journal of Southern African Studies* 22:4 (1996), 617–32.

Field, R. *Alex La Guma: A Literary & Political Biography*, Auckland Park: Jacana, 2010.

Fleming, T., and T. Falola. 'Africa's Media Empire: *Drum*'s Expansion to Nigeria', *History in Africa* 32 (2005), 133–64.

Fortune, L. *The House in Tyne Street: Childhood Memories of District Six*, Cape Town: Kwela Books, 1996.

Gordimer, N. *The Essential Gesture: Writing, Politics and Places*, ed. S. Clingman, Johannesburg: Taurus and Cape Town: David Philip, 1988.

'The Flash of Fireflies' [1968], in C. E. May (ed.), *Short Story Theories*, Athens: Ohio University Press, 1976, 178–81.

Occasion for Loving, London: Victor Gollancz, 1963.

A World of Strangers, London: Victor Gollancz, 1958.

Goudvis, B. *Little Eden [A novel]*, Cape Town: Central News Agency, 1949.

The Mistress of Mooiplaas and other Stories, Cape Town: Central News Agency, 1956.

Gray, S. 'A Tale Larger than the Sum of its Parts: Herman Charles Bosman's use of Short Fictional Forms', *Matatu* 3:5 (1989), 1–10.

Gready, P. 'The Sophiatown Writers of the 1950s – the Unreal Reality of Their World', *Journal of Southern African Studies* 16:1 (1990), 139–64.

Hannerz, U. 'Sophiatown – the View from Afar', *Journal of Southern African Studies* 20:2 (1994), 181–93.

Hart, D. M., and G. H. Pirie. 'The Sight and Soul of Sophiatown', *Geographical Review* 74 (1984), 38–47.

Head, B. *The Cardinals with Meditations and Short Stories*, ed. M. J. Daymond, Cape Town: David Philip, 1993.

   A Question of Power, London: Davis-Poynter, 1973.

Helgesson, S. 'Shifting Fields: Imagining Literary Renewal in *Itinerário* and *Drum*', *Research in African Literatures* 38:2 (2007), 206–26.

Hopkinson, T. *In the Fiery Continent*, London: Victor Gollancz, 1962.

   Under the Tropic, London: Hutchinson, 1984.

Jacobson, D. *A Dance in the Sun*, London: Weidenfeld & Nicolson, 1956.

   'Dan Jacobson Talks to Ian Hamilton', *New Review* 4:43 (October 1977), 25–9.

   The Evidence of Love, London: Weidenfeld & Nicolson, 1960.

   A Long Way from London, London: Weidenfeld & Nicolson, 1958.

   The Price of Diamonds, London: Weidenfeld & Nicolson, 1958.

   The Trap, London: Weidenfeld & Nicolson, 1955.

   The Zulu and the Zeide, London: Weidenfeld & Nicolson, 1959.

Jeppie, S., and C. Soudien (eds.). *The Struggle for District Six: Past and Present*, Cape Town: Buchu, 1990.

Johnson, D. *Shakespeare and South Africa*, Oxford: Clarendon, 1996.

La Guma, A. *A Walk in the Night*, Ibadan: Mbari, 1962.

Leveson, M. 'Bertha Goudvis: Time, Memory and Freedom', in C. Clayton (ed.), *Women and Writing in South Africa: A Critical Anthology*, Marshalltown: Heinemann, 1989, 61–71.

Lodge, T. *Black Politics in South Africa since 1945*, Johannesburg: Ravan, 1983.

Lukács, G. *The Meaning of Contemporary Realism*, trans. J. and N. Mander, London: Merlin, 1962.

   Studies in European Realism, trans. E. Bone, London: Hillway, 1950.

Maake, N. 'Publishing and Perishing: Books, People and Reading in African Languages in South Africa', in N. Evans and M. Seeber (eds.), *The Politics of Publishing in South Africa*, London: Holger Ehling Publishing and Scottsville: University of Natal Press, 2000, 127–62.

Manoim, I. S. 'The Black Press (1945–1963): The Growth of the Black Mass Media and their Role as Ideological Disseminators', MA thesis, University of the Witwatersrand, 1983.

Masilela, N. 'Sophiatown Renaissance 1952–1960', in 'New African Movement', http://pzacad.pitzer.edu/NAM/sophia/writers/sr.shtml, accessed 30 January 2010.

Matshikiza, J. 'Instant City', *Public Culture* 16:3 (2004), 481–97.

Matshikiza, T. *Chocolates for my Wife* [1961], Cape Town: David Philip, 1982.

Maughan Brown, D. '"The Anthology as Reliquary?"': Ten Years of *Staffrider* and *the Drum Decade*', *Current Writing* 1:1 (1989), 3–21.

Millin, S. G. *Two Bucks without Hair and other Stories*, Cape Town: Central News Agency, 1957.

Motsisi, C. *Casey & Co.: Selected Writings of Casey 'Kid' Motsisi*, ed. M. Mutloatse, Johannesburg: Ravan, 1978.

Mphahlele, E. *The African Image*, London: Faber, 1962.

  Down Second Avenue [1959], Gloucester, MA: Peter Smith, 1978.

  Man must Live and other Stories, Cape Town: African Bookman, 1946.

Mzamane, M. 'An Unhistorical Will into Past Times', *Current Writing* 1:1 (1981), 36–40.

Naidoo, R. *The Indian in Drum Magazine in the 1950s*, Cape Town: Bell-Roberts, 2008.

Nakasa, N. *The World of Nat Nakasa*, ed. E. Patel, Johannesburg: Ravan, 1975.

Ndebele, N. 'The Ethics of Intellectual Combat', *Current Writing* 1:1 (1989), 23–35.

Ngcelwane, N. *Sala Kahle District Six: An African Woman's Perspective*, Cape Town: Kwela Books, 1998.

Nicol, M. *A Good-looking Corpse*, London: Secker & Warburg, 1991.

Nixon, R. 'Harlem, Hollywood and the Sophiatown Renaissance', *Homelands, Harlem and Hollywood*, London and New York: Routledge, 1994, 11–41.

Nkosi, L. *Home and Exile and Other Selections*, London and New York: Longman, 1983.

Odendaal, A., and R. Field (eds.). *Liberation Chabalala: The World of Alex La Guma*, Bellville: Mayibuye Books, 1993.

Paton, A. *Cry, the Beloved Country*, London: Jonathan Cape, 1948.

  Tales from a Troubled Land, New York: Scribner, 1961; reprinted as *Debbie Go Home*, London: Jonathan Cape, 1961.

Pinnock, D. 'Ideology and Urban Planning: Blueprints of a Garrison City', in W. G. James and M. Simons (eds.), *The Angry Divide: Social and Economic History of the Western Cape*, Cape Town: David Philip, 1989, 150–68.

Rabkin, D. '*Drum* Magazine (1951–1961): and the Works of Black South African Writers Associated with it', Ph.D. thesis, University of Leeds, 1975.

Rive, R. 'District Six: Fact and Fiction', in S. Jeppie and C. Soudien (eds.), *The Struggle for District Six: Past and Present*, Cape Town: Buchu, 1990, 110–16.

Rive, R., and A. H. de Vries. 'An Interview with Richard Rive', *Current Writing* 1:1 (1989), 45–55.

S., H. V. L. Review of *The Dream and the Desert* by U. Krige, *The Lying Days* by N. Gordimer, and *A Time to Laugh* by L. Thompson, *African Affairs* 53:211 (1954), 173–4.

Sampson, A. *Drum: The Making of a Magazine* [1956], Johannesburg and Cape Town: Jonathan Ball, 2004.

Schadeberg, J., B. Gosani et al. *The Fifties People of South Africa*, Johannesburg: Bailey's Photo Archives, 1987.

Siebert, G. '"A More Sophisticated Bosman"', in S. Gray (ed.), *Herman Charles Bosman*, Johannesburg: McGraw-Hill, 1986.

Stein, P., and R. Jacobson (eds.). *Sophiatown Speaks*, Johannesburg: Bertrams Avenue Press, 1986.

Stein, S. *Second-Class Taxi*, London: Faber, 1958.

  Who Killed Mr Drum?, Johannesburg: Mayibuye Books, 1999.

Taylor, D. *Don't Tread on my Dreams*, Johannesburg: Penguin, 2008.

Themba, C. 'Through Shakespeare's Africa', *New African* 2:8 (1963), 150–3.

 The Will to Die [1972], Cape Town: David Philip, 1982.

 The World of Can Themba, ed. E. Patel [1985], Johannesburg: Ravan, 1990.

Titlestad, M. 'Jazz Discourse and Black South African Modernity, with Special Reference to "Matshikese"', *American Ethnologist* 32:2 (2005), 210–21.

Van Dyk, B. 'Short Story Writing in *Drum* Magazine, 1951–61: A Critical Appraisal', MA thesis, University of Natal, 1988.

Visser, N. W. 'South Africa: The Renaissance that Failed', *Journal of Commonwealth Literature* 9:1 (1976), 42–57.

West, N. *Miss Lonelyhearts* [1933], London: Livewright, 1949.

Willemse, H. (ed.). *More than Brothers: Peter Clarke & James Matthews at 70*, Cape Town: Kwela Books, 2000.

Winberg, C. 'Satire, Slavery and the *Ghoemaliedjies* of the Cape Muslims', *New Contrast* 19:4 (1992), 78–96.

Woodson, D. C. *Drum: An Index to 'Africa's Leading Magazine', 1951–1965*, Madison: University of Wisconsin Press, 1988.

20

Writing in exile

TLHALO RADITLHALO

Nineteen years I've roamed the continents / Renting one glasshouse after another / whence I've gazed and gazed / upon the wilderness of exile / all around me . . . / still turning round in circles / sowing seed / on borrowed land / for crops we'll always have to leave behind.

(Es'kia Mphahlele, 'A Prayer')

The initial impetus for exile by a South African writer was provided Peter Abrahams's decision in 1939 to skip the country in order to live a more fulfilling life in Britain. Abrahams's poignant ending of his memoir, *Tell Freedom* (1954), at a time when he is barely 21, touches on the core reasons why autobiographical writing seems to be especially made for the South African situation: alienation. Well before apartheid became state policy in May of 1948, the alienating effects of living in a racialising world touched on people such as Abrahams, presenting physical exile as a better option. He writes: 'I needed, not friends, not gestures, but my *manhood*. And the need was desperate . . . Also, there was a need to write, to tell freedom, and for this *I needed to be personally free*' (*Tell Freedom*, p. 311, emphasis added). The reader is drawn to a sense of emasculation that the alienated youth feels, as much as to the sense of a quest to be free by any means possible in order to be able to speak truth to power. He was actually shunned for being 'a dangerous radical' by newspapers such as *Bantu World* and *Umteteli wa Bantu* and, as he narrates, he was at one point 'homeless and near starvation' (*Return to Goli*, p. 14). In a sense, Abrahams's needs for exile provide the template within which to view much writing from the exilic condition: a repressed personality suffering from insistent infantilisation through racism and a sense of personhood. This quest to be racially unencumbered neatly reflects the kind of material and spiritual deprivation that was part of life for the majority of South Africans at the turn of the century.

According to Solomon T. Plaatje, this alienation was engineered and ought to be understood as a conscious act of political ill. As Plaatje observes in his unforgettable testament to deprivation, *Native Life in South Africa* (1916), the alienation of citizens of the country, much like the du Boisan declaration of the problem of the twentieth century, is alienation from South Africa: 'Awakening on Friday morning, June 20, 1913, the South African native found himself, not actually a slave, but a pariah in the land of his birth' (*Native Life in South Africa*, p. 21). In the decade to follow, black Africans were further deprived of land and hampered by legislation like the Apprenticeship Act (1922), the Natives (Urban) Areas Act (1923) and the Industrial Conciliation Act (1924). More than any other laws passed, these three statutes were to depress Africans' wages, depreciate their status and isolate them from the rest of the working class. They were followed by laws that circumscribed almost every other aspect of a black person's life; successive apartheid governments would, in effect, ensure that such legislation would unremittingly oppress black South Africans, making apartheid one of the most brutal (and successful) experiments in social engineering in the twentieth century.

The option of exile became a real possibility for writers and professional people, including politically inclined individuals, once the stranglehold of apartheid legislation became apparent. With the passing of such acts and the resistance that ensued, writers and activists were hard pressed to think of playing any meaningful role in a police state. The promulgation of the initial and draconian Internal Security Act (Suppression of Communism Act) No. 44 of 17 July 1950 allowed for the apartheid state to gradually, but with increasing malice, squeeze all forms of expression antagonistic to the state policy. Through its very broad definition of 'communism', the act was used to target any and all forms of independent thought and writing that placed authority in the spotlight. Crucially, this act allowed for a person deemed a threat to the state to be banned, and a banned person could not be quoted, could not have their writings read out in public, and thus was effectively silenced. It is this early act that was to lead, among others, to the general (but legal) lawlessness in the state of South Africa between 1960 and 1990, forcing a significant coterie of writers to flee the country.

One of the first writers to feel the might of the state was Es'kia Mphahlele. He had published his first collection of short stories, *Man must Live and other Stories* (1946), as the result of a compulsive impulse to write (*Down Second Avenue*, pp. 154–5). Whilst still a teacher at Orlando High School in Soweto,

Mphahlele, as secretary of the Transvaal African Teachers' Association, got wind of the Eiselen Commission on Bantu Education. Together with Zephania Mothopeng and Isaac Matlare, he campaigned against the commission's report, but the three were initially dismissed and subsequently charged with incitement of students. When the charges failed, they found that their dismissals came with the proviso that they could not teach anywhere in the Union (*Down Second Avenue*, pp. 158–9). The Bantu Education Act (1953) formalised the segregation of black education and became a lasting, if infamous, monument to Verwoerd as the then Minister for Bantu Administration.

Mphahlele initially sought refuge in Lesotho as a teacher, but could not really adapt to the quiet, rural background. He left Lesotho and went to Johannesburg to work for *Drum* magazine, before journeying on to Nigeria on 6 September 1957. The years of exile had begun in earnest.

In exile, Mphahlele began to thaw, and while he remained angry at the South African state, he launched himself into a most fruitful period of cultural engagement with Africa when he became the African division Director of Congress for Cultural Freedom (Congrès Pour la Liberté de la Culture) based in Paris. He financed the cultural renascences in west, east and southern African states, was connected to the Mbari Writers and Artists Club (Ibadan), and intricately involved in the influential journal *Black Orpheus: A Journal of African and Afro-American Literature* almost from its inception (Yesufu, 'Black Orpheus and Mbari', pp. 100–9). It is especially through *Black Orpheus* and Mbari's efforts that South African writers found an outlet for their works; two examples are Dennis Brutus and Alex La Guma, whose *Sirens, Knuckles and Boots* (1963) and *A Walk in the Night* (1962) respectively were published by Mbari. Arthur Nortje, to give another example, was initially published by Mbari after winning an Mbari prize for poetry in 1962. More crucially, it is as a result of the Congress for Cultural Freedom that the two seminal conferences that were to usher in African literature as a discipline were held in Makerere (1962) and Freetown (1963).

As Mphahlele's influence and critical interventions grew, so he was attacked on more than one occasion. The criticism he was to attract from no less a personality than Chinua Achebe – who sneeringly referred to Mphahlele as 'a VIP in African Literature' – points to how insecure people could be about his growing institutional authority (see Mphahlele, 'Letters to the Editor', p. 7).

Whilst it may be difficult to condense the entire gamut of Mphahlele's work in exile, it is germane to realise the extent to which he was seen as a spokesperson for Africa in general and South Africa in particular; his correspondence with figures like Colin Legum at the *Observer* (for instance, in a letter dated 22 May 1963) proves how much he insisted on Africa's proper appraisal from Europe.[1] Mphahlele, in the exile period of nineteen years, wrote for many influential journals, including *Transition, African Social Research, UNESCO Courier, Okike: An African Journal of New Writing, Ba Shiru, First World: An International Journal of Black Thought, New Statesman, Nation, Africa Today, New Letters, Ord och Bild, Harvard Educational Review, Encounter, Foreign Affairs, Black World, Black Books Bulletin* and the *Listener.* This was in addition to regular publications in academic journals, such as *Research in African Literatures* and the *Denver Quarterly.* His sheer intellectual output at the level of critical engagement with the African world and its relation to other continents remains unsurpassed by any of the other writers who were to follow in his footsteps.

The eternal alien: Bloke Modisane

The person who most epitomised the ravages of alienation in the late 1950s in South Africa was William 'Bloke' Modisane. Modisane was born in Sophiatown and came of age in this vibrant, multicultural community with all the ugliness and beauty of a ghetto. He truly loved and hated Sophiatown in that it stood for the African getting to grips with the twin polarities of modernity and aesthetic modernism. Whilst Afrikaner state philosophy saw modernity as inimical to African progression, townships such as Sophiatown and District Six in Cape Town proved the lie: art played a crucial role in the lives of such communities and Modisane's efflorescence was akin to that of the Renaissance man. His love of jazz and classical music, as well as literature, was legendary. His disillusion with the country's laws was compounded by the eventual forced scattering of the Sophiatown community under the dictates of the Blacks Resettlement Act (1954). Even earlier than this, his mind was already at odds with the circumstances of his life, and in his autobiography he captures this condition quite vividly in an acoustic metaphor: 'My life is like the penny whistle music spinning on eternally with the same repetitive persistence; it is deceptively happy, but it is all on the surface, like the melodic and harmonic lines of the kwela played by the penny whistle . . . But contained in it is a sharp hint of pain' (*Blame me on History*, p. 117). As he witnessed the destruction of Sophiatown the idea of an autobiography took hold, and it is perhaps correct to characterise this work as an unforgettable requiem for

1 For a comprehensive collection of Mphahlele's letters, see Manganyi and Attwell, *Bury me at the Marketplace.*

Sophiatown and its expressiveness. Through the psychological self-writing, Modisane bares his soul for scrutiny in a manner never attempted before by a South African writer, though the reading and reception of the text were to infuriate and delight in equal measure (see Nkosi, 'Sting in the Adder's Tail', pp. 54–5).

Modisane left South Africa over the Easter weekend of March 1959 after an encounter with Major Colonel Prinsloo of the Special Branch, who wanted, in exchange for a passport, for Modisane to inform on his colleagues at *Drum* magazine (*Blame me on History*, pp. 268–72). This forced him to leave behind his wife, Fikile, and daughter, Chris. Having arrived in London, he later appeared on television and, prophetically, warned of a bloodbath that was about to befall South Africa; while this was greeted with guffaws, a bloody massacre of sixty-nine protestors in Sharpeville did indeed happen almost a year after he had left South Africa. Modisane began a life of sorts, appearing as an actor in numerous films and televisions shows, as well as immersing himself in the kinds of questions that Mphahlele had begun to open up in the field of African literature. He was present, for instance, at the seminal conference of anglophone writers held in Kampala in 1962, as his report on the conference demonstrates ('African Writers' Summit', pp. 5–6).

An interesting correspondence between Modisane and the Legums – Margaret and Colin – shows how alienating exile was for him, experienced at its worst when he had to visit Potsdam to research the Maji Maji Resistance in Tanzania in what was then East Germany, an ordeal which he likened to 'an English tourist visiting Sophiatown' ('Letter to Margaret Legum', p. 1). Here the roles are reversed, in that Modisane is the one with material resources (money, food, comforts of travel, etc). An intricately sad moment is recounted in this letter, which reveals just how perceptive Modisane was to forms of exploitation. He relates how his lust for a waitress in Potsdam leads to an offer of sex and a marriage of convenience, just so she can escape to West Germany, a proposition which he refuses. This causes him anguish as he moves the scene to Sophiatown; in the process, he asks himself: if he had asked someone to help him move out of Sophiatown and been refused, would he have been able to understand the refusal? He describes his own fears and the matter as being 'a burden on my conscience' ('Letter to Margaret Legum', p. 3). Whatever else Modisane was, he was a prisoner, tied to the tyrannical hold South Africa exerted on him. His last letter to Colin Legum describes how East Germany conjures up several memories of Sophiatown, which he finds terribly depressing ('Letter to Colin Legum').

The making of a literary critic: Lewis Nkosi

A far more *literary* exile is that of Lewis Nkosi, one of the most accomplished critics of South African writing. Nkosi left South Africa after the Sharpeville massacre in 1960 and, on the strength of his journalistic credentials, went to London, where he quickly established himself as a literary editor of *The New African*. Although he never wrote his autobiography, Nkosi's oeuvre regarding writing by black South Africans in particular and Africans in general is truly impressive, even as he contrived, through the years, to make bitter enemies of every major writer from the continent, including Chinua Achebe, Wole Soyinka, Lenrie Peters, Es'kia Mphahlele, Dennis Brutus, Bloke Modisane and Richard Rive: the list is lengthy. His acerbic articles on literary matters, scattered in publications such as *Transition* and *Africa Report*, reveal an intellect as fearless as it was ruthless, and it is no surprise that his collection of essays, *Home and Exile* (1966), shared second prize with Ralph Ellison's *Shadow and Act* (1966) at the Dakar World Festival of Negro Arts in 1966. Consider, for instance, his review of *Long Drums and Cannons* by Margaret Laurence (1968) and *Whispers from the Continent: The Literature of Contemporary Black Africa* by Wilfred Cartey (1969), under the heading 'A Question of Literary Stewardship' (pp. 69–71). In it, he laments the sweeping form of literary criticism that was beginning to take hold in the form of surveys, and his savaging of Cartey's book is unremitting. He accuses Cartey of being 'one of the many examples of the eager stewardship of black academics in the new World', who, besides offering banal observations, are steeped in 'pseudo-profundity', resulting in 'warmed-over opinions' of little intellectual value. In the same breath, he castigates Laurence's text as a 'modest book', whose value lies in its assistance of students wishing to understand Nigerian fiction without too much effort. It is perhaps this degree of detachment when viewing African literary achievements and its criticism that allowed him, as early as 1966, to question the quality of what was being published, warning that bad writing, if unchecked, would slip through the dragnet of vigorous interrogation, especially in publications from Heinemann.

In his critique, 'Where does African Literature go from Here?' (pp. 7–11), he lambastes Flora Nwapa's *Efuru* (1966), Lenrie Peters's *The Second Round* (1965), and accuses Wole Soyinka's *The Interpreters* (1964) of abuse of the English language. He also has choice words for Ngugi's *The River Between* (1965), especially what he regards as its over-reliance on 'glib symbolism'. At the end, he asserts that genuine assessment of the literature from the continent 'is now taking place between writers, and this is all for the good. The romance has ended!' (p. 11). Nkosi's sensibility with regard to African literature is captured best in the collection of essays, *Tasks and Masks* (1981), and the retrospective appraisal of his complex contribution in *Still Beating the Drum: Critical Perspectives on Lewis Nkosi* (2006). Annie Gagiano, in reviewing his literary criticism, comments on 'the unmistakably exacting quality of most of the criticism – its seriousness, its trenchant ("non-nepotistic") tone, its prescience, and its constant evolution and expansion' ('Lewis Nkosi as Literary Critic', p. 5). Nkosi, it ought to be added, was the South African writer least affected by the traumas of exile. In one instance, he amusingly notes how he survived even homesickness, because of the 'undiminishing pleasure of the English woman'! ('Art Contra Apartheid', p. 69).

Exile and trauma: Arthur Nortje and Nathaniel 'Nat' Nakasa

Arthur Kenneth Nortje left South Africa as a result of having been awarded a scholarship to read English at Jesus College, Oxford in 1964–5. Nortje remains a fascinating figure in South African literature and his talent for poetry was established early in his publication by Mbari. His special interest lay in the poetry of Gerard Manley Hopkins, yet he bore the burden of existence as a bi-racial South African; the limitation of opportunities in his segregated home country troubled him deeply and is reflected in his poems, which could, nonetheless, be lyrical, colloquial, dramatic and complex. Hedy Davis records how, in December 1970, Nortje was caught in a bind: his passport was about to expire, and he faced deportation to South Africa, as he had been unable to obtain British citizenship. On the evening of 8 December he dined with college friends, and then watched the Cassius Clay fight on television at the local pub, seemingly enjoying the beers he had won on a wager on the result of the fight. He returned to his room and set down a final poem, entitled 'All hunger pass away'. Then he took a massive dose of barbiturates, choosing suicide rather than return to the country he loved above everything else (Davis, 'Forgotten South African Poet', pp. 5–7).

Another person who was to take his life at a young age was Nathaniel Nakasa, the assistant editor of *Drum* magazine, who, in 1964, was awarded the Nieman Fellowship to study at Harvard University. Nakasa had arrived in Johannesburg from Durban where he had eked out a meagre living and obtained a Junior Certificate before becoming a reporter. He quickly established himself as a columnist for the *Rand Daily Mail* in Johannesburg. His column, 'As I See It', provided a sober assessment of apartheid South Africa at the historical moment when the very might of the state seemed unassailable. What really made him come into his own was the new literary journal that he edited, *The Classic*. Aware of his limitations and the need to acquire skills, he set up a multiracial board of trustees and editorial advisors; he then set about the task of making *The Classic* the premier South African literary journal, even as he contemplated going to Harvard to correct what he perceived as real gaps in his intellectual formation. He was fortunate in having letters of recommendation from Helen Suzman, the white member of the South African Parliament who actively opposed the doctrine of apartheid, and Nadine Gordimer, his literary mentor. When the award duly came, the South Africa government refused him a passport as 'an opponent of apartheid' and left him with the option of an exit permit, which would forestall any attempt to return to the country of his birth. Difficult as the decision was, he chose exile and was to pay dearly for it.

His year at Harvard, while marked by nonchalance, hid the inner turmoil he suffered. As Lewis C. Clapp observes in *Harvard Reports* of 1993, at one point he underwent a complete breakdown as he attacked a lecturer who had initiated a discussion on race relations. It seemed Nakasa started well, 'but soon lost total control, shout[ing] incoherent statements about drinking blood and who is to judge civilization and how the white man can never really understand what goes on inside a black man' (Clapp, 'Will Nat Nakasa ever go Home?', p. 83). This outburst clearly indicated his inner turmoil and would later return with devastating results.

Nakasa is best remembered, perhaps, for his clear-sighted essays on race relations, which he wrote for the *New York Times*. Two of these, 'The human meaning of Apartheid' (pp. 42–9) and 'Mr Nakasa goes to Harlem' (pp. 48–61), stand in contrast to what he perceived as the two black worlds with as many similarities as differences. In 'The human meaning', Nakasa attempts to provide a succinct understanding for the reader by making a clear point: while African Americans in New York had the law on their side, the South African black was governed by 'a forest of legislation, countless laws which are often beyond the understanding of both the civilian and the law officer' (p. 42). He goes on to describe the pernicious nature of the pass laws, the effects on ordinary black South Africans and the lessening of opportunities. Crucially, he notes that even distinguished Africans cannot escape their black skin, which leads to increased frustration, and relates how, in having secured the Nieman Fellowship for 1960, Lewis Nkosi had to take the option of the exit permit, as he was denied a valid passport.

The profound alienation Nakasa was to feel in the United States had more to do with his non-acceptance of his exile position than with his lack of ambition or drive. Indeed, his Harlem article shows just how much he appreciated the progress of the African American, and the constant comparisons between Harlem and Sophiatown illustrate how deeply he felt the injustice of the South African polity. His despondency, brought on by thoughts of his mother in a mental hospital, illustrates how much of a depressive he had become, as he wondered aloud if he was also going mad (Clapp, 'Will Nat Nakasa ever go Home?', p. 83). At the home of John Thompson, the executive director of the Farfield Foundation, which had sponsored *The Classic* and paid for Nakasa's Harvard expenses, he took his life by jumping out of a bedroom window. His friends at home and in New York deeply mourned his passing, for he had shown what it meant to live 'without question and with easy dignity and natural pride in his Africanism' (Lelyveld, 'Friends honor black South African poet', p. 9). Nkosi provided the proper context in his observation that while Nakasa had shown flashes of brilliance in his writing, he was young and might have developed as he matured ('Notes on Transition', p. 40).

The survivalists: Dennis Brutus, Keorapetse Kgositsile and Mazisi Kunene

Other South African writers who were to make the United States their home away from home include Dennis Brutus, Keorapetse Kgositsile and Mazisi Kunene. Aside from Mphahlele, no other South African writers made a greater impact on black America than Brutus and Kgositsile. Both landed in the United States under interesting circumstances. Brutus was forced to take an exit permit after spending a year under house arrest. Prior to this, he had been dismissed from teaching in high schools after fourteen years' service and, as a banned person, could not be quoted. Despite all of this, in 1963 he agitated for the withdrawal of South Africa's right to participate in the Olympic Games, citing its charter as opposed to racism. He was duly arrested, tried and, while on bail, skipped the country by running away to Swaziland. He then made the error of proceeding to Mozambique, then still under Portuguese rule. The Portuguese secret police arrested him and gave him back to their South African counterparts, who drove him to Johannesburg. In Johannesburg, as he alighted from the car he took off and was promptly shot in the back. He was brought to Robben Island after recuperating and spent sixteen months breaking stones with a hammer. He became a sought-after speaker on the conditions on the island for the United Nations and the Red Cross. His activism found him working with Chicano groups in Chicago, Puerto Ricans, political prisoners in Chile and as an active opponent of the Greek colonels (Miller, 'Interview with Dennis Brutus', pp. 42–55).

Brutus's oeuvre, since the initial publication of *Sirens, Knuckles and Boots* (1963), was to grow exponentially in his exile years. Over his career he has endured the infamy of very bad reviews and criticism, while also enjoying what some critics see as undeserved praise heaped on him in a gesture of hero worship on account of his biographical details, rather than from serious consideration of his poems. In an insightful analysis, Bernth Lindfors takes on both sides of the divide and wonders, perceptively:

> When one critic praises a poet for his fortitude, calmness, restraint, control and precision and another condemns him for his undignified lapses in frenzied melodrama, raucous shouting and other insincere, tear-jerking theatrics, then something must be wrong with someone's perceptions. How else can two critics arrive at such diametrically opposed opinions about the same corpus of poetry?   ('Dennis Brutus and his Critics', pp. 137–44)

Lindfors charges critics with suffering from 'amateur psychologizing' when assessing Brutus's poetry, and with one even seeing the poet as a 'mentally unbalanced Christ-like figure' ('Dennis Brutus and his Critics', p. 143). What Lindfors discerns is that biographical criticism and sociological criticism are highly subjective and do not in any way do justice to Brutus's poetics. As if it were not enough already, his *Airs and Tributes* (1989) received a particularly savage attack from Amiri Baraka ('Review', pp. 621–6).

A very different assessment of Brutus's poetry appears in Gessler Nkondo's account of *Stubborn Hope: Poems* (1978) and *A Simple Lust: Collected Poems of South African Jail and Exile* (1973). It is such an erudite reading of the collections that one wonders if, perhaps, Brutus's overt political stance prejudiced reviewers and academic reappraisals of his works. Indeed, Nkondo avoids all the posturing addressed in the Lindfors article and concentrates on the influences he discerns in Brutus – Donne's metaphysics, the acoustic nature of his poetry – and notes his order, coherence of feeling and the precision of his presentation ('Dennis Brutus', pp. 32–40).

Brutus's stay in the United States was just as chequered: in the early 1980s he was involved in a protracted and debilitating fight with the State Department, which hoped to deport him. It turned out that, born in Rhodesia, he had travelled on a British passport which, with the attainment of Zimbabwe's independence in 1980, he was forced to return (Brutus, 'Shall I be Deported?', pp. 13–16). This, in a sense, was always one of the perils of exile that made even compatriots like Mphahlele shun African countries in later life and choose to remain aloof from all other cultural wars in their adopted countries. Mphahlele had resolved that he would engage with others' cultural struggles if he were invited to, but always with a clear definition of the limits of his involvement (Mphahlele, *Afrika my Music*, p. 100). An anthology of Brutus's poetry and criticism was published by the University of KwaZulu-Natal Press under the title *Poetry and Protest: A Dennis Brutus Reader* (2006).

Keorapetse Kgositsile, unlike Mphahlele, found his trajectory of engagement from 1962 at the coalface of the ferment of cultural and political revival in Harlem. When he started his studies at Lincoln University in Pennsylvania, he chose to immerse himself in the history of black America and, in this way, attained what he refers to as 'emotional placement' within literary production in the United States. As he explained in an interview, 'emotional placement' for him was about 'one's orientation to sound and its effect and everything else around them in an environment they are in' ('"With bloodstains to testify"', p. 28). Unlike other writers such as Nakasa, it was never a struggle for Kgositsile to be part of the black American milieu, so much so that his poetry was discussed as a bridge between Africa and black America. His erudite writings on literary production and the place of art in society regularly appeared in *Black World* (see 'Where is the Black Revolution?', pp. 16–21; 'Steps to Break the Circle', pp. 30–4; and 'Language, Vision and the Black Writer', pp. 25–7). Very rarely were African Americans so accommodating of a writer born outside their milieu, and Kgositsile's poetics, influenced by Aimé Césaire and Frantz Fanon among others, found resonance in a community struggling to assert itself in the cauldron of what was to be the volatile 1960s. His incisive contributions to various conferences, particularly those under the auspices of the African Literature Association (ALA), made serious interventions in the evolving critical appraisal of the discipline. The panel 'Literature and Commitment in South Africa', under the aegis of the Symposium on Contemporary African Literature and the First African Literature Association at Austin, Texas, brought to the fore the idea of compromise that Kgositsile was unwilling to countenance. For him, commitment was and is commitment. It was also at this conference, interestingly held in 1976, that Mphahlele questioned the validity of the ALA in light of its non-commitment to Africa. As he put it: 'When you've got a literature association going on in a country which has no commitment whatever to Africa, this is where my doubts come in. The association becomes a happy hunting ground for Africanists, for scholars and critics who want to gather material, for people who have absolutely no commitment to Africa' (quoted in Brutus, 'Panel on

South African Theater', p. 44). What irritated Mphahlele was the very notion that Africans were seen to parade themselves on foreign platforms, always performing to outside audiences with the ALA becoming a conveyor belt for those with no commitment to the continent.

It was such incisive cut and thrust discussions that allowed writers such as Kgositsile to be major figures regarding South Africa and the post-apartheid period. A well-regarded figure in the diaspora, he, like Nkosi, traversed the exilic condition far more easily than was the case with the rest of his compatriots. But surely the lion of the movement to outer environments remains Mazisi Kunene and what he stood for, namely the tenacity to assert an Africanist perspective without compromise, without doubt, and with fidelity to place and a people. Kunene's assertions regarding African literature in African languages reflect an old debate that, however, refuses to go away, and it is as a result, too, of his steadfastness to the ideal that he emerges as an important figure with due regard to writers in exile. Well before Ngũgĩ wa Thiong'o was to become famous for his stance on African languages and African writing, Kunene was actualising Obianjunwa Wali's distress call regarding what he perceived as 'The Dead End of African Literature' for as long as it was expressed in European languages. The polemics regarding Wali's criticism may well have waned with time, but at one point it occasioned some of the most electrifying literary critical debates, as illustrated by the letters to the *Transition* journal (Mphahlele, 'Polemics: The Dead End of African Literature', pp. 335–41).

Kunene's appraisal of his chosen medium was set out in many of the articles he wrote on the subject, and possibly the most engaging is that published in the special issue of *Research in African Literatures*, on the language question (Kunene, 'Problems in African Literature', pp. 27–44). Kunene's magisterial writing is as eloquent in this essay as it is in any of his defences for the choice of medium he works with, namely the richly idiomatic Zulu language, and in a sense it is an erudite reiteration of the main concerns of the Wali submission.

A key aspect of Kunene's work lies in what he perceives as the philosophical underpinnings of a language, and he goes on to write:

> For one to talk about the proper language to use in the creation of African literature, one must understand the fundamental realities of its philosophies. One must answer the question: what language or languages best serve the interests of cultural, social, and economic development within the African world? In other words, *the issue is not language at all but the philosophies and values that characterize the African world*.
>
> ('Problems in African Literature', p. 29)

In a sense, Kunene found himself in a position where he had to assert his position in what can only be described as a hostile environment – hostile, that is, to the possibility of African literature in African languages, since, more than ever, he sought to assert the idea that any language as a carrier of culture binds and rebinds a linguistic community. But, sadly, what he did not take into account, as Mphahlele had averred in 1962, is that the creative impulse does not wait for the linguistic solutions that should, in reality, emanate from both the educational sphere and the political one. Mphahlele asserted, then, that 'the creative impulse always runs ahead of social, political and economic developments; and the creative impulse cannot wait for such developments before it expresses itself... South African Bantu poetry dates back ninety years, Swahili poetry, in Arabic script, longer than that' ('Polemics: The Dead End of African Literature', pp. 336–7).

The Cardinals: Bessie Head, Alex La Guma and the exilic condition

Bessie Emory Head underwent an interesting but no less traumatic exilic condition in Botswana. She was born of black and white parents in Pietermaritzburg and sent to live with a foster family thereafter as she was unacceptable to her maternal relatives. Craig MacKenzie asserts that there is simply too much uncertainty regarding the early life of Bessie Head, and to make such a search would only be proof of 'the enigma of human prejudice' ('Introduction', p. ix). Head's life story encapsulated the trauma of a racial society. Her activism in the late 1950s to early 1960s was marked by constant harassment and several arrests, which resulted in her moving to Serowe in Botswana. Her writings examine existential themes of personal and societal alienation, political exile and sexual oppression. Her experiences in exile were extremely distressing, resulting in a nervous breakdown. But her writing remains a vibrant testimony to her exceptional talent, and the novels *When Rain Clouds Gather* (1969), *Maru* (1971), *A Question of Power* (1973) and her major non-fiction work, *Serowe: Village of the Rainwind* (1981), display her prodigious gifts and ability to enchant feminists, activists, scholars and social historians alike. Her fight for recognition as a Botswanan citizen was so long and protracted that at one point she truly was stateless, exacerbating an already fragile personality. Her legacy lies in the unflinching awesome honesty of her writing, and most evident in the brutal realisation of mental illness in *A Question of Power*. Some posthumous publications attest to her powerful writing: fictional short

writings collected as *Tales of Tenderness and Power* (1989), an autobiographical sketch titled *A Woman Alone: Autobiographical Writings* (1990), Randolph
Vigne's *A Gesture of Belonging: Letters from Bessie Head 1965–1979* (1991) and *The
Cardinals: With Meditations and Stories* (1993), which is a novella Head started
in the early 1960s while living in Cape Town.

Alex La Guma is another South African writer who endured persecution
before opting for exile. La Guma's strength lies in the short-story form.
His curiosity about the poverty, despair, oppression and hopes of humanity
combines with a deep concern about its sufferings and afflictions that inhabits
the minutest detail of the fictional environment: the physical state of buildings,
the rotting streets, the smells emanating from the beer halls and the lives lived
in such places. La Guma imagines his task as that of a storyteller long before
Njabulo Ndebele's call in 1984 for writers to 're-discover the ordinary', where
the ordinary is defined as the opposite of the spectacular, of sobering rationality
and the forcing of attention on necessary detail ('Rediscovery of the Ordinary',
p. 50). Whilst La Guma's tales provide entertainment, they also have a deep
moral grounding. In addition to the famous short-story collection *A Walk in
the Night and other Stories* (1962), he also wrote some ground-breaking novels:
And a Threefold Cord (1964), *The Stone Country* (1967), *In the Fog at the Season's
End* (1972) and *Time of the Butcherbird* (1979). He also wrote a travel book, *A
Soviet Journey* (1978), and a biography of his father, entitled *Jimmy La Guma*
(1997). He died in Havana, Cuba in 1985.

Other important figures on the South African literary scene forced into exile
were A. C. Jordan, Breyten Breytenbach and C. J. Driver. Jordan was educated
at the famous Lovedale missionary school in the Transkei and gained his Ph.D.
at Fort Hare in 1956. Political pressure saw him leave South Africa on an exit
permit in 1961 and settle in the United States, where he worked as a professor
of African languages and literature, first at the University of California and
later at Wisconsin. His classical novel, *Ingqumbo Yeminyanya* (The Wrath of
the Ancestors [1940], 1980), is still regarded as the best written in isiXhosa,
and is one which avoids easy solutions of the classical encounter between
coloniser and colonised. Posthumous publications include a collection of
African folk-tales, *Tales from Southern Africa* (1973), another collection of short
stories, entitled *Kwezo Mpindo zaTsitsa* (Along the Bends of Tsitsa, 1975), and
a critical study, *Towards an African Literature: The Emergence of Literary Form in
Xhosa* (1972).

Driver and Breytenbach provide a crucial aspect to exile in that, unlike the
many white South Africans whose flights were motivated by self-interest, they
left for the same reasons that had forced their black compatriots to flee, thus

nullifying the South African government's cherished excuse that those who opposed it were influenced from without its borders. Driver, in particular, was once imprisoned in 1964 for activities as the president of the National Union of South African Students (NUSAS) and held in solitary confinement. He immediately thereafter left for England. He endured statelessness for several years, as the British government refused to recognise his status before eventually doing so. He has published six collections of poems, among which feature the poignant collection *In the Water-Margins: Poems* (1994), five novels, *Elegy for a Revolutionary* (1969), *Send War in our Time, O Lord* (1970), *Death of Fathers* (1972), *A Messiah of the Last Days* (1974) and *Shades of Darkness* (2004), and contributed to a collection of short stories, *Penguin Modern Stories 8* (1971). He also published a biography of Patrick Duncan, titled *Patrick Duncan, South African and Pan-African* (1980). Breytenbach, like Brutus, proves to be an enduring rebel against forms of political obscurantism and centralisation while agreeing that life as an operative is more preferable as it allows a 'certain purity of thinking' (*Confessions*, p. 81). Educated in South Africa, Breytenbach had, as had André Brink, sought further education in Europe and thus he left South Africa in the early 1960s. He was then exposed to the full might of rebellion in the student protests of 1968, the cauldron that was Vietnam and its impact worldwide, and Palestine as part of his political education. These events fuelled his political commitment, which he explored in his poetry of the period; later he became a member of a left-leaning resistance group in exile, Okhela. This group, under the auspices of the ANC, was given the task of exposing European collaboration with apartheid and thereby enforcing trade sanctions (Nash, 'Zen Communist', p. 17). With the approval of the then ANC president, Oliver Tambo, Okhela was formed in order to attract 'white leftists within South Africa – more specifically . . . radical students, organisers in the emerging trade union movement, and dissident Afrikaner intellectuals' (Nash, 'Zen Communist', p. 17).

Breytenbach, as part of Okhela, undertook a secret mission in 1975 and was unfortunately captured by the state secret police. He was convicted of high treason and it was in prison that his poetry flourished. As Nash notes, imprisonment left him with no other identity than that provided by words. From his release in 1982, therefore, until at least 1989, he published four volumes of poetry regarding his imprisonment, a novel and a volume of literary reflection, a prison memoir, and a collection of political speeches. Breytenbach's reflections critique the central preoccupations of his years in Okhela: the idea of discipline, the goal of power, and the ostensible result of historical progress ('Zen Communist', p. 20).

Together with a growing number of South African writers and former activists, Breytenbach is at present showing signs of unease at a future they fought so hard to realise. His criticism of the South African polity is neatly captured in his trenchant article, 'Mandela's Smile: Notes on South Africa's Failed Revolution' (2008). He currently divides his time between continental Europe, Africa and the United States of America. He joined his alma mater, the University of Cape Town, as a visiting professor in the Graduate School of Humanities (from January 2000) and is also involved with the Goreé Institute in Dakar (Senegal) and with New York University, where he teaches in the Graduate Creative Writing Program.

The effects of exile on South African cultural life cannot be underestimated. By 1977, as a result of media oppression, academic timidity, bannings and generalised lawlessness in the form of continual harassment, many of the writers had slipped from popular memory. Institutions of higher education had little to add in making sure the writers were part of their students' cultural memory. As a discipline, South African literary studies was accused of regionalism, parochial choices of texts and an ingrained self-censorship (Grant, 'Silenced Generation', p. 40). The matter was not alleviated in any significant manner given the stringent application of censorship by the Publications Board under the auspices of the Publications Act (1974 and 1977). The dismal state of affairs was replicated in the school curricula, where learners were in some instances encouraged to write essays with England as a setting. A distinct two-streamed literature, of home and exile, was thus allowed to arise; slowly, South African literature is searching for new fictive, poetic and dramaturgical impulses in order to converge into a national literature.

Bibliography

Abrahams, P. *Return to Goli*, London: Faber, 1953.

    Tell Freedom, London: Faber, 1954.

Baraka, A. 'Review', *Black American Literature Forum* 23:3 (1989), 621–6.

Breytenbach, B. 'Mandela's Smile: Notes on South Africa's Failed Revolution', *Harper's Magazine* 317 (2008), 39–48.

    The True Confessions of an Albino Terrorist, Johannesburg: Taurus, 1984.

Brutus, D. 'In Memoriam: Arthur Nortje, 1942–1970', *Research in African Literatures* 2:1 (1971), 26–7.

    'Panel on South African Theater', *Issue: A Journal of Opinion* 6:1 (1976), 47–57.

    Poetry and Protest: A Dennis Brutus Reader, ed. Aisha Kareem and Lee Sustar, Chicago: Haymaker Books and Pietermaritzburg: University of KwaZulu-Natal Press, 2006.

    'Shall I be Deported from the USA?', *Index on Censorship* 3:83 (1983), 13–16.

A Simple Lust: Collected Poems of South African Jail and Exile, London and New York: Heinemann and Hill & Wang, 1973.

Sirens, Knuckles and Boots, Ibadan: Mbari, 1963.

Stubborn Hope: Poems, Washington DC: Three Continents, 1973.

Clapp, L. C. 'Nieman Notes: Will Nat Nakasa ever go Home?', *Nieman Reports* (1993), 82–3.

Davis, H. I. 'Arthur Nortje: A Forgotten South African Poet', *Reality* 11:4 (1979), 5–7.

Driver, C. J. *Death of Fathers*, London: Faber, 1972.

Elegy for a Revolutionary, London: Faber, 1969.

In the Water-Margins: Poems, Cape Town: Snailpress and London: Crane River, 1994.

A Messiah of the Last Days, London: Faber, 1974.

Patrick Duncan: South African and Pan-African, London: Heinemann, 1980.

Penguin Modern Stories 8, Harmondsworth: Penguin, 1971.

Send War in our Time, O Lord, London: Faber, 1970.

Shades of Darkness, Johannesburg: Jonathan Ball, 2005.

Gagiano, A. 'Lewis Nkosi as Literary Critic', in Stiebel and Gunner, *Still Beating the Drum*, 5–26.

Grant, J. 'Silenced Generation', *Index on Censorship* 6:3 (1977), 38–43.

Gunner, L., and L. Stiebel (eds.). *Still Beating the Drum: Critical Perspectives on Lewis Nkosi*, Johannesburg: University of Witwatersrand Press, 2006.

Head, Bessie. *The Cardinals: With Meditations and Stories*, ed. M. J. Daymond, Cape Town: David Philip, 1993.

A Gesture of Belonging: Letters from Bessie Head, 1965–1979, ed. R. Vigne, London: SA Writers and Portsmouth, NH: Heinemann, 1991.

Maru [1971], Oxford: Heinemann, 1995.

A Question of Power, London: Davis-Poynter, 1973.

Serowe: Village of the Rainwind, London: Heinemann, 1981.

Tales of Tenderness and Power, London: Heinemann, 1990.

When Rain Clouds Gather, London: Heinemann, 1968.

A Woman Alone: Autobiographical Writings, Oxford: Heinemann, 1990.

Jordan, A. C. *Ingqumbo Yeminyanya*, Alice: Lovedale Press, 1940.

Kwezo Mpindo Zetsitsa, Alice: Lovedale Press, 1975.

Tales from Southern Africa, Berkeley: University of California Press, 1973.

Towards an African Literature: The Emergence of Literary Form in English, Berkeley: University of California Press, 1973.

Killam, D., and R. Rowe (eds.). 'Bessie Emory Head (1937–1986)'; 'Jordan, A.C. (1906–1968); 'La Guma, Alex (1925–1985)', in *The Companion to African Literatures*, Oxford, Bloomington and Indianapolis: James Currey and Indiana University Press, 2000, 112–13, 123 and 131.

Kgositsile, K. 'In America and Africa: Where is the Black Revolution?', *Black World* 19:7 (1970), 16–21.

'Language, Vision and the Black Writer', *Black World* 21:8 (1972), 25–7.

'Panel on Literature and Commitment in South Africa', *Issue: A Journal of Opinion* 6:1 (1976), 34–46.

'Steps to Break the Circle', *Black World* 23:11 (1974), 30–4.

'"With bloodstains to testify": An Interview with Keorapetse Kgositsile', by C. H. Rowell, *Callaloo* 2 (1978), 23–42.

Kunene, M. 'Panel on South African Oral Traditions', *Issue: A Journal of Opinion* 6:1 (1976), 5–13.

'Problems in African Literature', *Research in African Literatures* 23:1 (1992), 27–44.

Lelyveld, J. 'Friends honor black South Africa poet who died in exile', *New York Times*, 3 April 1966, 9.

La Guma, A. *And a Threefold Cord*, Berlin: Seven Seas, 1964.

In the Fog of the Season's End, Oxford: Heinemann, 1992.

Jimmy La Guma: a Biography, ed. M. Adhikari, Cape Town: Friends of the South African Library, 1997.

A Soviet Journey, Moscow: Progress Publishers, 1978.

The Stone Country, Berlin: Seven Seas, 1967.

Time of the Butcherbird, London: Heinemann, 1979.

A Walk in the Night, Ibadan: Mbari, 1962.

A Walk in the Night and other Stories, London: Heinemann, 1967.

Lindfors, B. 'Dennis Brutus and his Critics', *West African Journal of Modern Languages* 2 (1976), 137–44.

MacKenzie, C. 'Introduction', in *Bessie Head – A Woman Alone*, London: Heinemann, 1990, ix–xix.

Mandela, N. *Long Walk to Freedom: The Autobiography of Nelson Mandela*, Randburg: MacDonald Purnell, 1994.

Manganyi, N. C., and D. Attwell (eds.). *Bury me at the Marketplace: Es'kia Mphahlele and Company: Letters 1943–2006*, Johannesburg: Witwatersrand University Press, 2010.

Miller, E. E. 'An Interview with Dennis Brutus', *Obsidian: Black Literature in Review* 1:2 (1975), 42–55.

Modisane, B. 'African Writers' Summit', *Transition* 5 (1962), 5–6.

Blame me on History (1963), Johannesburg: Ad Donker, 1986.

'Letter to Margaret Legum', Sunday, 1966 [n.d.], University of Cape Town, Libraries Archives. 'Letter to Colin Legum', Berlin, 28 May 1966, University of Cape Town, Libraries Archives.

Mphahlele, E. *Afrika my Music: An Autobiography 1957–1983*, Johannesburg: Ravan, 1984.

Down Second Avenue, London: Faber, 1959.

'Letters to the Editor: Peter Nazareth, Bill Court, Ezekiel Mphahlele', *Transition* 9 (1963), 5–8.

Man must Live and other Stories, Cape Town: African Bookman, 1946.

'Polemics: The Dead End of African Literature', *Transition* 75/76. *The Anniversary Issue: Selections from Transition, 1961–1976* (1997), 335–41.

'A Prayer', in *The Unbroken Song: Selected Writings of Es'kia Mphahlele*, Johannesburg: Ravan, 1981, 304.

Nakasa, N. 'The human meaning of apartheid', *New York Times*, 24 September 1961, 42–9.

'Mr Nakasa goes to Harlem', *New York Times*, 7 February 1965, 40–61.

The World of Nat Nakasa, ed. E. Patel, Johannesburg: Picador Africa, 2005.

Nash, A. 'Zen Communist: Breyten Breyetenbach's View from Underground', *Tydskrif vir Letterkunde* 46:2 (2009), 11–27.

Ndebele, N. 'The Rediscovery of the Ordinary: Some New Writings in South Africa', *The Rediscovery of the Ordinary: Essays on South African Literature & Culture*, Fordsburg: COSAW, 1991.

Nkondo. G. 'Dennis Brutus: The Domestication of a Tradition', *World Literature Today* (1981), 32–40.

Nkosi, L. 'Art Contra Apartheid: South Africa Writers in Exile', *Genève Afrique: Journal of the Swiss Society of Africa Studies* 18:2 (1980), 68–71.

'The Forbidden Dialogue', *UNESCO Courier* 20:3 (1967), 20–2.

Home and Exile, London: Longman, 1965.

'Notes on Transition', *Transition* 34 (1967/8), 40.

'A Question of Literary Stewardship', *Transition* 14:5–6 (1969), 69–71.

'The Sting in the Adder's Tail', *Transition* (1964), 54–5.

Tasks and Masks: Themes and Styles in African Literature, Harlow: Longman, 1981.

'Where does African Literature go from Here?', *Africa Report* 11:9 (1966), 7–11.

Plaatje, S. T. *Native Life in South Africa: Before and since the European War and the Boer Rebellion* [1916], Johannesburg: Ravan, 1982.

Sampson, A. *Mandela: The Authorised Biography*, London: HarperCollins, 2000.

Wali, O. 'The Dead End of African Literature?', *Transition* 10 (1963), 13–16.

Yesufu, A. '*Black Orpheus* and Mbari: The Matrix of an Artistic Culture and Es'kia Mphahlele', in S. Raditlhalo and T. lo Liyong (eds.), *Es'kia: May you Grow as Big as an Elephant*, Rivonia: Stainbank & Associates, 2006, 100–9.

21

Afrikaans literature, 1948–1976

HEIN WILLEMSE

The period 1948–76 is arguably the most significant in Afrikaans literature, a time that coincided with greater social privileges, better education and the rapid urbanisation of white Afrikaans-speaking South Africans. The electoral triumph of Afrikaner nationalism in 1948 enhanced the place of the Afrikaans language in the civil service, the educational system and the economy. New Afrikaans publishing houses were established and sustained through favourable changes in the macro-political and economic conditions of the country, symbiotic relationships with the major Nationalist-supporting Afrikaans newspaper houses and printers, youthful entrepreneurship and, most importantly, the fostering of close relationships with the decision makers in the newly established apartheid education system for which purpose-made schoolbooks were produced (see Steyn, 'Eerste Dekades'; 'Nederige Begin'). It was a time of the *embourgeoisement* of the Afrikaner, a social change that clearly resonated in Afrikaans literature.

The cultural consequences of this political ascendancy included early attempts at stabilising and canonising Afrikaner literary culture, such as the ambitious three-volume series *Kultuurgeskiedenis van die Afrikaner* (Cultural History of the Afrikaner, 1948–51); a new literary history, *Perspektief en Profiel* (Perspective and Profile, 1951; since 1998 updated into three volumes) and a new anthology, *Groot Verseboek* (Great Book of Verse, 1951). The same need for stocktaking is also reflected in the comprehensive literary histories of Dekker (*Afrikaanse Literatuurgeskiedenis* [Afrikaans Literary History, 1935]), Antonissen (*Schets van den Ontwikkelingsgang der Zuid-Afrikaansche Letterkunde* [Sketch of the Development of South African Literature, 1946]) and Kannemeyer (*Geskiedenis van die Afrikaanse Literatuur* [History of Afrikaans Literature, 1978,

I wish to thank Willie Burger, Ampie Coetzee and Helize van Vuuren for their critical and supportive comments on a draft version of this chapter.

1983]). Since these literary histories have described Afrikaans literature so comprehensively, it would be prudent to read them in conjunction with this chapter.

The publication and increased social capital of the *Groot Verseboek* is an instructive example of the convergence of Afrikaner political power, social hegemony, cultural assertion and economic entrepreneurship. This best-selling compilation of the 'best Afrikaans poetry' was published in 1951 and thereafter regularly updated right up to the twenty-first century. The *Groot Verseboek* was aimed at the university, teachers' college and the general market; the *Senior Verseboek* and the *Junior Verseboek* were prescribed at secondary and primary schools respectively and pre-schoolers were catered for with the *Kleuterverseboek* (Nursery Book of Verse) and *Klein Verseboek* (Small Book of Verse/Book of Verse for the Little One).

Apart from Afrikaans poetry, much of Afrikaans literature before 1948 was directed at modestly educated readers with popular tastes (see Steyn, 'Vet en Maer Jare'). The new generation of Afrikaans writers were highly educated, often well travelled and multilingual in European languages. In their writings they systematically deepened the complexity of their craft and the breadth of literary debates, and exhibited relationships with fashionable European philosophies and trends. In the 1930s writers such as N. P. van Wyk Louw and many Afrikaans literary critics were closely aligned with Afrikaner nationalism. However, by the late 1960s this close relationship between the Afrikaner Nationalist establishment and the apartheid government on the one hand, and leading Afrikaans writers on the other, had become less secure. Following the imprisonment of Breyten Breytenbach on terrorism charges, and especially after the 1976 uprisings, several younger Afrikaans writers lost confidence in an apartheid state that through its policies and actions had shaped a place for the Afrikaans language (and by extension its literature) but which was now perceived to be antipathetic to the interests of the majority black South Africans.

In this chapter leading Afrikaans writers will be discussed with reference to the distinct shifts in literary approaches that underscored Afrikaans literary development: from metaphysical concerns to Afrikaner nationalist or women's and activist anti-apartheid writing; from undemanding realism to literary experimentation influenced by contemporary philosophies such as existentialism – writerly sensibilities that created texts connected to modernist and postmodernist tendencies outside the confines of Afrikaans or South African literature.

Themes in postwar Afrikaans poetry

By the 1950s Van Wyk Louw (1906–70) had established his reputation as the major poet of Afrikaans literature (see also Chapters 15 and 17). Throughout the period under discussion he had produced twelve plays in verse of which the most significant is *Germanicus* (1956), a tragedy set against the background of the Roman Empire that explores the strains of a cultured, aristocratic leader who wants to remain true to his core values of intellectuality, compassion and humaneness amidst a society that demands brutal and base political leadership. This theme is a continuation of Van Wyk Louw's struggle with the role and function of the intellectual in society, a topic that he explored extensively in his critical writings on culture and society and that he would return to in *Tristia* (1962), his most complex and diverse collection of poetry. This volume contains some of his most memorable verses: love poems, odes, *ars poetica* and social commentary. Here, this erstwhile dabbler with national socialism and supporter of Afrikaner nationalism became disillusioned with what the ruling Afrikaner establishment had become: its 'gracious living', its corruption, self-indulgence and arrogance ('Being an Afrikaner is not Holy' ['Nuusberigte 1956' – News Reports 1956], *Tristia*, p. 115).

Overall, the postwar generation of Afrikaans poets concerned themselves with social issues as much as they explored modernist influences. The leading poet of his generation was D J Opperman (1914–85) who, as a journal editor and compiler of the *Verseboek* anthologies, played a major role in shaping the Afrikaans poetry canon. Besides some initial metaphysical concerns in his first collection, *Heilige Beeste* (Holy Cattle, 1945), he broke decisively with the overpowering poetic presence of Van Wyk Louw and his predilection for metaphysical enquiry. Opperman's earlier poetry is stark, multilayered and metaphor-rich, with the poetic voice exploring a multiplicity of histories. His poetry is often characterised as an attempt at finding what T. S. Eliot called 'objective correlatives'. Opperman explored in compact verse the contemporary social processes of rural migration, industrialisation and the alienation of the individual in the 'grey landscape' of the city in collections such as *Engel uit die Klip* (Angel from the Stone, 1950) and *Blom en Baaierd* (Flower and Chaos, 1956). An early example of his poetic methodology of dehistoricisation and the creation of an 'universal aesthetic' is *Joernal van Jorik* (Jorik's Journal, 1949), an epic poem which most Afrikaans critics have read as a symbolic treatment of the history of white settlement in South Africa interwoven with conceptions of right and wrong, mid-twentieth-century tensions between nationalism, communism and capitalism, and notions of the 'universal' human condition and western civilisation.

S. J. Pretorius (1917–95) expressed in his earlier volumes – *Vonke* (Sparks, 1943), *Die Arbeider en ander Gedigte* (The Worker and other Poems, 1945) – an identification with workers' struggles and a concern with rural migration and the difficult lives of the poor and marginalised, as did Opperman and several other South African writers across various writing traditions. If Pretorius's social concerns at times went beyond the struggles of the Afrikaner worker, then G. A. Watermeyer (1917–72) became known for his strident support of racial purity: 'Stay white, my people, stay white in spirit', especially in his privately issued volume, *Die Republiek van 'n Duisend Jaar* (The Republic of a Thousand Years, 1957). Most Afrikaans anthologies eschewed this part of his literary output and instead selected his personal lyrical poems or his best-known poem 'Ballade van die Bloeddorstige Jagter' ('Ballad of the Bloodthirsty Hunter') from *Sekel and Simbaal* (Sickle and Cymbal, 1948) that reflects an ecological sensitivity at variance with his chauvinist political views.

Much of Ernst van Heerden's (1916–97) earlier poetry in *Weerlose Uur* (Defenceless Hour, 1942) and *Verklaarde Nag* (Explained Night / Avowed Night, 1946) followed in the tradition of Van Wyk Louw's metaphysical poetry as well as late nineteenth and early twentieth-century English and Dutch poets, while his subsequent award-winning collections explored in stark verse a greater register of themes demonstrating a considerable range of world literary influences. Most notably, these included responses to the pastoral, religion, language, the act of writing, European classical music, eroticism, the achievement and physicality of the male sporting figure and its inevitable physical decline or confinement, while in his collections written in the 1980s the topicality of the South African apartheid experience is probed.

S. V. Petersen (1914–87) is considered to be the first coloured Afrikaans poet – a social appellation that he abhorred in later life. In a literary tradition that since the onset of the twentieth century had flourished with the demands and successes of Afrikaner nationalism, he was an early exception. In a sociopolitical sense his immediate forerunner was Peter Abrahams (also classified as coloured), who published poetry and short stories in English prior to Petersen's *Die Enkeling* (The Loner, 1944). As a teacher from a rural background, Petersen's collections often contain contemplative pastoral lyrics with reactions to an individualised, alienated urban existence. In his oeuvre he repeatedly protested against his social rejection and experiences of racial marginality.

Besides Petersen, a number of other black Afrikaans writers, among them P. J. Philander, Adam Small and Arthur Fula, began publishing their work during this period. Paul Roubaix (a pseudonym for Isaac Pfaff, 1920–2005), who published *Storm en Ander Eenbedrywe* (Storm and Other One-Act Plays, 1951), was the first black Afrikaans dramatist and some of his one-act plays were considered 'complicated' and 'original' with an ongoing tension between the perceived aesthetic demand for universalisation and social commitment.

The most interesting examples in the oeuvre of P. J. Philander (1921–2006) are his earlier collections published before his emigration to the United States. The texture and imagery of his post-emigration poetry lost the immediacy of a living language most clearly evident in his autobiographical novella *Rebunie* (the name of a mountain, literally 'Don't Call Me', 2000). Philander explored in three monologues the histories of the nineteenth-century (Namibian) historical figures of Jager Afrikaner, Jonker Afrikaner, Hendrik Witbooi or reinterpretations of Khoikhoi history in his second collection *Vuurklip* (Flint/Fire Stone, 1960) and the naturalist lyric or ancient master–slave relationships in his debut collection, *Uurglas* (Hourglass, 1955). Philander's poems are conscious attempts at writing the neglected history of indigenous and colonised people. Later he wrote an underrated work on the Phoenician myth in Africa, that is, the theory that Great Zimbabwe had been built by (Middle Eastern) foreigners. In Philander's rendering, the epic poem *Zimbabwe* (1968) becomes the tale of abortive colonisation, brought about by the settlers' insularity, a theme that could be interpreted as a barely disguised reference to the apartheid state (see Willemse, 'Insularity and Ambivalence', p. 144).

By the late 1950s and the beginning of the 1960s poets such as Peter Blum, Barend J. Toerien, Lionel Sheldon (*Weeklaag van die Wese* [Lament of the Orphans/Excluded], 1960) and Adam Small wrote poetry with revealing social sensitivity. Toerien (1921–2009) writes reminiscences of youth and an earlier pastoral existence, elegies of personal loss and, in well-developed rounded verse, poetry in which the excesses of apartheid privilege are explored. His later poetry, often written outside South Africa, reflects experiences of the traveller, the newness of foreign soils, the longing for the homeland and family and the concerns of the politically aware individual (see his collected poems *Om te Onthou* [To Remember], 2006).

Satire, neologism, multilingualism and a healthy disregard for political or social authority mark the poetry of Peter Blum (1925–90). Blum's work arose from an avowed cosmopolitanism and although he published only two books of poetry, *Steenbok tot Poolsee* (Capricorn to Polar Sea, 1955) and *Enklaves van die Lig* (Enclaves of Light, 1958), several of his poems are regarded as unique contributions to Afrikaans poetry. One set of three sonnets, 'Drie Uiterstes' ('Three Extremes'), tells of gradual degeneration: in the first increasing deafness, in the second blindness and in the third the pending madness in which language itself deteriorates into utter senselessness. In another series of light-hearted sonnets – 'Kaapse Sonnette' ('Cape Sonnets') – Blum employs the Cape Peninsula's working-class patois to send up stiff, middle-class Afrikaner values, social life and monuments.

In his most successful writings the poet-dramatist-philosopher Adam Small (1936–) uses the same Cape working-class patois to comical and ironic effect. In collections such as *Kitaar my Kruis* (Guitar my Cross, 1961) and *Sê Sjibbolet* (Say Shibboleth, 1963) the poet protests against the second-class status of those classified as coloured under apartheid and draws parallels with the Old Testament histories of Egyptian slavery and the leadership qualities of a modern-day Moses. Small's most outstanding and innovative work is the play *Kanna hy Kô Hystoe* (1965; translated as *Kanna, he's Coming Home*, 1992), in which some of the same linguistic and stylistic features of his poetry are present: the well-educated figure of whom so much is expected, but who has left his downtrodden family behind and only returns for one last time to bury his adoptive mother. The figure of Small, and the perceived black authenticity of his poetry, would influence a generation of black Afrikaans writers who associated themselves with Black Consciousness in the mid 1970s and 1980s (see Willemse, 'Emergent Black Afrikaans Poets').

Women poets in Afrikaans

When Elisabeth Eybers (1915–2007) published her first collection *Belydenis in die Skemering* (Confession in the Twilight, 1936) there was virtually no Afrikaans poetry written by women. At the time of her death women had come to dominate Afrikaans poetry. Today some of the most prominent and innovative poets are women and many of them regard Eybers as the doyenne of women's writing in Afrikaans. On her passing, one literary critic called Eybers a 'phenomenal poetess' who had lived exactly half her life in South Africa and the other half in her adopted country of the Netherlands, and had achieved the highest literary recognition in both (Ester, 'Met Elisabeth Eybers', p. 181). Over the course of her long career and in her many poetry collections (twenty-five in total) she chronicled in often direct, compact verse a wide range of personal topics: the adolescent awareness of a young girl, the experiences of motherhood, divorce, the invasiveness of mastectomy, the vagaries of life in a foreign country and approaching death. Even though she was an intensely private poet, she contemplates in her later collections the writer's artistic responsibilities or delivers critical social commentary. Her *Versamelde Gedigte* (Collected Poems, 2004) contains more than nine hundred poems.

Although a small number of Afrikaans women poets published texts after Eybers's ground-breaking debut, it was really Olga Kirsch's *Die Soeklig* (The Searchlight, 1944) and, ten years later, Ina Rousseau's *Verlate Tuin* (Abandoned Garden, 1954) that marked an upsurge of significant women's writing in Afrikaans literature. Kirsch (1924–97), the daughter of a Jewish-Lithuanian immigrant, explored, apart from her poetry of love and personal loss, the history of the Jewish diaspora, the impact of the Holocaust, her solidarity with the proverbial 'Wandering Jew' and matters of anti-apartheid social concern. Shortly after the publication of her second collection, *Mure van die Hart* (Walls of the Heart, 1948), she made *aliyah*, namely, emigrated to the newly created state of Israel. In her five post-*aliyah* collections she recalls the life and death of her parents, her youth in a rural South African town and the deep-rooted tensions of the ongoing strife in the Middle East.

The overall impression of the poetry of Rousseau (1926–2005) is her attention to her craft, her preference for traditional forms and her economical use of language. Her poetry reveals a wide interest in a variety of subjects. In *Verlate Tuin* the core theme refers to the abandonment of the Edenic garden of Judaeo-Christian mythology, while the biblical apocalypse dominates in *'n Onbekende Jaartal* (An Unknown Year, 1995). Her fascination with life forms and nature is apparent in the exploration of botanical classification and personal relationships in *Taxa* (1970), or the geological and ecological in *Kwiksilwersirkel* (Ring of Mercury, 1978).

When Nelson Mandela, in his first presidential speech in 1994, quoted 'Die Kind wat Doodgeskiet is deur Soldate by Nyanga' ('The Child who was Shot Dead by Soldiers at Nyanga') he made the name of Ingrid Jonker (1933–65) internationally recognisable for a poem that evokes the killing of a child in 'a location of the surrounded heart'. Although not primarily a public or activist poet, her concern in this poem (from her innovative volume, *Rook en Oker* [Smoke and Ochre], 1963) is illustrative of a younger generation of Afrikaans writers, the Sestigers, whose work showed increased awareness of the violence underscoring apartheid. To her followers her poetical legacy, apart from this poem, rests on her playful and light children's verse as well as her intense lyrical and love poetry, which has often been set to music by Afrikaans composers. Her tragic personal life and suicide at the age of 31 caused her to become a cult figure in South African literature, reminiscent of Sylvia Plath, Anne Sexton or Alejandra Pizarnik.

Beyond 'good-natured local realism'

Afrikaans authors of the early twentieth century wrote for a largely unassuming readership, producing didactic works mapped on to the idealised feudalism of a farm, the rigours of rural migration and the struggles of poor and impoverished (white) characters in unrelenting cities. Unlike the poetry of the late 1940s and 1950s, the prose fiction and dramatic output for the period were often regarded as undemanding. In postwar South Africa, leading literary critics increasingly demanded Afrikaans fictional or dramatic works that were aesthetically more challenging. By the end of the 1950s Van Wyk Louw's authoritative characterisation was that much of Afrikaans fictional (and dramatic) writing was *gemoedelike lokale realisme* ('good-natured local realism').

Short-story writers such as Boerneef (pseudonym for I. W. van der Merwe, 1897–1967), C. G. S. de Villiers (1894–1978) and M. I. Murray (1899–1983) excelled in their depiction of folksy characters in uncomplicated rural settings. Their unaffected characters tell of their experiences in regional argots, thereby providing insights into old traditions, folkloric beliefs or the marginalised world of black labourers, farmers, small-town types and reminiscing elderly narrators. In the best of these collections the reader gains an understanding of the constitutive forces or personal and social restraints that go beyond the retelling of interesting localised anecdotes.

White nationalist politicians often held out the vision of an independent republic. This promise came to fulfilment when the Republic of South Africa was established in May 1961 outside the Commonwealth. It is telling that prominent novelists such as Anna M. Louw and F. A. Venter underscored this political achievement with historical novels. Venter (1916–97) wrote a tetralogy – *Geknelde Land* (Land of Oppression, 1960), *Offerland* (Land of Sacrifice, 1963), *Gelofteland* (Land of the Covenant, 1966) and *Bedoelde Land* (The Promised Land, 1968) – recalling the Great Trek and the suffering, loss and triumph of the trekkers: a key event in the political mythology of Afrikaner nationalism. Venter is best remembered for his early prize-winning novels *Swart Pelgrim* (1952, translated as *Dark Pilgrim*, 1959) and *Man van Ciréne* (Man of Cyrene, 1957). These books were reprinted several times and set as prescribed works in high schools across the apartheid education system, including black and coloured schools. The latter novel recounts the life of Simon Niger, a non-believer of 'swarthy complexion' who was forced to carry Jesus's cross. He converted because of this experience and was ultimately crucified for propagating his new beliefs. In *Swart Pelgrim* a naive rural black man descends into urban criminality and steals from a white woman who rescues him from his evil ways; he eventually realises that a black man has no place in the white city. Some critics regard both novels as steeped in the racist ideologies associated with apartheid spatial planning, white authority and black subservience (Coetzee, 'Literature and Crisis', p. 338).

Across South Africa's literary traditions several novelists have written such 'Jim comes to Jo'burg' works; the best known of these are Alan Paton's *Cry, the Beloved Country* (1948) and Peter Abrahams's *Mineboy* (1946). Black Afrikaans writers including S. V. Petersen (*As die Son Ondergaan* [When the Sun Sets], 1945), Arthur Fula (*Jôhannie Giet die Beeld*, 1954; translated as *The Golden Magnet*, 1984) and Eddie Domingo (*Okkies op die Breë Pad* [Okkies on the Broad Road], 1955) have written similar novels. Fula had the distinction of being the first Xhosa mother-tongue speaker to use Afrikaans as a medium of literary expression (Willemse, *Aan die Ander Kant*, pp. 117–33). Most of these novels bear an anti-modernisation message of urban decay, personal neglect and debauchery, often ending with the redeeming insight that the city is a bad place.

Some of the more important prose fiction contributions in the first decade after 1948 are those of W. A. de Klerk (1917–96), Dolf van Niekerk (1929–) and Jan Rabie (1920–2001). De Klerk was known primarily as a playwright and also wrote several novels including *Die Uur van Verlange* (The Hour of Longing, 1953). In this novel a young Afrikaner goes off to study in America, the symbol of the new; in itself this personal decision is justified as an act of patriotism. On his return he becomes the archetypal *volks* capitalist, embodying the 'new [Afrikaner] nobility' that leads 'his people' from rural subsistence to industrial prosperity. Although the author allows one of his secondary characters to voice a humanist, anti-apartheid position that challenges the Afrikaner *embourgeoisement*, the novel remains largely ambivalent on these matters. In his best play *Die Jaar van die Vuur-Os* (The Year of the Fire-Ox, 1952), De Klerk is less circumspect in his support for greater social coexistence between all South Africans.

Like Rabie, Van Niekerk is often described as a forerunner of the Afrikaans modernising generation. His best-known novel, *Die Son Struikel* (The Sun Stumbles, 1960), is set against a period of war, resistance and a mine-worker strike with an outsider as the main character. He consistently creates outsider characters in his plays, short stories and novels. In later years he wrote successful youth novels and in his latest works, especially his poetry, explores the relationship between human beings and their natural environment.

In Rabie's *Ons, die Afgod* (Us, the Idol, 1958) there is none of the ambivalence that marks De Klerk's *Die Uur van Verlange*. Rabie unequivocally criticises the Afrikaner nationalist's 'idolatry of race' and the novel's main character advances views that support a common humanity: 'I hope anxiously with faith that my people will realise that the divinity resides in every being, that nobody dares to be someone else's superior or boss... give us the power to become South Africans' (Rabie, *Ons, die Afgod*, p. 145). Even if his literary contemporaries regarded the novel as overwritten didacticism, it gave rise to a fierce newspaper polemic in which Rabie was established as a socially engaged writer and the standard-bearer for 'detribalised' anti-apartheid Afrikaners (Kannemeyer, *Jan Rabie*, pp. 288–301). Whereas Venter's tetralogy focuses on a narrow white mythology, Rabie's *Bolandia* series – *Eiland voor Afrika* (Island in front of Africa, 1964), *Die Groot Anders-Maak* (The Great Make-Over, 1964), *Waar Jý Sterwe* (1966; translated as *A Man Apart*, 1969), *Ark* (1977) and *En Oseaan* (And Ocean, 1985) – promotes the kinship of white and coloured Afrikaans speakers and tells the story of the Afrikaans language as a creolisation narrative which explicitly repudiates apartheid orthodoxy.

A Parisian sojourn in the early 1950s and Rabie's acquaintance with contemporary French philosophy and European writing heavily influenced his earlier works, especially *21* (1956), a collection of short stories, and *Mens-Alleen* (Man-Alone, 1963), a novel of Kafkaesque qualities foreshadowing the existentialism of the Sestiger generation (Kannemeyer, *Geskiedenis*, p. 340). *21* is universally acknowledged as one of the more important short-story collections in Afrikaans literature. The collection of twenty-one short-short stories contains mostly surrealist or symbolic descriptions of degradation, perverted humanity and existential angst. The stories suggest a variety of sources and backgrounds, such as a warring Europe, a Southern African drought or Asian myths. For a subsequent generation of writers Rabie became the literary, if not intellectual, godfather in his radical break with the 'local realism' of an earlier generation, his adoption of modernist literary strategies and his anti-apartheid political stance.

The Sestigers and beyond

Following the events of 21 March 1960, when the South African police killed sixty-nine anti-pass protesters in Sharpeville, a group of Afrikaner clergy, among them Beyers Naudé, formally distanced themselves from the justification of apartheid on biblical grounds. On the whole, however, white society remained detached from the social upheaval, forced removals, treason trials and the intensification of state repression of black resistance that exemplified the black experience of the 1950s and 1960s. Precious little of this social ferment was reported in the Afrikaans writing of the preceding decade or the early 1960s. The enhanced support for the National Party and the increased prosperity of the white electorate overwhelmed the voices of mild concern that some Afrikaans writers occasionally expressed.

The National Party government extended its considerable hold on power to include stricter control over the media and publications when they enacted the Publications and Entertainment Act, Act 26 of 1963, which aimed to censor or ban material regarded as undesirable. The net result was that a number of writers were banned and/or had their books censored. In 1974 André P. Brink's *Kennis van die Aand* (1973; *Looking on Darkness*, 1974) was the first Afrikaans novel to be banned under this legislation. General political control was pervasive and extended well beyond the statutory provisions. Political acquiescence permeated most levels of Afrikaner cultural life: its churches, schools, universities and academic associations. For instance, when a prestigious prize was awarded to one of the Sestigers, Etienne Leroux (pseudonym for S. P. D. le Roux, 1922–89), fierce objections were raised on the grounds that the novel, *Sewe Dae by die Silbersteins* (Seven Days at the Silbersteins, 1962), was obscene, blasphemous and above all alien to the *volk*.

The Sestigers, named after a group of Afrikaans writers associated with the short-lived journal *Sestiger* (Sixtyer, 1963–5) became the signature Afrikaans grouping of the period after 1961. Writers such as Brink and Leroux, Breytenbach, Van Niekerk, Rabie, Abraham H. de Vries, Bartho Smit, Chris Barnard and Hennie Aucamp contributed to the journal, which quickly became known for its lively polemics, literary experimentation and pronounced aim that writers 'participate for change in literature; a change that . . . is necessary' (Anonymous, 'Redaksioneel', p. 1). The group consisted of mostly white male writers, with Adam Small the sole 'Black Sestiger'.

Leroux's *Sewe Dae by die Silbersteins* is a primary example of his *procédé*: seven chapters, seven days, seven sins and a tight structure with parallel or recurring (but ultimately progressive) events and themes; the Afrikaans literary trope of the farm novel is reinterpreted in line with the emergence of the Afrikaner nouveau riche. A naive young man, named van Eeden (literally 'from Eden') arrives on a highly industrialised estate for his arranged marriage; over a period of seven days his future, presumably Jewish, father-in-law initiates him into different social groupings and guides him through contemporary issues of good and evil, alienation and conformity, desolation, perversion, morality, myth, mysticism and modernity. This novel established Leroux as a major Afrikaans writer while it introduced Afrikaans readers and literary critics to the mysticism of the Jewish Kabbalah and Jung's exploration of 'archetypes', the 'collective unconscious' and 'individuation'. His subsequent novels, *Een vir Azazel* (One for Azazel – The Goat Demon, 1964) and *Die Derde Oog* (The Third Eye, 1966) complete the trilogy (published as *To a Dubious Salvation*, 1972), in which characters or themes from *Sewe Dae by die Silbersteins* reoccur but are developed or pursued in different directions. If Rabie's *21* was a clear indication that Afrikaans prose fiction was heading away from tried and tested naturalism, then this series of novels pointed to its new direction in symbolism, deliberate stylistic experimentation, intertextuality, iconoclasm and the conscious transgression of social mores. *Magersfontein, O Magersfontein!* (1976; translated under the same title in 1983), banned by the censors for its irreverence, is perhaps Leroux's most comic novel, a parody of the 1899 Battle of Magersfontein during the Anglo-Boer War in which the British Army suffered huge losses in a trench war against the Boer forces (see also Chapter 12).

Since his days as the editor of *Sestiger*, André P. Brink (1935–) has been the keenest proponent of literary innovation and one of the most outspoken anti-apartheid Afrikaans writers, although his earliest novellas – *Meul Teen die Hang* (Mill Against the Slope, 1958), *Die Gebondenes* (The Bounded, 1958) and *Eindelose Weë* (Unending Ways, 1960) – still bear the imprint of the unchallenging pastoralism of an earlier generation of Afrikaans novelists. He is one of the most prolific South African writers who, besides his novels, publishes poetry, plays, short stories, book club love stories, young adult fiction, travelogues, literary criticism, essays and translations.

Lobola vir die Lewe (Lobola for Life, 1962) was influenced by post-Second World War philosophies and the French *nouveau roman*. Along with Leroux's *Sewe Dae by die Silbersteins*, it has been identified as the epitome of the new Afrikaans novel: a demonstration of writerly experimentation, modernist and philosophical relativity, individual alienation and existentialism, and an explicit exploration of sexuality and religion. Although Brink's fifth novel, *Die Ambassadeur* (1963; translated as *The Ambassador*, 1964, 1985), is also strongly experimental in its presentation of narratological structures and inter-textuality, it has less of the overt insistence on the new that characterised the preceding novel.

Having tested the extravagances of novelistic modernism and experimentation (especially in *Orgie* [Orgy], 1965), Brink returned in *Kennis van die Aand* and *'n Oomblik in die Wind* (1975; *An Instant in the Wind*, 1976) to novels that are more realist and extended his writerly interests to works that are self-consciously political. In his critical writing he acknowledges his attraction to a Sartrean *littérature engagée* that prefigured his role as a socially committed writer, professing personal agency and the moral responsibility to contest apartheid oppression. Brink conceives of his coloured main character in *Kennis van die Aand*, a socially committed actor condemned to the gallows for the murder of his white girlfriend, as a transgressive figure whose actions deliberately invert notions of 'typical' racialised social behaviour. He becomes the accuser indicting consecutive local systems of historical and present injustice (see Gerwel, *Literatuur en Apartheid*, pp. 51, 82, 206). Written at a time when sexual relations between black and white people were prohibited in South Africa, this overtly political novel was bound to attract the attention of the censors. *'n Oomblik in die Wind* is an historical novel about the unfolding love relationship between a white woman lost in the wilderness and a runaway slave where the intricacies of journeying, as in so many of Brink's novels, becomes the real story. This is probably his most accomplished earlier novel and the first one in which he introduces a feminist female character, a feature that would mark his writing in the 1980s and 1990s.

Also closely aligned to the aesthetic experimentation of the Sestigers is the playwright Bartho Smit (1924–86), who in *Putsonderwater* (1962; translated as *Well-without-water or the Virgin and the Vultures*, 1968) drew on the examples of Samuel Beckett, Eugène Ionesco and the European tradition of the Theatre of the Absurd. For years local theatre organisations refused permission to stage his earlier social drama *Die Verminktes* (The Maimed, 1960), about a coloured man who passes for white and strikes up a relationship with a white woman. Many of his other plays were more successful and he achieved his greatest success with *Christine* (1971) and *Die Keiser* (The Emperor, 1977), the latter a reinterpretation of the naked emperor fairy-tale, this time set in tropical Africa. Other prominent dramatists of the period are P. G. du Plessis and Pieter Fourie, who both wrote plays in which they used innovative theatre techniques to explore social questions.

As a popular genre the short story has a long history in Afrikaans literature. Prominent short-story writers like Chris Barnard (1939–), Abraham H. de Vries (1937–) and Hennie Aucamp (1934–) responded in different ways to the Afrikaans modernist renewal. In some of Barnard's short stories in *Duiwel-in-die-bos* (Devil-in-the-bush, 1968) but especially in the novel *Mahala* (1971), the interrelationship between good and evil (with allusions to Conrad's *Heart of Darkness*) are created through the application of innovative narrative structuring. Both De Vries and Aucamp rework regionalist storytelling in new ways. Whereas Barnard's plays (for instance *Pa, Maak vir my 'n Vlieër, Pa* (Dad, make me a Kite, Dad, 1964) drew on the Theatre of the Absurd, his earlier short stories often have a dark, threatening feel. De Vries's short stories are mostly set in the recognisable settings of the Little Karoo, although their characters' lives are often more complicated and told with narrative competency and a refined sense of linguistic register. And whilst Aucamp also set his well-organised, well-told stories in recognisable settings, his writing became more encompassing in his exploration of the pressures on individuals in a variety of decadent, homosexual or regional settings. Another short-story writer of note is Henriette Grové (1922–2009). The collections *Jaarringe* (Year Rings, 1966), *Winterreis* (Winter Journey, 1971) and *Die Kêrel van die Pêrel of Anatomie van 'n Leuenaar* (The Gentlemen from the Pearl or Anatomy of a Liar, 1983) are generally considered her best work. She is known for her well-structured, intellectually sophisticated short stories, plays or novellas, which concentrate on the experiences of women or children against settings of complex, often gloomy, human relations that permit the exploration of notions of remembering or understanding past behaviour, the confrontation of opposing social values or the nature of reality and illusion, truth and deceit.

Anna M. Louw (1913–2003) started her career by writing short stories, travelogues and plays but made her mark with two early idealising historical novels, *Die Banneling: Die Lyfwag* (The Exile: The Bodyguard, 1964) and *Die Groot Gryse* (The Revered Grey One, 1968) on President Paul Kruger (1825–1904), also known in Afrikaner nationalist mythology as 'the father of the Afrikaner *volk*'. Although she received an important literary award for South African English writing for *Twenty Days that Autumn* (1964) – an exploration of the lives and interactions of four sets of South Africans between the date of the Sharpeville killings and the first attempt on the life of the South African prime minister, Hendrik Verwoerd, on 9 April 1960 – her more significant contribution was to longer Afrikaans fiction, especially the family farm epic *Kroniek van Perdepoort* (Chronicle of Perdepoort, 1975). This a-chronological, allegorical and symbolic tale on the morbid goings-on over the weekend of the reinterment of an immodest Afrikaner patriarch reveals the proverbial seven deadly sins of his family. The writer reinterprets the tradition of the Afrikaans farm novel and compellingly probes the narrow divide between good and evil.

Elsa Joubert, unlike her fellow Afrikaans travel writers, undertook extensive trips to eastern and northern Africa, Angola, Mozambique and several Indian Ocean islands. She wrote in her autobiography: 'It is not because I [was] brave, I [was] jumpy but I [knew] I had to go there' (*'n Wonderlike Geweld*, p. 385). Her travelogues informed her prose fiction, especially when history, geography and exoticism gave way to explorations of the essential humaneness of her characters or the giving of a voice to women in *Die Swerfjare van Poppie Nongena* or its Afrikaner family counterpart in *Die Reise van Isobelle* (1995; translated as *Isobelle's Journey*, 2002). Her novella *Ons Wag op die Kaptein* (We're Waiting on the Captain, 1963; translated as *To Die at Sunset*, 1982) is set in Angola and represents her first attempt at portraying the processes of decolonisation and posing the often asked question in Afrikaans literature of the place of the 'white man in Africa'. In her treatment the political and social are intertwined with a messianic judgement – the capitalised 'Captain' of the title – awaiting both coloniser and colonised. *Ons Wag op die Kaptein* introduced the trope of the South African apocalyptic novel - best exemplified by J. M. Coetzee's *Waiting for the Barbarians* (1980) and *Life & Times of Michael K* (1983) – where communities or individuals live on the cusp of radical social change or social disintegration.

During the final years of the period under discussion Joubert wrote her most committed work as literary non-fiction, a book that brought her international acclaim, namely *Die Swerfjare van Poppie Nongena* (1978; translated as *The Long Journey of Poppie Nongena*, 1980), the biography of a black woman's – Ntombizodumo Eunice Ntsatha (Joubert, *Reisiger*, p. 298) – unbearable struggle to keep her family together under the National Party's homeland policy. At the time of publication one commentator caused an uproar when he said that the book illustrated the 'institutional violence' of apartheid; that it would be impossible to say afterwards 'that we [the Afrikaners] never knew what the real state of affairs was and that we did not know that our laws caused this much devastation to people's lives' (Degenaar, *Voortbestaan*, pp. 65–6). Against this background it is perhaps more than ironic that the book won every available Afrikaans literary award.

As a literary persona Karel Schoeman (1939–) stands apart from his peers. In his early twenties he committed himself to Catholicism, against an Afrikaner cultural and social environment of the 1960s that did not embrace religious beliefs other than the Dutch Reformed Protestant tradition. He served several years as a novice in an Irish Franciscan monastery and although he published biographical works on St Francis of Assisi he did not finish his training as a priest and in later life became deeply interested in Buddhism. Schoeman is one of the most prolific Afrikaans writers. He has published novels, travelogues, biographical studies on, inter alia, Lucy Lloyd, Olive Schreiner and Irma Stern, autobiographies, translations from Gaelic, and historiographical monographs on the early Dutch colony, slavery, the Free State province, and a Griqua settlement in central Southern Africa.

Schoeman's Irish period resulted in *By Fakkellig* (By Torch Light, 1966), his first significant historical novel on the Irish resistance of the late eighteenth century. As in many of his subsequent novels, the main character is an outsider involved in an internal struggle over commitment. In this instance engagement translates into active political commitment, which is not the case in novels such as *Na die Geliefde Land* (1972; translated as *Promised Land*, 1978), *Om te Sterwe* (To Die, 1976) or *Die Hemeltuin* (The Heavenly Garden, 1979), where the main character remains an inactive observer. Schoeman's characters are often aesthetically sophisticated, socially alienated and asexual but keen observers of environments culturally alien to them. Even if his main characters are no paragons of physical action and the plot often relies on interiorised growth, Schoeman produces meticulously constructed prose with little of the experimentation that distinguished Afrikaans modernism in the early 1960s or postmodernism in the 1980s and 1990s.

Towards the end of the period under discussion violence in its brutal realistic forms was written into Afrikaans literature by P. J. Haasbroek and John Miles. Haasbroek's early short stories collections include *Heupvuur* (Fire of the Hip, 1974), *Roofvis* (Predator Fish, 1975) and *Skrikbewind* (Reign of Terror, 1976). His tales of military violence, terrorism and interrogation presage the *grensliteratuur* (border literature): a literature of war, military violence and white conscription that would dominate during the 1980s. Miles's short stories in *Liefs nie op Straat nie* (Preferably not on the Street, 1970) are reminiscent of Rabie's *21* and Breytenbach's *Katastrofes* in their exploration of blood and gore, while his thriller *Okker Bestel Twee Toebroodjies* (Okker Orders Two Sandwiches, 1973) involves espionage, kidnapping and political violence. These themes reoccur in his subsequent fictional texts, *Blaaskans* (Breathing Space, 1983) and *Kroniek uit die Doofpot* (1991; translated as *A Deafening Silence*, 1995); the latter is a fictionalised account of the actual killing in the late 1980s of a black policeman at the hands of his white colleagues.

The primary poet associated with the Sestigers is Breyten Breytenbach, whose career as a published poet was interrupted by a long prison sentence for anti-apartheid activities. His marriage to a Vietnamese woman gave rise to official unease and his wife was refused permission to visit South Africa where such marriages were prohibited by law. In the late 1980s Breytenbach played a key role in arranging strategic conferences between exiled South African liberation organisations and internal business, political and writers' groups that would partly pave the way to a democratic dispensation.

Breytenbach's poetry debut *Die Ysterkoei Moet Sweet* (The Iron Cow Must Sweat, 1964) made an immediate impression on publication. In a relatively conservative literary environment, his work drew on western classical, European literary and Protestant religious traditions, but also on eastern philosophies, especially a Taoist version of Zen Buddhism; his use of Afrikaans was innovative; his preferred poetical form was free verse with intuitive word, image, rhythmical or sound association; and as a painter his visual imagery was visceral with less of the neatly constructed metaphors of Opperman and his followers. Breytenbach wrote some of the most beautiful personal lyric and love poetry in Afrikaans literature in collections such as *Die Huis van die Dowe* (The House of the Deaf, 1967) and *Lotus* (1970). In much of his poetry he combines surrealist expression with a disarming playful directness or explores the recurring leitmotifs of life and death, growth and excretion, incarceration and freedom, as well as a love–hate relationship with the country of his birth.

The volume *Skryt. Om 'n Sinkende Skip Blou te Verf* (Skryt. To Paint a Sinking Ship Blue, 1972) was banned by the South African censorship board for its overt political verse. 'Skryt' is an Afrikaans neologism that hints at a number of derivations: writing, shouting or shitting. This collection also contains some of Breytenbach's most explicit political poetry, especially the poem 'Brief uit die Vreemde aan Slagter' ('Letter to Butcher from Abroad'), dedicated to the South African prime minister B. J. Vorster. *Voetskrif* (Foot Writing / Foot Script / Foot Deed [document], 1976), written during Breytenbach's pretrial incarceration, marked the beginning of an enforced seven-year silence. His subsequent publications, including his prison diary, *The True Confessions of an Albino Terrorist* (1984), and six individual prison poetry volumes compiled under the single title *Die Ongedanste Dans* (The Undanced Dance, 2005), would only be published after his release from prison in 1983.

Wilma Stockenström (1933–) is generally considered to be one of the more significant poetic voices in Afrikaans. Her early volumes include *Vir die Bysiende Leser* (For the Myopic Reader, 1970) and *Spieël van Water* (Mirror of Water, 1973); the latter notable for some poems critical of political and social pomposity, reminiscent of the satirical poetry of Peter Blum. Besides poetry she published plays and prose fiction including *Uitdraai* (Turn-Off, 1976), the farm novel revisited, and the critically acclaimed *Die Kremetartekspedisie* (1981; translated by J. M. Coetzee as *The Expedition to the Baobab Tree*, 1983). Her cryptic, stark verse often explores the primordiality of people and animals in the African landscape, most notably in *Van Vergetelheid en van Glans* (On Forgetfulness and Brilliance, 1976), that shows interesting folkloric and thematic correspondences with *Die Kremetartekspedisie*, in which a slave woman who gets lost during an expedition reconstructs in a delirious monologue her previous life and relationships with the indigenous people.

Apart from the towering presence of Breytenbach, a range of poets including Stephan Bouwer, Phil du Plessis, Marlise Joubert, Wilhelm Knobel, Freda
Plekker, Wessel Pretorius, Henk Rall and J. C. Steyn published 'competent . . . poetry . . . in the established aesthetic and monologic tradition' (Coetzee, 'Literature and Crisis', p. 358). Wopko Jensma, who published his first
Afrikaans poems in *Sestiger*, produced three avant-garde collections, *Sing for
our Execution* (1973), *Where White is the Colour/Where Black is the Number* (1974)
and *I Must Show you my Clippings* (1977) with mainly English and some Afrikaans
poetry, while M. M. Walters, Lina Spies and George Weideman wrote satire,
religious and regionalist poetry respectively. Sheila Cussons and Antjie Krog
published their first collections, poets who would develop into major literary figures producing their most accomplished work after 1976, a period
distinguished by prominent women writers.

During this period Afrikaans literature in scope and volume had developed
and grown far beyond the expectations of its first creative writers. By the
end of the 1930s the Dertigers had given Afrikaans readers a fillip with the
complexity of their poetry and their modernist sophistication. Three decades
later the Afrikaans writing tradition as a whole had gone through a steep
learning curve in which its writers had challenged traditional literary values
and adopted new worldly ways. At the base of these developments were not
only the writers' individual ingenuity but primarily a social, economic and
political system that affirmed the Afrikaans language and Afrikaans literature.
It is within this context that by the 1980s more Afrikaans books in all its variety
were published than in any other indigenous South African language. The
centrality of the Afrikaans language in the history of Afrikaner nationalist rule
was demonstrated in 1976 when thousands of students protested against the
enforced use of Afrikaans as a language of instruction in black schools. Whilst
for most Afrikaans speakers during the period 1948–76 the language and its
literature became two potent symbols of cultural empowerment, Afrikaner
establishment leaders regarded post-1960 anti-apartheid Afrikaans writing as
treason against their nationalist cause. At the same time the language became
the derided sign of black disempowerment.

Bibliography

Abrahams, P. *Mineboy*, London: Dorothy Crisp, 1946.
Anonymous, 'Redaksioneel', *Sestiger* 1:3 (1964), 1.
Antonissen, R. *Die Afrikaanse letterkunde van aanvang tot hede*, Cape Town: Nasou, 1955.
    Schets van den Ontwikkelingsgang der Zuid-Afrikaansche Letterkunde, Diest: Pro Arte, 1946.

Aucamp, H. *'n Bruidsbed vir Tannie Nonnie*, Cape Town: Tafelberg, 1970.

Dooierus, Cape Town: Tafelberg, 1976.

Die hartseerwals, Johannesburg: Afrikaanse Pers-Boekhandel, 1965.

Hongerblom, Cape Town: Tafelberg, 1972.

House Visits, Cape Town: Tafelberg, 1983.

Barnard, C. *Duiwel-in-die-bos*, Cape Town: Nasionale Boekhandel, 1968.

Mahala, Cape Town: Tafelberg, 1971.

Pa, Maak vir my 'n Vlieër, Pa, Johannesburg: Afrikaanse Pers-Boekhandel, 1964.

Beinart, W. *Twentieth-Century South Africa*, 2nd edn, Oxford University Press, 2001.

Beukes, W. D. (ed.). *Boekewêreld: Die Nasionale Pers in die Uitgewersbedryf tot 1990*, Cape Town: Nasionale Boekhandel, 1992.

Blum, P. *Enklaves van die Lig*, Cape Town: Nasionale Boekhandel, 1958.

Steenbok tot Poolsee, Cape Town: Nasionale Boekhandel, 1955.

Breytenbach, B. *Die Huis van die Dowe*, Cape Town: Human & Rousseau, 1967.

Katastrofes, Johannesburg: Afrikaanse Pers-Boekhandel, 1964.

Lotus, [Cape Town]: Buren, 1970.

Die Ongedanste Dans: Gevangenisgedigte 1975–1983, Cape Town: Human & Rousseau, 2005.

Skryt. Om 'n Sinkende Skip Blou te Verf, Amsterdam: Meulenhoff, 1972.

The True Confessions of an Albino Terrorist, Johannesburg: Taurus, 1984.

Voetskrif, Cape Town: Perskor, 1976.

Die Ysterkoei Moet Sweet, Johannesburg: Afrikaanse Pers-Boekhandel, 1964.

Brink, A. *Die Ambassadeur*, Cape Town: Human & Rousseau, 1963; *The Ambassador*, [Cape Town]: Central News Agency, 1964; London: Faber, 1985.

Eindelose Weë, Cape Town: Tafelberg, 1960.

Die Gebondenes, Johannesburg: Afrikaanse Pers-Boekhandel, 1958.

Kennis van die Aand, Cape Town: Buren, 1973; *Looking on Darkness*, London: W. H. Allen, 1974.

Lobola vir die Lewe, Cape Town: Human & Rousseau, 1962.

Meul Teen die Hang, Cape Town: Tafelberg, 1958.

'n Oomblik in die Wind, Johannesburg: Taurus, 1975; *An Instant in the Wind*, London: Allen, 1976.

Orgie, Cape Town. John Malherbe, 1965.

Coetzee, A. 'Literature and Crisis: One Hundred Years of Afrikaans Literature and Afrikaner Nationalism', in Trump, *Rendering Things Visible*, 322–66.

Coetzee, J. M. *Life & Times of Michael K*, London: Secker & Warburg, 1983.

Waiting for the Barbarians, Johannesburg: Ravan, 1980.

Degenaar, J. J. *Voortbestaan in Geregtigheid*, Cape Town: Tafelberg, 1980.

Dekker, G. *Afrikaanse Literatuurgeskiedenis*, Cape Town: Nasionale Boekhandel, 1935.

De Klerk, W. A. *Die Jaar van die Vuur-Os*, Cape Town: Nasionale Boekhandel, 1952.

Die Uur van Verlange, Cape Town: Nasionale Boekhandel, 1953.

De Vries, A. *Bliksoldate Bloei nie*, Cape Town: Human & Rousseau, 1975.

Briekwa, Cape Town: Perskor, 1973.

Dubbeldoor, Cape Town: Tafelberg, 1963.

Vliegoog, Cape Town: Tafelberg, 1965.

Volmoed se Gasie, Cape Town: Human & Rousseau, 1972.

Domingo, E. *Okkies op die Breë Pad*, Johannesburg: Afrikaanse Pers-Boekhandel, 1955.

Ester, H. 'Met Elisabeth Eybers (1915–2007) is een Fenomenale Dichteres Heengegaan', *Tydskrif vir Letterkunde* 45:1 (2008), 178–82.

Eybers, E. *Belydenis in die Skemering*, Bloemfontein: Nasionale Pers, 1936.

   Versamelde Gedigte, Cape Town: Human & Rousseau; 3rd edn, Cape Town: Tafelberg, 2004.

Fula, A. *Jôhannie Giet die Beeld*, Johannesburg: Afrikaanse Pers-Boekhandel, 1954. Translation by Carrol Lasker as *The Golden Magnet*, Washington DC: Three Continents Press, 1984.

Gerwel, G. J. *Literatuur en Apartheid*, Kasselsvlei: Kampen-uitgewers, 1983.

Giliomee, H. *The Afrikaners: Biography of a People*, Cape Town: Tafelberg, 2003.

Grové, H. *Jaarringe*, Cape Town: Tafelberg, 1966.

   Die Kêrel van die Pêrel of Anatomie van 'n Leuenaar, Cape Town: Tafelberg, 1983.

   Winterreis, Cape Town: Tafelberg, 1971.

Haasbroek, P. J. *Heupvuur*, Cape Town: Human & Rousseau, 1974.

   Roofvis, Cape Town: Human & Rousseau, 1975.

   Skrikbewind, Cape Town: Human & Rousseau, 1976.

Jensma, W. *I Must Show you my Clippings*, Johannesburg: Ravan, 1977.

   Sing for our Execution, Johannesburg: Ophir/Ravan, 1973.

   Where White is the Colour/Where Black is the Number, Johannesburg: Ravan, 1974.

Jonker, I. *Rook en Oker*, Johannesburg: Afrikaanse Pers-Boekhandel, 1963.

   Selected Poems, trans. Jack Cope and W. Plomer, Cape Town: Human & Rousseau, 1988.

Joubert, E. *Die Reise van Isobelle*, Cape Town: Tafelberg, 1995. Translation by Catherine Knox as *Isobelle's Journey*, Johannesburg: Jonathan Ball, 2002.

   Reisiger, Cape Town: Tafelberg, 2009.

   Die Swerfjare van Poppie Nongena, Cape Town: Tafelberg, 1978; *The Long Journey of Poppie Nongena*, Johannesburg: Jonathan Ball, 1980.

   Ons Wag op die Kaptein, Cape Town: Tafelberg, 1963. Translation by Klaas Steyler as *To Die at Sunset*, London: Hodder & Stoughton, 1982.

   'n Wonderlike Geweld: Jeugherinneringe, Cape Town: Tafelberg, 2005.

Kannemeyer, J. C. D. J. *Opperman: 'n Biografie*, Cape Town: Human & Rousseau, 1986.

   Geskiedenis van die Afrikaanse Literatuur, 2 vols., Cape Town: Academica, 1978, 1983.

   A History of Afrikaans Literature, Pietermaritzburg: Shuter & Shooter, 1993.

   Jan Rabie: Prosapionier en Politieke Padwyser, Cape Town: Tafelberg, 2004.

Kirsch, O. *Mure van die Hart*, Johannesburg: Afrikaanse Pers-Boekhandel, 1948.

   Die Soeklig, Pretoria: Van Schaik, 1944.

Leroux, E. (pseud. S. P. D. le Roux). *Die Derde Oog*, Cape Town: Human & Rousseau, 1966.

   Een vir Azazel, Cape Town: Human & Rousseau, 1964.

   Magersfontein, O Magersfontein!, Cape Town: Human & Rousseau, 1976. Translation by N. Roets as *Magersfontein, O Magersfontein!*, Wynberg: Hutchinson Group, 1983.

   Sewe Dae by die Silbersteins, Cape Town: Human & Rousseau, 1962. Translation by C. Eglington as *Seven Days at the Silbersteins*, Cape Town: Central News Agency, 1964.

   To a Dubious Salvation: A Trilogy of Fantastical Novels, trans. Charles Eglington and Amy Starke, Harmondsworth: Penguin, 1972.

Louw, A. M. *Die Banneling: Die Lyfwag*, Cape Town: Tafelberg, 1964.

   Die Groot Gryse, Cape Town: Tafelberg, 1968.

Kroniek van Perdepoort, Cape Town: Tafelberg, 1975.

Twenty Days that Autumn, Cape Town: Tafelberg, 1964.

Louw, N. P. van Wyk. *Germanicus*, Cape Town: Nasionale Boekhandel, 1956.

Tristia, Cape Town: Human & Rousseau, 1962.

Miles, J. *Blaaskans*, Emmerentia: Taurus, 1983.

Kroniek uit die Doofpot: Polisieroman, Bramley: Taurus, 1991. Translation by Eithne Doherty as *A Deafening Silence: Police Novel*, Cape Town: Human & Rousseau, 1995.

Liefs nie op Straat nie, Cape Town: Buren, 1970.

Okker Bestel Twee Toebroodjies, Cape Town: Buren, 1973.

Opperman, D. J. *Blom en Baaierd*, Cape Town: Tafelberg, 1956.

Engel uit die Klip: 1947–1950, Cape Town: Nasionale Boekhandel, 1950.

Groot Verseboek: 'n Bloemlesing uit die Afrikaanse Poësie, Cape Town: Nasionale Boekhandel, 1951.

Heilige Beeste, Cape Town: Nasionale Pers, 1945.

Joernal van Jorik, Cape Town: Nasionale Pers, 1949.

Junior Verseboek: 'n Bloemlesing uit die Afrikaanse Poësie vir die Middelbare Skool, Cape Town: Nasionale Boekhandel, 1951.

Klein Verseboek, Cape Town: Tafelberg, 1959.

Kleuterverseboek, Cape Town: Nasionale Boekhandel, 1957.

Senior Verseboek: 'n Bloemlesing uit die Afrikaanse Poësie vir die Hoërskool, Cape Town: Nasionale Boekhandel, 1951.

Paton, A. *Cry, the Beloved Country: A Story of Comfort and Desolation*, Harmondsworth: Penguin, 1948.

Petersen, S. V. *As die Son Ondergaan*, Port Elizabeth: Unie-Volkspers, 1945.

Die Enkeling, Port Elizabeth: Unie-Volkspers, 1944.

Philander, P. J. *Kebunie*, Cape Town: Human & Rousseau, 2000.

Uurglas, Cape Town: Nasionale Boekhandel, 1955.

Vuurklip, Cape Town: Nasionale Boekhandel, 1960.

Zimbabwe, Cape Town: Nasionale Boekhandel, 1968.

Pretorius, S. J. *Die Arbeider en ander Gedigte*, Pretoria: Van Schaik, 1945.

Vonke, Pretoria: Van Schaik, 1943.

Rabie, J. *21*, Cape Town: Balkema, 1956.

Ark, Cape Town: Human & Rousseau, 1977.

Eiland voor Afrika, Cape Town: Human & Rousseau, 1964.

Die Groot Anders-Maak, Cape Town: Human & Rousseau, 1964.

A Man Apart, London: Collins, 1969.

Mens-Alleen, [Johannesburg]: Afrikaanse Pers-Boekhandel, 1963.

Ons, die Afgod, Cape Town: Balkema, 1958.

En Oseaan, Cape Town: Human & Rousseau, 1985.

Waar Jý Sterwe, Cape Town: Human & Rousseau, 1966.

Roubaix, Paul (pseud. Isaac Pfaff). *Storm en Ander Eenbedrywe*, Johannesburg: Afrikaanse Pers-Boekhandel, 1951.

Rousseau, I. *Kwiksilwersirkel*, Cape Town: Human & Rousseau, 1978.

'n Onbekende Jaartal, Cape Town: Human & Rousseau, 1995.

Taxa, Cape Town: Human & Rousseau, 1970.

Verlate Tuin, Cape Town: Balkema, 1954.

Schoeman, K. *By Fakkellig*, Cape Town: Human & Rousseau, 1966.

Die Hemeltuin, Cape Town: Human & Rousseau, 1979.

Na die Geliefde Land, Cape Town: Human & Rousseau, 1972. Translation by Marion V. Friedmann as *Promised Land*, London: Friedmann, 1978.

Om te Sterwe, Cape Town: Human & Rousseau, 1976.

Sheldon, L. *Weeklaag van die Wese*, Johannesburg: Afrikaanse Pers-Boekhandel, 1960.

Small, A. *Kanna hy Kô Hystoe*, Cape Town: Human & Rousseau, 1965. Translation by Adam Small and Carrol Lasker as *Kanna, He is Coming Home*, New York: Garland, 1992.

Kitaar my Kruis, Cape Town: HAUM, 1961.

Sê Sjibbolet, Johannesburg: Afrikaanse Pers-Boekhandel, 1963.

Smit, B. *Christine*, Cape Town: Tafelberg, 1971.

Die Keiser, Cape Town: Perskor, 1977.

Putsonderwater, Johannesburg: Afrikaanse Pers-Boekhandel, 1962. Translation by A. Dawes as *Well-without-water or the Virgin and the Vultures*, Johannesburg: Dramatic, Artistic and Literary Rights Organization (Pty) Ltd, 1968.

Die Verminktes, Cape Town: Human & Rousseau, 1960.

Steyn, J. C. 'Die Eerste Dekades van die Nasionale Boekhandel', in Beukes, *Boekewêreld*, 119–58.

''n Nederige Begin vir Tafelberg', in Beukes, *Boekewêreld*, 160–77.

'Vet en Maer Jare', in Beukes, *Boekewêreld*, 86–115.

Stockenström, W. *Die Kremetartekspedisie*, Cape Town: Human & Rousseau, 1981. Translation by J. M. Coetzee as *The Expedition to the Baobab Tree*, Johannesburg: Jonathan Ball, 1983.

Spieël van Water, Cape Town: Human & Rousseau, 1973.

Uitdraai, Cape Town: Human & Rousseau, 1976.

Van Vergetelheid en Glans, Cape Town: Human & Rousseau, 1976.

Vir die Bysiende Leser, Cape Town: Reijger, 1970.

Toerien, B. *Om te Onthou*, Pretoria: Protea Book House, 2006.

Trump, M. (ed.). *Rendering Things Visible: Essays on South African Literary Culture*, Johannesburg: Ravan, 1990.

Van Coller, H. P. (ed.). *Perspektief en Profiel*, 3 vols., Pretoria: Van Schaik, 1998, 1999, 2005.

Van den Heever, C. M., and P. de V. Pienaar (eds.). *Kultuurgeskiedenis van die Afrikaner – Die Eerste Beskrywing van die Boere-volkslewe in al sy Vertakkinge*, 3 vols., Cape Town: Nasionale Boekhandel, 1948.

Van Heerden, E. *Verklaarde Nag*, Cape Town: Nasionale Pers, 1946.

Weerlose Uur, Cape Town: Nasionale Pers, 1942.

Van Niekerk, D. *Die Son Struikel*, Johannesburg: Dagbreek-Boekhandel, 1960.

Venter, F. A. *Bedoelde Land*, Cape Town: Tafelberg, 1968.

Geknelde Land, Cape Town: Tafelberg, 1960.

Gelofteland, Cape Town: Tafelberg, 1966.

Man van Ciréne, Cape Town: Tafelberg, 1957.

Offerland, Cape Town: Tafelberg, 1963.

Swart Pelgrim, Johannesburg: Boek-van-die-maand-klub, 1952. Translation by G. and W. Gordon as *Dark Pilgrim*, London: Collins, 1959.

Watermeyer, G. A. *Die Republiek van 'n Duisend Jaar*, Johannesburg: J. van Melle, 1957.

Sekel and Simbaal, Cape Town: Nasionale Pers, 1948.

Willemse, H. *Aan die Ander Kant: Swart Afrikaanse Skrywers in die Afrikaanse Letterkunde*, Pretoria: Protea Book House, 2007.

'Insularity and Ambivalence: The Case of the South African Poet P. J. Philander's Epic Poem, *Zimbabwe*', *Research in African Literatures* 39:1 (2008), 125–48.

'Die Skrille Sonbesies: Emergent Black Afrikaans Poets in Search of Authority', in Trump, *Rendering Things Visible*, 367–401.

22

Afrikaans literature after 1976: resistances and repositionings

LOUISE VILJOEN

Literature and history

The aim of this chapter is to give a selective overview of Afrikaans literature after 1976. It is customary in South African literary historiography to
accept that literary histories are shaped by contextual as well as aesthetic
factors and to use historical transitions as reference points for the periodisation of literature. It has also been argued that 'there is a growing consensus for a common periodization of contemporary South African literature which would use the dates of Sharpeville, Soweto, and the idea of
the interregnum to guide the organisation of the field' (Loflin, 'Periodization in South African literatures'). This is confirmed by the general practice in
Afrikaans literary historiography: Ampie Coetzee (*Letterkunde en Krisis* [Litera-
ture and Crisis], 1990) and J. C. Kannemeyer (*Die Afrikaanse Literatuur 1652–2004*
[Afrikaans Literature 1652–2004], 2005) as well as the writers of the overviews
in the different volumes of the collaborative literary history *Perspektief en
Profiel* (Perspective and Profile, 1998, 1999, 2005), edited by H. P. van Coller,
use these dates as reference points in their description of Afrikaans literary
history.

Afrikaans literature after 1976 can be divided into two phases, even though
certain discontinuities and overlaps occur. The first phase starts in 1976 when
the Soweto uprising against the enforced use of Afrikaans in schools signalled
the beginning of a more concerted resistance against the apartheid government. The ensuing stigmatisation of Afrikaans deeply affected Afrikaans literature and led Afrikaans authors to comment on the compromised status of
the language in which they wrote. The white Afrikaans poet Breyten Breytenbach expressed his ambivalent relationship with Afrikaans more than once,
referring to it on occasion as a 'gray reservist of more than a hundred years /
with its fingers stiffly around the triggers' in the poem 'Taalstryd' ('Language

Struggle', in *Lewendood* [Lifeanddeath], pp. 143–4). On the other hand, the black Afrikaans poet and academic Hein Willemse stated that one had to accept 'that Afrikaans is at once the language of the conqueror and the language of the oppressed' ('Black Afrikaans Writer', p. 239) and argued for the continued use of Afrikaans as an instrument in the struggle against apartheid. The second phase in the period after 1976 starts with the unbanning of the ANC and the release of Nelson Mandela from jail in the first months of 1990. That being said, one must concede that the years from 1990 to 1994 represent an interim stage in which some of the themes and preoccupations from the previous phase continued at the same time that new trends became apparent. The literary texts written and published in these years often reflected the uncertainty of this interim period that ended with the first democratic election on 27 April 1994.

Voices and countervoices of resistance, 1976–1990

Resistance to Afrikaner nationalism and related constructions of power was one of the strongest themes in Afrikaans literature in the period from 1976 to 1990. Various forms and degrees of resistance were articulated: there were texts expressing overt political resistance against the apartheid government as well as other bodies of writing that reacted against the patriarchal domination associated with the apartheid state, for instance writing about the war in Angola, women's writing, gay writing and various examples of protest theatre. Many of the writers involved in these forms of writing were influenced by poststructuralist and postmodernist thought, often engaging with the ideas of philosophers like Derrida, Foucault, Lyotard and Baudrillard and using the writerly techniques associated with postmodernism in their literary texts. As a result, these texts question master-narratives, emphasise the textual nature of reality, reflect on their own status as language constructs, merge fact with fiction, highlight intertextuality, reinstate the formerly marginalised, seek out connections with mass culture and rewrite history with a focus on the way it is lived by ordinary people. In the process, a localised and politically engaged version of postmodernism was developed in the work of Afrikaans writers like Breytenbach, Antjie Krog, Koos Prinsloo and others. Apart from the strong emphasis on resistance in this period, there were also a number of writers who insisted on their right to indulge the 'private ache' (that is, write about topics not related to the political context) as well as writers who raised voices running counter to the various kinds of resistance expressed in the majority of texts. The following overview will point out the most important trends and the most representative texts.[1]

Outspoken political resistance in different genres

At the time of the Soweto uprisings in 1976, several prominent Afrikaans writers found themselves at odds with the state: Breytenbach was serving a nine-year jail sentence after being found guilty on charges of terrorism in November 1975 and several Afrikaans authors began to experience the effects of state censorship so long suffered by authors writing in English and other South African languages. André Brink's novel *Kennis van die Aand* (Knowledge of the Night, 1973; Brink's own English version, *Looking on Darkness*, 1974) was banned in 1974, Breytenbach's volume of poetry *Skryt* (Shit/Write/Screech, 1972) in 1975, his poetry in translation *And Death White as Words* (1978) in 1978, Etienne Leroux's novel *Magersfontein, O Magersfontein!* (1976) in 1977 and, after that, a series of other Afrikaans literary texts until the mid 1980s (see McDonald, *Literature Police*, pp. 355–63). To contend with the problems caused by state censorship, the Afrikaanse Skrywersgilde (Afrikaans Writers' Guild) was founded in 1973 and the alternative publisher Taurus was set up in 1975 by literary academics Ernst Lindenberg, Ampie Coetzee and John Miles.

The strong presence of resistance in Afrikaans literature during this period is demonstrated by the fact that literary debates were preoccupied with the necessity of a *littérature engagée* in Afrikaans. Brink acted as spokesman for writers who felt they had the responsibility to engage with the sociopolitical context. He was often opposed by certain members of the literary establishment (A. P. Grové, T. T. Cloete, Elize Botha and others), who argued for the primacy of aesthetic principles in literature and literary studies. It is thus not surprising that Brink became one of the foremost writers of political resistance in Afrikaans in the late 1970s and 1980s. Novels like *Kennis van die Aand, Gerugte van Reën* (*Rumours of Rain*, 1978), *'n Droë Wit Seisoen* (*A Dry White Season*, 1979), *Die Muur van die Pes* (*The Wall of the Plague*, 1984), *States of Emergency* (1988) and *Die Kreef Raak Gewoond Daaraan* (The Lobster Gets Used to It, 1991; English version, *An Act of Terror*) react to political events of the time by representing political oppression, subversive political activity, relationships across the colour bar, the Soweto uprisings, torture and death in detention, exile, sabotage, espionage and revolutionary activity. Brink often uses the novelistic technique of a relatively detached narrator who is given

---

1 All Afrikaans titles are given with English translations; where there is a published English version, this title is given in italics. The bibliography lists available English translations.

documents (either personal or historical), which he, in turn, presents to the reader. The narrative about the relationship between an eighteenth-century black slave and a white woman stranded in the barren interior of South Africa in 'n Oomblik in die Wind (An Instant in the Wind, 1975) is also framed by a narrator who finds (fictionalised) historical documents containing information, which inspires him to 'imagine' the novel we then read. On the other hand, the novel Houd-den-bek (1982; English version, A Chain of Voices) is based on real historical documents, mostly court records about a slave rebellion that took place in the Cape Colony in 1825. The narrative makes use of a variety of narrating voices (the 'chain of voices' of the English title) to portray the views of participants in the slave rebellion, but deliberately structures the representation of historical events so as to reveal the parallels with the liberation struggle of the 1980s. Brink started translating his own novels in the 1960s, but since the late 1970s he has written and published the Afrikaans and English versions of his novels simultaneously.

When writing about the Afrikaans 'political' novel in the period 1976 to 1990, one also has to mention pivotal works by Etienne Leroux, Elsa Joubert and John Miles. Etienne Leroux was an established writer by the time he published Magersfontein, O Magersfontein! (1976), in which a film crew gathers to shoot a movie about the Battle of Magersfontein, which took place during the Anglo-Boer War. The whole project ends in disaster when the film set is flooded and everything dissolves into chaos. Although Leroux stated on more than one occasion that he wanted his novels to address modern man's spiritual destitution within a Jungian framework, rather than the specifics of South African politics, Magersfontein, O Magersfontein! is a carnivalesque send-up of Afrikaner history, ideology and values. It affronted political sensibilities to such an extent that the novel was banned in 1977. Elsa Joubert's early travel writing, as well as her first novels published in the 1960s, focused on the coexistence of black and white in different parts of Africa, thus preparing the way for the political focus of her most influential book, Die Swerfjare van Poppie Nongena (1978; The Long Journey of Poppie Nongena, 1980). This book is a non-fictional narrative in the first person about a black woman's day-to-day experience of the apartheid system as related to Joubert, so that there was some controversy about its packaging, as a novel rather than a collaborative autobiography or biography. Although the book raises complex questions about the relationship of power between the white Afrikaans writer Joubert and her black informant (whose name was changed to protect her identity), as well as their contradictory locations with regard to apartheid, the book played a significant role in raising political awareness amongst Afrikaans readers.

John Miles's novel *Donderdag of Woensdag* (Thursday or Wednesday, 1978) tells the story of a group of artists who want to kidnap the president. The narrative starts with the main character, Eksteen, travelling through Spain, but halfway through the novel the narrator gives up the pretence that he put up on behalf of political censors and admits that his novel is about South Africa. The novel was banned, as was *Stanley Bekker en die Boikot* (Stanley Bekker and the Boycott, 1980), in which Miles uses the format of a children's book to tell the story of racial discrimination and school boycotts from the perspective of a coloured child in Johannesburg. Miles is best known for his documentary novel *Kroniek uit die Doofpot* (Chronicle of a Cover-Up; translated as *Deafening Silence*, 1997), published in 1992 in the interim period between apartheid and majority rule. This novel tells the story of the policeman Tumelo John Moleko, who is persecuted and finally killed by members of the police force because he insists on a fair hearing after being wronged by his superiors. The novel is narrated by a writer who receives a shopping bag full of documents relating to Moleko's case, in the same way that John Miles received a bag full of documents relating to the real case of sergeant Richard Motasi from journalist Hans Pienaar. Two policemen later admitted to killing Motasi (alternative spelling Mutase) during the Truth and Reconciliaton Commission's hearings in 1996–7 (see Krog, *Country of my Skull*, pp. 82–9).

Apart from the above-mentioned novelists, Afrikaans poets also registered their political resistance. The best example of a protest poet in Afrikaans is Breytenbach, who defied literary, social and political conventions from the time of his debut in 1964. His most overtly 'political' volume of poetry, *Skryt* (1972), was banned because of its references to the names of prisoners who died in detention and a poem directed at the erstwhile prime minister, John Vorster, whom it addressed as 'butcher'. Breytenbach was himself a political prisoner from 1975 until the end of 1982, during which time he wrote five volumes of poetry. The first, *Voetskrif* (Foot-writing/Foot-script) was published in 1976 during his first year in prison; the other four prison volumes were published in quick succession by Taurus after he was released from jail in December 1982 (Breytenbach's prison poetry was subsequently collected in the anthology *Die Ongedanste Dans* [The Undanced Dance], published in 2005). When read against the background of the substantial body of South African prison poetry, Breytenbach's prison poems are less accessible that those of, for instance, Jeremy Cronin. They are marked by an intense degree of introspection, subtle reflections on the nature of poetry, sophisticated literary references and a densely textured play with words. Several Afrikaans poets reacted to Breytenbach's politics and imprisonment in their own poetry:

while a number of poets, like George Weideman, Wopko Jensma, Julian de Wette and Ernst van Heerden sympathised with his plight, others like M. M. Walters, Lina Spies and Wessel Pretorius were critical of the merciless way in which he criticised Afrikaners and the Afrikaner government. Fanie Olivier also produced memorable political poetry during this period, like the poem on the death of Hector Pieterson, 'die kind is nie dood nie' ('the child is not dead'), published in *Verklarings: 1967–1987* (Statements: 1967–87, 1988).

An important body of Afrikaans protest writing was the poetry written by black Afrikaans writers (although most of these writers were coloured, they made the ideological choice to refer to themselves as 'black', thereby putting their writing in the political arena). As Willemse argues, the mere fact that they wrote and published poetry from a position of racial oppression and exclusion was a form of 'resistance and protest' (*Aan die Ander Kant*, p. 198). These poets resisted exclusion by established publishers by making use of alternative publishers, like Taurus, and setting up their own publishing houses, like Prog and Domestica. Poets like Vernon February, Willie Adams, Jan Wiltshire and Clinton V. du Plessis rewrote the classics of the largely white Afrikaans literary canon in their poems. Others, like Peter Snyders and Marius Titus, expressed the experience of the working class in their poems and extended the range of poetic Afrikaans by using marginalised varieties in addition to standard Afrikaans, thus building on the practice of Adam Small in the 1960s. Some of these poets used their poetry as a vehicle for expressing private experience (for example, Vincent Oliphant, Richard Geldenhuys and Julian de Wette), whereas others employed it in the struggle against apartheid. In the preface to his debut volume *Amandla Ngawethu* (1985), Patrick J. Petersen articulates his belief that poetry can be an important 'weapon' in the political struggle. Anthologies like *Aankoms uit die Skemer* (Arrival From the Dusk, 1988), *Optog* (Protest March, 1990) and *I Qabane Labanthu. Poetry in the Emergency. Poësie in die Stryd* (1989) also expressed these writers' protest against apartheid.

Although the output of Afrikaans theatre texts has always been small compared to that of the other genres, the general sense of rebellion and resistance during the years 1976 to 1990 was also reflected in Afrikaans writing for the stage. Hennie Aucamp's cabaret texts, *Met Permissie Gesê* (With Permission, 1980) and *Slegs vir Almal* (Everybody Only, 1986), employed the tradition of the European *cabaret artistique* to satirise South African issues like censorship, the border war and racial conflict. Pieter Fourie experienced his most productive phase in the 1980s, with plays like *Die Joiner* (The Joiner, 1976), *Ek, Anna van Wyk* (I, Anna van Wyk, 1986) and *Die Koggelaar* (The Mimic, 1988), in which he interrogates Afrikaner obsessions with loyalty, guilt, treason, patriarchal control and racial purity. Pieter-Dirk Uys wrote plays and revues in both Afrikaans and English; important in Afrikaans is the play *Selle Ou Storie* (Same Old Story, 1983) and the revue *Die Van Aardes van Grootoor* (The Van Aardes of Grootoor, 1979), which parodied Afrikaans radio serials and the accompanying values. Deon Opperman's early play, *Môre is 'n Lang Dag* (Tomorrow will be a Long Day, 1986), is set in the border war with five conscripts in an army tent trying to come to terms with their feelings of guilt about the death of a comrade. His next play, *Stille Nag* (Silent Night, 1990), picks up on the political conflict in South Africa by setting two brothers on opposite ends of the political spectrum against each other. Reza de Wet also made her debut in the 1980s with *Diepe Grond* (Deep Earth, 1986), the most successful play in her *Vrystaat-trilogie* (Free State Trilogy, 1991). In the above-mentioned play, a brother and sister settle their account with traditional Afrikaner values and ideologies by murdering their parents and eventually also the lawyer who is sent to investigate. They maintain a perverted household in which the role of the black woman, Alina, is a throwback to the portrayal of the trusted maid-servant in early Afrikaans children's books (especially Alba Bouwer's *Stories van Rivierplaas* [Stories from River Farm], 1955).

Border literature

Strong resistance to the apartheid regime was also voiced in texts reflecting on South Africa's involvement in military conflicts in Rhodesia (Zimbabwe) and on the border between South West Africa (Namibia) and Angola. This body of texts became known – somewhat controversially – as *'grensliteratuur'* ('border literature'). A defining feature of these texts was that they were written by young men who were conscripted soldiers, either doing military service or fighting in the war. Their texts tended to be critical of the ideology underlying South African military action, to emphasise the inhumanity of the war and to subvert stereotypical views about heroism, valour and loyalty. Koos Prinsloo's short stories about the border war in the volumes *Jonkmanskas* (Youngman's Wardrobe, 1982) and *Die Hemel Help Ons* (Heaven Help Us, 1987) are characterised by a cool and emotionally detached style which contradicts its references to the trauma caused by militarisation and combat. The border war also features in Alexander Strachan's debut volume of short stories, *'n Wêreld Sonder Grense* (A World Without Borders, 1984), in which the stories are linked to give insight into different aspects of a conscripted soldier's experience: the brutality of military combat, the psychical trauma caused by war, the inability of ex-soldiers to adapt to civil life and the attraction of joining a renegade group operating outside military structures (with references to Coppola's film

Apocalypse Now). Etienne van Heerden published a volume of short stories, *My Kubaan* (My Cuban, 1983), and a novella, *Om te Awol* (To Awol, 1984), in which he evoked the experience of the conscripted soldier who is forced to become part of the military machine of the state. The story 'My Cuban' paints the picture of a young soldier brainwashed by the army to see the enemy as the ultimate representation of the other (animal-like, not white, son of a whore). He ostensibly tells his story to his Cuban prisoner, whom he keeps chained like a dog, but the ambiguous ending of the story reveals that in all likelihood there is no Cuban: the soldier-narrator is chained to a phantom image of his guilt and complicity in violence. Others in this category of soldier-writers are Louis Krüger (*'n Basis oorkant die Grens* [A Base Across the Border], 1984) and Gawie Kellerman, whose collection of short stories, *Wie de Hel Het Jou Vertel?* (Who the Hell Told You?, 1988), gives a cryptic and dispassionate rendering of war's violence.

These literary texts with their anti-war and anti-apartheid sensibilities must be set apart from a small body of popular literature in Afrikaans (novels, short stories and youth novels by writers like Adriaan Snyman, Maretha Maartens, Johan Coetzee and Pieter Pieterse) about the border war, in which the political status quo is affirmed, war is romanticised and stereotypes of heroism, valour and loyalty are upheld. The impact of the border war on serious Afrikaans literature is also visible in texts by writers who were not themselves part of the war but who explored war-related themes, like P. J. Haasbroek (*Roofvis* [Fish of Prey], 1975, and *Verby die Vlakte* [Past the Plain], 1982), Welma Odendaal (*Keerkring* [Tropic], 1977), J. C. Steyn (*Op Pad na die Grens* [On the Way to the Border], 1976) and Lettie Viljoen (*Klaaglied vir Koos* [Lament for Koos], 1983). Steyn's work, published before the first anti-war examples of border literature produced by soldiers, emphasises the parallels between the border war and the Anglo-Boer War. Although it paints a complex picture of the situation surrounding such wars, his handling of the themes of loyalty, resistance and heroism comes from within a framework of loyal, albeit critical, Afrikaner nationalism.

Women's writing

Another form of resistance, aimed not so much at apartheid as at the patriarchal structures embedded in South African society, became manifest in Afrikaans women's writing, which became increasingly gender-conscious and politicised after 1976. In the work of the writers selected for the purpose of this overview, the resistance against gender oppression often coincided with the resistance against racial oppression. Antjie Krog made her poetic debut at the age of 17 with the volume *Dogter van Jefta* (Daughter of Jephta) in 1970, but it was only from her fourth volume, *Otters in Bronslaai* (Otters in Cress, 1981), onwards that her work began to question patriarchal gender constructs. In this volume, she vividly expresses the frustration of the creative woman whose need to write comes into conflict with her roles as a wife, mother and housewife. In her next two volumes, *Jerusalemgangers* (Jerusalem Trekkers, 1985) and *Lady Anne* (1989), her poetry becomes increasingly political in the sense that she interrogates both racial and gender oppression. The latter of the two volumes is conceived as a postmodern epic in which the poet wants to use the Scottish noblewoman, Lady Anne Barnard, who lived at the Cape as wife of the Colonial Secretary from 1797 to 1802, as a guide or metaphor for her own life as white woman in South Africa in the 1980s. The volume is a collage of poems supplemented by citations, drawings, an ovulation chart, a property advertisement, an electoral poster and extracts from a diary, in which the power struggle between husband and wife, coloniser and colonised, white and black, the writer and her subject(s), the social responsibility of the poet and the difficult relationship between politics and aesthetics are explored. *Down to my Last Skin*, a selection and translation of Krog's poems by herself and others, was published in 2000 after Krog achieved international recognition for her seminal text on the Truth and Reconciliation Commission, *Country of my Skull* (1998).

The writer Wilma Stockenström has established herself in the canon of Afrikaans literature as an important poet, novelist and playwright. Although not an overtly political writer, her oeuvre is marked by an ironical gaze on all human enterprise that subtly undermines all systems of domination, whether based on gender, race or class. Her novel *Uitdraai* (Turn-Off, 1976) questioned the ideology underlying the traditional farm novel in Afrikaans (something also found in the work of male writers like Etienne van Heerden, Koos Prinsloo and Eben Venter). Her novel *Die Kremetartekspedisie* (translated by J. M. Coetzee as *The Expedition to the Baobab Tree*, 1981) is narrated by a woman captured as a child by slave traders in central Africa in the late fifteenth century and taken to a city on the East African coast to be sold as a slave. When her third owner dies, she accompanies his son and a wealthy merchant with whom she has fallen in love on a westward journey through Africa in search of a city of rose quartz. When everybody on the expedition dies, she takes refuge in the hollow trunk of a baobab tree (situated in the north of the present South Africa, as one can deduce by the references to the remains of the twelfth-century settlement Mapungubwe) until she drinks the poison left for her by the 'little people' who seem to revere her as a goddess. Both thematically (in its focus on a slave woman) and stylistically (through its lyricism, complex chronology, gaps and silences), the novel questions male-oriented representations of the past.

The writer Jeanne Goosen also defies conventional narrative strategies in her novella *Louoond* (Warming Oven, 1987). The epigraph of this work reads: 'Another book by a woman. Listen friends, the world of the kitchen is forsaken by man and by God. It is a condition of controlled hysteria'. The story is narrated from the conventionally female space of the kitchen, depicted as an anarchical but intensely creative space in which the narrator listens to her tapes of Maria Callas singing while she cooks and works on her manuscript, *Kombuis Blues* (Kitchen Blues), stored in the warming drawer of her oven. At the same time she has difficulty in dealing with the questions posed by the political emergency which seems about to erupt into her kitchen. She has heated discussions with her partner E. and friend Hermien about which course to take in the struggle against the regime. Another novella by Goosen, *Ons Is Nie Almal So Nie* (1990; *We're Not All Like That*, 2007), was hugely successful with the Afrikaans reading public and tells the story of a working-class Afrikaner family in the 1950s from the perspective of a young child. Her apparently guileless narrative reveals much about political tensions in the Afrikaner community, as well as the effect of forced removals of people of colour from certain neighbourhoods reserved for whites. Her mother bakes a cake for a coloured family who is forced to leave their neighbourhood in an attempt to relieve her feelings of guilt, and when they refuse her offering, she counters with the words: 'We're not all like that' (p. 122).

Apart from women whose writing addressed gender and racial politics, prominent writers like Sheila Cussons, Elisabeth Eybers, Anna M. Louw, Petra Müller, Ina Rousseau and Lina Spies kept on producing work that focused on broadly existential rather than political questions. By way of example, one can cite the work of poet Sheila Cussons, who made her debut in 1970 with the volume *Plektrum* (Plectrum). An extraordinarily productive period followed after Cussons suffered a debilitating accident with an exploding gas stove in 1974. Most exemplary of her poetic style and thematic concerns is the volume *Die Swart Kombuis* (The Black Kitchen, 1978), in which she transforms her own experience with fire into poems that draw on Greek mythology (as in the poem, 'Kombuis van Hera' ['Hera's Kitchen']), as well as Catholic mysticism (as in the poem 'Christ of the Burnt Men', which refers to the work of Thomas Merton). Cussons translated a selection of her poems into English under the title *Poems* in 1985.

Afrikaans women's writing in the 1980s also included the highly successful popular novels by Dalene Matthee. She published three novels set in the Outeniqua forest surrounding Knysna during the late nineteenth and early twentieth centuries, *Kringe in 'n Bos* (*Circles in a Forest*, 1984), *Fiela se Kind* (*Fiela's Child*, 1985) and *Moerbeibos* (*The Mulberry Forest*, 1987). A fourth 'forest' novel, *Toorbos* (*Dream Forest*), followed in 2003. All the 'forest' novels deal with the conflicts between the wealthy (the merchants who exploit the forest, the whites who make the rules for society) and the poor (the lumbermen in the forest, people of colour), and all emphasise the importance of conserving the indigenous forest. Another writer who has reached the same heights of popularity as Dalene Matthee is Marita van der Vyver, whose debut novel, *Griet Skryf 'n Sprokie* (Griet Writes a Fairy-tale; translated as *Entertaining Angels*), was published in 1992, but is set in the final months of 1989 and ends with the release of Nelson Mandela from jail in February 1990. The main character in this semi-autobiographical novel is Griet, whose analyst suggests that she should start writing the story of her life after a failed suicide attempt. Griet is also the compiler of a collection of fairy-tales in Afrikaans, so that her narrative becomes a Scheherezade-like attempt to survive the psychological trauma of her failed marriage by telling stories in which the facts of her life are skilfully interwoven with the fiction of the fairy-tales. The novel represents another (more popular and more accessible) face of the way in which Afrikaans women's writing resisted the conventions patriarchy imposed on women, especially through its frank and humorous depiction of Griet's sexual experiences.

Gay writing

The emergence of gay writing was also part of the resistance against the domination of patriarchal values in South African society. Although one can name several precursors in the Afrikaans literary tradition, it was only in the 1980s that the treatment of gay themes became more frank and open in Afrikaans writing. Building on the work of short-story writer Hennie Aucamp, younger male writers like Koos Prinsloo and Johann de Lange (also influenced by international writers such as David Leavitt, John Rechy, Thom Gunn and Edmund White, to name but a few) as well as female writers like Welma Odendaal, Jeanne Goosen, Joan Hambidge and Emma Huismans became increasingly explicit and questioning in their work. All these writers were political in the sense that they challenged the principles and values of the patriarchal, (hetero)sexist and racist society in which they lived. Koos Prinsloo, who died in 1994 of AIDS-related causes, left a small but powerful oeuvre consisting of four volumes of short stories in which he consistently attacked the abuse of power, be it by the militarised state, the police, the father or the literary establishment (represented by the mentor and the publisher). His challenge to patriarchal society reaches a climax in the volumes *Slagplaas* (Abattoir, 1992) and *Weifeling* (Wavering, 1993), in which he pushes the limits with his fictionalisation of (auto)biographical facts. The work of Emma Huismans (*Berigte van Weerstand* [Reports of Resistance], 1990) also places the lesbian experience in the midst of South African politics in the 1980s. These stories are derived from the author's experience as a journalist and challenge the priorities of struggle politicians who give precedence to racial over gender oppression. The early 1980s also saw the launch of the careers of poets Johann de Lange and Joan Hambidge, whose poetry embodies a wide variety of themes and techniques, but also introduced the first explicit representations of gay sexuality. In De Lange's work the focus is on the male body, gay sex and cruising (especially marked in *Nagsweet* [Night Sweats], 1991). In Hambidge's work, we find the first explicit renderings of lesbian sex in Afrikaans (for example, in *Hartskrif* [Heart Script], 1985, and *Bitterlemoene* [Bitter Oranges], 1986).

Although one can point to a steady production of literary texts by authors whose writing was not overtly political, the overwhelming impression one has when surveying Afrikaans literature in the period 1976 to 1990 is one of an anti-hegemonic literature in which voices of political protest were accompanied by a rebellion against the more widespread phenomena of racism, sexism and gay intolerance.

Repositionings after 1990

Whereas the period from 1976 to 1990 was characterised by resistance, the second phase, which starts in 1990, sees Afrikaans literature repositioning itself in various ways with regard to the changing political and social landscape. As in 1976, the political changes had an influence on the status of Afrikaans. It lost its privileged status as one of only two official languages in South Africa to become one of eleven official languages. Together with that, it also lost the state support that aided the growth of Afrikaans literature in the early years of the Afrikaner nationalist reign. For some writers, this loss of status signalled an opportunity for Afrikaans to free itself from the negative associations of the past. Antjie Krog said that she found new pleasure and freedom in writing in a language that suddenly found itself vulnerable (see Christiansë, "'Down to my last skin'", p. 16). Other writers, Breytenbach amongst them, increasingly came to fear for the continued existence of the language and its higher functions in the public domain. The most prominent trends in the literature of this period are the revisiting of history, the emergence of new voices and the appearance of a body of texts representing dystopic views on post-apartheid South Africa.

The return to the archive

In what can be described as a 'return to the archive', a variety of Afrikaans writers engaged with South African history in the light of events like the transition to democratic rule in 1994, the Truth and Reconciliation Commission and the centenary of the Anglo-Boer War from 1999 to 2002. In their engagement with various phases of South African history, these writers often focused on the injustices done to the indigenous peoples of the country by early colonisers. This, in turn, led to a renewed interest in the history and culture of the San and Khoikhoi in Afrikaans literature. More recent South African and Afrikaner history also came into focus in these texts in an attempt to revise official historiography and to bring to light suppressed histories. Eduan Swanepoel was the first to suggest that this interest in revisiting South African history can be seen as 'Afrikaans literature's own truth commission' ('Helende Terapie', p. 102). Van Coller points out that the tendency of some writers to dissect South African history with the aim of acknowledging the wrongs of the past and healing trauma (as in the case of Krog's account of her experience as reporter on the Truth and Reconciliation Commission in *Country of my Skull*, 1998) contrasts with the practice of writers like Alba Bouwer, J. C. Steyn and Engela van Rooyen, who in the same period write nostalgically about a lost past (Van Coller, 'Waarheidskommissie in die Afrikaanse Letterkunde', p. 13).

The first years of the Dutch settlement at the Cape in the seventeenth century is the focus of historian Dan Sleigh's novel *Eilande* (2002; *Islands*, 2004), which makes use of the narrative perspectives of ordinary people (amongst which the indigenous Khoi) who suffered under the governance of the Dutch East India Company (see Chapter 7). Karel Schoeman, who is known as a novelist and historian, published several novels after 1990 in which he explored nineteenth-century South African history. Especially significant is his *Stemme* (Voices) trilogy, consisting of *Hierdie Lewe* (1993; *This Life*, 2005), *Die Uur van die Engel* (The Angel's Hour, 1995) and *Verliesfontein* (1998). A quote from the German author Christa Wolf, in which she refers to the lifting of a sluice gate in front of a flood of formerly unheard voices, is used as epigraph for *Die Uur van die Engel*. It sets the tone for the trilogy, which concentrates on the lives of ordinary people who often moved on the periphery of the societies in which they lived. By way of example, one can refer to *Verliesfontein*, which tells the story of the Anglo-Boer War from the perspective of several characters who played a marginal role in the events. One of these is the magistrate's clerk in the town Verliesfontein in the Cape Colony, a settlement that was occupied for a short while by Boer troops from the Free State. When he looks back on events in old age, he is filled with remorse because he did not help a coloured man who was tortured and executed by the Boer troops (Schoeman bases this narrative on historical facts concerning Abraham Esau, who was executed in Calvinia during the Anglo-Boer War in 1901). In its emphasis on the difficulty of finding historical 'truth' and retrieving painful events from the past, the novel suggests parallels with the work of the Truth and Reconciliation Commission. Another novel that linked the Anglo-Boer War to the Truth and Reconciliation Commission is Christoffel Coetzee's *Op Soek na Generaal Mannetjies Mentz* (In Search of General Mannetjies Mentz, 1998). Central to the novel is the story of a revenge commando under the leadership of the immaculate General Mentz and his two henchmen, Niemannn and Vos. The commando attacks British troops to free Boer prisoners of war, and when the freed Boers do not want to return to the battlefield, they are executed together with the British. This novel raised a fair amount of controversy amongst readers and historians because of its free adaptation and fictionalisation of facts about the Anglo-Boer War. One can also cite the example of Ingrid Winterbach's novel *Niggie* (Niece/Cousin, 2002; English version *To Hell with Cronjé*, 2002), which firstly evokes the internal strife amongst Boer soldiers in the war and finally the devastating sense of loss when it becomes clear that the war has been lost. In general, the interest generated by the celebration of the Anglo-Boer War centenary from 1999 to 2002, as well as the important place it occupies in Afrikaner historiography, led to a significant increase in the production of literary texts on the war, including a range of popular novels and short stories.

Afrikaans novels from this period which focus on Afrikaner history have the tendency to preserve and dissect at the same time. Although Marlene van Niekerk's novel *Triomf* (1994) can be read on several levels, it can also be seen as a probing of certain moments in Afrikaner history. The novel evokes history through its focus on a family of poor white Afrikaners who live in the Johannesburg suburb of Triomf (Afrikaans for 'triumph'), built on the ruins of the black township Sophiatown demolished in the 1950s to create a suburb for the white working class. It is gradually revealed that the old man Pop, his 'wife' Mol and their 'relative' Treppie are actually siblings, while the epileptic Lambert is their son (it is not clear whether Pop or Treppie fathered him). On the one hand, the incestuous and inbred Benade family becomes symbolic of the extremes to which the apartheid philosophy of ethnic and racial exclusivity led; on the other hand, the novel is almost naturalistic in the way in which it depicts the detail of their everyday lives and reveals the specifics of the historical conditions that led to their situation (their ancestors were farmers forced off their land during an economic depression to become impoverished labourers in the railways and garment industry in Johannesburg).

Van Niekerk's second novel, *Agaat* (2004; international translation *The Way of the Women*, 2008), can also be interpreted as a reading of certain aspects of Afrikaner history, even though it is open to various other interpretations. The novel tells of the white woman Milla's complex relationship with the coloured woman Agaat, whom she took away from her parents when she was a young child. Even though the rural community of the 1950s frowns on her actions, she raises Agaat as her own child. When Milla unexpectedly falls pregnant, she moves Agaat into a room outside the house and into the position of a maidservant rather than a child in the house. Agaat eventually achieves a position of power over Milla when she is the one who nurses Milla through the final phases of motor neuron disease. After Milla's death, her son Jakkie makes over the farm to Agaat. The novel meticulously records certain details of Afrikaner history and Afrikaner life, whether it concerns farming, cooking, embroidery, gardening, religion or the structuring of relations with people of colour. As such, it highlights the archival impulse in which the specifics of Afrikaner history are preserved but at the same time subjected to critical scrutiny.

One can cite further examples: Joubert's *Die Reise van Isobelle* (1995; *Isobelle's Journey*, 1980) charts a hundred years of Afrikaner history up till 1994 from the perspective of four generations of female characters. Brink's *Duiwelskloof* (*Devils' Valley*, 1998) uses the techniques of magic realism to tell the story of an isolated and inbred community, intended to serve as an allegory of the Afrikaner nation. Etienne van Heerden also uses magic realism in *Die Swye van Mario Salviati* (2000; *The Long Silence of Mario Salviati*, 2002) to telescope two hundred years of history underlying the post-apartheid transformations, tensions and conflicts in the town of Tallejare. The attempt to examine Afrikaner history is not limited to the novel: playwright Deon Opperman's lengthy play *Donkerland* (Dark Land, 1996) dramatises the lives of six generations of the rather obviously named de Witt family ('wit' being the Afrikaans for 'white') in ten episodes that focus on key moments in Afrikaner history. The play starts with the first de Witt measuring out his farm in Natal in the nineteenth century and ends with his descendant having to surrender it to the original inhabitants of the land.

Revisiting the history and cultures of the San and Khoi peoples became a general trend in South African literature and academic studies in the 1990s.

Afrikaans literature after 1990 shared in this renewed interest shown by other literatures in South Africa (see Van Vuuren, 'Ek Hou 'n Troetelboesman Aan die Lewe', pp. 72–4.) The Namibian writer P. H. van Rooyen published several novels in which the interaction between white characters and contemporary San people is shown: *Die Spoorsnyer* (The Tracker, 1994), *Die Olifantjagters* (The Elephant Hunters, 1997) and *Gif* (Poison, 2001). He also published the autobiographical *Agter 'n Eland Aan* (Following an Eland, 1995), which tells of his work for a development trust in Namibia to help establish the Ju/'Hoan group as cattle farmers. Other novels that feature these indigenous groups are Dolf van Niekerk's *Koms van die Hyreën* (Coming of the He-rain, 1994), a novel about a struggle over land ownership, and Brink's novel *Bidsprinkaan* (Praying Mantis, 2005), which portrays a nineteenth-century Khoi man's vacillation between indigenous and Christian beliefs. Questions have, however, been raised about the issue whether the reworking of material from San, Khoi and Griqua culture by both English and Afrikaans writers (like Stephen Watson, Hans du Plessis, Thomas Deacon and Antjie Krog) might constitute an unacceptable form of appropriation of indigenous cultural goods.

New voices

The introduction of a range of new voices to Afrikaans literature after 1990 was partly the result of new strategies by Afrikaans publishers. The publishing house Kwela was set up by the media company Nasionale Pers in 1994 with the brief to focus on the development of new writers and to give voice to those South Africans who hitherto had not had the opportunity to make themselves heard. Together with the independent publisher Queillerie, Kwela was successful in developing the work of first-time writers like Abraham Phillips, A. H. M. Scholtz, E. K. M. Dido, Kirby van der Merwe and S. P. Benjamin in the 1990s; others, like Elias Nel, published with mainstream publisher Tafelberg. Whereas the black Afrikaans writers of the period 1976 to 1990 were mostly poets, these writers were mainly novelists. A. H. M. Scholtz achieved great success with his novel *Vatmaar* (1995; *A Place Called Vatmaar*, 2000), published when the author was 72 years old. Scholtz first wrote the novel in English because he did not have the confidence to publish in his mother tongue, Afrikaans. The novel tells how two of the founding members of the Vatmaar settlement, Uncle Chai and Corporal Lewis, got permission to settle in a spot close to the mining town of Dutoitspan in return for services rendered to the British government during the Anglo-Boer War. It makes use of a variety of narrating voices to tell the story of a hybrid community in which a wide variety of ethnic groups coexist, in a way which the author clearly sees as a model for South African society. He states in a preface addressed to the reader: 'I am going to tell a story of the coloured people of South Africa. They did not come from the North and also not from overseas. They originated here, true South Africans, who may one day be called Azanians'. E. K. M. Dido is the first black Afrikaans woman to establish herself as a successful novelist. Her first novel, *Die Storie van Monica Peters* (The Story of Monica Peters, 1996), related the story of an interracial couple's participation in the struggle against apartheid, their exile in Britain and their joyful return to South Africa in 1990. Her following novels often have a didactic slant and address a variety of social issues, including alcoholism, family violence, racial conflict between black and coloured, post-traumatic stress, crime and homelessness. Despite the introduction of the above-mentioned writers into the Afrikaans canon, the participation of black Afrikaans writers in the Afrikaans literary system still remains at a low level.

Dystopic views

Another trend that gradually emerged in Afrikaans literature after 1990, especially after the euphoria of the transition to democratic rule in 1994 dissipated, was the publication of literary texts that reflect on South African society with feelings of disillusion, moral uncertainty and the fear of a political and/or ecological disaster. In earlier Afrikaans literature, dystopian novels imagined a future after a bloody revolution in which Afrikaners lost their political and economic power. The best-known example is Karel Schoeman's novel *Na die Geliefde Land* (To the Beloved Country, 1972; English version, *Promised Land*, 1978), in which a man who left South Africa with his parents when he was a young child returns to the family farm, only to find the Afrikaner community of his youth living in fear and poverty after an unspecified change in the regime. Eben Venter's novel *Horrelpoot* (Club Foot, 2006; English version, *Trencherman*, 2008) is perhaps the strongest example of a dystopian novel in Afrikaans literature after 1990. The novel's main character is Marlouw, who lives in Australia and is asked by his sister to go and find her son Koert in South Africa (the names derive from the intertextual references to Joseph Conrad's *Heart of Darkness*). On his return to South Africa, Marlouw finds a country in decline: poverty is rampant, there are food shortages, AIDS has reached epidemic proportions, public services have ground to a halt, roads are in disrepair, corruption and opportunistic looting have become rife. When Marlouw finds Koert on the family farm (signed over to the black farm labourers when Marlouw and his sister left for Australia years before), he has degenerated

from powerful kingpin in a meat empire to a grotesquely disabled figure, inca-
pacitated by his obesity and a gangrenous leg. After a climax in which Koert
is killed during a carnivalesque party, the novel ends with a vision of the farm
as it might be after all human occupation has ceased: animals returning and
the veld gradually healing itself. Other Afrikaans novels that give a dystopic
future vision of South Africa are P. J. Haasbroek's *Oemkontoe van die Nasie*
(Umkhonto of the Nation, 2001), Jaco Botha's *Miskruier* (Dung Beetle, 2005)
and Koos Kombuis's *Raka: die Roman* (Raka: the Novel, 2005).

Afrikaans writing after 1990 has also seen a number of texts which reflect
critically on current rather than future or imagined scenarios. This trend
manifests itself in a variety of genres in Afrikaans, ranging from novels to
autobiographical fiction, short stories and poetry. The influence of J. M.
Coetzee's novel *Disgrace* (1999) is unmistakable in some of these texts. The
main character in Brink's novel *Donkermaan* (Dark Moon, 2000; translated by
the author with a title taken from Coetzee's novel, *The Rights of Desire*, 2000) is
Ruben Kruger, a librarian who is forced to retire to make way for a black man.
He indirectly experiences the effects of violent crime when his neighbour is
murdered and through the stories of his coloured housekeeper. As is often the
case in these texts, this novel's picture of post-apartheid South Africa as violent
and crime-ridden is accompanied by references to the country's violent past
in the narrative about the slave woman, Antje. Etienne van Heerden's novel
In Stede van die Liefde (In Love's Place, 2005) takes the dystopic view outside
the confines of South African society. The main character in Van Heerden's
novel is Christian Lemmer, whose travels as the owner of an internet company
dealing in African art, bring him into contact with the social ills of South Africa
as well as the larger global community: gangsterism, crime syndicates, drug
dealing and trafficking in humans. Hennie Aucamp's series of three writer's
diaries, *Gekaapte Tyd* (Cape Time / Hijacked Time, 1996), *Allersiele* (All Souls,
1997) and *In die Vroegte* (Early in the Morning, 2003) presents a sombre picture
of violence, moral degeneration and impending ecological disaster. In the first
of these diaries, the author contrasts his picture of the social, ecological and
cultural decline of the city of Cape Town, in which he lives with Sir Francis
Drake's reference to 'the fairest cape'. Whereas Aucamp's autobiographical
writing gives an urban perspective, Abraham H. de Vries's volume of short
stories, *Tot Verhaal Kom* (Recovering Your Wits / Story, 2003), concentrates on
the decline and deterioration visible in the rural areas. Stories like 'Bouvalle'
('Ruins') and 'Die Behoue Huis' ('The Preserved House') focus on issues such
as farm murders, but also emphasise the injustices of the past. In Afrikaans
poetry, the dystopic trend manifests itself in isolated poems in volumes by

poets such as Breytenbach, Krog, Barend Toerien and Louis Esterhuizen, rather than as the main theme of volumes. The anthology *Nuwe Verset* (New Resistance, 2000) also gathers together a collection of poems on this theme.

In conclusion, one must concede that an overview such as this is an homogenising construct imposed on a body of literature that has increasingly come to reflect the heterogeneity of the Afrikaans-speaking community in South Africa. As Pakendorf has suggested, it is precisely from its diversity of voices, sublanguages, genres and themes that Afrikaans literature derives its imaginative power and subversive potential as a minority literature in the larger South African context ('Kafka, en die Saak vir "'n Klein Letterkunde"', pp. 103–6).

Bibliography

Adams, N., et al. *Aankoms uit die Skemer*, St Helena Bay: Prog, 1988.

Adams, W., L. Koza and P. Petersen (eds.). *Optog*, Grassy Park: Domestica, 1990.

Aucamp, H. *Allersiele*, Cape Town: Tafelberg, 1997.

    Gekaapte Tyd, Cape Town: Tafelberg, 1996.

    Met Permissie Gesê, Cape Town: Tafelberg, 1980.

    Slegs vir Almal, Cape Town: HAUM-Literêr, 1986.

    In die Vroegte, Cape Town: Tafelberg, 2003.

Botha, J. *Miskruier*, Cape Town: Human & Rousseau, 2005.

Bouwer, A. *Stories van Rivierplaas*, Cape Town: Nasionale Boekhandel, 1955.

Breytenbach, B. *And Death White as Words: An Anthology of the Poetry of Breyten Breytenbach*, London: Rex Collings, 1978.

    Judas Eye and Self-Portrait/Deathwatch, London: Faber, 1988.

    Lewendood, Emmarentia: Taurus, 1985.

    Die Ongedanste Dans: Gevangenisgedigte, 1975–1983, Cape Town: Human & Rousseau, 2005.

    Skryt, Amsterdam: Meulenhoff, 1972.

    Voetskrif, Cape Town: Perskor, 1976.

Brink, A. *Bidsprinkaan*, Cape Town: Human & Rousseau, 2005; *Praying Mantis*, London: Secker & Warburg, 2005.

    Donkermaan, Cape Town: Human & Rousseau, 2000; *The Rights of Desire*, London: Secker & Warburg, 2000.

    'n Droë Wit Seisoen, Emmarentia: Taurus, 1979; *A Dry White Season*, London: W. H. Allen, 1979.

    Gerugte van Reën, Cape Town: Human & Rousseau, 1978; *Rumours of Rain*, London: W. H. Allen, 1978.

    Houd-den-bek, Bramley: Taurus, 1982; *A Chain of Voices*, London: Faber, 1982.

    Kennis van die Aand, Cape Town: Buren, 1973; *Looking on Darkness*, London: W. H. Allen, 1974.

    Die Kreef Raak Gewoond Daaraan, Cape Town: Human & Rousseau, 1991; *An Act of Terror*, London: Secker & Warburg, 1991.

Die Muur van die Pes, Cape Town: Human & Rousseau, 1984; *The Wall of the Plague*, London: Faber, 1984.

'n Oomblik in die Wind, Emmarentia: Taurus, 1975; *An Instant in the Wind*, London: W. H. Allen, 1976.

States of Emergency, London: Faber, 1988.

Christianse, Y. "'Down to my last skin": A Conversation with Antjie Krog', *Connect: Art Politics, Theory, Practice. Issue on Translation* (autumn 2000), 11–20.

Coetzee, A. *Letterkunde en Krisis: 'n Honderd Jaar Afrikaanse Letterkunde en Afrikanernasionalisme*, Bramley: Taurus, 1990.

Coetzee, A., and H. Willemse (eds.). *I Qabane Labantu: Poetry in the Emergency/Poësie in die Noodtoestand*, Bramley: Taurus, 1989.

Coetzee, C. *Op Soek na Generaal Mannetjies Mentz*, Cape Town: Queillerie, 1998.

Cussons, S. *Plektrum*, Cape Town: Tafelberg, 1970.

Poems, Cape Town: Tafelberg, 1985.

Die Swart Kombuis, Cape Town: Tafelberg, 1978.

De Lange, J. *Nagsweet*, Bramley: Taurus, 1991.

De Vries, A. H. *Tot Verhaal Kom*, Cape Town: Human & Rousseau, 2003.

De Wet, R. *Diepe Grond*, Pretoria: HAUM-Literêr, 1986.

Vrystaat-trilogie, Pretoria: HAUM-Literêr, 1991.

Dido, E. K. M. *Die Storie van Monica Peters*, Cape Town: Kwela Books, 1996.

Fourie, P. *Die Joiner*, Cape Town: Tafelberg, 1984.

Ek, Anna van Wyk, Pretoria: HAUM-Literêr, 1986.

Die Koggelaar, Pretoria: HAUM-Literêr, 1988.

Goosen, J. *Louoond*, Pretoria: HAUM-Literêr, 1987.

Ons Is Nie Almal So Nie, Pretoria: HAUM-Literêr, 1990. Translation by A. Brink as *We're Not All Like That*, Cape Town: Kwela Books, 2007.

Haasbroek, P. J. *Oemkontoe van die Nasie*, Pretoria: Protea Boekhuis, 2001.

Roofvis, Cape Town: Human & Rousseau, 1975.

Verby die Vlakte, Cape Town: Human & Rousseau, 1982.

Hambidge, J. *Bitterlemoene*, Cape Town: Human & Rousseau, 1986.

Hartskrif, Cape Town: Human & Rousseau, 1985.

Hugo, D., L. Rousseau and P. du Plessis (eds.). *Nuwe Verset*, Pretoria: Protea Boekhuis, 2000.

Huismans, E. *Berigte van Weerstand*, Bramley: Taurus, 1990.

Joubert, E. *Die Reise van Isobelle*, Cape Town: Tafelberg, 1995. Translation by C. Knox as *Isobelle's Journey*, Johannesburg: Jonathan Ball, 2002.

Die Swerfjare van Poppie Nongena, Cape Town: Tafelberg, 1978. Translation by E. Joubert as *The Long Journey of Poppie Nongena*, Johannesburg: Jonathan Ball, 1980.

Kannemeyer, J. C. *Die Afrikaanse Literatuur 1652–2004*, Cape Town: Human & Rousseau, 2005.

Kellerman, G. *Wie de Hel Het Jou Vertel?*, Cape Town: Tafelberg, 1988.

Kombuis, K. *Raka: die Roman*, Cape Town: Human & Rousseau, 2005.

Krog, A. *Country of my Skull*, Johannesburg: Random House, 1998.

Dogter van Jefta, Cape Town: Human & Rousseau, 1970.

Down to my Last Skin, Johannesburg: Random Poets, 2000.

Jerusalemgangers, Cape Town: Human & Rousseau, 1985.

Lady Anne, Bramley: Taurus, 1989.

Otters in Bronslaai, Cape Town: Human & Rousseau, 1981.

Krüger, Louis. *'n Basis Oorkant die Grens*, Cape Town: Tafelberg, 1984.

Leroux, E. *Magersfontein, O Magersfontein!*, Cape Town: Human & Rousseau, 1976. Translation by N. Roets as *Magersfontein, O Magersfontein!*, Wynberg: Hutchinson, 1983.

Loflin, C. 'Periodization in South African Literature', *Clio* 26:2 (1997).

Matthee, D. *Fiela se Kind*, Cape Town: Tafelberg, 1985. Translation by D. Matthee as *Fiela's Child*, Harmondsworth: Penguin, 1986.

Kringe in 'n Bos, Cape Town: Tafelberg, 1984. Translation by D. Matthee as *Circles in a Forest*, Harmondsworth: Penguin, 1984.

Moerbeibos, Cape Town: Tafelberg, 1987. Translation by D. Matthee as *The Mulberry Forest*, Harmondsworth: Penguin, 1989.

Toorbos, Cape Town: Tafelberg, 2003. Translation by D. Matthee as *Dreamforest*, Johannesburg: Penguin, 2004.

McDonald, P. D. *The Literature Police: Apartheid Censorship and its Cultural Consequences*, Oxford University Press, 2009.

Miles, J. *Donderdag of Woensdag*, Emmarentia: Taurus, 1978.

Kroniek uit die Doofpot, Bramley: Taurus, 1991. Translation by E. Doherty as *Deafening Silence*, Cape Town: Human & Rousseau, 1997.

Stanley Bekker en die Boikot, Emmarentia: Taurus, 1980.

Odendaal, W. *Keerkring*, Cape Town: Perskor, 1977.

Olivier, F. *Verklarings: 1967–1987*, Cape Town: Human & Rousseau, 1988.

Opperman, D. *Donkerland*, Cape Town: Tafelberg, 1996.

Môre is 'n Lang Dag, Cape Town: Tafelberg, 1986.

Stille Nag, Cape Town: Tafelberg, 1990.

Pakendorf, G. 'Kafka, en die saak vir "'n klein letterkunde"', *Stilet* 5:1 (1993), 99–106.

Petersen, P. J. *Amandla Ngawethu*, Genadendal: Morawiese Boekhandel, 1985.

Prinsloo, K. *Die Hemel Help Ons*, Emmarentia: Taurus, 1987.

Jonkmanskas, Cape Town: Tafelberg, 1982.

Slagplaas, Cape Town: Human & Rousseau, 1992.

Weifeling, Groenkloof: Hond, 1993.

Schoeman, K. *Hierdie Lewe*, Cape Town: Human & Rousseau, 1993. Translation by E. Silke as *This Life*, Cape Town: Human & Rousseau, 2005.

Na die Geliefde Land, Cape Town: Human & Rousseau, 1972. Translation by M. V. Friedman as *Promised Land*, New York: Summit Books, 1978.

Die Uur van die Engel, Cape Town: Human & Rousseau, 1995.

Verliesfontein, Cape Town: Human & Rousseau, 1998.

Scholtz, A. H. M. *Vatmaar*, Cape Town: Kwela Books, 1995. Translation by C. van Wyk as *A Place Called Vatmaar*, Cape Town: Kwela Books, 2000.

Sleigh, D. *Eilande*, Cape Town: Tafelberg, 2002. Translation by A. Brink as *Islands*, London: Secker & Warburg, 2002.

Steyn, J. C. *Op Pad na die Grens*, Cape Town: Tafelberg, 1976.

Stockenström, W. *Die Kremetartekspedisie*, Cape Town: Human & Rousseau, 1981. Translation by J. M. Coetzee as *The Expedition to the Baobab Tree*, London: Faber, 1983.

Uitdraai, Cape Town: Human & Rousseau, 1976.

Strachan, A. *'n Wêreld Sonder Grense*, Cape Town: Tafelberg, 1984.

Swanepoel, E. 'Helende Terapie', *De Kat* (April 1995), 102.

Uys, P-D. *Selle Ou Storie*, Johannesburg: Ad Donker, 1983.

Die Van Aardes van Grootoor, Emmarentia: Taurus, 1979.

Van Coller, H. P. 'Die Waarheidskommissie in die Afrikaanse Letterkunde: die Afrikaanse Prosa in die Jare Negentig', *Stilet* 9:2 (1997), 9–21.

Van Coller, H. P. (ed.). *Perspektief en Profiel*, vols. i–iii, Pretoria: Van Schaik, 1998, 1999, 2005.

Van der Vyver, M. *Griet Skryf 'n Sprokie*, Cape Town: Tafelberg, 1992. Translation by C. Knox as *Entertaining Angels*, London: Michael Joseph, 1994.

Van Heerden, E. *In Stede van die Liefde*, Cape Town: Tafelberg, 2005.

My Kubaan, Cape Town: Tafelberg, 1983.

Om te Awol, Cape Town: Tafelberg, 1984.

Die Swye van Mario Salviati, Cape Town: Tafelberg, 2000. Translation by C. Knox as *The Long Silence of Mario Salviati*, London: Sceptre, 2002.

Toorberg, Cape Town: Tafelberg, 1986. Translation by M. Hacksley as *Ancestral Voices*, Harmondsworth: Penguin, 1989.

Van Niekerk, D. *Koms van die Hyreën*, Cape Town: Tafelberg, 1994.

Van Niekerk, M. *Agaat*, Cape Town: Tafelberg, 2004. Translation by M. Heyns as *Agaat*, Johannesburg: Jonathan Ball, 2006; *The Way of the Women*, London: Abacus, 2008.

Triomf, Cape Town: Queillerie, 1994. Translation by L. de Kock as *Triomf*, Johannesburg: Jonathan Ball, 1999.

Van Rooyen, P. *Agter 'n Eland Aan*, Cape Town: Queillerie, 1995.

Gif, Pretoria: Protea Boekhuis, 2001.

Die Olifantjagters, Cape Town: Tafelberg, 1997.

Die Spoorsnyer, Cape Town: Tafelberg, 1994.

Van Vuuren, H. '"Ek Hou 'n Troetelboesman aan die Lewe": Die Boesman-drieluik van Piet van Rooyen', *Stilet* 14:1 (2002), 72–99.

Venter, E. *Horrelpoot*, Cape Town: Tafelberg, 2008. Translation by L. Stubbs as *Trencherman*, Cape Town: Tafelberg, 2008.

Viljoen, L. *Klaaglied vir Koos*, Emmarentia: Taurus, 1984.

Willemse, H. *Aan die Ander Kant. Swart Afrikaanse Skrywers in die Afrikaanse Letterkunde*, Pretoria: Protea Boekhuis, 2008.

'The Black Afrikaans Writer: A Continuing Dichotomy', *Triquarterly* 69 (1987), 237–47.

Winterbach, I. *Niggie*, Cape Town: Human & Rousseau, 2002. Translation by E. Silke as *To Hell with Cronjé*, Cape Town: Human & Rousseau, 2007.

23

The liberal tradition in fiction

PETER BLAIR

To speak of any 'tradition', let alone a 'liberal' tradition, in South African English fiction requires caution. In 1979 Stephen Gray considered that 'tradition-making, in English South Africa, has often occurred fortuitously, rather than by any planned consciousness through which the writer has fused his or her own literature's past with contemporary stimuli' (*Southern African Literature*, p. 7), and in 1994 Stephen Clingman concluded that there is 'no aim or sense of building a novelistic tradition', only 'patterns of thematic accumulation' ('Novel', p. 1148). If the critical consensus has resisted the notion of a tradition, it has nevertheless ascribed a certain shape to the literary history of liberal fiction. Richard Rive, himself a liberal author, is one of many who consider Alan Paton's *Cry, the Beloved Country* (1948) a 'watershed', soon after which 'liberal writing was on the wane' ('Liberal Tradition', pp. 31, 21). Paul Rich argues that between *Beloved Country* and Nadine Gordimer's *The Late Bourgeois World* (1966) a 'crisis at the heart of post-war South African liberalism' gave rise to 'a progressive loss of literary self-confidence' that 'produced an internal crisis of literary form' (*Hope and Despair*, pp. 119–20; see also Rich, 'Liberal Realism'), while Michael Vaughan describes the overturning of liberal hegemony in the 1970s by modernism and popular realism, represented respectively by J. M. Coetzee and Mtutuzeli Matshoba ('Literature and Politics'). Whereas these appraisals explain literary development primarily in terms of historical context, Tony Morphet's 'patricidal' account of 'trajectories in the liberal novel' foregrounds immanent factors, highlighting decisive cleavages between Paton (a backward-looking Christian and traditional liberal, whose allegiance is to the rural and to religion) and Gordimer (a forward-looking secular and radical liberal, whose allegiance is to the urban and to history); and between Gordimer and Coetzee (an 'epistemological liberal', who rejects

I would like to thank Jacques Berthoud for the many generous conversations, over a number of years, that helped shape my understanding of the texts discussed in this chapter.

linearity, whether nostalgic or utopian, for a spatialising scrutiny of colonial and novelistic discourses) (Morphet, 'Stranger Fictions').

Whilst Rive, Rich and Vaughan in various ways resist crude historical determinism, and Morphet's notion of 'trajectory' fights shy of 'tradition', stressing key inter-author dissonances rather than comprehensive intertextual resonance, what emerges from both emphases is a three-part narrative suggesting a pre-apartheid elaboration of what might be termed 'classic' liberal fiction, followed by a period of transition, and a transformation in the 1970s in what David Attwell notes was 'a literary-intellectual moment that became generally understood as "postliberal"' (*J. M. Coetzee*, p. 26).[1] Although this teleology, and its periodisation of the fiction into discrete phases, could well be problematised, this chapter will use it as a serviceable framework, as well as outlining its sociohistorical context and a fourth, post-apartheid, stage.

Liberalism in politics and civil society

If it is problematic to speak of a 'tradition', then the term 'liberal' raises even more acute difficulties, since liberalism has meant different things at different times to different South Africans. In 1973 Paton offered a well-known seven-fold definition that was, however, expressly transhistorical: 'By liberalism I don't mean the creed of any party or any century. I mean a generosity of spirit, a tolerance of others, an attempt to comprehend otherness, a commitment to the rule of law, a high ideal of the worth and dignity of man, a repugnance for authoritarianism and a love of freedom' (Alexander, *Alan Paton*, p. 383). In 1998 David Welsh listed seven (broadly cognate) 'core values of liberalism': 'a commitment to fundamental human rights and those procedural safeguards known as the rule of law'; 'a commitment to constitutionalism'; 'a belief in equality'; 'an emphasis on the primacy of the individual'; 'tolerance of conflicting viewpoints'; 'an optimistic belief in the possibilities of individual and social "improvement"'; and 'compassion' ('Liberal Inheritance', p. 2). For the purposes of this chapter, the last four may be taken, along with Paton's writerly 'attempt to comprehend otherness', as the criteria that distinguish liberalism from other ideologies that also promote equality, constitutionalism and the rule of law; but these distinguishing principles, while seductively

---

1 Richard Peck suggests a similar three-stage model of liberal fiction: represented by Alan Paton and Laurens van der Post; undermined by Dan Jacobson, Phyllis Altman and Mary Benson; and superseded by Nadine Gordimer and André Brink (Peck, *A Morbid Fascination*).

humanistic, are notoriously elusive and their implications uncertain. In particular, as Welsh acknowledged, democracy is conspicuously absent from his 'core values'. He considered that their 'cumulative consequence . . . would be a democratic system', yet, as he had conceded in 1987, 'the conjunction of the two words "democratic" and "liberal" . . . has not always been true of the whole of the South African liberal tradition' (Butler, Elphick and Welsh, 'Editors' Introduction', *Democratic Liberalism*, p. 7).

This tradition developed from a liberal paternalism imported into the Cape Colony as part of the cultural baggage of British administrators (from 1795) and the 1820 Settlers. A significant minority challenged the local conditions of slavery (abolished 1834, with manumission in 1838), and humanitarian polemics against the mistreatment of indigenous peoples appeared in the 1820s and 1830s, including Thomas Pringle's *Narrative of a Residence in South Africa* (1834) (see Chapter 9). Liberals also established a democratic marker in the colourblind franchise entrenched in the Colony's 1853 constitution, though its whittling down by registration acts in 1887, 1892 and 1894 left Cape liberalism somewhat tarnished (Davenport, 'Cape Liberal Tradition', pp. 32–3).

After the Union of South Africa in 1910, and under a United Party intent on tightening and codifying segregation, liberals were active in welfare work and social research, through the Joint Councils in the 1920s and, from 1929, the Institute of Race Relations. They made important contributions to the debate about segregation, their analyses ranging from (usually separatist) group-based multiracialism, theorised as cultural idealism, to (ultimately assimilationist) individual-based non-racialism, which stressed common humanity. But as Hertzog's administration (1924–39) appropriated liberals' terminology to justify a brand of segregation that was repressive rather than benevolent, many distanced themselves from the policy and concentrated on ameliorating its effects. (See Dubow, *Racial Segregation*; Rich, *White Power*; Rich, *Hope and Despair*.)

The Smuts government of 1939–48 relaxed segregation, but the election of Malan's Nationalists under the banner of apartheid, and their re-election in 1953, prompted liberals, led by Paton, to form the Liberal Party. Hoping to secure the support of white voters, the party initially adopted the Cape principle of 'civilised' suffrage, but in 1954 it ratified a policy of universal suffrage to be progressively introduced, and in 1960 accepted that it should be introduced without delay. The party also radicalised in other ways, supporting boycotts (1959) and advocating land redistribution (1961). Black membership had increased, and 1960–1 saw the party 'at the height of its achievement'

(Robertson, *Liberalism in South Africa*, p. 215; see also Vigne, *Liberals Against Apartheid*). Meanwhile, the Black Sash (founded 1955) enhanced liberalism's profile as campaigner and mediator.

In the wake of the Sharpeville massacre (1960) and the establishment of the Republic (1961), however, liberalism looked impotent. The Liberal Party went into decline, precipitated by the exposure in 1964 of young, rogue members who had abandoned non-violence for the sabotage activities of the African Resistance Movement (1961–4). In 1968, when non-racial political organisations were outlawed, the party dissolved itself. Party-political liberalism became the prerogative of the Progressive Party (founded 1959), the relative conservatism of which allowed it to achieve the parliamentary representation that had eluded the Liberal Party; while Helen Suzman was its sole MP in the 1960s, as the Progressive Federal Party it became the official opposition (1977–86).

By this stage, however, liberalism was regarded by most blacks and leftist whites as a quietist ideology complicit with colonialism rather than a disinterested mediator or credible oppositional strategy. Dialogist approaches had manifestly failed, and liberal faith in the 'self-correctibility' of the individual, and of society, looked misplaced (Vaughan, 'Literature and Politics', p. 120). Critics derided the idealism of appealing to errant consciences to correct themselves and debunked the belief of economic liberals that capitalism would erode apartheid. Black Consciousness, emerging in the late 1960s, anyway rejected non-racialism, and the 1976 Soweto uprising made liberals' gradualism seem irrelevant. In the 1950s figures such as Paton and Suzman had been denounced as liberals by the Right, but 'in the 1980s the Left freely used "liberal", as well as "humanist", as terms of abuse' (Coetzee, 'South African Liberals', p. 322).

The fortunes of South African PEN, the 'most straightforwardly liberal' writers' group in the country (McDonald, *Literature Police*, p. 166), followed a similar trajectory. The South African branch of PEN was launched in Johannesburg in 1927 by Sarah Gertrude Millin, whose fiction obsessively denigrates 'miscegenation', but as the group became increasingly anti-racialist Millin felt marginalised and in 1960 resigned. By this stage PEN had a second branch in Cape Town and around eighty members (p. 166). PEN's 1955 yearbook had sufficiently upset the government for it to withdraw a grant supporting the publication (Sowden, 'PEN'), and in 1964–8 a series of editorials by Tony Fleischer protested against censorship and depicted the membership as 'embattled', under pressure from both Left and Right to tow an 'official line'; but Fleischer also dismissed 'ideological distinctions' as 'tiresome', prizing such qualities as sincerity and individuality (Fleischer, 'Editorial'). PEN was thus variously regarded as a 'white liberal advocacy group' and a 'belletristic bourgeois club' (McDonald, *Literature Police*, p. 168). In the mid 1970s PEN was challenged by the newly formed Artists' and Writers' Guild (AWG), a radical group frustrated with the 'relatively passive tradition of liberal protest' embodied by PEN (p. 177), and in 1978 the Johannesburg branch merged with the AWG and other groups to be reconstituted, under black leadership, as Johannesburg PEN. However, tensions between those who believed that a non-racial guild was 'inimical to the black consciousness movement' and 'inhibit[ed] the writing of literature "relevant" to the struggle' (Wentzel, *Liberal Slideaway*, p. 13) and non-racialists such as Lionel Abrahams, who was concerned that concentrating on the 'populist utterance' neglected 'techniques and individual self-realisation' (Abrahams, 'From Shakespeare House', pp. 10, 16), led to disbandment in January 1981, many members forming the exclusively black African Writers' Association.

It would be wrong, though, to assume that liberal writing had been, or would become, the preserve of white English speakers. The first novel by a black South African, Sol Plaatje's *Mhudi* (1930; written *c.* 1917–20), was in some key respects liberal, depicting the destructive effect on interpersonal relations of tribal and racial chauvinisms in the 1830s, during the *mfecane* and Great Trek; and this chapter will discuss writers who were coloured (Peter Abrahams, Richard Rive) and Afrikaans (André Brink), as well as two post-apartheid black writers. Nevertheless, liberalism's entanglement with the stubborn self-image of English speakers as frontier innocents caught 'in the middle' between the competing nationalisms of *laager* and *kraal* – which Mike Kirkwood, in a swingeing 1974 attack, branded 'Butlerism', after the poet Guy Butler ('Colonizer') – helped ensure the predominant Englishness of the tradition, and its demise.

In 1979 the editor of *The Liberal Dilemma in South Africa* pronounced the book an 'epitaph' for liberalism (van den Berghe, 'Introduction', p. 8), and in 1984 Rich concurred that liberalism had 'failed politically' (*White Power*, p. 123). In 1993, however, Rich conceded that liberalism had 'acquired an unforeseen relevance' (*Hope and Despair*, p. 211). Proponents hailed the 'ironic victory' that saw liberal values 'rise phoenix-like' to be enshrined in the post-apartheid constitution and the Truth and Reconciliation Commission (Johnson and Welsh, *Ironic Victory*; Vigne, *Liberals Against Apartheid*, p. 224). Rich subsequently argued the revisionist case that 'since at least the late 1970s' liberalism was being reinvented, all but losing its 'distinct political identity' in the 'merging of liberal, democratic and non-racial discourses' during the 1980s and early 1990s ('New South African Liberal Conscience?', pp. 1, 14, 16). The terms 'liberal' and 'liberalism', however, remain widely pejorative.

Classic liberal fiction, 1883–1948

If British settlers established liberalism at the Cape, then Olive Schreiner is generally credited with founding the 'liberal-concerned' tradition in the South African novel (Parker, 'South African Novel', p. 7), her preface to the second edition of *The Story of an African Farm* (1883) renouncing the imperial romance (see Chapter 11 above), as the mode of the outsider, and inaugurating an indigenous tradition of liberal realism. This foundation in contradistinction to another fictional mode was salutary, for the later development of liberal fiction can be charted against writing that was variously illiberal, anti-liberal or simply uninterested in liberalism, ranging from the racist schematics of Millin to the social(ist) realism of Alex La Guma, and from Black Consciousness writing (see Chapter 24) to fiction in the 'experimental line' (see Chapter 37). More important, though, is the realist mode that Schreiner's inaugural text adopts and adapts, being clearly marked by the affinity between the novel as it developed in nineteenth-century Britain and a liberal outlook, with its emphasis on interiority and choice, grounded in a paradoxical conception of the individual as embedded in sociohistorical context yet essentially free of social determinants.

African Farm is generically complex, but this liberal aesthetic drives its exploration of the bleak struggles for self-realisation of its two Cape-born protagonists, Lyndall (a proto-feminist) and Waldo (an eventual pantheist), against the boorish colonials and harsh landscape of the Karoo. For all its much vaunted liberalism, however, the novel is only marginally concerned with race. Black characters are also peripheral in the posthumously published *Undine* (1928) and *From Man to Man* (1926), and their representations tainted with the scientific racism that fascinated Schreiner in her 1890s essay 'The Problem of Slavery' (*Thoughts on South Africa*, 1923). Schreiner's most straight-forwardly liberal works are *Trooper Peter Halket of Mashonaland* (1897), an allegory attacking Rhodes and the treatment of Rhodesia's indigenous people by his Chartered Company, and the pamphlet *Closer Union* (1909), which argued for the extension of the Cape franchise to the new federation. The anti-imperial humanitarianism of *Peter Halket* is evident in Schreiner's eulogising of the Boers in *Thoughts* and the short story 'Eighteen Ninety-Nine' (1923; written *c.* 1901–4), but the contradiction in her advocacy of both African and Afrikaner remained unresolved; as in her three novels and *Woman and Labour* (non-fiction, 1911), she is often more interested in the position of women and the construction of gender (see Chapter 36). Schreiner's inauguration of the 'liberal-concerned' tradition is therefore ethically as well as formally complex, compromised by a conservative ethnography and complicated or even displaced by other, broadly liberal, concerns.

Like *African Farm*, Pauline Smith's *The Beadle* (1926) largely occludes the black labour on which the white farm depends, but where Schreiner found colonial society cruelly trammelling, Smith is nostalgic for its feudal paternalism – despite the poor-white tragedies of *The Little Karoo* (1925) (see Chapter 18). Most liberal fiction after Schreiner, however, stemmed from a domestication of the European 'social-problem' novel, race being substituted for class, and two key aspects of the local 'Colour Problem' were compulsively fictionalised: black migration to the cities giving rise to the 'Jim comes to Jo'burg' theme, and interracial sex producing the 'miscegenation' novel.

The first anti-miscegenation law had been passed in 1685, but subsequent laws (including legislation of 1902 and the Immorality Act of 1927) provoked liberal protest. Among the earliest examples are Perceval Gibbon's *Souls in Bondage* (1904) and *Margaret Harding* (1911), but in neither does miscegenation occur. *Souls in Bondage* merely raises the possibility of marriage between a white man and a coloured woman (then legal) as an act of paternalistic charity, while *Margaret Harding*'s more daring exploration of unconsummated desire in the illicit, doubly-taboo conjunction of black man and white woman amounts, finally, to a cautious plea for legal and attitudinal reform. The prurient Millin, in contrast, is unequivocally condemnatory, though 'the mild liberalism of her early years' (Rubin, *Sarah Gertrude Millin*, p. 74) produces aberrant, empathetic moments in *God's Step-Children* (1924) (Blair, 'That "ugly word"'). Self-contradiction is thematised in William Plomer's *Turbott Wolfe* (1925), which has been described as 'a forerunner of the "liberal novel" and at the same time a critique of liberalism' (Rabkin, 'Race and Fiction', p. 86); Wolfe becomes enthusiastically involved in a pro-miscegenation society, only to find himself unable to approve of, or engage in, an interracial affair. Plomer gives the theme more considered treatment in 'The Child of Queen Victoria' (1933). Peter Abrahams's *The Path of Thunder* (1948), in which love takes Lanny Swartz and his white partner 'above and beyond colour' (p. 91), until others intervene, offers perhaps the strongest liberal protest. But the novel also interrogates contradictions in liberal ideology, Swartz's self-immolation in the doomed affair arguably symptomatic of a 'crisis of the liberal subject', produced when the incorporationist project that underpins his identity as a teacher – a candidate for, and acculturating agent of, eventual assimilation – is rendered obsolete by an illiberal system (Wade, 'Peter Abrahams's *The Path of Thunder*').

Tensions within liberalism also emerge in the 'Jim comes to Jo'burg' sub-genre, which was 'essentially concerned with the rural black man's encounter with the white-controlled industrial city' (Gray, 'Third World Meets First World', p. 61). The 'Jim' typically journeys from naivety to depravity, via bewilderment, wonder, dissolute peers, white injustice and brutal employment (often including traumatic entombment in the mines), while the fiction looks to liberal patronage and/or retribalisation as possible remedies. This subgenre was pioneered by Douglas Blackburn's *Leaven: A Black and White Story* (1908), in which Bulalie suffers the inevitable corruption, despite the endeavours of the missionary David Hyslop (the liberal 'leaven'). Bulalie, who redeems himself in his final moments, is both a parody of Umslopogaas from Haggard's *Allan Quatermain* (1887) (Coetzee, Couzens, and Gray, 'South African Literatures', p. 193) and 'the first credible black figure in our fiction' (Chapman, *Southern African Literatures*, p. 141), and Blackburn's probing of the system that destroys him ironises Hyslop's resilient faith in paternalism. *Leaven* thus anticipates key concerns of the liberal-realist tradition – the (often self-conscious) representation of otherness; individual- versus system-based social analyses; the limits of trusteeship – as well as reflecting Blackburn's foundation of an alternative, if intermittent, tradition of satire, in which his most significant successor was Herman Charles Bosman (see Chapter 18 above).

A number of subsequent 'Jim' narratives explore the prospects for retribalising the migrant. In W. C. Scully's *Daniel Vananda: The Life Story of a Human Being* (1923), Vananda's urban dissolution is redeemed by the intervention of Stephen Vardy; but Vardy's death leaves Vananda exposed, driven to the Reef where he contracts phthisis, a ravaging lung disease that symbolises the city's contamination of the black migrant. Scully's protest is passionate, and he clearly demonstrates the inadequacy of ad hoc liberal interventions; but he explores no alternative urban solution, and when Vananda retreats to his birthplace to die he finds the once 'delectable land, rich of soil and murmurous with many streams' (p. 17) blighted by drought and taxes. In two shorter, contrasting works of 1927, R. R. R. Dhlomo's novella *An African Tragedy* (a mission morality tale) and Plomer's 'Ula Masondo' (a quizzical short story), no liberal patron intervenes, and the return of the deracinated migrant has catastrophic consequences for others. Dhlomo's Robert Zulu returns a drunken philanderer who infects his wife and, fatally, his child with venereal disease, while the estrangement of Masondo, who returns with a pregnant prostitute on his arm, is such that he disowns his mother, driving her to suicide. These anxieties are absent, however, from Frank Brownlee's *Ntsukumbini: Cattle Thief* (1929), in which Ntsukumbini, having returned from the city unscathed, indulges in nostalgic reminiscences about his youthful tribal exploits, with Brownlee (in a conceit both deferential and appropriative) his amanuensis.

Later works reluctantly accept detribalisation, and in the absence of a viable segregationist solution reflect self-consciously on black proletarianisation and its challenge to liberal ideology. In Laurens van der Post's *In a Province* (1934) the migrant story of Kenon Badiakgotla is subsumed in a loaded portrayal of trade union activity in the 1920s, represented by Burgess, a rabble-rousing Marxist who rejects liberalism's 'inevitability-of-gradualness nonsense' (p. 187) for revolution. Afrikaner Johan van Bredepoel voices the classic liberal riposte: 'The system is only a garment round the human heart; it doesn't give the shape to the heart, it takes its own shape from the heart' (p. 334). Abrahams's *Mine Boy* (1946), in contrast, engages in an heuristic spirit with Marxist, Africanist and liberal analyses, but is ultimately unresolved, Xuma's vision of 'man without colour' (pp. 173–4) melding the three ideologies uneasily into a 'radical populist liberalism' (Wade, '*Song of the City*', p. 99).

The high-water mark of the subgenre is of course Paton's *Beloved Country*, a 'hypercanonical' text (Van der Vlies, *South African Textual Cultures*, pp. 71–105) often taken as metonymic of South African liberalism and liberal fiction, as well as a potential '"great national novel"' (Attwell, 'South African Literature', p. 516) and a malleable icon of South Africa in the global imaginary (see Chapter 33). In 1946 Stephen Kumalo, a humble parson from rural Natal, journeys to Johannesburg in search of three relatives: his sister Gertrude, a prostitute; his brother John, a reckless demagogue; and his son Absalom, who has murdered liberal activist Arthur Jarvis during a bungled burglary. Paton's novel documents the harsh city conditions as well as the rural degradation that ensures urbanisation, but it rejects black mass politics, caricatured in John Kumalo, endorsing the dignified long-suffering of his brother and valorising trusteeship, represented by a plethora of white liberals. Meanwhile, Kumalo's moving odyssey and reconciliation with Arthur's father seems designed to induce a change of heart in the complacent or illiberal reader, on the model of Jarvis's heart-changing, which moves him to charity. The novel's 'one great fear', voiced by a black clergyman, 'that one day when they turn to loving they will find we are turned to hating' (p. 235) ominously undercuts this approach, and the ironic coincidence of *Beloved Country*'s publication with the Nationalists' election made it seem outdated;[2] far from turning to loving, whites

---

2 For discussion of *Beloved Country*'s early publication history, and the contrast between its reception in South Africa and abroad, see Chapter 33 below.

had elected a party seemingly bent on turning blacks to hating. As apartheid deepened, *Beloved Country* would look increasingly inadequate, exemplary of 'the failure of the liberal vision' (Watson, '*Cry, the Beloved Country*'), and it continued to be dismissed as 'an appeal to the lump in the throat' (Peck, *Morbid Fascination*, p. 95). Properly historicised, however, *Beloved Country*'s social analysis looks more credible and its political gradualism less wishful than its detractors have alleged (Foley, '"Considered as a social record"'), and from a post-apartheid perspective its theme of interracial reconciliation appears more relevant. But its paternalism and sentimentality may long forestall coronation as 'great national novel'.

Liberal fiction during apartheid, 1948–70

Phyllis Altman's *The Law of the Vultures* (1952) offered an alternative, socialist analysis of the 'Jim' scenario, depicting liberals as ultimately unreliable and presenting black collectivist action sympathetically, but in most fiction the greenhorn 'Jim' was superseded by the urbanised black, whose experience was vividly represented by the *Drum* writers (see Chapter 19). Liberal fiction also moved away from its pastoral affiliations, though the earlier line persisted in Paton and in Jack Cope, whose novels include *The Fair House* (1955), *The Golden Oriole* (1958), *Albino* (1964) and *The Rain-Maker* (1971). At the same time, the erosion of the peaceful non-racial activism of the 1950s, as the entrenchment of apartheid radicalised opposition, pushed liberal fiction towards critical self-scrutiny.

The development of Gordimer, whose novels offer a remarkably prompt, even prescient articulation of 'history from the inside' (Clingman, *Novels of Nadine Gordimer*), is in many respects paradigmatic. *The Lying Days* (1953), a *Bildungsroman* straddling the 1948 election, traces Helen Shaw's awakening to, and rejection of, her racist society; but her disillusionment with the bohemian lifestyle-liberalism of friends and the embattled liberal-trusteeship of her lover leaves her unaligned, craving the escape represented by Europe. Dan Jacobson's novella *A Dance in the Sun* (1956) also depicts young English-speaking South Africans struggling to translate liberal inclination into practical action. Two student hitch-hikers are appalled by the feudal family drama that unfolds at a ramshackle Karoo guesthouse, where the Afrikaner brother-in-law of the English-speaking proprietor has fathered a child with the sister of a black servant, but they are left smarting and bemused by the servant's indifference to their offer of help. These early works by two writers of a new generation relocated the liberal dilemma to a young urban consciousness, in styles whose often ironic detachment was quite different from the passionate lyricism of Paton.

In Gordimer's *A World of Strangers* (1958) such detachment is incomplete, for, as critics writing in the wake of South Africa's post-liberal 'moment' observed, this novel was one of several in which Gordimer both exemplified and critiqued the 'pitfalls of' or 'strains in' liberalism (Parker, 'Nadine Gordimer'; R. Green, 'Nadine Gordimer's *A World*'). English narrator Toby Hood moves between Johannesburg's white suburbs and the black township of Sophiatown, associating in each with politically uncommitted 'private livers' and committed 'public livers' (pp. 122–3), until the death of his hedonist black friend Steven Sitole pushes him towards the latter. The novel depicts an exhilarating Sophiatown and asserts the Forsterian humanist paradigm that one need 'only connect'; but it also ironises Hood's immersion in shebeen jazz culture, which is never far from voyeuristic urban safari, as well as his subsequent declaration of political solidarity. Athol Fugard, whose major contribution to the liberal tradition is in drama (see Chapter 27), sets his only novel, *Tsotsi* (1980; written 1960–2), beneath the *faux* underworld that is Hood's Sophiatown. 'Tsotsi', a murderous gang leader who goes by the generic term for a black street thug, has repressed feelings of sympathy, along with the memory of his childhood and name, since a police raid removed his mother for a pass violation. A series of emotive encounters – with an innocent victim, a probing gang member, a newborn taken from a woman he intended raping, a coerced wet nurse, a legless beggar he intended killing and a church gardener – restores his memory and compassion, which prompts the redemptive act in which he dies, attempting to save the baby from government bulldozers razing Sophiatown. *Tsotsi*, 'the first South African novel with a black protagonist to fully engage with the tradition of the *Bildungsroman*' (Barnard, 'Tsotsis', p. 551), thus implicates the white brutality that frames and circumscribes David Madondo's *Bildung* and exemplifies in the most damaged of blacks a capacity for self-reformation that might also be embraced by the damaging whites. This 'proto-*Bildungsroman*' (p. 555) straddles divergences in liberal fiction, for while its Freudian underpinnings suggest some affinity with Gordimer, whose 'political' novels can be read as 'at core . . . Freudian family romances' (Chapman, *Southern African Literatures*, p. 235), its Christian overtones and moral example align Fugard with Paton.

Redemption of *tsotsis* by Christian-liberal methods is indeed the keynote of Paton's *Debbie Go Home: Stories* (1961), which draws on Paton's experience as principal of the Diepkloof black reformatory (1935–48), recounted in the first of his two volumes of autobiography, *Towards the Mountain* (1980) and

Journey Continued (1988); these are important contributions to liberal prose, as are his biographies of prominent liberals, *Hofmeyr* (1964) and *Apartheid and the Archbishop* (1973). Other notable short-story writers in the liberal tradition include Jacobson ('*A Long Way from London*', 1958; '*Beggar my Neighbour*', 1964; *Inklings: Selected Stories*, 1973); Cope (*The Tame Ox*, 1960; *The Man who Doubted*, 1967; *Alley Cat*, 1973; *Selected Stories*, 1986); Rive (*African Songs*, 1963; *Advance, Retreat: Selected Short Stories*, 1983); and Gordimer, whose ten collections are represented in *Selected Stories* (1975) and *Life Times: Stories, 1952–2007* (2010).

Miscegenation, the crux of Jacobson's *Dance*, had also attracted direct treatment. Paton's *Too Late the Phalarope* (1953), which appeared soon after the 1950 extension of the Immorality Act, focuses on the downfall of idolised police lieutenant Pieter van Vlaanderen. The story, set in a Transvaal *dorp*, is narrated by Pieter's chorus-like aunt as a tragedy, his miscegenetic 'error' prompted by a character flaw that makes him deviate from his strict Afrikaner-Calvinist upbringing; but unbending adherence to Afrikaner-Calvinism produces a further tragedy in his father's striking of Pieter's name from the family Bible, race ideology disabling compassion for his son. Jacobson's *The Evidence of Love* (1960) details the contrasting upbringings of white liberal Isabel Last and coloured student Kenneth Makeer, and the ways in which these (and a hypocritical benefactress) complicate their falling in love in London, as well as their defiant gesture of returning home married, where they are imprisoned for 'Immorality'. Gordimer's *Occasion for Loving* (1963) does not directly invoke the act, but extends Jacobson's attention to the psychological effects of apartheid, which cause the affair between Gideon Shibalo and Ann Davis to fail, even though it takes place within the most liberal of social circles.

Besides this generational, rural–urban split in literary liberalism, a startlingly different liberal voice emerged from 'popular' writing. Between 1946 and 1974 Daphne Rooke published eight South African novels that together cover the country's major events from 1868 to 1961, often retaining the sense – renounced by Schreiner, and absent from the puritanical liberal mainstream – of history as pioneering adventure. Rooke uses a 'popular' romance mode, which has been dubbed 'colonial Gothic' (Voss, 'Story', p. 13), to 'serious historical effect' (M. Green, 'Difference and Domesticity', p. 130), largely because of her broad imaginative sympathy. Particularly noteworthy are *Mittee* (1951), set in the rural Transvaal of 1890–c. 1902 and narrated by a coloured female servant; *Ratoons* (1953), which includes sustained focus on Natal's Indian community in the early 1900s; *Wizards' Country* (1957), set in 1870s Zululand and narrated by a tribal Zulu; and *The Greyling* (1962), set in 1960–1, mostly in a Transvaal *dorp*, and narrated by an Afrikaner woman.

Mittee and *The Greyling* share Paton's interest in rural Afrikanerdom, and present miscegenation as the displaced colonialism that is perhaps latent in the white man–black woman scenario of *Phalarope*, rather than as the thwarted humanism explored in the black man–white woman relationships of *Evidence* and *Occasion*. They also focus on the experience of the subject woman, in contrast to *Phalarope*, where Stephanie remains a cipher. *Mittee* depicts a sadomasochistic affair between Mittee's husband and her coloured servant Selena, as well as exploring the ambivalences of cross-racial sisterhood, while *The Greyling* explores an equally sadomasochistic relationship between Maarten Delport and the coloured Bokkie Sipho (the titular 'greyling'), but with a twist: Maarten comes to love Bokkie, murders her out of self-disgust, and is executed because the apartheid state is even less able than he to acknowledge his mitigating emotion. In reaction, his parents and the narrator undergo their own changes of heart. In *Phalarope*, Afrikaner hearts were not for changing. *Mittee* epitomised Rooke's predominant narrative mode, but the sombre *Greyling*, though it retains 'popular' elements, was a departure from it. Whilst Rooke's darkly exuberant romances might broaden the liberal canon, *The Greyling* – Rooke's only contemporary and 'political', as opposed to 'historical', novel – thus sits, if a little awkwardly, within its agonistic mainstream.[3]

The Sharpeville shootings and inauguration of the Republic set the mood of *The Greyling*, but in their aftermath, as the 'armed struggle' was launched, the issue of political commitment became more prominent and problematic. Rive's *Emergency* (1964), set during three days in March 1960, between Sharpeville and the declaration of a State of Emergency, examines a crisis or 'emergency' in the political development of Andrew Dreyer, a coloured teacher who becomes involved in Cape Town's anti-pass laws campaign; the focus on the ethical dilemma of the individual, and his hesitancy about commitment, set Rive apart from other black protest writers. The subsequent rise and crushing of the first wave of sabotage activity, particularly that of the African Resistance Movement, shapes Gordimer's novella *The Late Bourgeois World* (1966). Like Rive, Gordimer uses a compressed timescale to concentrate on a moment of decision, in this case a single day which begins with Elizabeth van den Sandt receiving news that her ex-husband Max, a young saboteur turned state witness, has committed suicide. Though Max betrayed his liberal principles, and then his ex-liberal co-conspirators, Elizabeth concedes that he

3 For discussion of the liberalism of another 'popular' writer, Joy Packer, see Stotesbury, *Apartheid, Liberalism and Romance*.

at least *did* something. Consequently, she considers Luke Fokase's suggestion that she help channel overseas funding to his militant black resistance organisation; but the dilemma is unresolved, Elizabeth's liberal principles leaving her stalled at a bleak impasse. The scorn Elizabeth's sardonic narrative directs at 'bathed and perfumed and depilated white ladies' (p. 38), herself included, is a recurrent feature of Gordimer's fiction, and of Jillian Becker's trilogy *The Keep* (1967), *The Union* (1971) and *The Virgins* (1976); *The Virgins*, for example, exposes the colossal vanity and liberal sanctimony of an affluent Johannesburg matriarch, against which her adolescent daughter rebels.

Two novels of 1969 revisit the crisis period of the 1960s and examine more decisive breaks with liberalism. C. J. Driver's *Elegy for a Revolutionary*, which explores the African Resistance Movement and its betrayal from within, might almost be read as *The Late Bourgeois World*'s back story; while Mary Benson's *At the Still Point*, in which liberal journalist Anne Dawson, radicalised by the political trials of 1965, decides to help an escaped prisoner cross the border for guerrilla training, culminates in the kind of decision on the verge of which Gordimer left Elizabeth. In Gordimer's *A Guest of Honour* (1970), set in an unnamed African post-colony, liberal ex-colonial administrator James Bray is persuaded to defect from the anti-colonial revolutionaries he helped bring to power and back a left-wing coup; though this is a complex novel addressed only obliquely to South Africa, Bray's double radicalisation, his acceptance of non-dialogist strategies and collectivist policies, does indicate a move beyond liberalism.

Post-liberal fiction during apartheid, 1970–90

By the early 1970s Gordimer was referring to herself as a 'radical', repudiating 'liberal' as a 'dirty word' (Ratcliffe, 'South African Radical', p. 21), and her novels of the period she christened the 'interregnum' (Gordimer, 'Living in the Interregnum'), from the mid 1970s to 1990, depict various liberalisms as redundant, often subjecting them to hostile irony. *The Conservationist* (1974) exposes the complicity of Johannesburg industrialist and weekend 'farmer' Mehring, a 'mining-house' liberal who dismisses the left-liberalism of his ex-mistress and teenage son as naive self-righteousness and who is in denial of what the novel's powerful symbolic and intertextual devices intimate is inevitable: black repossession of the land. In *Burger's Daughter* (1979), Gordimer provides one last, sympathetic account of the soul-searching of a young liberal idealist, but relocates it from a context of bourgeois complacence to one of radical dissidence. Rosa Burger, growing up the daughter of a celebrated communist between Sharpeville and Soweto, finds in the aftermath of Soweto that the commitment crisis has been transformed by Black Consciousness into a rejection crisis; though Rosa finally feels impelled to return from a European sojourn to contribute to 'the struggle', she can do so only in a peripheral role. Thereafter, liberalism is given short shrift. In *July's People* (1981), set in an imagined revolution in an imminent future, the scruples that guided Maureen Smales in her treatment of her servant July are shown, in retrospect, to be demeaning and self-serving. In *A Sport of Nature* (1987), which ranges from the mid 1940s to the projected inauguration of a post-apartheid state, a revisiting of the early 1960s also finds self-satisfaction in the more proactive liberalism of Hillela's guardian-aunt Pauline, from whom Hillela soon departs to join the ANC in exile. These acerbic valedictions are quite a contrast to Paton's retrospective celebration of 1950s liberals in *Ah, but your Land is Beautiful* (1981). The life of radical action chosen by Hillela is further valorised by Gordimer, in the forms of underground resistance and the pragmatic politics of transition, in *My Son's Story* (1990) and *None to Accompany Me* (1994).

This rejection of liberalism had its aesthetic corollary in a move away from liberal realism, anticipated by Plomer's proto-modernist *Turbott Wolfe* and apparent in Sheila Fugard's *The Castaways* (1972). In Gordimer, history is usually refracted by an individual subjectivity itself shaped by family psycho-dynamics, but in this phase both history and its subjective refraction are problematised by unreliable, multiple and limited perspectives, the most extreme of which produces the lacunae-ridden 'biography' of *A Sport of Nature*. At the same time, Gordimer rewrote the liberal tradition's four most significant forms: *The Conservationist* followed Jacobson's *Dance* in subverting the farm novel of Schreiner and Smith; *July's People*, in which the Smales family flees Johannesburg for their servant's village, inverted the 'Jim comes to Jo'burg' narrative; *A Sport of Nature*, in which Hillela marries two black revolutionaries, recast the miscegenation novel as something other than tragedy; and *Burger's Daughter* updated the commitment-quandary *Bildungsroman*. However, the greatest challenge to the liberal novel, as well as to the broader politicisation of fiction, came from Coetzee, whose allegorical and metafictional works deconstructed colonial discourses and turned even more self-consciously to literary tradition. Whilst *Dusklands* (1974) rewrote the eighteenth-century anthropological travelogue to expose the link between discursive and physical violence and *In the Heart of the Country* (1977) reworked the farm novel and Afrikaans *plaasroman* as disorienting anti-pastoral, *Waiting for the Barbarians* (1980), *Life & Times of Michael K* (1983), *Foe* (1986) and *Age of Iron* (1990) reprised the liberal novel of philanthropic concern, re-examining the relevance of liberal values in thoroughly illiberal times. What was remarkable, too, was the confessional mode of Coetzee's first-person narrators, which took liberal self-criticism to a new, excoriating level.

A recurring situation in these novels is an encounter between a philanthropic liberal, who is clearly implicated in the structures of power, and an often wilfully inarticulate other whose victimhood is symbolised by a physical disfigurement. In *Barbarians* the liberal magistrate of an imperial outpost in an unspecified place and time is disturbed by the torture of indigenous prisoners and their construction as the 'barbarians' on which empire is predicated. The Magistrate shelters a torture-scarred 'barbarian' girl, but his compulsive sexual exploitation of her figures liberalism's complicity with empire and the fetishisation of victimhood, while his subsequent public stand demonstrates liberalism's impotence before, and vulnerability to, imperial violence. In *Michael K*, set like *July's People* in a future revolutionary South Africa, the hare-lipped K rejects the Medical Officer's attempts to help and understand him, while in *Foe*, a metafictional prequel to *Robinson Crusoe*, a tongueless (and possibly castrated) Friday likewise resists the impositions of a self-appointed patron, Susan Barton. In *Age of Iron* the scenario is replayed in Mrs Curren's relationship with the vagrant Vercueil, whose crippled hand betokens his withheld story; but Mrs Curren also bears a mark of apartheid – cancer of the (liberal) heart - and it is she who is pressed to answer questions now asked by the other. *Age of Iron* locates this examination in the Cape Town unrest of 1986, and has Mrs Curren's charitable actions and humanitarian pronouncements rebutted not just by the taciturn Vercueil but by forthright characters from Guguletu township, meanwhile subjecting her thoughts to self-scrutiny. The novel has thus been regarded as liberalism's 'death rattle', or its elegy (see Marais, 'J. M. Coetzee', p. 146); but it can also be argued that Mrs Curren's very lack of authority, her stark marginality and political irrelevance, paradoxically validates her opinions (Attwell, *J. M. Coetzee*, p. 122).

If *Age of Iron* does salvage ethical values from the wreckage of liberalism, one which remains irrecoverable is the liberal-humanist belief that the other is fundamentally knowable. Vercueil is only marginally less opaque for Mrs Curren than was the 'barbarian' girl for the Magistrate, K for the Medical Officer, and Friday for Barton (though the third-person narratives that frame the Medical Officer's bafflement do, tentatively, enter K's inner world). Where Gordimer had reluctantly set bounds to her belief in the hyper-perceptive powers of the artist (Gordimer, 'Novel and the Nation'), Coetzee's response to the ethical imperative to represent otherness without appropriating it was

to provide extensive but limited portrayals while at the same time conveying the portrayed others' resistances to, and disruptions of, the discourses –
colonial, liberal and novelistic – within which they are constituted. For Mike
Marais, these are 'meta-representational strategies of excession' which provide
'a *sense* of that which exceeds the novel's representational protocols', inducing
'an "epiphany" of the infinitude of the other' that has an ethical effect on the
reader and, therefore, on history ('Writing with Eyes Shut', pp. 49, 56). For
others, however, these strategies fixate the reader unhealthily upon difference,
ironically reinscribing the societal exclusions they critique and neglecting the
historical-material conditions that produce those exclusions (see, for example, Parry, 'Speech and Silence'); this criticism of Coetzee thus echoes that
of the tradition he rewrites, allegedly heart-changing novels being attacked
for inadequate representations of others and inattention to social forces. The
'(post)modernist' Coetzee is often also placed in literary-critical opposition
to the 'realist' Gordimer, despite Gordimer's experimentation and Coetzee's
own creation of a strong realist illusion that generally survives its destabili-
sation. A perhaps more useful distinction is that Coetzee's rewriting of the
liberal novel, influenced by Beckett and Kafka, produces a literature of ethical
implication rather than saturation. In this, he bears unlikely comparison with
Rooke.

André Brink, many of whose novels are avowedly postmodernist, brings
another distinctive voice to the liberal tradition, though he might more properly be placed within the tradition of Afrikaner dissidence (see Chapters 21
and 22). Brink comes closest to the liberal novel with *A Dry White Season*
(1979), in which an idealistic Afrikaner teacher, Ben du Toit, is shaken out
of naive complicity by the deaths in police detention of a school janitor and
his son, and makes a determinedly courageous attempt to expose the perpetrators. In an exposition of the powerlessness of individuals to challenge the
apartheid state by peaceful means, which would find allegorical expression in
Coetzee's *Barbarians*, he is harassed and murdered by the Security Police; but
his story survives, supposedly reconstructed by a pulp fiction writer, to bear
testamentary witness.

Whilst irony had been one factor distinguishing writers like Gordimer,
Jacobson and Becker from the sentimental and tragic tone of many of their
predecessors, liberal fiction, however excoriating or experimental, remained
prone to self-aggrandising melodrama and was largely humourless. Satire
again provided an alternative form of dissidence, with Tom Sharpe's *Riotous
Assembly* (1971) and *Indecent Exposure* (1973) lampooning the police, and Christopher Hope's *A Separate Development* (1980), *Kruger's Alp* (1984) and *The Hottentot*

Room (1986) casting their mordant net more widely to expose the cruel and corrupting absurdities of racial stratification; the latter focuses on political exiles in London, while liberals are amongst Hope's catch in, for example, 'Hilton Hits Back' (*'Private Parts' and other Tales*, 1981). Another tack was taken by Sheila Roberts, whose first two volumes of stories, *Outside Life's Feast* (1975) and *This Time of Year* (1983), explore, with uncompromising realism, the privations and prejudices of South Africa's white working class. Roberts (whose novels *He's my Brother*, 1977, and *The Weekenders*, 1981, are also noteworthy) thus charts territory largely beyond the compass of Gordimer, Jacobson and Becker, avoiding the middle-class guilt that pervades white liberal writing.

Meanwhile, Rive produced *Writing Black* (1981), an anecdotal and anti-racialist autobiography, and juxtaposed reminiscence with fictional recreation in *'Buckingham Palace', District Six* (1985), a eulogy to the Cape Town coloured community in which he grew up and a protest against its removal in the late sixties. The postmodernist turn was reflected in the intertextual and metafictional dimensions of Rive's final novel, *Emergency Continued* (1990), which places characters from *Emergency* in the political turmoil of three Cape Town days in 1985. Dreyer again tries to keep alive the sanctity of an individual response, resisting involvement and documenting as a 'personal history' (p. 5) what he witnesses, but the marginality that the city's youths required of white pedagogues in Menán du Plessis's *A State of Fear* (1983) and Coetzee's *Age of Iron* proves impossible for the coloured teacher; the pressure to reconsider his liberal principles and embrace active solidarity is made finally irresistible by his son's assassination. Metafiction and the quandary of commitment feature also in John Conyngham's 'Natal Trilogy', *The Arrowing of the Cane* (1986), *The Desecration of the Graves* (1990) and *The Lostness of Alice* (1998). *Arrowing*, in which a 'pragmatic liberal' sugar planter is besieged by unseen arsonists, places the African farm under the threat of expropriation that was only symbolised in *The Conservationist*, capturing the sense of imminent catastrophe realised in the future histories of *July's People* and *Michael K*. In *Desecration* a novice biographer's research into the Anglo-Boer (or South African) War is interrupted by the more pressing conflict it might illuminate when he encounters a black fugitive; but his decision not to report his sighting and thereby, as he sees it, join 'the struggle', constitutes the most tenuous of solidarities. By this stage, the commitment quandary had clearly had its day. The real interest of Conyngham's trilogy lies in a broader issue of belonging, the 'lostness' of the unradicalised liberal in time of transition (see Blair, 'Of Lostness and Belonging').

(Post-)liberal fiction after apartheid

Conyngham's *Lostness*, in which the protagonist chooses exile, can be read as an expression and/or exploration of 'liberal funk' – liberal fear of post-apartheid marginalisation and violent crime. This vein is epitomised by Coetzee's *Disgrace* (1999) (see Marais, 'Very Morbid Phenomena'), in which the disgraced academic David Lurie and his lesbian daughter Lucy are attacked on Lucy's smallholding by three black men, who burn David and rape Lucy, leaving her pregnant. Lucy's agreeing to a polygamous marriage (and the forfeiture of her farm) to her former labourer Petrus, who seems to be connected to the attackers, suggests an acceptance of white marginality and an abandonment of the liberal ethic of reciprocity, curtailed in Coetzee's earlier fiction, for one of sacrifice; though this sacrificial ethic is explicitly critiqued in the novel, the prospects for reciprocity remain bleak. Similarly bleak are Justin Cartwright's *White Lightning* (2002), in which a middle-aged man returns from England and attempts to transform a rundown farm into a benevolent Arcadia, and Damon Galgut's *The Good Doctor* (2003), in which an idealistic young doctor is posted to a dilapidated and remote rural hospital. Gordimer's *The House Gun* (1998) is also concerned with the ethical inheritance of the 'new' South Africa, but is relatively sanguine about whites' post-apartheid position. Violence, normalised by apartheid, is not, here, an external, retributive threat, but has been internalised by a bisexual man who murders his former gay lover; and the adaptation of his affluent liberal parents to the new dispensation, reassuringly represented by an urbane black lawyer, requires trust rather than abasement.

Gordimer's *The Pickup* (2001) and Phaswane Mpe's *Welcome to our Hillbrow* (2001) bring different, essentially liberal perspectives to bear on the opening up of South Africa to transnational migration. Gordimer's apartheid-era concern with the shaping of personal relations by inequality is refocused on a cross-cultural affair between a young white woman and an Arab (see Blair, 'Anxiety of Affluence'), while Mpe reprises the 'Jim' theme to produce a harrowing tale that indicts xenophobia and HIV prejudice, pleading for tolerance (see Blair, 'Moral and the Macabre'). Equally discomfiting are K. Sello Duiker's *Thirteen Cents* (2000) and *The Quiet Violence of Dreams* (2001), in which a street child and a student, respectively, struggle to make sense of traumatic pasts, become involved in male prostitution, and seek salvation in personal epiphanies. Duiker, like Abrahams, wants to live in a world 'above and beyond colour', but race repeatedly intrudes, even in moments of homosexual solidarity, pushing the novels toward the more self-conscious non-racialism of Rive (see Viljoen, 'Non-racialism Remains a Fiction'). Given the emphases on tolerance, non-racialism and the individual's inner world (including a new explicitness, for liberal fiction, about sexuality), these might be considered works of reconstructed liberalism.[4]

The intense rendering of interior lives, and resistance to formative histories, also characterise Henrietta Rose-Innes's *Shark's Egg* (2000), *The Rock Alphabet* (2004) and *Homing: Stories* (2010). Whilst *Shark's Egg*, which traces the growth of a girl to adulthood, turns away from public themes, in *The Rock Alphabet* the attempt to domesticate two boys of uncertain racial ancestry found wild – and having developed a language of their own – in the mountains, again problematises benevolence and suggests that it is possible to live, as Coetzee's K attempted to do, outside identities pre-formed by history.

The recentring of the personal is apparent, too, in Gordimer's *Get a Life* (2005), and in a turn from the present to the past in a spate of autobiographical writing about childhood under apartheid, including Coetzee's *Boyhood* (1997) (see Chapter 34). In fiction, Barbara Trapido's *Frankie and Stankie* (2003) refreshed the liberal *Bildungsroman*, following Dinah de Bondt from a 1940s liberal childhood to her 1964 exile with a dissident lover, and reflecting on the absurdities of apartheid with dark irony, and on those of adolescence and young adulthood with sparkling wit. Shaun Johnson's *The Native Commissioner* (2006), in contrast, is a sombre autobiographical novel in which author-surrogate 'Sam Jameson' reconstructs the story of his father George, an accomplished Africanist whose moderate liberalism is increasingly at odds with the system he serves from the 1930s.[5] Though disheartened by the degeneration of trusteeship into brutal social engineering, George is unable to embrace 'ultra-liberalism' (p. 186), regarding majority rule as premature. The narrative traces, as tragedy, the consequent disintegration of a man who could neither forgive his own complicity nor extricate himself from a paternalist mindset that prevented opposition, his depressions and breakdowns culminating, in 1968, in suicide. That George's death comes mere months before the dissolution of the by then 'ultra-liberal' Liberal Party is indicative of liberalism's broader demise. This novel is not the first discussed here to revisit liberalisms of the past, or to demonstrate the inability of ameliorist wait-and-see liberals to make history happen; but it goes behind and beyond

---

4 For discussion of the urbanism of Duiker and Mpe, see Chapter 32 below.
5 Compare Marguerite Poland's *Recessional for Grace* (2003), in which a postgraduate student attempts to complete a lexicon of metaphorical names for indigenous Nguni cattle begun by an academic in 1946, and finds herself reconstructing his life. Poland has published numerous children's books based on African and Khoi-San folklore. Her other fiction for adults includes the novels *Train to Doringbult* (1987), *Shades* (1993) and *Iron Love* (1999).

this, providing a sustained, historicised and personal account of the inevitable defeat by apartheid of even the most informed and tenacious 'decency'. Like Coetzee's *Age of Iron*, *The Native Commissioner* can thus be considered an elegy for liberalism, but its retrospective laying to rest of a different cast and vintage of that ideology might also be regarded as an indispensable countersign to the new, reconstructed liberalisms exemplified here by Gordimer, Duiker, Rose-Innes and Mpe.

Bibliography

Abrahams, L. 'From Shakespeare House to the Laager: The Story of PEN (Johannesburg)', *Sesame* 3 (summer 1983/4), 5–19.

Abrahams, P. *Mine Boy*, London: Dorothy Crisp, 1946.

   The Path of Thunder, New York: Harper, 1948; Cape Town: David Philip, 1984.

Alexander, P. F. *Alan Paton: A Biography*, Oxford University Press, 1994.

Altman, P. *The Law of the Vultures*, London: Jonathan Cape, 1952.

Attwell, D. *J. M. Coetzee: South Africa and the Politics of Writing*, Berkeley and Los Angeles: University of California Press and Cape Town: David Philip, 1993.

   'South African Literature in English', in F. A. Irele and S. Gikandi (eds.), *The Cambridge History of African and Caribbean Literature*, 2 vols., Cambridge University Press, 2004, vol. II, 504–29.

Barnard, R. 'Tsotsis: On Law, the Outlaw, and the Postcolonial State', *Contemporary Literature* 49:4 (2008), 541 72.

Becker, J. *The Keep*, London: Chatto & Windus, 1967.

   The Union, London: Chatto & Windus, 1971.

   The Virgins, London: Victor Gollancz, 1976.

Benson, M. *At the Still Point*, Boston: Gambit, 1969.

Blackburn, D. *Leaven: A Black and White Story*, London: Alston Rivers, 1908.

Blair, P. 'The Anxiety of Affluence: Gordimer's *The Pickup*', *Current Writing: Text and Reception in Southern Africa* 15:1 (April 2003), 178–82.

   'The Moral and the Macabre' [review of Mpe's *Welcome to our Hillbrow*], *Current Writing: Text and Reception in Southern Africa* 14:1 (April 2002), 163–8.

   'Of Lostness and Belonging: Interview with John Conyngham', *Current Writing: Text and Reception in Southern Africa* 15:1 (April 2003), 74–90.

   'That "ugly word": Miscegenation and the Novel in Preapartheid South Africa', *Modern Fiction Studies* 49:3 (autumn 2003), 581–613.

Brink, A. *A Dry White Season*, London: W. H. Allen, 1979.

Brownlee, F. *Ntsukumbini: Cattle Thief*, London: Jonathan Cape, 1929.

Butler, J., R. Elphick and D. Welsh (eds.). *Democratic Liberalism in South Africa: Its History and Prospects*, Middleton, CT: Wesleyan University Press and Cape Town: David Philip, 1987.

Cartwright, J. *White Lightning*, London: Hodder & Stoughton, 2002.

Chapman, M. *Southern African Literatures*, London: Longman, 1996.

Clingman, S. 'Novel (South Africa)', in E. Benson and L. W. Conolly (eds.), *Encyclopedia of Post-Colonial Literatures in English*, 2 vols., London: Routledge, 1994, vol. II, 1148–52.

The Novels of Nadine Gordimer: History from the Inside, Johannesburg: Ravan, 1986.

Coetzee, A. J., T. Couzens and S. Gray. 'South African Literatures to World War II', in A. S. Gérard (ed.), *European-Language Writing in Sub-Saharan Africa*, 2 vols., Budapest: Akadémiai Kaidó, 1986, vol. I, 173–213.

Coetzee, J. M. *Age of Iron*, London: Secker & Warburg, 1990.

Boyhood: Scenes from Provincial Life, London: Secker & Warburg, 1997.

Disgrace, London: Secker & Warburg, 1999.

Dusklands, Johannesburg: Ravan, 1974.

Foe, Johannesburg: Ravan, 1986.

In the Heart of the Country, London: Secker & Warburg, 1977.

Life & Times of Michael K, London: Secker & Warburg, 1983.

'South African Liberals: Alan Paton, Helen Suzman', in *Stranger Shores: Essays 1986–1999*, London: Vintage, 2002, 318–31.

Waiting for the Barbarians, London: Secker & Warburg, 1980.

Conyngham, J. *The Arrowing of the Cane*, Johannesburg: Ad Donker, 1986.

The Desecration of the Graves, Johannesburg: Ad Donker, 1990.

The Lostness of Alice, Johannesburg: Ad Donker, 1998.

Cope, J. *Albino*, London: Heinemann, 1964.

Alley Cat, London: Heinemann, 1973.

The Fair House, London: Heinemann, 1955.

The Golden Oriole, London: Heinemann, 1958.

The Man who Doubted, London: Heinemann, 1967.

The Rain-Maker, London: Heinemann, 1971.

Selected Stories, Cape Town: David Philip, 1986.

The Tame Ox, London: Heinemann, 1960.

Davenport, R. 'The Cape Liberal Tradition to 1910', in Butler, Elphick and Welsh, *Democratic Liberalism*, 21–34.

Dhlomo, R. R. R. *An African Tragedy*, Alice: Lovedale Press, 1927.

Driver, C. J. *Elegy for a Revolutionary*, London: Faber, 1969.

Dubow, S. *Racial Segregation and the Origins of Apartheid in South Africa, 1919–36*, Houndmills: Macmillan, 1989.

Duiker, K. S. *The Quiet Violence of Dreams*, Cape Town: Kwela Books, 2001.

Thirteen Cents, Cape Town: David Philip, 2000.

Du Plessis, M. *A State of Fear*, Cape Town: David Philip, 1983.

Fleischer, T. 'Editorial', in T. Fleischer (ed.), *New South African Writing*, 5 vols., Johannesburg: Purnell, 1964–8, vol. II (1965), v–vii.

Foley, A. '"Considered as a social record": A Reassessment of *Cry, The Beloved Country*', *English in Africa* 25:2 (October 1998), 63–92.

Fugard, A. *Tsotsi*, Johannesburg: Ad Donker, 1980.

Fugard, S. *The Castaways*, London: Macmillan, 1972.

Galgut, D. *The Good Doctor*, New York: Grove Press, 2003.

Gibbon, P. *Margaret Harding*, London: Methuen, 1911.

Souls in Bondage, Edinburgh: Blackwoods, 1904.

Gordimer, N. *Burger's Daughter*, London: Jonathan Cape, 1979.

The Conservationist, London: Jonathan Cape, 1974.

Get a Life, Cape Town: David Philip, 2005.

A Guest of Honour, New York: Viking, 1970.

The House Gun, Cape Town: David Philip, 1998.

July's People, Johannesburg: Ravan, 1981.

The Late Bourgeois World, London: Jonathan Cape, 1966.

Life Times: Stories, 1952–2007, London: Bloomsbury, 2010.

'Living in the Interregnum', in S. Clingman (ed.), *The Essential Gesture: Writing, Politics and Places*, London: Jonathan Cape, 1988, 261–84.

The Lying Days, London: Victor Gollancz, 1953; Harmondsworth: Penguin, 1994.

My Son's Story, Cape Town: David Philip, 1990.

None to Accompany Me, Cape Town: David Philip, 1994.

'The Novel and the Nation in South Africa', in G. D. Killam (ed.), *African Writers on African Writing*, London: Heinemann, 1973, 33–52.

Occasion for Loving, London: Victor Gollancz, 1963.

The Pickup, Cape Town: David Philip, 2001.

Selected Stories, London: Jonathan Cape, 1975.

A Sport of Nature, Cape Town: David Philip, 1987.

A World of Strangers, London: Victor Gollancz, 1958.

Gray, S. *Southern African Literature: An Introduction*, New York: Barnes & Noble, 1979.

'Third World meets First World: The Theme of "Jim Comes to Joburg" in South African English Fiction', *Kunapipi* 7:1 (1985), 61–80.

Green, M. 'Difference and Domesticity in Daphne Rooke's *Wizards' Country*', *English in Africa* 21:1–2 (July 1994), 103–39.

Green, R. 'Nadine Gordimer's *A World of Strangers*: Strains in South African Liberalism', *English Studies in Africa* 22 (1979), 45–54.

Haggard, H. R. *Allan Quatermain*, London: Longmans, Green & Co., 1887.

Hope, C. *The Hottentot Room*, London: Heinemann, 1986.

Kruger's Alp, London: Heinemann: 1984.

'*Private Parts' and other Tales*, Johannesburg: Bateleur, 1981. Revised as *Learning to Fly*, London: Minerva, 1990.

A Separate Development, Johannesburg: Ravan, 1980.

Jacobson, D. '*Beggar my Neighbour' and other Stories*, London: Weidenfeld & Nicolson, 1964.

A Dance in the Sun: A Novel, London: Weidenfeld & Nicolson, 1956.

The Evidence of Love, London: Weidenfeld & Nicolson, 1960.

Inklings: Selected Stories, London: Weidenfeld & Nicolson, 1973.

'*A Long Way from London' and other Stories*, London: Weidenfeld & Nicolson, 1958.

Johnson, R. W. and D. Welsh (eds.). *Ironic Victory: Liberalism in Post-Liberation South Africa*, Cape Town: Oxford University Press, 1998.

Johnson, S. *The Native Commissioner: A Novel*, Johannesburg: Penguin, 2006, 2007.

Kirkwood, M. 'The Colonizer: A Critique of the English South African Culture Theory', in P. Wilhelm and J. A. Polley (eds.), *Poetry South Africa: Selected Papers from Poetry '74*, Johannesburg: Ad Donker, 1976, 102–33.

Marais, M. 'J. M. Coetzee', in P. A. Scanlon (ed.), *South African Writers*, Dictionary of Literary Biography, ccxxv, Detroit: Bruccoli Clark Layman, 2000, 131–49.

'Very Morbid Phenomena: "Liberal Funk", the "Lucy-Syndrome" and J. M. Coetzee's *Disgrace*', *Scrutiny2* 6:1 (2001), 32–8.

'Writing with Eyes Shut: Ethics, Politics, and the Problem of the Other in the Fictions of J. M. Coetzee', *English in Africa* 25:1 (May 1998), 43–60.

McDonald, P. D. *The Literature Police: Apartheid Censorship and its Cultural Consequences*, Oxford University Press, 2009.

Millin, S. G. *God's Step-Children*, London: Constable, 1924.

Morphet, T. 'Stranger Fictions: Trajectories in the Liberal Novel', *World Literature Today* 70:1 (winter 1996), 53–8.

Mpe, P. *Welcome to our Hillbrow*, Pietermaritzburg: University of Natal Press, 2001.

Parker, K. 'Nadine Gordimer and the Pitfalls of Liberalism', in Parker, *South African Novel in English*, 114–30.

'The South African Novel in English', in Parker, *South African Novel in English*, 1–26.

Parker, K. (ed.) *The South African Novel in English: Essays in Criticism and Society*, London: Macmillan, 1978.

Parry, B. 'Speech and Silence in the Fictions of J. M. Coetzee', in D. Attridge and R. Jolly (eds.), *Writing South Africa: Literature, Apartheid and Democracy, 1970–1995*, Cambridge University Press, 1998, 149–65.

Paton, A. *Ah, but your Land is Beautiful*, Cape Town: David Philip, 1981.

Apartheid and the Archbishop: The Life and Times of Geoffrey Clayton, Archbishop of Cape Town, Cape Town: David Philip, 1973.

Cry, The Beloved Country: A Story of Comfort in Desolation, New York: Scribner, 1948; Harmondsworth: Penguin, 1988.

Debbie Go Home: Stories, London: Jonathan Cape, 1961. Also published as *Tales from a Troubled Land*, New York: Scribner, 1961.

Hofmeyr, Oxford University Press, 1964.

Journey Continued: An Autobiography, Cape Town: David Philip, 1988.

Too Late the Phalarope, London: Jonathan Cape, 1953.

Towards the Mountain: An Autobiography, Cape Town: David Philip, 1980.

Peck, R. *A Morbid Fascination: White Prose and Politics in Apartheid South Africa*, Westport, CT: Greenwood Press, 1997.

Plaatje, S. T. *Mhudi: An Epic of South African Native Life a Hundred Years Ago*, Alice: Lovedale Press, 1930.

Plomer, W. 'The Child of Queen Victoria', in *'The Child of Queen Victoria' and other Stories*, London: Jonathan Cape, 1933.

Turbott Wolfe, London: Hogarth Press, 1925.

'Ula Masondo', in *I Speak of Africa*, London: Hogarth Press, 1927.

Poland, M. *Iron Love*, Johannesburg: Viking, 1999.

Recessional for Grace, Johannesburg: Viking, 2003.

Shades, Johannesburg: Viking, 1993.

Train to Doringbult, London: Bodley Head, 1987.

Pringle, T. *Narrative of a Residence in South Africa*, London: E. Moxon, 1835. First published jointly with *Poems Illustrative of South Africa* as *African Sketches*, London: E. Moxon, 1834.

Rabkin, D. 'Race and Fiction: *God's Stepchildren* and *Turbott Wolfe*', in Parker, *South African Novel in English*, 77–94.

Ratcliffe, M. 'A South African Radical Exulting in Life's Chaotic Variety' [interview with Gordimer], *Times* (London), 29 November 1974, 21.

Rich, P. B. *Hope and Despair: English-Speaking Intellectuals and South African Politics, 1896–1976*, New York: St Martin's Press, 1993.

   'Liberal Realism in South African Fiction, 1948–66', *English in Africa* 12:1 (May 1985), 47–81.

   'A New South African Liberal Conscience?', *Current Writing: Text and Reception in Southern Africa* 9:2 (October 1997), 1–20.

   White Power and the Liberal Conscience: Racial Segregation and South African Liberalism, 1921–60, Manchester University Press, 1984.

Rive, R. *Advance, Retreat: Selected Short Stories*, Cape Town: David Philip, 1983.

   African Songs, Berlin: Seven Seas, 1963.

   'Buckingham Palace', District Six, Cape Town: David Philip, 1986.

   Emergency, London: Faber, 1964.

   Emergency Continued, Cape Town: David Philip and London: Readers International, 1990.

   'The Liberal Tradition in South African Literature', *Contrast* 14:3 (July 1983), 19–31.

   Writing Black, Cape Town: David Philip, 1981.

Roberts, S. *He's my Brother: A Novel*, Johannesburg: Ad Donker, 1977. Also published as *Johannesburg Requiem*, New York: Taplinger, 1980.

   Outside Life's Feast: Short Stories, Johannesburg: Ad Donker, 1975.

   'This Time of Year' and other Stories, Johannesburg: Ad Donker, 1983.

   The Weekenders, Johannesburg: Bateleur, 1981.

Robertson, J. *Liberalism in South Africa, 1948–1963*, Oxford: Clarendon Press, 1971.

Rooke, D. *The Greyling*, London: Victor Gollancz, 1962.

   Mittee, London: Victor Gollancz, 1951.

   Ratoons, London: Victor Gollancz, 1953.

   Wizards' Country, London: Victor Gollancz, 1957.

Rose-Innes, H. *Homing: Short Stories*, Cape Town: Umuzi, 2010.

   The Rock Alphabet, Cape Town: Kwela Books, 2004.

   Shark's Egg, Cape Town: Kwela Books, 2000.

Rubin, M. *Sarah Gertrude Millin: A South African Life*, Johannesburg: Ad Donker, 1977.

Schreiner, O. *Closer Union*, London: Fifield, 1909.

   'Eighteen Ninety-Nine', in *Stories, Dreams and Allegories*, London: T. Fisher Unwin, 1923.

   From Man to Man; or, Perhaps Only . . . , London: T. Fisher Unwin, 1926.

   The Story of an African Farm, London: Chapman & Hall, 1883.

   Thoughts on South Africa, London: T. Fisher Unwin, 1923.

   Trooper Peter Halket of Mashonaland, London: T. Fisher Unwin, 1897.

   Undine, New York and London: Harper, 1928.

   Woman and Labour, London: T. Fisher Unwin, 1911.

Scully, W. C. *Daniel Vananda: The Life Story of a Human Being*, Cape Town: Juta, 1923.

Sharpe, T. *Indecent Exposure*, London: Secker & Warburg, 1973.

   Riotous Assembly, London: Secker & Warburg, 1971.

Smith, P. *The Beadle*, London: Jonathan Cape, 1926.

   The Little Karoo, London: Jonathan Cape, 1925.

Sowden, L. 'The PEN and the Government', in L. Sowden (ed.), *South African PEN Year Book 1956–1957*, Cape Town: Howard B. Timmins, 1957, 7–17.

Stotesbury, J. A. *Apartheid, Liberalism and Romance: A Critical Investigation of the Writing of Joy Packer*, Uppsala: Swedish Science Press, 1996.

Trapido, B. *Frankie and Stankie*, London: Bloomsbury, 2003.

Van den Berghe, P. L. 'Introduction', in P. L. van den Berghe (ed.), *The Liberal Dilemma in South Africa*, London: Croom Helm, 1979, 7–16.

Van der Post, L. *In a Province*, London: Hogarth Press, 1934.

Van der Vlies, A. *South African Textual Cultures: White, Black, Read all Over*, Manchester University Press, 2007.

Vaughan, M. 'Literature and Politics: Currents in South African Writing in the Seventies', *Journal of Southern African Studies* 9.1 (October 1982), 118–38.

Vigne, R. *Liberals Against Apartheid: A History of the Liberal Party of South Africa, 1953–68*, Houndmills: Macmillan and New York: St Martin's Press, 1997.

Viljoen, S. 'Non-Racialism Remains a Fiction: Richard Rive's "Buckingham Palace", District Six and K. Sello Duiker's *The Quiet Violence of Dreams*', *English Academy Review* 18:1 (2001), 46–53.

Voss, T. 'The Story of an African Femme', *Reality* (March 1989), 13.

Wade, J. 'Peter Abrahams's *The Path of Thunder*: The Crisis of the Liberal Subject', *English in Africa* 16:2 (October 1989), 61–75.

'*Song of the City* and *Mine Boy*: The "Marxist" Novels of Peter Abrahams', *Research in African Literatures* 21:3 (autumn 1990), 89–101.

Watson, S. '*Cry, the Beloved Country* and the Failure of the Liberal Vision', *English in Africa* 9:1 (May 1982), 29–44.

Welsh, D. 'The Liberal Inheritance', in Johnson and Welsh, *Ironic Victory*, 1–21.

Wentzel, J. *The Liberal Slideaway*, Johannesburg: South African Institute of Race Relations, 1995.

24

Black Consciousness poetry: writing against apartheid

THENGANI H. NGWENYA

> We have set out on a quest for true humanity, and somewhere on the
> distant horizon we can see the glittering prize. Let us march forth with
> courage and determination, drawing strength from our common plight and
> our brotherhood. In time we shall be in a position to bestow upon South
> Africa the greatest possible gift – a more human face.
> (Biko, quoted in Van Wyk, *We Write What We Like*, p. 24)

This chapter seeks to explore the interconnections between the philosophy of
Black Consciousness in South Africa and English poetry published in the 1960s
and 1970s by the four black African poets who, over the years, have been given
the status of representing Black Consciousness by critics and editors of poetry
anthologies. Taking the form of a wide-ranging critical overview, the chapter
focuses on selected poems illustrating particular themes and perspectives, as
well as poetic techniques and conventions in the poetry of this era.

Steven Bantu Biko's prophetic words quoted above remind us that Black
Consciousness is essentially a philosophy of humanity (*ubuntu*) and national
redemption. In line with his conception of Black Consciousness as a regenerative and redemptive philosophy, Biko's definition of blackness is both
pragmatic and all-embracing:

> We have in our policy manifesto defined blacks as those who are by law
> or tradition politically, economically and socially discriminated against as a
> group in the South African society and identifying themselves as a unit in the
> struggle towards the realisation of their aspirations.
> (Biko, *I Write What I Like*, p. 62)

For Biko and other proponents of Black Consciousness, blackness does not
merely denote skin pigmentation but is 'a reflection of a mental attitude'. It
is as a consequence of this unambiguous and strategic conception of 'blackness' that Indian, coloured and black African poets wrote poems tackling
various aspect of 'black experience' in apartheid South Africa. Essentially, the

ideology of apartheid and the discriminatory legislation it spawned negated the humanity of all South Africans regardless of race. Biko understood the inherently demeaning and emotionally corrosive effect of the apartheid ideology on the psyche of all South Africans. He cautions against narrow and negative interpretations of the philosophy underlying Black Consciousness: 'It [Black Consciousness] works on the knowledge that "white hatred" is negative, though understandable, and leads to precipitate and shot-gun methods which may be disastrous for black and white alike' (quoted in Arnold, *Steve Biko*, p. 20).

Richard Rive, the author of a memoir entitled *Writing Black: An Author's Notebook* (1981), whose work is firmly grounded in his awareness of 'blackness', sets the tone for the poetry of brotherhood that was to follow in the following poem, 'Where the Rainbow Ends: 1950–1960', which served as a prologue to a short story published in *Drum* magazine in May 1955:

> Where the rainbow ends,
> There's going to be a place brother,
> Where the world can sing all sorts of songs,
> And we're going to sing together, brother,
> You and I,
> Though you're White and I am not.
> It's going to be a sad song, brother,
> 'Cause we don't know the tune,
> And it's a difficult tune to learn,
> But we can learn it, brother,
> You and I,
> There's no such tune as a Black tune,
> There's no such tune as a White tune,
> There's only music, brother,
> And it's the music we're going to sing,
> Where the rainbow ends.
>
> (Couzens and Patel, *Amasi Bird*, p. 155)

Although, for various reasons, literary scholars have tended to focus on the work of Mafika Gwala, Oswald Mbuyiseni Mtshali, Sipho Sepamla and Mongane Wally Serote, there is a more inclusive group of poets of all races who were committed to the task of liberating all South Africans from the ideology of apartheid and its concomitant warped values, attitudes and patterns of behaviour. This group includes white, Indian and coloured poets such as Peter Horn, Jeremy Cronin, Richard Rive, Abdullah Ibrahim (commonly known as a jazz musician), James Matthews, Essop Patel, Don Mattera, Achmat Dangor, Chris van Wyk, Fhazel Johennesse, Shabbir Banoobhai and Farouk Asvat.

Echoing Biko, the critic Achille Mbembe explains why South Africans of all races stood to benefit from what he sees as the forward-looking and inherently positive philosophy of Black Consciousness:

> In a context in which the possibility of being human was foreclosed for both blacks and whites the concept of 'Black Consciousness' became the name of a different life to come – it was from the start, a philosophy of life and a philosophy of hope.   (quoted in Van Wyk, *We Write What We Like*, p. 137)

The studies of literary critics such as Jacques Alvarez-Pereyre (*The Poetry of Commitment*), David Attwell (*Rewriting Modernity*), Ursula Barnett (*A Vision of Order*), Michael Chapman (*Soweto Poetry, South African English Poetry* and *Southern African Literatures*), Tim Couzens ('Politics and Black Poetry in South Africa'), Jeremy Cronin ('The Law that Says/Constricts the Breath-line'), Nadine Gordimer (*The Black Interpreters*), Mbulelo Vizikhungo Mzamane ('The Impact of Black Consciousness' and 'Mtshali, Sepamla, Gwala and Serote'), Piniel Viriri Shava (*A People's Voice*), Jane Watts (*Black Writers from South Africa*), and myself ('Mafika Gwala', 'The Poetry of Mafika Gwala' and 'Interview with Sipho Sepamla') have confirmed the status of Black Consciousness poetry as a distinctive category of creative writing by black South African poets who chose or were forced by historical circumstances to write in English during the 1960s and 1970s. Apart from the four established poets mentioned earlier there were, of course, other, lesser-known poets whose work appeared in the various anthologies of South African black English poetry, including André Brink's *A World of their Own: Southern African Poets of the Seventies* (1976); Couzens and Patel's *The Return of the Amasi Bird: Black South African Poetry 1891–1981* (1982); Chapman and Dangor's *Voices from Within: Black Poetry from Southern Africa* (1982); Chapman's *A Century of South African Poetry* (1981) and the revised version of that anthology, *The New Century of South African Poetry* (2002); Stephen Gray's *Modern South African Poetry* (1984) and from the Writers' Forum, *Exiles Within: Seven South African Poets* (1986). Although connections between political ideologies and artistic products are, at best, tenuous, it cannot be gainsaid that Black Consciousness as a philosophy and a political ideology inspired – in direct and indirect ways – the work of the poets who came into prominence in the late 1960s, flourished in the 1970s and continued to contribute to literary magazines such as *The Classic, The Purple Renoster, Staffrider, Contrast, Bolt, Ophir, New Coin Poetry, SASO Newslettter, MEDU Newsletter* and other publications.

Critical reappraisal: themes and perspectives

Defying critical essentialism and easy pigeonholing, the poetry that constitutes the subject of this chapter has been variously referred to as 'Post-Sharpeville Poetry', 'Soweto Poetry', 'New Black Poetry' and 'Protest Poetry'. In the introduction to the collection of short stories *Hungry Flames* (1986), South African writer and literary scholar Mbulelo Mzamane offers the following characterisation of the poetry emanating from what he describes as a 'cultural renaissance' in black South African writing:

> Black Consciousness and the literature it inspired emerged in the midst of political and cultural repression after Sharpeville. The new wave of writers who emerged in South Africa after 1967 appeared to shy away at first from the more explicit medium of prose and took up poetry, after the manner of established literary figures such as James Matthews . . . Between 1967 and 1974 the cultural renaissance which accompanied the rise of Black Consciousness produced, at an unprecedented rate in the literary history of South Africa, many outstanding poets of the calibre of Dollar Brand (Abdullah Ibrahim), Oswald Mbuyiseni Mtshali, Mongane Wally Serote, Sipho Sepamla, Mafika Gwala, Mafika Mbuli, Mandlenkosi Langa and Njabulo Ndebele.
>
> (Mzamane, *Hungry Flames*, pp. xx–xxi)

If one is looking for a particular book of poetry that set the stage for the introduction of the poetry of the so-called New Black Poets, then Mtshali's *Sounds of a Cowhide Drum* (1971) (published by Renoster Books, owned by Lionel Abrahams) is without a doubt that book. Mtshali's seminal volume was soon followed by the debut collections of his contemporaries: Serote (*Yakhal'inkomo*, 1972), Sepamla (*Hurry Up to It!*, 1975) and Gwala (*Jol'iinkomo*, 1977), all published by Ad Donker. The publication of their poetry by these progressive white-owned publishing houses gave them an opportunity to express their anger and frustration while redefining their personal and communal identities in a manner that was in stark contrast to the way they were labelled by the apartheid regime and its functionaries.

In its deliberate foregrounding of the theme of racial pride and of the need to acknowledge the humanity of black people, Black Consciousness poetry exhibits some striking thematic affinities with the poetry associated with negritude as espoused by Aimé Césaire, Léopold Sédar Senghor and Leon Damas. It is, however, worth pointing out that the former was a direct response to the relatively unique South African political situation and was more of a liberation strategy than a philosophical outlook. In line with its conception as a transformative philosophy, Black Consciousness took, as its point of departure and *raison d'être*, the need for political freedom rather than hankering for a return to some mythical and untouched glorious past regarded as defining the essence of being African. As a political liberation strategy, Black Consciousness had a direct impact on political mobilisation in the various sectors of the South African black community, including various forms of cultural expression such as sculpture, painting, music and literature.

Both revisionist historiography and collective identity reappraisal function as organising principles and defining themes in the poetry of associated Black Consciousness in South Africa. In line with this approach, the process of rewriting history, whether this denotes a re-evaluation of the past or strategising for the future, is a central preoccupation of the Black Consciousness poets. With regard to the theme of historical revisionism, which characterises much of Black Consciousness poetry, there are poems that deal with the well-known and well-documented historical upheavals such as the Bulhoek and Sharpeville massacres (1921 and 1960 respectively), and the Soweto students' uprisings of 1976, as well as the assassination of political leaders. Poets also challenge what they see as the deliberate distortion or outright erasure of particular events from the collective memory of South Africans. It would not be an exaggeration to say that the literary – and sometimes the deliberately anti-literary – (re)writing of South African history constitutes the all-pervading and perhaps ineluctable theme of Black Consciousness poetry. The first three stanzas of Gwala's poem 'Afrika at a Piece (On Heroes Day)' capture the value and significance of the reappraisal of history both in and beyond the poetic text:

> You can't think of a solution
> Without your mind spelling revolution
> Unless your mind is steamed with pollution
> So much that you drop the notion
>
> As our heroes die
> As our heroes are born
> Our history is being written
> With the black moments given
> Looking the storm in the eye
> Our hope is not gone
>
> Our blackman's history
> is not written in the classrooms
> on wide smooth boards
> Our history shall be written

at the factory gates
at the Unemployment offices
in the scorched queues of dying mouths.
>> (Couzens and Patel, *Amasi Bird*, pp. 358–9)

Engaging directly with the contested notion of history, the speaker in the final stanza of Sepamla's 'History-books, Amen!' explains the responsibilities of the black poet, who is not only a creator of aesthetic beauty but also an astute student of history:

I know my history damn well
I'd need to have you stand back so I tell it
by God you've breathed down my neck for too long
your ominous shadow cast over all my events blurring details of it
this same history of bloody wars and bitter tears
whose pain sears through the body of our nation.
>> (Sepamla, *Selected Poems*, p. 123)

As argued in the rest of this chapter, the poetry of this era in the history of black South African literature exemplifies, in a direct and graphic way, the complex interconnections between literature, history and politics. The poetry of Black Consciousness constantly reminds the reader of its status as both 'literary' and 'historical' text. Eschewing the formalist conception of poetry as marked by technical complexity, a predetermined structure and sometimes obscure imagery and symbolism, Black Consciousness poets move with relative ease from the exhortatory language of the political rally to the standard western poetic discourses they were taught at school. Thus, from the New Historicist critical perspective, it could be argued that Black Consciousness poets seek to textualise history while simultaneously historicising poetry. Elaborating on the role of the poet as historian, Mtshali announces the recognisably historical and political nature of this poetry in the author's note to his second volume of poems, *Fireflames* (1980), which on publication was instantly banned by the apartheid government:

These poems, written during the past few years, were inspired by personal, social, economic and, most especially, political events in South Africa. The situation has been in a state of flux since the early sixties, from which period we have been writhing with increasing momentum through the most crucial period in our relentless, tear-stained and blood-soaked struggle for our total liberation from racism, exploitation and dehumanisation.

Confirming Mtshali's words above, Michael Chapman (*Art Talk, Politics Talk*), a respected scholar of South African literature, points out that it is not always easy for critics and general readers alike to distinguish between 'art talk' and 'politics talk' in the work of most South African writers, especially those who were primarily writing against apartheid.

In its stated mission to redeem the human dignity of all South Africans and in particular black people and to give expression to various forms of racial oppression, Black Consciousness poetry resonates with the work of the African American poets of the Harlem Renaissance of the 1920s – poets such as Claude McKay and Langston Hughes – as well as with the fiercely revolutionary rhetoric of Stokely Carmichael's Black Power of the 1960s and 1970s. Rather as Biko's essays (appearing in various publications during the 1960s and 1970s and collected in *I Write What I Like* after his assassination) have an inspirational resonance with Black Consciousness poetry, so too the seminal essay by Alain Locke (1886–1954), *The New Negro* (1925) – rightly described as 'the central text of the Harlem Renaissance' (and quoted in full in Gates and McKay, *African American Literature*, pp. 960–70) – has resonance for the poets associated with the Harlem Renaissance in the USA of the 1920s. When Langston Hughes says, 'I, too, sing America / I, too, am America' (Gates and McKay, *African American Literature*, p. 1258), he is affirming his humanity, which he is certain his white fellow citizens will acknowledge at some point. The thematic affinity between Rive's poem quoted at the beginning of this chapter and Hughes's well-known poem is striking, to say the least. Similarly, Claude McKay's poem 'If We Must Die' (1919) captures the spirit of revolutionary defiance in the African American community, which was to culminate in the sometimes violent and disruptive civil rights campaigns of the 1960s in the United States:

> If we must die, let it not be like hogs
> Hunted and penned in an inglorious spot,
> While round us bark the mad and hungry dogs,
> Making their mock at our accursed lot.
> If we must die, O let us nobly die,
> So that our precious blood may not be shed
> In vain; then even the monsters we defy
> Shall be constrained to honour us though dead!
>
> (Gates and McKay, *African American Literature*, p. 984)

Like Gwala's poem quoted earlier, McKay's angry poem is essentially about the anticipated revolution and the heroic sacrifices associated with it. For both

Gwala and McKay the main preoccupation is reclaiming the honour, pride and dignity of black people. The social and historical contexts may differ but the concerns of the two poets are strikingly similar.

Irrepressible feelings of revolutionary anger characterise Mtshali's poem written for the memorial service in honour of Onkgopotse Tiro, a student leader murdered by government forces, at the Regina Mundi Church in Soweto on 17 February 1974:

> A new order will be forged
> on the anvil of our sorrows;
> the flame in our furious hearts will flash
> all the nocturnal conspiracies
> at which deadly devices are made and sent,
> to wound, to maim, and to kill,
> and spatter your sacrificial blood
> on the door to freedom.
>
> But no bomb can ever kill
> the spirit of a fearless fighter,
> no gun can shoot it,
> no jail can hold it,
> not even the grave will seal it off
> from a people aroused to action.   (Mtshali, *Fireflames*, p. 31)

Like African American poetry associated with the Harlem Renaissance, Black Consciousness-inspired poetry is patently ideological, decidedly literalist and political in its themes, diction and imagery. It is primarily for this reason that some critics have found it banal and lacking in sophistication (Livingstone, 'Critical Evaluation'; Watson, 'Shock of the Old'). The response to the criticisms of literary scholars is often given directly in the poems themselves, with Gwala's poem 'In Defence of Poetry' summing up the poet's disdain for the literary small-mindedness of some critics:

> What's poetic
> about Defence Bonds and Armscor?
> What's poetic
> about long-term sentences and
> deaths in detention
> for those who 'threaten state security'?
> Tell me,
> What's poetic
> about shooting defenceless kids
> in a Soweto street?

Can there be poetry
in fostering Public Relations?
Can there be poetry
in the Immorality Act?
What's poetic
about deciding other people's lives?
Tell me brother,
What's poetic
about defending herrenvolkish rights?

As long as
this land, my country
is unpoetic in its doings
it'll be poetic to disagree.

(Gwala, *No More Lullabies*, p. 10)

Gwala provides what could be seen as a poetic manifesto for the poetry associated with Black Consciousness. The label 'anti-poets' has been used by some critics (Chapman, *South African English Poetry*; McDonald, *Literature Police*) to refer to what seems to be a deliberate decision on the part of the black poets of this era to challenge inherited poetic conventions. In a slim collection entitled *Exiles Within* (1986), Achmat Dangor's poem accounts for the degeneration of what could have been subtle, carefully structured, ironic or symbolic poetic texts into uncontrolled ejaculations of anger and defiance. Again, as in Gwala's poem, Dangor anticipates the standard criticism of predominantly white critics in 'Once there was a Poem':

These bitter words
tumble from me
like a flood

Do not wonder at this:
you it was who
milked the udders
of my love,
and left me nothing
but the venomous
dredges of despair

Come,
search the emptiness
of my heart,
and ignite
the dry tinder
of its substance,

and say:
Once there was
a poem here.
(quoted in Writers' Forum, *Exiles Within*, p. 9)

The recurrent themes that characterise the poetry of the four main Black Consciousness poets are black pride, the tactical foregrounding of positive aspects of African traditional culture, communal self-respect and a rejection of imposed identities and roles. As one critic puts it, all these themes affirm an overriding humanistic ethos : 'The humanistic ethos of the poetry is expressed by the articulation of a black poet's fear that he may become as brutal, as insensitive, and as callous as the white oppressor, and in doing what is needed he might lose his essential humanity' (Wa Bofelo, 'Influences and Representations', p. 197). Evident in the work of all four poets mentioned above are attempts to bolster a new and radically politicised collective identity of the black community by citing examples of immediately recognisable instances of racial oppression and the prominent features of multifaceted black urban culture. In order to ensure accessibility, the poems, written in stark unadorned idiom, were published in literary magazines and newsletters and recited at political gatherings, such as those of the South African Student Organisation and the Black People's Convention, and at the meetings of community development organisations linked to the Black Consciousness movement. Serote's 'Burning Cigarette', a poem that revolves around the fate of black youth with no prospect of a meaningful life in a racially segregated country, has a direct resonance with the experience of the black community in the South Africa of the 1970s and 1980s:

This little black boy
Is drawn like a cigarette from its box,
Lit.
He looks up at his smoke hopes
That twirl, spiral, curl
To nothing.
He grows like cigarette ashes
As docile, as harmless;
Is smothered.   (Serote, *Selected Poems*, p. 30)

This remarkably taut poem captures with striking verbal economy and expressive imagery the fate of millions of young people whose lives were 'smothered' in various ways by the inhuman system of apartheid. The combined effect of the poem's diction and imagery and the organising simile of a burning cigarette is to reinforce the boy's utter helplessness and the complete hopelessness of his situation. In terms of its portrayal of young people trapped in debilitating social conditions, this poem is comparable to Serote's other poems on the fate of the black youth of the 1970s, such as 'My Brothers in the Street' and 'A Sleeping Black Boy'.

Nowhere is the social entrapment of young black people under apartheid more aptly captured than in Mtshali's 'Boy on a Swing'. In the poem the swing functions as a metaphor for the overwhelming, dizzying and confusing social environment in which the boy and his family find themselves. The bewildered, directionless boy in the poem represents what has come to be called 'the lost generation' of the 1970s and 1980s in South Africa. I quote the last two stanzas:

> The world whirls by:
> east becomes west,
> north turns to south;
> the four cardinal points
> meet in his head.
>
> Mother!
> Where did I come from?
> When will I wear long trousers?
> Why was my father jailed?
>
> (Chapman, *New Century*, p. 193)

Both Serote's and Mtshali's poems recall Peter Abrahams's 'The Negro Youth' written in the typical protest mode and first published on 5 December 1936 in *Bantu World*. Significantly, the young man who is the subject of the poem could be South African or American, as he is not immediately recognisable as belonging to either context:

> He stood alone,
> A Negro youth.
> What of his future?
> His cap was worn,
> This Negro youth.
> Why was he born?
> Born to lead an empty useless life,
> Born to mar the record of his race,
> Or born to lead his race?

Locked are the doors,
Locked – the doors of his future.
His burden to bear,
To suffer pain of life's cruel ways,
That is why he was born.

(Couzens and Patel, *Amasi Bird*, p. 85)

As noted above, it has now become a critical commonplace to regard the Sharpeville massacre (21 March 1960) as signalling the beginning of black protest poetry, which was directly and stridently critical of the apartheid regime. It is, however, worth pointing out that the themes, imagery and symbolism of what is generally referred to as Black Consciousness poetry in South African creative writing have their origins in the 1930s and 1940s, in the work of Peter Abrahams and H. I. E. Dhlomo, both of whom were continuing a trend initiated by J. J. R. Jolobe, S. E. K. Mqhayi, B. W. Vilakazi and other politically aware black poets who preceded them. Like the Black Consciousness poets of the 1970s, their poetry tackled the dehumanising effect of discriminatory legislation on the black community. Jolobe's 'The Making of a Servant', Mqhayi's 'The Prince of Britain' and Vilakazi's 'The Gold Mines' are more than just protest poems; they mark an unprecedented political consciousness and self-assertiveness on the part of black poets. The following lines from 'The Gold Mines' by Vilakazi could have been written by any of the four Black Consciousness poets mentioned above:

O see how day by day this land
Is being plundered by those who seized it
The foreigners who enrich themselves
While I and my deprived black brothers
Are landless, penniless, empty-handed!

(Chapman and Dangor, *Voices from Within*, p. 47)

However, it was Peter Abrahams and H. I. E. Dhlomo who dealt directly with the issues that were to become the defining themes of black poetry after Sharpeville and the subsequent banning and exile of writers who could have served as role models for Black Consciousness poets. For example, the conception of the poet as the self-appointed spokesperson of the oppressed black community, which was to become a common feature of the poetry of the 1970s and 1980s, is nowhere better articulated than in the final stanza of Abrahams's poem 'Self' from his *A Blackman Speaks of Freedom* (1940):

I'm a poet,
And through hunger
And lust for love and laughter
I have turned myself into a voice,
Shouting the pain of the People
And the sunshine that is to be.
                              (Chapman and Dangor, *Voices from Within*, p. 49)

All four of the poets who, like Abrahams, saw themselves as the voices of the black community began their careers as poets by publishing in the literary magazines mentioned above in the late 1960s and early 1970s. The first collection that featured the work of all the major Black Consciousness poets is the volume edited by R. Royston, *To Whom it May Concern: An Anthology of Black South African Poetry* (1973). The book derives its title from a bitingly satirical poem written by Sipho Sepamla decrying the impact of the pass laws on the lives of black South Africans. In the first six lines of the poem the reader is introduced to a nameless and faceless entity that is hardly recognisable as a human being. Moreover, as is implicit in the title, the movement of this entity must be 'processed' clinically by an impersonal government bureaucratic system. This poem exemplifies Sepamla's uncanny ability to combine direct political protest with carefully targeted satire and irony. It is precisely this quality that makes his work stand out within the work of Black Consciousness poets.

Bearer
Bare of everything but particulars
Is a Bantu
The language of a people in southern Africa
He seeks to proceed from here to there
Please pass him on
Subject to these particulars
He lives
Subject to the provisions
Of the Urban Natives Act of 1925
Amended often
To update it to his sophistication
Subject to the provisions of the said Act
He may roam freely within a prescribed area
                              (Royston, *To Whom it May Concern*, p. 96)

Most of the poets represented in this seminal poetry collection subsequently established themselves as writer-activists who, according to the common phrase of the time, regarded 'writing as a cultural weapon' (p. 37). In their attempts to tackle the all-embracing theme of 'black experience', the poets played on the literal and symbolic meanings of blackness and its antithesis, whiteness. It goes without saying that whiteness, like blackness, also went beyond denoting skin pigmentation to connote an attitude or state of mind. As the speaker in Serote's poem 'The Actual Dialogue' aptly reminds us, one of the key concerns of the Black Consciousness movement was to initiate a 'dialogue' between the two modes of being (blackness and whiteness), which could help in eliminating distrust, fear and insecurity:

> Do not fear Baas.
> It's just that I appeared
> And our faces met
> In this black night that's like me.
> Do not fear –
> We will always meet
> When you do not expect me.
> I will appear
> In the night that's black like me.
> Do not fear –
> Blame your heart
> When you fear me –
> I will blame my mind
> When I fear you
> In the night that's black like me.
>
> (Sepamla, *Selected Poems*, p. 19)

Genuine rapprochement between races is only possible through frank dialogue in what is essentially a battle of hearts and minds. Interestingly, in his first collection which, characteristically, bristles with irony and satire, *Hurry Up to It!* (1975), Sepamla also explores the theme of fear and mistrust in 'Darkness':

> yes sir i have arrived
> walk the night if you dare
> there i reign over death
> 'swonder you legislate the night
> i walk erect in the night
> you crouch in retreat
> crowding each nook in fear
> of the stench of my blackness
> agitated by a darkness
>
> (Sepamla, *Selected Poems*, p. 24)

Black Consciousness poetry is the poetry of anger, declamations and warnings about portending danger. As shown in the examples quoted above, the speaker in most of these poems is addressing an unidentified interlocutor in an incongruous scenario of a one-sided dialogue. Perhaps the poem that best typifies the anger, militancy and self-assertion of the black community is Serote's 'What's in this Black "Shit"'. In this frequently anthologised poem exploring the pervasive theme of 'black experience' in the post-Sharpeville era, Serote turns his gaze, in the final stanza, on the notorious pass laws:

> I'm learning to pronounce this 'Shit' well,
> Since the other day,
> At the pass office,
> When I went to get employment,
> The officer there endorsed me to Middleburg,
> So I said, hard and with all my might, 'Shit!'
> I felt a little better;
> but what's good, is, I said it in his face,
> A thing my father wouldn't dare do.
> That's what's in this black 'Shit'.
>
> (Sepamla, *Selected Poems*, p. 42)

In this poem 'Shit' becomes a metaphor for the anger and frustration of the black community. As suggested in Serote's poem, the black poetry of this era sought to reclaim the humanity of black people, not only articulating their anger and frustration but also signalling to the oppressor that the anger of the black community could explode at any time. The speaker in Serote's poem alerts us to the differences between the different generations of black people, the deferential and subservient older generation and the militant and angry generation of the 1970s. Similarly, in Gwala's long poem suggestively titled 'Getting off the Ride', the use of revolutionary self-transformation features throughout. The speaker states in explicit terms that one aspect of 'getting off the ride' entails a profound process of self-examination followed by a militant confrontation of the political and ideological discourses that construct black people in a new negative way:

> I ask again, what is Black?
> Black is when you get off the ride.
> . . .
> Black is energetic release from the shackles of Kaffir, Bantu, non-white.
>
> (Chapman and Dangor, *Voices from Within*, p. 138)

Whilst firmly anchored in the present of black experience in both its rural and urban contexts, the poets of Black Consciousness also consciously adopted backward-looking or historical perspectives in some of their poems. Their conscious attempts to link the past with the present are also evident in the titles of their first collections: Mtshali invokes that quintessentially African symbol, the drum; Serote and Gwala both use the title of Miriam Makeba's song about cattle. Without romanticising traditional African culture and values, they highlight the heroism, national cohesiveness and relative peace that characterised precolonial communities in southern Africa. A careful examination of the poems on African traditions reveals that they use symbols, myths and traditional cultural practices to bolster self-affirmation or assist black people in regaining self-respect. This is illustrated in poems such as Sepamla's 'To Makanna and Nongqawuse'; Mtshali's 'Back to the Bush' and 'The Birth of Shaka'; and Gwala's 'The Children of Nonti'. For example, Gwala points to the indomitable qualities of African people, in particular their ability to adapt to difficult conditions of living, in 'The Children of Nonti':

> Nonti Nzimande died long, long ago
> Yet his children still live.
> Generation after generation, they live;
> . . .
> Sometimes a son rises above the others
> of the children of Nonti. He explains the workings
> and the trappings of white thinking.
> The elders debate;
> And add to their abounding knowledge
> Of black experience.
> The son is still one of the black children of Nonti
> For there is oneness in the children of Nonti.
> > (Chapman and Dangor, *Voices from Within*, pp. 131–2)

Despite all the ongoing cultural changes, the children of Nonti (black people) have retained the virtue of African humanism (*ubuntu*), the central principle of which is that a human being is a human being because of other human beings (*umuntu ngumuntu ngabantu*). As noted above, recognising and acknowledging the essential humanity of each human being is at the core of the Black Consciousness philosophy. It is therefore not surprising that the ideal of *ubuntu* characterises the poetry inspired by this philosophy.

In 'To Makanna and Nongqawuse', another poem that links the past to the present, Sepamla appeals to the spirits of Makanna and Nongqawuse, well-known figures in Xhosa history, to sustain him and his people in this modern warfare, which 'demand[s] briefcases and cotton ties':

> O! spirits of my ancestors awake
> I hear the whizz of bullet words
> and I am felled as many times as I listen
> give me the silence of your graves
>
> O! spirits of the departed prophets
> Let me meet you instead at a street corner
> And from the brow of your unwrinkled face
> I'll learn the secrets of this life.
>
> (Gray, *Modern South African Poetry*, p. 201)

Similarly in 'The Birth of Shaka', Mtshali finds reassurance in the figure of King Shaka, a well-known African warrior-king:

> His baby cry
> was of a cub
> tearing the neck
> of the lioness
>
> . . .
>
> The gods
> boiled his blood
> in a clay pot of passion
> to course in his veins.
>
> His heart was shaped into an ox shield
> to foil every foe.
>
> (Gray, *Modern South African Poetry*, p. 165)

Although Black Consciousness was clearly a phenomenon of its time, it drew its inspiration, at least in part, from a common conception of a traditional past, which was not without its flaws but which had been erased from the memory of 'enlightened' and 'educated' Africans, who were encouraged to look up to the West for progress and excellence. The reader is alerted to some of the problems associated with a civilising discourse that demonised African traditions but failed to provide viable alternatives in Mtshali's 'Back to the Bush'. The speaker in this poem grapples with the dilemma of being an 'enlightened black man' in a country where he is prevented by legislation from demonstrating his discriminating taste and sophistication:

I have gone back to where I came from,
and then I heard you, Father Cockerel
telling your fellow priests
that your sermons have been in vain;
'These people have hardly come out of the bush,
they are reverting to barbarism.'

That may be true, Father Cockerel,
I have definitely gone back to the bush, Father Cockerel.
What do you expect me to do, Father Cockerel?
Where am I supposed to go, Father Cockerel?

There is 'No Admittance' for me in the strip joints
that proliferate in the red light districts of cities;
I am not wanted in your nudist colonies,
I cannot even take a stroll on the 'Euro-penis Only' Clifton Beach,
because I will see naked White women.   (Mtshali, *Fireflames*, p. 48)

A remarkable feature of the poetry of Black Consciousness is the way the poets dealt with the issue of gender. In poems such as 'This Old Woman', 'The Three Mothers', 'Beerhall Queen', 'The Auntie Otherside' (Serote); and 'Come Duze Baby', 'Song of Mother and Child', and 'The Black Girl' (Sepamla), women are shown to be key participants in the resilient and complex township culture. Serote captures the femininity of black woman beautifully in a poem inspired by a sculpture by Dumile Feni:

Kneel down woman . . .

(Saluting Mother and Child sculpture by Dumile)

Kneel down woman, naked as you are,
Let your heavy head hang down,
And the milk of your breast
And the weight of your back
Pull you down;
Take a look at the thighs
And see.
The world that God wrote with his big fingers,
Were they hesitant fingers?
They wrote a story that we live but do not understand.
Kneel down, woman,
We the born shall lie and hide on your back,
While you take a look.

The truth is that you are seeing an arrangement,
There's water, is it salty? There's blood,
That is salty.
Kneel down woman, naked as you are.
We are waiting, we want to know.

(Chapman, *Paperbook*, p. 165)

Betraying an awareness of some technical shortcomings of their art, Black Consciousness poets kept returning to the issue of 'literariness' to justify the approaches and themes they had chosen. As shown in the few excerpts quoted above, the language, form and structure of Black Consciousness poetry reflect the poets' attempts to merge the traditional oral forms with both contemporary township forms of cultural expression and modern western poetic forms. It is important to bear in mind that some of these poems were specifically composed for performance or recitation at political gatherings such as trade union rallies, student meetings and the meetings of community development organisations. It would be incongruous to have such poems written in complex diction and imagery as they were meant to have an immediate appeal to and response from an audience. For this reason most of the poetry associated with the Black Consciousness movement may not be carefully crafted artefacts in terms of the standard conventions of English poetry as defined in the narrowest, national or canonical sense, but rather clear and unambiguous and sometimes angry political statements. The language of Black Consciousness poetry seeks to approximate the actual speech patterns in black residential areas and the musical rhythms of jazz and blues. This is evident in the poetry of all four of the major Black Consciousness poets but is particularly noticeable in Sepamla's poetry, where 'township English', *tsotsitaal* and standard English are used to good effect. Of the four poets, Sepamla stands out in his experimentation with the languages of the slums, the township and the rural village. His poems 'Come Duze Baby', 'Da Same Da Same' and 'Statement: The Dodger' all illustrate his creativity and skill in this regard. The following three stanzas from 'Statement: The Dodger' demonstrate his talent:

Hayi ke mos
This world inento zawo

This fellow-ndini ndithi-speak about
Ndimqhelile, I'm used to him ngaloo way
Yokumthi-see everyday on the street

He comes to me one day
You know nge-same way
Ka-I'll be alright tomorrow Jack
He says ndimthi-borrow i-five bob
Uzandithi-fixup on a Friday
Xa sithi-meet again on the way.

(Sepamla, *Selected Poems*, p. 57)

Black Consciousness poets saw art in the broadest conception of the term as having a crucial role to play in both the psychological and physical liberation of black people in South Africa. As if confirming its close thematic and structural associations with other art forms such as painting, music and visual art, Black Consciousness poetry is replete with references to other art forms. Serote, Gwala and Sepamla make direct references to South African jazz musicians such as Dollar Brand (Abdullah Ibrahim), Winston Monwabisi 'Mankunku' Ngozi, Mackay Davashe and others. Mtshali's second volume contains illustrations by such artists as Mzwakhe Mhlabatsi and Epraim Ziqubu, among others.

As if responding to critics who expect aesthetic beauty in his poetry, Serote provides a graphic explanation of the effect of content on form in his poem 'Prelude', published in *Tsetlo* (1974):

When i take a pen,
my soul bursts to deface the paper
pus spills –
spreads
deforming a line into the figure that violates my love,
when i take a pen,
my crimson heart oozes into the ink,
dilutes it
spreads the gem of my life
makes the word i utter gasp into the world, –
my mother, when i dance your eyes won't keep pace
look into my eyes,
there, the story of my day is told.   (Serote, *Selected Poems*, p. 45)

Because of its shocking imagery, Serote's poem conveys its meaning by creating its own standards for aesthetic beauty. It is the almost inarticulate beauty of physical pain and emotional turmoil. Essentially, the poem revolves around the difficulty the poet is having in composing 'aesthetically beautiful' poems for poets who have been denied the social capital to do so.

Black Consciousness poets were not unaware of how their unapologetically political work would be received by literary critics, as Mtshali reminds us in his poem 'Literary Critics', from which I quote the first and final stanzas:

> Critics are enemies of the truth
> and lovers of pomposity and falsity
> which they parade with all the inanities of
> intellectual tripe and sanctimonious sob-songs.
>
> . . .
>
> They write in ornate style
> and pick your work with a fine tooth-comb.
> But I write what I please
> as I huddle in these crummy rooms
> infested with rats and roaches.   (Mtshali, *Fireflames*, p. 62)

As I have tried to show, the South African Black Consciousness movement took its impetus from political and cultural movements with similar goals in the USA and in post-independence Africa. The poetry emanating from Harlem, Senegal, Algeria and the Caribbean islands at the time attested to the growing need for black people around the world to be recognised as human beings. In the South African context the poetry has been shown to be self-referential, politically direct and based on the realities of the black experience in an unjust political system. These poems lend themselves to analysis as historical-literary texts and surely add a unique and provocative element in the writing of South African literary history.

Bibliography

Alvarez-Pereyre, J. *The Poetry of Commitment in South Africa*, London: Heinemann, 1979.

Arnold, M. W. (ed.). *Steve Biko: No Fears Expressed*, Johannesburg: Skotaville, 1987.

Attwell, D. *Rewriting Modernity: Studies in Black South African Literary History*, Pietermaritzburg: University of KwaZulu-Natal Press, 2005.

Barnett, U. *A Vision of Order: A Study of Black South African Literature in English (1914–1980)*, Cape Town: Maskew Miller Longman, 1983.

Biko, S. B. *I Write What I Like*, ed. A. Stubbs, London: Bowerdean, 1978.

Brink, A. (ed.). *A World of their Own: Southern African Poets of the Seventies*, Johannesburg: Ad Donker, 1976.

Chapman, M. *Art Talk, Politics Talk*, Pietermaritzburg: University of KwaZulu-Natal Press, 2006.

South African English Poetry: A Modern Perspective, Johannesburg: Ad Donker, 1984.

Southern African Literatures, London and New York: Longman, 1996.

Chapman, M. (ed.). *A Century of South African Poetry*, Johannesburg: Ad Donker, 1981.

The New Century of South African Poetry, Johannesburg: Ad Donker/Jonathan Ball, 2002.

The Paperbook of South African English Poetry, Johannesburg: Ad Donker, 1986.

Soweto Poetry, Johannesburg: MacGraw-Hill, 1982.

Chapman, M., and A. Dangor (eds.). *Voices from Within: Black Poetry from Southern Africa*, Johannesburg: Ad Donker, 1982.

Couzens, T. 'Politics and Black Poetry in South Africa, 1930–1950', *African Perspective* 7 (1978), 1–15.

Couzens, T., and E. Patel (eds.). *The Return of the Amasi Bird: Black South African Poetry 1891–1981*, Johannesburg: Ravan, 1982.

Cronin, J. 'The Law that Says/Constricts the Breath-line: South African English Poetry Written by Blacks in the 1970s', *English Academy Review* 3:1 (1985), 25–49.

Daymond, M. J., J. U. Jacobs and M. Lenta (eds.). *Momentum: On Recent South African Writing*, Pietermaritzburg: University of Natal Press, 1984.

Gates Jr, H. L., and N. Y. McKay (eds.). *The Norton Anthology of African American Literature*, New York: W. W. Norton, 1997.

Gordimer, N. *The Black Interpreters*, Johannesburg: Sprocas/Ravan, 1973.

Gray, S. (ed.). *Modern South African Poetry*, Johannesburg: Ad Donker, 1984.

Gwala, M. *Jol'iinkomo*, Johannesburg: Ad Donker, 1977.

No More Lullabies, Johannesburg: Ad Donker, 1983.

'Writing as a Cultural Weapon', in Daymond et al., *Momentum*, 1984, 37–53.

Livingstone, D. 'The Poetry of Mtshali, Serote, Sepamla and Others in English: Notes Towards a Critical Evaluation', in Chapman, *Soweto Poetry*, 1982, 57–61.

McDonald, P. D. *The Literature Police: Apartheid Censorship and its Cultural Consequences*, Oxford University Press, 2009.

Mtshali, O. M. *Fireflames*, Pietermaritzburg: Shuter & Shooter, 1980.

Sounds of a Cowhide Drum, Johannesburg: Renoster Books, 1971; Johannesburg: Ad Donker, 1982.

Mzamane, M. V. *Hungry Flames and other South African Short Stories*, Harlow: Longman, 1986.

'The Impact of Black Consciousness on Culture', in B. Pityana et al. (eds.), *Bounds of Possibility: The Legacy of Steve Biko and Black Consciousness*, Cape Town: David Philip, 1991, 179–93.

'Mtshali, Sepamla, Gwala and Serote and other Poets of the Black Consciousness Era in South Africa, 1967–1984', in M. Chapman, C. Gardner and E. Mphahlele (eds.), *Perspectives on South African English Literature*, Johannesburg: Ad Donker, 1992, 352–77.

Ngwenya, T. 'Mafika Gwala: Towards a National Culture' (interview by Thengamehlo Ngwenya), *Staffrider* 8:1 (1989), 69–74.

'The Poetry of Mafika Gwala', *Staffrider* 11:2 (1992), 44–51.

'Interview with Sipho Sepamla: 2 September 1993', *English Academy Review* 1 (1994), 73–82.

Rive, R. *Writing Black: An Author's Notebook*, Cape Town: David Philip, 1981.

Royston, R. (ed.). *To Whom it May Concern: An Anthology of Black South African Poetry*, Johannesburg: Ad Donker, 1973.

Sepamla, S. *The Blues is You in Me*, Johannesburg: Ad Donker, 1976.

Children of the Earth, Johannesburg: Ad Donker, 1983.

From Goré to Soweto, Johannesburg: Ad Donker, 1988.

Hurry Up to It!, Johannesburg: Ad Donker, 1975.

Selected Poems, ed. M. V. Mzamane, Johannesburg: Ad Donker, 1984.

The Soweto I Love, Cape Town: Africa Book Centre, 1977.

Serote, M.W. *Behold Mama, Flowers*, Johannesburg: Ad Donker, 1978.

No Baby Must Weep, Johannesburg: Ad Donker, 1974.

Sekected Poems, ed. M. V. Mzamane, Johannesburg: Ad Donker, 1982.

Tsetlo, Johannesburg: Ad Donker, 1974.

Yakhal'inkomo, Johannesburg: Renoster Books / Ad Donker, 1972.

Shava, P. V. *A People's Voice: Black South African Writing in the Twentieth Century*, London: Zed Books, 1989.

Van Wyk, C. (ed.). *We Write What We Like*, Johannesburg: Witwatersrand University Press, 2007.

Wa Bofelo, M. 'The Influences and Representations of Biko and Black Consciousness in Poetry in Apartheid and Post-Apartheid South Africa / Azania', in A. Mngxitama, A. Alexander and N. Gibson (eds.), *Biko Lives: Contesting the Legacies of Steve Biko*, New York: Palgrave Macmillan, 2008, 191–212.

Watson, S. 'Shock of the Old: What's Become of Black Poetry? (1987)', in *Selected Essays 1980–1990*, Cape Town: Carrefour Press, 1990, 82–7.

Watts, J. *Black Writers from South Africa*, London: Macmillan, 1989.

Writers' Forum. *Exiles Within: Seven South African Poets. An Anthology of Poetry*, Johannesburg: Writers' Forum, 1986.

25

Popular forms and the United Democratic Front

PETER HORN

'Protest art' – political art – 'struggle poetry'

The 1960s witnessed a massive clampdown by the government on protest writing (and black writing in general – see Horn, 'Right of the People'), resulting in authors being silenced and driven into exile. In the year 1963, the South African government introduced the Publications Act, 'an extensive and repressive "security" apparatus [that was] levelled against literary production' (Ryan, 'Literary-Intellectual Behavior', p. 293), which wiped out the writing of many important South African writers (see Kunene, 'Ideas under Arrest'). And when black literature revived in the following decade, it looked quite different. As it was based now on the concepts of Black Consciousness, white literary orientations were no less denounced than the political values of whites: in fact, this new generation of blacks conceived of the western literary conceptions as an integral part of western imperialism.

In September 1968, *Ophir: Journal for Poetry* published one of the first poems of Oswald Mtshali ('The Master of the House', p. 7), followed by 'What's in this Black "Shit"' by Wally Mongane Serote (p. 16) in 1969, while *Ophir* issue 11 featured seven poems by Pascal [Mafika] Gwala ('Kwela Ride', 'Things', 'Promise', 'An Attempt at Communication', 'Food for the Couple', 'Election Pincers', 'When it's all Double-You'). By the time *Ophir* published its last issue, in spring 1976, black poetry in English had again become a force no longer to be overlooked.[1] When *Staffrider* was launched in 1978, there was a chorus of black voices in poetry. New voices of the 1960s and 1970s were, among others, Jennifer Davids (*Searching for Words*, 1974), Fhazel Johenesse (*The Rainmaker*, 1979), Madlenkosi Langa, Ingoapele Madingoane (*Africa my Beginning*, 1979), James Matthews (*Black Voices Shout*, 1974; *Pass me a Meatball, Jones*, 1977), Donald Parenzee (*Driven to Work*, 1985), Essop Patel (*They Came at*

---

1 Black poets had featured prominently in 1974 at the Poetry South Africa Conference at the University of Cape Town. See Chapman, *Soweto Poetry*.

Dawn, 1980), Sipho Sepamla (*Hurry Up to It!*, 1975; *The Blues is You in Me*, 1976; *The Soweto I Love*, 1977), Gladys Thomas (*Cry Rage!*, with James Matthews, 1972) and Christopher van Wyk (*It is Time to go Home*, 1979). But from the 1960s to the late 1980s among the growing chorus of powerful black protest poets and resistance poets there were always also white poets, whose contribution was considerable: among them Jeremy Cronin, Ingrid de Kok, Keith Gottschalk, Antjie Krog, Wopko Jensma, Ari Sitas and Kelwyn Sole.

A radical rethinking of the art of poetry

The 1970s was the time of Black Consciousness.[2] Black Consciousness poetry, while asserting the resources of Africa and directing itself to a black and oppressed audience, did not always escape the gesture of protest (see Chapter 24).[3] By postulating a 'Black Aesthetics' or an 'African Aesthetics', it rigorously cut itself loose from liberal and radical white tutelage and associated attempts to steer black poetry into safe channels of British aesthetics, 'which had more to do with dictating to Blacks how they should think and feel than with telling them how to write good poetry' (Maughan Brown, 'Black Criticism', p. 47). Those who had equated their partial (white) aesthetics with aesthetics as such were suddenly challenged by another, equally partial but powerful aesthetics, or by the total disregard of those they disregarded. James Matthews pre-emptively rejected the label 'poetry' and those who set themselves up to bestow it: 'To label my utterings poetry and myself a poet would be as self-deluding as the planners of parallel development. I record the anguish of the persecuted whose words are whimpers of woe wrung from them by bestial laws' (Matthews and Thomas, *Cry Rage!*, p. 70). Mafika Gwala argued that 'the majority of our literary critics are intellectual propagandists. They prefer the language of the elite' (*No More Lullabies*, p. 10). Gwala is, however, not content with this merely negative stance, which leaves the accolade 'poetry' in the hands of the enemy. After asking 'What's poetic / about long-term sentences and / deaths in detention', he postulates against the 'unpoetic' reality of the apartheid state an 'aesthetics of resistance' (see Horn, 'Aesthetics and the Revolutionary Struggle'), which appropriates the term 'poetry' for a revolutionary praxis:

2 In 1968, SASO (South African Students' Organisation) was formed with Steve Biko as its first president. See Horn, '"When it rains, it rains"'; Horn, 'A Radical Rethinking of the Art of Poetry'.
3 See Horn, 'Struggle Poetry'; Alvarez-Pereyre, *The Poetry of Commitment*; Alvarez-Pereyre, 'Peter Horn's *Civil War Cantoes*'.

As long as
this land, my country
is unpoetic in its doings
it'll be poetic to disagree
(Gwala, *No More Lullabies*, p. 10)

In the late 1970s and early 1980s the mood changed. Trade unions engaged in illegal strikes in Natal; the schoolchildren of Soweto rose up in revolt; the Mass Democratic Movement (MDM) reformed and the United Democratic Front (UDF) appeared openly on platforms. Njabulo Ndebele wrote: 'Serote came with *No Baby Must Weep*', and that after this, poetry which portrayed the oppressed as weeping could only falsify the historical reality. Protest poetry turned into struggle poetry, the poetry of those participating in one way or another in the fight against apartheid. It is no longer a poetry 'waiting to be asked what the problem is'. It is, in the words of Njabulo Ndebele, 'the poetry of a fighting people'. The Soweto uprising of 16 June 1976 meant that the people were no longer prepared to allow themselves to be pushed around: 'people said: "Enough, our patience, it has limits"' (Ndebele, 'Life-Sustaining Poetry', pp. 44–5.) This poetry proclaims a new truth:

Our blackman's history
is not written in classrooms
on wide smooth boards
Our history shall be written
at the factory gates
at the Unemployment offices
in the scorched queues of dying mouths

Our history shall be our joys
           our sorrows
           our anguish
scrawled in dirty Third Class toilets
Our history will be the distorted figures
and bitter slogans
decorating our ghetto walls
where flowers found no peace enough to grow
(Gwala, *No More Lullabies*, p. 44)

In a reaction that paralleled discussions by other Africans and black Americans about creating a black aesthetic, as opposed to a white aesthetic, black South African authors returned to traditional African models of literature. And one of the most important aspects of their black aesthetic was to reject the western idea of a division of labour between the various genres (Zander, 'Prose-Poem-Drama'). Mothobi Mutloatse coined the term 'proemdra' and wrote a kind of manifesto in the introduction of the anthology *Forced Landing* (1980):

> We are involved in and consumed by an exciting experimental art form that I can only call, to coin a phrase, 'proemdra': Prose, Poem and Drama in one! We will have to donder conventional literature: old-fashioned critic and reader alike. We are going to pee, spit and shit on literary convention before we are through; we are going to kick and pull and push and drag literature into the form we prefer. We are going to experiment and probe and not give a damn what the critics have to say. Because we are in search of our true selves – undergoing self-discovery as a people.
>
> (quoted in Zander, 'Prose-Poem-Drama', p. 16)

This also meant renouncing the western credo according to which 'good' literature has to abstain from all political goals and is to pursue only literary aims of its own. In the black tradition, it was contended, literature always had distinct social functions. Zakes Mda points out:

> I have dismally failed to respond to the strange aesthetic concepts so cherished in the western world that profess that artistic creation is an end in itself, independent of politics and social requirements. I draw from the traditional African aesthetics where art could not be separated from life. In our various African societies the artist was a social commentator.
>
> ('Extracts', p. 296; see also Gwala, 'Writing as a Cultural Weapon', pp. 37–53)

Black South Africans claimed that black literature, under the conditions of apartheid, had to serve the resistance against white oppression; they declared that 'good' black literature necessarily had to be politically committed. As Mbulelo Mzamane put it: 'Since the most important lessons for South Africans are in the political sphere, a writer in that land is unimportant, irrelevant and probably alienated unless he is political' ('Literature and Politics', p. 150). The very instability of a society founded on a repressive minority rule – in which polarised forces fought violently to institute their polarised visions of the future – meant that both black and white writing became future-obsessed, 'for our future is a poem which says so' (Serote, *Tough Tale*, p. 39). South Africa post 1976 felt like a provisional society poised on the brink of the unimaginable (Nixon, 'Aftermaths', p. 73). In his long poem 'Promised Land', Kelwyn Sole takes stock of this devastated present, 'chewing its gum of acid rain' (*Projections in the Past Tense*, p. 85), in an intricate weaving of 'prosaic' declaration and 'poetic' intensity. 'Our promised land' is an upside-down land, a land where all relationships have been inverted, 'where the dead / give birth to their own mothers', 'where brave men seek their own murders / to free themselves from any guilt' (*Projections in the Past Tense*, pp. 86–7; see also Horn, 'Where we Stride', pp. 14–15).

'no letter / containing a poem / shall be forwarded'

The apartheid security forces were well aware of the power of poems to convey revolutionary messages. Keith Gottschalk's poem, 'War Memorial', celebrates the victory of the poetry of Jeremy Cronin and Breyten Breytenbach against conditions of imprisonment:

> they probably don't know it yet,
> but this place
> has a calligraphic,
> a sort of war memorial,
> to Jeremy Cronin
> (marxist, seven years),
> Breyten Breytenbach
> (buddhist, seven & a half years).
>
> . . .
>
> I mean, that yellowed paper
> onto which they've glued the new Regulasie 4(f):
> 'no letter
> containing a poem
> shall be forwarded
> from a prisoner
> to the outside
> or from outside
> to a prisoner'   (Gottschalk, *Emergency Poems*, p. 25)

Jeremy Cronin reported on a 'treason trial of sixteen United Democratic Front and trade union leaders', where 'the apartheid prosecutor produced a weighty indictment running to over three hundred pages'. Amongst the material presented were 'quotations and translations of songs sung and slogans chanted. There is also evidence on the wording on banners, T-shirts, buttons, pamphlets and flyers. Among this mass of forensic detail, as part of the allegedly treasonable material, there are a few poems.' Ironically, he notes, the 'state prosecutor has understood more about current black poetry in South Africa than many an academic commentator' ('"Even under the Rine of Terror . . . "', p. 12). He points out that

> this is a poetry that can only be understood and analysed in its relationship to a range of traditional and contemporary oral and verbal practices: songs, chants, slogans, funeral orations, political speeches, sermons and graffiti. It can be understood only in terms of the context of its major mode of presentation and reception. ('"Even under the Rine of Terror . . . "', p. 12)

Whilst some of these poems are preserved in books and small magazines, this is the exception rather than the rule. One needs to understand the unique context and its auditory dimensions: the improvisational riffs and verbal tone colours, the gestural and phatic elements, the linguistic energy which sometimes spills into the pure sound of glossolalia. As one example of this cultural phenomenon, Cronin describes the national conference of AZASO, the black university and college students' organisation, in July 1984:

> 'Poem! Poem!' is a request that gets called out fairly frequently between breaks in the days' sessions. The poetry of the two Turfloop students consists in a set of chanted refrains, one voice leading: 'Cuppa-ta-lismmmma! cuppa-ta-lismmma! cummmma to me-e-e-e!' with the other voice weighing in behind in response, 'I-I-I-I a-m-m-m-m-a cuppa-ta-lismmma' . . . They then call to each other across the heads of the five hundred delegates: 'Cuppa-ta-lismmmma, cuppa-ta-lismma A spectre is a hauntinnnga you This accordinnnnga the gospel Of Marx and Engels Cuppa-ta-lissssmmma!' The interplay continues for some time with the second voice ('Capitalism') finally fading away with a long groan to enthusiastic foot stomping from those present.

Cronin does not only note the content of these 'poems', he points out that the manner in which the perfomance uses language and melody, the 'slow lilt', the 'phonetic exaggeration', the 'increased stress' and the 'the repeated nasal sounds' contribute essentially to the enjoyment of the audience. This gives the English a pronounced, indeed, an exaggerated African texture. The poetic thickening of language carries a playfulness, as well as implications of appropriation and nationalisation (Cronin, '"Even under the Rine of Terror . . . "', pp. 12ff).

In the acute phase of the struggle, many townships and rural areas were turned into only nominally undeclared war zones.[4] Political funerals, the site around which many of these forms are clustered, are described by Mike Kirkwood as 'harbingers of a secular future (in terms of the content of funeral

---

4 See Bauer and Powell, 'Culture as you don't see it at the City Hall', and a letter criticising this article by Kelwyn Sole.

oratory, funeral poetry, icons, photographic images, etc.), at the same time as "looking back" to the centrality of funeral arrangements, wakes, processions, memorialising and grave-tending in the cultural past' ('Literature and Popular Culture', p. 659). One of the contexts of this poetry was the founding of the UDF.

The founding of the UDF and COSATU

On 20 August 1983 the United Democratic Front was launched in a new era of mass mobilisation against apartheid in the Rocklands community hall, Mitchell's Plain, near Cape Town, as a proxy for the banned African National Congress (ANC) in the 1980s (Swilling, *United Democratic Front*). Seekings argues about the perceived shortcomings of the UDF that '[its] priorities during 1983–84 were national rather than local, focusing on the state's constitutional reforms and in particular the Tricameral Parliament' ('"Trailing behind the masses"', p. 94). This meant that its focus was more in the coloured and Indian areas, and not on direct involvement in the local struggles that were central to politics in African townships. Nevertheless, the UDF was seen 'as a structure for the more permanent linking of township struggles and organisations into a national framework'. Through its very existence, 'the UDF had an important indirect organisational and ideological impact on African township politics' (Seekings, '"Trailing behind the masses"', pp. 93–114).

Kenneth W. Grundy points out that there was, at the time, a veritable multiplication of progressive cultural groups. It was a fluid collection of organisations, subject to shifting bases of support, personality and leadership turnover and uncertain responsibility and undefined reach. In the absence of a national mass-based cultural organisation that could serve to coordinate the democratisation of the arts, a number of Johannesburg-based disciplinary organisations came together in May 1987 to form the Transvaal Interim Cultural Desk. Its driving force was a firebrand young poet, Mzwakhe Mbuli. The Desk may have been Mbuli's idea, but it was established under the umbrella of the United Democratic Front (Grundy, 'Politics', p. 398). It was charged with organising cultural workers, and 'it sought to enlist progressive elements in the artistic community in the struggle to end apartheid, and in some fashion make decisions and impose a modicum of order on the "cultural boycott" then unmethodically enforced' (Grundy, 'Politics', p. 398).

In a poem, first called 'Praise Poem of the United Democratic Front' and later published as 'Praise Poem of the African National Congress', Gottschalk celebrates the new political organisation of the 1980s:

Our shouts are peaks in a range of voices,
Our hands harvest fruit from fields of strength,
Our comrades are a million men and women.
(*Emergency Poems*, pp. 122–3; see also Horn,
'Written Poetry for Performance')

It is in this context of uprisings, mass stayaways, political strikes, consumer boycotts, political funerals (involving anything up to seventy thousand mourners at a time), factory occupations, rent boycotts, school and university boycotts, mass rallies and physical confrontation over barricades with security forces that we must understand the political poetry of the 1980s. Some organisations allied to the UDF consisted of cultural workers, for example the Screen Training Project, Community Arts Project and *Staffrider* magazine, launched in 1977 (see *Staffrider*, issue for March 2008).

After the police shot the Langa demonstrators in 1985,[5] protests turned to insurrection; South Africa was engulfed in a black youth uprising. Young activists, using military and militant songs, gestures, guns, *toyi-toyi*, rhythms and khaki attire saw themselves as soldiers of the liberation (Sitas, 'Making of the "Comrades" Movement', pp. 630–1, 635). Sandile Dikeni's poem about the molotov cocktail, 'Guava Juice' (Coetzee and Willemse, *I Qabane Labantu*, p. 55), inciting the young lions to 'throw that liquid of capitalist invention' and to 'Dance around the fire of resistance', was a poem in constant demand at rallies. Personal strife is translated into an act of defiance and a call to arms; 'I am guilty in South Africa / I am destroyed in South Africa / I must be arrested whenever I am not satisfied / I live like a dog in South Africa' incants a youth from KwaMashu; after a tirade of how the Boere, the *amabhunu* and 'Gatsha' (Buthelezi) are killing the nation, he asserts himself with 'aka' (AK47 automatic gun) and 'TNT' (explosive) (Sitas, 'Making of the "Comrades" Movement', p. 636). Kirkwood describes the 'militant dance forms – such as the Eastern Cape's *toyi-toyi* with its ritualised "hand-grenade", "bazooka" and other movements – and the reworking of traditional resistance songs to render the sharpened context of today's struggle' ('Literature and Popular Culture', p. 659).

Closely connected to the struggle against apartheid is the theme of exile, which is part of the experience of most MK soldiers (Mkhonto we Sizwe, or

---

5 The shooting in Langa Township, Uitenhage, on 21 March 1985 was in the context of the school boycotts in the Eastern Cape (Port Elizabeth, Grahamstown, Port Alfred, Graaf Reinet and Uitenhage). The unrest has been attributed to a number of factors, such as inferior education for blacks, the increase in the price of foodstuffs and bus fares, and the arrest of community leaders (Majodina, 'A Short Background', p. 488).

Spear of the Nation, was the ANC's guerrilla army). It can be found in poems of suffering: Qabula's 'Dearest', a poem to his lover, describes how he became a 'wanderer', a 'sailor' travelling the continent strumming his guitar, learning from nature and from the heritage of other African traditions. And the return: he strummed his guitar at Messina and Sasol and the 'in-laws' danced and fell. Similar themes run through the self-evocations of youth: suffering and then return. A youth from Greytown recites how, on his return, he sits on the hill observing how the Western Industrial township, which he rebaptises as 'Worstmeat Towncheat', stares at him. He has returned from his wanderings with his AK47, and this is the night before the storm (Sitas, 'Making of the "Comrades" Movement', p. 639).

At the launch of the Congress of South African Trade Unions (COSATU) in a Durban sports stadium in 1985, the male worker poets Qabula and Hlatshwayo delivered their praise poem, translated here from the isiZulu and isiXhosa:

> We have
> Come from the sparkling kitchens
> Of our bosses.
>
> We have arrived from the exhausting
> Tumult of factory machines.
>
> Victory eludes us still!
>
> . . .
>
> Here is COSATU
> Who knows no color
> Here then is our tornado-snake-inkanyamba
> Helele
> COSATU
>
> Helele
> Workers of South Africa
>> (Bunn and Taylor, *From South Africa*, p. 286)

The event of the launch was also the event of the poem: the *imbongi*, a traditional Zulu oral praise singer, now composes while driving a forklift at Dunlop; the union and the poets deal with ethnicity by embodying non-ethnic politics in traditional forms and imagery (O'Brien, 'Literature in Another South Africa', p. 80). Nise Malange, a woman COSATU poet, wrote 'Long Live Women':

You have given birth to the leaders of this earth
and they have robbed you of your rights.

Don't cry, don't cry women.
History will judge them.

When I talk to women words become stuck in my throat
Because I am woman

. . .

Probably all the meetings and organisations will be silenced
And my voice will not reach you.
It does not matter
You will continue to hear my voice

. . .

Let's stand up and fight!
I am talking to you women of our country peasant women
who believed in the struggle for equal rights,
to the working women
who worked more, to the mothers who knew
of our concern for her
children, to the women who have sacrificed their lives for our rights.
(Goldner, *South African Mail-Messages from Inside*, p. 81)

Ari Sitas speaks about the 'comrades' political economy of martyrdom':

> The dead martyrs, larger than life, are sung about, remembered in poems and committed to lineage, to memory: from 'comrade Sipho . . . who was forced / to swallow / cooking bullets / and the angry sound of gunfire' to Solomon Mahlangu, the Mxenges, Sibiya and Ngubane and so on.
> ('Making of the "Comrades" Movement', p. 639)

Even in the work of one of the most cautious of the worker poets, Mi Hlatshwayo, one finds a stunning and defiant eulogy on Mahlangu. According to one youth from Kwa Mashu, 'They killed Eric Gumede. I was angry. They killed Jonathan Sithole. I was angry again. They killed Vusumuzi Ndlovu. They must kill me now. The murderers' (E. Bhengu, KwaMashu, April 1990, quoted in Sitas, 'Making of the "Comrades" Movement', p. 639). Finally, Rob Nixon pointed out that the brutal prohibitiveness of apartheid was making some writers obsessed with the spectacle of oppositional violence ('Aftermaths', p. 69).

The Congress of South African Writers (COSAW)

'The most committed writings of the late 1980s furnish evidence of a dramatic break with the work of the 1970s' (Ménager-Everson, 'Albie Sachs Debate',

p. 60). In 1981 South African PEN was disbanded and shortly after that the African Writers' Association (AWA), a Pan-Africanist and Black Conscious-ness organisation, was founded. COSAW was launched in July 1987. It arose out of the need for a grass-roots writers' organisation that sought to pro-mote literature and redress the imbalances of apartheid education. COSAW organised literary events, conducted research, liaised with literacy organisa-tions, established writing groups, facilitated workshops for aspirant writers from disadvantaged communities and published materials (Combrinck, *South African History Archive*). The COSAW constitution stated:

> We, the writers of South Africa, pledge ourselves and our total creative resources to advance the struggle for the creation of a non-racial, non-exploitative, non-sexist, united and democratic South Africa. We recognise that writers and cultural workers, generally, are products of and belong to the community. As such they have a responsibility to serve the community. We recognise the critical role that literature and the other arts must play in the struggle for liberation.   (17 July 1988, COSAW)

The particular form of poetry chosen to be performed in the context of the political struggle between 1980 and 1990 and the form of its communication were closely related both to the fact that South Africa was in a permanent state of emergency and to the political style of the UDF. As an imagination of an insurrection, this poetry was directly opposed to the State of Emergency (see Voss, 'Emerging Literature', pp. 25ff, and Brink, 'Writer in a State of Siege', pp. 172–95).

One such form of communication, highlighted by Cronin, is the *umrabulo*. *Umrabulo* is a term that exists in several South African languages and cultures, used to describe the customary passing round of beer and the proverbial conversation that accompanies it; *umrabulo* has also been used as the title of a series of ANC pamphlets and discussion documents, taken from the word's adaptation amongst political prisoners on Robben Island to 'inspire political discussion and debate'. As the back cover on one such pamphlet describes it, 'this concept is being revived to assert our fundamental adherence to the necessity for enriched discussion at all levels of organisation. In this way, the programmes that we implement will be based on a solid understanding of our options and our principles' (Cronin, *Even the Dead*). Cronin provides, in the opening poem of *Even the Dead*, 'three reasons for a mixed, *umrabulo*, round-the-corner poetry': (1) the 'mud of its production'; (2) the 'shift out there / From lyric to epic'; and (3) that 'Here it is safe to assume / Nothing at all. Niks' (Cronin, *Even the Dead*, p. 20).

A notion of performance as the creation of metaphors of self is the base of Sitas's paper on 'Traditions of Poetry in Natal'. Re-examining the work of H. I. E. Dhlomo, Masizi Kunene and that of a younger generation of worker poets such as Lawrence Zondi, Alfred Qabula and Mi Hlatshwayo, Sitas sees in their poetry a 'bold imaginative relocating of self vis-à-vis the black past and the nationalist present' (quoted in Erlmann, 'Review', pp. 675–7).

In all these works we find evidence of, on the one hand, a decisive break with the hegemonic culture of South Africa's colonial past and, on the other, the forging of new continuities with past epochs of cultural resistance (see Kirkwood, 'Literature and Popular Culture', p. 657). Mzwakhe Mbuli's texts incorporate numerous images favoured by Black Consciousness writers, Gwala in particular, whose concepts of the township poet and Mother Africa and whose accusations of Bantustan corruption are echoed by Mbuli. Mbuli is representative of all those artists who have attempted to bring a new dimension to literary expression within the context of the South African struggle against apartheid and white domination (Ménager-Everson, 'Albie Sachs Debate', p. 61). The poems in the anthology *Black Mamba Rising: South African Worker Poets in Struggle* (ed. Sitas, 1986) were all originally performed at collective gatherings, at May Day rallies and at services for fallen workers in soccer stadiums, hostels and township halls. In this context, the *imbongi* oral poetry, thought by many to be a dead tradition or the preserve of chiefly praises,[6] resurfaced as a voice of ordinary black workers and their struggles from about 1984. Of course, the techniques and rhythms of the *imbongi* tradition had never really been dead. 'The traditional praise-singer, the imbongi, is at work in the name of a new chief – the union' (Willemse, 'Poems speak of militant working class', p. 18).

Mi Hlatshwayo, a union member who in the Black Consciousness period had attended political meetings at which poems were read, was discouraged, because these poets wrote in English, a language in which his own proficiency was limited. Then one day at a union meeting he heard Alfred Qabula *bonga* (compose or recite praises) in Zulu. In Qabula's version, the chief was replaced by the black trade union movement. What he praised was its struggle and the strength it offered through solidarity (see Chapter 4 above). A poem like 'The Black Mamba Rises Again in Victory' celebrates the victory of the Dunlop workers after an uphill fight with management and records the main events of this chapter in the recent history of the trade union movement

---

6 In 'New Words Rising', Kelwyn Sole points out that both Kaizer Matanzima and Buthelezi had their traditional praise poets, as has the Zulu king and many other Inkatha officials and chiefs (p. 108).

(Kirkwood, 'Literature and Popular Culture', p. 661). The totemic animal symbols which figure in many praise poems are freed from the specific weight of clan histories, and now carry associative bonds that have been created in the popular memory of national oppression and struggle: black mamba, black buffalo and black ants. Imagery of this kind, as well as references to 'our heroes on the Island', evokes both the historic national struggle of black South Africans and its contemporary socialist content.

Worker *izibongo*, while they need to be located in a wider cultural context than a purely literary one, do not claim attention in a literary vacuum. The poems of Qabula or Hlatshwayo need to be assessed, for instance, in relation to the transformation of the Zulu epic tradition by Mazisi Kunene in his *Emperor Shaka the Great* (1979) and *Anthem of the Decades* (1981), Mongane Serote's choice of the long poem as the vehicle of his more recent work, Ingoapele Madingoane's *Africa my Beginning* (1979) and *Black Trial* (1979), and Modikwe Dikobe's *Dispossessed* (1983). All these works together have been described as indicating a cultural watershed (Kirkwood, 'Literature and Popular Culture', pp. 662–3).

At the launch of COSAW's Women's Forum (24 September 1989), Dumi Mafokeng stated that women 'must combat competitiveness and individualism. Let us speak for domestic workers and farm workers. Let us also write about our dreams and our commitment, about women's rights'. According to her, the woman writer 'will never write outside her community'. She emphasised the need 'to challenge the old traditions and attitudes that prevent women from participating in our structures' (Phipson, 'Launch of COSAW Women's Forum', p. 75).

At one stage, COSAW decided to have 'Local' structures, so as to interact more closely with the writers' communities. One of the more active groups within COSAW, but otherwise typical of this kind of structure, is the Lansdowne Local (still in existence in 2010), whose work has been published in three issues of *Under Lansdowne Bridge* (1991, 1992 and 1995). In a limited sense, *Under Lansdowne Bridge* continued the Western Cape tradition of local publications, including *Arthur Nortje and other Poets* (1988), *17 July 1988* (1988), *Season of Bars* (1989), *Utterings in the Garden* (1988) and the short-lived journal, *Akal*.

Speaking places: prison, poetry and nation

Apartheid ('separateness') worked by regulating the mobility of black South Africans. It is no wonder, then, that the prison looms large in South African literature produced under apartheid: the cell stands as a synecdoche for a vast system of confining, quarantining, containing, controlling and segregating human beings. But the history of the struggle has shown that the potential for transformation can be born from a geography of oppression: even enforced movements through a country's territories (e.g., commuting from a black township to a white city, or from a rural 'homeland' to a mine compound) have the potential of being converted into mobilising collective experiences and of being narrated as 'national allegory' (see Jameson 'Third World Literature') or 'cognitive mapping': a 'grasping of the social totality [that] is structurally available to the dominated rather than the dominating classes' (Barnard, 'Speaking Places', pp. 157–8).

Among the few critics who have begun to measure the dimensions of this refashioning, the former political prisoner, poet and activist Jeremy Cronin has so far made the most decisive contribution. Cronin's understanding of the politics of place represents the struggle as an opening up of spaces. Again and again in the 1980s, Cronin celebrated the resistance movement's creation of 'liberated zones': places that, in a reversal of apartheid's restrictions on mobility, have become 'no-go areas for the . . . regime' and where the people, however precariously, could begin to govern themselves – 'yes,' Cronin adds, 'even to write their own poetry.' Cronin compares these 'liberated zones' to the rural areas in Angola and Mozambique that served the MPLA (People's Movement for the Liberation of Angola) and FRELIMO (Liberation Front of Mozambique) as bases of operation. But 'liberated zones' are also experimental sites in which one may imagine and act out the possibility of a wholly liberated land. Given the utopian and imaginative dimension of this spatial contestation, it is fitting that Cronin should attend as closely as he does to the literary and linguistic aspects of the emergent democratic culture. His thinking about politics and space includes – indeed, repeatedly insists on – the need to find a 'speaking place' for all citizens, especially those who have been 'deprived of a voice in the land of [their] birth' (Cronin, 'Law that Says', pp. 25–30). In his essay 'No Unnecessary Noises, OK?', he boldly asserts that 'the achievement of liberation will inevitably also be a major linguistic event' (p. 11). It must be so, he argues, precisely because linguistic acts and attitudes have been part of the mechanism of oppression: that is, of considering certain languages more authoritative than others. Just as the liberated zones in Mozambique served as 'laboratories' for the new, so too, in Cronin's view, can the aesthetic realm serve as a kind of rehearsal space, a site for a different kind of political practice (Barnard, 'Speaking Places', p. 159; see also Chapter 26 below).

The debate about political poetry and standards

One of the major debates of the 1980s revolved around the question: When dealing with 'popular' poetry, do we have to suspend conventional aesthetic judgements? Lionel Abrahams, in a letter to the *Weekly Mail* (3 April 1987), referring to *Black Mamba Rising*, argues that to praise 'passages of very minor achievement' is harmful, 'not least to black poets, both accomplished and aspirant. Its main message to them is: "The best is not for you"'. In the same issue of the *Weekly Mail*, Farouk Asvat argues: 'But if Cronin, and many like him (both black and white) would lead us to believe that the mere mouthing of political slogans and rhetoric is sufficient to make anything written by blacks or workers poetry, then they must have a serious rethink, if they have the advancement of our people in mind.' 'Slogan poetry,' he continues, 'merely stunts the growth of our people. If poetry is to be meaningful, it must not only capture the complex humanity of peoples' emotions, it must also interpret peoples' lives so that they can have a better insight into themselves.'

Because of their use as agitprop, many critics implied that these political poems were aesthetically inferior. Now there is no doubt that a lot of poetry of the 1980s was deliberately designed to be politically useful, and that its art value was of less concern in the politics of protest and defiance of the liberation movements as the people sought to render the apartheid state 'ungovernable'. The conditions of war demanded that, in the words of Sipho Hlati, a local artist, 'here in this country, one has got to take sides, you either collaborate with the state or you are together with the people' (Steinberg, 'Albie Sachs', p. 195). Keorapetse Kgositsile made the point that there is not one single writer who would claim to be committed to the typewriter; because you are committed to certain values, you are committed to life, long before you sit at the typewriter (Kgositsile et al., 'Panel on Literature', p. 34). Dennis Brutus agreed that there is no uncommitted writing. Commitment, he maintains, does not exist as an abstraction; it exists in action. When one examines literature, or when one creates literature, one is either following an established order and functioning within it, or one is challenging that order. Therefore the irritation which African writers feel when they are subjected to western criticism is symptomatic of something much deeper. It is not just the rejection of a set of literary values: it is a questioning of a whole social order, of the western way of life and its values (Kgositsile et al., 'Panel on Literature', p. 35; Brutus, 'Literature and Change', pp. 101–4).

Proponents of the 'Great Tradition' in the (English) literature departments still largely believed that there was one standard for all literature, and they believed that they were able to define that standard: if you agree that there is only one 'Great Tradition', you must reject everything else as inferior. But the slightest knowledge of cultures other than one's own will demonstrate that there is always and was always a plurality of values, more or less different from nation to nation, from class to class, and from epoch to epoch. Whilst the culture of peasants, workers and other ruled classes was usually devalued, it existed and had its own implicit set of values, although these were seldom formulated in an aesthetic.

One of the ways of fighting against the hegemony of the ruling class is to make fun of it, to portray it in a comical or satirical manner. What is central to *satire* is the sudden flash-like insight into the incongruous. Of course, 'the riotous dreams amendment act / section 7 / brrrrrackets beeeeeeeeee' (Gottschalk, 'Forbidden Dreams', *Emergency Poems*, p. 51) is funny both in the pompousness of the original and its subversive rewriting. But its *satirical* quality derives from both the incongruity of this armed invasion into the most guarded sphere of privacy, the dream, and the frightening possibility that that is what the state aims at: 'I order your dream / loudly / in both official languages: / DISPERSE FORTHWITH!' (Gottschalk, 'Forbidden Dreams', *Emergency Poems*, p. 51).

On the other hand, as Orenna Krut, a speaker at a COSAW meeting, argued, 'even without knowing it, [we have] created a culture of what is acceptable . . . as long as you've said the right slogans in your poem, everyone else approves of your work even if it is boring, badly written, and completely unoriginal' (see Steinberg, 'Albie Sachs', p. 195). The debate about 'standards' thus was a debate between different cultures and classes in a warlike situation. 'During the 1980s, therefore, the main concern of committed South African writers has been to determine if one can still employ creative forms that the liberal writers of the 1970s had adopted, or if these forms had become obsolete because of the radical nature of the fight against the apartheid regime' (Ménager-Everson, 'Albie Sachs Debate', p. 61).

The Albie Sachs debate

The stance adopted by Albie Sachs and presented at an ANC in-house seminar in 1989 unleashed a violent controversy and statements like 'our members should be banned from saying that culture is a weapon of struggle. I suggest a period of, say, five years', explaining that this slogan 'results in an impoverishment of our art'. Whilst admitting that 'in the case of a real instrument of struggle, there is no room for ambiguity: A gun is a gun is a gun, and if it were full of contradictions, it would fire in all sorts of directions and be useless for its purpose', Sachs maintains that 'the power of art lies precisely in its capacity to expose contradictions and hidden tensions' (Sachs, 'Preparing Ourselves', pp. 239–40).

Sachs's opposition to the violence advocated by so many of his comrades provoked an almost immediate reaction.

> Ari Sitas's openly aggressive response was in strict accordance with the ANC's hardline approach to culture. Sitas underscored the reassuring nature of Sachs's reflections, which, he feels, give comfort to the liberal white intellectual elite which had been previously discomfitted by the revolutionary slogans that advocated a people's culture and the use of literature as a weapon . . . He regrets Sachs's failure to define the theoretical principles underlying the search for higher standards in the arts, and he is irritated by references to a 'good taste' which Sitas, citing the French sociologist Pierre Bourdieu, decries as a form of violence perpetrated by the powerful against the weak. The appeal to 'good taste' had been used, for example, against Herbert I. E. Dhlomo or Steve Biko, both of whom were victims of white liberal patronage . . . Although he agrees that artistic practices need to be modified, he wonders whether Sachs is not simply pandering to the whims of the petty bourgeoisie. (Ménager-Everson, 'Albie Sachs Debate', pp. 62–3)

Rushdy Siers's biting response ('Vampire Bats', pp. 57ff) articulated this groundswell of anger. Siers, a COSAW member, a poet and a writer of short stories, rebuked Sachs, a long-term exile, for assuming that those living inside the country understood it as little as he did. The members of the Culture and Working Life Project (in 'Albie Sachs Must not Worry', pp. 99ff) reclaimed the concept of 'struggle' from what they saw to be Sachs's narrow interpretation of the term: 'We see struggle as part of us, part of our everything – you wake up in the morning and it starts coming to you, if it has let you sleep at all, it is about surviving, being resilient, living, singing, and fighting' (p. 99; see also Steinberg, 'Albie Sachs', p. 195). Whilst the writers from COSAW argued for artistic independence and attacked political leaders who demanded that artists comply with the stated goals of the latest party campaign, some acknowledged that the attempt to change people into 'perfect struggling machines', full of hatred and anger, only resulted in works of questionable value. Nevertheless, the COSAW writers could not conceal their allegiance to a particular ideology and their antipathy to works that promoted 'values [they] could not support – like, for example, writings and novels that promoted traditional authoritarianism and capitalism' (Ménager-Everson, 'Albie Sachs Debate', p. 63). Their conclusion is ambiguous, for although they encourage non-hegemonic cultural practices, they fear that such practices might prove incapable of bringing about the political goals they are seeking to realise, especially because they would only be adopted by 'an articulate and already tolerant creative elite – primarily drawn from the middle classes' (Ménager-Everson, 'Albie Sachs Debate', p. 63). Their response reaffirms the assumption that 'one is first part of the struggle and then a cultural worker' (Ménager-Everson, 'The Albie Sachs Debate', p. 63). Questioned individually, the majority of South African artists have generally reacted more positively to Sachs's remarks. For example, Frank Meintjies ('Albie Sachs and the Art of Protest', pp. 30ff), a member of the COSAW Committee, supports Sachs's contention that arts and literature need to be varied and rich in expression and removed from narrow dogmatism. Njabulo Ndebele has long been one of the most vocal critics of the reactive orthodoxies that permeated South African literature. He deplores 'the overt political nature and journalistic reportage of some post-1984 black South African fiction', thereby aligning himself with Sachs's attack upon the lack of originality in some committed literature of the period (Ménager-Everson, 'Albie Sachs Debate', p. 64).

The excitement generated by the events surrounding Mandela's release was clearly reflected in the Albie Sachs debate, which unequivocally demonstrated there existed a will to find new ways of establishing a harmony that seemed to have been precluded by centuries of oppression and the more recent history of apartheid (Ménager-Everson, 'Albie Sachs Debate', p. 65). But Mandela's election brought fewer deep changes than many had hoped for. For artists steeped in the resistance mode – like playwright Maishe Maponya and performance poet Sandile Dikeni – this has proven to be not just a bewildering period, but a vexing one. They have both maintained that, whatever the political gains, this half-baked situation was not the revolution they had been creating for. Many had the feeling that 'The future has arrived and therefore disappeared. A great source of dreaming has ended, and with it, a great source of dread' (Nixon, 'Aftermaths', pp. 70, 74).

Bibliography

Alvarez-Pereyre, J. 'Peter Horn's *Civil War Cantoes*', in G. V. Davis (ed.), *Crisis and Conflict. Essays on Southern African Literature*, Essen: Die Blaue Eule, 1988, 215–27.
   The Poetry of Commitment in South Africa, London: Heinemann, 1984.

Barnard, R. 'Speaking Places: Prison, Poetry, and the South African Nation', *Research in African Literatures* 32:3 (2001), 155–76.

Bauer, C., and I. Powell. 'Culture as you don't see it at the City Hall', *Weekly Mail*, 21–27 November 1986.

Brink, A. 'The Writer in a State of Siege', in *Mapmakers: Writing in a State of Siege*, London: Faber, 1983, 172–95.

Brutus, D. 'Literature and Change in South Africa', *Research in African Literatures* 24 (1993), 101–4.

Bunn, D., and J. Taylor (eds.). *From South Africa: New Writing, Photographs and Art*, Evanston, IL: Northwestern University Press, 1987.

Chapman, M. (ed.). *Soweto Poetry*, Johannesburg: McGraw-Hill, 1982.

Coetzee, A., and H. Willemse. *I Qabane Labantu· Poetry in the Emergency/Poësie in die Noodtoestand*, Bramley: Taurus, 1989.

Combrinck, L. *South African History Archive*, www.saha.org.za/collections.htm? collections/AL2606.htm, accessed November 2010.

Coplan, D. B. *In Township Tonight! South Africa's Black City Music and Theatre*, Johannesburg: Ravan, 1985.

COSAW. *17 July 1988*, Athlone: COSAW, 1988.

Arthur Nortje and other Poets, Athlone: COSAW, 1988.

Season of Bars, Athlone: COSAW, 1989.

Under Lansdowne Bridge: A Publication of the Lansdowne Local of the Congress of South African Writers, Cape Town, 1991, 1992, 1995.

Utterings in the Garden, Athlone: COSAW, 1988.

Cronin, J. *Even the Dead: Poems, Parables and a Jeremiad*, Cape Town and Johannesburg: David Philip/University of the Western Cape and Mayibuye Books, 1997.

'"Even under the Rine of Terror . . ."': Insurgent South African Poetry', *Research in African Literatures* 19 (1988), 2–23.

Inside, Johannesburg: Ravan, 1983.

Inside and Out, Cape Town: David Philip, 1999.

'"The law that says/Constricts the breath line": South African English Language Poetry Written by Africans in the 1970s', *English Academy Review* 3 (1985), 25–30.

'No Unnecessary Noises Allowed, OK?', *Ingolovane* 1 (n.d.), 8–12.

Culture and Working Life Project. 'Albie Sachs Must not Worry', in De Kok and Press, *Spring is Rebellious*, 99–103.

Davids, J. A. *Searching for Words*, Cape Town: David Philip, 1974.

Daymond, M. J., J. U. Jacobs and M. Lenta (eds.). *Momentum: On Recent South African Writing*, Pietermaritzburg: University of Natal Press, 1984.

De Kok, I., and K. Press (eds.). *Spring is Rebellious: Arguments About Cultural Freedom*, Cape Town: Buchu, 1990.

Dikobe, M. *Dispossessed*, Johannesburg: Ravan, 1983.

Erlmann, V. 'Review', *International Journal of African Historical Studies* 30:3 (1997), 675–77.

Goldner, J. *South African Mail-Messages from Inside: Women Artists in Resistance*, New York: Soho 20 Gallery, 1990.

Gottschalk, K. *Emergency Poems*, introduced by P. Horn, Bellville: Mayibuye Books, 1992.

Grundy, K. W. 'The Politics of South Africa's National Arts Festival: Small Engagements in the Bigger Campaign', *African Affairs* 93:372 (July 1994), 387–409.

Gwala, M. *No More Lullabies*, Johannesburg: Ravan, 1982.

'Towards a National Culture. Interview by Thengamehlo Ngewenya', *Staffrider* 8 (1989), 72.

'Writing as a Cultural Weapon', in Daymond, Jacobs and Lenta, *Momentum*, 37–53.

Harlow, B., and J. Cronin. 'A Chapter in South African Verse: Interview with Jeremy Cronin', *Alif: Journal of Comparative Poetics* 21 (2001), special issue on the Lyrical Phenomenon/الظاهرة الشعرية, 52–270.

Hlatshwayo, M. 'The Black Mamba Rises Again in Victory', *Staffrider* 6:3 (1986), 8–10.

Horn, P. 'Aesthetics and the Revolutionary Struggle: Peter Weiss's Novel "The Aesthetics of Resistance"', *Critical Arts* 3:4 (1985), 7–54.

'Art is Like Breathing Freely: The Necessity of a People's Culture', in Coetzee and Willemse, *I Qabane Labantu*, 167–76.

'A Radical Rethinking of the Art of Poetry in an Apartheid Society', *Journal for Commonwealth Studies* 29:1 (1993), 97–113.

'The Right of the People to Censor the Arts', in National Union of South African Students (eds.), *Dead in One's Lifetime*, Cape Town: NUSAS, 1979, 92–105.

'Struggle Poetry' [Sandile Dikeni, *Guava Juice*, and Barry Feinberg, *Gardens of Struggle*], *Southern African Review of Books* (March/April 1993), 9–10.

'"We all sat round a faia" – A Critique of the Methods used to Analyse South African Texts. An Essay in the Sociology of Literature', *UCT Studies in English* 7 (1977), 28–36.

'"When it rains, it rains": US Black Consciousness and Lyric Poetry in South Africa', in Chapman, *Soweto Poetry*, 162–8.

'Where we Stride Above the Fading, Insistent Mutter of the Dead', *Southern African Review of Books* (January/February 1993), 14–15.

Writing my Reading: Essays on Literary Politics in South Africa, Amsterdam: Rodopi, 1994.

'Written Poetry for Performance (Jeremy Cronin, Keith Gottschalk)', in R. Nethersole (ed.), *Emerging Literatures*, Bern: Peter Lang, 1990, 71–181.

Jameson, F. 'Third World Literature in the Era of Multinational Capitalism', *Social Text* 15 (autumn 1986), 65–88.

Johenesse, F. *The Rainmaker*, Johannesburg: Ravan, 1979.

Kgositsile, K., D. Brutus, C. Achebe and A. A. Mazrui. 'Panel on Literature and Commitment in South Africa', *Journal of Opinion* 6:1 (spring 1976), proceedings of the symposium on Contemporary African Literature and First African Literature Association Conference, 34–46.

Kirkwood, M. 'Literature and Popular Culture in South Africa', *Third World Quarterly* 9:2 (April 1987), *After Apartheid*, 657–71.

Kunene, D. P. 'Ideas under Arrest: Censorship in South Africa', *Research in African Literatures* 12 (1981), 421–39.

Kunene, M. *Anthem of the Decades*, London: Heinemann, 1981.

Emperor Shaka the Great, London: Heinemann, 1979.

Madingoane, I. *Africa my Beginning*, Johannesburg: Ravan, 1979.

Black Trail, Johannesburg: Ravan, 1979.

Majodina, T. 'A Short Background to the Shooting Incident in Langa Township, Uitenhage', *Human Rights Quarterly* 8:3 (August 1986), 488–93.

Matthews, J. (ed.). *Black Voices Shout*, Athlone: Blac, 1974.

Pass me a Meatball, Jones, Athlone: Blac, 1977.

Matthews, J., and G. Thomas. *Cry Rage!*, Johannesburg: Sprocas-Ravan, 1972.

Maughan Brown, D. 'Black Criticism and Black Aesthetics', in Chapman, *Soweto Poetry*, 46–55.

Mda, Z. 'Extracts', in Daymond, Jacobs and Lenta, *Momentum*, 295–7.

Meintjies, F. 'Albie Sachs and the Art of Protest', in de Kok and Press, *Spring is Rebellious*, 30–6.

Ménager-Everson, S. V. 'The Albie Sachs Debate', *Research in African Literatures* 23 (1992), 59–66.

Mutloatse, M. 'Introduction', in M. Mutloatse (ed.), *Forced Landing: Africa South: Contemporary Writings*, Johannesburg: Ravan, 1985, 1–7.

Mzamane, M. 'Literature and Politics among Blacks in South Africa', in Chapman, *Soweto Poetry*, 150–6.

Ndebele, N. S. 'Artistic and Political Mirage: Mtshali's *Sounds of a Cowhide Drum*', in Chapman, *Soweto Poetry*, 190–3.

'Life-Sustaining Poetry of a Fighting People', *Staffrider* 5:3 (1983), 44–5.

Rediscovery of the Ordinary, Manchester University Press, 1994.

Nixon, R. 'Aftermaths', *Transition* 72 (1996), 64–78.

O'Brien, A. 'Literature in Another South Africa. Njabulo Ndebele's Theory of Emerging Culture', *Diacritics* 22:1 (spring 1992), 67–85.

Parenzee, D. *Driven to Work*, Johannesburg: Ravan, 1985.

Patel, E. *They Came at Dawn*, Athlone: Blac, 1980.

Phipson, L. 'Launch of COSAW Women's Forum', *Agenda* 6 (1990), 73–5.

Ryan, R. 'Literary-Intellectual Behavior in South Africa', *boundary 2* 15 (1988), 283–304.

Sachs, A. 'Preparing Ourselves for Freedom', paper prepared for an ANC in-house seminar on culture [1989], in D. Attridge and R. Jolly (eds.), *Writing South Africa. Literature, Apartheid and Democracy, 1970–1995*, Cambridge University Press, 1998, 239–48.

Seekings, J. '"Trailing behind the masses": The United Democratic Front and Township Politics in the Pretoria-Witwatersrand-Vaal Region, 1983–84', *Journal of Southern African Studies* 18 (1992), 93–114.

Sepamla, S. *The Blues is You in Me*, Johannesburg: Ad Donker, 1976.

Hurry Up to It!, Johannesburg: Ad Donker, 1975.

The Soweto I Love, London: Collins, 1977.

Serote, W. M. *A Tough Tale*, London: Kliptown Books, 1987.

Siers, R. 'Vampire Bats of Ambiguous Metaphors', in De Kok and Press, *Spring is Rebellious*, 57–67.

Sitas, A. 'The Making of the "Comrades" Movement in Natal, 1985–91', *Journal of Southern African Studies*, special issue on 'Political Violence in Southern Africa', 18:3 (1992), 629–41.

'The Sachs Debate: A Philistine's Response', in de Kok and Press, *Spring is Rebellious*, 91–8.

Sitas, A. (ed.). *Black Mamba Rising: South African Worker Poets in Struggle*, Johannesburg: Worker Resistance and Culture Publications, 1986.

Sole, K. *Projections in the Past Tense*, Johannesburg: Ravan, 1992.

Steinberg, C. 'Albie Sachs: Our Shakespearian Fool', *Drama Review* 35 (1991), 194–9.

Swilling, M. *The United Democratic Front and Township Revolt: Interview with Johnny Issel, Key UDF Western Cape Leader, 2003*, www.sahistory.org.za/pages/governence-projects/organisations/udf/udf-frameset.htm, accessed June 2010.

Van Wyk, C. *It is Time to go Home*, Johannesburg: Ad Donker, 1979.

Vaughan, M. 'A Critique of Dominant Ideas in Departments of English in the English Speaking Universities of South Africa', *Critical Arts* 3 (1984), 48.

Voss, T. 'Emerging Literature: The Literature of Emergency', in R. Nethersole, *Emerging Literatures*, ed. Bern: Peter Lang, 1990, 25ff.

Willemse, H. 'Poems speak of militant working class', *South*, 19 March 1987, 18.

Zander, H. 'Prose-Poem-Drama: "Proemdra": "Black Aesthetics" versus "White Aesthetics" in South Africa', *Research in African Literatures* 30 (1999), 12–33.

26

Writing the prison

DANIEL ROUX

As a body of work, South African prison literature intersects strongly, but not completely, with the languages of political activism in this country. At least since 1948, with the Nationalist Party's ascension to government, the prison was fundamental to the coercive power of the state. Leaders of resistance movements, artists, writers, intellectuals and rights campaigners were routinely imprisoned, often under the flimsiest of pretexts. Between 1960 and 1990 approximately 80,000 people were detained without trial, in addition to the large number of charged and sentenced political prisoners (Gready, *Writing as Resistance*, p. 1). When the first democratic cabinet was announced under Nelson Mandela's presidency in 1994, nine of its thirty members had spent time in prison and most had lived in exile at some point to avoid imprisonment.

South Africa's prisons were inescapably part of the national imagination, representing and performing the disproportionate and capricious authority of the government over many aspects of its citizens' public and private lives. In 1996 the South African Constitutional Court moved its headquarters to the old Johannesburg Fort, one of apartheid's most notorious prisons, shrewdly symbolising the displacement of a coercive, brutal state power by a different, more democratic ideal of governance and also underscoring the massive importance of the penal system to the maintenance of apartheid rule. In prison, successive generations of activists defined the nature and form of resistance against apartheid policies, laid down some of the basic coordinates of a democratic nation, interrogated and redefined the nature of citizenry, defined a particular notion of politicised collectivity and raised the complex question of an emergent democratic national identity. If the Constitutional Court literally and figuratively displaced the apartheid prison, its values and disposition were also largely the *effect* of the intellectual and creative labour of prisoners: the cultures that were formed in and around apartheid's prisons constitute a foundation for the official post-apartheid constitution and its formal arbitration.

In this chapter I attempt, broadly, to demonstrate the ways in which writing from and about prison resisted the power of the apartheid state, even while it was conditioned and mediated by the rituals and architecture of apartheid penal institutions. My corollary aim is simply to insist on the heterogeneous nature of South African prison literature: a diversity that is often muted, or deliberately forgotten, in the service of new hegemonic narratives about the post-apartheid state.

Before attempting a survey of South Africa's apartheid-era prison literature, it is useful to foreground a tension that is common to prison literature, and especially to political prison writing, as an international genre. On the one hand, the prison enjoins a preoccupation with interiority and self, if only because it wrests people out of their organic communities, restricts the mobility of bodies and discourages solidarity between prisoners. Moreover, South Africa inherited something of the idea of the Enlightenment prison – the European penitentiary, with its philosophy of individualisation, discipline and reform – and perhaps more so than elsewhere in Africa (Bernault, 'Politics of Enclosure', pp. 7–8). To varying degrees, the South African prison countered the formation of group identities and punished infractions of its rules with the deployment of reward-based classificatory systems and with the use of solitary confinement. It attempted, in a rather haphazard way, to apply a system that atomised its inmates, used their labour and combined punishment and reform. One should, however, qualify the idea that South African prisons enjoyed anything more than a superficial resemblance to the Benthamite ideal that John Montagu is widely credited for introducing to the Cape in the nineteenth century (Smit, *South African Prison Law and Practice*, pp. 10–11; Deacon, *Island*, p. 108). In fact, the idea of the prison as a potentially benign site working to individualise and reform its inmates in the service of the public good never really took root in South Africa, and was all but abandoned by the apartheid government, which used prisons largely as a means to enforce a dictatorial form of social control. In the twentieth century prisons for black inmates tended to be modelled on mining work compounds, which were in turn simply prisons under a different name. As William Worger points out, 'free' black workers were compelled to live in the compound 'for the duration of their six-month contracts, fenced and guarded and not permitted to leave the company premises at any time except to enter the mines' ('Convict Labour', p. 76). Nonetheless, South African prisons paid lip service to the idea of 'reform', frequently used solitary confinement as a form of punishment and banned the use of the word 'we' in any correspondence.[1] If the confessional, self-focused autobiography as it emerges in the West in the eighteenth century can be linked to the analogous disciplinary procedures that produced the modern penitentiary (with its focus on minute classifications, its individualising processes and even a notion of *bildung* as one progresses from one clearly defined 'status' to another until freedom – the right to rejoin society – is obtained), then even a loose appropriation of the Benthamite prison enjoins or at least facilitates a personal, confessional voice. The prison, as material institution, cultivates an individualised confessional form of experience.

On the other hand, as David Schalkwyk remarks, 'It is one of the reiterated and paradoxical platitudes of prison writing and its criticism that prison both depersonalises the individual and renders communality indispensable' ('Writing from Prison', p. 280). The prison's interdiction of solidarity and of the kinds of discourses that enable cohesion among inmates means that the most effective language of resistance insists precisely on an 'I' that speaks for others. In the case of *political* prison writing, this propulsion towards a collective voice is made even more urgent and inescapable, because, as a political prisoner, you cannot, by definition, apprehend yourself as merely part of a mass of disordered people, a throng of individuals who fall, for different reasons, outside the boundaries that are drawn by the polity. To the contrary, you represent an *alternative* polity *in posse*, a system, and you are required to speak on its behalf. In prison, as a political prisoner, you encounter the state as a condition – the state of the people in a country, to revert to an Early Modern use of the word 'state' – and your response is necessarily to the condition of the people rather than the self, or rather to the condition of the self as it synecdochically stands for the state of the people. In his *Long Walk to Freedom* (1994), Mandela makes the point that collective identity is an obvious and important precondition for effective resistance, and that the prison is, in fact, capable of ambiguously *occasioning* the very solidarity it apparently seeks to undermine:

> Our survival depended on understanding what the authorities were attempting to do to us, and sharing that understanding with each other. It would be very hard, if not impossible, for one man alone to resist. I do not know that I could have done it had I been alone. But the authorities' greatest mistake was to keep us together, for together our determination was reinforced. We

---

1 According to Indres Naidoo, 'department policy for warders was the same as it was for us: no one talked in terms of "we". Only in terms of "I"' (*Island in Chains*, p. 230). In many ways, the warders on Robben Island were treated rather like the prisoners, with severe punishments for infractions and a poor diet for bachelor guards.

supported each other and gained strength from each other. Whatever we knew, whatever we learned, we shared, and by sharing whatever courage we had individually.   (p. 463)

The idea that South African prison writing inexorably straddles these contrary but profoundly interlinked impulses towards self-reflection and confession, on the one side, and towards forging a self-effacing collective identity, on the other, can be a useful way to establish a loose thematic and stylistic connection between the widely divergent examples of the genre of prison writing as we encounter it in apartheid South Africa. At the one pole, we encounter the tortured interiority of Breyten Breytenbach in his influential prison memoir, *True Confessions of an Albino Terrorist* (1984), which is characterised by its self-reflexivity, rejection of the conventional registers of documentary realism, philosophical digressions, formal experimentation and the insistence on the deeply personal nature of experience. For Breytenbach, communality remains a chimera, a deeply felt psychological need that can never be effectively accomplished, and always presents the dangers of coercion and self-betrayal in its realisation. At the other pole, we encounter Caesarina Makhoere, who in effect forecloses the dimension of a private subjectivity altogether in her *No Child's Play: In Prison under Apartheid* (1988), or Jeremy Cronin, who incessantly uses the confessional impulse to manufacture a sense of collective agency in his celebrated collection of poems, *Inside* (1983).

Michael Dingake, in his autobiography *My Fight against Apartheid* (1987), makes a useful point with regard to the tension that I am trying to elucidate here. Dingake writes in some detail about the censorship of letters from Robben Island, and focuses in particular on the prohibition against the use of the word 'we'. After recounting the frustration caused by this kind of censorship, he notes: 'If "we" was objectionable as the plural of "I", many ways, varied construction in syntax and grammar, existed to convey the same "we" concept. In the long term self-censorship was self-defeating. It was an exercise in futility' (p. 168). Dingake's point here is astute: as much as the separation of prisoners from one another is effected physically (through isolation cells and prohibitions against communication), it is effected symbolically, through language. But language is flexible and inexhaustibly expressive: in this case, resisting individualisation takes the form of a grammatical detour, a form of expression that inhabits the oppressive grammar of the prison even as it eludes it. A subversive communal voice is in a sense always available in the interstices and equivocations of the language of the prison. Simultaneously, as Dingake's autobiography makes clear, community has its practical uses, its political valency, but in actual fact, in prison, the 'community' very easily slips into the more unruly, dangerous 'crowd'. Below, he describes a weekend in the Johannesburg Fort in a cell with 'common law' (non-political) prisoners:

> During the weekend I witnessed some of the most callous bullying of prisoners by fellow prisoners in the communal cells. Hardened prisoners, for sheer sport, bullied, terrorized and assaulted newcomers to prison . . . When the ganging up against the cheeky ones took place, an impromptu choir would be organised to sing some tune. Harmony or discord in the music did not matter, what mattered was the noise to drown the heartrending cries of the victims of assault. I escaped the assaults, not through Saint's intercession but thanks to the 'clevers' who knew me in Sophiatown or Alexandra.   (p. 124)

Dingake's community is fractured and constantly shifting. The prison affords the possibility for a kind of community, but it is a community held together by strategic alliances and pulled apart by power play. In practice, especially in prisons for black inmates, overcrowding meant that 'individualisation' was really something that was experienced only in an abstract way, except in solitary confinement. In this sense, Dingake's ability to enunciate a shared identity by varying syntax and grammar construction is enabled not merely by the polysemic quality of signs, but also by the fundamental indifference of the prison to the purported purpose of its own rules. The prohibition against the use of 'we', in other words, is purely formal: as Dingake implies, the rule is enforced in a mechanical way so that its purpose is more to inflict 'humiliation upon humiliation' (p. 167) on the prisoners than to effect individualisation.

In political prison writing, then, the self that speaks is caught between contrary impulses: to speak from the 'inside' of the self, inescapably encountered in the deracinated 'inside' of the prison, and to speak as a 'we', a category that is officially forbidden by the penal system and yet also produced by it.

To make another general point, related to the above: prison writing, especially political prison writing, represents a laboratory for examining the encounter between the autobiographical 'I' and the powers that seek to contain and regulate the subject. It speaks not just from some interior, individual location, but rather reflects on the very processes that constitute and limit the specific contours of that individuality in a given space and at a given time. Moreover, it is easy to think of South African post-apartheid freedoms as born out of a defiant encounter with the apartheid state – through words and actions directed against power in the form of prisons, the military and other institutions. But what prison literature also shows us is that the material conditions that underpin resistance play a role in shaping the language of resistance. The relationship between prison writing and the power represented by the prison is therefore not entirely agonistic: rather, the logic of the penitentiary pervades the language of resistance and shapes and informs it in a variety of ways. The 'modernist' agenda of freedom movements in South Africa and elsewhere (a belief that society can be reshaped through a collective political and cultural endeavour) is not entirely inimical to the 'modernist' foundation of the prison, which is seen as a site where individuals can be 'recreated' to accord with social norms: thus, as I suggest later in this chapter, Mandela's version of a free South Africa in *Long Walk to Freedom* looks suspiciously like a benign Enlightenment penitentiary. At a more banal level, the rituals, day-to-day preoccupations, material deprivations and humiliations of the prison inevitably determine the terms through which the self and the political are apprehended; the claustrophobic enclosure of the prison provides a tightly delimited repertoire of preoccupations and metaphors that become enmeshed with pre-existing political ideas to form what Bakhtin called a 'chronotope', or a distinctive blending of time and space in language.[2]

One of the first important South African prison memoirs, Herman Charles Bosman's *Cold Stone Jug* (1949), is interesting because, while it in many ways founds the genre of 'South African prison writing', it is relentlessly *unpolitical* in any explicit way. Nonetheless, it cleared the ground for subsequent South African prison writing, both in terms of its disquieting realism and in its anecdotal, non-chronological form. It also establishes the autobiography as the dominant literary mode for representing the prison.

Bosman was really also the first South African prisoner to write about a prison that was designed to be a 'total institution' with an explicitly reformative, rather than a punitive, function. When Bosman was imprisoned in 1926 for the murder of his stepbrother, the Benthamite prison had a history of shorter than thirty years in South Africa. For many South Africans, public executions were still in living memory. Against this background, Pretoria Central was one of the first recognisably 'modern' prisons in South Africa: the blueprint allocated single cells to long-timers, and provided for workshops

---

2 In *The Dialogic Imagination*, Bakhtin defines the chronotope as referring to 'the intrinsic connectedness of temporal and spatial relationships that are artistically expressed in literature' (p. 84) and continues to explain that the chronotope is essential to the notion of *genre*. Following Bakhtin, we can say that prison literature, *as genre*, is characterised by the particular way in which the *prison* as material space 'knots together' or informs the *literary* representation of space and time. Schalkwyk explores an analogous idea in some detail in his 'Chronotopes of the Self'.

where prisoners could also receive skills training (Gray, 'Introduction', *Cold Stone Jug*, p. 16).

When Hugh Lewin entered Pretoria Central some decades later as a political prisoner, the institution had hardly changed at all. In his prison autobiography *Bandiet* (1974), he notes:

> Forty years before we arrived there, Bosman had been sent to Central for murdering his step-brother: condemned to be hanged, he was later reprieved and spent eight years in Cold Stone Jug. He wrote an absorbingly funny book of his experiences at Central – *Cold Stone Jug*, which I read for the first time inside Cold Stone Jug. In forty years, very little had changed. (p. 83)

Lewin's comment invites a number of observations. First, it shows the influence of Bosman's account on subsequent South African prison writers. Lewin's account of Pretoria Central, and his memory of the space, is constructed through self-conscious reference to Bosman's memoir. As much as Lewin inhabits the same prison as Bosman, he also takes up residence in his predecessor's literary form. Second, it shows the extent to which the apartheid state sustained pre-apartheid forms of control and coercion with only small amendments. The apartheid government did not really invent new modalities of discipline and punishment to reflect its new ideological disposition, it simply used the forms of compulsion that it inherited and extended their use dramatically. As the state's actions became more violent and illegal, it sustained a recognisably Benthamite facade that screened the existence of other, more sinister rituals of punishment and oppression: the interrogation room, secret death farms, police holding cells and so on. It never abandoned the outward show of the reformative penitentiary: even Robben Island, one of the apartheid state's harshest prisons for black inmates, could be transformed overnight, like a Potemkin village, into a benign rehabilitative institution for the benefit of visitors from the Red Cross. The apartheid government had a particular iniquitous genius for preserving and using the material and ideological resources that it had become heir to on its accession to power. In this sense, Herman Charles Bosman could write about his experience of prison in South Africa in the 1930s in a way that is entirely resonant with the experiences of (mainly white) prisoners throughout the remainder of the twentieth century.

The Nationalist government's criminalisation of a wide range of political activities, coupled with an increasingly organised and militant resistance to its rule, resulted in a surge of prison autobiographies after 1960, especially when detention without trial became widespread with the passing of the

General Law Amendment Act in 1963. In *Writing as Resistance*, Paul Gready identifies three waves of political imprisonment. The first stage is heralded by the Sharpeville shooting of 1960, and the subsequent state of emergency and outlawing of the African National Congress (ANC) and the Pan African-ist Congress (PAC). The second stage is introduced by the Soweto uprisings of 1976, sparked by a government decision to force black schools to adopt Afrikaans as the medium of instruction. The third stage is characterised by various states of emergency between 1985 and 1989 (Gready, *Writing as Resistance*, p. 3).

Important prison autobiographies that emerged during the first wave of imprisonment include Ruth First's *117 Days* (1965) and Albie Sachs's *Jail Diary* (1966). Dennis Brutus published two significant collections of prison poems in the 1960s: *Sirens, Knuckles and Boots* (1963) and *Letters to Martha and other Poems from a South African Prison* (1968). His collection *A Simple Lust* (1973) can be grouped with his work from this period. Hugh Lewin's memoir *Bandiet*, published in 1974, also reflects on resistance politics and incarceration during the 1960s. The most significant prison novel to appear during the first wave of protest and imprisonment is probably Alex La Guma's *The Stone Country* (1967), a novel that clearly draws on La Guma's own experience of prison. D. M. Zwelonke published his unremittingly grim catalogue of tortures in *Robben Island* (1973), an autobiography thinly disguised as fiction. Indres Naidoo published his Robben Island memoir, *Island in Chains*, in 1982. Naidoo describes his incarceration from 1963 to 1973 in a similarly grim fashion, although he also takes care to represent Robben Island as a place of debate and learning: the outlines of the influential trope of Robben Island as 'university' are sketched here (but certainly without the sanguinity or nostalgia of some later accounts). Breyten Breytenbach, one of South Africa's best-known Afrikaans poets, was arrested at the airport as he was about to flee the country, and sentenced to nine years in 1975. Whilst in prison he penned some semi-fictional autobiographical sketches that were later published under the title *Mouroir* (1983) and published his well-known prison memoir, *True Confessions of an Albino Terrorist*, in 1984, while in exile in France. Moses Dlamini's memoir *Hell Hole, Robben Island*, first published in 1984 while Dlamini was living in exile in Tanzania, recounts his harrowing stay on Robben Island from 1963 to 1966 for furthering the aims of the PAC. Michael Dingake was sentenced to prison for fifteen years in 1966 and published an autobiography, *My Fight against Apartheid*, a couple of decades later in 1987.

The 1976 uprisings brought a wave of young, militant activists to South Africa's prisons. These prisoners were strongly influenced by the new Black

Consciousness movement associated with Steve Biko, and possessed an uncompromising militant sensibility that distressed some of the older generation of political prisoners. This militancy is reflected in the spurt of prison autobiographies that emerged after the events of 1976. Notable among these are Caesarina Kona Makhoere's *No Child's Play: In Prison under Apartheid* (1988), Emma Mashinini's *Strikes have Followed me all my Life* (1989) and Molefe Pheto's *And Night Fell: Memoirs of a Political Prisoner in South Africa* (1985). The same period saw a proliferation of short stories, dramas and novels that centre around the experience of prison: notably Mtutuzeli Matshoba's collection of short stories, *Call me not a Man* (1979), and the prison poetry of James Matthews.

The dismantling of apartheid and the demise of apartheid censorship saw a veritable explosion of retrospective prison memoirs, starting with Nelson Mandela's iconic *Long Walk to Freedom* (1994) and rapidly followed by the memoirs of, for instance, Jean Middleton (1998), Mac Maharaj and others in an edited collection (2001), Fatima Meer (2001), Raymond Suttner (2001), Stanley Mmutlanyane Mogoba (2003) and Ahmed Kathrada (2005). Whilst not really in the scope of this chapter, the demise of apartheid has seen the emergence of interest in the prison experiences of 'non-political' prisoners: Jonny Steinberg's biography *The Number* (2004) stands out for its sustained, reflective account of the life of Magadien Wentzel as he moves between prison and civilian life, and also for the discerning way it uses Charles van Onselen's pioneering work on the historical origins of South African prison gangs and the development of a gang mythology.

The overwhelming bulk of prison writing in South Africa was written in English, partly because English was seen as the language of political struggle: the events of 1976 engendered a sense that the adoption of English over Afrikaans and other indigenous languages was an important strategy for resisting the marginalisation of black South Africans from mainstream political, cultural and intellectual life (Kangwangamalu, 'English and the Politics of Language', pp. 238–9). The use of English also played an important role in the internationalisation of the plight of South Africans under apartheid. Breyten Breytenbach, however, wrote a series of poetry anthologies in Afrikaans after his release from prison, and Frank Anthony's Afrikaans poems, collected as *Robbeneiland: my Kruis my Huis* (Robben Island, my Cross, my House) appeared in 1983. The paucity of prison writing in languages other than English does not mean, of course, that writers were not acutely aware of South Africa's linguistic diversity, or of the fact that South African English has been deeply influenced by the country's many languages. In *Inside*, Cronin makes the following point under the heading 'Geography of the Mouth': 'South Africa is a multilingual country; even the English we speak is many Englishes, layered with occupation, defiance and conquest. To speak South African is to disturb history, the tongue bumping against repressed parts' (p. 51). Cronin's formulation is provocative, because it suggests that commonality, in this case a commonality predicated on a shared language, does not necessarily preclude difference and contestation: a common language is, in practice, always already divided against itself and marked by its history.

David Schalkwyk takes Sheila Roberts to task for suggesting that there is a 'homogeneity of substance, tone and mood' in South African prison writing, and points out that such a view negates the heterogeneous social and historical forces that carry the narratives ('Confession', p. 24). Indeed, given the allegorical potency of the prison, it stands to reason that certain commonalities of content and structure belie the widely divergent notions of incarceration that one encounters in prison writing. Thus, for instance, as Riouful observes, post-apartheid representations of Robben Island have tended to background painful and divisive aspects of life on Robben Island in favour of descriptions of the prison as a place of community, resistance, survival and triumph ('Behind Telling', pp. 24–7). Riouful's division between apartheid and post-apartheid understandings of the prison is echoed in a great deal of the critical literature on Robben Island (see Grunebaum-Ralph, 'Replacing Pasts, Forgetting Presents', and Nuttall and Michael, 'Autobiographical Acts'). Beyond the broad mediation of national history, party-political ideology also refracts the narrative. Mandela, for instance, finds the behaviour of the 1976 generation shocking because of their absolute rejection of the structure of the prison and their refusal to treat any of its disciplinary mechanisms with anything other than contempt. 'In a way that even the authorities acknowledged,' Mandela observes, 'order in prison was preserved not by the warders but by ourselves' (Long Walk to Freedom, p. 464). The new generation of young prisoners on Robben Island, strongly influenced by the militancy of Black Consciousness and increasingly sceptical of negotiation with the authorities, threatened precisely this self-regulated order of the prison. For Mandela, the prison as a space of reform, where both prisoners and warders strive towards a form of normative 'humanity' under the gracious and understated guidance of the ANC, is essentially a blueprint for a new nation. In this sense, Long Walk to Freedom is marked both by a leader's anxieties about an ungovernable populace and by the arguably more moderate political rhetoric of the ANC.

In contrast, Caesarina Makhoere, a 1976 prisoner, is inflexible in her understanding of the prison as a radically antagonistic space, with prisoners and prisoner officials locked in a battle that must terminate in victory for one side or the other, or not at all. In a review of Makhoere's autobiography, Dorothy Driver expresses some disquiet at Makhoere's lack of self-doubt and the absence of an 'interrogative' self-reflexivity ('Review Article', p. 351). One should nonetheless make the point that this uncompromising stance is born out of the turbulent political landscape of 1976.

Given the strong ideological positions that many prisoners carried with them to prison, one could argue that any attempt to uncover the everyday texture of life in South African prisons under apartheid, to penetrate the demagoguery and censorship that obscured 'real life' in prison, is necessarily misguided. In the South African parlance of resistance, for instance, Robben Island enjoyed importance as an almost spiritual site of pilgrimage and suffering, as attested by stories like Matshoba's 'A Pilgrimage to the Isle of Makana' (1979). Prisoners were well aware that they were entering a space of exceptional symbolic significance, a 'place of martyrs' (Zwelonke, *Robben Island*, p. 13). From the outset, they adapted their identity to accord with the status of the island: as much as the island is retrospectively reinvented in prison memoirs, the lives that are described by these autobiographies are always already invented, their subjectivities oriented towards the role imposed by the island as metaphor for resistance and survival. It is simply not possible to isolate some anterior, authentic experience of the prison, because such an 'authentic' experience is from the outset anticipative of historical judgement and marked by an element of the fictional.

Having made the point that the prison cannot appear in 'authentic' guise in prison narratives, because these narratives are produced under specific social and historical conditions, it is also necessary to emphasise that the prison is *itself* one of the sociohistorical structures that govern how the individual subject becomes knowable in prison writing. The prison, to borrow Foucault's formulation, is a 'machine for altering minds' (*Discipline and Punish*, p. 125). The penitentiary is not an objective phenomenon that becomes assimilated into and mediated by pre-existing local and global information flows, but is itself productive of particular subjectivities. One of the few academic studies of South African prisons to make an analogous point is Fran Buntman's *Robben Island and Prisoner Resistance to Apartheid*. Buntman's text stands out from other histories of Robben Island for its willingness to engage the key role of political imprisonment in forming – and sustaining – strategies for resistance. Moreover, the text is attentive to the ways in which the prison's 'impact resonated beyond anti-apartheid opposition to the politics of negotiating a transition and creating and governing a democratic state' (*Prisoner Resistance to Apartheid*, p. 4).

Given the role that the prison space and prison culture has played in the formation of languages of resistance and emerging nationhood, one should reiterate that South African prisons also historically treated prisoners very differently based on their race, their gender and their political persuasion. Indeed, one of the functions of the apartheid prison was precisely to reinscribe notions of separate cultures and discrete races in the face of a mass struggle that attempted to remove these barriers. Thus Fatima Meer comments: 'We were all women, but so classified and separated that we could not be women together' (*Prison Diary*, p. 209).

Describing her cell at the Gezina police station, Jean Middleton notes her relative privilege as a white prisoner who is allowed more than one blanket and four felt mats (*Convictions*, p. 38). Later, she comments that the warders' upbringing 'had taught them to speak to whites as equals, in a courteous, friendly way' (p. 88) and recalls a wardress who burst into tears because she couldn't bring herself to treat Middleton and her colleagues with contempt, since they were 'just ordinary women' (p. 88).

It is clear from the writing of women like Helen Joseph, First and Middleton, imprisoned in the 1960s, that the apartheid prison found it difficult to interpellate them as delinquent or iniquitous. In fact, their very presence in prison precipitated a crisis of perception: one of the sentimental justifications of racial oppression hinged on the figure of the vulnerable white woman, a kind of bearer of civilised culture, whose protection necessitated the practice of apartheid. In the figure of the white woman freedom fighter, the apartheid state encountered an impossible conflation of the object of its self-justifying chivalric fantasy and the very enemy it had sworn to safeguard her from.

This deference to white women increasingly evaporated as the apartheid carceral system became more entrenched and the pretence of legality was abandoned in the 1970s and 1980s, as is shockingly evidenced by the letter bomb that killed First in 1982.

One way of approaching the dialogue that emerges between the prison's imposed categories and narrative responses to prison life is by way of the prison's complex and inconsistent attitude towards collective identity. In an article on women's prison writing under apartheid, Schalkwyk makes the point that Ruth First, because of her educational and cultural background, had access to a more nuanced language with which to describe interiority than writers such as Emma Mashinini (Schalkwyk, 'Chronotopes', p. 9). As a consequence, for Schalkwyk, Mashinini struggles to relate her experience of solitary confinement, while First can devote considerable space to the experience of isolation. Unlike Mashinini, she can employ what Schalkwyk terms 'freely discursive and speculative modes' of self-consciousness ('Chronotopes', p. 25). Whilst there is truth to this argument – writers do, indeed, enter prison with a particular kind of orientation to the world and a specific constellation of discourses – it is necessary to point out that the apartheid prison itself treated white and black prisoners completely differently, and that differences in self-representation attend at least as much on the material conditions of imprisonment as on a writer's discursive repertoire. Penal discourse in South Africa saw black and white subjects as belonging to entirely different moral, social and legal spheres. Stephen Peté and Annie Devenish observe that 'African subjects in the colonies were separated from the realms of law, civilisation and social contract . . . which governed the development of "modern" penal ideas in Britain. Under indirect rule, black criminals, unlike their white counterparts, did not belong to a "shared moral universe"' ('Flogging, Fear and Food', p. 12). Notions of 'reform' were simply not applied to black prisoners, but remained an important rationale for the imprisonment of white subjects. In fact, before prisons were officially segregated in 1959, the social stigma of being incarcerated with black prisoners was seen as a serious obstacle to the prison's rehabilitative function (Peté and Devenish, 'Flogging, Fear and Food', p. 17). Thus, for instance, Emma Mashinini's experience of prison is marked from the outset by humiliation. The most basic markers of politeness and reciprocity that would allow her some sense of dignity and self are lacking from the language of the prison officials and the security agents.

In marked contrast, First is from the outset addressed as someone with interiority. The prison addresses her in its guise as a penitentiary, and invokes a Benthamite language of contrition and reform that is altogether absent in Mashinini's case. First is troubled by the romantic undertone of her relationship with Viktor, her interrogator, who treats her as someone with subjective depth who is not identical to her role as political prisoner. In her autobiography, she describes how he sexualises both her mockery of him and the violence and inequality implicit in their relationship: 'When his fist clenched I tilted my chin upward in mock acceptance of the blow. He had regained control. "I'd rather kiss it," he said' (First, 117 Days, p. 138). A kind of je ne sais quoi arises as a supplement to their relationship, as interrogator and prisoner, an excessive, sexual quality born out of the mutual recognition of each other's inner qualities. However, it is this same excess, this sexualised fantasy of subjective depth, that brings First dangerously close to confession: 'I loathed myself but it seemed I could not resist taking part in this exchange with another human being, talking, responding, proving I was not a caricature, a prototype, but a person' (First, 117 Days, p. 138).

In this instance, First's femininity and her 'inner self' are simultaneously excessive to the 'normal' relationships that govern the prison and, paradoxically, constitute the very forms through which the prison fulfils its particular purpose. It is precisely by treating First as more than 'just' a prisoner and by suggesting that he is more than 'just' her interrogator that Viktor compels her to comply to the interrogation sessions. First's voice is not merely individualised and self-reflective because of some literary, cultural or political predisposition, although all of these elements undoubtedly play a role. She enters a space that is recognisably aligned to the western tradition of confessional autobiographies *because* she is treated as a confessional subject by the prison. As with Breytenbach, her experience of incarceration, and therefore the literary devices that serve to reconstruct this experience, is strongly determined by the way the apartheid penal institution understood her, categorised her and addressed her.

The fact that, on balance, black prison writers are more inclined to adopt a strong collective voice than white prisoners can be approached in a similar manner. Rather than simply reflecting a more communal political identity, it also attends on the real conditions of incarceration. Black prisoners were much more likely to occupy overcrowded communal cells than white prisoners, leading both to serious tensions and to a sense of solidarity. Black prisoners were *enjoined*, in a sense, to negotiate a collective 'we' by their conditions of incarceration, and the communal voices that emerge under apartheid are marked by the tensions and contradictions that characterised such a construction of collective identity in an enclosed space.

Similarly, the material circumstances of Mandela's confinement mediate both his autobiographical voice in *Long Walk to Freedom* and determine the possibilities for political action. It is essentially Mandela's isolation from the other imprisoned leaders in a single cell that allows him to start negotiating with the apartheid government in the late 1980s. 'As a leader,' he notes, 'one must sometimes take actions that are unpopular, or whose results will not be known for years to come' (*Long Walk to Freedom*, p. 464). Mandela puts this philosophy into practice when he starts negotiations with the apartheid government. His description of how he takes this decision is quite extraordinary:

> I chose to tell no one what I was about to do. Not my colleagues upstairs nor those in Lusaka. The ANC is a collective, but the government had made collectivity in this case impossible. I did not have the security or the time to discuss these issues with my organization. I knew that my colleagues upstairs would condemn my proposal, and that would kill my initiative even before it was born. There are times when a leader must move out ahead of the

flock, go off in a new direction, confident that he is leading his people the right way. Finally, my isolation furnished my organization with an excuse in case matters went awry: the old man was alone and completely cut off, and his actions were taken by him as an individual, not a representative of the ANC.   (p. 627)

In retrospect, *Long Walk to Freedom* can posit this deeply individual decision as the realisation of the will of the ANC, or the 'right way' of historical necessity. The profoundly unrevolutionary (or perhaps post-revolutionary), nation-building agenda of *Long Walk to Freedom* necessitates this kind of understanding of South African history, where the 'will of the people' is exercised in a logical, progressive and intelligible way through its individual agent-instruments. However, Mandela's decision becomes the will of the people only after it has been made; it is the collective will only from the post-apartheid framework that this very same decision inaugurates. The individual choice, in a sense, creates the context that will allow the decision to be reinterpreted as communal. In fact, his 'splendid isolation' (*Long Walk to Freedom*, p. 626) from the ANC enables these negotiations, which he presents to Oliver Tambo, the actual leader of the ANC, as a *fait accompli* (*Long Walk to Freedom*, p. 632). Mandela could act in a unilateral way because he was effectively isolated from the structures of the ANC. His decision is an unpredictable – and perhaps characteristically – individual choice, in part enabled by the physical space of the prison.

As much as the employment of a collective voice is an effect of the generic demands of prison writing, it also attends on the specific conditions of incarceration. In this sense, the penal space *produces* specific versions of and attitudes towards communality. Mandela's nation-building agenda insists on a rather idealised and all-embracing notion of a prison community that is conspicuously lacking in works such as Dlamini's *Hell Hole, Robben Island* or D. M. Zwelonke's *Robben Island* (both written by members of the PAC). Dlamini and Zwelonke both construct a militant but fraught and internally divided 'we' that hardly ever extends to the ordinary 'common law' prisoners that inhabited Robben Island in the early 1960s. Zwelonke, for instance, describes the criminal convicts as 'servile, ignorant, selling each other for favours, full of fear, every man for himself' (*Robben Island*, p. 68). As I have argued elsewhere (Roux, 'Jonny Steinberg's *The Number*'), these 'uncanonised' prison autobiographies demonstrate the historical processes of hierarchisation and exclusion that underpin the deceptively neutral and all-inclusive 'prisoner's voice' that has come to represent the voice of the people in the hegemonic narratives of the post-apartheid nation. In particular, the 'we' of the political activist in these texts is born out of the anxious exclusion of common law prisoners, who are incessantly placed outside the ambit of solidarity and the political. It is apparent, in the few prison life stories that reflect on the post-apartheid prison, that the plight of prisoners is no longer really regarded as an eminently *political* question, but rather as a consequence of personal life choices (see, for instance, Julia Landau's *Journey to Myself: Writings by Women from Prison*, published in 2004, or Heather Parker Lewis's *The Prison Speaks: Men's Voices / South African Jails*, published in 2003). Without the overt category of the 'political prisoner', we find the rapid post-apartheid depoliticisation of the experience of the prison and its role in South African life.

Scholarship in the area of South African prison writing therefore confronts an interesting situation. South African prison literature participates in a particular *global* discourse of human rights. Mandela's *Long Walk to Freedom* ranks with Egyptian Nawāl Sa'dāwī's *Memoirs from the Women's Prison* (1994) and Kenyan Ngugi wa Thiong'o's *Detained* (1981) as a seminal text about the state's abuse of power, the predicaments of the developing world and the meanings of personal and national freedom. In political prison writing, one of the modern state's technologies of 'localisation' – the prison – is opened to, and in fact motivates, a global rights culture where specific national predicaments are translated into abstractions about civil liberties that enjoy universal currency. Simultaneously, the prison memoir is compelled to comment on its local conditions and to include those most marginalised and stationary of people, ordinary convicts. In this way, the victims of an extreme form of localisation find their way back into history, the official stories of nation-building and the language of universal human rights. To be sure, such convicts often appear under erasure: as unpredictable, singular entities that have yet to be converted into a group by the nobility of struggle, as inhuman grotes-queries that defy categorisation, as a formless and dangerous mob, and so on. Nonetheless, reading South African prison writing widely and carefully also demonstrates the ways in which the valorised and globally marketable identity of the freedom fighter is produced through a *contestation* of identity: a day-to-day interaction with the subaltern, with people who have disappeared into the normally invisible spaces of social exclusion. More than that, it insists on the idea of human rights as materially grounded in a close and messy immersion in local conditions.

In conclusion, we can say that South African prison writing is doubled in two ways. Firstly, it is split between individuated introspection and the need to speak in a communal way about the events that propel an individual life. If this is an effect of the genre itself – the exigencies of encountering and writing about the prison as a politicised subject – it is also an effect, in South Africa, of the way the prison understands community, subjectivity and responsibility through unequivocal categories of race and gender, and organises the penal space accordingly. Secondly, it is split between the manufacture of an empowered collective 'we' – the authoritative and globally meaningful voice of the activist – and the uneasy but necessary inscription of those eminently local 'others' that the 'we' posits itself against and often seeks to exclude. It is perhaps to those others, the ordinary prisoners, that new research in the field of apartheid-era prison writing could direct some of its attention.

Bibliography

Anthony, F. *Robbeneiland: My Kruis, My Huis*, Kasselsvlei: Kampen, 1983.

Bakhtin, M. M. *The Dialogic Imagination: Four Essays*, ed. M. Holquist, trans. C. Emerson and M. Holquist, Austin: University of Texas Press, 2004.

Bernault, F. 'The Politics of Enclosure in Colonial and Post-Colonial Africa', in F. Bernault and J. L. Roitman (eds.), *A History of Prison and Confinement in Africa*, Portsmouth, NH: Heinemann, 2003.

Bosman, H. C. *Cold Stone Jug: The Anniversary Edition*, ed. S. Gray, Cape Town: Human & Rousseau, 1999.

Breytenbach, B. *Mouroir: Bespiëelde Notas van 'n Roman*, Johannesburg: Taurus, 1983.

The *True Confessions of an Albino Terrorist* [1985], San Diego: Harcourt Brace, 1994.

Brutus, D. *Letters to Martha and other Poems from a South African Prison*, London: Heinemann, 1968.

A Simple Lust, London: Heinemann, 1979.

Sirens, Knuckles and Boots, Ibadan: Mbari and Evanston, IL: Northwestern University Press, 1963.

Buntman, F. *Robben Island and Prisoner Resistance to Apartheid*, Cambridge University Press, 2003.

Cronin, J. *Inside*, London: Jonathan Cape, 1987.

Deacon, H. *The Island: A History of Robben Island, 1488–1990*, Cape Town: David Philip, 1996.

Dingake, M. *My Fight against Apartheid*, London: Kliptown Books, 1987.

Dlamini, M. *Hell Hole, Robben Island*, Nottingham: Spokesman, 1984.

Driver, D. 'Review Article: *No Child's Play*, *Strikes have Followed Me all My Life*, *A Far Cry*: The Making of a South African', *Journal of Southern African Studies* 17:2 (1991), 337–54.

First, R. *117 Days: An Account of Confinement and Interrogation under the South African 90-day Detention Law*, Harmondsworth: Penguin, 1965.

Foucault, M. *Discipline and Punish: The Birth of the Prison*, trans. A. Sheridan, Harmondsworth: Penguin, 1991.

Gray, S. 'Introduction', in H. Bosman, *Cold Stone Jug: The Anniversary Edition*, ed. S. Gray, Cape Town: Human & Rousseau, 1999.

Gready, P. *Writing as Resistance: Life Stories of Imprisonment, Exile, and Homecoming from Apartheid South Africa*, Lanham, MD: Lexington Books, 2003.

Grunebaum-Ralph, H. 'Replacing Pasts, Forgetting Presents: Narrative, Place and Memory in the Time of the Truth and Reconciliation Commission', *Research in African Literatures* 32:3 (2001), 198–212.

Joseph, H. *If this be Treason*, Johannesburg: Contra, 1998.

Kangwangamalu, N. 'When 2 + 9 = 1: English and the Politics of Language Planning in a Multilingual South Africa: South Africa', in C. Mair (ed.), *The Politics of English as a World Language: New Horizons in Postcolonial Cultural Studies*, Amsterdam: Rodopi, 2003.

Kathrada, A. *A Free Mind: Ahmed Kathrada's Notebook from Robben Island*, Johannesburg: Jacana, 2005.

Landau, Julia (ed.). *Journey to Myself: Writings by Women from Prison in South Africa*, Cape Town: Footprints Publishers, 2004.

La Guma, A. *The Stone Country*, Cape Town: David Philip, 1991.

Lewin, H. *Bandiet out of Jail* [1974], Johannesburg: Random House, 2002.

Lewis, H. Parker. *The Prison Speaks: Men's Voices/South African Jails*, Cape Town: Ihilihili, 2003.

Maharaj, M. (ed.). *Reflections in Prison: Voices from the South African Liberation Struggle*, Cape Town: Zebra, 2001.

Makhoere, C. K. *No Child's Play: In Prison under Apartheid*, London: Women's Press, 1988.

Mandela, N. R. *Long Walk to Freedom: The Autobiography of Nelson Mandela* [1994], London: Abacus, 1996.

Mashinini, E. *Strikes have Followed me all my Life: A South African Autobiography*, London: Women's Press, 1989.

Matshoba, M. *Call me not a Man: The Stories of Mtutuzeli Matshoba*, Johannesburg: Ravan, 1979.

'A Pilgrimage to the Island of Makana', in *Call Me not a Man*, 92–142.

Meer, F. *Prison Diary*, Cape Town: Kwela Books, 2001.

Middleton, J. *Convictions: A Woman Political Prisoner Remembers*, Johannesburg: Ravan, 1998.

Mogale, D. W. *Prison Poems*, Johannesburg: Ad Donker, 1992.

Mogoba, M. S. *Stone, Steel, Sjambok: Faith Born on Robben Island*, Johannesburg: Ziningweni Communications, 2003.

Naidoo, I. *Island in Chains: Ten Years on Robben Island by Prisoner 885/63*, Harmondsworth: Penguin, 1982.

Newman, W. A. *Biographical Sketch of John Montagu*, London: Harrison, 1855.

Nuttall, S., and C-A. Michael. 'Autobiographical Acts', in S. Nuttall and C-A. Michael (eds.), *Senses of Culture: South African Cultural Studies*, Oxford University Press, 2000, 298–317.

Peté, S., and A. Devenish. 'Flogging, Fear and Food: Punishment and Race in Colonial Natal', *Journal of Southern African Studies* 31:1 (2005), 3–21.

Pheto, M. *And Night Fell: Memoirs of a Political Prisoner in South Africa*, London: Heinemann, 1985.

Riouful, V. 'Behind Telling: Post-Apartheid Representations of Robben Island's Past', *Kronos* 26:1 (2000), 22–41.

Roux, D. 'Jonny Steinberg's *The Number* and Prison Life-Writing in Post-Apartheid South Africa', *Social Dynamics* 35:2 (2009), 231–43.

Sachs, A. *The Jail Diary of Albie Sachs*, Cape Town: David Philip, 1990.

Schalkwyk, D. 'Chronotopes of the Self in the Writings of Women Political Prisoners in South Africa', in N. Yousaf (ed.), *Apartheid Narratives*, Amsterdam: Rodopi, 2001, 1–36.

'Confession and Solidarity in the Prison Writing of Breyten Breytenbach and Jeremy Cronin', *Research in African Literatures* 25:1 (1994), 23–45.

'Writing from Prison', in Nuttall and Michael, *Senses of Culture*, 278–97.

Smit, D. v. Z. *South African Prison Law and Practice*, Durban: Butterworths, 1992.

Steinberg, J. *The Number: One Man's Search for Identity in the Cape Underworld and Prison Gangs*, Johannesburg: Jonathan Ball, 2004.

Suttner, R. *Inside Apartheid's Prison: Notes and Letters of Struggle*, Durban: University of Natal and Ocean Press, 2001.

Worger, W. H. 'Convict Labour, Industrialists and the State in the US South and South Africa, 1870–1930', *Journal of Southern African Studies* 30:1 (2004), 63–86.

Zwelonke, D. M. *Robben Island*, London: Heinemann, 1989.

27

Theatre: regulation, resistance and recovery

LOREN KRUGER

Although twentieth-century literary drama in English and Afrikaans appeared in separate milieus in print, on stage or in informal circulation, theatrical practice mixed indigenous forms like *izibongo* (praises) and *ingoma* (music) with modern inventions like vaudeville, minstrelsy and the jazz musical. This diversity reflected a syncretic history and hinted at an integrated future, despite the entrenchment of segregation. Whilst segregationists would have denied these facts, supporters of an integral South Africa found in theatre a place and occasion for staging unity in diversity and an alternative public sphere in a hostile state. Theatrical forms identified with South Africa in the last half-century have been thoroughly hybridised, whether in variations of international forms like satirical skits or intimate confessionals or in distinctly local transformations:

- the musical fuses *ingoma ebusuku* (literally: 'music by night'; analytically: performance by professionals or aspirants in urban settings for cash) and the African American jazz revue to produce multilingual drama with songs, dance and dialogue.
- the testimonial play or theatre of witness, protest or resistance, testifies to individual and collective struggle, blending dialogue, narrative, and polemical statements; its trajectory includes Herbert Dhlomo's *The Pass* (1942), Athol Fugard's *No-Good Friday* (1958), as well as *Survival* (1976) and other collectively created plays, culminating in *Born in the RSA* (1986). The best bear powerful witness, but the relative authority and authorship of witness and interpreter remain controversial. (For these and other South African theatrical genres, see Kruger, *Drama of South Africa*, pp. 1–34, 86–99, 154–209)

Significant variations emerged within these categories – activists asserted a sharp break between 'protest' and 'resistance' while critics distinguish Soweto musicals from Cape Town forms using carnival and Afrikaans rather than *ingoma* and (mostly) Nguni languages. Distinctions between local testimony and transnational literature may be blurred, especially given Fugard's overseas reputation. Finally, textual and visual experiments at the limits of theatre, once eclipsed by anti-apartheid testimony, now challenge received definitions and practices.

The evolution of theatrical forms and functions does not follow a tidy chronology, but can be mapped according to three overlapping movements; each highlights different relationships among theatre, society, the state and cultural institutions, and informal groups:

(a) *regulation* tracks the supervision of theatre by the apartheid state through the censorship apparatus and the Performing Arts Councils (PACs, 1962–98) but includes the National Theatre Organisation (NTO, 1949–62) and present-day regulation through parastatals like the National Arts Council (NAC), the South African Broadcasting Corporation (SABC) and the National Lottery.

(b) *resistance* highlights theatre that challenged apartheid not only in critical content but in flouting Group Areas and other segregation laws. It dominated anti-apartheid culture in the 1970s and 1980s as well as the perception of this culture at home and abroad; but it also includes integrated theatre in the 1950s, before apartheid suppressed associations across the colour line, satire and other anti-state performances in post-apartheid contexts.

(c) *recovery* refers to post-apartheid performance of local and regional histories suppressed by apartheid, and of topics sidelined by the anti-apartheid movement, especially gender violence and the lives of sexual and ethnic minorities. Theatrical recovery may also be complicated when multiple media modify live performance and theatre must coexist with other forms, whether live (dance/informal spatial practices) or mediated, including radio, which launched several playwrights, and television, which has lured theatre writers and directors.

Three determinants prevail over time: (1) theatre has been predominantly *urban*; (2) participants have usually understood theatre as *modern*, even if New Africans defined modernity differently from Afrikaners defending 'western civilisation'; (3) playmakers remain mostly *male*. Women of all groups have struggled with family demands for domestic labour as well as with limited access to education and training; while black men seized the spotlight in the anti-apartheid period, black women have not emerged in numbers to compete either with them or with white men and women.

Even when apartheid legislation segregated education and other amenities and suppressed legitimate opposition as 'communist', private institutions remained relatively open until the 1960s. The 1950s signified both the end of a period that Lewis Nkosi called an 'intercultural bohemia' associated with Sophiatown, and, retrospectively, a model of integrated culture that would be revived in the 1980s (Nkosi, *Home and Exile*, p. 24). Both musical and testimonial play saw key developments. *King Kong* (1959), based on the life and death of boxer Ezekiel Dhlamini (as profiled in *Drum*), represented in part the culmination of variety traditions that had blended the talents of writers and musicians since Dhlomo and Griffiths Motsieloa collaborated with Joint African European Councils for the Emancipation Centenary Celebration (1934), and in part an attempt by white liberals to 'improve' this tradition by importing the 'jazz opera' of George Gershwin, himself indebted to African American music. Under Union Artists, which produced jazz and drama at Dorkay House and other Johannesburg venues, *King Kong* brought together established composer / writer Todd Matshikiza, known for *Uxolo* (Peace, 1956), the cantata commissioned for Johannesburg's seventieth anniversary, and his *Drum* column 'Music for Moderns', with amateur writer, Harry Bloom, who took credit for a collective script directed by Leon Gluckman. It celebrated the volatile mixture of dissidence and lawlessness in Sophiatown and launched newcomers like Miriam Makeba but could not resist the government's assault on integrated culture. Despite Union Artists musicals like Ben Masinga's *Back in your own Backyard* (1960) and Kente's first show, *Manana Jazz Prophet* (1963), many *King Kong* principals and Sophiatown intellectuals emigrated and apartheid legislation made integrated performances very difficult. By 1964 the 'intercultural bohemia' was over.

Regulation

Even before *King Kong* played the bohemian swan song, apartheid regulation favoured segregated institutions. The NTO attempted, as a (whites only) 'people's theatre' to bridge the divide between Afrikaans and English and between South African and European repertoires on small town tours as well as urban stages. Although it supported segregation mostly by omission, the NTO overtly countenanced apartheid ideology by participating in state occasions such as the Van Riebeeck Tricentenary (1952). The NTO's plays did not quite match the myth-making pageant (written by Gerhard Beukes; directed by Anna Neethling-Pohl, who also directed N. P. van Wyk Louw's *Die Dieper Reg* [The Deeper Right] for the Voortrekker Centenary), which treated Van Riebeeck, historically an indifferent colonial bureaucrat, as an heroic pioneer (Witz, *Apartheid's Festival*, pp. 30–83). In dramatising an Afrikaner farmer's response to government allocation of white land for blacks, W. A. de Klerk's *Die Jaar van die Vuur-os* (Year of the Fire-ox) inverted the historical fact of *white* appropriation of black land. Witnessed by silent blacks, the conflict pits farmer Pieter against his cosmopolitan brother Martin and a liberal MP defending African rights. Despite this dissent, Martin finally endorses Pieter's view that Afrikaners are the only nation in the region with a history and his marriage with Gillian suggests that English speakers should join this *volk*. *The Dam* by Guy Butler also uses marriage between English and Afrikaner to signify national unity but betrays, through farmer Long's futile attempt to transform the arid land, prevailing white anxiety about civilisation in a 'primitive' wilderness.

When the four provincial Performing Arts Councils, PACT (Transvaal), PACOFS (Orange Free State), CAPAB (Cape Province) and NAPAC (Natal), replaced the NTO, they joined other institutions like the subsidised presses to promote white 'western civilisation' in the Afrikaner mould. In the first decade, only CAPAB produced local English drama, including Fugard's *People are Living There* (1966), in a repertoire dominated by imports from Europe and North America. British plays were prohibited by the Equity playwrights' boycott. The Afrikaans repertoire mixed European translations with original plays, from Van Wyk Louw's revisionist Anglo-Boer War drama *Die Pluimsaad Waai Ver* (The Plumed Seed Blows Far, PACT 1966) to P. G. du Plessis's poor white tragicomedy in *Siener in die Suburbs* (Seer in the Suburbs, 1971) and Chris Barnard's dark farce about a clerk in delusional rebellion against unseen bosses in *Die Rebellie van Lafras Verwey* (The Rebellion of Lafras Verwey, SABC radio 1971; PACT 1974). Although Afrikaner playwrights received support from the PACs, several challenged Nationalist notions of patriotism. Van Wyk Louw clashed with Verwoerd, and Bartho Smit saw plays postponed or cut. Whilst these setbacks pale in comparison to the exile, banning and harassment of black writers, they signal dissidence even in the *volk*. In *Die Verminktes* (The Maimed, 1960), Smit exposed the hypocrisy of apartheid assertions of racial purity in the face of so-called miscegenation. Performed promptly in Belgium and in English translation in London, it was staged in South Africa only in 1977; in its original form, an Afrikaner politician barely acknowledges his overseas-educated coloured son, Frans, and responds to Frans's desire to marry the politician's ward by castrating him (cut in the 1977 version). This scenario is melodramatic, finally dispatching Frans by turning him into a *skollie* (petty criminal) talking *gamtaal* (gangster Afrikaans), but its very excesses express the repressed truth of hybridity with greater intensity than English plays on love across the colour line, such as Basil Warner's *Try for White* (Cockpit Players) or Lewis Sowden's *Kimberley Train* (Johannesburg Library Theatre), both

1958. Whilst *Die Verminktes* circulated in print, *Blood Knot* launched Fugard on a national scale. Staged in 1961 at Dorkay House by Fugard and Zakes Mokae, it toured segregated venues countrywide in 1962, the first local play to receive such exposure. The conflict, set in a coloured township shack, between articulate but neurotic 'play-white' Morrie and his stronger blacker brother Zach, escalates from role play to violence in frustrated response to the way each misunderstands the other's aspirations. Although Nkosi criticised it for replicating stereotypes (*Home and Exile*, p. 139), he recognised that *Blood Knot* showed the impact of racial typing on intimate experience, a theme Fugard revisited in his third 'Port Elizabeth' play *Boesman and Lena* (1969) and, later, in his autobiographical '*Master Harold' and the . . . Boys* (1984).

Although produced by contrasting institutions, Fugard and Smit both challenged legal and cultural prohibitions on interracial association to expose the consequences of racial and sexual repression in Afrikaner Calvinism. Fugard writes in English, but he has said that his characters often speak Afrikaans. Unlike Morrie and Zach, the siblings in *Hello and Goodbye* (Library Theatre 1965) are classified white but their privileges (Johnnie's house and pension) are negated by their abjectness. Johnnie appears so obsessed by his dead father that he encourages Hester to believe the latter is alive in the next room and, after the illusion is exposed, retreats on the dead man's crutches. Hester, returning to Port Elizabeth to demand her inheritance, invokes her experience as a 'whore' in Johannesburg to dismiss the rhetoric of sin as merely fathers' fairy-tales. Hester thus initiates a series of women battling Calvinist patriarchy, which would culminate in *The Road to Mecca* (1986), Fugard's tribute to outsider artist Helen Martins, who was hounded to suicide by the Church. Smit's *Putsonderwater* (Well-without-water, 1962), staged in Belgium and at Rhodes University (1968) and by PACOFS (1969), takes the seduction and betrayal of a woman both sensual and naive from Georges Bernanos's *Sous le soleil de Satan* (Under Satan's Sun) but locates Maria and her predators, a doctor, a policeman and a *dominee* (pastor), in an arid South African *dorp*. The men woo Maria with fine words, but Smit portrays them as hypocrites who treat her as a dumb creature whose murder of the *dominee* in self-defence, like her fantasy of flight to Johannesburg, invokes their patronising disbelief.

Although better known for *Christine* (PACT 1973), a play made notorious by stage undress and, in an overblown extension of Brecht's *Jewish Wife*, a self-pitying old Nazi fleeing the memory of the wife he abandoned to the SS (Brink, *Aspekte*, pp. 144–8), Smit's best work exposed home-grown duplicity. The full force of *Putsonderwater* resonated only a generation later. In *Die Teken* (The Sign, 1984), Deon Opperman defied Calvinist dogma to portray a patriarch who would kill his grandchild rather than confront his daughter's claim to bear the messiah, and in *Diepe Grond* (1985; English title *African Gothic*), Reza de Wet mined southern Gothic as well as Afrikaans morality tales in explicit tribute to Smit and indirect to Tennessee Williams to create a surreal drama of two *enfants terribles* on a decaying farm who mix infantile attachment to their nanny and murderous manipulation of a lawyer who disrupts their idyll. Although the PACs later revived *Verminktes* (PACT 1977) and also staged *Die Teken* (PACOFS 1985), *Diepe Grond* went from the ATKV student production to the Market Theatre instead. By the 1990s the PACs had become sites of conspicuous consumption while newer companies were doing more with less but, before closing, produced significant work like Charles Fourie's *Don Gxubane onner die Boere* (PACT 1995), a post-apartheid riposte to Smit's *Don Juan onner die Boere* (NTO 1960), Opperman's *Donkerland* (Dark Land, PACT 1996), and De Wet's *Drif* (Crossing, CAPAB 1994) and *Drie Susters 2* (1997), a sequel to Chekhov's *Three Sisters*.

Apartheid enabled lavish productions of white theatre in the PACs and curtailed integrated projects in town and township, and black and brown authors had little support. Adam Small's *Kanna, Hy Kô Hystoe* (Kanna, He's Coming Home, 1965), hailed by André Brink as a major play (*Aspekte*, p. 168), was staged in (coloured) Athlone only in 1972 and with white PAC casts in 1974. The attempt to make Cape Afrikaans stage-worthy continued locally in the 1980s and received national audiences with David Kramer and Taliep Petersen's *District Six* musical (1987 and 1990s revivals) and Oscar Petersen and David Isaacs's *Joe Barber* series (from 2000). Kramer and Petersen's final collaboration (before Petersen's murder in 2006) was their crowning achievement; *Ghoema* revived ballads from the colonial Dutch and slave repertoire in combination with new songs commenting on the history of slavery and its aftermath in the Cape and celebrating the rich musical and linguistic legacy of the Cape. In the black townships, a few entrepreneurs created show businesses in the 1960s. Gibson Kente was one, and his endurance, expertise and flair for combining jazz, melodrama and *ingoma* made him influential and relatively well off. *Sikhalo* (Lament, 1966) established Kente's trademark fusion of sentimental dialogue in English and songs in his native Xhosa or other local languages when on tour, about township people confronting adversity – poverty, handicaps, loss of love or money usually stolen by township toughs – and finding redemption in faith. Only with *How Long?* (1974) and *Too Late!* (1975), his single published text, did Kente address the resurgent political struggle by suggesting that apartheid, from the pass laws to job restrictions, rather than moral failings, was responsible for wrecked lives; both plays were promptly banned. In *Sekunjalo* (Now is the Time, 1985), however, he favoured Christian forbearance in a drama of civil war with an allegedly godless ANC. Whilst he appealed to conservative blacks in the 1960s (many of them first-generation urban dwellers) and made enough money by selling cosmetics as well as tickets to pay his employees better than factory workers, by the 1980s a new militant generation preferred political poetry and theatre of resistance.

Resistance

Although the Market Theatre in Johannesburg was for years *the* institution of theatrical resistance, theatre indicting white supremacy began much earlier. Motsieloa's shows used African American plays to condemn local segregation in the 1930s and the African National Theatre joined unionists such as Guy Routh (later of Union Artists) to produce plays like Ivan Pinchuk's *Tau* (1941) about the rebellious peasant later documented by Charles van Onselen (*The Seed is Mine*, p. 3), and to read texts like Dhlomo's *Pass* (1942). And while integrated associations were under threat, Dorkay House survived long enough to produce plays such as *No-Good Friday* (1958). Fugard is sometimes credited with founding political theatre, but *No-Good Friday*'s depiction of Sophiatowners caught between *tsotsis* and the police draws on Routh's example and on the insights of actor-writers Nkosi and Bloke Modisane. Nkosi later wrote several plays in exile. Whilst some read *The Rhythm of Violence* (1964) as a drama of student militancy, its tone is by turns surreal and satirical; its racial and sexual wordplay recalls 'stunts' like 'White America, my hand is on your thigh' by Black Beatnik Ted Joans, whom Nkosi admired in New York. 'We can't all be Martin Luther King' (BBC Radio 1969) and 'Virgin Malcolm, look not so pale' (ICA, London 1970) (Gunner, 'Contaminations', pp. 51–66) cultivated the ironic treatment of politics that characterised Nkosi's later fiction.

After detention without trial and the banning of mass opposition pushed resistance underground, Fugard worked in New Brighton near Port Elizabeth with the Serpent Players. More disciplined than the Dorkay House group, they produced collective plays, in particular *The Coat*, which deployed the spare staging and narrative clarity of Brecht's learning plays to present a situation based on their experience. A man sentenced to prison for political activity gives a stranger his coat to return to the prisoner's wife, urging her to make use of it; the players then present alternative scenarios for the audience to choose between. Performed for the New Brighton community as well as a white 'drama appreciation' group in 1966, this play presented dilemmas confronted by ordinary people in impossible situations; its value was recognised in revivals by the South African Black Theatre Union (SABTU) in 1972 and by students and others since. *The Coat* reminds us that the enabling conditions for Fugard's better-known collaborations, *Sizwe Bansi is Dead* and *The Island*, were political as well as theatrical and that Fugard is only the most visible of many contributors. Written with John Kani and Winston Ntshona, these plays drew on the lives of Serpent players. The opening monologue in *Sizwe* echoed Kani's experience at the Ford Motor plant; the performance of *Antigone* in *The Island* drew on Norman Ntshinga's staging on Robben Island (with Mandela as Creon) even though the *Island* cast was reduced to two and the location disguised by the initial title, *The Hodoshe Span*.

These plays received critical notice when they appeared at the Space in Cape Town, which opened in 1972 with Fugard's *Statements after an Arrest under the Immorality Act*. Operating as a private club to avoid prosecution by the Publications Control Board or the Group Areas Act, the Space accommodated integrated audiences but had little contact with Black Consciousness militants who saw all-black organisation as the only way to rebuild self-respect. Even before *Sizwe* opened in October, Mulligan Mbikwana directed the Serpent Players at the SABTU festival in Durban in June in *The Coat* and *The Just* (after Albert Camus), which appeared alongside Mtuli Shezi's *Shanti* (about African and Indian student militants) directed by the People's Educational Theatre and others including Ronnie Govender's *Lahnee's Pleasure* (about men in an Indian back bar confronted by a militant stranger and shadowed by the unseen *lahnee* [white boss]). Despite appearing in Cape Town in December, SABTU went unnoticed by the Space; its associates were dead (Shezi) or detained by the time *The Island* appeared in 1973. The Space nonetheless broke new ground, challenging the repression of sexual minorities, as in Jean Genet's *Maids* with Pieter-Dirk Uys and Vincent Ebrahim, and also in Uys's own *Selle ou Storie* (Same Old Story, 1975); it drew attention to the lives of apparently unoppressed minorities, like the Jewish children in Geraldine Aron's *Bar and Ger,* and also staged occasional history plays, like Fatima Dike's *The Sacrifice of Kreli* (1976). It featured topical domestic drama like Uys's *Paradise is Closing Down* (1977), in which white bohemians confront the former (coloured) occupant of their inner-city house, or Dike's *The First South African* (1977), which depicted a coloured man's dilemma between black and white demands as the national condition. When founders Brian Astbury and Yvonne Bryceland emigrated, the (People's) Space under Rob Amato staged testimonial plays like Kessie Govender's *Working Class Hero* (about Indian / African class tension in Durban) as well as Zakes Mda's *Dark Voices Ring* (1979) and *The Hill* (1980).

Before the Market Theatre became the pre-eminent venue for theatre resisting apartheid, it drew on existing organisations, not only the Space, whose combination of liberal capital and black and white playmakers it emulated, but also smaller groups like Workshop 71, an intellectual/worker collective based at Witwatersrand (Wits) University, and others in Soweto. Workshop 71 created memorable pieces like James Mthoba's *Uhlanga* (Reed) but *Survival* became the exemplary testimonial play. Four young, angry men explain in terse English punctuated by jokes and songs in Zulu their reasons for landing in prison, from overt political activity to confronting a white policeman while trying to get to hospital. Performed to vocal audiences in university and township venues in May 1976, before the June uprising, and briefly thereafter, it was banned for allegedly inciting riots. Its creators led by Robert McLaren left the country, but others, including Mthoba and Ramalao Makhene, shared their skills with black groups like the Federated Union of Black Artists (FUBA) and Soyikwa, as well as integrated organisations like Junction Avenue Theatre Company and the Market. Market director Barney Simon had developed similar workshops from diverse sources, including Joan Littlewood in 1950s London, Black Power in 1960s New York, and health education skits with black nurses in 1970s Transkei. But it was the explosion of Workshop 71 and the return to the stage of the Dorkay House generation, as well as the commitment of white progressives, that brought to Market playmakers who could revive the syncretic forms and integrated politics of Sophiatown and transform that legacy for the task of bearing witness to apartheid and creating liberated zones of production and assembly.

Although the Market opened in the heat of the uprising with Chekhov's *Seagull*, it became known for workshopped testimonial plays as well as shaping single author work in rehearsal. Initiated with *Call Me Woman* (1977), which staged performers' testimony by turns raw and lyrical to show both differences and commonalities in the sexual and social lives of women, this work included *Black Dog* (1984), which juxtaposed mostly male testimonies as far apart as a township youth leader and an anti-terrorist operative to recall the turmoil of the uprising, but reached its most powerful expression in *Born in the RSA*. Performed at the height of the Emergency (1986), the play not merely depicted this turbulent moment but also illuminated it. Under Simon's direction, co-writers including Fiona Ramsey as an anti-apartheid Afrikaans lawyer, Thembi Mtshali as her activist client tortured by police, Gcina Mhlope as the latter's sister attempting vainly to escape politics, and Neil McCarthy as a police interrogator masquerading as an activist, researched, scripted and portrayed characters in a dialectical manner, demonstrating the force of politics and society on their actions while acknowledging the subjective truth of each character. Although *Born in the RSA* was unequalled for interweaving conflicting stories of apartheid society, this decade included significant collaborations on quite different topics, such as middle-class domestic violence in *This is for Keeps* (1982) by Vanessa Cooke and Danny Keogh, or an African land claim to the Cape in *The Native who Caused all the Trouble* by Cooke, Keogh and Nicholas Haysom (1983).

Perhaps the Market's most revived play, *Woza Albert* by Mbongeni Ngema and Percy Mtwa collaborating with Simon (1981), blended the comic gags and stage types of Mtwa and Ngema (drawn from their time with Kente) together with Simon's work using the body techniques of poor theatre and the research practice of testimonial theatre. The result was a very funny play about Christ's second coming to a South Africa whose authorities treat him as a dangerous subversive. Whilst Jesus never appears on stage, Mtwa and Ngema play a range of characters who encounter him, from white bureaucrats (signified by pink noses) to township people such as coal sellers and an old man recalling the death of the Boers at the hand of Dingaan's warriors. Revived into the twenty-first century, the play's traces could also be seen in skits on community stages across the country.

Despite some cliched reiterations, the best testimonial plays transformed the formula – terse delivery in English of personal stories made political by apartheid injustice; angry posture of the defiant actor, and the leavening of this anger with hymns, songs and jokes in the vernaculars – with the force of an individual story made vividly present to audiences of diverse backgrounds. Matsamela Manaka's *Egoli* (1979), began at the Soweto YMCA, evolved at the People's Space and exploded at the Market. As in *The Island*, two men struggle with each other and with their confinement, in this case, the hostel and the mine – but *Egoli* fleshed out *The Island*'s abstraction in the visceral embodiment of brutalisation. John (Ledwaba, who co-wrote the script) responds to a narrow escape from a shaft collapse by drinking until he vomits, and is restored, after a disembodied voice announces his son's death in that accident, by the ceremonial cleansing of his face by his roommate. Manaka's later plays became more ceremonial, from *Pula* (1982; about drought and the blessing of rain) to *Goree* (1990; on the slave island and its pan-African resonance). *Egoli*'s strongest successors, such as Maishe Maponya's diptych *Gangsters* and *Dirty Work* (1984), matched testimonial urgency with precise embodiment, in contrast to the wordy militancy of plays like Ngema's *Asinamali* (1982). *Gangsters* borrowed its scenario from Beckett's *Catastrophe*, but the author's experience of detention and his ability as an actor to render corporal responses to torture gave the performance an immediacy acknowledged even by the censors who banned it. In *Dirty Work*, a security expert gives a lecture on torture techniques in a space increasingly subject to unexplained tampering; his ever tetchier response mirrors the siege mentality that gripped many whites in the emergency years.

Although Maponya was one of few black male playmakers to write credible female roles (in *uMongikazi/Nurse* for example), not many women filled the gap. Gcina Mhlope's autobiographical *Have you Seen Zandile?* (1986; with Maralin van Reenen and fellow actor Thembi Mtshali), which follows Zandile from a childhood idyll with her Zulu grandmother to abduction in preparation for marriage by her father's Xhosa family and finally to her self-realisation as a writer, received acclaim for its portrayal of childhood as well as its criticism of the impact of 'customary' law on women, but Mhlope left the theatre to tell and publish stories for young readers. Mtshali tapped her own story of love and separation in *Woman in Waiting* (1999) but, in contrast to *Zandile*, publication in *Theatre of Witness* gave primary authorship to adaptor Yael Farber. Dike wrote several plays, but she too left the theatre (and country) between her autobiographical *Glasshouse* (1979) and *So What's New?* (1991), which juxtaposed bosom-buddy chat and nostalgic songs to dramatise four women's responses to domesticity, criminality and *The Bold and the Beautiful* in interregnum Soweto, followed much later by *The Return* (2009), about a repatriated exile haunted by his dead brother. *Sarafina* (1986), Ngema's musical about the high school alleged to have started the Soweto uprising, featured two central women – Sarafina and her inspiring teacher – but this representation of female agency was compromised by the cheery display of short-skirted legs that had more in common with the vacuous revue *Ipi Tombi* (Where are the Girls?, 1974) than with student activists.

Many authors wrote only a single testimonial play, but two stand out as writers of several plays that simultaneously express resistance and impress readers with complex characters and evocative dialogue. Although their subjects differ, Paul Slabolepszy and Zakes Mda depict people left out of grand anti-apartheid struggles and take on untried topics, from the impunity of violent racists to the impact on individuals of globalisation after apartheid. Slabolepszy debuted with *Saturday Night at the Palace* (1982), which depicted with horrifyingly plausible intensity two white thugs (the first of several played by the author) who torment and kill a black fast-food employee, and deepened the portrayal of white belligerence in *Smallholding* (1989), in which 'a Boere-Rambo' abuses hapless intruders in a more adult but no less insane way than the murderously overgrown children in *Diepe Grond*. Slabolepszy shares interest in white male frustration with dramas about military conscripts like Opperman's *Môre is 'n Lang Dag* (Tomorrow is a Long Day, 1984), James Whyle's *National Madness* (1983) and Greig Coetzee's *White Men with Weapons* (1994) but extends its range. *Mooi Street Moves* (1992) ends in the death (by an unseen enforcer) of the streetwise black man in the edgy city at the end of apartheid, but its centre is the poignant confusion of the white naif who, in reversal of the 'Jim comes to Jo'burg' scenario, wanders into black Hillbrow. *Fordsburg's Finest* (1998) tracks the conflict between Thandi, the Americanised daughter of exiles who returns to Fordsburg to find her family home, and Freddie, an Afrikaner former policeman who runs a used-car shop on the site, but, in the truce between them against Freddie's thuggish brother, also stages the provisional reclamation of Johannesburg from the disorder of the interregnum.

Written in exile in Lesotho, Mda's *Dark Voices Ring* (1979) and *The Hill* (1980) dramatise apartheid's impact on the poorest, in rural South Africa and in Lesotho, but use dialogue that weaves together documentary clarity and lyrical, even allegorical, elements, thus challenging the primacy of urban set and emphatic delivery in testimonial theatre. Revived in 1980 at FUBA and often since, *The Hill*'s portrayal of desperate men waiting in vain for jobs in the goldmines captures not only the dehumanising effects of apartheid exploitation but also the persistence of structural inequity and other assaults on human dignity after liberation. *And the Girls in their Sunday Dresses* (1989) develops these themes, as two women, one poor, one apparently rich, wait in an endless queue for rice from UN coffers already depleted by local officials. Mda revisited postcolonial corruption in *The Nun's Romantic Story* (1995) and post-liberation depression in *The Bells of Amersfoort* (2002), but these lack the satirical power of his first play, *We shall Sing for the Fatherland*. Performed by FUBA in 1979, by Soyikwa and others in the 1980s, and by the state-subsidised Windybrow in 1995, the drama portrays two liberation army veterans who haunt a central park in an unnamed postcolonial capital. They resemble the drifters in Soyinka's satire *The Road* but their vain petition to a newly rich businessman, their death by exposure, and their summary burial by prison labour bring their story home as veterans' destitution is exploited today by regional politicians for their own gain.

Recovery

Mda's play looked through post-apartheid euphoria to the limits of recovery, but even before the end of apartheid playmakers had begun to rewrite its history. Junction Avenue Theatre Company (JATC) produced critical history plays from *Randlords and Rotgut* (1978; on English capitalists and Afrikaner republicans colluding to sell alcohol to blacks in early Johannesburg) to their most famous, *Sophiatown* (1986), which recalled in song and dialogue the 'intercultural bohemia' and its brutal demolition as well as the hope of new cultural integration. This critical edge distinguished JATC's work from nostalgic treatments such as *Bloke* (1994), a sentimental musical drawn from Modisane's more bitter than sweet memoir, *Blame me on History* (1964). The edge returned in other Sophiatown revivals, especially the stage adaptation of *The Suit* (1993), Can Themba's caustic tale of infidelity and abuse, and in Kramer and Petersen's last musical, *Ghoema* (2005), discussed above.

Although the most spectacular, *Ghoema* was not the only attempt to recover minority histories overshadowed by the grand anti-apartheid narrative. Muthal Naidoo, whose *We 3 Kings* offered a classic anti-apartheid critique of segregated Indian elections in 1983, turned in *Flight from the Mahabharath* (1994) to a feminist parody not only of the Indian epic but also of gender relations in the local Indian community. *At the Edge* (1991) and *1949* (1994) moved Ronnie Govender beyond the class and ethnic stereotyping of *Lahnee's Pleasure* (and the even broader imitations by a generation of Durban comedians) to examine apartheid's impact on Indian South Africans in the demolition of Cato Manor in the 1950s and especially the trauma of 1949, when Zulu rioters abetted by whites assaulted, killed and dispossessed Indian merchants. Vivian Moodley updated Kessie Govender's treatment of Indian exploitation of blacks with *Got Green Chillies, Makoti!* (1994) about Indian madams. Like Moodley and Govender, others used single performers to deepen the intimacy of testimony. In Ismael Mahomed's *Purdah* (1993), a Muslim woman accused of killing her abusive husband defends herself, while in *Cheaper than Roses* (1996) a woman who passed for white during apartheid remembers her abandoned family while criticising post-apartheid racial typing. Whilst *Purdah* was the first to dramatise Indian Muslim characters, *At her Feet* by Nadia Davids (2002) uses the *hadith* 'paradise at the feet of mothers' as a point of departure for vignettes of Cape Muslim women; these include a critical student, her middle-aged aunt, a fashion-slave cousin and a hip-hop militant who enact diverse responses to the veil, the post-apartheid persistence of hair prejudice and the 'honour killing' of a young woman in Jordan, enlivened by the performer's embodiment of different characters through fabric, coiffure and music.

The single-hander and two-hander also lend themselves to satire which, while it may not produce publications, has drawn larger audiences than literary drama. Robert Kirby's savage shredding of high-level politicians and low-level bureaucrats earned him banning orders in the 1970s, while Uys and his alter ego Evita Bezuidenhout mocked the same politicians in the 1980s and new ones in the 1990s and 2000s. Uys remains effective as well as popular because he satirises his fans as well as the government. Mike van Graan moved from skits in the 1990s to longer-form but no less critical plays, especially *Green Man Flashing* (2004), its drama of rape and intimidation by politicians not only uncannily anticipating the trials of Jacob Zuma but also resonating in print with the ongoing debate about democratic ideals and political impunity. Younger playmakers like James Cairns and Rob van Vuuren have blended satiric dialogue with vigorous mimicry to expose the absurdity as well as the harm of bureaucrats in *Brother Number* (2007). Although not always in formal theatres, satire and comedy dominate festivals from the flagship National Arts in Grahamstown to its many competitors.

Whilst overseas readers remain more fascinated by Truth and Reconciliation Commission (TRC) testimony about apartheid than satiric exposure of post-apartheid ills, South Africans have been preoccupied with violent crime, the growing wealth gap that exacerbates it, and the struggles of state, civil society and individuals to make the country whole. Therapeutic performance has occasionally reached the theatre, as in *The Story I am About to Tell* (1998) by the Khulumani survivors' group, including Duma Khumalo, who was reprieved at the last minute after international protest against the Sharpeville Six's death sentence for 'terrorism'; but TRC themes have not, despite attempts like Kani's *Nothing But the Truth* (2003) or *He Left Quietly* (Farber's dramatisation of Khumalo's prison testimony with his and other voices; 2003), generated theatre to match the complexity of prose such as Antjie Krog's *Country of my Skull*. In contrast, several plays dealing with violence done to individuals by people they know or even love capture both particular stories and their social implications. After his *Top Down* (with Muntu wa Bachaki; 1988) exposed corrupt teachers and *Golden Gloves* (1992) critiqued the lure of boxing, Themba Mtshali's *Weemen* (1996) dramatised one woman's resistance to her husband's abuse as well as his attempts to justify his behaviour to his female boss and a sceptical *sangoma* (traditional diviner) more subtly than Aubrey Sekhabi's hyped *On my Birthday*, to show conflicting viewpoints about violence against women. Lara Foot-Newton's *Tshepang* (2002) shows no stage violence but the stark depiction of village people wasted by poverty, alcohol and hopelessness deepened understanding of the case of a baby raped that shocked a nation apparently inured to sexual assault. Foot-Newton's *Reach* (2007), like Fugard's *Victory* (2006) and Craig Higginson's *Dream of the Dog* (2007), dramatises the intimacy of fear in encounters between ageing white liberals and black protégés turned intruders. Where *Victory* favoured an old curmudgeon who lectured his former housekeeper's daughter and her criminal boyfriend about self-improvement through books and was criticised locally for its remoteness from real people, Foot-Newton and Higginson create complex characters, in particular elderly white women and young black men and women, whose conflicts stem from intimate association as well as profound misunderstanding, and so underscore the legitimacy and irreconcilability of their positions. Whyle offers a more reconciliatory picture of similar characters in *Rejoice Burning* (BBC Radio 2003); white householders employing a Zimbabwean gifted in voice and handiwork become his care-givers as he dies of AIDS.

Whilst these domestic dramas depict intimate encounters in suburban or rural settings, others tackle the post-apartheid city in scenes ranging from naturalistic interiors to improvised street spaces. As early as 1989, Susan Pam-Grant's *Curl up and Dye* dramatised in the interaction of white and black women in an inner-city salon the changing neighbourhood demography as well as surprising alliances across race, class and age that heralded shifts in urban life. Only a decade later did Slabolepszy's *Fordsburg's Finest* and JATC's *Love, Crime and Johannesburg* (1999) catch up with representations of Johannesburg as the edgy city of unpredictable encounters between strangers. Whereas these 1990s plays attempt to analyse current ills, some younger playwrights imply that pervasive amorality resists analysis. Paul Grootboom's *Cards* (2005), *Relativity* (2006) and *Foreplay* (2009) have drawn fire for overdramatising extreme violence against women in a country with the world's highest reported rape rates, but Grootboom counters that his plays reflect real brutality in town and township and are no more graphic than educational TV serials on city youth.

After 2000 some pieces highlighted uncivil disorder in Johannesburg and environs, while others heralded the urban renewal, when planners and artists joined forces to reclaim the city for civil, purposeful and playful collaboration. Although choreographed interactions between professionals and pedestrians – from *Tour Guides for the Inner City* by Stephen Hobbs and artists including William Kentridge and *City Scapes* by Jay Pather, JazzArt dancers and participating videographers (2000) to *Cascoland* by European and local visual and performance artists at the Drill Hall and *Hillbrow/Dakar* by Hobbs and associates working with the Senegalese in, and assorted visitors to, Hillbrow (2007) – may not yield paper publications or full urban transformation, they and many similar events enact changing relationships between text and image, live performance and mediated representation, fictional stories and factual developments, and thus reinvent spatial as well as literary practices. They also tap new funding sources, including city government, transnational foundations and corporations. These acts may be ephemeral but they anticipate more durable text-based installations such as the voiced environments in new museums like Constitution Hill (2004), and they haunt prose on the city from Ivan Vladislavić to Phaswane Mpe.

These performances deserve attention not only because they realign text in relation to other media but also because they challenge insular national culture by including incidental migrants as well as overseas guests in transnational acts. Whilst the collaborations between Handspring Puppets and Kentridge (himself associated with JATC since 1976), especially *Woyzeck on the Highveld* (1993) and *Faustus in Africa* (1995), and his later transformations of opera such as Mozart's *Magic Flute* (2007), staged spectacular fusions of South African text and image with classical stories of suffering, hubris and redemption (enlivened by Handspring's lifesize marionettes and Kentridge's animations of dreams and nightmares from the national imaginary), several playmakers have effectively combined transnational themes and local material on a scale ranging from poor theatre's minimal body work to multimedia extravaganzas. In 1988 Nicholas Ellenbogen, Ellis Pearson and others launched Theatre for Africa with *Horn of Sorrow* and other ecological parables that used mime, minimal props and dialogue to dramatise the tension among wildlife preservation, human survival and cultural claims to products like rhino horn. Although Ellenbogen turned to eco-documentary film, Pearson collaborated with Bheki Mkhwane on *A Boy Called Rubbish* (1996) to engage township children and parents not only with recycling and reuse but also with struggles for scarce resources, and Mkhwane later dramatised the conflict between Zulu cosmology and modern corporate man in *Born Through the Nose* (with Greig Coetzee, 2006). Andrew Buckland and First Physical Theatre have blended satire, the precise mime of Le Coq and other international schools, and ecological catastrophe in plays from *The Ugly Noo-Noo* (1988) through *Blood Stream* (1992) and *Feedback* (1994) to *Well-being* (2002) and *Fuse* (2004). Mark Fleischman, Jenny Reznick and Magnet Theatre used similar techniques to dramatise the plight of displaced people from *So Loep Ons Nou Nog* (And So We Go On, 1994) to *Everyday, Every Year I Am Walking* (2006) and, with Pather's JazzArt, *Cargo* (2007). The last two link South Africa to transnational themes and performers; *Everyday* deploys a musician, a single suitcase of props and two women performing in English, French, Afrikaans and Xhosa to tell a story both particular and general: drawing on refugee testimonies from Congo to Ethiopia, they plot the journey of a mother and her surviving daughter from the scene of a lost daughter's death in a house set alight by neighbours in a civil war, through camps and other dubious refuges to Cape Town and humiliation by Home Affairs bureaucrats. *Cargo*'s dance drama depicts South Africa at the intersection of slave routes between the Indian Ocean and the Atlantic Ocean and so, on similar terrain but with a more sombre note than *Ghoema*, it challenges the northern bias of black Atlantic slave narratives.

Post-apartheid recovery has renewed links between classical texts and modern crises. On a large, perhaps hubristic scale, Brett Bailey and Third World Bunfight have assembled professional and community performers to dramatise local stories as well as transhistorical classics. *Zombie* (1996) tackled the Bhongweni community's response to the 1995 death by minibus crash of several boys, from the denunciation of local women as murderous witches to the clash not only between Christians and traditionalists but also between older citizens and disgruntled youth who envy their elders' resources, often merely meagre pensions, that the youth demand as their post-liberation due. Mobilising church choirs, sangomas and children, *Zombie* invested this powerful tragedy of lost generations and the fear of change with the awe of a mystery play or a cleansing ritual, but its revival as *Ipi Zombi?* (1997) and successors, from *iMumbo Jumbo* (1998), about the alleged appropriation of Xhosa king Hintsa's head by British authorities, to *Big Dada* (2001), about Idi Amin, preferred a mix of shamanism, showman hocus-pocus and cartoonish satire anchored uneasily by campy lead performers. In *Orfeus* (2007), the ancient fable and atmospheric open-air sites added gravitas to the enactment and, in the title role, Congolese Bebe Lueki gave topical resonance to Orpheus's fate – torn asunder as a foreigner – but Bailey could not resist grotesquerie, as in Hades' cabinet of horrors that trapped Eurydice and other women behind minstrel make-up. In contrast, Farber's *Molora* (Ash; 2007) revived the practice of critically revising Greek tragedy, but, while anti-apartheid adaptors from Serpent Players in the 1960s to the Theatre Council of Natal (TECON) in the 1970s and Peter Sepuma in the 1980s had found lessons in *Antigone* about political revolt and civil war, Farber tempered retribution in the Atreide saga from the *Oresteia* to *Elektra* with the ethical renewal of *ubuntu* and its vocal expression in the overtone singing (*umNgqokolo*) of the Ngqoko Cultural Group, whose choral intervention stops this Orestes and Elektra in the act of matricide and begins the process of healing. Although the miked testimony in the opening and closing scenes and the reiteration of known torture techniques by (white) Klytemnestra on (black) Elektra recall the TRC hearings, the play and its title evoke not only global atrocities from the death camps to the exploded twin towers but also the colour donned by Xhosa initiates celebrating manhood.

Framing Xhosa practices and Mycenaen legend with a Sotho title, *Molora* has both deep roots and worldly resonance.

These explorations reflect not only an experimental thrust beyond text and stage but also critical engagement with transnational performance ventures. Whereas anti-apartheid theatre magnified the global imaginary by feeding struggle images to overseas consumers, and so inadvertently stoking their self-righteousness, post-apartheid playmakers like Magnet Theatre and Third World Bunfight counter with interventions in the *transnational symbolic*. In other words, they explode the simplified image repertoires that constitute 'South Africa' abroad and create new representations weaving manifold strands of text, theatre and testimony to link different South Africas with one another and with points on the continent from Mali to Zimbabwe as well as with international traditions and vanguards. This recovery of transnational links transforms early twentieth-century connections between Africa and African America and between Europeans abroad and 'Europeans' at home. Twenty-first-century transnationalism enables writers, performers and audiences to animate regional roots and routes while at the same time to re-envisage South Africa through multiple media in the wider world.

Bibliography

Aron, G. *Bar and Ger*, Cape Town: Oxford University Press, 1975.
    'Bar and Ger', in H. S. Houghton-Hawksley (ed.), *Play Spectrum: Short Plays for High School*, Cape Town: David Philip, 1986.
Bailey, B., and Third World Bunfight. 'Big Dada', unpublished play script, 2001.
    'iMumbo Jumbo', in *The Plays of Miracle & Wonder*, Cape Town: Double Storey, 2003.
    'Ipi Zombi?', in D. Graver (ed.), *Drama for a New South Africa*, Bloomington: Indiana University Press, 1999.
    'Ipi Zombi?', in *The Plays of Miracle & Wonder*.
    'Orfeus', unpublished play script, 2007.
Barnard, C. *Die Rebellie van Lafras Verwey*, Cape Town: Tafelberg, 1971.
Beukes, G. *Van Riebeeck Tricentenary Pageant 1952*, Cape Town: National Library of South Africa Collection.
Bloom, H., and T. Matshikiza. *King Kong – An African Jazz Opera*, London: Collins, 1961.
Brink, A. *Aspekte van die Nuwe Drama*, Cape Town: Human & Rousseau, 1986.
Buckland, A. 'Blood Stream', unpublished play script, 1992.
    'Feedback', unpublished play script, 1994.
    'Fuse', unpublished play script, 2004.
    'The Ugly Noo-Noo', in Kani, *More Market Plays*.
    'Well Being', unpublished play script, 2002.
Butler, G. *The Dam*, Cape Town: Balkema, 1953.

Coetzee, G. 'Born Through the Nose', unpublished play script, 2006.
'White Men with Weapons', in G. Coetzee, *Johnny Boskak is Feeling Funny and other plays*, Pietermaritzburg: University of Kwazulu-Natal Press, 2009.

Cooke, V., J. Honeyman and D. Keogh. 'This is for Keeps', in S. Gray (ed.), *Market Plays*, Johannesburg: Ad Donker, 1986.

Davids, N. *At her Feet*, Cape Town: Oshun, 2006.

Davis, G. V. (ed.). *Beyond the Echoes of Soweto*, Amsterdam: Harwood Academic Publishers, 1997.

De Klerk, W. A. *Die Jaar van die Vuur-os*, Cape Town: Tafelberg, 1952.

De Wet, R. 'African Gothic', in *Plays Two*, London: Oberon Books, 2007.
'Crossing', in R. De Wet and S. Stead (trans.), *Plays One*, London: Oberon Books, 2000.
'Three Sisters 2', in *A Russian Trilogy*, London: Oberon Books, 2002.

Dhlomo, H. I. E. 'The Pass', in N. Visser and T. Couzens (eds.), *Collected Works*, Johannesburg: Ravan, 1985.

Dike, Fatima. *The First South African*, Johannesburg: Ravan, 1979.
'Glass House', in M. Banham et al. (ed.), *African Theatre Women*, Oxford: James Currey, 2002.
'The Return', unpublished play script, 2009.
'The Sacrifice of Kreli', in S. Gray (ed.), *Theatre One*, Johannesburg: Ad Donker, 1978.
'So What's New?', in Mda, *Four Plays*.
'So What's New?', in Perkins, *Black South African Women*.

Du Plessis, P. G. *Siener in die Suburbs*, Cape Town: Tafelberg, 1971.

Ellenbogen, N. 'Horn of Sorrow', in Graver, *Drama for a New South Africa*.

Farber, Y. *Molora*, based on *Oresteia* by Aeschylus, London: Oberon Books, 2008.

Farber, Y., with D. Kumalo. 'He Left Quietly', in *Theatre as Witness*, London: Oberon Books, 2008.

Farber, Y., with T. Mtshali-Jones. 'A Woman in Waiting', in *Theatre as Witness*, London: Oberon Books, 2008.

Foot-Newton, L. *Reach*, in Homann (ed.), *At this Stage*.
Tshepang, London: Oberon Books, 2005.

Fourie, C. J. 'Don Gxubane Onner die Boere', in *Vrygrond, Die Eend, and Don Gxubane Onner die Boere*, Cape Town: Tafelberg, 1994.

Fourie, C. J., and G. Mhlophe (eds.). *New South African Plays*, London: Aurora Metro Press, 2006.

Fugard, A. 'Blood Knot', in *Blood Knot and other Plays*, New York: Theatre Communications Group, 1987.
'Blood Knot', in *Selected Plays*, intro. D. Walder, Oxford University Press, 1987.
Boesman and Lena, Oxford University Press, 1973.
'The Coat', in Walder, *Township Plays*.
'The Coat', in Malan, *The Distance Remains*.
'Hello and Goodbye', in Hauptfleisch and Steadman (eds.), *South African Theatre*.
'Master Harold . . . and the Boys*, Oxford University Press, 1983.
'Master Harold – and the Boys*, New York: Penguin, 1984.
'No-Good Friday', in Walder, *Township Plays*.
People are Living There, Oxford University Press, 1970.

The Road to Mecca, New York: Theatre Communications Group, 1991.

'Statements after an Arrest under the Immortality Act', in *Statements: Three Plays*, Oxford University Press, 1974; New York: Theatre Communications Group, 1991.

Township Plays, ed. D. Walder, Oxford University Press, 1993.

'Victory', unpublished play script, 2007.

Fugard, A., J. Kani and W. Ntshona. *Statements: Three Plays [Sizwe Banzi is Dead, The Island* and *Statements after an Arrest under the Immorality Act]*, New York: Theatre Communications Group, 1986.

Govender, K. *Working Class Hero*, in N. Bose (ed.), *Beyond Bollywood and Broadway: Plays from the South Asian Diaspora*, Bloomington: Indiana University Press, 2009.

Govender, R. G. '1949', in *At the Edge and other Cato Manor Stories*, Pretoria: R. G. Govender and MANX, 1996.

The Lahnee's Pleasure, Johannesburg: Ravan, 1977.

The Lahnee's Pleasure, in N. Bose (ed.), *Beyond Bollywood and Broadway: Plays from the South Asian Diaspora*, Bloomington: Indiana University Press, 2009.

Graver, D. (ed.). *Drama for a New South Africa: Seven Plays*, Bloomington: Indiana University Press, 1999.

Graver, D., and L. Kruger. Synopsis of Bachaki Theatre's 'Top Down', *Maske und Kothurn* 35:1 (1989), 81–5.

Grootboom, P. 'Cards', unpublished play script, 2005.

Foreplay. Based on *Der Reigen* by A. Schnitzler, London: Theatre Royal Stratford East, 2009.

Grootboom, P., and P. Chweneyagae. *Relativity: Township Stories*, Johannesburg: Dung Beetle Dramas, 2006.

Gunner, L. 'Contaminations: BBC Radio and the Black Artist: Lewis Nkosi's "The Trial" and "We can't all be Martin Luther King"', in L. Gunner and L. Stiebel (eds.), *Still Beating the Drum: Critical Perspectives on Lewis Nkosi*, Johannesburg: Witwatersrand University Press, 2006, 51–66.

Handspring Puppet Company and W. Kentridge. 'Faustus in Africa' and 'Woyzeck on the Highveld', in *William Kentridge & Handspring Puppet Company: 15 Minute Excerpts from 4 Productions*, DVD, South Africa: Handspring Puppet Company, 2007.

Hauptfleisch, T., and I. Steadman (eds.). *South African Theatre*, Pretoria: HAUM, 1983.

Higginson, C. *Dream of the Dog*, in Homann, *At this Stage*.

Hobbs, S., et al. *Hillbrow/Dakar*, installation and walk documented at www.onair.co.za [Tour Guides for the Inner City], assessed 6 June 2011.

Homann, G. (ed.). *At this Stage: Plays from Post-Apartheid South Africa*, Johannesburg: Witwatersrand University Press, 2009.

Junction Avenue Theatre Company. *Love, Crime and Johannesburg*, Johannesburg: Witwatersrand University Press, 2000.

'Randlords and Rotgut', in M. Orkin (ed.), *At the Junction: Four Plays by the Junction Avenue Theatre Company*, Johannesburg: Witwatersrand University Press, 2001.

'Sophiatown', in Graver, *Drama for a New South Africa*.

Sophiatown, Cape Town: David Philip in association with Junction Avenue Press, 1988.

Kani, J. *Nothing but the Truth*, Johannesburg: Witwatersrand University Press, 2002.

Kani, J. (selector). *More Market Plays*, Johannesburg: Ad Donker, 1994.

Kavanagh, R. M. (ed.). *South African People's Plays*, London: Heinemann, 1981.

Kente, G. 'How Long?', unpublished play script, 1974.

'Sekunjalo' (Now is the Time), unpublished play script, 1985.

'Sikhalo' (Lament), unpublished play script, 1965.

'Too Late!', in Kavanagh, *South African People's Plays*.

Keogh, D., V. Cooke and N. Haysom. 'The Native who caused all the Trouble', in Kani (selector), *More Market Plays*.

Khulumani. 'The Story I am about to Tell', unpublished play script, 1997.

Kramer, D., and T. Petersen. *District Six – the Musical*, Cape Town: Blik Music, 1986.

Ghoema, Cape Town: Blik Music, 2005.

Kruger, L. *The Drama of South Africa: Plays, Pageants and Publics since 1910*, London: Routledge, 1999.

Magnet Theatre. 'Everyday, Every Year I Am Walking', unpublished play script, 2007.

'So Loep Ons . . . Nou Nog' (And so We go on), unpublished play script, 1994.

Louw, N. P. van Wyk. *Die Dieper Reg*, Cape Town: Nasionale Pers, 1947.

Die Pluimsaad Waai Ver, Cape Town: Human & Rousseau, 1972.

Mahomed, I. 'Cheaper than Roses', in Perkins, *Black South African Women*.

'Purdah', in Graver, *Drama for a New South Africa*.

Malan R. (ed.). *The Distance Remains and other Plays*, Cape Town: Oxford University Press, 1996.

Manaka, M. 'Egoli', in Davis, *Beyond the Echoes of Soweto*.

'Pula', in Gray, *Market Plays*.

'Pula', in Davis, *Beyond the Echoes of Soweto*.

Maponya, M. *Doing Plays for a Change*, Johannesburg: Witwatersrand University Press, 2001.

'Gangsters', in Ndlovu, *Woza Afrika!*.

'Umongikazi / The Nurse', in Perkins, *Black South African Women*.

Market Theatre. 'Call Me Woman', unpublished play script, 1977.

Matshikiza, T. 'Uxolo', unpublished cantata, 1956.

Mda, Z. 'The Bells of Amersfoort', in *Fools, Bells and the Habit of Eating*, Johannesburg: Witwatersrand University Press, 2002.

'Dark Voices Ring', in *Plays of Zakes Mda*.

'And the Girls in their Sunday Dresses', in *And the Girls in their Sunday Dresses and other Plays*, Johannesburg: Witwatersrand University Press, 1993.

'And the Girls in their Sunday Dresses', in Graver, *Drama for a New South Africa*.

'The Hill', in *Plays of Zakes Mda*.

'The Nun's Romantic Story', in Mda, *Four Plays*.

Plays of Zakes Mda, Johannesburg: Raven Press, 1990.

'We Shall Sing for the Fatherland', in *Plays of Zakes Mda*.

Mda, K. (compiler). *Four Plays*, Florida Hills: Vivlia, 1996.

Mhlophe, G., M. Vanrenen and T. Mtshali. 'Have you Seen Zandile?', in Malan, *The Distance Remains*.

'Have you Seen Zandile?', in Perkins, *Black South African Women*.

Mkhwane, B., and E. Pearson. 'A Boy Called Rubbish', unpublished play script.

Moodley, V. 'Got Green Chillies, Makoti', unpublished play script, 1994.

Mtshali, T. 'Golden Gloves', unpublished play script, 1996.

'Weemen', in Perkins, *Black South African Women*.

Mtwa, P., M. Ngema and B. Simon. *Woza Albert!*, London: Methuen, 1990.

'Woza Albert!', in M. Banham and J. Plastow (eds.), *Contemporary African Plays*, London: Methuen, 1999.

Naidoo, M. 'Flight from the Mahabarath', in Perkins, *Black South African Women*.

We 3 Kings, Durban: Asoka Theatre Publications, University of Durban Westville, 1992.

Ndhlovu, D. (ed.). *Woza Afrika!*, New York: Braziller, 1986.

Ngema, M. 'Asinamali!', in D. Ndlovu (ed.), *Woza Afrika!. Mbongeni Ngema's Sarafina!*, Cape Town: Nasou, 2006.

Nkosi, L. *Home and Exile*, 2nd edn, London: Longman, 1983.

The Rhythm of Violence, in G. Wellwarth (ed.), *Themes in Drama*, New York: T. Crowell, 1973.

Opperman, D. *Donkerland*, Cape Town: Tafelberg, 1996.

Môre is 'n Lang Dag and Die Teken, Cape Town: Tafelberg, 1986.

Pam-Grant, S., with D. J. Grant. 'Curl Up and Dye', in A. P. Barr (ed.), *Modern Anglophone Drama by Women*, New York: Peter Lang, 2007.

'Curl up and Dye', in S. Gray (ed.), *South African Plays*, London: Nick Hern, 1993.

Pather, J. 'Cargo', unpublished choreography, 2007.

'City Scapes', unpublished choreography 2006; video in possession of choreographer.

Perkins, K. A. (ed.). *Black South African Women: An Anthology of Plays*, London: Routledge, 1998.

Petersen, O., and D. Isaacs. *Joe Barber*, VHS, Cape Town: Djamaqua Productions, 2003.

Pillay, K. *Looking for Muruga*, Durban: Asoka, 1995.

Sekhabi, A. 'On My Birthday', unpublished play script, 1996.

Serpent Players. 'The Coat', *Classic* 2:3 (1967), 50–68.

'The Just', unpublished play script, 1972.

Shezi, M. 'Shanti', in Kavanagh, *South African People's Plays*.

Simon, B., and the Market Theatre cast. 'Born in the RSA' and 'Black Dog/Inj'emnyama', in *Born in the RSA: Four Workshopped Plays*, Johannesburg: Witwatersrand University Press, 1997.

Slabolepszy, P. 'Fordsburg's Finest', unpublished play script, 1998.

Mooi Street and other Moves, Johannesburg: Witwatersrand University Press, 1994.

'Mooi Street Moves', in Graver, *Drama for a New South Africa*.

Saturday Night at the Palace, Johannesburg: Ad Donker, 1985.

Small, A. *Kanna Hy Kô Hystoe*, Cape Town: Tafelberg, 1980. Translation by C. Lasker as *Kanna – He is Coming Home*, New York: Garland, 1992.

Smit, B. *Christine*, in Hauptfleisch and Steadman, *South African Theatre*.

Don Juan Onner die Boere, Cape Town: Human & Rousseau, 1967.

Putsonderwater, Cape Town: Tafelberg, 1979.

Die Verminktes, 2nd edn, Johannesburg: Perskor-uitgewery, 1976.

Themba, C. 'The Suit', in E. Patel (ed.), *The World of Can Themba*, Johannesburg: Raven, 1985.

Themba, C., and C. van Wyk (stage adaptor). *The Suit*, Johannesburg: Viva Books, 1994.

Uys, P-D. *Paradise is Closing Down and other Plays*, Harmondsworth: Penguin, 1989.

Selle Ou Storie, Johannesburg: Ad Donker, 1983.

Van Graan, M. 'Green Man Flashing', in Fourie and Mhlophe, *New South African Plays*.

Van Onselen, C. *The Seed is Mine: The Life of Kas Maine, African Sharecropper, 1894–1985*, Cape Town: David Philip, 1996.

Van Vuuren, R., and J. Cairns. 'Brother Number', unpublished play script, 2007.

Whyle, J. 'National Madness', in Gray, *Market Plays*.

'Rejoice Burning', in Fourie and Mhlophe, *New South African Plays*.

Witz, L. *Apartheid's Festival: Contesting South African's National Pasts*, Bloomington: Indiana University Press, 2003.

Workshop '71 Theatre Company. 'Survival', in Kavanagh, *South African People's Plays*.

'Uhlanga', unpublished play script, 1971.

28

The lyric poem during and after apartheid

DIRK KLOPPER

Poetics and politics of the lyric poem

Distinguished by the expression of personal observations and feelings, the lyric poem is an introspective and self-reflexive form that seeks to give direct voice to individual consciousness, articulating its singular patterns of cognitions, desires and doubts. This self-expressive impulse is closely associated with Romanticism, and specifically with the Romantic projection of the internal life of a subject who is estranged from existing political institutions and social structures, turns to nature and natural philosophy for alternative systems of meaning and value, and takes this subjective revolt as the very material of poetry, striving, against the limits of language itself, for spontaneous and sincere utterance. For all their conceptual and stylistic differences, Wordsworth's 'Tintern Abbey' and Shelley's 'Adonais' have in common the self-expressive impulse of a subject who seeks in nature an aesthetic understanding of the mind's symbolic relation with the real.

Whilst Romantic aspiration towards authentic individual expression has been subjected to the dislocations and ironic perspectives of modernism, it has continued to haunt modernism as an elusive possibility, a transitory achievement of consciousness, even where, as in Eliot's 'Waste Land', the myths that inform western culture are invoked in fragmentary form to constitute an aesthetic of loss. A more systematic challenge to Romantic subjectivity was formulated by late twentieth-century literary theory, specifically poststructuralist deconstructions of the expressive self and post-Marxist exposures of the ideological investments of poetic discourse. The latter, in particular, was influential in determining attitudes to the lyric poem in the apartheid period. During the political struggle of the 1970s and 1980s, a poetics of resistance drew on post-Marxist thought in claiming, as Jeremy Cronin does in his reading of Campbell's poem 'Rounding the Cape', that the focus on self-expression in the South African lyric poem does not elude ideology so much as mask it (Cronin, 'Turning Around').

Undoubtedly, the South African lyric poem in English emerges out of the tradition of Romantic and post-Romantic self-expression in British literature, and its early development adheres closely to the forms, styles and habits of mind introduced by English-language immigrants of the nineteenth century, a poetics derived from shifting practices within English literature, exemplified, early in the century, by the picturesque attentiveness to local detail found, for example, in the poetry of Wordsworth, and, later in the century, by the commanding, even imperial viewpoint found, for example, in the poetry of Tennyson. Speaking the language of western intellectual culture, and projecting its systems of understanding, the settler poet unsurprisingly looked to the British literary tradition for an understanding of the subject's place in the world.

Nevertheless, from the outset, in Thomas Pringle's *Poems Illustrative of South Africa* (1834) as much as in Francis Carey Slater's *Dark Folk and other Poems* (1935), there is a tension between the metropolitan origins of the writing, its European forms and styles, and the geographical, historical and social contexts of its enunciation. This tension creates a crisis of authority in the South African lyric poem, leading, with gathering momentum since the 1950s, to an internal questioning of its poetics.

So the South African lyric poem in English did not suddenly, in the 1970s, find itself challenged by the conceptual rigours of literary theory or the political exigencies of the anti-apartheid struggle. It was challenged from the outset not only by the uneasy articulation of its literary language and tradition with the social and natural landscapes of South Africa, but also by its status as the language of political and cultural power, the language of British imperial rule. Through its rapid globalisation in the nineteenth and twentieth centuries, the commanding status of English has survived the end of empire and has continued as a dominant language in South Africa, despite Afrikaner nationalism on the one hand and African nationalism on the other. Certainly, Afrikaans and African-language literatures have had an ambiguous relationship with English-language literature, not only because global English threatens minority languages, but also because English is the repository of an extensive, highly developed, influential and seductive body of literary works. The literary traditions of Afrikaans and of African languages have cultivated an identity independent of that of the British tradition, following different trajectories and articulating different concerns, insisting, in their different ways, upon their difference.

Following defeat of the Boer republics and fears among Afrikaans speakers of a loss of cultural independence, early Afrikaans poetry of the post Anglo-Boer War period was employed as vehicle of an emergent Afrikaner nationalist identity. Even in the introspective turn of the poetry from the 1930s onwards, associated with writers such as N. P. van Wyk Louw, D. J. Opperman, Elizabeth Eybers and Ingrid Jonker, and later Breyten Breytenbach and Antjie Krog, there is not so much a departure from Afrikaner identifications as a pursuit of these in subjective terms, as the life-world of the Afrikaner (see above, Chapters 13, 15 and 21). Like the English lyric poem, the Afrikaans lyric poem is broadly concerned with individual consciousness and its apprehension of the natural world, its intersubjective relation with others and its metaphysical self-questionings. Nevertheless, while its concerns resonate with the English lyrical tradition, it runs parallel to this tradition rather than entering into dialogue with it. The two traditions are aware of one another, but whereas English poets were grappling with their split heritage, growing increasingly conscious of a disarticulation between the European language they used and the world they inhabited, Afrikaans poets were developing a language that was increasingly severed from the language of its European origins, becoming less like Dutch and more like an indigenous language articulating a local sensibility.

Likewise, the lyrical form of expression in African literature is different, despite the use of English by its exponents (see Chapters 16 and 29). The lyrical voice in African literature draws on the English lyrical tradition, but also seeks to articulate a distinctive African world-view. The poetry might invoke a Romantic discourse of subject and nature, but it uses this discourse not to express a private vision but to assert an ancestral right to the land and a communal identification with it, as in H. I. E. Dhlomo's 'Valley of a Thousand Hills' (1941) and Mazisi Kunene's *The Ancestors and the Sacred Mountain* (1982). The relation to the land as mediated by an African sensibility, a sensibility conscious of itself as African and cognisant of the ancestral world, is also evident in more recent work, such as Mzi Mahola's *Strange Things* (1994).

In short, the South African English lyric poem may be voiced in a dominant language and informed by a substantial tradition, but its purchase on local literary sensibility has nevertheless been uncertain. The next section discusses how this poetic form is seen by scholarship to project a split between metropolitan affiliations and local identifications. Whilst an ideological criticism might argue that the South African lyric poem in English is therefore an inauthentic literary form, such is not the drift of the argument pursued here.

The intention, rather, is to provide an analytical framework from which the poetic form of the South African lyric poem in English may be seen to engage with the very problematic of authenticity.

Imperialism, double consciousness and authenticity

The post-Second World War period of the 1950s and the liberation struggle of the 1980s were periods of particularly acute political crises for the South African English writer, with the 1950s ushering in a period of Afrikaner nationalist rule and the 1980s witnessing the climax of African nationalist resistance. Unable fully to identify with either Afrikaner or African nationalist ideals, the South African English writer used the lyric poem as a vehicle to imagine an alternative order of existence, located not in nation but in nature, not in political relations but in interpersonal relations, an order of existence apprehended through a visionary epistemology that employs the associative logic of metaphor rather than the analytical logic of disputation.

In his paper 'On Being Present where you are' (1976), delivered at the Poetry '74 conference at the University of Cape Town, Guy Butler identifies what he describes as an existential and political dilemma, a disjunction between the white English-speaking South African poet's identification, on the one hand, with the local landscapes and communities, and, on the other hand, his affiliation to western cultural history. This disjunction is evident, says Butler, in the twentieth-century poetry of South African writers such as Francis Carey Slater, Roy Campbell, William Plomer, Ralph Currey and Anthony Delius, as well as in his own work. But while they may be writing in 'the imperial twilight', these poets are nevertheless 'harbingers', he says, 'of the African dawn'. However, they are set apart from the Africa they celebrate, as 'their time-scale', says Butler, 'is essentially European'. For Butler, the problem is that of different histories, ways in which 'the various communities in our society are not present to each other because they are not present in the same history' (p. 95).

The disjunction between local experience and metropolitan structures of thought is seen by Butler to create a split consciousness. The challenge, for him, is to learn to speak the language of the land and its people, to compel the material and social environment to yield an inclusive symbolic in which the African context and the Europe inheritance merges. This requires openness, receptivity to the here and now. Poets who exemplify this receptivity, says Butler, are 'startled' into the 'miraculous present' through 'someone or something which is suddenly, nakedly present to them' (p. 96). These are moments of epiphany, visionary moments, when encounters with natural landscapes, or with the people of the land, assume an emblematic significance.

But even as Butler was presenting this view of the liberating power of the visionary imagination as a solution to an existential and political impasse, at the same conference he stood accused of epitomising a cultural theory that is oblivious of its own discourse of authority and control. In his paper 'The Coloniser: A Critique of the English South African Culture Theory' (1976), Mike Kirkwood argues that the double consciousness Butler speaks of does not issue in a merging of Africa and Europe but in an assertion of European cultural hegemony over the African. He maintains that double consciousness requires not synthesis but transcendence, and transcendence comes when the coloniser relinquishes cultural and political authority over the colonised. The coloniser, says Kirkwood, ceases to be a coloniser when the colonised ceases to be the colonised. He uses the term 'Butlerism' to identify an essentially conservative English South African culture theory, which he says will be overcome only through 'an art for liberation' (p. 131), one that involves not merely an art technique but also a technique of living (p. 132).

Critique of the South African lyric poem in English continued well into the 1980s. J. M. Coetzee's pronouncements have probably been most influential in determining how this poetry is now read. Coetzee similarly sees Butler as failing to reconcile the disjunction between a local identification and an imperial upbringing, saying, in his essay 'Reading the South African Landscape' (1988), that Butler may treat 'the relation of the poet to his landscape historically' (p. 169) but he ends up merely playing out 'themes from the English tradition' against 'an African backdrop' (p. 171). A more radical response to what Coetzee describes as 'the burden of finding a home in Africa for a consciousness formed in and by a language whose history lies on another continent' is to eschew what he calls 'the prospect position' employed by earlier South African poets and to opt instead for 'an unsettled habitation *in* the landscape' (p. 173). The distinction Coetzee draws between the complacency of the prospect position and the unsettlement of an embedded habitation is apt but somewhat dualistic in conception. Elsewhere, Coetzee suggests that tension between distance and immanence, generality and specificity, outside and inside, characterises any attempt at invoking the subject's place in the world. In his early novels, for example, which are set in the South African hinterland, immanence, conceived as a merging of subject and world, is shown to be unthinkable, as such merging would entail the collapse of the very psychic structures that enable separation and identity, a fate contemplated by Magda in *In the Heart of the Country*.

Coetzee cites the work of Sydney Clouts to exemplify how poetry might inhabit the South African landscape in an unsettled kind of way. Certainly, there is a persistent sense in this poetry that the world is resistant to language, but there is also the sense that it is language that renders the world present to consciousness. For example, the poem 'After the Poem' describes the tenuousness but also the necessity of this relation if there is to be any consciousness of the world at all. The poetry may be more oblique in its representational strategies than is characteristic of South African lyric poetry, but it is not exceptional in its projection of a consciousness located uneasily between perception and its object, between the idea and its representation, between word and world.

Lionel Abrahams's poem 'Place', for example, may be more conventional in its representational strategies than Clouts's 'After the Poem', but it similarly renders possession of the landscape uncertain. The location which the poem describes is a material place, a mine dump in Johannesburg, but also a place of language. It is a geographical location as well as the location of a poetry reading where two eastern European writers, Herbert of Warsaw and Holub of Prague, are brought 'strangely home' to a place described as having a 'very local savour / . . . thin, durable as tin'.

When the relation between self and world is rendered suddenly strange, by social revolution but also by the revolutionary potential of a poetic language that seeks to constitute the world afresh, the uneasy location of consciousness is made visible, and the problematic of authentic being is reopened for negotiation. The remainder of this chapter will focus on the way in which lyric poetry of the apartheid and post-apartheid periods is framed by the problematic of an authentic South African consciousness. If the lyric poem is fundamentally concerned with consciousness, with the observations and feelings of the self in relation to the world, then a perceived disjunction in consciousness between self and world – that is, a crisis of authenticity – would necessarily register significantly in the poetry. Critical scholarship suggests that the problematic of authenticity was a salient concern of the lyric poem in the disruptive context of the apartheid period. It is no less of a concern, though, in the post-apartheid period, where the question of selfhood, of what constitutes an authentic way of being in South Africa, remains unsettled.

Taking the problematic of authenticity as a primary motif of the lyric poem during and after apartheid, the chapter will trace the elaboration of this motif from the 1950s to the present, through reference to four groupings of poets arranged approximately in chronological order. The question of authenticity is taken up explicitly in the poetry of Guy Butler and Patrick Cullinan, where it is explored primarily in relation to consciousness of place and of family. In the poetry of Ruth Miller and Douglas Livingstone, geography and personal history remain entangled, but authenticity is now addressed specifically with reference to the biological world, especially the place of the human in relation to the animal. The sense of disjunction, if anything, is even more acute in the poetry of Stephen Watson and Kelwyn Sole, where personal relationships and attachments to place, which might have provided some purchase on the world, are rendered ambivalent and tenuous, and give way to post-Romantic disenchantment and melancholia. The discussion concludes with the poetry of Joan Meteleikamp and Rustum Kozain, who render the intimate spaces of gender and race especially visible, with the subject emerging, in this post-apartheid moment, as an uncanny doubling of personal and political histories.

These poets exemplify a concern with consciousness that is clearly evident also in a number of other poets writing in the apartheid and post-apartheid periods. Aside from Sydney Clouts and Lionel Abrahams, there are, for example, Peter Horn, Tatamkulu Afrika, Don Maclennan and Ingrid de Kok. This chapter does not aim, however, at a comprehensive survey of the field. Rather, it focuses on representative viewpoints within it and attempts to provide a sense of the relations between these various positions.

Ancestral sites: Guy Butler and Patrick Cullinan

Given Guy Butler's (1918–2001) preoccupation with the contribution European culture has made to South Africa, it is not surprising that his poetry should frequently invoke the figure of the pioneer. In the early poem 'The Last Trekker', the figure is generalised, drawn from the imaginary of the imperial romance, projecting a solitary self at one with nature and at odds with modernity. Celebrating the spirit of Dutch settlers who left the domestication of the Cape to explore the interior of the land, the poem describes the historical anomaly of a willed reversion from settlement to unsettlement, seeing this as an heroic expression of personal independence, a cutting loose from conventional social practice and a sovereign exercise of power. 'He is a great reaction', declares the speaker, 'keeping his freedom unconquered'. Even in contemporary times, in the disposition of descendants inhabiting the 'waste places' of the land, he is to be found 'evading the established law, the well-worn road / and the new machine economy'.

In later poems such as 'Sweetwater' and 'Farmer', the pioneer figure is particularised, most commonly in the person of an elderly relative or acquaintance, more especially a farmer. 'Sweetwater' provides a portrait of an uncle who represents an older rural order, where the individual engaged directly with the elements, took sustenance from the earth and exhibited a reverential attitude to the land. The poem employs dialogue to invoke the living context of the uncle's life, describing him leaving the farm in his old car with his family to attend a church bazaar and stopping en route at a new causeway over the Kwaai River to drink, as he had done as a boy, from the stream, leaving the young speaker to wonder 'to what stream I could take whom / and kneel like that, and say: / Taste how sweet it is'. In 'Farmer', the rural figure is not a beloved relative but a somewhat coarse and unloving neighbour, severe in his dealings with family and workers, but who nevertheless evinces a close and even tender bond with the land. The speaker acknowledges the dangers of presenting a man such as this as either a caricature of the reactionary settler-type or a sentimental figure of rural simplicity, but observing him on his veranda gazing out at the veld, the speaker reflects how the farmer had 'taken all that he saw into himself', absorbing 'the distance through his eyes', establishing a relationship that, from the point of view of the speaker's 'public, urban world', seemed remarkably 'real'.

These poems suggest that while the pioneer may, from the contemporary perspective, appear uncouth and bigoted, he nevertheless inhabits his world in a legitimate way, largely through an intimate relationship with the land. The formative influence of landscape is evident also in poems that deal with Butler's childhood in Cradock, particularly the mountainous terrain around the town, his early experience of this area comprising the grammar of his existence. In 'Cradock Mountains', the ancient abiding presence of these always visible masses of rock and scrub keep dispassionate watch over the rural existence of farming and hunting that defined the speaker's early life. The sensual experience of youth is figured as a kind of love, where, 'after the dizzy, blinding, first dive of a kiss', the speaker surfaces 'gasping' to find the mountain 'floating remote, impassive as dreadnoughts through the winter air'. The imagery of a battleship says something about the imaginary of the displaced European child in Africa, with his love of the history of European wars, but also points ahead to the young adult's enlistment in the South African contingent of the British Army during the Second World War. The poem 'Homecoming' describes the speaker's return to the landscape of his childhood after the war and the resurgence of Afrikaner nationalism it precipitated, having suffered loss of innocence and faith, a heart 'fogged with lies' and the 'open hand' become 'a fist'.

Increasingly in the poetry, landscape is recognised also as land. Alongside the transcendent visionary attachment to place of the earlier poems, derived from a poetics of the beautiful and the sublime, there is another kind of attachment evident in the later poems, an attachment derived from history, from the intertwining of personal lived experience and rival communal experiences. In the poem 'From Elegy II', competing historical claims to the land between Englishman and Afrikaner are rendered meaningless by a sudden awareness, in the presence of an anonymous grave, of the temporary and solitary condition of the self, while in the poem 'Grave Robbers' the dead Xhosa pastor encountered by the young boys haunts the living, representing the return of a disremembered history, a return of the repressed.

Butler's best-known work is probably the clutch of poems that deal most directly with the ambivalent consciousness of the European in Africa. The poem 'Myths' presents a symbolic event in childhood that heralds the end of a sense of integration with the domestic settler world in which he has been reared and the beginning of a sense of separateness and unbelonging. The killing of the snake at the beginning of the poem transforms the youngster's world, bringing the African landscape close and vivid while rendering the landscape of the homestead alien and uncertain. Caught as he is in a double consciousness marked by sensory awareness of the African landscape and intellectual awareness of the inherited English cultural landscape, the possibility of a reconciliation of these contending continents is revealed in a moment of vision at the end of the poem, when the 'ghosts' that books had put in his 'brain' slip from behind his eyes 'to take on flesh, the sometimes curious flesh / of an African incarnation'. The division between Africa and Europe is imagined in 'Home Thoughts' as a struggle between sensuous Dionysus and intellectual Apollo, with the reconciliation of these ancient foes projected as a form of psychic reintegration.

Patrick Cullinan (1932–2011) echoes many of Butler's concerns, though his subject position – as a writer of a younger generation who grew up in urban Pretoria rather than in rural Cradock – is different. Like Butler, Cullinan evinces awareness of imperial history and the imperial perspective. His attitude to history, however, is more detached. In the poem 'François le Vaillant', Cullinan returns to late eighteenth-century South African history, sketching a portrait of this humane and idealistic Enlightenment figure who travelled in the Cape in 1780–5 (see Chapter 8). Le Vaillant reflects in the course of the poem that his account of his travels sought to establish truth in the place of the fabulous. He acknowledges now, in old age, that this form of empirical truth – which makes 'a country real, a normal place', and shows that 'men in skins' move in a 'certain landscape', and are 'men like us, have names' – may nevertheless constitute a betrayal of what actually exists. He suggests that things may be different from what we routinely see. They may be other, as in a landscape rendered fluid in moonlight.

Like Butler, Cullinan is concerned with what it means to be native, and similarly employs the trope of the disjunctive position of the European inhabitant. His sense of the significance of Africa, however, is different, arising from the political context of the 1970s rather than the 1950s. The poem 'Exiles' treats the aspiration to being native ironically, with the belief that intimate knowledge could be attained from a position of privilege and power revealed as paternalist. 'We knew them well enough', says the speaker, 'to want their good'. Nevertheless, the experience of attachment, to land if not to people, remains as a formative experience, an internal topography, like the night the headlights of the truck driving through long grass revealed an 'Africa within' as much as an 'Africa beyond'.

Cullinan also writes of his family, though with less sympathy. The patriarchs are moneyed autocrats who instil obedience and fear rather than affection and respect, and inhabit urban centres of commercial power as opposed to the rural Karoo of feudal relations. In the poem 'The Billiard Room', the conflict between father and son is attached to a specific location, which contains tokens of power of the father and his caste and where 'the cues glitter like weapons' and war memorabilia of 'steel and brass' comprise 'records of dead encounter'. Standing by a half-opened window, the grown son recalls 'unbreaking love, unfinished war'.

In 'Sir Tom', the grandfather, a wealthy autocrat who made his money in diamonds, is pictured by his grandson in demented old age, tormented by delusion, pathetically dependent on his servants, oppressive towards family members, cruel with children. Enduring the monthly Sunday luncheon in a room in which all 'style' and 'energy' were 'broken' by this decrepit and perverted power, the boy witnesses the old man's collapse into 'the awful nonsense raving' of hell 'seething in his head'.

The locations Cullinan invokes are urban, apprehended not as visionary ground of being but as sites of political contestation. The poem 'Johannesburg' invokes the city as an existence within which an uneasy love resides, the beauty of flowers turned to putrefaction, domesticity become violence, the heat of summer a flame of revolution invading the suburbs. Even when the natural world is directly evoked, history is present, as in the poem 'A Word in the Ear', where the visible interlinking of animal and human worlds around orchard and house is mirrored by a mingling of living bodies and the spiritual presences of the dead.

Concerned with a thematic of belonging not unlike that of Butler's post world war generation, Cullinan's poems nevertheless speak from a different place and moment. The speaker does not evince the sense of a retiring, settled rural order but a commanding, affluent, restless urban order. He resolutely maintains an ironic distance from notions of kinship with family and land while nevertheless exploring the familiar terrain of the displaced European consciousness in Africa. Reading Butler and Cullinan alongside one another, one has the sense of a poetics that stretches from Wordsworth's evocations of the spirit of place to W. H. Auden's evocations of the consciousness of place.

A biological perspective: Ruth Miller and Douglas Livingstone

The physical presence and iconographic force of Africa is vividly present in the 1960s poetry of Ruth Miller (1919–69). Although she writes from the suburbs of Johannesburg, and her voice evinces a metropolitan sensibility, Miller nevertheless projects a strong connection with the land and its animals, presenting them in a sparse, imagist style that is at times brutally direct.

The exploration of an inner landscape, an 'Africa within', is dramatically performed in Miller's work. The journey to the interior of the land, the principal theme of early South African writing, is undertaken in the modern world not by wagon but by mechanised transport. Where the emphasis fell earlier on external features, on details of geography, animals and plants, it now falls, in Miller's poem 'Long Journey', on the inner aspect of travel, the distances covered and locations discovered within the mind. The trip from Cape Town to Johannesburg is distinguished not by scenic interest but by a sense of the indeterminacy of a land that cannot be deciphered, a land that draws the speaker into the incertitude of her own apprehension of life and evokes a vague sense of something malevolent, fateful, where yellow rivers gather the provinces into a 'shrivelled pouch' within which 'cunning bones of witchcraft', the inhabitants of the estranging land, are seen to 'Shake and stir'.

The land is engaged through the geography of evolution, one in which the subject is identified with a history that is older than the clash of cultures. In the poem 'Pebble', the core of self is not expansive spirit but irreducible stone, corroded by life to inert material existence, devoid of desire and meaning. The poem 'Sterkfontein' invokes the underground caves that contain the remains of the earliest hominids, who are seen to communicate with the living from within the earth, connecting past and present.

In several poems the relation to the land is mediated through the emblematic figure of an animal, typically described in an unpredictable environment where survival is tenuous. 'The Floating Island' uses the image of a frieze of terrified buck, stranded on a small piece of land torn from the banks of the Zambezi River in flood and hurtled down to the Falls, to invoke the displaced and doomed European in Africa. 'Indigenous' portrays drought and renewal as perennial symbols of both the inhospitality and the promise of the land, where scorpions and snakes seek out the shade of an ancient fig and the land remembers 'Before the wagons' creak the scream of spears, / Before the spears, the formidable silences'. The poem 'Sea Idyll' opens with a beach at sunset where 'flushed waves' break 'heart-breaking' on the sand. A landscape conventionally associated with an aesthetics of harmony yields suddenly images of disfigurement and death, 'a black blind / Dog with its eyes white stone' and a 'smashed seagull, one headlong half / In a dull spray, the other / Spreading in the speechless dark / Of its dry blood'.

In Miller's poems, European culture continues, however elusively, to inhabit the poetic consciousness as heritage, even though, as in the poem 'Travellers', this heritage is accessible only as tourist destination for the displaced white South African. As both the origin and the destination of European culture, the Acropolis is presented to the eye of the speaker as a timeless point of reference, an ideal glimpsed from a distant aeroplane window, indistinguishable from model replicas found in curio shops. The poetry continues to register a metropolitan consciousness aware of its essential estrangement from the world, confessional in a way that was to characterise metropolitan poetry of the 1960s, particularly the work of female writers such as Anne Sexton.

Miller's poems reveal a European sensibility even as they invoke images of Africa. They eschew the actual historical encounter between Europe and Africa in favour of a timeless biological process of territorial aggressivity. In contrast, Douglas Livingstone's (1932–96) poems, which likewise focus on the biological, bring to these concerns an historical awareness of the colonial perspective and locate the South African versions of it with ironic detachment. The poem 'Sjambok' describes how this whip of 'plaited leather terminating / in a single thong', which used to be employed as instrument of subjugation of man and beast, and to which countless tales of colonial heroism and horror are attached, is now reproduced as a kitsch tourist ornament at the Victoria Falls and any other 'tourist trap'. 'The Heritage' draws attention to a 'psychic break' that occurred between the rural past and the urban present, the colonial world of territorial expansion and warfare versus the modern world of managerial control, institutional healthcare and safe recreational pursuits, and sees in the past a repository of myths of indigenisation for the displaced European.

In poems such as these Livingstone's poetic voice is masculine, chauvinistic even, as he seeks to articulate the attitudes and speech habits of a colonialism driven by the will to tame the wilderness, an unsentimental evolutionist imperative. This evolutionist notion, of existence as struggle and survival, is evident also in the more overt nature poetry. Like Miller, Livingstone portrays an animal world governed by instincts and driven by a struggle to survive. But while Miller produces a fiercely emotional and visceral bond with the South African landscape, and renders it as a disturbing site of biological struggle, Livingstone is more detached than she is, more self-possessed, and projects the voice of the curious naturalist, an observer whose emotional participation is slightly more distant, at once compassionate and dispassionate.

In the poem 'Gentling a Wildcat', the savagery of the wild is made present one night in the bush, when the speaker discovers a wildcat lying in moonlight on a heap of dusty leaves, 'open from chin to loins; / lower viscera missing; truncated tubes / and bitten-off things protruding'. The wildcat had been caught in mid-confinement by a jackal, which had disembowelled her to get to the unborn kittens. The speaker is made vividly aware of the cycles of death and renewal in nature, the 'lifetimes of claws, kaleidoscopes; / moon-claws, sun-claws, teeth after death, / certainly both at mating and birth', and sits with the cat, tentatively and then more assuredly gentling her with his hand. Calmed, the cat allows the speaker to 'ease her claws, the ends of the battle', and to pull off 'the trapped and rancid flesh' of her adversary before she dies.

The poetic voice characteristically seeks unity with the world, at times through the vestiges of an evolutionary history contained in the subject at a microbiological level. 'Reciprocals' shows how the rhythms of the human body are mirrored in the rhythms of nature, in the rise and fall of ocean tides, suggestive of heartbeat and breathing. Such reciprocity, governed by lunar influence, provides intimation of reciprocity between material nature and the intellectual and affective orders, between matter and electromagnetic waves, 'the inhalation and the exhalation of felt but unseen spirit'. 'An Evolutionary Nod to God' describes how the vestiges of evolutionary history are carried within a self who apprehends the failures and successes of natural selection, its 'unstrung mutations' and 'random nightmares', but also perhaps an 'enigmatic principle', a kind of shaping spirit of the universe.

The Africa Livingstone invokes in many poems is a mythic Africa of magic and wilderness, imaginatively richer than contemporary African modernity impoverished by the globalisation of instrumentalist reason. 'The Sleep of my

Lions' employs an elegiac but also mischievous voice to decry the destruction of the ancient world by contemporary progress, domestication and mechanisation, the 'violation' of the old 'pastory' and ensuing diminishment of experience, of 'quagga' and 'dodo', 'moon-rites and rain-dances'. In 'Eland' the hidden cave containing rock paintings evokes the ancient Bushman world of human and animal relations, of shamanistic practices and rites of passage, but also calls to mind the history of colonial brutality and injustice that all but wiped out these first people of southern Africa. As homage to their inviolate memory, the least the speaker can do, he says, is to keep this cave hid, 'mounting no sign and exacting no due, / having called, stroked and dreamed into eland'.

Livingstone's training as a microbiologist confers on his animal and nature poems a precision of observation, an understanding of relevant ecological contexts and an unsentimental sense of the reduced scale of human history in relation to biological time. In this it echoes the kinds of concerns found in the poetry of Ted Hughes. The place of the human in nature has been a consistent preoccupation of the South African lyric poem, in Butler's evocation of a rural community as much as in Miller's sense of an elemental life. But nature also inhabits the cities, and Cullinan evokes its somewhat different presence in the urban context. As the poetry becomes increasingly urban-based, nature as ground of being remains a powerful motif, but the European involvement with Africa has shifted from a relationship with land to a relationship with its people, to the terrain, that is, of political struggle.

Livingstone refused to engage in what he called 'Polit-Lit', saying, in his essay '"Africa within us" . . . ?' that modern literature has not changed the heart of one politician, and that the function of this literature is merely to demonstrate that 'One's Heart is in the Right Place' (p. 142). But pressure to make the right kinds of political statements in the literature of the struggle years was intense, with the very existence of the lyric poem as medium of subjective consciousness put into question.

Melancholic landscapes: Stephen Watson and Kelwyn Sole

Like Livingstone, Stephen Watson (1954–2011) resisted pressure to write poetry that was overtly political, focusing instead on his immediate environment of Cape Town and the Cape peninsula. Whilst this landscape is minutely anatomised and carefully described, it is infused with subjectivity, with affect, with personal history. Landscape emerges here as an ambivalent presence. On the one hand it is rendered atmospherically bleak and culturally impoverished, a landscape bereft of history. In the poem 'Thinness' the absence of a sense of fullness in the physical environment, the poverty that inheres in daily activities and language, confer a kind of inconsequentiality on life, an intuition of inevitable disappointment and ultimate meaninglessness. This was evident even to the 5-year old, when the speaker first intimated, he says, that 'there was no point', that this desolation was there already, 'and would return / in the skeletal cloud, the diluted skies, in the air-thinned blues of wind years on'. On the other hand the landscape is vivid and elemental, a landscape of rock and wind and sea that returns the self to an embodied sensory experience. 'The Sea Close By' presents the immediacy of the experience of summer light and heat to which the body responds and which it assimilates as a memory of itself, of its sensory responsiveness, its being in the world and of the world, its desire to live 'in the salt of its own blood'.

In Watson's poetry this desire is performed within the geographical coordinates of an intensely realised physical environment, creating an intimate emotional connection between subject and place, an entanglement of psyche and topography. When Watson writes about family, it is the psychoanalytic family that interests him rather than the ancestral family. 'Ties of Blood' presents this domestic sphere of family, this site of 'crazy-paving', 'tea-cosies' and shabby festive entertainment as the source of passions that animate the soul, however devoid of pleasure the family and demeaning its struggle for existence. That which prevails in the family, says the speaker, 'these ties of sadness', are stronger and more desperate 'than all the other ties of blood'. The poem 'In a Nearly Empty Hotel Bar' employs details of location, of interior decor and exterior features of landscape, as signifiers of a meaning that remains elusive, an experience that exists beyond the reach of language, a desire that cannot be fulfilled, an absence sensed by the lovers as they gaze out on the garden of the hotel, 'where the most that could be seen, in the playground's clearing, / was a swing that moved, its seat empty, ropes barely trembling / in the grey'.

The meaning of nature increasingly becomes an explicit concern in the poetry, with the vision of a transfiguring presence of the earth giving way to a vision of its destruction. 'The Mountain Light at Kromrivier' offers a detailed evocation of the numinous quality of evening light in autumn in the Cederberg mountains, a light in which 'all things are stilled / into their own' and which returns the observing self to its own presence in and of the earth. 'After Reading *The End of Nature*' offers a contrasting vision of the sacramental bounty of nature on the one hand and its imminent ruination through the mechanical and industrial on the other. As in many of Watson's poems, this one explores simultaneously the relation between language, presence and loss. The mind, like the seeping rain outside the window, falls and is pulled deep down, still feeling 'to reach a place, a world, that's not yet left the earth behind, / to find those words still left, that haven't left the earth behind'.

In contrast, the landscapes of Kelwyn Sole's (1951–) poems are characteristically the terrain of a politics of the domestic, a politics of the meaning of home in a context where home is rendered uncertain and the subject unsettled. 'Love Poem' offers an ironic projection of the Romantic impulse to seek a home in the wilderness, invoking not the solitary splendour of sparsely inhabited land and confrontation with a sublime other, but the forlorn ennui of a lonely, marginal and bored life, where the speaker welds poems under a vast sky that 'mocks' him, and where he gets drunk and falls 'monotonously' in love. 'Home' takes a voyeuristic look at the suburban life of a neighbour who works at creating a secure and insular existence divorced from the surrounding urban contestations of the liberation struggle, painting gutters, sawing planks, hammering nails, while at evening, when the house curtains are drawn, sirens begin to 'stammer' and riot vans 'nudge' the footsteps of 'the lost / in the street'.

But there are also poems that have a broad compass, invoking a sprawling geography of history. 'Another Version of Melancholia' provides an ironic response to Watson's melancholic invocations of the Cape Town urban environment, satirising the poetic voice Watson employs and projecting it as petulantly self-aggrandising. 'Momentoes for a Birthday' juxtaposes the intimate embrace of lovers and the proximate violence of the streets during political unrest, the anguish and anger of the people out there in the 'dove-like pulse' of the night 'beating soft'.

Despite the imperatives of revolutionary change, landscapes retain the signifiers of cultural memory, even if the meanings of this culture are more ambivalent than anticipated. Rather than pay reverential tribute to Olive Schreiner, 'A Visit to Schreiner's Grave' satirises such invocation of iconic loyalty. The sarcophagus on top of Buffelskop, a mountain outside Cradock, remains a destination of literary pilgrimage, but the girlfriend treats the speaker's high-minded declarations of belonging to land and literary tradition with appropriate irreverence, covering him with dry winter grass as a symbol, she, says, 'to enclose the meaning of your poem', the one he wishes to write to commemorate the experience. 'Presence' employs the voice of an Herero subject to invoke the mythology of the primordial tree which gave birth to the first man and his wife, and uses this invocation to ruminate on both the otherness of God and his proximity with the human, so that looking for God, he will appear as a pool of water in the Namib desert, and then transform into a mirage in which what you see is 'your own face'.

Watson may eschew direct political statement, evident in Sole's poetry, but his poems are as incisive in capturing the incertitude of the European consciousness in postcolonial Africa. The challenge posed by the political struggle to European cultural codes does not escape Watson. He simply seeks, more single-mindedly perhaps than any of his contemporaries, to retain the reflective potential of the lyric voice and aims at an intertwining of word and world, reaching beyond the immediate political context to embrace an aesthetic vision, in the manner of poets he admires such as Czesław Miłosz. Sole, on the other hand, seeks rather to speak directly to the political context and to show its impact on the personal life.

The return of history: Joan Metelerkamp and Rustum Kozain

From the 1950s to the 1990s white South African English poetry was concerned with the problematic of an authentic South African consciousness. This problematic continues to inform South African lyric poetry of the post-apartheid era. Nevertheless, the contrast between a European intellectual tradition and an African experiential world is no longer as stark as it appeared to Butler and Cullinan. Nor do poets necessarily turn to the African wild to affirm a biological connection with place, as in the work of Miller and Livingstone. Like their contemporaries Watson and Sole, Joan Meterlerkamp (1956–) and Rustum Kozain (1966–) entertain a complex sense of their lived relationship with Africa, and specifically the way in which history, body and place converge.

Metelerkamp's 'A New Language' is characteristic of the way in which much of her poetry takes the form of a seemingly unpremeditated and random musing, as if the reader is privy to the speaker's innermost thoughts. The poem takes up the motif of a return to the land and interweaves this with a sense of the proximity of childhood, with the speaker recalling, from her newly obtained home, 'a tenant's cottage' located 'up against the mountains', how, as a girl, she became suddenly aware of 'the way the wind blows, / the cricket, / the fly, / the cattle in the heat, / the trapped bee on the pane'. But the return to the countryside of her childhood 'is no returning', she says, and has no clear meaning other than 'something / like instinct', an endeavour perhaps to imagine 'a new way of speaking, way of being'.

Kozain's 'This Carting Life' uses the image of an archival search through boxes in the British Museum as a form of remembrance of the speaker's imagined Khoisan ancestry. Kneeling in the dust of the museum's base-ment before an unopened box, on a 'pilgrimage' of sorts into a colonial past enshrined in this national institution, the speaker imagines what the box might hold. Could the box perhaps contain the shears and whetstone his father, an itinerant Khoikhoi sheep-shearer in the dry farmlands of the Karoo, had lost somewhere on the road? Or could the box, more traumatically, contain the decapitated heads of a band of San who had been massacred by a colonial commando sent out to exterminate them? The boxes remain unopened as the speaker deliberates whether he should not rather escape from the tomblike interior of the building and 'break / into a brisk walk into damp London'. If Butler and Cullinan had been concerned with the attachment of history to remembered bodies, Kozain, in this poem, is concerned with the attachment of history to those who have been 'disremembered'.

The post-apartheid period has opened up opportunities for self-expression by extending the imaginative range of individual consciousness across pre-viously patrolled boundaries of race, modes of consciousness, locations of culture. As awareness of the heterogeneous positioning of self has emerged, the kinds of claims made about belonging have changed. Meterlerkamp and Kozain explore ways of living with local memories and attachments within a globalising cultural context of diverse discursive possibilities, the local sited within a postcolonial cosmopolitan order rather than an imperial metropolitan order.

A local habitation

In his Jerusalem Prize acceptance speech, Coetzee claims that white South Africans suffer from a 'failure of love'. Even their professed love of the land is attenuated, he says, by their inability to embrace the land's inhabitants. This failure of love has resulted in a literature whose expressions of the inner life are marked, he says, by 'stuntedness and deformity', an inadequacy that cannot simply be overcome by an act of the imagination ('Jerusalem Prize', p. 97).

It is unclear whether Coetzee sees the imagination as inherently limited or whether it is limited specifically by the structures of authority and power that govern South African life. From his wider literary and critical writings we may infer that he sees power relations as unavoidable, though their forms may vary. If the imagination is unable to operate outside power relations, unable to transcend them, then the only recourse open to the writer is to interrogate his own position of authority within such relations. In 'A Note on

Writing', Coetzee suggests this might be achieved through a poetics of the middle voice, where the relation between subject and object is not as clearly specified as it is in the case of the active voice, where the subject is sovereign, or the passive voice, where the subject is acted upon (p. 95). The middle voice both affirms and negates its authority by foregrounding its discursive conditions.

Given the context of cultural difference in South Africa, lyric poets have been compelled to interrogate their discursive authority, or at least evince awareness that their discursive authority cannot be taken for granted. Such performance of the conditions of possibility of speech troubles the Romantic desire for a merging of consciousness and world precisely because it entails an acknowledgement of the constitutive function of language in establishing relations with land and with people. The local habitation, as Butler himself kept pointing out, is a place of language. What poets writing after him were to explore more intensively is the indeterminacy of this ground, how language confers familiarity but also estrangement, exposing a consciousness located uneasily between crisis and understanding.

Bibliography

Abrahams, L. *A Reader*, ed. Patrick Cullinan, Cape Town: Ad Donker, 1988.

Afrika, T. *Nightrider*, Plumstead: Snailpress, 2003.

Breytenbach, B. *Die Hand Vol Vere*, Cape Town: Human & Rousseau, 1995.

Butler, G. *Collected Poems*, ed. L. Wright, Cape Town: David Philip, 1999.

    'On Being Present where you are: Some Observations on South African Poetry, 1930–1960', in P. Wilhelm and J. Polley (eds.), *Poetry South Africa*, Cape Town: Ad Donker, 1976, 82–101.

Clouts, S. *Collected Poems*, Cape Town: David Philip, 1984.

Coetzee, J. M. 'Jerusalem Prize Acceptance Speech' and 'A Note on Writing', in D. Attwell (ed.), *Doubling the Point: Essays and Interviews*, Cambridge, MA: Harvard University Press, 1992.

    'Reading the South African Landscape', in *White Writing: On the Culture of Letters in South Africa*, New Haven, CT: Yale University Press, 1988.

Cronin, J. 'Turning Around: Roy Campbell's "Rounding the Cape"', *English in Africa* 11:1 (May 1984), 65–78.

Cullinan, P. *Escarpments: Poems 1973–2007*, Roggebaai: Umuzi, 2008.

De Kok, I. *Familiar Ground*, Johannesburg: Ravan Press, 1988.

Dhlomo, H. I. E. 'Valley of a Thousand Hills' [1941], in *Collected Works*, ed. N. Visser and T. Couzens, Johannesburg: Ravan, 1985.

Eybers, E. *Versamelde Gedigte*, Cape Town: Human & Rousseau, 1990.

Horn, P. *Poems 1964–1989*, Johannesburg: Ravan, 1991.

Jonker, I. *Black Butterflies*, trans. A. Krog and A. P. Brink, Cape Town: Human & Rousseau, 2007.

Kirkwood, M. 'The Coloniser: A Critique of the English South African Culture Theory', in Wilhelm and Polley (eds.), *Poetry South Africa*, 102–33.

Kozain, R. *This Carting Life*, Plumstead: Snailpress, 2005.

Krog, A. *Down to my Last Skin*, Johannesburg: Random House, 2000.

Kunene, M. *The Ancestors and the Sacred Mountain*, London: Heinemann, 1982.

Livingstone, D. '"Africa Within Us" . . . ?', in Wilhelm and Polley, *Poetry South Africa*, 142–4.

    Selected Poems, ed. M. Chapman, Johannesburg: Ad Donker, 2004.

Louw, N. P. Van Wyk. *Versamelde Gedigte*, Cape Town: Human & Rousseau, 2002.

Maclennan, D. *Letters*, Cape Town: Carrefour Press, 1992.

Mahola, M. *Strange Things*, Plumstead: Snailpress, 1994.

Metelerkamp, J. *Into the Day Breaking*, Scottsville: Gecko Poetry, 2000.

Miller, R. *Poems, Prose, Plays*, ed. L. Abrahams, Cape Town: Carrefour Press, 1990.

Opperman, D. J. *Versamelde Poësie*, Cape Town: Tafelberg, 1987.

Pringle, T. *Poems Illustrative of South Africa* [1834], Cape Town: Struik, 1970.

Slater, F. C. *Dark Folk and other Poems*, Edinburgh: Blackwood, 1935.

Sole, K. *The Blood of our Silence*, Johannesburg: Ravan, 1987.

    Projections in the Past Tense, Johannesburg: Ravan, 1992.

Watson, S. *The other City: Selected Poems 1977–1999*, Cape Town: David Philip, 2000.

Wilhelm, P. and J. Polley (eds.). *Poetry South Africa*, Cape Town: Ad Donker, 1976.

29

Writing and publishing in African languages since 1948

CHRISTIAAN SWANEPOEL

In his 1966 study, *Neo-African Literature*, Janheinz Jahn refers to 'the tragedy of Southern Bantu literature' (p. 100), a linguistic category that comprises nine of the country's eleven official languages: isiZulu, isiXhosa, Sesotho, Setswana, Sepedi, Tshivenda, Xitsonga, siSwati and isiNdebele. Can it be said that this 'tragedy' persists today? If it does, is it because the development of at least five of the literatures came about through the initiatives of missionaries who had actually come to southern Africa to spread the Gospel – an act that lured Africans away from their traditional religious roots? Did the 'tragedy' persist and deepen after 1948, when the National Party seized power and the literatures ran into the repressive powers of the apartheid system which held them captive for the greater part of the following five decades, both sponsoring and censoring them into insignificance? And is the 'tragedy' continuing in the present under the African National Congress's democratic dispensation, whose brave constitutional acknowledgement of eleven official languages, in current practice, is amounting to little more than the selection of one language of record, thereby inhibiting development in the others?

In Jahn's view, the literatures must by 1948 already have suffered from the 'pettiness of that simple pious world' under the missionaries. However, it was the National Party's Bantu Education Act No. 47 of 1953 'that swept away the mission schools and with them the sparse remains of a semi-free literature. Anything allowed to appear since then scarcely deserves to be called literature: it is merely reading matter for beginners' (p. 100). Literary writing in isiXhosa, Sesotho, isiZulu and Setswana did, however, develop under the guiding eyes of the missionaries. Ironically, apartheid's equally unjust dealings under the catchphrase of 'separate development' led to the growth of literatures in Sepedi, Tshivenda and Xitsonga, and later also in siSwati and isiNdebele, while enabling further development of the others.

The apartheid regime will deserve to go down in history as a despicable miscarriage, yet its pursuit of ethnically defined language policies and mother-tongue education for young children contributed to the rise of a body of literature of considerable size which is difficult to dismiss. From the Publishers' Association of South Africa's laudable 2009 *Writings in Nine Tongues*, a catalogue of literature and readers in nine African languages for South Africa, a rough count indicates a total of well over 2,000 titles of creative writing, including novels, short stories and dramas as well as collections of poetry, of the people's folklore and folk-life, and of accounts of national heroes. The PASA catalogue carries numerous titles on subject matter that had either been censored by the previous regime or which has emerged since the new dispensation came into power in 1994. The catalogue only includes titles that are in print, which means that those out of print are excluded from the figure, and the sizeable number of readers for the young has not been counted. The figure also excludes creative writing produced and published in South Africa's neighbour states of Lesotho, Botswana, Swaziland and Mozambique, where Sesotho, Setswana, siSwati and Xitsonga are recognised as official languages alongside English or Portuguese. Counted together with the output across South Africa's borders, the figure for examples of creative writing could well rise to over 3,000.

As to the question of whether Jahn's statement should be read as conclusion (that the tragedy has already happened by 1966), prophecy (that a tragedy is in the offing), or statement (that the tragedy is happening under our eyes), the jury is still out. Whilst investigations are underway, it might be untimely to foreclose on the possibility of such misfortune. The missionaries may have engaged the potential of the fledgling literatures in order to protect their narrow-minded objectives. Apartheid must have shattered hopes for greater works the missionary epoch may have foreshadowed. Today's democratic dispensation, presumably in its zeal to break out of the perceived Balkanisation of language ghettos, has been undecided about which way to go with the language implications of the Constitution. However, if staying power is anything to consider, it may well be found one day that the literatures have emerged, grown and are continuing to develop through the zeal of creative minds who have been writing against the many obstacles that three epochs have rolled on to their pages.

The purpose of this chapter is to map out writing and publishing in the African languages since 1948. The years 1948 and 1994 are markers of political change which impacted on the literary history of the African languages, and these dates are accordingly useful for arranging the material under discussion, although, as will become clear, significant overlapping of subject matter and of authors occurs, complicating any rigid mapping of literary history. A logical starting point for this overview would have been the so-called 'missionary period' which, for lack of space, will be touched on only very briefly here (see also above, Chapters 10, 14 and 16).[1]

African-language literatures under apartheid, 1948–94

A number of factors characterise the condition of the literatures during this period. Some of them relate to the government's policy of separate development and its controlling measures, others to the socioeconomic condition of Africans in rural areas and on white-owned farms; others to the inevitable thrust of urbanisation that rapidly increased after 1948. Considered together with the consequential disintegration of firm family ties and social structures generally, all these impacted on the problem of readership, which is continuing to this day. They also impacted on the kind of subject matter that would emerge in the literary output of African-language writers.

Change is often foreshadowed before it actually happens. Signals of a looming hazard are to be detected in African-language writing during the last decades of the missionary period. A thematic case in point is 'relevant' or 'committed' writing. Political commitment is an area in which the literatures have been found wanting for the greater part of their existence. However, during the outgoing years of the missionary period protestation was in fact audible. It is also not surprising that the first protestations came from two sites of labour that had been in contestation for a long time: the farm and the mine.[2] In *Umyezo* (Eden, 1937), J. J. R. Jolobe published his famous poem 'Ukwenziwa konkhonzi' ('The Making of an Ox'), in which the training of a worker is likened to the relentless breaking-in of a young yoke-ox. In 1942 the Catholic Book Centre at Mazenod in Lesotho published Albert Nqekhu's *Arola, naheng ya Maburu* (Arola in the Country of the Boers), an outspoken novel about racial tension on eastern Free State farms. B. W. Vilakazi, composing under the influence of both the *izibongo* and the British Romantic poets in *Inkondlo kaZulu* (Zulu Songs, 1935) and *Amal'eZulu* (Zulu Horizons, 1945), produced his

1 For concise overviews of the missionary period with regard to the literatures, see Albert S. Gérard et al., *Comparative Literature and African Literatures*, and D. B. Ntuli and C. F. Swanepoel, *Southern African Literature in African Languages*. Further see Swanepoel, 'The *Leselinyana* Letters', pp. 145–53 and Jeff Opland, 'Xhosa Literature in Newspapers, 1837–1909', pp. 110–28. Recommended as well is 'Constructing South African Literary History', which appeared in *Englischsprachige Literaturen Afrikas*, vol. XIV (ed. E. Lehmann, E. Reckwitz and L. Vennarini). For a contemporary study of missionary journals, see Chapter 10 above.
2 Much of the material included in this section has been informed by the work the present writer has co-authored with D. B. Ntuli (see Bibliography below).

famous poem 'Ezinkomoni' ('In the Mine Camps') expressing the grievances of miners under white supervision. Indeed, the black miner's predicament is a subject that would reoccur in isiZulu and the other literatures in years to come, both in written and oral poetry.[3] It has given rise to a prominent oral genre in isiXhosa, Sesotho and isiZulu (see Chapter 3 in particular).

Readership, prescription and publishing

The Bantu Education Act of 1953 commissioned the relevant department to encourage reading on the one hand, and, on the other, to control what learners at all levels should read. The prescribing of textbooks, subjected to the censorship rules of the country, the regulations of the Department of Bantu Education (established in 1958), its language boards and screening committees, became crucial for both author and publisher. This contributed to the paucity of adult readers in at least two ways. Firstly, the freedom of authors to choose themes as they saw fit, and to develop them in an appropriate language, was severely curtailed. Secondly, serious readers lost interest in reading material that was filtered to appease a political agenda. Reading habits inculcated within the walls of schools, colleges and universities did not succeed significantly in contributing to a reading culture thereafter, nor did those habits spread significantly to a broader spectrum of the public. Reading habits furthermore relate to lifestyle and living conditions conducive to such style. In the urban areas where black Africans were forced to reside in segregated townships far from work, with inadequate free time, low wages and a general feeling of want and non-belonging, even the bare essentials were hardly affordable and reading was subject to the struggle for survival.

Between writer and reader stands the publisher, in a complex cycle of interdependent agencies. Publishers need budgets before they can proceed. Missionary publishing houses worked according to their own revenue and budgeting processes. The situation changed rapidly when private, commercial publishing houses appeared on the scene, since income-driven businesses are dependent on sales. To gain access to a market, books had to be prescribed. With a dearth of adult readers of African-language literature, the school market inevitably became the targeted area. Despite the glaring deficiencies, the secondary school syllabus of the time did make ample provision for the reading and studying of prescribed works in all prominent genres, eventually in most of the African languages. Ntshangase could state in 1996: 'Today, publishing in African languages is one of the largest and financially most

3 J. K. Ratau's *Khirimpana* (1955) is an extensive written poem of seventy-seven pages entirely devoted to the life of a miner whose name serves as title of the volume.

viable enterprises within the educational publishing industry' ('Publishing in African Language', p. 48). On prescription procedures he goes on to say:

> The apartheid system which established language boards (homeland-attached government structures created to develop African languages and recommend books to be prescribed by the education departments) also aimed at exposing readers to works that glorified the state. This political role of the language boards resulted in stifled thematic development. In the end writing was almost totally restricted to members of these boards, known to publishers as 'contacts'. This inevitably led to corruption in the prescription procedures. (p. 51)

Publishing companies such as Afrikaanse Pers Boekhandel (APB), Nasionale Pers with its branches Via Afrika and Nasou, Shuter & Shooter, Juta, Maskew Miller Longman, J. L. van Schaik, and De Jager-HAUM, and later Kagiso, Heinemann, Macmillan South Africa, the Witwatersrand University Press and a number of other university presses (some from overseas, such as Oxford University Press) entered the market. Sasavona, a less commercial press attached to the Swiss mission in South Africa, did much for the development of the literature in Xitsonga. Not all of these publishers supported state policy, especially those with overseas roots, but they all operated in a regulated market.

The pull of the city, modern education and their consequences

The magnetism of the industrial areas was bound to be significantly reflected in the writings that emerged by the middle of the twentieth century. The city here not only implies a place of glittering attractions, the possibility of work and a lucrative income; it also implies education. In simplest terms the migration to the city as reflected in the literatures has been described as the 'Jim goes to Jo'burg' or the 'prodigal son' theme. In the Sotho languages and Tshivenda this writing became known as the *Makgoweng/Makhuwani* (To the Whites) motif. Writing in 1968, Marivate refers to this kind of work as 'a young man leaving his rural area to look for work in town, then while there, is corrupted by town life and later goes back home; or sometimes just an account of experiences' ('Tsonga Literature', p. 39). The label may apply to an early Sesotho novel such as *Molahlehi* (The Lost One, 1946) by S. S. Matlosa, M. O. M. Seboni's Setswana novel *Rammone wa Kgalagadi* (Rammone of Kalahari, 1947), E. S. Madima's Tshivenda novel *A si ene* (It is not Him, 1955), E. P. Ndhambi's Xitsonga novel *Mambuxu* (1950), or C. L. S. Nyembezi's *Mntanami! Mntanami!* (My Child! My Child!, 1950), a novel in isiZulu. Serudu refers to writing on what he calls 'contact themes' in Sepedi, stating: 'Writers such as Phalane in his book *Motangtang*, Madiba in his books *Tsiri* and *Nkotsana*, and Sehlodimela in *Moelelwa* and *Tša maabane*, made the 'makgoweng' motif a popular theme during this period' ('Northern Sotho Literature', pp. 158–9). Another slant on the relation between city and country is provided by Nyembezi's novel *Inkinsela yase Mgungundlovu* (1961; translated by S. Ngidi as *The Rich Man of Pietermaritzburg*, 2008); it tells of a city conman who at first fools, but then is routed by, a rural community. R. C. Bodibe's Sesotho translation of this gem appeared in 1983 under the title *Kgabane ya Mokokotlofo*.

A closer look at the criticism on works of this kind indicates that the works are often dismissed for reasons other than the subject matter they share. With their rather stereotyped structures, less than credible solutions to serious problems and simplified and often moralistic endings, many works failed to provide the serious reader with much to enthuse about. But not all of the works deserve to be brushed aside in this way. On Nyembezi's *Mntanami! Mntanami!*, for example, Ntuli notes that it 'deals with the prodigal-son theme, but the writer fills his story with so much power and life that it is one of the most moving works of prose in the Zulu language' ('Zulu Literature', pp. 143–4). Offering an approach to this kind of subject matter that same year, Ntuli and Swanepoel ventured this opinion:

> Even the hardliner critic will perhaps be prepared to admit that these works are, in fact, documents of devastating disruption. As a body of works they tell the story of a century-long Diaspora of more than half of a nation, whose effects can be seen in present-day South Africa. They speak of the countless journeys made to hold body and soul together. And they show how, in the end, the body may have been saved, but the soul was lost, despite the conversion to a new religion. The biographical nature of these works, to which P. S. Groenewald has referred, may signal a concealed autobiography – told in collective commiseration with the multitudes that have withered away. (*Southern African Literature*, p. 82)

Seen this way, the motif relates to a complex constellation of themes which should perhaps be viewed within an overarching thematic architecture or taxonomy, with, as capstone, the confrontation between traditional African life and westernisation. The meeting of diverse cultures activated a process of acculturation, often with dire consequences. It is probably the need for a somewhat wider perspective that compelled contemporary scholars to opt for a wider formulation. Kaschula, for example, refers to the country–city divide

('Xhosa Literary History', p. 60),[4] while Zulu refers to the city versus village theme ('Literary History of Sesotho', p. 79).

The wider perspective enables accommodation of the more sophisticated novel where the confrontation is addressed at a deeper level and where novelistic skills reach a different level of artistry altogether. Ntuli's view of Nyembezi's *Mntanami! Mntanami!*, referred to above, is a case in point. Ten years earlier A. C. Jordan's *Ingqumbo yeminyanya* (1940; translated as *The Wrath of the Ancestors*, 1980) appeared at Lovedale. This is a novel that belongs to the sophisticated category as well. Written in the missionary period and published by a missionary press, it not only straddles the periodisation literary historians are fond of making, but reaches forward to debate the issue of acculturation. Setting his novel in the princedom of the Mpondomise people, Jordan works with two sides of the clash of cultures: the conflict between modern education and traditional values; and individual, Christian marriage against traditional, polygamous marriage. The wrath of the ancestors ensues when the traditional is abandoned in favour of the modern. Given the inescapable fact of change, tragedy seems inevitable.

Based on the same conflict between modern education and traditional values is B. M. Khaketla's *Mosali a nkhola* (A Woman Lands me in Trouble), a Sotho novel published by the Afrikaanse Pers-Boekhandel in 1960, although Khaketla states in his *Selelekela* (Foreword) that the work was completed in June 1951. Set in the heyday of British colonial rule in Lesotho, with an over-elaborate system of local administration through traditional chiefs, the novel explores the consequences when a young ruler, who has had a wide education and who values freedom of choice, has to face the prejudice of conservative traditionalists. Khaketla's young ruler, Mosito, accepts the choice of spouse made by his father, but with dire consequences for his reign and life. The wife is also conservative and an easy tool in the hands of the courtiers. Being at war, the British administration in Maseru decides to rationalise the system of local administration and decrees that the local chiefs and headmen are to receive salaries based on the number of taxable subjects. After a complaint about this decision is rejected, the traditional counsellors persuade a reluctant Mosito that a medicine man be called in. He requires human body parts, implying the necessity for *seretlo* (ritual murder). The police get wind of the murder and Mosito is arrested. In the high court in Maseru, Mosito and some of his collaborators are condemned to the gallows. The work's message is evident in the tragic conclusion: ritual murder is not justifiable as

4 Kaschula in this regard acknowledges the work of R. Williams, *The Country and the City* (1973) ('Xhosa Literary History', p. 61).

a means of retaining power in a world which has outgrown ancient beliefs. Khaketla's work continues to attract scrutiny from contemporary literary scholars. Among them is T. Selepe, who prefers to interpret the theme against the background of deculturation.[5] Selepe comments:

> What should be noted further here is that in spite of Khaketla's expressed intention of writing to expose the despicable practice of *diretlo* [i.e., *seretlo*], this seems to be of lesser importance in the novel. Rather, the dichotomies between justice and injustice, educated and uneducated people, backward and advanced culture all contribute to one central idea, namely that if a foreign culture is imposed on a people, it is bound to disrupt the social fabric of their lives, thus causing mental dislocation, emotional displacement as well as confusion of self-knowledge among them. This is in short what deculturation amounts to.   ('Deculturation', p. 152)

With the myriad frustrations many black migrants to the city have had to endure during their ventures, counter-reactions were to be expected, one which was a re-evaluation of home and the values associated with it. Home in this sense was not necessarily, or only, a physical place; it was also a spiritual space. A writer who has become known for pursuing this reaction was O. K. Matsepe. Writing in Sepedi, he produced nine novels from 1954, the last published posthumously in 1981. He is acknowledged as a towering figure in African-language literature. Matsepe wrote about royal life in traditional Kopa society prior to its substantial contact with whites. His kings, chiefs and headmen are fictitious characters involved in typical traditional feuds around the court. Among his best works are *Kgorong ya Mošate* (In the Court of the King, 1962), *Lešitaphiri* (The Umbilical Cord, 1963), *Megokgo ya bjoko* (Tears of the Mind, 1969) and *Letšofalela* (A Thorny Problem, 1972). In *Kgati ya moditi* (The Cane of the Initiation Leader, 1974) he poses difficult problems: Mmatshepho's ambition to become queen, and an albino's to become king – both in opposition to tradition. Serudu points out that Matsepe's work is a counter to the *Makgoweng* (To the Whites) movement, and can be called a *Magaeng* (At Home) motif. He quotes P. S. Groenewald: 'During this struggle (cultural survival) the past was looked at as a period of peace and tranquillity,

---

5 Selepe bases his interpretation of 'deculturation' on the views of D. P. Kunene, who states: 'You are in danger of undergoing "deculturation", a neologism coined by the present writer to refer to a process whereby, at the meeting of two cultures, one consciously and deliberately dominates the other and denies it the right to exist, by both directly or indirectly questioning its validity as a culture, denigrating it, making its carriers objects of ridicule and scorn, and thus finally leading to its questioning by the very people whom it has nurtured and given its identity and a positive being' (*Heroic Poetry*, p. xi).

and the Northern Sotho author then took to writing about those days gone by' (Serudu, 'Survey of Northern Sotho Literature', p. 160).

Critics are in agreement that Matsepe's novels have complex structures with an almost complete disregard for chronology. Grobler, using Gérard Genette's terminology, interprets this disregard as a particular attitude towards past and present ('Time Order', p. 299). The narrator deals with features of simultaneity given in concepts such as 'coexistence', 'co-presence', 'interpenetration' and 'specious present'. His texts are designed to reflect a milieu in which 'time as a linear order' is superseded by a 'reality of simultaneity'. The deliberate distortion of chronology renders a narrated world in which the temporal succession of events becomes insignificant – what is of importance is the multiplicity and often simultaneity of events. In this sense the reader experiences a 'timeless' world in which man, floating in the inevitable stream of time, attends to what comes his way in his own time, says Grobler (p. 300). (See also Ntuli and Swanepoel, *Southern African Literature*, pp. 112–13.)

Still related to the confrontation between traditional African life and westernisation are a number of related themes contributing to yet another network of social issues. There is a sizeable body of literature on the problems attached to parental privilege in the choice of a marriage partner, a custom that came under severe pressure through exposure to the alternatives brought by modernity (Milubi, 'Tshivenda Literature', p. 203), enlightenment or innovation (Marivate, 'Tsonga Literature', p. 223). Also connected to this theme is a web of subjects which relate to love affairs, marriage and unmarried motherhood. Another relates to witchcraft as a means to success, often for leadership positions in traditional communities, or what Milubi has called 'the struggle for chieftainship' ('Tshivenda Literature', p. 202). D. P. Moloto, a pioneer of the 1940s of the novel in Setswana based his *Manyobonyobo* (Complicated Matters, 1984) on the power struggle at local government level. The conflict is well captured in a realistic setting. In addition, there emerged subjects typical of urban township life such as crime, blackmail, general social instability and the plight of having to carry a 'pass'. S. M. Mofokeng in his Sesotho collection of short stories *Leetong* (On the Road, 1952) gave vent to this in the story 'Mona pela tsela' ('Here by the Roadside') which is a subtle yet convincing portrayal of the 'blind' administering such offensive regulations.

Parental privilege in the choice of spouse has been handled in all literatures, with work of varying quality, from the mid century onwards. Noteworthy are four novelists in isiZulu, two dramas in the literature of siSwati, and a particularly prominent figure in Setswana. J. K. Ngubane led the field in isiZulu with his *Uvalo lwezihlonzi* (Fear of the Frown, 1956), in which he ridiculed this forced-love practice. The demand for a bride-price (*ilobolo*) is similarly satirised. E. E. N. T. Mkhize (1969), Z. Khuzwayo (1969) and I. S. Kubheka (1973) then followed suit. Kubheka's *Kungavuka AbaNguni* (Over my Dead Body) blends plot, characterisation and setting well. According to Makhambeni, these contribute 'to give a united whole' ('Zulu Novels', p. 39). In siSwati, M. S. Mbuyane's drama *Ungatihluphi* (Don't Worry Yourself, 1990) is about Ncobile's success in marrying a young man of her choice against her parent's wishes. S. M. Magagula's *Tentile* (1990) ends in a tragedy when Tentile's lover is murdered and she, too, dies (Ntuli and Swanepoel, *Southern African Literature*, p. 133).

The Setswana novelist D. P. S. Monyaise also criticises this custom in his *Bogosi Kupe* (Supremacy is a Holy Cow, 1967), a novel which is remembered also for its intricate structure. As Ranamane indicates, Monyaise 'criticises the old Batswana tradition of parents choosing a wife for a man [and] maintains that such a marriage will fail because the husband marries a lady who is deeply in love with someone else' ('Setswana Literature', p. 181). Shole explains that most of Monyaise's stories begin in the middle, detail comes in the form of flashbacks, and the plot does not unfold in any chronological way ('Setswana Literature', p. 112). Monyaise was born in Soweto, where some of his plots are situated. Because of illness, he spent two years in the Baragwanath hospital (now the Chris Hani-Baragwanath), where he started working on his first work, *Omphile Umphi Modise* (1960). According to Malepe, the work depicts the turbulent life of an unmarried mother in search of her son, whom she had taken to an orphanage shortly after his birth ('Tswana Literature', pp. 70–1). Her effort to find the child after she has married another man fails, since the child has already been adopted and taken to the countryside. A turning point comes when the reader realises that the mother's new husband and her son's stepfather are running a business together. The mother falls ill, and her son, now called Modise, goes to see her. Recognising him by a birthmark behind the ear, she faints and dies of shock.

Monyaise's *Marara* (Confusion, 1961) is situated in the township of Lichtenburg, depicting its fights, robbery and murder 'as a result of low morals' (Malepe, 'D. P. S. Monyaise', p. 71). His *Ngaka, mosadi mooka* (Doctor, the Woman is an Acacia Tree, 1965), deals with life at the Baragwanath hospital and works with 'the typical raw township life of crime, love squabbles, kidnapping and corruption, without necessarily touching the sociopolitical implications' (Shole, 'Setswana Literature', p. 99). At the same time, according to Ranamane, the book satirises the attitudes of the educated, who seem 'to regard love as fun or the satisfaction of one's sexual desires' ('Setswana Literature', p. 179).

In Tshivenda, N. A. Milubi pursued aspects of the subject matter quite forcefully in four dramas appearing in the 1980s. Education and economic, political and religious issues form the conflict in *Mukosi wa lufu* (Cry of Death, 1983). The African is depicted as being caught between the western and the traditional. If the western is chosen, most of your people will tend to shun you. If you keep to your traditional culture, you may be regarded as backward (Ntuli and Swanepoel, *Southern African Literature*, p. 129). His *Ndi mitodzi muni?* (What Tears are These?, 1985) addresses the problem of corruption in modern African states. The dramatist himself wrote: 'The publication appears to have found its way to the hearts of many of the Vhavenda readers who were disenchanted with their government, which was corrupt to the core' (Milubi, 'Tshivenda Literature', p. 207). 'Government' in this case was the Venda homeland authority, which disappeared when a united South African state was formed in 1994 under the democratic dispensation. *Zwo lungwa* (It has been Tampered With, 1989) deals with unfaithfulness between the clergy and some of their congregants. Milubi states the following about the problem of publishing for the schools market:

> In Tshivenda literature, Milubi is, so far, the single author who has written without the schoolchild in mind. His writings deal with controversial topics such as corruption, bribery and detention. Since publishers were not willing to publish such materials, Milubi became his own publisher.
>
> ('Tshivenda Literature', p. 211)

This long period saw a continuation of works dealing with historical figures and battles in isiZulu, adding to those of H. I. E. Dhlomo. Jessie Gwayi published three gripping novels during the 1970s: *Bafa Baphela* (They all Died, 1973) is about the legendary Basia woman ruler, Mmanthathisi, while *Shumpu* (Chopping Down, 1974) depicts the fall of Dingiswayo, the great Mthethwa monarch, and *Yekanini* (Oh, My!, 1976) deals with Shaka's young days until his inauguration as king. Critics such as Ntuli view Gwayi as a highly imaginative writer of well researched historical works ('Zulu Literature', pp. 148–9). Exploring drama as genre, E. Zondi's *Ukufa kukaShaka* (The Death of Shaka, 1962) was followed many years later by *Insumasumane* (A Mysterious Flow of Events, 1986). Basing his work on the Bambatha rebellion of 1906, the dramatist makes a committed stand, using historical material to suggest that rebellion is a way of dealing with an hegemonic situation, with national autonomy as the ultimate goal (see Groenewald, 'Zondi's Scenario', p. 12). C. T. Msimang is another writer who explores Zulu history with considerable sensitivity. His *Izulu eladuma eSandlwana* (Stormy Weather over Isandlwana, 1976) is based on the battle between the Zulus and the British at Isandlwana in 1879, while his novel *Buzani kuMkabayi* (Ask Mkabayi, 1982) has as subject matter the influence of Mkabayi, Shaka's kinswoman, who was the kingmaker during more than fifty years of Zulu history (Killam and Rowe, *Companion to African Literatures*, p. 315).

Between the years 1960 and 1980 Hubert Sishi, one of the most prolific pioneer writers of radio plays in isiZulu, wrote about one hundred and thirty thirty-minute one-act plays under the title '*Imilando yakwaZulu*' ('Historical Accounts of Zululand'). According to Ntuli, Zulu kings such as Shaka, Dingane and Mpande, and generals such as Mdlaka and Ndlela, feature prominently in the plays ('Hubert Sishi', p. 250). Some of the episodes are independent of each other, while others are consequentially linked in 'what could almost be regarded as mini-series within the whole range of the production'.

During the years 1990 to 1994 (the years of democratic change) S. S. Masondo enriched isiZulu literature with six detective novels and an anthology of detective short stories, inspired more by James Hadley Chase than Sherlock Holmes. According to I. J. Mhlambi ('African Discourses', pp. 82–109), these novels together form a set of two trilogies in which Masondo's naming of characters across the works overlap. However, the strategy can be regarded as extraordinary in that it disrupts expectations, says the researcher.

The early 1990s also saw translations of some of the Nigerian novelist Chinua Achebe's masterpieces into African languages. His *Things Fall Apart* (1958) became available in a Setswana version by D. P. S. Monyaise in 1992 and in a Sepedi version by M. S. Serudu in 1993. K. S. Bongela's isiXhosa translation of the same work was also published in 1993, and C. T. Msimang's isiZulu translation in 1995. Achebe's *No Longer at Ease* (1960) appeared in isiXhosa, translated by H. Motlhabane, in 1992 and in isiZulu, translated by M. N. Makhambeni, in 1993. Translations from Africa heralded a trend that would soon expand into a survival and strengthening strategy for the literature.

Towards the end of this period, when the apartheid government's control measures had run out of steam, more committed work saw the light of day. The trials and tribulations of the black person under the oppressive apartheid regime is the focus of the seasoned P. T. Mtuze's isiXhosa *Alitshoni lingaphumi* (The Sun Never Sets Forever, 1986). The master–servant relationship, the Group Areas Act, the high unemployment rate and forced removals from home contributed to making life extremely difficult for the ordinary black person.

The literatures beyond 1994

National expectancies were high when the African National Congress won the first democratic election in South African history on 27 April 1994. They rose even higher on 10 May that year when Nelson Mandela was inaugurated as the first black president of the Republic of South Africa. Fighter jets slicing through serene blue skies over the Union Buildings at presidential inaugurations was not a new sight. What was new were the two *izimbongi* (praise-singers) Sthembile Mlangeni and Zolani Mkiva, who showered the new president and his guests of honour with traditional praises in the laureate's home language, isiXhosa (see Chapter 2).[6] History was in the making; it included literary history.

African-language writers and critics followed in a spirit of relief and expectation and participated in envisioning a worthier future in a free land. Among the things they were looking forward to were the prospect of writing in an environment unobstructed by the restrictions of the past, a similarly enabling publishing regime, a market that reached the sought-after adult readership, and an African-language literature finding recognition as part and parcel of South African literary history, neither through cooption nor as afterthought, only on its own merit. Ranamane predicted that there was going to be an exploration of the so-called controversial and thorny themes in the literature. These themes had been forbidden in the literature because they dealt with politics. The authorities feared that the treatment of such themes could cause an uprising. The changing social order, from apartheid to democracy, was certainly going to cause their exploration (Ranamane, 'Setswana Literature', p. 192).

Milubi looked forward to a literature beyond that of the schoolchild: 'Vhavenda authors . . . should develop an eagerness to write on thorny issues, not for the purpose of making propaganda but for the sake of literary and aesthetic expression' ('Tshivenda Literature', p. 211). Ntuli and Swanepoel conclude their book with the comment:

> The anticipated political changes in South Africa will undoubtedly result in educational, social, economic and other changes as well. These will present the African writer with new challenges. Will the writer now feel free to produce worthwhile works of art? We look forward to seeing how such challenges will be met. (*Southern African Literature*, p. 143)

---

6 For discussion of the *izibongo* of that historic day, see M. W. Jadezweni, 'The Inauguration of President Nelson Mandela', pp. 67–70.

Grobler further detailed the expectations by asking,

> Will African-language writers be able to prove beyond doubt that the restraints were indeed the reason for the 'immature' state of African-language writing in South Africa? Will the abolition of the hateful restrictive measures necessarily result in the emergence of masterpiece after masterpiece? Will black writers who have abandoned their mother tongue for English, return to the languages of their birth to help improve the quality of their literatures? And if so, how will they be received by their alienated audiences? Will African-language writers succeed in uplifting their literatures to a level of maturity to the world *even if it means criticising the new government?* Can African-language literature obtain the status of maturity simply by picking the bones of apartheid?   ('Writers Unshackled', p. 58)

Writing five years into the new democratic dispensation, Zulu, after acceding to the general perception that the African-language literatures lacked maturity, states:

> However, not all the criticism is justified. Because of the laws of segregation, South African literary histories developed separately, and as a result, few South Africans knew very much about South African literature in general. Much of the negative comment still tends to come from people who have no direct knowledge of literature written in the African languages. ('African Literature in the New Millennium', p. 291)

Summarising new developments, he continues:

> After the unbanning of the political organisations in 1990, writing about socio-political and economic issues such as the liberation struggle and the effects of apartheid no longer offended the censorship board. Apparently taking advantage of the situation, large publishing companies such as Kagiso, Maskew Miller Longman and Naspers, amongst others, established prestigious literary competitions . . . It is important to note that the publishers who set up literary competitions indicated that writers were free to write on any subject – including the effects of apartheid – which is an indication that the subject matter was being preferred.   (p. 300)

Response to liberation

Post-1994 writing indeed shows that writers did much to 'write open the country', so to speak. Life under apartheid, solidarity with the struggle, frustrated expectations of the new regime; the HIV / AIDS pandemic, society and crime, rape, gayness, unrest and xenophobia; love affairs across what was called 'the colour bar' and many others soon became visible as subject matter. Writing on labour relations on the farm continued, perhaps with more openness than before. Hero admiration, particularly focused on president Mandela, continued. In the field of broadcasting, where multilingualism is surviving – there are dedicated language stations on radio and time and channel sharing between languages on television – the contribution towards a literary culture continued to be quite considerable. For more than half a century now radio dramas, and since 1976 television series, have reached and captivated large adult audiences on all African-language stations and channels in a manner literary writers would have envied. Studies such as those of Lubbe ('Evaluering'), Van Heerden ('Radiovervolgverhaal'), Ntuli ('Function of the Narrator') and Gunner ('Wrestling with the Present'), and the publishing of radio drama texts such as those edited by Moeketsi (*Seyalemoya* 1996), Masondo (*Inkundlanye*, 1997) and Ntuli (*Imilando YakwaZulu*, 2000) are likely to continue.

In the field of television and film in African languages, the first half-decade of the new millennium saw an imaginative recycling of themes already referred to, such as arranged marriages and youth migration to the metropoles, in the Zulu drama series *Gaz' Lam* (Cousins), by A. Yazbek, that ran on a South African Broadcasting Corporation television channel in consecutive series from 2002 to 2005. I. J. Mhlambi's research demonstrates how 'the drama series in the post-apartheid context not only retrospectively reviews and dispels received meanings, but also offers fresh new readings in line with the socio-economic and political realities of the post-apartheid African society' ('Thematic Re-engagements', p. 119). Her discussion of some of the novels by authors in isiZulu already referred to lays bare an intriguing degree of intertexuality between literature and film. Her approach and findings are likely to introduce a similarly enriching re-evaluation of apartheid and post-apartheid literature in their response to the realities of their times.

Several novels and plays in isiXhosa, isiZulu, Tshivenda, Sesotho and the other literatures catch the eye.[7] A prompt response to the possibilities of the

---

7 The material condensed in this section was obtained through five research processes. Firstly, a questionnaire compiled by the present writer for the purposes of this chapter, to which the following critics have kindly responded and whose contributions are gratefully acknowledged: Professors N. N. Mathonsi, M. J. Mafela, H. C. Groenewald, and Doctors J. Sukumane, W. M. Tšiu and V. A. Mhlakaza. Professors N. S. Zulu, T. J. Selepe, M. R. Madiba, R. N. Madadzhe, Dr I. J. Mhlambi and Mr X. E. Mabaso responded equally helpfully in other respects. Secondly, much of the bibliographic information was pieced together from the PASA catalogue *Writings in Nine Tongues* (2007–9) with follow-up enquiries addressed to the relevant publishers; PASA and these publishers are likewise gratefully acknowledged. Thirdly, information was drawn from scholarly articles that appeared mainly in the *South African Journal of African Languages* and its predecessor at the University of South Africa, *Limi*; and from Master's dissertations and doctoral theses. Fourthly, I am indebted to the websites of Dr K. P. D. Maphalla, Professors P. T. Mtuze, D. B. Z. Ntuli and Mazisi Kunene for indispensable help in focusing the argument. And fifthly, to Mr Mzwakhe Maseko from Heinemann South Africa and Mrs Mathabo Kunene for working English translations of the titles of the late Mazisi Kunene's isiZulu texts.

new dispensation came from the Sesotho writer N. P. Maake (the author of Chapter 3 above). His absorbing novel *Kweetsa ya pelo ya motho* (Depth of the Human Heart, 1995) is a narrative of human behaviour in political turmoil. Deeply rooted in the political struggle of the late 1980s and early 1990s, and in moral considerations underlying the justness of the cause, the novel explores human behaviour from four different points of view, each represented by a main character. Interpersonal relations in times of trouble, such as suspicion (of conspiracy, collaboration and betrayal) and blackmail, sensitive social issues such as backyard abortion, as well as the human need to love and be loved – these contribute to define an admirable narrative that looks back. As is the case with the other works referred to here, this work marks a significant rupture with past African-language literary history (Swanepoel, 'Narrative of Human Behaviour', p. 52). Maake is a prolific contemporary Sesotho writer, critic and academic.

Ncedile Saule is a well-published contemporary writer of isiXhosa. His *Ukhozi olumaphiko* (The Champion, 1996) is also set in the pre-1994 South Africa. Mfazwe refuses to become a police informant and subsequently becomes their target. Prescribed for the Western Cape Education Department's Grade 12 examination, this novel received an uncommon reception from a candidate who wrote the isiXhosa paper on literature. Journalist Marelize Potgieter reported in the Afrikaans newspaper *Die Burger* of 26 November 2010 that one of the candidates she had spoken to remarked: 'For the prescribed book *Ukhozi* by Ncedile Faule [sic] learners had to know the history of Hector Pieterson in order to handle the questions with insight' (present author's translation from the Afrikaans). (Hector Pieterson was killed by the police during the mass youth uprising on 16 June 1976, now a public holiday in the country.) In N. S. Puleng's Sepedi novel *Ba ikgethetše motsotso* (They Chose the Moment Themselves, 2000) a group of young people led by a young woman plan to overthrow the government. Zulu expresses high regard for J. M. Mngadi's isiZulu novel *Asiko ndawo bakithi* (We Are No Good People, 1996), its plot structure, characters, narrators, narrative time and space and theme ('African Literature', p. 291). The novel is about the anguish of survival in the oppressed society of the mid 1980s when the notorious 'people's court' hearings and necklace executions with motor vehicle tyres occurred. Zulu comments:

> What is ironic about the burning of Thabekhulu by Nkosana is that Nkosana is a victim of these people who burn others with tyres. When they first arrive in the slum he is forced to kill people, and this torments him. But

later, after seeing his father being killed by his mother and Thabekhulu, he becomes the judge and leader of just such rabble, and uses his position to wreak vengeance . . . This is where the moral of the story lies – people call themselves freedom fighters but they victimise the very same oppressed people; the situation is so desperate that the victims of the system use it for their own ends. In this game of survival, son kills mother, and mother kills son; husband kills wife, if wife does not kill husband.   (p. 294)

Written in Tshivenda, R. N. Madadzhe's *Tshelede ndi mavhulaise* (Money is the Root of all Evil, 1994) takes as its context the wave of bank robberies that has hit the country the past three decades. S. Yawa's isiXhosa *Ubunzulu bentliziyo* (The Whirlpool, 2005) is also about the sad escalation of crime, including cash in-transit hauls with innocent people becoming victims. L. L. Ngewu's *Koda kube nini na?* (How Long?, 1998), written in isiXhosa, courageously examines the aftermath of the struggle. For Themba, returning home from years in exile, the new democracy falls short of expectations. Uneducated and believing that he has been abandoned by his leaders, he resorts to crime for survival. M. G. Mdliva portrays the political change in a one-act isiXhosa play *Uthini na Dlalani?* (What do you Say, Dlalani?, 2002), working with cultural diversity in former white areas and exposure of street children to difficulties such as drug abuse.

In isiZulu, M. V. Bhengu's *Itshwele lempangele* (The Guineafowl's Chicken, 1998) explores intercultural love between a young Zulu man and a young woman of Indian descent. Both eventually overcome the stereotypical prejudice of their parents to fasten the knot for a successful marriage. Zulu concludes that 'the author repudiates commonly held Indian and Zulu stereotypes, and thus strengthens racial harmony' ('Racial Relations', p. 286). M. Sikosana's Ndebele novel *Kungavuk'amaJali* (I Swear by my Ancestors, 2008) deals with a similar dilemma, which turns out to be less fortunate for the parties involved.

Another writer of the new South Africa, writing in isiZulu, is N. G. Sibiya, who celebrates the opportunity to address contemporary societal conundrums openly and in both the novel and in drama. His *Kuxolelwa Abanjani?* (Who Deserves to be Forgiven?, 2002), mainly deals with HIV/AIDS. Given that the widespread disease can be contracted through unfaithfulness and multiple relationships, the novel poses the question as to whether partners can forgive each other when they are infected during a relationship. Sibiya's drama *Kwaze Kwalunkhuni* (It is very Difficult, 2003) looks at the myth surrounding virginity and the HIV/AIDS issue in South Africa. Mathonsi writes:

A released prisoner who arrives home to discover that his brother is dead, forces himself on his brother's wife and unknowingly infects her with the HIV virus. When the ex-prisoner realises that he is HIV positive he rapes a virgin who is coming from the Reed Dance, because he believes that if a positive person has sexual intercourse with a virgin he becomes HIV negative.

('Response to Questionnaire', p. 5)

Sibiya's isiZulu *Bengithi Lizokuna* (I Thought it would Rain, 2008) deals with homosexuality and transexuality. Groenewald explains:

In the first chapter Mhlengi Ngidi is presented, at the age of 24, as a gay man. He has come to the conclusion that he cannot live as a man any longer. He visits his girl friend, Nontobeko, for the last time and tells her that he is leaving her after which he visits his father to tell him that he is gay. After this he leaves for Cape Town where he undergoes operations to change his sex and his appearance. No crime or immorality has been committed but the character's change from Mhlengi to Mahlengi leads to the same consequences as one would find in a moral story.   ('Response to Questionnaire', pp. 5–6)

The Vhavenda scholar, critic and writer M. J. Mafela's novel *Lwendo lwashu* (Our Journey, 2004) also deals with the dilemma of the unfaithfulness that can cause the spread of the HIV/AIDS virus: a woman who indulges in extramarital affairs becomes infected and eventually both she and her husband are victims. A prolific Xitsonga writer is C. M. Lubisi, whose drama *Byi le tintihweni* (In the Fingers, 2005) is about Professor Xirilo, a philanderer of note. As a result he picks up HIV/AIDS, a misfortune which leads to his demise. In *Muthulata* (1999) Milubi situates his plot in the more affluent society where HIV/AIDS results from the philandering of a medical doctor with one of his patients: even medical doctors can be infected if they do not take good care of themselves.

The white-owned farm as site of conflict is one of the themes that returns in this period with novels in Sesotho and Xitsonga, amongst others. This is not surprising, since, as much as the new government has succeeded in transferring power from white to black in numerous sectors of the country's economy, land restitution has remained one of the most vexed of outstanding issues. Decent human relations between farm labourers and their farm owners are forever in the balance, despite consistent interventions from the government and equally regular assurances from organised agriculture. Both N. S. Zulu's *Nonyana ya tshepo* (The Bird of Hope, 1997) and T. W. D. Mohapi's *Lehlaba la lephaku* (The Pain of Hunger, 1999) are in Sesotho and take the confrontation to an interpersonal level; for Zulu during the apartheid era, with brutality on the part of white bosses mixed with disagreement among black labourers; for Mohapi, between the labourers and their black supervisor, a position he has acquired in the spirit of the black economic empowerment policy after 1994. N. B. Mkhari, a zealous Xitsonga writer, likewise bases *Ndzi tswaleriwe kwala* (I was Born Here, 1995) on unfair labour practices and living conditions on farms. Workers are dismissed on a whim and even treated worse when they are aged. For V. A. Mhlakaza, however, this is a time for reconciliation and interpersonal support: in his Sesotho short-story collection *Tikamotse* (1999), 'Lemo tse 95' ('The Year 95') is about a bewildered white female postal assistant being calmed down by the polite Modiehi, who intervenes and breaks the language barrier between an elderly African woman being served and the assistant.

The past decade has seen the continuation of work in the field of translation that bridges the late apartheid–early post-apartheid period with three initiatives. Nelson Mandela's *Long Walk to Freedom* (1994) was translated into Sepedi, isiXhosa and isiZulu, by S. M. Serudu, P. T. Mtuze and D. B. Z. Ntuli, all of them gifted wordsmiths. An abridged version of the autobiography by C. Cachalia and colleagues appeared in all the other languages. In 1999 the now inactive All African Languages Redevelopment Institute of Southern Africa initiated the translation of Zakes Mda's *The Plays of Zakes Mda* (1990). The volume comprises five one-act plays by Mda that appeared between 1979 and 1982. Translations in nine South African languages appeared by Unisa Press in 2002, with M. R. Madiba the series editor. The third initiative comes from the national Department of Arts and Culture. Under the overarching objective of 'Advance and Elevate Official African Languages', a workshop was held in February 2009 in Pretoria. Several papers inspired a follow-up in September that year. An action plan was drafted for the further development and promotion of African literature, with particular emphasis on intra-African language translation in the spirit of the Asmara Declaration (January 2000). The plan aligns with the trend we have noted earlier and is likely to expand the horizons of authors and readers.

Four key figures

Mazisi Kunene (1930–2006) is remembered for his *Emperor Shaka the Great* (1979), an epic praise poem of 438 pages which was originally written in isiZulu. The original is expected to appear in 2011. Kunene's return to South Africa in 1993 enabled him once again to publish in his home language, which he celebrated with the publication of *Isibusiso sikamhawu* (Blessings of Sympathy, 1994), *Impepho* (Incense, 1994; a collection of essays), *Indida yamancasakazi* (The Puzzle of the Ncasakazi, 1995; a collection of 209 poems), *Izigigaba nezingameko zamhlaba* (Affairs and Events of the World, 1996; short stories), *Umzwilili wama-Afrika* (Sweet Melody of the Africans, 1996), *Igudu likaSomcabeko* (The Smoking Pipe of SoMcabeko, 1997), *Iziyalo zomtanami* (Counsel to my Child, 2007; posthumously) and *Amalokotho kaNoMkhubulwane* (NoMkhubulwane's Dare, 2007; short stories). Earlier works in English include *Anthem of the Decades* (1981), an epic dedicated to the women of Africa, and *The Ancestors and the Sacred Mountain* (1982), a collection of elegiac poems. These achievements respond in no uncertain terms to some of Grobler's questions quoted earlier: a 'returnee' whose self-exile of thirty-four years reinforced deep dedication to land and language. Kunene was awarded the status of 'poet laureate' by UNESCO in 1993 and by the South African government in 2005. Given his output and commitment to language and heritage, it is expected that he will remain a major voice in African literature.

D. B. Z. Ntuli (1940–) is a writer in isiZulu whose creative output straddles both periods. Starting with a novel at the age of 21, it was in the fields of poetry (eight volumes), short stories / essays (sixteen volumes) and drama (ten texts, including radio drama) that he made an indelible mark on African literature. His poetry is rich in imagery and symbolism (See Mncube, 'Weather Symbolism', p. 147), while his short stories are known for their surprising endings. In addition, Ntuli has co-authored and edited eight anthologies of poetry, led numerous workshops for aspiring authors and served as a mentor for many. His anthology *Ugqozi olumaphiko* (Winged Inspiration, 2002) includes a number of Mazisi Kunene's poems. He is also a keen translator, amongst others of Nelson Mandela's *Long Walk to Freedom* under the title *Uhambo olude aluya enkululekweni*. A commemorative anthology consisting of a selection of Ntuli's poems, edited by H. C. Groenewald, was published by Shuter & Shooter in 2002. In 2008 a biography of Ntuli by Sibiya and Makhambeni appeared under the title *U-DBZ Ntuli Usiba lwaseGcotsheni* (D. B. Z. Ntuli the Scribe of Gcotsheni). He has been awarded many literary prizes and is a sought-after participant at the national multilingual literary festivals, which have become popular in the new South Africa.

P. T. Mtuze (1941–), a bard of repute working in isiXhosa, contributed to African literature in multiple respects, including oral and written literature and in scholarly work in collaboration with scholars such as Opland and Kaschula. His creative output includes more than thirty books, including novels, short stories, essays, poetry, dramas and translations. Court interpreter, radio announcer / producer, publisher, minister of religion, lexicographer, professor of African languages and head of isiXhosa at Rhodes University, his perspective on the chequered transformation of South Africa is unique and equally uniquely captured in his autobiography *An Alternative Struggle* (2007).

K. P. D. Maphalla (1955–) is a Sesotho author with forty titles to his credit. Foremost a gifted lyrical poet in awe of the natural environment and human nature, which comprise more than half of his output, he also writes novels, short stories and the occasional drama of a local realist kind. *Sentebale* (Forget Me Not, 1986) is a collection of poetry that depicts the persona in relation to the divine, fellow human beings and ephemeral life, while *Ha maru a rwalellana* (When Rain Clouds Gather, 2007) is a novel whose title is reminiscent of Bessie Head's novel (1968). His first English novel appeared in 1996 under the title of *A Tale of Two Fathers*. Maphalla's output of about two works per year gave rise to the unfounded rumour that he is a 'syndicate' (Khotseng, 'Maphalla').

A number of preliminary conclusions may be drawn from this chapter, although its brevity has prevented a fuller history of African-language writing since the middle of the twentieth century, let alone of individual literatures or of authors. Such an exercise would require more than one volume, especially when links with the literatures in Afrikaans and English are considered. A second conclusion is that Jahn's notion of a tragedy that has happened, is happening, or will happen appears to be overstated. Jahn intended to sound the death knell for African-language literatures under apartheid, but the idea of a 'tragedy' must be dismissed as an illusion. The literatures are alive, as we have seen, undoubtedly responding to their freedom, to societal realities, and doing so with imagination and assertion.

The literatures are being hampered more by external factors than by intrinsic ones. Many of those are carry-overs from the apartheid era; others are of recent making. The school still being the mainstay of the market, readership has not improved. It may even have shrunk after the introduction of outcomes-based education, the reduction in the number of prescribed works and the waning of serious reading in favour of a popular approach. Since the dismantling of apartheid, the number of students of African languages at universities has started to dwindle. With access now open for black learners to attend previously white schools, the perception is that African-language study at school level is also declining. Some observers say the situation is one of stagnation.

However, the intentions of the National Curriculum Statement, numerous circulars from the provincial education departments and announcements regarding major funding injections by the Department of Arts and Culture are worthy of praise. National priorities benefiting the country's community libraries and centres for the book have been outlined. With the HIV/AIDS pandemic, creative writing has become an instrument for social intervention, with the schoolchild now being approached as a young adult. Further imaginative responses are to be expected with regard to the upward aspirations of citizens, as creative minds engage with the full range of human existence. With this challenge to be faced in a free country and this responsiveness of writers and their associations, with an active critical fraternity and fresh plans on national level, it is possible to hope that new boundaries will be crossed and new horizons explored.

Bibliography

Achebe, C. *No Longer at Ease*, London: Heinemann, 1960. *Akusekho konkwaba*, isiXhosa translation, trans. H. Motlhabane, London: Heinemann, 1992. *Kwakwenzenjani?*, isiZulu translation, trans. N. Makhambeni, London: Heinemann, 1993.

　Things Fall Apart, London: Heinemann, 1958. *Dilo di masoke*, Setswana translation, trans. D. P. S. Monyaise, London: Heinemann, 1992. *Di wele makgolela*, Sepedi translation, trans. M. S. Serudu, London: Heinemann, 1993. *Lwadilik'Udonga*, isiXhosa translation, trans. K. S. Bongela, London: Heinemann, 1993. *Kwafa gula Linamasi*, isiZulu translation, trans. C. T. Msimang, London: Heinemann, 1995.

Bhengu, M. V. *Itshwele lempangele*, London: Heinemann, 1998.

Gérard, A. S. *Comparative Literature and African Literatures*, Goodwood: Via Afrika, 1983.

Gérard, A. S., et al. *Comparative Literature and African Literatures*, rev. edn, ed. C. F. Swanepoel, Pretoria: Via Afrika, 1993.

Grobler, G. M. M. 'Creative African-Language Writing in South Africa: Writers Unshackled after Apartheid', *South African Journal of African Languages* 15 (1995), 56–9.

　'Time Order in Three Novels of O. K. Matsepe', D.Lit and Phil. thesis, University of South Africa, 1989.

Groenewald, H. C. '*Insumasumane*: Zondi's Scenario for Today', *South African Journal of African Languages* 9 (1989), 6–13.

　'Response to Questionnaire for CHSAL chapter, including manuscript of "Theme, Emplotment and Narration in the novels of NG Sibiya"', unpublished, October 2010.

Groenewald, H. C. (ed.). *Imibhalo ka DBZ Ntuli*, Pietermaritzburg: Shuter & Shooter, 2002.

Groenewald, P. S. 'Periode van Nostalgie', *South African Journal of African Languages* 7 (1987), 58–63.

Gunner, L. 'Wrestling with the Present, Beckoning to the Past: Contemporary Zulu Radio Dramas', *Journal of Southern African Studies* 26:2 (June 2000), 223–37.

Gwayi, J. J. *Bafa Baphela*, Pietermaritzburg: Shuter & Shooter, 1973.

　Shumpu, Pietermaritzburg: Shuter & Shooter, 1974.

　Yekanini, Pietermaritzburg: Shuter & Shooter, 1976.

Jadezweni, M. W. 'The Inauguration of President Nelson Mandela on 10 May 1994: The Dawn of a New Era in Xhosa Praise Poetry', *Southern African Journal for Folklore Studies* 11:2 (2000), 67–77.

Jahn, J. *A History of Neo-African Literature: Writing in Two Continents*, London: Faber, 1966.

Jordan, A. C. *Ingqumbo yeminyanya*, Alice: Lovedale Press, 1940.

Kaschula, R. H. 'Xhosa Literary History: Towards Transformation in Selected Xhosa Novels', *South African Journal of African Languages* 23 (2003), 60–76.

Khaketla, B. M. *Mosali a nkhola*, Johannesburg: Afrikaanse Pers-Boekhandel, 1960.

Kubheka, I. S. *Kungavuka AbaNguni*, Pietermaritzburg: Shuter & Shooter, 1973.

Khotseng, R. 'K. P. D, Maphalla', http://blackafricanliterature.blogspot.com, accessed January 2010.

Killam, D., and R. Rowe (eds.). *The Companion to African Literatures*, Oxford: James Curry and Bloomington: Indiana University Press, 2000.

Kunene, D. P. *Heroic Poetry of the Basotho*, Oxford University Press, 1971.

Kunene, M. *Amalokotho kaNoMkhubulwane*, Cape Town: Nasou Via Afrika, 2007.

  The Ancestors and the Sacred Mountain, London: Heinemann, 1982.

  Anthem of the Decades, London: Heinemann, 1981.

  Emperor Shaka the Great: A Zulu Epic, London: Heinemann, 1979.

  Igudu likaSomcabeko, Pretoria: Van Schaik, 1997.

  Impepho, Cape Town: Nasou Via Afrika, 1994.

  Indida yamancasakuzi, Pietermaritzburg: Shuter & Shooter, 1995.

  Isibusiso sikamhawu, Cape Town: Nasou Via Afrika, 1994.

  Izigigaba nezingameko zomhlaba, Cape Town: Macmillan South Africa, 1996.

  Iziyalo zomtanami, Durban: Kunene Foundation and Brass, 2007.

  Umzwilili wama-Afrika, Cape Town: Maskew Miller Longman, 1996.

Lehmann, E., E. Reckwitz and L. Vennarini (eds.). 'Constructing South African Literary History', in *Englischsprchige Literaturen Afrikas*, vol. xiv, Essen: Die Blaue Eule, 2000, 7–193.

Lubbe, H. J. P. 'Evaluering van Suid-Sotholuisteraars se voorkeure ten opsigte van radio-dramas', MA thesis, Rand Afrikaans University, 1968.

Lubisi, C. M. *Byi le tintihweni*, Cape Town: Maskew Miller Longman, 2005.

Maake, N. P. *Kweetsa ya pelo ya motho*, Cape Town: Maskew Miller Longman, 1995.

Madadzhe, R. N. *Tshelede ndi mavhulaise*, Cape Town: Via Afrika, 1994.

Madima, E. S. *A si ene*, Johannesburg: Bona Press, 1955.

Mafela, M. J. *Lwendo lwashu*, Pietermaritzburg: Shuter & Shooter, 2004.

Magagula, S. M. *Tentile*, Pietermaritzburg: Shuter & Shooter, 1990.

Makhambeni, M. N. 'An Analysis of Certain Prominent Themes in Zulu Novels', *South African Journal of African Languages* 8 (1988), supplement 1.

Malepe, A. T. 'Biographical Sketches – D. P. S. Monyaise', *Limi* 2:1 (1974), 7–8.

  'A Brief Survey of Modern Literature in the South African Bantu Languages: Tswana', *Limi* 6 (1968), 68–75.

Mandela, N. *Long Walk to Freedom: The Autobiography*, Randburg: Macdonald Purnell, 1994. *Leetotelele go ya Tokologong*, Sepedi translation, trans. M. S. Serudu, Florida Hills: Vivlia, 2001. *Uhambo olude oluya Enkululekweni*, isiZulu translation, trans. D. B. Z. Ntuli, Florida Hills: Vivlia, 2001. *Indlela ende eya Enkululekweni*, isiXhosa translation, trans. P. T. Mtuze, Florida Hills: Vivlia, 2001.

Maphalla, K. P. D. *Ha maru a rwalellana*, Pietermaritzburg: Shuter & Shooter, 2007.

  Sentebale, Pretoria: Acacia Books, 1986.

  A Tale of Two Fathers, Johannesburg: Kwela Books, 1996.

Marivate, C. T. D. 'Tsonga Literature', *Limi* 6 (June 1968), 36–44.

'Tsonga Literature', in Gérard et al., *Comparative Literature and African Literatures*, 213–25.

Masondo, S. S. *Ingalo Yomthetho*, Pietermaritzburg: Shuter & Shooter, 1994.

Ingwe Nengonyama, Midrand: Educum, 1994.

Inkundlanye: A Collection of One-Act Stage, Radio and TV plays, Pretoria: Academia, 1997.

Iphisi Nezinyoka, Johannesburg: Educum, 1991.

Isigcawu Senkantolo, Johannesburg: Educum, 1990.

Kanti Nawe, Pietermaritzburg: Shuter & Shooter, 1994.

Ngaze Ngazenza, Pretoria: De Jager-HAUM, 1994.

Mathonsi, N. N. 'Response to Questionnaire for CHSAL chapter', unpublished, October 2010.

Matlosa, S. S. *Molahlehi*, Morija: Morija Sesotho Book Depot, 1946.

Matsepe, O. K. *Kgati ya moditi*, Pretoria: Van Schaik, 1974.

Kgorong ya mošate, Pretoria: Van Schaik, 1962.

Lešitaphiri, Pretoria: Van Schaik, 1963.

Letšofalela, Pretoria: Van Schaik, 1972.

Megokgo ya bjoko, King Williams Town: Thanda Press, 1969.

Mbuyane, M. S. *Ungatihluphi*, Pietermaritzburg: Shuter & Shooter, 1990.

Mda, Z. *The Plays of Zakes Mda*, Johannesburg: Ravan, 1990. *Diterama tsa ga Zakes Mda*, Setswana translation, trans. P. M. Sebate, Pretoria: Unisa Press, 2002. *Ditiragalo tsa Zakes Mda*, Sepedi translation, trans. D. M. Mampuru, Pretoria: UNISA Press, 2002. *Ditshwantsho tsa Zakes Mda*, Sesotho translation, trans. M. W. Tšiu, Pretoria: UNISA Press, 2002. *Dzidirama dza Zakes Mda*, Tshivenda translation, trans. T. Madima, Pretoria: UNISA Press, 2002. *Mintlangu ya Zakes Mda*, Xitsonga translation, trans. D. J. Risenga, Pretoria: UNISA Press, 2002. *Imidlali kaZakes Mda*, Isizulu translation, trans. D. B. Z. Ntuli, Pretoria: UNISA Press, 2002. *Imidlalo kaZakes Mda*, Isindebele translation, trans. A. Mnguni, Pretoria: UNISA Press, 2002. *Imidlalo yaZakes Mda*, siSwati translation, trans. Z. T. Motsa, J. M. Khumalo and J. H. Nkosi, Pretoria: UNISA Press, 2002. *Imidlalo kaZakes Mda*, Isixhosa translation of *The Plays of Zakes Mda*, trans. K. Moropa, Pretoria: UNISA Press, 2002.

Mhlakaza, V. A. *Tikamotse*, Cape Town: Maskew Miller Longman, 1999.

Mhlambi, I. J. 'African Discourses: The Old and the New in Post-Apartheid isiZulu Literature and South African Black Television Dramas', Ph.D. thesis, University of the Witwatersrand, 2008.

Mhlambi, I. J. 'Thematic Re-engagements in the Television Drama *Gaz' Lam* and isiZulu Literature', *South African Journal of African Languages* 30 (2010), 119–34.

Milubi, N. A. *Mukosi wa lufu*, Pietersburg: NAM Publishers, 1983.

Muthulata, Pietersburg: NAM Publishers, 1999.

Ndi mitodzi muni?, Pietersburg: NAM Publishers, 1985.

'Tshivenda Literature: A Thematic Appraisal', in Gérard et al., *Comparative Literature and African Literatures*, 197–212.

Zwo lungwa, Pietersburg: NAM Publishers, 1989.

Mkhari, N. B. *Ndzi tswaleriwe kwala*, Cape Town: Maskew Miller Longman, 1995.

Mncube, G. J. G. 'Weather Symbolism in D. B. Z. Ntuli's Literature', MA thesis, University of South Africa, 2006.

Mngadi, J. M. *Asikho ndawo bakithi*, Pietermaritzburg: Shuter & Shooter, 1996.

Moeketsi, R. H. (ed.). *Seyalemoya*, Pretoria: Van Schaik, 1996.

Mofokeng, S. M. *Leetong*, Johannesburg: Witwatersrand University Press, 1952.

Mohapi, T. W. D. *Lehlaba la lephaku*, Moreleta Park: S & W Promotions, 1999.

Moloto, D. P. *Manyobonyobo*, Pretoria: Educum, 1984.

Monyaise, D. P. S. *Bogosi Kupe*, Pretoria: Van Schaik, 1967.

Marara, Pretoria: Van Schaik, 1961.

Ngaka, mosadi mooka, Pretoria: Van Schaik, 1965.

Omphile Umphi Modise, Pretoria: Van Schaik, 1960.

Msimang, C. T. *Buzani kuMkabayi*, Pretoria: Van Schaik, 1982.

Izulu eladuma eSandlwana, Pretoria: Van Schaik, 1976.

Mtuze, P. T. *Alitshoni lingaphumi*, Cape Town: Maskew Miller Longman, 1986.

An Alternative Struggle, Florida Hills: Vivlia, 2007.

Ndliva, M. G. *Uthini na Dlalani?* Pietermaritzburg: Shuter & Shooter, 2002.

Ndhambi, E. P. *Mambuxu*, Johannesburg: Sasavona, 1950.

Ngewu, L. L. *Koda kube nini na?*, London: Heinemann, 1998.

Ngubane, J. K. *Uvalo lwezihlonzi*, Pietermaritzburg: Shuter & Shooter, 1956.

Ntshangase, D. K. 'Publishing in African Languages', in B. van Rooyen (ed.), *How to Get Published in South Africa: A Guide for Authors*, Halfway House: Southern Book Publishers, 1996.

Ntuli, D. B. 'The Function of the Narrator in Hubert Sishi's *Imilando YakwaZulu*', *South African Journal of African Languages* 19 (1999), 250–7.

'Zulu Literature', in Gérard et al., *Comparative Literature and African Literatures*, 139–54.

Ntuli, D. B. (ed.). *Imilando YakwaZulu* [by H. Sishi], Pretoria: UNISA Press, 2000.

Ugqozi olumaphiko, Pietermaritzburg: Shuter & Shooter, 2002.

Ntuli, D. B., and C. F. Swanepoel. *Southern African Literature in African Languages: A Concise Historical Perspective*, Pretoria: Acacia, 1993.

Nyembezi, C. L. S. *Inkinsela yase Mgungundlovu*, Pietermaritzburg: Shuter & Shooter, 1961. Translated by S. Ngidi as *The Rich Man of Pietermaritzburg*: Laverstock: Aflame Books, 2008. *Kgabane ya mokokotlofo*, Sesotho translation, trans. R. C. Bodibe, Pietermaritzburg: Shuter & Shooter, 1983.

Mntanami! Mntanami!, Pietermaritzburg: Shuter & Shooter, 1950.

Opland, J. 'Xhosa Literature in Newspapers, 1837–1909', in J. A. Smit, J. van Wyk and J-P. Wade (eds.), *Rethinking South African Literary History*, Durban: Y Press, 1996.

Potgieter, M. '. . . Xhosa lewer geen probleme op nie', *Die Burger*, 26 November 2010.

Publishing Association of South Africa, *Writings in Nine Tongues: A Catalogue of Literature and Readers in Nine African Languages for South Africa*, Cape Town, 2007, 2008, 2009.

Puleng, N. S. *Ba ikgethetše motsotso*, Pietersburg: NAM Publishers, 2000.

Qangule, Z. S. 'A Brief Survey of Modern Literature in the South African Bantu Languages: Xhosa', *Limi* 6 (1968), 14–28.

Ranamane, D. T. 'A Survey of Setswana Literature', in Gérard et al., *Comparative Literature and African Literatures*, 1969–95.

Ratau, J. K. *Khirimpana*, Morija: Morija Sesotho Book Depot, 1955.

Satyo, S. C. 'A Short History of Xhosa Literature', in Gérard et al., *Comparative Literature and African Literatures*, 65–89.

Saule, N. *Ukhozi olumaphiko*, Cape Town: Nasou Via Afrika, 1996.

Seboni, M. O. M. *Rammone wa Kgalagadi*, Pretoria: Via Afrika, 1947.

Selepe, T. 'Deculturation: An Afrocentric Critique of B. M. Khaketla's *Mosali a nkhola*', *Literator* 30:3 (2009), 135–56.

Serudu, S. M. 'A Survey of Northern Sotho Literature', in Gérard et al., *Comparative Literature and African Literatures*, 155–67.

Shole, J. S. 'Setswana Literature: A Perspective', in Gérard et al., *Comparative Literature and African Literatures*, 97–105.

Sibiya, N. G. *Bengithi lizokuna*, Pietermaritzburg: Nutrend, 2008.

   Kuxolelwa abanjani?, Pietermaritzburg: Shuter & Shooter, 2002.

   Kwaze kwalunkhuni, Florida Hills: Vivlia, 2003.

Sibiya, N. and N. Makhambeni. *U-DBZ Ntuli Usiba lwaseGcotsheni*, Pietermaritzburg: New Dawn Publishers, 2008.

Sikosana, M. *Kungavuk'amaJali*, Pietermaritzburg: Shuter & Shooter, 2008.

Sishi, H. 'Imilando yakwaZulu', unpublished tapes, Durban: South African Broadcasting Corp., 1966–8.

Swanepoel, C. F. 'B. M. Khaketla's *Mosali a nkhola*', in P. J. Wentzel (ed.), *Third African Language Congress of UNISA*, Pretoria: University of South Africa Press, 1980.

   'Echoes of Commitment: Race Relations in Three Southern African Literatures', in C. Malan (ed.), *Race and Literature/Ras en Literatuur*, Pinetown: Owen Burgess Publishers, 1987; 60–76.

   'Kweetsa ya pelo ya motho (N. P. Maake): Narrative of Human Behaviour in Political Turmoil', *South African Journal of African Languages* 19 (1999), 52–9.

   'The *Leselinyana* Letters and Early Reception of Mofolo's *Chaka*', *South African Journal of African Languages* 9 (1989), 145–53.

Van Heerden, T. 'Die Radiovervolgverhaal in Noord-Sotho', M.A. thesis, Rand Afrikaans University, 1971.

Williams, R. *The Country and the City*, London: Chatto & Windus, 1973.

Yawa, S. *Ubunzulu bentliziyo*, Pietermaritzburg: Shuter & Shooter, 2005.

Yazbek, A. *Gaz' Lam*, vol I, Johannesburg: South African Broadcasting Corp., 2002–5.

Zondi, E. *Insumasumane*, Johannesburg: Witwatersrand University Press, 1986.

   Ukufa kukaShaka, Johannesburg: Witwatersrand University Press, 1962.

Zulu, N. S. 'African Literature in the New Millennium', *South African Journal of African Languages*, 19 (1999), 291–301.

   'The Literary History of Sesotho Literature in Social Transition: A Survey of Prominent Themes and Trends after 1990', *South African Journal of African Languages* 23 (2003), 77–94.

   Nonyana ya tshepo, Cape Town: Maskew Miller Longman, 1997.

   'Racial Relations and Intercultural love in *Itshwele lempangele*', *South African Journal of African Languages* 20 (2000), 277–87.

30

Writing the interregnum: literature and the demise of apartheid

STEPHEN CLINGMAN

In a celebrated series of essays written in a burst of intellectual and creative energy in the mid 1980s, Njabulo Ndebele set out some key terms for considering the history, trajectory and imperatives of South African literature.[1] Some of these terms – 'spectacle', 'interiority', 'information', 'counsel' – will come up again for discussion in this chapter, as will the wider resonances of Ndebele's contribution. Beyond the terms themselves, however, there is a deeper – one might say foundational – aspect in Ndebele's approach, which may be even more significant in considering writing in South Africa in the 1980s and early 1990s – the long decade of its 'interregnum' through the final years of apartheid. It is an aspect on one level simple, but nonetheless profound – that Ndebele established a perspective for considering the history of South African literature on *formal* grounds. Moreover, these were not the formal or generic grounds of standard literary history – realism, romanticism, experimentalism – though such terms can and do have their place. Rather, these formal terms had to do with what *informed* South African writing – what shaped it, gave it perspective: its own versions of 'interiority', as it were.

The implicit challenge in Ndebele's formal approach has not much been taken up in the writing of South African literary history, but along with a number of other patterns in the period, it does allow us to reach towards certain features at the heart of the era. In his essay 'The Rediscovery of the Ordinary', for instance, Ndebele pointed out that the history of black South African writing had 'largely been the history of the representation of spectacle' (*Rediscovery*, p. 41). To some degree this was coterminous with what was commonly designated 'protest literature', though the implications of the spectacular went deeper as a matter of psychic and political as well as fictive practice. The literature of spectacle was a literature of recognition, of predetermined (and overdetermined) moral images, which for the most part returned

1 These essays were collected in Ndebele, *South African Literature and Culture: Rediscovery of the Ordinary*, cited in this chapter as *Rediscovery*.

the surface of South African reality to itself without disrupting, questioning or disturbing it. It did not allow for versions of interiority that would concern process rather than product. It did not allow identity to shift or change, except in designated categories of demonstration, protest or revolution. Because of its preordained nature, it was strangely anti-democratic in formal terms, even as it proclaimed its democratic intentions at the level of content.

How does this help us understand the South African interregnum of the 1980s and early 1990s and the particular roles of writing through the demise of apartheid? Mainly it does so by allowing us to discern a set of patterns and a mutually informing definition. This is not the place to give an exhaustive account of South African history during the period, yet even the most sum-mary listing gives a sense of its tumult. This was the era of the rise of the United Democratic Front (UDF) and sustained grass-roots resistance throughout the country; of major strikes and insistent labour activism; of people's culture, worker poets and union plays; of successive States of Emergency; of secret and unsecret wars in Namibia and Angola; of no education without libera-tion; of state terrorism, assassinations, dirty tricks and third forces; of people's courts, mass funerals, the *toyi-toyi*, of necklacing;[2] of the myriad horrific acts of brutality and inhumanity that characterised apartheid in its last throes. Ultimately there was the release of the African National Congress (ANC) prisoners towards the end of 1989, and of Nelson Mandela on 11 February 1990, followed by the Convention for a Democratic South Africa (CODESA) negotiations and the election of 1994, which formally brought apartheid to an end. But who, in the earlier years, could have foreseen the latter? And who, in the latter years, would have escaped the trauma and after-images of the former? The South African world during these years was so foreboding that cataclysm was as easily imaginable an outcome as peace.

In this light, a number of principles emerge. One is that the 'interregnum' in South Africa went through phases, as different aspects of its dynamic unfolded; this pattern will be an intrinsic part of this chapter. A second concerns the seeming paradox that in such a period of momentous and inescapable spectacle, a writer and critic of Ndebele's perspicacity should have called for an end to the literature of the spectacular. But the paradox is resolved if we see it from a different angle. For if a literature of spectacle concerned a set of predetermined images and perspectives, then who in this era could see

2 The *toyi-toyi* was a quasi-martial jog or dance which became part of resistance culture, while 'necklacing' was the practice among some black communities of killing a suspected collaborator by putting a tyre around his or her neck and setting it alight.

anything like the true nature of reality? This was an era in South Africa when reality itself was becoming loosed from its moorings; like shifting tectonic plates, a gap was opening up between the 'real' and any pre-existing apparatus for discerning or codifying it. To represent it in accustomed forms was not a *means* to vision, but its prevention. Perhaps it is no accident, then, that Ndebele's dissatisfaction with an aesthetics of recognition came into being at such a time; it may not have been the primary or only *reason* it came into being, but it was one among many markers of the period which it addressed.

Beyond these principles, however, there is another, also of a formal character. If, in these terms, the South African interregnum is defined as an era in which the nature, dynamic and future of South African reality became intrinsically problematic – in some sense invisible, present only as the shadowed and uncanny – then, by the same token, the literature of the interregnum was writing whose intrinsic form was to register that very loosening or unmooring, the problematics of reality itself. The ways in which South African writing did so took on varied inflections, but this is where the mutually informing definition comes into play: the writing of the interregnum was a writing that approached, whether directly or by way of deferral, the cracks in an aesthetics of recognition. It was, in a way, writing which *defined* the interregnum, sometimes in advance of, but often obliquely to, standard forms of political recognition, across its own fault lines of the visible.[3]

As I have suggested, there were phases in such a movement; after the stresses of the 1980s, and as the prospect – still precarious – of a more tangible future approached in the 1990s, so too the forms of South African writing began to cool, to take on more recognisable or even familiar shapes. But particularly in the 1980s we see an intrinsic and telling shift. And so we arrive at yet a further underlying pattern. Precisely because it was not clear how reality could or should be represented, some of the key writing of the interregnum moved *from the representation of history*, understood as a concern not so much with the past but with an unfolding present – which had perhaps been the dominant form of writing until then – into *a history of representation*, in which the problematics of representing the South African reality came to the fore. Such a shift was not unprecedented, nor was it invariable, but it was heightened during this period, when a number of the country's major writers (mainly of fiction) were active at a particular pitch of intensity and

---

3 Elleke Boehmer's argument that the writing of the era involved mainly a sense of closure (see 'Endings') should perhaps be seen in tandem with this formal perspective.

accomplishment.[4] In their work, the modes of writing South Africa were at issue. It was not so much that they responded to a predefined interregnum, but their writing helped create the sense of an interregnum whose lineaments we now see in retrospect.

Living in the interregnum

In this regard, it is significant that the South African interregnum was defined in the literary world long before it was in the political. It was Nadine Gordimer, in an essay entitled 'Living in the Interregnum' (1983), who established some of its essential characteristics. 'I live at 6,000 feet,' she wrote, 'in a society whirling, stamping, swaying with the force of revolutionary change . . . The city is Johannesburg, the country South Africa, and the time the last years of the colonial era in Africa' (p. 262). This was a view that few might have ventured at the time – that South Africa was *already* in a state of revolution – but for Gordimer it concerned not only the politics of the present, but the graspable nature of her world. The past, as she put it, had begun 'to drop rapidly out of sight' and 'historical co-ordinates don't fit life any longer' (pp. 262–3). Vision too had been compromised in the very instruments of its possibility; she spoke of 'the successfully fitted device in the eye of the beholder' inducing distortions even as there was a need to believe 'in our ability to find new perceptions, and our ability to judge their truth' (p. 266). Any claim on the future on the part of whites opposed to apartheid would depend on 'how to offer one's *self*' (p. 264). But self, time, co-ordinates, vision, the pressure of the future – in these categories Gordimer set out some of the major markers of the interregnum, indicating how they were exactly what had become problematic. It was not for nothing, Gordimer wrote, that she had chosen as the epigraph to her novel *July's People* a quotation from Antonio Gramsci: 'The old is dying, and the new cannot be born; in this interregnum there arises a great diversity of morbid symptoms' (p. 262).

July's People was published in 1981, and in it we see a number of the features of interregnum writing. Time, for one thing, is dislodged from its moorings, as the novel is set in an indeterminate future moment of putative revolution, following the Smales family as they flee a collapsing Johannesburg to take up residence in the rural village of their servant, July. If the setting suggests the pressure of an absent future, then, by the same token, that future loops back on past and present, as Gordimer uses it to scrutinise the once

---

4 In this chapter I deal primarily with fiction in English or translation into English, cross-referring to other chapters in the volume where relevant.

'normal' – now abnormal – life of the Smaleses.[5] Particularly telling is that the Smales family are what might be regarded as good liberals, believing in an essentially humane creed and the procedural triumph of rationality. But it is exactly the imbrications of their humanity and rationality in the distorting mirror-world of apartheid that is in question, particularly in the life of Maureen Smales. This is where Gordimer dissects the 'morbid symptoms' of the interregnum world, where no gesture is uncompromised, where July, as much as Maureen or her husband, Bam, is imprinted with the mental frameworks of the past. The village, then, becomes another motif in a broader matrix of the interregnum, for it is a site of containment. Open to the past, fringing on yet virtually sealed to the future, the novel gives the sense of enclosure without any clear possibility of transition. It is fitting that the ending of the novel is apocalyptic: a translation out of 'real' time into mythic time as Maureen abandons the entrapment of the interregnum by running towards an unmarked helicopter, which might equally bring life or death.[6] Here are the signs of interregnum writing: 'unreal' time, the problematic self, closed environments, unstable vision, the press of an insistent but unknowable future, and apocalyptic presentiments.

J. M. Coetzee's work is, of course, very different from Gordimer's, but it is intriguing that his novels from this period suggest some of the same patterns. In *Waiting for the Barbarians* (1981), time and space are dislodged from anything like the 'real', as the novel is set in indeterminate territory on the frontier of an empire whose lineaments could derive from regimes as diverse as the Roman, Soviet or South African, or the Gestapo torture chambers. In this respect, its relation to the South African world is at most one of the uncanny – shadowed, looming, yet also evasive. Here again – in a novel which begins with the question of eyesight and filters – vision is at issue, as the central character and narrator, the Magistrate, finds it impossible to discern clear markers in time or space, and – even more importantly – any clear location for himself in moral time and space. He is the Magistrate administering the law, but under empire law is unhinged from justice much as signs are decoupled from reference, and so the Magistrate faces another key measure of the interregnum, namely the inescapability of complicity. In his relationship with a barbarian woman, he discovers that torture may be indistinguishable from the underlying intrusions of a compulsion to read its

5 For the relationship between present and future in the novel, see Clingman, *The Novels of Nadine Gordimer*, pp. 201–2. For the novel's 'epistemological unhousing . . . of white South Africa', see Barnard, *Apartheid and Beyond*, p. 31.
6 Readings of the ending have varied widely. For three approaches, see Visser, 'Beyond the Interregnum', Boehmer, 'Endings' and Clingman, *Grammar of Identity*, chapter 6.

marks. Though his fortress is on the outpost of empire, empire is a total environment which allows no escape at all, and while ultimately the novel foretells empire's inevitable demise, the Magistrate himself can see no way forward, no redemption, no differentiation from its undifferentiated space. In that way, the novel is poised between the sense of an ending and the sensation of endless suspension (see Boehmer, 'Endings', p. 48). Coetzee, who in an article entitled 'The Novel Today' wrote urgently of the need for fiction to rival history,[7] has written a novel which, though it may not be 'about' the South African interregnum, has, in its very alterity, captured haunting evocations from its heart.

In *Life & Times of Michael K* (1983), Coetzee returned more overtly to the South African world, but still in a defamiliarised and defamiliarising form. As in *July's People*, the setting was some indeterminate point of breakdown in the future, and part of the underlying purpose was to engage with the present. But where Gordimer's characters flee towards the margins of their time and space, Coetzee's Michael K makes his way into the interior towards a half-memorialised, half-imagined point of origin, the birthplace of his mother. It is a point that slips away as he approaches, an ungraspable source. Yet, in a shift as he buries his mother's ashes, he discovers an identity for himself as cultivator – a different relationship to the earth than the male regimes of possession and conflict that surround him. Michael himself is defamiliarised: with his hare lip, he does not speak the language of his world, and yet his mouth will also never close; nothing can quite close the gap in which he seems to live. A medical officer in an internment camp develops a compulsion to pin down his 'meaning', yet as the Magistrate discovers in *Waiting for the Barbarians*, to claim meaning is also to imprison it. As for Michael, detained in one location after another in a war-torn country, his aim is to be 'out of all the camps at the same time' (Coetzee, *Life & Times*, p. 248). In a novel with Foucauldian echoes, the Medical Officer intuits Michael's scandal: of how 'a meaning can take up residence in a system without becoming a term in it' (*Life & Times*, p. 228). Michael's way of doing so is through versions of anorexia: non-participation in the cycles of the world, a search for ethical purity which may lead to his death. Yet in his commitment to start from the essentials – of seeds, growth, nurturing, being 'a tender of the soil' (*Life & Times*, p. 156) – there is just the slightest sense of new versions of beginning. At

---

7 Coetzee's comments were first presented at the *Weekly Mail* Book Week in Cape Town in 1987. Later he was clear that his article should be read primarily in the context of a moment when he felt the novel to be under attack by the 'colonising' discourse of history in South Africa. Yet not all historical approaches to fiction discounted its intrinsic modes of operation, and they too should be read in the context of the period.

once archaic and resistant, there is also allegiance that is in its own way quite radical. Michael's time is not the time of South African history; if the novel was 'writing the interregnum', then it was a different form of the interregnum than the political world might have imagined.[8]

In this still early phase of interregnum writing, a novel such as Mongane Wally Serote's *To Every Birth its Blood* (1981) offered its own complex contribution by being fragmented in at least two dimensions. The first, in part one of the novel, is explored through the narrative of Tsi Molope, a journalist who has suffered a traumatic assault at the hands of the police and whose general perceptual reality under the oppressions of apartheid borders on nightmare – dispersed, chaotic, paratactic in its underlying structures. The novel's focus in this section – emerging partly from a Black Consciousness ethos – is *experiential*: the traumatised stream of consciousness under the brutalities of apartheid. David Attwell has pointed out that experimental writing of this kind is not unprecedented in black South African literature (*Rewriting Modernity*, pp. 169–77), but here again we see motifs heightened in the interregnum: the problematic self, dislodged versions of time and space, an unanchored reality and the search for a language to register it. Yet in a countermove, part two of the novel adopts a different modality. Tsi Molope drops away and a new 'collective' identity takes over – an underground group active in 'The Movement'. Tsi's problematic behaviour – particularly his violence towards women – is overcome, and the chaos of his life is resolved in the larger and stabilising commitment to the political struggle. Though the novel makes it clear that the price of such commitment is high, the shift nonetheless resolves problems of self, time, future and reality, sublimating them in a political script. There is a paradox here worth contemplating. If, in a political frame, the novel proceeds from dissociation towards revolution, then formally its trajectory is more conservative, proceeding in the direction of normalisation. This split in the aesthetics of the novel becomes its own sign: in this interregnum, which represented the 'reality'? It was a world in which the chaotic, the experiential and the political were in serious contention, often fragmented and sometimes indistinguishable.

New aesthetics, altered visions

To focus only on writing that allowed itself to register the formal disruptions of the South African ethos is perhaps to do other kinds of fiction a disservice.

8 For a most nuanced account of the novel in these terms, see Attwell, *J. M. Coetzee*, chapter 4.

And it is true that writers responded to the intensities of the period in varied ways, both political and cultural. So, for instance, Menán du Plessis's *A State of Fear* (1985) magnifies the self-consciousness of its white protagonist, Anna Louw, in relation to the turmoil of the early 1980s in the Cape townships, finding its narrative trajectory in that gap. Richard Rive's *'Buckingham Palace', District Six* (1986) is an act of memorialisation and retrieval set in the coloured community of Cape Town's District Six before it was demolished under apartheid. Rose Zwi's trilogy, *Another Year in Africa* (1980), *The Inverted Pyramid* (1981) and *Exiles* (1984), explored with great empathy the Jewish immigrant and political experience in South Africa and (in the third novel) Israel. In stories from the late 1970s and 1980s, collected in *Noorjehan and other Stories* (1990), Ahmed Essop brought his delicate yet vivid depictions of the Indian-South African experience, in works such as *The Hajji and other Stories* (1978) and *The Emperor* (1984), into the more politicised circumstances of the decade (see Rastogi, *Afrindian Fictions*, chapter 2). In a very different form, a journal such as *Staffrider* presented the virtually unmediated voices and images of writers, poets, photographers and artists around the country to a public sphere unused to such voluminous, democratic, communal and insistent manifestations – work that was at once both political and cultural.[9]

Yet it was in this moment, with its seemingly unending political demands, that Njabulo Ndebele offered his critique of the dominant forms of South African writing – work whose primary tendency only returned the surface of the 'political'. Ndebele's views have in turn been criticised for an intrinsic formal conservatism and uninspected humanism – always a possibility in the South African setting – yet it is equally important to avoid any mimetic fallacy in considering them.[10] Though the forms he recommended may *look* recognisable, to short-circuit their complexity may be to miss their deeper dynamics. Starting with his essay 'Turkish Tales and some Thoughts on South African Fiction', first published in *Staffrider* in 1984 (reprinted in *Rediscovery*), Ndebele developed a sophisticated and dialectical account. Part of his address came out of the Black Consciousness movement, in which Ndebele had participated as a poet, particularly the concern with 'consciousness' and 'interiority'. Ndebele was also attempting to rehabilitate a form of narrative *counter* to the dominant modes of western realism, exploring an oral mode of storytelling,

9 On the orientation of *Staffrider*, see Kirkwood, 'Remembering Staffrider', and Van Wyk, 'Staffrider and the Politics of Culture'.
10 For a thoughtful critique of both Ndebele and Albie Sachs, see Sole, 'The Role of the Writer'. For Ndebele's underlying focus on 'an authentic version of a familiar world', see Parry, 'Some Provisional Speculations', p. 17.

whether in Yashar Kemal's *Turkish Tales* or in South African culture. At the same time, these ideas were linked, via Walter Benjamin's 'The Storyteller', to forms of understanding which cut through the 'realisms' of information (which Ndebele tied, a little forcedly, to liberal hegemony in South Africa) towards alternative modes of apprehension: wisdom, counsel and the unfolding logic of narrative itself. Where 'interiority' – which Ndebele emphasised the need for – may have appeared to be 'humanist', via Herbert Marcuse it was intrinsically connected to a dialectical form of liberation from the dominant enforcements of the 'real'. It also entailed a refusal of the anonymity to which black South Africans were consigned under apartheid. In this context, fictional characters whose interiority was the subject of *process* in a story both transcended predetermined moral allegories and involved their readers in a democratic mode of participation in the work of making meaning. As Ndebele wrote in much quoted words, 'The challenge is to free the entire social imagination of the oppressed from the laws of perception that have characterised apartheid society' ('Redefining Relevance', in *Rediscovery*, p. 67). Such a formulation reversed the standard ratios between the aesthetic and the political, allowing the latter to emerge from the former, rather than vice versa. It was a formulation designed to reach a different version of the political itself.

How such principles might be achieved in practice began to be evident in Ndebele's *Fools and other Stories* (1983). For one thing, the volume was not so much a story 'collection' as a 'cycle' with threaded motifs, whose gaps and continuities invite a process of readerly involvement. In *Fools and other Stories*, Ndebele also writes a world virtually devoid of white characters. Here black characters, in all their imperfections and foibles, enter into the exact opposite of the anonymity assigned to them under apartheid – the radical possibility inherent in the exploration of 'interiority'. So, in 'The Test', all that appears to be at stake is whether a young boy playing soccer will go running in the rain against what he knows would be the wishes of his mother. Yet transgression against authority is a version of liberation – a first step towards individuation, and towards new forms of immanent agency and knowledge (see Attwell, *Rewriting Modernity*, p. 184). In 'The Prophetess', another young boy finds that he himself has the healing power his mother needs – though it involves a different kind of transgression. There may be few short stories in the world as genuinely celebratory as 'Uncle', in which joy, freedom and discipline are finely balanced, and which ends with a quite magical collective musical epiphany. In the volume's title story, 'Fools', Ndebele deliberately chooses a figure of authority – a teacher – living in disgrace (the term will resonate later in South African fiction): he has stolen money, raped a student and is unfaithful to his wife. Yet the story is a first-person narrative: we see Zamani's world from the inside, participate in his degradation and his conflict with a younger and highly political alter ego, Zani, and contemplate his partial redemption at the end. Here is character as process rather than product; here readers are fully absorbed in negotiations of sympathy and disgust; here are some of Ndebele's most telling ruminations on 'the obviousness of analysis' (*Fools*, p. 262), of how revolutionary fervour can paradoxically negate the depth and wisdom of other forms of investigation (p. 236). By the end, as Zamani stands up to a 'boer' who is whipping him, in a setting somewhere between farce and heroism, he is nothing if not a complex and full human being. In various ways, the surface of South African reality, and its characteristic forms of political representation, have been altered.

If anyone took up this mantle in an even more inventive way, it was Zoë Wicomb in another short-story cycle, *You Can't Get Lost in Cape Town* (1987). In part, the fictional brief of the cycle concerns interstitial identities in the coloured community of Little Namaqualand, caught between black and white, English and Afrikaans, country and city; in part, it is to introduce a feminist perspective into the South African narrative of race, class, language and region. But in following the first-person narrator, Frieda Shenton, from the smallholding where her father is a teacher, to Cape Town, England and back, one of the major concerns of the stories is to complicate any notion of the 'real', as well as the artificialities of narrative itself. The opening story, 'Bowl Like Hole', raises the question of identity, but also that of a narrator who describes more about the 'real' than she could possibly have known. In the small masterpiece, 'Jan Klinkies', what is at stake in a world governed by racial identification is nothing less than the regime of the sign under apartheid, and the radical, if apparently 'mad', gesture of the character who resists it. As narrator, Frieda kills off her mother – only to revive her in a later story; then it is her father who is dead. In the abortion she opts for in the title story she also finds individuation through transgression, accepting for herself a condition both abandoning and abandoned, whether of the child she might have had or the patriarchal laws of God. In 'A Trip to the Gifberge', Frieda's return to South Africa ultimately revolves around language and landscape, evoking forms of representation and mapping much older than apartheid, as if some counternarrative is always there to be retrieved. The cycle as a whole angles into such counternarratives, prising open the regimes of the real.

The interregnum in Afrikaans

Two Afrikaans writers – or writers who originally worked in Afrikaans – deserve particular mention in this setting, precisely because of the issue of formal disruption. Both had their beginnings in the 'Sestiger' period and, as Afrikaners, both were quite familiar with the need to splinter the veneer of cultural as well as political normalcy.[11] They did so in different ways – André Brink producing a string of novels across more than four decades in South Africa; Breyten Breytenbach with his poetry, painting, travelogue and memoir from exile in Paris and then prison in Pretoria and Pollsmoor. For Breytenbach, especially, the 'experimental' line was second nature; but the work of both writers in the 1980s accorded strongly with interregnum patterns.

In André Brink's work, this is most visible in *States of Emergency* (1988), a novel written, as its title suggests, in the context of the political turmoil of the decade. On one level, the work hews closely to the fierce concentration of historical events, such as the Cradock Four and Mxenge murders;[12] on another, it is dotted with references to theorists, such as Saussure, Barthes, Wittgenstein and Gadamer. The key feature is that the work purports *not* to be a novel, but rather 'notes towards a love story', in which the legitimacy of writing any such account in these circumstances can only be in serious question. There is a postmodern modus operandi, with the 'novelist' – part Brink, part not – juggling multiple narratives; a 'real' love story from the 1960s migrating into an 'unreal' (but no more or less fictive) love story from the 1980s, all set against the political backdrops of both periods and the writer's 'personal' musings. The 'novel' – if there is one – is nothing less than the totality of these narratives, but in lieu of an ending – for there cannot be one in the midst of this writerly *crise de conscience* in relation to a present of surplus intensity – there are only multiple options, each of them equally suspect. If there is a core for the writer of/in this novel, it is primarily one of double vision: 'As if he is staring at two altogether different scenes at the same time, superimposed on one another, the lines incongruous' (Brink, *States of Emergency*, p. 190). There is a fault line between text and history, the 'real' and

---

11 For more on the Sestigers and the writings of both Brink and Breytenbach, see chapters 21 and 22 in this volume. On the 'self-consciously critical' nature of white South African writing, see Lazarus, 'Modernism and Modernity', p. 134.

12 The Cradock Four – Mathew Goniwe, Fort Calata, Sparrow Mkhonto and Sicelo Mhlauli – were seized by South African security forces while returning from Port Elizabeth to Cradock in June 1985; they were then murdered and their bodies burned. Anti-apartheid lawyers Griffiths and Victoria Mxenge were also brutally murdered by the security forces, he in 1981 and she in 1985.

the 'fictive', and a future both necessary and impossible; the cracked poetics of the South African interregnum.

In 1975, Breyten Breytenbach was arrested after a somewhat half-baked attempt to visit South Africa in secret and set up a form of underground resistance – a quest perhaps as much 'fictive' as political. Sentenced to nine years in prison and initially kept in isolation in Pretoria, he was, strangely, permitted to write. The books which resulted – *The True Confessions of an Albino Terrorist* (1984) and *Mouroir: Mirrornotes of a Novel* (1983) – can be considered from the perspectives both of prison writing and experimental narrative; but for the purposes of this chapter, the salient aspect is the *conjunction* of the two so that, from the heart of the South African edifice, its reality is both emphasised and dissolved. Whereas in most South African prison writing of a political nature there are twin impulses towards realism and solidarity, in *True Confessions* there is an equal focus on writing and the impossibilities of 'confession'. In this context, as David Schalkwyk has suggested, for Breytenbach writing itself becomes doubled – the only pathway to the 'real', yet also the dreamwork of the writer recognising the impossibility of reference ('Confession and Solidarity'). In *Mouroir* – originally published in alternating sections of Afrikaans and English, and mixing modalities of parable, allegory and the surreal – the 'mirror' becomes the central image, not in any standard form as the reflection of reality, but rather the other way round: 'Reality is a version of the mirror image' (*Mouroir*, 1984 edition, p. 62). There are other forms of doubleness: the book's title combines the French *miroir* (mirror) and *mourir* (to die), and Breytenbach presents a searing account of prison executions, to which he was the proximate yet 'absent' mirror during his years in Pretoria Central. J. M. Coetzee suggests that Breytenbach's ultimate mirror image is himself ('Breyten Breytenbach', p. 232). Facing his own interregnum in prison – though he does not put it that way – Breytenbach writes a book of the real/unreal/surreal in a form that evokes the South African world from the other side of its habitual mirrors.

Towards the end of apartheid

On another level, a fierce debate had been raging through the literary world of the 1980s, partly as a legacy of Black Consciousness, partly in response to the urgencies of the decade. At its core were questions of political affiliation and the proper ratios of priority between politics and culture. So, organisations formed and disbanded: the Johannesburg branch of PEN fracturing under Black Consciousness pressure, the African Writers' Association competing with the Congress of South African Writers (COSAW), affiliated with the broader Congress organisations. In December 1987, Amsterdam was host to the Culture in Another South Africa (CASA) conference, dedicated to the emergence of a non-racial and democratic culture in a liberated South Africa (Campschreur and Divendal, *Culture*). In the midst of it all was the Cultural Desk, associated with the ANC/UDF movement, operating as both political and cultural arbiter and at times as a form of censor.

It was in this context that, in 1989, Albie Sachs presented a paper, titled 'Preparing Ourselves for Freedom', at an in-house ANC seminar, soon after published to widespread debate inside the country. In a new spirit of openness – and in the light of new political openings – Sachs called for the intrinsic dispositions of art to be set free. Beginning with the idea that 'we all know where South Africa is, but we do not yet know what it is', he proposed a moratorium of five years on ANC members 'saying that culture is a weapon of struggle' (Sachs, 'Preparing Ourselves', p. 19).[13] A purely 'instrumental and non-dialectical view of culture', he suggested, was damaging not only to art, but also to 'the struggle itself' (p. 22). What was the ANC fighting for, he asked, 'if not the right to express our humanity in all its forms' (p. 21)? South African art was strangely governed by its oppressors, but rather than being 'subject' to the political – from whatever direction – the political could and should be instructed by culture. To many, Sachs's pronouncements came as a breath of relief; to others – worker and community poets, those who had been involved in both the political and cultural struggles of the decade inside the country – it felt like a betrayal. To some there was serious irony, summarised by Graham Pechey: 'A movement that believes the freedom of artists is somehow in its gift cannot, the argument goes, truly believe in their freedom' ('Introduction' to Ndebele, *Rediscovery*, p. 5). There was also the point that although Sachs's formulation was committed to the independence of art, it offered relatively little in the way of aesthetic or theoretical content. By contrast, Ndebele's views, offered in a similar vein, appeared much more developed, substantial and intricate.

That there was no necessary contradiction between political and literary commitments is suggested by the fact that some major figures were involved in the developments of the period: Ndebele and Gordimer as founding figures in COSAW; Gordimer in attending political funerals in solidarity, presenting testimony for the defence in political trials and continuing to bear witness in her essays. Yet, in a new phase in which the demise of apartheid was

---

13 For a wide range of responses to Sachs, see the full volume from which this essay is drawn.

approaching, fiction continued to tell its story in forms that ran not so much parallel to the political, but in tension and articulation with it. Gordimer's unusual venture in 1987 was *A Sport of Nature*, a picaresque political romance that followed its central character, Hillela, through a series of global events and love affairs, culminating in an imagined freedom celebration in South Africa which she attends as wife to an African general and leader of his country. Here the trajectory may have seemed fanciful, yet if Gordimer had a deeper topic it was the correlation between an unconstrained bodily drive and the irrepressibility of political liberation. A related juxtaposition in the novel, between its utopian romance and themes of the darker realities of power, suggested more unsettling questions for a South Africa on the brink of change – how far power and utopia would infuse and complicate one another.

In a more subdued yet structurally intricate vein, Gordimer's *My Son's Story* (1990) opened up those ambiguities even further. Here, in the story of a coloured teacher and lover of literature turned political orator, doubleness is all. In taking on the loyalties of politics, Sonny betrays his wife in an affair; later his wife will return the favour in the opposite direction, becoming an underground cadre in the liberation struggle without his knowledge. Their son, Will, is the writer as 'traitor', secretly telling this story of father and mother. But beyond these levels, doubleness is compounded. Sonny becomes 'Sonny', the orator – split from himself; the political rhetoric he speaks is shallow and alien to him, especially when he recognises that the language of liberation in South Africa has also been the language of oppression in Eastern Europe. Gordimer – who had written in 'Living in the Interregnum' that 'nothing I say here will be as true as my fiction' (p. 264), and who added in 'The Essential Gesture' that 'art is on the side of the oppressed' (p. 291) – puts those two principles in dialogue. What she discovers is that the art of liberation may have to be one that tangles with liberatory politics itself.

Yet if any novel left a haunting imprint in this last phase prior to the years of a negotiated settlement in South Africa, it was most likely Coetzee's *Age of Iron* (1990). Here too was surprise, for in this novel Coetzee engaged with the stark textures of South African realities – particularly conflict in the townships around Cape Town – in a way he never had before. But that was only, in a way, to turn them inside out. The novel's central character is Mrs Curren, a retired classics professor whose recently discovered cancer, from which she will soon die, seems coterminous with the disease in South African society. Mrs Curren – non-political yet engaged with all her might in a sense of human responsibility – is writing a letter (the text of the novel) to her daughter in the USA, who may never receive it. At her house arrives Mr Verceuil, a derelict tramp, who becomes her only companion, Angel of Death or what passes for saviour. Her maid's child is involved in the township uprising and is killed; a trip to the township becomes a journey to Virgil's underworld without any notion of redemption or resolving destiny. Insistently remaining at home, Mrs Curren is in exile; looking for grace, she understands 'how one must live from now on: in a state of shame' (Coetzee, *Age of Iron*, p. 86). With extraordinary power, Coetzee brings the South African world into Mrs Curren's landscape of the soul, placing it there for her to live with and inspect. Her comment on shame seems like a true judgement on the apartheid years, though in his own way Coetzee would bring that idea into the post-interregnum world as well.

In transition

'Somewhere between November 1989 and February 1990,' wrote Nicholas Visser, 'South Africa's future changed' ('Politics of Future Projection', p. 62). This certainly made sense in political terms, as, following the unbanning of the ANC and other movements and the release of political prisoners, South Africa entered a new phase of negotiations around and about the future dispensation of the country. Similarly, the sense of an absent future, invoked largely through its looming pressure yet essential unknowability, began to transform in the South African imagination, emerging into a domain of the practical and the real. This was the final phase, so to speak, of the interregnum. It was an actual interregnum in political terms, as parties and constituencies jockeyed for power or sought the essential compromises that would make a future possible. Yet at every level, residual features of the 1980s endured or even intensified, evident in myriad forms: in conflict between Inkatha and the ANC or (sometimes tied to this) between hostel dwellers and township residents; in martial threat by neo-fascist Afrikaner movements; in the sustained brutal stealth politics of the South African 'security' machinery; in the massacres of Boipatong and Bisho; and in the rise of the militant 'Young Lions'. These, the last years of South Africa's 'pre-post-apartheid' era, were an extraordinary fusion of horror and promise, of past, present and future combining in unprecedented ways.

In these circumstances, it is perhaps no surprise that the literature examined territory now familiar, yet also raised new perspectives and registered new moods. André Brink explored extreme possibilities in *An Act of Terror* (1991), specifically a plot by an underground group to blow up the President of South Africa during a visit to the Castle in Cape Town. The novel becomes the occasion for a soul-searching inspection of Afrikaner responsibility, in that the character directly involved in the plot is an Afrikaner; yet there is a retreat from the formal experimentalism of *States of Emergency*. In a different vein, Lauretta Ngcobo's *And They Didn't Die* (1990) took on new themes in looking back to campaigns of the late 1950s, meshing a rural focus with a feminist emphasis in exploring the intersection of traditional African culture with the structures of apartheid in the struggles of women.[14] Sindiwe Magona explored a range of female experiences in her short-story collection, *Living, Loving and Lying Awake at Night* (1991). Richard Rive revisited his earlier novel, *Emergency*, in *Emergency Continued* (1990). Mike Nicol rewrote the contours of South African reality through forms of magical realism (see Chapter 37). Elleke Boehmer, in *Screens Against the Sky* (1990) and *An Immaculate Figure* (1993), explored gendered versions of white South African vacuity and complicity.

Yet if any two works registered the new moods of the era, they would probably be Gordimer's *None to Accompany Me* (1994) and Zakes Mda's *Ways of Dying* (1995). For a writer who, for some years, had revealed herself as allied with the ANC, Gordimer's novel is notably contemplative in the very year of liberation, inspecting transitional themes with her usual clinical eye, but also with compassion. As much as the novel concerns the new, it also concerns ageing, particularly in the life of its central character, Vera Stark, and there are various crossings: of love with politics and politics with love; of exiles returning home – some not to find the place or placement they expected; of gender hierarchies in change; of both insiders and outsiders abandoning old roles in the complex search for new. A marital relationship falters and there are new morphologies: Vera in a (non-sexual) affiliation with an African man, her lesbian daughter as mother to an adopted African child. There are the issues of the day: land rights, violence, constitutional negotiations and questions of empowerment as against justice. But new configurations of the political also allow new versions of the personal, and there is a focus in Vera's mind on a different revelatory dimension: 'Everyone ends up moving alone towards the self' (p. 306). *None to Accompany Me* becomes a story of transitional identities at a time when the identity of South Africa itself was in flux, with quite unknown shapes to come.

In *Ways of Dying*, Mda took Coetzee's Mr Verceuil and turned him into a most remarkable character: a highly principled derelict who has invented the vocation of professional mourner.[15] Dressed in his theatrical costume, somewhere between carnival and the grotesque, Toloki is the performer offering

---

14 For gender politics in the novel, see Daymond, 'To Write Beyond the "Fact"', and Hunter, '"We have to defend ourselves"'.

15 For the connection between Toloki and Verceuil, see Attwell, *Rewriting Modernity*, p. 193.

the dead their due lamentations. His occupation matches the extraordinary circumstances of the day – Toloki as their inner image, as it were. As he tells Noria, his 'home girl' from the village with whom he now connects in her informal settlement surroundings, 'our ways of living are our ways of dying' (p. 98). For her part, in a novel which fuses magical realism with the forms of oral culture, Noria has lost her son twice – the second time at the hands of the Young Tigers who necklace him as a putative 'sell out'. Noria becomes a kind of divine mother to the abandoned children of the settlement, and Toloki joins her there. Each feels the other 'knows how to live', and in this there is serious critique as well as assertion. The critique is of the Young Tigers and their destructive solidarity, of their aesthetic (political songs which incite to violence and death), and of political leaders who betray ordinary people in the interests of 'the struggle'. In contrast, the novel asserts a different vision of art: of the shack which Noria and Toloki construct and fill with imagined objects and decorations, and of the pictures Toloki draws for children, eliciting their unadulterated joy. The novel has been criticised on the grounds of its 'abstentionist' form of politics (Farred, 'Mourning the Postapartheid State Already?'). But here too is a version of Ndebele's earlier perspective: the refusal of anonymity on the part of the oppressed, and their humanisation in the face of circumstances which continue to constrict it; the creativities of resistance as well as the resistance of creativity; a different construction of the political. In its mixed modes and visions, again a novel of the interregnum interrupts the surface of the real. *Ways of Dying* ends poised between this vision and the smell of burning rubber.

Bibliography

Attwell, D. *J. M. Coetzee: South Africa and the Politics of Writing*, Berkeley: University of California Press and Cape Town: David Philip, 1993.

    Rewriting Modernity: Studies in Black South African Literary History, Pietermaritzburg: University of KwaZulu-Natal Press, 2005.

Barnard, R. *Apartheid and Beyond: South African Writers and the Politics of Place*, New York: Oxford University Press, 2007.

Boehmer, E. 'Endings and New Beginning: South African Fiction in Transition', in D. Attridge and R. Jolly (eds.), *Writing South Africa: Literature, Apartheid, and Democracy, 1970–1995*, Cambridge University Press, 1998, 43–56.

    An Immaculate Figure, London: Bloomsbury, 1993.

    Screens Against the Sky, London: Bloomsbury, 1990.

Breytenbach, B. *Mouroir: Bespieëlende Notas van 'n Roman*, Johannesburg: Taurus, 1983.

    Mouroir: Mirrornotes of a Novel, New York: Farrar, Straus & Giroux, 1984.

    The True Confessions of an Albino Terrorist, Johannesburg: Taurus, 1984.

Brink, A. *An Act of Terror*, New York: Summit, 1991.

    States of Emergency, New York: Summit, 1988.

Campschreur, W., and J. Divendal (eds.). *Culture in Another South Africa*, New York: Olive Branch Press, 1989.

Clingman, S. *The Grammar of Identity: Transnational Fiction and the Nature of the Boundary*, Oxford University Press, 2009.

    The Novels of Nadine Gordimer: History from the Inside, 2nd edn, Amherst: University of Massachusetts Press, 1992; London: Bloomsbury, 1993.

Coetzee, J. M. *Age of Iron*, New York: Random House, 1990.

    'Breyten Breytenbach and the Reader in the Mirror', in *Giving Offense: Essays on Censorship*, University of Chicago Press, 1996, 215–32.

    Life & Times of Michael K, Harmondsworth: Penguin, 1985.

    'The Novel Today', *Upstream* 6:1 (1988), 2–5.

    Waiting for the Barbarians, New York: Penguin, 1999.

Daymond, M. J. 'To Write Beyond the "Fact": Fictional Revisions of Southern African Women in History by Yvonne Vera and Lauretta Ngcobo', *African Literature Today* 24 (2004), 138–55.

Du Plessis, M. *A State of Fear*, Cape Town: David Philip, 1985.

Essop, A. *The Emperor*, Johannesburg: Ravan, 1984.

    The Hajji and other Stories, Johannesburg: Ravan, 1978.

    Noorjehan and other Stories, Johannesburg: Ravan, 1990.

Farred, G. 'Mourning the Postapartheid State Already? The Poetics of Loss in Zakes Mda's *Ways of Dying*', *Modern Fiction Studies* 46:1 (2000), 183–206.

Gordimer, N. 'The Essential Gesture', in S. Clingman (ed.), *The Essential Gesture: Writing Politics and Places*, New York: Knopf and London: Jonathan Cape, 1988, 285–300.

    July's People, London: Jonathan Cape, 1981.

    'Living in the Interregnum', in S. Clingman (ed.), *The Essential Gesture: Writing Politics and Places*, New York: Knopf and London: Jonathan Cape, 1988, 261–84.

    My Son's Story, New York: Farrar, Straus & Giroux, 1990.

    None to Accompany Me, New York: Farrar, Straus & Giroux, 1994.

    A Sport of Nature, London: Jonathan Cape, 1987.

Hunter, E. '"We have to defend ourselves": Women, Tradition, and Change in Lauretta Ngcobo's *And They Didn't Die*', *Tulsa Studies in Women's Literature* 13:1 (1994), 113–26.

Kirkwood, M. 'Remembering Staffrider', in A. W. Oliphant and I. Vladislavić (eds.), *Ten Years of Staffrider 1978–1988*, Johannesburg: Ravan, 1988, 1–9.

Lazarus, N. 'Modernism and Modernity: T. W. Adorno and Contemporary White South African Literature', *Cultural Critique* 5 (winter 1986/7), 131–55.

Magona, S. *Living, Loving and Lying Awake at Night*, New York: Interlink, 1994.

Mda, Z. *Ways of Dying*, New York: Picador, 1995.

Ndebele, N. *Fools and other Stories*, London: Readers International, 1993.

    South African Literature and Culture: Rediscovery of the Ordinary, introduced by G. Pechey, Manchester University Press and New York: St Martin's Press, 1994.

Ngcobo, L. *And They Didn't Die*, New York: George Braziller, 1991.

Parry, B. 'Some Provisional Speculations on the Critique of "Resistance" Literature', in E. Boehmer, L. Chrisman and K. Parker (eds.), *Altered State? Writing and South Africa*, Sydney: Dangaroo, 1994, 11–24.

Rastogi, P. *Afrindian Fictions: Diaspora, Race, and National Desire in South Africa*, Columbus: Ohio State University Press, 2008.

Rive, R. *'Buckingham Palace', District Six*, Cape Town: David Philip, 1986.

Emergency Continued, Cape Town: David Philip, 1990.

Sachs, A., 'Preparing Ourselves for Freedom', in I. de Kok and K. Press (eds.), *Spring is Rebellious: Arguments about Cultural Freedom / by Albie Sachs and Respondents*, Cape Town: Buchu, 1990, 19–29.

Schalkwyk, D. 'Confession and Solidarity in the Prison Writing of Breyten Breytenbach and Jeremy Cronin', *Research in African Literatures* 25:1 (1994), 23–45.

Serote, M. *To Every Birth its Blood*, Johannesburg: Ravan, 1981.

Sole, K. 'The Role of the Writer in a Time of Transition', *Staffrider* 11:1–4 (1993), 90–8.

Van Wyk, C. 'Staffrider and the Politics of Culture', in A. W. Oliphant and I. Vladislavić (eds.), *Ten Years of Staffrider 1978–1988*, Johannesburg: Ravan, 1988, 165–70.

Visser, N. 'Beyond the Interregnum: A Note on the Ending of *July's People*', in M. Trump (ed.), *Rendering Things Visible: Essays on South African Literary Culture*, Johannesburg: Ravan, 1990, 61–7.

'The Politics of Future Projection in South African Fiction', *Bucknell Review* 37:1 (1993), 62–82.

Wicomb, Z. *You Can't Get Lost in Cape Town* [1987], New York: Feminist Press, 2000.

Zwi, Rose. *Another Year in Africa*, Johannesburg: Bateleur, 1980.

Exiles, Johannesburg: Ad Donker, 1984.

The Inverted Pyramid, Johannesburg: Ravan, 1981.

31

Rewriting the nation

RITA BARNARD

National dreams

With the release of Nelson Mandela in 1990 and, even more decisively, with his election as president in April 1994, South Africa set off on a new course. This did not mean that a unified national culture, bridging earlier divisions between black and white, between literary and linguistic traditions, between expatriate and local writers, or between the privileged and the deprived immediately came into being. Indeed, while optimistic terms like the 'rainbow nation' or 'the new South Africa' pervaded political discourse during the 1990s, more cautious literary commentators always preferred to use those terms in scare quotes. Loren Kruger, for one, suggested that much South African writing from this period should be termed 'post-anti-apartheid' rather than 'post-apartheid' literature *tout court* ('"Black Atlantics"', p. 35). More recently, scholars have found a need to mark a distinct shift in mood that occurred in the course of Mbeki's presidency. Some have even proposed the term 'post-transition' to describe the more disenchanted writing that has emerged in the new millennium. The implication is that we can no longer – nearly two decades after the official end of apartheid – rely on the magic word 'transition' as 'a convenient label to positively connote an evolution and to make and justify a social, economic, or political "lack"' (Popescu, *South Africa*, p. 162). The experience of rampant poverty and crime, AIDS and AIDS denialism, and the erosion of the new democracy's moral authority in the international sphere has proven too dark for that.

It is no surprise, therefore, that several accounts of the literary culture of post-apartheid South Africa (like those of Attwell and Harlow, Lazarus and Irlam) have started out by insisting that many features of the past linger on. Economic inequalities, they point out, have remained, as has racism and sexism – to the point where the dream of liberation comes to seem not 'a dream deferred' but 'a dream derailed', as Cyril Ramaphosa once put it (Russell,

Machine Gun, p. 23). From this point of view, Chris van Wyk's neglected 1996 novel, *The Year of the Tapeworm*, emerges as uncannily predictive in its deep ambivalence about the political transition it records. Whilst celebrating the accession to power of the once imprisoned President Sibisi, Van Wyk's protagonist envisages the possibility that Sibisi, who dines with the oppressive white leader De Vries, might be contaminated with the latter's tapeworm and thereby with the old colonial belly politics of greed. The novel is criss-crossed with allusions to Ayi Kweyi Armah's disillusioned novel, *The Beautyful Ones are not yet Born* (1973) – and appropriately so, for South Africa has not proven immune to the troubles of other African post-colonies: a grasping national bourgeoisie, dangerous forms of ethnic assertion, dire poverty and mismanaged disease.

And yet it would be a mistake for the literary historian to retrospectively minimise the extent to which the political transition marked a true watershed, and one that left an ineradicable thematic and formal imprint on South African writing. *SA 27 April 1994*, André Brink's compilation of essays by forty-five important authors about the day of the historic election, remains a fascinating testament to the elation of national belonging and liberation that characterised that moment. Nadine Gordimer's reflections are among the most poignant:

> Of course nearby in city streets there were still destitute black children sniffing glue as the only substitute for nourishment and care; there were homeless families existing in rigged-up shelters in the crannies of the city. The law places the ground of equality underfoot; it did not feed the hungry or put up a roof over the head of the homeless today, but it changed the base on which South African society was for so long built. The poor are still there, round the corner. But they are not The Outcast . . . They *count*.
>
> (*SA 27 April 1994*, p. 52)

Eschewing the triumphalism – the ejaculating cannons and billowing flags – that marred her rendering of the end of apartheid in *A Sport of Nature* (1987), Gordimer here meditates on the 'X', the mark of the illiterate, now trans-formed into the mark of citizenship: 'The day has been captured for me by the men and women who couldn't read or write, but underwrote it, at last, with their kind of signature' (*SA 27 April 1994*, p. 52). She ends with a prayer that we, as literary scholars, can still endorse: 'May it be the seal on the end of illiteracy, of the pain of imposed ignorance, of the deprivation of the fullness of life' (*SA 27 April 1994*, p. 52).

For cultural production in South Africa, this changed social base meant, first of all, that the rhetoric of urgency, the doctrinaire validation of the overtly political over the aesthetic, could be set aside. A characteristic work of the transition era, therefore, is Zakes Mda's *Ways of Dying* (1995), a novel in which the after-effect of violence – the smell of burnt rubber – still lingers, but one that nevertheless affirms the protagonist's discovery of creativity and peaceful domesticity amidst the poverty of the shacklands. It is a novel of aesthetic education, in which national politics have moved to the sidelines, terror has been replaced with laughter and the capacity for change is celebrated – most joyously so in the New Year's carnival parade with which the novel closes. Whilst Mda's Janus-faced novel is set in the run up to the election, other novels of the transition, including E. K. M. Dido's *Die Storie van Monica Peters* (The Story of Monica Peters, 1996), Rayda Jacobs's *Sachs Street* (2001), Marlene van Niekerk's *Triomf* (1999) and André Brink's *Sandkastele* (*Imaginings of Sand*, 1995), stage their affirmative climaxes on election day 1994. (An earlier novel, Marita van der Vyver's 1992 feminist fairy-tale, *Griet Skryf 'n Sprokie* [*Entertaining Angels*], similarly worked the release of Mandela – recast as a clever Hansel who fools his jailors – into its comic denouement.) Of the works I have listed here, Van Niekerk's and Brink's have – rightly – received the most critical attention. Both are, on some level, national allegories, in which domestic spaces (in the former, a decrepit house in the white suburb of Triomf and, in the latter, an ostrich-era mansion in the Little Karoo, replete with secret rooms, strange murals and magical fauna) are transformed, along with the social space of the entire country. Brink's novel concludes with his expatriate heroine's reassimilation into the nation, as she goes to the polling station to cast her vote along with her grandmother's farm workers, who are finally recognised as family. Whilst *Sandkastele* is marred by Brink's rather presumptuous attempt to recover South Africa's 'herstory' on behalf of its silenced women, it nevertheless has the merit of yoking the need for an inclusive national community to the need for more enlightened gender relations. Moreover, in its adoption – however heavy-handed – of magical realist tropes, Brink's novel joins Mda's in ushering in a richer array of generic possibilities for the post-apartheid novel than the formerly dominant modes of realism and documentary witness.

Van Niekerk's novel, a tour de force of stream-of-consciousness narration and bravura dialogue, may feel claustrophobically focused on an inept and incestuous family of poor white Afrikaners, the Benades. But the novel also offers a sardonic account of the atmosphere and political manoeuvrings in the months preceding the historic election. Van Niekerk skewers both the patronising attempts of the National Party's yuppy canvassers to rally the constituents they once took for granted and the gung-ho efforts of the right-wing AWB (Afrikaner Resistance Movement) to recruit white males with military training. Whilst the hapless Benades think of 26 April 1994 more as their misbegotten son Lambert's fortieth birthday, the first occasion on which he will – thanks to the availability of prostitutes in the new chaos of Johannesburg – have sex with a woman other than his mother, the day turns out to be both catastrophic and liberatory in unexpected ways. When a bustling team of painters arrive to give the Benades' derelict house a spanking new coat of white paint, the allegorical implications can only be read ironically: the novel has made it abundantly clear that 'the house of the white race', to steal a term from Gordimer (Bazin, *Conversations*, p. 9), has collapsed, precisely because of its emphasis on ethnic purity and national kinship. And yet the Benades adapt to the new dispensation; they are even granted a moment of utopian belonging when they are accidentally swept up in a peace march and blissfully hold hands with those they were taught to think of as *klimmeide* (servant-girls) and *kaffirs*.

Of the transition-era novels written in English, two have emerged as particularly important: Nadine Gordimer's *None to Accompany Me* (1994) and Ivan Vladislavić's *The Restless Supermarket* (2001). Both of these thematise the emergence of new social relations and new subjectivities by charting the shifting racial demographics of the South African city and, in the case of Vladislavić's novel, its shifting linguistic fabric as well. Gordimer's novel is a restrained reworking of her abiding interests in the politics of place. Foregrounding the transformed erotic and domestic arrangements of two married couples (a pair of white liberal professionals and a pair of returned ANC activists), the novel also engages with the ongoing struggle to redress the legacy of apartheid's geographic iniquities. The concerns of Vladislavić's novel are not unrelated, though in its comic verve it is closer in spirit to Van Niekerk's work than to Gordimer's. The novel's narrator, Aubrey Tearle, a crabby retired proof-reader with a hatred of error and irregularity, is facing the demise of his social world, symbolised by the closing of his beloved haunt, the Café Europa. By the novel's end, however, he is forced into a grudging yet hopeful accommodation with the new urban scene and its inhabitants, whose languages – 'squirming and wriggling' like the myriad lights that surround the city – are ones he will never be able to 'put to the proof' (p. 304). He is confronted, in short, with the unpredictability, uncontrollability and the irrepressible energy of change.

These two novels are clearly major works: stylistically inventive accounts of the transformation of everyday life and ordinary subjects in the wake of political transition. But if we also consider, as the literary historian must, works that are less likely than these to make it into university syllabi, we may find that the most characteristic writing of the period took the fairly conventional form of autobiography, a genre that merges two of the most marketable forms of postcolonial writing: the *Bildungsroman* and the national allegory. Many works in this genre (discussed also in Chapter 34) record the lives of struggle veterans and other political figures, like Nelson Mandela, Ahmed Kathrada, Ronny Kasrils, Ismael Meer, Alex Boraine, Zubeida Jaffer, Rusty Bernstein, F. W. de Klerk and even General Magnus Malan (see bibliography below). The category also includes the life stories of actors, writers and survivors of struggles other than the one for national liberation (child abuse, poverty, illness and displacement): stories that cumulatively enlarge and refine our sense of the range of subject positions opened up with apartheid's demise. Among the most successful books in this vein are Julian Roup's *Boerejood* (2005), Chris van Wyk's *Shirley, Goodness, and Mercy* (2006), Pregs Govender's *Love and Courage* (2008), Denis Hirson's *White Scars* (2006) and Antjie Krog's *A Change of Tongue* (2009). As Annie Gagiano has noted, these autobiographies share a number of common attributes. They are addressed, in the first instance, to an inclusive national reading public, they describe experiences of adjustment as their protagonists negotiate a changed social world, they assess their authors' contributions to South African society and they present the lessons of the past as guides to a shared future ('To Remember', p. 261). These stories are, in a sense, unwriteable without the dramatic turn – the potentialities for narrative development, closure and address provided by 'the new South Africa'; their very proliferation attests to the real change wrought in individual lives by the transition to democracy.

Collective memories

The political events of the 1990s not only invited new dreams for South Africa's future, but a radical reimagination of its past. 'The passage of time which brought forth our freedom', announced Njabulo Ndebele in 1998, 'has given legitimacy and authority to previously silenced voices. It has lifted the veil of secrecy and state-induced blindness . . . Where in the past the state attempted to compel the oppressed to deny the testimony of their own experience, today that experience is one of the essential conditions for the emergence of national consciousness' ('Memory, Metaphor', p. 21). Many writers and critics have sounded a more cautionary note, reminding us, as Jeremy Cronin does in his satirical 'Jeremiad' (1999), that triumphal national master-narratives tend to create their own zones of amnesia. But it is nevertheless true that national memory – not only its contents, but the manner in which it is created, inscribed and preserved – became one of the most important preoccupations in post-apartheid literature. According to Shane Graham, the most characteristic and pervasive tropes in the writing of the period have been the archive, the palimpsest and the excavation (even, more concretely, digging and holes) – all of which are concerned with the retrieval and revelation of what is latent and repressed (see *Mapping Loss*). Against the dangers of oblivion, so characteristic of the global geographies of consumerism, South African writers have insistently revisited the loci of memory – sites where the legacy of the past can still be traced.

Whilst Ndebele rightly emphasises the silencing and discrediting of black voices under apartheid, Brink has observed that apartheid produced other lacunae as well: not only did it compel writers to focus on the present, it also disavowed and repressed such matters as slavery, the creole origins of Afrikaans, the role of women and outsiders, and, more generally, the intimate entanglement of black and white experience in the nation's history. Brink's own post-apartheid novels have attempted to fill these gaps, albeit in a way that leaves him open to charges of appropriation and of giving a self-serving twist to the stories of the marginalised and oppressed. (A case in point is his novel *Rights of Desire* [2000], where the ghost of a decapitated female slave ultimately gives her benediction to the white man who owns the house she has haunted since the seventeenth century.) Fortunately, Brink has been joined in his exploration of the 'silent places' of South African history by a diverse crop of younger writers. We may think, for instance, of Rayda Jacobs, whose historical romance *The Slave Book* (1998) revisits the Cape wine farms of the nineteenth century, not only to document the past but also to reverse a long history of racist denigrations through its heroic depiction of Muslim and mixed-race characters. A related novel, Yvette Christiansë's *Unconfessed* (2006), takes its inspiration from early nineteenth-century court records in order to recreate the figure of Sila van den Kaap, a Mozambiquan slave condemned to hard labour on Robben Island for the murder of her son. Though reminiscent of Toni Morrison's *Beloved*, the work's address to the dead child connects it to other post-apartheid writings (e.g., Phaswane Mpe's *Welcome to our Hillbrow* [2001]) in which an experimental use of the second person seems to be a defining feature, revealing the work's elegiac perspective on its subject matter. Such revisions of apartheid's official histories were no doubt to be expected in the new democracy. More surprising and perhaps bolder are those works that have addressed the shameful lacunae of the resistance struggle. Works like Mandla Langa's *The Naked Song and other Stories* (1997), Zoë Wicomb's *David's*

Story (2000) and Lewis Nkosi's *Underground People* (2002) have complicated the heroic narrative of liberation traced in more affirmative works like the struggle autobiographies. Thus, while both Brink and Ndebele associate the 'archival turn' (see above, Chapter 22) with the recuperation of silent voices and the creation of a national narrative of reconciliation and healing, several novels of historical retrieval have proven to be rather more fractious and counterhegemonic.

Central to any account of the treatment of the past in post-apartheid South African literature is the work of the Truth and Reconciliation Commission (TRC): a body founded with the express aim of excavating the secrets of an ugly past with a view to healing and national unity. Both Brink and Ndebele (and important critics like Mark Sanders) have characterised the modus operandi of the TRC as essentially literary; it was, in Ndebele's words, 'a living example of people reinventing themselves through narrative' ('Memory, Metaphor', p. 27). For Brink, this reinvention must exceed factual testimony: unless the work of the TRC is 'extended, complicated and intensified in the imaginings of literature', he declares, 'society cannot sufficiently come to terms with its past to face the future' ('Stories of History', p. 30). Insofar as this declaration is an invitation to literary creativity, it has surely been accepted by other writers, though many (especially J. M. Coetzee, Achmat Dangor and Wicomb) would probably balk at the use of the phrase 'coming to terms', with its implication of finality and closure. The TRC has been the subject of a vast body of writing. This includes scholarly reflections like that of Sanders; plays like Jane Taylor and William Kentridge's *Ubu and the Truth Commission* (1997), Zakes Mda's *The Bells of Amersfoort* (2002) and John Kani's *Nothing but the Truth* (2002; see Chapter 27); poetry like Ingrid de Kok's *Terrestrial Things* (2000) and Jeremy Cronin's *Even the Dead* (1999); novels like Gillian Slovo's *Red Dust* (2000); and a slew of memoirs by TRC participants and observers, the most famous of which is unquestionably Antjie Krog's lyrical and often heart-rending *Country of my Skull* (1998). The literary quality of these works is as varied as their generic forms. *Red Dust*, for example, is revealing about the actual operation of the TRC, the requirements for amnesty and its work of excavation, but it remains ultimately a legal thriller with no great understanding of the nuances of South African languages and locales. Other works, most notably *Country of my Skull*, are far more experimental and sophisticated, formally and personally risky in their confrontation of the ethical, narrative and linguistic challenges surrounding the commission's work. The TRC's literary ramifications, however, need to be traced far beyond works that deal with it as their overt subject matter. We must remember that the hearings, in which both perpetrators and victims of human rights violations narrated their stories in public, were broadcast daily, so that confession was, so to speak, in the air. It became the pervasive discursive form in South Africa from the mid to late 1990s. The impact of the commission's myriad public revelations can be registered in a sizeable body of quasi-confessional fiction concerned with traumatic family secrets buried in the apartheid past. Following Michiel Heyns, we might divide this body of work into two loose categories. The first is a set of lugubrious, even nostalgic confession narratives, in which the focal character's guilty abjection becomes an all too easy plea for absolution. For Heyns, this category includes Jo-Anne Richards's *The Innocence of Roast Chicken* (1996), Jann Turner's *Heartland* (1997) and the confessed spy Mark Behr's compelling but sensationalistic *The Smell of Apples* (1997). But there is another set of far more morally strenuous quasi-autobiographical fictions, which view the complicities of the racist past with an unflinchingness that does not presume (or implicitly ask for) forgiveness or reconciliatory transcendence. Among these works we may list Jeanne Goosen's *Ons is Nie Almal so Nie* (*We're Not all Like That*, 1990), Etienne van Heerden's *Kikoejoe* (*Kikuyu*, 1996), Tony Eprile's *The Persistence of Memory* (2005) and, most famously, J. M. Coetzee's third-person 'autrebiography' *Boyhood* (1997), which, while in no way hiding its young protagonist's furtive arrogance and coldness, tends to question rather than court the satisfaction and closure of confession.

There are also several novels set in contemporary South Africa – including Coetzee's *Disgrace* (1999), Achmat Dangor's *Bitter Fruit* (2005), Zoë Wicomb's *Playing in the Light* (2006), Sindiwe Magona's, *Mother to Mother* (1999), Njabulo Ndebele's *The Cry of Winnie Mandela* (2004) and J. M. Gilfillan's underrated *Pouoogmot* (Emperor Moth, 1997) – where the TRC features as a marginal yet activating presence, providing the characters with an impetus for examining or reliving the past, for confronting or containing repressed trauma. These novels, moreover, do not necessarily subscribe to the TRC's premise that making the dark secrets of the past public is *ipso facto* healing or therapeutic. With its recurrent meditations on the perfective form of the verb, *Disgrace* implicitly questions the idea that past trauma may be wrapped up and put to rest; it also problematises – in a scene where the focal character is urged to make a confession before a university committee on sexual harassment – the exchange of sincere testimony for amnesty in which the TRC essentially traded. Dangor's *Bitter Fruit* (a novel divided into sections headed 'Memory', 'Confession' and 'Retribution') sharply questions the therapeutic validity of making private wounds public. Focused on the family of Silas Ali, a former activist and the current liaison officer between Mandela's Justice Department and the TRC, the novel shows that remembered violence does not necessarily lead to reconciliation. In this case, a chance encounter with the policeman who raped Ali's wife leads to her self-mutilation, the family's disintegration and, ultimately, to an act of revenge: Mikey, the product of the rape, kills his biological father, adopts an Islamic *nom de guerre* and moves towards reconnection, not with fellow South African citizens but with his Indian ancestry.

Lewis Nkosi is therefore correct when he says that the kind of harking back to a golden age that often characterises nationalist culture seems absent from South African writing in the Mandela era ('Republic of Letters', p. 248). Except perhaps for a handful of nostalgic works in Afrikaans, the past is represented as troubled and painful – often so painful that testimony and recollection seem rife with betrayal. In novels like *Bitter Fruit* and Wicomb's *David's Story*, the past – especially the traumatic experience of women – remains dangerous, beyond consolation and retrieval: this leaves its mark on the novels' complicated narrative structures. It is therefore not quite accurate to say that while apartheid-era literature tended to be focused on the future, post-apartheid literature has been focused on the past, though literary historians have sometimes made this broad periodising gesture. The truth is that past, present and future are not so readily disentangled when historical experience is particularly painful. It is for this reason that several of the more formally inventive post-apartheid novels, including Anne Landsman's *The Devil's Chimney* (1998), Etienne van Heerden's *Die Swye van Mario Salviati* (2000; translated as *The Long Silence of Mario Salviati*, 2002), Zakes Mda's *The Heart of Redness* (2003), Marlene van Niekerk's *Agaat* (2004) and, again, Wicomb's *David's Story*, have multilayered plot lines. Their forms, one might say, are palimpsestic; the narrative oscillates between contemporary events and parallel (or originary) events in the past. The temporality of post-apartheid writing (as I have already hinted at in connection with Christiansë) is perhaps most characteristically traumatic: marked by recurrences, melancholia and an elegiac affect that is not readily brought to term. The present, one might say, bears the scars of the past. Indeed, that very metaphor is given concrete expression by both Mda in *The Heart of Redness* (which engages with genocidal colonial wars and disastrous millenarian prophecy) and by Wicomb in *David's Story* (which engages with histories of migration and exile, ethnic pride and ethnic shame, and sexual violence, with its unspeakable, ineradicable marking of the female body).

Damon Galgut's Booker shortlisted *The Good Doctor* (2003), set in a rural, neglected hospital in a former 'homeland', is another novel suffused with a past that continues to menace the present, but in ways that cannot easily be isolated and articulated, given the cynicism and vested interests of the narrative voice. Galgut's work charts the uneasy relationship between the narrator and a new arrival, the young, idealistic doctor Laurence Waters, of whom we hear in the novel's opening line: 'The first time I saw him I thought, *he won't last*' (p. 1). Compared by reviewers to Albert Camus, J. M. Coetzee and Graham Greene, *The Good Doctor* explores the grim consequences of an encounter between post-national, postcolonial ennui and a dangerously naive commitment to the new national project, all of it set in a compelling locale where orderlies strip the clinic of its fittings at night, reluctant Cuban medical professionals serve out their placements and the Brigadier, once a self-styled dictator from the days of apartheid, returns at night to mow the lawns of his old residence.

Imagined families

One of the pioneering features of South Africa's 1996 constitution was the banning of discrimination not only on the basis of race and gender, but also of sexual orientation. Whilst this historic achievement did not mean that prejudicial attitudes towards gays and lesbians evaporated overnight, it spoke volumes about the importance of the discourse of rights in the liberation struggle. It implied, as Brenna Munro puts it, 'a rejection of a regime that regulated both straight and gay people's sexuality in the name of racial purity' ('Queer Family', pp. 401–2). And it allowed for yet another optimistic and allegorical reading of the South African transition – as a 'coming-out story'. Albie Sachs, for one, affirmed the parallel between the homosexual's transition from repression towards self and social acceptance with South Africa's transition from its pariah status towards its liberation and inclusion in the global community of nations: 'It's not just the gay and lesbian community that is coming out', the freedom fighter turned judge declared on occasion. 'The truth has been coming out . . . We're all coming out . . . we've become a better nation' (in Trengrove-Jones, 'Fiction and the Law', pp. 114–15).

Post-apartheid literature has registered this change – and not only in the emergence of many gifted gay and lesbian writers (like Mark Behr, Damon Galgut, Stephen Gray, Michiel Heyns, Marlene van Niekerk, Joan Hambidge and K. Sello Duiker), or in the prominent inclusion of gay and lesbian characters in major novels like Gordimer's *None to Accompany Me* and *The House Gun* and Coetzee's *Disgrace*. At stake, more broadly, in the literary treatment of sexuality, reproduction and sexual violence – crucial themes in post-apartheid writing – are questions of how the nation can be and has been represented.

After all, the imagined community of the nation has traditionally been thought of in familial and domestic terms (of one's *'vaderland'* or 'mother tongue') and its iconographies and myths have been gendered ones – of founding fathers, mothers of the nation and brothers of the land. Nations are always 'born', it seems; their origins biologised. The new South Africa has not been an exception to this rule (we may recall that one of the most celebrated struggle novels, Mongane Serote's *To Every Birth its Blood* [1989], ends with the words 'push, push, push' – signalling the painful parturition-in-progress of a new political order). Consequently, the fiction of the transition has been open to feminist critique, like that of Samuelson, who has explored the problematic ways in which female icons from the past have been retrieved in post-apartheid fiction, replete with allegorical resonances, but deprived on their own voices and agency. These figures include Krotoä-Eva, the first Khoi woman to marry a settler, Sarah Baartman, the ill-fated 'Hottentot Venus', put on display as a sexual curiosity in Europe, and Nongqawuse, the young prophetess whose millenarian visions led to the Xhosa Cattle-Killing of 1856–7. The prominence of these figures in post-apartheid writing raises a pressing question: must the origins of the new democracy only be 'remembered' in a way that, as Samuelson puts it, 'dismembers women', reduces them to wombs? (An obvious case in point is Brink's aforementioned *Sandkastele*, which seems obsessed with bodily matters like menstruation, childbearing, and, most problematically, transracial rape.) Whilst the deployment of female figures to represent the nation (the Virgin Queen in England, Jeanne d'Arc in France, la Malinche in Mexico, and so forth) is certainly a transnational matter, it is important to note that, in a hyperpatriarchal and racist county like apartheid South Africa, questions of national and ethnic identity were associated all the more powerfully with biological reproduction and racial endogamy. It makes sense, therefore, that Van Niekerk should represent the humiliating demise of Afrikaner culture, with its obsessive valuation of the *'volkseie'* (ethnically exclusive cultural property), via the incestuous Benades of Triomf. It also makes sense that the liminal figure of the homosexual should, as Munro has argued, perform some of the work of racial reconciliation during the early years of the transition. One might think here of the prominent actor-activist Pieter-Dirk Uys's ever glib, ever hypocritical alter ego, Evita Bezuidenhout, who enabled both South Africans to laugh at serious political matters and served, Munro observes, as a campy 'Tannie' (Auntie), rather than 'Mother' of the nation ('Queer Family', p. 407).

The negotiation of gendered, sexual and raced identities and desires – love, marriage and so forth – has ever been the stuff of literature, and it is certainly so in contemporary South African literature. What Michiel Heyns once wryly termed 'the political efficacy of sexual intercourse' ('Whole Country', p. 48) was a familiar trope in apartheid-era fiction: most famously so, perhaps, in the work of Nadine Gordimer, but also in novels like Lewis Nkosi's *Mating Birds* (1986) and Arthur Maimane's *Victims* (1976, republished in 2000 as *Hate no More*), where distortions of gender identity and sexual relationships function as key indictments of the apartheid state. This trope does not disappear exactly from post-apartheid fiction: it is, instead, ironised in Etienne van Heerden's *Casspirs en Camparis* (Casspirs and Camparis, 1991), played out on a global terrain in Gordimer's *The Pickup* (2001) and evacuated – perhaps forever – of redemptive potency in the obsessive interracial couplings of Kleinboer's *Kontrei* (translated as *Midnight Missionary*, 2006). Anxieties about the history and the future of race relations, moreover, have been dramatised in a sizeable set of novels where an interracial rape is the crisis event, including Dangor's *Bitter Fruit* (2005), Farida Karodia's *Other Secrets* (2000), Beverly Naidoo's *Out of Bounds* (2003) and Sipho Sepamla's *Rainbow Journey* (1996). Of these fictions of rape, Coetzee's troubling novel *Disgrace* is by far the most controversial and best known. It is a novel where the political transition is explored in relation to a discomfiting shift (at least for its white male protagonist) in the dominant sex-gender system with its familiar institutions like romantic love and (more furtively) prostitution. Charged with sexual harassment, David Lurie's profoundly literary, masculinist and European erotic notions run aground: first against the new, more politically correct and historically aware gender codes of the contemporary academic establishment and then against the violent practices of a rising, grasping and vengeful black patriarchy. The latter finds its agents not only in the three rapists who attack Lurie's daughter and, like dogs (as the novel's metaphor would have it), mark her as their property, but also in the former handyman Petrus, the *novus homo* of the new South Africa, intent on gaining status and land through a cynical redeployment of polygamous traditions.

Without diminishing either its dark history or the alarming threat that sexual violence continues to pose in South African society, I would observe here that rape has traditionally served as figure for imagining new, exogamous national beginnings (the rape of the Sabine women, Europa and the bull and Leda and the Swan are all cases in point). This is, arguably, also the case in *Disgrace*, where Lurie, at the end of the novel, accepts the idea that the issue of the rape will be an authentic 'child of this earth' (p. 216). Indeed, the fact that in almost all of these rape-centered novels the violation is productive of mixed-race offspring (rare in actual rape cases) is a sign that we are dealing here, in various degrees of subtlety and explicitness, with national allegory: one that dramatises the possibility of a creolised cultural identity but that stops short of queering the national family or breaking away from the old reproductive, biologistic, filiative tropes in favour of more affiliative, artificial and voluntary ones. In this respect Gordimer's *None to Accompany Me* is exceptional: the domestic arrangement validated at the end of the work is the household of two lesbians who have adopted a black child. It is also interesting, in this context, to contemplate the prevalence of miraculous pregnancies and births in post-apartheid literature. Two major novels, Magona's *Mother to Mother* and Mda's *The Heart of Redness*, for example, feature immaculate conceptions – perhaps the single sure way in which newness may be figured biologically, but without bringing such inevitably fraught matters as sex, race, paternity, desire and violence into play.

The importance of a few innovative works of fiction from the transition era may be assessed against this background. Njabulo Ndebele's peculiar novel *The Cry of Winnie Mandela* (which, along with Gilfillan's *Pouoogmot*, takes the form of a symposium in which a range of female voices participate in a formally disjointed, but thematically unified, colloquy) is a rigorously experimental work. The four speakers meet in a purely fictional – indeed, purely conjectural – space in order to testify to their sufferings under apartheid and, more specifically, under the distorted familial and sexual relationships that its segregated spatial regimes imposed. Excluded from epic events, like the patient Penelope of old, they wait on the sidelines as the grand narrative of national liberation plays out elsewhere. Their imagined audience and eventual interlocutor is, appropriately, Winnie Madikizela-Mandela, a woman who, like them, was compelled to wait for her husband, but who, unlike them, was heroically inscribed in the story of the nation (though, of course, as its 'mother'). The resolution of the novel is comic and integrative in a way that eschews the symbolic trappings of marriage, sexuality and family. The four women, joined by Winnie sporting her trademark designer sunglasses, set off on a road trip together. They pick up a white hitch-hiker, who turns out to be none other than Penelope, on the run from her boring role as the archetype of all faithfully waiting women. The collectivity imagined here is voluntary, freed from the constraints of family – indeed, of time and nation. And it is in motion: the women claim their citizenship and openness to the future by adopting the new roles of tourist and adventurer.

No less of a break with the old, but operating on darker terrain, are the novels of the late K. Sello Duiker: *Thirteen Cents* (2000) and *The Quiet Violence of Dreams* (2001). Both are remarkable in their depiction of male bodies as rapeable, something that is also the case in Behr's earlier novel *The Smell of Apples*. But where the latter novel explores the function of rape and pederasty in social reproduction (the young male protagonist is initiated by violence, secrecy and shame into the militaristic, hypermasculine domain of Afrikaner nationalism), the male rapes in Duiker's work point to the complete failure of the post-apartheid state to protect its children. Whilst Azure, the 13-year-old protagonist of *Thirteen Cents*, is unable to escape and control his own violation and commodification (the title underscores both his young age and the small value he commands in the brutal world of commercialised sex), the older protagonist of *The Quiet Violence of Dreams* is able to trace out a vulnerable but more affirmative personal trajectory in South Africa's newly fluid urban spaces. In the course of the novel, Duiker's Sipho moves beyond the fantasy of a non-racial if thoroughly commercialised club culture, to the discovery of a temporary brotherhood among the hustlers of Cape Town, to an eventual embrace of Hillbrow's foreign migrants: 'I feel at home with them because they are trying to find a home in our country', he asserts. 'In their eyes, I see Africa. I feel like I live in Africa when I walk out in the streets and hear dark-skinned beauties rapping in Lingala or Congo or a French patois that I don't understand' (p. 454).

With this vision of a tenuous belonging among outsiders, Duiker's harrowing *Bildungsroman* suggests how post-apartheid fiction might not only be sundered from the bonds – real and symbolic – of the hetero-normative family, but how these may be transcended in favour of a radical new openness and inclusivity. Perhaps sexual intercourse continues to have a certain 'political efficacy', but it is sexual intercourse of a very different sort from that featured in the 'sex across the colour bar' fictions of earlier times.

Global realities

It is fair to say, then, that an important body of work written after 1990 has taken on the task of assessing the character of the new 'rainbow nation' and redescribing its past. But as Shaun Irlam has observed, post-apartheid literature has also testified to the rainbow's unravelling. According to Irlam, a new interest in the personal and the local (and we might add the transnational and global) has emerged, to the detriment of the strictly national. So, too, have new modes of identity politics, including more American-style, 'multicultural' configurations of race and ethnicity. The canny work of Zoë Wicomb is a particularly complex case in point: *David's Story* both entertains and mocks the possibility of a Griqua identity, while *Playing in the Light* – the title is clearly a nod to Toni Morrison's *Playing in the Dark* – exposes the constructedness of racial categories, even as it explores the characteristically coloured experience of passing for white: a familiar trope in African American literature. A body of recent Afrikaans writing in the genealogical vein has engaged in what Wicomb has sardonically called a 'scramble for alterity' ('Five Afrikaner Texts', p. 365): an attempt to reclaim the Afrikaans language and Afrikaner ethnicity as somehow authentically mixed and authentically indigenous. This broadly genealogical impulse is shared by a number of talented Indian South African writers, including Imraan Coovadia (*The Wedding*, 2001) and Aziz Hassim (*The Lotus People*, 1997), who have traced out the experiences of immigrant families from the subcontinent, thereby complicating the simple black–white dichotomies of the past. In moving deftly between Pakistan, Durban and New York, Coovadia's second novel, *Green-Eyed Thieves* (2006), explores an intriguing new set of international triangulations and trajectories for fiction from South Africa. But if his first two works are comic novels that are occasionally reminiscent of Rushdie and Nabokov, his third book *High Low In-Between* (2009) is a more sombre meditation on HIV/AIDS denialism and the politicisation of medical science in contemporary South Africa.

Emerging black middle-class subjectivities, assertive and ironic, savvy about the self-making potentialities of affirmative action, have been articulated by younger writers like Niq Mhlongo in *Dog Eat Dog* (2007) and Kopano Matlwa in *Coconut* (2007). These ethnically particular fictions have cumulatively – perhaps against their best intentions – exceeded or fractured a unified (or even a prismatically encompassing) South Africanness.

If, then, as Leon de Kock has argued, the term 'South African literature' has historically named a collective attempt to suture a racial seam or fracture, post-apartheid writing is beginning to ignore this seam ('Global Imaginary', pp. 275–7; 'South African Literature is Dead'). Contemporary novelists of all stripes seem to be abandoning the project of forging the broad horizontal fraternities of an imagined national community and are instead seeking affiliations and connections at will with various international trends – be it magical realism, the US immigrant narrative, the genealogical novel, chick lit or more experimental forms. At the same time, in the work of writers like Ken Barris (*Small Change*, 1988), Ashraf Jamal (*The Shades*, 2002), David Medalie (*The Shooting of the Christmas Cows*, 1990; *The Mistress's Dog*, 2010) and Henrietta Rose-Innes (*Homing*, 2010), the short story has enabled attention to smaller, more local ways of meaning – to region, interiority, the single encounter – because as a form it is less subject to the pressure of being interpreted as national allegory (or at least, state-of-the nation report) than the novel. In an afterword to Medalie's most recent collection, Michael Titlestad even suggests that in its potential for suspension and indeterminacy, the (modernist) short story has proved particularly apt to map the contours of contemporary South African experience, even as that experience becomes less distinctive, more transnational and translatable (*Mistress's Dog*, p. 191).

There is, in other words, a sense in which 'South African literature' has ceased to exist at the precise historical moment when the old obstacles to a unified national identity (or at least some of them) have been eliminated. That this should be so is hardly surprising. As Jean and John Comaroff have often reminded us, the new South Africa, along with other democracies founded in the wake of the cold war, was presented from the outset with a challenging and even paradoxical task: that of shaping a sense of nationness at the very moment when global economic, cultural and demographic conditions combined to render national boundaries porous ('Nurturing the Nation', pp. 632–7). The result has not been the disappearance of the nation, or even of nationalism in its more toxic forms, as the bloody anti-immigrant riots of May 2008 sadly demonstrated. It meant, rather, that concepts of national culture, citizenship and the state have been reconceptualised and deployed in historically new ways. As many of the state's once quasi-monopolistic functions (education, broadcasting, the provision of utilities and the like) have come to be shared with or delegated to private enterprises, it has come to be thought of largely as a provider of services, especially security; or, perhaps, as a kind of joint stock company in which all citizens are shareholders. In this context, national culture is an increasingly commercialised matter; it becomes, in fact, a globally marketable 'heritage' or 'Ethnicity, Inc.', as the Comaroffs put it. This shift, which has obvious implications for literature, is captured in the contemporary sections of Zakes Mda's *The Heart of Redness* (which is, in this respect, too, a key post-apartheid text). An exploitative casino development is forestalled when the coastal village in which the novel takes place is declared a 'national heritage site' and rival cultural and eco-tourism projects end up vying for legitimacy – and tourist dollars.

The vulnerability of the South African state has also produced an overemphasis on one of its functions: policing. This is, of course, an ironic turn of events, given the fact that the ANC government took over from a racist police state. But the prevalence of crime, along with the counter-discourse of law and order it has provoked, has become one of the most important features of post-apartheid society and one that has had a profound impact on literary production. Crime writing and detective fiction have flourished since 1994. The Afrikaans writer Deon Meyer has acquired a substantial international readership in translation, and Mike Nicol (*Payback*, 2007), Patrick Williams (*The Eighth Man*, 1999), David Dison (*Death in the New Republic*, 2007) and Margie Orford (*Like Clockwork*, 2006) have local followings. As with other postcolonial detective novels, these books reveal what Franco Moretti has described as the tendency in world literature to merge global forms with local contents ('Conjectures on World Literature', p. 65).[1] But the local contents that make their way into these novels seem particularly revealing and socially diagnostic. One can do a lot worse than read Meyer's *Infanta* (translated as *Devil's Peak*, 2008) for a sense of the pressing issues in contemporary South Africa (sexual violence, generational relationships, affirmative action, the fate of Afrikaans, and so forth) – even if the inevitable Colombian drug dealers have to be dragged in for an exciting denouement. The thematics of crime or law and order have also generated of a great variety of serious works, including Antjie Krog's *Relaas van 'n Moord* (Account of a Murder, 1995), Breyten Breytenbach's *Dog Heart* (1999), Rozena Maart's *The Writing Circle* (2007), Nadine Gordimer's *The House Gun* (1998) and, in the domain of literary journalism, Jonny Steinberg's *Midlands* (2002) – a gripping work of reportage about a farm murder, which would significantly enrich an international reader's understanding of the social resonances of Coetzee's *Disgrace*. Along with *The House Gun*, *Midlands* is particularly striking in the way in which it uses the events leading up to and following a murder to probe the changes – new vulnerabilities, new micro-geographies, new social and (un)employment structures – brought about by the end of apartheid. Mark Seltzer's observation that public spheres are 'increasingly constituted today around the scene of a crime' (*Serial Killers*, p. 254) seems particularly pertinent to South African literature in this neoliberal era, where a postcolonial state with weakened power needs to enact its legitimacy in dramatic ways.

The most salient feature of globalisation – the accelerated flux of capital, goods and people – has also left its mark on recent South African writing. The mobility of capital and its impact on localities is perhaps best illustrated in Damon Galgut's curious novel, *The Imposter* (2008). The work seems, at first, to revisit one of the well-worn tropes about locality in South Africa: namely, whether the landscape of South Africa's semi-arid interior – desolate, barren, featureless, prehistoric – can be turned into poetry. A middle-aged man with the symbolic name of Adam retreats to a house in a Karoo town to

---

1 More accurately, Moretti sees a triangulation of foreign forms, local materials and local form: 'Simplifying somewhat: foreign plot; local characters; and local narrative voice' ('Conjectures', p. 65). The formula applies well to the genre of novels I am referring to here, especially to Meyer, whose handling of free indirect point of view and treatment of traumatised masculinity is sophisticated.

write, but, overcome by the isolation, begins to question whether 'the soul of South Africa' isn't perhaps 'a crooked property developer, obsessed with cheap fittings' rather than a poet. The plot then begins to turn on precisely the kind of destruction of the local we associate with global capitalism at its worst: a game reserve in a verdant *kloof* is sold off to become a golf course and resort. The deal involves members of the new political elite (puppet figures who satisfy the dictates of black economic empowerment), a professional golfer, and – the master mind – a shady Eastern European called Genov, who is eventually identified as involved in international crime: drug smuggling, human trafficking and money laundering. Indeed, the whole scheme turns out to be a kind of money-laundering operation: Genov is interested in the development 'for tax reasons' or 'to move money around', and intends for it to go belly up.

With its interest in the machinations of the post-apartheid elites, *The Imposter* (along with Etienne van Heerden's *In Stede van die Liefde* [Instead of Love, 2005], which also features legal and illegal global trade) may still be unusual. But the culture of global mobility is also registered – by negation – in a myriad imaginative works that focus on marginalised localities and on people who are bound to a given out of the way place, whether in affection or in frustration. We might think here of, say, A. H. M. Scholtz's folk novel *Vatmaar* (translated as *A Place Called Vatmaar*, 2001) about a small community near Kimberly, Brink's *Duiwelskloof* (translated as *Devil's Valley*, 1998), or even popular music (e.g., the songs of the ethno-musicologist and performer David Kramer, which often deal with outmoded, marginal, rural people, who are essentially stuck in place). The culture of global mobility is evident, above all, in the spate of writings about urban space (see Chapter 32) that has been such a rich and distinctive feature of post-apartheid literature and criticism and is best represented by Ivan Vladislavić's extraordinary triad of fictions on Johannesburg's transformation: *The Restless Supermarket*, *The Exploded View* (2004) and *Portrait with Keys* (2009). We may note here that cities generate an improvisational mode of being and belonging, quite different from that proposed by nationalism: national belonging is inevitably an ideological and abstract matter involving 'relations of disembodied extension', while urban subjectivities are existential and concrete (Robins, 'Becoming Anybody', p. 87). Urban life is about immersion in a world of multiplicity, where one can – theoretically at least – become anybody, make oneself anew. In this conceptual framework, simultaneously global and intensely local, the contribution of novels like Duiker's *The Quiet Violence of Dreams*, Phaswane Mpe's *Welcome to our Hillbrow* and Patricia Schonstein Pinnock's *Skyline* (2000) is readily grasped:

all of them deal with urban wanderers and confront issues of displacement, migration and xenophobia. Read more optimistically, these novels also hint at a new cosmopolitanism, however fragile, in which South Africa becomes part of Africa, just as Africa – in the shape of those thousands of migrants and refugees seeking new lives in what Schonstein Pinnock's characters call 'Mr. Mandela's country' – becomes part of South Africa.

An important new development, therefore, is the publication in 2008 of Simão Kikamba's *Going Home*. The novel addresses the travails of a refugee from Congo and Angola who is confronted with a state bureaucracy and citizenry intent on guarding the exclusive claim of autochthonous South Africans to the nation's resources. But welcome or not (we may recall here the generous address of Mpe's title), migrants from elsewhere in Africa will remain a permanent feature of South African social life, and their very presence raises questions about the future of 'South African literature' as a category. With, for example, an estimated 30,000 francophone Congolese in Johannesburg alone, it is conceivable that South African life will, in future, find literary expression in French or Portuguese or Lingala, and by writers born beyond its boundaries. The contemporary mobility of intellectuals, likewise, will affect the obvious 'South Africanness' of their literary production: after all, many writers of South African origins now write and earn their livelihoods abroad. J. M. Coetzee has emigrated to Australia, Breyten Breytenbach lives in Paris and Dakar, Anne Landsman and Yvette Christiansë in New York, Zakes Mda in Ohio, Marita van der Vyver in Provence and Eben Venter (whose *Horrelpoot* [*Trencherman*], 2006, not only rewrites Conrad's *Heart of Darkness* but also gestures towards the new reality of a dispersed, international Afrikanerdom) commutes between Prince Albert and Melbourne. Whereas South African writers during the apartheid era often spanned the dual imaginary locations of home and exile, they are now fully and voluntarily diasporic; the geographical and thematic range of their work has been broadened accordingly.

Thus, as De Kock has noted, there is a new freedom, a new cosmopolitanism in 'South African' writing that is tending to make the word 'post-apartheid' – a word I have often used in this chapter – obsolete ('Does South African Literature Still Exist?'). Many of the best novels of recent years, de Kock observes, including Henrietta Rose-Innes's *The Rock Alphabet* (2005), Finuala Dowling's *What Poets Need* (2006), Landsman's *The Rowing Lesson* (2007), Heyns's *Bodies Politic* (2008) and van Heerden's *30 Nagte in Amsterdam* (2008) have moved so far beyond the national concerns of the struggle years that a new conceptual framework – perhaps one that operates, as Franco Moretti suggests, on the macro level of genre or on the micro level of devices, metaphors or words

('Graphs, Maps', p. 50) – will be needed to replace our ultimately politically motivated critical project of viewing works by South African-born writers as contributing to an (only theoretically and tenuously unified) national canon.

Bibliography

Armah, A. *The Beautyful Ones are not yet Born*, London: Heinemann, 1973.
Attwell, D., and Harlow, B. (ed.). 'Introduction: South African Fiction after Apartheid', *Modern Fiction Studies* 46:1 (2000), 1–9.
Barris, K. *Small Change*, Johannesburg: Ad Donker, 1988.
Bazin, N., and Seymour, M. (ed.). *Conversations with Nadine Gordimer*, Jackson: University Press of Mississippi, 1990.
Behr, M. *The Smell of Apples*, New York: Picador, 1997.
Bernstein, R. *Memory Against Forgetting: Memoirs from a Life in South African Politics*, New York: Viking, 1999.
Bethlehem, L. '"A primary need as strong as hunger": The Rhetoric of Urgency in South African Literary Culture under Apartheid', *Poetics Today* 22:2 (2001), 365–89.
Borainc, A. *A Life in Transition*, Cape Town: Struik, 2008.
Breytenbach, B. *Dog Heart: A Memoir*, New York: Harcourt, 1999.
Brink, A. *Donkermaan*, Cape Town: Human & Rousseau, 2000; *Rights of Desire*, New York: Harcourt, 2001.
  Duiwelskloof, Cape Town: Human & Rousseau, 1998; *Devil's Valley*, London: Secker & Warburg, 1998.
  SA 27 April 1994: An Author's Diary = 'n Skrywersdagboek, Cape Town: Queillerie, 1994.
  Sandkastele, Cape Town: Human & Rousseau, 1995; *Imaginings of Sand*, London: Secker & Warburg, 1996.
  'Stories of History: Reimagining the Past in Post-Apartheid Narrative', in S. Nuttall and C. Coetzee (eds.), *Negotiating the Past: The Making of Memory in South Africa*, Cape Town: Oxford University Press, 1998, 29–42.
Christiansë, Y. *Unconfessed*, New York: Other Press, 2006.
Coetzee, J. M. *Boyhood*, London: Secker & Warburg, 1997.
  Disgrace, London: Secker & Warburg, 1999.
Comaroff, J., and J. L. Comaroff. *Ethnicity, Inc.*, University of Chicago Press, 2009.
  'Nurturing the Nation: Aliens, Apocalypse, and the Postcolonial State', *Journal of South African Studies* 27:3 (2001), 627–55.
Coovadia, I. *Green-Eyed Thieves*, Johannesburg: Umuzi, 2006.
  High Low In-Between: A Novel, Cape Town: Umuzi, 2009.
  The Wedding, New York: Picador, 2001.
Cronin, J. *Even the Dead: Poems, Parables, and a Jeremiad*, Johannesburg: Mayibuye Books, 1999.
Dangor, A. *Bitter Fruit*, New York: Black Cat, 2005.
De Klerk, F. W. *The Last Trek: A New Beginning*, Philadelphia: Trans-Atlantic Publications, 2000.
De Kok, I. *Terrestrial Things*, Cape Town: Kwela Books, 2000.

De Kock, L. 'Does South African Literature still Exist? Or: South African Literature is Dead, Long Live Literature in South Africa', *English in Africa* 32:2 (2005), 69–83.

'South Africa in the Global Imaginary: An Introduction', *Poetics Today* 22:2 (2001), 263–98.

Dido, E. K. M. *Die Storie van Monica Peters*, Cape Town: Kwela Books, 1996.

Dison, D. *Death in the New Republic*, Johannesburg: Jacana, 2007.

Dowling, F. *What Poets Need*, Cape Town: Penguin Global, 2006.

Duiker, K. S. *The Quiet Violence of Dreams*, Cape Town: Kwela Books, 2001.

Thirteen Cents, Cape Town: David Philip, 2000.

Eprile, T. *The Persistence of Memory*, New York: W. W. Norton, 2005.

Gagiano, A. '"... To Remember is Like Starting to See": South African Life Stories Today', *Current Writing* 21:1–2 (2009), 261–85.

Galgut, D. *The Good Doctor*, Johannesburg: Viking, 2003.

The Imposter, New York: Black Cat, 2008.

Gilfillan, J. M. *Pouoogmot*, Cape Town: Human & Rousseau, 1997.

Goosen, J. *Ons is Nie Almal so Nie*, Pretoria: HAUM-Literêr, 1990. Translation by A. Brink as *We're Not all Like That*, Cape Town: Kwela Books, 2007.

Gordimer, N. *The House Gun*, New York: Farrar, Straus & Giroux, 1998.

None to Accompany Me, New York: Farrar, Straus & Giroux, 1994.

The Pickup, New York: Farrar, Straus & Giroux, 2001.

A Sport of Nature, New York: Knopf, 1987.

Govender, P. *Love and Courage: A Story of Insubordination*, Cape Town: Jacana, 2008.

Graham, S. *South African Literature after the Truth Commission: Mapping Loss*, New York: Palgrave, 2009.

Hassim, A. *The Lotus People*, Johannesburg: STE Publications, 1997.

Heyns, M. *Bodies Politic*, Cape Town: Jonathan Ball, 2008.

The Children's Day, Johannesburg: Jonathan Ball, 2002.

'The Whole Country's Truth: Confession and Narrative in Recent White South African Writing', *Modern Fiction Studies* 46:1 (2000), 42–66.

Hirson, D. *White Scars: On Reading and Rites of Passage*, Cape Town: Jacana, 2006.

Irlam, S. 'Unravelling the Rainbow: The Remission of Nation in Post-Apartheid Literature', *South Atlantic Quarterly* 103:4 (2004), 696–718.

Jacobs, R. *The Slave Book*, Cape Town: Kwela Books, 1998.

Sachs Street, Cape Town: Kwela Books, 2001.

Jaffer, Z. *Our Generation*, Cape Town: Kwela Books, 2005.

Jamal, A. *The Shades*, Howick: Brevitas, 2002.

Karodia, F. *Other Secrets*, Johannesburg: Penguin, 2000.

Kasrils, R. *'Armed and Dangerous': My Underground Struggle Against Apartheid*, Portsmouth, NH: Heinemann, 1995.

Kathrada, A. *Memoirs*, Cape Town: Zebra, 2004.

Kikamba, S. *Going Home*, Cape Town: Kwela Books, 2008.

Kleinboer. *Kontrei*, Johannesburg: Praag, 2003. Translation by J. Fouché as *Midnight Missionary*, Cape Town: Zebra, 2006.

Krog, A. *A Change of Tongue*, Cape Town: Struik, 2009.

Country of my Skull: Guilt, Sorrow, and the Limits of Forgiveness in the New South Africa, New York: Times Books, 1998.

Relaas van 'n Moord, Cape Town: Human & Rousseau, 1995.

Kruger, Loren. '"Black Atlantics", "White Indians", and "Jews": Locations, Locutions, and Syncretic Identities in the Fiction of Achmat Dangor and others', *Scrutiny2* 7:2 (2002), 34–50.

Landsman, A. *The Devil's Chimney*, Cape Town: Jonathan Ball, 1998.

The Rowing Lesson, London: Soho, 2007.

Langa, M. *The Naked Song and other Stories*, Washington DC: Three Continents, 1997.

Lazarus, N. 'The South African Ideology: The Myth of Exceptionalism, the Idea of Renaissance', *South Atlantic Quarterly* 103:4 (2004), 607–28.

Maart, R. *The Writing Circle*, Toronto: Toronto South Asian Review, 2007.

Magona, S. *Mother to Mother*, Boston, MA: Beacon Press, 1999.

Maimane, A. *Hate no More* [2000], Cape Town: Kwela Books, 2004.

Malan, M. *My Life with the SA Defence Force*, Pretoria: Protea, 2006.

Mandela, N. *Long Walk to Freedom*, Boston, MA: Little, Brown, 1994.

Matlwa, K. *Coconut*, Cape Town: Jacana, 2007.

Mda, Z. *Fools, Bells, and the Habit of Eating: Three Satires* [2002], Johannesburg: Witwatersrand University Press, 2003.

The Heart of Redness, New York: Picador, 2003.

Ways of Dying [1995], New York: Picador, 2004.

Medalie, D. *The Mistress's Dog: Short Stories, 1996–2010*, Johannesburg: Picador, 2010.

The Shooting of the Christmas Cows, Cape Town: David Philip, 1990.

Meer, I. *A Fortunate Man*, Cape Town: Struik, 2003.

Meyer, D. *Infanta*, Pretoria: Lapa, 2004. Translation by K. Seegers as *Devil's Peak*, New York: Little, Brown, 2008.

Mhlongo, N. *Dog Eat Dog*, Cape Town: Kwela Books, 2007.

Moretti, F. 'Conjectures on World Literature', *New Left Review* 1 (2000), 54–68.

'Graphs, Maps, Trees: Abstract Models for Literary History – 3', *New Left Review* 28 (2004), 43–63.

Mpe, P. *Welcome to our Hillbrow*, Pietermaritzburg: University of Natal Press, 2001.

Munro, B. 'Queer Family Romance: Writing the "New" South Africa in the 1990s', *GLQ* 15:3 (2009), 397–439.

'Queer Futures: The Coming-out Novel in South Africa', in T. Olaniyan and A. Quayson (eds.), *African Literature: An Anthology of Criticism and Theory*, Malden, MA: Blackwell, 2007, 753–64.

Naidoo, B. *Out of Bounds: Seven Stories of Hope and Conflict*, New York: Harper Collins, 2003.

Ndebele, N. *The Cry of Winnie Mandela*, Boulder, CO: Lynne Rienner, 2004.

'Memory, Metaphor, and the Triumph of Narrative', in S. Nuttall and C. Coetzee (eds.), *Negotiating the Past*, Cape Town: Oxford University Press, 1998, 19–28.

Nicol, M. *Payback*, London: Old Street, 2007.

The Waiting Country: A South African Witness, London: Victor Gollancz, 1995.

Nkosi, L. *Mating Birds*, New York: Harper & Row, 1986.

'The Republic of Letters after the Mandela Republic', *Journal of Literary Studies* 18:13–14 (2002), 240–58.

Underground People, Cape Town: Kwela Books, 2002.

Nuttall, S., and Coetzee, C. (eds.). *Negotiating the Past: The Making of Memory in South Africa*, Cape Town: Oxford University Press, 1998.

Orford, M. *Like Clockwork* [2006], London: Atlantic, 2010.

Pinnock, P. Schonstein. *Skyline*, Cape Town: David Philip, 2000.

Popescu, M. *South African Literature Beyond the Cold War*, New York: Palgrave, 2010.

Richards, J. *The Innocence of Roast Chicken*, London: Headline Review, 1996.

Robins, K. 'Becoming Anybody: Thinking Against the Nation and through the City', *City* 5:1 (2001), 78–90.

Rose-Innes, H. *Homing*, Cape Town: Random House / Umuzi, 2010.

The Rock Alphabet, Cape Town: Kwela Books, 2005.

Roup, J. *Boerejood*, Cape Town: Jacana, 2005.

Russell, A. *Bring me my Machine Gun: The Battle for the Soul of South Africa from Mandela to Zuma*, New York: Public Affairs, 2009.

Samuelson, M. *Remembering the Nation, Dismembering Women? Stories of the South African Transition*, Pietermaritzburg: University of KwaZulu-Natal Press, 2007.

Sanders, M. *Ambiguities of Witnessing: Law and Literature in the Time of a Truth Commission*, Palo Alto, CA: Stanford University Press, 2007.

Scholtz, A. *Vatmaar: 'n Lewendagge Verhaal van 'n Tyd wat Nie Meer is Nie*, Cape Town: Kwela Books, 2001. Translation by C. van Wyk as *A Place Called Vatmaar: A Living Story of a Time that is no More*, Cape Town: Kwela Books, 2001.

Seltzer, M. *Serial Killers: Death and Life in America's Wound Culture*, New York: Routledge, 1998.

Sepamla, S. *Rainbow Journey*, Johannesburg: Vivlia, 1996.

Serote, M. *To Every Birth its Blood*, New York: Thunder's Mouth Press, 1989.

Slovo, G. *Red Dust*, London: Virago, 2000.

Steinberg, J. *Midlands*, Johannesburg: Jonathan Ball, 2002.

Trengrove-Jones, T. 'Fiction and the Law: Recent Inscriptions of Gayness in South Africa', *Modern Fiction Studies* 46:1 (2000), 114–36.

Turner, J. *Heartland*, London: Orion, 1997.

Van der Vyver, M. *Griet Skryf 'n Sprokie*, Cape Town: Tafelberg, 1996. Translation by C. Knox as *Entertaining Angels*, New York: Dutton, 1995.

Van Heerden, E. *30 Nagte in Amsterdam*, Cape Town: Tafelberg, 2008. Translation by M. Heyns as *30 Nights in Amsterdam*, Johannesburg: Penguin, 2011.

Casspirs en Camparis, Cape Town: Tafelberg, 1991. Translation by C. Knox as *Casspirs and Camparis*, New York: Viking, 2003.

In Stede van die Liefde, Cape Town: Tafelberg, 2005.

Kikoejoe, Cape Town: Tafelberg, 1996. Translation by C. Knox as *Kikuyu*, Cape Town: Kwela Books, 1999.

Die Swye van Mario Salviati, Cape Town: Tafelberg, 2000. Translation by C. Knox as *The Long Silence of Mario Salviati*, London: Sceptre, 2002.

Van Niekerk, M. *Agaat*, Cape Town: Tafelberg, 2004. Translation by M. Heyns as *Agaat*, Johannesburg: Jonathan Ball, 2006; and by M. Heyns as *The Way of the Women*, London: Little, Brown, 2007.

Triomf, Cape Town: Queillerie, 1999. Translation by L. de Kock as *Triomf*, London: Little, Brown, 1999.

Van Wyk, C. *Shirley, Goodness, & Mercy: A Childhood in South Africa*, London: Macmillan, 2006.

The Year of the Tapeworm, Johannesburg: Ravan, 1996.

Venter, E. *Horrelpoot*, Cape Town: Tafelberg, 2006. Translation by L. Stubbs as *Trencherman*, Cape Town: Tafelberg, 2008.

Vladislavić, I. *The Exploded View*, Cape Town: David Philip, 2004.

Portrait with Keys: The City of Johannesburg Unlocked, New York: W. W. Norton, 2009.

The Restless Supermarket, Cape Town: David Philip, 2001.

Wicomb, Z. *David's Story*, Cape Town: Kwela Books, 2000.

'Five Afrikaner Texts and the Rehabilitation of Whiteness', *Social Identities* 4:3 (1998), 363–83.

Playing in the Light, New York: New Press, 2006.

Williams, M. *The Eighth Man*, Cape Town: Oxford University Press, 1999.

32

Writing the city after apartheid

MICHAEL TITLESTAD

Prior to the late 1980s, South African urban geography expressed the ambitions of apartheid ideologues: the identity of black South Africans was essentialised along a rural–urban axis (casting them as 'temporary sojourners' in 'white' cities), and zoning, forced removals, curfews, influx control generally and the *dompas* in particular were used to establish and entrench racial divisions in the cities.[1] To the extent that urbanisation was permitted, it occurred in a uniquely constrained and regulated way: cities came to comprise a combination of dormitory (black) townships, (white) suburbs and industrial areas, all gathered around a central business district (CBD) which coordinated the flows of capital. Apartheid parochialism, economic sanctions and the cultural boycott made these cities increasingly anachronistic and disjunctive. They were shielded – by a formidable apartheid bureaucracy – from the political, economic and social realities of their African and global context.

These cities figure in South African literature centrally as destinations for migrant labourers. 'Jim comes to Jo'burg' is an organising trope of representations of black urban experience before and during apartheid. In this regard, novels such as R. R. R. Dhlomo's *An African Tragedy* (1928), an allegory of the corruption of its protagonist 'Robert Zulu', Alan Paton's *Cry, the Beloved Country* (1949) and F. A. Venter's *Swart Pelgrim* (1958), which won the Hertzog Prize in 1961, are paradigmatic. Each develops a version of the convention of the 'greenhorn': an uncorrupted black man arrives from a rural ('traditional') context and discovers a mesmerising but overwhelming Johannesburg. In each novel the city resonates alternately with Jerusalem and the Cities of the Plain: it is both an inspirational site and one of louring corruption in which the innocent are led astray.

---

1 The Pass Laws Act of 1952 made it compulsory for all black South Africans over the age of 16 to carry a pass book or *dompas* in which their right to be in a white urban area was documented, and the duration of their 'legitimate' sojourn detailed.

Literature of the 1950s – much of it associated with the 'Sophiatown Renaissance' – asserted the essentially urban experience and priorities of black South Africans. City life, in these representations, entails, in addition to an *élan vital*, a perpetual tension between the emergence of enclaves of relative (black) autonomy – Sophiatown, District Six, Fordsburg, and so on – and apartheid social engineering. Communities fight for their right to be part of cities from which they are being systematically excluded.

By the 1970s and 1980s protest literature reflected a world that had been effectively divided, and in which black townships were becoming sites of militant resistance. Monganc Scrote's *To Every Birth its Blood* (1981) includes some of the most resonant descriptions of this division:

> From the centre of the Golden City to the centre of the Dark City is a mere nine miles. Where one starts the other ends, and where one ends, the other begins . . . Everything that says anything about the progress of man, the distance which man has made in terms of technology, efficiency and comfort: the Golden City says it well; the Dark City, by contrast, is dirty and deathly. The Golden City belongs to the white people of South Africa, and the Dark City to the black people. (p. 25)

The 'deregulation' of these divided cities since 1989 has been spectacular. With first the collapse of apartheid bureaucracy and then the regime change in 1994, South African cities were compelled to engage African and global modernity. For a period at least, it seemed as if planners had lost their hold on the arrangement of the polity. Let us take, as our example, Johannesburg, the largest and economically most significant metropolis, which Meg Samuelson describes as 'the crucible of a new national culture' ('City Beyond the Border', p. 247). Most accounts of Johannesburg's transformation emphasise the northward migration of office space (into suburban office nodes) and the ongoing decentralisation of retail, which has increasingly aggregated in suburban shopping malls. These shifts are both symptoms and causes of the decline of the CBD. In the early to mid 1990s an influx of poorer black South Africans into the city began, most of whom sought cheap accommodation in buildings that had been vacated during the 'laissez-faire greying process' (Beavon, *Johannesburg*, p. 244). Various initiatives sought to stem the tide, but the critical point had long since passed. By 1995 shacks and squats dominated areas of the city, and at the same time vacant apartment buildings in the inner-city residential zone were 'invaded'. These 'invasions', and the proliferation of informal settlements within the city, led increasingly to strained relations between tenants and landlords. Residential blight escalated dramatically, with parts of the inner city, Hillbrow, Berea and Newtown, becoming derelict.

In addition, apartheid parochialism gave way to an accelerated African-isation of the cities. An influx of migrants from Nigeria, the Democratic Republic of the Congo (DRC), Cameroon and Zimbabwe – who have been met with South Africans' notorious xenophobia – has made Johannesburg cosmopolitan: it is now a major urban hub of the continent.

This account may seem to suggest that post-apartheid cities have integrated. However, the envisaged desegregation has not occurred at either the rate or to the extent that was anticipated; the spectre of Serote's Golden and Dark Cities continues to haunt the present. Beavon indicates that, 'although there has been a noticeable movement of African people into formerly whites-only suburbs, in most sectors [of Johannesburg] the actual numbers and percentages of African buyers in the total pool of property transactions have remained low' (*Johannesburg*, p. 267). The net result is a city that it still segre-gated along race and class lines: the 'combined population of Soweto, Diep-kloof, South and Orange Farm districts is 1.6 million, 59% of the city's total population', while blacks (if we exclude Alexandra) comprise only 37 per cent of people living in the north (Tomlinson et al., *Emerging Johannesburg*, p. 13). The 'post-apartheid city' is, therefore, a phrase one should treat with caution.

The simultaneous transformation of apartheid cities and their vestigial divi-sions have made these concatenations primary sites for literary engagements with the simultaneous utopian promise and crippling contradictions of con-temporary South Africa. Perhaps for the first time in our history a complex and complicating literature of the urban has emerged.

It is impossible to identify a dominant aesthetic in representations of post-apartheid cities. Revealingly, though, a recurrent preoccupation – in both South African literary criticism and literature itself – has been with the writing of Michel de Certeau. His essay, 'Walking the City', distinguishes two incli-nations in representation which usefully frame this chapter – the cartographic and the peripatetic. The essay begins with him gazing down on Manhattan from the 110th floor of the World Trade Centre. The sweep of the eye reduces this 'most immoderate of human texts' (p. 92) to a 'panorama-city', a 'visual simulacrum' (p. 93). Manhattan, in his mind's eye, is transformed into a plan of itself by his gaze, which is that of the surveyor, the rationalist 'voyeur-god' (p. 93), who reduces the complexities and contingencies of the world in terms of the logic of a 'scopic or gnostic drive' (p. 92).

This perspective depends on disentangling oneself from 'the ordinary prac-titioners of the city' (p. 93), on overlooking the countless ways in which the city is experienced in the quotidian. The alternative, with which Certeau is centrally concerned, sets aside this cartographic turn in favour of the multiple stories told, at ground level, in terms of *practices*, *operations* and *tactics*. Walkers, he argues, are consumers who produce, 'through their signifying practices . . . "errant" trajectories obeying their own logic' (p. xviii). Even while their meanings derive from the established vocabularies of their context (in the sense that they are embedded in the prevailing *episteme*), 'they trace out the ruses of other interests and desires' (p. xviii). The capacity to rearrange the vocabulary at one's disposal implies that meanings are not 'determined or captured by the systems in which they develop' (p. xviii). Rather, by using the available elements in an almost parasitic relation (through appropriation, rearrangement, manipulation, substitution, diversion and superimposition), individuals leave what Jeremy Ahearn calls, 'the irreducible mark of the human subject within [the] order [in which they operate]' (*Michel de Certeau*, p. 159).

These two perspectives suggest different ways of attempting to come to terms with the excess of post-apartheid cities. One can either aspire to a rational overview of social, economic, cultural and political change (as do many in the social sciences committed to materialist and sociological analysis) or one can emphasise the multiple (often 'hybridising' or 'Afropolitan')[2] ways in which people 'make do' in the increasingly globalised environments of South African cities. Many of the studies that adopt this second approach are concerned with self-styling and sub-cultural styling; the logic and micropolitics of the ways in which individuals and communities assemble, manipulate and perpetuate their identities and their practices of belonging.

Literature is well placed to mediate between analytical maps and particular pathways of meaning. The diversity of engagements discussed below suggests a range of such mediations which affirm the psycho-geographical understanding that each city is manifold: it comprises Italo Calvino's 'invisible cities' or Jonathan Raban's 'soft cities' depending on how and why one approaches the city, one's race, class and gender, personal and political history, or whether one's priority is commerce, survival, politics, sanctuary, exile, narration, medical treatment, evangelism or some eccentric desire. Some represented cities, we will see, are fashioned from fear, others by strangers; some out of nostalgia, others in terms of imported, generic conventions. Five organising tropes are explored (transition, discrepancy, insinuation, ontology and genre). These are not mutually exclusive. Given the diversity of post-apartheid writing, this

---

2 For an explanation of this term, see Nuttall and Mbembe, 'Introduction: Afropolis', *Johannesburg*, pp. 1–33.

approach is inevitably speculative. Each trope is a pathway of the literary imagination: the post-apartheid city is too immoderate and unresolved to be mapped.

Transitional cities

Various South African novels engage the transformation of South African cities by describing the simultaneity of history and emergent post-apartheid possibilities. Three important discrepant engagements are Marlene van Niekerk's *Triomf* (1994), which describes the moribund world of Afrikaner nationalism, Zakes Mda's *Ways of Dying* (1995), one of the first portraits of the prospects of freedom, and Ivan Vladislavić's comic masterpiece, *The Restless Supermarket* (2001), a portrait of anxious white social demotion.

Triomf signalled the arrival of a major presence on the post-apartheid literary scene. Set against the backdrop of the first democratic election, the novel is a portrait of the lives of the Benades – Pop, Mol, Treppie and Lambert – who live at 127 Martha Street in Triomf, a suburb of western Johannesburg. Triomf was built after Sophiatown was destroyed and its population forcibly removed to the nascent Soweto and its houses graded. Sophiatown – although it is often difficult to discern the truth through the mythology – was a vibrant, largely freehold suburb and a black cultural and intellectual hub in Johannesburg in the 1950s. Triomf ('Triumph') was named for its decimation, celebrating the National Party's pyrrhic segregationist victory.

The ideological 'triumph', in apartheid's terms, entailed 'purification': urban blight was being eradicated, and the needs of landless white working-class Afrikaners, for whom Triomf was intended, were being met. The Benades, however, are anything but pure: their incestuous history (all the men have sex with Mol, and Lambert is the genetically impaired, monstrous offspring of siblings – either Pop or Treppie and Mol) has extinguished any hope of a future. Lambert is a 'cul-de-sac': the end point of the introversion of an Afrikaans community driven by its own isolationist logic. The action of the novel – the self-destructive, often farcical, but surprisingly poignant exploits of the Benades – accentuates this dynamic of self-destruction; while they are victims of the state's failed planning, they are really their own worst enemy. Nationalism, the novel suggests, like Kronos, devours its children.

Triomf does not represent a post-apartheid city. It expresses the result of building (cities, identities and lives) on the ruins of suppressed black history. In the novel, the dogs of Sophiatown still howl and fragments of the bulldozed past keep resurfacing; the repressed, constantly returning, is on the verge of returning with a vengeance. All subsequent literature about the city has to contend with the death this novel inscribes as constitutive.

If *Triomf* captures the moribund apartheid order, Mda's *Ways of Dying*, which concerns the life of Toloki, a 'professional mourner', presents an imagined freedom. Rita Barnard argues that the novel is 'forward-looking, insofar as it provides a springboard for speculations about new urban subjectivities and semantic topographies that may emerge with apartheid's demise' (*Apartheid and Beyond*, p. 150). Toloki improvises, not only an eccentric ascetic subjectivity, but ways of inhabiting the unnamed port city that he has – itinerant, with his worldly possessions in a shopping trolley – made his own. Contrary to the 'Jim comes to Jo'burg' trope, Mda represents a peripatetic practice of making meaning through which Toloki transforms, among other things, the wretchedness of Noria's shack in the informal settlement into a magical (realist) world of luxury and possibility. Barnard points out that the 'social divisions so starkly expressed [in Serote's aesthetic] are no longer in evidence' (pp. 154–5); rather Toloki's aesthetic engagement with the possibilities of everyday life represents an 'imaginative reaching out to distant horizons' (p. 155) that contradicts the ghetto logic of apartheid. Toloki's 'creative urbanity' (p. 155), in Certeau's terms, cuts across the plans and schemes of the ideologues; the walker trumps the 'fixed and tyrannical topography' intended to regulate his identity (*Apartheid and Beyond*, p. 154).

Vladislavić's writing, to which we return later, is arguably the most sustained imaginative investigation of post-apartheid urban life. *The Restless Supermarket* expresses, in certain senses, the opposite of Mda's peripatetic, quotidian liberation. The novel tells the story of Aubrey Tearle, a retired proofreader of telephone directories who is regularly ensconced in the Café Europa in Hillbrow bemoaning the emergence of the 'New South Africa'. He considers himself 'an incorrigible "European"' (p. 15) – although he has never been to Europe – who is facing the country's ineluctable deterioration: 'Decline with a capital D' (p. 81). The Café is a metonym for a white habitus that is being challenged at the Convention for a Democratic South Africa, occurring across town, at which the first democratic election and the post-apartheid dispensation are being plotted.

'Change' for the recalcitrant narrator equates only to a decline in 'standards of correctness' (p. 63), a 'general malaise'. He faces political transformation with the anxious disposition of a compulsive proofreader. As Marais notes, 'Vladislavić collapses the distinction between his protagonist's *linguistic* proofreading and his *social* proofreading, that is, the obsessive manner in which Tearle detects "errors" in the world around him as he goes about his daily business' ('Reading Against Race', p. 283). He weaves these errors – or 'corrigenda', 'things to be corrected, especially in a printed book' (p. 61) – into his grand opus, 'The Proofreader's Derby' (which comprises the second part of the novel). This surreal narrative describes a pastiche European city, 'Alibia', and its decline into chaos as the 'Members of the Society of Proofreaders' strive to stem the entropy.

Tearle's Alibia is an eloquent expression of white transitional anxieties: that the post-apartheid order would entail nothing other than disorder, disorientation and loss. The English language (settled in the *Oxford Pocket Dictionary* the narrator always carries with him) proves inadequate to the task of maintaining the order of things in a context that seems to Tearle increasingly cacophonous (in fact, multilingual and transnational), which he is unable to regulate – to proofread. Helgesson describes *The Restless Supermarket* as staging the *'minoritisation'* or devolution of South African English ('"Minor disorders"', p. 778): the entire semiotic order of the proofreader's comprehension is facing appropriation, transformation and marginalisation. The swirling, collapsing, paradoxical and unpredictable Alibia is an expression of the historical grounds of white hegemony giving way.

Discrepant cities

The lives of many black South Africans and African immigrants to post-apartheid cities remain particular: townships, inner-city suburbs and informal settlements have their own ethnographies and their own economies of exchange, possibility and threat. If we compare Phaswane Mpe's *Welcome to our Hillbrow* (2001), K. Sello Duiker's novel, *The Quiet Violence of Dreams* (2001), his novella, *Thirteen Cents* (2000), and the picaresque novels of Niq Mhlongo, we can discern three different modes in which black urbanity is represented.

Mpe's *Welcome to our Hillbrow* constructs Hillbrow as a nodal point in the national imaginary and in transnational networks (Samuelson, 'City Beyond the Border', p. 248). The densely populated inner-city suburb is linked – by the pathways of migrancy – to a South African and African hinterland. The lives of its inhabitants are constitutively mobile; comprising endless practices of translating one's origins into the idiom of the city and of redescribing one's 'home' (in the case of the novel's narrator and its protagonists, the rural settlement of Tiralong) into the languages of the urban and the global. Unlike the 'Jim comes to Jo'burg' trope, Mpe's novel collapses the conventional binaries: the city (though plagued by AIDS, xenophobia, grime and crime) is part of the same moral order as that of Tiralong, and the lives of its characters are woven from the relational stories they tell in their efforts to make their lives cohere.

Much of the novel is addressed to the dead Refentše by an unnamed narrator. Refentše, who has come from Tiralong to attend the University of the Witwatersrand, develops, street by street, a cognitive map of Hillbrow and Braamfontein; his interiority and the city begin to merge, and he elects to remain beyond his undergraduate years to complete a postgraduate degree and to take up a teaching post at the university. His lover's betrayal and his unsuccessful efforts to capture the contesting worlds of the city in fiction leave him despairing, and he commits suicide. The last sections of the narrative are addressed to Refilwe – who has followed a similar route from Tiralong to the city. She is employed by a publishing house as a commissioning editor of Sepedi texts, travels to Oxford to continue her studies, but returns when her HIV infection develops into full-blown AIDS.

Sarah Nuttall suggests that the title of the novel – 'welcome to . . .' is a refrain throughout the novel, and its concluding sentence is 'Welcome to our Heaven . . .' (p. 124) – implies a disavowal of 'a politics of hatred in favor of an ethics of hospitality' ('Literary City', p. 203). *Welcome to our Hillbrow* is a novel of fraught loves, of the complications of the heart and of the hopes and aspirations of those living with pressing post-apartheid realities. Even though its pages bear witness to prejudice (particularly against AIDS sufferers and the *makwerekwere*, as foreigners in South Africa are pejoratively known) and depict the effects of crime, Mpe describes a world of complicated civility in which strangers can arrive and learn their way. Whilst in Aubrey Tearle's city all seems lost, in Mpe's Hillbrow the quotidian experiences of evolving lives consists in losses and gains.

If *Welcome to our Hillbrow* revises apartheid representations of migration and asserts the complicated imbrication of cities and rural contexts, Duiker's novel *The Quiet Violence of Dreams* captures the purely urban world of many young South Africans. It concerns the vicissitudes of the daily life of Tshepo, a student who abandons his studies following a spell in Valkenberg, a psychiatric hospital – the official diagnosis is 'cannabis induced psychosis' (p. 13) – and who journeys towards both the discovery of his true sexuality and a qualified optimism. In his portrait of Tshepo's friendships and social milieu, his cohabitation – and increasingly homoerotic fascination – with the ex-convict Chris, his violent rape by Chris and two of his cronies, and his subsequent experiences in the world of male prostitution, Duiker elaborates a new urbanity.

The identities of the novel's cast of characters seem more vested in patterns of consumption and practices of self-styling than in historically constituted racial and cultural categories. Mmabatho, Tshepo's confidante, declares at a point that she 'came to Cape Town so that [she] could run away from the whole race thing' (p. 33). At another point she avers that she '[refuses] to blame history' (p. 63). This first generation of 'new South Africans' is intent on escaping the determinations of the past: theirs is a world of overlapping and intersecting realities that cut across the previous regimes of identity, and the city they inhabit is, at least superficially, post-political, comprising interrelated subcultures and new dynamics of circulation and affiliation.

But several of the main characters, including Tshepo and Mmabatho, come to recognise the tenacity of the history and categories they believe they can slough off. There are finally no 'blank spaces' (p. 31) that individuals can fill at will. Mmabatho finds herself the subject of conventional essentialisation: 'If you're black and you don't do the darkie thing then they say you're trying to be white' (p. 33). She finds herself repeatedly labelled 'a coconut' (p. 39),[3] an epithet that describes a black person who is 'white on the inside'. The endless circulation of this metaphor in the post-apartheid public sphere demonstrates that faith in a utopian postracial order has proved naive.

But despite the persistence of racial determination, the overall trajectory of *The Quiet Violence of Dreams* is quietly optimistic. At the novel's conclusion Tshepo has begun to edge away from the anomic condition and the unresolved haunting by his past that drove him to Valkenberg. He experiences an oceanic compassion, and resolves to live in terms of the 'treasures' that lie within him (p. 457): 'When I think about Cape Town and all the experiences I had with the many coloured faces I met, I become suspicious and curious. Perhaps life was giving me a hint. Perhaps the future of mankind lies in each other, not in separate continents with separate people. We are still evolving as a species, our differences are merging' (p. 456).

Whilst *The Quiet Violence of Dreams* touches on the wretchedness of poverty in Cape Town – on the desperate attempts of the homeless and victims of violence and xenophobia to survive – these concerns are central to Duiker's first novella, *Thirteen Cents*. It tells of the life of Azure, a homeless orphan who lives rough in Cape Town, of the unspoken realities of a city that is so often presented as a tourist and investment mecca. The world of Azure – of sleeping under bridges, foraging for food and clothing, prostituting himself, most commonly to white bourgeois men, of pimps and paedophiles – is marked by the violence of a drug-riddled city divided among rival criminal gangs. He constantly seeks protection from the seemingly powerful; only

---

3 A recent, more playful interrogation of the 'coconut' is presented in Kopano Matlwa's *Coconut*.

to have them either exploit his vulnerability or visit violence upon him in pursuit of their own, often inscrutable, ends. The city of the homeless – as Jonathan Morgan also reveals in *Finding Mr Madini* (1999) – is one of live-saving improvisation in the face of spectacular inhospitality.

Niq Mhlongo is the author of two novels, *Dog Eat Dog* (2004) and *After Tears* (2007). Often described as 'the novelist of the *kwaito* generation',[4] Mhlongo's works confront the realities of being a young black man in a transforming South Africa. His first, *Dog Eat Dog*, set in 1994, describes the daily challenges faced by a Johannesburg university student for whom the financial pressures of studying are as real as the promise of the first democratic election. His more recent *After Tears* is a picaresque account of a student, Bafana Kuzwayo, who drops out of the law programme at the University of Cape Town and returns to Soweto. Since he has neglected to inform anyone that he has failed, Bafana is expected to assume the responsibilities of a township lawyer.

Many of the issues engaged by Mpe and Duiker (AIDS, crime, xenophobia and so on) recur in Mhlongo's novels. The difference is tone: both *Dog Eat Dog* and *After Tears* playfully indulge the local colour of *Loxion Kulcha* (commodified 'township/location culture'), generally eschewing gravity in favour of narrative momentum.

Insinuated cities

Among other writers, Vladislavić and Heinrich Troost are concerned with the ways in which their characters contend with the cacophonous possibilities of the post-apartheid dispensation. How, in other words, do they assemble trajectories of meaning in the face of the disruption or abandonment of the schemes of meaning in terms of which their perception and subjectivity have been fashioned? Both writers represent a new tendency in post-apartheid literature: the reflection of a peripatetic assemblage of meaning from diverse, even contending, systems of meaning.

Vladislavić's *The Exploded View* (2005) comprises four interwoven stories: 'Villa Toscana' concerns Budlender, a statistician seconded from the Development Bank by Statistical Services to assist in redrafting questionnaires for the national census, after 'those used in the census of 1996, the first non-racial headcount in the country's history, had flummoxed half the population' (p. 5); 'Afritude Sauce' recounts an inspection visit by a sanitary engineer, Egan, to a

---

4 *Kwaito* refers to a local variation of house, which incorporates elements of South African music, and which typically rests on a deep bassline. It emerged in South African townships in the 1990s.

Reconstruction and Development Programme (RDP) housing project, Hani View, which compels him to dwell on the disjunction between plans and reality; 'Curiouser' reflects the improvisatory practices of a black artist, Simeon Majara, whose installations have addressed various genocides (the Holocaust, Bosnia, Rwanda), but whose most recent work entails the physical and conceptual dissection of African curios (hence 'curio-user'); and, 'Crocodile Lodge', the final narrative, describes a catastrophic day in the life of Gordon Duffy, whose small company erects billboards, particularly those depicting artists' impressions of new housing developments.

The novel presents improvisations on a number of themes. Reminiscent of Aubrey Tearle's attachment to Oxford English, Budlender's faith in statistics represents the talismanic possibility that the world can be quantified, its meanings ordered and rendered legible. Egan, whose favourite aphorism is 'Blame the plans. Shoot the planners' (p. 71), comes to believe that planners lack 'realism': they are committed to cartographic overviews fashioned from a desire for an ordered and predictable world that denies the actual rivalries, expectations, conflicts, histories and vested interests that comprise the ways in which individuals inhabit cities. Duffy's ideal world is reflected in the pages of *Popular Mechanics*, which he read compulsively in his youth. In it, the 'surfaces [are] airbrushed to perfection, gleaming with old-fashioned optimism; the inner working laid bare, frankly and practically, as the product of enterprise and effort' (p. 171). The graphic device through which the 'inner working' of the world is 'laid bare' is 'the exploded view'. The detailed precision of the exploded view reveals a world of planning, order, proportion and precise combination. It is a view in which the plan of the real is revealed; in which everything is poised, waiting to be put in its place, nothing is lacking and in which every element is essential to the integrity of the assembly.

Each of the four narrators experiences a moment of vertiginous disorientation when the world of swirling signs cannot be ordered in terms of the system of meaning on which he depends. A slippage occurs – and, for each, the real begins to recede beneath a tide of signifiers that have become detached from their signifieds. Vladislavić's Johannesburg is the unreality of its limits: its boundaries 'are drifting away, sliding over pristine ridges and valleys, lodging in tenuous places, slipping again. At its edges, where the city fades momentarily into the veld, unimaginable new atmospheres evolve' (p. 6). In this space of unstable meaning, of Budlender's simulated Tuscan villa, complete with 'medieval treatment' (p. 7), of Duffy's 'artists' impressions' of simulated villas and game lodges, and Egan's European letrasets and an 'African themed' restaurant, meaning is everywhere deferred, comprising only pastiche and palimpsest. But the city they occupy – which endlessly disrupts the static binary oppositions of Africa–Europe, tradition–modernity, local–global (Helgesson 'Johannesburg as Africa', p. 34) – while it confounds all familiar schemes and taxonomies, is also a context in which the creativity of Simeon Majara can generate not just artworks but entire lineages of meaning. A groundlessness of meaning, *The Exploded View* suggests, is not only a reason to panic.

Vladislavić's most recent work, *Portrait with Keys: Joburg & What-What* (2006), which won the Sunday Times Alan Paton Award for Non-Fiction in 2007, takes aspects of its form and philosophy from, among other sources, Italo Calvino's *Invisible Cities* (1997) and the writing of Michel de Certeau. Like Calvino's layered portrait of Venice, it meditates on the many 'cities' that constitute the variety of ways in which Johannesburg is understood and inhabited. It also elaborates the pedestrian epistemology detailed by Certeau, exploring not only the ways in which the narrator and others walk parts of the city into trajectories of meaning, but also the multiple paradoxes, contradictions and generative possibilities that can be improvised by those at ground level. This philosophy is further performed in 'Itineraries', an appendix that suggests various 'pathways' through the linked vignettes (essays, short stories) comprising the text. In counterpoint to this sense of improvisatory potential in *Portrait with Keys* is a poignant presentation of loss and decline. This soft nostalgia – which is so different from the comic rendition of Aubrey Tearle's reactionary sentiments in *The Restless Supermarket* – faces (through a version of autobiography) the loss of familiar maps.

Heinrich Troost's debut novel, *Plot Loss* (2007), is the story, in free indirect discourse, of Harry van As, a legal consultant in an insurance firm who, in the wake of the death of his wife and children in a motor car accident, has been seconded from Cape Town to one of its Pretoria offices. Given that the narrative mimics the Russian doll logic of free-associative thinking, of nested stories linked by their subjective or discursive relations, it is difficult to summarise. Broadly, the novel traces van As's *flâneur*-like rediscovery of the city of his youth and of his emerging relationships with an eclectic group of friends.

His return to the capital, a city traditionally identified with the parochialism of apartheid nationalism, occasions a re-examination of his ties to the archives of Afrikaner identity and an engagement with the discontinuities of his life. Growing up, van As experienced only alienation in this heart of Afrikaner nationalism – Pretoria was 'a city where people were strange and he was a stranger' (p. 15). Rather than the anomie and transitional anxiety we might anticipate he will experience in the post-apartheid context, he 'finds relief, solace, confirmation in the tumbling icons he despised in his youth' (p. 15). Whilst the contemporary cacophony – the clash of the historical, the African and the global – may at times be deafening, Van As experiences it as infinitely productive in contrast to the engineered silences of the past.

As the novel proceeds, events become increasingly dreamlike, culminating in an excursion to the 200,000-year-old Tswaing meteoric crater outside Pretoria to celebrate the summer solstice. Events take first a Dionysian and then a surreal turn. This surreality is then explained. The first line, 'He lies facing upwards, drifting in and out of sleep, eyes opening now and then' (p. 7), the refrain 'pillow talk', the occasional moments when the narrative is interrupted by electronic beeps, have all indicated the actual state of affairs. The story is a sustained hallucination of the comatose Harry van As, who, rather than losing his wife and children, has himself sustained critical injuries in a car accident. We have been witnessing an instance of near death dreamwork.

Van As occupies, rather than some tainted past of Afrikanerdom, the bohemian world of Café Riche, not Church Square; the flea market, not Melrose House. Grafted on to the ponderously historical is a city of dissonant possibilities, evanescent connections and affiliations, and emergent and incomplete selves. Losing the plot – when it simply confines and confirms – is, *Plot Loss* suggests, the most generative thing we can do. Only then ('plotless') do we have the potential to take ourselves, and others, by surprise.

Ontological cities

Afrikaans novelists have contended with the ontological reorientation necessitated by their political and social demotion within the post-apartheid dispensation. The city, in much new Afrikaans literature, figures simultaneously as a site for engaging this shift and as a domain of creative prospects for assembling non-hegemonic alternatives. Any comprehensive survey of representations of the city in post-apartheid Afrikaans literature would have to take account of, among others, recent writing by André Brink, Koos Kombuis, Rachelle Greeff, Jaco Botha, P. J. Haasbroek, Jaco Fouché, Hermann Wasserman, Elsa Joubert, Ingrid Winterbach and Johann de Lange. This literature is worldly; it is best interpreted in the context, not just of national literary history, but also of the multiple ways in which city life is being constructed in other postcolonial and postmodern literatures. Let us consider just three novels, by Etienne van Heerden, Kleinboer and Eben Venter respectively, in which this changing textuality is manifest.

Central among new globalised Afrikaans writing is Etienne van Heerden's *In Stede van die Liefde* (2005), which translates as 'in cities/instead of love'. This intricately plotted work of psycho-geography alternates between an account of the life of Christian Lemmer (who runs a web-based African art dealership) and the story of a small community (and a violin) in Matjiesfontein, a Karoo town. It is concerned, like much post-apartheid writing, with repressed histories, African immigrants and xenophobia, but also addresses the metaliterary questions of artistic production and the ontology of artworks.

The story of Christian and his various relationships is definitively urban. The novel begins with one of those moments, not untypical in contemporary South African writing, when two worlds collide· returning to Stellenbosch from Cape Town airport, Christian's car is shot at by a gang member. He escapes narrowly, but is plagued for the remainder of the novel by an arbitrary 'death sentence'. In order to address this bizarre reality, Christian taps into another world that he inhabits: without the knowledge of his wife, Christine, he keeps a flat in Sea Point, indulges a severe cocaine habit (despite recent heart surgery), and has a network of friends and associates far removed from the relatively genteel world of Stellenbosch and art dealers. The novel culminates in a decision to explore this bifurcation of his life with Christine, at the same time as they are both forced to confront her repressed memories and elided past, which link to the world of Matjiesfontein.

Not only does the novel juxtapose Christian's Sea Point and Stellenbosch – both of which Van Heerden describes in luxuriant detail – but his professional nomadism takes him to Johannesburg, Manhattan, Vienna, Antwerp, Berlin and eventually Harare. He inhabits each city in terms of a range of memories, priorities, desires and anxieties, shifting identities across each cityscape. The versatility, even indeterminacy, of a global city life is expressed in the trope of '*verglyding*' ('slideout'/slippage), repeated often in the text: reality slips away from under us and we find ourselves living across the surface of a world of contending stories, each with its own setting, cast of characters and provenance.

Kleinboer's *Kontrei* (2003), translated as *Midnight Missionary* (2006), exists in the tradition of libidinal epistemology that links George Bataille to Michel Houellebecq. It is a confessional account of the white narrator's multiple sexual encounters (almost all with black prostitutes), as well as his complicated relationship with his partner, Thembi. Its title, *Kontrei*, alludes simultaneously to 'country' and 'cunt-ry'; the English translation plays on the ambiguity of 'missionary': an evangelist (the narrator weaves his iconoclastic interpretation of Bible verses into his eroticism) and the 'missionary position'. Collapsing the nation into the sexual – the political into the intimate – allows Kleinboer to provide a refreshing map of the Johannesburg he inhabits, but also of the possibilities of post-apartheid identity.

His is a phallic world driven by its own voracious logic, which cuts across all Calvinist precepts, as well as the racial and gender stereotypes in which representations of Afrikaner men are trapped. Behind the jouissance of the novel is a significant dissembling of received notions of whiteness and masculinity. Kleinboer's Johannesburg is a string of brothels and pubs; his cartography a sexual itinerary. Coming at a familiar world at an angle, he defamiliarises, by embodying, both the city and the ways in which it can be occupied.

Eben Venter's award-winning *Horrelpoot* (2006), translated into English as *Trencherman* (2008), is a shatteringly dystopic vision of a future South Africa in which the state has collapsed and in which criminal syndicates rule. The infrastructure has collapsed entirely (roads have disintegrated, there is no water or electricity provision and the economy has been reduced to desperate barter), bribery and corruption are routine and AIDS infection is universal. A retelling of Conrad's *Heart of Darkness*, the novel recounts Marlouw's arrival from Melbourne, at the instigation of his sister, to find his nephew Koert, who has transformed himself from a suburban teenager into a sickly, gangrenous, perspiring and bed-ridden overlord who, Nintendo control in hand, also controls the distribution of meat and whiskey to the region surrounding the erstwhile family farm, 'Ouplaaas'. Like Kurtz, he rules through his able-bodied minions who revere, fear and loathe him in equal measure. And, like Kurtz, he is rotting from within, his moral corruption expressed in the meat he consumes excessively and which oozes from his every pore.

The climax of Venter's depiction of white (South) African deterioration is a scene in which Marlouw transports Koert, strapped to a bed on the back of a *bakkie*, to the family graveyard, where they discover grave robbers digging up their forebears. This final 'invasion' indicates symbolically the end point of the *plaasroman* tradition; it is impossible to have a farm (or even a grave) in Africa. But, even as Koert is finally carved to death by his followers, we realise that he embodies the fears at the heart of whiteness: his decadence (evident in his corrupted language as much as in his bloated body) is the hyperbolic expression of the corruption of everything on which Afrikanerdom in particular, and African whiteness more generally, depends.

As this brief synopsis suggests, the primary scene of *Horrelpoot* is rural. Marlouw, though, does land in Johannesburg, and bribes his way on to a connecting flight to Bloemfontein. The fourth chapter of the novel includes a nightmarish vision of a city of desperate poverty and starvation, barricaded buildings, arbitrary militia roadblocks, mass HIV infection and roaming criminal gangs. This gothic vision of doom calls white readers to confront the literary manifestation of their paranoia.

Generic cities

Post-apartheid cities also exist in popular genres quite conventionally fashioned. This is perhaps most apparent in that post-apartheid publishing phenomenon, the crime novel. Given the centrality of crime in the social imaginary, and in many of the works discussed in this chapter, it is unsurprising that South African authors have turned their hands to writing thrillers, whodunnits and police procedurals.

Deon Meyer is by far the most widely read South African crime thriller author. His novels have been translated into fifteen languages and are published both locally and internationally. These include *Feniks* (1996, translated as *Dead Before Dying*), *Orion* (2000; *Dead at Daybreak*, 2000), *Proteus* (*Heart of the Hunter*, 2003), *Infanta* (*Devil's Peak*, 2005), *Onsigbaar* (*Blood Safari*, 2007), and most recently *13 Uur* (2008), which continues the story of Meyer's main police detective, Bennie Griessel. Meyer's exhausted, existential, alcoholic policemen are forced to navigate a city of sinister rivalries and embedded histories, at the same time as they are called upon to contend with globalised crime. The lives of impoverished black prostitutes are folded into the world of Colombian drug dealers; survivors of the apartheid security forces end up in daily transactions with both ex-activists and petty criminals of the Cape Flats.

Meyer's writing has spawned a tradition. Notable among recent crime titles by other authors are: Michael Williams, *Hijack City* (1999); Richard Kunzmann, *Bloody Harvests* (2004); Andrew Brown, *Coldsleep Lullaby* (2005), which won the *Sunday Times* Fiction Prize in 2006; Mike Nicol and Joanne Hichens, *Out to Score* (2006); Margie Orford, *Like Clockwork* (2006) and *Blood Rose* (2007); Angela Makholwa, *Red Ink* (2007); Jassy Mackenzie, *Random Violence* (2008); and Mike Nicol, *Payback* (2008). In *Moxyland* (2008) and *Zoo City* (2010), Lauren Beukes creates dystopian but lingusticially inventive versions of Cape Town and inner Johannesburg respectively, in which elements of the corporate thriller and the *noir* crime novels of Raymond Chandler are combined with other, more flamboyant modes – science fiction, cyberpunk, gonzo journalism, Afro-futurism – as well as a dense array of references to online and pop culture.

It is impossible to generalise about such a diversity of novels. Each, though, engages South African city life by describing the national and international networks of criminality in which post-apartheid cities are enmeshed and the challenges facing the South African police force and security establishment. Writing crime novels in crime-saturated societies raises particular difficulties: one cannot represent – especially in light of South Africa's lumbering and leaky criminal justice system – an uncomplicated restoration of order; the usual dynamics of the police procedural have no credibility in a context in which the capacity of the police is stretched to breaking point, and in which the force is riddled with corruption; and crime novels and thrillers circulate in a milieu in which spectacular violence is ubiquitous and routine. A further complication is that crime in South Africa is ineluctably historical: most people would argue that one cannot divorce the current tide of criminality from colonial and apartheid inequalities and injustices. As a consequence of these realities, local writers have been forced to adapt and stretch the conventions of the crime novel. Some have done so with compelling results.

South Africa's post-apartheid cities – in all of their emergent complexity – have proved to be the key sites for engaging and representing the nation's transformation. The abolition of racial segregation, in principle if not in reality, combined with the integration of South Africa's cities into the region, the continent and the world, has made them contexts of rivalries, contestations, threats and opportunities. The discrepant engagements – the pathways – detailed in this chapter suggest that white and black South Africans contend with discrepant histories and realities of urban life, and that authors have developed distinct vectors of representation to capture this difference. What they share, though, is the recognition of the shock of the new; that our habitual maps – the tropes, devices and conceits of an earlier literary history – are inadequate to the representational challenges posed by the lived urban realities of the post-apartheid dispensation. The novels that have been discussed in this chapter suggest collectively a spirit of heurism, which is simultaneously attached to the history of apartheid literature and which is seeking new ways of seeing and coming to terms with a fluid and often excessive, fullness of life.

Bibliography

Ahearn, J. *Michel de Certeau: Interpretation and its Other*, Cambridge: Polity Press, 1995.
Barnard, R. *Apartheid and Beyond: South African Writers and the Politics of Place*, Oxford University Press, 2007.

Beavon, K. *Johannesburg: The Making and Shaping of the City*, Pretoria: UNISA Press, 2004.

Beukes, L. *Moxyland*, Johannesburg: Jacana, 2008.

    Zoo City, Johannesburg: Jacana, 2010.

Bremner, L. 'Crime and the Emerging Landscape of Post-Apartheid Johannesburg', in H. Judin and I. Vladislavić (eds.), *blank ___: Architecture, Apartheid and After*, Rotterdam: NAi, 1998, 49–61.

Brown, A. *Coldsleep Lullaby*, Cape Town: Zebra, 2005.

Calvino, I. *Invisible Cities*, trans. William Weaver, London: Vintage, 1997.

Certeau, M. de. *The Practice of Everyday Life*, trans. Steven Randall, Berkeley: University of California Press, 1984.

De Kock, L. 'South Africa in the Global Imaginary: An Introduction', *Poetics Today* 22:2 (summer 2001), 263–98.

Duiker, K. Sello. *The Quiet Violence of Dreams*, Cape Town. Kwela Books, 2001.

Helgesson, S. 'Johannesburg as Africa: A Postcolonial Reading of *The Exploded View* by Ivan Vladislavić', *Scrutiny2* 11:2 (2006), 27–35.

    '"Minor disorders": Ivan Vladislavić and the Devolution of South African English', *Journal of Southern African Studies* 30:4 (December 2004), 777–87.

Kleinboer. *Kontrei*, Johannesburg: Uitgewery Praag, 2003. Translation by Jaco Fouché as *Midnight Missionary*, Cape Town: Zebra, 2006.

Kunzmann, R. *Bloody Harvests*, Houndmills: Macmillan, 2004.

Mackenzie, J. *Random Violence*, Cape Town: Umuzi, 2008.

Makholwa, A. *Red Ink*, Johannesburg: Pan Macmillan, 2007.

Marais, M. 'Reading Against Race: J. M. Coetzee's *Disgrace*, Justin Cartwright's *White Lightning* and Ivan Vladislavić's *The Restless Supermarket*', *Journal of Literary Studies* 19:3–4 (December 2003), 271–89.

Matlwa, K. *Coconut*, Johannesburg: Jacana, 2007.

Mda, Z. *Ways of Dying*, Cape Town: Oxford University Press, 1995.

Meyer, D. *Feniks*, Cape Town: Human & Rousseau, 1996.

    Infanta, Cape Town: Human & Rousseau, 2005.

    Onsigbaar, Cape Town: Human & Rousseau, 2007.

    Orion, Cape Town: Human & Rousseau, 2000.

    Proteus, Cape Town: Human & Rousseau, 2003.

    13 Uur, Cape Town: Human & Rousseau, 2008.

Mhlongo, N. *After Tears*, Cape Town: Kwela Books, 2007.

    Dog Eat Dog, Cape Town: Kwela Books, 2004.

Moele, K. *Room 207*, Cape Town: Kwela Books, 2006.

Morgan, J. *Finding Mr Madini*, Cape Town: David Philip. 1999.

Mpe, P. *Welcome to our Hillbrow*, Pietermaritzburg: University of Natal Press, 2001.

Nicol, M. *Payback*, Cape Town: Umuzi, 2008.

Nicol, M., and J. Hichens. *Out to Score*, Cape Town: Umuzi, 2006.

Nuttall, S. 'Literary City', in Nuttall and Mbembe, *Johannesburg*, 195–218.

Nuttall, S., and A. Mbembe (eds.). *Johannesburg: The Elusive Metropolis*, Johannesburg: Witwatersrand University Press, 2008.

Orford, M. *Blood Rose*, Cape Town: Oshun, 2007.

    Like Clockwork, Cape Town: Oshun, 2006.

Raban, J. *Soft City*, London: Picador, 2008.

Samuelson, M. 'The City Beyond the Border: The Urban Worlds of Duiker, Mpe and Vera', *African Identities* 5:2 (2007), 247–60.

Thirteen Cents, Cape Town: David Philip, 2000.

Serote, M. *To Every Birth its Blood*, Johannesburg: Ravan, 1981.

Tomlinson, R., R. A. Beauregard, L. Bremner and X. Mangcu (eds.). *Emerging Johannesburg: Perspectives on the Postapartheid City*, New York: Routledge, 2003.

Troost, H. *Plot Loss*, Cape Town: Umuzi, 2007.

Van Heerden, E. *In Stede van die Liefde*, Cape Town: Tafelberg, 2005.

Van Niekerk, M. *Triomf*, Kaapstad: Queillerie, 1994. Translation by L. de Kock as *Triomf*, Johannesburg: Jonathan Ball, 1999.

Venter, E. *Horrelpoot*, Cape Town: Tafelberg, 2006. Translation by L. Stubbs as *Trencherman*, Cape Town: Tafelberg, 2008.

Vladislavić, I. *The Exploded View*, Johannesburg: Random House, 2004.

The Folly, Cape Town: David Philip, 1993.

Missing Persons, Cape Town: David Philip, 1989.

Portrait with Keys: Joburg & What-What, Cape Town: Umuzi, 2006.

Propaganda by Monuments and other Stories, Cape Town: David Philip, 1996.

The Restless Supermarket, Cape Town: David Philip, 2001.

Williams, M. *Hijack City*, Cape Town: Oxford University Press, 1999.

PART VI

*

SOUTH AFRICAN LITERATURE:
CONTINUITIES AND
CONTRASTS

The final part of this book is devoted to a series of topics traced across the period divisions that structure Parts II to V; they are not the only imaginable subjects that could be examined in this way, but they constitute some of the most important continuities from the beginnings of South African literature to the present day.

For the popular imagination in the metropolitan centres of the world, South Africa has been as much an idea as a reality, albeit a complex and changing idea, or series of ideas: the beautiful but dangerous Cape, the far-flung and exotic colony, the dwelling place of native savagery, the land of untold mineral riches, the stronghold of the plucky / rebellious Boers, the international pariah and the unexpected success story. Many aspects of these various constructs have been discussed in earlier chapters; in Chapter 33, Andrew van der Vlies attends in particular to the later twentieth century in charting the role of literature in the global representation of South Africa. Chapter 34, jointly authored by Margaret Daymond and Andries Visagie, traces the place of life-writing and confessional narrative in South Africa's literary production since the eighteenth century, culminating in the extraordinary prominence given to the autobiographical mode by the Truth and Reconciliation Commission.

As we noted in the Introduction, South Africa's linguistic diversity has had a major effect on the country's literary production, and the practice – and question – of translation has been central to the entire history traced in this volume. Leon de Kock considers this issue in Chapter 35. Also central to South Africa's literary history has been writing by women, from Olive Schreiner to Nadine Gordimer and Antjie Krog and, as Meg Samuelson shows in Chapter 36, women's place in the political and social fabric has frequently been the subject of their literary ventures. Michael Green, discussing experimental fiction in Chapter 37, takes as his first example Sol Plaatje's *Mhudi*, written in 1919/20, though the bulk of the chapter necessarily focuses on formal innovation in recent writing, reflecting the lessening of political urgency and an increasing commitment to a variety of stylistic and generic models.

A concern with the material conditions of publication animates Peter D. McDonald's account of 'The Book in South Africa' in Chapter 38, complementing the earlier chapters' discussions of particular genres and linguistic traditions. Book history is a new field in South African literary scholarship, and one in which a comparative perspective is invaluable, as this chapter demonstrates. Finally, David Johnson offers an account of the long and fruitful tradition of literary and cultural criticism in South Africa, beginning with the newspapers and periodicals that circulated in the Cape in the 1820s and ending with the burgeoning of the critical literature on South African writing since the demise of apartheid. South African critical and theoretical positions have always been articulated in the context of global movements as well as local pressures, and this chapter traces the shifting perspectives and practices that have emerged in response to this double demand.

33

South Africa in the global imaginary

ANDREW VAN DER VLIES

'South Africa' has long meant different things to different people. As a discursive construction, the term has traded on – and been influenced by –
contending representations and performances across a range of media, the
reception of which, both within the region and 'abroad', has necessarily had
an effect on what this label is taken to name. Reception is always *interested*,
influenced by ideological or psychological imperatives, whether by apologists
for or subjects of empire, members of anti-colonial or anti-apartheid movements, exiles and émigrés, or by only apparently disinterested outsiders for
whom the region's vicarious rewards have been – and are – many. Thus
'South Africa', once no more than a descriptive geographical term of convenience, has served for disaggregated global communities of interest variously
to signify a site of adventure, sport or recuperation, a space marked by vitality
or cruelty, reconciliation and redemption, and been mediated or contested
as a kind of home. During the second Anglo-Boer or South African War, it
named the location of one of imperial Britain's most serious moments of crisis,
while simultaneously providing occasion for transnational identifications by
such diverse groups as Irish nationalists and aristocratic tsarist Russians,[1] who
shared little with the proto-Afrikaner Boers besides opposition to the British
Empire. For much of the second half of the twentieth century it served in a
global imaginary largely as the domain of a white nationalist regime whose
policies propelled the word 'apartheid' into the global lexicon.[2] By the end
of the millennium, South Africa had come to 'matter' (in the words of an
editorial introducing a 2001 special issue of *Daedalus*, the journal of the American Academy of Arts and Sciences) 'for itself, for the rest of Africa, but also

---

1 Davidson and Filatova describe widespread Russian enthusiasm for the Boer cause, including
naming places for Boer heroes or towns (Kharkov gained a Joubertovskaia and Krugerovskaia;
two Mennonite villages were called Pretoria) and decorating inns and cafés in 'Boer' style; see
The Russians and the Anglo-Boer War, pp. 183–4.
2 On other South African words that have migrated into global discourse, see Pechey, 'On
Trek'.

for a larger world community that has invested such hope in its democratic prospects as a multiracial state' (Graubard, 'Preface', p. vi).

Such investments can be read in the subjects of writing about South Africa and in the particular fates of work by writers who have negotiated relationships of affiliation to the place. (They also necessarily structure the manner in which such writing is regarded *as* literature, the status of the literary being by no means uncontested in the cultural politics of the region.) Quite how literature has served or contested – and indeed in part been defined through – these investments is the central concern of this chapter. Veit Erlmann, in a study of South African music at key moments of global entanglement, conceives of a 'global imagination' less as a foreign interpreter appropriating a local product than 'an epistemological symbiosis', a set of located modes of engagement resulting from processes by which local and imported modernities become imbricated in articulating common styles and interests (*Music, Modernity*, pp. 3–4). Leon de Kock and colleagues use the phrase 'global imaginary' to refer both to external impositions of 'identity-forming global discourses' as well as to 'forms of self-fashioning, from within, either in the image of a greater world "out there" or in defiance of it' ('Global Imaginary', p. 8). These conceptualisations draw on Arjun Appadurai's sense of an imaginary as 'a collective, social fact' (*Modernity at Large*, p. 31), while gesturing towards the manner in which local and global senses of place and politics might serve each other's interests. Some writing is clearly amenable to international take-up, whether or not it is so intended, while other writing engages global strategies of expression or performance for ends directed locally. This chapter is unable to encompass the variety in local and varied global imaginaries: rather, it comments on certain of the means by which some cultural texts have been constructed as 'South African' – why, by whom, and with what effects.

Sites of reading: 'Metropolitan' expectation and vicarious identification

In South African-born Scottish resident Zoë Wicomb's second novel, *Playing in the Light* (2006), Marion Campbell, a Cape Town travel agent holidaying in the United Kingdom, reads two novels recommended by Clarke's Bookshop on Long Street: Nadine Gordimer's *The Conservationist* (1974) and J. M. Coetzee's *In the Heart of the Country* (1977). Neither is quite what Marion expects, although she at first finds Coetzee's title 'inspiring' and, in 'alien' surroundings and thinking herself 'a colonial at heart', feels an immediate connection with her country through the book – or at least through its title. She takes it up with a sense of 'pride', considers the cover's 'accolades and the photograph of a kindly author', and anticipates being 'lured into identification' with the woman pictured on the front cover (p. 197). This encounter is highly suggestive of the processes involved in acts of reading: of the manner in which texts are identified (almost always too neatly) in relation to national categories premised on an author's origins or the work's setting; and in gesturing towards the operation of variously local and global technologies of aesthetic or sociocultural validation in the reception of literary works. It also draws attention to the fact that all such encounters involve a particular material instantiation of the text in question: in this case, identifiably a Penguin paperback edition of Coetzee's novel. Although Marion is South African, Wicomb stages an international encounter with writing marked and marketed as 'South African', suggesting the manner in which such writing's labelling has so often been refracted through foreign constructions of the place and its cultural products, *and* that many of the country's most high-profile writers long sought to publish their work in London or New York before Cape Town or Johannesburg.

For readers of the most famous literary exports, 'South Africa' signified a limited affective range. Consider Julie Kramer's suggestion in the *New York Review of Books* in December 1982 – in a review of Coetzee's *Waiting for the Barbarians* (1980) and André Brink's *A Chain of Voices* (1982) – that, for American readers, apartheid had replaced the Gulag as 'the revealed outrage of the literary season', providing the kind of 'guilty reading' that was an 'armchair ritual among the bourgeoisie' ('In the Garrison', p. 8). Such reading required little discrimination and merely a 'vague appetite for self-chastisement', she quipped, the label 'literature of apartheid' had come to designate a broad range of work by 'writers of wildly various sensibilities and talent, proving only how much easier it is to tell good from bad than to tell good books from bad books', she continued (p. 8). In this self-consciously high-literary and cosmopolitan organ of discrimination, conscious of its placement at the centre of global networks of cultural production and validation (the review is published alongside advertisements for publishing firms and the Bell corporation, speaking awkwardly of divergent investments in literariness *and* pragmatic globalisation), Kramer identifies the attraction of such work for American readers in the early 1980s: 'white South Africans' appeared as proxies for concerned (and implicitly white) American readers, she argued; they had placed 'the wall of their own dissidence between ourselves and the black Africa we praise and fear', offering themselves as 'surrogates in resistance' (p. 8). This is not to suggest that Kramer does not venture aesthetic judgement: she praises Coetzee's novel, while dismissing Brink's. Rather, she muses on the difficulty – or, ironically, the ease – of separating aesthetic judgements from those made on other grounds, finding that writing 'mortgaged' to apartheid tended to be judged less as literary works – picked out by the cultural arbiters, published by leading northern-hemisphere trade presses, appreciated in the leading broadsheets and reviews – than as opportunities for vicarious disavowal by those who might abhor apartheid but not question the Reagan administration's pragmatic accommodation of the Pretoria regime.

Similar comments were made thirty-five years previously about Alan Paton's *Cry, the Beloved Country* (1948), still perhaps the best-selling and most widely translated book of South African authorship and theme (although written in Norway and North America, and published first in New York). A reviewer in the *Southwest Review*, for example, wrote that Paton's novel was 'a mirror in which the American South may be seen reflected in dispassionate perspective'; it presented 'the most acceptable and effective expression on the subject of race relations for American readers' (Burns, 'Mirror to the South', pp. 408–10). This expression suggested an attractive gradualist and non-confrontational solution to the so-called problems of racial inequality and discrimination that appealed to American readers wary of Communism and of direct threats to white hegemony (Van der Vlies, *South African Textual Cultures*, pp. 73–6). As Lesley Cowling puts it, Paton's novel 'allowed for a collective imagining of a narrative of race, trauma and Christian reconciliation in an imagined world (the beloved country) that was not [Americans'] own' ('Beloved South African', p. 89). Paton's Christian humanist parable was thus highly amenable for widespread circulation in the United States: it was one of the first four books abridged for the *Reader's Digest Condensed Books* series launched in 1950; a stage musical adaptation (by Maxwell Anderson, with music by Kurt Weill) followed in 1949. The London Film Company released an adaptation, directed by Zoltan Korda, in 1951.[3] The novel also clearly appealed to readers elsewhere: Norwegian, Danish, Swedish, Finnish, Dutch and French translations were contracted in the same year as the novel's American and British publication, with, amongst others, Portuguese, Italian, German and Icelandic editions following within a decade (and many subsequently, including Zulu in 1957). We should recall, however, that as Paton's

3 On the abridgement in the *Reader's Digest Condensed Books* series, see Van der Vlies, *South African Textual Cultures*, pp. 88–91. On film, see Beittel, '"What sort of memorial"?', and Davis, *In Darkest Hollywood*, pp. 39–42. The novel was adapted for screen once more in 1995 (dir. Darrell Roodt), with a screenplay by South African-born playwright Ronald Harwood. On the trans-national nature of 'South African' film production, see Flanery, 'What National Cinema?'

novel was feted abroad, its vision of white trusteeship was immediately questioned by black and radical white intellectuals in South Africa. Rob Nixon
notes that the novel provided Sophiatown writers and intellectuals associated
with *Drum* magazine a book against which to write (Nixon, *Homelands*, p. 25).
Murray Carlin noted as early as October 1948 that Paton glossed over 'the
real savagery of the situation in South Africa'; Carlin blamed the novel's local
success on a 'reigning artistic-patriotic fervour' in the country 'whereby anything South African is automatically good' ('Review', p. 11). Kramer might
have concurred about foreign readers in metropolitan America in the early
1980s.

Displaced anxieties similar to those that explain, in part, the success of
Paton's novel in the United States, have been suggested as reasons for the consistent popularity of Athol Fugard's plays there for at least the last thirty years.
As Jeanne Colleran suggests, whatever one might say about its aesthetic merit
or artistic singularity, Fugard's drama in American production has been readily received as participating in 'agonized conversations about race in America',
Fugard's white South African characters appearing as 'long-lost cousins who
have reappeared just in time to remind us', Colleran (an American) continues,
'that despite our tepid political response to both apartheid and to domestic
racism, our capacity for moral outrage is still intact' ('South African Theatre',
p. 228). Fugard has premiered many of his plays in the United States since the
early 1980s, and his work remains in almost constant rehearsal and performance in that country. In March 2010 a new play, *The Train Driver*, premiered
at a theatre – named for the playwright – in a converted textile warehouse
in Cape Town's iconic District Six / Zonnebloem neighbourhood, and ran to
excited reviews. Fugard continues to have a considerable reputation in South
Africa, at least amongst some white audiences – if not always amongst critics (Chapman, *Southern African Literatures*, pp. 364–5). Paton's, by contrast, is
a starker example of the possible divergence of local and global validation.
Another, from the end of the following decade, is provided by responses to
Todd Matshikiza and Harry Bloom's jazz musical *King Kong* (1959), particularly on the eve of its transfer to London in 1961, when local white English
journalists seemed unwilling to believe that metropolitan audiences might
take seriously a representation of what one called 'cola-colonization in the
locations and townships' (Titlestad, *Making the Changes*, p. 98).

Yet another example is provided by another *New York Review of Books*
review, published two decades after Kramer's, in this case of editions of two
novels by Zakes Mda published in the United States: a Picador paperback
of *Ways of Dying* (2002; original South African edition 1995), and a hardback

edition of *The Heart of Redness* (2002; originally 2000).[4] Novelist and National Book Award winner Norman Rush argued that Mda seemed too little interested in the social realities of the new South Africa; his work was too fabular, 'escapist' and insufficiently scripted by the spectacle of continuing deprivation or – more significantly for Rush – the spectre of HIV/AIDS ('Apocalypse When?', p. 31). If the white reviewer of 1982 praises white South African writers for their surrogate suffering of an apparently intractable political situation, this later (white) reviewer of fiction by a black South African demands realism, that the black writer should take responsibility for a new dispensation in which a black majority government must deal with pressing social problems (which no longer stand metonymically for American dilemmas, but are brutally, indisputably *themselves*). Rush even reads Mda's sensitive exploration of the relative epistemologies and technologies of self and communal definition in the bi-temporal plot of *Heart of Redness* as coming down on the side of the past, as 'a literary gesture against modernity' (p. 31). This is post-9/11 American criticism: there are geopolitical emergencies that must be attended to in a newly unstable world, one ironically less apparently stable – in its antagonisms, in knowledge of one's antagonists – than the cold war world of the early 1980s (or the late 1940s). Deprived of the spectacle of apartheid, South African writers should, Rush seems to suggest, turn to others, like poverty and HIV/AIDS.

There are two imperatives operating in uneasy balance in these instances of 'metropolitan' reception (which admittedly is circumscribed – the *New York Review of Books* does not speak for the world, but does offer a useful barometer for the consistent engagement by northern anglophone readers with 'South African' writing): on the one hand a desire for 'relevance' (other essays in this volume engage with the rhetoric of urgency advanced or contested in relation to the country's literary representations); on the other a desire to read allegorically (however disingenuous the disavowal of the significance of the local, 'South African' background of the work, a background that in fact makes *possible* such allegorical interpretative imperatives). An example of the former is a 1978 American librarian and teachers' sourcebook guide to building a collection of South African literature, which warned that critics referred habitually 'to the literature *vis à vis* content rather than form alone, maintaining that the quality of writing results from the fusion of propaganda or social commentary with the aesthetics of literary creativity' (Gorman,

---

4 South Africa's Oxford University Press paperback of *The Heart of Redness*, though positioning the novel as fiction, also marked it as expressly educational (the local imprint's major market). For further discussion, see Van der Vlies, *South African Textual Cultures*, pp. 159 and 166–70.

South African Novel, p. 15). In relation to the latter, Clive Barnett has suggested that foreign non-academic reviewers tended to read Coetzee's early novels as positive allegories with 'universal, moral' resonances no less than was the case for Paton's *Cry, the Beloved Country*: South Africa is invoked as 'context and referent' in these readings, he notes, but simultaneously 'idealised' as a stage for more general moral dramas of human suffering and violence' ('Constructions of Apartheid', pp. 292, 294, 290). Some recently successful examples include, inter alia, Pumla Gobodo-Madikizela's *A Human Being Died that Night* (2003) and Antjie Krog's *Country of my Skull* (1998). It is worth noting, in relation to Krog's creative non-fiction account of the Truth and Reconciliation Commission (TRC), that the American trade edition differs in key respects from the UK and South African editions in omitting some of the indications that the narrative is part fictionalised: in the 'American' imaginary, this editorial intervention would suggest, there is little room for confusion about the 'truth' in relation to moral dramas of trauma and suffering (see Moss, '"Nice audible crying"'). Such changes amongst different editions of a number of South African books often go unmarked,[5] although 'consequential changes' can reflect the expectations of different markets and allow multiple versions of the same work to circulate – sometimes with unintended consequences. These words are from a letter from Sheila Hodges, a Gollancz employee, to Daphne Rooke, about changes to the latter's *Mittee* (1951) (quoted in Graham, 'Consequential Changes', p. 43). Lucy Graham examines how the first British edition of the novel included a scene in which a black man rapes a black servant. The first American edition, by contrast, included a typical 'black peril' narrative featuring the rape of a white woman by black men. Graham's research suggests that Rooke initially wrote the latter, but Gollancz, fearful of South African censorship, compelled the change – which was not made to the American edition (p. 45). As Graham demonstrates, J. M. Coetzee's assertion – in an afterword to *Mittee*, published in a 1991 Penguin paperback edition – that Rooke avoided a black peril narrative, is accurate in relation to the Penguin (which reprints the Gollancz) text, but not when included in a recent edition that reprints the 1952 Houghton Mifflin text ('Consequential Changes', pp. 44–5).

Several critics have observed how many mainstream international representations of South Africa convert particular moments of the country's history into a timeless backdrop suggestive of the long anti-apartheid struggle

5 Some other examples include the Afrikaans dialogue in the 1978 Ravan edition of J. M. Coetzee's *In the Heart of the Country*, which does not appear in the 1977 British or American editions. See Van der Vlies, *South African Textual Cultures*, pp. 134–50.

or, increasingly, conditions in the post-apartheid nation. Rob Nixon has written about the manner in which such strategies operated in 1980s anti-apartheid films like *Cry Freedom* (dir. Richard Attenborough, 1987) and *A Dry White Season* (dir. Euzhan Palcy, 1989), which utilised outdated snapshots of history frozen in time – especially the Soweto uprising of 1976 – as backdrop for affective representations reflecting the emotional investments of foreign (and particularly American) audiences rather than necessarily engaging with any South African reality (Nixon, *Homelands*, pp. 77–97).[6] Recent internationally successful films like *Yesterday* (dir. Darrell Roodt, 2004), *U-Carmen eKhayelitsha* (dir. Mark Dornford-May, 2005) and *Tsotsi* (dir. Gavin Hood, 2005),[7] while sometimes more complex in attempting to offer local points of view, still engage to a greater or lesser degree with simplified – and reified – post-1994 South African scenarios that might be said to appeal to particular global sensibilities.

Local responses and global expectations

Accepting the Central News Agency (CNA) Literary Award for *Waiting for the Barbarians* in early 1981, Coetzee offered his thoughts on the place of an anglophone South African literature in a global cultural landscape. 'Our relation . . . to the West European and North American centres of the dominant world civilization remains that of province to metropolis', he stated, adding that if he was correct in suggesting that South African writers were extending 'an established provincial literature' rather than 'building a new national' body of work, it seemed to him that a response 'more constructive' than pity at a 'provincial lot' (or 'plotting an escape to the metropolis') would be to rehabilitate – indeed embrace – 'the notion of the provincial' ('SA authors', p. 16). Coetzee clearly had in mind the kind of 'white' writing to which the title of his 1988 collection on the European culture of letters in South Africa would refer. He implies that writers looking to northern – anglophone or European – models and expectations would inevitably have to accept a marginal status in relation to metropolitan literary production, their work enjoying a kind of curiosity value in the north. An embrace of the provincial might then suggest that local white writing could aspire to the condition of a respectable

6 Loren Kruger has argued similarly about so-called 'protest plays' that 'take on the characters of a "national allegory", the overarching category to which Fredric Jameson loftily assigns "all Third World texts"' ('Apartheid on Display', p. 191, referring to Jameson, 'Third-World Literature').
7 On *Tsotsi*, see the following: Barnard, 'Tsotsis', pp. 541–72; Graham, 'Save us all', pp. 114–16; Flanery, 'What National Cinema?', p. 240. Dornford-May is director and his wife Pauline Malefane (star of *uCarmen*) co-music director of Isango Portobello, the theatre company in residence at the new Fugard Theatre in Cape Town.

minor Europhone literature (like Dutch or Danish); it would also inevitably appear parochial. By contrast, Njabulo Ndebele, in a keynote address at the Commonwealth Institute in London two years later (in November 1984), suggested that such parochialism had powerful protonational possibilities: Ndebele called famously for 'black South African literature' to engage in an anticipatory national project of 'rediscovering the ordinary' ('Rediscovery of the Ordinary', p. 55). Rather than reflecting the spectacle of apartheid brutality, a local literature that had its eye on a post-apartheid future might find alternative narratives in the mundane, Ndebele argued, and so avoid producing narratives effectively scripted by the state. Such narratives, of course, might not hold quite the same interest for international readers.

Olive Schreiner's 'Preface' to the second edition of *The Story of an African Farm*, published in July 1883, is in some ways the *locus classicus* of self-conscious engagement with metropolitan horizons of expectation in relation to South Africa and an assertion of the claims of the ordinary. Schreiner sought to distance her first novel, then still published under a male pseudonym (although widely known to be by a young woman from the colonies), from the expectation that such writing should adhere to a certain pattern. In her case, the metropolitan expectation was for 'a history of wild adventure; of cattle driven into inaccessible "krantze" by Bushmen', or 'encounters with ravening lions, and hair-breadth escapes'– literature, Schreiner famously suggested, which was 'best written in Piccadilly or in the Strand' ('Preface', pp. viii–ix). In its claim that a more authentic 'local' product should trade more in realism than romance, Schreiner's assertion also anticipates debates about commitment, reportage and literariness that structured literary academic discourse about South African writing in the second half of the twentieth century. Imperial romances of the type Schreiner invokes as counterexample frequently staged Britain's colonies as the sites of possible rejuvenation. Charles W. Wood, contributing dispatches on his South African travels to Bentley's magazine, *The Argosy*, in late 1894, described a region 'full of capabilities and resources', and suggested that while 'over-population appears to be journeying hand in hand with diminishing resources' in Europe, South Africa appeared 'destined to be the future antidote for this great evil' ('Letters', p. 516).[8] This trope, drawing on eugenics and proto-fascism, would dominate a strand of popular British representations of the region until at least the end of the first quarter of the twentieth century.

8 See Katz, *Rider Haggard*, pp. 30–1.

The writer who became a reluctant – though also typically self-aggrandising – poster-boy for this view of the country and its (white) literary production was Roy Campbell. He and William Plomer were included in selections of dominion writing by the likes of Hector Bolitho, a New Zealand-born anthologist who worked briefly in South Africa in the 1920s and made a career of promoting writers from what he called *The New Countries* (the title of one of his anthologies, published by Jonathan Cape) (Bolitho, *Restless Years*, pp. 107–15). Campbell came to distance himself from Bolitho, satirising in his poem 'A Veld Eclogue' the '"nameless something" which Bolitho traces / To gazing out across the "open spaces"' (Campbell, *Adamastor*, p. 23), although he clearly benefited from the association. By 1945, Campbell had become the most readily identifiable 'South African' writer in English, at least for British readers, despite his dalliance with Franco and fascism in the 1930s. Sarah Gertrude Millin enjoyed a similar – though arguably not as elevated – status, chiefly on the strength of *God's Step-Children* (1924), although one that drew on similar tropes of eugenics and catastrophe. She was author of, amongst others, the novels *The Dark River* (1919), *Adam's Rest* (1922), *The Jordans* (1923), *Mary Glenn* (1925), *An Artist in the Family* (1928), *Three Men Die* (1934), *What Hath a Man?* (1938), *The King of the Bastards* (1949), *The Burning Man* (1952) and *The Wizard Bird* (1962), as well as biographies of Cecil Rhodes (1933) and Jan Smuts (1936), a popular history entitled *The South Africans* (1926, expanded as *The People of South Africa*, 1951), two autobiographies and a series of diaries.

Plomer disavowed the regional associations Campbell occasionally championed, choosing instead to remake himself as a comparatively parochial *English* man of letters, though always acknowledging his status as a 'sort of doubly displaced person', 'simultaneously a South African writer and an English reader, but also an English writer and a South African reader' (Plomer, 'South African Writers', p. 55). One might speculate about which combination most informed his judgement as publisher's reader for Cape, who published Paton's *Cry, the Beloved Country*[9] and Phyllis Altman's *The Law of the Vultures* (1953), amongst other novels regarded as 'South African'. Laurens van der Post, who worked briefly with Campbell and Plomer on the self-consciously avant-garde journal *Voorslag* in the mid 1920s, did trade on associations of southern Africa with vitality and alternative (even mystical) values, particularly in a series of books – including *Flamingo Feather* (1955) and *A Story Like the Wind* (1972), both novels, and *The Lost World of the Kalahari* (1958) (all published in Britain by Hogarth Press, which published his first novel, *In a Province*, in 1934) – about

9 Plomer was, contrary to received opinion, not enthusiastic about Paton's novel; see Van der Vlies, *South African Textual Cultures*, p. 76.

the San peoples of the Kgalagadi (or the 'Bushmen' of the Kalahari), which propelled him to international prominence as supposed spokesperson for this collection of autochthonous communities, as well as for a kind of new-age spiritualism that found high-profile adherents amongst western celebrities. There are lines to be drawn, too, between Van der Post's work and the long tradition of adventure from Rider Haggard to Wilbur Smith (Zambian-born, but surely an honorary South African), popular films like *The Gods Must be Crazy* (1980) (see Nicholls, 'Apartheid Cinema', pp. 20–32), Credo Mutwa and others' pan-African mysticism, recent memoirs and novels that romanticise Khoi-San wisdom (Rupert Isaacson's *The Healing Land: A Kalahari Journey*, 2001), and some representations of *ubuntu* in the context of the Truth and Reconciliation Commission.

Global sites of 'South African' publication

Many of the writers discussed above sought publication outside of South Africa, their publication histories illuminating the extent to which the institutions of publishing – and other forms of cultural production and validation – have been responsible for the construction of a notional national literature, and how these operations have often been transnational. Publication by the northern anglosphere's leading publishing houses brought wider reviewing opportunities, better sales and access to reader's club or prize endorsements. For most South African writers, these were the London trade presses; few sought publication first or exclusively with North American presses (Paton is the earliest significant example; Nadine Gordimer's short stories in the *New Yorker* began appearing in the 1950s and 1960s), and British publishers enjoyed exclusive sales rights in the Commonwealth, including South Africa, after the Traditional Markets Agreement divided the English-speaking world into zones of interest in 1947.

Some leading writers developed long-running relationships with particular presses, enjoying the support of assiduous editors or readers (some of these, like Plomer at Cape, themselves South African-born). Breyten Breytenbach has long been published by Faber, which also publishes Brink (who ended a long-running association with Allen under acrimonious circumstances in the early 1980s – see Brink, *Fork in the Road*, pp. 315–20), and also published Peter Abrahams, Es'kia Mphahlele and C. J. 'Jonty' Driver. Coetzee has long been published by Secker & Warburg (now Harvill Secker), while Gordimer's principal associations have been with Gollancz (who also published Daphne

Rooke and, initially, Bessie Head), Cape, and with Bloomsbury. Other smaller or less self-consciously literary British presses with particular associations (about which one should be careful to generalise) included Collins (Stuart Cloete, Harry Bloom), Hodder & Stoughton (Todd Matshikiza), Heinemann (Jack Cope, Wilbur Smith), Weidenfeld & Nicholson (Dan Jacobson, who later published with Secker), and MacGibbon & Kee (Cope; David Lytton,[10] who later published with Bodley Head). Some titles by these authors later found their way into Penguin paperback editions, and several were published by American trade presses.

By the early 1960s there had been a growth in publishing writing from Commonwealth countries, including in magazines like the *London Magazine* under Alan Ross (after 1961), which included regular contributions from Gordimer, Douglas Livingstone and Christopher Hope. Other firms with interests in the field included André Deutsch, Hutchinson, Thomas Nelson and Oxford University Press, but perhaps the most influential was the African Writers Series (AWS). Established in 1962 by Alan Hill and Van Milne at Heinemann Educational Books (a subsidiary of the trade press William Heinemann), the AWS was aimed primarily at educational markets in Africa, but it enjoyed a niche market in Britain, flourishing under the direction of Keith Sambrook and then James Currey, the latter director from 1967 to 1984 (Hill, *In Pursuit*, pp. 122–6, 168–71, 144; Currey, *Africa Writes Back*, pp. 1–24). Over a 42-year history it published some 350 titles, including reprints of previously published material and also original work; a number were by South African writers, including an early reprint of Abrahams's *Mine Boy* (original 1946) in 1963, Alex La Guma's *A Walk in the Night and other Stories* in 1967, and the anthologies *Quartet* (ed. Richard Rive, 1965) and *Seven South African Poets* (ed. Cosmo Pieterse, 1971). In May 1973, at an event at the Africa Centre in London's Covent Garden, several titles were launched, including Dennis Brutus's *A Simple Lust*, D. M. Zwelonke's *Robben Island*, Modikwe Dikobe's (Marks Rammitloa's) *The Marabi Dance* and a reissue of Nelson Mandela's *No Easy Walk to Freedom*. By the 1980s works like Mongane Serote's *To Every Birth its Blood* (Ravan edn 1981) were subcontracted from the lists of local oppositional publishers, facilitating the promotion of their lists to wider audiences (Currey, *Africa Writes Back*, pp. 189, 213, 185, 196).

Graham Huggan suggests that the AWS, despite serving as a 'valuable promoter of cross-cultural understanding', was also an 'ironic purveyor of

---

10 Lytton's work includes novels *The Goddam White Man* (1960), *A Place Apart* (1961), *The Paradise People* (1962), all published by MacGibbon & Kee and then in Penguin paperback, and *The Grass won't Grow till Spring* (1965) and *The Freedom of the Cage* (1966), both Bodley Head, with US publication by Panther.

exoticist modes of cultural representation' (*Postcolonial Exotic*, pp. xi, 50). Nonetheless, it came to be a key promoter of some South African writing in a particular global imaginary, which not insignificantly included substantial pan-African marketing and circulation. Its publication of Brutus's 1973 collection (of earlier work; AWS had published *Letters to Martha* in 1968) illustrates the transnational networks involved in this global interpolation. Currey, in deference to Brutus's desire not to be 'pigeonholed in the category of "African poet writing in English" but simply as someone writing poetry in English', was keen to arrange a hardback edition of the collection under the Heinemann imprint, and to follow with an AWS paperback. Brutus, however, also explored other options, including having a selection of his poetry made by Bernth Lindfors for American publication by Doubleday or Northwestern University Press (to whom approaches were made on Brutus's behalf by John Povey, South African-born academic). Doubleday turned down the selection, though it was accepted by Hill & Wang and subsequently published by Heinemann in London (Currey, *Africa Writes Back*, pp. 210–13). These negotiations reveal the extensive network of expatriate South Africans involved in such publishing: Currey, himself born to South African parents in Britain, employed Arthur Ravenscroft, South African academic and pioneer of African studies at the University of Leeds, as publisher's reader for Brutus's selection. Others in the field included Caroline de Crespigny, exiled activist and founder of the Picador imprint in London; Ros Ainslie, better known under her married name, Ros de Lanerolle, managing director of the Women's Press; Ronald Segal, erstwhile editor of *Africa South* and in exile in London, who, with Ruth First, selected South African titles for Penguin paperback publication; Randolph Vigne, Cosmo Pieterse, C. J. 'Jonty' Driver, Myrna Blumberg, Mary Benson, and Clive Wake, who all promoted or reviewed work in British publications (Currey, *Africa Writes Back*, pp. 224, xix).

La Guma's writing, too, suggests the other imaginaries – and complex cultural politics – in which South African writing was involved, unwittingly or not. *A Walk in the Night* was published in 1962 by Mbari, a literary and artistic collective in Ibadan, Nigeria, run by Ulli Beier, an expatriate German and a founding editor of *Black Orpheus* (1957), a magazine in which fiction by La Guma, Rive and James Matthews appeared (Mphahlele, *Afrika my Music*, p. 26; see Benson, '"Border Operators"'). Beier's operations were funded by money raised in part by Mphahlele, then head of the Paris-based Congress for Cultural Freedom (established 1950), itself funded by the Ford and Farfield foundations, and covertly through the latter by the United States's Central Intelligence Agency (see McDonald, *Literature Police*, p. 123). If this fact of publication associated La Guma with cold war cultural politics, so too (though on the opposite front) did the publication of *And a Threefold Cord* (1964) and *The Stone Country* (1967) by Seven Seas Press in East Berlin. Seven Seas, a firm founded in 1958 by an American (Gertrude Gelbin) married to a dissident East German author (Stefan Heym), ran for twenty years, promoting progressive or overtly socialist English-language writing neglected or proscribed in its countries of origin (see advertisements in La Guma, *And a Threefold Cord*, pp. 174–5, and *The Stone Country*, pp. 170–1). Other South African titles included Bloom's *Transvaal Episode* (1959; originally 1956), Mphahlele's *Down Second Avenue* (1962; originally 1959) and Cope's *The Fair House* (1960; originally 1955). Seven Seas aimed to distribute throughout the Communist Bloc, but struggled against restrictive export quotas and so had its primary markets in Britain and the United States (through progressive bookstores), although its books were available elsewhere – including in India. South African writing did circulate in the Soviet Union, mostly in translation: Victor Ramzes, later secretary of the Writers Union of the USSR, noted in 1966 that *A Walk in the Night*, along with Abrahams's *The Wreath of Udomo* and *The Path of Thunder* (the latter a particular success, 'screened, used for a ballet', and having 'had no less than twelve printings'), Bloom's *Transvaal Episode*, Altman's *The Law of the Vultures* and Cope's *The Fair House* were all available there ('African Literature in Russia', p. 41).

Changing imaginaries

Clearly, what 'South Africa' has meant for readers of the region's literary and other cultural production has been in constant flux. Viewed from a metropolitan (London-centred and lingeringly imperial) perspective, a proto-national South African identity was slow to be disaggregated from a more capacious colonial identity, although by the later 1920s British commentators were welcoming the development of indigenous traditions. An enthusiastic survey by Winifred Holtby in the London *Bookman* in September 1929, for example, praised familiar writers – Schreiner she called 'first and the greatest of South African writers', Millin 'the most interesting of modern realists' ('Writers of South Africa', pp. 280, 281) – but noted writers who have faded from the popular consciousness, like Ethelreda Lewis (who wrote under the pseudonym R. Hernekin Baptist, and was well known in her day for facilitating the stories of adventurer Aloysius 'Trader' Horn in books selected as Books of the Month in the United States) and Marie Linde, whose novel, *Among Privileged People*, Holtby calls 'the first translated Afrikaans novel'

(p. 282). Nearly three decades later, Anthony Sampson, writing (anonymously) in the *Times Literary Supplement* in August 1957, and drawing comparisons with both Cold War powers (South African literature seemed 'more involved in its country's affairs than that of any other country west of the Iron Curtain', he charged, and echoed increasingly common comparisons with writing of the American 'Deep South'), observed a shift in expectations of writing from a region in which the 'scene' was 'changing very rapidly' and writing had increasingly to consider the political ('South African Conflicts', p. xxxvi).[11]

Expectations continue to change: a reader obtaining a Seven Seas edition of Bloom's *Transvaal Episode* at the Calcutta Book Fair in the early 1970s would have had a quite different expectation of writing about South Africa than a Nigerian purchasing Mazisi Kunene's *Emperor Shaka the Great* in AWS paperback (1979) from a bookshop in Lagos in 1980, or a Canadian reading a second-hand American (Farrar, Straus & Giroux, 1998) hardback edition of Nadine Gordimer's *The House Gun* at the turn of the millennium. For each of these, 'South Africa' would signify differently, or not at all. Developing her argument in response to remarks about the fate of Paton's *Cry, the Beloved Country* on the Oprah Winfrey show in 2003, Rita Barnard suggests that nations like South Africa may come increasingly, in the new conditions of globalisation and a flattening of affect in relation to the West's others, to function 'as mediascapes, occasions for certain kinds of stories, and (to be sure) certain kinds of touristic experiences' (Barnard, 'Oprah's Paton', p. 99).

Arjun Appadurai noted in 1986, in an analysis of the cultural life of things, that 'as commodities travel greater distances (institutional, spatial, temporal), knowledge about them tends to become partial, contradictory, and differentiated', and that, perhaps paradoxically, 'such differentiation may itself (through the mechanisms of tournaments of value, authentication, or frustrated desire) lead to the intensification of demand' ('Commodities and the Politics of Value', p. 56). As the spectre of apartheid recedes, representations of South Africa continue to be circulated in global imaginaries, but perhaps in forms that are as yet not adequately described or theorised. Appadurai's observation might, for example, be true in unexpected ways as a growing South African diaspora, animated by fragmentary recollections or nostalgic impressions of their homeland, engages with, circulates and demands new kinds of affective representations.[12]

---

11 On Paton's *Cry, the Beloved Country*, Sampson noted: 'To-day [in 1957] it is regarded by many who would have praised it then [in 1948] as an old-fashioned paternalist book, which portrays Africans in a sentimental and unrealistic light' (p. xxxvi).
12 See Van der Vlies, section ii of 'Introduction: Annexing the Global', p. 10.

Bibliography

Abrahams, P. *Mine Boy*, London: Dorothy Crisp, 1946; London: Heinemann Educational, 1963.

The Path of Thunder, London: Faber, 1952.

The Wreath of Udomo, London: Faber, 1956.

Altman, P. *The Law of the Vultures*, London: Jonathan Cape, 1953.

Anderson, M. *Lost in the Stars: The Dramatization of Alan Paton's Novel* Cry, the Beloved Country [1950], London: Jonathan Cape and Bodley Head, 1951.

Appadurai, A. 'Introduction: Commodities and the Politics of Value', in A. Appadurai (ed.), *The Social Life of Things: Commodities in Cultural Perspective*, Cambridge University Press, 1986, 3–63.

Modernity at Large: Cultural Dimensions of Globalization, Minneapolis: University of Minnesota Press, 1996.

Attenborough, R. (dir.). *Cry Freedom*, prod. Universal Pictures, 1987.

Barnard, R. 'Oprah's Paton, or South Africa and the Globalization of Suffering', *English Studies in Africa* 47:1 (2004), 85–107.

'Tsotsis: On Law, the Outlaw, and the Postcolonial State', *Contemporary Literature* 49:4 (winter 2008), 541–72.

Barnett, C. 'Constructions of Apartheid in the International Reception of the Novels of J. M. Coetzee', *Journal of Southern African Studies* 25:2 (1999), 287–301.

Beittel, M. '"What sort of memorial?" *Cry, the Beloved Country* on Film', in Isabel Balseiro and Ntongela Masilela (eds.), *To Change Reels: Film and Film Culture in South Africa*, Detroit, MI: Wayne State University Press, 2003, 70–87.

Benson, P. '"Border Operators": *Black Orpheus* and the Genesis of Modern African Art and Literature', *Research in African Literatures* 14:4 (winter 1983), 431–73.

Bloom, H. *Episode*, London: Collins, 1956. Reprinted as *Transvaal Episode*, Berlin: Seven Seas, 1959.

Bolitho, H. *My Restless Years*, London: Max Parrish, 1962.

Bolitho, H. (ed.). *The New Countries: A Collection of Stories and Poems by South African, Australian, Canadian and New Zealand Writers*, London: Jonathan Cape, 1929.

Brink, A. *A Chain of Voices*, New York: William Morrow and London: Faber, 1982.

A Fork in the Road: A Memoir, London: Harvill Secker, 2009.

Brutus, D. *Letters to Martha, and other Poems from a South African Prison*, London: Heinemann Educational, 1968.

A Simple Lust, London: Heinemann Educational, 1973.

Burns, A. 'Mirror to the South', *Southwest Review* (autumn 1948), 408–10.

Campbell, R. *Adamastor*, London: Faber, 1930.

Carlin, M. 'Review', *Student Review: A Journal for Liberals* (29 October 1948), 10–11.

Chapman, M. *Southern African Literatures* [1996], rev. edn, Pietermaritzburg: University of Natal Press, 2003.

Coetzee, J. M. *In the Heart of the Country*, Johannesburg: Ravan, 1977; London: Secker & Warburg, 1978; Harmondsworth: Penguin, 1982; as *From the Heart of the Country*, New York: Harper & Row, 1977.

'SA authors must learn modesty', published text of address on receiving the CNA Prize for 1980, *Vaderland* (1 May 1981), 16.

Waiting for the Barbarians, Johannesburg: Ravan and London: Secker & Warburg, 1980; Harmondsworth: Penguin, 1982.

White Writing: On the Culture of Letters in South Africa, New Haven: Yale University Press, 1988.

Colleran, J. 'South African Theatre in the United States: The Allure of the Familiar and of the Exotic', in D. Attridge and R. Jolly (eds.), *Writing South Africa: Literature, Apartheid and Democracy, 1970–1995*, Cambridge University Press, 1998, 221–36.

Cope, R. K. (Jack). *The Fair House*, London: MacGibbon & Kee, 1955; Berlin: Seven Seas, 1960.

Cowling, L. 'The Beloved South African: Alan Paton in America', *Scrutiny2: Issues in English Studies in Southern Africa* 10:2 (2005), 81–92.

Currey, J. *Africa Writes Back: The African Writers Series & the Launch of African Literature*, Oxford: James Currey, 2009.

Davidson, A., and I. Filatova. *The Russians and the Anglo-Boer War 1899–1902*, Cape Town: Human & Rousseau, 1998.

Davis, P. *In Darkest Hollywood: Exploring the Jungles of Cinema's South Africa*, Randburg: Ravan and Athens: Ohio University Press, 1996.

De Kock, L. 'South Africa in the Global Imaginary: An Introduction', in L. de Kock, L. Bethlehem and S. Laden (eds.), *South Africa in the Global Imaginary*, Pretoria: UNISA Press and Leiden: Koninklijke Brill, 2004, 1–31.

Dikobe, M. (Marks Rammitloa). *The Marabi Dance*, London: Heinemann Educational, 1973.

Dornford-May, M. (dir.). *U-Carmen eKhayelitsha*, prod. Spier Films, 2005.

Erlmann, V. *Music, Modernity, and the Global Imagination: South Africa and the West*, New York: Oxford University Press, 1999.

Flanery, P. D. 'What National Cinema? South African Film Cultures and the Transnational', *Safundi: The Journal of South African and American Studies* 10:2 (April 2009), 239–53.

Gobodo-Madikizela, P. *A Human Being Died that Night: A South African Story of Forgiveness*, Boston: Houghton Mifflin, 2003; as *A Human Being Died that Night: Forgiving Apartheid's Chief Killer*, London: Portobello Books, 2006.

Gordimer, N. *The Conservationist*, London: Jonathan Cape, 1974.

The House Gun, London: Bloomsbury and New York: Farrar, Straus & Giroux, 1998.

Gorman, G. E. *The South African Novel in English since 1950*, Boston: G. K. Hall, 1978.

Graham, L. '"Consequential changes": Daphne Rooke's *Mittee* in America and South Africa', *Safundi: The Journal of South African and American Studies* 10:1 (January 2009), 43–58.

'"Save us all": "Baby rape" and Post-Apartheid Narratives', *Scrutiny2: Issues in English Studies in Southern Africa* 13:1 (2008), 105–19.

Graubard, S. R. 'Preface to the Issue: "Why South Africa Matters"', *Daedalus* 130:1 (winter 2001), v–viii.

Hill, A. *In Pursuit of Publishing*, London: John Murray, 1988.

Holtby, W. 'Writers of South Africa', *The Bookman* 74:456 (September 1929), 279–83.

Hood, Gavin. (dir.) *Tsotsi*, prod. UK Film and TV Production Company, Industrial Development Corporation of South Africa, National Film and Video Foundation of South Africa, Moviworld, Tsotsti Films, 2005.

Huggan, G. *The Postcolonial Exotic: Marketing the Margins*, London: Routledge, 2001.

Isaacson, R. *The Healing Land: A Kalahari Journey*, London: Fourth Estate, 2001.

Jameson, F. 'Third-World Literature in the Era of Multinational Capitalism', *Social Text* 15 (autumn 1986), 65–88.

Katz, W. R. *Rider Haggard and the Fiction of Empire: A Critical Study of British Imperial Fiction*, Cambridge University Press, 1987.

Korda, Z. (dir.). *Cry, the Beloved Country*, prod. London Films, 1951.

Kramer, J. 'In the Garrison', *New York Review of Books*, 2 December 1982, 8–12.

Krog, A. *Country of my Skull*, Johannesburg: Random House, 1998; London: Jonathan Cape, 1999. Edited version as *Country of my Skull: Guilt, Sorrow, and the Limits of Forgiveness in the New South Africa*, New York: Times Books, 1999.

Kruger, L. 'Apartheid on Display: South Africa Performs for New York', *Diaspora* 1:2 (1991), 191–208.

Kunene, M. *Emperor Shaka the Great: A Zulu Epic*, London: Heinemann, 1979.

La Guma, A. *And a Threefold Cord*, Berlin: Seven Seas, 1964.

   The Stone Country, Berlin: Seven Seas, 1967.

   A Walk in the Night, Ibadan: Mbari, 1962.

   A Walk in the Night and other Stories, London: Heinemann, 1967.

Lewis, E. (ed.). *The Life and Works of Alfred Aloysius Horn*, London: Jonathan Cape, 1927–9.

Linde, M. *Among Privileged People: A Novel from the Afrikaans*, trans. E. M. Arderne and G. A. Tomlinson, London: Stanley Paul, 1927.

Lytton, D. *The Freedom of the Cage*, London: Bodley Head, 1966; New York: Panther, 1969.

   The Goddam White Man, London: MacGibbon & Kee, 1960; Harmondsworth: Penguin, 1962.

   The Grass won't Grow till Spring, London: Bodley Head, 1965; New York: Panther, 1968.

   The Paradise People, London: MacGibbon & Kee and New York: Simon & Schuster, 1962.

   A Place Apart, London: MacGibbon & Kee, 1961.

Mandela, N. *No Easy Walk to Freedom: Articles, Speeches, and Trial Addresses of Nelson Mandela*, ed. R. First, London: Heinemann, 1965; London: Heinemann Educational, 1973.

Matshikiza, Todd, Harry Bloom, Pat Williams, et al. *King Kong, an African Jazz Opera*, London: Collins, 1961.

McDonald, P. D. *The Literature Police: Apartheid Censorship and its Cultural Consequences*, Oxford University Press, 2009.

Mda, Z. *The Heart of Redness*, Cape Town: Oxford University Press, 2000; New York: Farrar, Straus & Giroux, 2002.

   Ways of Dying, Cape Town: Oxford University Press, 1995; New York: Picador, 2002.

Millin, S. G. *Adam's Rest*, London: W. Collins Sons, 1922.

   An Artist in the Family, London: Constable, 1928.

   The Burning Man, London: Heinemann, 1952.

   The Dark River, London: W. Collins Sons, 1919,

   General Smuts, 2 vols., London: Faber, 1936.

   God's Step-Children, London: Constable, 1924.

   The Jordans, London: W. Collins Sons, 1923.

   The King of the Bastards, New York: Harper, 1949; London: Heinemann, 1950.

   Mary Glenn, London: Constable, 1925.

   The People of South Africa, London: Constable, 1951.

Rhodes, London: Chatto & Windus, 1933.

The South Africans, London: Constable, 1926.

Three Men Die, London: Chatto & Windus, 1934.

What Hath a Man?, London: Chatto & Windus, 1938.

The Wizard Bird, London: Heinemann, 1962.

Moss, L. '"Nice audible crying": Editions, Testimonies, and *Country of my Skull*', *Research in African Literatures* 37:4 (2006), 85–104.

Mphahlele, E. *Afrika my Music: An Autobiography 1957–1983*, Johannesburg: Ravan, 1984.

Down Second Avenue, London: Faber, 1959; Berlin: Seven Seas, 1962.

Ndebele, N. S. 'The Rediscovery of the Ordinary: Some New Writings in South Africa', in *South African Literature and Culture: Rediscovery of the Ordinary*, introduced by G. Pechey, Manchester University Press, 1994, 37–57.

Nicholls, B. 'Apartheid Cinema and Indigenous Image Rights: The "Bushman myth" in Jamie Uys's *The Gods Must Be Crazy*', *Scrutiny2: Issues in English Studies in Southern Africa* 13:1 (2008), 20–32.

Nixon, R. *Homelands, Harlem and Hollywood: South African Culture and the World Beyond*, New York: Routledge, 1994.

Palcy, E. (dir.) *A Dry White Season*, prod. Davros Films, Star Partners II, Sundance Productions, 1989.

Paton, Alan. *Cry, the Beloved Country: A Story of Comfort in Desolation*, New York: Scribner's and London: Jonathan Cape, 1948; *Gråt, mitt elskede land*, trans. F. Aasen, Oslo: Gyldendal Norsk, 1948; *Ve, mit elskede land*, trans. V. Bloch, Copenhagen: Gyldendal, 1948; *På lösan sand*, trans. B. and Å. Leander, Stockholm: Ljus, 1948; *Tranen over Johannesburg*, trans. B. Majorick, Amsterdam: Elsevier, 1948; *Itke, rakastettu maa*, trans. J. Linturi, Helsinki: Tammi, 1948; *Pleure, ô pays bien-aimé*, trans. D. van Moppès, Paris: Albin Michel, 1948; *Chora, terra bem amada!*, trans. A. d. S. Matias, Lisbon: Minerva, 1949; *Piangi, terra amata*, trans. M. S. Ferrari, Milan: Bompiani, 1949; *Denn sie sollen getröstet werden*, trans. M. Hackel, Hamburg: Wolfgang Kruger, 1951; *Gråt Ástkæra Fosturmold*, trans. A. Björnsson, Reykjavik: Almenna Bókafélagid, 1955; *Lafa elihle kakhulu*, trans. C. L. S. Nyembezi, Pietermaritzburg: Shuter & Shooter, 1957.

Pechey, G. 'On Trek', *Times Literary Supplement*, 30 April 2004, 14–15.

Pieterse, C. *Seven South African Poets*, London: Heinemann Educational, 1971.

Plomer, W. 'South African Writers and English Readers', in *Proceedings of a Conference of Writers, Publishers, Editors and University Teachers of English*, Johannesburg: Witwatersrand University Press, 1957, 54–72.

Ramzes, V. 'African Literature in Russia', *Transition* 25 (1966), 40–2.

Rive, R. (ed.). *Quartet: New Voices from South Africa*, New York: Crown, 1963; London: Heinemann Educational, 1965.

Roodt, D. (dir.). *Cry, the Beloved Country*, prod. Alpine, Distant Horizons, Miramax Films, Videovision Entertainment, 1995.

Yesterday, prod. Distant Horizon, Dv8, Exciting Films, HBO Films, M-Net, Nelson Mandela Foundation, Videovision Entertainment, 2004.

Rooke, D. *Mittee*, London: Victor Gollancz, 1951; Boston: Houghton Mifflin, 1952; Harmondsworth: Penguin, 1991; New Milford: Toby Press, 2007.

Rush, N. 'Apocalypse When?', *New York Review of Books*, 16 January 2003, 29–32.

[Sampson, A.]. 'South African Conflicts', *Times Literary Supplement*, 16 August 1957, xxxvi.

Schreiner, O. 'Preface', in *The Story of an African Farm*, 2nd edn, London: Chapman & Hall, [July] 1883, viii–ix.

The Story of an African Farm, London: Chapman & Hall, 1883 [as Ralph Iron]; Oxford University Press, 1992.

Serote, M. *To Every Birth its Blood*, Johannesburg: Ravan, 1981; London: Heinemann Educational, 1983.

Titlestad, M. *Making the Changes: Jazz in South African Literature and Reportage*, Pretoria: UNISA Press and Leiden: Koninklijke Brill, 2004.

Uys, J. (dir.). *The Gods must be Crazy*, prod. CAT Films, Mimosa, 1980.

Van der Post, L. *Flamingo Feather: A Story of Africa*, London: Hogarth Press, 1955.

In a Province, London: L. and V. Woolf [Hogarth Press], 1934.

The Lost World of the Kalahari, London: Hogarth Press, 1958.

A Story Like the Wind, London: Hogarth Press, 1972.

Van der Vlies, A. *South African Textual Cultures: White, Black, Read all Over*, Manchester University Press, 2007; Johannesburg: Witwatersrand University Press, 2011.

Van der Vlies, A., with P. D. Flanery. Section II of 'Introduction: Annexing the Global, Globalizing the Local', *Scrutiny2: Issues in English Studies in Southern Africa* 13:1 (2008), 3–17.

Voorslag: A Magazine of South African Life and Art 1, 2 and 3 (1926), ed. R. Campbell, W. Plomer and L. van der Post, facsimile reprint, Pietermaritzburg: University of Natal Press, 1985.

Weill, K. *Lost in the Stars*, words by Maxwell Anderson, New York: Chappell, 1949.

Wicomb, Z. *Playing in the Light: A Novel*, New York: New Press, 2006.

Wood, C. W. 'Letters from South Africa', *The Argosy* 344 (December 1894), 496–520.

Zwelonke, D. M. *Robben Island*, London: Heinemann, 1973.

34

Confession and autobiography

M. J. DAYMOND AND ANDRIES VISAGIE

A confessional mode dominated white South African autobiography in English in the 1990s; this followed the emphasis on bearing witness in black writing of the previous two decades. More recently, confession has entered black writing too. In Afrikaans writing, the modes of apologia (a defence of individual beliefs and actions) and auto-ethnography (a form of life-writing that relates the personal to the broader cultural and sociopolitical context) are still generally favoured.[1] Since 1994, writing in English by black and white has presented a continuing desire to speak truthfully about the impact of power relations on selfhood (as confession met witness-bearing), but self-reflection has become less anguished in the context of a vision of nation building for which the new constitution and the Truth and Reconciliation Commission (TRC) were the public faces. Although nearly all the political parties and many communities in South Africa have subsequently withheld complete support from the TRC's procedures (Johnson, *SA's Brave New World*, pp. 272–93) and findings,[2] hopeful interactions between a newly inclusive vision and autobiography are evident and individual stories continue to reflect and perhaps shape the macrohistory.

Before discussing particular post-1994 autobiographies, this chapter will indicate some of the earlier, but comparably symbiotic, relationships between life-writing and the elements of the national imaginary that can be traced across South African history. Then it will take up the suggestion that in the past fifteen years of potentially inclusive democracy there is emerging a more

---

1 While some autobiography has been translated into an African language (e.g., Peter Mtuze has translated Mandela's *Long Walk to Freedom* into isiXhosa), the only autobiography in another official language is in isiXhosa, namely *U-Mqhayi wase-Ntab'ozuko* (Mqhayi of the Mountain Beauty, 1939) by the *imbongi* S. E. K. Mqhayi, who lived from 1875 to 1945. Extracts were translated into English by W. G. Bennie (see Scott, *Mqhayi*), and this 'formed the basis of a translation into German' (Opland, *Xhosa Oral Poetry*, p. 90) by Westermann (see *Afrikaner Erzählen*). Coullie et al. introduce the interviews in *Selves in Question* with a valuable survey of South African life-writing.

2 On the difficulties of an official translation of one TRC testimony, see Krog et al., *There was this Goat* (2009).

open, less guilt-ridden mode of confessional writing, in which, particularly in the case of black writers, the representation of selfhood raises fresh questions about community.

Life-writing, 1652–1990[3]

The writing produced in South Africa in Dutch in the seventeenth century, notably the 1651–62 journal of Jan van Riebeeck and the 1661 travel account of Pieter van Meerhof ('Naar Het Land van de Namaqua's'), testifies to the struggle for European survival on a foreign continent and is motivated by the trade objectives of the Dutch East India Company (see Chapters 7, 9 and 13). In the eighteenth century the autobiographical strand in the writings in English of explorers, hunters, traders and some colonial officials is imbued with a spirit of heroic adventure and conquest (see Chapter 8).[4] These writings were also motivated by an empiricist desire to describe the uncharted territory and its inhabitants (Huigen, 'Nederlandstalige Suid-Afrikaanse Letterkunde', pp. 12–13). Today one could speculate that the masculine heroics of these narratives, written largely for consumption in Europe, would find a counterpart in what Buthelezi (in Chapter 4) calls the 'patriarchal' tradition of Zulu praises. Some writing by missionaries also enjoyed an adventurous spirit, as in Catherine Barter's 1855 account (*Alone Among the Zulus*) of travelling alone to the Phongolo River in Natal to rescue her brother, while Christianity fostered a confessional mode in the diaries of Voortrekkers such as Louis Trichardt (1836–8) and the cleric Erasmus Smit (1836–9). With organised British settlement in the early nineteenth century, more prosaic accounts of farm and frontier-town life were kept in the journals and letters of those who came to the Eastern Cape (Chapman, *Southern African Literatures*, pp. 90–1). These texts also contain a new note: the anxieties of a 'problematic appropriation' of the land (Van Wyk Smith, *Grounds of Contest*, p. 2), a note which would develop into one of the enduring themes of South African fictional and autobiographical writing in English (see Coetzee, *White Writing*). In fiction, the response to the strangeness of the land took a compensatory turn as the quest romance could imply a right

---

3 Used of texts from the past, 'life-writing' embraces memoirs, diaries, journals and travel writing, as well as autobiography. Nowadays its reference is much wider. Eakin has pointed to the global appeal of confession in the late twentieth century, suggesting that it is invited by a range of communicative forms: 'interviews, profiles, ethnographies, case studies, diaries, Web pages, and so on', and using 'life-writing . . . to cover [these] protean forms' (*Ethics of Life Writing*, p. 1).

4 The major travellers and explorers are discussed in Gray (*Southern African Literature*) and van Wyk Smith (*Grounds of Contest*), as are hunter-explorers. Lady Anne Barnard recorded her eighteenth-century Cape travels in her journals (1797–8) and diaries (1799–1800).

to the land and its riches (See Chapter 11 above, and McClintock, 'Maidens, Maps and Mines').

Quest romance is boastful and the stuff of thrills; a sober counterpart claims factual reliability. The attractions of each mode could be taken up by the same writer: for example, Percy Fitzpatrick assumes in both his romance, *Jock of the Bushveld* (1907), and in his report, *Through Mashonaland with Pick and Pen* (1892), a right to invade and trade in the territory of others. The self-vaunting note of the quest romance survived for at least another century, surfacing in Roy Campbell's two volumes of autobiography, *Broken Record* (1934) and *Light on a Dark Horse* (1951), and in Laurens van der Post's blend of myth-making, adventure and big-game hunting in *Venture to the Interior* (1952) and *The Lost World of the Kalahari* (1958). The fantastical element in Van der Post is counterbalanced by Guy Butler's more scrupulous account in *Karoo Morning* (1977) of living in a beloved land while knowing that the sons of settlers could not make straightforward claims to ownership, and by Dan Jacobson's careful scrutiny of his memories of Kimberley (*Time and Time Again*, 1985).

In the early twentieth century the letters and diaries of Boers produced during the Great Trek and the South African War, particularly accounts of suffering in British concentration camps,[5] were instrumental in the rise of Afrikaner nationalism. Victimhood served as justification for the struggle to attain language and cultural rights. The war diaries (*Oorlogsdagboek*, 1978) of writer and poet Jan F. E. Celliers and of poet and theologian 'Totius' (Du Toit), published in 1977 as *Vier-en-Sestig Dae te Velde* (Sixty-Four Days on the Battlefield), are representative. Writer and politician C. J. Langenhoven presented his life in *U Dienswillige Dienaar* (Your Willing Servant, 1932) as one of service to the Afrikaans language and its struggle for recognition. Novelist M. E. Rothmann (M. E. R.)[6] embraced apologia in her autobiography, *My Beskeie Deel* (My Humble Contribution, 1972), while she and the first Afrikaner woman doctor, Petronella van Heerden, in *Kerssnuitsels* (Candle Snuffings, 1962) and *Die Sestiende Koppie* (The Sixteenth Cup, 1965), involved women in the project of nation building (Viljoen, 'Nationalism, Gender and Sexuality').

The discovery of diamonds and then gold in the late nineteenth century brought a dramatic rise in the demand for migratory labour, and with it came

---

5 A rare black South African's perspective of part of the war ordeal is given by Plaatje in *The Boer War Diary of Sol T. Plaatje: An African at Mafeking* (1973). For life-writing in Afrikaans and Dutch from this time, see Jansen and Jonckheere, *Boer en Brit*. For women's accounts of British concentration camps, see Emily Hobhouse's *War Without Glamour* and Van Niekerk ('"Finding my own voice"'). See also Chapter 12 above.

6 Rothman was instrumental in founding the Afrikaanse Christelike Vrouevereniging (ACVV) and served on the Carnegie Commission's inquiry into the poor white question.

a shift from a rural to an urban life-writing. The new focus tended to be on 'private, inner and agonized space' (Van Wyk Smith, *Grounds of Contest*, p. 37), rather than on the self in relation to a limitless land. Then, out of the polarising exploitation of black labour, there emerged in the mid twentieth century a line of black autobiography in English in which a spirit of defiance, based in the counter-assertion of identity, is strong (see, in particular, the discussion of Bloke Modisane and Es'kia Mphahlele in Chapter 20). Arguably, the political column 'Straatpraatjes' (Street Talk) by Piet Uithalder (thought to be a pseudonym of Dr Abdullah Abdurahman) that appeared from 1909 to 1922 in the magazine *APO* (African Political Organisation) represents the beginnings of autobiographical writing by coloured people in Afrikaans (Willemse, *Aan die Ander Kant*, pp. 62–88). As all of this writing demonstrates, South Africa was becoming 'a battleground of identities, identities that were changing, forced upon, demanded, created, invented, dictated, used and abused' (Coullie et al., *Selves in Question*, p. 411). The life stories of black writers in English, active in the 1940s and 1950s, usually end in the emptiness of exile (see Chapter 20). It was the next generation who stayed and in which black women autobiographers appeared.

The pioneering account of black women's lives is Ellen Kuzwayo's *Call me Woman* (1985; see Chapter 36), while Mamphela Ramphele's *A Life* (1995) gives an early indication of how gender comes to disturb the required unanimity of resistance movements in the 1960s. After 1994 the publications in Afrikaans by coloured life-writers – *Staan uit die Water Uit* (Emerge from the Waters, 1996) by Karel Benjamin, Joseph Marble's *Ek, Joseph Daniel Marble* (I, Joseph Daniel Marble, 1999) and *Met 'n Diepe Verlange* (With Deep Longing, 2000) by Catherine Willemse – were followed by autobiographical essays by novelist E. K. M. Dido, whose 'My Lewe op 'n Wipplank' (My Life on a See-saw) appeared in 2001, and poet Diana Ferrus's 'Liefste Daddy' (Dear Daddy) in 2006. In all of these texts, black and coloured writers give unquestioned primacy to the community within and through which selfhood is created. A recovered sense of community becomes the vital source of counter-asserted identity (Driver, 'Women as Mothers, Women as Writers', p. 237) and a ratification of belonging.

Several white radical opponents of the regime who were active in the early years of apartheid have written memorably about their lives: Breyten Breytenbach (*True Confessions*, 1984); Hilda Bernstein (*The World that was Ours*, 1989); Rusty Bernstein (*Memory against Forgetting*, 1999); Helen Joseph (*Side by Side*, 1986); Norma Kitson (*Where Sixpence Lives*, 1987); AnnMarie Wolpe (*The Long Way Home*, 1994) and the family biography by Gillian Slovo (*Every Secret*

Thing, 1997). These memoirists show that their beliefs gave them a validated site for utterance from which they could reject white racist supremacy. In the next generation and during the tumultuous decades that preceded the unbanning of the African National Congress (ANC) in 1990, this confidence would evaporate as the search of white writers in English became one for a viable site from which to speak. Significantly for the argument later in this chapter, J. M. Coetzee attested to this search in his fiction rather than his autobiographical writing. In *Age of Iron* (1990), the dying Mrs Curren's lengthy letter to her daughter stages both her demand for utterance (suggesting her right to it, and even its value), as well as the uncertainties of its reception.

An increase in Afrikaans life-writing since 1994 is attributed by Henriette Roos to Afrikaners' prevailing perception of their political marginalisation ('Afrikaanse Prosa 1997 tot 2002', p. 65), while, in a more dramatic pronouncement, Hennie Aucamp regards it as an extended elegy for a once dynamic culture ('Vaal Kransies', p. 4).[7] Afrikaans writers such as Breytenbach, in *True Confessions* (1984), and Antjie Krog, in *Country of my Skull* (1998), ventured into the confessional mode, but chose to publish in English, presumably because Afrikaans had as yet relatively few confessional practitioners. Although there has been some recent confessional life-writing in Afrikaans,[8] most writers in this language still prefer auto-ethnography, thereby emphasising their cultural affiliations and avoiding what might be regarded as evidence of political or cultural dissidence.

Besides Rian Malan's autobiographical lament, *My Traitor's Heart* (1990), some important inaugurators of the confessional line deploy fiction: Mark Behr's novel *The Smell of Apples* (1995) represents a boy's being drawn into complicity with the oppressor, and Antjie Krog fictionalises aspects of her account of reporting the TRC hearings in *Country* (1998). Fiction allows Krog to depict an extramarital romance which 'is a figure for the larger loyalty to others that Krog proposes, an acknowledgement of others that feels like a betrayal of all that one knows' (Rostan, 'Ethics of Infidelity', p. 144). Fictionalising is also a reminder that autobiography itself is a confluence of fiction and fact (Coullie, '"Not quite fiction"', pp. 1–23), in that all life-writing

---

7 Biographies by J. C. Kannemeyer and J. C. Steyn heralded a revival of life-writing in Afrikaans after the transition to an inclusive democracy in 1994. Kannemeyer published six comprehensive biographies: *D. J. Opperman* (1986), *Langenhoven* (1995), *Leipoldt, Die Goue Seun* (The Golden Boy, 1999), *Jan Rabie* (2004) and *Leroux* (2008). At present he is at work on a biography of J. M. Coetzee. J. C. Steyn wrote *Van Wyk Louw* (1998) and *Die 100 Jaar van MER* (The 100 Years of MER, 2004).
8 For example, Koos Kombuis's *Seks & Drugs & Boeremusiek* (Sex, Drugs and Boer Music, 2000), *It's Me, Anna* (2005) by Elbie Lötter (the pseudonym of novelist Anchien Troskie), and *Midnight Missionary* (2006) by Kleinboer.

'invents its object, whether or not it declares its fictionality' (Attwell in Coullie, ed., *Selves in Question*, p. 214).

In order to inquire what may be evolving out of these factual and fictional confessions of material, personal and spiritual guilt, this chapter now concentrates on selected authors, other than political figures, who have produced both kinds of autobiographical writing in the last two decades. (Barnard discusses political autobiographies and fiction in relation to national memory; see Chapter 31.) These writers are (in English) J. M. Coetzee, Tatamkulu Afrika, Rayda Jacobs and Fred Khumalo, and (in Afrikaans) Karel Schoeman, Elsa Joubert, J. C. Steyn and Breyten Breytenbach. Comparative reference is also made to André Brink and Sindiwe Magona. Writers in both languages set up a complementary relation between their volumes of factual and fictional writing so as to re-engage with and even revitalise their stories. In the cases of Coetzee and Breytenbach, as with Krog, the distinction between fact and fiction is deliberately challenged or dissolved within one work.[9]

Autobiographers, 1990–2009

J. M. Coetzee's 1985 essay, 'Confession and Double Thoughts: Tolstoy, Rousseau and Dostoevsky', written when South Africa was in a state of near civil war, asks whether the revelations of a self-conscious, secular confessant who can invoke no higher authority than the writing self, can ever achieve truth, let alone envisage redemption. The autobiographical volumes which followed the essay, *Boyhood* (1997), *Youth* (2002) and *Summertime* (2009), are informed by these concerns, but their narrative modes mean that it is the reader who must find and apply the tests of truth. The first two volumes use a self-estranging third-person present-tense narration, a combination which allows the narrating self no retrospective self-insights and leaves the reader to function as priest-confessor, psychoanalyst and judge without overt textual guidance.

The story of *Boyhood* is one of conflicted desire. Guilts which the child cannot articulate, despite his early habits of self-examination, arise as he gradually repudiates his parents and their families' cultural affinities.[10] Only

9 As Hermione Lee observes, J. M. Coetzee's *Youth* was read by many British reviewers as a novel (*Body Parts*, pp. 167–76). Attridge (*Ethics of Reading*) considers the implications of this possibility.

10 Autobiographical writing in which the focus is exclusively on childhood may explore the 'fictional convention that children are "innocent" in a generally unspecified sense' (Heyns, 'The Whole Country's Truth', p. 50). Many of these texts, such as Patrick Cullinan's *Matrix* (2002) and Chris van Wyk's *Shirley, Goodness and Mercy: A Childhood Memoir* (2004), rely on a reader's

when he is alone on his paternal uncle's farm does he have a sense that he 'belong[s]' – 'the secret and sacred word' (p. 95) at the heart of his desires. Apart from his favourite cousin, Agnes (renamed Margot in *Summertime*, allowing fiction to disturb the claims of memory), his self-validating bond is with place, reinforcing the boy's solitude. Even his mother, with whom he has a close tie, is in many respects a repudiated presence because her love, being fundamentally self-sacrificial (p. 47), weighs too heavily on him in his quest for selfhood. These failed connections shape the boy's dawning understanding that he occupies what Coetzee would later call 'a totally untenable historical position' (*Doubling the Point*, p. 250).

The narration of *Youth* again holds the reader within the perspectives of its protagonist, thereby matching the protagonist's own desire as a writer to inhabit the inevitable limits of a particular horizon of knowledge (p. 138). As a would-be writer who reads for guidance, he binds himself unquestioningly to the literary tastes of Ezra Pound with comic and sometimes terrible results. His voluntary subservience is an extreme version of cultural affiliation, so it is a relief when he is released, through reading Beckett's *Watt* (p. 159), by the discovery that fine sensibilities may differ. The frankness with which Coetzee presents his protagonist's failures is not a measuring of self against an established set of standards (Attridge, *Ethics of Reading*, pp. 144–5), but a never-ending enquiry into appropriate and authentic responses to events in their historical contexts.

The culmination of each volume lies in the prospect of writing. In *Boyhood*, the child recognises the importance of 'keeping in his head, all the books, all the people, all the stories' (p. 166). In *Youth*, the moment that signals that some continuity between past and present and between writer and protagonist might be achieved occurs when, in response to reading Burchell's early nineteenth-century account of his travels, the protagonist imagines himself taking up the story of South Africa (p. 138). This story-telling enterprise does not, however, hold the redemptive promise that through it past wrongs might fade, a hope that to some extent the TRC would hold out to those who confessed, testified or observed its proceedings. In *Summertime*, testimony (in the TRC's terms) is again without consolation. It is juxtaposed with confession as a would-be biographer interviews five people who had known a famous and now dead writer called John Coetzee and their reports are ranged alongside the

---

text-external knowledge of what awaits their protagonists. They contrast, on the one hand, with Coetzee's treatment of his anxious child protagonist, and with, for example, Christopher Hope's *White Boy* (1988) and Mark Mathabane's *Kaffir Boy* (1986), on the other, where the narrative's perspective is that of the knowing adult.

writer's own life notes. As the biographer promises his informants that he will remove what they find uncomfortable when he reads their testimonies back to them (but there is no indication that he has done so), the reader is brought up against the former's mediating function and reminded of the potential fictionality of biography. The 'countervoices released by writing' (Attwell, in Coullie et al., *Selves in Question*, p. 215) and the notes both require as much critical assessment by a reader as would fiction. The questions that variously occupy each biographical informant echo the final pages of *Youth* where the young protagonist despairingly asks himself how 'life, love, poetry' (p. 168) can serve each other when he cannot rise to the intensity that each demands. In *Youth* the protagonist's requirement of himself is both touching and youthfully arrogant, but in *Summertime* the informants' related requirements are a measure of their (mis)shaping of the writer they knew.

Positioning itself as distant from the healing ethos of the TRC, Tatamkulu Afrika's confessional autobiography, *Mr Chameleon* (2005), uses its narration to disorient the reader in a flurry of clashing and confusing possibilities, but not to indicate its fictionality. Its first-person, retrospective narration relishes the possibilities of self-doubt and self-regard, but these can also deflect certain crucial questions. These emerge, for example, when the narrator is told that his birth-mother was Turkish and his father Egyptian. His first inclination is to fall into 'the honey trap of romanticizing' (p. 42) his origins so as to explain to himself why, within white South Africa, he has always felt different. Then, when his adoptive mother assures him that she will always love him 'as though we were of one blood' (p. 43), but warns him that he must keep secret his parentage, the narration indicates the cruelty of a loving embrace which instructs the child to know himself as forever marginalised.

There is one positive that stands against the narrator's corrosive self-doubt: his friendship with the Ovambo miner, Simon, whom he meets in Tsumeb, Namibia. But his romantic-heroic portrait of this man, which tries to deny a strong sexual attraction in favour of the bond of warriors (p. 255), raises questions about the honesty of his depictions of himself. The friendship affords the narrator, for the first time and against the norms of his world, the mutual recognition of equals and so it may be that Afrika's evasions are an attempt to protect these memories from much that he feels has been sordid in his life.

Afrika's broaching his bisexuality is historically important (Stobie, *Double Rainbow*, pp. 105–30), but the tensions surrounding it are matters he seems unable to resolve. The autobiography ends sadly as Afrika's rapidly increasing blindness causes his own words simply to slip off the page; more tellingly, his autobiographical fiction also ends without resolution. The central relationship in *Mr Chameleon* is with an English soldier, Danny, when they are prisoners in an Italian and then a German camp. Their undeclared love is revisited in the novel *Bitter Eden* (2002), where the narrator-protagonist suggests that wartime prison camps encouraged male prostitution, making it impossible for men to acknowledge feelings of love. Immediately after the war, however, it is mere chance that prevents the sexual union that both men want. Although fiction offered him an opportunity, Afrika does not imagine a resolution of these issues and so the novel becomes a dramatisation of his own dilemma in actual life.[11]

Karel Schoeman's autobiography, *Die Laaste Afrikaanse Boek* (The Last Afrikaans Book, 2002), combines a novelist's skills with his achievements as an historian, gathering all three salient aspects of recent life-writing in South Africa: confession, apologia and auto-ethnography. In fact, Schoeman's frank confessions of his homosexuality (p. 459) – which he feels should have featured more openly in his novel *Die Noorderlig* (Northern Lights, 1975) – and of his failure to raise his voice against racial discrimination during the rule of the National Party are remarkable within the tradition of Afrikaans life-writing.

Die Laaste Afrikaanse Boek is further innovative as auto-ethnography in presenting the narrating self primarily as a Free Stater and a South African, rather than an Afrikaner. Schoeman emphasises the fact that during his isolated childhood, his mother, the daughter of the Dutch consul in Bloemfontein, spoke only Dutch to him and that he had limited contact with the Afrikaans-speaking relations of his father, who had virtually disappeared from his life after his parents' divorce in 1943 when he was 3 years old. Indeed, he attempted his first novels in Dutch and English before deciding to write in Afrikaans. Although he grew up in Paarl in the Western Cape, Afrikaner nationalism was not part of his frame of reference and it was only when he converted to Catholicism that he paid attention to his other cultural roots: 'With my entry into the Catholic Church I became aware of my Afrikaner identity for the first time, or if that goes too far, let me rather say the ties that I have with Afrikaners through my father and the moral duty resting on me to work towards bringing them back to the only true Mother Church' (p. 323). It is conceivable that Schoeman's life as a Catholic monk in Ireland, between 1961 and 1964, influenced his adoption of a confessional mode. At the age of 50 he realised that his reserved nature was a defence mechanism that he had acquired when his father disappeared from his life. Writing his autobiography

11 Afrika's first novel, *The Innocents* (1994), is based on his activity as an MK freedom fighter. It depicts an all-male (but political) context in which emotional allegiances are again unresolved.

enables him to achieve greater clarity about his pain and to heal the emotional trauma of separation from his father that had haunted him throughout his adult life.

André Brink is critical of Schoeman's defence of his relative absence from the anti-apartheid struggle: 'Certainly it was perfectly in order for him (as a writer, not necessarily as a citizen) to refrain from political action or activism and to focus exclusively on writing – but then he should not attempt to either represent himself or his work as something it patently never was' ('Afrikaans is bound to outlive', p. 7). Yet Schoeman openly admits that he benefited from a life of white privilege and claims that his apartheid testimony had to be that of 'an observer from a distance', as he had no 'talent for protest or demonstration' (*Afrikaanse Boek*, pp. 104, 390). He claims that his greatest criticism of apartheid is contained in his novel, *Promised Land* (1978).

Although Elsa Joubert's novel, *The Long Journey of Poppie Nongena* (1980), attests to her later critical stance towards the apartheid regime (see Chapter 22), the first volume of her autobiography, *'n Wonderlike Geweld* (A Wonderful Violence, 2005), gives no sign of these views, for it covers only the first twenty-six years of her life, which coincided with the rise of Afrikaner nationalism, from 1922 to 1948.[12] Like Coetzee, Joubert writes in the third person, enabling her to signal the distance between her later views and her passionate beliefs as a teenager and a student. Extracts from her diaries ensure an immediate sense of the young girl's thoughts and experiences. Her second volume, *Reisiger* (Traveller, 2009), is written in the first person, suggesting a confluence of the elderly narrator and the younger self who forms the subject of the narration. Joubert writes frankly about her relationship with an Indian man and, reminiscing about her travels through Madagascar, she isolates an incident which enabled her to overcome her fear of other Africans. When a child on a bus accidentally kicks her softly in her side, she is filled with a feeling of unity with the African continent.

Joubert was the child of an educated family of Huguenot descent who lived in Paarl in the Western Cape. Her father repeatedly reminded her of the historical documents produced by the Genootskap van Regte Afrikaners (GRA) (Association of True Afrikaners; see Chapter 13) that had been discovered in the loft of their home. The young Joubert resolved to follow in the footsteps

---

12 Joubert's book, J. C. Steyn's books *Hoeke Boerseuns ons Was* ('The Afrikaner Boys we once were') and *Sonkyker* ('Sungazer'), as well as *Kambro-Kind: 'n Jeugreis* ('Kambro Child: A Journey through Childhood') by F. A. Venter, are instances of Afrikaans writers' memories of childhood and youth. Their focus was preceded by two compilations, *My Jeugland: Jeugherinneringe van Afrikaanse Skrywers* ('Country of My Youth: Childhood Memories of Afrikaans Writers'), edited by C. M. van den Heever, and the anonymously edited *Herinnering se Wei* ('Memory's Pastures').

of the GRA and to become an Afrikaans writer (*Geweld*, p. 54). Her resolve resulted in a play about the Great Trek, which was produced at her school. As a student at Stellenbosch University, she joined the Ossewabrandwag,[13] participated in the semi-military marches of this nationalist movement and shared its pro-German sentiments during the Second World War. It was later, while working as a journalist for the magazine *Huisgenoot*, that the true horror of the German concentration camps began to dawn on her: 'If we could have been so mistaken about the Germans, how can we in future have confidence in our own judgement? Our own lives are wavering' (p. 359). Auto-ethnography diminishes towards the end of this volume when Joubert embarks on a long journey through Africa, motivated by the urge to escape the prescriptions that marked her youth and to find her own voice.

Novelist and biographer J. C. Steyn overtly frames his autobiography *Sonkyker: Afrikaner in die Verkeerde Eeu* (Sungazer: An Afrikaner in the Wrong Century, 2008) within the history of the Afrikaner. In the preface he decides, possibly with Hermann Giliomee's 'biography of a people', *The Afrikaners* (2003), at the back of his mind, that 'My book is, like so many others, neither an autobiography, nor a biography of a people but an "in-betweener"' (p. ix). As auto-ethnography, Steyn's book offers a compelling apologia, not only for his own life as a journalist, poet, novelist, linguist and cultural historian, but for all Afrikaners of his generation.

Steyn's title refers to the giant girdle-tailed lizard, or sungazer, which quietly surveys the world and scurries for shelter at the slightest suspicion of approaching danger. He grew up as the son of a Free State farmer and characterises himself as a timid country bumpkin who, throughout his life, struggled to communicate. Steyn becomes elusive whenever he broaches the subject of his sexuality, hinting only occasionally at homosexual relationships, so that his writing both conceals and reveals.

Steyn became known as progressive in his political views, but in his auto-biography he openly professes his allegiance to an Afrikaans nationalism (as distinct from Afrikaner nationalism), because only a modern form of nationalism will prevent the Afrikaans language from total disintegration. He remains critical of the proceedings of the TRC and, in 1990, he fervently opposed André Brink, who argued that Afrikaans had to sacrifice its status as an official language in order to shed its political baggage. Steyn believes that the adoption of eleven official languages in South Africa, in 1993, would privilege English and effectively marginalise the other ten. He quotes Rothmann: 'One does not

13 The 'Oxwagon Sentinel', whose goal was to establish a republic modelled on the defunct Boer republics.

only live as an individual but through and with one's own group or people. If the life and work of a people become stymied, the individual also suffers' (*Sonkyker*, p. 373).

Steyn's opposition to André Brink gives a glimpse of the outspoken political-critical role that Brink has played in recent decades in the Afrikaans-speaking world. In his memoir, *A Fork in the Road* (2009), Brink reports his trangressions against cultural orthodoxy, his painful break with his family, and the forces that created the rebel group of Afrikaans writers, the Sestigers. But these departures appear to leave him unscarred, for his narrating persona in the memoir is stable and sometimes self-satisfied, apparently unmarked by what others have seen as treachery. It seems that Brink leaves the note of anguished confession to his fiction. One of the factors that might have given complexity to the reading of his memoir – his identifying his new wife, Karina, as the motivating force behind the writing of his life story and his primary reader – is kept until the Postscript and so the implications of a mediating presence are not taken up.

In contrast to J. C. Steyn's attachment to the Afrikaner people, Breyten Breytenbach, in his autobiographical *Woordwerk* (Wordwork, 1999), bluntly refuses to acknowledge the Afrikaner nation as a fait accompli. He has had a tumultuous relationship with the Afrikaner establishment, consistently resisting attempts to co-opt him into any cultural configuration. He wrote many of his autobiographical texts in English, as part of his frequent attempts to sever his bonds with Afrikaans and with Afrikaners. In *Woordwerk*, he positions himself as the *'swerwer'* (drifter) of his subtitle, a nomad whose attachments are primarily to friends and family and not to any larger ethnic grouping. *Woordwerk* gathers the 'stories' (p. 224) and fragments that Breytenbach hopes to share with his daughter, Gogga, who may eventually learn to understand Afrikaans, the language that her father chose in this case for his reminiscences about his life as a wanderer who divided his time between Paris, Catalonia, South Africa and the West African island of Gorée.

As in much of Breytenbach's writing, *Woordwerk* problematises the boundaries between fact and fiction in the fantasies and dreamlike sequences that alternate with more factual material. Breytenbach describes his text as a 'novel of the self' (p. 125), casting doubt on the ontological status of the autobiographical 'I'. The narrating voice consistently undermines the identity of the self by creating a range of alternative personae that all resemble, to some extent, the author. As pointed out by Viljoen in "'n "Tussenin-Boek"' (An In-between Book, p. 10), the 'I' is dispersed, reappearing as Walker (who also features quite prominently in the autobiographical *Return to Paradise* [1993] and *Dog Heart* [1998]), as the black writer Dog, and as the somewhat enigmatic *kek*, presumably a contraction of the Afrikaans words *ek* (I) and *kak* (shit).

The fascination with death and suicide in *Woordwerk* becomes a dramatisation of Breytenbach's desire to undermine the self as a fixed entity. He is torn between an intractable fear and an intense longing for death. As his text negotiates these conflicting impulses, it becomes apparent that the more philosophical Buddhist preoccupation with non-being that is present throughout his writings is challenged by the painful reality of death when the narrator has to witness the passing away of Loup, a friend whom he first met in 1968 in the aftermath of the student protests in Paris. He decries Loup's death, although not suicide, as 'a crime against himself, against his friends. Self-destruction. Egoistic and narcissistic. Without any reason' (p. 42).

The recurrence of interrogation rooms and spaces of execution in *Woordwerk* may still point to Breytenbach's processing of the trauma of his captivity during the apartheid period. However, in response to a question by Saayman about such spaces in his memoir, *A Veil of Footsteps* (2008), Breytenbach observes that they have always been present in his writing: 'References to prisons and interrogators are metaphors, gateways and gatekeepers into and out of the respective stages of the one world of layered consciousness. Maybe they represent nothing more than the need for patternmaking!' ('"Writing is travelling"', p. 203). (In Chapter 26, Roux includes Breytenbach's *True Confessions* and *Mouroir* in his overview of prison writing.)

The search for community that Rayda Jacobs narrates in her autobiography and her fiction continues the concern of earlier black writers, but the accompanying desire for a fusion of religious and secular life is unusual in South African autobiographical writing. Both collections of short stories, *The Middle Children* (1994) and *Postcards from South Africa* (2004), as well as her autobiography, *Masquerade* (2008), represent the events that led to her emigration to Canada and her return years later to the Muslim community in the Western Cape, into which she was born. This subject matter is confessional,[14] but, unlike the secular confessants discussed here, Jacobs is able to entertain as she writes the promises of absolution and an ending for her story.

Jacobs's novel, *Confessions of a Gambler* (2003), is her fictional counterpart of the self-examination in *Masquerade*, and is her most powerful depiction of confession's uncertain processes. The narrator-protagonist, Abeeda, begins with 'The first thing I have to confess is that I'm a Muslim woman' (p. 7), follows this with 'I like risk' and then confesses her efforts to hide her growing

14 This claim includes *The Mecca Diaries* (2005), but not Jacobs's historical fiction, *Eyes of the Sky* (1996) and *Slave Book* (1998).

addiction to gambling from herself and her friends. This ordering confirms Gallagher's view that religious confession is primarily a declaration of faith or grace, and only then an owning up to sin (*Truth and Reconciliation*, pp. 3–4). In *Masquerade*, Jacobs writes: 'Addiction doesn't choose a particular culture or race, it's a disease' (p. 315), but her fiction allows her to explore addiction as a matter of personality too. Fiction also allows Jacobs to counterbalance Abeeda's addiction with her youngest son's homosexuality and his dying of AIDS-related illnesses (Kearney, 'Representations of Islamic Belief and Practice', pp. 150–1). For his 'transgression', he has been rejected by his father and the religious community who refuse all knowledge of his dying. The community's failure leads to Abeeda's shrewd and challenging observation that 'mothers will do what they must and tread where fathers fear to go. For our children we will do anything. It's easier to face God than to have the community know your business. God forgives. A community never forgets' (*Confessions*, p. 25).

Gender crystallises Jacobs's analysis of the community, and it plays a part in her account of institutionalised religion. The subordination of women in all communities is also central to her account of her unhappy early family life, her long exile in Canada, her return to South Africa and her gradual reversion to Islam. The inclusiveness of her concern for women is also indicated by her choice of topics for the third-person cameos which punctuate the narration of *Masquerade*. These revisit milestones and difficult issues in most women's lives: the birth of a child, the death of a parent, the breakdown of family life, divorce and the contested guardianship of children, accidents and the mortality of children, patriarchal power, the linguistic hegemony of English, exile and marriage outside one's religious community.[15]

For some black writers, confession offered, even in the darkest days before the unbannings of 1990, a note of playful self-deprecation, as well as blame, angst or anger. Sindiwe Magona begins *Forced to Grow* (1992), the second volume of her autobiography, with the confession that 'I was a has-been at the age of twenty-three' (p. 1). As the ending of *To my Children's Children* tells it, she is husbandless and jobless, with three children to support and only her mother to help. Some luck, her resilience and her humour carry her out of township despair, into an education and eventually a job in America.[16]

15 Jacobs reports that her publisher wanted more politics in *Masquerade*, and that a journalist friend criticised *Confessions* for the absence of politics. She defends her elisions by saying that while her own struggle was created by the political context into which she was born (*Masquerade*, p. 120), the binary divisions of racial oppression and resistance could not reflect her sense of self.
16 Much of Magona's autobiographical writing relies on her fine ear for the robust wit of township women. It is also present in her story collection, *Living, Loving and Lying Awake at*

Another black writer who records his escape and who seems to have drawn some strength from laughter is Fred Khumalo. Of the writers discussed here, only he explicitly aligns his autobiography, *Touch my Blood* (2006), with the TRC (p. 196). Like Magona, he begins with a partly playful confession: on the 'spur of the moment' he silenced an obnoxious countryman by reaching under the table, 'grab[bing] his testicles . . . and squeez[ing] viciously' (pp. 9–10). For all its violence, the moment is presented as comic, and Khumalo is disarmingly self-deprecating. He is serious too, saying he still 'needed to deal with the demons from my past' (p. 12). He has emerged from the largely 'hidden civil war' of the 1980s, fearing that its *mores* will grip him forever (p. 12), wherever he goes. In this respect, Khumalo's confession can be compared with Rian Malan's earlier *My Traitor's Heart* (1990), in which he too asks whether racial violence will mark him forever. But Khumalo, like Magona, does not see the issue in the Manichean terms that Malan takes from the 1980s. Whilst much of Khumalo's narrative laments the bitter and reductive allegiances that were imposed on the inhabitants of Mpumalanga (a township near Durban) when ANC-aligned forces battled the Inkatha Freedom Party for territorial control, he signals his wish to move beyond division: 'For so many of us the past is a place of hurt' (p. 196). Reconciliation is what Malan desired but could not envisage in the circumstances within which he wrote in the late 1980s; like Magona, Khumalo has been released from the self-accusatory and self-distrusting note of Malan's confessional mode.

As Magona does in *Mother to Mother* (1998), so Khumalo turns to fiction to explore some of the personal and communal self-destructiveness that has troubled his own life. In *Bitches' Brew* (2006),[17] the narration is conducted largely through an exchange of confessional letters between Lettie and Zakes, lovers who do not trust each other because, like many energetic and intelligent people of their generation, they have turned to living off sex, drugs and crime. So criminalised are ordinary activities in township life, that the concept of wrongdoing has little meaning to them. Magona's confessing mother feels that in her circumstances (a life of deprivation and denial, much like Magona's own) she was made unable to protect her son when he joined a political group that would eventually resort to violence (the action is based on the killing of Amy Biehl, an American student). Her cry is 'where did we go wrong?', a question which shapes Khumalo's writing too.

Night (1991) which, in 2002, was voted one of 'Africa's 100 Best Books of the Twentieth Century' (Daymond, 'Sindiwe Magona').

17 Khumalo's novel and autobiography were 'written almost concurrently' (interview with Chris van Wyk, 4 April 2009, www.litnet.co.za/cgi-in/giga.cgi?cmd=cause_dir_new).

'Family' is not an option for the lovers in Khumalo's novel, and 'community' fails in his autobiography. In the epilogue to *Touch my Blood*, dated 2005, he records a gathering for the funeral of his younger brother who has died of HIV / AIDS. The ritual eating of meat 'goes down well to stories seasoned with dark humour, hyperbole' (p. 195). As the storytellers turn from the conflicts of the past to their own crime-ridden present, his friends congratulate Khumalo on his good fortune. When he confesses that he too has known despair and has had to consult a psychiatrist in order to cope, they laugh in derision. Their repudiation of self and community healing seems to overwhelm Khumalo at this point, for he turns away from the evidence of 'a younger generation, meaner, more lost than ever we were' and simply reaffirms his pride in the past, in 'people who have impacted on my life and made me who I am today' (p. 196). The autobiography forgoes an ending; so too does the fiction. It might be that Khumalo feels that his writing cannot go beyond the truth of his community's condition – until he sees resolution being sought around him, he will not imagine one for his fictional characters either.

The loss or rejection of land and community and a consequent search for belonging has been a constant theme in South African autobiography. In the 1980s in black writing in English, community became the revered source of a counterasserted identity. In white writing in English, the anguish of inherited guilt led to a more self-isolating confessional approach, as in J. M. Coetzee's autobiographical writing. More recently, for black writers in English, autobiographical work is leading to a questioning of community and particularly to the requirements of a necessary self-healing. In Rayda Jacobs's work issues of self and community find some resolution; in Tatamkulu Africa and Fred Khumalo they do not.

A comparable trend in Afrikaans writing is evident. After the exclusivity of desired nationhood implicit in the life-writing which lasted for most of the twentieth century, a new note has gradually developed. The trend is not yet a dominant one, for apologia and auto-ethnography continue, and, since the language policy formulated in the post-1994 nation building, many Afrikaners have reanimated a protectionist view of their own language and culture. But writers such as Schoeman, Breytenbach and Krog provide, in their various ways, indications of another line of thinking. One of its early manifestations comes in the first autobiographical text by Breyten Breytenbach, *A Season in Paradise* (1980), originally published in Afrikaans in 1976. After criticising Afrikaners for their complicity with the then governing National Party, he writes: 'What I discover myself means nothing. What we realise as a group, as a society – that is important, for that is a shared possession, it has value because it is on the way to truth. We are all involved in this tragedy together' (pp. 156–7). Breytenbach ends with the even more pointed wish 'that we may break away, both in our perception and conduct, to a broader South African identity' (p. 179). Enquiring into how a broader identity might emerge across communities, Krog, who calls her second major work in English *A Change of Tongue* (2003), stages a conversation between herself and two colleagues, Ghangha and Mamukwa, about race, identity and belonging. Consensus seems impossible, but Krog gives the last word of their interrupted conversation to Ghanga: 'The point is . . . we do not have to be hugging one another all the time, as long as we live together amicably and caringly' (p. 275).

Such a view of potential healing is cautiously hopeful; the search for it can be related to an earlier example of divisions within the autobiographical self and between self and community. In the concluding interview in *Doubling the Point*, Coetzee speaks of what his writing self will need in order to relate 'amicably and caringly' to his experiencing self. He hopes for a condition of 'grace' in which, in the act of self-representation, the 'truth can be told clearly, without blindness' (p. 392). Working towards 'grace', he says earlier that he hopes to achieve 'unflinchingness' and then 'forgivingness' (p. 29), as well as 'a measure of charity', which is how 'grace allegorises itself in the world' (p. 249). The spiritual connotations of these terms may seem difficult to reconcile with Coetzee's having presented himself as a secular confessant, and, in the character of Elizabeth Costello, as caught in the paradox that a writer 'cannot afford to believe' (*Costello*, p. 213), but must strive for fidelity. But, however taxing, his terms undertake to articulate what will be involved if South African autobiographers are to continue to move with assurance beyond the self-recriminations of the confessional mode and into exploring possibilities of a shared future.

Bibliography

Afrika, T. *Bitter Eden*, London: Arcadia Books, 2002.
  The Innocents, Cape Town: David Philip, 1994.
  Mr Chameleon, Johannesburg: Jacana, 2005.
Anon. *Herinnering se Wei*, Pretoria: Afrikaanse Pers Boekhandel, 1966.
Attridge, D. *J. M. Coetzee and the Ethics of Reading: Literature in the Event*, Pietermaritzburg: University of KwaZulu-Natal Press, 2005.
Aucamp, H. 'Vaal Kransies op Vergange Kultuur', *Rapport*, 12 July 2009, p. 4.
Barnard, Lady A. *The Cape Diaries of Lady Anne Barnard 1799–1800*, vols. I and II, ed. M. Lenta and B. le Cordeur, Cape Town: Van Riebeeck Society, 1999.

The Cape Journals of Lady Anne Barnard 1797–1798, ed. A. M. Lewin-Robinson, Cape Town, Van Riebeeck Society, 1994.

Barter, C. *Alone Among the Zulus* [1855], Pietermaritzburg: University of Natal Press, 1995.

Behr, M. *Die Reuk van Appels*, Cape Town: Queillerie, 1993; *The Smell of Apples*, London: Abacus, 1995.

Benjamin, K. *Staan uit die Water Uit: 'n Kaapse Jeug*, Cape Town: Kwela Books, 1996.

Bernstein, H. *The World that was Ours*, London: SA Writers, 1989.

Bernstein, R. *Memory against Forgetting: Memories from a Life in South African Politics, 1938–1964*, London: Viking, 1999.

Breytenbach, B. *Dog Heart: A Travel Memoir*, Cape Town: Human & Rousseau, 1998.

Mouroir: Mirrornotes of a Novel, London: Faber, 1984.

Return to Paradise, Cape Town: David Philip, 1993.

A Season in Paradise, trans. R. Vaughan, London and Boston, MA: Faber, 1980.

The True Confessions of an Albino Terrorist, Johannesburg: Taurus, 1984.

A Veil of Footsteps: Memoir of a Nomadic Fictional Character, Cape Town and Pretoria: Human & Rousseau, 2008.

Woordwerk: Die Kantskryfjoernaal van 'n Swerwer, Cape Town: Human & Rousseau, 1999.

Brink, A. 'Afrikaans is bound to outlive its "last book"', *Sunday Independent*, 2 March 2003, 7.

A Fork in the Road, London: Harvill Secker, 2009.

Butler, G. *Karoo Morning: An Autobiography 1918–1935*, Cape Town: David Philip, 1977.

Campbell, R. *Broken Record*, London: Boriswood, 1934.

Light on a Dark Horse, London: Hollis & Carter, 1951.

Celliers, J. F. E. *Oorlogsdagboek van Jan F. E. Celliers 1899–1902*, Pretoria: Human Sciences Research Council, 1978.

Chapman, M. *Southern African Literatures*, London: Longman, 1996.

Coetzee, J. M. *Age of Iron*, Harmondsworth: Penguin, 1990.

'All Autobiography is *Autre*-biography' (interview with D. Attwell), in. Coullie et al., *Selves in Question*, 213–18.

Boyhood: Scenes from Provincial Life, London: Secker & Warburg, 1997.

'Confession and Double Thoughts: Tolstoy, Rousseau, Dostoevsky', in Attwell, *Doubling the Point*, 251–93.

Doubling the Point: Essays and Interviews, ed. D. Attwell, Cambridge, MA: Harvard University Press, 1992.

Elizabeth Costello, London: Vintage Books, 2004.

Summertime, London: Harvill Secker, 2009.

White Writing: On the Culture of Letters in South Africa, Johannesburg: Radix and New Haven: Yale University Press, 1988.

Youth, London: Secker & Warburg, 2002.

Coullie, J. L. '"Not quite fiction": The Challenges of Poststructuralism to the Reading of Contemporary South African Autobiography', *Current Writing: Text and Reception in Southern Africa* 3 (1991), 1–23.

Coullie, J. L., S. Meyer, T. H. Ngwenya and S. Olver (eds.). *Selves in Question: Interviews in Southern African Auto/biography*: Honolulu, University of Hawai'i Press, 2006.

Cullinan, P. *Matrix*, Plumstead: Snailpress, 2002.

Daymond, M. J. 'Sindiwe Magona: Writing, Remembering, Selfhood and Community in *Living, Loving, and Lying Awake at Night*', in C. O. Ogunyemi and T. J. Allan (eds.), *Twelve Best Books by African Women: Critical Readings*, Athens: Ohio University Press, 2009.

Dido, E. K. M. 'My Lewe op 'n Wipplank', in E. van Heerden (ed.), *Briewe Deur die Lug: LitNet/Taalsekretariaat-skrywersberaad 2000*, Cape Town: Tafelberg, 2001, 67–74.

Driver, D. 'M'a-Ngoana O Tšoare Thipa ka Bohaleng – The Child's Mother Grabs the Sharp End of the Knife: Women as Mothers, Women as Writers', in M. Trump (ed.), *Rendering Things Visible: Essays on South African Literary Culture*, Johannesburg: Ravan, 1990, 225–55.

Du Toit, J. D. ['Totius']. *Vier-en-Sestig Dae te Velde: 'n Oorlogsdagboek*, Cape Town: Tafelberg, 1977.

Eakin, J. P. (ed.). *The Ethics of Life Writing*, Ithaca, NY: Cornell University Press, 2004.

Ferrus, D. 'Liefste Daddy', in McKerron and Ferrus, *Slaan Vir My 'n Masker, Vader*, 7–14.

Fitzpatrick, P. *Through Mashonaland with Pick and Pen* [1892], Johannesburg: Ad Donker, 1973.

Jock of the Bushveld [1907], London: Longmans, Green, 1949.

Gallagher, S. V. *Truth and Reconciliation: The Confessional Mode in South African Literature*, Portsmouth, NH: Heinemann, 2002.

Giliomee, H. *The Afrikaners: Biography of a People*, Cape Town: Tafelberg, 2003.

Gray, S. *Southern African Literature: An Introduction*, Cape Town: David Philip, 1979.

Heyns, M. 'The Whole Country's Truth: Confession and Narrative in Recent White South African Writing', *Modern Fiction Studies* 46:1 (2000), 42–66.

Hobhouse, E. *War Without Glamour: Women's War Experiences Written by Themselves, 1899–1902*, trans. E. Hobhouse, Bloemfontien: Nasionale Pers Beperk, 1924.

Hope, C. *White Boy Running: A Book about South Africa*, London: Secker & Warburg, 1988.

Huigen, S. 'Nederlandstalige Suid-Afrikaanse Letterkunde, 1652 tot 1925', in Van Coller, *Perspektief en Profiel*, 3–42.

Jacobs, R. *Confessions of a Gambler: A Novel*, Cape Town: Kwela Books, 2003.

Eyes of the Sky, Cape Town: Kwela Books, 1996.

Masquerade: The Story of my Life, Cape Town: Umuzi, 2008.

The Mecca Diaries, Cape Town: Double Storey, 2005.

The Middle Children, Toronto: Second Story Press, 1994.

Postcards from South Africa, Cape Town: Double Storey, 2004.

The Slave Book, Cape Town: Kwela Books, 1998.

Jacobson, D. *Time and Time Again: Autobiographies*, London: Andre Deutsch, 1985.

Jansen, E. and Jonckheere, W. (eds.). *Boer en Brit. Afrikaanse en Nederlandse Tekste Uit en Om die Anglo-Boereoorlog*, Pretoria: Protea Boekhuis, 1999.

Johnson, R. W. *South Africa's Brave New World: The Beloved Country since the End of Apartheid*, London: Allan Lane, 2009.

Joseph, H. *Side by Side. The Autobiography of Helen Joseph*, Johannesburg: Ad Donker, 1986.

Joubert, E. *The Long Journey of Poppie Nongena*, trans. E. Joubert, Cape Town: Jonathan Ball, 1980.

Reisiger, Cape Town: Tafelberg, 2009.

'n Wonderlike Geweld, Cape Town: Tafelberg, 2005.

Kannemeyer, J. C. D. J. *Opperman: 'n Biografie*, Cape Town, Human & Rousseau, 1986.

Die Goue Seun: Die Lewe en Werk van Uys Krige, Cape Town: Tafelberg, 2002.

Jan Rabie: Prosapionier en Politieke Padwyser, Cape Town: Tafelberg, 2004.

Langenhoven: 'n Lewe, Cape Town: Tafelberg, 1995.

Leipoldt: 'n Lewensverhaal, Cape Town: Tafelberg, 1999.

Leroux: 'n Lewe, Pretoria: Protea Boekhuis, 2008.

Kearney, J. 'Representations of Islamic Belief and Practice in a South African Context: Reflections on the Fictional Work of Ahmed Essop, Aziz Hassim, Achmat Dangor and Rayda Jacobs', *Journal of Literary Studies* 22:1–2 (2006), 138–57.

Khumalo, F. *Touch my Blood: The Early Years*, Cape Town: Umuzi, 2006.

Bitches' Brew, Johannesburg: Jacana, 2006.

Kitson, N. *Where Sixpence Lives*, London: Hogarth Press, 1987.

Kleinboer. *Midnight Missionary*, trans. J. Fouché, Cape Town: Zebra, 2006.

Kombuis, K. A. *Seks & Drugs & Boeremusiek. Die Memoires van 'n Volksverraaier*, Cape Town: Human & Rousseau, 2000.

Krog, A. *A Change of Tongue*, Johannesburg: Random House, 2003.

Country of my Skull, Johannesburg: Random House, 1998.

Krog, A., N. Mpolweni and K. Ratele. *There was this Goat: Investigating the Truth Commission Testimony of Notrose Nobomvu Konile*, Pietermaritzburg: University of KwaZulu-Natal Press, 2009.

Kuzwayo, E. *Call me Woman*, London: Women's Press, 1985.

Langenhoven, C. J. *U Dienswillige Dienaar*, Cape Town: Nasionale Pers, 1932.

Lee, H. *Body Parts: Essays in Life-Writing*, London: Chatto & Windus, 2005.

Lötter, E. *It's me, Anna*, trans. M. Thamm, Cape Town: Kwela Books, 2005.

Magona, S. *Forced to Grow*, Cape Town: David Phillip, 1992.

Living, Loving, and Lying Awake at Night, Cape Town: David Philip, 1991.

Mother to Mother, Cape Town: David Philip, 1998.

To my Children's Children, Cape Town: David Philip, 1990.

Malan, R. *My Traitor's Heart: Blood and Bad Dreams: A South African Explores the Madness in his Country, his Tribe and Himself*, London: Vintage Books, 1990.

Marble, J. *Ek, Joseph Daniel Marble*, Cape Town: Kwela Books, 1999.

Mathabane, M. *Kaffir Boy: Growing out of Apartheid* [1986], London: Bodley Head, 1987.

McClintock, A. 'Maidens, Maps and Mines: *King Solomon's Mines* and the Reinvention of Patriarchy in Colonial South Africa', in C. Walker (ed.), *Women and Gender in Southern Africa to 1945*, Cape Town: David Philip and London: James Currey, 1990, 97–124.

McKerron, S., and Ferrus, D. (eds.). *Slaan Vir My 'n Masker, Vader*, Bellville: Diana Ferrus, 2006.

Opland, J. *Xhosa Oral Poetry: Aspects of a Black South African Tradition*, Cambridge University Press, 1983.

Plaatje, S. T. *The Boer War Diary of Sol T. Plaatje: An African at Mafeking*, London: Sphere Books, 1976.

Ramphele, M. *A Life*, Cape Town: David Philip, 1995.

Roos, H. 'Die Afrikaanse Prosa 1997 tot 2002', in Van Coller, *Perspektief en Profiel*, 43–104.

Rostan, K. 'The Ethics of Infidelity in *Country of my Skull*', *Current Writing: Text and Reception in Southern Africa* 19:2 (2007), 144–62.

Rothmann, M. E. *My Beskeie Deel: 'n Outobiografiese Vertelling*, Cape Town: Tafelberg, 1972.

Saayman, S. '"Writing is travelling unfolding its own landscape". A Discussion with Breyten Breytenbach on *A Veil of Footsteps*', *Tydskrif vir Letterkunde* 46:2 (2009), 201–12.

Schoeman, K. *Die Laaste Afrikaanse Boek: Outobiografiese Aantekeninge*, Cape Town: Human & Rousseau, 2002.

Die Noorderlig, Cape Town: Human & Rousseau, 1975.

Promised Land: A Novel, trans. M. V. Friedman, London: J. Friedmann, 1978.

Scott, P. E. *Samuel Edward Krune Mqhayi, 1875–1945: A Bibliographic Survey*, Communication 5, Grahamstown: Department of African Languages, Rhodes University, 1976.

Slovo, G. *Every Secret Thing: My Family, my Country*, New York: Little, Brown, 1997.

Smit, E. *The Diary of Erasmus Smit*, Cape Town: Struik, 1972.

Steyn, J. C. *Die 100 Jaar van MER*, Cape Town: T. Fafelberg, 2004.

Hoeke Boerseuns ons Was, Cape Town: Tafelberg, 1991.

Sonkyker: Afrikaner in die Verkeerde Eeu, Cape Town: Tafelberg, 2008.

Van Wyk Louw, 'n Lewensverhaal, Cape Town: Tafelberg, 1998.

Stobie, C. *Somewhere in the Double Rainbow: Representation of Bi-Sexuality in Post-Apartheid Novels*, Pietermaritzburg: University of KwaZulu-Natal Press, 2007.

Trichardt, L. *Die Dagboek van Louis Trigardt*, ed. T. H. le Roux, Pretoria: Van Schaik, 1966.

Van Coller, H. P. (ed.). *Perspektief en Profiel: 'n Afrikaanse Literatuurgeskiedenis*, vol. III, Pretoria: Van Schaik, 2005.

Van der Post, L. *The Lost World of the Kalahari* [1958], London: Vintage, 2004.

Venture to the Interior [1952], Harmondsworth: Penguin, 1957.

Van Heerden, P. *Kerssnuitsels*, Cape Town: Tafelberg, 1962.

Die Sestiende Koppie, Cape Town: Tafelberg, 1965.

Van den Heever, C. M. *My Jeugland*, Pretoria: Afrikaanse Pers Boekhandel, 1953.

Van Meerhof, P. 'Naar Het Land van de Namaqua's', in V. Roeper and R. van Gelder (eds.), *In Dienst van de Compagnie. Leven Bij de VOC in Honderd Getuigenissen (1602–1799)*, Amsterdam: Athenaeum-Polak and Van Gennep, 2002, 90–5.

Van Niekerk, A. '"Finding my own Voice?" Women's Ego Texts from the South African War – A Genre Exploration', *Stilet* 13:2 (2001), 103–22.

Van Riebeeck, J. *Journals of Jan van Riebeeck*, 3 vols., ed. and trans. H. B. Thom, Cape Town: Van Riebeeck Society, 1952–8.

Van Wyk, C. *Shirley, Goodness and Mercy: A Childhood Memoir*, Johannesburg: Picador, 2004.

Van Wyk Smith, M. *Grounds of Contest: A Survey of South African English Literature*, Cape Town: Jutalit, 1990.

Venter, F. A. *Kambro-kind, 'n Jeugreis*, Cape Town: Tafelberg, 1979.

Viljoen, L. 'Nationalism, Gender and Sexuality in the Autobiographical Writing of Two Afrikaner Women', *Social Dynamics* 34:2 (2008), 186–202.

''n "Tussenin-Boek": Enkele Gedagtes oor Liminaliteit in Breyten Breytenbach se *Woordwerk*', *Stilet* 17:2 (2005), 1–25.

Westermann, D. 'Samuel Edward Krune Mqhayi, ein Südafrikanischer Dichter', in D. Westermann (ed. and trans.), *Afrikaner Erzählen ihr Leben*, Essen: Essener Verlagsanstalt, 1938.

Willemse, C. *Met 'n Diepe Verlange*, Cape Town: Human & Rousseau, 2006.

Willemse, H. *Aan die Ander Kant: Swart Afrikaanse Skrywers in die Afrikaanse Letterkunde*, Pretoria: Protea Boekhuis, 2007.

Wolpe, A. *The Long Way Home*, London: Virago, 1994.

35

'A change of tongue': questions of translation

LEON DE KOCK

Speaking from a South African point of view, translation, or a 'change of tongue' (in the words of the multilingual poet and self-translator Antjie Krog) is both a mode of being in the colony/postcolony as well as a form of writing. That is to say, before one is able to talk meaningfully about translation as an act of writing and as a way of delivering literary-symbolic goods, one must first go into what Zoë Wicomb, relying on J. M. Coetzee, calls the 'yard of Africa' ('Translations', p. 209) and pick one's way through the uneven trading of identity via language and the fraught 'translation' of subjectivities in that 'yard' of colonisation and its aftermath.

Indeed, colonisation and its cognate, conflict, are what yield writing in Southern Africa, as Michael Chapman has argued (*Southern African Literatures*, pp. 1–16). It is an established article of knowledge in southern African studies that prior to the 350 or so years of colonial and neocolonial rule in this region, non-literate or oral cultures held sway. And, when the Book arrived on the shores of the Cape, along with the printing press, it was centrally implicated in a process of 'conversion' that by now has been well documented: 'heathens' and 'barbarians' had to be pacified and induced into a culture in which they would, by indoctrination, inculcation and violence, both physical and epistemic, become receptive to book learning. The very identities of various others, indeed the flesh of their subjectivities, had to be 'translated' in such a way that they could become participants in a culture of book learning, of writing and ultimately of a broad form of translation. Identities, modalities of cognition and culture, indeed the very accents of being, its language and its expressive forms, were implicated in this process.

Two modes of translation

It is thus necessary to speak about two principal and co-implicated modes of translation. The first, as suggested, is what we may wish to call identity or subjectivity translation. In consequence of this momentous sociohistorical, cultural and material event, what we may call writerly translation emerges as a dominant mode of expression in southern Africa. The two modes of translation are thoroughly implicated in each other. Coming out of an oral culture (if one were to compress history into storyline), one does not simply take up the quill and calmly commence writing, seamlessly moving on, or away, from the base camp of indigenous, other than literate culture. On the contrary, along with the quill in hand, and the printing press in sight, most often, come a change of tongue, a new set of clothes, altered forms of social organisation and religious or spiritual observation, and, at base, transformed and transforming modes of being in the midst of such restructured or reinterpellated subjectivity. That is, by the time that quill comes to be taken up, an entire, although uneven (some would say messy, only half-successful, asymmetrical, 'hybrid' or 'syncretic') translation of subjectivity into socially constituted identities will in most cases have partially occurred and still be in process. Like all translations, however, the original text, or the source code, is never obliterated, and it continues to talk, in implicit dialogue, with its translated versions – or what some might call its transculturated versions of itself within a 'rewriting', an appropriation, of modernity.[1]

It should be fairly obvious, then, that writing out of cultures other than 'English', in Southern Africa, into English, whether through translation or self-translation (about which, more below), involves in its very substrate of content, the (mostly asymmetrical) translations of subjectivity between what one might style, for the sake of shorthand, English and non-English (although other coordinates of translation, not altogether as frequent, also exist in Southern Africa). I say this not only because this chapter is about questions of translation in a region dominated by English, but also because the textures in the space of 'trans' – translation, transformation, transfiguration – become the very ground of the region's various and many acts of writing.

Literary processes in southern Africa

A related point was made in 1989 by Stephen Gray, a key figure in South African literary historiography, when he argued that South African literature,

1 See Attwell, *Rewriting Modernity*. On the terms 'subjectivity' and 'identity': in the wake of much twentieth-century work on the idea, 'subjectivity' is here seen as related to questions of power, historical period and culture, in that these factors establish *structures or conditions of possibility* for the nature of subjectivity in a general sense. One might think of subjectivity (or possible subject positions) standing in relation to the concept of 'identity' as deep structure does to surface structure or *langue* to *parole* – even more simply as something like what is meant by the form / content distinction. I am grateful to Susan van Zyl in helping me to formulate the distinction between subjectivity and identity.

though similar to other literary systems, did in fact have a certain claim to exceptionalism. '*Unlike* other literary systems,' he wrote in an essay called 'Some Problems of Writing Historiography in Southern Africa', adding the emphasis to the word 'unlike' himself, 'the total literary production of our system stretches across a vast spectrum of cultural manifestations, from Stone Age to TV.' And he added, once again italicising for causal emphasis,

> *therefore* our system does have some norms peculiar to it . . . the writer is always forced into a position of having to negotiate between extremes, into crossing the language-colour barrier; he or she can only be a syncretist and hybridiser. And *therefore* the basic act of writing is one of carrying information across one or another socio-economic barrier, literally of 'trading'.

This led Gray to come up with the following 'identikit portrait': 'The writer exists at any of several boundaries (*not* at the centre of one self-enclosed group); his or her act of making literature is part of transferring data across that boundary, from one audience to another – an act which in its broadest sense may be termed "translation"' ('Some Problems', pp. 20–1).

If one accepts Gray's argument, then translation must be seen as central to the literary processes of southern Africa. And, in consequence of that argument, one of the key sources of identity 'trading' is surely to be found in print-based missionary interaction, where a form of modality translation saw persistent attempts to transcode oral expressive modes, and diverse, often non-Christian spiritual practice, as well as practices of material culture, into forms of culture and daily life located in the predominantly Protestant ethos brought to southern Africa by missionaries (see also Chapter 10 above).

Further, processes such as these relied to a very great extent on the existence and continued refinement of a growing culture of print, and on the reification of the book as a pre-eminent source of both knowledge and human understanding in a normative sense.

That is to say, a widespread culture of the book, and of print, made it possible both to inscribe in the subjectivities of 'captive' audiences – in mission schoolrooms, mission school debating societies, newspapers edited by missionary graduates for African consumption, mission book culture, mission-educated social networks and so on – behavioural blueprints and to encode such attempts at behavioural and spiritual modification within deterministic modes of *literary* representation.

Translation and asymmetrical 'trading'

Translation in such a context means a lot more than the mere writerly act of rendering a work in one language into another. Translation, here, occupies the transitive space, where 'transitive' is understood as 'passing over to or affecting something else; operating beyond itself' and is 'characterised by or involving transition, in various senses' (shorter *OED*, 1973).

However, it must be understood that such transitive 'trading' is by no means a practice that is as technically neutral, as reciprocal and systemically equal, or as balanced, as Gray's description (above) would seem to suggest. Indeed, as Zoë Wicomb, a South African writer who is herself engaged in continuing acts of cultural translation in her own fiction, writes in her essay 'Translations in the Yard of Africa', despite theories of ethical translation (based on trust, where she cites George Steiner on the 'enactment of reciprocity' as the core matter of interlingual translation), and despite Homi Bhabha's notion of 'newness [coming] into the world' (where migrant subjectivity in the process of transition/translation retains something of the residual of the source text), the evidence suggests that (1) the intersubjectivity necessary for the Steiner model of translation (given an 'asymmetry of domination' in the colony) does not properly exist; and (2) the 'invariants of the old regime [are] horribly present in the new translations' (p. 222), weakening Bhabha's 'newness' hypothesis. Wicomb makes this conclusion about so-called 'post-apartheid' culture in relation to J. M. Coetzee's novel *Disgrace*, which, for her, 'declares the failure of transition as a crossing over to democracy' (p. 222). Wicomb argues that in Coetzee's 'desolate yard in Africa' (where David Lurie's banjo 'squawks' rather than sings), Bhabha's 'conflation of translation and an emancipatory transition is unthinkable' (p. 222). For Wicomb, too, Lawrence Venuti's dissident cultural politics of 'abusive fidelity' in the act of postcolonial translation is 'impossible to map on to the condition of migrancy' (p. 211). For her, such happily transgressive 'abusive fidelity' in the southern African scene is by no means easily or optimistically achievable.

Eva-Krotoä

To make the point, Wicomb recalls the story of Eva-Krotoä. Wicomb frames her account in the context, or against the grain, of Bhabha citing Fanon on a 'liberatory people' constructing their culture 'from a national text translated into modern western forms of information technology, language, dress', or, as Wicomb paraphrases the position, '[assuming] agency in the process of translation', where the 'act of sartorial transformation does not compromise the native's cultural integrity' (p. 212). This is a familiar strain in postcolonial renditions of transculturated subjectivity in which notions of hybridity and syncretism have been invoked in emancipatory, affirmative, resistance talk. Krotoä was an indigenous Khoikhoi woman who was taken up by the Dutch authorities after their arrival at the Cape in 1652. She learnt to speak Dutch and Portuguese and became known as 'Eva, the interpreter', developing a reputation as a mediator between the Dutch and the indigenous people. However, Krotoä's story of identity translation is characterised by what Wicomb calls 'psychic violence'. She married Pieter van Meerhof in 1664, engaging in the first native–settler marriage, but he died early and Krotoä is subsequently said to have 'degenerated into drunkenness and prostitution'. Crucial to Wicomb's argument, against subsequent attempts to install Krotoä as 'originary Mother of the Afrikaner' by contemporary cultural theorists, is the act that leads to her being expelled to Robben Island. Wicomb writes: 'Her story climaxes in an exquisite moment on February 8, 1669, at a grand colonial gathering where, in a classic Calibanesque gesture, she hurls drunken abuse "within the hearing of the Commander"' (p. 215). This event, which eventuates in her banishment to the famous island, is, for Wicomb a speech-act which 'falls between her two names, pushing them asunder: the assimilated Eva who is admitted to the Governor's presence, and Krotoä, the indigene who asserts her otherness by disturbing the grand event'. In addition, 'Krotoä the "savage" asserts her untranslatability, refusing to be the source text for Eva, the "citizen"'. Similarly, in Wicomb's reading of *Disgrace*, 'pathologies can be read as elements of the untranslatable, the residue of apartheid – an overarching intertext – that continues its vulgar influences on its subjects'. Where translation does appear to operate, writes Wicomb, 'it inevitably carries the residue of apartheid'. She concludes: 'We are then according to *Disgrace* hamstrung by the double bind of translatability and untranslatability, and the modalities of the past – sex, race, violence – continue to prevail, carrying with them the echo of Eva-Krotoä's curses' (pp. 221–2). Wicomb means this conclusion to carry well beyond merely an interpretation of the novel *Disgrace*. The practices of translation in South African writing, one may suggest, are more generally implicated in the kind of double bind Wicomb describes, often imparting a particular urgency – and pathos – to the literature of the region.

Interstitial writing and the seam

Wicomb's argument speaks to the idea that South African writing should be characterised as *interstitial*, in that it carries a perpetual sense of emergence from within division and difference: multiple language streams, polyglot cultural difference, and incommensurate bodies of material and cultural practice (illustrated in the fact that the country has eleven official languages). The only way to bridge the gap from the first-person singular to the first-person plural, from 'I' to 'us' (and therefore from subject to nation in political terms), is via the transitive zone, where literary acts cross over, trying to suture the fissures of language, culture, class, race, ethnicity and gender. But in doing so, the mark of the suture remains: a representational seam, inscribing difference in the same moment that it seeks to smooth it out, conjoin it or resolve it. This transitive–translational seam, I would argue, in its various forms has come to mark, to scar, one might say, what we today talk about as 'South African' writing.[2]

So, were one to seek a symbolic source object, a moment of origin, in the what we now call 'South African literature', one might variously cite the (translated) oral San trance song invoking the shamanic power of hunted animals, the (translated) epic account of Portuguese seafaring around the Cape, the (translated) Dutch register of occupation (for example, Jan van Riebeeck's diary), the imperial English explorer's travel journal, the (translated) French naturalist/scientific narrative of the Eastern Cape (François le Vaillant) or the Scottish Romantic ballad (for example, Thomas Pringle's 'The Bechuana Boy'). The two English texts in this list occupy the colonial master-language, and therefore need no literal translation, but they remain, unavoidably, accounts of cultural translation, as are the rest. The search for origins in South African literature, then, takes one up and down the loops of the transitive–translative experiential and representational trace, or seam.

The 'Bushman' archive and cultural
cross-appropriation

Another emblematic case of cultural translation conjoined with interlingual translation is the famous Bleek-Lloyd archive of San orality. It is impossible to write any kind of account of the multiply constellated concept of 'South African writing' or 'South African culture' without weaving through the Bleek-Lloyd story, and it is a story of translation at several critical levels of

2 For a full discussion of the 'seam' theory, see De Kock, 'South Africa in the Global Imaginary'.

procedure (see Chapter 1 in this volume for a more detailed discussion). The shorter route is via Bleek and Lloyd's *Specimens of Bushman Folklore*, published in 1911 and republished as a facsimile reprint by a South African publisher, Struik, in 1968. This book contains what it calls mythology, fables, legends, and poetry.

What is crucial here is that the Bleek-Lloyd archival restitution of a large oral cultural trace, implicated as it was in interlingual as well as cultural translation, has been compulsively reappropriated, and retranslated, from a (now somewhat archaic) Victorian English transcript, into various contemporary registers and idioms. Not only has South African writing seen such appropriations of the |Xam lyrics and stories (for example, by poets Stephen Watson, Alan James and Antjie Krog),[3] but these very appropriations have become the subject of culture wars involving allegations of (improper) appropriation of other writers' material, within an even larger context of public accusations of cultural vampirism in memorialising and feting the Bushman (for example, in the *Miscast* exhibition, curated by Pippa Skotnes in 1996 in Cape Town).

In an important sense, then, the trace of origins and of emergence in what has become known as 'South African' writing, very often takes its shape, or finds its track, within the transitive–translational seam. This accounts for the fact that what people most often mean when they use the term 'South African writing' is actually 'South African writing *in English*', which, in a bland systemic account, is really just one of several 'literatures', written in several languages, in and of South Africa. However, the English stream has accrued arguably the most weight and come to stand in for the other literatures because it carries the greatest burden of 'crossing over', or is the most common and widely read language in the process of South African transitive seaming/seeming, in which, one must add, *seeming* to be *not other to itself* is a central conceit, that is, implicitly seeking to deny its translational nature. Alternatively, in its inaugural phases, the writing celebrates actually being other to everything 'English' in the British sense, despite being written in a language native to England, and so stories about deluded Boers, anthropomorphised animals, 'wild' heathens and savages, and exotic treasures and tropics, abound.

Crossovers

If a 'national' culture can be seen to exist in South Africa, then, it exists in translation, in a literature of compulsive crossing over.

3 See Alan James, *The First Bushman's Path* (2001); Stephen Watson, *Return of the Moon* (1991); and Antjie Krog, *the stars say 'tsau'* (2004).

So, one of the most widely taken up works in South African writing in any language or genre, Antje Krog's multigenre, many-voiced act of narrative ventriloquism, *Country of my Skull* (1998), is a book which, essentially, seeks to translate the experience of pain and trauma from barely reachable repositories of subjectivity and cultural specificity into a more generally accessible idiom. In doing this, Krog is implicated in various acts of translation: her own native-tongue registers of Afrikaans into English, the more general, literal translation of testimony at the Truth and Reconciliation Commission (TRC) from various languages into English; the translation, or recasting, of pain-inflected utterance into the substrate of literary record and aesthetic statement; the interpretative 'translation' of this testimony, and its effect/affect, into a national imaginary, a shared language, of mutuality.

However, preceding Krog in the historical record of literary work in the transitive zone of translational writing, of crossing over, were similar acts of socially burdened translation, freighted with momentous experiential transition, such as the massive undertaking to translate the Bible into isiXhosa and other indigenous languages, preceded by great and onerous labours among missionaries and their agents to settle upon orthographies for the written renditions of indigenous languages. Between 1833, for example, when the first isiXhosa translation of a section of the Bible was published by Wesleyans William Boyce and Barnabas Shaw, and 1864, when the first complete Bible in isiXhosa was published (by the British and Foreign Bible Society), sustained work was ploughed into these acts of translation because they were seen as key to creating a form of commonality out of the materials of difference. (On various other Bible translation histories involving vernacular languages, see Hermanson, 'Brief Overview', pp. 13–16; see also Doke, 'Scripture Translation'.)

In more recent times, the impetus to engage in translational crossovers as a compulsive seeking after common ground has found expression in multiple translations of Nelson Mandela's *Long Walk to Freedom*, in a coordinated project which saw Antje Krog render the text into Afrikaans (*Lang Pad na Vryheid*, 2000), D. B. Z. Ntuli into isiZulu (*Uhambo olude oluya enkululekweni*, 2001), S. M. Serudu into Sepedi (*Leetotelele go ya tokologong*, 2001) and Peter Mtuze into isiXhosa (*Indlela ende eya enkululekweni*, 2001). A similar initiative was launched through UNISA Press, which saw the production of multiply translated Zakes Mda plays. These plays, written in English but speaking to black experience in cosmopolitan settings, were then translated into isiZulu, isiXhosa, SiSwati, isiNdebele, Sesotho, Sepedi, Setswana, Tshivenda and Xitsonga. Although this publishing exercise, according to information conveyed to me during my tenure as a member of the governing board of UNISA Press, was not a commercial success, the desire to cross and re-cross every possible bridge of language and experience speaks resonantly to the condition of a 'national' culture finding its measure most urgently, most iteratively and compulsively, in the seam of translation.

Complexities of translation in the work of Marlene van Niekerk

The translation of the work of Marlene van Niekerk, a leading contemporary writer currently working from within South Africa, brings to the fore several of the complexities of translation described in this chapter. In this section, I discuss some of the dynamics inherent in my own translation of Van Niekerk's iconoclastic novel, *Triomf*, which is widely regarded as a dissident, comic explosion of the sanctities of Afrikanerdom – and its pious myths of cultural purity.

Triomf was written on the eve of democratic transition and first published in 1994; its translation posed severe challenges because the novel incorporates both code-breaking and code-switching. That is, it breaks the primary rule, for a serious work in the Afrikaans literary tradition, of linguistic purity; it will not participate in the refusal to translate itself, or the refusal to concede an inherent bastardisation. Not only is the Afrikaans spoken by *Triomf*'s characters studded with slang, foul language and gross impurities of diction, it also combines English words and phrases in a form of low-life Afrikaans, committing a deliberate calumny upon the culturally sanctified ideal of 'civilised' ('algemeen beskaafde') Afrikaans, or ABA. Needless to say, the ABA ideal of linguistic fencing-off amid a Babel of tongues in the wilderness of Africa was an ideological priority in whose name the very institution of 'Afrikaans literature' came into being. It was a 'literature' constructed from within a white ideological camp which mustered a 'pure' form of Afrikaans to draw iron-tight boundaries of race and class against 'black' influences on its language. From the very beginning of its official life as a politically and culturally sanctified white African language, Afrikaans had repressed its linguistic origins in admixtures of Malay and 'unwhite' Cape 'impurities', including the broad tributary of coloured Afrikaans. In view of this conservative tradition, the importance of Van Niekerk's code-breaking should be clear: as a fiery Afrikaner dissident she was determined to reveal just how contaminated such putative purity was in the mouths of the Afrikaner working class, the 'white trash' who were the voting fodder of Afrikaner Nationalist politicians. In Van Niekerk's novelistic vision, these politicians were looting the national treasury prior to selling out the white working class, whose 'culture' they had vowed to protect against the black peril, but in the end they ran off with the money instead, leaving their lower-class voting dupes to deal with democracy all on their own, a moneyless minority with neither power nor legitimacy. The entire edifice of Afrikaans literature, for Van Niekerk, had been built on just such a deception of privileged purity, and so as an Afrikaans writer she felt impelled to turn the language inside out, to give air to its actual, bastardised state, to give the lie to everything the vaunted tradition of Afrikanerdom had constructed so painfully since the rise of white nationalism in the early twentieth century. (Revealing the underlying 'bastardisation' of Afrikaner identity, indeed celebrating it, is a major impulse in the work of celebrated Afrikaans dissident poet Breyten Breytenbach, too.)

Van Niekerk's characters in *Triomf* therefore speak in a bastardised urban sociolect in which English and Afrikaans are mixed up in a degenerate, rich patois. How, then, does one 'translate' this kind of code-switching between Afrikaans and South African English, when such 'switching' itself is usually the work of the translation but is here used as a key device in the source text itself to signify cultural creolisation? This is an example in which 'cultural translation' is incorporated into the primary language of the original text in 'already-translated' passages of writing, or half-translated segues across the linguistic and experiential seam, freely code-switching between what would normally be the 'source language' and the 'target language'. Here, for me, was a supreme example of *traduttore, traditore* – to translate is to betray. In the end, I refused to betray, meaning I refused, in certain instances, to translate, to render the heteroglossic text monoglossic, or to translate monolingually. Assuming a South African publisher and an audience that would understand the code-switching in *Triomf* from within a reasonably bilingual culture (in terms of English and Afrikaans), I allowed, for example, the supremely syncretic, culturally hybrid character Sonnyboy in chapter 13 of the novel to enunciate his multiply mixed identity in his own, untranslatable South African argot. This pivotal passage of (non)translation reads as follows:

> 'Kyk, daai's nou my luck in Jo'burg gewies, nè! Ek's 'n Xhosa, ek kom van die Transkei af. En ek's maar so.' He touches his face. 'Toe dag die Boesmans ek's ok 'n Boesman, toe kry ek 'n room in Bosmont tussen hulle. En hulle praat met my regte coloured Afrikaans. En toe leer ek maar so on the sly en ek sê fokol, want hoe minder 'n Boesman van jou af weet, hoe beter. Dis 'n bad scene, die Boesmanscene. Hulle lê dronk en suip en steel en steek jou met messe en goed . . . ' (van Niekerk, *Triomf* [SA version], pp. 227–8)

The only sentence I translated in this entire passage was 'He touches his face.' The passage represents a moment of utterly candid self-description which struck me as untranslatable in a sense that goes beyond linguistic or idiomatic untranslatability. I felt that Sonnyboy's description of himself *enacted* the hybridity of identity into which he had been inducted in the course of surviving outside of South Africa's white camps. Sonnyboy can talk Xhosa (and, in all probability, other indigenous languages, too), and when addressing Lambert he can adjust his lexicon to an Afrikaans in which he both mixes in English ('luck', 'on the sly', 'room', 'bad scene') and in which he distances himself from what he calls 'Coloured Afrikaans', a dialect he is telling the white character Lambert he picked up 'on the sly' while pretending to be coloured as a result of what he claims is the yellowish pallor of his 'Xhosa' skin. By contrast, Lambert can speak only Afrikaans and broken English. They are both low-life characters, and although Lambert *thinks* he is superior because he is white, the events of the chapter show that he is not, and that Sonnyboy is more resourceful, agile and in touch with the complexities of his shifting environment, not to mention a good deal more intelligent. If any character in *Triomf* is a 'true South African', it is Sonnyboy, culturally hybrid, linguistically diverse, street-smart and fully indigenised. His enunciations enact these characteristics. To some extent, Sonnyboy's very being – his irremediable hybridity, his means of survival – rests on the tip of his versatile tongue. To *translate* such a mélange of mixed speech into the pallid registers of 'standard English' struck me as a monstrous betrayal, a denaturing of Sonnyboy's necessary specificity. If Sonnyboy stands in for an interracial South African self that proposes an alternative, to some extent, to single-stranded ethnic impositions and machinations of political identity, then how does one blandly go and strip him of precisely his multivocality in the name of translation? I would not do it.

But I was forced to do it, in the end, when a British multinational publisher (Little, Brown) offered the author a contract for the English translation of *Triomf*. Realising that there was now no way out, I approached the author and suggested that I present *two* versions of the translation, one for the South African publisher Jonathan Ball, and a 'fully translated' version for Little, Brown. Van Niekerk agreed, and so the translation now exists in two variants, a 'South African' version and an 'international' version. In the international version, the above passage is rendered as follows:

> 'Look, that's how the dice fell for me here in Jo'burg. I'm a Xhosa, I come from the Transkei, and some of us are yellow.' He touches his face. 'That's why

the bladdy Bushmen thought I was one of them, so I got a room in Bosmont right in among them. And they began talking real Coloured Afrikaans to me. So I got the hang of it on the sly, and I didn't say nothing, 'cause the less a Bushman knows about you, the better. It's a bad scene, the Bushman scene. They drink themselves stupid and then they rob and stab you and leave you for dead . . .' (Van Niekerk, *Triomf* [international version], p. 275)

The losses in this particular passage of translation are incalculable, but such is the compromise when a deep, compacted form of transculturation is rendered back into the so-called master-language, the source code, the site of inscription whose overweening registers of control inspired the rebellious bastardisation reflected in the barely translatable source text (previous quotation) in the first place.

It is interesting to note that in the translation of Van Niekerk's subsequent novel, *Agaat*, translator Michiel Heyns broke the codes of translation too, but in a different way. Heyns extended the allusive range of the Afrikaans original, explicitly adding T. S. Eliot's *The Four Quartets* as an additional intertext in the translated version of the novel, among other allusive additions (for a fuller discussion of this, see De Kock, 'Found in Translation', p. 18). The text of *Agaat* enabled this extension to its range of reference because its assemblage was always already inter-referential, in dialogue with texts and ideas outside of its immediate experiential range (although intensely rendered from within that range) in a way that speaks to Van Niekerk's writerly imperative to break through limit conditions and to create cascading frames of understanding and reading, in contradistinction to the frames in which her characters are often trapped. Van Niekerk's texts embody a condition of cultural and linguistic fluidity – a crossing and recrossing of fences and boundaries of all kinds – that render translation both problematic and potentially transgressive. Her fiction speaks to the need to translate at a deeper level of complexity than is normally associated with the already great difficulties of literary translation from source language to target language. Specifically, the co-implicated conditions of, on the one hand, what I have called cultural translation, and 'regular' translation on the other, come together in Van Niekerk's fiction in a manner that speaks resonantly of the peculiarly transitive conditions of writing in and of South Africa.

Afrikaans writing

English, one might say, is the language that, ironically, today carries the greatest burden of transitive convergence. For an Afrikaans novel to be translated into English, for example, has become a special mark of success. Why? Because it potentially globalises the novel's reception, and it means the novel gets written twice: once in the writer's native language, redolent of the younger, arguably less trodden registers of indigenous Afrikaans, and once in the now enriched and transcoded registers of an ever so slightly transformed English. Even if one were fully to take Wicomb's point about the 'double bind of translatability and untranslatability', translation into English for a non-English text means that the text now enjoys a double life, both in terms of communities of readers, and in the sense that the text is doubled, in representational terms, and comes to reside in a mirror condition. It perpetually mirrors another version of itself, and displays the play and torsion of that cross-appropriation. At the same time, it consists of writing that, in itself (that is, before interlingual translation) is implicated in cultural translation, in a perpetual contestation with otherness. It is surely no accident that two of the best writers the country has yielded, Breyten Breytenbach and Marlene van Niekerk, use the mirror-concept as pivots in their work (Breytenbach, explicitly in his prison narrative, *Mouroir: Mirrornotes of a Novel* (1984), and van Niekerk as a leading structural motif in *Agaat*).

Breytenbach (1983) is probably the most skilful Afrikaans poet alive, and his writing of *Mouroir* at first partly in English and then entirely so (1984) marks a choice, a change of tongue willingly undertaken, within the transitive–translational seam. One could speculate why Breytenbach chose neither to have this work translated from an Afrikaans original nor to write the work himself separately in both English and Afrikaans (there are all manner of possible political, aesthetic and contextual reasons), but it remains remarkable that, from the publication of *Mouroir* to the present day, Breytenbach's writing has more or less bifurcated: lyrical prose (often memoirist writing) has emerged in English, while his poetry has continued to appear in Afrikaans (some of it translated, although the untranslatability level is very high in Breytenbach's Afrikaans poetry as a result of its intricate wordplay and the rootedness of its expression). Such a willed bifurcation in the language of writing is not unique (compare Joseph Conrad and Vladimir Nabokov), but it is most unusual to *continue* to write in two languages, one language for one genre, another for a second genre, as a habit, and it says a lot about the location of the writer in and of South Africa in a necessarily transitive space.

Two other major Afrikaans writers, André P. Brink and Antjie Krog, occupy this space in a slightly different way. Brink is renowned for his 'simultaneous' novel writing in both English and Afrikaans, a process in which he composes novels in both languages more or less at the same time, and then releases them in both languages simultaneously, evincing a most extraordinary versatility of writing that has emerged from the transitive condition. Krog, on the other hand – at least in the case of her most internationally famous book, *Country of my Skull* – reworks her own Afrikaans text into English before publication. However, in her more recent book, *A Change of Tongue* / *'n Ander Tongval*, she self-translated her original Afrikaans text for the English version, which appeared in 2002, and then subsequently allowed the original Afrikaans text to be published (in 2005). The intricacies of this process, both sociopolitical and aesthetic, could take up a study all on its own.

These maestros of the interstitial writing space, these auto-translators, have a distinct advantage over other writers precisely because they have seized the full potential of the transitive nature of the South African writing context. Not only do they refuse to surrender their texts to delegated translators, in whose hands their works could easily slip out of their own writerly control and design, but they also appropriate to themselves the double-agency of writing not once, but twice, for two distinct audiences – one local (including the global locals) and one global (including the local globals) – thereby striking two drums in an alternation of dialogic, interreferential textuality.

Black writing

It would be a mistake, however, to imagine that the multilayered complexities of translation as a condition of writing are restricted to the play of English and Afrikaans. To the contrary, most of the country's historical negotiations of identity have occurred in a translational politics situated at the intersection of English and several indigenous languages flowing from the Nguni and Sotho mainstreams. This has yielded what we have come to think of as 'black' writing in English, although in several cases English has also been translated back into indigenous languages, mostly in the form of canonical instructional texts such as Bunyan's *The Pilgrim's Progress*, some of Shakespeare's plays, the Bible and other Christian texts. Famous examples include Sol T. Plaatje's translations of Shakespeare into Setswana and the rendering of the King James Bible into indigenous languages.[4] A. C. Jordan's rendering into English of Xhosa folklore (*Tales from Southern Africa*) and the Bleek-Lloyd archive, condensed to some extent in *Specimens of Bushman Folklore*, illustrate the co-implication

---

4 On Plaatje's translations of Shakespeare, see Willan, *Sol Plaatje*, p. 308. Plaatje translated four of Shakespeare's plays, two of which were published: *Diposho-phoso* (*A Comedy of Errors*, Morija: Morija Printing Works, 1930); and *Dintshontsho tsa bo-Juliuse Kesara* (*Julius Caesar*, Johannesburg: Witwatersrand University Press, 1937). The two translations that appear to have been lost are *Much Ado About Nothing* and *The Merchant of Venice*.

of literal or writerly translation with cultural translation. Black writers all the way from the nineteenth through to the twentieth centuries have been engaged in similar acts of cultural translation into English, translating both their senses of self as well as specific texts between indigenous languages and English. A list of such figures would start with Tiyo Soga, the first ordained black minister in the Cape, stretching through to and beyond figures as diverse as John Tengo Jabavu, D. D. T. Jabavu, John Dube, Magema Magwaza Fuze, Isaac Wauchope, John Knox Bokwe and Sol T. Plaatje: all writers who were often forced into polemic in English in periodicals and books simply to hold a line of perceived accuracy in a transitive zone where cultural mistranslations were legion. In the twentieth century more explicitly creative writers such as the Dhlomo brothers, the so-called 'Drum' writers of the 1950s, and the many writers who were forced into exile, including Es'kia Mphahlele, Lewis Nkosi, Peter Abrahams, Dennis Brutus, Mazisi Kunene and scores more, were chronically engaged in acts of representational seaming in English, re-presenting the South African 'case' to an international audience. The successors of these writers, figures such as Zakes Mda, Njabulo Ndebele, K. Sello Duiker, Phaswane Mpe and others, would take this project further by grasping the possibilities of experimentalism in black writing in English, once again retranslating the idioms of writing in 'English' from a 'black' point of view.

An emblematic example of 'black' writing in the transitive–translational seam is A. C. Jordan's literary classic, *The Wrath of the Ancestors* (1980). Its original appearance was as the novel *Ingqumbo Yeminyanya* (1940), in which the story is told, in isiXhosa, of the 'wrath of the ancestors' when Xhosa subjects turn their back on traditional forms of culture in the face of modernisation. As such, the novel speaks to the complexities of cultural cross-appropriation. This impetus, so pronounced in this case, to give voice across difference is taken further when Jordan, with the help of his wife, Phyllis Jordan, auto-translates the novel into English as *The Wrath of the Ancestors*. In 1995 an Afrikaans translation, *Die Toorn van die Voorvaders* (trans. S. J. Neethling) appeared, capturing a South African Translators' Institute translation award in 2000.

As in the case of Afrikaans writing, translation serves here not only to facilitate crossovers in a literary-cultural field crucially defined by difference, it also signals a second-order existence for selected works, usually the more memorable acts of writing in a given literary field, since the demand for translation also has much to do with the perceived centrality or importance of particular works of writing. In black South African writing, it is often the doubly published writers (once in an indigenous language, once in English, in rare cases triply or multiply translated into other languages, too, such as Mandela and Mda) who rise to prominence. So, for example, black writers who stand out for this reason, apart from A. C. Jordan, and who merit a mention in Moses N. Nintai's entry in the *Encyclopedia of Literary Translation into English* are Mazisi Kunene (translations into English of *Emperor Shaka the Great: A Zulu Epic* and *Anthem of the Decades: A Zulu Epic*); S. E. K. Mqhayi (translated by various scholars, including Jeff Opland); John Dube (his historical novel *Insila kaTshaka* translated into English as *Jege the Bodyservant of King Tshaka*); Magema Fuze (his historical work *Abantu Abamnyama Lapa Bavela Ngakhona* translated into English as *The Black People and Whence they Come: A Zulu View*); and Benedict W. Vilakazi, whose poetry, including *Inkondlo kaZulu* and *Amal' Ezulu*, has been translated into English (see Nintai, 'African Languages'). These are examples of black writers who have 'hit the seam', so to speak, and whose works have been multiply read and rewritten.

In the movement known as the 'Sestigers' (see Chapter 21) Afrikaans writers such as Brink, Breytenbach, Jan Rabie, Etienne le Roux and a number of others were reappropriating Afrikaans for an avant-garde, modernist practice that involved cultural translation from European influences back into the indigenous tradition of (often pastoralist, sentimentalist and nationalistic) Afrikaans writing. In all, such cultural and interlingual translations go to the core of the transitive zone in which subjectivities are lured into transitional modalities of cultural and material practice, belief and value systems. What is at stake in such translations is so much more than a literary act alone; the very matter of subjectivity and identity are under translation, in transit, a shuttling of being which is engaged in complex trade-offs and double binds, promises and compromises. There remains rich material for deeper and further research in areas such as this. And, as suggested above, it is not in the more explicit literary acts alone (that is, published books) that such processes can be detected. The history of 'modernisation' in what was to become known as 'South Africa' in the nineteenth and twentieth centuries, particularly in its cultural and educational guise under the supposedly benign custodianship of missionaries and educational agents, has left in its wake an enormous archive of writing in missionary periodicals, in books penned by indigenous subjects in transition / translation, in poems scattered in various forms of publication, all of which attest to a certain 'dislocation', a certain remove in which modernity is 'rewritten', transculturated precisely in the transitive–translational seam in which language and being are engaged in a process of continuous translation and retranslation.

In this sense the term translation comes into full play, across the whole range of its torsions and tensions, not to mention its scope for creative variability and 'abusive fidelity', within an overall, rich problematic of the double bind of translatability and untranslatability. It is, in many senses, the story of South African literature writ large.

Bibliography

Attwell, D. 'The Experimental Turn: Experimentalism in Contemporary Fiction', in *Rewriting Modernity: Studies in Black South African Literary History*, Pietermaritzburg: University of KwaZulu-Natal Press, 2005, 169–204.

Bleek, W. H. I., and L. C. Lloyd. *Specimens of Bushman Folklore*, London: G. Allen, 1911.

Breytenbach, B. *Mouroir: Bespieëlde Notas van 'n Roman*, Johannesburg: Taurus, 1983.

   Mouroir: Mirrornotes of a Novel, London: Faber, 1984.

Chapman, M. *Southern African Literatures*, 2nd edn, London: Longman, 2003.

De Kock, L. *Civilising Barbarians: Missionary Narrative and African Textual Response in Nineteenth-Century South Africa*, Johannesburg: Witwatersrand University Press and Alice: Lovedale Press, 1996.

   'Found in Translation' (essay on *Agaat* translation, interview with Michiel Heyns and Marlene van Niekerk), *Sunday Times Lifestyle*, 28 January 2007, 18.

   'South Africa in the Global Imaginary: An Introduction', *Poetics Today*, special issue on 'South Africa in the Global Imaginary', 22:2 (2001), 263–98; reprinted in L. de Kock, L. Bethlehem and S. Laden (eds.), *South Africa in the Global Imaginary*, Pretoria: UNISA Press and Leiden: Brill, 2004.

Doke, C. M. 'Scripture Translation into Bantu Languages', *African Studies* 17:2 (1958), 82–99.

Gagiano, A. 'Just a Touch of the Cultural Trophy-Hunter', *Die Suid-Afrikaan* (April–May 1992), 78.

Gray, S. 'Some Problems of Writing Historiography in Southern Africa', *Literator* 10:2 (1989), 16–24.

Hermanson, E. A. 'A Brief Overview of Bible Translation in South Africa', *Acta Theologica Supplementum* 2 (2002), 6–18.

James, A. *The First Bushman's Path: Stories, Songs and Testimonies of the |Xam of the Northern Cape*, Pietermaritzburg: University of Natal Press, 2001.

Jordan, A. C. *Tales from Southern Africa*, Berkeley: University of California Press, 1973.

Krog, A. *A Change of Tongue*, Johannesburg: Random House, 2003.

   Country of my Skull, Johannesburg: Random House, 1998.

Krog, Antjie (selected and adapted). *the stars say 'tsau': |Xam Poetry of Diä!kwain, Kweiten-ta-//ken, /A!kunta, /Han≠kass'o and //Kabbo*, Cape Town: Kwela Books, 2004.

Mandela, N. *Long Walk to Freedom: The Autobiography*, Randburg: Macdonald Purnell, 1994; *Lang Pad na Vryheid*, Afrikaans translation, trans. Antjie Krog, Florida Hills: Vivlia, 2000; *Leetotelele go ya Tokologong*, Southern Sotho translation, trans. M. S. Serudu, Florida Hills: Vivlia, 2001; *Uhambo olude oluya Enkululekweni*, isiZulu translation, trans. D. B. Z. Ntuli, Florida Hills: Vivlia, 2001; *Indlela ende eya Enkululekweni*, isiXhosa translation, trans. P. T. Mtuze, Florida Hills: Vivlia, 2001.

Montrose, L. A. 'Professing the Renaissance: The Poetics and Politics of Culture', in H. A. Veeser (ed.), *The New Historicism*, New York: Routledge, 1989,

Nintai, N. 'African Languages', in Olive Classe (ed.), *Encyclopedia of Literary Translation into English*, vol. 1, Chicago: Fitzroy Dearborn, 2000, 19–22.

Van Niekerk, M. *Agaat*, Cape Town: Tafelberg, 2004. Translation by M. Heyns as *Agaat*, Johannesburg: Jonathan Ball, 2006. Translation by M. Heyns as *The Way of the Women*, London: Little, Brown, 2007.

   Triomf, trans. L. de Kock (SA version), Johannesburg: Jonathan Ball, 1999. Translation by L. de Kock as *Triomf* (international version), London: Little, Brown, 1999 and New York: Overlook Press, 2004.

Watson, S. *Return of the Moon: Versions from the |Xam*, Cape Town: Carrefour Press, 1991.

Wicomb, Zoë. 'Translations in the Yard of Africa', *Journal of Literary Studies* 18:3–4 (2002), 209–23.

Willan, B. (ed.). *Sol Plaatje: Selected Writings*, Johannesburg: Witwatersrand University Press and Athens, OH: Ohio University Press, 1996.

36

Writing women

MEG SAMUELSON

Women's writing spans the periods, concerns, genres, languages and media addressed in this collection. The purpose of this chapter is not so much to provide a detailed overview of women's writing in South Africa – an impossible task within the space constraints – as to sketch out landmark publications, attending to the emergence of the female autograph and the ways in which women write women within and/or against feminist and national discourses, while exploring the following questions: Through what devices, tropes and reconstructed genealogies have women writers laid claim to artistry, authorship and textual authority? How do they represent the category of 'women' and inscribe national identity within a fractured, divided and heterogeneous polity? What representational strategies do they develop to unpick the 'patchwork quilt of patriarchies' (Bozzoli, 'Marxism', pp. 149, 155) in South Africa? [1]

The female autograph and the nation: Schreiner and Mgqwetho

Situated on opposite sides of the colonial divide, taking up different generic approaches and grappling with divergent concerns, Olive Schreiner (1855–1920) and Nontsizi Mgqwetho (published during the 1920s; date of birth and death unknown) enter into print culture an emergent national and feminist consciousness, while negotiating female authorship. The fate of their respective oeuvres is indicative of the differential challenges women have faced in coming into and remaining in print in South Africa. Schreiner's first novel, *The Story of an African Farm* (1883), was an immediate success and has achieved

---

1 More extensive representations of, or engagements with, women's writing in South Africa can be found in Clayton, *Women and Writing in South Africa*; Daymond et al., *Women Writing Africa: The Southern Region*; Daymond (ed.), *South African Feminisms*; Govinden, 'Sister Outsiders'; Coullie, *The Closest of Strangers*.

canonical status, yet it was first published under a male pseudonym (Ralph Iron). Schreiner was unable to complete the novel many regard as her magnum opus, *From Man to Man; or, Perhaps Only* . . . (1926), posthumously edited by her husband, Samuel Cronwright-Schreiner and out of print for much of the past three decades. Nonetheless, Schreiner's oeuvre and literary life has been appraised in numerous studies and biographies and her letters have been anthologised. Mgqwetho, in contrast, after 'explod[ing] on the scene' (Mgqwetho in Opland, *Nation's Bounty*, p. 252) of South African print culture in 1920, vanished from critical view until her rediscovery by Jeff Opland, who has gathered her 102 poems and short prose pieces into a translated and annotated collection. Biographical information on Mgqwetho is thin, and her fate, following the publication of her last poem in January 1929, unknown. Like Schreiner, however, she too claimed the authority of authorship – of both texts and the nation they represent – by taking up and adapting a masculine voice.

Schreiner's foreword to the second edition of *African Farm* reveals that she consciously positioned herself against the colonial romance to inscribe a grounded view of an emergent nation (see Chapter 33 above). With its evocative descriptions of the Karoo and its spirited female character, Lyndall, who rails against a stultifying social environment at odds with the expansive landscape, the novel established Schreiner as a founding figure in South African letters and a leading light of the Anglo-American women's movement. The narrative is technically innovative, moving between realism, allegory and impassioned feminist statements about how 'the world makes men and women' (*African Farm*, p. 176) as it forges a literary language with which to represent and open up a circumscribed colonial and patriarchal sphere and reach towards new horizons.

From Man to Man develops the insights of *African Farm* and Schreiner's feminist polemic, *Woman and Labour* (1911). Its title points to the traffic in women, which for Schreiner occurred in two spheres: the socially sanctioned exchange by which women entered wedlock and the transactional sex work Victorian discourse marked as its antithesis. Through the story of two sisters, Rebekah and Bertie, Schreiner deconstructs this binary of public versus private women. At the same time, the title alludes to the desire to transcend gender difference so that woman and man could commune as 'man to man', even as the novel stages the failure of such communion in the refusal of a man to read his wife's letter. Whilst inter-gender relations are central to the plot, those between women variously located across the colonial divide also figure prominently. The letter in which Rebekah catalogues her husband's infidelities and issues her appeal for intellectual intercourse between men and women is written after she sees him leaving 'the servant girl's room' (p. 246). When she enters this room herself, the markers of similarity and difference between women become fraught: Rebekah's gaze lingers on racialising signs, while acknowledging that the woman's apparent defiance is an attempt to mask her fear; finally, the pregnant Rebekah realises 'that it was with that girl even as it was with herself that day' (p. 301). After the woman's departure, Rebekah whitewashes the room and takes in her child, Sartjie. Dorothy Driver reads the confrontation between the two women as a 'racist rupture [that] stands as an extraordinarily self-conscious moment in Schreiner's writing' at the point where Rebekah's feminism is made to confront race, 'produc[ing] for our scrutiny the rupture within white feminism itself' ('Reclaiming Schreiner', pp. 117, 120).

Four other African women play significant, if apparently minor, parts in the novel: the 'old Ayah', who Anne McClintock reads as a boundary marker on to whom Schreiner displaces her rage at the 'cult of domesticity' (*Imperial Leather*, p. 268); Griet, the 'Bushman girl, whom Bertie had got from her drunken mother' (Schreiner, *From Man to Man*, p. 104); and two 'Kafir' women, whose stories shape the young Rebekah, and which she later relates to Sartjie and her sons as she forges a 'maternal vision of social and economic equality between men and women, white and black' (Driver, 'Reclaiming Schreiner', p. 119) – one martyrs herself in a confrontation between African assegais and English canons; the other jumps from a mountain with her children strapped under her arms. Rebekah empathises keenly with the 'Kafir' women, shifting her prior identification with Queen Victoria on to them and employing them as guides in her attempts to interpret the intersecting structures of patriarchy and colonialism.[2] Similarly, the shift from third-person to second-person narrative voice in the short chapter devoted to Griet suggests that the subversion she introduces into the represented world, and particularly her rage against the 'cult of domesticity', is an authorial one. Griet's 'hither and thither' (*From Man to Man*, p. 104) movements across the text anticipate also the 'protean' subject and form of Zoë Wicomb's post-apartheid novel, *David's Story* (p. 35), while Schreiner's efforts to locate the authority of authorship – of texts and of new social visions – in women's productive and reproductive labour advances strategies that a number of women writers later take up.

---

2 In her introductory framing of *Woman and Labour*, a feminist polemic that denounces 'sex-parasiticism' and hails the emergence of the 'New Woman', Schreiner similarly casts an African woman, 'a person of genius' (p. 13), as the interpretive subject who becomes a formative influence on her thinking around gender and race.

In the decade following Schreiner's death, Mgqwetho published poetry and short prose pieces in isiXhosa in the Crown Mines newspaper *Umteteli wa Bantu*, where she produced as autograph 'a woman poet Nontsizi Mgqwetho' (Opland, *Nation's Bounty*, p. 452). Her output was and remains extraordinary: although women began to publish prose fiction in isiXhosa a decade before Mgwetho's poetry entered print,[3] no volume of poetry in isiXhosa has as yet been published by a woman. Opland ascribes this to 'the fact that women are prominent participants in the tradition of *intsomi*, the Xhosa folk-tale, but, although women are as active as men as composers and transmitters of personal and clan praises, the *imbongi*, the court poet, is always a male' ('Nontsizi Mgqwetho', p. 162). Employing print as her medium, Mgqwetho appropriates this gendered voice, performing it as a woman poet, while distancing herself from its traditional function of recording history in the form of royal patrilineal genealogies through her reiterated disclaimer: '(The names of kings confuse me)' (in Opland, *Nation's Bounty*, pp. 248 ff).

Fluctuating between masculine and feminine positions, Mgqwetho's idiom and imagery also deconstruct binaries of oral versus print culture, rural versus urban, traditionalist versus Christian or 'red' versus 'school'.[4] Her adroit movements back and forth between such dichotomous terms enable various authorial interventions: assuming the 'martial tone' of the *imbongi*, she is 'outspoken in rallying blacks to organise against their oppressors and exploiters' (Opland, 'Nontsizi Mgqwetho', p. 169), while harnessing print culture to address a larger national group than the *imbongi*; shifting between Christian and traditionalist registers, she advances a God later evoked by liberation theology, while rejecting the colonising culture that introduced Christianity to Africa (Opland, 'Nontsizi Mgqwetho', p. 175); articulating the voice of the woman poet in a performative appropriation of the traditionally male-authored *izibongo*, she negotiates the competing and complementary demands of an emergent feminist and nationalist consciousness.

Mgqwetho's desire, 'as a poet singing praises to Africa', to recover the continent 'abandoned on the battlefield by our forefathers' (in Opland, *Nation's*

---

3 The earliest published novels by women in isiXhosa are Latitia Kakaza's *Intyantyambo Yomzi* (1913) and *UThandiwe wakwaGcaleka* (1914) (see chapter 14 of this volume) and V. N. M. Swaartbooi's *UMandisa* (1934; a translated excerpt with an introductory note by V. M. Sisi Magaqi appears in Daymond et al., *Women Writing Africa*, p. 205–9). Commentary by Peter Mtuze and Magaqi suggests that Swaartbooi shares Schreiner's concern with how 'society predetermines what roles girls must play' (Mtuze p. 49) and with representing 'the emergence of a new type of woman' (Magaqi in Daymond et al., p. 206).

4 Applying to the Eastern Cape region, this binary distinguishes between 'heathen' traditionalists and Christian converts, who typically were absorbed into mission schools and adopted westernised dress.

Bounty, p. 252) sets her at odds with urban modernity. At the same time, the city, which has rent the social fabric she aims to restore, enables the emergence of the woman poet: 'no female poet / came from our house', she states in her first poem; 'the poet who rouses the court / and censures the king's always male' (in Opland, *Nation's Bounty*, p. 3). The critical licence of the praise poet becomes available to her as a woman only within urban modernity, even as this voice is taken up to critique urban mores: 'We first encountered these female poets / here in this land of thugs and booze' (in Opland, *Nation's Bounty*, p. 3). Widening the cultural crack introduced by colonialism in order to issue her voice on a national scale,[5] while using print as her medium and evoking the Bible as one of her central sources, Mgqwetho simultaneously assumes the voice of a 'Red', castigating Africans for forsaking their traditional cultures. Negotiating deftly between 'modernity' and 'tradition', her poetry is outspoken about its awe-inspiring power: 'you strip poetry bare to the bone / and the nation's mountains swivel as you sway from side to side' (in Opland, *Nation's Bounty*, p. 76).

The innovations and concerns of Schreiner and Mgqwetho reverberate through women's writing under apartheid: Lauretta Ngcobo, as a black woman writer, lays an ambivalent claim on Schreiner as a foremother (see 'Black South African Woman'), while Nadine Gordimer critiques her refusal to relegate gender concerns to 'a secondary matter' ('Review', p. 18); Ngcobo, Ellen Kuzwayo and Sindiwe Magona elaborate the maternal voice Schreiner forged and, along with Bessie Head, follow Mgqwetho in reappraising traditional cultures; similarly to Mgqwetho, Gcina Mhlophe and the worker poet Nise Malange take up *izibongo* conventions in written poetry; and the assertive autograph of the woman writer forged in Mgqwetho's and Schreiner's oeuvres reappears in Miriam Tlali's *Muriel at Metropolitan* (1975), echoes in the title of Kuzwayo's *Call me Woman* (1985), and is problematised in the creation of Elsa Joubert's *The Long Journey of Poppie Nongena* (1978; English translation 1980).

Women writing under apartheid: hearing the 'variety of discourses'

Some women writing under apartheid resist the state's dichotomous, discriminatory logic through various counter-discourses; others speak through forked

5 Mgqwetho records the critique she is subject to for 'producing poetry on a national scale (the preserve of the male *imbongi*)' (Opland, *Nation's Bounty*, p. 457) when she states: 'You were thrashed by kieries on Ngqika plains / for praising chiefs and *not* commoners' (p. 80).

tongues or a 'double-voiced discourse' (Showalter, 'Feminist Criticism in the Wilderness', p. 34), enfolding their critiques of patriarchal structures deep within anti-apartheid plots. Such works demand a reading practice engaged in what Wicomb terms 'hear[ing] the variety of discourses' ('To Hear') – that is, 'hearing' gendered discourses within a context dominated by the national liberation struggle, while acknowledging the heterogeneity of gendered subjectivity and inviting readers to trace the complex intersection of discourses within the subject of writing. Bessie Head provides a touchstone in Wicomb's analysis.

An avatar of Schreiner's visionary stance and Mgqwetho's revisioning of rural, traditional culture, Bessie Head (1937–86) went into exile in Botswana in 1964, where she completed the works published in her lifetime (see Chapter 20 above). *When Rainclouds Gather* (1968) transposes the exilic experience onto the central male character, while *A Question of Power* (1973) presents an intimate portrayal of mental breakdown through the first-person narrator, Elizabeth. In its enquiry into the nature of power, the novel presents a provocative response to oppositional struggles articulated through the 'black power' salute, which is contrasted to the 'soft drooping hand' of the Buddha (*Question of Power*, pp. 133–4). As a transitional text between the two, *Maru* (1971) exemplifies 'double-voiced discourse' in its presentation of a 'dominant' and 'muted' story (Showalter, 'Feminist Criticism', p. 34).

The surface of *Maru* centres on Margaret, a Masarwa ('Bushman') orphan in a Botswana village. The Basarwa are rejected and reviled as a tribe, but Margaret, with her extraordinary soul power and artistic creativity, is selected by Maru, a member of the Tswana aristocracy, to be his wife in a gesture that decolonises the minds of the subjugated Basarwa. Driven by its concern with combating racial prejudice, this plot is premised on a vision of the power of love to shatter oppressive structures. The novel's subterranean currents, in contrast, articulate the female self and women's artistry by critically engaging the plots into which women are written through generic convention (the romance novel) along with the political prioritisation of national liberation. Presenting a double ending in the opening prolepsis (the prefatory pages are set after the conclusion of the story, thus functioning also as an epilogue) and the closing scene, Head reveals a subtle resistance to romance plots that circumscribe women's subjectivity, creativity and desire, thus subverting the representational modes through which she conveys her message of liberation.[6]

6 Head's awareness of romance conventions, and her own resistance to their constraining effects on women's subjectivity, is shown in Colette Guldimann's research into her journalism for the *Golden City Post* before her departure from South Africa ('Bessie Head's *Maru*', pp. 47–69).

The opening pages suggest that Maru's dream of a better world will not be realised until the doors enclosing Margaret are opened, enabling her to experience as a woman and an artist the liberation offered to the Basarwa as a tribe (see Driver, 'Transformation through Art'; Wicomb, 'To Hear'). Margaret's paintings act as metaphors of the kind of writing Head performs. Both have prophetic qualities, authorising visions and dreaming up futures yet to be realised; both shatter binary structures and celebrate the resilience of the oppressed and the vitality and majesty of ordinary village women; both draw out of the figures of love-sick women the alternative image of a woman 'who sat alone and aloof and stared with deep, penetrating eyes on the value of her own kingdom' (Head, *Maru*, p. 108).

Whereas Head began to publish only after leaving South Africa, *Muriel at Metropolitan* by Miriam Tlali (1933–) was the first novel in English to be written and published in South Africa by a black woman. Completed in 1969, it was issued six years later in a '"censored" version' by Ravan Press (interview by Schipper, p. 62; see Chapter 38 below); the delay was largely due to Tlali and her husband's refusal to accept African women's minority status, which required that her husband sign the publishing contract on her behalf (Ngcobo, 'Miriam Tlali', p. 382). In 1979, Longman published what Tlali terms 'the integral text' (interview by Schipper, p. 62).

Eschewing the domestic as the proper sphere for women's stories of self, *Muriel at Metropolitan* is set almost entirely within Muriel's workplace, a hire purchase radio and furniture outlet wherein she negotiates the contradictions of her employment, which depends on the exploitation of black city dwellers and enacts the 'divided' realities of apartheid (Tlali, *Muriel at Metropolitan*, p. 11). (The novel's alternative title is 'Between Two Worlds'.) The novel is explicitly counter-discursive, refuting white representations of urban Africans and, more subtly, the dichotomous portrayal of black city women as either 'maternal' or 'independent' and thus 'suspect' (interview by Schipper, p. 64). As in *Maru*, the politics of gender are, however, often muted. Tlali has since stated that she 'did not want to overemphasize' conflict between African men and women, because 'the success of the struggle depended on how united we were against it' (interview by Jolly, p. 146). Yet, in both Head and Tlali the strategic decision to 'mute' the female voice is subject to self conscious reflection.

When Muriel is asked to make tea for her white co-workers, reducing her horizons as black urban woman to the role of domestic worker, her husband urges her to quit and drafts her a letter of resignation; in his eyes, Muriel is 'a goddess', rather than 'a mere black nanny' (p. 118). This reimagining recalls Head's presentation of Margaret's British foster mother reinscribing her dead Masarwa mother from 'low, filthy nation' to 'goddess' (Head, *Maru*, p. 7, 10). Both are presented as positive moments; yet both also muffle the black woman's voice, which is spoken over by white woman and black man respectively. Persuaded by her employer to withdraw this letter of resignation, Muriel eventually arrives at her own decision to stop functioning as a cog in the machinery of apartheid capitalism and, in the denouement, 'scribble[s] [her] formal letter of resignation': 'My hand just glided over the sheet . . . My handwriting had never looked so beautiful' (p. 190). Thus does Tlali encode black women's writing *as refusal*. Given the publication history of the novel, this assertive autograph is orientated not only against the apartheid state, but also specifically against its construction of African women as perpetual minors and helpmeets.

Accounting for the dearth of black women novelists in apartheid South Africa, Tlali states that they 'do not have time to dream' (in Lockett, 'Interview', p. 71). Lauretta Ngcobo (1931–) also identifies the conditioning of women into social gender roles (what Schreiner describes as how 'the world makes men and women' [*African Farm*, p. 176]) and points to complicities between African patriarchies and the apartheid state in silencing women's voices: 'Years of conditioning had taught us that only men have a voice and are worth listening to. This, over and above the intolerance engendered by Apartheid South Africa in all spheres of life. That tutored feeling of "less worthiness" has been a crippling factor in all my creative thinking' ('My Life', p. 86). Ngcobo shares with Mgqwetho a complex reception of and ambivalent response to the values encoded in the oral tradition: 'In our male-dominated societies our oral traditions extolled the virtues of humility, silent endurance and self-effacing patterns of behaviour for our girls, while young boys received all the encouragement to go out there and triumph and survive' ('African Woman Writer', p. 81).

It is precisely this sense of struggling on more than one front that has led Wicomb to render audible 'the variety of discourses': 'I can think of no reason why black patriarchy should not be challenged alongside the fight against Apartheid' ('To Hear', p. 37). Yet this challenge was often a difficult one to issue under the urgencies of apartheid. Reflecting on her first novel, *Cross of Gold* (1981), in which the woman activist dies at the end of the first chapter, Ngcobo relates: 'I had intended writing about my own life – the role of women in the struggle. But for reasons I cannot understand, my main character kept dying. In the end I let her, and the story in *Cross of Gold* became a story about the son' (Ngcobo, 'Women under Pressure', p. 51).

Ngcobo's second novel, *And They Didn't Die* (1990), positions black women and their struggles centre stage. Unable to support herself and her children on the depleted lands of a rural Bantustan, Jezile Majola seeks domestic work in the city, where she is raped by her white employer and falls pregnant. Ngcobo presents the absence of empathy between women when Jezile fails to evoke a sympathetic response from her rapist's wife. At the same time, Jezile is also ostracised by her husband's family on her return home (and particularly by her mother-in-law, as senior women within the patriarchal hierarchy are shown to oppress those beneath them). Jezile is cast as a vessel of reproduction by the contradictory but intersecting demands of traditional patriarchy and the apartheid capitalist state: women like her 'produce migrant labour – [their] children are the labour resource of this government' (Ngcobo, *And They Didn't Die*, p. 42); when her husband's family claim her children after her rape, Jezile recognises also that she 'had been a mere vessel . . . to carry the Majolas and only the Majolas [and] was now unable to claim for herself her own flesh and blood' (p. 227).

Jezile reclaims 'her own flesh and blood' when she saves her daughter from rape. Whereas her own rape is represented only with the terse statement 'He had his way with her' (p. 205), she is able to articulate a symbolically vocal response when she later encounters a white soldier attempting to rape her daughter. Her resistance is enacted as a mother in a manner that limits her resistance to this domain, while expanding its definition to encompass a militant subject position in ways that mirror the political mobilisation of many South African women.[7] Rather than a patriarchal institution casting Jezile as 'vessel', motherhood is reconceived in opposition to 'the father's law' that props up the apartheid state (Daymond, *South African Feminisms*, p. xxvii). Entering the scene of rape, Jezile notes the phallic power of the soldier's gun, but chooses instead as her weapon the knife left over from the evening meal, denoting the sustaining power of maternal care. Turning from the symbolic conjunction of tumescent penis and gun that identifies the authorship of the apartheid state, she locates in the domestic sphere the authority with which to inscribe her refusal on the soldier's body, 'pale as white paper' (p. 241).

The assertion of authorship concluding both *Muriel at Metropolitan* and *And They Didn't Die*, and the maternal authority Jezile inscribes, appears also in *Call me Woman* (1985), the autobiography of Ellen Kuzwayo (1914–2006), whose

---

7 See Walker, 'Conceptualising Motherhood'; Wells, 'The Rise and Fall of Motherism'; Fester, 'Merely Mothers'.

title has been read as a rejoinder to Mtutuzeli Matshoba's account of the emas-culating effects of apartheid in *Call Me Not a Man* (1979). Carole Boyce Davies finds the autobiography to be shot through with 'double-voiced discourse': 'locat[ing] the self more directly within the larger historical context of the collective struggle for freedom', it simultaneously 'conceal[s] the individual woman's story' such that the personal story, which narrates familial rejection, domestic abuse and divorce, is 'truncated' ('Private Selves', pp. 111, 117). This textual reticence mirrors that within the represented world when Kuzwayo opts for an out-of-court settlement to her divorce in order to avoid having to 'wash [her] dirty linen in public' (*Call me Woman*, p. 140) – a strategy that secures her access to her children. On a textual level, the muting of personal, gendered struggles similarly shores up her self-proclaimed identity as 'Mother of Soweto', placing her 'in a position of authority over the younger genera-tion' (Driver, 'M'a-Ngoana O Tšoare Thipa ka Bohaleng', p. 229) and entering motherhood into the public sphere of political engagement. The silencing of the personal story, moreover, enables the text to accommodate within the pages of an autobiography the stories of many women. Judith Coullie also finds that Kuzwayo elaborates subjectivity through the conventions of praise poetry, producing an understanding of selfhood at odds with the individual-ism encoded in the western autobiographical form ('Space Between Frames', pp. 139–41); only after inserting herself into an ancestral genealogy does Kuzwayo assert: 'I am the author of this book' (*Call me Woman*, p. 55).[8]

Whereas Kuzwayo 'hosts' the voices of women in her act of self-writing, 'collaborative auto/biography', as exemplified by Elsa Joubert's *Die Swerf-jare van Poppie Nongena* (1978; *The Long Journey of Poppie Nongena*, 1980), has been charged with appropriation and misrepresentation. Like *And They Didn't Die*, *Poppie Nongena* foregrounds the apartheid apparati of pass laws, influx control regulations and migrant labour practices, detailing their effects on black women's lives and exploring the ways in which the 'institution of mar-riage' functions as a 'direct weapon of state control' (McClintock, *Imperial Leather*, p. 324). *Poppie Nongena* advanced Afrikaner readers' awareness of the evils of apartheid by lending the authority of Joubert's signature (that of a well-established Afrikaans novelist) to a story of a black woman's travails under apartheid (see Chapter 22 above). Yet this autograph has also seen it labelled a 'scandalous book' (McClintock, *Imperial Leather*, p. 300). Its conceit is

---

8 Similar constructions of the autobiographical voice appear in Noni Jabavu's *The Ochre People* (1963) and Sindiwe Magona's *To my Children's Children* (1990). Magona textualises the voice of a Xhosa grandmother, preserving histories and passing them on to future generations, while in the preface to the second edition of her autobiography (1982), Jabavu also performs the voice of 'grandmother'.

that Poppie Nongena (a pseudonym used at her request) arrived at Joubert's home one evening in 1976 and Joubert, presenting her own role as being no more than 'a tape-recorder, a mouthpiece', 'realised she had found the woman who could speak for the black women of the Cape' (Lenta, 'Break in the Silence', pp. 147–8). Joubert's posturing as 'tape-recorder' has, however, been questioned by critics. Desiree Lewis, for instance, points to 'the overtly manipulating role of a fictionalizing story-teller in relation to her subjects' voices' ('Constructing Lives', pp. 171–2); in the text's ethnographic moments, such as when Joubert represents Poppie's entry into the unfamiliar world of the rural Eastern Cape, Lewis notes that 'the biographical subject' becomes 'a medium through which the biographer confirms preconceived views of a "strange world"' ('Constructing Lives', p. 175).

After 'Poppie's' death, Joubert revealed her identity: far from arriving unannounced on her doorstep, the woman whose story she presents was, in fact, her domestic servant. Here, too, lies some of the scandal of the text, for it is in the exploitative labour relation between 'madam and maid' that the category of 'women' has come under the greatest strain. Sindiwe Magona (1943–) was herself employed as a domestic worker, having found herself ensnared in the 'patchwork quilt of patriarchies' and forced to defer her aspirations when falling pregnant and being abandoned by her migrant labourer husband. Her two-part autobiography, *To my Children's Children* (1990) and *Forced to Grow* (1992), charts her movement from childhood innocence through apartheid's brutalisations and deprivations to her final escape from its structures, which cast her, as Tlali's protagonist found, in the figure of servant. In a cycle of stories in *Living, Loving and Lying Awake at Night* (1991), Magona grants first-person narrative voice to a group of domestic workers, enabling them to speak back to the 'madams' who deny their subjectivity. Gladys Thomas similarly calls the category of 'women' into crisis in her earlier poem, 'Leave me Alone' (1972):[9] 'I tear my hungry babe from my breast / To come and care for yours / Yours grows up fine / But, oh God, not mine'. The poet's final question – 'What have I done that you won't leave me alone?' – deals the death knell to sentimental notions of 'sisterhood'. In 'Small Passing' (1989), Ingrid de Kok, writing from the other side of apartheid's racial divide, abandons the easy assumption of a 'sisterhood' between women in favour of forging hard-earned coalitions between women, drawing on shared biological and social experiences of mothering to build bridges across apartheid's chasms without erasing the legislated differences between women.

9 Published in *Cry Rage!*, the collection Thomas co-authored with James Matthews, which was the first volume of poetry to be banned by the apartheid government.

The female signature, then, is overwritten by racial classification. Lewis has critiqued the binary casting of black women as figures of *experience* and white women as *interpreters* of black experience in South African feminist reading practices (see 'Politics of Feminism'). Wicomb, who has commented wryly on the critical expectation that black women only write autobiographically, evokes this expectation only to confound it in her collection of stories *You Can't get Lost in Cape Town* (1987), which apparently maps out Wicomb's lived experience, only to emphasise the text's fictionality in the cunning narrative strategy of killing off the mother and then resurrecting her in the final story (see Chapter 30).

In the face of apartheid's racialising regime, Nadine Gordimer (1923–), who was awarded the Nobel Prize for literature in 1991 and is South Africa's most famous and prolific woman writer,[10] resisted this label and declared that the 'feminist battle must come after . . . the real battle for human rights' (in Gardner, 'Story for this Place and Time', p. 33). Many have nonetheless found in her oeuvre detailed attention to gender politics, not least in her persistent exploration of the relation between the personal and the political. *Burger's Daughter* (1979), in particular, is seen as 'an appealing book for feminists' (Gardner, 'Story for this Place and Time', p. 30). Here Gordimer stages a confrontation between what some might call a feminist, or at least 'female', consciousness and Black Consciousness. Rosa, who has been exploring her identity as a woman following the death of her revolutionary father, has a chance encounter with a man she grew up thinking of as her 'black brother'. In response to his challenge, she is seen as taking up 'the social commitment her father left off' (Clingman, 'Subject of Revolution', p. 68), while others note that – as is the case in *My Son's Story* (1990) – her search is not so much for her father as for her mother, the 'real revolutionary'. Driver argues also that Gordimer '*is* to be commended for illustrating various ways in which [white] South African women participate and benefit by racial oppression . . . and for insisting, not on women's passivity, but on their responsibility' ('Nadine Gordimer', p. 198).

In her first poem, originally written for her school magazine, 'My Beautiful Land' (1969; English translation 2000), Afrikaans poet Antjie Krog (1952–) also explores the relation between the personal and the political, and between the apartheid state and the patriarchal ordering of society: 'look, I build myself a land / where skin colour doesn't count . . . where I can love you, / can lie beside you in the grass / without saying "I do"' (*Down to my Last Skin*, p. 11).

10 She was the first South African and seventh woman to be awarded a Nobel Prize for literature (Newman, *Casebook*, p. 3).

Krog later became closely associated with the post-apartheid nation-building project, through her work on the Truth and Reconciliation Commission and her translation into Afrikaans of Nelson Mandela's *Long Walk to Freedom*, as did Ingrid Jonker (1933–65), whose poem 'Die Kind' ('The Child', 1963) was read in Afrikaans by Mandela at the historic opening of Parliament in 1994.

The question of white women's political responsibility is addressed in Krog's poetic negotiation of the voice of two precursors: the Boer woman, Susanna Smit (1799–1863), who challenged both her male counterparts and the British colonial administrator of Natal (on Smit, see Chapters 7 and 13), in a collection published in 1981; and Anne Barnard (1750–1825), the Scottish noblewoman who spent five years at the Cape (1797–1802) and whose journal, letters and sketches pen parts of the region of South Africa (in *Lady Anne* [1989]).[11] Evoking Anne Barnard 'as guide' to 'show it is possible / to hone the truth by pen / to live an honourable life in an era of horror' (*Down to My Last Skin*, p. 73), Krog traces the implications of her literary voice through engagements with this historical foremother before finally rejecting her 'frivolous life' (p. 73). (On other women writing in Afrikaans during this period, particularly Wilma Stockenström, Jeanne Goosen and Reza de Wet, see Chapter 22).

Gcina Mhlophe (who writes and performs in English, isiXhosa and isiZulu) refuses the 'choice' between two front lines that saw Gordimer retreating from an explicitly feminist position: 'When they give you a back seat / in the liberation wagon / say No / Yes Black Woman / A Big NO' ('Say No', pp. 351–2). Like Mgqwetho, Mhlophe has adapted the conventions of the *izibongo* to express her concerns as a black woman writer. Echoing Virginia Woolf's claim that the woman writer 'thinks back through her mothers' (Woolf, *Room of One's Own*, p. 96), she inserts herself into a range of genealogies in 'Praise to our Mothers' (1989). Her short story, 'The Toilet' (1987), picks up on Krog's enquiry into the extent to which metropolitan women are able to function as guides to South Africa. 'The Toilet' transposes the Woolfian 'room of one's own' on to the claustrophobic, segregated realities of apartheid South Africa. In the kind of double gesture Mgqwetho honed, Mhlope offers a complicated response to Woolf, who emphasised the woman writer's experience of being excluded from the library and her need for a room with a lock and key.

---

11 Poems from the *Lady Anne* collection have been published in English translation in *Down to my Last Skin* (2000). In her note on translation, Krog says: 'Some of the poems, like the Susanna Smit series with its clipped or ecstatic language, didn't work at all [in translation] and had to be abandoned' (*Down to my Last Skin*, p. 3).

'The Toilet' is located in the margins of the 'maid and madam' relationship: the protagonist shares a backyard room with her sister, who is employed as a domestic worker in the white suburbs. A figure of the emergent writer, Mhlophe's protagonist reads whatever she can lay her hands on: old copies of *Fair Lady*, *Women's Weekly* and *Drum* – publications produced for and about white women and black men respectively. No literary space, or viable tradition, is presented to her as a black woman, nor does she have access to a room of her own. To avoid her sister's employers, she has to vacate the room before they wake up each day and occasionally finds herself locked out on the street. The forces of exclusion are not the guardians of the male literary canon but the white 'madam', and also her sister, who questions her reading habits and wonders what kind of a wife she will make. Simultaneously locked out of the home and cast as home-maker, the protagonist finds a public toilet that she transforms into a private refuge. The toilet becomes the enabling 'room of her own', fostering the emergence of her writing self. One morning she finds herself locked out of even this sanctuary, but, internalising the creative space, she moves to a park bench, where she 'wrote [her] story anyway' (p. 18).[12] Thus does Mhlophe reiterate Woolf's argument, while moving beyond it to consider the plight and potential of women who do not have access to 'five hundred pounds a year and a room with a lock on the door' (Woolf, *Room of One's Own*, p. 109) and yet who still write. As a trope, the toilet recalls also *Muriel at Metropolitan*, where the lack of a toilet marked 'black women', shows up the absurdity of apartheid's racial and gender divisions, and erases the figure of 'black woman' between the constructs of gender and race. It is indeed this muted figure that the act of 'hearing the variety of discourses' aims to render audible.

Women writing after apartheid: engaging with past and present

Much writing by women in the early post-apartheid era participates in, or challenges, the nation-building project and engages with the attempt by the Truth and Reconciliation Commission (TRC) to construct a new nation by creating discursive space for silenced voices and reviewing the past conflict; such texts are attentive in particular to the 'women's work' (De Kok, 'Mending',

---

12 Similarly to 'The Toilet', her play *Have you Seen Zandile?* (1986) culminates in 'her self-realisation as a writer' (see chapter 27 of this volume); Miki Flockemann suggests that the play articulates a 'counter-discourse' to 'protest theatre' in its focus on 'personal life and experience' (in Blumberg, 'Revaluing Women's Storytelling', p. 142).

p. 35) of mourning and mending through acts of bearing witness. Other writers, such as Yvette Christiansë, turn to more distant pasts. Some, such as Gordimer in *None to Accompany Me* (1994), suggest that the new nation opens up empowering positions for women, while Wicomb maps out in *David's Story* (2000) various 'recursions' (p. 184) between past and present representations and experiences of women's bodies. The arrival of democracy has also seen the emergence of new writers as well as new emergencies to which women writers are addressing themselves.

Country of my Skull (1998), Krog's partly autobiographical account of the TRC hearings, is crafted as an intricate quilt of voices and registers. Some have flung the charge of 'appropriation' at her (see Cook, 'Metaphors for Suffering' and Ruden, 'Guilt and Sorrow'), while Mark Sanders reads the text as a performative act of 'hospitality', accommodating the voices silenced by the brute force of apartheid and 'set[ting] to work an ethics of advocacy, the task of giving the domain of words over to the other' ('Truth, Telling', p. 17). Magona's *Mother to Mother* (1998) and Elleke Boehmer's *Bloodlines* (2000) reiterate the TRC scene by presenting two mothers testifying on behalf of their sons. *Mother to Mother* stages an address to the mother of Amy Biehl, a Fulbright scholar killed in South Africa in 1993, by the mother of one of Biehl's killers. Mandisa's story, which she relates while addressing Biehl's mother to make her 'understand her son', reveals once more exploitative relations between women – like the younger Magona, she is employed as a domestic worker. Yet, the act of telling her story, and her recognition of the sorrow shared by another mother, enables her to reach across racial boundaries and address her white counterpart as her 'Sister-Mother' (*Mother to Mother*, pp. 198, 201).

The most complex response to the new nation, and the project of recovering voices and revisiting pasts, appears in *David's Story*, which is preoccupied with questions of representation and authorship. The preface by the narrator, the fictional amanuensis who claims to have written David's story, highlights the implications of the female autograph, before proceeding to present David's attempt to write about one of South Africa's most iconic female figures, Saartje Baartman. David's writing on Baartman takes place when the narrator asks him to pin down the elusive character of Dulcie, a female guerrilla who is described as a 'scream' through his story. Yet the very attempt to write Dulcie, like Baartman, enacts violence on her body, 'mutilat[ing her] on the page' (p. 205). The novel, in contrast, presents itself with the challenge of not pinning Dulcie down as interpretable subject, of permitting the discordance her unstable presence introduces into the text. Thus does it frustrate both nationalist desires for narrative coherence and biological continuity and feminist appeals to the authentic experience of women. Rather than 'simply "giv[ing] voice" to those who were marginalised, oppressed, and disinherited . . . *David's Story* dramatises the literary, political, philosophical, and ethical issues at stake in any attempt at retrieval of history and voice' (Driver, 'Afterword', p. 216).

Wicomb attributes her ability 'to speak and write' to both Black Consciousness and feminism (in Hunter and MacKenzie, *Between the Lines II*, p. 88; see Driver, 'Afterword', pp. 238–9; Samuelson, 'Disfigured Body'). The exchange set up within the novel between David and the narrator is presented as one between a radical, militaristic discourse that has in part emerged from Black Consciousness and a liberal humanist discourse associated with certain strands of feminism; oscillating between the two, the novel negotiates the demands of both gender and race. What the exchange dramatises is the inability of either discourse to accommodate the figure of the woman warrior as the 'hither and thither' movements of Dulcie's 'protean' (p. 35) form fluctuate between them (while Schreiner's Griet might be said to fluctuate between a discourse of gender subversion and one of racial othering). In a national context dominated by the ritualistic act of 'giving voice', *David's Story* explores the limitations of discourse in articulating topics such as sexual violence or figures such as the female guerrilla, thereby clearing space in which to re-evaluate women's contributions to the nation. (For other representations of women as activists and freedom fighters, see Kagiso Lesego Molope's *Dancing in the Dust* [2002] and autobiographies by Zubeida Jaffer, Pregs Govender and Mamphela Ramphele; for accounts by women political prisoners, see Chapter 26 above).

Concerns about retrieving voice in and through available discourses also structure Christiansë's volume of poems, *Castaway* (1999), and her novel, *Unconfessed* (2006). *Castaway*, she says, 'began with what is by now a familiar gesture for writers and theorists of anti- and postcoloniality – namely, an argument with history. This argument was staged in personal terms in that I had wanted to bring to the fore a voice for which there is no discursive place in any formal history' ('Selections', p. 303). Readers are invited to rustle through the poems in search of this voice; yet, as Christiansë says elsewhere,

> My grandmother never speaks. She never materialized despite my listening, and what I hear is utterly untranslatable . . . as if to say, "This is not right, this prying, no matter how much your longing pays me respect." And so, obedient, I learned to listen to this absence and now consider it a resistance.
>
> ('Selections', pp. 304–5)

In *Unconfessed*, Christiansë undertakes another act of retrieval: that of Sila van den Kaap, a slave woman brought from Mozambique to the Cape, where she is later incarcerated for *kindermoord* (the murder of her son). Sila is entered into the colonial archive at the moment of her court confession. Christiansë, in contrast, presents Sila as an unconfessing character: refusing to be known, and instead engaging the power-knowledge regimes that produce her as subjugated, Sila is treated in similar ways to Christiansë's grandmother.

Other kinds of silences structure Marlene van Niekerk's *Agaat* (2004; English translation 2006 – outside South Africa, this translation appears under the title *The Way of the Women*), a profound exploration of communication across the yawning betrayals and intense intimacies of the domestic relation (on Van Niekerk's earlier novel, *Triomf*, see Chapters 22, 31 and 32; on the translation of both novels, see Chapter 35). Milla, the white protagonist, is on her deathbed, reduced to bare life by the ravages of motor neuron disease. Her companion, caretaker and interpreter is Agaat, a coloured woman she had adopted as a child only to recast as servant when she herself fell pregnant. The structures of dependency have now been reversed, and Milla, able only to 'speak' through the almost imperceptible movements of her eyes, is read and spoken for by Agaat, who also subjects Milla to recitations of her old diaries, revisiting their painful history in a communion both tender and tormenting. *Agaat* bristles with undercurrents of violence – physical and psychic – between men and women, and women and women, as well as charges of love. As Agaat and Milla peer into one another's 'throats in search of a word' (p. 43), a new 'language of women' (p. 212) emerges. Subverting the ideological demands of the 'farm novel' and following rather a tradition of writing the farm/land that stems from Schreiner's *Story of an African Farm* and passes through Gordimer's *The Conservationist* (1974), *Agaat* concludes by bequeathing Milla's farm to Agaat.

Writing in English, Anne Landsman similarly subverts the 'farm novel' in *Devil's Chimney* (1997). Revisiting the past by presenting acts of narrative reconstruction between two sisters, one of whom is deaf and between whom lies a bitter betrayal, *Devil's Chimney* exploits a similar conceit as *Agaat*. In the narrative of the past that Connie constructs, we also find a charged and treacherous encounter between a white and a coloured woman. Landsman's *The Rowing Lesson* (2009) invests its political engagements almost fully in the personal and intimate as it traces an expatriate daughter's memories of her dying father and of the country of her childhood.

This turn to the intimate, and the consequent opening up of the domain of the 'political', is a feature also of much post-apartheid poetry by women. Gabeba Baderoon's collections – *The Dream in the Next Body* (2005) and

A Hundred Silences (2006) – are exemplary here. Baderoon's poetry, particularly 'War Triptych: Silence, Glory, Love', also extends the geopolitical range of South African writing and its engagements, which encompass here Iraq and Palestine. Playwright Nadia Davids, in *At her Feet* (2002; published 2005), similarly weaves together the voices of a Jordanian woman and Muslim women in Cape Town. In *Cissie* (2008), Davids recreates the life of activist Cissie Gool, suggesting that the act of 'thinking back through their mothers' remains an important one for women writers. A similar act of homage is performed by literary critic Devarakshanam Govinden, who recreates the story of her grandmother's arrival in South Africa as an Indian indentured labourer, and uses this as the basis for retrieving the often ignored literary voices of Indian South African women and for theorising the interplay between 'identity and difference' (see *'Sister Outsiders'*).

Kopana Matlwa's *Coconut* (2007) tackles the muting of black women's voices from the perspective of a post-apartheid generation. The novel unfolds in two parts, each narrated by a young black woman negotiating identity in the erstwhile white suburbs and revealing the damaging inscription of whiteness on her interior world. Her voice clipped and pruned to sound out the proper accent, Olfilwe reveals the costs of inhabiting the English language, and at the end of her story painstakingly begins to relearn her mother's tongue. Other forms of violence lurking within the home are presented in Nadine Gordimer's *The House Gun* (1998), Zazah Khuzwayo's autobiographical *Never Been at Home* (2004) and Zukiswa Wanner's *The Madams* (2006). Billed as a 'wildly provocative novel', *The Madams* develops the emergent form of 'chick lit' to explore new terrains of connection and conflict between women and women, and women and men, within domestic structures both surprisingly persistent and newly reconfigured. The central event is the decision of a black woman to employ a white maid. Presenting their relationship, as well as other female friendships and hetero- and homosexual unions, the novel engages a number of contemporary themes, including domestic violence, infidelity and HIV/AIDS.

Another genre taken up by women writers with which to engage gender violence in post-apartheid South Africa is the thriller: Angela Makholwa in *Red Ink* (2007) and Margie Orford in *Like Clockwork* (2006) present women reading the clues left by serial rapist-murderers to avert further carnage of female bodies. The other state of emergency women writers are urgently tackling is that of the HIV/AIDS pandemic. Magona's *Beauty's Gift* (2008), narrated in the first person by the dying eponymous heroine, leaves Beauty's four female friends with the 'gift' of awareness and optimism for the future (see also her collection of poetry, *Please, Take Photographs* [2009]), while De Kok's poetry presents a sobering image of the ravages AIDS has wrought on family structures in 'a girl of thirteen / children in her arms / house balanced on her head' ('The Head of the Household', p. 59).

Bibliography

Baderoon, G. *The Dream in the Next Body: Poems*, Cape Town: Kwela Books/Snailpress, 2005.

A Hundred Silences. Poems, Cape Town: Kwela Books, 2006.

Blumberg, M. 'Revaluing Women's Storytelling', in M. Blumberg and D. Walder (eds.), *South African Theatre as/and Intervention*, Amsterdam: Rodopi, 1999, 137–46.

Boehmer, E. *Bloodlines*, Cape Town: David Philip, 2000.

Boyce Davies, C. 'Private Selves and Public Spaces: Autobiography and the African Woman Writer', *Neohelicon: Acta Comparationis Litterarum Universarum* 17:2 (1990), 183–210.

Bozzoli, B. 'Marxism, Feminism and South African Studies', *Journal of Southern African Studies* 9:2 (1983), 139–71.

Christiansë, Y. *Castaway*, Durham, NC: Duke University Press, 1999.

'Selections from *Castaway*', in S. Pierce and A. Rao (eds.), *Discipline and the other Body: Correction, Corporeality, Colonialism*, Durham, NC: Duke University Press, 2006, 303–15.

Unconfessed, New York: Other Press, 2006.

Clayton, C. (ed.). *Women and Writing in South Africa: A Critical Anthology*, Marshalltown: Heinemann, 1989.

Clingman, S. 'The Subject of Revolution', in J. Newman (ed.), *Nadine Gordimer's Burger's Daughter: A Casebook*, Oxford University Press, 2003, 55–79.

Cook, M. 'Metaphors for Suffering: Antjie Krog's *Country of my Skull*', *Mosaic: A Journal for the Interdisciplinary Study of Literature* 34 (2001), 73–90.

Coullie, J. L. 'The Space Between Frames: A New Discursive Practice in Ellen Kuzwayo's *Call me Woman*', in Daymond, *South African Feminisms*, 131–53.

Coullie, J. L. (ed.). *The Closest of Strangers: South African Women's Life Writing*, Johannesburg: Witwatersrand University Press, 2004.

Daymond, M. J. (ed.), *South African Feminisms: Writing, Theory, and Criticisms, 1990–1994*, New York: Garland, 1996.

Daymond, M., et al. (eds.). *Women Writing Africa: The Southern Region*, Johannesburg: Witwatersrand University Press, 2003.

Davids, N. *At her Feet: The Playscript* [2005], Cape Town: Oxford University Press, 2009.

Cissie: The Playscript [2008], Cape Town: Oxford University Press, 2009.

De Kok, I. 'The Head of the Household', in *Terrestrial Things*, Cape Town: Kwela Books/Snailpress, 2002, 59.

'Mending', in *Transfer*, Cape Town: Snailpress, 1997, 35.

'Small Passing', in *Familiar Ground: Poems*, Johannesburg: Ravan, 1988, 49.

Driver, D. 'Afterword' to Z. Wicomb, *David's Story*, New York: Feminist Press, 2000, 215–71.

'M'a-Ngoana O Tšoare Thipa ka Bohaleng – The Child's Mother Grabs the Sharp End of the Knife: Women as Mothers, Women as Writers', in M. Trump (ed.), *Rendering*

Things Visible: Essays on South African Literary Culture, Johannesburg: Ravan, 1990, 225–55.

'Nadine Gordimer: The Politicisation of Women', in R. Smith (ed.), *Critical Essays on Nadine Gordimer*, Boston: G. K. Hall, 1990, 180–204.

'Reclaiming Olive Schreiner: A Re-Reading of *From Man to Man*', in E. Reckwitz, K. Reitner and L. Vennarini (eds.), *South African Literary History: Totality and/or Fragment*, Essen: Blaue Eule, 1997, 111–20.

'Transformation through Art: Writing, Representation and Subjectivity in Recent South African Fiction', *World Literature Today* 70:1 (1996), 45–53.

Fester, G. 'Merely Mothers Perpetuating Patriarchy? Women's Grassroots Organizations in the Western Cape, 1980 to 1990', in A. Gouws (ed.), *(Un)Thinking Citizenship: Feminist Debates in Contemporary South Africa*, Aldershot: Ashgate, 2005, 199–218.

Gardner, S. 'A Story for this Place and Time: An Interview with Nadine Gordimer about *Burger's Daughter*', in J. Newman (ed.), *Nadine Gordimer's 'Burger's Daughter': A Casebook*, Oxford University Press, 2003, 27–40.

Gordimer, N. *Burger's Daughter*, New York: Viking Press, 1979.

The Conservationist, New York: Viking Press, 1974.

The House Gun, Cape Town: David Philip, 1998.

My Son's Story, Cape Town: David Philip, 1990.

None to Accompany Me, Cape Town: David Philip, 1994.

'Review of *Olive Schreiner: A Biography* by Ruth First and Ann Scott', in M. van Wyk Smith and D. Maclennan (eds.), *Olive Schreiner and After: Essays on Southern African Literature in Honour of Guy Butler*, Cape Town: David Philip, 1983, 14–19.

Govender, P. *Love and Courage: A Story of Insubordination*, Johannesburg: Jacana, 2007.

Govinden, D. *'Sister Outsiders': The Representation of Identity and Difference in Selected Writings by South African Indian Women*, Leiden: Brill, 2008.

Guldimann, C. 'Bessie Head's *Maru*: Writing after the End of Romance', in M. Sample (ed.), *Critical Essays on Bessie Head*, Westport, CT: Praeger, 2003, 47–69.

Head, B. *Maru* [1971], London: Heinemann, 1995.

A Question of Power, London: Davis-Poynter, 1973.

When Rainclouds Gather, London: Heinemann, 1968.

A Woman Alone: Autobiographical Writings, London: Heinemann, 1990.

Hunter, E., and MacKenzie, C. (eds.). *Between the Lines II: Interviews with Nadine Gordimer, Menán du Plessis, Zoë Wicomb and Lauretta Ngcobo*, Grahamstown: National English Literary Museum, 1993.

Jabavu, N. *The Ochre People: Scenes from a South African Life*, London: John Murray, 1963.

Jaffer, Z. *Our Generation*, Cape Town: Kwela Books, 2003.

Joubert, E. *Die Swerfjare van Poppie Nongena*, 1978; translated as *The Long Journey of Poppie Nongena*, London: Hodder & Stoughton, 1980.

Khuzwayo, Z. *Never been at Home*, Cape Town: David Philip, 2004.

Krog, A. *Country of my Skull: Guilt, Sorrow, and the Limits of Forgiveness in the New South Africa*, Johannesburg: Random House, 1998.

Down to my Last Skin: Poems, Johannesburg: Random House, 2000.

Kuzwayo, E. *Call me Woman*, Johannesburg: Ravan, 1985.

Landsman, A. *Devil's Chimney*, Johannesburg: Jonathan Ball, 1997.

The Rowing Lesson: A Novel, Cape Town: Kwela Books, 2007.

Lenta, M. 'A Break in the Silence: The Long Journey of Poppie Nongena', in M. J. Daymond, J. U. Jacobs and M. Lenta (eds.), *Momentum: On Recent South African Writing*, Pietermaritzburg: University of Natal Press, 1984, 147–58.

Lewis, D. 'Constructing Lives: Black South African Women and Biography under Apartheid', in N. Yousaf (ed.), *Apartheid Narratives*, Amsterdam: Rodopi, 2001, 163–89.

'The Politics of Feminism in South Africa', *Staffrider* 10:3 (1992), 15–29.

Magona, S. *Beauty's Gift*, Cape Town: Kwela Books, 2008.

Forced to Grow, Cape Town: David Philip, 1992.

Living, Loving and Lying Awake at Night, Cape Town: David Philip, 1991.

Mother to Mother, Cape Town: David Philip, 1998

Please, Take Photographs, Cape Town: Modjaji, 2009.

To my Children's Children, Cape Town: David Philip, 1990.

Makholwa, A. *Red Ink*, Northlands: Pan Macmillan, 2007.

Matlwa, K. *Coconut*, Johannesburg: Jacana, 2007.

Matshoba, M. *Call me not a Man and other Stories*, Johannesburg: Ravan, 1979.

McClintock, A. *Imperial Leather: Race, Gender and Sexuality in the Colonial Context*, New York: Routledge, 1995.

Mhlophe, G. *Have you Seen Zandile? A Play Originated by Gcina Mhlophe, Based on her Childhood*, Braamfontein: Skotaville, 1988.

'Praise to our Mothers' [1989], in *Love Child*, Scottsville: University of Kwa-Zulu Watal Press, 2002, 26.

'Say No', in *Breaking the Silence: A Century of South African Women's Poetry*, ed. C. Lockett, Johannesburg: Ad Donker, 1990, 351–2.

'The Toilet', in A. Oosthuizen (ed.), *Sometimes when it Rains*, London: Pandora, 1987, 1–7.

Molope, K. L. *Dancing in the Dust*, Toronto: TSAR, 2002.

Newman, J. *Nadine Gordimer's 'Burger's Daughter': A Casebook*, Oxford University Press, 2003.

Ngcobo, L. *And They Didn't Die*, New York: Feminist Press, 1990.

'The African Woman Writer', *Kunapipi* 7:2–3 (1985), 81–2.

'A Black South African Woman Writing Long after Olive Schreiner', in I. Vivan (ed.), *The Flawed Diamond: Essays on Olive Schreiner*, Sydney: Dangaroo Press, 1991, 189–99.

Cross of Gold, London: Longman, 1981.

'Miriam Tlali', in B. Lindfors (ed.), *Twentieth-Century Caribbean and Black African Writers*, 3rd series, Detroit, MI: Gale, 1996, 381–8.

'My Life and my Writing', *Kunapipi* 7:2–3 (1985), 83–6.

'Women under Pressure', in R. Granquist and J. Stotesbury (eds.), *African Voices: Interviews with Thirteen African Voices*, Sydney: Dangaroo Press, 1991.

Nuttall, S. 'Literature and the Archive: The Biography of Texts', in C. Hamilton et al. (eds.), *Refiguring the Archive*, Cape Town: David Philip, 2002, 283–300.

Opland, J. 'Nontsizi Mgqwetho: Stranger in Town', in G. Furniss and L. Gunner (eds.), *Power, Marginality and African Oral Literature*, Cambridge University Press, 1995, 162–84.

Opland, J. (ed.). *The Nation's Bounty: The Xhosa Poetry of Nontsizi Mgqwetho*, Johannesburg: Witwatersrand University Press, 2007.

Orford, M. *Like Clockwork*, Cape Town: Oshun, 2006.

Peires, J. *The Dead will Arise: Nongqawuse and the Great Xhosa Cattle-Killing Movement of 1856–7*, Johannesburg: Ravan, 1989.

Ramphele, M. *Mamphela Ramphele: A Life*, Cape Town: David Philip, 1995.

Rich, A. *Of Woman Born: Motherhood as Experience and Institution*, London: Virago, 1976.

Ruden, S. '*Country of my Skull*: Guilt and Sorrow and the Limits of Forgiveness in the New South Africa', *Ariel* 30:1 (1999), 165–79.

Samuelson, M. 'The Disfigured Body of the Female Guerrilla: (De)Militarization, Sexual Violence and Re-Domestication in Zoë Wicomb's *David's Story*', *Signs: Journal of Women in Culture and Society* 32.4 (2007), 833–56.

Sanders, M. 'Truth, Telling, Questioning: The Truth and Reconciliation Commission, Antjie Krog's *Country of my Skull*, and Literature after Apartheid', *Modern Fiction Studies* 46:1 (2000), 13–41.

Schreiner, O. *From Man to Man; or, Perhaps Only . . .* [1926], London: Virago, 1982.
  The Story of an African Farm [1883], New York: Schocken Books, 1976.
  Woman and Labour [1911], London: Virago, 1978.

Showalter, E. 'Feminist Criticism in the Wilderness', in E. Abel (ed.), *Writing and Sexual Difference*, University of Chicago Press, 1982, 9–35.

Smiley, T. 'Yvette Christiansë', interview, 15 February 2007, http://www.pbs.org/kcet/tavissmiley/archive/200702/20070215christianseuml.html, accessed 8 December 2007.

Thomas, G., and J. D. Matthews. *Cry Rage!*, Johannesburg: Spro-cas Publications, 1972.

Tlali, M. Interview by Cecily Lockett, in C. Mackenzie and C. Clayton (eds.), *Between the Lines: Interviews with Sheila Roberts, Ellen Kuzwayo, Miriam Tlali*, Grahamstown: National English Literary Museum, 1989, 69–85.
  Interview by Mineke Schipper, in M. Schipper (ed.), *Unheard Words: Women and Literature in Africa, the Arab World, Asia, the Caribbean and Latin America*, trans. B. P. Fasting, London: Allison & Busby, 1985, 59–68.
  Interview by Rosemary Jolly, in D. Attridge and R. Jolly, eds., *Writing South Africa: Literature, Apartheid, and Democracy, 1970–1995*, Cambridge University Press, 1998, 141–8.
  Muriel at Metropolitan, Johannesburg: Ravan, 1975.

Van Niekerk, M. *Agaat* [2004], Johannesburg: Jonathan Ball, 2006.

Walker, C. 'Conceptualising Motherhood in Twentieth-Century South Africa', *Journal of Southern African Studies* 21:3 (1995), 417–37.

Wanner, Z. *The Madams*, Cape Town: Oshun, 2006.

Wells, J. 'The Rise and Fall of Motherism as a Force in Black Women's Resistance Movements', Conference on Women and Gender in Southern Africa, University of Natal, Durban, 1991.

Wicomb, Z. *David's Story*, Cape Town: Kwela Books, 2000.
  'To Hear the Variety of Discourses', *Current Writing* 2 (1990), 35–44.
  You Can't get Lost in Cape Town, New York: Feminist Press, 1987.

Woolf, V. *A Room of One's Own*, London: Harcourt, 1929.

The experimental line in fiction

MICHAEL GREEN

This chapter will consider what J. M. Coetzee has called 'the experimental line' within the works of black and white writers in English and Afrikaans, showing how, during the apartheid years, its playfulness and experimentalism was often passed over in critical accounts intent on identifying a literature of witness and solidarity. It will also trace the continuing 'line' of experimentation in post-apartheid literature.

'What value does the experimental line in modern Western literature hold for Africa?', asks Coetzee in 'Alex La Guma and the Responsibilities of the South African Writer' (p. 117), an essay first published in 1971. The question is prompted by Lewis Nkosi's 1966 essay, 'Fiction by Black South Africans', in which he argues that, 'With the best will in the world it is impossible to detect in the fiction of black South Africans any significant and complex talent which responds with both the vigour of the imagination and sufficient technical resources to the problems posed by conditions in South Africa.' 'If black South African writers have read modern works of literature', Nkosi states, name-checking Dostoevsky, Burroughs, Kafka and Joyce, 'they seem to be totally unaware of its most compelling innovations'. 'What we get most frequently,' he argues, 'is the journalistic fact parading outrageously as imaginative literature' (p. 246).

Coetzee's response presents a prescient sketch of the main issues that have congregated around the kind of fiction he would go on to write. Setting aside any prescriptivism as to what kind of fiction Africans 'ought' to write, Coetzee frames the question of experimentalism and responsibility within related questions concerning the literary and the social ('does not the Western experimental line assume *and perpetuate* a rift between the writer and society at large which is a fact of life in the West but need not become a fact of life in Africa?'); the assumption that innovations in aesthetic form are necessarily progressive in terms of both literary expression and ideological allegiance ('does homage to Western experimentalism not involve a rather simple-minded view of an absolute "technique" which, as in the myth of our science, can only progress, never regress . . . ?'); and the political and ethical dimensions of electing to work in a particular fictional mode in a specific context ('are we not entitled to ask . . . whether there might not be a whole spectrum of valid literatures open to Africa, and to suggest that the writer should not, so to speak, choose his tradition at random, but rather choose it with some sense of the social implications of his choice?' [p. 117]).

Working through these questions as they apply to La Guma's fiction, Coetzee shows that La Guma's work, whilst clearly not related to the strategies of high modernism Nkosi finds absent as an influence on black South African writing, moves well beyond the limits of naturalism into the European traditions of critical or social realism. Even though Coetzee closes his response to Nkosi by keeping the whole question of form and responsibility open (there can be no '"correct" mode' for a society 'in search of an identity it may never find' [p. 124]), the conclusions he reaches concerning La Guma still feed into the tropes governing the reception of apartheid-period black South African writing: that its predominant method is that of documenting the atrocities of colonialism and apartheid through the realist mode.

The argument that La Guma's work can be read productively in relation to a specifically European line of realism is something of an anomaly in the critical consensus of the time – so much so that Coetzee sees La Guma's socially progressive critical realism as a form of experimentalism that avoids the conservatism into which Nkosi's argument lapses. Significantly, the more 'naive' versions of local realism criticised by both Coetzee and Nkosi from their different perspectives in this exchange were, within a few years, to take on the status of a principled choice and an ethical imperative. Variously ascribed to the deprivation and isolation of black South African writers, the influence of popular fiction or the impact of a vigorous period of local journalism in the 1950s, the kind of writing that, in Es'kia Mphahlele's words, 'extracts experience from raw life and does little to impose an aesthetic on the material' (cited in Bethlehem, Skin Tight, p. 3) was, as the brutality of apartheid suppression and the militancy of opposition escalated, soon to become practically a mandatory mode for progressive writing. The realist ideal of capturing the human subject as embedded in a full political, social and economic context, which emerged in relation to the rise of nineteenth-century industrial capitalism, has lent itself to a number of ideological programmes, from György Lukács's views on the socialist realist novel to the British liberal literary tradition. Adopted by and adapted to the South African context, the claims made for the moral authority of realism as the primary mode of bearing witness to the truth of South Africa infused the cultural activism of the late 1970s and 1980s, as is clear in Mothobi Mutloatse's ringing assertion in an interview of 1981: 'We need a writing that records exactly the situation we live in, and any writing which ignores the urgency of political events will be irrelevant' (cited in Bethlehem, *Skin Tight*, p. 2).

Mutloatse's assertion was echoed in any number of pronouncements by the Congress of South African Writers and the cultural desks of the African National Congress, the United Democratic Front and the Congress of South African Trade Unions. This 'rhetoric of urgency' (Bethlehem, *Skin Tight*, p. 3) is indeed dominant, although with less consistency than one would expect, in the poetry, theatre, novels and short stories written by black writers of the period. Nadine Gordimer, the most prominent of white literary activists, would go so far in a 1973 essay as to reject outright the formal literary experimentation of the European kind Nkosi criticises African writers for ignoring. Whilst Gordimer defined her own sophisticated exploration of the realist novelistic tradition to some degree against the more direct representational modes she believed appropriate for black writers, her opposition to the 'hyperintrospective' (Bethlehem, *Skin Tight*, p. 7) experimental text as a suitable mode for engaging with the heightened political context of South Africa would be extended to all South African writers, a prime target being the fiction of J. M. Coetzee (see 'The Idea of Gardening', p. 6). The fiction Coetzee began writing within a few years of setting out the 'responsibilities of the South African writer' appears to fly in the face of each of the points he raises in his response to Nkosi. Certainly a good number of his critics have chosen to use criteria implicitly related to these or similar points against Coetzee's work. A few representative examples must suffice: that Coetzee's work perpetuates a rift between the writer and society is central to Vaughan's comment that 'Coetzee's language can say next to nothing, and certainly nothing reliable, about experiences outside the modality of its own racial-historical dialectic' ('Literature and Politics', p. 128). That the novels overemphasise 'technique' is registered in Chapman's charge that both Coetzee and the critics who espouse his work 'confirm the suspicions of many black writers that literary pursuit in white South Africa has rather more to do with the gratifications of libidinal language than the fulfilments of fighting political injustice' ('Writing of Politics', p. 338), whilst Coetzee's experimentalism is denied any 'progressive' merit in JanMohamed's assertion that it 'epitomizes the dehistoricizing, desocializing tendency of colonialist fiction' ('Economy of Manichean Allegory', p. 73) in a postcolonial context. And that Coetzee has disregarded the social constraints upon a writer's choice of 'tradition' is evident for Rich, who holds that Coetzee's novels demonstrate precisely how 'literary postmodernism in a postcolonial context as South Africa . . . is a moral dead end' ('Apartheid and the Decline of the Civilization Idea', p. 389).

Modernism and its posts

Comparatively early in his career Coetzee's work would find an audience that recognised a different kind of responsibility and engagement, one predicated on interrogating just such discursive horizons in the South African critical and creative landscape. In the first full-length study of Coetzee's work, *The Novels of J. M. Coetzee: Lacanian Allegories* (1988), Teresa Dovey argued that the novels were a form of 'criticism-as-fiction, or fiction-as-criticism' (p. 9) that pre-empted naive readings on essentially referential terms. David Attwell, in his *J. M. Coetzee: South Africa and the Politics of Writing*, attempted to cut through the 'considerably oversimplified polarization' between the claims of political resistance and poststructuralist sophistication in a reading of the novels as 'a form of situational metafiction' that takes into account both '*reflexivity* and *historicity*' (pp. 2–3).

More recently, Derek Attridge has challenged the compulsion to define the 'postmodern' paradigm in terms of either reactionary aestheticism or radical innovation by reinvesting the discursive strategies of modernism with an ethical dimension particularly appropriate to the postcolonial context. Attridge allies the self-reflexiveness of modernist writing with 'a new apprehension of the claims of otherness, of that which cannot be expressed in the discourse available' (*J. M. Coetzee and the Ethics of Reading*, p. 4). For him, Coetzee's self-reflective, allusive, metafictional strategies are not so much postmodern as late or neomodern (p. 2), in that his 'handling of formal properties is bound up with the capacity of his work to engage with – to stage, confront, apprehend, explore – otherness' (p. 6). Combining a consistent denial of 'any ethical guidance from an authoritative voice or valorizing metalanguage' with narrating figures insistently presented as 'selves mediated by a language which has not forgotten its mediating role' (p. 7), Coetzee's novels produce a 'continued, strenuous enterprise in acknowledging alterity' (p. 12).

The Vietnamese and native South Africans linked through the violence of the imperial and colonial projects paralleled in the two novellas making up Coetzee's first novel, *Dusklands* (1974); the farm servants of *In the Heart of the Country*'s (1977) obsessive, hallucinatory, antipastoral interrogation of the tradition of the farm novel; the barbarians in the no time/no place of *Waiting for the Barbarians* (1980), where the moral and political basis for the liberal-humanist attempt at distancing itself from the coloniser–colonised relationship is interrogated in its most intimate confessional form; the atopian figure of the protagonist in *Life & Times of Michael K* (1983) whose distilled minimalism disrupts dystopian and utopian projections alike at a moment of historical impasse; Friday, whose silence/silencing both generates and undercuts *Foe*'s (1986) intertextual engagement with a founding work in a canon the novel subverts and extends; the impenetrable figure of Vercueil in *Age of Iron* (1990), to whom the dying Mrs Curren entrusts the passing on of the letter to her daughter in which she has attempted to put down the truth of how she has lived in a time of acute civil unrest; the absent son – absent beyond the fact of his death – at the heart of *The Master of Petersburg*'s (1994) historic-biographical play around Dostoevsky during the genesis of *The Possessed*; the author himself as the oblique subject of the third-person, present-tensed 'autobiographies', *Boyhood: Scenes from Provincial Life* (1997), *Youth: Scenes from Provincial Life* (vol. II, 2002), and the resistance the figure of the author presents to his biographer's efforts in *Summertime* (2009); Lucy as the daughter whose surrender to the violent displacement of the new the father fails to understand, even in the midst of his own acts of abasement in *Disgrace* (1999); the lessons making up *Elizabeth Costello* (2003) which the writer as protagonist can never master; each of these 'figures of alterity' – figures who continue to recur in Coetzee's ongoing fictional output – convey a resistance, says Attridge (in terms not necessarily related to those presented here), to 'the discourses of the ruling culture': 'the culture, that is, which has conditioned the author, the kind of readers which the novels are likely to find, and the genre of the novel itself' (p. 13).

The evident achievements of these novels rapidly took Coetzee from the marginality Edward Said suggests is the natural place of the 'public intellectual' (the descriptor most recently revived as a way of positioning Coetzee) to one of the most highly recognised and rewarded of South African writers. The 'experimental line', then, has clearly not been 'passed over' in the reception of South African fiction for some time ('It is difficult to be a so-called successful writer and to occupy a marginal position at the same time, even in our day and age', responds Coetzee to Jane Poyner's attempts to manoeuvre him back into such a position ['J. M. Coetzee in Conversation', p. 23]), but it is important to note at this point that the figure of the line, in Coetzee's sense of both a specific approach to or type of writing and a continuous, interconnected series, cannot be left in the singular.

Writing white / writing black

In *J. M. Coetzee: South Africa and the Politics of Writing*, David Attwell made a major contribution to the case for seeing Coetzee as an exemplary figure in the history of experimental 'white writing' in South Africa; his more recent study, *Rewriting Modernity: Studies in Black South African Literary History*, is implicitly complementary in its analysis of South African black writing. In the final chapter, Attwell mounts a specific rebuttal of Nkosi's insistence 'that in South Africa there exists an unhealed... split between black and white writing, between on the one side an urgent need to document and bear witness and on the other side the capacity to go on furlough, to loiter, and to experiment' ('Postmodernism and Black Writing in South Africa', p. 75). Entitled, in an overt invocation of the early Coetzee, 'The Experimental Turn', it opens up a rich field for critical consideration when, by way of clearing the ground for his analysis of 'experimentalism in contemporary fiction', Attwell sets out a number of examples illustrating that 'black writing is indeed replete with instances of aesthetic self-consciousness, not excluding the very kinds of experimentalism that we associate with modernism' (p. 172).

Attwell cites Njabulo Ndebele's experimenting with Joycean internal monologues in isiZulu while a student; the spirit of the modernist manifesto in Muthobi Mutloatse's introduction to the collection of Black Consciousness-inspired short fiction, *Forced Landing* (1980); the overtly experimental 'Interludes' in Esk'ia Mphahlele's autobiography, *Down Second Avenue* (1959); the informing voices of Albert Camus and Richard Wright in Nkosi's own *Mating Birds* (1979); Dugmore Boetie's *Familiarity is the Kingdom of the Lost* (1969), in which the distinction between the artist and con man is blurred; and the narrative mode of Part One of Mongane Serote's *To Every Birth its Blood* (1981), modelled as it is on the compositional and performance techniques of jazz.

He then moves on to a thorough and detailed reading of the implicit experimental dimensions in Ndebele's *Fools and other Stories* (1983) and the more overt display of this in Zakes Mda's *Ways of Dying* (1995) and *The Heart of Redness* (2000). In something of a reprise of Coetzee's analysis of La Guma, Attwell argues that in *Fools*, Ndebele 'redeploys realism's resources in an experimental intervention' (p. 192). In 'drawing on the symbolic goods of realism long after the effects of modernism have been widely felt' (p. 182), Ndebele makes of realism an experimental mode that recovers, in the intense and fraught context of 1980s South Africa, 'some of the epistemological freshness that once adhered to realism itself' (p. 183) in the nineteenth century.

Ndebele's later fiction expands into the radically hybrid form of *The Cry of Winnie Mandela* (2003), a two-part work in which fiction, essay and biography merge within overtly metafictional structures. In the first part the separate stories of four southern African women – 'Penelope's descendants' – separated from their husbands by circumstances common during the apartheid period are told. In the second part the women share their stories and then decide to address them to the Mother of the Nation, Winnie Mandela, the archetypal South African figure of a woman who spent much of her life waiting for her husband to return. Winnie herself responds in a variety of voices overtly mediated by the narrator-as-author, meditating on the public nature of her separation, her failure to live up to the ideal of the patient wife, and her refusal to be turned into a symbolic figure of post-apartheid national reconciliation. Woven around journeys through an evocatively rendered South African landscape, the novel ends with Winnie joining the four women coming into their respective identities as they drive to the coast for a holiday. En route they pick up a hitch-hiker who turns out to be Penelope; she gives her blessing to the women's 'pilgrimage to eternal companionship' (p. 121).

Mda's fiction is smoother in its development within the experimental line. There is an almost palpable sense of relief in Attwell's claim that the intertextuality Mda sets up between his early fiction and that of Coetzee is evidence of a 'movement of modernist practice across the racial divide of authorship in South Africa' (p. 194). Certainly by the time Mda – best known through the struggle years as a playwright – turned to the novel form in the 1990s, a critical climate had been created in which the fictional modes he adopted were welcomed largely on grounds won in earlier debates concerning primarily white writers in the 'experimental line'. *Ways of Dying* (1995), written in the transitional period of the early 1990s, tells the story of Toloki, a self-appointed professional mourner who creates in his improvised funerary performances a dynamic relationship between traditional forms and uneven urban modernities that points towards the symbolic shifts necessary for anything like a new South Africa. Dual narratives in *The Heart of Redness* (2000) reposition the past in relation to the present, with the split allegiances of the traumatic 1856–7 Cattle-Killing movement in the Eastern Cape resounding in the choices facing a community at the time of the first democratic South African election in 1994. In the process the struggle years lose their obsessive centrality in South African writing, becoming simply 'the middle generations' in an ongoing negotiation between tradition and modernity. This somewhat controversial deprivileging of the anti-apartheid period carries through into Mda's embracing of the new stylistic freedoms available in the post-apartheid context evident in *The Madonna of Excelsior* (2002), where the narrative mode through which an historical interracial sex scandal of the 1970s is depicted draws upon the expressionist work of a European-born local painter-priest. In *The Whale Caller* (2005) it is Mda's choice of subject – 'a relationship of loving biosociality between a human being and a whale' (Woodward, 'Whales, Clones', p. 334) – as much as style that displays its break with the dominant modes and themes of post-apartheid literature. In the overt metafictionality of *Cion* (2007), Toloki, the lead character in *Ways of Dying*, returns to join his creator in an exploration of his writing in relation to a wide repertoire of storytelling traditions, a vital resource which he is also concerned should never inhibit imaginative creativity. 'The degree of self-reflexivity in Mda's novels,' conclude David Bell and J. U. Jacobs, 'positions them in the same category as the metafictional discourses of J. M. Coetzee, just as their imaginative inventiveness is matched perhaps only in the fictional works of Ivan Vladislavić or Etienne van Heerden' ('Introduction', *Ways of Writing*, p. 1).

The significance of this claim takes on its full force if we consider an apparently truncated example of a text by a black writer about which similar claims could have been made in an earlier, more fraught, period. 'When *To Every Birth its Blood* appeared in 1981,' writes Nick Visser, 'it seemed to resolve a long-standing dilemma in South African literary studies . . . Here at last . . . was a novel by a black South African which . . . could stand alongside the work of Nadine Gordimer and of J. M. Coetzee' ('Fictional Projects and the Irruptions of History', p. 67). The experimental form employed in *To Every Birth its Blood* motivated this view, but the alienated, fragmented, individual perspective that dominates the first part of the two-part work gives way to more conventional multiple perspectives in Part Two. In Visser's opinion, this stylistic shift was the result of an 'irruption of history'. Serote, he says, 'apparently started out to write . . . a novel fully immersed in modernist and existentialist narrative practices', but 'the events and aftermath of June 1976 . . . compelled him to abandon not just one fictional project for another but one kind of novel for another, and one kind of politics for another' (p. 72). Run into a single narrative, the chaotic narrative perspective of the first person in Part One, the reflex of the protagonist's existential collapse, is ordered into an orchestrated pattern in the third person, realist mode – the embodiment of the People's Culture campaign of the mid 1980s with its emphasis on concrete, documentary form – of Part Two by the democratisation of narrative perspective and its accompanying recuperation of the individual self within a communal subject. The neatness of this argument hides a hint of frustration, a frustration not easily admitted to in the early 1980s by a critic of a pronounced historical-materialist bent and realist affiliations. One cannot help but sense something of Visser's own response to the novel behind the thinly veiled generalisation buried in his endnotes: 'Some may feel that the change in fictional projects involved losses as well as gains: the shift to radical political fiction in the second fictional project cost us one of our first modernist novels by a black South African writer' (p. 76).

Experimentalism and modernity

If Mda is held to represent this guilty secret of even Leftist desire coming to fruition, we should not let this erase ways of reading that allow us to see in much earlier black writing expressions of an experimentalism as defined by Attwell, following Charles Taylor: 'self-consciously aesthetic practices . . . that try to initiate an epistemological renewal in response to conditions we associate with modernity' (*Rewriting Modernity*, p. 175). Temporally such practices are, in western literary histories, associated with the late nineteenth and early twentieth centuries and the period conventionally identified by the term 'modernist', but imposing either the conventional attributes of modernism or its periodisation directly on South African writing produces serious distortions in our understanding of the literary cultures of the region.

It is in any event a truism of southern African literary history that no sustained modernist tradition was produced here in chronological relation with the metropolitan modernist period. The trio of writers who collaborated as the editors and principal contributors to the overtly modernist *Voorslag* literary journal in the mid 1920s – Roy Campbell, Laurens van der Post and William Plomer – were largely self-marginalised through a deliberately elitist and romantically isolated posturing; this is perhaps more true of Campbell and Van der Post than Plomer, but all three would in any event leave South Africa by 1926 and return only sporadically. Campbell's notable early attempts at infusing his colonial background into metropolitan experimentalism trailed off into modernism's tendencies towards a fascist rejection of liberalism and democracy, while Van der Post made a career out of merging psychoanalytic theory with African primitivism to create a somewhat suspect mystical, ethno-mythographic, humanism. Plomer's novel *Turbott Wolfe* (1926), written when he was just 19, is perhaps the strongest legacy of this explicitly modernist moment in South Africa. The hallucinatory mode Plomer uses (the fevered narrator is on his deathbed) provides the novel's exploration of racialised sexuality with a self-referential, parodic frame for its own socially indecisive aestheticism. In this, it is the nearest thing to a precursor for the explicitly modernist narrative forms Coetzee is usually credited with introducing to South African fiction.

Another South African text produced during the period usually identified as modernist but rarely associated with the kinds of experimentalism practised at the time can extend usefully our sense of the 'experimental line'. Written between 1919 and 1920 but published only in 1930, Solomon Tshekisho Plaatje's *Mhudi* took on a renewed significance for South African cultural life in the 1970s when the emergence of the social history movement, which impacted strongly on southern African literary studies, swept figures like Plaatje back to prominence. Committed in particular to bringing the excluded perspective of black experience into the writing of history, the literary scholars who aligned themselves with this form of historiographical revisionism were guided to some degree by social historians' interest in the lived effects of the dehumanising structures of segregation and apartheid. In both content and form, social history reinforced literary realism's interests in what Bethlehem calls 'representational literalism' (*Skin Tight*, p. 7), a focus that has tended to isolate *Mhudi* from a serious consideration of its modernist qualities.

Mhudi is a flagrantly hybrid work, a mélange of not only 'western' literary forms ranging across the romance, epic and historical novel, but also 'indigenous' oral modes, including the folk-tale, proverbs, praise poems and prophecy, at times only awkwardly held together by Edwardian prose. The social historical interests that gave *Mhudi* its renewed attention tended to emphasise certain of its stylistic features, particularly those, such as its use of oral modes, that gave it an 'indigenous' representational authenticity. If, however, we read *Mhudi* into Robert Pippin's definition of modernism as a 'dawning sense of a failure in the social promise of modernisation' (*Modernism as a Philosophical Problem*, p. 36), then the novel's central concerns – its ambivalent attitude to the modernisation that the colonising technology embodies, the clear sense of all the cultures it represents being appropriated into the progressive march of 'History', the overpowering awareness of the entrance of southern Africa into 'national time' simultaneously with the failure of the region to achieve the 'confidence of community' that Benedict Anderson (*Imagined Communities*, p. 40) perceives as essential to the nation – all mark the work, beyond any purely formal concerns or essentialist genre identifications, as a very immediate expression of the defining features of modernist literary expression. Its complex formal strategies, then, may be considered as 'experimental' in the strong sense of being materially located in relation to an historically situated literary category.

'Magical realism'

The intimate relation between varying forms of experimentalism and their specific material contexts is an important consideration to keep in mind as we return to more contemporary works and their relation to the experimental lines we are tracing. A common term often associated with experimental fiction, particularly in postcolonial contexts, is 'magical realism'. Notoriously loose as a descriptor – Brenda Cooper asks if it is 'a mode, a genre, a style, a politics?' (*Magical Realism in West African Fiction*, p. 15) – the term has carried over from Latin America precisely on the basis of what Gerald Gaylard calls 'vaguely congruent "post-colonial" antinomies' ('Meditations on Magical Realism', p. 93). In the process, however, it requires constant reconsideration in relation to the texts and contexts to which it is applied.

In his study of magical realism in the works of Zakes Mda, Christopher Warnes defines the term as 'a mode of narration that naturalises the supernatural, representing real and non-real in a state of equivalence and refusing either greater claim to truth' ('Chronicles of Belief and Unbelief', p. 74), adding that it is commonly identified as emerging out of contexts in which preindustrial and postindustrial modes, the 'traditional' and the 'modern', coexist. Such a relation of a formal definition to a material context, even if not reductively applied, presents problems for South Africa however; as Warnes notes, there is little literary expression of this sort in the country despite its being marked more than most by just such uneven development. Indeed, Zakes Mda's comparatively recent plays and the novels referred to above have been credited with virtually single-handedly introducing the mode into South African literature.

In a move common amongst African writers, Mda distances himself from any direct relation to the term. He stresses that his use of expressive features identified as magical realist were drawn initially from the African tale-telling traditions with which he was familiar rather than consciously modelled on a style associated with origins further afield. Although Mda says he later aimed at a more conscious understanding of the mode (*Ways of Writing*, p. 9), Warnes illustrates just how few examples of overt magical realism there are to be found in Mda's early novels, and how the defining supernatural element is often ironically deployed.

The term shifts significantly from anything like the definition given by Warnes above when it is extended – as it regularly is – to writers such as Mike Nicol, Ivan Vladislavić and, to a certain extent, J. M. Coetzee. Shaken free of its serious invocation of and deep investment in forms of cultural otherness, it is difficult to know what precise lines may be drawn between magical realism and a wide range of playful, self-conscious texts. One could argue that there is little of the overtly fabulous or fantastical in Coetzee (*In the Heart of the Country* comes closest to displaying some of these features), and, while Vladislavić is widely celebrated for the fantastic transmutations the historical and the ordinary undergo in his fiction, this is a result of the release of the full multivalency of their modes of representation rather than the playing off of various cultural systems against each other.

André Brink sees Mike Nicol's first novel, *The Powers That Be* (1989) – which he describes as 'an exorbitant imaginative recapturing of apartheid as a school of Jarryesque violence, intrigue, and corruption' (*Writing South Africa*, p. 27) – as 'a rediscovery of African magical realism' (p. 26). Critics strained to find a suitable category for Nicol's next novel, *This Day and Age* (1991), using terms ranging from allegory to fable to parable or folk-tale to identify the mode of its interwoven story lines, metafictional conceits and multiple, layered genres. Nicol's third novel, *Horseman* (1994), a reimagining of the Book of Revelation in a postcolonial context, joins its predecessors in exhibiting, as Warne has it, 'a tendency to use [magical realism] for playful, self-conscious, critical purposes', with nothing of the 'investment in cultural otherness' that is to be found in the 'faith-based magical realism' of a writer like Ben Okri ('Chronicles of Belief and Unbelief', p. 89).

Derek Alan Barker expands Warnes's sense of the 'irreverent magical realism' ('Chronicles of Belief and Unbelief', p. 89) he identifies in Vladislavić and Nicol to include, as the original German coinage of *Magischer Realismus* attempted to do in finding a position between expressionism and realism, 'a felt need in the South African context for a mode of art which moves away from ingenuous realism but stops short of the existential flight of overly abstract modes of art' ('Escaping the Tyranny of Magic Realism?', p. 5).

In Nicol's work, this tendency is emphasised in his conscious shift away from magical realism in *The Ibis Tapestry* (1998). Written in a high post-modern mode, the narrator's quest to reconstruct the death of an apartheid arms dealer finds an intertextual mirror in the death of Renaissance playwright Christopher Marlowe and quickly becomes, in the words of Ken Barris, 'a referential maze more closely resembling hypertext search than that most sequential of genres, the thriller' ('Hunting the Snark', p. 8). Possibly in response to the relative critical neglect of his overtly experimental work, Nicol has in more recent novels like *Payback* (2008) moved towards popular crime fiction and the conventional realism associated with this genre.

We may note a distantly related shift in the more recent work of Vladislavić. In his earlier work, particularly the short-story collections *Missing Persons* (1989) and *Propaganda by Monuments* (1996), the style is overtly postmodern, foregrounding the representation of the domestic, the political and the historical signifiers of South African life by opening them up to radical acts of fantastical re-representation. This is true too of the more sustained allegorical mode of *The Folly* (1993), where a vacant patch of veld is taken over by a mysterious figure who constructs an imaginary house that takes on a contested reality, and peaks in the *The Restless Supermarket* (2001), where English as a South African mode of communication, caught between a fading Euro café society and an emerging Afro-chic, becomes less representation than a materialisation of its own etymology. In later works like *The Exploded View* (2004), the slippage of the real away from its signifiers at moments of extreme disorientation links the protagonists of each of the four parts of the novel, but the overall effect depends upon our first having a sense of what constitutes their reality, conveyed through a strongly realistic mode of representation. *Portrait with Keys* (2006) verges on the hyperrealistic in its exploration of the ways in which various pedestrian trajectories through a city create both a meaningful 'portrait' of a place and bring out its paradoxes and contradictions.

What the various forms of neorealism emerging in South Africa illustrate is, as we saw in Coetzee's analysis of La Guma and Attwell's reading of Ndebele, that modes considered 'conservative' in one context may take on 'experimental' dimensions when deployed in circumstances other than those with which they are normally associated. This is particularly true of conventionalised subgenres – like the detective and crime thriller forms currently being used not only by Mike Nicol but also other South African authors like Deon Meyer, Angela Makholwa and Margie Orford – currently being adopted by South African authors. These forms are able to sit quite comfortably, in post-1994 South African literature, alongside a novel like Anne Landsman's debut, *The Devil's Chimney* (1997), which is widely celebrated for using 'magical realism' to open up the South African national narrative to a fluid, many layered, ambiguous array of voices. André Brink hails the novel, which centres on a multiply signifying cave in which the past interpenetrates the present through the novel's alcoholic, creatively unreliable narrator, as belonging 'exuberantly within a burgeoning new kind of writing which has begun to displace the novel of realism and commitment that marked the dark years of political oppression in South Africa' ('Real and Magical *Devil*'). At the same time, he challenges Coetzee's assertion on its cover that this is 'the first time' South Africa is seen 'through the lens of magic realism'. For Brink, the term refers 'to an already well established genre characteristic of a young society in a stage of transition and in search of a new identity'. South Africa, he says, is 'fortunate in being able to draw on at least two indigenous traditions of magic realism . . . the rich oral narratives of the indigenous peoples; but also an old tradition of Afrikaner narrative' ('Real and Magical *Devil*').

Afrikaans experimentalism

Tracing the Afrikaner tradition of narrative through C. Louis Leipoldt, C. J. Langenhoven and Herman Charles Bosman to 'the taken-for-granted interaction between the living and the dead in Etienne van Heerden's *Toorberg*' (1986), Brink could well have gone on to include a number of contemporary writers in Afrikaans, pre-eminently Marlene van Niekerk's widely praised *Triomf* (1994) and *Agaat* (2004; translated outside South Africa as *The Way of the Women*). Brink is himself, of course, a significant figure in a broader 'experimental line' in Afrikaans fiction, for which Etienne Leroux's highly patterned, fantastical *Sewe dae by die Silbersteins* (1962; translated as *Seven Days at the Silbersteins*) could be considered seminal. Leroux would, like the young Brink, associate himself with the Sestigers (literally Sixtiesers), the literary movement generally considered to have introduced a spirit of 'renewal' into writing in Afrikaans (see Chapter 21 above). The majority of its most productive writers – who also included Breyten Breytenbach, Jan Rabie and Bartho Smit – brought their formative experiences as students and sojourners in France back to a South Africa in which they became increasingly politicised and opposed to the Nationalist establishment. For Ampie Coetzee, the period these writers spent in the 'decolonized space' of France liberated their writing 'from the essentially realist and esthetic tradition that had developed in Afrikaans literature. They came into contact with Surrealism, the absurd, protest literature, and a completely different literary landscape'. Coetzee sees in this a direct link between the aesthetic and the political: 'Not only did they introduce different techniques, styles, and metaphors in prose and poetry, but they contested the hegemony into which they had been born' ('Literature in Afrikaans', p. 414).

Brink's *Kennis van die Aand* (1973; translated into English as *Looking on Darkness*, 1974) would become the first Afrikaans work to be found 'undesirable' under the Publications and Entertainment Act introduced in 1963. A powerful series of politically engaged novels would follow, although Derek Attridge who, as we have seen, is quite ready to acknowledge the effectiveness of the 'reworking of modernism's methods' in contexts like those of South Africa, feels that Brink's 'use of modernist (or postmodern) techniques contributes much less to the success of his fiction than the essentially realist storytelling they sometimes mediate'. Novels like *A Chain of Voices* (1982), in which multiple perspectives on an historical event are presented without 'a totalizing and adjudicating central voice', and *States of Emergency* (1988), a narrative generated by the self-reflexivity of a novelist attempting to write a love story in a time of political crisis, have, says Attridge, 'a slight air of modernism-by-numbers' (*J. M. Coetzee and the Ethics of Reading*, pp. 4–5).

Although Breyten Breytenbach's work was never banned, he served seven years of a nine-year prison sentence after illegally re-entering South Africa from his exile in France on a botched clandestine mission. Two books came directly out of experience, *The True Confessions of an Albino Terrorist* (1985) and *Mouroir: Mirrornotes of a Novel* (published in 1983 in South Africa partly in English but mainly in Afrikaans, and entirely in English in 1984), both of which run counter to the realist mode of most South African prison writing (see Chapter 26). *True Confessions* is written from a comparatively conventional single, retrospective vantage point, although it does foreground the act of writing and the fraught nature of confession. *Mouroir*, however, takes its highly experimental form from the material circumstances of its composition. Barred from painting, Breytenbach was allowed to write in prison, although anything he wrote was taken from his cell to be examined by the authorities as soon as it was written. Returned to him after his release, it is this writing that makes up the thirty-eight discrete sections of *Mouroir*, which range from surreal to hyperrealistic fragments, impressions and stories about his experiences in prison. Their dense, allusive and elliptical style perhaps owes as much to Breytenbach's frustrating the prison officials' attempts at finding incriminating evidence as to the surrealist prose poetry it resembles.

More recent Afrikaans fiction in the experimental line consciously participates in the magical realism praised by Brink. Etienne van Heerden, for example, regularly referred to as a 'South African Marquez', weaves the fantastical with the everyday in *Die Swye van Mario Salviati* (2000; translated as *The Long Silence of Mario Salviati*, 2002). Here, as in most of his novels, a remote rural community is disrupted by the arrival of an outsider who exposes a hidden history the community has jealously guarded. In this case, a young arts administrator, Ingi Friedländer, who has come to buy a sculpture for the new Houses of Parliament, is taken up by the feuding Pistorius and Bergh families. They draw her into a welter of stories which add mysterious layers to the historical record; as in Van Heerden's *Toorberg* (1986; translated into English as *Ancestral Voices*, 1989), the dead interact with the living or comment on their actions, and in *The Long Silence* two hundred years of history swirl around the transition to a post-apartheid society. The story of Salviati himself, the deaf, dumb and now blind Italian stonecutter brought to South Africa as a prisoner of war, is just one of the stories Ingi is told, but it serves to focus the novel on the nature of art, which the bureaucrat has to learn anew before returning to Cape Town.

Experimentalism and essentialism

A tendency to essentialise form in relation to social historical circumstance has held strong sway within the history of South African literary reception. Chapman has been far from alone in tending, as he does in *Southern African Literatures*, towards the view that it is only a writer like 'the "unschooled" Matshoba' who 'can quite unselfconsciously be less than an artist with his testimony claiming authenticity as the representation of his life condition'. White novelists, in any language, seem fated by the privileges of 'race, education, income, and reputation' to feel 'the need to be enormously self-conscious about the truth of their fiction' (*Southern African Literatures*, p. 386).

Michael Cawood Green's *Sinking: A Verse Novella* (1997) exemplifies this self-consciousness in its representation of a 1960s mining disaster as an event – something approximating Benjamin's 'Messianic time', 'a simultaneity of past and future in an instantaneous present' (*Illuminations*, p. 265) – rather than an unfolding narrative. Treated as a multidimensional image, the sinkhole that opens up beneath an Afrikaans mining family's home is presented through a chorus of voices (the family, their servant, neighbours, workers on the mine, a semi-omniscient authorial voice mediating reportage, historical discourse and a web of intertextual references) that swirl around it. In the case of *For the Sake of Silence* (2008), a heavily researched account of a group of monks from a strictly contemplative community who come from Europe to South Africa in the 1880s only to be expelled from their order after giving in to the temptation to engage in the mission work forbidden to them, Cawood Green uses the high realism of the nineteenth-century novel as something of an experiment in itself, in which the form is ultimately resisted by the material it tries to contain (see Green's *Novel Histories*).

In 1991 Njabulo Ndebele warned that the essentialised black identity of 1970s and 1980s liberationist writing should not replicate the reductive binaries of white hegemony (see *South African Literature and Culture*, 1991). One particular codification of identity produced by South African sociopolitical discourse provides a tempting place from which to subvert the racialised classifications informing Ndebele's concern, even as it is in many ways the victim of them. Coloured authors write out of a fluid, contingent and indeterminate process of racial identity formation which, when brought into the related critiques of gender to be found in the work of writers like Zoë Wicomb, presents a powerful challenge to essentialism in general – as long as one reads this, of course, as the result of a particular cultural and historical positioning, rather than a siting between or outside 'purer' categorisations.

Wicomb's *You Can't get Lost in Cape Town* (1987) gave renewed prominence to the short-story cycle as an important form in contemporary South African fiction. Linked though the stories are through a common narrator / focaliser, a young coloured woman attempting to define her identity in relation to friends, lover and family, the coherence of the stories – along with the narrator's fragmented coming of age – is undermined by the gaps between them. In the novel that followed, *David's Story* (2000), the tension between the search for a coloured identity based upon a common history and an identity defined by difference and discontinuity is expressed in a more overtly metafictional text, one in which any number of stories collide with and collapse into each other, and meaning – individual and historical – is provisional and unreliable. The form of the novel itself actively resists any hope of a cohesive cultural identity, much as the radical fragmentation of the narrative voice in Yvette Christianse's *Unconfessed* (2006) refuses to respond to the lack of direct, first-person slave narratives of the Cape Colony by providing 'a complete, consoling recuperation of the colonial record' (Christianse, 'About this Book').

Wicomb specifically acknowledges Bessie Head as a precursor, and in doing so emphasises the relation between experimental form and identity as a socially fraught construct. Born in a mental hospital to a white woman with a history of mental illness who was reinstitutionalised when her parents found that she was pregnant with the child of a black man, a series of personal and political pressures resulted in Head becoming a political refugee in Botswana. *When Rain Clouds Gather* (1968), the novel she wrote about the newly independent country in which she was so precariously placed, gave glimpses of the innovative techniques that would set her apart from other African writers being published at that time, but it is the overtly autobiographical *A Question of Power* (1973) that places Head most clearly in an 'experimental line'.

Written during a period in which she had suffered a number of mental breakdowns, the novel follows roughly the course of her own life. At the point where the protagonist begins to suffer attacks of mental illness, the narrative shifts back and forth, without any overt correlation, between the horrors of her inner torment and the details of daily life in a small rural village. Hallucinatory sequences clearly drawing on her experience as a rejected mixed race child coming of age in an intensely racist context slowly give way to her involvement in the communal gardening which forms the central focus of the world she inhabits. This humble, caring, communal activity provides the basis for the novel's concluding affirmative vision – an ending that would elude Head herself; after a period of heavy drinking and ill health, she died in a coma in 1986. This begs the question of the relationship between literary form and lived experience, particularly when the broken life behind the fractured form can be read back so directly into a specific sociopolitical context. The line between experimentalism and breakdown in the much debated 'special case' of South Africa, emblematic on a global scale for its formalisation of ruptures and disjunctures, can be especially tenuous, but it is a suitable reminder of how hard-won have been the achievements of the experimental line in South African writing.

Bibliography

Anderson, B. *Imagined Communities: Reflections on the Origin and Spread of Nationalism* [1983], London: Verso, 1991.

Attridge, D. *J. M. Coetzee and the Ethics of Reading: Literature in the Event*, Pietermaritzburg: University of KwaZulu-Natal Press and University of Chicago Press, 2005.

Attridge, D., and R. Jolly (eds.). *Writing South Africa: Literature, Apartheid, and Democracy, 1970–1995*, Cambridge University Press, 1998.

Attwell, D. *J. M. Coetzee: South Africa and the Politics of Writing*, Berkeley: University of California Press and Cape Town: David Philip, 1993.

    Rewriting Modernity: Studies in Black South African Literary History, Pietermaritzburg: University of KwaZulu-Natal Press, 2005 and Athens: Ohio University Press, 2006.

Barker, D. A. 'Escaping the Tyranny of Magic Realism? A Discussion of the Term in Relation to the Novels of Zake Mda', *Postcolonial Text* 4:2 (2008), 1–20.

Barris, K. 'Hunting the Snark,' review of *The Ibis Tapestry, Mail and Guardian*, 7–13 August 1998, 8.

Bell, D., and J. U. Jacobs. 'Introduction', in Bell and Jacobs, *Ways of Writing*, 1–14.

Bell, D., and J. U. Jacobs (eds.). *Ways of Writing: Critical Essays on Zakes Mda*, Pietermaritzburg: University of KwaZulu-Natal Press, 2009.

Benjamin, W. *Illuminations*, ed. Hannah Arendt, trans. Harry Zohn, London: Fontana, 1973.

Bethlehem, L. *Skin Tight: Apartheid Literary Culture and its Aftermath*, Pretoria: University of South Africa Press, 2006.

Boetie, D. *Familiarity is the Kingdom of the Lost*, London: Arena, 1969.

Brink, A. *A Chain of Voices*, London: Faber, 1982.

    Kennis van die Aand, Cape Town: Buren, 1973.

    Looking on Darkness, London: W. H. Allen, 1974.

'A Real and Magical *Devil*', review of *The Devil's Chimney*, *Leadership*, August 1997, www.annelandsman.com/index.php?mode=objectlist&section_id=138&object_id= 246, accessed August 2009.

States of Emergency, London: Faber, 1988.

Chapman, M. 'The Writing of Politics and the Politics of Writing: On Reading Dovey on Reading Lacan on Reading Coetzee', *Journal of Literary Studies/Tydskrif vir Literatuur-wetenskp* 4:3 (1988), 327–41.

Christiansë, Y. *Unconfessed*, New York: Other Press, 2006; Cape Town: Kwela Books, 2007.

'*Unconfessed*: About this Book – Author's Note', www.randomhouse.com/catalog/ display.pperl?isbn=9781590512814&view=rg, accessed October 2010.

Coetzee, A. 'Literature and Crisis: One Hundred Years of Afrikaans Literature and Afrikaner Nationalism', in M. Trump (ed.), *Rendering Things Visible: Essays on South African Literary Culture*, Johannesburg: Ravan, 1990, 322–66.

'Literature in Afrikaans', in F. A. Irele and S. Gikandi (eds.), *Cambridge History of African and Caribbean Literature*, vol. I, Cambridge University Press, 2004, 408–23.

Coetzee, J. M. *Age of Iron*, London: Secker & Warburg, 1990.

'Alex La Guma and the Responsibilities of the South African Writer', in J. Okpaku (ed.), *New African Literature and the Arts*, vol. III, New York: Third Press, 1973, 116–24.

Boyhood: Scenes from Provincial Life, London: Secker & Warburg, 1997.

Disgrace, London: Secker & Warburg, 1999.

Dusklands, Johannesburg: Ravan, 1974.

Elizabeth Costello: Eight Lessons, London: Secker & Warburg, 2003.

Foe, London: Secker & Warburg, 1986.

In the Heart of the Country, London: Secker & Warburg, 1977. Published in the USA as *From the Heart of the Country*, New York: Harper & Row, 1977.

'J. M. Coetzee in Conversation with Jane Poyner', in J. Poyner (ed.), *J. M. Coetzee and the Idea of the Public Intellectual*, Athens: Ohio University Press, 2006, 21–41.

Life & Times of Michael K, London: Secker & Warburg, 1983.

The Master of Petersburg, London: Secker & Warburg, 1994.

Summertime: Scenes from a Provincial Life, London: Harvill Secker, 2009.

Waiting for the Barbarians, London: Secker & Warburg, 1980.

White Writing: On the Culture of Letters in South Africa, New Haven, CT: Yale University Press, 1988.

Youth, London: Secker & Warburg, 2002.

Cooper, B. *Magical Realism in West African Fiction: Seeing with a Third Eye*, London: Routledge, 1998.

Dovey, T. *The Novels of J. M. Coetzee: Lacanian Allegories*, Johannesburg: Ad Donker, 1988.

Gaylard, G. 'Meditations on Magical Realism', *Current Writing* 11:2 (1999), 92–109.

Gordimer, N. 'The Idea of Gardening', *New York Review of Books*, 2 February 1984, 3–4.

Green, M. *Novel Histories: Past, Present, and Future in South African Fiction*, Johannesburg: Witwatersrand University Press, 1997.

Green, M. Cawood. *For the Sake of Silence*, Roggebaai: Umuzi, 2008; London: Quartet Books, 2010.

Sinking: A Verse Novella. Johannesburg: Penguin, 1997.

Head, B. *A Question of Power*, New York: Pantheon, 1973; London: Heinemann, 1974.

When Rain Clouds Gather, New York: Simon & Schuster, 1968; London: Victor Gollancz, 1969.

JanMohamed, A. 'The Economy of Manichean Allegory: The Function of Racial Difference in Colonialist Literature', *Critical Inquiry* 12 (1985), 59–87.

Landsman, A. *The Devil's Chimney*, New York: Soho, 1997.

Leroux, E. *Sewe Dae by die Silbersteins*, Cape Town: Human & Rousseau, 1962. Translation by C. Eglington as *Seven Days at the Silbersteins*, Johannesburg: Central News Agency, 1964.

Mda, Z. *Cion*, Johannesburg: Penguin, 2007.

    The Heart of Redness, Cape Town: Oxford University Press and New York: Farrar, Strauss & Giroux, 2002.

    The Madonna of Excelsior, Cape Town: Oxford University Press and New York: Farrar, Strauss & Giroux, 2004.

    She Plays with the Darkness, Florida Hills: Vivlia, 1995; Trenton, NJ: Africa World Press, 1999.

    Ways of Dying, Cape Town: Oxford University Press, 1995; New York: Picador, 2002.

    The Whale Caller, Johannesburg: Penguin, 2005.

Mphahlele, E. *Down Second Avenue* [1959], London: Faber, 1971.

Mutloatse, M. (ed.). *Forced Landing: Africa South: Contemporary Writings*, Johannesburg: Ravan, 1980.

Ndebele, N. *The Cry of Winnie Mandela: A Novel*, Cape Town: David Philip, 2003.

    Fools and other Stories, Johannesburg: Ravan, 1983.

    South African Literature and Culture: Rediscovery of the Ordinary [1991], Manchester University Press, 1994.

Nkosi, L. 'Fiction by Black South Africans' [1966], in L. Stiebel and L. Gunner (eds.), *Still Beating the Drum: Critical Perspectives on Lewis Nkosi*, Johannesburg: Witwatersrand University Press and Amsterdam: Rodopi, 2006, 245–55.

    Mating Birds, Johannesburg: Ravan, 1979.

    'Postmodernism and Black Writing in South Africa', in Attridge and Jolly (eds.), *Writing South Africa*, 75–90.

Nicol, M. *Horseman*, London: Bloomsbury, 1994.

    The Ibis Tapestry, New York: Knopf, 1998.

    Payback, Cape Town: Umuzi, 2008.

    The Powers That Be, London: Bloomsbury, 1989.

    This Day and Age, London: Bloomsbury, 1992.

Pippin, R. B. *Modernism as a Philosophical Problem: On the Dissatisfactions of European High Culture*, Cambridge, MA, and Oxford: Blackwell, 1991.

Plaatje, S. T. *Mhudi: An Epic of Native Life a Hundred Years Ago* [1930], London: Heinemann, 1978.

Plomer, W. *Turbott Wolfe* [1926], London: Hogarth Press, 1965.

Rich, P. 'Apartheid and the Decline of the Civilization Idea: An Essay on Nadine Gordimer's *July's People* and J. M. Coetzee's *Waiting for the Barbarians*', *Research in African Literatures* 15:3 (1984), 365–93.

Serote, M. *To Every Birth its Blood*, Johannesburg: Ravan, 1981.

Van Heerden, E. *Toorberg*, Cape Town: Tafelberg, 1986. Translation by M. Hacksley as *Ancestral Voices*, London: Allison & Busby, 1989.

Die Swye van Mario Salviati, Cape Town: Tafelberg, 2000. Translation by C. Knox as *The Long Silence of Mario Salviati*, London: Hodder & Stoughton, 2002.

Van Niekerk, M. *Agaat*, Cape Town: Tafelberg, 2004. Translation by M. Heyns as *The Way of the Women*, London: Little, Brown, 2007.

Triomf, Cape Town: Queillerie, 1994. Translation by L. de Kock as *Triomf*, Johannesburg: Jonathan Ball, 1999.

Vaughan, M. 'Literature and Politics: Currents in South African Writing in the Seventies', *Journal of Southern African Studies* 9:1 (1982), 118–38.

Visser, N. 'Fictional Projects and the Irruptions of History: Mongane Serote's *To Every Birth its Blood*', *English Academy Review* 4 (1987), 67–76.

Vladislavić, I. *The Exploded View*, Johannesburg: Random House, 2004.

The Folly, Cape Town and Johannesburg: David Philip, 1993.

Missing Persons, Cape Town and Johannesburg: David Philip, 1989.

Portrait with Keys – Joburg & What-What, Roggebaai: Umuzi, 2006.

Propaganda by Monuments, Cape Town and Johannesburg: David Philip, 1996.

The Restless Supermarket, Cape Town and Johannesburg: David Philip, 2001.

Warnes, C. 'Chronicles of Belief and Unbelief: Zakes Mda and the Question of Magical Realism in South African Literature', in Bell and Jacobs, *Ways of Writing*, 73–90.

Wicomb, Z. *David's Story*, New York: Feminist Press; Cape Town: Kwela Books, 2000.

You Can't get Lost in Cape Town, London: Virago, 1987.

Woodward, W. 'Whales, Clones and Two Ecological Novels: *The Whale Caller* and Jane Rosenthal's *Souvenir*', in Bell and Jacobs, *Ways of Writing*, 333–53.

38

The book in South Africa

PETER D. MCDONALD

In 1980 the University of Cape Town offered its final-year undergraduates a specialist option entitled 'The Book in Africa' as part of its new African Literature programme. In his prospectus, the convenor, J. M. Coetzee, noted that it was a novel and potentially risky choice for students:

> We will be exploring some of the determinants of literary production not often dealt with in literary studies: environmental pressures of all kinds on writers, the economics of publishing and distributing literary works, the nature of the readership of literary works, etc. Since much of the information required for this kind of study is not readily available, students are forewarned that the course will entail a certain amount of bibliographical ferreting and a certain amount of practical investigative research.   ('Book in Africa')

There was, indeed, much ferreting. Among other things, Coetzee encouraged students to investigate 'the location of bookstores in the Cape Peninsula and the types of clientele they serve'; 'the library services in the black residential areas of the Cape'; the histories and editorial policies of a number of 'South African literary magazines', including *Bolt* (1970–5), *Classic* (1963–71), *Contrast* (1960–), *Izwi* (1971–4), *New Classic* (1975–8), *New Coin* (1965–), *Ophir* (1967–76), *Purple Renoster* (1956–72) and *Staffrider* (1978–93). In addition, he suggested they might consider which 'works by black South African writers' the apartheid censors 'tended to proscribe' and which ones they 'let through'; the 'origin and development of the Heinemann African Writers series'; and, given the emphasis on South and West African contexts, he suggested that students might 'compare and contrast Onitsha market literature with the South African *fotoroman* [photo-novel] in terms of themes and readership'.

In the same year, the new, state-sponsored Centre for South African Litera-ture Research (CENSAL), then under Charles Malan's directorship, launched

For their generous research assistance, my thanks go to Donald Powers, Peter Johnston and the staff at the National English Literary Museum in Grahamstown; and for permission to quote from unpublished materials, I would like to thank John Coetzee.

its *SA Literature* series, an annual survey of the literary activities across all South Africa's languages, which called for a comparable historiographical shift towards the 'socio-political' context of literary production, albeit one that begged a number of large questions to which Coetzee was already alert. For all its comparative ambitions, the series implicitly perpetuated aspects of apartheid thinking by treating all South Africa's literatures as separate linguistic systems. Each volume was divided into three distinct sections, covering 'English Literature', 'Black Literature (Vernacular)' and 'Afrikaanse Literatuur' (Galloway, *SA Literature/Literatuur*, pp. 9–10). Because the first volume, covering 1980, appeared only in 1982, Coetzee did not refer to this series in his course outline. What is worth noting about this unintended conjunction, however, is that neither CENSAL nor Coetzee mentioned the emergent interdisciplinary field now generally known as the history of the book. Whilst Coetzee included on his extensive reading list Richard D. Altick's *The English Common Reader* (1957), Robert Escarpit's *The Book Revolution* (1966), Q. D. Leavis's *Fiction and the Reading Public* (1932) and John Sutherland's *Fiction and the Fiction Industry* (1978), all of which made important, though indirect, contributions to the new field, he did not cite the work of the more self-consciously pioneering book historians of the 1960s and 1970s, such as Roger Chartier, Robert Darnton, Elizabeth Eisenstein, Lucien Febvre, Henri-Jean Martin or D. F. McKenzie. Tellingly, he was drawn to the field not by an interest in the history of the book as such but by a range of questions concerning the predicament of African writers in the second half of the twentieth century. His reading list gave special prominence to essays by, among others, Chinua Achebe, Ali Mazrui, Es'kia Mphahlele, Ngugi Wa Thiong'o, Emmanuel Obiechina and Wole Soyinka. Pointing to a further research topic based on these source materials, he suggested students might wish to 'outline the argument for writers in newly independent African states to throw themselves into the activity of nation-building and national identity formation' and to reflect on 'some of the positions that African writers and intellectuals take up on this question'. Having said this, he also cited the Chicago sociologist Edward Shils, whose work informed another suggested topic on 'the tension between a metropolitan orientation and a provincial orientation in the cultural life of Cape Town, as revealed in its cultural organs'.

Given the history of its advent during the era of European colonisation and its role as an agent for change in Africa, *the book* lay at the heart of these large issues for Coetzee. Though this downplayed the influence of Islamic scribal culture, which, as more recent scholarship has shown, spread into sub-Saharan Africa in the course of the thirteenth century, it nonetheless remains the case that the arrival of the book, and print culture generally, from Europe after the fifteenth century represented a decisive event for African cultures in which dance, the visual arts, music and varieties of orature constituted the traditionally dominant expressive media (see Jeppie and Diagne, *Meanings of Timbuktu*). In Coetzee's view, the consequences of this were not just cultural or political. 'If we accept (following Ong, McLuhan, Goody) that print changes modes of thought', he remarked in his preparatory notes for the course, 'then printing can be seen as the agent whereby the world is modernized' ('Book in Africa'). Echoing McLuhan's arguments in *The Gutenberg Galaxy* (1962), he added that 'it is the print quality of the artefact, not its content (the medium rather than the message) that is of prime importance'. To understand this, and so to grasp the full implications of the linkage between literacy and modernity, it was essential to attend not just to the history of the book in Africa or to 'mundane social factors in the study of the growth of the reading habit, e.g., availability of light, of seating space in trains, etc.' It was necessary to analyse 'the class structure of so-called emergent African nations' and, above all, the place of the 'intelligentsia' in that structure, since this particular social faction was the 'prime modernising agent' for whom newspapers, periodicals and books of all kinds were essential media.

This broader sociopolitical analysis, which took the publishing industry as its starting point, raised a number of pressing questions for aspirant African-ists. 'As long as African writers remain bound into a supranational system of publication (in the broadest sense)', Coetzee commented in his notes, 'the old splits in consciousness (which may or may not aid production) will persist':

> Writing for a national audience versus writing for an international audience; writing to foster nationalist values versus writing to foster internationalist values (the values of the international intelligentsia); writing after African models versus writing after metropolitan models; writing by African standards versus writing by metropolitan standards.

Indeed, at one level, 'The Book in Africa' was designed to highlight the value of developing an indigenous 'system of publication' for the future. Coetzee did not intend his course to address Africanists only, however. Making the book the initial point of departure also opened up some key methodological questions for literary students in general. As he noted, the course presupposed that 'the unit of historical meaning is not who writes what at what time, but that, at a certain time, someone should write X, someone should publish it, someone should bring it to the attention of readers, and someone should read it'. The primary object was 'the complete act of transmission'. For literary students, or scholars for that matter, schooled in one or another tradition of 'close reading', who considered the 'words on the page' or more ambitiously 'discourse' to be their chief concern, or, indeed, for those more interested in contextual questions, this entailed a radical shift in orientation. 'From this point of view', Coetzee continued,

> it is not the publishing industry in isolation that must be examined, and certainly not the activity of writing (or texts in isolation), but the total industry that involves the sponsorship of texts (in part by the creation of a climate, in part by educational processes), the dissemination of texts (publishing, distribution, selling and lending), and the criticism of texts.

At a time when Literary Studies was expanding its conception of its primary object, shifting from a canon of great works to ideas of, say, 'colonial discourse', Coetzee's emphasis on the 'total industry', and his effort to displace attention away from the 'activity of writing', was as challengingly novel as it was demanding. In addition to acquiring some expertise in a wide range of disciplines, including literary criticism, sociology, cognitive psychology, cultural history, politics and economics, he expected his students to have a firm grounding in bibliography and to develop an appreciation of its relevance to African studies and humanistic scholarship generally. Given all the ferreting involved, not to mention the fact that the course tested the limits of Literary Studies at the time, it is perhaps unsurprising that it was not a success. Though the University of Cape Town's embattled African Literature programme continued, despite opposition from its traditionalist English Department, Coetzee's option attracted few takers and it was shelved after the first year. He did consider reviving it in the mid 1990s, as part of a new interdisciplinary Masters in Literary Studies, but this never came to anything. If the course had little appeal to students eager to fashion a more affective, rather than scholarly, connection with Africa, it was evidently also ahead of its time. Indeed, despite important ground-clearing efforts by a new generation of scholars, writing a history of the book in Africa in the comprehensive way Coetzee first envisaged in 1980 remains a task for the century ahead (see Beukes, *Boekewêreld*; Galloway and Venter, *Stilet*; Hofmeyr, *Portable Bunyan*; van der Vlies, *South African Textual Cultures*). What follows, then, is at best a suggestive series of notes towards a study of the book in South Africa, mapping the main coordinates of a still largely unexplored territory, developing aspects of Coetzee's ambitious venture and focusing on its value as a tool for literary scholars.

Books in African languages

The deceptively elementary bibliographical question 'Who publishes?', which underpinned Coetzee's analysis of the African writers' immediate predicament post independence, had a special inflection in South Africa, where the fraught history of European domination intersected with a peculiarly complex multilingual environment. Whilst writers who chose English as their literary medium were until the 1940s, and, indeed, well into the 1970s, bound mainly to a 'supranational system' of book publication – periodicals always created other, more localised openings – those who chose Afrikaans or one of South Africa's many African languages depended on very different publishing networks that formed part of a national and, in some cases, regional system, which began to take shape in the course of the nineteenth century. It follows that no single or simple history of literary publishing in South Africa can be told. Since these multiple systems evolved within a political and economic context that was until 1994 deformed by the realities of white minority rule, it is also impossible to tell a pure version of this history. Yet, for all the entanglements and highly contested divisions, there was at least one common dilemma faced by all South African writers. Whilst the large problems of economic ownership remained particularly intractable for black writers, at least until the first major black-owned publishing house was established in 1982, all writers had to contend with the fact that publishers were at one and the same time vital intermediaries, who helped to create a public for their work, and sometimes questionable guardians, who were driven by their own cultural and other imperatives. This dilemma was, of course, not unique to South African writers. Given the particularities of South African history, however, the pressures it created were especially acute. Since this was most evident to those who wrote in African languages, it is to them that I turn first.

Writing in 1945, R. H. W. Shepherd, then director of Lovedale, the oldest mission press in South Africa, remarked that 'the mass of the vernacular literature published in the past emanated, and still today emanates, from missionary presses, and naturally such literature has sought to fulfil the aims of missionary societies' (Peires, 'Lovedale Press', p. 71). This obscured the extent to which more independent secular spaces had begun to open up by the 1880s, especially in the newspapers founded by the educated Xhosa elite aligned to the emergent anti-tribalist New African movement (see Chapters 10 and 16). Yet Shepherd did capture the central problem African writers faced while the mission presses dominated book publishing. To begin with, the challenge was simply to get books produced at all, given the doubts most presses had about their commercial viability. In 1907, for instance, the great isiXhosa *imbongi* S. E. K. Mqhayi found himself having to pay Lovedale to print *USamson*, his (now lost) politically inflected retelling of the biblical Samson story. Despite this, as Opland notes, Mqhayi's own promotional notices for the book pointedly drew attention to the fact that it was published not by Lovedale but by *Izwi labantu* (The Voice of the People, 1897), the independent isiXhosa newspaper to which he contributed regularly (Opland, 'First Novel in Xhosa', pp. 96–8). For the most part, though, the difficulties centred on the more predictable conflicts between writers, who sought to rethink the encounter between tradition and modernity on their own terms, and the mission presses, who remained committed to their evangelising aims. As a consequence, literary modernity was, as *USamson* and Thomas Mofolo's celebrated Sesotho novel *Chaka* (1925) testified, all but inseparable from Christian modernity. *Chaka* was first published by Morija, which was in modern-day Lesotho, one of the main rivals to Lovedale, which was in the Eastern Cape.

By the 1930s the situation had begun to change as new spaces opened up within and outside the mission presses. By agreeing to issue *Mhudi* in 1930, the novel, written in English, which Sol T. Plaatje had been trying to get published for almost ten years, and A. C. Jordan's *Ingqumbo Yeminyanya* (The Wrath of the Ancestors) in 1940, Shepherd showed that he was, as White put it, 'more broadly sympathetic to the needs of literature than to the narrow concerns of the missionary' ('Lovedale Press', p. 71). Both novels, which are critical of European and missionary thinking, stand as powerful testaments to what Masilela has called the 'the secularisation of the New African intellectual and literary imagination' (Gikandi, *Encyclopaedia of African Literature*, p. 509). Unlike Lovedale, the Mariannhill Mission Press, based in what is now KwaZulu-Natal, generally kept to the mainstream traditions of missionary publishing – religious and educational books – though it did bring out B. W. Vilakazi's early isiZulu fictions *Noma-nini* (Forever and Ever, 1935) and *Nje-nempela* (Really and Truly, 1944). At around this time, however, new independent outlets began to have a more significant impact on the system. In 1935 the University of Witwatersrand Press, which was founded in 1922, launched its long-running Bantu Treasury series under Clement Doke's astute editorship. By publishing many of the major contemporary African-language poets – notably Mqhayi, J. J. R. Jolobe and Vilakazi – Doke established himself as the most pre-eminent guardian of modern African literature of his time. The other key publisher to support the new trends was Shuter & Shooter, a commercial firm established in Pietermaritzburg in 1925. Primarily an educational publisher, Shuters none the less developed a strong isiZulu literary list, beginning with John Dube's

Insila ka Shaka (The Bodyservant of King Shaka, 1930) and the early fictions of E. H. A. Made and R. R. R. Dhlomo, which first appeared in the 1940s.

During the next sixty years, which saw the rise and fall of the apartheid state, the African-language literary revolution that began in the 1880s was sidelined, if not wholly derailed. This was in part a result of direct governmental intervention. It is significant, for instance, that Mazisi Kunene, in many ways Vilakazi's direct literary successor, published his two major epic poems of this period in self-translated English editions and abroad. Both *Emperor Shaka the Great* (1979) and *Anthem of the Decades* (1981) were first published as part of the Heinemann African Writers series. What effectively removed Kunene, who went into exile in 1960, not just from the African-language tradition but also from the public domain in South Africa, however, was the personal ban imposed on him throughout the apartheid era (see Chapter 20). Along with a number of other writers, he was formally declared a 'listed communist' in April 1966, which made it illegal to quote or publish any of his writings. The censors compounded this blanket ban by specifically suppressing *Anthem of the Decades* as well. The other black writers affected by the 1966 banning order – Todd Matshikiza, Bloke Modisane, Es'kia Mphahlele, Lewis Nkosi and Can Themba – all of whom wrote in English, suffered a similar double fate.

Since the number of African-language books submitted to the censors was actually negligible, such direct repressive measures were not the greatest threat to this developing tradition of modern writing during the apartheid years. What proved most damaging were the monopolistic ambitions of the Afrikaner-owned publishing houses that began to take over the African-language market in the 1950s and to refashion it along apartheid lines. Working closely with the school inspectors who controlled the selection of prescribed books firms like Afrikaanse Pers-Boekhandel (APB), which had direct links to the Afrikaner political elite, made the most of the new commercial opportunities 'Bantu' and later 'Homeland' education afforded. For a writer like Sibusiso (C. L. S.) Nyembezi, this quickly made working with them impossible. Having started out as an APB author with his first novel *Mntanami! Mntanami!* (My Child! My Child!, 1950), he moved to Shuter & Shooter the following decade with *Inkinsela yase Mgungundlovu* (1961; translated as *The Rich Man of Pietermaritzburg*), where he stayed and also took up a position as African-language literary editor. By the 1980s, though Shuters retained a share of the isiZulu market, and though Lovedale, multinationals like Oxford University Press and local university presses remained active on the margins, the system was dominated by J. L. van Schaik, Via Africa and Educum. The last two were the educational African-language subsidiaries of the giant Afrikaner conglomerates that emerged in the 1970s, Nasionale Pers and Perskor. For commercial and political reasons, these publishing houses were committed to promoting literature and serving a curriculum that reinforced, or at least did not unsettle, apartheid thinking.

Books in Afrikaans

As with the four major African languages – isiXhosa, isiZulu, Setswana and Sesotho – Afrikaans began to be self-consciously adopted as a literary language in the last decades of the nineteenth century, with newspaper and then book publishers playing an influential role in the process. D. F. du Toit, a Paarl-based publisher aligned to the First Afrikaans Language Movement, led the way, launching his *Afrikaanse Gedigte* (Afrikaans Poems) series in 1878 and bringing out the work credited with being the first novella in Afrikaans, C. P. Hoogenhout's *Catharina*, a year later. Given the specific circumstances that influenced the overdetermined evolution of Afrikaans (see Chapter 13) – in particular, the tensions among a nationalist-inspired linguistic separatism versus the ineluctable historical ties to Dutch and numerous other languages – this politico-literary struggle was always fraught and often conflicted, as the names of the first major Afrikaans literary publishers suggest. After the Hollandsch-Afrikaansche Uitgeversmaatschappij (HAUM, or the Dutch-Afrikaans Publishing Company), which had offices in Cape Town and Amsterdam, was founded in 1894, the next major company to emerge was pointedly called Nasionale Pers (National Press). Established in 1915, Nasionale, which also had substantial newspaper interests, focused on Afrikaans titles, which it published out of Bloemfontein and Cape Town. Though the founder of the other key literary imprint of this period, J. L. van Schaik, was Dutch-born, he was no less committed to the nationalist cause. Van Schaik, which was based in Pretoria, also opened for business in 1915. The ascendancy of the separatist ideals, which was officially confirmed in 1925 when Afrikaans replaced Dutch as the Union's other official language alongside English, was reflected in two important developments within the new national publishing system in the 1930s: the emergence of the Pretoria-based Afrikaanse Pers (Afrikaans Press) in 1932, and the creation of the long-running periodical *Ons Eie Boek* (Our Own Book) three years later. Though Afrikaanse Pers, like Nasionale, began by publishing books and newspapers, it separated out its two main activities in the mid 1940s. Nasionale followed suit in 1950.

Even though most early Afrikaans writers were just as dedicated to the idea of the Afrikaner as a self-determining *volk* – though there were always dissenting voices – their relations with the publishers who came to dominate the system were not always harmonious. This was especially true for the generation that emerged in the 1930s. Whilst, some, notably the novelist C. M. van den Heever, who became a key champion of the Afrikaner's cultural and linguistic 'apartheid', worked happily with the system – he had a long and productive relationship with van Schaik, Nasionale and Afrikaanse Pers – others, most notably the poet N. P. van Wyk Louw, who was the leader of a minority faction I have called the *volk* avant-garde, felt frustrated by the prevailing commercialism, parochialism and narrow moralism of the dominant publishing houses. Finding himself increasingly at odds with the mainstream guardians of *volk* culture, Van Wyk Louw, together with a small group of like-minded writers, including J. du P. Scholtz and 'Boerneef' (I. W. van der Merwe), formed a subscription publishing venture called the Vereniging vir die Vrye Boek (VVB or Coalition for the Free Book) in 1935. Though united by their desire to sidestep firms like van Schaik and Nasionale, which focused on the school book market where profits were to be made, the VVB, like so many writers' groups, was riven by internal disagreements, impeded by financial difficulties, and short-lived. It lasted five years, during which time it published only four titles, including a translation of Flaubert's Sadean tale of parricide *The Legend of Julian Hospitator* (1877) and Van Wyk Louw's second volume of poems, *Die Halwe Kring* (The Half Circle, 1937). Despite this, the VVB was, according to Kannemeyer, 'more important for the development of Afrikaans literature' than the more narrowly *volk*-oriented Afrikaanse Skrywerskring (Afrikaans Writers' Circle), which was formed in 1934 under Van den Heever's chairmanship (Kannemeyer, *Literatuur*, p. 122). Van den Heever was also the founding editor of the group's magazine *Tydskrif vir Letterkunde* (1951–).

In the years ahead Van Wyk Louw continued to defend the freedom of the Afrikaans book and the kind of literary republicanism to which he was dedicated, first through *Standpunte* (Standpoints), the combative literary periodical he co-founded in 1945, and then, more problematically, by ensuring that various literary academics and writers sympathetic to his *volk* avant-garde ideals took control of the apartheid censorship bureaucracy in the 1960s. Following the unpredictable twists and turns of literary history during the apartheid years, this particular 'fatal compromise', as Ampie Coetzee called it – the consequences of which I have detailed in *The Literature Police* (2009) – led to a revival of the VVB in 1975, when Ampie Coetzee, Ernst Lindenberg and

John Miles, all of whom had been colleagues of Louw's at the University of the Witwatersrand, formed Taurus, a clandestine subscription publishing venture that went on to become the most important dissident Afrikaans imprint of the late apartheid era (Trump, *Rendering Things Visible*, p. 345). Unlike the original VVB, which attempted to create space for the *volk* avant-garde, Taurus was aligned to a new, anti-*volk* faction within Afrikaans literary and intellectual culture, which set itself against apartheid and the Nationalist government as well as the censors and the overly compromised publishers of the early 1970s. Distinguishing themselves from Human & Rousseau (H & R, 1959), the leading publisher of the emergent *volk* avant-garde in the 1960s, they 'gave writers the assurance that [Taurus] would publish any manuscript of value without any form of pre-censorship being exercised' (Gordimer, *What Happened to 'Burger's Daughter'*, back cover; Venter, 'Inventing an Alternative'). In order to bypass the censors and avoid the financial costs publishers incurred when books were banned, Taurus initially mailed its titles directly to subscribers. By that point H & R already had a record of rejecting politically controversial works, partly for financial reasons and largely on the advice of their chief reader, the poet D. J. Opperman. Whilst it is possible to describe other Afrikaans publishers of the apartheid era as interventionist – the small firm Buren, for instance, which enjoyed a precarious existence in the late 1960s and early 1970s, and Prog, a poetry imprint launched in 1988 – Taurus was the most prominent and successful.

The 1970s was an epochal decade in the history of Afrikaans literary publishing in a number of respects. In the first place, following global trends in the industry towards increased concentration, Afrikaanse Pers, which had already merged with Dagbreekpers (Dawn Press) in 1962, amalgamated with Voortrekkerpers (Voortrekker Press) in 1971 to form the conglomerate Perskor. In a simultaneous process, Nasionale Pers began to reconstitute itself as a rival, acquiring a series of major literary imprints, starting with Tafelberg (1951) in 1970, H & R in 1977 and van Schaik in 1986. These two giants dominated the Afrikaans publishing scene throughout the rest of the apartheid era, while, as we have seen, also making significant inroads into the African-language and 'Bantu education' markets. The apartheid censors also contributed to the cultural shift in the 1970s by breaking the pact regarding Afrikaans literature, which they had kept throughout the previous decade. They banned André Brink's *Kennis van die Aand* (*Looking on Darkness*, 1973) in 1974 and Breyten Breytenbach's *Skryt* (1972) a year later. This marked a decisive change in the relations between Afrikaans writers and the apartheid state, signalled by, among other things, the formation of Taurus and the multiracial Afrikaans

Skrywersgilde (Writers' Guild), again in 1975. It also exposed a deep rift within the publishing world, a rift which had been growing in the course of the previous decade. Tellingly, neither Brink's *Kennis* nor Breytenbach's *Skryt* were issued by mainstream Afrikaans publishers. Whilst the former came out under the imprint of the small firm Buren after H & R rejected it, the latter was published in Amsterdam by Breytenbach's Dutch publisher Meulenhoff after he had rejected H & R. Following a heated public dispute in 1968, which centred on political issues, Breytenbach broke all ties with the firm, moving first to Buren and then to Taurus. The fallout from all this – further disputes over how best to confront the scourge of censorship, wrangles about the collaborationist stance of the major conglomerates, questions about H & R's independence within Nasionale, and so on – would continue to divide the Afrikaans literary world for the rest of the apartheid era.

Books in English

Because they had access to a 'supranational system of publication', centred mainly in London but also in New York, writers who adopted English as their main literary medium were always in a different position to their peers who chose to write in one or other of South Africa's minority languages. By the 1940s and 1950s, however, which saw the founding of a number of new local commercial firms, this situation gradually began to change. Though most were generalists with an interest in marketable Africana (popular histories, biographies, travel, bird and cook books), they also contributed to the postwar boom in literary publishing, which centred on Cape Town. A. A. Balkema, who initially published out of Amsterdam as well as Cape Town, produced English and Afrikaans titles, launching the poet Guy Butler's career with *Stranger to Europe* (1952); Howard Timmins focused on the English-language market and became the principal publisher for the prolific best-seller Lawrence Green after bringing out *Where Men Still Dream* (1945); while Purnell contributed to the development of a local literary scene by publishing *New South African Writing* (1964–), an annual selection produced by South African PEN, the oldest writers' group in the country, which was established in 1927. The most significant project of the 1940s, however, was Julian Rollnick's multilingual African Bookman, which inaugurated the local interventionist publishing tradition. Though short-lived – the imprint survived only from 1943 to 1948 – Rollnick produced over sixty titles, including his low-cost Sixpenny Library series, mainly in English, but also with translations in isiXhosa, isiZulu and Setswana, many of which offered an African perspective on social and political questions. Among the more notable titles in the Sixpenny series were Govan Mbeki's *Let's do it Together* (1944), about co-operative societies, Jacob Nhlapo's *Bantu Babel* (1944), about the future of African languages, and Pauline Podbrey's *Famous American Negroes* (1944), about, among others, Langston Hughes, Paul Robeson and Booker T. Washington. Rollnick also achieved distinction by inaugurating Es'kia Mphahlele's literary career with *Man Must Live and other Stories* (1946).

Periodicals of various kinds, including *Drum* (1951–), *Africa South* (1956–61), *Fighting Talk* (1942–63), *New Age* (1954–62), *Purple Renoster* (1956–72), *Contrast* (1960–) and *Classic* (1963–71), sustained this interventionist tradition throughout the 1950s and 1960s. It was only with the emergence of three new white owned imprints in the early 1970s – David Philip (1971) in Cape Town, and Ravan Press (1972) and Ad Donker (1973), both in the Johannesburg area – that the focus shifted to book publishing. The smaller Renoster Books imprint, which issued Mbuyiseni Mtshali's *Sounds of a Cowhide Drum* (1971) and Mongane Serote's *Yakhal'inkomo* (1972), also contributed to this shift, as did Bateleur Press (1974). Though these new publishers did not start exporting books abroad on a large scale, reversing the well-established trade relations of the colonial era, they did enter into various co-publishing or sub-licensing arrangements with British and US publishers, ranging from small specialist firms like Rex Collings in London and Third World Press in New York to larger-scale Africanist projects like Longman's Drumbeat Series and Heinemann's African Writers Series. Depending on the agreements negotiated, they tended to retain exclusive selling rights in South or southern Africa. In practice, this meant that from the early 1970s local English-language writers could potentially reach any one or more of five overlapping markets within the increasingly complex global Anglosphere: South Africa, southern Africa, anglophone Africa, the Commonwealth or North America.

These new English-language publishers, all of whom took a firm stand against censorship, though Ravan was the worst affected by the system, gave new life to the interventionist publishing tradition Rollnick initiated in the 1940s. David Philip launched his important Africasouth paperback series, which included a number of previously banned works, with a reprint of Harry Bloom's *Transvaal Episode* in 1982, while Ad Donker went on to become a leading poetry publisher of the Black Consciousness generation, and Ravan gave Wopko Jensma, J. M. Coetzee and Miriam Tlali their first break with, respectively, *Sing for our Execution* (1973), *Dusklands* (1974) and *Muriel at Metropolitan* (1975). Yet the transformation they effected in the literary marketplace was far from straightforward. This was not just because they were white-owned or because they continued to depend on the network of generally cautious established booksellers. It was also because they worked within what Peter Randall, the first director of Ravan, later called the 'framework of a dominant white liberal culture' and obliged authors 'to write and publish within that culture as well' (Gardner, *Publisher/Writer/Reader*, p. 14). This changed only in 1977 when the poet and literary academic Mike Kirkwood, whose political sympathies lay with a broadly Marxist tradition, took over as director of Ravan and set about attempting to address the problem of white liberal guardianship. Over the next decade he developed a more collectivist ownership structure within Ravan, working together with a number of leading black writers, notably Mothobi Mutloatse and Jaki Seroke, while also adopting a more co-operative editorial policy, especially for his two flagship projects, *Staffrider* (1978–93) and the related low-cost paperback Staffrider series (1979–86). In order to overcome the racialised system of distribution, which meant bypassing the traditional booksellers, all of whom were located in white residential areas, Kirkwood also helped to set up an informal network of sellers to get *Staffrider* magazine and the books directly into the townships.

Kirkwood's innovative strategies, some of which were a source of contention among writers, were not always successful and they were, in any case, simply part of what he saw as a 'transitional culture' (Kirkwood, '*Staffrider*', p. 31). To deal convincingly with the problem of white guardianship, which was inseparable from the larger underlying crisis of white minority rule, it was necessary to create a wholly independent, black-owned publishing house. This eventually happened in 1982, when Mutloatse and Seroke, with the support of the newly formed African Writers Association, founded Skotaville, the last major literary publisher to emerge during the apartheid era. James Matthews had led the way with his small, largely one-man BLAC (Black Literature and Arts Congress) publishing house in the early 1970s, which published in English and occasionally in Afrikaans (see Chapter 21). Though other outlets emerged in the late 1980s, notably Dinah Lefakane's feminist press Seriti sa Sechaba (1987–90) and COSAW (1988–95), the imprint of the Congress of South African Writers, Skotaville remained the largest and most diverse of the black-run imprints. As Seroke noted, it was named after Mweli Skota (1893–1976), not just because he was a new African moderniser, a founding figure in the early ANC and a prominent journalist on the black-owned newspapers of the 1920s and 1930s, but because 'throughout his life he wanted to establish a publishing house, an independent publishing house, that would put a positive image of African people right through the continent' (Seroke, 'Voice of the Voiceless', p. 201).

Like COSAW and Ravan, Skotaville was heavily dependent on foreign donor support. Whereas the former received substantial backing from the Dutch, Swedish and Norwegian governments, often via their own national writers' groups, Skotaville was funded by local corporate sponsors, the Rockefeller and Ford Foundations, and the South African Council of Churches. The last came about as a result of its close association with Desmond Tutu. In keeping with Skota's legacy, Mutloatse and Serote began by publishing a revived version of *The Classic*, the Pan-Africanist magazine Nat Nakasa had originally founded in 1963. Their more general ambition to establish continuities across the various moments in the history of an alternative African cultural modernity was reflected in the efforts they made to reclaim African-language publishing from the Afrikaner-dominated educational publishers, working in conjunction with the SACHED (South African Committee for Higher Education) Trust, a non-governmental educational organisation, and in the anthology *Umhlaba Wethu: An Historical Indictment* (the title meant 'Our Country or Earth'), which they published in 1987. This was the last volume in Mutloatse's three-part series of anthologies dedicated to archiving black cultural history, the first two volumes of which – *Forced Landing* (1980) and *Reconstruction* (1981) – had been published as part of Ravan's Staffrider series. To put these anthologies in perspective, it is worth comparing them to the kinds of books Perskor was producing for the 'Bantu Education' market at around this time. *Literary Gems*, a frequently reprinted collection of short stories Perskor first published in 1978, is a notable example. Whereas *Forced Landing* included stories by James Matthews, Mbulelo Mzamane, Bessie Head and Mtutuzeli Matshoba, *Literary Gems* made no mention of any black writers, focusing instead on Nadine Gordimer, Alan Paton, Jack Cope and Doris Lessing. Like all the major interventionist imprints founded in the 1970s, Skotaville was affected by censorship as well as other forms of official harassment, and often hampered by financial and managerial difficulties, but it survived to contribute to the end of apartheid, as did Ravan, David Philip and Ad Donker.

The future of the Book in South Africa

The massive process of political, cultural and economic transformation that got underway in South Africa in the 1990s inevitably had an impact on the smaller world of literary publishing. Whilst the withdrawal of foreign donor support affected the local interventionist publishing tradition, the more mainstream firms faced new challenges as the government's reform of the educational system made the lucrative school book market less predictable. Other developments within the 'supranational system of publication' also played a part, as multinationals like Random House in the UK, which was itself part of Bertelsmann AG, the German-based multimedia conglomerate, began to grant more editorial autonomy to their local offices. In 2005 Random founded Umuzi, which 'publishes accessible literary fiction with a South African flavour, and non-fiction that offers a fresh, culturally significant perspective on the country', mainly in English but also in Afrikaans (Umuzi). Their first titles included Antjie Krog's *Verweerskrif/ Body Bereft*, Lewis Nkosi's *Mandela's Ego*, Ivan Vladislavić's *Portrait with Keys* and Zoë Wicomb's *Playing in the Light*, all of which appeared in 2006. In a similar devolutionary spirit, Penguin launched its English-language SA Modern Classics series in 2005 with a reprint of Sol T. Plaatje's *Mhudi* as a complement to its more established list, SA Fiction. Under Stephen Gray's imaginative editorship, this series also included Alfred Hutchinson's *Road to Ghana* and A. Mopeli-Paulus's *The World and the Cattle*. Throughout the transitional period a number of small, alternative local publishers, notably Hond (1993–8) and Buchu Books (1987–97), came and went, while other new independents like Jacana (1991), Queillerie (1991) and Protea Boekhuis (1997) stayed for the longer term and established firms like Shuters and Lovedale continued to operate. The dismantling of the apartheid censorship bureaucracy, which was replaced by an unevenly modernised Film and Publication Board (FPB) in 1996, was another significant internal development. Reflecting its new role as a classificatory body, and the constitutional commitment not just to the 'freedom of expression' but to the 'freedom of artistic activity', the FPB has the following motto on its website: 'We inform. You choose' (accessed 13/7/11). (Given amendments to the legislation introduced in 2009, which open the way for a new form of censorship by imposing a form of pre-publication vetting, it remains to be seen whether or not the FPB continues to live up to this ideal.) For the most part, however, the transformation of the national publishing system was effected through various mergers and acquisitions, as the industry began to restructure itself for a post-apartheid future and a new multimedia age.

By 2008 most of the publishers that shaped the literary cultures of South Africa in the twentieth century had either ceased to exist or they had been absorbed into larger groups, surviving only as imprints (Evans and Seeber, *Politics of Publishing*). The most radical developments were in Afrikaans publishing. Whilst Perskor folded, selling off part of its business to the black-owned Kagiso Publishers in 1996, van Schaik became part of the large educational conglomerate Nasou Via Afrika in 2005. H & R, which acquired Taurus's list after it ceased in 1992, stayed with Nasionale, now reinvented as the large multi-lingual firm NB Publishers, alongside other imprints, including Tafelberg and Kwela Books. The latter, which focused on black writing, was founded in 1994. In the same year Ravan Press ended its three decades as an independent when Hodder & Stoughton Educational Southern Africa acquired a majority share-holding. Two years later it was wholly absorbed by Hodder, which had by then itself become part of Hodder Headline, and in 2000 it was sold to Macmillan SA. In 2004 Pan Macmillan, a subsidiary of the parent firm, began to reissue some Ravan titles as part of its new Picador Africa series. Whilst another major commercial firm, Jonathan Ball, which had been active since the late 1970s, acquired Ad Donker in 1992, David Philip continued as an independent until the founders, David and Marie Philip, retired in 1999. In 2000 New Africa Media, a division of the black empowerment group NAIL, acquired a major share in the firm, and five years later it became a key imprint of New Africa Books. In 1992, after Seroke and Mutloatse failed to agree on the best way forward in the new circumstances, Skotaville briefly became part of Nolwazi Publishers, which was owned by Macmillan, before being revived in 1999 in a joint venture with, among others, Juta, the well-established South African educational publisher, and the Black Management Forum. BLAC, which had been dormant throughout much of the 1990s, re-emerged in 2000 as Realities, once again under the direction of the indefatigable James Matthews, albeit this time with state support. In an effort to address one of the main challenges facing literary publishers in a democratic South Africa, which is committed to protecting all minority languages under the Constitution, Matthews launched Realities Xhosa in 2005, focusing on the work of Sindiwe Magona. A further testament to the state's concern to promote literacy and minority literatures in African languages was the appearance of the new South African Classics reprint series in 2009. Among the titles included in the first phase of this series, which was produced by the Department of Arts and Culture working jointly with the National Library of South Africa, were S. E. K. Mqhayi's collection of isiXhosa stories *Ityala Lamawele*, A. C. Jordan's isiXhosa novel *Ingqumbo Yeminyanya*, and Sibusiso Nyembezi's isiZulu novel *Inkinsela yase Mgungundlovu*.

Many factors contributed to J. M. Coetzee's interest in 'The Book in Africa' in 1980. At that point, while apartheid censorship was going through the darkest phase of its history, a new generation of Black Consciousness intellectuals who were critical of the way their work was being produced sought to break all ties with the white-dominated publishing industry in South Africa. As Coetzee was aware, these quarrels often centred on his own local publisher, Ravan

Press, which was then under Mike Kirkwood's engaging but embattled directorship. More or less simultaneously, albeit in different ways, Coetzee began to take issue with the way his own books were being presented and read. Having first aired his concerns when he received the CNA award for *Waiting for the Barbarians* (1980) in 1981, he returned to his theme in an interview two years later: 'I sometimes wonder whether it isn't simply that vast and wholly ideological superstructure constituted by publishing, reviewing and criticism that is forcing on me the fate of being a "South African novelist"' (Morphet, 'Two Interviews', p. 460; see also McDonald, *Literature Police*, pp. 303–8).

These concerns, and, indeed, the questions he raised in his prospectus for 'The Book in Africa', left their mark on his fictions as well, perhaps most explicitly in *Foe* (1986), which is, among other things, a sustained reflection on the origins of the 'English' novel as a product of the emergent bourgeois public sphere in eighteenth-century England and on the intimate linkage between ideas of authorship and the material trade in books. Yet, as we have seen, understanding the production, dissemination, sponsorship and criticism of texts – Coetzee's 'total industry' – has always had a particular urgency given the complex sociopolitical life of the book in South Africa. Whether as a product of the mission presses in the nineteenth century or of the supranational (post)colonial publishing system, as a vital medium of Afrikaner Nationalism or the New African movement, or, indeed, as a threat to the apartheid regime, the book has always been part of the larger histories that have shaped and reshaped the space of the literary in South Africa. As the new state-sponsored South African Classics series suggests, not to mention the latest initiatives of the various commercial publishers currently operating in South Africa, such questions are no less compelling today. That they will remain so in the century ahead is clear. What will be different, however, is that any future study of literary production in South Africa, or elsewhere, will need to come to terms not just with the material history of books but also with their changing place in the virtual, almost borderless, world of our now not so new digital age.

Bibliography

Beukes, W. D. (ed.). *Boekewêreld: Die Nasionale Pers in die Uitgewersbedryf tot 1990*, Cape Town: Nasionale Boekhandel, 1992.

Coetzee, J. M. 'The Book in Africa' (seminar), National English Literary Museum, Grahamstown, South Africa, 2002, 13:2.1.1.

'Two Interviews with J. M. Coetzee, 1983 and 1987', interview by T. Morphet, *TriQuarterly* 69 (spring/summer 1987), 453–64.

Evans, N., and S. Seeber (eds.). *The Politics of Publishing in South Africa*, Scottsville: University of Natal Press, 2000.

Galloway, F. (ed.). *SA Literature/Literatuur 1980*, Johannesburg: Ad Donker, 1982.

Galloway, F., and Rudi M. R. Venter (eds.). *Stilet*, special issue on book studies, 20:2 (2008).

Gardner, S. (ed.). *Publisher/Writer/Reader: Sociology of Southern African Literature*, Johannesburg: University of Witwatersrand Press, 1986.

Gikandi, S. (ed.). *Encyclopaedia of African Literature*, London: Routledge, 2003.

Gordimer, N., et. al. *What Happened to 'Burger's Daughter' or How South African Censorship Works*, Emmarentia: Taurus, 1980.

Hofmeyr, I. *The Portable Bunyan*, Johannesburg: Witwatersrand University Press, 2004.

Jeppie, S., and S. B. Diagne (eds.). *The Meanings of Timbuktu*, Cape Town: Human Sciences Research Council Press, 2008

Kannemeyer, J. C. *Die Afrikaanse Literatuur, 1652–2004*, Cape Town: Human & Rousseau, 2005.

Kirkwood, M. 'Staffrider: An Informal Discussion', *English in Africa* 7:2 (1980), 22–31.

McDonald, P. D. *The Literature Police: Apartheid Censorship and its Cultural Consequences*, Oxford University Press, 2009; www.theliteraturepolice.com, accessed 15 June 2009.

Opland, J. 'The First Novel in Xhosa', *Research in African Literatures* 38:4 (2007), 87–110.

Peires, J. 'Lovedale Press: Literature for the Bantu Revisited', *English in Africa* 7:1 (1980), 71–85.

Seroke, J. 'The Voice of the Voiceless', *African Book Publishing Record* 10:4 (1984), 201–6.

Trump, M. (ed.). *Rendering Things Visible*, Johannesburg: Ravan, 1990.

Van der Vlies, A. (ed.). 'Histories of the Book in Southern Africa', special issue of *English Studies in Africa* 47:1 (2004).

  South African Textual Cultures: White, Black, Read all Over, Manchester University Press, 2007.

Venter, R. M. R. 'Inventing an Alternative through Oppositional Publishing: Afrikaans Alternative Book Publishing in Apartheid South Africa – The Publishing House Taurus (1975–1991) as Case Study', *Innovation* 35 (2007), 86–114.

White, T. 'The Lovedale Press During the Directorship of R. H. W. Shepherd, 1930–1955', *English in Africa* 19:2 (1992), 69–84.

39

Literary and cultural criticism in South Africa

DAVID JOHNSON

Nineteenth-century origins

Many enduring characteristics of South African literary and cultural criticism are evident in the very first articles, book and theatre reviews and lectures that appeared in the small-circulation newspapers and periodicals of the Cape. These early newspapers included John Fairbairn and Thomas Pringle's *South African Commercial Advertiser* (1824–69), William Bridekirk's *South African Chronicle* (1824–6), Frederick Brooks's *South African Grins; or, The Quizzical Depot of General Humbug* (1825–6), Joseph Suasso de Lima's *De Verzamelaar/The Gleaner* (1826–7), C. E. Boniface and C. N. Neethling's *Zuid-Afrikaan* (1830–71), A. J. Jardine's *Cape of Good Hope Literary Gazette* (1830–5), and Robert Godlonton's *Graham's Town Journal* (1831–1919) (Huigen, 'Nederlandstalige', pp. 7–11; Lewin Robinson, *None Daring*). The periodicals of this period – Fairbairn and Pringle's *South African Journal* (1824), Abraham Faure's *Het Nederduytsch Zuid-Afrikaansche Tydschrift* (1824–43), Andrew Smith and James Adamson's *South African Quarterly Journal* (1830–7) and James L. Fitzpatrick's *Cape of Good Hope Literary Magazine* (1847–8) – were dominated by articles on the natural sciences, history and travel, and there were only occasional pieces of literary or cultural criticism, like Fairbairn's two-part essay 'On the Writings of Wordsworth' in the *South African Journal* (1 [1824], pp. 12–16, and 2 [1824], pp. 107–17), and the anonymous 'On the Sources of Shakespeare's Plots' in the *Cape of Good Hope Literary Magazine* (2, 10 [1848], pp. 571–92). Other noteworthy literary criticism took the form of public lectures organised by the literary and scientific societies in Cape Town and Grahamstown, like James Adamson's philosophically inflected *Modern Literature* (1844), and Nathaniel Merriman's *On the Study of Shakespeare* (1857) and *Shakespeare as Bearing on English History* (1858) (Johnson, 'Violence and Philosophy', pp. 68–73).

Arguably the most striking feature of this early criticism was its proximity to religious discourse, with the reading of the Bible taken as the key and guide to reading literature. All the intellectuals at the Cape who wrote about literature and culture were devout Christians, and many, including Adamson and Merriman, were also ministers of religion. Adamson's long essay *Modern Literature* follows A. W. Schlegel in surveying all literatures of all ages, but concludes that although certain truths might be revealed through literature, 'the knowledge of God is the highest knowledge, – the most enriching and most inspiring' (Adamson, *Modern Literature*, p. 19). In his first lecture, Merriman argues that 'the faculties which we bring into exercise in studying Shakespeare . . . are the self same faculties which we are required to use in a far higher pursuit – I mean, in studying that one Divine Book' (Merriman, *On the Study of Shakespeare*, p. 1). In the second lecture, he concludes that Shakespeare 'everywhere sets up the most unmistakeable fingerposts pointing to the moral government and the retributive justice of God in the affairs of men' (Merriman, *Shakespeare*, p. 16). Merriman does not believe that *all* English literature has the capacity to do God's work; Byron, for example, is quite unsuitable, as 'his diseased and unhappy mind . . . [is unable] to create a single healthful impersonation of humanity' (Merriman, *On the Study of Shakespeare*, p. 15).

Three further characteristics of South African criticism are evident in the poetry reviews of the period, namely the impulse to promote the work of writers from the Cape (and later, South Africa); the readiness to disagree ferociously over literary judgements; and the urge to quarantine literature off from politics. All the newspapers published the work of local poets, and R. J. Stapleton assembled an anthology of Cape poems, declaring that 'it is impossible not to be struck with the beauty of some of [these] poetical effusions' (Stapleton, *Poetry*, preface). Stapleton's assessment of the Cape's poets and his attempt to promote their work was challenged, however, by Frederick Brooks in *South African Grins; or, The Quizzical Depot of General Humbug*, as he rhymed, 'You'd hardly think in this distant land, / That *Poets* as thick as mushrooms stand! / Some of whom, in their own conceit, / Think no one can with them compete; / But if I may judge from their works, / Most of them are dull as *Turks*' (1:1 [1825], p. 15). The vast majority of poems concerned the beauties of nature; reviewers commented mostly on their imagery and style and only occasionally applied political criteria. For example, a week after a sympathetic notice of Byron's death in the *South African Chronicle*, a correspondent, 'Veritas', submitted an attack on Byron, asking, 'How cold and feeble are his acknowledgments of the triumph of British valour at Waterloo?', and then lamented that Byron had 'strayed into the wilderness of sensuality [and] the torch of talent was dimmed by the contamination of vice' (8 September 1824, p. 2). An even sharper polemical edge is evident in reviews of poets at the Cape, as for example in C. J. Gray's comments on Thomas Pringle's poems in the *Grahams Town Journal*:

> Do, my good Mr Pringle, please to explain the following lines, and show how far you were ever justified in penning them:
>
> > 'The sea which heaved them up at first
> > For Amakosa's curse and bane,
> > Howls for the progeny she nursed,
> > To swallow them again.'
>
> Please to shew how the British whom you so contemptuously call 'progeny', have been 'Amakosa's curse and bain'. Would to God, Sir, that the seas had never heaved you, or *such* as you, to the shores of South Africa, to be the British Colonists' 'curse and bane!'   (9 January 1835, p. 4)

In his long articles on Wordsworth, Fairbairn resisted reading poetry through politics and expands upon Wordsworth's style, but he concedes that 'the spirit of the age' makes it difficult for 'the genuine poet' to transcend politics, 'when war, and party, and private distress had contracted the man into the mere citizen, the citizen into the politician, and wrapt the latter up in a fleece of utter selfishness – it was not possible that Wordsworth's refined meditations and expansive charities could be made intelligible' (*South African Journal* 1 [1824], pp. 13, 15, 16).

Another persistent concern is the tension between high and popular culture, especially in the early theatre reviews. English melodramas, farces and Shakespeare comedies made up the majority of productions, but the works of other European playwrights were also performed (Fletcher, *Story of Theatre*, and Bosman, *Drama en Toneel*). Theatre reviews were generally appreciative, although mild criticism was sometimes expressed, as in the comment on an otherwise excellent *Rob Roy* that 'we were sorry to see the memory of several of the performers prove treacherous' (*South African Chronicle*, 18 August 1824, p. 2). Reviewers were always swift to emphasise the importance of appealing to popular tastes. Following an evening combining a farce and a melodrama, the 'Correspondent' writing for the *South African Commercial Advertiser* asked, 'Do the Managers not think, that the selection of Melo-dramas is rather injudicious? Our advice would be, to choose light, laughable Comedies' (14 April 1824, p. 2). The dangers of deviating from farces and comedies were explained further in a review of an unsuccessful performance of *Hamlet*: 'The climate is against Tragedy. The flagging spirits require constant novelty and excitement to rouse them into action' (*Sam Sly's African Journal*, 27 August 1846, p. 3).

Implicit in all the early nineteenth-century South African criticism was an unwavering deference to the cultural standards of London, Oxbridge and Edinburgh. This deference – what Australian historians have termed 'cultural cringe' – moderated slightly after the establishment in 1854 of representative government and in 1872 of responsible government at the Cape, as the Cape's settler (as opposed to colonial) elite asserted its autonomy from Britain. In this period, most criticism focused on English-language literature, but both Afrikaans- and African-language literatures also started attracting attention. Reviews continued in the newspapers of the Cape, but the most extensive English-language criticism appeared in the *Cape Monthly Magazine (CMM)*.

Edited from 1857 to 1881 by Alfred Whaley Cole and the brothers John and Roderick Noble, the *Cape Monthly* published articles on the natural sciences, philosophy, religion, geology, anthropology and travel, and at its peak had a subscription list of 350 (Dubow, *Commonwealth of Knowledge*, pp. 71–120). The regular 'Literary Review' column reflected the Cape's cultural dependency; it only reviewed novels recently arrived from England, subjecting them to plot-and-character summaries and confident assessments of their literary and moral value. For example, W. Harrison Ainsworth's *Jack Sheppard. A Romance* (1839) was compared unfavourably to *Oliver Twist* (1838): 'The one only panders to the lowest passions, and renders vice and crime something almost heroic. The other aims at great social reforms, and pictures crime . . . as intensely odious, and to be condemned' (*CMM* 1 [1857], p. 382).

There was far less deference to European authority in Afrikaans criticism. The aspirations of the First Afrikaans Language Movement, spearheaded by S. J. du Toit, C. P. Hoogenhout and J. Lion Cachet, were expressed through the monthly newspaper *Afrikaanse Patriot* and the magazine *Zuid Afrikaan*. Dominated by political and religious opinion, episodes from *volk* history and debates about language, these papers also published cultural criticism (broadly conceived). The anonymous article 'De Zuid-Afrikaanse Litteratuur en hare opkomst' ('South African Literature and its future') in the magazine *Ons Tijdschrif. Geillusteeerd Familieblad voor Zuid-Afrika* (3 [1898/9], pp. 7–11, 61–4) declared that South African literature dated from 1806 (the second British occupation of the Cape) but had only assumed any real significance in the 1880s. For South African literature to thrive, the article argued, the example of Holland's rebellion against Spain needed to be followed and English influence expelled from South Africa.

Under the patronage of missionaries, two traditions of African-language criticism emerged: an anthropological criticism recording African oral literatures, and a book review criticism passing judgements on new African literary works. The leading proponent of the former was the German linguist W. H. I. Bleek, who translated the Nguni and Khoi-San languages of Southern Africa but drew a distinction between their respective literary capacities: 'in the faculty of imagination Bushmen (the San) certainly . . . far exceed anything that we meet with among the Negroes' (Bleek, 'On Inquiries', 1; Moran, *Representing Bushmen*, pp. 114–27; see also Chapter 1 above). Bleek's assessment of the imaginative capacity of Southern Africa's 'Negroes' was contradicted by the collections of folklore like Henry Callaway's *Nursery Tales, Traditions and Histories of the Zulus* (1866), Azariele Sekese's *Makhoa ea Basotho le Maele le Litsomo* (Sotho Customs, Proverbs and Tales, 1893) and Walter Rubusana's *Zemk' iinkomo magwalandini* (There go the Cattle, you Cowards, 1906), as well as by the vigorous literary culture in late nineteenth-century Xhosa newspapers. After the final Frontier War of 1879, Xhosa intellectuals such as Isaac Williams Wauchope saw writing as an important means of resistance. In a poem in the newspaper *Isigidimi samaXhosa* (Xhosa Messenger) in June 1882, Wauchope declared 'Yishiy' imfakadolo, / Putuma ngosiba' (Lay down the musket, / Take up the pen) (Opland, 'Fighting with the Pen', p. 10). This combative spirit was evident in the second tradition of African-language criticism, notably in the first reviews of isiXhosa poetry published in the two competing newspapers *Izwi labantu* (Voice of the People) and *Imvo zabantsundu* (Black Opinions). *Izwi* spoke for the nationalist aspirations of the Xhosa and Thembu, whereas *Imvo* spoke for the assimilationist Mfengu, and their political antipathy extended to aesthetic differences: *Izwi* championed verse written in the form of traditional Xhosa *izibongo*, and *Imvo* favoured western poetic styles. These differences were to the fore in Jonas Ntsiko's attack on S. E. K. Mqhayi's poetry published in *Imvo* (20 November 1900); for Ntsiko, Mqhayi's observance of Xhosa oral conventions was misconceived, as he should rather have used Alexander Pope's couplets as his poetic model (Opland, *Xhosa Poets*, pp. 243–4).

The Union of South Africa

The first half of the twentieth century saw several new developments in South African literary and cultural criticism. In English-language criticism, two well-received books on Shakespeare by South African critics (Arnold Wynne's *The Growth of English Drama* [1914] and F. C. Kolbe's *Shakespeare's Way: A Psychological Study* [1930]) were published. Of greater significance were two overviews of South African writing, namely Sidney Mendelssohn's *South African Bibliography* (1910) and Manfred Nathan's *South African Literature: A General Survey* (1925). Most criticism, however, continued to appear in periodical literature, and the wave of new journals which appeared around the time of Union in 1910 provided fresh impetus – *African Monthly* (1906–10), *The State* (1909–12), and the two journals of the South African Home Reading Union, *The Bulletin* (1909–10) and *South African Bookman* (1910–15) (Merrington, 'Staggered Orientalism', pp. 323–64). Despite an emphasis on books by canonical British authors, these journals did shift towards reviewing South African writers like Pringle, Olive Schreiner, Percival Gibbon and Douglas Blackburn (*Bulletin* 1 [October 1909], pp. 187–91). The *Bulletin*'s reviewer argued that 'there appears to be no writer of recent years whose literary skill has developed in a really South African direction', and bemoaned the fact that South African novelists remain 'too fond of classics of bygone days and other civilisations . . . [and are] not sufficiently self-reliant' (*Bulletin* 1 [October 1909], p. 190).

This emergent South African literary nationalism was also expressed in critical assessments of European writers of the past, as in John Purves's appropriation of Camões: '*The Lusiads* is then . . . not only the first but also the greatest of South African poems. It is our portion of the Renaissance' (*State* 2:12 [December 1909], p. 745). The ideal of building an independent South African literature continued in journals like *Voorslag* (1926–7), edited by Roy Campbell, William Plomer and Laurens van der Post. Campbell, for example, expressed the hope that in South Africa 'we are gradually approaching a promised era . . . when the Rudyards cease from Kipling / and the Haggards Ride no more' (1:1 [June 1926], p. 45).

Another development was the appearance of articles on women writers, including Elizabeth Gaskell (*African Monthly* 1:1 [December 1906], pp. 31–8); Harriet Martineau (*South African Bookman* 3 [June 1911], pp. 152–5); and Schreiner (*South African Bookman* 2 [January 1911], pp. 66–71, and *African Monthly* 1:1 [December 1906], pp. 69–73). These articles were complemented by E. L. McPherson's short study *Women Letter Writers and Diarists of South Africa, 1710–1862* (Cape Town, 1918). Their efforts led to the appearance in 1930 of *The Bluestocking*, an interdisciplinary journal dedicated to the interests of women, which published a significant amount of literary criticism. The frustrations of these critics are captured in E. E. Drennan's observation that 'we are slow movers in South Africa, and . . . it is one of Life's Little Ironies, that though South Africa had the honour of giving birth to Olive Schreiner, she has been the slowest Dominion to concede women the dues that Olive Schreiner advocated' (*Bluestocking* 3:2 [May 1933], p. 19).

From the 1920s onwards there appeared a number of popular radical journals, which published short stories, poems, literary reviews and longer essays on culture and literature. These included: *Forward* (1924–57), the official organ of the South African Labour Party; Stephen Black's *Sjambok* (1929–31); Bernard Sachs's *South African Opinion* (1934–47); Herman Charles Bosman, John Webb and A. J. Blignaut's *Touleier* (1930–1); Jacques Malan's bilingual *Trek* (1939–54); Lily Rabkin's *Forum* (1938–64); the African National Congress and South African Communist Party papers *The Guardian* (1937–52), *Advance* (1952–1954) and *New Age* (1954–62); the Non-European Unity Movement's *Torch* (1946–1963); and the University of Cape Town journal *The Critic* (1932–9). Constituting what Oskar Negt and Alexander Kluge define as 'a counterpublic sphere' (*Public Sphere*, p. 91), these publications afforded a space for writers to challenge the political and cultural establishment. Critics writing for these publications included 'Kees Konyn' (Jan Greshoff) (Kannemeyer, *Koléperas van Kees Konyn*), the controversial Afrikaans literary reviewer on *Trek*; Ruth Schechter (Hirson, *Cape Town Intellectuals*), prolific reviewer and champion of Olive Schreiner; Mary Morison Webster, novelist and for forty years book reviewer at the *Rand Daily Mail*; and the Trotskyist Dora Taylor (Sandwith, 'Dora Taylor', pp. 5–27), who wrote over seventy book reviews for *Trek*, as well as many longer essays.

In the first half of the twentieth century two books were published that discussed Dutch-South African literature, Gerrit Besselaar's *Zuid-Afrika in de Letterkunde* (1914) and Elizabeth Conradie's *Hollandse Skrywers uit Suid-Afrika: 'n Kultuur-historiese Studie, Deel 1 (1652–1875)* (1934). With Afrikaans attaining official status in 1925, a number of studies of Afrikaans literature appeared: D. F. Malherbe's *Afrikaanse Letterkunde: 'n Bloemlesing* (1922); E. C. Pienaar's *Taal en Poësie van die Tweede Afrikaanse Taalbeweging* (1922); P. C. Schoonees's *Die Prosa van die Tweede Afrikaanse Beweging* (1922); Rob Antonissen's *Die Afrikaanse Letterkunde van Aanvang tot Aede* (1926); and Gerrit Dekker's *Afrikaanse Literatuurgeskiedenis* (1935). Associated with the Second Afrikaans Language Movement, and complementing popular histories like Gustav Preller's *Piet Retief* (1906), these works constructed an Afrikaans literary canon centred upon C. J. Langenhoven, J. D. du Toit (Totius), Jan F. E. Celliers, Louis Leipoldt and Eugene Marais. More influential than these books, however, were the many articles on literary matters in popular magazines like *Huisgenoot*, *Brandwag* and *Boerevrou*. Craig Calhoun has argued that 'the institutionalization of a public sphere was at the heart of the project of defining the nation' ('Nationalism and the Public Sphere', p. 97); in the case of the Afrikaner nation in the 1920s and 1930s, this function was fulfilled by these magazines, whose abundant cultural commentary on literature, art, architecture, interior design, fashion, music and sport cumulatively constituted an Afrikaner national identity (Hofmeyr, 'Building a Nation from Words', pp. 95–123). Less concerned with literary analysis or aesthetic judgements, the criticism in these magazines offered hagiographic articles on Afrikaans writers, thereby inscribing them as *volksdigters* (the people's poets).

Criticism of African-language literatures continued along the lines laid down in the late nineteenth century, with exegeses on African folklore and proverbs and reviews of new works by African writers in newspapers. Of the former, the most wide-ranging was Solomon T. Plaatje's *Sechuana Proverbs with Literal Translations and their European Equivalents* (1916), which included 732 proverbs, with English translations and their closest English equivalents. Plaatje's declared object was 'to save from oblivion, as far as this can still be done, the proverbial expressions of the Bechuana people' (Willan, *Sol Plaatje*, p. 214). The same ambition drove other such works, like Isaac Williams Wauchope's many articles on Xhosa proverbs and folklore in *Imvo Zabantsundu* between 1889 and 1903 (Opland and Nyamende, *Isaac Williams Wauchope*, pp. 236–311), and Edouard Jacottet's two-volume *Treasury of Ba-Suto: Being Original Sesuto Text, with a Literal English Translation and Notes* (1908, 1911).

A survey of the extant publications on African-language literatures was provided in 1921 by D. D. T. Jabavu's *Bantu Literature. Classification and Reviews*, which classified all works in Sotho, Xhosa, Zulu and Tswana and concluded with critical discussions of books by Thomas Mofolo, Azariele Sekese, Everrit Segoete, Samuel Mqayi and Tiyo Soga. Jabavu applauded literary works which are 'imaginative' (p. 15), 'coherent', 'credible' and display 'stylish idiom and proverbial expression' (p. 20), but rebuked authors when their moral purpose is 'too bluntly applied' (p. 20) and when they 'offend modern ideas of decency' (p. 24). Jabavu's disapproving judgements are relatively mild compared to the robust objections of other critics. For example, Wauchope's two-part review of Mqhayi's short novel *uSamson* (1907) in *Imvo Zabantsundu* on 12 and 19 November 1907 (Opland, 'First Novel in Xhosa', pp. 98–102) castigated the novel's lack of fidelity to the original Bible story. Three decades later Herbert Dhlomo's review of B. W. Vilikazi's Zulu poetry in *South African Outlook* criticised (among other things) Vilikazi's rigid rhyme scheme and his failure to learn from the example of Shakespeare, whose blank verse 'comes naturally and without effort to the African writer [and] is native to our genius' (1 April 1939, p. 90).

Although much of this criticism was characterised by reverence for the Bible and Shakespeare, these critics also expressed the desire for an independent South African literature. In 1923 a 'Special Correspondent' in an article 'Towards our Own Literature' in *Ilanga Lase Natal* declared that a national literature should avoid a 'narrow or racial spirit', and seek rather to establish a 'brotherhood of the heart [through] the precision of Zulu and the elasticity of English' (2 December 1923, p. 4). Also indicative of a shift away from European religious and literary standards were Herbert Dhlomo's sympathetic critical introductions to black South African writers – Mqhayi, Plaatje, Mofolo, Vilikazi, Sulyman Ismail, R. R. R. Dhlomo and J. J. R. Jolobe – in the four issues of his small circulation periodical *The Reader's Companion* in 1938 (see Couzens, *New African*; Attwell, *Rewriting Modernity*, pp. 77–100; Masilela, *Cultural Modernity*; see also *English in Africa*'s special issue on H. I. E. Dhlomo, 4:2 [1977]).

Apartheid

The black South African critics who wrote under apartheid rule followed Dhlomo in celebrating the literary achievements of black South African writers. Between 1958 and 1960 A. C. Jordan wrote a series of articles in the journal *Africa South*, which were republished after his death in 1968 as *Towards an African Literature: The Emergence of Literary Form in Xhosa* (1973). Lindi Nelani Jordan has described Jordan's criticism as committed to a 'dialectical approach to literature [which] requires the literary critic . . . to know the historical forces that shaped that society' (*Towards an African Literature*, p. x). Of a different temper were Es'kia (Ezekiel) Mphahlele's two books, *The African Image* (1962) and *Voices in the Whirlwind and other Essays* (1972), which ranged widely across African, North American and European literatures and expressed reservations about both the ideology of negritude and Jean-Paul Sartre's model of the politically committed writer.

With regard to South African writers, Mphahlele praised early writers like Plaatje, but was less generous with his contemporaries at *Drum* magazine, as he found their short stories poorly plotted and too derivative of American models. Mphahlele's doubts about 1950s and 1960s black South African writing were amplified by Lewis Nkosi, who invoked European literary standards in *Home and Exile* (1965) to argue that his South African contemporaries were unequal to the task of describing their society, as they lacked both 'vigour of imagination' and 'sufficient technical resources' (Nkosi, *Home and Exile*, p. 125.) In contrast to Mphahlele's and Nkosi's criticism, with its concern with the formal imperfections of black South African writing, Steve Biko's cultural theory emphasised the imperative of reversing European cultural imperialism and proclaiming African culture. In a 1971 lecture 'Some African Cultural Concepts', Biko affirmed the urgent need for a 'culture of defiance, self-assertion and group pride and solidarity. This is a culture which emanates from a situation of common experience of oppression. Just as it now finds expression in our music and our dress, it will spread to other aspects' (Biko, *I Write What I Like*, p. 46).

Biko's Black Consciousness ideology did indeed 'spread to other aspects', and especially to literature, as a number of writers and critics rejected Eurocentric aesthetic values. Mothobi Mutloatse declared 'we are going to pee, spit and shit on literary convention before we are through; we are going to kick and push and drag literature into the form we prefer' (Mutloatse, *Forced Landing*, p. 5; Sole, 'Culture, Politics and the Black Writer', pp. 37–84). At around the same time that this polemical criticism appeared, a number of academic studies of African literatures in vernacular languages were published, notably Isaac Schapera's *Praise Poems of Tswana Chiefs* (1965), Samson Guma's *The Form, Content and Technique of Traditional Literature in Southern Sotho* (1967), Trevor Cope's *Izibongo: Zulu Praise Poems* (1968), Daniel Kunene's *The Heroic Poetry of the Basotho* (1971), Albert Gérard's *Four African Literatures: Xhosa, Sotho, Zulu, Amharic* (1971), Mosebi Damane and P. B. Sanders's *Lithoko: Sotho Praise Poems* (1974) and Harold Scheub's *The Xhosa Ntsomi* (1975). Retrospective and anthropological in character, most of these studies were published in England and aimed – in Gérard's words – 'to trace, collect, record, and so to preserve and make generally available, as much evidence as possible' (Gérard, *Four African Literatures*, pp. 10–11) about the African language literatures of Southern Africa, with a particular focus on the oral and precolonial literatures.

Afrikaans criticism in the 1940s and 1950s was dominated by the literary journals *Standpunte* and *Tydskrif vir Letterkunde*. *Standpunte* was edited by N. P. van Wyk Louw, W. E. G. Louw and H. A. Mulder, and ran from December 1945 to August 1986 (see Chapter 17 above). The editors' declared intention was to 'serve the free spiritual and intellectual life' (1:1 [1945], p. 1; my translation), and in particular to 'serve serious literature in South Africa' (p. 3). The only criterion to be applied in assessing poetry and prose would be 'quality', and the journal was determinedly independent – 'independent of both political parties and the large publishing companies' (p. 3). The majority of articles were in Afrikaans, and they consolidated the canon of white Afrikaans writers centred upon the major literary figures of the 1930s.

Complicating the project of constituting an Afrikaner high culture were a number of articles in both Dutch and English which considered other literatures. The quarterly *Tydskrif vir Letterkunde*, the official journal of the Afrikaanse Skrywerskring (Writers' Circle), first appeared in March 1951, having evolved from the *Jaarboek van die Afrikaanse Skrywerskring* (founded in 1936), and was edited by C. M. van den Heever. Like the editors of *Standpunte*,

Van den Heever placed great emphasis on championing 'quality' in Afrikaans writing: in his first editorial, he cited T. S. Eliot's warning against 'untrained readers being taken in by the sham and adulterate . . . indeed preferring them, for they are more assimilable than the genuine article' (1:1 [March 1951], p. 5). The antidote is for the good critic to 'seek out quality honestly and fearlessly and to establish the truth in the work of a writer' (p. 7). *Tydskrif vir Letterkunde* differed from *Standpunte* in that it only published Afrikaans articles, poems and short stories, and it also received financial backing from the state.

Van den Heever concluded his first editorial by thanking the Department of Education, the South African Academy for Science and Art and the former prime minister, General J. B. M. Hertzog, for their support. The constitution of a literary canon of white Afrikaans writers by these two journals was further consolidated by Gerhard Beukes and Felix Lategan's *Skrywers en Rigtings* (1952), D. J. Opperman's *Digters van Dertig* (1953), Rob Antonissen's *Die Afrikaans Letterkunde van Aanvang tot Hede* (1955) and Ernst Lindenberg's edited collection *Inleiding tot die Afrikaanse Letterkunde* (1965). None of these critics ever attended to the literary works of either white working-class Afrikaans writers or black Afrikaans writers (Van Wyk, *Constructs of Identity*; Willemse, *Aan die Ander Kant*).

The next generation of white Afrikaans writers and critics, the Sestigers (Jan Rabie, Etienne Leroux, Bartho Smit, Breyten Breytenbach, Ingrid Jonker, André Brink and Chris Barnard) defined themselves in opposition to inherited religious, moral and political values, and their iconoclasm provoked heated critical debate within white Afrikaner literary circles. The Sesigters repeated the Dertigers' successful strategy of self-canonisation, as favourable reviews of their own work in Smit and Brink's journal *Sestiger* (1963–5), and in monographs like Brink's *Aspekte van die Nuwe Prosa* (1967), swiftly cemented their literary reputations (Cope, *Adversary Within*). The congruence of interests announced by Van den Heever in 1951 between the state and the literary critic, however, was broken, as was evident in 1979 with Etienne Leroux's novel *Magersfontein, O Magersfontein!* being simultaneously banned by the Censor Board and awarded the prestigious Hertzog Prize for prose.

Compared to the oedipal disputes in Afrikaans literary criticism in the 1960s, and the ill-tempered debates triggered by Nkosi's and Biko's pronouncements, South Africa's English literary critics produced a relatively sedate body of criticism from the 1940s to the 1970s. In the late 1940s Cambridge-educated graduates like Geoffrey Durrant returned to South Africa and promoted the practical criticism of I. A. Richards and the cultural diagnoses of F. R. Leavis (Johnson, *Shakespeare and South Africa*, pp. 148–61). The journals publishing practical criticism were the Pietermaritzburg-based *Theoria* (1947–), Witwatersrand University's *English Studies in Africa* (1958–) and *Unisa English Studies* (1963–96). In the editorial of the first issue of *Theoria*, Durrant stated that the journal's task was 'to discover those successful patterns of symbols that we call "good poems", to live the experience of them as fully as we can, and to help others to the same experience' (1 [1947], p. 5).

A number of monographs written in this spirit were also published, including J. Y. T. Greig's *Thackeray: A Reconsideration* (1950), D. R. C. Marsh's *The Recurring Miracle* (1962), W. H. Gardner's *Gerard Manley Hopkins* (1966), D. G. Gillham's *Blake's Contrary States* (1966), Laurence Lerner's *The Truth-Tellers: Jane Austen, George Eliot, D. H. Lawrence* (1967) and Durrant's *Wordsworth* (1969). The relationship between this literary-critical discourse and apartheid politics is perhaps best conveyed by the example of Marsh, who completed his study of *Cymbeline* while imprisoned for his activities on behalf of the South African Liberal Party. Aside from a wry comment by Durrant on the flyleaf of *The Recurring Miracle* about Marsh's imprisonment, the book makes no reference to apartheid South Africa. Sharing the same formalist methodology as Durrant and Partridge, Guy Butler at Rhodes University argued for the inclusion of South African writing (including his own) in literature syllabuses (Watson, *Guy Butler*). Also unusual for this period in its focus on South African literature was J. P. L. Snyman's *The South African Novel in English, 1880–1930* (1952).

Less restrained criticism appeared in the many small literary magazines which appeared between the 1950s and 1970s. Publishing mainly poems and stories, these magazines included articles and reviews reflecting diverse critical opinions. They included Lionel Abrahams's *Purple Renoster* (1956–72), Jack Cope's *Contrast* (1960–89; subsequently *New Contrast*), Nat Nakasa and Barney Simon's *The Classic* (1963–71), Smit and Brink's *Sestiger* (1963–5), Guy Butler and Ruth Harnett's *New Coin* (1965–), P. A. de Waal Venter, Phil du Plessis and Marié Blomerus's *Wurm* (1966–70), Peter Horn and Walter Saunders's *Ophir* (1967–76), John Miles's *Kol* (1968–9), Christopher Hope, Mike Kirkwood and Tony Morphet's *Bolt* (1970–5), Phil du Plessis, Stephen Gray and Wilma Stockenstrom's *Izwi* (1971–4), Joyce Ozynscki's *Snarl* (1974–7), Sipho Sepamla's *New Classic* (1975–8) and Welma Odendaal's *Donga* and *Inspan* (1976–8) (Gardner, *South African Literary Magazines*, and *English in Africa* 7:2 [1980]). Most the magazines targeted particular language readerships – *Purple Renoster* and *Contrast* aimed at English readers, *Sestiger* and *Kol* at Afrikaans readers – but they also challenged the apartheid state's racial and language boundaries. The short-lived *Donga*, for example, published essays ranging from Ampie

Coetzee on 'Politiek en Poësie' (1 [July 1976], p. 1) to Bessie Head on Miriam Makeba (4 [February 1977], p. 6). Arguably the most significant of the 'small magazines' came after the Soweto uprising – *Staffrider*, which achieved distribution figures of 7,000, ran from 1978 to 1993 under the collective editorship of Mike Kirkwood and Mothobi Mutloatse, and later Chris van Wyk and Andries Oliphant, and published short stories, poems and photographs as well as essays and manifestoes on literature, culture and politics.

New international literary journals publishing articles on South African literature appeared in this period, notably the *Journal of Commonwealth Literature* (UK, 1965–), *Research in African Literatures* (US, 1970–), *Ariel* (Canada, 1970–), *World Literature Today* (US, 1977–), *Kunapipi* (Denmark, 1979–), the series *African Literature Today* (UK, 1977–), *Third World Quarterly* (UK, 1979–), and *Wasafiri* (UK, 1984–). Much more such criticism appeared in South African journals: the Grahamstown-based *English in Africa* (1974–), which carried special issues republishing out of print work of neglected South African writers; *Communiqué* (1974–86), which was published by the University of the North and which included articles in English and Afrikaans; the *Annual Review (English Academy)* (1974–9; from 1980, *English Academy Review*), which sought originally to serve the interests of the English language in South Africa, but now declares a broader remit; the theoretically ambitious culture and media studies journal, *Critical Arts* (1980–) under the editorship of Keyan Tomaselli; *Literator* (1980–), the Afrikaans literary journal from the University of Potchefstroom; *Journal of Literary Studies / Tydskrif vir Literatuurwetenskap* (1985–), which is based at the University of South Africa (UNISA) and publishes in English and Afrikaans, with a substantial component critical theory and literary history; the bilingual *South African Theatre Journal* (1987–); the University of KwaZulu-Natal (Durban) journal *Current Writing* (1989–), which has published exclusively on Southern African writing; the University of Cape Town's journal *Pretexts* (1989–2003), which published interdisciplinary research combining literary, historical and theoretical reflection; and the Afrikaans journal *Stilet: Tydskrif van die Afrikaanse Letterkundevereneiging* (1989–), the declared intention of which is to publish articles on the 'scientific study of Afrikaans literature'. The most widely read journal of the period was Rob Turrell's interdisciplinary magazine the *Southern African Review of Books* (1987–96), which included long essays on South African literature and hosted entertaining literary-critical debates in its letters pages.

These trends were reinforced by several book-length studies: Christopher Heywood's edited collection *Aspects of South African Literature* (1976), J. C. Kannemeyer's two-volume *Die Afrikaanse Literatuur 1652–1987* (1978, 1983), Stephen

Gray's *Southern African Literature: An Introduction* (1979), Albert Gérard's *European-Language Literature in Sub-Saharan Africa* (1986), and Malvern van Wyk Smith's *Grounds of Contest: A Survey of South African English Literature* (1990). Complementing these surveys were a number of studies – some biographical, others literary-critical – on individual South African writers like Schreiner (Ruth First and Ann Scott [1980], Cherry Clayton [1983], Karel Schoeman [1989]); Sol Plaatje (Brian Willan [1984]); Herbert Dhlomo (Tim Couzens [1985]); D. J. Opperman (J. C. Kannemeyer [1986]); Nadine Gordimer (Michael Wade [1978], Stephen Clingman [1986], Judie Newman [1988]); Athol Fugard (Temple Hauptfleisch [1982], Dennis Walder [1984])]; and J. M. Coetzee (Teresa Dovey [1988]). Studies of categories of South African writing demarcated by race, gender or genre also started appearing – Vernon February's *Mind Your Colour: The 'Coloured' Stereotype in South African Literature* (1981), Ursula Barnett's *A Vision of Order: A Study of Black South African Literature in English* (1983), J. M. Coetzee's *White Writing: On the Culture of Letters in South Africa* (1988); Cherry Clayton's collection *Women and Writing in South Africa* (1989); Kenneth Parker's collection *The South African Novel in English* (1978); Jacques Alvarez-Pereyre's *The Poetry of Commitment in South Africa* (1984); Michael Chapman's *South African English Poetry: A Modern Perspective* (1984); Robert Kavanagh's *Theatre and Cultural Struggle in South Africa* (1985) and Martin Orkin's *Shakespeare Against Apartheid* (1987). Another new forum for literary-critical exchanges was created by the annual conferences of the Association of University English Teachers of South Africa, which commenced in 1988.

Accompanying the shift towards criticism focused on South African literatures was a theoretical assault on the hegemony of formalist criticism. South Africa's version of the 'theory wars' was played out over a couple of decades, with those challenging the South African literary-critical establishment drawing upon social history, critical theory and the ideas of anti-colonial intellectuals. The temper of these often acrimonious exchanges is captured in the newsletter reporting on the inaugural conference in January 1977 of South African university English teachers:

> Prof. [David] Gillham offered a closely reasoned and dispassionate statement of the classical 'prac. crit' approach, expressing his concern to 're-instate criteria that are in danger of being attenuated'. He expressed his conviction that 'really great works of art have the habit of providing their own relevant knowledge . . . the work will itself suggest the criteria by which it should be judged. Prof. [Peter] Horn put the cat firmly among the pigeons by arguing for the interpretation of literature in terms of the complex social, political, and

other relevant contexts in which it has been produced – the classical Marxist position . . . In the course of the following two days speakers and delegates found themselves returning to the above issues.

(Couzens, 'Criticism of South African Literature', pp. 45–6)

In the 1970s Gillham's ideas still prevailed, but in the succeeding decades Horn's arguments – supplemented by other varieties of critical theory – have become hegemonic. The pace and nature of the changes in critical discourse have varied widely from institution to institution, but by 1994 only a few adherents of the Leavis / Gillham position continued to publish. Key interventions in these debates include: Mike Kirkwood's 1976 book chapter on South African English culture ('The Colonizer', pp. 102–33), the 1977 articles by Tim Couzens ('Criticism', pp. 44–52), Isabel Hofmeyr ('Problems of Creative Writers', pp. 31–7) and Kelwyn Sole ('Problems of Creative Writers', pp. 4–25) in *Work in Progress* (1977), Michael Vaughan's 1984 article in *Critical Arts* ('A Critique of the Dominant Ideas in Departments of English', pp. 35–51), Anne McClintock and Rob Nixon's 1986 exchange with Jacques Derrida in *Critical Inquiry* ('No Names Apart', pp. 140–54), Ampie Coetzee's 1988 book *Marxisme en die Afrikaanse Letterkunde* and Cicely Lockett's 1990 article (and the responses to it) in *Current Writing* ('Feminisms and Writing in English in South Africa', pp. 1–21). Afrikaans-language literary critics in this period were also engaging with literary theory, but the fiercest arguments centred specifically on J. C. Kannemeyer's two-volume *Geskiedenis van die Afrikaanse literatuur* (1978 and 1983), and more generally upon what constituted 'Afrikaans literature' (Van Vuuren, 'Introduction', pp. 261–78).

Post-apartheid

Polemical exchanges between South African critics continued to enliven South Africa's literary and cultural journals in the early 1990s. See, for example, the debates following Albie Sachs's ANC cultural policy paper 'Preparing ourselves for freedom' (1989) and Njabulo Ndebele's *Rediscovery of the Ordinary* (1991) (De Kok and Press, *Spring is Rebellious*, and Brown and Van Dyk, *Exchanges*); the interventions on postapartheid literature and culture hosted in *Current Writing* (6:2 [1994]); and the debates between 1992 and 1997 about poststructuralism and Marxism in postcolonial theory (McClintock, 'Angel of Progress', pp. 84–98; Bhabha, interview, pp. 100–13; Carusi, 'Postcolonial Other', pp. 228–38; De Kock, 'Postcolonial Analysis', pp. 44–69; Chrisman, 'Inventing Post-Colonial Theory,' pp. 205–12; Sole, 'South Africa Passes the

Posts', pp. 116–51; Parry, 'Postcolonial', pp. 3–21; and Visser, 'Postcoloniality of a Special Type', pp. 79–94). By the end of the millennium, however, South African literary and cultural criticism was increasingly characterised by a strategically polite professionalism. The only debate to interrupt this consensus centred upon cultural rather than specifically literary issues, namely the disagreements triggered by former president Thabo Mbeki's Pan-Africanist ideology of the African Renaissance, which inspired articles restating certain Black Consciousness ideals and provoked responses questioning inter alia their interpretation of history and their readings of class and gender relations (Makgoba, *African Renaissance*; Moloka and Le Roux, *Problematising the African Renaissance*).

With access to and promotion within university careers increasingly determined by publications, there has been a sharp increase in the number of scholarly monographs on South African literature and culture. South African literature has also been the focus of more critical attention than ever before in scholarly journals, notably *World Literature Written in English* (UK, 1970–) under its new title *Journal of Postcolonial Writing* (UK, 2005–), *Postcolonial Studies* (Australia, 1998–), and *Interventions* (UK, 1998–). Access to many of these journals via web-based resources like JStor and EBSCO Host has increased the availability of their material. In South Africa itself, two new academic journals publishing literary and cultural criticism have appeared. *AlterNation* (1994–), which was based at the University of Durban-Westville (since integrated into the University of KwaZulu-Natal), has an interdisciplinary remit and has introduced the research of a new generation of critics. *scrutiny2* (1996–), which is based at UNISA, appealed in its first editorial for 'submissions that break the mould of dreary "accredited" articles'. It challenged readers to 'write their hearts out, not for the prospect of some distant portion of subsidy money, but for the sake of good writing and knife-point scrutiny of our intellectual and moral quandaries' (*scrutiny2* 1/2 [1996], p. 1). Several new small magazines publishing both creative writing and critical reviews and articles, and aimed at academic and non-academic audiences, have appeared: Johan Marais's Afrikaans culture and literature magazine *Ensovoort* (1993–); the magazine of the Johannesburg-based poetry collective *Botstotso* (1994–); Port Elizabeth-based *Kotaz* (1998–) edited by Mxolisi Nyezwa; Limpopo-based *Timbila* (2000–) edited by Vonani Bila and Mark Waller; the Pan-Africanist *Chimurenga* (2002–) edited by Ntone Edjabe; and *South Africa Writing* (2005–), from Cape Town. Of these small magazines, *Chimurenga* is closest in spirit to the radical cultural politics of the small magazines of the 1930s and the 1970s; a piece by Louis Chude-Sokei and Victor Gama, 'Dr Satan's Echo Chamber', for example, starts with an intricate photo montage dominated by the slogan 'Read Fanon you Fucking Bastards' (13 [2008], p. 1).

Another lively forum for literary-critical debate has been the website Lit-Net (www.litnet.co.za/cgi-bin/giga.cgi), which focuses predominantly on Afrikaans literature but also includes substantial coverage of literature in other South African languages. By contrast, book reviews in South African newspapers – aside from occasional exceptions in the *Sunday Independent* and *Mail & Guardian* – are largely uncritical, and function as free advertising for the publishing houses.

There is a temptation to read the history of South African literary and cultural criticism as a happy if uneven journey from modest, persecuted, parochial and amateurish beginnings in the nineteenth century to a confident, unfettered, international and professional present. There are at least two reasons to question this complacent *telos*. The first relates to the professionalisation of literary and cultural criticism, a process which in other contexts has had the effect of diminishing and containing the influence of literary critics beyond their immediate elite constituencies. Reflecting upon the social history of criticism in the United States, Rosa A. Eberly has argued that 'throughout the twentieth century . . . the power and agency of citizen critics have diminished . . . largely through the mechanisms of commodified public opinion and corporate capitalism . . . Marketing has turned texts usually considered literary into commodities and . . . legal, aesthetic, corporate, and other expert discourses have come to determine which books are published, who reads them, and how they are read' (*Citizen Critics*, p. xi). South African criticism in the last two decades has been subject to similar pressures, and any claims as to its achievements should be framed accordingly.

The second reason for resisting an optimistic reading of the history of South African criticism is that contemporary criticism continues to rest upon a contradictory nineteenth-century cultural residue. Beyond the sophisticated theoretical vocabularies and elongated footnotes, conservative assumptions continue to underwrite much South African criticism: that literature functions as an alternative secular religion, containing (like the Bible) unique truths, which critics (like priests) explicate for obedient worshippers; that as a matter of national pride South African writers and their work should be published and promoted; that the divisions between literary and popular literature and high and low culture should be observed; and that cultural authority derives from the universities and publishing houses of the (neo)colonial masters. However, certain other nineteenth-century impulses have also survived, and they continue to produce more interesting criticism. This minority tradition is characterised by a keen appetite for polemic and critical debate, a desire to relate literature to 'the political' (broadly conceived), and a related concern with how South African literatures articulate with South African nationhood. It is this second tradition I have tried to highlight in this chapter.

Bibliography

Adamson, J. *Modern Literature: An Address Delivered at the Fifteenth Annual Meeting of the Subscribers to the Public Library*, Cape Town: J. H. Collard, 1844.

Attwell, D. *Rewriting Modernity: Studies in Black South African Literary History*, Pietermaritzburg: University of KwaZulu-Natal Press, 2005.

Bhabha, H. Interview by D. Attwell, *Current Writing* 52 (1993), 100–13.

Biko, S. *I Write What I Like*, London: Heinemann, 1979.

Bleek, W. H. I. 'On Inquiries into Australian Aboriginal Folklore', *Cape Monthly Magazine* 9 (1874), 1–8.

Bosman, F. C. L. *Drama en Toneel in Suid-Afrika*, Cape Town: HAUM, 1928.

Brown, D., and B. van Dyk (eds.). *Exchanges: South African Writing in Transition*, Pietermaritzburg: University of Natal Press, 1991.

Calhoun, C. 'Nationalism and the Public Sphere', in J. Weintraub and K. Kumar (eds.), *Public and Private in Thought and Practice: Perspectives on a Grand Dichotomy*, University of Chicago Press, 1997, 75–102.

Carusi, A. 'The Postcolonial Other as a Problem for Political Action', *Journal of Literary Studies* 7:3–4 (1993), 228–38.

Chrisman, L. 'Inventing Post-Colonial Theory: Polemical Observations', *Pretexts* 5:1–2 (1995), 205–12.

Coetzee, A. *Marxisme en die Afrikaanse Letterkunde*, Bellville: University of the Western Cape Press, 1988.

Cope, J. *The Adversary Within: Dissident Writers in Afrikaans*, Cape Town: David Philip, 1982.

Couzens, T. 'Criticism of South African Literature', *Work in Progress* 2 (1977), 44–52.

  The New African: A Study of the Life and Work of H. I. E. Dhlomo, Johannesburg: Ravan, 1985.

De Kok, I., and K. Press (eds.). *Spring is Rebellious*, Cape Town: Buchu, 1990.

De Kock, L. 'Postcolonial Analysis and the Question of Critical Disablement', *Current Writing* 5:2 (1993), 44–69.

Dubow, S. *A Commonwealth of Knowledge: Science, Sensibility, and White South Africa, 1820–2000*, Oxford University Press, 2006.

Eberly, R. A. *Citizen Critics: Literary Public Spheres*, Urbana: University of Illinois Press, 2000.

English in Africa, special issue on 'H. I. E. Dhlomo', 4:2 (1977).

  Special issue on 'Literary Magazines' 7:2 (1980).

Fletcher, J. *The Story of Theatre in South Africa: A Guide to its History from 1780–1930*, Cape Town: Vlaeberg, 1994.

Gardner, M. *South African Literary Magazines 1956–1978*, Johannesburg: Warren Sieberts, 2004.

Gérard, A. *Four African Literatures: Xhosa, Sotho, Zulu, Amharic*, Berkeley: University of California Press, 1971.

Hirson, B. *The Cape Town Intellectuals: Ruth Schechter and her Circle, 1907–34*, Johannesburg: Witwatersrand University Press, 2001.

Hofmeyr, I. 'Building a Nation from Words: Afrikaans Language, Literature and Ethnic Identity, 1902–1924', in S. Marks and S. Trapido (eds.), *The Politics of Race, Class and Nationalism in Twentieth-Century South Africa*, London and New York: Longman, 1987, 95–123.

'Problems of Creative Writers: A Reply', *Work in Progress* 2 (1977), 31–7.

Huigen, S. 'Nederlandstalige Suid-Afrikaanse Letterkunde, 1652 tot 1925', in H. P. van Coller (ed.), *Perspektief en Profiel: 'n Afrikaanse Literatuurgeskiedenis*, vol. III, Pretoria: Van Schaik, 2005, 3–42.

Johnson, D. *Shakespeare and South Africa*, Oxford: Clarendon Press, 1996.

'Violence and Philosophy: Jack Cade, A. W. Schlegel, and Nathaniel Merriman', in J. Joughin (ed.), *Philosophical Shakespeares*, London: Routledge, 2000, 68–73.

Jordan, A. C. *Towards an African Literature: The Emergence of Literary Form in English*, Berkeley: University of California Press, 1973.

Kannemeyer, J. C. *Geskiedenis van die Afrikaanse Literatuur*, 2 vols., Cape Town and Pretoria: Academica, 1978, 1983.

Die Koléperas van Kees Konyn, Emmerentia: Taurus, 1983.

Kirkwood, M. 'The Colonizer: A Critique of the English South African Culture Theory', in P. Wilhelm and J. Polley (eds.), *Poetry 74*, Johannesburg: Ad Donker, 1976, 102–33.

Lewin Robinson, A. M. *None Daring to make us Afraid: A Study of the English Periodical Literature of the Cape from 1824–1834*, Cape Town: Maskew Miller, 1962.

Lockett, C. 'Feminisms and Writing in English in South Africa', *Current Writing* 2:1 (1990), 1–21.

Makgoba, M. W. (ed.). *African Renaissance: The New Struggle*, Cape Town: Tafelberg, 1999.

Masilela, N. *The Cultural Modernity of H. I. E. Dhlomo*, Trenton, NJ: Africa World Press, 2007.

McClintock, A. 'The Angel of Progress: Pitfalls of the Term "Postcolonialism"', *Social Text* 31/32 (1992), 84–98.

McClintock, A., and R. Nixon. 'No Names Apart: The Separation of Word and History in Derrida's "Le Dernier mot du racisme"', *Critical Inquiry* 13:1 (1986), 140–54.

Merriman, N. *On the Study of Shakespeare*, Grahamstown: General Institute, 1857.

Shakespeare as Bearing on English History, Grahamstown: General Institute, 1858.

Merrington, P. 'A Staggered Orientalism: The Cape-to-Cairo Imaginary', *Poetics Today* 22:2 (2001), 323–64.

Moloka, E., and E. le Roux (eds.). *Problematising the African Renaissance*, Pretoria: Africa Institute of South Africa, 2000.

Moran, S. *Representing Bushmen: South Africa and the Origin of Language*, New York: University of Rochester Press, 2009.

Mutloatse, M. *Forced Landing: Africa South – Contemporary Writings*, Johannesburg: Ravan, 1980.

Negt, O., and A. Kluge. *Public Sphere and Experience: Toward an Analysis of the Bourgeois and Proletarian Public Sphere* [1972], trans. P. Labanyi, J. Owen Daniel and A. Oksiloff, Minneapolis: University of Minnesota Press, 1993.

Nkosi, L. *Home and Exile*, London: Longman, 1965.

Opland, J. 'Fighting with the Pen: The Appropriation of the Press by Early Xhosa Writers', in J. A. Draper (ed.), *Orality, Literacy, and Colonialism in Southern Africa*, Pietermaritzburg: Cluster, 2003, 9–40.

'The First Novel in Xhosa', *Research in African Literatures* 38:4 (2007), 98–102.

Xhosa Poets and Poetry, Cape Town: David Philip, 1998.

Opland, J., and A. Nyamende (eds. and trans.). *Isaac Williams Wauchope, Selected Writings 1874–1916*, Cape Town: Van Riebeeck Society, 2008.

Parry, B. 'The Postcolonial: Conceptual Category or Chimera?', *Yearbook of English Studies* 27 (1997), 3–21.

Sandwith, C. 'Dora Taylor: South African Marxist', *English in Africa* 29:2 (2002), 5–27.

Sole, K. 'Culture, Politics and the Black Writer: A Critical Look at Prevailing Assumptions', *English in Africa* 10:1 (1983), 37–84.

'Problems of Creative Writers in South Africa', *Work in Progress* 1 (1977), 4–25.

'South Africa Passes the Posts', *Alternation* 4:1 (1997), 116–51.

Stapleton, R. J (ed.). *Poetry of the Cape of Good Hope Selected from the Periodical Journals of the Colony*, Cape Town: G. Greig, 1828.

Van Vuuren, H. 'Introduction: Literary Historiography, with specific reference to the problems of the South African context', *Journal of Literary Studies* 10:3–4 (1994), 261–78.

Van Wyk, J. *Constructs of Identity and Difference in South African Literature*, Durban: University of Durban-Westville, 1995.

Vaughan, M. 'A Critique in the English-Speaking Universities of South Africa', *Critical Arts* 3:2 (1984), 35–51.

Visser, N. (ed.). 'Postcoloniality of a Special Type: Theory and its Appropriations in South Africa', *Yearbook of English Studies* 27 (1997), 79–94.

Watson, S. (ed.). *Guy Butler: Essays and Lectures 1949–1991*, Cape Town: David Philip, 1994.

Willan, B. (ed.). *Sol Plaatje: Selected Writings*, Johannesburg: Witwatersrand University Press, 1996.

Willemse, H. *Aan die Ander Kant: Swart Afrikaanse Skrywers in die Afrikaanse Letterkunde*, Pretoria: Protea, 2007.

Index